TERRORISM AND THE LAW

TERRORISM AND THE LAW

Professor Clive Walker
Professor of Criminal Justice Studies, School of Law, University of Leeds

Consultant Editors
Lord Carlile of Berriew QC
Lord Ken McDonald QC
Sir David Omand

OXFORD
UNIVERSITY PRESS

OXFORD
UNIVERSITY PRESS

Great Clarendon Street, Oxford ox2 6DP

Oxford University Press is a department of the University of Oxford.
It furthers the University's objective of excellence in research, scholarship,
and education by publishing worldwide in

Oxford New York

Auckland Cape Town Dar es Salaam Hong Kong Karachi
Kuala Lumpur Madrid Melbourne Mexico City Nairobi
New Delhi Shanghai Taipei Toronto

With offices in

Argentina Austria Brazil Chile Czech Republic France Greece
Guatemala Hungary Italy Japan Poland Portugal Singapore
South Korea Switzerland Thailand Turkey Ukraine Vietnam

Oxford is a registered trade mark of Oxford University Press
in the UK and in certain other countries

Published in the United States
by Oxford University Press Inc., New York

British Library Cataloguing-in-Publication Data
Data available

Library of Congress Cataloging in Publication Data
Data available

Typeset by Glyph International, Bangalore, India

Printed in Great Britain on acid-free paper by
CPI Antony Rowe

ISBN 978-0-19-956117-9

PREFACE

A law academic could enjoy a fulfilling but hectic career devoted entirely to the consumption of the prodigious amount of laws and public policy which has been fashioned in response to terrorism. Such has been the fate of your author, who, since taking up the subject of 'The Prevention of Terrorism in British Law' for a PhD study in 1979, has suffered few dull moments. It remains a daunting task to keep pace with, and to derive meaning from, the astonishing and complex events and legal responses which have unfolded during the ensuing three decades, not least since 11 September 2001.

Whilst this long experience of legal development helps to deepen understandings of purpose and meaning, the core mission of this project is to provide an authoritative and comprehensive description and analysis of the counter-terrorism laws which impact within the United Kingdom today. The book is designed to be of prime utility as an accumulation of knowledge, analysis, and critique to practitioners (legal practitioners and law enforcement), academics, researchers, students, policy-makers, administrators, and anyone interested in looking behind the rhetoric about counter-terrorism.

Compared to other works on terrorism laws, this book features two distinct advantages. First, it provides coverage and depth beyond previous works, ranging well beyond just the principal anti-terrorism legislation. As well as delving deeper into domestic law, aspects of comparative and international laws are also covered. Secondly, the book assumes a practical orientation by paying full regard to implementation and practice. This aspect benefits from extensive fieldwork in the form of visits and interviews, as detailed below.

In substance, the book will focus upon domestic laws and practices in relation to terrorism. As mentioned, the prime sources of law remain the extensive anti-terrorism legislation, and these key texts will be dissected in full. The current crop of special legislation is founded upon the Terrorism Act 2000, which represents a considered, comprehensive, and principled code whose period of gestation goes back to the Lloyd Report[1] as well as the government's broadly supportive response.[2] The Act primarily reflects a criminal prosecution approach, but executive alternatives soon reappeared, following the September 11 attacks, via Pt IV of the Anti-terrorism, Crime and Security Act 2001. The mechanism of detention without trial soon incurred fierce criticism from the Newton Report[3] and was dealt a final blow by the House of Lords in *A v Secretary of State for the Home Department*.[4] As a result, Pt IV was replaced by the no less controversial 'control orders' in the Prevention of Terrorism Act 2005. Later legislation, the Terrorism Act 2006 and the Counter-Terrorism Act 2008, has principally involved a refinement and thickening of the criminal prosecution approach, in part driven by the London bombings of 7 July 2005 and in part by international developments.

---

[1] *Inquiry into Legislation against Terrorism* (Cm 3420, London, 1996).
[2] *Legislation Against Terrorism* (Cm 4178, London, 1998).
[3] *Privy Counsellor Review Committee, Anti-Terrorism, Crime and Security Act 2001 Review Report* (2003–04 HC 100).
[4] [2004] UKHL 56.

Finally, aspects of financial counter-measures were reformed by the Terrorist Asset-Freezing etc. Act 2010.

The other principal legislative development has occurred in Northern Ireland, reflecting the advancement of the Peace Process. Part VII of the Terrorism Act 2000, allowing for the continuance of the non-jury 'Diplock' trials and various special policing powers, has been replaced by the Justice and Security (Northern Ireland) Act 2007, which retains the essence of these measures but on a more confined basis (covered in Chapter 11).

By these successive pieces of legislation, anti-terrorism laws are being worked into an overarching collection, covering criminal prosecution, executive measures, police powers, sentencing, and target-hardening. But the anthology remains unprincipled, incomplete, and disjointed.

Aside from this fragmented assortment of special terrorism legislation, other laws against terrorism had accumulated well before the passage of the Terrorism Act 2000. Beyond its remit are the offences in the Explosive Substances Act 1883 and international treaty-based offences against terrorism. Within the spheres of investigations and policing, important sources of law of relevance to terrorism include the surveillance powers under the Regulation of Investigatory Powers Act 2000, while other outlying policing and executive powers reside in the Police and Criminal Evidence Act 1984, common law rules (such as on lethal force), and the immigration and asylum rules. Finally, a wide variety of legal and administrative sources govern the regulation of munitions, aviation, nuclear and biological security, other public protection, and support for victims.

Increasingly important sources of the law on terrorism within the United Kingdom are the European Union, the United Nations, international human rights, and international humanitarian law. The notion that security is the exclusive concern of sovereign states is no longer tenable. All countries value the facility of international cooperation against 'their' terrorists, and most recognize that they must comply with international law requirements and restraints if this cooperation is to be secured. These outside influences will not be treated as subjects in themselves, for their activities with respect to terrorism are now too voluminous. However, their direct impacts on United Kingdom law—as hard rather than 'soft' law—will be fully documented. The influence of international human rights under the European Convention on Human Rights is particularly pervasive and will be mentioned in every chapter.

Just as international law about terrorism has proliferated, so other national jurisdictions have begun to emulate the British torrent of special laws. It would pack another very substantial volume to delineate fully these foreign developments. Therefore, for present purposes, the comparisons will be narrowed to those jurisdictions which either reflect the closest relations to British legal traditions—Australia, Canada, Ireland, and the United States (Federal aspects only)—or are influential within the European Union (France, Germany, and Spain). Comparisons will be utilized selectively to underline trends and to suggest alternatives (both desirable and undesirable).

Building upon these various sources, the book will comprise the following elements. Part I (Chapter 1) is introductory and will concentrate upon meanings of 'terrorism' both in political science and also in law. An understanding of the phenomenon and the legal concept, including its statutory definitions, is essential to the assessment of the strategies and tactics adopted in the codes of laws which follow. Equally vital is an appreciation of counter-terrorism strategies, now conveniently rehearsed in the CONTEST documents.[5] Every aspect of the strategy will be considered, though this book's focus on law inevitably entails priority for 'Pursue' rather than 'Prevent', 'Prepare', or 'Protect'. Normative constraints, such as human rights, will also be evaluated, including notions of balance with concepts such as security. The legislature and judiciary must ensure accountability and respect for constitutionalism in these special circumstances, and their efforts in those directions will be assessed. Overall conclusions as to the current legal disposition will be offered here.

Part II begins the survey of law by taking up the agenda of 'Investigation and Policing'. In this way, the book follows an ordering which reflects criminal justice process. One might argue that 'Investigation and Policing' should in any event enjoy pre-eminence by signifying the most frequent and important activity under terrorism laws. The catalogue of Pt II includes investigatory powers of search, stop, or surveillance (Chapter 2), legal demands for the disclosure of information (Chapter 3), and the investigation of persons through their arrest, detention, and sampling, including the use of force in the implementation of these purposes and international policing cooperation (Chapter 4).

The outcomes of investigation and policing may remain hidden as intelligence-gathering or as disruptive intervention. More overt actions by way of criminal law and criminal process are the subject of Pt III. Chapter 5 embarks upon the offences which are used against terrorism. Some are enshrined in special domestic legislation, and international law also provides an extensive array of offences against terrorism. However, many commonly used offences do not derive from these sources. Therefore, it is important to offer a sense of what is 'normal' in terrorism cases as well as what is 'special'. Chapter 6 correspondingly covers the processes by which offences are applied against terrorists—at pre-trial, trial, and post-trial (sentence and post-sentence) stages. Aspects of the management of court cases and other practices will be addressed, plus international cooperation for judicial purposes.

As well as criminal justice resolutions, other legal approaches will be considered in Pt IV. These share the strategic objective of pre-emptive responses against potentially indiscriminate, substantial, and suicidal attacks on civilian targets. The first such measure, in Chapter 7, concerns 'Executive Controls over Individuals' which comprises not only control orders but also the application of deportation and exclusion powers. Chapter 8 moves on to consider the broad range of laws taken against 'Extreme Organizations and Speech'. Part of that agenda consists of criminal offences, but additional legal pathways include proscription, and election and media controls. The chapter will also consider the extent to which groups which may be categorized as sub-revolutionary, such as animal rights extremists, are treated as terrorists or are subjected to other legal treatment. Chapter 9 reflects a similar range of possibilities when responding to 'Terrorist Funding and Property'. Criminal offences form part of the equation, but various other forms of freezing, restraints, and regulations have been implemented, including highly complex regimes adapted from sanctions regimes by the United Nations. Chapter 10, on 'Protective Security' considers both general themes of general public protection and resilience and also protective measures for special sectors such as aviation and materials of potential mass impact (chemical, biological, radiological, and nuclear). Counter-terrorism here relies in part upon criminal offences but additionally sets

---

[5] Home Office, *Countering International Terrorism* (Cm 6888, London, 2006) and *Pursue, Prevent, Protect, Prepare: The United Kingdom's Strategy for Countering International Terrorism* (Cm 7547, London, 2009).

up extensive regulatory schemes. The chapter also considers the victims of terrorism, characteristically left to the end, as is historically their fate in law.

Part V considers the 'Other Jurisdictions' of relevance, which for these purposes means Northern Ireland and Scotland (Chapter 11).

The research behind this book has been extensive and enjoyable in equal measure. With the benefit of an Arts & Humanities Research Council fellowship,[6] I have been enabled to make visits and attend events as follows during 2009 and 2010: Stanford University Law School (with thanks to Professors Kathleen Sullivan and Laura Donohue); the 25 Bedford Row conference at the Law Society's Hall; the Police National Legal Database Annual Conference, Birmingham; the British Society of Criminology Conference, Cardiff, where I organized a panel on 'The Prosecution of Terrorism' alongside Professor John Jackson (University College Dublin) and Francesca Laguardia (New York University Law School); the Society of Legal Scholars Annual Conference, Keele; the European Consortium for Political Research General Conference, Potsdam; the American Society of Criminology Meeting, Philadelphia; the Institute of Advanced Legal Studies at the University of London (as visiting fellow which also enabled access to the British Library and the National Archives); the University of Minnesota Law School conference on 'Exceptional courts and military commissions', with thanks to Professor Oren Gross and Professor Fionnuala Ní Aoláin; the Robert S. Strauss Center for International Security and Law, University of Texas School of Law (with thanks to Professor Robert Chesney); the conference on 'The impact of contemporary security agendas' at the Max Planck Institute, Freiburg i.Br. (with thanks to Professors Ulrich Sieber, Mordechai Kremnitzer, and Yuval Shany); the European Union Institute, Florence; the 'Counter-terrorism and Human Rights Conference' of JUSTICE (with thanks to Eric Metcalf); the 'Future Terrorism Conference' at the Royal United Services Institute; and the Centre for the Study of Terrorism and Political Violence, St Andrews' University (with thanks to Professor Max Taylor).

Aside from these set events, I have benefited greatly from the discussions with: the Hon. Mr Justice David Calvert-Smith, Murray Hunt (Joint Committee on Human Rights), Carmi Lecker (Public Committee Against Torture in Israel), Professor Andrew Lynch (University of New South Wales), Professor Kent Roach (University of Toronto), DS Andrew Staniforth (NECTU), DI Neil Smith (CTC), and Sgt Bob Steele (Paddington Green). My colleagues at the School of Law in the University of Leeds have continued to provide excellent support, as have Jane Kavanagh, Katie Heath, and Faye Judges on behalf of the publishers. Above all, I thank Lord Carlile, Lord Ken McDonald, and Sir David Omand who acted as consultants, though the opinions expressed herein remain entirely my own responsibility.

The book takes account of developments up to 31 October 2010, save that the passage of the Terrorist Asset-Freezing etc. Act 2010 has been plotted for longer and assumed to have been completed.

Clive Walker
School of Law
University of Leeds

---

[6] Fellowship grant no AH/G00711x/1.

CONTENTS

III CRIMINAL LAW AND CRIMINAL PROCESS

5. Criminal Offences and Terrorism

6. Court Processes, Punishment, and Terrorism

TABLE OF CASES

TABLE OF LEGISLATION

Northern Ireland

*This list includes legislation passed for Ireland as a
whole before 1922.*

LIST OF ABBREVIATIONS

ATCSA 2001	Anti-terrorism, Crime and Security Act 2001
Baker Report	*Review of the Operation of the Northern Ireland (Emergency Provisions) Act 1978* (Cmnd 9222, London, 1984)
Bennett Report	*Report of the Committee of Inquiry into Police Interrogation Procedures in Northern Ireland* (Cmnd 9497, London, 1979)
Colville Report	*Review of the Operation of the Prevention of Terrorism (Temporary Provisions) Act 1984* (Cm 264, London, 1987)
CTA 2008	Counter-Terrorism Act 2008
Diplock Report	*Report of the Commission to Consider Legal Procedures to Deal with Terrorist Activities in Northern Ireland* (Cmnd 5185, London, 1972)
EPA 1973, 1978, 1987, 1991, 1996, 1998	Northern Ireland (Emergency Provisions) Act 1973, 1978, 1987, 1991, 1996, 1998
Home Office Response to Lloyd Report	Home Office and Northern Ireland Office, *Legislation against Terrorism* (Cm 4178, London, 1998)
Home Office Response to Newton Report	Home Office, *Counter-Terrorism Powers: Reconciling Security and Liberty in an Open Society* (Cm 6147, London, 2004)
Jellicoe Report	*Report of the Operation of the Prevention of Terrorism (Temporary Provisions) Act 1976* (Cmnd 8803, London, 1983)
JSA 2007	Justice and Security (Northern Ireland) Act 2007
Lloyd Report	*Inquiry into Legislation against Terrorism* (Cm 3420, London, 1996)
Newton Report	*Privy Counsellor Review Committee, Anti-Terrorism, Crime and Security Act 2001 Review Report* (2003-04 HC 100)
PACE	Police and Criminal Evidence Act 1984
PACE(NI)	Police and Criminal Evidence (Northern Ireland) Order 1989, SI 1989/1341
PT(TP)A 1974, 1976, 1984, 1989	Prevention of Terrorism (Temporary Provisions) Act 1974, 1976, 1984, 1989
PT(AP)A 1996	Prevention of Terrorism (Additional Powers) Act 1996
PTA 2005	Prevention of Terrorism Act 2005
RIPA	Regulation of Investigatory Powers Act 2000
Rowe Report	*Review of the Northern Ireland (Emergency Provisions) Act 1991* (Cm 2706, London, 1995)
Shackleton Report	*Review of the Operation of the Prevention of Terrorism (Temporary Provisions) Acts 1974 and 1976* (Cmnd 7324, London, 1978)
TA 2000	Terrorism Act 2000
TA 2006	Terrorism Act 2006
T(NI)A 2006	Terrorism (Northern Ireland) Act 2006
UNSCR	United Nations Security Council Resolution

Part I

INTRODUCTION

1

TERRORISM

A. Introduction

This chapter provides both an introduction and a conclusion. It will first examine the **1.01** phenomenon of terrorism, seeking to build an analytical setting in terms of strategy and counter-strategy. The legal implications of terrorism will be addressed in general terms, including the normative considerations which should govern the design and application of law within this fraught enterprise. Having set the scene, it will then be possible to return in more detail to the definition of terrorism, before reaching some overall conclusions about how law and terrorism have interacted.

B. The Phenomenon of Terrorism

Concept of terrorism

Images of aircraft crashing into skyscrapers, suicide bombings, and public spaces shrouded **1.02** by barricades have dramatized contemporary perceptions of terrorism. The attacks of 11 September 2001, reinforced by subsequent attacks on transportation, hotels, and public gatherings, have also constructed a compelling trigger for official rejoinders through security activity and legislation, even extending to the world's superpower declaration of 'the first war of the twenty-first century'.[1] Yet, the relationship between terrorism and the legal system has been more unremitting and less impulsive than these recent dramas imply. '*A luta continua*'

---

[1] <http://georgewbush-whitehouse.archives.gov/news/releases/2001/09/20010916-2.html.>

('the struggle continues') was the revolutionary slogan voiced by movements against Portuguese colonialism, and 'terrorism' has indeed endured as a recurrent idiom in political struggle since at least the French Revolution. Counter-terrorism laws can match this longevity and adaptability.[2]

1.03 Attempts at a precise definition will be considered later in this chapter. For the moment, terrorism can be conceptualized as a sub-set of political violence—the application of certain forms of violence for specified political ends. The invariable essence is a tripartite relationship whereby the actors (terrorists) seek to impact on a target (specific victims) with a view to influencing a political audience (typically the government or the general public).[3] There is often a fourth aspect, whereby terrorists wish to influence their potential recruiting base or existing supporters, though some are entirely self-generating and perpetuating.

1.04 Whether such action is justifiable historically, politically, or morally is a vital question. The commonplace mantra, indicating moral relativism, is: 'One man's terrorist is another man's freedom fighter'. The careers of Éamonn de Valera, Menachim Begin, and Nelson Mandela bear witness to the fluidity of the label, as does the career of the FBI's most wanted terrorist:[4] '. . . Osama bin Laden was a freedom fighter for Reagan but a terrorist for Bush. One can change sides without changing tactics . . .'.[5] However, progress has been made in international law by distinguishing between political objectives, which remain forever contestable, and specific techniques, such as the bombing of civilians, which have become depicted as unpardonable wrongs for all actors at all times.[6] Since this book is concerned with positive law, the moral vindication of terrorists or of the opposing state will not be measured. [7] Positive laws cannot morally resolve that dispute since their very authority is disputed by state opponents. It follows that the label 'terrorism' will be used in this book to describe any action correlating to its legal description and is not meant to convey pejorative implications.

Categories of terrorism

1.05 A categorization of terrorism may be constructed around the ends being pursued and can be depicted as: revolutionary and counter-revolutionary; sub-revolutionary; or statist. It is assumed in this categorization that terrorism can generally be understood as a form of rational choice. Individual circumstances and motives may be more varied, but the contention that terrorists suffer from psychological dysfunction or collective hysteria has generally not been sustained.[8]

---

[2] See Walker, C, 'Terrorism and criminal justice' [2004] *Criminal Law Review* 311.

[3] See Crelinsten, RD, 'Analysing terrorism and counter-terrorism: a communication model' (2002) 14 *Terrorism & Political Violence* 77.

[4] <http://www.fbi.gov/wanted/terrorists/fugitives.htm>.

[5] Nielsen, K, 'On the moral justifiability of terrorism (state and otherwise)' (2003) 41 *Osgoode Hall Law Journal* 427 at 430.

[6] See International Convention for the Suppression of Terrorist Bombings, adopted by the General Assembly of the United Nations on 15 December 1997 (37 ILM 249).

[7] See Honderich, T, *After the Terror* (McGill-Queen's University Press, Montreal, 2003); Coady, CAJ, 'Terrorism and innocence' (2004) 8 *Journal of Ethics* 37; Primoratz, I, *Terrorism: The Philosophical Issues* (Palgrave, Basingstoke, 2004); Waldron, J, 'Terrorism and the Uses of Terror' (2004) 8 *Journal of Ethics* 5; Scheffler, S, 'Is terrorism morally distinctive?' (2006) 14 *Journal of Political Philosophy* 1 (2006); Goodin, R, *What's Wrong With Terrorism?* (Polity Press, Cambridge, 2006); Steinhoff, U, *On the Ethics of War and Terrorism* (Oxford University Press, New York, 2007); Meisels, T, *The Trouble with Terror* (Cambridge University Press, Cambridge, 2008). Many of these commentaries misleadingly rely upon distinctions between combatants and non-combatants, regardless of the existence of 'conflict'.

[8] See Sageman, M, *Understanding Terrorist Networks* (University of Pennsylvania Press, Philadelphia, 2004); Horgan, J, *The Psychology of Terrorism* (Routledge, Abingdon, 2005); Richardson, L, *What Terrorists Want* (John Murray, London, 2006); Silke, A, 'Holy warriors' (2008) 5 *European Journal of Criminology* 99.

Revolutionary terrorism arises where a group or movement seeks to implement a change **1.06**
which can be counted as 'revolutionary'—a change in state allegiance or a fundamental
constitutional change within that state. This tactic of terrorism may be adopted as an end
in itself, for example, by anarchists or nihilists. However, terrorism is more frequently
undertaken as a tactic based upon the conditions of endemic political and military weakness. There are two contexts in which the weak commonly resort to revolutionary terrorism:
within independent states or within a decolonization campaign.[9] The latter format seeks
to increase the economic and political costs of retaining the external territory and to exert
international pressure. Within independent states, the terrorists seek to trigger a spiral of
governmental repression and consequent loss of popularity and authority. It may be
counted as a partial terrorist success if governmental victory is achieved at the expense of
political fragmentation or deep unpopularity, thus paving the way for future conflict.
Consequently, 'the issue is not merely survival, but the way in which society chooses to
survive'.[10]

The United Kingdom can assuredly claim to have encountered more configurations **1.07**
and episodes of revolutionary terrorism than most other polities. This thrasonical statement is founded upon several elements.[11] The first relates to the bygone era of British
Empire, when multiple nationalist movements fighting colonialism applied political violence, mainly confined to the territory of the colony but occasionally spilling into the
'motherland'.[12] In succession to these conflicts, Britain has been the locus for the plotting
and perpetration of terrorism based on foreign or international causes, especially Palestinian
and Sikh factions.

The second and most prominent element of experience arises from the intermittent, **1.08**
irredentist campaigns of terrorism in Ireland against colonization and then incorporation
within the British state over a period of more than three centuries. The Provisional Irish
Republican Army announced in 2005 a permanent end to its violence, though splinter
Republican groups remain active.[13] The Irish context has generated counter-revolutionary
terrorism by equally enduring Loyalist groups such as the Ulster Volunteer Force and Ulster
Defence Association.[14]

The advent in Britain of Al-Qa'ida[15] has developed a variant of revolutionary terrorism which **1.09**
cannot be depicted as entirely 'foreign' or 'international', since its political aims and membership contain domestic and foreign elements. Some relate to British involvement in Iraq and
Afghanistan, some relate to Palestine, Middle Eastern governments, and the treatment of
Muslims throughout the world. Thus, Al-Qa'ida is sometimes categorized as a wholly novel
form of terrorism—'Third Millennium Terrorism'—with features such as religious and cultural motivations and the cataclysmic use of suicide attacks alongside predominantly late

---

[9] See Wilkinson, P, *Terrorism Versus Democracy* (2nd edn, Routledge, Abingdon, 2006) p 4.
[10] Friedlander, RA, *Terrorism: Documents of International and Local Control*, Vol I (Oceana, New York, 1979)
p 108.
[11] See Hoffman, B, *Inside Terrorism* (2nd edn, Columbia University Press, New York, 2006) chs 2, 3.
[12] See Andrew, C, *The Defence of the Realm* (Allen Lane, London, 2009) p 352.
[13] Independent Monitoring Commission, *Eighth Report* (2005–06 HC 870). See Neumann, PG, *Britain's
Long War* (Palgrave, Basingstoke, 2003); Alonso, R, *The IRA and the Armed Struggle* (Routledge, Abingdon,
2007); Dingley, J, *Combating Terrorism in Northern Ireland* (Routledge, Abingdon, 2009).
[14] Wood, IS, *Crimes of Loyalty* (Edinburgh University Press, Edinburgh, 2006).
[15] Versions of this Arabic name vary, but the above represents the form adopted in the Terrorism Act 2000
(Proscribed Organisations) (Amendment) Order 2001, SI 2001/1261.

modern structures, methods, and communications.[16] Whether these features amount to an entirely 'new' form of terrorism remains debatable,[17] but the threat is certainly perceived as demanding the enhancement of the ability to anticipate and pre-empt through legal means but not the total abandonment of pre-2001 counter-terrorism laws. Though its core structure has degraded since 2001,[18] Al-Qa'ida remains a vanguard under which some of the most destructive acts of terrorism in history have been committed. Notorious above all were the 11 September 2001 attacks, but the litany also includes bombings in East Africa in 1998, Yemen in 2000, Bali in 2002, Jakarta in 2003 and 2004, Madrid in 2004, and London in 2005.[19]

1.10 Two further categories of 'terrorism' remain. Sub-revolutionary terrorism seeks a political end which does not involve a fundamental change to the existence or nature of the state but is confined to a particular policy or aspect of policy. Animal liberationists who have resorted to violence may provide an illustration, though their activities are rarely treated under the rubric of terrorism.

1.11 Next, terrorism as a tactic adopted by a state is the most prevalent and devastating form of all. Notable protagonists of terror tactics during the last century were Hitler and Stalin whose regimes resulted in far more deaths than all revolutionary terrorism since that time.[20] Of course, state terrorism is not just the preserve of the great dictators. It is a distressingly commonplace accusation that even democracies abandon restraints during terrorism emergencies, though not, it should be emphasizsed, on the scale of totalitarian dictators. Engagement in 'Dirty Wars' is a charge made against the UK government not only during its historical colonial campaigns, but also in contemporary times, with the use of degrading and inhuman treatment against suspects,[21] alleged policies of shoot-to-kill,[22] and collusion with counter-revolutionaries.[23]

---

[16] See Gunaratne, R, *Inside al Qaeda* (Columbia University Press, New York, 2002); Gray, J, *Al Qaeda and What It Means to Be Modern* (Faber and Faber, London, 2003); Sageman, M, *Understanding Terror Networks* (University of Pennsylvania Press, Philadelphia, 2004); Gerges, FA, *The Far Enemy* (Cambridge University Press, New York, 2005); Greenberg, KJ, *Al Qaeda Now* (Cambridge University Press, Cambridge, 2005).

[17] Lia, B, *Globalisation and the Future of Terrorism* (Routledge, London, 2005); Neumann, P, *Old and New Terrorism* (Polity, Cambridge, 2009).

[18] Cabinet Office, *The National Security Strategy of the United Kingdom: Update 2009: Security for the Next Generation* (Cm 7590, London, 2009) paras 4.19, 6.30 and (Cm 7953, London, 2010) para 1.3.

[19] See National Commission on Terrorist Attacks upon the United States, *The 9/11 Commission Report* (GPO, Washington DC, 2004); Intelligence and Security Committee, *Inquiry into Intelligence, Assessments and Advice prior to the Terrorist Bombings on Bali 12 October 2002* (Cm 5724, London, 2002); *Inquiry into Intelligence, Report into the London Terrorist Attacks on 7 July 2005* (Cm 6785, London, 2005); Home Office, *Report of the Official Account of the Bombings in London on the 7th July 2005* (2005–06 HC 1087).

[20] See Conquest, R, *The Great Terror* (Oxford University Press, Oxford, 2007).

[21] See (Compton) *Report of an Enquiry into allegations against the security forces of physical brutality in Northern Ireland arising out of arrests on the 9 August 1971* (Cmnd 4828, London, 1972); (Parker) *Report of the Committee of Privy Counsellors appointed to consider authorised procedures for the interrogation of persons suspected of terrorism* (Cmnd 4901, London, 1972); (Bennett) *Report of the Committee of Inquiry into Police Interrogation Procedures in Northern Ireland* (Cmnd 7497, London, 1979); *Ireland v United Kingdom* App no 5310/71, Ser A 25 (1978); (Aitken) *Investigation into cases of Deliberate Abuse and Unlawful Killing in Iraq in 2003 and 2004* (Ministry of Defence, London, 2008).

[22] See Bloody Sunday Inquiry (<http://www.bloody-sunday-inquiry.org.uk>); Stevens Inquiry on UDA/RUC collusion (*The Times* 18 April 2003, pp 4, 5); de Menezes inquires (IPCC, *Stockwell One and Stockwell Two* (London, 2007)).

[23] See Rolston, B, 'An effective mask for terror' (2005) 44 *Crime Law & Society* 181; Police Ombudsman for Northern Ireland, *Statement by the Police Ombudsman for Northern Ireland on her investigation into the circumstances surrounding the death of Raymond McCord Jr and related matters* (Belfast, 2007); Police Ombudsman for Northern Ireland, *RUC Investigation of the alleged involvement of the late Father James Chesney in the bombing of Claudy on 31 July 1972* (Belfast, 2010).

Whilst terrorism in all forms is seen as a security risk, often the prime threat of all, it is by no **1.12** means the sole or most common threat. Contextualization as to types of emergency and their constitutive factors is offered by the Civil Contingencies Act 2004.[24] 'Emergencies' are therein defined by ss 1 and 19 as events or situations which threaten serious damage to human welfare or serious damage to the environment, or amount to war or terrorism which threatens serious damage to national security. Terrorism is thereby counted as just one potential emergency, with floods being in fact the most common source of emergency. A corresponding panoply of potential disasters (with terrorism in the top tier) is listed in the Cabinet Office's papers on *The National Security Strategy of the United Kingdom*.[25] These broader conceptions of emergency may be redolent of a culture of fear which spawns increasing risk aversion, whereby public policy becomes hostage to perceived risks which are inconsistent with our unprecedented levels of personal safety so that security policy supplants social policy.[26] The allegation that governments overplay the risk of terrorism, with excessive security budgets and even offensively paranoid public announcements,[27] also reflects contemporary theoretical approaches to the centrality of risk, in particular, the management of diffuse and complex risks that even threaten the notion of 'modernity' itself. The 'risk society' (the idiom of Ulrich Beck) is therefore 'an epoch in which the dark sides of progress increasingly come to dominate social debate'.[28] Terrorism is one of these 'dark sides' in which the growth of Al-Qa'ida is a reflexive aspect of more positive features of late modernity such as globalized travel and technology.

Counter-terrorism

The UK government published a clear, clever, and comprehensive counter-terrorism strategy **1.13** (CONTEST) in 2006 which was revised in 2009.[29]

Delivery of the strategy continues to be organized around four principal workstreams as follows:

- Pursue: to stop terrorist attacks
- Prevent: to stop people becoming terrorists or supporting violent extremism
- Protect: to strengthen our protection against terrorist attack
- Prepare: where an attack cannot be stopped, to mitigate its impact.

The 'Protect' and 'Prepare' elements are very much the province of the Civil Contingencies **1.14** Act 2004. The Act seeks to bolster through planning and networking the resilience of responders to potential emergencies.

'Prevent' has come to the fore since the July 2005 bombings, which obliged the government **1.15** and public to confront the unpalatable fact that the terrorism was not the work of alien

---

[24] See Walker, C and Broderick, J, *The Civil Contingencies Act 2004* (Oxford University Press, Oxford, 2006).

[25] Cm 7291, London, 2008, para 1.3 and (Cm 7953, London, 2010,) p 27. See also Cabinet Office, National Risk Register 2008 and 2010 (London) p 5.

[26] Furedi F, *Culture of Fear* (rev. edn, Continuum, London, 2002), *Invitation to Terror* (Continuum, London, 2007). See further Mythen, G. and Walklate, S, 'Criminology and terrorism' (2006) 46 *British Journal of Criminology* 379.

[27] See Advertising Standards Association, *Adjudication on the Association of Chief Police Officers* (122211, 2010).

[28] Beck, U, *Ecological Enlightenment* (Humanities Press, New Jersey, 1995) p 2.

[29] Home Office, *Pursue, Prevent, Protect, Prepare: The United Kingdom's Strategy for Countering International Terrorism* (Cm 7547, London, 2009) para 7.07. See also Home Office, *Countering International Terrorism* (Cm 6888, London, 2006), *The United Kingdom's Strategy for Countering International Terrorism* (Cm 7833, London, 2010). Compare the previous absence of campaign planning under *Operation Banner* (Army Code 71842, London, 2006) paras 409, 536.

foreigners but involved attacks by their erstwhile neighbours.[30] Therefore, efforts must be made to reduce this propensity, adding to the emphasis on anticipatory risk and pre-emption rather than aftermath response.[31]

1.16 As for 'Pursue', an element often stressed is the importance of intelligence-gathering.[32] It can form the basis not only for pre-emptive action in general but also for the individual application of criminal justice disposals or alternative executive measures. Which path to 'Pursue' is preferable? Where there is sufficient evidence of criminal activity, then a criminal prosecution is the more legitimate response.[33] A criminal justice path formed the core of the most important report on terrorism legislation, the *Diplock Report,* in 1972. This approach does not mean that criminal justice cannot adapt to allow for early intervention, and the very use of the term 'terrorism', interrogations under special arrest powers with special detention periods, special courts without juries, and special 'precursor' offences have all been implemented. These changes can become so numerous and so profound that they endanger the legitimacy of the criminal justice process, and thereby produce 'political prisoners' in the minds of defendants and their communities. The dangers were dramatized by the hunger strikes in the Maze Prison H Blocks in 1981 in resistance to the ascription of criminalization.[34] Further problems are that the criminal justice process, however modified, may remain unappealing to the security services who wish to avert the hazard of potentially devastating attacks and to avoid disclosure of methods and sources in a public courtroom. Hence, there emerge executive alternatives to prosecution such as internment and control orders.

1.17 British dalliance with a 'war model' has been confined to military operations in Afghanistan and Iraq. Even in this sphere, the operative rules have remained the regular international humanitarian and human rights laws. In this way, there has emerged no British 'legal black hole'[35] equivalent to the facilities and processes at Guantánamo Bay.[36] Nor has there been any overt emulation of programmes of executive domestic surveillance[37] or rendition for interrogation.[38] Instead the UK government has rejected even the terminology of the 'war on

---

[30] See Walker, C, '"Know Thine Enemy as Thyself": Discerning friend from foe under anti-terrorism laws' (2008) 32 *Melbourne Law Review* 275. The extent to which foreign influences continue remains unclear, but see Hayman, A, *The Terrorist Hunters* (Bantam Press, London, 2009) p 286; Hoffman, B, 'Radicalisation and subversion' (2009) 32 *Studies in Conflict & Terrorism* 1100.

[31] See Dershowitz, A, *The Case for Preemption* (W.W. Norton, New York, 2006); Suskind, R, *The One Per Cent Doctrine* (Simon & Schuster, New York, 2007).

[32] Walker, C, 'Intelligence and anti-terrorism legislation in the United Kingdom' (2006) 44 *Crime, Law and Social Change* 387; Gill, P, 'Security intelligence and human rights' (2009) 24 *Intelligence & National Security* 78.

[33] Kentridge, S, 'The pathology of a legal system: criminal justice in South Africa' (1980) 128 *University of Pennsylvania Law Review* 603 at 612; Zedner, L, 'Securing liberty in the face of terrorism' (2005) 32 *Journal of Law & Society* 507 at 533; Gearty, C, *Can Human Rights Survive?* (Cambridge University Press, Cambridge, 2005) p 139.

[34] See Walker, C, 'Irish Republican prisoners—political detainees, prisoners of war or common criminals?' (1984) 19 *Irish Jurist* 189; von Tangen Page, M, *Prisons, Peace and Terrorism* (Macmillan, Basingstoke, 1998); Williams, J, 'Hunger-strikes: a prisoner's right or a "wicked folly"?' (2001) 40 *Howard Journal of Criminal Justice* 285; McEvoy, K, *Paramilitary Imprisonment in Northern Ireland* (Oxford University Press, Oxford, 2001) ch 4.

[35] Steyn, J, 'Guantanamo Bay' (2003) 53 *International & Comparative Law Quarterly* 1. See also Sands, P, *Lawless World* (Allen Lane, London, 2005); Duffy, H, *The 'War on Terror' and the Framework of International Law* (Cambridge University Press, Cambridge, 2005); *R (Al-Skeini) v Secretary of State for Defence* [2007] UKHL 27.

[36] US Presidential Order, Detention, Treatment, and Trial of Certain Non-Citizens in the War Against Terrorism, 13 November 2001 (66 Federal Register 57831).

[37] US Department of Justice, *White Paper on NSA Legal Authorities, Legal Authorities Supporting the Activities of the National Security Agency Described by the President, 19 January 2006* (Washington DC, 2006).

[38] See Walker, C, 'The treatment of foreign terror suspects' (2007) 70 *Modern Law Review* 427.

terror' and claims instead that 'prosecution is—first, second, and third—the government's preferred approach when dealing with suspected terrorists'.[39]

The CONTEST strategy is measured according to the related Public Service Agreement 26[40] **1.18** and is overseen by a National Security Council.[41] Alongside the Home Office, the Ministry of Defence is concerned with the overseas aspects of 'Prevent' and 'Pursue'.[42] As well as governmental actors, there is increasing partnership with, and reliance upon, the private sector.[43] One illustration is the involvement of private military companies in all aspects of security work, especially logistics, guarding, and training. Another involves private protective security which arises since the private sector now controls most of the critical national infrastructure. Such a corporatist approach was evident when a 'Ring of Steel' was formed around the City of London, backed by state guarantees for commercial properties through the Reinsurance (Acts of Terrorism) Act 1993.[44] In 2007, the Centre for the Protection of the National Infrastructure was established to offer security advice and cooperation to a wider range of commercial sectors.[45]

Strictly speaking, CONTEST addresses international terrorism only, but the principles are **1.19** wider in the National Policing Plan 2005–08 which depicts domestic counter-terrorism as 'an overarching imperative'.[46]

In a liberal democracy at least, the ultimate test of success or failure of strategies against **1.20** terrorism is the maintenance of public support while at the same time respecting the fundamental values on which legitimacy and consensus cohere:[47]

> Few things would provide a more gratifying victory to the terrorist than for this country to undermine its traditional freedoms, in the very process of countering the enemies of those freedoms.

The corresponding aim of CONTEST is not victory but 'to reduce the risk from international terrorism, so that people can go about their daily lives freely and with confidence'.[48]

The European Union has adopted a very similar strategic response following 11 September **1.21** 2001.[49] Its initial rejoinder was a Plan of Action on Combating Terrorism on 21 September

---

[39] Hansard HC vol 472 col 561 (21 February 2008), Tony McNulty.

[40] HM Treasury, *PSA Delivery Agreement 26: reducing the risk to the UK and its interests overseas from international terrorism* <http://www.hm-treasury.gov.uk/d/pbr_csr07_psa26.pdf>, 2007.

[41] Home Office, *A Strong Britain in an Age of Uncertainty: The National Security Strategy* (Cm 7953, London, 2010) p 5.

[42] Ministry of Defence, *Defence Plan including the Government's Expenditure Plans 2008–2012* (Cm 7385, London, 2008) pp 5, 6, 14, 15, 19.

[43] See Cabinet Office, *The National Security Strategy of the United Kingdom* (Cm 7291, London, 2008) para 2.5. See also *Update 2009: Security for the Next Generation* (Cm 7590, London, 2009) and *A Strong Britain in an Age of Uncertainty: The National Security Strategy* (Cm 7953, London, 2010).

[44] See Walker, C, 'Political violence and commercial risk' (2004) 56 *Current Legal Problems* 531.

[45] See Walker, C, 'The governance of the Critical National Infrastructure' [2008] *Public Law* 323.

[46] (Home Office, London, 2004) para 1.3.

[47] Hansard HC vol 833 col 634 (29 November 1974), Roy Jenkins.

[48] Home Office, *Pursue, Prevent, Protect, Prepare: The United Kingdom's Strategy for Countering International Terrorism* (Cm7547, London, 2009) para 0.17.

[49] See Monar, J, 'Anti-terrorism law and policy: the case of the European Union' in Ramraj, VV, Hor, M, and Roach, K, *Global Anti-Terrorism Law and Policy* (Cambridge: Cambridge University Press, 2006); Bures, O, 'European Union counter-terrorism policy' (2006) 18 *Terrorism & Political Violence* 57; de Cesari, P, 'The European Union' in Nesi, G (ed), *International Cooperation in Counter-Terrorism* (Ashgate, Aldershot, 2006); O'Neill, M, 'A critical analysis of the European Union legal provisions on terrorism' (2008) 20 *Terrorism & Political Violence* 26; Wahl, T, 'The European Union as an actor in the fight against terrorism' in Wade, M and Maljevic, A, *A War on Terror?* (Springer, New York, 2010).

2001, which has been updated in 2004, 2005, and 2007,[50] and supplemented by its Action Plan on Radicalisation and Recruitment 2005.[51] These fragmented to-do lists have persisted, but the policy vacuum has gradually been filled. Under the auspices of a British Presidency, the Council of the European Union in 2005 issued the European Union Counter Terrorism Strategy which commits the European Union 'To combat terrorism globally while respecting human rights, and make Europe safer, allowing its citizens to live in an area of freedom, security and justice'.[52] While Member States retain the primary responsibility for combating terrorism, the EU role is important and comprises: strengthening national capabilities; facilitating European cooperation; developing collective capability; and promoting international partnership. The Strategy is divided into the four pillars—Prevent, Protect, Pursue, and Respond. This taxonomy sounds very redolent of the CONTEST approach and in substance is identical since 'Respond' covers the 'Prepare' agenda. While this duality may have pleased the British proponents, the strategy still fails to capture the distinctive role of the European Union or to identify priorities.[53]

1.22   Other countries have also pursued the more holistic response mapped out by CONTEST. For example, the 9/11 Commission in the US demanded action on protection and preparation,[54] and the mammoth Department for Homeland Security, founded in 2002,[55] represents the engine for change. The National Strategy for Combating Terrorism adopts short-term goals, including killing or capturing terrorists, denying havens and material resources, as well as strengthening resilience; the long-term project is to win the battle of ideas, ultimately by 'the advancement of freedom and human dignity through effective democracy'.[56]

Pathways out of terror

1.23   The more modest aim of CONTEST suggests that exit from terrorism requires more elements than the four 'P's. Thus, the resolution of terrorism often resides in a concoction of social, political, and economic retorts which ambitiously seek the delivery of 'abiding human needs',[57] alongside security attrition.[58] The precise mixture will be specific to the circumstances of each conflict and society, will be demanding, and will be distasteful. Governments do not relish negotiations with terrorists: 'The enemy of the moment always represented absolute evil, and it followed that any past or future agreement with him was impossible.'[59]

---

[50]   SN 140/01, 7906/04, 10586/04, 16090/04, 9809/1/05, 7233/07. See Bossong, R, 'The Action Plan on Combating Terrorism' (2007) 46 *Journal of Common Market Studies* 27.

[51]   COM (2005) 0313 final, 14781/05, 14782/05.

[52]   (14469/05, Strasbourg, 2005) p 2. See further the six monthly reports of the Counter-Terrorism Coordinator on the Implementation of the Strategy and Action Plan to Combat Terrorism (9809/1/05, 14734/1/05, 15704/05, 9589/06, 15266/06, 9666/07, 15411/07, 9416/08, 14862/08, 15912/08, 9715/09, 15538/09) and the EU Counter-Terrorism Strategy—discussion paper (15359/09).

[53]   Heisbourg, F (2005) 'The "European Security Strategy" is not a security strategy' in Everts, S et al (eds), *A European Way of War* (Centre for European Reform, London, 2005). Compare the United Nations Global Counter Terrorism Strategy (UNGA Res 60/288) which places a greater emphasis on addressing the conditions conducive to the spread of terrorism.

[54]   National Commission on Terrorist Attacks upon the United States, *Report* (GPO, Washington DC, 2004) p 383.

[55]   Homeland Security Act of 2002 (PL 107-296).

[56]   (Washington DC, 2006) p 8. The original version was published in 2003.

[57]   Gray, J, *Al Qaeda and What It Means to Be Modern* (Faber and Faber, London, 2003) p 4.

[58]   Jones, SG and Libicki, MC, *How Terrorist Groups End* (RAND, Santa Monica, 2008); Cronin, AK, *How Terrorism Ends* (Princeton University Press, Princeton, 2009).

[59]   Orwell, G, *Nineteen Eighty-Four* (Penguin, Harmondsworth, 1954) p 31.

Nevertheless, it is possible to find some common themes, which will be illustrated by the example of the Northern Ireland Peace Process, with the caveat that the same mixture does not necessarily translate to non-regional and non-ethnic terrorism.

The components of the Peace Process are both rational and irrational, and not all have been fully played out. One significant factor was the growing confidence, maturity, and authority of Sinn Féin. The second was the growing impact of counter-forces in the shape of the security forces and also Loyalist paramilitaries. The third was the willingness of the UK government to cooperate with the Irish government in constitutional terms.[60] The fourth was the malleability of the agreements being devised, thereby easing the pain of concessions. The fifth concerned the attitude of the largest paramilitary constituency—prisoners who were facing sacrificed lives.   **1.24**

The elements of settlement in Northern Ireland, in common with deals in other jurisdictions, involved an overall constitutional covenant, demilitarization, prisoner release, police and criminal justice reform, attention to victims, and the quest for truth and reconciliation. Implementation is detailed, and often deliberately complex and obtuse, and (as illustrated by dissident groups) incomplete. No more than an outline can be offered here.[61]   **1.25**

Many terrorist campaigns have simply fizzled out without being sanctified by any constitutional concessions. Many of the radical European movements of the 1970s met this fate. But more substantial and militarily intractable campaigns in Ireland and Latin America have produced outcomes with two common features. First, no side clearly wins or loses, and, second, coalition-style government with guaranteed involvement and representation is installed (sometimes referred to as consociationalism).[62] The Northern Ireland Peace Settlement—the Belfast Agreement of 1998 or the 'Good Friday Agreement'[63]—followed this pattern. As implemented by the Northern Ireland Act 1998, it includes: guarantees for the continuance of the Union with Britain at the same time as institutional involvement by the government of the Republic; a power-sharing executive and legislature; and a general emphasis on the recognition and enforcement of human rights for all.[64]   **1.26**

Decommissioning has continued under an international Decommissioning Commission. It was established by the Northern Ireland Arms Decommissioning Act 1997, which allows the grant of amnesty for the turning in of weapons or the process of 'putting them beyond use'. So as to check on progress towards decommissioning by paramilitary groups and their adherence to ceasefires and desistence, another body was set up under the Northern Ireland (Monitoring Commission etc) Act 2003, namely the Independent Monitoring Commission. Demilitarization has also been applied to the British Army presence in Northern Ireland. The Army is reducing to 5,000 (at the height of the 'Troubles' in 1972, the total reached 28,000), and many of its bases and installations have closed.   **1.27**

---

[60] See Anglo-Irish Agreement 1985 (Cmnd 9657); Downing St Declaration 1993 (Cm 2442); Northern Ireland Office, *Frameworks for the Future* (Cm 2964, 1995).

[61] See further Wilford, R (ed), *Aspects of the Belfast Agreement* (Oxford University Press, Oxford, 2001); Campbell, C et al, 'The frontiers of legal analysis: reframing the transition in Northern Ireland' (2003) 66 *Modern Law Review* 317; Cox, M et al (eds), *A Farewell to Arms?* (2nd edn, Manchester University Press, Manchester, 2006); Bew, P, *The Making and Unmaking of the Good Friday Agreement* (Liffey Press, Dublin, 2007); Barton, B and Roche, PJ (eds), *The Northern Ireland Question* (Palgrave Macmillan, New York, 2009).

[62] See McGarry, J and O'Leary, B, *The Northern Ireland Conflict: Consociational Engagements* (Oxford University Press, Oxford, 2004).

[63] British Irish Agreement reached in the multi-party negotiations (Cm 3883, London, 1998).

[64] See Bell, C, *Peace Agreements and Human Rights* (Oxford University Press, 2000).

1.28   Prisoners are often the most vital constituency in a paramilitary movement, and it was clear that concessions would have to be made to them. These reforms were some of the most unpalatable aspects of the Peace Process, because convicts, including mass murderers, were released under the terms of the Northern Ireland (Sentences) Act 1998 (described further in Chapter 11). A total of 447 were released within a couple of years, and the most potent symbol of paramilitary imprisonment, the Maze Prison, closed in 2000.[65]

1.29   The reform of criminal justice and policing remains one of the most sensitive and intractable issues. Following the Belfast Agreement, the *Patten Report* on policing was issued in 1999.[66] Changes were implemented by the Police (Northern Ireland) Act 2000, which abolished the Royal Ulster Constabulary and set up the Police Service of Northern Ireland which was designed to be more representative of, and responsive to, the Catholic community. However, Sinn Féin's refusal to support the new police disrupted the new Northern Ireland Executive which was suspended in 2002 until the accord enshrined in the Northern Ireland (St Andrews Agreement) Act 2006. The result was a new executive once Sinn Féin agreed in January 2007 to support police institutions. There was a further Northern Ireland Act 2009 to pave the way for devolution of policing and justice powers, which was secured in 2010 and implemented further by the devolved Department of Justice Act (Northern Ireland) 2010.

1.30   On criminal justice reform, the Justice (Northern Ireland) Act 2002 and the Justice (Northern Ireland) Act 2004 implement the recommendations of the Criminal Justice Review Group in its report, *Review of the Criminal Justice System in Northern Ireland* in 2000. The main outcomes of the legislation are to update the system in line with English modes, but there are some special provisions about appointments and oaths to demonstrate equality.

1.31   Victims and their treatment have been prominent items on the agenda of the Peace Process as each former protagonist vies for recognition of its special sense of grievance. The implementation of this agenda will be more fully described in Chapter 11. The victims' agenda is currently being advanced through the Commission for Victims and Survivors Act (Northern Ireland) 2008.[67]

1.32   The final element of the Peace Process is truth and reconciliation, an idea most associated with South Africa.[68] The (Bloomfield) Report of the Northern Ireland Victims Commissioner, *We Will Remember Them*,[69] was doubtful about such a vast enterprise and the mixed outcomes of the South African precedent. There is usually no agreed history of conflict, and so the platform given to one set of participants can serve to antagonize the other side, without any greater empathy being engendered. Nevertheless, the United Kingdom government has experimented with various levels of 'truth' inquiries. The most ambitious has been the Bloody Sunday Inquiry,[70] set up in 1998 under Lord Saville to re-examine the events considered by

---

    [65] See McEvoy, K et al, 'Resistance, transition and exclusion' (2004) 16 *Terrorism & Political Violence* 646; Shirlow, P and McEvoy, K, *Beyond the Wire* (Pluto Press, London, 2008).
    [66] The Independent Commission on Policing for Northern Ireland, *New Beginning: Policing in Northern Ireland* (Northern Ireland Office, Belfast, 1999). See Conway, V, 'Lost in translation' (2008) 54 *Northern Ireland Legal Quarterly* 417.
    [67] The appointment of a single Commissioner under the Victims and Survivors (Northern Ireland) Order 2006 was challenged: *In re Downes* [2006] NICA 24, [2007] NIQB 1.
    [68] South Africa Truth and Reconciliation Commission, <http://www.doj.gov.za/trc>. See Campbell, C and Ní Aoláin, F, 'Local meets global–transitional justice in Northern Ireland' (2003) 26 *Fordham International Law Journal* 871; Bell, C et al, 'Justice discourses in transition' (2004) 13 *Social & Legal Studies* 305.
    [69] Northern Ireland Office, Belfast, 1998.
    [70] *Report of the Bloody Sunday Inquiry* (2010–11 HC 29).

the Widgery report on the shootings of thirteen civilians at a demonstration in Londonderry in 1972.[71] The Inquiry reported in 2010 and was accompanied by a fulsome Prime Ministerial apology for the loss of life.[72] More specific inquiries were established under retired Canadian Judge Peter Cory. His reports, issued in 2003 and 2004, into the deaths of Pat Finucane, Rosemary Nelson, Robert Hamill, and Billy Wright, have resulted in the commitment to hold ongoing public inquiries.[73] The Inquiries Act 2005 limits the scope of these inquiries, which Cory has criticized, and has prevented any progress in the case of Finucane because of objections by relatives. The costs and delays of the Bloody Sunday Inquiry have deterred the government from promising any further grand inquiry.[74] The future model is the Inquiries Act 2005, despite criticisms that it unduly limits and controls investigations.[75]

Alongside these 'truth' inquiries, policing investigations have been resumed into the many **1.33** unsolved cases from the 'Troubles'. An Historical Enquiries Team was set up in 2005 as a unit of the Police Service of Northern Ireland to investigate 3,269 murders committed between 1968 and 1998 in connection with the Troubles.[76] It is staffed by police officers and civilian staff recruited both within Northern Ireland and externally, with the latter in command. There are also investigations by the Police Ombudsman for Northern Ireland.[77]

Killings and attacks have reduced substantially in Northern Ireland. On 28 July 2005, the **1.34** IRA called for an end to the armed campaign: 'The leadership of *Oglaigh na hEireann* has formally ordered an end to the armed campaign.' But the 'Peace' comprises an absence of overt violence, especially against the state, rather than communal harmony, with a slide from paramilitarism into organized crime.

C. Legal Strategies for Counter-Terrorism

Types of legal counter-terrorism

The counter-strategy to terrorism must aim at both political and violent aspects of the **1.35** phenomenon, but by means which respect fundamental values and retain legitimacy. Fundamental values will be explored later. Within those parameters, the following elements of legal policy are in play: the rule of law; proportionality; international cooperation; and criminalization and control.

---

[71] See *Report of a Tribunal appointed to inquire into the events on Sunday 30th January, 1972* (1971–72 HC 220).

[72] Hansard HC vol 511 col 739 (15 June 2010), David Cameron.

[73] See *Cory Collusion Inquiry Reports*, Billy Wright (2003–04 HC 472) and Billy Wright Inquiry (2010–11 HC 431 and <http://www.billywrightinquiry.org/>); Pat Finucane (2003–04 HC 470); Robert Hamill (2003–04 HC 471) and Robert Hamill Inquiry (<http://www.roberthamillinquiry.org/>); Rosemary Nelson (2003–04 HC 473) and Rosemary Nelson Inquiry (<http://www.rosemarynelsoninquiry.org/>). See further *Finucane v United Kingdom*, App no 29178/95, 2003-VIII.

[74] Hansard HC vol 511 col 741 (15 June 2010), David Cameron. See further Blom-Cooper, L, 'What went wrong on Bloody Sunday' [2010] *Public Law* 61.

[75] See Joint Committee on Human Rights, *Scrutiny: First Progress Report* (2004–05, HL 26/HC 224) ch 2; Requa, M, 'Truth, transition and the Inquiries Act 2005' [2007] *European Human Rights Law Review* 404; Gay, O, *Investigatory inquiries and the Inquiries Act 2005* (SN/PC/02599, House of Commons, London, 2009).

[76] <http://www.psni.police.uk/historical-enquiries-team>; Northern Ireland Affairs Committee, *Policing and Criminal Justice in Northern Ireland: the Cost of Policing the Past* (2007–08 HC 333 and *Government Response* HC 1084).

[77] See *RUC Investigation of the alleged involvement of the late Father James Chesney in the bombing of Claudy on 31 July 1972* (Belfast, 2010).

1.36 The rule of law principle can be illustrated in various ways. One is a willingness to ensure there are express rules rather than vague discretion. Thus, legislation is preferable to ancient prerogative powers (other than in 'particularly extreme and urgent circumstances')[78] or to administrative guidance. Second is a determination to ensure that action against terrorism complies with those rules, to articulate reasons for action, to investigate possible breaches, and to allow effective challenges to excesses. As expressed in *R v Wilkes*: 'We must not regard political consequences; however formidable soever they may be; if rebellion was the certain consequence, we are bound to say "*fiat justitia, ruat caelum*".' ('Though the heavens fall, let justice be done.')[79] Third is an acceptance of constitutionalism—principles which reflect the values of individual rights, democratic and legal accountability (discussed later in this section). It also embodies a principle of 'normalcy'—that the overall purpose should be the restoration of normal existence without the regular invocation of special powers.

1.37 Proportionality will also be considered more precisely later. For now, it is sufficient to avoid a situation where anti-terrorism efforts divert from other pressing social policies, where the expense becomes ruinous, and where the inconvenience and intrusion of security serve as constant reminders of insecurity. It was Michael Chertoff, Secretary of the Department for Homeland Security, who stated: 'We do not want a regime in which we are so focused on risk to the exclusion of all else that we lock everything down and we destroy our country.'[80]

1.38 International cooperation has been increasingly harnessed since the mid 1990s, when there began to be a change of attitude over support for 'freedom-fighters' at a time when almost all overt colonialism had been dismantled. There was at the same time a perception of the growing sophistication of terrorist groups and the concern that international boundaries were being exploited against the interests of sovereign states. These trends were exemplified by the multi-national team which attacked on 11 September 2001. International cooperation was in turn boosted by the UNSCR 1373 of 28 September 2001, which required compliance with international laws against terrorism financing, demanded no safe havens, and set up the Counter-Terrorism Committee to oversee national implementation. Other aspects of international cooperation include a range of extra-jurisdictional offences, cooperation between policing, security, and judicial authorities, and the greater willingness to extradite suspects.

1.39 Having determined to take action against terrorism in line with the foregoing principles, state responses can broadly be categorized as falling under four models: criminalization, executive, war, and exit.[81] In all cases, the seriousness and complexity of terrorism will demand that the state's resources for intelligence-gathering are fully deployed, and the availability of intelligence will in turn ensure that all four approaches are available.

1.40 As will be explained in Part III, the criminal prosecution model is expressed to be the preference, and it has been actively pursued even in adverse conditions such as in Northern Ireland.[82] Though prosecution has been the fate of many, this criminal justice model is not

---

[78] See Ministry of Justice, *The Governance of Britain: Review of Executive Royal Prerogative Powers* (London, 2009) para 72. See for history, Rubin, GR, 'The royal prerogative or a statutory code?' in Eales, R and Sullivan, D, *The Political Context of Law* (Hambledon, London, 1987).

[79] (1770) 98 ER 327 at 347 per Lord Mansfield. See further, Mathews, AS, *Freedom, State Security and the Rule of Law* (Sweet & Maxwell, London, 1988).

[80] *Financial Times* 13 March 2006, p 1.

[81] There is correspondence here with the inward and outward facing typology of Tapia Valdes, JA, 'A typology of national security policies' (1982) 9 *Yale Journal of World Public Order* 10.

[82] See *Diplock Report*.

for all. The peril of contemporary terrorism, characterized by wanton mass attacks on civilians, demands intervention at an anticipatory stage of the criminal enterprise. But early intervention at the stage of preparatory actions might also pre-empt the criminal justice demand of proof beyond reasonable doubt, and it may in any event be unappealing to the security services to reveal in the public domain of a courtroom their methods and sources. Therefore, models of executive measures have persisted alongside criminal prosecution for all but a few months during the past three decades.

The 'executive model' includes measures such as disruptive operations and detention with-   **1.41** out trial, which was used frequently in Northern Ireland and was last revived under Part IV of the ATCSA 2001 until replaced by control orders by the PTA 2005. The other such measure was exclusion under successive Prevention of Terrorism (Temporary Provisions) Acts 1974–96.[83] As well as individual measures, the executive approach also comprises more general policies, such as pressure through communal engagement, diplomatic engagement, and economic means.[84]

The opposite of a criminal justice approach is to take the suspects entirely out of criminal   **1.42** justice or even beyond the realms of individual executive measures. One might depict this approach as the 'war' model. The 'war on terror' was in part adopted by the US, after the September 11 attacks,[85] not just as a rhetorical device[86] but also as engendering operative codes on detention, interrogation, trial, and surveillance. This policy strand is exemplified by the abyss of 'the legal black hole'[87] that appeared in the detention and trial regimes at Guantánamo Bay. This mode of approach is highly controversial because of its real incursions upon liberty and due process and because it does not match international law as understood by others. It is now to be dismantled in the US,[88] and has been rejected by the UK government. Former Foreign Secretary, David Miliband, stated that 'the notion is misleading and mistaken. The issue is not whether we need to attack the use of terror at its roots, with all the tools available. We must. The question is how.'[89] This rejection certainly pertains to domestic law, though not without the appearance of some elements of implementation, such as the arming of specialist police units. In addition, 'counter-insurgency' abroad is practised in Afghanistan[90] as a form of counter-terrorism.[91]

---

[83] See Walker, CP, 'Constitutional governance and special powers against terrorism' (1997) 35 *Columbia Journal of Transnational Law* 1.

[84] See Forst, B, *Terrorism, Crime, and Public Policy* (Cambridge University Press, New York, 2009) ch 9.

[85] See Presidential Order, Detention, Treatment, and Trial of Certain Non-Citizens in the War Against Terrorism, of the 13 November 2001 (66 Federal Register 57831).

[86] Compare Forst, B, *Terrorism, Crime, and Public Policy* (Cambridge University Press, New York, 2009) p 18; Ward, I., *Law, Text, Terror* (Cambridge University Press, Cambridge, 2009) pp 20–21.

[87] Steyn, J., 'Guantanamo Bay' (2003) 53 *International & Comparative Law Quarterly* 1. See further Scraton, P (ed), *Beyond September 11* (Pluto, Cambridge, 2002) p 8; Strawson, J (ed), *Law After Ground Zero* (Glasshouse Press, London, 2002) p xi; Greenwood, C, 'War, terrorism and international law (2003) 56 *Current Legal Problems* 505; Lowe, V, '"Clear and present danger": Response to terrorism' (2005) 54 *International and Comparative Law Quarterly* 185.

[88] Review and Disposition of Individuals Detained at the Guantánamo Bay Naval Base and Close of Detention Facilities and for a Review of Detention Policy Options Executive Orders 13492 and 13493 (74 Federal Register 4897 and 4901).

[89] *The Guardian* 15 January 2009, p 29.

[90] Home Office, *Pursue, Prevent, Protect, Prepare: The United Kingdom's Strategy for Countering International Terrorism* (Cm 7547, London, 2009) paras 7.15–7.16.

[91] Cabinet Office, *The National Security Strategy of the United Kingdom: Update 2009: Security for the Next Generation* (Cm 7590, London, 2009) paras 2.27, 6.47.

1.43   Military deployment against terrorism may enjoy some advantages. It meets some public and media expectations for severe and punitive action, which may foment dissent and deterrence amongst the terrorists. Conversely, military operations are conducive to a diminution of the safeguards of normal civil society[92] and commonly incur in practice disproportionate and escalating responses, which may stimulate sympathy for the terrorists and loss of support from international allies. Military intervention may also produce false expectations amongst the general public that terrorism can be defeated solely on a security basis.

1.44   The fourth approach is the 'exit model'. It seeks the removal of foreign terrorist suspects without criminal or executive legal resolution. It instead averts their threat by way of deportation or exclusion, perhaps further based on a withdrawal of citizenship. The 'exit model' has been pursued with vigour after the 7 July 2005 bombings, which in part were blamed on the malign influence of foreign demagogues, but has been restrained by court action as shall be described in Chapter 7.

Justifications for special laws against terrorism

1.45   Implicit in the TA 2000 is the claim that extensive legislation against political violence and the sense of emergency it can create is needed now and for ever after. Sunset clauses attached only to Pt VII and to some successor provisions in 2007. Renewal without limit has also been applied to control orders under the PTA 2005 and to 28-day police detention under the TA 2006. Amongst the disadvantages of special laws are that they are unnecessary adjuncts to 'normal' laws relating to police powers, such as those in PACE, and regular criminal offences, that they engender abuses, and that they damage the country's international reputation.[93] Therefore, the implicit claim to an ongoing need for distinct anti-terrorist laws should be tested. It can be answered at three levels which, for a century or so, have regularly convinced the ruling elites of many countries to resort to special laws.[94]

1.46   The first level concerns the powers and duties of states. In principle, it is justifiable for liberal democracies to be empowered to defend their existence, for 'The first priority of any Government is to ensure the security and safety of the nation and all members of the public'.[95] A democracy is not a suicide pact,[96] and exceptional measures have long been recognized as a legitimate reaction of a liberal democracy to clear and present dangers.[97] This approach is reflected in the European Convention on Human Rights. Article 17 prohibits the engagement

---

[92] See Allen, FA, *The Habits of Legality* (Oxford University Press, New York, 1996) pp 37–40.

[93] *Lloyd Report*, paras 5.6–5.9.

[94] See Porter, B, *The Origins of the Vigilant State* (Weidenfeld & Nicolson, London, 1978) p 192; Walker, C, 'Clamping down on terrorism in the United Kingdom' (2006) 4 *Journal of International Criminal Justice* 1137.

[95] Home Office, *Pursue, Prevent, Protect, Prepare: The United Kingdom's Strategy for Countering International Terrorism* (Cm 7547, London, 2009) p 4.

[96] *Terminiello v Chicago* (1949) 337 US 1 at 37 per Douglas J.

[97] See Chowdhury, SR, *The Rule of Law in a State of Emergency* (Pinter, London, 1989); Finn, JE, *Constitutions in Crisis* (Oxford University Press, Oxford, 1991); Oraa, J, *Human Rights in States of Emergency in International Law* (Clarendon Press, Oxford, 1992); Fitzpatrick, JM, *Human Rights In Crisis* (University of Pennsylvania Press, Philadelphia, 1994); Sajó, A (ed), *Militant Democracy* (Eleven International Publishing, Utrecht, 2004); Ferejohn, J and Pasquino, P, 'The law of exception' (2004) 2 *International Journal of Constitutional Law* 210; Agamben, G, *The State of Exception* (University of Chicago Press, Chicago, 2005); Gross, O and ní Aoláin, F, *Law in Times of Crisis* (Cambridge University Press, Cambridge, 2006); Dyzenhaus, D, *The Constitution of Law* (Cambridge University Press, Cambridge, 2006); Thiel, M (ed), *The 'Militant Democracy' Principle in Modern Democracies* (Ashgate, Aldershot, 2009).

in any activity or performance of any act aimed at the destruction of rights and freedoms. Article 15 affords the power of derogation in time of emergency threatening the life of the nation.[98] In the context of Northern Ireland terrorism, this derogation facility was repeatedly invoked up to 1984, and from 1988 until 2001. It was upheld in relation to a scheme of seven days' police detention in *Brannigan and McBride v United Kingdom*.[99] One of the express purposes of the TA 2000 was to allow the notice of derogation to be withdrawn (which happened on 26 February 2001), though it continued in respect of the British Islands until 5 May 2006. A further derogation was entered in respect of the detention measures in Pt IV of the ATCSA 2001 but that in turn was withdrawn on 14 March 2005.[100]

Aside from any power to take action, there is a state responsibility to act against violence in order **1.47** to safeguard the protective right to life of citizens. Security is a 'broadly shared social good', and the state has a pre-eminent security role in delivering it.[101] This duty principally arises as an aspect of Article 2 of the European Convention on Human Rights, though the right to life does not entail absolute guarantees of safety.[102] In addition, states should more generally implement the enjoyment of rights and democracy (under Article 1 of the Convention). According to various United Nations instruments, states must not harbour or condone terrorism.[103]

In summary, state security and personal security are valuable to society. However, they must **1.48** not wholly subsume other values, as encapsulated in the wider concept of human security.[104] Therefore, 'security' may be viewed either as instrumental (as a condition for the securing of higher values such as individual rights)[105] or as a cipher for a bundle of rights, such as the right to life or liberty,[106] rather than as an independent and conflicting value.

The second level of justification for special laws is more morally grounded. This argument **1.49** points to the illegitimacy of terrorism as a form of political expression. Many of its emanations are almost certainly national or international crimes, even if the political cause of the terrorist is deemed legitimate.

Thirdly, terrorism may be depicted as a specialized form of criminality which presents peculiar **1.50** complications in terms of policing and criminal process by reference to its structure, capacity

---

[98] Emergencies must be 'existential' in this sense, but Article 15 does not exhaust the range of legitimate anti-terrorism laws. Compare: Ackerman, B, *Before the Next Attack* (Yale University Press, New Haven, 2006) p 172.

[99] App nos 14553/89, 14554/89, Ser A 258-B. See further *Marshall v United Kingdom*, App no 41571/98, 10 July 2001; *Kerr v United Kingdom*, App no 40451/98, 10 July 2001.

[100] See Human Rights Act (Amendment Order) 2005, SI 2005/1071.

[101] Loader, I and Walker, N, *Civilizing Security* (Cambridge University Press, Cambridge, 2007) pp 70, 171, 194; Zedner, L, *Security* (Routledge, Abingdon, 2009) p 66.

[102] See *Lloyd Report*, para 5.15; Hornle, T, 'Hijacked airplanes' (2007) 10 *New Criminal Law Review* 582; *X v Ireland*, App no 6040/73, 16 YB 388 (1973); *W v UK*, App no 9348/81, 32 DR 190 (1983); *X v UK*, App no 9825/82, 8 EHRR 49 (1985); *M v UK and Ireland*, App no 9837/82, 47 DR 27 (1986); *K v UK and Ireland*, App no 9839/82, 4 March 1986.

[103] See United Nations General Assembly Resolutions 40/61 of 9 December 1985; 49/60 of 9 December 1994; UNSCR 1368 of 12 September 2001 and UNSCR 1373 of 28 September 2001.

[104] See UN Commission on Human Security, *Human Security Now* (United Nations, New York, 2003); Commission on Human Security; Annan, K, *In Larger Freedom* (United Nations, New York, 2005); Callaway LR and Harrelson-Stephens, J, 'Toward a theory of terrorism: human security as a determinant of terrorism' (2006) 29 *Studies in Conflict and Terrorism* 773.

[105] Téson, FR, 'Liberal security' in Wilson, RA (ed), *Human Rights in the 'War on Terror'* (Cambridge University Press, Cambridge, 2005).

[106] Lazarus, L, 'Mapping the right to security' in Goold, BJ and Lazarus, L, *Security and Human Rights* (Hart, Oxford, 2007) p 344.

to intimidate, and sophistication. It therefore demands a specialist response to overcome the complications posed for normal detection methods and processes within criminal justice. Just as variations have been adopted against, for example, rapists, serious fraudsters, and drug traffickers,[107] so terrorists may warrant variant treatment because of their atypical organization, methods, and targets. As for organization, paramilitary groups can typically hinder the re-establishment of public safety and democratic processes because of their sophistication, the transnational scale of their activities, and the difficulty of obtaining assistance from paramilitary-affected communities because of the impact of intimidation or even popularity.

1.51 One must expect that 'democracies respond when there is blood on the streets',[108] and there is righteous justification for them to do so based on the international law duties to combat terrorism and the duty in national and international law to protect individual life. The *Newton Report* found the response model of the TA 2000 'compelling'—it is desirable to have on a permanent basis, 'considered, properly regulated counter-terrorism legislation' with its own 'tailored safeguards'.[109]

1.52 Whilst emergency laws have allure, they also entail dangers. There arises pressure to respond quickly and decisively, which can produce ill-considered 'panic' emergency law-making. Secondly, fear is consciously or unconsciously amplified because of the vividness of the terrorist damage or injury and its strange provenance,[110] and this exaggeration may even be fostered by political elites to bolster their legitimacy and powers, as already noted. In addition, the apparent immediate and tangible gain of present security will be preferred to the possible future and rather intangible losses, such as a loss of legitimacy. The ill-design arising from these two grounds may result in legislation which is ineffective and merely symbolic, or it may impact excessively or inappropriately given that terrorism is rarely an existential threat. Thirdly, 'emergency' laws regularly linger beyond the original emergency. Fear and risk are endemic, not transitory, so normality is hard to reassert. The fourth point is that the executive branch of the state will become unduly dominant. People expect action not words, and the ability to take action is held by the executive not the courts or Parliament. In addition, the executive has the detailed information and intelligence and so appears better placed to act. Fifthly, emergencies are the time of greatest threat to individual rights. Individual rights are often depicted as obstacles to public safety and security. Sixthly, even if Parliament does provide new laws, sweeping though they may be, there remains the grave danger that the executive or the security forces, will exceed them. Seventhly, emergency or special laws will provide a dangerous precedent which will result in contagion—that special powers will be adapted to unintended situations or the adoption within 'normal' laws of measures which become commonplace incursions onto liberty. This charge is commonly lodged against special powers in Northern Ireland becoming a proving ground for Britain,[111]

---

[107] Sexual Offences (Amendment) Act 1976; Drug Trafficking Offences Act 1994; Criminal Justice Act 1987.

[108] Collins, JM, 'And the walls came tumbling down' (2002) 39 *American Criminal Law Review* 1261 at 1261.

[109] *Newton Report*, paras 14, 107, 111.

[110] See Gross, O, 'Chaos and rules' (2003) 112 *Yale Law Journal* 1011; Posner, EA and Vermeule, A, 'Accommodating emergencies' (2003) 56 *Stanford Law Review* 605 and 'Emergencies and democratic failure' (2006) 92 *Virginia Law Review* 1091; Marks, JH, '9/11 + 3/11 + 7/7 =? What counts in counterterrorism?' (2006) 37 *Columbia Human Rights Law Review* 559; Sunstein, CR, *Worst-Case Scenarios* (Harvard University Press, Cambridge, 2007).

[111] See Hillyard, P, 'The normalisation of special powers: From Northern Ireland to Britain' in Scraton, P (ed), *Law, Order and the Authoritarian State* (Open University Press, Milton Keynes, 1987).

but the evidence is equivocal since British distaste for policy transfer has been evident.[112] Eighthly, security laws tend not to be applied evenly. Ethnic minorities or aliens will suffer most either through discriminatory implementation or through the higher chances of abuse and error.[113] Thus, the legislation will trigger disaffection and discontent, for example among young Muslim males.[114] The causes of violent *jihadist* terrorism[115] seem less dependent on the abusive exercise of security powers than was the position in Northern Ireland.[116] Nonetheless, the targeting of suspect communities might hinder the identification and detection of terrorists by encouraging sympathy for their cause and a reduction of voluntary assistance.

The cumulative outcomes of these features is an inclination towards overuse—that instead **1.53** of a 'break glass in case of emergency' law model, there will be too much smashing of the glass to take out the special laws in preference to serviceable normal laws. A debate is therefore necessary about balance and limits.

Balance and limits

There has long been official and academic debate around the appropriate 'balance' between **1.54** security and liberties, with the assumption that liberties in an emergency are 'strictly luxury products'.[117] Thus, the Home Office paper, *Counter-Terrorism Powers: Reconciling Security and Liberty in an Open Society*, stated:[118]

> There is nothing new about the dilemma of how best to ensure the security of a society, while protecting the individual rights of its citizens. Democratic governments have always had to strike a balance between the powers of the state and the rights of individuals.

It is rational to react to the consequences of terrorism and to the risks of upholding rights in **1.55** changed circumstances. It is rational to reassure the public in times of crisis.[119] What is less rational is the assertion that security and liberty can be 'balanced' in a causal 'hydraulic' relationship,[120] having regard also to the difficulties of cognitive measurement and the dubious validity of consequentialist arguments when weighing deontic values which cut across both liberty and security. In short, security is a value for liberty, and liberty is a value for security.[121]

In reality, experienced commentators have long eschewed any simplistic balance between **1.56** security and rights and have sought to develop more intellectually rational, structured, and

---

[112] See Mulcahy, A, 'The other lessons from Ireland' (2005) 2 *European Journal of Criminology* 185.

[113] Cole, D, *Enemy Aliens* (New Press, New York, 2006). Compare Posner, EA and Vermeule, A, 'Emergencies and democratic failure' (2006) 92 *Virginia Law Review* 1091.

[114] See Home Affairs Committee, *Terrorism and Community Relations* (2003–04 HC 165) para 43.

[115] '*Jihadist* terrorism' reflects the adaptation of the Qu'ranic concept of 'struggle' or 'striving' which is commonly invoked by such groups: see Rehman, J, *Islamic State Practices, International Law and the Threat from Terrorism* (Hart Publishing, Oxford, 2005).

[116] See Hussein, E, *The Islamist* (London: Penguin, 2007).

[117] Rossiter, CL, *Constitutional Dictatorship* (Princeton University Press, Princeton, 1948) p 5.

[118] *Home Office Response to Newton Report*, p i.

[119] Ackerman, B, 'The emergency constitution' (2004) 113 *Yale Law Journal* 1029 at 1037.

[120] Ashworth, A, 'Security, terrorism, and the value of human rights' in Goold, BJ, and Lazarus, L, *Security and Human Rights* (Hart, Oxford, 2007) p 208.

[121] See Waldron, J, 'Security and liberty: the image of balance' (2003) 11 *Journal of Political Philosophy* 191; Zedner, L, 'Securing liberty in the face of terror' (2005) 32 *Journal of Law & Society* 507 at 511; Roach, K, 'Must we trade rights for security?' (2006) 27 *Cardozo Law Review* 2157; Meisels, T, *The Trouble with Terror* (Cambridge University Press, Cambridge, 2008) ch 3. Compare Posner, RA, *Not a Suicide Pact* (Oxford University Press, New York, 2006).

finely attuned mechanisms for choice even if there remains ultimately a 'tragic choice'.[122] An example is Lord Lloyd, who set four principles against which the legislation should be judged in his 1996 review:[123]

(i) Legislation against terrorism should approximate as closely as possible to the ordinary criminal law and procedure.[124]

(ii) Additional statutory offences and powers may be justified, but only if they are necessary to meet the anticipated threat. They must then strike the right balance between the needs of security and the rights and liberties of the individual.

(iii) The need for additional safeguards should be considered alongside any additional powers.

(iv) The law should comply with the UK's obligations in international law.

1.57 Likewise, the 'guiding principles' behind the *National Security Strategy* comprise 'human rights, rule of law, legitimate and accountable government, justice, freedom, tolerance, and opportunity for all'.[125] Building upon these precepts and upon other formulations in these directions,[126] the normative setting should be understood as 'constitutionalism' which can be understood according to three parameters. As well as these principled concerns, 'policy relevance and impact' must be assured. Legislation should meet demands of efficacy and efficiency, and these attributes should be judged in the light of the CONTEST strategy. Indeed, these tests ought to be the first to be applied, for if a measure does not sensibly advance the chosen strategy, there is no point in subjecting that design to further tests.

Rights audit

1.58 There is first a need for a 'rights audit'.[127] Whilst there have been episodes of official angst about the imputed hindrance of rights on terrorism operations,[128] almost all official reviewers of the legislation, from Lord Diplock in 1972 onwards, have been enjoined to take account of human rights which have even proven resilient under the challenge of supreme emergencies.[129] Thus, the principle here advanced is that the rights of individuals must be respected according to traditions of the domestic jurisdictions and the demands of international law. For the United Kingdom, the two are largely assimilated by the Human Rights Act 1998.[130] The 1998 Act has had positive impacts in shaping and promoting political debate, in emboldening the courts, and in creating new pathways for rights discourse to become more explicit and prominent.[131]

---

[122] See Ackerman, B, 'The emergency constitution' (2004) 113 *Yale Law Journal* 1029 at 1077.

[123] *Lloyd Report*, para 3.1.

[124] See further *Newton Report*, para B1. Lloyd's principles are otherwise accepted: para C94.

[125] Cm 7291, London, 2008, para 2.1, and see also (Cm 7953, London, 2010,) para 0.9.

[126] See Walker, CP, 'Constitutional governance and special powers against terrorism' (1997) 35 *Columbia Journal of Transnational Law* 1; Cotler, I, 'Terrorism, security and rights' (2002) 14 *National Journal of Constitutional Law* 1; Loader, I and Walker, N, *Civilizing Security* (Cambridge University Press, Cambridge, 2007) p 216.

[127] See Marks, JH, '9/11 + 3/11 + 7/7 =? What counts in counterterrorism?' (2006) 37 *Columbia Human Rights Law Review* 559.

[128] See Department for Constitutional Affairs, *Review of the Implementation of the Human Rights Act* (London, 2006). Suggested reforms are not intended to affect the anti-terrorism laws: Ministry of Justice, *Rights and Responsibilities* (Cm 7577, London, 2009) para 4.26.

[129] See Statman, D, 'Supreme emergencies revisited' (2006) 117 *Ethics* 58; Cole, D, 'Human rights and the challenge of terror' in Weinberg, L, *Democratic Responses to Terrorism* (Routledge, Abingdon, 2008) p 159.

[130] See Warbrick, C, 'The principles of the ECHR and the response of states to terrorism' [2002] *European Human Rights Law Review* 287; Sottioux, S, *Terrorism and the Limitation of Rights* (Hart, Oxford, 2008).

[131] See Gearty, C, '11 September 2001, counter-terrorism and the Human Rights Act' (2005) 32 *Journal of Law & Society* 18; Hiebert, JL, 'Parliamentary review of terrorism measures' (2005) 65 *Modern Law Review* 676.

Since rights values focus on the treatment of individuals, there is a special role for the courts **1.59**
as the prime deliberative forum. The concept of 'proportionality' will often be invoked to
resolve the permissible incursions of security interests. In *A v Secretary of State for the Home
Department*,[132] the House of Lords explained that when assessing whether an incursion into
individual rights is arbitrary or excessive, the court must ask itself, 'whether: (i) the legislative
objective is sufficiently important to justify limiting a fundamental right; (ii) the measures
designed to meet the legislative objective are rationally connected to it; and (iii) the means
used to impair the right or freedom are no more than is necessary to accomplish the objective'.
A fourth test has sometimes been added: (iv) whether the measure strikes a proper balance
between the gains for the policy purpose and the incursion into individual rights.[133] In
Huang and others v Secretary of State for the Home Department, this formula was rendered as
a balance between the interests of the community and the right of the individual.[134] These
tests of proportionality correspond to Lord Lloyd's initial three tests and can be elaborated
further. In respect of (i), the perceived nature and level of threat to security should be
examined, with the expectation that it should be clear and present in order to warrant
intervention. In respect of (ii), the question is whether the security measures are fit for the
purpose addressing that particular threat at that particular level. As for (iii), one should ask
whether there are 'adequate and effective guarantees against abuse'[135] and whether there are
workable, less intrusive alternative responses. On (iv), are the drawbacks of the measure, for
example in terms of success rate or impact on wider security concerns such as community
cooperation, so great as to outweigh any benefits?

Proportionality in the context of terrorism laws must be appreciated in relation to different **1.60**
categories of rights. For those rights which are treated as absolute (such as Article 3), no
balance or model of accommodation is permitted by law.[136] As stated in *Chahal v United
Kingdom*: 'in protecting their communities from terrorist violence . . . the Convention
prohibits in absolute terms torture or inhuman or degrading treatment or punishment,
irrespective of the victim's conduct'.[137] Rights to liberty and due process under Articles 5
and 6 may be termed 'fundamental' rather than absolute. Here, the language of proportionality is recited[138] but applies only to the limited circumstances where these rights might be
curtailed for the sake of the rights of others, such as victims or witnesses. Other rights
(Articles 8 to 11) are provisional and may be proportionately balanced not only against
other rights but also, according to those Articles, against specified societal interests. Here,
the broad language of balance between security and rights finds some resonance but is still
not left as a balance beyond the language of rights.

When there is derogation under Article 15, reflection must be given to the existence of the **1.61**
emergency and to whether any measure in pursuance of it is 'strictly required' (which appears

---

[132] [2004] UKHL 56 at para 30.
[133] *R v Oakes* (1986) 1 SCR 103 at 139.
[134] [2007] UKHL 11 at para 19.
[135] *Klass v Germany*, App no 5029/71, Ser A 28 (1978) para 50.
[136] See Dershowitz, A, *Why Terrorism Works* (Yale University Press, New Haven, 2002); Ignatieff, M, *The
Lesser Evil* (Edinburgh University Press, Edinburgh, 2005); Gross, O, 'Are torture warrants warranted?'
(2004) 88 *Minnesota Law Review* 1481; Ginbar, V, *Why Not Torture Terrorists?* (Oxford University Press,
Oxford, 2008).
[137] App no 22414/93, Reports 1996-V, para 79.
[138] See *Brogan v United Kingdom*, App nos 11209, 11234, 11266/84, 11386/85, Ser A 145-B, (1989) para 61;
R (Gillan) v Commissioner of Police for the Metropolis [2006] UKHL 12, para 64.

more demanding than 'proportionate').[139] The review of emergency causes acute problems both in terms of the standard of review and also as to the very justiciability of the question. Many have criticized undue judicial deference towards executive emergency decision-making.[140] The English judges have now accepted that review is proper, albeit that they have warned of the continuance of some 'deference'[141] to executive assessments in the implementation of counter-measures which is warranted by the superior information and expertise held by the executive. At the same time, the judges are no more 'amateurs' in the taking of complex security decisions than are the politicians who ultimately authorize them.[142] They may, on the one hand, have the disadvantage of less frequent engagement with security issues (though that feature can be counteracted by specialization) but, on the other hand, have advantages of focus and calm to balance against a relative deficit of information. Thus, Lord Bingham warned that 'While any decision made by a representative democratic body must of course command respect, the degree of respect will be conditioned by the nature of the decision'.[143] A more vivid formulation was offered by Lord Justice Laws in *International Transport Roth GmbH v Secretary of State for the Home Department*,[144] whose guideline is that 'greater deference will be due to the democratic powers where the subject-matter in hand is peculiarly within their constitutional responsibility, and less when it lies more particularly within the constitutional responsibility of the courts. . . . There are no tanks on the wrong lawns.' He posited the further useful guideline that 'greater deference is to be paid to an Act of Parliament than to a decision of the executive or subordinate measure'.[145]

Accountability

1.62 The second aspect of constitutionalism demands 'accountability' which includes attributes such as information provision, open and independent debate, and an ability to participate in decision-making. These attributes conduce against contentions that a dictatorial regime is best fitted to respond to a crisis and instead seek to ensure the continuance of parliamentary (in other words, public and partisan) scrutiny.[146] This process can be aided by stating explicitly some of the desirable limiting principles adduced earlier. So, for each part of anti-terrorism legislation, there should be expressed criteria by which to judge its value or dispensability and its proportionality, with a distinct vote on each part.

1.63 Vigilance through democratic accountability should be undertaken not simply by Parliament but also by independent permanent expert review which enriches its scrutiny. The tailored need for special scrutiny contends against the mixing of 'normal' and 'special' provisions such as has occurred in the ATCSA 2001.[147] As well as democratic and expert accountability, the mechanism of accountability to the courts plays an important role

---

[139] See Ashworth, A, 'Security, terrorism, and the value of human rights' in Goold, BJ and Lazarus, L, *Security and Human Rights* (Hart, Oxford, 2007) p 215.

[140] See Dyzenhaus, D, *The Constitution of Law* (Cambridge University Press, Cambridge, 2006).

[141] See *Huang v Secretary of State for the Home Department* [2007] UKHL 11 at para 16; *al-Jedda v Secretary of State for Defence* [2010] EWCA Civ 758; Lord Steyn, 'Deference: a tangled story' [2005] *Public Law* 346.

[142] Compare Posner, EA and Vermeule, A, *Terror in the Balance* (Oxford University Press, Oxford, 2007) p 31.

[143] [2004] UKHL 56 at para 39.

[144] [2002] EWCA Civ 158 at paras 85, 86.

[145] Ibid para 83.

[146] See House of Lords Constitution Committee, *Counter-Terrorism Bill: The role of ministers, Parliament, and the Judiciary* (2007–08 HL 167). The idea of escalating super-majorities in Ackerman, B, *Before the Next Attack* (Yale University Press, New Haven, 2006) p 80 wrongly assumes a chronologically finite threat and thereby engineers needless and successive panics.

[147] *Newton Report*, paras C111–113.

consistent with democracy.[148] The role of the judiciary will mainly arise on the basis of rights jurisprudence, as already described, but accountability to concepts such as legality should equally be applied.

Constitutional governance

The third and broadest aspect of constitutionalism demands 'constitutional governance'. **1.64** This aspect includes the subjection of governmental action to a lawfulness requirement that terrorism laws 'indicate with reasonable clarity the scope and manner of exercise of the relevant discretion conferred on the public authorities'.[149] Next, the 'constitutional' mode of governance demands respect for meta-norms—tenets of national constitutional law and also international law, as indicated by Lord Lloyd's fourth point, the impact of which ensures that the response to terrorism will be conducted within a liberal and democratic framework. The norms must reflect the need for rationality and proportionality, including the overall purpose of the restoration of fundamental features of constitutional life. These considerations of constitutional governance also point towards the delineation of special powers in advance of an emergency. The repeal of all emergency laws is likely to abnegate the influence of the legislative and judicial branches and to gift absolute power to the executive. Contingent threats are also worthy of consideration but are already the subject of the Civil Contingencies Act 2004, Pt II, which entails a range of further restraints under its 'triple lock'. Contingent or precautionary risk, such as that detention without charge of suspects might be required for more than twenty-eight days, ought not to be the basis for measures in the terrorism legislation unless there is a willingness to match the safeguards in the 2004 Act.

Factual triggers

Is existing political or paramilitary violence in the United Kingdom of such severity as to warrant **1.65** the severe departures from normal standards which are now perpetrated by anti-terrorism legislation? A precise econometric calculation of where the advantage lies is tricky.[150] For instance, there were 2,645 road deaths in the United Kingdom in 2008,[151] whereas the highest annual loss in the modern era from terrorism was 502 in 1972.[152] The legislative reactions to faulty driving and terrorism are very different. Yet, this comparison (which might also apply to diseases such as influenza) is facile, since there are significant qualitative differences. First, terrorists aim to terrorize, and, especially if through repeated attacks, this outcome can achieve a widespread, destabilizing impact, potentially causing deep social cleavages, economic depression, and political instability. Secondly, prevention is implemented both for the sake of road safety and security from terrorism, but the latter has secured an unusually generous allocation of resources which interdicted the plots, for example, of Dhiren Barot,[153] Omar Khyam,[154] and Abdulla Ahmed Ali,[155] thereby affecting the figures revealed in Table 1.1.

---

[148] [2004] UKHL 56 at para 42 per Lord Bingham.

[149] *Malone v United Kingdom*, App no 8691/79, Ser A 82 (1984) para 79.

[150] But see Posner, RA, *Not a Suicide Pact* (Oxford University Press, New York, 2006); Enders, W and Sandler, T, *The Political Economy of Terrorism* (Cambridge University Press, Cambridge, 2006).

[151] Department for Transport, *Road Casualties Great Britain 2008* (2009); PSNI, *Road Traffic Collision Statistics Annual Report 2008* (2009) p 7. See further Wolfendale, J, 'Terrorism, security and the threat of counter terrorism' (2007) 30 *Studies in Conflict and Terrorism* 75; Sunstein, CR, *Worst-Case Scenarios* (Harvard University Press, Cambridge, 2007) ch 1.

[152] McKittrick, D et al, *Lost Lives* (Mainstream, Edinburgh, 1999) p 1473.

[153] *The Times* 13 October 2006, p 1.

[154] *The Times* 1 May 2007, p 11.

[155] *The Times* 9 September 2008, p 6.

Table 1.1 Terrorism related deaths in UK 2001–2009[a]

	2001	2002	2003	2004	2005	2006	2007	2008	2009
GB	0	0	0	0	57	1	1	0	0
N Ire.	17	15	7	4	6	4	1	5	2

[a] Sources: PSNI, Statistics on the Security Situation (Belfast); *Report of the Official Account of the Bombings in London on 7th July 2005* (2005–06 HC 1087) para 2. These totals include the deaths of Jean Charles de Menezes, Alexander Litvinenko, and five suicide bombers.

The threat is also underlined by attacks abroad, especially in New York in 2001 (sixty-seven British victims) and Bali in 2002 (twenty-four British deaths).

1.66 Overall, it is plausible to conclude that UK governments have been justified in invoking anti-terrorism laws for at least three reasons. Most important is the evidence just given of a clear and present danger, far more prescient than in February 2001 when the TA 2000 came into force. The main focus is *jihadist* terrorism,[156] but dangers remain in Northern Ireland,[157] more in line with most other European jurisdictions where separatist terrorism still predominates in quantitative terms.[158] Conversely, other forms of terrorism originating within the United Kingdom, including animal rights violence, are deemed to be not so severe or complex as to warrant special laws.[159]

1.67 Secondly, total abolition of special legislation without replacement throws the baby out with the bath-water. In other words, safeguards and restraints, which have painstakingly been fought over, conceded, and honed over a period of years, will be lost alongside more reviled instruments of coercion.[160]

1.68 Thirdly, it is illogical to oppose all conceivable forms of special laws on a platform of concerns for human rights. Rather our collective concern for human rights should lead to the utmost protection of citizens against either zombie-like paramilitary organizations or maddened security forces and that to vacate the field to either faction is to abdicate rather than to exercise responsibility for the governance of special powers. There is ample evidence to suggest that governments of wholly different complexions will, in a tight corner, wish to resort to much the same measures and react in much the same ways. Thus, if the legal field is left unattended, the power elite will very soon fill it with architecture which, in the circumstances of an emergency, will be rather ugly. One cannot coherently complain about 'panic' legislation but then deny to the state the principled and refined means to defend itself and to fulfil its duty to safeguard its population.

1.69 The government claims that the terrorism threat remains so severe as to justify derogation under Article 15 of the European Convention,[161] though there is no present intention to

---

[156] The Prime Minister revealed there are 2,000 such suspects, and 75 per cent have links to Pakistan: *The Times* 15 December 2008, p 33.

[157] Independent Monitoring Commission, *Twenty Second Report* (2008–09 HC 1085).

[158] See Europol, *EU Terrorism Situation and Trend Report TE-SAT 2009* (Brussels, 2009).

[159] *Lloyd Report*, para 1.24; *Home Office Response to Lloyd Report*, para 3.10.

[160] Brennan, WJ, 'The American experience', in Shetreet, S, *Free Speech and National Security* (Nijhoff, Dordrecht, 1991) pp 16–17.

[161] Joint Committee on Human Rights, Counter-Terrorism Policy and Human Rights (Seventeenth Report): *Bringing Human Rights Back In* (2009–10 HL 86/HC 111) para 11.

lodge a notice. In justification of this stance, the European Court of Human Rights did not demur from the derogation issued in 2001,[162] and terrorism on home soil has become evidently more deadly since that time.

D. Institutions, Review, and Accountability

Institutions

The executive unit responsible for legislative development and administration is the **1.70**
Home Office's Office for Security and Counter Terrorism. The policing and security agencies working alongside this structure will be described further in Chapter 10. The Home Office was split into two in 2007 to allow for a greater concentration of effort on security and policing (not including justice) and thereby gave greater prominence to the Office. The departmental split seems to have bedded in well.[163]

The Prime Minister chairs the National Security Council which was established in May **1.71**
2010, with a Minister of Security and National Security Advisor to lead delivery and is based in the Cabinet Office.[164] Its relationship to reviews of the terrorism legislation is yet to be clarified.[165] The Council is successor to the Ministerial Committee on National Security, International Relations and Development, which sets policy at a higher level than the Weekly Security Meeting chaired by the Home Secretary, as well as sub-committees on Tackling Extremism and Intelligence.[166] Adding to the mix, the Cabinet Office handles emergency planning through its Civil Contingencies Secretariat,[167] but there is clear linkage to the National Security Secretariat.

There is little enthusiasm for the creation of an equivalent to the unwieldy US Department **1.72**
of Homeland Security,[168] though the House of Commons Select Committee on Defence felt that a more modest body along the lines of a National Counter-Terrorism Service merited further attention.[169] The British approach has been to shuffle key backroom departmental formations, at least until the advent of the National Security Council. It has also relied upon sectoral and specialist agency formations. These include the Joint Terrorism Analysis Centre (JTAC), which handles the analysis and assessment of intelligence relating to international

---

[162] *A v United Kingdom*, App no 3455/05, 19 February 2009, paras 219, 220. For justifications in 2001, see Walker, C, *The Anti Terrorism Legislation* (1st edn, Oxford University Press, Oxford, 2002) pp 8–11.

[163] Compare Hayman, A, *The Terrorist Hunters* (Bantam Press, London, 2009) p 222.

[164] Cabinet Office, *A Strong Britain in an Age of Uncertainty: The National Security Strategy* (Cm 7953, London, 2010) p 5.

[165] Lord Carlile, *Report on the Operation in 2001–2009 of the Terrorism Act 2000* (Home Office, London) para 13.

[166] See Intelligence and Security Committee, *Annual Report 2007–08* (Cm 7542, London, 2009) para 120; House of Commons Home Affairs Committee, *The Home Office's Response to Terrorist Attacks* (2009–10 HC 117) para 7 and Government Reply (Cm 7788, London, 2010) p 6.

[167] See Walker, C and Broderick, J, *The Civil Contingencies Act 2004* (Oxford University Press, Oxford, 2006) ch 8.

[168] Homeland Security Act 2002 (PL 107-296). See Gregory, F, 'National governance structures to manage the response to terrorist threats and attacks' in Wilkinson, P (ed), *Homeland Security in the UK* (Routledge, Abingdon, 2007).

[169] Defence Committee, Defence and Security in the UK (2001–02 HC 518) para 81; *Government Reply to the House of Commons Science and Technology Committee, The Scientific Response to Terrorism* (Cm 6108, London, 2004) para 44.

terrorism, including the setting of the threat level. Although based within the Security Service, its governance structure is through a joint board in which the Cabinet Office, Ministry of Defence, Home Office, Foreign Office, and other interested departments are represented, and its prime feature is to conduct its own intelligence analysis on an all-source basis derived from the intelligence agencies, the police, and government departments.[170]

1.73 One of the disadvantages of the incremental British approach has been the absence of a focal point. However, the National Security Council and Minister of Security (Baroness Neville-Jones) and National Security Advisor (Sir Peter Ricketts) are intended to command more prominence than the former and very active 'Parliamentary Under-Secretary for Security and Counter-terrorism' (Lord West).

1.74 In the European Union, a prominent role is undertaken by the Counter-Terrorism Coordinator who was appointed under the Declaration on Combating Terrorism on 25 March 2004 in the wake of the Madrid bombings.[171] The Counter-Terrorism Coordinator seeks to facilitate the implementation of the policies of the European Union on terrorism and acts as a representative of the Union but is confined by national sovereignty as represented through the Council of Ministers.

1.75 Next, in the United States, the National Counterterrorism Center was established in 2004 in line with the wishes of the 9/11 Commission.[172] The Center is situated within the Office of the Director of National Intelligence, whose Director (John Brennan) serves as the head of the intelligence community and acts as the principal advisor to the President, the National Security Council, and the Homeland Security Council. The mission of the Center is to analyse terrorist threats, integrate the efforts of different agencies, and ensure that information is shared. In this way, the body has some key functions, as well as dealing with strategic operational planning and integration and leading Interagency Task Forces.[173]

1.76 Given the tendency to overreact to terrorism incidents, as already outlined, it is important next to consider review and accountability mechanisms.

Review mechanisms within the anti-terrorism legislation

Mechanisms adopted

1.77 Since the TA 2000 is otherwise a permanent code, responding to a permanent threat to national security and the right to life of individuals, there is no requirement for periodic renewal or re-enactment.[174] According to former Home Office Minister, Charles Clarke:[175]

> We have had so-called temporary provisions on the statute book for 25 years. The time has come to face the fact of terrorism and be ready to deal with it for the foreseeable future.

---

[170] See Intelligence and Security Committee, *Annual Report 2002–03* (Cm 5837, London, 2003) para 62 and *Annual Report 2003–04* (Cm 6240, London, 2004) para 92.

[171] 7906/04. See House of Lords European Union Committee, *After Madrid* (204-05 HL 53). There is also an Australian 'Ambassador for Counter Terrorism': Counter Terrorism White Paper, *Securing Australia: Protecting Our Community* (Canberra, 2010) para 5.6.2.

[172] See National Commission on Terrorist Attacks upon the United States, *The 9/11 Commission Report* (GPO, Washington DC, 2004) p 403; Executive Order 13354 (69 FR 53989); Intelligence Reform and Terrorism Prevention Act 2004 (PL 108-458) s 1021.

[173] Aspects of foreign coordination are dealt with by the Office of the Coordinator for Counterterrorism in the Department of State: <http://www.state.gov/s/ct>.

[174] See *Lloyd Report,* paras 1.20, 17.6.

[175] Hansard HC vol 346 col 363 (15 March 2000).

We need to make the powers permanently available, although the fact that those powers are available does not mean that they have to be used.

While it is logical that there should be no requirement of renewal, the level of ongoing scrutiny applied otherwise to extreme incursions into the rights of individuals is disappointing. Section 126[176] simply requires that the Secretary of State shall lay before both Houses of Parliament at least once in every twelve months a report on the working of the legislation. This formulation pointed towards past application rather than future need. It also gave no promise as to Parliament's reaction to the report. There is no guarantee of an annual debate on the floor of the House—the Minister pointed rather to possible select committee scrutiny.[177] Neither has actually occurred. **1.78**

The loss of the annual renewal mechanism is not decisive. There is no serious chance that any part of the legislation will be struck down or seriously analysed in a debate lasting an hour and a half. What is regrettable is the lack of initiative from Parliament to keep the legislation under systematic scrutiny. Yet, extraordinary powers should be subjected to extraordinary scrutiny. Select committees have filled the gap to a limited extent, with an inquiry into impacts on community relations[178] and attention to detention powers in the context of legislative proposals to extend them in 2005–06 and 2007–08. Proscription (with the exception of the People's Mujahideen Organisation of Iran), financial measures, and criminal offences have largely passed unnoticed. The annual report, which has been diligently compiled by Lord Carlile,[179] has been formalized by the TA 2006, s 36, though without substantive change in its prominence. **1.79**

A more complex array of limits and reviews were inserted into the 2001 Act. By s 122, the Home Secretary was required to appoint a committee of no fewer than seven members, all Privy Counsellors, to conduct a review of the entire Act. But the government emphasized that the review was a one-off exercise which would report within two years[180] with a copy to be laid before Parliament. In the event, the Newton Committee reported at the end of 2003. Its thorough report recommended the end of detention without trial as well as detailed changes in other areas. The government's initial response was unenthusiastic. Its hand on detention without trial was forced by the House of Lords judgment in *A v Secretary of State for the Home Department*.[181] Otherwise, many other recommendations were rejected.[182] The idea of a general two-year sunset clause was resisted: 'We are not convinced of the need for sunset clauses on . . . the bread-and-butter precautionary anti-terrorist measures in this Bill.'[183] **1.80**

As for more limited reviews under the ATCSA 2001, Parliament insisted on limits in ss 28 and 29 on the duration of Pt IV by way of annual renewal by order and a review by an independent person (Lord Carlile was appointed).[184] But no review specific to other parts of the legislation was set up. **1.81**

---

[176] Hansard HC Standing Committee D col 312 (8 February 2000), Charles Clarke.
[177] Ibid col 315.
[178] Home Affairs Committee, *Terrorism and Community Relations* (2003–04 HC 165).
[179] *See Reports on the Operation of the Terrorism Act 2000* (Home Office, London, 2002–10).
[180] Hansard HL vol 629 col 1536 (13 December 2001), Lord Rooker.
[181] [2004] UKHL 56.
[182] *Home Office Response to Newton Report.*
[183] Hansard HL vol 629 col 634 (3 December 2001), Lord Rooker.
[184] See Lord Carlile, *Anti-terrorism, Crime and Security Act 2001 Part IV Section 28, Reviews 2001–2005* (Home Office, London).

1.82   Another limit as to duration applied in Pt XI in connection with the retention of communications data, which was allowed to persist on a mandatory basis under s 104 for two years at a time. This scheme has now been replaced by permanent legislation, as detailed in Chapter 2.

1.83   The third limit, in s 111, allowed the implementation of European Union Third Pillar measures by order. The purpose of s 111 was to avoid legislative delay in the implementation of urgent counter-measures. Rather than primary legislation, there could be secondary legislation, roughly equivalent to the precedent in Common Market matters to s 2(2) of the European Communities Act 1972. The power was hugely controversial, not least because it was not confined to anti-terrorism measures, and so was time-limited to 1 July 2002. In the event, while progress was made at European level, notably with the implementation of the European arrest warrant scheme,[185] it was implemented by the Extradition Act 2003 in line with the pace of European partners and the original intention of the government.[186] The other major development, the Council Framework Decision on Combating Terrorism of 2002,[187] was not interpreted to require any immediate domestic response.

1.84   Under the PTA 2005, annual independent review is required under s 14,[188] and s 13 provides for expiration after one year whereupon there can be a renewal order and debate upon it. This extra scrutiny reflects the controversial nature of control orders and the bitter Parliamentary opposition to the passage of the legislation, in contrast to the broad consensus in 2000 and 2001.

1.85   The extension of detention provisions under the TA 2006, s 23, is uniquely in that legislation subject to annual renewal under s 25. In addition, an independent review is required under s 36 for the whole of Pt I of the Act (much of Pt II being subject already to review as amendments to earlier legislation). Lord Carlile has duly obliged, with his reports rolled up in those for the 2000 Act.

1.86   There is no review under the JSA 2007, ss 1 to 9 (non-jury trials), but a time limit of two years (renewable) is imposed. The special police and army powers (derived from Pt VII of the 2000 Act) are without specific time duration, but are subject to a power to repeal by order and to annual review under s 40 (by Robert Whalley).

1.87   There is no extra time limit or review scheme in this 2008 Act, which is a startling omission, though the Independent Reviewer has chosen to accord scrutiny to some of this Act.

1.88   As illustrated by this survey, the mechanisms for review by Parliament are muddled, and the coverage of independent review is beset by 'pragmatic incrementalism'.[189] The 2000 Act reviewer can also be commissioned to undertake thematic reviews and has reported on proposals in 2005 and 2007 for extended detention of 90 days and then 42 days under s 41, on the definition of terrorism in 2007, and on Operation Pathway in 2009 (all described in Chapter 4).

---

[185] See Council Framework Decision 2002/584/JHA of 13 June 2002.

[186] Hansard HL vol 629 col 1142 (10 December 2001), Baroness Symons.

[187] 2002/475/JHA of 13 June 2002. See further Council Framework Decision amending Framework Decision 2002/475/JHA on combating terrorism (6561/08); House of Commons European Scrutiny Committee, *Seventh Report* (2007–08 HC 16-vii).

[188] See *Reports of the Independent Reviewer pursuant to Section 14(3) of the Prevention of Terrorism Act 2005* (Home Office, London, 2006–09).

[189] Lord Carlile, Conference on the Regulation of Criminal Justice (Manchester, 9 April 2008).

Assessment

To some extent the obstacles thus presented are overcome by appointing the same person   **1.89**
to undertake virtually all independent reviews. Thus, Lord Carlile was appointed on
11 September 2001 under the TA 2000 and has subsequently shouldered all the later
reviews[190] with the exception of the JSA 2007 review which is handled by Robert
Whalley.[191] The review reports are always accurate and helpful, but more could be achieved
by a structure which relied less upon happenstance and the capacity of just one person, no
matter how able.

The reviews should therefore be strengthened in order to meet standards of accountability   **1.90**
and to improve the rights of audit and constitutional governance.[192] First, the invocation of
powers should be subject to pre-announced and expressly invoked criteria, in order that the
reviewers and Parliament can assess the desirability of the provisions. Secondly, there should
be an independent review panel, not just one or two persons, so as to incorporate a range of
views, to cope with the burgeoning workload, and to adopt a rolling system of appointments
which would constantly infuse fresh ideas and avoid institutional capture.[193] The idea was
rejected by the (Rowe) *Annual Report on the Prevention of Terrorism Act* in 1996 on grounds of
insecurity for information and complexity in the consultation process and in drafting reports.
But the complexity argument equally rejects the virtue of deeper and more nuanced
approaches. Lord Carlile views himself as a watchdog and commentator whose main
constituency is Parliament and the government; he seeks success principally in terms of relevance to, and improvement of, debates. One implication of the target audience is that reports
must be short and relatively shorn of arguments and data. However, a panel could address
different audiences—Parliament and government may be the prime audience, but the communities most affected by the legislation, the lawyers who work with it, and even the general
public, all have legitimate interests in greater knowledge about the entire legislation. The
panel should investigate and report on any proposed institution of anti-terrorism legislation,
its working while in force, its renewal, and its compatibility with policy and standards. It
should be able to draw upon the resources of specialists. Thirdly, there should be a specialist
review committee in Parliament as its chief correspondent.[194] Under the current disposition
of Parliamentary committees, the function of reviewing anti-terrorism legislation is clearly
either of insufficient priority or of excessive bulk.

The annual review system was reflected upon in Lord Carlile's final report. He called for a   **1.91**
full-time reviewer and staff; while not endorsing a panel of reviewers, an advisory group of
experts is endorsed.[195]

Another two forms of review have operated in the past in Northern Ireland. One was the   **1.92**
Independent Assessor of Military Complaints Procedures, latterly established under the

---

[190] See also Lord Carlile, *First Annual Review of Arrangements for National Security in Northern Ireland* (Northern Ireland Office, Belfast, 2008).

[191] See Reports of the Independent Reviewer: *Justice and Security (Northern Ireland) Act 2007* (Northern Ireland Office, Belfast, 2008–09).

[192] These ideas were rejected by the government: Joint Committee on Human Rights, *Government Responses to the Committee's 20th and 21st Reports and other correspondence* (2007–08 HL 127, HC 756) p 20.

[193] (Home Office, London, 1997) p 4.

[194] See Joint Committee on Human Rights, *Terrorism Policy and Human Rights: Annual Review of Control Orders Legislation 2008* (2007–08 HL 57/HC 356) para 33.

[195] Lord Carlile, *Report on the Operation in 2009 of the Terrorism Act 2000 and Part I of the Terrorism Act 2006* (Home Office, London) paras 306–7.

TA 2000, s 98, but terminated in 2007 with the substantial decline in military involvement. More significant was the Office of the Independent Commissioner for Detained Terrorist Suspects which will be discussed in Chapter 4.

1.93 The most recent major independent review was the *Newton Report* in 2003. The government response was very negative and major parts are yet to be implemented. Perhaps as a result of this experience, the government has resisted granting any further inquiry of this kind and has preferred the more regular reviews by Lord Carlile, even though those reviews are more limited in scope and arguably carry less political weight.

1.94 A system of periodic review on the Newton model, especially to audit the impact of new legislation, would be helpful. A review of six aspects of terrorism laws was announced by the Home Secretary in July 2010; the reviewer is Lord Macdonald.[196] Under review are:

> six key powers: control orders; section 44 stop-and-search powers and the use of terrorism legislation in relation to photography; the use of the RIPA by local authorities and access to communications data more generally; extending the use of deportations with assurances in a manner that is consistent with our legal and human rights obligations; measures to deal with organisations that promote hatred or violence; and the detention of terrorist suspects before charge.

The review will also inform the debates about asset freezing legislation (as described in Chapter 9).

1.95 There has been debate in Australia about effective review structures, with interest in the Sheller Review[197] and support from a Private Member's Independent Reviewer of Terrorism Laws Bill 2008.[198] Under the Bill, the reviewer would be selected by the Prime Minister but could also be tasked by the Parliamentary Joint Committee on Intelligence and Security and be accorded full statutory powers to access and obtain information. The Reviewer's reports would always be considered by the Minister, by Parliament, and by the specialist committee.

Parliament

1.96 The performance of Parliament[199] in response to proposals of anti-terrorism legislation conforms to a recurrent 'classical' pattern. A significant attack occurs. Then the government reveals its proposals (sometimes prepared in advance, sometimes in haste afterwards), warns Parliament of the need for a firm and decisive response, and condemns any opponents as 'weak on terrorism'. This 'security theater'[200] has been followed on many past occasions. Two clear instances are the PT(TP)A 1974 (passed within a few days of the Birmingham bombings)[201] and the Criminal Justice (Terrorism and Conspiracy) Act 1998 (passed

---

[196] Hansard HC vol 513 col 797 (13 July 2010) Theresa May.

[197] *Report of the Security Legislation Review Committee* (Canberra, 2006) ch 18.

[198] See Senate Standing Committee on Legal and Constitutional Affairs, *Independent Reviewer of Terrorism Laws Bill 2008 [No. 2]* (Canberra, 2008).

[199] See Hiebert, JL, 'Parliamentary review of terrorism measures' (2005) 68 *Modern Law Review* 676; Gearty, C, 'Human rights in an age of counter-terrorism' (2005) 58 *Current Legal Problems* 25.

[200] Schneier, B, *Beyond Fear* (Springer, New York, 2003) p 38.

[201] See Walker, CP, *The Prevention of Terrorism in British Law* (2nd edn, Manchester University Press, 1992) ch 4; Bonner, D, 'Responding to crisis' (2006) 122 *Law Quarterly Review* 602. Compare Vermeule, A, 'Emergency lawmaking after 9/11 and 7/7' (2008) 75 *University of Chicago Law Review* 1155.

within two days after the recall of Parliament in response to the Omagh bombing).[202] Amongst the current legislation, the ATCSA 2001 was passed within just over one month, which should be put in the context of a substantial document, much of which was never debated. The next extraordinary process involved the PTA 2005, passed within two weeks under the whip of the pending expiration of detention without trial.

There have been two occasions when determination was shown to break this cycle. The fruits **1.97** of one of the most enduring studies, the *Diplock Report* in 1972, were delivered sedately by the EPA 1973. The paradox of a time of greatest threat from terrorism being the backdrop for some of the calmest and most rational debates may in part be explained by the fact that other special legislation was already in force and that the objectives of the *Diplock Report* were not viewed as attainable in the short term. The other major exception is the TA 2000, which followed a leisurely timetable in pursuance of the *Lloyd Report* in 1996. It helped enormously that there was no terrorism crisis while the Northern Ireland Peace Process gathered pace. The fact that much legislation was already extant assisted the rational passage of the 2006 and 2008 Acts. On these occasions, Parliament stood out against the wilder claims to increase detention after arrest but did sanction a 28-day period which is well beyond the norm of four days.[203]

Virtually no detailed work was undertaken by any specialist parliamentary committee on the **1.98** anti-terrorism legislation, until the ATCSA 2001. However, beginning with that legislation and thereafter, select committees have become more major players in the scrutiny of the passage of proposed legislation and, to a lesser extent, in the subsequent administration and working of enacted measures. The relevant reports will be cited frequently in this book. There are too many reports to mention, but the main committees to undertake this work have been the Joint Committee on Human Rights and the House of Commons Home Affairs Committee, with many others joining in from time to time. Their impact has not been dramatic but has been beneficial. Their main advantage is to provide a depth of expert evidence and measured findings which can then be relayed to Ministers and cited in debates.

Select committee scrutiny should be encouraged further. A specialist Joint Committee on **1.99** National Security Strategy was created in 2010.[204] But the reform process shows a 'lack of dynamism',[205] given that the idea was promised in 2008, alongside a reformed Intelligence and Security Committee which has yet to be fully delivered.[206] Other mechanisms to improve the performance of Parliament include pre-legislative scrutiny, the fuller publication of legal advice about compliance with the European Convention, and the requirement of periodic post-enactment review and a statement of principles by which such review can be judged.[207] Whether a 'sunset clause' is required depends on the circumstances of passage. Certainly, if there has been rushed legislation in a crisis, then a sunset clause is helpful, but for well-considered legislation, a sunset clause can invite later accretions and amendments in unfavourable circumstances.

---

[202] See Walker, C, 'The bombs in Omagh and their aftermath' (1998) 62 *Modern Law Review* 879; House of Lords Constitution Committee, Fast Track Legislation (2008–09 HL 116) para 75.

[203] Police and Criminal Evidence Act 1984, Pt IV.

[204] *A Strong Britain in an Age of Uncertainty: The National Security Strategy* (Cm 7953, London, 2010) p 5. See further IPPR, *Commission on National Security in the 21st Century, Shared Responsibilities* (London, 2009).

[205] House of Commons Home Affairs Committee, *The Home Office's Response to Terrorist Attacks* (2009–10 HC 117) para 55.

[206] See Ministry of Justice, *The Governance of Britain—Constitutional Renewal* (Cm 7342, London, 2008) paras 235–244; Intelligence and Security Committee, *Annual Report 2007–08* (Cm 7542, London, 2009) para 13.

[207] See House of Lords Constitution Committee, *Fast Track Legislation* (2008–09 HL 116).

Courts

1.100 The attitudes of the courts to security or emergency legislation have been closely scrutinized in literature, especially their degree of deference to the executive or to Parliament.[208] For present purposes, it is sufficient to offer an overview and then to examine the practice in later chapters.

1.101 During the last century, the UK judges adopted a high degree of deference in times of emergency. There was a great reluctance to question at all the existence or declaration of an emergency, with the broad issue being deemed to be non-justiciable and specific applications being accepted without any degree of objective proof.[209] As regards the executive, this stance flows from respect for the expertise and privileged information of the acting Minister as well as respect for the Minister's political and democratic credentials. There is recognition of the constitutional position—the Minister is accountable to Parliament and Parliament conferred these powers upon this Minister. Finally, there is concern for the sensitive nature of the information. Though the judges sought to recant the high water mark of this approach, in *Liversidge v Anderson*,[210] a stance of extensive deference persisted in terrorism-related cases.[211]

1.102 The European Court of Human Rights has not in the meantime developed a markedly more demanding standard for the review of the existence of, or response to, emergencies, including terrorism. Indeed, the Court has the added arguments for reticence that it is an international court which must show respect for the sovereignty of nation states and their wide legal diversity.[212] Its approach is reflected in reliance upon the doctrine of the 'margin of appreciation', especially in determining whether an emergency exists for the purposes of Article 15.[213] On this point, the Court has accepted that a 'public emergency' can cover situations which are unlikely to overthrow a government, such as low-intensity terrorism, and can be confined to one area of the country (such as Northern Ireland), and, despite the nomenclature of emergency, can endure for many years.[214] Sustained breaches of Article 15 or measures based on it are few and far between.[215] But Convention review does embody two differences from the British common law approach: there is review in substance; and some rights are absolute even in

---

[208] See Dyzenhaus, D, *The Constitution of Law* (Cambridge University Press, Cambridge, 2006); Feldman, D, 'Human rights, terrorism and risk' [2006] *Public Law* 364; Gross, O and Ní Aoláin, F, *Law in Times of Crisis* (Cambridge University Press, Cambridge, 2006); Posner, EA and Vermeule, A, *Terror in the Balance* (Oxford University Press, New York, 2007).

[209] See Simpson, AWB, *In the Highest Degree Odious* (Clarendon Press, Oxford, 1992); Ewing, KD and Gearty, CA, *The Struggle for Civil Liberties: Political Freedom and the Rule of Law in Britain 1914–1945* (Oxford University Press, Oxford, 2000).

[210] [1942] AC 206. Compare *Nakkuda Ali v Jayaratne* [1951] AC 66.

[211] *McEldowney v Forde* [1971] AC 632; *R v Secretary of State for the Home Department, ex parte Brind* [1991] AC 696; *Re Williamson* [2000] NI 281; *R v Secretary of State for Home Affairs, ex parte Stitt* (1987) *The Times* 3 February (QBD); *R v Secretary of State for the Home Department, ex parte McQuillan* [1995] 4 All ER 400; *R v Secretary of State for the Home Department, ex parte Adams (No 1)* [1995] All ER (EC) 177.

[212] See Bates, E, 'A "public emergency threatening the life of the nation"?' (2005) 76 *British Yearbook of International Law* 245.

[213] See *Lawless v Ireland (No 3)* App no 332/56, Ser A 3; *Marshall v United Kingdom*, App no 41571/98, Judgment 10 July 2001; *Kerr v United Kingdom*, App no 40451/98, 10 July 2001; *A v United Kingdom*, App no 3455/05, 19 February 2009.

[214] *Ireland v UK*, App no 5310/71, Ser A 25 (1978).

[215] *Denmark, Norway, Sweden, and the Netherlands v Greece*, App nos 3321/67, 3322/67, 3323/67, 3344/67, (1969) 12 *Yearbook of the European Convention on Human Rights* 1.

emergencies, especially the right to life (Article 2), freedom from torture (Article 3), and freedom from retrospective penalties (Article 7).

Whether the measures taken under a declaration of emergency are strictly proportionate to the exigencies of the situation, the European Court still asserts that the Court stated that national authorities are '. . . in a better position than the international judge to decide both on the presence of such an emergency and on the nature and scope of derogations necessary to avert it. Accordingly, in this matter a wide margin of appreciation should be left to national authorities.'[216] But it has been readier to sustain breaches in application.[217]

1.103

Returning to British law, the passage of the Human Rights Act 1998 provided a strong legislative signal that a new judicial culture should be developed in which challenges to the executive on grounds of rights were to be permissible. The result has been a much greater willingness to review in factual detail. Though the notion of deference remains,[218] the courts have dared to defy security policies and decisions on a scale and to a degree which is unprecedented in history.[219] The change of stance was illustrated most forcefully in *A v Secretary of State for the Home Department*,[220] when detention without trial in Belmarsh Prison was declared incompatible with s 4. Reactions to control orders have also been striking (as detailed in Chapter 7).

1.104

The headlines about some of these executive reverses may create the impression of a judicial revolt, but a new era of obdurate judicial activism has not dawned for several reasons. First, there remain the vast majority of instances where executive decisions have been upheld. Secondly, even in the *Belmarsh* case, the House of Lords did sustain the finding of emergency. It also did not require the courts to demand a fresh look at the original evidence. In the *Belmarsh* case, the defects were inherent in the legislative policy from the face of the Act—but what if the defects had been more personal and latent? Variables affecting judicial intervention may include the maturity of the terrorism threat; when a threat first emerges, the judges fall into line behind the executive, but as time goes on, independent assessments emerge. Next, there is variation according to the rights affected, with the judges more trenchant about matters of due process than on liberty and privacy. The judges are next affected by prevailing political and public pressures, such as growing hostility to the Human Rights Act.[221]

1.105

Nevertheless, a jurisprudence of the control of security powers has begun to develop.[222] The judges have forcefully resisted 'legal back holes'. Shades of grey remain, but the executive can no longer count on judicial indulgence.

1.106

---

[216] *Brannigan and McBride v United Kingdom*, App nos 14553/89, 14554/89, Ser A 258-B (1994) para 43. A stricter standard was arguably imposed in *A v Secretary of State for the Home Department* [2004] UKHL para 42.

[217] See *Klass v Germany*, App no 5029/71, Ser A 28; *Brogan v United Kingdom*, App nos 11209, 11234, 11266/84, 11386/85, Ser A 145-B (1988) para 48; *Fox, Campbell and Hartley v United Kingdom*, App nos 12244, 12245, 12383/86, Ser A 182 (1990) para 44; *Aksoy v Turkey*, App no 21987/93, 1996-VI; Warbrick, C, 'The principles of the ECHR and the response of states to terrorism' [2002] *European Human Rights Law Review* 287.

[218] *R v Director of Public Prosecutions, ex parte Kebilene* [1999] 3 WLR 972 at 1000 per Lord Hope; *Secretary of State for the Home Department v Rehman* [2001] UKHL 47 at para 62 per Lord Hoffmann.

[219] See Campbell, C, '"War on terrorism" and vicarious hegemons' (2005) 54 *International & Comparative Law Quarterly* 321; Kavanaugh, KA, 'Policing the margins: rights protection and the European Court of Human Rights' [2006] *European Human Rights Law Review* 422; Dickson, B, 'The House of Lords and the Northern Ireland conflict—a sequel' (2006) 69 *Modern Law Review* 383.

[220] [2004] UKHL 56. See Tierney, S, 'Determining the state of exception' (2005) 68 *Modern Law Review* 668; Walker, C, 'Prisoners of "war all the time"' [2005] *European Human Rights Law Review* 50.

[221] See *R v Horncastle* [2009] UKSC 14.

[222] See Walker, C, 'Counter-terrorism and human rights in the UK' in Breen-Smyth, M, *Ashgate Companion to Political Violence* (Ashgate, Abingdon, forthcoming).

E. Definition of Terrorism

Elements

1.107   The basic definition of 'terrorism' given earlier will now be examined more technically.[223] Arising from controversies engendered by the passage of the TA 2006, the United Kingdom government initiated a review of the legal definition of 'terrorism', as set out in s 1 of the TA 2000. The inquiry was conducted by Lord Carlile, who produced a comprehensive and thoughtful review in 2007.[224] However, his report sparked only minor change, in accordance with the Home Office view that the definition remains 'comprehensive and effective'.[225] This recent debate has reignited longer-standing apprehensions about the span of special police powers and offences, as well as the more deep-seated political quandary inherent in the task of defining 'terrorism'. Powerful polities have long sought to exercise hegemonic control over the ascription of legitimacy in emergencies.[226] One may recall the vehemence of Margaret Thatcher, commenting on the Republican hunger-strikes of 1981, that 'Crime is crime is crime. It is not political.'[227] In this way, the label can become an opportunistic and pejorative ascription rather than a simple description of a tactic. No doubt, 'counter-hegemonic political violence'[228] would not have the same ring to it, though it might reduce charges of acting as 'the rhetorical servant of the established order'.[229]

1.108   So what is meant by 'terrorism'? One author has surmised: 'Above the gates of hell is the warning that all that enter should abandon hope. Less dire but to the same effect is the warning given to those who try to define terrorism.'[230] Another author has compared the task to the search for the Holy Grail.[231] Nevertheless, wide currency is given to the following 'academic consensus' formula proffered by Schmid and Jongman:[232]

> Terrorism is an anxiety-inspiring method of repeated violent action, employed by (semi-) clandestine individual, group, or state actors, for idiosyncratic, criminal, or political reasons, whereby—in contrast to assassination—the direct targets of violence are not the main targets.

Three common denominators might be distilled from this excerpt, relating to purpose, target, and method. Each warrants some elaboration.

1.109   As for purpose, there is a political end in sight and the belief that it can be facilitated through instilling terror, though terrorization is not the end in itself. Criminals such as armed bank robbers might also terrorize, so it is useful to distinguish by purpose those who instil fear on

---

[223] See further Saul, B, *Defining Terrorism in International Law* (Oxford University Press, Oxford, 2006); Walker, C, 'The legal definition of "Terrorism" in United Kingdom law and beyond' [2007] *Public Law* 331.

[224] Lord Carlile, *The Definition of Terrorism* (Cm 7052, London, 2007).

[225] *Government Reply* (Cm 7058, London, 2007) p 5.

[226] See Campbell, C, '"War on terrorism" and vicarious hegemons' (2005) 54 *International & Comparative Law Quarterly* 321 at 353.

[227] Levin, B and Donosky, L, 'Death wish in Ulster' (1981) *Newsweek* 40.

[228] Butko, T, 'Terrorism redefined' (2005) 18 *Peace Review* 145 at 145.

[229] Gearty, C, 'Terrorism and morality' [2003] *European Human Rights Law Review* 377 at 380.

[230] Tucker, D, *Skirmishes at the Edge of Empire* (Praeger, Westport, 1997) p 51.

[231] Levitt, G, 'Is "terrorism" worth defining?' (1986) 13 *Ohio Northern University Law Review* 97 at 97.

[232] Schmid, A and Jongman, A, *Political Terrorism* (North-Holland, Amsterdam, 1987) p 28. See further Schmid, A, '"Terrorism on trial": terrorism—the definitional problem' (2004) 36 *Case Western Reserve Journal of International Law* 375 and 'Frameworks for conceptualising terrorism' (2004) 16 *Terrorism & Political Violence* 197.

a grander scale through their ability to terrorize populations or their representatives rather than selected victims and for public rather than private gain.

The target element draws out the instrumentality, or communicative nature, of the violence. **1.110** The direct victims of attack are not the sole objects in sight. The aim is to generate terror in a broader audience (such as the public). The broader audience may thus differ from the ultimate target audience for the political end (often a government).

As regards method, the core is violence, and terrorism involves types of violence which cause **1.111** terror, often amplified through devices such as media threats. Violence is usually conceived as perpetrating harm to human beings. Property destruction can also be 'violent' in common parlance and even in legal parlance,[233] though without accompanying human terror, one doubts it should qualify as 'terrorism'. By contrast, the UK government asserts that, excepting trivial damage such as graffiti,[234] 'people have lost their lives in [property] attacks. It would be rash simply to exclude property, even though a terrorist organization could say that its intent was not to threaten life.'[235]

The roles of a legal definition

Before delineating what is or should be the legal definition of 'terrorism', one should first **1.112** reflect upon the roles that any definition might play. After all, why agonize over the word if it is not to be put to any significant use in counter-terrorism strategy? If there is to be a law on terrorism, then legal definition is unavoidable,[236] but its roles within law should be the subject of careful reflection.

Leaving aside any denunciatory function, legal support can be a relevant tactic in all **1.113** four aspects of the CONTEST formulation. There are two of its themes which conduce towards legal reliance upon the term 'terrorism'. One is that, in view of the serious threat posed by terrorism to the public and constitutional order, prevention often outweighs after-the-event pursuit.[237] This factor conduces towards widening the definition of 'terrorism' within dependent all-encompassing powers and offences so that early interventions become more possible than when dealing with 'ordinary decent criminals',[238] thereby allowing some margin of error.[239] The second theme is that preventive strategies require advance targeting of individuals, events, and places. Therefore, effective intelligence-gathering becomes vital so as to facilitate prevention, contingency planning, or even prosecution.[240] An abundance of information further allows a government to criticize rebels, to gauge the strength of political opposition, and to make cogent social reforms.

---

[233] See Public Order Act 1986, s 8.

[234] Hansard HL vol 613, col 235 (16 May 2000), Lord Bassam. The definition of terroristic attacks on property is narrower in s 57 since it expressly requires an endangerment of life.

[235] Hansard HC Standing Committee D, col 20 (18 January 2000), Charles Clarke. See also Lord Carlile, *The Definition of Terrorism* (Cm 7052, London, 2007) para 50 and *Government Reply* (Cm 7058, London, 2007) p 6.

[236] Compare Fletcher, G, 'The indefinable concept of terrorism' (2006) 4 *Journal of International Criminal Justice* 894.

[237] See further Joint Committee on Human Rights, Counter-Terrorism Policy and Human Rights: Prosecution and Pre-Charge Detention (2005–06 HL 240, HC 1576) para 6.

[238] *Baker Report*, para 136.

[239] Hansard HC vol 346 col 410 (15 March 2000), Charles Clarke.

[240] See Kitson, F, *Low Intensity Operations* (Faber, London, 1971) chs 6, 7; Walker, C, 'Intelligence and anti-terrorism laws in the United Kingdom' (2006) 44 *Crime, Law and Social Change* 387.

1.114   One conclusion which flows from the foregoing discussion is that if indulgence through the use of the term 'terrorism' is to apply anywhere, then it is better utilized in the anticipatory aspects of criminal justice—the tasking of the police and security officials rather than in criminal offences and trials where, to retain legitimacy, harm to others is key and process must remain solemn and fair. On both scores, a restrictive rather than an expansive definition would seem advisable within criminal justice, focusing on particular tactics without reference to agent or cause being served.[241] Nevertheless, the task is worthwhile: 'By defining terrorism, it is possible to structure and control the use of a term . . .'[242]

The current legal formulation

1.115   The following version of the definition of 'terrorism' was advanced by s 20(1) of the PT(TP) A 1989: '. . . "terrorism" means the use of violence for political ends and includes any use of violence for the purpose of putting the public or any section of the public in fear'.

1.116   The current definition (in s 1 of the Terrorism Act) states with much greater length and detail as follows:[243]

(1) In this Act 'terrorism' means the use or threat of action where
    (a) the action falls within subsection (2),
    (b) the use or threat is designed to influence the government or an international governmental organisation or to intimidate the public or a section of the public, and
    (c) the use or threat is made for the purpose of advancing a political, religious, racial or ideological cause.
(2) Action falls within this subsection if it
    (a) involves serious violence against a person,
    (b) involves serious damage to property,
    (c) endangers a person's life, other than that of the person committing the action,
    (d) creates a serious risk to the health or safety of the public or a section of the public, or
    (e) is designed seriously to interfere with or seriously to disrupt an electronic system.

1.117   The essence lies in s 1(1), which contains three conjunctive legs, all of which must normally be satisfied. An exception is in s 1(3) which designates the use of firearms or explosives as terrorism regardless of s 1(1)(b)). This exception was invoked by the claimants in *R (Islamic Human Rights Commission) v Civil Aviation Authority*[244] to challenge the governmental and public authorities for allowing weapons to transit through British airports to Israel during its conflict with Hizbollah in southern Lebanon in 2006. Ouseley J viewed as 'a misconception' the implication that s 1(3) encompasses lawful acts of war.[245] A more clear-cut basis for rejection would have been the confused assumption that 'terrorism' amounts to an offence.[246]

1.118   Later legislation also largely relies upon this TA 2000 definition, though variants may arise in the enforcement of international law or European Union obligations. It will be noted from s 1(1)(b) that terrorism may be directly targeted at either the government

---

[241] See Meisels, T, *The Trouble with Terror* (Cambridge University Press, Cambridge, 2008) p 28.
[242] Saul, B, *Defining Terrorism in International Law* (Oxford University Press, Oxford, 2006) p 68.
[243] TA 2006, s 34 added the reference to international governmental organisations. See European Union Framework Decision on combating terrorism (2002/475/JHA, 13 June 2002) art 1; International Convention for the Suppression of Acts of Nuclear Terrorism 2005 (Cm 7301, London, 2007) art 1.5.
[244] [2006] EWHC 2465 (Admin).
[245] Ibid para 44.
[246] Ibid para 41.

(including its agents such as the police) or the public, though the ultimate aim is broadly political (s 1(1)(c)).

Section 1 is purposefully wider than its predecessor, aside from two points.[247] First, s 1 demands a 'serious'[248] level of violence (and also 'serious' damage or risks to health and safety or electronic disruption). But s 1 also encompasses any endangerment of life without qualification, 'other than that of the person committing the action' (s 1(2)(c)).[249] Next, as originally drafted, the Terrorism Bill entirely dropped the alternative objective in the previous definition of 'putting the public or any section of the public in fear', which may sometimes result from non-political hooliganism or individual acts of aggression. However, it is sufficient that the use or threat is 'to intimidate the public or a section of the public' (s 1(1)(b)).[250]   **1.119**

In more aspects, s 1 is significantly broader than its predecessor. A wider scope is given to the word 'violence'.[251] Section 1(2) addresses (b) risks to property, (d) risks to safety, and (e) interference with computer systems. In a late modern society, the state is 'hollowed out' and power is diffused across both public and private sectors. Power relates more to finance, knowledge, and security, and so the likely targets of terrorists shift in line with the new concentrations of power and the new power-holders. Next, as well as the listed actions, s 1 mentions the 'threat' of them, which correspondingly expands upon the meaning of violence.   **1.120**

Section 1 next offers some widening of the relevant purposes or motives of terrorism. The definition is not limited by actors, so that state agents engaging in terrorism (unauthorized force for political ends) are caught. The forbidden activities comprise, first, influencing the government and, secondly, religious or ideological causes. It could be argued that 'influence' is too wide, especially having regard to rights to political action under Articles 10 and 11 of the European Convention,[252] and a better word might be 'intimidate'.[253] This adjustment has been rejected by the government.[254] As for religious and ideological causes, whether these really amount to any extension over 'political' is debatable.[255] Inclusion of the word 'religion' may avoid some fine debates over motives but might also cause problems by blurring into personal disputes, such as family or clan disputes about an arranged marriage or a dowry.[256] Secondly, single issue ideological organizations, such as 'eco-terrorists' or anti-abortion groups, could also count as political campaigners even if their prime impact is upon private individuals (such as genetic crop farmers or abortionists) rather than the state, especially when their tactics fall within s 1(3). Rather than tightening the definition, the definition was   **1.121**

---

[247] See *Lloyd Report*, para 5.22; *Home Office Response to Lloyd Report*, para 3.16; Hansard HL vol 611 col 1484 (6 April 2000) and vol 614 col 1448 (4 July 2000), Lord Bassam; Hansard HC Standing Committee D col 31 (18 January 2000), Charles Clarke.

[248] See Hansard HL vol 614 col 1451 (4 July 2000), Lord Bassam.

[249] See Hansard HL vol 614 col 1451 (4 July 2000), Lord Bassam.

[250] The mention of a 'section of the public' may serve to protect minorities within groups or sects: Lord Carlile, *The Definition of Terrorism* (Cm 7052, London, 2007) para 57.

[251] *Home Office Response to Lloyd Report*, para 3.16.

[252] Tomkins, A, 'Legislating against terror' [2002] *Public Law* 205 at 211.

[253] See Lord Carlile, *The Definition of Terrorism* (Cm 7052, London, 2007) para 59; (New Zealand) Terrorism Suppression Act 2002, s 5(2)(b).

[254] *Government Reply* (Cm 7058, London, 2007) p 6.

[255] Edge, P, 'Religious organisations and the prevention of terrorism legislation' (1999) 4 *Journal of Civil Liberties* 194 at 198.

[256] These arguments were rejected by Lord Carlile, *The Definition of Terrorism* (Cm 7052, London, 2007) para 53.

extended by the CTA 2008 to allow for racial causes, to reflect recent international documents, and to reassure minorities.[257]

1.122 The references to purposes and especially to motives have been challenged. First, it is said to be contrary to criminal law principle to mention motive. Secondly, it makes conviction of terrorists more difficult by adding an extra leg of proof. Third, there is an unwelcome emphasis on political goals rather than criminality.[258]

1.123 One response to the first point is that the definition serves not just the purposes of criminal law but also the tasking of state agencies. Another reply is that whilst motive is traditionally of relevance to sentencing rather than offence elements, there is no strict division between motive and the delineation of intent (especially specific intent). In addition, motive is relevant to inquiries as to dishonesty and defences such as provocation and is expressly embraced in offences against racism.[259] Thus, no firm doctrinal or constitutional principle of irrelevance arises, but distinctions are made *ad hoc* to clarify the elements of a crime and to disqualify claims troubling to public policy (such as pleas of poverty or religious dogma).[260]

1.124 A response to the second challenge is that the inclusion of motive does not in practice make proof of terrorist offences much more arduous. The focus remains on the intentions of the defendant, and motives are easily rolled up within that inquiry in evidential terms.[261] In so far as more work is imposed on the prosecution, then that burden is justifiable as reflecting more serious charges often carrying more serious consequences, though, if the attempt fails, there is often the option of an alternative in terms of 'normal' police powers or criminal offences. [262] Conversely, the absence of motive unduly relieves the Crown of a burden.

1.125 The inclusion of motive in the definition of 'terrorism' was also criticized along these lines by the Hederman Commission in Ireland on grounds of the creation of complexity and uncertainty:

> Suppose, for example, that the Gardaí believed that persons carried out a bank robbery using firearms at the behest of an illegal organisation, but it transpired following the arrest of the suspects under section 30 that they had robbed the bank for their own purposes. Alternatively, suppose that the Gardaí believed that a particular person had been shot dead by a known paramilitary, but suspected that the killing had taken place for reasons of private revenge.[263]

---

[257] s 75. See Hansard HL vol 705, col 607 (11 November 2008), Lord West; Lord Carlile, *The Definition of Terrorism* (Cm 7052, London, 2007) para 65. See also Criminal Justice Act 2003, Sch 21, para 4(2)(c).

[258] For differing views, see Saul, B, 'The curious element of motive in definitions of terrorism' and Roach, K, 'The case for defining terrorism with restraint and without reference to political or religious motives' in Lynch, A et al, *Law and Liberty in the War on Terror* (Federation Press, Sydney, 2007); Plaxton M, 'Irruptions of Motive in the War on Terror' (2007) 11 *Canadian Criminal Law Review* 233; Carter, M, 'R v Khawaja, the definition of "terrorist activity" and the irrelevance of motive doctrine' (2009) 42 *University of British Columbia Law Review* 197.

[259] Crime and Disorder Act 1998, ss 28–32.

[260] See Norrie, A, *Crime, Reason, and History* (2nd edn, Butterworths, Toronto, 2001) pp 37–9; Binder, G, 'The Rhetoric of Motive and Intent' (2002) 6 *Buffalo Criminal Law Review* 1.

[261] *R v Williams (CI)* (1986) 84 Cr App R 299.

[262] See for example, *R v Zeky Mallah* [2005] NSWSC 317, 358 (the defendant was acquitted of terrorism offences but convicted of making threats).

[263] *Report of the Committee to Review the Offences against the State Acts, 1939–1998 and Related Matters* (Dublin, 2002) para 7.27.

However, the motive element must be established on the standard of reasonable suspicion in the case of a lawful arrest. If the basis of the arrest is undermined by later investigation, then either the person should be released or rearrested on another basis.

As for the third argument, the recital of motive does regrettably emphasize the political **1.126** nature of the offence, contrary to the objective of criminalization under 'Pursue'. But at the same time, to remove all reference to motive would extend the special provisions to an over-inclusive range of circumstances, such as robbery, rape, and homicide. Such is the potential result in the Canadian case of *R v Khawaja*,[264] where the Ontario Supreme Court struck down as an unconstitutional interference with free expression the reference in the Criminal Code, s 83.01(1) to 'a political, religious or ideological purpose, objective or cause'. Of course, the fact that there is reference to constitutionally relevant objectives does not mean that the state should indulge violent means for their achievement. Indeed, a more accurate reading of *Khawaja* is that Rutherford J was primarily concerned with the inclusion of non-violent objectives within the formulation of motive (such as essential services which are not mentioned within s 1) rather than with motive per se as an element of crime, especially as the other motive (or purpose) element of intimidating the public or compelling the government was not impugned.[265]

In conclusion, the three conjunctive legs should all have relevance to the s 1 approach to the **1.127** definition of 'terrorism', and limits (perhaps including s 1(3)) are of doubtful assistance.[266] A sounder approach than the Canadian reformulation would be to delimit or to avoid altogether reference to the term, 'terrorism', an issue considered later.

As for the feared methods, these are limited in s 1(1) to actions, and so cannot include, for **1.128** example, the omissions of going on strike (withdrawing labour or services) or passive forms of civil disobedience (refusing to pay taxes). There is some room for doubt, however, on this score. For instance, the refusal to pay a tax is an omission, but it may also amount to the commission of an offence.

Assessing this definition against the prerequisites of purpose, target and method, the first and **1.129** second aspects are largely secured by the TA 2000, s 1(1)(b) and (c). Purpose (motive) has already been examined. As regards target, the terrorism violence should be an attack on the collective, subject to the exception of s 1(3). The idea behind this exception is to allow for the label of 'terrorism' to be ascribed in all cases to attacks by explosives or firearms upon political or public figures, even if the purpose of the assailant is not clear and may even be personal rather than political: '. . . we do not want the police to feel hindered in any way from acting in situations that most, if not all of us would regard as terrorism—such as assassinations—because it was not clear that either of those elements was present'.[267] However, this exception remains subject to the requirement of a purpose as in s 1(1)(c), and it is limited to attacks with explosives or firearms whereas attacks by drowning, poisoning, or strangulation remain within s1(1)(b).

As regards method, the core is violence of a kind which causes terror. It was argued earlier that **1.130** one more readily thinks in terms of attacks on humans than on property (as allowed by s 1(2) (b) and (e)). But the prime problem here is that the core term, 'violence', is left unrefined and

---

[264] (2006) 214 CCC (3d) 399, 2008 ON.C.LEXIS 4226.
[265] Ibid, paras 49, 50, 52.
[266] See further Lord Carlile, *The Definition of Terrorism* (Cm 7052, London, 2007) para 55.
[267] Hansard HL vol 614, col 160 (20 June 2000), Lord Bach.

malleable. It is true that in many, perhaps most, cases, 'violence' can readily be translated into established offences. The European Court of Human Rights in *Brogan v United Kingdom* accepted 'terrorism' as within the Convention's notion of an 'offence' for the purposes of Article 5,[268] though that judgment must be read in the context of specific offences of membership of a proscribed organization founding the arrest of the applicant.[269] Nevertheless, one can still conceive of some situations where the current formulation goes further than necessary:[270]

> One is where the person's action in committing suicide [as a form of protest] endangers other people's lives. One might call it the 'Emily Davison case', although no one, not even the horse, was seriously damaged except Emily herself . . . The second issue relates to what one might call the 'Swampy case', where the protester may be thought to cause danger to other people because he tempts them to rescue him.

1.131 The point is that these actions may fall within s 1(2)(c) of the TA 2000 by endangering a person's life, other than that of the person committing the action, as well as satisfying s 1(1)(a) and (c). Another example might be derived from the installation of the artist, Cornelia Parker, whose *Cold Dark Matter: An Exploded View*, is composed of the fragments of a garden shed.[271] Since the explosion was courtesy of the British Army's School of Ammunition, one might assume lawful authority for that particular detonation. But if another artist had undertaken a do-it-yourself explosion, as a representation not just as a parody of the creation of the universe and the subsequent human folly contained within it but also of the brutality of British military force, then s 1 might apply in a disproportionate way and reliance upon prosecutorial good sense would not avert the chilling effect.[272]

Foreign comparisons

International endorsement

1.132 Three points may be made about the definitions of 'terrorism' in other jurisdictions.[273] The first is that the need for a workable legal concept is internationally endorsed. At the same time, international law has not furnished a generic definition either by treaty or customary law,[274] despite substantial efforts to do so since the time of the attacks on the athletes at the Munich Olympics in 1972.[275] Instead, international law has proceeded piecemeal, preferring

---

[268] App nos 11209, 11234, 11266/84, 11386/85, Ser A 145-B (1988) para 50. See also *Ireland v United Kingdom*, App no 5310/71, Ser A 25 (1978) para 196.

[269] Hansard HL vol 613 col 677 (16 May 2000), Lord Lloyd. In response, see Hansard HL vol 613, cols 681–2 (16 May 2000), Lord Bassam.

[270] Hansard HL vol 614 col 1446 (4 July 2000), Lord Beaumont.

[271] Lord Carlile, *The Definition of Terrorism* (Cm 7052, London, 2007) para 34.

[272] Compare Lord Carlile, *Report on the Operation in 2002 and 2003 of the Terrorism Act 2000* (Home Office, London, 2004) para 25.

[273] See Lord Carlile, *The Definition of Terrorism* (Cm 7052, London, 2007) para 18.

[274] But see the Geneva Convention for the Prevention and Punishment of Terrorism (League of Nations, 1937).

[275] See Cassese, A, 'Terrorism as an international crime' in Bianchi, A (ed), *Enforcing International Norms Against Terrorism* (Hart, Oxford, 2004); Dugard, J, 'The problem of the definition of terrorism in international law' and Subedi, SP, 'The war on terror and UN attempts to adopt a comprehensive convention on international terrorism' in Eden, P and O'Donnell, T, *11 September 2001* (Transnational Publishers, Ardsley, New York, 2005); Lim, CL, 'The question of a generic definition of terrorism under general international law' in Ramraj, VV, Hor, M, and Roach, K (eds), *Global Anti-Terrorism Law and Policy* (Cambridge University Press, Cambridge, 2006); Saul, B, *Defining Terrorism in International Law* (Oxford University Press, Oxford, 2006) chs 3–5; Gioia, A, 'The United Nations Conventions on the prevention and suppression of international terrorism' in Nesi, G (ed), *International Cooperation in Counter-Terrorism* (Ashgate, Aldershot, 2006).

to deal with specific unconscionable actions, such as hijacking or hostage-taking.[276] Reasons which conduce against an international crime of terrorism include the desire for flexibility in the definition, the difficulty of distinguishing legitimate force for self-determination/liberation, and the unease that state military actions will be tarred with the same brush. However, the proliferation of sectoral treaties on terrorism, including more ambitious attempts at condemnation in the form of the Civilian Bombing Convention and the Terrorist Finance Convention,[277] have edged the international community towards a workable conglomerate concept of terrorism.

In particular, the (United Nations) International Convention for the Suppression of the Financing of Terrorism 1999, Article 2(1),[278] contains the following definition: **1.133**

> Any person commits an offence within the meaning of this Convention if that person by any means, directly or indirectly, unlawfully and wilfully, provides or collects funds with the intention that they should be used or in the knowledge that they are to be used, in full or in part, in order to carry out: (a) An act which constitutes an offence within the scope of and as defined in one of the treaties listed in the annex; or (b) Any other act intended to cause death or serious bodily injury to a civilian, or to any other person not taking an active part in the hostilities in a situation of armed conflict, when the purpose of such act, by its nature or context, is to intimidate a population, or to compel a Government or an international organization to do or to abstain from doing any act.

This formula was described as 'catching the essence of what the world understands by "terrorism"' in *Suresh v Canada*.[279] Its relevance has grown because of the demands for enforcement in the UN Security Resolution 1373 of 28 September 2001. As a result, most national legal systems make some reliance upon the term 'terrorism', and many exceed the implementation of international conventions.

This trend has been furthered by UN Security Council Resolution 1624 of 14 September   **1.134**
2005, which 'Calls upon all States to adopt such measures as may be necessary and appropriate and in accordance with their obligations under international law to: (a) Prohibit by law incitement to commit a terrorist act or acts . . .' A further tranche of legislation has ensued in several states, including, as will be explained in Chapter 8, Germany and the United Kingdom. For the latter, Prime Minister Blair pulled off the neat hegemonic trick of being the principal mover of this resolution in New York, when he spoke forcefully for action against 'poisonous propaganda',[280] while at the same time citing in aid the Security Council Resolution as one justification for the suppression of speech by what became the TA 2006.

---

[276] The various international Conventions are addressed mainly in Chapters 5 and 10 where they form the basis for domestic crimes and protective action. See Bassiouni, MC, *International Terrorism: Multinational Conventions (1937–2001)* (Transnational Publishers, Ardsley, 2001).

[277] International Convention for the Suppression of Terrorist Bombings, adopted by the General Assembly of the United Nations on 15 December 1997 (37 ILM 249); International Convention for the Suppression of the Financing of Terrorism, adopted by the General Assembly of the United Nations on 9 December 1999 (39 ILM 270).

[278] 39 ILM 270, 1999.

[279] 2002 SCC 1 at 98. See also *Fuentes v Canada (Minister of Citizenship and Immigration)* [2003] 4 FC 249.

[280] UNSC (S/PV.5261) p 9.

Emulation in comparable jurisdictions

1.135   The second point about definitions in other jurisdictions is that the TA 2000, s 1 has set a persuasive precedent for comparable jurisdictions, its faults notwithstanding.[281] For instance, the Australian Criminal Code Act 1995, Division 100.1, states that a terrorist act means an action or threat of action where the action causes listed harms or interferences and the action is done or threatened with the intention of advancing a political, religious, or ideological cause and with the intention of (i) coercing, or influencing by intimidation, the government of the Commonwealth or a State, Territory, or foreign country, or (ii) intimidating the public or a section of the public. The listed harms or interferences are very similar to those in the TA 2000, s 1(2), though the purview is wider still and encompasses financial systems, essential government services or public utilities, and any transport system.

1.136   In Canada, the definition of 'terrorist activity' introduced into the Criminal Code, s 83.01(1), by the Anti-terrorism Act 2001 falls into two parts. First, 'terrorist activity' is defined to include any act or omission committed, threatened, attempted, or counselled, inside or outside of Canada, that amounts to a terrorist offence referred to in any of ten anti-terrorist international conventions. The second part is more redolent of the British precedent. By s 83.01(1)(b), 'terrorist activity' consists of an act or omission, in or outside Canada, that is committed for a political, religious, or ideological purpose, objective, or cause, and with the intention of intimidating the public, with regard to its security, including its economic security, or compelling a person, a government or a domestic or an international organization to do or to refrain from doing any act. In addition, there must be the intention to cause harms or interferences which are similar to the TA 2000, s 1(1)(b), save that any 'essential service, facility or system' is protected. This definition has, as already noted, been found invalid in so far as it relies upon motivation, but 'terrorism' is not necessarily unconstitutionally vague.[282]

1.137   Though the South African Protection of Constitutional Democracy against Terrorism and Related Activities Act 2004 has rightly been touted as generally much more restrained than the foregoing examples,[283] its definition of terrorism in s 1 represents a significant lapse from this standard.[284] 'Terrorist activity' is defined as any act which involves the systematic, repeated, or arbitrary use of violence or dangerous substances; the endangerment of life; the causing of serious risk to the health or safety of the public; the destruction of or substantial damage to any property, natural resource, or the environmental or cultural heritage; the serious interference with or serious disruption of an essential service, facility, or system, or the delivery of any such service, facility, or system; the causing of any major economic loss or extensive destabilization of an economic system; or the creation of a serious public emergency situation or a general insurrection. The intention must be to threaten the territorial unity or integrity, to intimidate or terrorize the public, or to coerce the government or public. The motive must be for the purpose of the advancement of an individual or collective political, religious, ideological, or philosophical motive, objective, cause, or undertaking.

---

[281] See Roach, K, 'Sources and trends in post 9/11 anti terrorism laws' in Goold, BJ and Lazarus, L, *Security and Human Rights* (Hart, Oxford, 2007) p 244. Before 2000, earlier British precedents along the same lines have an equally pervasive influence; see for example: Israeli Prevention of Terrorism Ordinance 1948 (no 33) s 1.

[282] *Suresh v Canada* 2002 SCC 1 at 99.

[283] Compare South African Law Commission, *Project no.105: Report on the Review of Security Legislation* (Pretoria, 2002).

[284] See Schonteich, M, 'Back to the future?' (2002) 14 *Terrorism & Political Violence* 1.

These foreign formulations venture even further than the British precedent and further than is **1.138** necessary. All seriously confuse potential civil emergencies through industrial or even political disruption [285] with terrorism which should concentrate on the infliction of personal violence.[286]

There is no emulation in the USA and, instead, multiple definitions of 'terrorism' may be **1.139** found.[287] This apparent manipulation of different definitions serving different purposes can be illustrated by the US annual surveys of terrorism, whereby 'terrorism' is confined to 'premeditated, politically motivated violence perpetrated against noncombatant targets by subnational groups or clandestine agents, usually intended to influence an audience'.[288] Thus, state terrorism is excluded. A variety of other definitional approaches range from listing specific criminal activities or types of criminal activities through to broader definitions which are indiscriminate as to crimes and instead emphasize dangerous acts which appear intended to intimidate or coerce a civilian population or to influence or affect a government.[289]

'Scheduled offence' approach

The third point about comparative definitions is that some other jurisdictions have instead **1.140** adopted a 'scheduled offence approach'. This alternative approach was also adopted by the Northern Ireland (Emergency Provisions) Acts 1973–96 and then in Pt VII of the TA 2000.[290] Under this model, counter-terrorism laws are designed by reference to a catalogue of specified offences commonly involved in terrorism.

This scheduling approach has long been the model for the Irish Republic's Offences against **1.141** the State Act 1939, both for special policing powers and for trial without jury in the Special Criminal Court.[291] The *Hederman Report* in 2002 endorsed the scheduling approach for policing powers in the absence of a satisfactory definition of terrorism but was critical of ministerial powers to alter the scope of the schedule.[292] However, the Report recommended that at the point of trial a more discerning decision should be made on the merits of the case rather than on the preconceived view that certain types of offences are inevitably terroristic.[293] The German Penal Code, s 129a, which provides for the criminalization of 'terrorist organizations' also relies purely upon listed offences without reference to ulterior intent or motive.

Next, the approach has been emulated in international law by the Council of Europe, **1.142** which has defined terrorism primarily by reference to specific international offences in the

---

[285] Compare Civil Contingencies Act 2004, ss 1, 19.

[286] Proposals vary in their support of this suggestion. See Special Senate Committee on the Anti Terrorism Act, *Fundamental Justice In Extraordinary Times* (Ottawa, 2007) ch 2; *Response of the Government of Canada to the Final Report of the House of Commons Standing Committee on Public Safety and National Security Sub-Committee on the Review of the Anti-terrorism Act* (Ottawa, 2007) pp 2–7; Attorney General, *National Security Legislation Discussion Paper* (Canberra, 2009) pp 43–9.

[287] See Blakesley, CL, *Terror and Anti-Terrorism* (Transnational, New York, 2006) chs 2, 3.

[288] See US Department of State, *Patterns of Global Terrorism* (<http://www.state.gov/s/ct/rls/pgtrpt>) and the National Counterterrorism Center, *Reports on Terror* (<http://www.nctc.gov/>), as regulated by 22 USC s 2656f(a), with the definition set in s 2656f(d).

[289] See 18 USC ss 1956(c)(7), 2331, 2332a(a), 2332(b), 2339A, 2339B, as amended by the USA PATRIOT Act 2001 s 802.

[290] See further Walker, C, *The Anti-Terrorism Legislation* (Oxford University Press, Oxford, 2002) ch 7; Golder, B and Williams, G, 'What is terrorism' (2004) 27 *University of New South Wales Law Journal* 270.

[291] But note the additional Criminal Justice (Terrorist Offences) Act 2005, which implements the European Union approach described later.

[292] *Report of the Committee to Review the Offences against the State Acts, 1939–1998 and Related Matters* (Dublin, 2002): paras 7.24–7.27.

[293] Ibid para 9.57.

European Convention on the Suppression of Terrorism of 1977 and the Convention on the Prevention of Terrorism of 2005.[294]

1.143 The European Council Framework Decision on Terrorism[295] requires Member States to ensure that terrorist offences are enacted. Under Article 1, the activities to be defined as offences under national law are those which may seriously damage a country or an international organization where committed with the aim of seriously intimidating a population, unduly compelling a government or international organization to perform or abstain from performing any act, or seriously destabilizing or destroying the fundamental political, constitutional, economic, or social structures of a country or an international organization. This relatively vague formula is then given more substance by reference to a range of types of offences which comprise: personal attacks, kidnapping or hostage taking; causing extensive destruction to governmental or public facilities, transport systems, infrastructure (information systems), a fixed platform, a public place or private property likely to endanger human life or result in major economic loss; the seizure of aircraft, ships, or other means of transport; involvement with weapons, explosives, or nuclear, biological or chemical substances; the release of dangerous substances, or causing fires, floods, or explosions the effect of which is to endanger human life; or interfering with or disrupting the supply of water, power, or any other fundamental natural resource the effect of which is to endanger human life. Article 2 goes on to require a further set of offences (such as participation) in a 'terrorist group' which is defined as 'a structured group of more than two persons, established over a period of time and acting in concert to commit terrorist offences'. Article 3 covers offences linked to terrorist activities, including, since 2008, public provocation to commit a terrorist act.

1.144 In this way, much of the document follows the scheduled offence approach, but in Article 2 there emerges a 'scheduled offence in context approach' in which the offence is indicative but must be associated with elements of sustained group activity for political purposes. The latter is also adopted by the French Penal Code art 421-1, by which 'acts of terrorism' are constituted by a listed range of offences but only where they are committed intentionally in connection with an individual or collective undertaking the purpose of which is seriously to disturb the public order through intimidation or terror.

1.145 A 'scheduled offence' approach better complies with fundamental requirements as to legal certainty and emphasizes the goal of responding with 'normal' laws rather than adopting a political, religious, ethnic, or racial framework.[296] Next, the scheduling approach can better differentiate between terrorism at home and abroad by devising different crime inventories, the foreign list by reference to global international instruments which address aspects of terrorism. To avoid the dangers of overbreadth, as identified by the *Hederman Report*, the 'scheduled offence in context approach' is preferable.

---

[294] CETS No 90, arts 1 and 2; CETS 196, Appendix.

[295] European Union Council Framework Decision on Combating Terrorism (2002/475/JHA), as amended by Framework Decision 2008/919/JHA.

[296] See *Report of the Special Rapporteur on the promotion and protection of human rights and fundamental freedoms while countering terrorism* (E/CN.4/2006/98, 2005) para 33; Cole, D, and Dempsey, JX, *Terrorism and the Constitution* (3rd edn, New Press, New York, 2006) p 249.

The Home Office view is that to limit the application of the definition of terrorism to actions **1.146** contrary to the criminal law will not suffice.[297] It would hamper police discretion, and it would create uncertainties when dealing with international terrorism. It also alleges that there may be occurrences designed to terrify which are not unlawful—such as a refusal to perform a duty to keep others safe,[298] provided the refusal is for political rather than industrial motives.[299]

Assessment and conclusions

Reformulation

Lord Carlile pronounced in 2007 that s 1 is 'practical and effective'.[300] His preference was to **1.147** structure more carefully the discretion of the Attorney General to allow prosecutions.[301] Limits are now enshrined in the TA 2006, s 36, and the Counter Terrorism Act 2008, s 29. However, the reliance upon prosecution barriers only highlights the underlying promiscuity of the syntax and has less impact on policing practices. One worrying trend is the application to individual extremists who lack the threat and sophistication for the proportionate invocation of special measures. Another is the influence of foreign relations, as evidenced by the treatment of the Libyan Islamic Fighting Group.[302]

Limits by context

Where the TA 2000 may be condemned as particularly lax in comparison with its pre- **1.148** decessor is not much in the terms of its core elements of purpose, target, and method but in the circumstance of how these components are applied in the body of the legislation—the context. Thus, it is the decoupling of the legislation from its historical grounding in the undoubtedly serious conflict in Ireland that permits the overuse of draconian provisions in circumstances where ordinary policing and laws might suffice. To cater for this broader context, there should be emphasis upon not only the types of seriously threatening and destabilizing offences being perpetrated but also the nature of the perpetrators, for it is that context which renders less capable 'normal' criminal justice processes and thereby justifies special laws. The position is made much worse because s 1(4) makes explicit that the scope of the definition includes action outside the United Kingdom against foreign governments. There were unsuccessful attempts in Parliament to confine the foreign coverage of the TA 2000 to 'designated countries' rather than regimes which might be viewed as 'odious'.[303] But the implication of labelling some terrorism as officially acceptable was unpalatable to the government.

Consequently, if the legislation is to be disestablished from its Irish grounding, further quali- **1.149** fications ought to be inserted to ensure that specially designed counter-laws really offer a proportionate response. A prime reason why special laws might be justifiable is if the political violence occurs in the context of a secretive and organized group—it is the collective para-military nature which makes the action so threatening and difficult to police. Therefore, s 1

---

[297] Hansard HL vol 611 col 1484 (6 April 2000), Lord Bassam.
[298] Hansard HL vol 614 col 1448 (4 July 2000), Lord Bassam.
[299] Hansard HC Standing Committee D, col 31 (18 January 2000), Charles Clarke.
[300] Lord Carlile, *Report on the Operation in 2005 of the Terrorism Act 2000* (Home Office, London, 2006) para 32.
[301] Lord Carlile, *The Definition of Terrorism* (Cm 7052, London, 2007) para 81.
[302] See Chapter 8. Compare the non-prosecution of Simon Mann and associates for the attempted over-throw of the government of Equatorial Guinea: *The Independent on Sunday* 8 November 2009, p 32.
[303] Hansard HC Standing Committee D, col 26 (18 January 2000), David Lidington. That s 1 protects the Libyan government was confirmed in *R v F* [2007] EWCA Crim 243 (see Chapter 6).

should specify that the political violence must involve concerted action by a group of people acting in an organized and secretive way.

1.150　This context for violence is more clearly recognized in the alternative definition of 'terrorism' in s 2 of the Reinsurance (Acts of Terrorism) Act 1993, which establishes a scheme for reinsurance for commercial property damage resulting from terrorism:[304]

> (2) In this section 'acts of terrorism' means acts of persons acting on behalf of, or in connection with, any organisation which carries out activities directed towards the overthrowing or influencing, by force or violence, of Her Majesty's government in the United Kingdom or any other government *de jure* or *de facto*.
>
> (3) In subsection (2) above 'organisation' includes any association or combination of persons.

1.151　In practice, this need for context is recognized by the United Kingdom authorities[305] who have declined to treat animal rights extremists as 'terrorists' even though they fit the definitional profile[306] and have been described as replicating 'a quasi-terrorist cellular structure'.[307] Conversely, the additional elements of definition would not fail to apply the bite of special laws to loose collectives inspired by a 'franchise' like Al-Qa'ida. For instance, the facts that the perpetration of the 7/7 London bombings involved at least four people, deploying sophisticated techniques, and possibly with support from confederates abroad,[308] does raise elements of complexity and danger which defy the application of 'normal' law.

1.152　A further issue of context is the 'Kosovo problem'—the concern that British soldiers in conflicts abroad could be labelled as terrorists. The government's response to this point unsatisfactorily relied on the alleged 'general principle in law that statutes do not bind the Crown unless by express provision or necessary implication'.[309] Since it is clear that the definition of terrorism can apply to state actors and that soldiers in Northern Ireland have fallen foul of it,[310] a better approach might have been a more explicit statement about when force is 'lawful' under either domestic or international law.

Protest rights

1.153　An additional safeguard in the legal definition of 'terrorism' might be an additional proviso for the proportionate respect for individual freedoms of belief, expression, and association (as in Articles 9 to 11 of the European Convention on Human Rights). Its purpose would be to offer 'symbolic reassurance'.[311] However, its practical utility where implemented elsewhere is not evident.[312] It therefore remains a concern that the term,

---

[304] See Walker, C, 'Political violence and commercial risk' (2004) 56 *Current Legal Problems* 531.

[305] *Government Reply* (Cm 7058, London, 2007) p 5.

[306] See Home Office, *Animal Rights Extremism* (London, 2001) para 3.75.

[307] Department of Trade and Industry, *Animal Welfare—Human Rights: protecting people from animal rights activists* (London, 2004) para 43.

[308] See Intelligence and Security Committee, *Report on the London Terrorist Attacks on 7 July 2005* (Cm 6785, London, 2005); Home Office, *Report of the Official Account of the Bombings in London on 7 July 2005* (2005–06 HC 1087).

[309] Hansard HL vol 613 col 241 (16 May 2000), Lord Bach. See also *Re Lockerbie Air Disaster, The Times*, 20 May 1992 (CA).

[310] See further Lord Carlile, *The Definition of Terrorism* (Cm 7052, London, 2007) para 83.

[311] Roach, K, 'Canada's response to terrorism' in Ramraj, VV, Hor, M, and Roach, K, *Global Anti-Terrorism Law and Policy* (Cambridge University Press, Cambridge, 2006) p 520.

[312] See Australian Criminal Code 1995, Div 101(3); Canadian Anti-terrorism Act 2002, s 83.01; New Zealand Terrorism Suppression Act 2001, s 5(5).

'terrorism' is inimical to protesters, cranks, and fantasists as much as to terrorists, recognizing at the same time that these catgeories must sometimes be subject to firm policing action.

Conclusions

A number of changes have been suggested which would improve the usage of the term   **1.154**
'terrorism' in United Kingdom law. The more radical approach would be to redesign the term 'terrorism' around a combination of the types of seriously threatening and destabilizing offences commonly perpetrated, all of which should harm human welfare. The context of the offences should be added, and it should emphasize the presence of collective, complex, and sustained enterprises. A more timid approach would be to apply this 'scheduled offence in context' approach only to criminal offences about terrorism, where the need for certainty and equality is greatest, leaving a broader definition of 'terrorism' along the current lines for the purposes of the accentuation of anticipatory action through policing powers. The effect of the emphasis upon context is to insert within the law a 'principle of normalcy'—that reflection should be given to normal powers, procedures, and offences in priority to special counter-terrorism laws.[313] If the 'scheduled offence in context' approach is not adopted as such, then a free-standing principle of normalcy should be added to the special legislation, for it reminds us of the fundamental lesson that the instrument of law should be used in proportion. The danger otherwise is that the likes of the Terrorism Acts will foster the very extremism they were meant to prevent.

F. Conclusions

For reasons adduced in this chapter, the generation of permanent anti-terrorism laws can be a   **1.155**
worthwhile exercise in practical and ethical terms. But, as delivered, some commentators view the laws in the United Kingdom as 'an unmitigated disaster' for 'the motherland of liberty'.[314] Even the Archbishop of York, John Sentamu, has warned about the development of a police state.[315] Though Lord Carlile dismissed this language as 'extravagant',[316] terrorism policing certainly extends into political life, with proscription and offences about the encouragement of terrorism. It impinges on civil life, with restrictions on liberty through arrest, stop and search, port controls, and, for the few, control orders. The routines of travel and economic life have also been affected by surveillance. Has this effort delivered the goal of CONTEST— 'so that people can go about their daily lives freely and with confidence'?[317] With an emphasis upon prevention and the management of risk, where non-occurrence is the desired result and where full information is never divulged, quantitative measures are problematic. It is accepted that terrorism has been prevented during the past decade through factors such as the incompetence of the terrorists, the vigilance of the public, and also the anticipatory work of the intelligence agencies and the police, sometimes aided by anti-terrorism laws.[318]

---

[313] Rossiter, CL, *Constitutional Dictatorship* (Princeton University Press, Princeton, 1948) p 7.

[314] Ackerman, B, *Before the Next Attack* (Yale University Press, New Haven, 2006) p 70.

[315] *The Times* 5 February 2007, p 26.

[316] Lord Carlile, *Report on the Operation in 2006 of the Terrorism Act 2000* (Home Office, London, 2007) para 30.

[317] Home Office, *Pursue, Prevent, Protect, Prepare: The United Kingdom's Strategy for Countering International Terrorism* (Cm 7547, London, 2009) para 0.17.

[318] See Klausen, J, *Al-Qaeda-affiliated and 'Homegrown' Jihadism in the UK: 1999–2010* (Institute for Strategic Dialogue, London, 2010).

Though statistics will be presented throughout this book, they do not give a full sense of achievement.[319] So, qualitative impressions will now be added.

1.156 The survey in this book suggests that a legal model of accommodation of special measures[320] can be worthwhile in two senses. One is that there can be tangible policy gains. The laws will be scored in this book against CONTEST. While many claims will not be sustained and while others may be exaggerated, neither is a universal finding. The other sense in which the exercise is worthwhile is that the policy outcomes can be achieved without always sacrificing societal values. Once again, it is not claimed that there is entire normative compliance, but there are many instances of genuine attempts to secure protection for rights and to avoid undue usage of anti-terrorism laws. This imperfect model of accommodation is surely preferable to a 'business as usual' model which pretends that law cannot help against the modes of attack presented by terrorism. Equally, it is preferable to the 'extra-legal measures model' of *ex post facto* reckoning and possible punishment or indemnity of officials who are more likely to lie about their misdeeds and have them covered up in solidarity than to face any reckoning. Even when a public reckoning is applied, the model assumes absolution and so becomes a 'business as usual model' with institutional indulgence for excess.

1.157 Moving from general assessments to specific legislation, the TA 2000 represents a valuable attempt to fulfil the role of a code against terrorism, though it fails to meet the desired standards in every respect. The 2001 and 2005 Acts have proven much less satisfactory either in substance or as polished legislative performances. Part IV of the 2001 Act was a dubious artifice which rightly foundered. Many other parts of that Act owe more to opportunism than terrorism.[321] For its part, the 2005 Act fosters the abhorrent process of allowing the executive to sit in judgment over individual freedoms. Perhaps the best that can be said of control is that it avoids worse outcomes—either another variant of detention without trial or the emulation the American concept of the 'war on terror'. The 2006 and 2008 Acts have reverted to a more calculated approach in which criminalization is prioritized. But their accretion underlines the sobering thought, proffered by the Home Affairs Committee, that the overall result is that 'this country has more anti-terrorist legislation on its statute books than almost any other developed democracy'.[322]

1.158 Aside from the extension of the anti-terrorism legislation, other persistent trends are manifested by the materials in this book. One is the permanence of the special provisions against terrorism. This permanence is increasingly unremarkable. The twenty-first century concept of normality in criminal justice embodies the contingency and reality of 'special' powers dealing with 'special' situations or risks,[323] whether terrorism, serious frauds, sex offenders, or the anti-social. This trend towards fragmentation and specialization may be warranted, provided sensible safeguards and scrutiny are secured. One should not confuse the construction of such a specialist code in modern democracies with a bout of transient 'emergency law' in

---

[319] Home Affairs Committee, *Policing in the 21st Century* (2007–8 HC 364) para 40.
[320] Gross, O, and Ni Aolain, F, *Law in Times of Crisis* (Cambridge University Press, Cambridge, 2006) chs 1–4.
[321] See Hansard HL vol 629 col 633 (3 December 2001) Lord Rooker.
[322] *Report on the Anti-terrorism, Crime and Security Bill 2001* (2001–02 HC 351), para 1.
[323] See Gross, O, and Ni Aolain, F, 'To know where we are going we need to know where we are' in Hegarty, A and Leonard, S, *Human Rights* (Cavendish, London, 1999) p 82.

a Roman dictatorship.[324] In addition, permanence is not the same as the 'normalization' of special powers or the 'contamination' of 'normal' laws.[325] It is true that special laws are difficult to confine in temporal, geographical, or functional terms,[326] and there is overlap with 'normal' laws, such as in regard to asset confiscation and restrictions on the right against self-incrimination. Nonetheless, one can equally point to many instances of British distaste for Northern Irish anti-terrorism legislation and efforts to curtail their excesses.

The second trend concerns the emphasis upon anticipatory risk and the proactive countering of terrorism. The result is an emphasis on intelligence-gathering, demonstrated not only by the perseverance with 'executive measures' (ministerial legal powers such as control orders) but also by the proliferation of precursor criminal offences. This trend is encouraged by the more holistic approach to terrorism represented by the CONTEST strategy. The culmination of 'Prevent' may be a welcome emphasis on the generation of conditions which encourage resort to terrorism, though reliance upon more holistic concepts such as human security do raise the equally alarming prospect of the undue 'securitization of political issues and public policy'.[327]   **1.159**

A third trend concerns the growing influence of international law. As terrorism is successfully depicted by western states as a universal scourge, so it is increasingly possible to base state action on international accords.[328] Evidence for this trend includes the international crimes mentioned in Chapter 5, and the more pervasive influence since 11 September 2001 of the European Convention on Human Rights, the European Union, and the United Nations.   **1.160**

A fourth unrelenting theme has been the troubled relationship between anti-terrorism laws and human rights. Almost all official reviewers of the legislation, from Lord Diplock in 1972 onwards, have been enjoined to take account of human rights, and so the concept has been to the fore, even though its application has often failed to satisfy human rights advocates. It follows that the Human Rights Act 1998 was not necessarily destined to have a major impact in this area, given that legislation had been 'Strasbourg-proofed' for some years and given that the European Convention on Human Rights shows considerable indulgence towards anti-terrorism legislation.[329] Indeed, the application of human rights discourse has been a two-edged sword, with failed challenges resulting sometimes in entrenchment and legitimation and the insertion of human rights safeguards encouraging the grant of more extreme powers.[330] Nevertheless, human rights have become the pre-eminent standard for review.   **1.161**

This point leads to the fifth, more positive, trend—the rising assertion of judicial and parliamentary review. This trend towards greater assertiveness in security disputes challenges the   **1.162**

---

[324] See Frerejohn, J, and Pasquino, P, 'The law of the exception' (2004) 2 *International Journal of Constitutional Law* 210.

[325] See Hillyard, P, 'The normalisation of special powers: From Northern Ireland to Britain' in Scraton, P (ed), *Law, order and the authoritarian state* (Open University Press, Milton Keynes, 1987).

[326] See Gross, O, 'Chaos and rules' (2003) 112 *Yale Law Journal* 1011.

[327] Zedner, L, *Security* (Routledge, Abingdon, 2009) p 45.

[328] See Bowring, B, 'The degradation of international law?' in Strawson, J, (ed), *Law After Ground Zero* (Glasshouse Press, London, 2002).

[329] See Council of Europe, *The Fight against Terrorism* (3rd edn, Strasbourg, 2005); Warbrick, C, 'The principles of the ECHR and the response of states to terrorism' [2002] *European Human Rights Law Review* 287.

[330] For example, judicial review of TA 2000, s 41 detention became a safeguard which made more palatable the doubling of the period of detention by the Criminal Justice Act 2003, s 306.

assertion that anti-terrorism legislation represents naked power—rule by law and not the rule of law.[331] A more principled and controlled approach towards anti-terrorism legislation, which is shared in fair part by the executive itself, is far from that of a totalitarian state of exception which operates in a legal vacuum.[332] The government has not declared an all-encompassing 'war on terror' which rivals or replaces regular laws, nor has it produced a 'zone of anomie in which all legal determinations are deactivated'.[333] Those commentators who peddle such a picture appear ignorant of the efforts of the international community since 1945 to determine that no such state of anomie or Hobbesian state of savagery can be authorized again under the contemporary codes of international humanitarian and human rights laws. The modern rulers of liberal democracies who seek to draw upon the poisonous old doctrines of executive authority have rightly (as was the eventual fate of the Presidency of George Bush) faced concerted legal opposition and unprecedented unpopularity. Most norms have not at any time been suspended, as with the 'war on terror' or 'criminal law of the enemy',[334] but society has adapted to a new normality of terrorism. As the former Foreign Secretary, David Miliband, has declared: 'We must respond to terrorism by championing the rule of law, not be subordinating it, for it is the cornerstone of the democratic society.'[335] There is much room for disagreement on the outcomes, but the trend towards strategic action and constitutionalism at least demonstrates that the principles set out earlier in this chapter are becoming 'not a mask but the true image of our nation'[336] and offer protection from naked state power.[337] The law thereby has demonstrated capacity through its normative power and through the independence of its institutions to respond to executive claims to power.[338]

1.163 A sixth feature concerns the symbolic role of anti-terrorism laws. For instance, some offences which were the subject of intense debate, such as indirect incitement, have hardly been used. This feature may also betray the difficulties of gathering intelligence which is translatable into public action and also the sensitivities of imposing every conceivable legislative burden upon communities which are suspicious in equal measure to their being suspect.[339] The public is also sceptical of the assurance being offered by symbolic legislation. Polling on the 42-day proposal suggested scepticism about the gain from the loss of liberty and suspicion of the motives of politicians.[340]

---

[331] See Agamben, G, *The State of Exception* (University of Chicago Press, Chicago, 2005).

[332] Compare Schmitt, C, *Political Theology* (MIT Press, Cambridge, 1985).

[333] Agamben, G, *The State of Exception* (University of Chicago Press, Chicago, 2005) p 50.

[334] See Jakobs, G, and Melia, MC, *Criminal Law of the Enemy* (2nd edn, Civitas, Madrid, 2006).

[335] *The Guardian* 15 January 2009, p 29.

[336] Ignatieff, M, *The Lesser Evil* (Edinburgh University Press, Edinburgh, 2005) p 144.

[337] See Marks, S, 'State centrism, international law and the anxieties of influence' (2006) 19 *Leiden Journal of International Law* 339; Campbell, C and Connelly, I, 'Making war on terror? (2006) 69 *Modern Law Review* 935 at 939; Vaughan, B and Kilcommins, S, *Terrorism, Rights and the Rule of Law* (Willan, Cullompton, 2008) p 13.

[338] Campbell, C and Connelly, I, 'Making war on terror? (2006) 69 *Modern Law Review* 935 at 939.

[339] See Fenwick, H, *Civil Liberties and Human Rights* (4th edn, Routledge-Cavendish, Abingdon, 2007) p 1233.

[340] Only 36 per cent supported the extension: Joseph Rowntree, British Policies Survey (York, 2008). Compare the ICM poll in 2006 which found 73 per cent favoured the more abstract proposition of loss of rights in return for greater security: Landman, T, 'The continuity of terror and counterterror' in Brysk, A and Shafir, G, *National Insecurity and Human Rights* (University of California Press, Berkeley, 2007).

It follows that the anti-terrorism laws are often largely peripheral in effect. An unusually **1.164** frank insight is the Intelligence and Security Committee's report, *Could 7/7 have been Prevented?*[341] For all the powers and resources of the police and security services, the bombers were not detected save as very peripheral figures in the machinations of others. But if every possible contact became subject to close scrutiny, then the kind of police state dreaded by some would indeed come about.[342] Resources have since been increased and liaison between agencies improved, but failings are 'understandable and reasonable' given the desire for an ethical response and given the determination of the terrorists.[343] A more macro-level indicator of achievement might be the official threat level whereby, once again, despite rising levels of resources, liaison, and experience, the state's combined efforts have managed to reduce the level from 'severe' or 'critical' to 'substantial' for just six months out of the four years when the information has been published.[344]

More important factors in dealing with terrorism will comprise normal police powers and **1.165** criminal offences and regular techniques of investigation and securitization. These must operate alongside cooperation and vigilance on the part of the public who provide, even in terrorist cases, much of the policing capability of society. International cooperation is also of growing importance in response to more fluid and global vulnerabilities. Above all, there must be a vibrant and inclusive democracy which can discern the difference between vituperative and politically immature hot air and violence with the potential to spill blood and which holds its nerve and its cherished values in the face of the heat and light of the terrorist spectacular. That democracy must even remain willing to speak to its enemies, as explained in the analysis of the Northern Ireland Peace Process. In an asymmetric conflict, the terrorists cannot destroy Western polities.[345] But they may provoke Western polities to destroy their own spirits and cultures through the politics and practices of fear, discrimination, and intolerance.

It would be a fine development if, having been fortified with these sweeping powers, the UK **1.166** government and its security forces could have the confidence and ability to rely primarily on 'normal' policing powers and upon their extensive contingency planning and networks. However, as they perceive themselves to live in an extraordinarily and increasingly threatening epoch, terrorism laws can anticipate a long and active life. The emphasis should therefore be upon the standards of constitutionalism so that the persistence of special measures does not corrode the values of society and so that a return to normality is not lost from sight. With due regard for those values, attention will now be turned towards the detailed contents of the anti-terrorism laws.

---

[341] Cm 7617, London, 2009.
[342] Ibid para 143.
[343] Ibid para 212.
[344] See <https://www.mi5.gov.uk/output/threat-levels.html>.
[345] This point was made by Leon Trotsky ('Why Marxists oppose individual terrorism' (1911) *Der Kampf*) long before contemporary pundits alighted upon the idea (*A v Secretary of State for the Home Department* [2004] UKHL 56 at para 97 per Lord Hoffman; Ignatieff, M, *The Lesser Evil* (Edinburgh University Press, Edinburgh, 2005) p 80).

PART II

INVESTIGATION AND POLICING

2

TERRORIST INVESTIGATIONS

A. Introduction

It is an article of faith within CONTEST that good intelligence is 'vital to defeating terrorism' **2.01**
as well as being a 'currency' more important than firepower.[1] This elevated importance
derives from the sophisticated, secretive, and committed nature of terrorist groups, which
render them difficult to infiltrate or to monitor, and the value of focused state responses.
The importance of intelligence has also been reflected in institutional terms with the conferment of intelligence lead on the Security Service (in 1992 for Britain and in 2007 for
Northern Ireland),[2] the growth in expenditure on the intelligence community,[3] and the
establishment of the Joint Terrorism Analysis Centre[4] and regional offices within the
Security Service.[5]

---

[1] Home Office, *Countering International Terrorism: The United Kingdom's Strategy* (Cm 6888, London,
2006) para 65; *Operation Banner* (Army Code 71842, London, 2006) para 818.
[2] See Hollingworth, M and Fielding, N, *Defending the Realm* (Andre Deutsch, London, 2003) ch 5;
Andrew, C, *The Defence of the Realm* (Allen Lane, London, 2009) pp 600, 644, 683, 734, 799, 813.
[3] See Intelligence and Security Committee, *Report into the London terrorist attacks on 7 July 2005* (Cm 6785,
London, 2006) para 118.
[4] See Intelligence and Security Committee, *Annual Report 2002–03* (Cm 5837, London, 2003) para 62 and
Annual Report 2003–04 (Cm 6240, London, 2004) para 92.
[5] Hansard HC vol 418 col 303 (25 February 2004), David Blunkett.

2.02   The anticipatory risk of mass terrorism casualties has deepened this emphasis. Pre-emptive intervention involves intelligence-led special investigative techniques which add to the range of more overt police detection aids, such as CCTV, and the collection of data about movements, communications, and finances.

2.03   The effect of 9/11 terrorism has been 'to speed up and spread out' surveillance techniques[6] whereby 'successive UK governments have gradually constructed one of the most extensive and technologically advanced surveillance systems in the world'.[7] A further consequence is to accord unprecedented centrality to the secret security agencies which puts them under an unaccustomedly harsh spotlight.

2.04   The interventions resulting from investigation may involve prosecution or executive measures such as control orders. However, most anti-terrorism operations do not produce formal legal process but more commonly involve monitoring, physical disruption (such as modifying explosives), or indirect disruptive intervention (by deceptions, lies, or stings).

2.05   Intelligence arises from manifold sources and techniques.[8] The sources of greatest interest to this chapter will comprise human sources and physical observations, as well as communications, signals, and electronic data gathering. Of course, a great deal of intelligence is collected from open sources such as newspapers and web pages without the intercession of special powers. But legislation can assist the process by providing for pretexts for contact with human sources and can also authorize technical intrusions into private data. Those latter techniques have been endorsed by the European Court of Human Rights in *Klass v Germany*, on the basis that 'Democratic societies nowadays find themselves threatened by highly sophisticated forms of espionage and by terrorism, with the result that the State must be able, in order effectively to counter such threats, to undertake the secret surveillance of subversive elements operating within its jurisdiction'.[9]

2.06   This chapter will examine the laws about the investigation of terrorism in three sets. First, there are powers which allow access to, and search of, documents and places. These powers are relatively focused in terms of the objectives or targets (or both) of the investigation. The second set of investigatory powers involves 'surveillance'. This term is often associated with electronic devices but also encompasses human agency. Thirdly, there are investigatory powers which might be said to reflect 'all-risks policing'. Into this category fall measures such as powers to stop and search and ports controls.

2.07   The topic of investigation, the core of this chapter, is so vast that some relevant measures must be consigned to other chapters. Offences and powers which are designed to elicit the disclosure of relevant information are considered in Chapter 3. The interrogation and testing of suspects in police detention are set out in Chapter 4. Some specialist financial investigative powers are consigned to Chapter 9.

---

[6] Lyon, D, *Surveillance after September 11* (Polity, Cambridge, 2003) p 1.
[7] House of Lords Select Committee on the Constitution, *Surveillance: Citizens and the State* (2008–09 HL 18) para 1.
[8] See Council of Europe, *Terrorism: Special Investigation Techniques* (Strasbourg, 2005) p 13; Gill, P and Pythian, M, *Intelligence in an Insecure World* (Polity Press, Cambridge, 2006) ch 4.
[9] App no 5029/71, Ser A 28 (1987) para 48.

B. Investigation of Places and Documents

Introduction and background

A definition of 'terrorist investigations' appears in the TA 2000, s 32,[10] as a peg on which to **2.08** hang other powers to investigate documents and places within Pt IV:

> ... 'terrorist investigation' means an investigation of—
>
> (a) the commission, preparation or instigation of acts of terrorism,
> (b) an act which appears to have been done for the purposes of terrorism,
> (c) the resources of a proscribed organisation,
> (d) the possibility of making an order under section 3(3), or
> (e) the commission, preparation or instigation of an offence under this Act or under Part 1 of the Terrorism Act 2006 other than an offence under section 1 or 2 of that Act.

The purpose of the 'terrorist investigation' concept is to allow pre-emption and wide discretion. Therefore, it does not require the authorities to await the occurrence of any proven crime or proven link to terrorism and will allow investigations into preparatory work relevant to terrorism.

The main tranche of measures is introduced by s 37 and Sch 5 of the TA 2000.[11] Schedule 5 **2.09** essentially offers variants upon the already compendious powers in Sch 1 of PACE and PACE(NI). The main differences relate not only to the triggering criteria but also to the extent of powers so triggered. However, in many details, the terminology of the PACE legislation is followed.[12]

In so far as these powers (or any others in the TA 2000) involve the search of premises, then, **2.10** by s 116(1), a power to search premises allows the search of any container within it. A small pool of judges handles applications, and they are located in court buildings with secure storage facilities.[13]

Provisions: premises search

The first search power, to enter premises, to search the premises or any person found there, **2.11** and to seize and retain any relevant material, is in Sch 5, para 1(1): 'A constable may apply to a justice of the peace for the issue of a warrant under this paragraph for the purposes of a terrorist investigation.' The premises to be targeted may be particular (for a 'specific premises warrant') or, following amendment by the TA 2006, s 26,[14] they may comprise any or sets of premises occupied or controlled by a specified person (an 'all premises warrant').[15] To make an application, the constable must have reasonable grounds under para 1(3) for believing

---

[10] As amended by the TA 2006, s 37(1). The exclusion of the TA 2006, ss 1 and 2 was to delimit those controversial offences: Hansard HL vol 677, col 1242 (25 January 2006), Lord Bassam.

[11] For earlier legislation, see Walker, CP, *The Prevention of Terrorism in British Law* (2nd edn, Manchester University Press, Manchester, 1992) p 187. Prior Northern Ireland legislation was decanted into the TA 2000, Pt VIII, now replaced by the JSA 2007 ss 21–42 (see Chapter 11).

[12] PACE, ss 21, 22 are directly applied by Sch 5, para 17.

[13] Lord Carlile, *Report on the Operation in 2001 of the Terrorism Act 2000* (Home Office, London, 2002) para 4.5.

[14] This was inspired by the Serious Organised Crime and Police Act 2005, ss 113, 114.

[15] A warrant may incorporate both formats: *Redknapp v Metropolitan Police Commissioner* [2008] EWHC 1177 (Admin).

that the evidence is likely to be of substantial value[16] to a terrorist investigation, and that it must be seized in order to prevent it from being concealed, lost, damaged, altered, or destroyed. In turn, the justice may grant an application only if 'satisfied' under para 1(5): (a) that the warrant is sought for the purposes of a terrorist investigation; (b) that there are reasonable grounds for believing that there is material on the premises which is likely to be of substantial value to a terrorist investigation; (c) that the issue of a warrant is likely to be necessary in the circumstances of the case; and (d) in the case of an all premises warrant, that it is not reasonably practicable to specify all the premises. 'Excepted material' may not be the subject of an application. Paragraph 1 includes in the definition of 'terrorist investigation' anything likely to be of substantial value to 'a', and not 'the', terrorist investigation so that where material relevant to a different terrorist investigation is discovered, there is no need to return to court for another warrant.

2.12 Arising from Operation Pathway, the searches of property under Sch 5 para 1 were challenged in *Sher v Chief Constable of Greater Manchester Police*[17] on the ground that the police occupied the premises for some days. However, this action could still amount to a search 'on one occasion' as specified by the search warrant. The High Court was determined that the police should not be hamstrung but warned that the police would not have been entitled to leave and come back later.[18]

2.13 Additional powers to seize and sift materials elsewhere are generally enabled under the Criminal Justice and Police Act 2001, ss 50, 51, and 55. These powers have been expanded by the CTA 2008 which allows the removal of documents[19] for examination in the context of a police search under existing terrorism legislation search powers.[20] Thus, there is power, backed by the deterrence of an offence of obstruction under s 2,[21] to remove a document from premises so that the police can examine it elsewhere, where it is not possible to examine it effectively at the search site because of its bulk or inextricable link to other material.[22] Before this amendment, the sifting power applied only in relation to the search powers in the TA 2000 Sch 5 in relation to paras 1, 3, 11, and 15.[23] Section 1 of the CTA 2008 grants this power in relation to a much wider range of search powers[24] in order that the police can examine back at base materials such as foreign language documents and computer data so as to ascertain whether they may be seized. The other major change brought about by s 1 is that it lowers the threshold for seizure. Reliance on the 2001 Act scheme required reasonable suspicion that the extra seized materials were relevant evidence in relation to the offence justifying the search. The standard of reasonable suspicion is removed by s 1—it is sufficient that an officer might merely 'think' that what appears to be a restaurant bill from Peshawar is in fact an Al-Qa'ida document.[25] Thus, s 1 intercedes where the document is 'entirely obscure', though

---

[16] Under PACE, Sch 1, para 2, it should be 'relevant evidence'.

[17] [2010] EWHC 1859 (Admin).

[18] Ibid paras 110, 115.

[19] 'Documents' can mean information stored in electronic form (s 9) but do not include computers: Hansard HL vol 704 col 344 (9 October 2008), Lord West.

[20] There were 347 seizures over a five-year period to 2008: Hansard HL vol 704 col 358 (9 October 2008), Lord West. Powers to examine documents in the TA 2000, s 87, expired in 2007.

[21] Compare Police Act 1996, s 89.

[22] It is promised that PACE Codes will explain further: Hansard HC Public Bill Committee on the Counter-Terrorism Bill col 177 (29 April 2008), Tony McNulty.

[23] Criminal Justice and Police Act 2001, Sch 1, para 70.

[24] It adds: TA 2000, s 43, Sch 5, paras 28, 31, PTA 2005, ss 7A, 7B, or 7C, and TA 2006, s 28.

[25] Hansard HC Public Bill Committee on the Counter Terrorism Bill col 169 (29 April 2008), Tony McNulty.

it is not to encourage 'fishing expeditions' as will be clarified by PACE Code B.[26] The Act also more clearly regulates seizures without reference back to the 2001 Act. In particular, the power is subject to the protection under s 3[27] of documents that are, or may be, legally privileged, where the constable has reasonable cause to believe the item has that status. If it is later discovered that a removed document is an item subject to legal privilege, it must be returned immediately unless it cannot be separated from other parts. By s 4, there must be a written record of the removal as soon as is reasonably practicable and in any event within twenty-four hours. Section 5 limits the retention for examination to forty-eight hours unless further retention for an extra forty-eight hours is authorized by a chief inspector. Supervised access or a copy may be granted under s 6. Copying of the material is restricted under s 7.

Greater latitude is allowed in the second search power in Sch 5, in para 2, because the application does not relate to residential premises.[28] There is no equivalent to this power in PACE, and the origins of this power reside in the PT(AP)A 1996,[29] s 2. The purpose of para 2 is to facilitate mass searches, such as of lock-up premises in a given area where it is suspected that bomb-makers are active but without sufficient knowledge as to the precise location of their premises. Such a warrant is exercisable only within twenty-four hours of issuance of the warrant. Under para 2, the premises must be specified, but there is an 'all premises' variant under para 2A.[30] The application is made by a police officer of at least the rank of superintendent to a justice of the peace, and, in contrast to para 1 applications, the justice of the peace need not be concerned that the issue of a warrant is likely to be necessary in the circumstances of the case. Area searches would normally be invalid because of generality,[31] so it is surprising that a lowly justice of the peace should have the task of scrutinizing these applications.   **2.14**

The third search power relates to cordoned areas, including residential premises. There is no equivalent in PACE 1984. Sch 5, para 3 empowers a police officer of at least the rank of superintendent, with reasonable grounds for believing that there is material to be found on the premises, to authorize by a written and signed authority a search of specified premises which are wholly or partly within a cordoned area. To cater for dire emergencies, perhaps within the first few minutes after cordoning off, any constable may give an authorization (presumably to himself) if he considers it necessary by reason of urgency. The search may be repeated at any time during designation. The limitations as to materials which may be seized are the same as in para 1, and the power to seize and sift elsewhere under the Criminal Justice and Police Act 2001 also apply. It is a summary offence wilfully to obstruct a search under para 3.[32]   **2.15**

Provisions: powers of production and access to materials

The fourth investigative power, under para 5, deals with the production of, or access to, excluded and special procedure material which are defined together (along with legally privileged materials) as 'excepted materials' in para 4 for the whole of the first part of   **2.16**

---

[26] Hansard HL vol 704 cols 339, 343 (9 October 2008), Lord West.

[27] Compare Criminal Justice and Police Act 2001, s 54.

[28] Classification as 'non-residential' depends on reasonable belief: para 2(4), 2A(4).

[29] See Reid, K, 'Prevention of Terrorism (Additional Powers) Act 1996' [1996] 4 *Web Journal of Current Legal Issues*; Jason-Lloyd, L, 'The Prevention of Terrorism (Additional Powers) Act 1996—a commentary' (1996) 160 *Justice of the Peace* 503.

[30] See TA 2006, s 26.

[31] See *Entick v Carrington* [1765] 95 ER 807; *R v Atkinson* [1976] Crim LR 307; *Redknapp v Metropolitan Police Commissioner* [2008] EWHC 1177 (Admin); *R (Bhatti) v Croydon Magistrates' Court* [2009] EWHC 3004 (Admin).

[32] The penalty will increase to 51 weeks: Criminal Justice Act 2003, s 280, Sch 26, para 55.

Sch 5 by reference to PACE 1984. These materials are excepted from the objectives of the foregoing three powers, though it is only legally privileged materials which may not be seized and retained under those powers if found by chance rather than design. The search power under para 5 for excluded material sharply contrasts with PACE. By para 8, only legally privileged material is exempt from the clutches of para 5 which overrides all other statutory restrictions, even, according to para 9, to material held by government departments.

2.17   By para 5(1), a constable may apply to a circuit judge[33] for an order to access excluded or special procedure material (including, under para 7, material coming into existence within twenty-eight days) for the purposes of a terrorist investigation. There is no requirement that notice be given to the possessor of the materials or that the material must be potential 'evidence' for a court case. An application may also relate to a person who is likely to have possession of such material within twenty-eight days. If granted, the order may require under para 5(3) a specified person normally within seven days: (a) to produce to a constable within a specified period for seizure and retention any relevant material; (b) to give a constable access to relevant material within a specified period; and (c) to state to the best of his knowledge and belief the location of relevant material if it is not in, and will not come into, his possession, custody, or power within the period specified under (a) or (b). An order may also require any other person who appears to the judge to be entitled to grant entry to the premises to allow entry and access.

2.18   The circuit judge may grant an order[34] if 'satisfied' of two criteria in para 6. The first condition relates to the relevance to the purposes of a terrorist investigation as well as the need for 'reasonable grounds for believing that the material is likely to be of substantial value'. The second condition demands reasonable grounds for believing that it is in the public interest that the material should be produced. There is no reference to demonstrating that other methods of access have been unsuccessful or are doomed to failure.

2.19   Much of the consequent litigation under the TA 2000 and equivalent predecessors has considered journalistic materials. In *R v Middlesex Guildhall Crown Court, ex parte Salinger*,[35] the police sought from prominent US journalist, Pierre Salinger, and his employers records of interviews conducted in Libya with the two prime suspects of the Lockerbie bombing in 1988. It was held by the High Court that on the initial *ex parte* application, the police should provide to the judge a written statement of the material evidence, including the nature of the available information for which disclosure would be sensitive. The applicant police officer should appear before the judge to provide oral evidence. The judge could then decide on the grant of the order and also on what information might be served on the recipients. In turn, the recipient is entitled to be given, preferably in writing and at the time of service of the order, as much information as could properly be provided as to the grounds for the order but it would rarely be appropriate or necessary for disclosure of the source or details. A subsequent application to discharge or vary should be made to the same judge with the same police officer who gave oral evidence being present. On this application, the judge will reconsider the order on its merits, and there is no onus on the recipient to satisfy the judge that

---

[33] A District Judge (Magistrates' Courts) may also act once the Courts Act 2003, s 65, Sch 4, para 9(a) comes into force; this change will affect all the powers in Sch 5. In Northern Ireland, a Crown Court judge acts in this capacity (substituted for a county court judge by the ATCSA 2001, s 121, to bring it in line with the Proceeds of Crime Act 2002, s 343). This switch to the Crown Court removed the availability of judicial review in Northern Ireland, but a process to discharge or vary is still implied: *Re Morris* [2003] NICC 11.

[34] Under para 10, it is treated as an order of the Crown Court.

[35] [1993] QB 564.

the order was wrongly made. The processes were further clarified in *Re Morris*.[36] Appearance at the *ex parte* stage by the possessors should be rare but could be allowed by discretion of the court where it did not impede the investigation and could be of assistance to the court, which might be especially true in difficult and complex cases involving the media.[37]

Journalistic material was at issue in 1991, when Box Productions compiled a programme, **2.20** broadcast by Channel 4, which alleged that there was collusion between members of the Royal Ulster Constabulary and Loyalist terrorists which was presided over by a secret committee of prominent people.[38] The police sought the production of documents connected with the programme. A redacted dossier of material was handed to the police, but it was claimed that further sensitive material had either been destroyed or removed from the jurisdiction and that the only person who knew the whereabouts of the material was a researcher employed by Box Productions. The judge then directed that the material sent abroad should be brought back and produced to the police. The respondents refused to comply and thereby put themselves in contempt of court. The Divisional Court could not review the judge's exercise of his discretion to make the order, and it therefore proceeded to impose a fine of £75,000 for the contempt.[39]

In *Re Moloney's Application*,[40] the Northern Ireland editor of the *Sunday Tribune* newspaper **2.21** was required to produce any notes of an interview with William Stobie, who was later accused (and acquitted) of the murder of lawyer Patrick Finucane. Quashing the Recorder's order, the High Court stated:[41]

> ... the police have in our view to show something more than a possibility that the material will be of some use. They must establish that there are reasonable grounds for believing that the material is likely to be of substantial value to the investigation.

In *Re Jordan*,[42] the police sought materials from a BBC Panorama programme, *Gangsters at* **2.22** *War*, which showed an announcement by a masked man on behalf of the Ulster Freedom Fighters. He was identified through voice analysis as Dennis Cunningham.[43] According to the Crown Court in Belfast, any arguments about the chilling effect of disclosure on the ability to carry out investigative journalism were outweighed by 'the unmasking of terrorists and bringing them to justice'.[44]

In *Malik v Manchester Crown Court*,[45] a production order was granted under para 6 in **2.23** connection with a book manuscript written about Hassan Butt, entitled, *Leaving Al-Qaeda*. The police believed materials possessed by Malik, who helped to write the book, might disclose evidence of crimes by Butt. It was held that 'likely' under para 6(2)(b) demanded a high standard—'probable'; but 'substantial value' required only a value more than minimal.[46]

---

[36] [2003] NICC 11 at para 35.
[37] Ibid para 35.
[38] See further McPhilemey, S, *The Committee* (Roberts Rinehart, Boulder, 1999).
[39] *DPP v Channel 4 & Box Productions* [1993] 2 All ER 517. See further Costigan, R, 'Further dispatches' (1992) 142 *New Law Journal* 1417.
[40] [2000] NIJB 195.
[41] Ibid 207.
[42] [2003] NICC 1.
[43] He was later convicted on this evidence: *R v Cunningham* [2005] NICC 45.
[44] [2003] NICC 1 at para 21 per Judge Hart.
[45] [2008] EWHC 1362 (Admin).
[46] Ibid para 36.

Being 'satisfied' required a firm belief rather than a suspicion.[47] On review, it was determined that the grant of the order could not be faulted, though the terms were altered. The High Court indicated that a court could of its own motion exceptionally appoint a special advocate to appear at the *ex parte* hearing or on an application for variation or discharge.[48]

2.24 There was another battle between journalists and police in *Re Galloway*, concerning an application by the PSNI sought for records and materials of the Northern Editor of the *Sunday Tribune* newspaper relating to claims of responsibility for the murders by Republican dissidents of two soldiers in 2009.[49] The application was refused. The Court endorsed the approach that the public interest in the investigation and prosecution of serious crime is important, so the level of proof of overriding interests must attain a very high threshold of a substantial risk—in this case the threat to the right to life (Article 2 of the Convention) of the journalist and her family. That standard was met by the journalist.

2.25 Two issues not yet adequately litigated are first, whether compliance with the production order might involve forcible self-incrimination contrary to Article 6 of the European Convention. The offences of withholding information about terrorism offences committed by another under s 19 or 38B of the TA 2000 (both described in Chapter 3) might be engaged by production orders. It was indicated in *R v Central Criminal Court, ex parte Bright*[50] that the statutory powers of production override the right against self-incrimination. The production of physical materials with an existence independent of the will of the defendant has been treated as distinct from demanding information from the knowledge of the defendant.[51] The second factor yet to be fully rehearsed is the impact of s 12(4) of the Human Rights Act 1998, which requires particular regard for the importance of freedom of expression before any order is granted.

2.26 Should a production order under para 5 be viewed as inappropriate for the purposes of the investigation (perhaps because it would tip off a potential collaborator), then under para 11, a constable may apply to a circuit judge (or in Northern Ireland, a Crown Court judge) for the issuance of a warrant to permit entry, search, and seizure. This variant procedure may be selected where, under para 12, a circuit judge is satisfied that a production order (whether on specified premises or an 'all premises' type) has not been complied with (para 12(1)) or where satisfied (under para 12(2)–(4)) that there are reasonable grounds for believing there is present material likely to be of substantial value but that it is not appropriate to proceed by way of production order. The power to seize and retain materials attracts additional powers to seize and retain articles for sifting elsewhere enabled under the Criminal Justice and Police Act 2001.

Provisions: ancillary powers

2.27 The fifth type of investigative power is ancillary to the foregoing. By Sch 5, para 13, a constable may apply to a circuit judge (or in Northern Ireland, a Crown Court judge) for an order requiring any person specified in the order to provide an explanation of any material

---

[47] Ibid para 37.
[48] Ibid para 99.
[49] [2009] NICty 8.
[50] [2001] 2 All ER 244. Compare *Inner West London Coroner v Channel 4 Television Corporation* [2007] EWHC 2513 (QB).
[51] See *Brown v Stott* [2000] UKPC D3; *R v Allen* [2001] UKHL 45; *O'Halloran and Francis v United Kingdom*, App nos 15809/02, 25624/02, 29 June 2007; *R v S* [2008] EWCA Crim 2177.

seized, produced, or made available under paras 1, 5, or 11. There is no equivalent invasive power in PACE 1984. Though the usual exception as to legal privilege applies, a lawyer may be required to provide the name and address of his client. There is no express immunity against revealing information concerning other excepted materials. It is an offence under para 14 knowingly or recklessly to make a false or misleading statement. By para 13(4)(b), and in deference to Article 6, a statement in response to a requirement imposed by an order under this paragraph may be used in evidence against the maker only on a prosecution for an offence under para 14 but not for any other offence.[52]

The sixth investigative power, under Sch 5, para 15, deals with cases of urgency. A police **2.28** officer of at least the rank of superintendent may give written authority equivalent to a warrant or order under para 1 or para 11. The officer must have reasonable grounds for believing that the case is one of great emergency and that immediate action is necessary. Particulars of the case shall then be notified as soon as is reasonably practicable to the Secretary of State, though no particular response is then required. Wilful obstruction of a search is a summary offence.[53] There is no defence of reasonable excuse, but the requirement that the obstruction be 'wilful' performs part of its job. The power to seize and retain materials attracts additional powers to seize and sift under the Criminal Justice and Police Act 2001.

There is a corresponding emergency equivalent to the compulsory disclosure power under **2.29** Sch 5, para 13 for materials under para 15. By para 16, a police officer of at least the rank of superintendent who has reasonable grounds for believing that the case is one of great emergency may by a written notice require any person specified in the notice to provide an explanation of any material seized in pursuance of an order under para 15. It is a summary offence to fail to comply with a notice. It is a defence for a person charged with such an offence to show that he had a reasonable excuse for his failure (perhaps relating to the difficulty of accessing or amassing information within a required time scale); s 118 does not apply.

Finally, there are some variants for Northern Ireland and Scotland. The adaptations for **2.30** Northern Ireland are minor,[54] since erstwhile special executive powers of the Secretary of State by Sch 5, paras 19, 20, and 21, have now been repealed.[55]

Part II of Sch 5 provides for Scottish powers equivalent to those in England and Wales. **2.31** Part II represents a considerable extension of police powers since PACE does not apply in Scotland. Powers corresponding to the first category are found in para 28; the procurator fiscal may apply to the sheriff to grant a warrant for the purposes of a terrorist investigation.[56] There is no direct equivalent to the second or third search powers. However, similar to the fourth power, by para 22, the procurator fiscal may apply to the sheriff for a production order which can relate to material of any specified description (the concepts of special procedure and excluded materials not being part of Scottish law). Explanations, as in the fifth power, can be required under para 30 on application by the procurator fiscal to the sheriff. Police powers, dealing with urgent situations in the sixth category, are granted by paras 31 and 32.

---

[52] See *Saunders v United Kingdom*, App no 19187/91, 1996-VI; *IJL v United Kingdom*, App nos 29522/95, 30056/96, 30574/96, 2000-IX.

[53] The penalty is to increase to 51 weeks: Criminal Justice Act 2003, s 280, Sch 26, para 55.

[54] See Sch 5 para 18.

[55] T(NI)A 2006, s 5, Sch.

[56] All premises warrants are provided for by the TA 2006, s 27.

Implementation

2.32 Accountability is woefully weak for the exercise of Sch 5. Regular statistical returns for Great Britain are not available, though it was revealed that 694 production orders were issued in 2006,[57] and that few applications are denied.[58] The picture in Northern Ireland is a little clearer, as indicated in Table 2.1:

Table 2.1 **Premises searched under warrant under s 37 and Sch 5 of the TA 2000 in Northern Ireland**[a]

Year	Premises searched
2001	94
2002	181
2003	278
2004	416
2005	223
2006	133
2007	237
2008	108

[a] Source: Northern Ireland Office, Statistics on the Operation of the Terrorism Act 2000 (Belfast).

2.33 Although scrutiny by the independent reviewer (Lord Carlile) is applicable, attention by him (and by Parliament) has been minimal.

Foreign comparisons

2.34 The most directly comparable jurisdiction is the Republic of Ireland. Special search powers are granted by the Offences against the State Act 1939, s 29 (as substituted by the Criminal Law Act 1976, s 5). Where an officer of the Gárda Síochána, not below the rank of superintendent is satisfied that there is reasonable ground for believing that evidence relating to a scheduled offence may be found in any place, the officer may issue to a police officer not below the rank of sergeant a search warrant. Unlike under the Terrorism Act, there is no need for any emergency circumstances to justify passing the authority from judicial to police officer. However, the Hederman Committee endorsed s 29 as a 'vital weapon in the armoury of the Gardaí in their fight against the activities of illegal organisations'.[59]

Assessment and conclusions

2.35 Schedule 5 seeks cumulatively to enable the 'Pursue' element of CONTEST but achieves that goal by lowering safeguards normally available in PACE and without consideration of whether PACE powers could suffice. In so far as reliance is deemed unavoidable, whether

---

[57] HM Treasury, *The Financial Challenge to Crime and Terrorism* (London, 2007) para 2.64. The figure used to be around 100: (Rowe) *Report of the Operation in 1998 of the Prevention of Terrorism (Temporary Provisions) Acts* (Home Office, London, 1999) para 70.

[58] Lord Carlile, *Report on the Operation in 2001 of the Terrorism Act 2000* (Home Office, London, 2002) para 4.6.

[59] (Hederman) *Report of the Committee to Review the Offences against the State Acts, 1939–1998 and Related Matters* (Dublin, 2002) para 6.141.

because of the additional powers offered by the Terrorism Act or because of its broader notion of 'terrorist investigation', three departures from PACE cause most disquiet. One is that the powers under paras 1, 5, and 11 are subjectively worded.[60] Secondly, the police can issue their own authorizations under para 15, without subsequent reporting and confirmation by a judicial officer. The third departure concerns the extension of powers to excepted material under paras 5 and 13. The high standard set in *Re Galloway* for the protection of investigative journalism materials suggests that insufficient weight has been accorded to Article 10.[61]

Various criticisms of specific measures in Sch 5 may be mounted. The implication that non-residential premises should attract virtually no privacy protection misreads the European Convention.[62] Therefore, the power in paras 2 and 3 should be confined to emergencies and should be strictly limited in time. **2.36**

The necessity for the powers should also be scrutinized. As well as PACE, the field of financial criminal investigations is also occupied by the Proceeds of Crime Act 2002, Pt VIII. Part VIII investigations are narrower since they relate to whether someone has derived 'benefit from his criminal conduct' (s 341), but the enforcement measures otherwise closely resemble Sch 5, including production orders (ss 345 and 380, but not extending to excluded material by ss 348 and 383), search warrants (ss 352 and 387), and disclosure orders (ss 357 and 391). The criteria for issuance under s 358 are notably stricter, and the courts have imposed sensible limits when dealing with external activities on behalf of the foreign authorities who had deliberately chosen not to seek an order in their own country.[63] Consolidation would be beneficial to ensure unity of terminology and coverage of the 2002 Act's extensive guidance,[64] and to improve constitutional governance. **2.37**

As for constitutional governance under Sch 5, the laws are detailed, and the possibility of judicial challenge does exist. **2.38**

C. Cordons

Introduction and background

Part IV of the TA 2000 allows the setting up of cordons and reproduces powers first enacted after the 1996 Docklands bombings.[65] The typical scenario will be where the police suspect that a bomb has been planted or wish to take control over the vicinity of an actual explosion or arrest operation. **2.39**

Provisions

By s 33 of the TA 2000, a police officer can designate a 'cordoned area' if considered 'expedient for the purposes of a terrorist investigation'.[66] The acting officer must by s 34 be **2.40**

---

[60] Compare PACE, Sch 1.

[61] See *Goodwin v United Kingdom*, App no 17488/90, 1996-II, para 39.

[62] Compare *Chappell v United Kingdom*, App no 10461/83, Ser A 152-A (1989); *Halford v United Kingdom*, App no 20605/92, 1997-III.

[63] *Serious Fraud Office v King* [2008] EWCA Crim 530 at para 59.

[64] See Proceeds of Crime Act 2002 (Investigations in England, Wales and Northern Ireland: Code of Practice) Order 2008, SI 2008/946.

[65] See PT(AP)A 1996, ss 4, 5.

[66] 'Expedient' should be interpreted as in *R (Gillan) v Commissioner of Police for the Metropolis* [2006] UKHL 12.

of at least the rank of superintendent, unless there is urgency, in which case any constable may step in. An amendment under the ATCSA 2001[67] allows a superintendent (but not other officers even in an emergency) in the British Transport Police[68] and Ministry of Defence Police to designate cordon areas in places within their jurisdiction.

2.41 The power is unusually broad and is expressed in terms of 'expedience' to cater for confused situations:[69]

> An example might be where a bomb warning was imprecise, or the police believed it was inaccurate—deliberately or otherwise. In such a case the necessity for a cordon might be debatable, but it makes good sense to have one. Similarly, in the case of stop and search or parking restriction powers, there could be cases where a cordon might not be considered 'reasonably necessary' but could be to the general advantage.

2.42 Because of the circumstances of grave emergency in which such operations arise, the designation may be oral in the first instance (ss 33(3) and 34(3)), but it must be confirmed in writing as soon as reasonably practicable. Once an order has been issued under s 33, the police must demarcate the cordoned area, so far as is reasonably practicable, by means of tape marked with the word 'police' or in such other manner as a constable considers appropriate.

2.43 By s 35, a designation has effect as specified in the order, but it must not endure longer than the end of the period of fourteen days beginning with the day on which the designation is made, renewable for up to a further fourteen days. While an area remains designated, any constable in uniform may, under s 36(1) order physical evacuation of persons and vehicles, arrange for the removal of parked vehicles, and prohibit or restrict access to a cordoned area by pedestrians or vehicles.

2.44 A person commits a summary only offence under s 36(4) by failing to comply with an order, prohibition, or restriction.[70] It is a defence under s 36(3) for a person to prove a reasonable excuse for the breach; lack of clear specification of the designated area might be one ground. Section 118 does not apply to this defence.

Implementation

2.45 Police cordoning activities centre upon London, but otherwise practices appear erratic. In 2008, there were no cordons in the Metropolitan Police area but one lasting twenty-eight days in Derbyshire. No clear explanation exists for either feature, and record-keeping is 'casual' (see Table 2.2).[71]

Foreign comparisons

2.46 Cordoning is not commonly granted as a specific anti-terrorism power elsewhere, but one example is in the South African Terrorism and Related Activities Act 2004, s 24. If, on written request under oath to a judge in chambers by a police director, it appears to the judge that it is necessary in order to prevent any terrorist or related activity, the judge may issue a

---

[67] Sch 7, para 30.
[68] This power does not apply in Northern Ireland: Railways and Transport Safety Act 2003, s 31.
[69] Hansard HL vol 613 col 660 (16 May 2000), Lord Bassam.
[70] Note the pending changes as to penalty: Criminal Justice Act 2003, s 280, Sch 26, para 55.
[71] Lord Carlile, *Report on the Operation in 2009 of the Terrorism Act 2000 and Part I of the Terrorism Act 2006* (Home Office, London) para 121.

Table 2.2 Cordoning powers[a]

Year	Met Police		City London		Other Eng/Wales		Scot		NI	
	n	Ave mins	n	Ave mins	n (forces)	Ave mins	n	Ave mins	n	Ave mins
2001	30	118	0	0	1 (1)	4,320	0	0	62	n/a
2002	14	184	0	0	12 (2)	260	0	0	239	n/a
2003	16	158	0	0	8 (4)	2,295	0	0	175	n/a
2004	4	60	17	47	0	0	0	0	126	n/a
2005	68	408	11	40	0	0	0	0	72	n/a
2006	13	67	8	30	8 (1)	4,716	0	0	38	287
2007	52	81	22	43	0	0	0	0	29	n/a
2008	0	0	7	40	10 (2)	6,584	0	0	59	n/a
2009	34	58	8	37	1	7,200	0	0	n/a	n/a

[a] Sources: *Carlile Reports* (the duration prior to 2004 is expressed only in full hours); NIO Statistics & Research Branch (from 2001 to 2005) and then from the PSNI.

warrant for the cordoning of a specified area for ten days. The judicial pre-authorization is a notable contrast to the UK process.

Assessment and conclusions

The imposition of cordons is a sensible adjunct to the strategies of 'Pursue' and 'Protect'. **2.47** As for efficiency and efficacy, Table 2.2 suggests that many police operations proceed by negotiation rather than imposition.

Accountability for cordons is under-developed. It is not specified what detail must be given **2.48** in the written confirmation nor to whom the confirmation is to be given nor where the written document is to be lodged. Unlike under s 44 (discussed later in this chapter) no ministerial oversight is required, nor review by a senior police officer. There is no guidance as to mediation with the community. Judicial review is available, but many cordons will have been lifted by the time the lawyers assemble in court. Given current divergent practices, a limit of, say, twenty-four hours should apply beyond which judicial authorization should be obtained.

Moving to a rights audit, the fleeting and incidental nature of the impact on liberty is **2.49** probably not sufficient to infringe Article 5.[72] Freedom of movement is certainly affected but is not yet recognized under the Human Rights Act 1998. As for rights to family life and enjoyment of property, proportionality will be the issue.[73] Most vulnerable to challenge is the initial trigger of 'expedience', which may be deemed to be inadequate to ensure necessity and proportionality related to terrorism rather than police convenience.[74]

As for alternative methods of achieving the same goal, common law powers were invoked **2.50** against Alan Clark, MP,[75] who was convicted of obstruction of the police in the execution of

---

[72] See *R (Gillan) v Commissioner of Police for the Metropolis* [2006] UKHL 12; *R (Laporte) v Chief Constable of Gloucestershire* [2006] UKHL 55; *Austin v Commissioner of Police for the Metropolis* [2009] UKHL 9.

[73] *(Margaret) Murray v United Kingdom*, App no 14310/88 Ser A 300A (1994) para 90.

[74] Compare *Gillan and Quinton v United Kingdom*, App no 4158/05, 12 January 2010.

[75] *The Times*, 14 June 1996, p 5.

their duty at Bow Street Magistrates' Courts for breaching a police cordon during a bomb alert. In addition to common law protective powers, common law forensic protection powers have since been developed. In *DPP v Morrison*,[76] police officers were held to be entitled to erect a cordon to investigate a crime and to preserve evidence. They could even assume that that there was always consent to do so on private land over which a public right of way existed, such as a shopping mall.[77] Another relevant power is s 22(3)(d) of the Civil Contingencies Act 2004, by which regulations may prohibit, or enable the prohibition of, movement to or from a specified place. Thus, a cordon can be imposed around an area affected by, say, a 'dirty' bomb, assuming an emergency can be established to activate Pt II of the Act.[78] In summary, alternative powers do exist, but the common law lacks the clarity of the terrorism legislation,[79] and the Civil Contingencies Act applies only to catastrophic incidents after a declaration of emergency.

D. Surveillance

Introduction and background

2.51 Several deep-seated factors have impelled policing and intelligence agencies in late modern societies towards techniques of surveillance. One is the growing reliance of society on technology, which unlocks new possibilities for investigative techniques. Another is the growing capacities of computers to record and to analyse huge amounts of data, well beyond the capacities of paper records. There is also the factor of transborder linkages which can be impractical to track on the ground. In short, 'Surveillance is key . . .'.[80]

2.52 'Surveillance' is defined in the RIPA,[81] s 48 as monitoring, observing, or listening to persons, their movements, their conversations, or their other activities or communications; recording in the course of that surveillance; and surveillance by a device. The application of the RIPA has given rise to a complex legal edifice, only selections of which are relevant for the purposes of this book.[82]

Provisions: electronic surveillance

2.53 If surveillance is generally of importance to terrorism investigations, then electronic surveillance seems to be first amongst equals. For example, it has been said that 'Telecommunications interception is of crucial importance . . . Telecommunications interception is one of the most efficient and low risk counter-terrorism investigative techniques . . .'.[83] An array of legal

---

[76] [2003] EWHC Admin 683.

[77] The assumption is also made in PACE Code B, para 2.3.

[78] See Walker, C and Broderick, J, *The Civil Contingencies Act 2004* (Oxford University Press, Oxford, 2006) ch 5.

[79] Lord Carlile, *Report on the Operation in 2008 of the Terrorism Act 2000* (Home Office, London) paras 103, 104.

[80] Hayman, A, *The Terrorist Hunters* (Bantam Press, London, 2009) p 247.

[81] Note also the Regulation of Investigatory Powers (Scotland) Act 2000.

[82] See Lustgarten, L and Leigh, I, *In From the Cold* (Clarendon Press, Oxford, 1994); Lyon, D, *Surveillance after September 11* (Polity, Cambridge, 2003); Williams, V, *Surveillance and Intelligence Law Handbook* (Oxford University Press, Oxford, 2006); Harfield, C and Harfield, K, *Covert Investigation* (Oxford University Press, Oxford, 2008); Colvin, M and Cooper, J (eds), *Human Rights and the Investigation and Prosecution of Crime* (Oxford University Press, Oxford, 2009) chs 2–5.

[83] Australian Government, Counter Terrorism White Paper, *Securing Australia: Protecting Our Community* (Canberra, 2010) p 58.

powers outside the specialist anti-terrorism legislation has been developed to allow for investigation through electronic surveillance.

The catalogue elsewhere begins with statutory powers of surveillance granted to the **2.54** security agencies (the Security Service, the Secret Intelligence Service, and the Government Communications Headquarters).[84] The Intelligence Services Act 1994, s 5 (replacing the Security Service Act 1989, s 3, and as amended by the Security Service Act 1996, s 2) allows entry on, or interference with, property or with wireless telegraphy under a warrant issued by the Secretary of State if considered necessary and proportionate to the functions of the agencies. Those purposes include safeguarding 'national security', which in the case of the Security Service expressly includes the threat of terrorism.[85] Special restrictions apply to warrants interfering with property within the jurisdiction: they can be issued only to the Security Service and must investigate specified serious offences.

A more generic tasking authorization may be issued by the Foreign Secretary of State under **2.55** s 7 to the Intelligence Service or GCHQ in order to excuse actions for which the agent could otherwise be liable in the United Kingdom for any act done outside the British Islands.[86] The actions must be undertaken for the proper discharge of a function of the Intelligence Service and their nature and likely consequences must be reasonable. The intention is not to grant 'a licence to kill' but to allow, for instance, conspiracy, forgery, and bribery which might otherwise contravene the Criminal Justice Act 1948, s 31.

An equivalent power of property interference for police officers is granted under the **2.56** Police Act 1997, Pt III.[87] There may be police 'interferences' with property or wireless telegraphy, such as to plant bugging devices, and these operations are authorized under s 93 by a chief police officer or deputy. Interferences with dwellings and office searches must be approved by a judge (a Surveillance Commissioner) under s 97. This special regime of prior Surveillance Commissioner approval also applies under ss 98 to 100 to legally privileged, personal confidential, and confidential journalistic material no matter where located.

The RIPA responds to privacy rather than property encroachments. It first deals with the **2.57** interception of communications in Pt I, chapter 1.[88] Interception of communications under Pt I involves intrusion into the contents of communication and requires authorization by warrant and observance of the general safeguards in s 15. Some interceptions can be lawful

---

[84] See Wadham, J, 'The Intelligence Services Act 1994' (1994) 57 *Modern Law Review* 916; Andrew, C, *The Defence of the Realm* (Allen Lane, London, 2009) p 753; Regulation of Investigatory Powers (Covert Surveillance and Property Interference: Code of Practice) Order 2010, SI 2010/463.

[85] Security Service Act 1989, s 1(2). The term was held to be sufficiently precise in *Hewitt and Harman v United Kingdom (No 2)* App no 20317/92, 1 September 1993; *Esbester v UK*, App no 18601/91, 2 April 1993; *Christie v United Kingdom*, App no 21482/93, DR 78A, 119 (1994). But the notion was rejected in *Amann v Switzerland*, App no 27798/95, 2000-II.

[86] But where the property is discovered to be in the UK, the action may continue: TA 2006, s 31. A similar amendment relating to apparatus had been made by the ATCSA 2001, s 116.

[87] See *Govell v United Kingdom*, App no 27237/95, 14 January 1998; *R v Khan (Sultan)* [1997] AC 558; *Khan v United Kingdom*, App no 35394/97, 2000-V.

[88] See further Home Office, *Interception of Communications Code of Practice* (London, 2007); Akdeniz, Y et al, 'Regulation of Investigatory Powers Act 2000: Bigbrother.gov.uk' [2001] *Criminal Law Review* 73; Benjamin, VO, 'Interception of internet communications and the right to privacy' [2007] *European Human Rights Law Review* 637. For Scotland, see Regulation of Investigatory Powers (Scotland) Act 2000.

without warrant under ss 3 and 4, including those in prisons[89] and those made for certain business purposes.[90]

2.58 These powers are mainly constructed in terms of individual surveillance, but blanket strategic monitoring of 'external communications' is permitted by s 8(4) under a ministerial warrant. Government pleas that these powers are essential to counter 'a growing threat from terrorism' were rejected as conferring unfettered discretion in *Liberty v United Kingdom*.[91] That case arose from a blanket authorization for foreign intelligence gathering (of all telephone traffic to, and from, Ireland) between 1990 and 1997. The British approach was compared unfavourably with the German 'G10 Act' (*Gesetz zur Beschränkung des Brief-, Post- und Fernmeldegeheimnisses* 1968, as modified by the *Verbrechensbekämpfungsgesetz* 1994) which requires biannual ministerial reports to a Bundestag supervisory board and a Commission which must consent to interceptions, as well as restrictions in search terms in relation to identifiable individuals or addresses.[92] The Home Secretary has since asserted by letter to the Chair of the Joint Committee on Human Rights[93] that the passage of the RIPA (with some added safeguards in s 16 to delimit content) and Codes offer sufficient protection.[94]

2.59 The foremost feature under Pt I which has become entwined in debates about terrorism powers is that, under the RIPA, s 17, neither the process of interception nor intercepted material can form admissible evidence in legal proceedings, subject to several uncertainties and anomalies.[95] This stance raises two difficulties.

2.60 The first is that exculpatory materials cannot reach the attention of the defence. Instead, full faith must be placed in the prosecutor under s 18(7)(a) who may receive the material and then determine what is required to secure fairness,[96] including the dropping of charges or evidence or the making of admissions.[97] The worries remain that a partial picture may mislead the jury and that much original intercept evidence never even reaches the purview of the prosecutor.[98]

2.61 The second problem is that the material cannot be used as part of the prosecution evidence, thereby causing undue reliance upon devices such as control orders or extended police detention. Inadmissibility is exceptional in comparative terms,[99] and intercepted material figures as important evidence elsewhere.[100] Any direct claim of pertinence to British terrorism cases

---

[89] See Prison Rules 1999 r 35A (SI 1999/728, as amended).

[90] Telecommunications (Lawful Business Practice) (Interception of Communications) Regulations 2000 (SI 2000/2699).

[91] App no 58243/00, 1 July 2008. See Goold, B, 'Liberty v United Kingdom' [2009] *Public Law* 5.

[92] Ibid paras 53, 68. See *Weber and Saravia v Germany*, App no 54934/00, 29 June 2006.

[93] <http://www.parliament.uk/documents/upload/Johnson_Liberty140709.pdf>, 2009.

[94] See also *Report of the Interception of Communications Commissioner for 2004* (2004–05 HC 549) paras 40–41.

[95] See Ormerod, D and McKay, S, 'Telephone intercepts and their admissibility' [2004] *Criminal Law Review* 15. The system was upheld in *Preston v United Kingdom*, App no 24193/94, 2 July 1997.

[96] See Attorney General's Section 18 RIPA Prosecutors Intercept Guidelines England and Wales (CPS, London, 2003).

[97] Home Office, *Interception of Communications Code of Practice* (London, 2007) para 7.13.

[98] See *Natunen v Finland*, App no 28552/05, 8 December 2009.

[99] See JUSTICE, *Intercept Evidence: Lifting the Ban* (London, 2006); Horne, A, *The Use of Intercept Evidence in Terrorism Cases* (SN/HA/5249, House of Commons Library, London, 2009). The Council of Ministers Committee of Ministers, *Special Investigative Techniques* (Rec (2005) 10, Strasbourg, Art 7) recommends the production of intercept evidence in court.

[100] See *US v Narseal* 2007 US Dist LEXIS 61186; *US v Abu Jihaad* 531 F Supp 2d 299 (2008); *R v Benbrika* [2009] VSC 21; *R v Elomar* [2010] NSWSC 10.

has, however, been denied by Lord Carlile and by independent senior criminal counsel.[101] Nonetheless, it seems highly improbable that surveillance should be so coveted for intelligence-gathering and yet should prove so useless for evidence-gathering only in the United Kingdom.

The danger of revealing or compromising methods of interception,[102] the creation of **2.62** conflicting objectives as between intelligence agencies and police, and the added burdens of cataloguing and disclosure were accepted as important but surmountable factors by the *Chilcot Report*.[103] But strict boundaries were set for the *Chilcot Report*, including the injunction that the intercepting agency retains a veto over prosecutorial usage so that interception remains the ultimate property of the intelligence services. Therefore, they do not necessarily have to collect data in a way which maintains integrity of the provenance of evidence, nor need they fret about disclosure claims (including the incidental disclosure of techniques far more sophisticated than telecommunications intercepts). The subsequent Advisory Group of Privy Counsellors concluded that the objectives cannot viably be secured by the 'Public Interest Immunity Plus' system.[104] Further studies continue, but there remains much opposition to any change,[105] and it seems unlikely that a positive outcome will result unless the conditions of ownership to be met are altered[106] so as give more priority to the interests of individual justice and less to collective risk.[107] A change may require some reassessment of the 1992 Directive which transferred the lead in terrorism investigations from the police to the Security Service,[108] followed in Northern Ireland in 2007.[109]

The next surveillance technique, the acquisition of communications data, is dealt with in Pt I, **2.63** chapter 2 of the RIPA.[110] The police (plus around 900 public authorities) can by s 22 access the record (but not the transmission or content: s 21) of telephone calls[111] and electronic communications. This surveillance is said to be vital in four cases: building a background picture of suspects and networks, with terrorists a prominent example; providing evidence in court; assisting vulnerable persons; and shaping a more focused interception intervention.[112]

---

[101] See *Second Report of the independent reviewer pursuant to section 14(3) of the Prevention of Terrorism Act 2005* (Home Office, London, 2007) paras 34–35; Government, *Reply to the Fourth Report of the Independent Reviewer Pursuant to Section 14(3) of the Prevention of Terrorism Act 2005* (Cm 7624, London, 2009) p 6.

[102] See Sir Peter Gibson, *Review of Intercepted Intelligence in relation to the Omagh Bombing of 15 August 1998* (Northern Ireland Office, Belfast, 2009) para 26 (mentioned also in his *Intelligence Services Commissioner Report for 2008* (2008–09 HC 902) para 36.

[103] Privy Council Review, *Intercept as Evidence* (Cm 7324, London, 2008). See Spencer, JR, 'Telephone-tap evidence and administrative detention in the UK' in Wade, M and Maljevic, A, *A War on Terror?* (Springer, New York, 2010).

[104] *Intercept as Evidence* (Cm 7760, London, 2009).

[105] See *Reports of the Interception of Communications Commissioner for 2005–06* (2006–07 HC 315) para 42 and for 2008 (2008–09 HC 901) para 2.7; Lord Carlile, Operation Pathway (Home Office, London, 2009) para 105.

[106] See Joint Committee on Human Rights, *Counter-Terrorism Policy and Human Rights (Seventeenth Report): Bringing Human Rights Back In* (2009–10 HL 86/HC 111) paras 100–102.

[107] As required by Art 6: *Natunen v Finland*, App no 21022/04, 31 March 2009; *Janatuinen v Finland*, App no 28552/05, 8 December 2009.

[108] House of Commons Debates, vol 207, col 297, 8 May 1992. See further Security Service Act 1996; ATCSA 2001, s 116; Andrew, C, *The Defence of the Realm* (Allen Lane, London, 2009) p 773.

[109] See Lord Carlile, *First Annual Review of Arrangements for National Security in Northern Ireland* (Northern Ireland Office, Belfast, 2008).

[110] See further Regulation of Investigatory Powers (Communications Data) Order 2010, SI 2010/480.

[111] See Sir Peter Gibson, *Review of Intercepted Intelligence in relation to the Omagh Bombing of 15 August 1998* (Northern Ireland Office, Belfast, 2009) para 31.

[112] See Home Office, *Protecting the Public in a Changing Communications Environment* (Cm 7586, London, 2009) p 9.

2.64 Next, the RIPA Pt II[113] creates three systems of authorizations. Unlike for interception, it is not an offence to proceed without authorization but immunity from privacy claims is granted under s 27 only to operations which are authorized.

2.65 One aspect is directed surveillance which, under s 26(2), is covert and undertaken as part of a pre-planned specific investigation which is likely to gather private personal information.[114] Directed surveillance may be authorized by a police superintendent under s 28.

2.66 When the directed surveillance shifts to private residential property or vehicles through the presence of an individual on the premises or in the vehicle or is carried out by means of a surveillance device (but not the tracking of vehicles), then it becomes 'intrusive surveillance' under s 26(3). Authorization must be by a senior authorizing officer (a chief constable or equivalent) or by the Secretary of State (s 32(1)) and the authorization cannot be implemented without the approval of a (judicial) Surveillance Commissioner under s 36 (with an appeal against refusal to the Chief Surveillance Commissioner under s 38). Where Part II surveillance overlaps with the Police Act 1997, combined authorization will apply.[115]

2.67 Intrusive and directed surveillance authorizations were issued for prison visits to Babar Ahmed, including by his solicitor who later became a Member of Parliament. Sadiq Khan held these roles successively, but the police and prison authorities claimed ignorance of his election.[116] It was revealed that MPs have exemption from monitoring in prisons under the terms of the Approved Visitor Scheme, and the 'Wilson Doctrine' of 1966 provides that interception under ministerial warrant of the communications of MPs should be exceptional. The Chief Surveillance Commissioner concluded that the surveillance had been lawfully conducted but that the concessions should be clarified. The Interception of Communications Commissioner has called for an end to the Wilson Doctrine.[117]

2.68 The surveillance of lawyers arose again in *Re McE*.[118] A solicitor was charged with incitement to murder and perverting the course of justice, the evidence being provided through covert surveillance of conversations held with various clients in the serious crime suite at Antrim Police Station. The five applicants in *Re McE* were subsequently arrested or remanded on unrelated terrorism and other charges. They were refused assurances that their conversations with solicitors or with a medical examiner would not be monitored. The House of Lords concluded that directed surveillance under Pt II extended to lawyer/client consultations ordinarily protected by legal professional privilege. A breach of Article 8 followed since only a level of authorization equivalent to that for intrusive surveillance would provide a sufficient safeguard. The government was rebuked for not passing an order under

---

[113] See further Regulation of Investigatory Powers (Covert Surveillance and Property Interference: Code of Practice) Order 2010, SI 2010/463; Regulation of Investigatory Powers (Directed Surveillance and Covert Human Intelligence Sources) Order 2010, SI 2010/521.
[114] Overt photography during an arrest operation was upheld in *(Margaret) Murray v United Kingdom*, App no 14310/88, Ser A 300-A (1994).
[115] See *Report of the Commissioner for 1999, Security Service Act 1989* (Cm 4779, London, 2000) para 24.
[116] Sir Christopher Rose, *Report on two visits by Sadiq Khan MP to Babar Ahmad at HM Prison Woodhill* (Cm 7336, London, 2008).
[117] See *Report of the Interception of Communications Commissioner for 2005–06* (2006–07 HC 315) paras 47–57.
[118] [2009] UKHL 15.

s 47(1)(b) of the RIPA to implement this recategorization.[119] Evidence from such surveillance might be excluded from any trial as unfair.[120]

Stricter guidance on the monitoring of lawyers has since imposed additional requirements **2.69** that must be satisfied before an authorization is granted.[121] A further order issued in 2010 ensures that directed surveillance that is carried out in any specified premises used for the purpose of legal consultations is to be treated as intrusive surveillance.[122] Even the intrusive surveillance authorization scheme might be inadequate for this most sensitive private information since the circumstances of grant are very wide and there is no restriction of the usage of the product.[123] More generally, the distinction between directed and intrusive surveillance remains unsatisfactorily based on an assumption that location and privacy interests always correlate.[124]

Various other surveillance techniques do not sit easily within these frameworks, including **2.70** overt surveillance, such as photography at demonstrations[125] and CCTV, such as the mass of cameras installed secretively in predominantly Asian suburbs of Birmingham in 2010.[126] Keylog programs in rootkits and Remote Administration Trojans may also skirt existing regulations by harvesting or duplicating data rather than intercepting any communication.[127] Regulation may in those situations arise more from the installation of the software, while any intrusion which gathers data may potentially breach the Computer Misuse Act 1990. The European Union Council of Ministers has asked for any cross-border surveillance to be based on clear legal authorization.[128]

Provisions: data retention and disclosure

Information technologies are of value to investigators not only for facilitating communica- **2.71** tions which might be monitored but also for capturing records which are traceable and searchable. This potential avenue of investigation was exploited by the ATCSA 2001, Pt XI, which concerned the retention of communications data.[129] In this way, data which had been gathered for other purposes, arising from commercial billing or legal enforcement,[130] had to be retained in case data-mining was later to be performed. The measure responded to the inconvenience in a late modern society that many important sources of information are no longer held by compliant public authorities but rest within the clutches of private

---

[119] See Chief Surveillance Commissioner, *Annual Report for 2007–08* (2007–08 HC 659) para 3.4.

[120] See *R v Grant* [2005] EWCA Crim 1089.

[121] Regulation of Investigatory Powers (Covert Human Intelligence Sources: Matters Subject to Legal Privilege) Order 2010, SI 2010/123.

[122] Regulation of Investigatory Powers (Extension of Authorisation Provisions: Legal Consultations) Order 2010 SI 2010/461. See *Re RA* [2010] NIQB 99.

[123] *Re McE* [2009] UKHL 15 at para 66.

[124] Compare *Halford v UK*, App no 20605/92, 1997-III; *Perry v United Kingdom*, App no 63737/00, 2003-IX.

[125] *Wood v Commissioner of Police of the Metropolis* [2009] EWCA Civ 414.

[126] Thornton, S, *Project Champion* (Thames Valley Police, Kidlington, 2010).

[127] See Wall, D, *Cybercrime* (Polity Press, Cambridge, 2007) pp 60, 77.

[128] See Council Presidency Note of 11 July 2008 (EU Doc 13567/08).

[129] See House of Commons Research Paper on Communications Data: Access and Retention, 02/63, 21 November 2002; Walker, C, *The Anti Terrorism Legislation* (1st edn, Oxford University Press, Oxford, 2002) ch 5; Walker, C and Akdeniz, Y, 'Anti-Terrorism laws and data retention: war is over?' (2003) 54 *Northern Ireland Legal Quarterly* 159; Levi, M and Wall, DS, 'Technologies, security, and privacy in the post-9/11 European Information Society' (2004) 31 *Journal of Law & Society* 194.

[130] Telecommunications (Data Protection and Privacy) Regulations 1999, SI 1999/2093. There is a power but no obligation to retain on national security and crime prevention grounds (rr 32, 33).

Communications Service Providers (CSPs) who have no interest in retention for public purposes.[131] Those CSPs were asked to retain communications data during a specified period for an investigatory rainy day.

2.72 Should access for investigatory purposes later be required for terrorism investigation purposes, attention must be turned to other measures, since the ATCSA 2001 did not deal with access or disclosure. Those issues fall under the exemption from non-disclosure which allows voluntary disclosure for crime prevention or investigation purposes under s 29(3) of the Data Protection Act 1998. If detailed records of substance are demanded, then resort may be made either to the RIPA powers of compulsory disclosure in relation to communications data, or to Sch 1 of PACE.[132] The decision in *R (NTL Group Ltd) v Ipswich Crown Court*[133] suggests that access to data (content data in this case) under Sch 1 of PACE is a possibility to be borne in mind by a CSP. Therefore, pending the making of an order under para 4 of Sch 1, the relevant material should be preserved in accordance with para 11. Retention of such data by a CSP would not amount to an offence under the RIPA, s 1.

2.73 Part XI was fiercely criticized as a threat to privacy. It depicted the entire population as potentially suspect and was a blanket measure which did not respond to any specific 'terrorist investigation'. Furthermore, the mass snooping was not confined to terrorism but encompassed criminal investigations because it was said to be impractical to limit the measure to terrorism data.[134] Attempted amendments to limit the purpose were repelled.[135]

2.74 To allay concerns, Pt XI initially proceeded under s 102 by way of a voluntary code of practice.[136] Just in case the CSPs 'don't volunteer enough',[137] compulsory directions could have been issued under s 104. The voluntary scheme worked tolerably well: data retention rose from 25 per cent prior to the 2001 Act to 95 per cent by 2007.[138] The Privy Counsellor Review Committee recorded that in the 12 months after 11 September 10,000 requests for communications data related to terrorism.[139] The Report viewed the policy as proper but called for the time of retention to be limited to one year and for there to be oversight by the Information Commissioner.[140]

2.75 The Pt XI system has since been replaced by compulsory European Union rules which ensure uniformity in the competitive CSP marketplace and increase the opportunities for

---

[131] Home Office, Home Office Regulatory Impact Assessment: *Retention of Communications Data* (2001) para 6.

[132] For criticisms, see All Party Parliamentary Internet Group, *Communications Data* <http://www.apcomms.org.uk/apig/archive/activities-2002/data-retention-inquiry/APIGreport.pdf>, 2003.

[133] [2002] EWHC 1585 (Admin).

[134] House of Lords Deb vol 629 col 774 (4 December 2001), Lord Rooker. See further Joint Committee on Human Rights, Draft Voluntary Code of Practice (2002–03 HL/181/HC 1272).

[135] Home Office, Home Office Regulatory Impact Assessment: *Retention of Communications Data* (2001), para 6 col 981 6 December 2001, col 1479, 13 December 2001; HC Debs vol 376 col 1111 (13 December 2001).

[136] The Code (Retention of Communications Data under Part 11: Anti-Terrorism, Crime & Security Act 2001, (Home Office, London, 2003)) was issued under the authority of the Retention of Communications Data (Code of Practice) Order 2003 SI/3175. See further Retention of Communications Data (Extension of Initial Period) Order 2003, SI 2003/3173; Retention of Communications Data (Further Extension of Initial Period) Order 2005, SI 2005/3335.

[137] 'The net's eyes are watching' *Guardian Online*, 15 November 2001.

[138] Hansard HL vol 694 col 762 (24 July 2007).

[139] *Newton Report*, para 380.

[140] Ibid para 396.

cross-border exchanges of data. The European Union Directive 2002/58/EC concerning the processing of personal data and the protection of privacy in the electronic communications sector (Directive on privacy and electronic communications) was the first step.[141] The relevant provision on data warehousing, Article 15, allowed for (but did not require) the retention of data for a limited period to safeguard national security, defence, public security or the prevention, investigation, detection, and prosecution of criminal offences or of unauthorized use of the electronic communications system, as referred to in Article 13(1) of Directive 95/46/EC. The United Kingdom government had strongly lobbied for this development.[142]

Under further pressure from the UK government, this first step was reinforced by Directive **2.76** 2006/24/EC on 'the retention of data generated or processed in connection with the provision of publicly available electronic communications services or of public communications networks and amending Directive 2002/58/EC'.[143] The Directive requires Member States to ensure that public communications providers must retain, for a period of between six months and two years, communications data about traffic and location and allow access by competent national authorities. In *Ireland v European Parliament and Council of the European Union*,[144] an application for annulment of the Directive was rejected on the basis that the Directive properly sought to limit national disparities which might either affect fundamental freedoms or market competition. The European Court of Justice also emphasized the limited nature of the harmonization in that it did not impinge on access rules or on data exchange.[145]

The Directive began to be enforced in the United Kingdom by the Data Retention (EC **2.77** Directive) Regulations 2007[146] which covered land and mobile telephony and demanded retention for twelve months. Following a further Home Office Consultation in 2008, the Data Retention (EC Directive) Regulations 2009 replaced the 2007 version and supplanted entirely the Pt XI scheme.[147] Data about internet access, internet e-mail, and internet telephony are also now covered.[148] A standard retention period of twelve months applies across the board, meaning that internet communications data will have to be retained by notified public communications providers[149] longer than under the Pt XI scheme. The government justifies this extension by reference to a two-week survey undertaken on behalf of ACPO in 2005 which showed there had been 231 requests for data aged between six and twelve months, with 60 per cent of the cases relating to murder or terrorism.[150]

One way or another, many more terabytes of data will have to be stored by CSPs as a result **2.78** of the operation of the Data Retention (EC Directive) Regulations 2009. Whether this

---

[141] 12 July 2002, OJ [2002] L201/37–47, 31.7.2002.

[142] See, for example, House of Commons European Scrutiny Committee, *Thirty-Second Report*, HC 152–xxxii, Session 2001–02, July 2002 (19 DTI (23528) Personal data and privacy in telecommunications).

[143] See Maras, H-M, 'From targeted to mass surveillance' in Goold, BJ and Neyland, D, *New Directions in Surveillance and Privacy* (Willan, Cullompton, 2009).

[144] Case C-301/06, 10 February 2009.

[145] See Konstadinides, T, 'Wavering between centres of gravity' (2010) 35 *European Law Review* 88.

[146] SI 2007/2199. See Hansard HC vol 694 col 762 (24 July 2007).

[147] SI 2009/859. See Home Office, Transposition of Directive 2006/24/EC (London, 2008).

[148] See Directive, Art 5.

[149] See SI 2009/859, reg 10. No list of those notified has been disclosed. Some services may be excluded where they are primarily based abroad or where the provider might be considered a subsidiary gateway (as in the case of Hotmail or Gmail).

[150] Home Office, *Transposition of Directive 2006/24/EC* (London, 2008) para 5.5.

indiscriminate interference with private information is 'necessary' and 'proportionate' within Article 8(2)[151] seems doubtful since at any one time the vast majority of those affected are bound to be non-terrorists and the intrusion is without any form of judicial authorization or oversight.[152] A blanket approach to data retention of innocent individuals has been condemned in the contexts of DNA samples[153] and the photographing of demonstrators against an arms trade fair.[154] One suitably restrained approach would have been to adopt 'data preservation' (storing only the data of suspects identified to CSPs)[155] or perhaps to resort to blanket retention for a specified period around a specified operation.

2.79 These changes to the data retention rules coincided with an alleged plan to 'pull' this and other data into central storage rather than to access it piecemeal from service providers. A proposed draft Communications Data Bill was vaguely outlined in 2008.[156] However, this 'Interception Modernisation Programme'[157] was later modified in the light of criticism on cost and privacy grounds. In its 2009 paper, *Protecting the Public in a Changing Communications Environment*, the Home Office emphasizes that it does not seek to create a central database but does require more prescriptive rules about the retention of internet-based communications data, and extends that term to a potentially vast range of third party data.[158]

2.80 Finally, data retention may be limited as an investigative technique against terrorism for two practical reasons. The first is the doubt whether it can beyond reasonable doubt link a technical occurrence to personal identity, though this is more an impediment to formal prosecution than to other forms of response.[159] The second practical obstacle is that evasion is relatively simple. One example is Zacarias Moussaoui, who was charged as a conspirator in the September 11 attacks.[160] The FBI only discovered that Moussaoui had utilized three Hotmail accounts through his written court pleadings. Detection difficulties can be multiplied by using a public internet terminal, the use of more sophisticated anonymized web browsing systems, and the use of foreign-based information society service providers.

Provisions: encrypted data

2.81 Encryption can in theory delay or nullify investigations in terrorist cases. However, the verdict from the oversight commissioners is that 'the use of information security and encryption

---

[151] Compare *Rotaru v Romania*, App no 28341/95, 2000-V; All Party Parliamentary Internet Group, *Communications Data* (London, 2003) para 141.

[152] See Lyon, D, *Surveillance after September 11* (Polity, Cambridge, 2003) p 103; Civil Liberties, Justice and Home Affairs, *Electronic communications: personal data protection rules and availability of traffic data for anti-terrorism purposes* (COD/2005/0182, 2006); Scheinin, M, *Reports of the Special Rapporteur on the promotion and protection of human rights and fundamental freedoms while countering terrorism* (A/HRC/10/3, United Nations, 2009) para 32.

[153] *S and Marper v United Kingdom*, App nos 30562/04, 30566/04, 4 December 2008. The Crime and Security Bill 2009–10, cl 16, applies a normal retention period of six years in terrorism cases.

[154] *R (Wood) v Commissioner of Police for the Metropolis* [2009] EWCA Civ 414.

[155] See All Party Parliamentary Internet Group, *Communications Data* (London, 2003) para 182.

[156] See Danby, G, *Draft Communications Data Bill* (SN/HA/4884, House of Commons Library, London, 2009).

[157] See Home Office, *Security and Counter Terrorism Science and Innovation Strategy* (London, 2007) p 14; Hansard HL vol 703 col wa76 (8 July 2008), Lord West. The government set up the Communications Capabilities Directorate to consider the issue further.

[158] Home Office, *Protecting the Public in a Changing Communications Environment* (Cm 7586, London, 2009) pp 25, 26.

[159] Bowden, C, 'CCTV for inside your head' (2002) 8 *Computer and Telecommunications Law Review* 21.

[160] See Walker, C, 'Cyber-terrorism' (2006) 110 *Penn State Law Review* 625 at 636.

products by terrorist and criminal suspects is not . . . as widespread as had been expected'.[161] Nevertheless, the threat is recognized by Pt III of the RIPA.[162]

2.82 The authorities may in the interests of national security or for the purpose of preventing or detecting crime issue under s 49 a notice to the person believed to have possession of the encryption key and impose a disclosure requirement in respect of the protected information. Judicial authority for the issuance of a notice must be granted under Sch 2 of the RIPA, though the police and security agencies may self-authorize in some circumstances, including for materials seized under the TA 2000, s 44. The recipient of the s 49 notice must then convey the information in an intelligible form (under s 50(1)(b)) or may pass on any private keys which are capable of decrypting the protected information (s 50(2)(a)). Under s 50(3), disclosure of the key may be the directed response, provided under s 51(4) the official believes that there are special circumstances for requiring the key itself and that the giving of the direction is proportionate.

2.83 A person to whom a s 49 notice has been given will be guilty of an offence under s 53 (with a maximum penalty of two years' imprisonment) if he knowingly fails to make the disclosure required. If it is shown that that person was in possession of a key at any time before the giving of the notice, that person shall be taken for the purposes of those proceedings to have continued to be in possession of that key, unless it is shown otherwise. Thus, the burden of proof is placed on defendants to show that they no longer hold a key that they may previously have held. However, by s 53(3), a person shall be taken to have shown that he was not in possession of a key to protected information at a particular time if: '(a) sufficient evidence of that fact is adduced to raise an issue with respect to it; and (b) the contrary is not proved beyond a reasonable doubt'. So, the defendant bears an evidential burden only.

2.84 In *R v S and A*,[163] the accused were alleged to have conspired to help another person to breach a control order. Having been arrested, they refused to allow access to encrypted files and argued that the requirement was a form of self-incrimination contrary to Article 6. In line with Strasbourg jurisprudence, it was held that the keys (and data) were distinct from the will of the defendants, though demands about the knowledge of the existence of the keys could be an incriminating fact which might trigger PACE, s 78.

2.85 Part III was not activated until 1 October 2007,[164] following the paradoxical amendment by the TA 2006, s 15, to increase the penalty (to five years for national security cases) for this long dormant crime.[165]

2.86 Implementation involves the National Technical Assistance Centre (NTAC), first located in the Security Services London headquarters but now subsumed into the Government Communications Headquarters (GCHQ).[166] It provides technical support to law enforcement

---

[161] *Report of the Information Commissioner for 2004–05* (2005–06 HC 549) para 7; *Report of the Intelligence Services Commissioner for 2005–06* (2006–07 HC 314) para 7.

[162] See also Regulation of Investigatory Powers (Investigation of Protected Electronic Information: Code of Practice) Order 2007 (SI 2007/2200).

[163] [2008] EWCA Crim 2177.

[164] See Home Office, *Investigation of Protected Electronic Information* (London, 2006).

[165] This limit was based on respect for the principle that anti-terrorism legislation should not make general changes. Hansard HC vol 677 col 653 (17 January 2006), Charles Clarke.

[166] See Hansard HC vol 378 col 829w (22 January 2002), David Blunkett, and vol 451 col 11ws (31 October 2006), Margaret Beckett.

agencies and the intelligence services. Under the Code of Practice for the Investigation of Protected Electronic Information 2007, no public authority can serve a notice under s 49 without the consent of NTAC.[167]

Provisions: human agents

2.87 Covert human intelligence sources (CHIS), such as informants and undercover operatives, are regulated by the RIPA, s 26(7). The necessity for legal regulation flows from the need to protect privacy rights, highlighted in *Teixeira de Castro v Portugal*.[168] Authorization for the conduct or use of covert human intelligence sources is on the same grounds as for directed surveillance, therefore authorization is by a police superintendent under ss 29 and 30.[169] It is arguable whether this non-judicial approval will satisfy the European Court.[170] In addition, s 29 demands arrangements to ensure that the source is independently managed and supervised and that records are kept.

2.88 The history of human agents in connection with Irish terrorism has witnessed an extensive and vital source of investigation, disruption,[171] and engagement. One might expect the pattern to be mirrored eventually with *jihadi* groups now that some derive from the ranks of citizens rather than distinctive bands of émigrés. Four negative impacts have also been evident.

2.89 In ascending level of seriousness, the first problem arises from the quality of the testimony of agents in court, as illustrated by the 'supergrass' trials which operated in Northern Ireland between 1982 and 1985.[172] It was denied that there ever was a 'system',[173] but its forensic failure became patent when the Northern Ireland Court of Appeal serially rejected the testimony of the supergrasses as inherently dangerous and unlikely to be reliable without other evidence. The lessons pronounced by the Attorney General were that clear and compelling corroboration or supportive evidence would normally be required, the number of defendants per trial would not exceed ten, and full immunity for serious offences would not normally be granted to the witness.[174] Though these supergrasses petered out in Northern Ireland,[175] more modest cases occasionally arise, including Patrick Daly (recruited as an informant against the INLA),[176] David Rupert (an agent of both US and UK agencies, who provided

---

[167] (Home Office, London, 2007) paras 3.10, 9.3.

[168] *Teixeira de Castro v Portugal*, App no 25829/94, 1998-IV. See further *Allan v United Kingdom*, App no 48539/99, 5 November 2002; Gillespie, AA, 'Regulation of internet surveillance' [2009] *European Human Rights Law Review* 552 at 560.

[169] See further Regulation of Investigatory Powers (Covert Human Intelligence Sources: Code of Practice) Order 2010, SI 2010/462; Regulation of Investigatory Powers (Directed Surveillance and Covert Human Intelligence Sources) Order 2010, SI 2010/521.

[170] Compare *Lüdi v Switzerland*, App no 12433/86, Ser A 238 (1992); *A v France*, App no 14838/89, Ser A 277-B (1993); *MM v Netherlands*, App no 39339/98, 8 April 2003; *R v Rosenberg* [2006] EWCA Crim 6.

[171] Dillon, M, *The Dirty War* (Hutchinson, London, 1990) p 17.

[172] See Greer, S, *Supergrasses* (Clarendon, Oxford, 1995); Gilmour, R, *Dead Ground* (Warner Books, London, 1998).

[173] Hansard HC vol 47 col 3 (24 October 1983).

[174] Hansard HC vol 94 col 185 (19 March 1986). But formal warnings under *Davies v DPP* [1954] AC 378 ceased to be required by the Criminal Justice and Public Order Act 1994, s 32(1)(a).

[175] See Collins, E, *Killing Rage* (Granta, London, 1997) (an informant who was murdered: *The Times* 28 January 1999, p 1); O'Callaghan, S, *The Informer* (Corgi, London, 1999); McGartland, M, *Fifty Dead Men Walking* (Blake, London, 1999) (he was also seriously injured: *The Times* 18 June 1999, pp 1, 8); Fulton, K, *Unsung Hero* (John Blake, London, 2008).

[176] *The Times* 20 November 1993, p 3, 17 December 1993, p 5.

testimony against the Real IRA),[177] and the Stewart brothers (whose conscience induced them to inform against former UVF colleagues).[178]

The second problem is that a CHIS may step over the line from providing passive insider **2.90** reports to active encouragement to crime as an agent provocateur who engages in entrapment.[179] The legal boundaries of entrapment have been drawn on a case law basis.[180] Sting operations for the purchase of missiles were related in the extradition request in *R v Governor of Belmarsh Prison, ex parte Martin*.[181] O'Farrell, Rafferty, and McDonald were convicted in May 2002 of attempting to acquire weaponry for the Real IRA after being lured to a meeting in Slovakia with British Security Service agents, pretending to represent the Iraqi government.[182]

The third problem arises from the criminal participation of the CHIS. So that they can **2.91** operate effectively, they may unavoidably condone or participate in criminality by their confreres. The most prominent illustration concerned Brian Nelson,[183] who, as the Army's top Loyalist (Ulster Defence Association) agent from 1987 to 1990, committed serious offences. However, his criminality was considered to be self-directed as well as in the service of the Crown, and he pleaded guilty in 1992 to twenty charges, including conspiracy to murder. He was sentenced to ten years, taking into account a character reference from Brigadier Gordon Kerr who said he had saved many lives. A Republican high-level agent equivalent to Nelson was alleged in 2003 to be Freddie Scappaticci—'Stakeknife'—who was said to be involved in internal disciplinary procedures for the IRA.[184] He denied these allegations, but the government has followed its usual security information policy of 'Neither Confirm Nor Deny'.[185] Another example is Joe Fenton who, in order to divert IRA attention away from his status as an informant, provided the names of two other informants who were murdered in 1985, Fenton being murdered himself in 1989.[186] The other top-level Republican informant to be unmasked is Denis Donaldson, whose role in spying within Stormont on behalf of Sinn Féin was not prosecuted in the public interest in 2005.[187]

The misdeeds of Brian Nelson are alleged to have spilt over into the fourth problem area, that **2.92** of criminal collusion between handlers and agents. The handlers are here deploying the agent as an offensive weapon, to ensure that the enemies of the state are attacked, such as by giving details of Republican targets to Loyalist terror groups. Sir John Stevens reported in 2003 on collusion between the security forces and the UDA (especially the agent, Brian Nelson, who was convicted of conspiracy to murder but nevertheless received praise for his work with the

---

[177] See *McKevitt v DPP* [2003] IESC 9/03; *Breslin v McKenna* [2005] NIQB 18; *People (DPP) v McKevitt* [2008] IESC 51; *DPP v McKevitt* [2009] IESC 29; *R v Hoey* [2007] NICC 49. It is alleged that Rupert was paid $1.25 million by the FBI: *The Daily Telegraph* 7 August 2003, p 1. See Mooney, J, and O'Toole, M, *Black Operations* (Maverick House, Ashbourne, 2003).

[178] *R v Stewart and Stewart* [2010] NICC 8.

[179] See *US v Duggan* 743 F2d 59 (1984); *US v Lakhani* 480 F3d 171 (2007); Stevenson, D, 'Entrapment and terrorism' (2008) 49 *Boston College Law Review* 125.

[180] See *R v Looseley* [2001] UKHL 53.

[181] [1995] 1 WLR 412.

[182] [2005] EWCA Crim 1945, [2005] EWCA Crim 1970.

[183] *The Times* 30 January 1992, pp 1, 2.

[184] Ingram, M and Harkin, G, *Stakeknife* (O'Brien Press, Dublin, 2004).

[185] See *Re Scappaticci* [2003] NIQB 56.

[186] See Dillon, M, *The Dirty War* (Hutchinson, London, 1990) pp 321–5; Moloney, E, *A Secret History of the IRA* (Penguin, London, 2002) p 28.

[187] *The Sunday Times* 18 December 2005, p 13. He was murdered in 2006.

Army Force Research Unit).[188] Even graver allegations were made of the systemic provision of police death squads and direction by 'The Committee', as claimed in the book of that title by Sean McPhilemy, which was subject to contempt and libel proceedings.[189] These allegations were not accepted by an earlier *Stevens Report* in 1990, which found that collusion was not institutionalized at a high level. More localized evidence of collusion with the Mount Vernon Ulster Volunteer Force was sustained by the Police Ombudsman for Northern Ireland report surrounding the death of Raymond McCord Junior and related matters.[190]

2.93　Because of the impetus of the Peace Process, because of the (unpublished) findings of the 2003 *Stevens Report*, and also because it was sustained in *Finucane v United Kingdom*[191] that neither the inquest nor the initial *Stevens Report* satisfied Article 2, a range of other inquiries have been undertaken into allegations of collusion, some related to Nelson's activities. The initial work was undertaken by Judge Peter Cory who studied four murders in the Republic of Ireland, namely, the cases of Chief Superintendent Breen and Superintendent Buchanan, and Lord Justice Gibson and Lady Gibson.[192] Cory found sustainable allegations in the Northern Ireland killings assigned for his scrutiny: Patrick Finucane, Robert Hamill, Rosemary Nelson, and Billy Wright.[193] All were then referred for forms of public inquiry. Inquiries into the cases of Rosemary Nelson, Robert Hamill, and Billy Wright opened in 2005.[194] The government also announced an inquiry into the Pat Finucane case. It has yet to open because of legal proceedings in connection with his murder[195] and because the Inquiries Act 2005 would, in the view of his relatives, unduly limit the investigation.

2.94　Tighter controls under the RIPA should avert some of the excesses of the past, but the absence of independent oversight for CHIS activity offers little confidence that this outcome is assured. In addition, the fact that the informants, again *jihadis*, may be run by overseas agencies, such as the CIA, is a new twist which again increases scepticism that British security authorities and courts will receive a full and fair representation of this evidence. Nevertheless, a survey by HM Inspectorate of Constabulary found in 2008 arrangements for CHIS in Northern Ireland which were 'robust, effective, and comply with all the necessary legislation'.[196]

---

[188] Stevens, J, Stevens Enquiry: *Overview and Recommendations* (Metropolitan Police Service, London, 2003). See Stevens, J, *Not for the Faint-Hearted* (Weidenfield & Nicholson, London, 2005); Rolston, B, 'An effective mask for terror' (2005) 44 *Crime Law & Society* 181. For other instances, see also *R v Browne, Jones and Smith* (1993) 6 NIJB 64.

[189] (Roberts Rinehart, Boulder, 1999). See *DPP v Channel Four Television* [1993] 2 All ER 517; McPhilemy won substantial damages against *The Sunday Times* for claiming the allegations were a hoax: *The Times* 31 March 2000, p 10. See also Bruce, S, 'Loyalist assassination and police collusion in Northern Ireland' (2000) 23 *Studies in Conflict & Terrorism* 61.

[190] Police Ombudsman for Northern Ireland, *The Circumstances surrounding the death of Raymond McCord Junior and related Matters* (Belfast, 2007).

[191] App no 29178/95, 1 July 2003.

[192] See *Cory Collusion Inquiry Reports*: Chief Superintendent Breen and Superintendent Buchanan, (Department for Justice, Equality and Law Reform, Dublin, 2003), Lord Justice Gibson and Lady Gibson (Department of Justice, Equality and Law Reform, Dublin, 2003). See also Barron, H, *Report of the Independent Commission of Inquiry into the Dublin and Monaghan Bombings* (Taoiseach's Office, Dublin, 2003).

[193] See Patrick Finucane (2003–04 HC 470), Robert Hamill (2003–04 HC 471), Billy Wright (2003–04 HC 472) and Rosemary Nelson (2003–04 HC 473).

[194] See <http://www.roberthamillinquiry.org/>, <http://www.billywrightinquiry.org/> (with conclusions reported at 2010–11 HC 431), <http://www.rosemarynelsoninquiry.org/>; *In re X and the Rosemary Nelson Inquiry* [2008] NIQB 65; *Re Hamill* [2008] NIQB 73.

[195] Kenneth Barrett pleaded guilty in 2004: *R v Barrett* [2004] NICC 28. William Stobie was acquitted of complicity in the murder of Finucane but then murdered: *The Independent* 13 December 2001, p 9.

[196] HM Inspectorate of Constabulary, *Management and Handling of Covert Human Intelligence Sources in Terrorist Networks* (London, 2009).

Implementation

Limited data on implementation can be garnered from the reports of the various commis- **2.95**
sioners, though the Intelligence Services Commissioner refuses to divulge any. Most of the
statistics are given in global terms and without reference to terrorism (which is not a term of
art in the RIPA).

The data suggest a peak around 2003 which in part may have related to terrorism inves- **2.96**
tigations but probably more reflected a growing recognition of the need to record existing
practices and a first flush of enthusiasm to try out new powers (see Table 2.3). That
enthusiasm has waned, probably because of complexity and bureaucracy. The vagaries of
recording practices also affect the returns.

Foreign comparisons

Intercept powers have grown in many other jurisdictions.[197] Ireland alone allows the **2.97**
exclusion of evidence of intercept warrants under the Interception of Postal Packets
and Telecommunications Messages (Regulation) Act 1993 and the Postal and
Telecommunications Services (Amendment) Act 1999. Evidence may be used in court in
principle, but the police and prosecution always choose not to do so and disclosure may be
forbidden under s 12 of the 1993 Act.

Data retention was implemented after 2001 under a secret directive under the Postal Packets **2.98**
and Telecommunications Act 1993, s 110, but attacks as to its legality by the Data Protection
Commissioner and concerns arising from the prosecution of Colm Murphy[198] have resulted
in an overt statutory scheme under Pt VII of the Criminal Justice (Terrorist Offences) Act
2005. It is very helpful to combine the rules on retention and access in this way, but in

Table 2.3 Surveillance powers[a]

Year	Police Act 1997 Pt III: Property interference/ terrorism related	RIPA Pt I: Intercept warrants issued[b]	RIPA Pt I: Communications data requests	RIPA Pt II: Directed surveillance authorization (only law enforcement)	RIPA Pt II: Intrusive surveillance/ terrorism related	RIPA Pt II: CHIS recruits	RIPA Pt III: Encrypted data application/ orders/ compliance
2001–02	2,519/116	1,445	n/a	28,000	493/12	5,400	n/a
2002–03	2,511/170	1,605	n/a	26,400	475/25	5,900	n/a
2003–04	2,483/177	1,983	n/a	26,986	447/22	5,907	n/a
2004–05	2,210/221	1,973	n/a	25,518	461/18	4,980	n/a
2005–06	2,310/224	2,407	n/a	23,628	435/14	4,559	n/a
2006–07	2,311/116	1,435	253,557	19,651	350/1	4,373	n/a
2007–08	2,493/120	2,026	519,260	18,767	355/12	4,498	n/a
2008–09	2,681/18	1,712	504,073	16,118	384/1	4,278	26/15/4
2009–10	2,705/14	1,706	525,130	15,285	384/2	5,320	38/22/6

[a] Sources: Chief Surveillance Commissioner, *Annual Reports*; Interception of Communication Commissioner, *Annual Reports*.
Reporting periods have altered in some cases.
[b] These statistics do not encompass warrants issued by the Foreign Office or in Northern Ireland.

---

[197] See JUSTICE, *Intercept Evidence: Lifting the Ban* (London, 2006).
[198] *People (DPP) v Murphy* [2005] IECCA 1.

substance, the legislation achieves legality rather than effective regulation.[199] Following the passage of Directive 2006/24/EC and amending Directive 2002/58/EC, Pt VII will be replaced by the Communications (Data Retention) Bill 2009.

2.99 Other forms of surveillance are mostly regulated by the Criminal Justice (Surveillance) Act 2009.[200] Unlike under the RIPA, most authorizations are judicial.

2.100 The (Australian) Telecommunications (Interception and Access) Act 1979 allows for interceptions under judicial warrant for law enforcement purposes and under the warrant of the Attorney General for intelligence-gathering purposes.[201] The Telecommunications Interception Legislation Amendment Act 2002 amended the Telecommunications (Interception) Act 1979 to permit law enforcement agencies to seek telecommunications interception warrants in connection with the investigation of terrorism offences and other purposes. An amendment in 2006 extended the legislation to any stored communications such as e-mail. Where the purpose of the surveillance under the 1979 Act is law enforcement, then the product may be used as evidence in court. The prosecution will provide an 'Evidentiary Certificate' under s 61 which is *prima facie* evidence of lawfulness, authenticity, and integrity. In so far as the intercept process is then impugned, there may be special hearings under the terms of the National Security Information (Criminal and Civil Proceedings) Act 2004.[202] The material is made available to the judge, prosecution, and defence counsel (subject to vetting, which is routinely refused) but not to the defendant, and the burden is shifted towards suppression since 'the greatest weight' must be given to the views of the Attorney General (s 31). The Chilcot Review found Australia to be a 'compelling example',[203] but whether the 2004 Act observes the standards of Article 6 of the European Convention would depend on whether disclosure is sufficient to allow the effective briefing of counsel.[204]

2.101 The Surveillance Devices Act 2004 establishes procedures for officers to obtain warrants or emergency authorizations for the installation and use of data (including key logging), optical, listening, and tracking surveillance devices in relation to criminal investigations and other operations. However, there is no need for an external warrant if the operation can be completed without property interference.

2.102 The USA has long relied on telephone intercepts to combat organized crime. The Omnibus Crime Control and Safe Streets Act 1968, Title III,[205] requires a judicial warrant process for full intercepts, and communications data can be obtained by 'pen register' under the Electronic Communications Privacy Act 1986, which also covers access to stored data.[206] Foreign powers or their agents are handled under the Foreign Intelligence Surveillance Act 1978 (FISA) without a court order (but with notification to the Foreign Intelligence

---

[199] See McIntyre, TJ, 'Data Retention in Ireland' (2008) 24(4) *Computer Law and Security Report* 326.
[200] For CCTV, see An Garda Siochána Act 2005, s 38.
[201] See also the Australian Security Intelligence Organisation Act 1979 for intelligence warrants.
[202] See *R v Lodhi* [2006] NSWSC 586; Donaghue, S, 'Reconciling security and the right to a fair trial' and Boulten, P, 'Preserving national security in the courtroom' in Lynch, A et al, *Law and Liberty in the War on Terror* (Federation Press, Sydney, 2007).
[203] (Chilcot) Privy Council Review, *Intercept as Evidence* (Cm 7324, London, 2008) para 156.
[204] *AF (No 3)* [2009] UKHL 28.
[205] PL 90-351. Interception for national security purposes was excepted: *US v US District Court* 407 US 277 (1972).
[206] PL 99-508.

Surveillance Court).[207] To cater for the fragmented and stateless nature of *jihadi* terrorism, a 'lone wolf' exception in 2004 allows for action against international terrorism without connection to a foreign power.[208] The PATRIOT Act 2001, Title II,[209] widened the opportunities for electronic surveillance. Interception warrants are made available in respect of terrorism offences (s 201) and can be made on a national basis (s 220). The pen register and trap and trace powers (dialled numbers and caller identification) are applied to the internet (s 216). The Act also makes the Foreign Intelligence Surveillance Act 1978 available where the foreign target is a significant purpose but not the primary purpose of the investigation (s 218). Special encryption measures equivalent to the RIPA Pt III have not been passed, but keystroke logging can be applied under warrant.[210]

When intercept evidence is at issue, disclosure issues are handled under the Classified Information Procedure Act 1980,[211] which allows for close judicial management and offers the prosecution the chance to make representations and to drop charges. **2.103**

Even this extensive surveillance regime was not, however, thought sufficient in the view of the US executive which conferred upon itself more programmatic powers under the National Security Agency's secret warrantless Terrorist Surveillance Program from 2001 onwards and revealed only by the *New York Times* in late 2005.[212] Because of challenges to the legality of this programme, the Protect America Act of 2007 (as renewed by the FISA Amendments Act 2008)[213] extended warrantless surveillance on Presidential authority of communications that begin or end in a foreign country even if intercepted within the US, with certification to the FISA Court which considers only general agency compliance rather than individual application. Even beyond these systems lies the surveillance network known as ECHELON, based on the sharing of signals intelligence under a British-US Communication Intelligence Agreement 1946 involving a National Security Agency post at Menwith Hill as well as other state participants.[214] **2.104**

Administrative rules for human surveillance also underwent amendment after September 11. The Attorney General Guidelines of 1976 were altered in 2002 so as to remove restrictions on the surveillance of lawful political or religious activities by the FBI and lowering the threshold of suspicion for commencing operations.[215] A variety of other tasking guidelines **2.105**

---

[207] PL 95-511. See *US v Duggan* 743 F2d 59 (1984); *US v bin Laden* 126 F Supp 2d 264 (2000); *In re Sealed Case* 310 F3d 717 (2002); *US v Hassoun* 2007 US Dist LEXIS 25086.

[208] Intelligence Reform and Terrorism Prevention Act of 2004, s 6001 (PL 108-458).

[209] PL 107-56. See Donohue, LK, *The Cost of Counterterrorism: Power, Politics, and Liberty* (Cambridge University Press, Cambridge, 2008) ch 4.

[210] See *US v Scarfo* 180 F Supp 2d 572 (2001).

[211] PL 96-456 of 1980, 18 USC App III ss 1-16. See further Chapter 6.

[212] See Offices of the Inspectors General, *The President's Surveillance Program* (Washington DC, 2009); Schwartz, PM, 'Reviving telecommunications surveillance law' (2008) 75 *University of Chicago Law Review* 287; Wittes, B, *Law and the Long War* (Penguin, New York, 2008) ch 8; Wagner, M, 'Warrantless wiretapping' (2009) 78 *Geo Washington Law Review* 204.

[213] PL 110-55, PL 110-261. See Barnum, DG, 'Foreign intelligence surveillance in the United States' [2008] *European Human Rights Law Review* 633.

[214] National Archives HW/80/4. See European Parliament resolutions on the existence of a global system for the interception of private and commercial communications (ECHELON interception system) (2001/2098(INI), dated 5 September 2001, and 7 November, 2002 (B5-0528/2002); Bedan, M, 'Echelon's effect' (2007) 59 *Federal Criminal Law Journal* 425.

[215] Attorney General's Guidelines for Reporting on Civil Disorders and Demonstrations Involving a Federal Interest 1976; Attorney General's Guidelines on General Crimes, Racketeering Enterprise and Terrorism Enterprise Investigations 2002. These guidelines do not apply to the growing body of state police capabilities such as the NYPD Counterterrorism Bureau.

have been altered, especially by the issuance in 2003 of the National Security Investigations and Foreign Intelligence Collection Guidelines which were combined in 2008 as the Attorney General Consolidated Guidelines for FBI Domestic Operations covering investigation of crimes and threats to the national security and collection of foreign intelligence; assistance and information to other agencies; and intelligence analysis and planning functions. Published rules about tasking are valuable modes of governance, and there is a distinct lack of published British counterparts.[216] On the other hand, the European recognition of rights to privacy provides a backstop which is lacking in the US.[217]

2.106   Within European jurisdictions, one of the main controversies has concerned data-mining. The *Rasterfahndung* (grid search) of databanks under German Länder laws was revived after 9/11,[218] whereby profiling based on the 9/11 perpetrators was applied to alien and resident registration and university records, resulting in 32,000 'hits' which were reduced to 1,689 suspects with relevant knowledge or access. No prosecutions followed, and the database was deleted in 2003. This operation (though not the laws themselves) was found to be in breach of the constitutional right to the fundamental right to informational self-determination by the Federal Constitutional Court (*Bundesverfassungsgericht*) in 2006.[219] Nevertheless, there remain broad powers under the *Gesetz zur Bekämpfung des Internationalen Terrorismus* (Second Counter-Terrorism Act) of 2002 to access integrated public data for directed investigations and also to carry out security checks.

2.107   The Federal Constitutional Court has also struck down the German law which implements the Data Retention Directive of 2006, finding it unacceptable on grounds of the insecurity of retained data and also the lack of safeguards and rights which should include judicial oversight over release (a far cry from the permissive Data Protection Act 1998, s 29(3)) and notification to the person affected.[220]

2.108   Surveillance has next become of interest to the European Union which has promoted networked pooling mechanisms, the most notable of which is the Schengen Information System.[221] The system has records of 930,000 people. While most relate to unwanted aliens, there is a category of nearly 33,000 who are within the borders of the European Union and are being kept under 'discreet surveillance' for the purposes of crime prevention or national security under Article 99 of the Schengen Agreement.[222] Cross-border surveillance operations are permitted under Article 40 and are authorized in the United Kingdom by the Crime (International Cooperation) Act 2003, s 83.

---

[216] See Gill, P, 'Security and intelligence services in the United Kingdom' in Brodeur, JP et al, *Democracy, Law and Security* (Ashgate, Aldershot, 2003) p 293. One acute example concerns the guidelines issued to the Security Service on the treatment and interview of detainees: Intelligence and Security Committee, *Annual Report 2008–09* (Cm 7807, London, 2010) para 158.

[217] Ross, J, 'The place of democratic societies' (2007) 55 *American Journal of Comparative Law* 493.

[218] See Oehmichen, A, *Terrorism and Anti-Terror Legislation* (Intersentia, Antwerp, 2009) pp 253, 259, 271.

[219] 1 BvR 518/02, No 40/2006, 4 April 2006. See Capoccia, G, 'Germany's response to 9/11' in Crenshaw, M (ed), *Consequences of Counterterrorism* (Russell Sage, New York, 2010).

[220] BVerfG, 1 BvR 256/08, 2 March 2010. See DeSimone, D, 'Pitting Karlsruhe against Luxembourg?' (2010) 11 *German Law Journal* 291.

[221] Schengen acquis—Convention implementing the Schengen Agreement of 14 June 1985 (L239, 22/09/2000, 19). See House of Lords European Union Committee, *Schengen Information System II* (SIS II) (2006–07 HL 49); Mathieson, T, 'Lex vigilatoria' in Deflem, M (ed), *Surveillance and Governance* (Emerald, Bingley, 2008).

[222] Council of the European Union, *Schengen Information System Database Statistics* (6162/10, Brussels, 2010).

Building on the Schengen Acquis, the Prüm Treaty 2005 provides for the compilation of a **2.109** database of DNA profiles, fingerprints, and vehicle registration numbers.[223] Core elements of Prüm were transferred into the European Union legal framework by Council Decision in 2008.[224]

Council Framework Decision 2006/960/JHA of 18 December 2006, commonly known **2.110** as the 'Swedish Initiative', seeks to simplify the exchange of information and intelligence regarding serious criminal matters (not including national security data).[225] It establishes the rules (and proformas) but does not impose any obligation. The instrument was implemented by Home Office Circular 030/2008 and EU Council Framework Decision 2006/960/JHA. A Member State must make available information on the same basis it would make it available to other law enforcement agencies within its own jurisdiction.

Assessment and conclusions

An investigation can deliver several goals under the CONTEST strategy. The most obvious **2.111** is 'Pursue', but criminal justice outcomes are not always in mind. Intercepts cannot be used as evidence, and, regardless of this rule, intelligence-based outcomes, monitoring, and disruption are more common.

Effectiveness is very difficult to judge without fuller disclosure of the state's innermost **2.112** secrets. As a generalization, human sources appear to be particularly effective against hierarchical and disciplined organizations, and infiltration in Northern Ireland probably achieved significant disruptive and stabilizing impacts.[226] The more heterarchical disposition of Al-Qa'ida seems less promising ground, and the police complained in 2007 of the lack of 'community intelligence',[227] though the absence of discipline in these looser groupings may be a weakness for them. By contrast, scepticism has been most loudly voiced about blanket methods of data mining.[228] There are also potential inefficiencies when ultimate decision-making about surveillance is vested in politically motivated government Ministers and not detached judges. However, the dangers identified by the *Butler Report*[229] can be countered to some extent by the formalities required by the RIPA.

The ethics of intelligence-gathering through surveillance have primarily revolved around **2.113** privacy interests, though rights of expression and association are also engaged. According to *Klass v Germany*, the objective of defeating terrorism will count as a justified limit on privacy, but that case also reiterates the need for adequate and effective guarantees against abuse,

---

[223] See House of Lords European Union Committee, *Prüm: an effective weapon against terrorism and crime?* (2006–07 HL 90).

[224] See Council Decision 2008/615/JHA and 2008/615/JHA.

[225] See Grief, N, 'EU law and security' (2007) 32 *European Law Review* 752.

[226] Moran, J, 'Evaluating Special Branch and the use of informant intelligence in Northern Ireland' (2010) 25 *Intelligence & National Security* 1 at 17. See also Bamford, BWC, 'The role and effectiveness of intelligence in Northern Ireland' (2005) 20 *Intelligence & National Security* 581.

[227] Clarke, P, 'Learning from experience' (Metropolitan Police Service, London, 2007).

[228] See Committee on Technical and Privacy Dimensions of Information for Terrorism Prevention and Other National Goals, National Research Council, *Protecting Individual Privacy in the Struggle Against Terrorists* (National Academies Press, Washington DC, 2008); Brown, I and Korff, D, 'Terrorism and the proportionality of internet surveillance' (2009) 6 *European Journal of Criminology* 119.

[229] See Committee of Privy Counsellors, *Review of Intelligence on Weapons of Mass Destruction* (2003–04 HC 898).

which can be difficult to apply to covert action.[230] Even the basic standards of constitutional governance—the reliance on express laws rather than vague administrative discretion—have regularly been breached by security practices. The RIPA has addressed the problem of constitutional governance and has done so without mention of the term 'terrorism'. But its substantive terms are less effective or sophisticated in securing proportionality, for it still relies on broad triggers such as 'national security' which are mostly authorized by police superiors rather than independent judges. There is also no provision for subsequent redress through notification of the operation to the subject, a device which is seen as desirable though not obligatory.[231] Nevertheless, the intercept system has been upheld by the European Court of Human Rights in *Kennedy v United Kingdom*[232] as sufficiently clear and sufficiently supervised by the Commissioner and the Investigatory Powers Tribunal to meet the standards of Article 8.

2.114 In terms of accountability, so far as police oversight goes, the HMIC view is that the measures are running smoothly.[233] Otherwise, much faith is placed in the work of the various judicial commissioners who audit under Pt IV the surveillance measures under the RIPA as well as the Intelligence Services Act 1994 and the Police Act 1997.[234] There should also be an Investigatory Powers Commissioner for Northern Ireland under s 61, but it is surely a disgrace that no appointment has been made.[235] A tribunal under s 65 hears individual complaints. But few powers are subject to issuance by a judicial officer which could be argued to be desirable not necessarily to assist with admissibility[236] but rather to ensure that decisions are taken with forensic precision and proportionality.[237]

2.115 Oversight is also offered by the Intelligence and Security Committee under the Intelligence Services Act 1994, s 10. The Committee examines the expenditure, administration, and policy of the security agencies and has privileged access to information. Its performance has been considered wanting even by the government.[238]

2.116 The courts are increasingly prepared to scrutinize surveillance activities in contrast to prior doctrines of non-justiciability.[239] The litigation surrounding Binyam Mohamed has highlighted the defiance of executive arguments and threats.[240]

---

[230] App no 5029/71, Ser A 28 (1987) paras 49–50. See further Council of Ministers Committee of Ministers, *Special Investigative Techniques* (Rec (2005) 10, Strasbourg) Arts 2–5; Council of Europe, *Terrorism: Special Investigation Techniques* (Strasbourg, 2005) p 20; Walker, C, 'The pursuit of terrorism with intelligence' in Moran, J and Phythian, M, *Intelligence, Security and Policing Post-9/11* (Palgrave Macmillan, Basingstoke, 2008) p 73.

[231] See *Redgrave v United Kingdom,* App no 20271/92, 1 September 1993; *Leander v Sweden*, App no 9248/81, Ser A 116 (1987) para 66.

[232] App no 26839/05, 18 May 2010. A form of intrusive surveillance regulated by subsequent judicial review was upheld in *Uzun v Germany*, App no 35623/09, 2 September 2010.

[233] HM Inspectorate of Constabulary, *A Need to Know: HMIC's Thematic Inspection of Special Branch and Ports Policing* (Home Office, London, 2003) para 3.39.

[234] See House of Lords Select Committee on the Constitution, *Surveillance: Citizens and the State* (2008–09 HL 18) para 252 and *Government Response* (Cm 7616, London, 2009) p 3.

[235] See Chief Surveillance Commissioner, *Annual Report for 2007–08* (2007–08 HC 659) para 3.3.

[236] Compare Schenin, M, *Report of the Special Rapporteur on the promotion and protection of human rights and fundamental freedoms while countering terrorism* (A/HRC/10/3, United Nations, 2009) para 29. See also A/HRC/14/46, 2010.

[237] House of Lords Select Committee on the Constitution, *Surveillance: Citizens and the State* (2008–09 HL 18) para 263.

[238] *The Governance of Britain—Constitutional Renewal* (Cm 7342, London, 2008) paras 235 *et seq.*

[239] See Walker, C, 'The threat of terrorism and the fate of control orders' [2010] *Public Law* 3.

[240] *R (Mohamed) v Secretary of State for Foreign and Commonwealth Affairs* [2010] EWCA Civ 65.

A rather bleak view is that 'Privacy is the terrorist's best friend . . .'.[241] On that score, everyone **2.117** must become the object of eternal suspicion. This widespread surveillance might be more tolerable if public authorities could demonstrate evident success and could be trusted to act in a discerning and considerate way. But governmental departments have been culpable of massive data losses[242] and have found it difficult to delimit broad surveillance powers. There is the further danger that even weak controls over state agencies will be evaded by passing responsibility to private communications providers whose priority is commercial success and not public values.[243] These tendencies should be countered with 'data minimization' at the outset,[244] more attention to the quality of data being mined and the premise behind any operation,[245] and a firmer recognition of accountability to courts for any intrusion into private lives.

E. All-Risks Policing

Introduction and background

Because of the complexities of distinguishing friend and foe, security and insecurity, or **2.118** even war and peace, terrorism appears to be an insidious, endemic, pervasive, and endless risk. The embedded nature of terrorism risk therefore provokes the demand for 'all-risks' security and policing measures.[246] Their application owes more to an intelligence-led approach than to the collection of evidence, and will reflect 'a new and urgent emphasis on the need for security, the containment of danger, and the identification and management of any kind of risk'.[247] The effect of these pervasive tactics is to treat anyone and everyone as a risk on the basis of leads even more vague and haphazard than suspicion. The reason for attention is not so much the suspicion falling on any given individual but the nature of a particular site or some other perceived vulnerability. Thus, a degree of rational risk calculation is still present, but it shifts from the personal to the positional. At the same time, all-risks policing is rarely applied evenly. While mathematical models of profiling might be used, they embody preconceptions or skewed application, both of which result in 'targeted governance' directed at 'risky' groups.[248]

Two aspects of 'all-risks' policing as applied to persons will be considered here with reference **2.119** to terrorism: stop and search powers and port controls. Identity cards also fall into this category but have not yet been adopted on an all-risks basis.[249] Protective security of places will be left to Chapter 10.

---

[241] Posner, RA, 'Privacy, surveillance and law' (2008) 75 *University of Chicago Law Review* 245.

[242] See further Cabinet Office, *Data Handling Procedures in Government* (London, 2008).

[243] Compare Balkin, SM, 'The constitution in the national surveillance state' (2008) 93 *Minnesota Law Review* 1; Kerr, OS, 'The national surveillance state' (2009) 93 *Minnesota Law Review* 2179.

[244] Information Commissioner's Office, *Annual Report 2007–08* (2007–08 HC 670) p 8.

[245] See Cate, FH, 'Government data mining' (2008) 43 *Harvard Civil Rights-Civil Liberties Law Review* 435.

[246] See Walker, C, 'Neighbor terrorism and the all-risks policing of terrorism' (2009) 3 *Journal of National Security Law & Policy* 121.

[247] Garland, D, *The Culture of Control* (Oxford University Press, Oxford, 2001) p 12.

[248] See Amoore, L and de Goede, M, 'Governance, risk and dataveillance in the war on terror' (2005) 43 *Crime, Law and Social Change* 149.

[249] See Identity Cards Act 2006; Identity Documents Bill 2010–11.

Stop and search

Introduction and background

2.120 The powers of stop and search in s 44 of the TA 2000 were said to be required to afford a chance to intercept munitions or to thwart plans.[250] Thus, objectives of prevention and protection through disruption, intelligence-gathering, and public reassurance rather than 'Pursue' though criminal justice are to the fore.

2.121 The powers to stop and search for munitions had long existed in Northern Ireland, but their contemporary life can be traced to the Irish Republican Army truck bombs in the City of London in 1992 and 1993 and then in Docklands in 1996. The Criminal Justice and Public Order Act 1994, s 81, extended to Britain some of the Northern Irish powers.[251] The 1994 Act was applied to pedestrians by the PT(AP)A 1996.[252]

Provisions[253]

2.122 Armed with an authorization under s 44, any police constable in uniform can stop a vehicle and search the vehicle, the driver, or any passenger, and also stop and search a pedestrian, if located within an area or at a place specified in an authorization. It is made clear in s 45(1)(b) that the power 'may be exercised whether or not the constable has grounds for suspecting the presence of articles of that kind'. Subsequent amendments allow the British Transport Police, Ministry of Defence Police, and Civil Nuclear Constabulary to exercise these powers,[254] as well as designated Police Community Support Officers.[255] By amendment in the TA 2006, s 30, the powers apply to internal waters.[256] The use of s 44 by the British Transport Police (typically at railway stations) has caused some friction with police authorities who complain that they are not adequately informed of operations in their jurisdiction.

2.123 There are three different offences under s 47(1) for non-compliance with stops and searches.

2.124 There are several limits to the exercise of these powers. By s 45, powers must be exercised only for the purpose of 'searching for articles of a kind which could be used in connection with terrorism' (s 45(1)(a)). They may not involve a person being required 'to remove any clothing in public except for headgear, footwear, an outer coat, a jacket or gloves' (s 45(3)). A further safeguard is that a driver or pedestrian may apply within twelve months for a written statement as to the legal basis for the stop (s 45(5)). In line with other stop and search powers under Code A, Form 5090[257] should be completed for every stop at the time, or if there are exceptional circumstances which would make it wholly impracticable then once it becomes practical. This record of the search or a receipt must be offered to the person searched.[258]

---

[250] *Lloyd Report*, paras 10.14, 10.21.

[251] Hansard HC Standing Committee B col 721 (10 February 1994), David Maclean.

[252] See Reid, K, 'Prevention of Terrorism (Additional Powers) Act 1996' [1996] 4 *Web Journal of Current Legal Issues*; Jason-Lloyd, L, 'The Prevention of Terrorism (Additional Powers) Act 1996—a commentary' (1996) 160 *Justice of the Peace* 503.

[253] See further Walker, C, 'Know thine enemy as thyself' (2008) 32 *Melbourne Law Review* 275.

[254] ATCSA 2001, Sch 7, paras 29, 31; Energy Act 2004, Sch 23. See further Home Office Circulars 24/2002 and 25/2002 (London, 2002).

[255] Police Reform Act 2002, Sch 4, para 15.

[256] For the definition, see Home Office Circular 8/2006 (London, 2006) para 69.

[257] See MacPherson, W, *The Stephen Lawrence Inquiry* (Cm 4262-I, London, 1999); Flanagan, R, *Independent Review of Policing* (Home Office, London, 2008).

[258] PACE Code A para 4.1. The officer may be identified by warrant number only: paras 3.8(b), 4.4.

By s 44(5), any detention must be carried out 'at or near the place where the person or vehicle   **2.125**
is stopped'. In *Mooney v Ministry of Defence*,[259] the claimant was stopped en route to the
airport under equivalent powers in Northern Ireland at a vehicle checkpoint (VCP) and
detained for twenty minutes. His vehicle was then removed to police premises some miles
away for a search which took eighty-five minutes, and the claimant was obliged to accompany the vehicle. The claimant missed his flight and was awarded damages of £1,200 on the
basis that, though the incidental detention of a stopped person is lawful, the detention and
search powers must be exercised only at the site of the stop.

Next, when exercising stop and search powers, police officers must have regard to PACE   **2.126**
Code A. First, according to para 1.1, powers to stop and search must be used 'fairly, respon-
sibly, with respect for people being searched and without unlawful discrimination'. Secondly,
para 1.2 provides that the 'intrusion on the liberty of the person stopped or searched' has to
be brief and that any detention 'must take place at or near the location of the stop'. On the
other hand, since the power is not applied on the basis of reasonable suspicion, there may be
some doubts as to the applicability of the warning in para 2.2 not to exercise the powers based
on 'generalisations or stereotypical images [or a] person's religion'. The Stop and Search
Manual published in 2005 by the Stop and Search Action Team in the Home Office makes
clear that reasonable suspicion does not apply to s 44.[260]

The precondition for exercise, an authorization, may be granted only if the senior police   **2.127**
officer giving it considers it 'expedient' for the prevention of acts of terrorism (s 44(3)).
An authorization, which may be valid for up to twenty-eight days under s 46 and can be
renewed, may be given by an Assistant Chief Constable or a Commander of a London force.
Section 46 requires the police to inform the Secretary of State as soon as is reasonably
practicable. The authorization must be confirmed (or amended or rejected) within forty-
eight hours. Forces are encouraged by Home Office guidance to be specific and limited on
area coverage.[261] Though the authorization processes are clear, they have been breached on
forty occasions.[262] There is also criticism of the slow pace of Home Office authorizations,[263]
though the forty-eight-hour period of grace surely caters for reasonable operational
uncertainties. No data are released as to refusals.

The broad powers in s 44 contrast with the other stop and search power in s 43. By s 43(1),   **2.128**
a constable may stop and search a person reasonably suspected to be a 'terrorist' to discover whether the person possesses anything which may constitute evidence that he is a
terrorist. This power can apply in public and private places, provided in the case of the
latter that there is some other legal basis for entry. There is no prior authorization process,
but under s 43(3), a search of a person under this section must be carried out by someone
of the same sex.

Stop and search powers in the Act are subject to s 116(2), by which a power to stop a person   **2.129**
includes power to stop a vehicle (other than an aircraft which is airborne). By s 116(3), a
person commits a summary offence when there is a failure to stop a vehicle as directed. The
power to seize and retain materials under subsection (4) on reasonable suspicion that they

---

[259] (1994) 8 BNIL n 28 (QBD).
[260] (Home Office, London, 2006) para 66.
[261] Home Office Circular 03/01 (London, 2001) para 5.6.2.
[262] Hansard HC vol 511 col 23ws (10 June 2010).
[263] Hayman, A, *The Terrorist Hunters* (Bantam Press, London, 2009) p 54.

may constitute evidence that the person is a terrorist attracts additional powers to seize, retain, and sift articles elsewhere under the Criminal Justice and Police Act 2001, s 51.

Implementation

2.130   Five manifest patterns have occurred since 2001: a sustained increase in usage of s 44, a low rate of consequent terrorist arrests, a higher rate of non-terrorist arrests, a disproportionate impact on ethnic minorities, and uneven geographical delivery (see Table 2.4).

2.131   The overall usage has increased substantially since 2000. The powers had been used twenty-nine times in five police areas (twenty-two in London alone) from 1994 to 1996,[264] with a diminution thereafter. There were on average 14,060 stops per annum (70,300 in total, with 43,700 in 1996–97) between 1994 and 2000. After 2000, there was a spike in 2007–08, which presumably related to fears of further attacks after the Haymarket bombing, though it may also relate to more careful recording practices since the 2005 total was not so high. Resultant arrests of relevance to terrorism are rarities (well under 1 per cent). There are many more non-terrorist arrests, but these must be discounted since these extraneous impacts cannot possibly justify the s 44 powers. Assistant Chief Constable Beckley defended (on behalf of the Association of Chief Police Officers) the lack of consequent arrests by stressing that 'this is a power to be used to put people off their plans, hence it is used in a pretty random way'.[265] In this way, the disruptive potential is more important than its interdictory or prosecutorial potential, though whether disruption is effectively achieved is very difficult to gauge in empirical terms because it amounts to proof of a negative and also because of secrecy surrounding operations. It is also tenable that intelligence-gathering can be part of the purpose, and police craft can turn a power to stop and search into a de facto power to stop and question. But the diffuse nature of the locations and populations affected by s 44 are quite distinct from practices in Northern Ireland where a 'suspect community' could be targeted.[266]

Table 2.4 Usage of s 44[a]

Year	Stops			Terrorism/other arrests			Ethnicity (if recorded)			Location %		
	Vehicle	*Pedestrian*	*Total*	*Vehicle*	*Pedestrian*	*Totals*	*White*	*Black*	*Asian*	*MPS (London)*	*City (London)*	*Other*
2001/2	7,604	946	8,550	20/149	0/20	20/169	6,629	529	744	49	32	19
2002/3	16,761	4,774	21,577	11/280	7/79	18/359	14,429	1,745	2,989	61	21	18
2003/4	21,287	8,120	29,407	14/358	5/112	19/470	20,637	2,704	3,668	53	25	23
2004/5	21,121	10,941	32,062	35/240	24/153	59/393	23,389	2,511	3,485	40	20	40
2005/6	25,479	19,064	44,543	46/246	59/212	105/458	30,837	4,155	6,805	51	15	35
2006/7	23,485	13,712	37,197	14/246	14/205	28/451	25,962	3,602	5,505	68	6	26
2007/8	65,217	52,061	117,278	34/665	38/515	72/1180	73,967	15,218	20,768	87	2	11
Ave	25,851	15,660	41,516	25/312	21/185	46/497	27,979	4,352	6,281	58	17	25
(% of total)	(62)	(38)		(7/93)	(10/90)	(8/92)	(67)	(10)	(15)			

[a] Home Office and Ministry of Justice, *Statistics on Race and the Criminal Justice System* (London, 2002–09).

---

[264] *Lloyd Report*, para 10.16.

[265] Home Affairs Committee, *Terrorism and Community Relations* (2003–04 HC 165) para 54.

[266] Compare Pantazis, C, and Pemberton, S, 'From the "old" to the "new" suspect community' (2009) 49 *British Journal of Criminology* 646 at 655.

One can appreciate that arrests for non-terrorist offences can arise from the genuinely **2.132**
unexpected detection of drugs or offensive weapons. But there is a fear of the transposition
of terrorism powers more widely than is proper. Some notable instances include Walter
Wolfgang, an 82-year-old party activist, who was ejected from the Labour Party's 2005
annual conference after he heckled Foreign Secretary Jack Straw and then was stopped under
s 44 when he tried to re-enter the venue.[267] A woman in a harbour area of Dundee was
stopped for walking along a cycle path.[268] Another example might be Nicholas Gaubert, who
was disabled by a Taser after acting 'strangely' on a Leeds bus shortly after the July 7
bombings. Police thought he might be a suicide bomber, but he was a diabetic who was
entering a coma.[269]

Analysis in terms of ethnicity reveals an over-representation of minorities,[270] given the **2.133**
overall composition of the United Kingdom population which comprises 92 per cent white,
4 per cent Asian, and 2 per cent Black.[271] The extent of these racial inequalities, also very
evident in non-terrorism stop and search powers, is disputed because of the inaccuracy of
recording practices and the nature of the users of public spaces.[272] In addition, 'Asian' should
not be translated as 'Muslim', since only half of those belonging to this ethnic group are in
fact Muslims, though this proportion rises to 92 per cent for those of Pakistani or Bangladeshi
origins. [273] The data for terrorism-related arrests following a stop accentuates this trend. Out
of 72 arrests in 2007–08, there were 18 persons of white, 20 Asian, and 15 black ethnic
appearance. What emerges is a pattern of ethnic disparities which may stem from the endemic
ethnic presumptions on the part of police officers which are reflected in the stops of persons
of black ethnic appearance (up 322 per cent in 2007–08, a higher rate than for Asians).

That ethnicity is taken into account has been admitted from time to time. The point was **2.134**
starkly admitted in 2005 by Ian Johnston, Chief Constable of the British Transport Police:
'We should not waste time searching old white ladies. It is going to be disproportionate. It is
going to be young men, not exclusively, but it may be disproportionate when it comes to
ethnic groups.'[274] The Home Office Minister, Hazel Blears, concurred that the sources of the
terrorist threat 'inevitably means that some of our counter-terrorist powers will be dispro-
portionately experienced by people in the Muslim community'.[275] The apparent conserving
of resources and selection as targets of the politically marginal may further explain
patterning.[276]

At the same time, there is a reminder from the ethnicity data that the powers remain of the **2.135**
'all-risks' variety in that the 'white' population still provide the largest number of those
stopped. Some have vainly attempted to explain this fact by reference to the targeting of Irish

---

[267] *The Guardian*, 29 September 2005, p 1.
[268] *The Times*, 17 October 2005, p 8.
[269] *Yorkshire Post* 7 July 2008.
[270] It is not considered seriously disproportionate in London: Metropolitan Police Authority, *Counter-Terrorism: The London Debate* (London, 2007) p 49.
[271] See Office for National Statistics, *National Statistics: Ethnicity* (London, 2003).
[272] See Bowling, B and Phillips, C, 'Disproportionate and discriminatory' (2007) 70 *Modern Law Review* 936.
[273] Home Affairs Committee, *Terrorism and Community Relations* (2005–06) HC 165-I para 63.
[274] *The Guardian* 17 August 2005, p 6.
[275] Home Affairs Committee, *Terrorism and Community Relations* (2003–04 HC 165) para 46.
[276] See *Report of the Special Rapporteur on the promotion and protection of human rights and fundamental freedoms while countering terrorism* (A/HRC/4/26, 2007); Moeckli, D, *Human Rights and Non-Discrimination in the 'War on Terror'* (Oxford University Press, Oxford, 2008) pp 198, 200.

dissident Republicans[277] or radical demonstrators or that 'compensatory stops' are made to even out the ethnicity profiles.[278] These factors do contribute to the totals, but the basic feature of the 'all-risks' nature of the power is a better explanation.

2.136   The power is also distributed highly selectively in terms of location. Overwhelmingly, its usage has been concentrated in London, where it has been in force on a rolling basis from 2001 until 2009.[279] It was always envisaged that authorizations might last 'for a considerable time'.[280] Elsewhere, only a minority of force areas issue authorizations.[281] This variation has become the subject of some criticism, and the idea of national blanket usage has been proposed as necessary but hampered by the erratic independence of local chief constables.[282] However, even after serious attacks such as in 2005 and 2007, the universal application of s 44 would have been disproportionate to the nature of the threat.

2.137   The magnified usage in London in part arises because the Metropolitan Police Service operated from April 2001 through to July 2009 a 'rolling', force-wide authorization of s 44. Lord Carlile criticized the absence of a more tailored and 'patchwork' approach.[283] Therefore, a pilot scheme was commenced in July 2009 in four boroughs before being rolled out force-wide in August 2009, in the expectation that rates will be significantly reduced.[284] The pilot scheme divides each borough into three 'levels'. In Level 1 'security zones', s 44 is continuously in force. Designated within such zones are 'iconic' and 'high risk' targets. 'Level 2' areas are where s 44 is applied in response to a specific occurrence, such as a large social event. 'Level 3' areas are not protected by s 44, though s 43 still applies by default.

2.138   The usage of s 43 has increased in the shadow of the consequent decline of s 44, but not so much as to become interchangeable. Thus, there were 1,247 stops in 2008, and 1,450 in 2009.[285]

2.139   The increasing use of s 44 in Northern Ireland since 2006 has led to serious alarm being expressed by the Northern Ireland Policing Board,[286] which resulted in a decision to halt recourse to s 44 in 2010. No data are disclosed before 2005, but the supposition would be that usage of s 44 was then modest because of the availability of powers under Part VIII of the TA 2000. Many of those alternative powers still remain under the JSA 2007, but the impetus towards normalization has encouraged a switch to s 44 (see Table 2.5).

---

[277]   In 2007–08, the Irish amounted to 1,296 stops out of 73,967 (1.75%). According to the 2001 Census, there were almost 691,000 White Irish people in Great Britain (1.17% of the population).

[278]   Pantazis, C, and Pemberton, S, 'From the "old" to the "new" suspect community' (2009) 49 *British Journal of Criminology* 646 at 656.

[279]   Lord Carlile, *Report on the Operation in 2007 of the Terrorism Act 2000* (Home Office, London, 2008) paras 125, 129.

[280]   Hansard HC Standing Committee B col 718 (10 February 1994), David Maclean.

[281]   Lord Carlile, *Report on the Operation in 2007 of the Terrorism Act 2000* (Home Office, London, 2008) at para 99.

[282]   See Hayman, A, *The Terrorist Hunters* (Bantam Press, London, 2009) pp 54, 278.

[283]   See Lord Carlile, *Report on the Operation in 2008 of the Terrorism Act 2000 and of Part I of the Terrorism Act 2006* (Home Office, London, 2009), para 147.

[284]   The author thanks Genevieve Lennon, PhD Leeds, for this information. See further Yates, J, *Section 44 Terrorism Act 2000: Tactical Use Review* (Metropolitan Police Authority, London, 2009).

[285]   Lord Carlile, *Report on the Operation in 2001–2009 of the Terrorism Act 2000* (Home Office, London) para 189.

[286]   See Northern Ireland Policing Board, *Human Rights Annual Report 2008* (Belfast, 2009) p 50.

Table 2.5 Section 44 in Northern Ireland[a]

Year	Persons	Vehicles	Total
2005	204	156	360
2006	948	791	1,739
2007	2,167	1,801	3,968
2008	6,922	6,016	12,938

[a] Source: Northern Ireland Office, *Statistics on the Operation of the Terrorism Act 2000: Annual Statistics 2008* (Research and Statistical Bulletin 10/2009, Belfast).

There have been several attempts to provide better guidance on the exercise of the powers. **2.140** The fullest explanation is now in the National Policing Improvement Agency's *Practice Advice on Stop and Search in Relation to Terrorism*,[287] which must be read alongside Home Office Circular 027/2008.[288]

Foreign comparisons

In the Republic of Ireland, powers to stop and search include the Offences against the State **2.141** Act 1939, s 30. It differs from s 44 by requiring suspicion by a member of Garda Síochána. More comparable to s 44 is s 8 of the Criminal Law Act 1976, which is designed to be exercised against vehicles.[289] It differs from s 44 (and is stricter even than PACE, s 4) by being based on reasonable cause to suspect a specified offence on the part of a member of Garda Síochána. No further suspicion is then required for any search of the vehicle, but a search of persons accompanying it can only be carried out on reasonable cause against that particular person. These stops short of arrest were upheld as constitutional in *O'Callaghan v Ireland*.[290]

The Australian Protective Service Amendment Act 2003 gives the Australian Protective **2.142** Service and Australian Federal Police powers to request a person's personal details, stop and search a person suspected of possessing a weapon, seize weapons, and other initiatives.

Under the South African Terrorism and Related Activities Act 2004, s 24, there can be an **2.143** application for a judicial warrant to stop and search vehicles and persons within a specified area for a period which may not exceed ten days. The judicial involvement contrasts with the UK approach.

Though a right against unreasonable searches (without 'probable cause') generally prevails **2.144** under the US Constitution Fourth Amendment, the Court in *MacWade v Kelly* upheld the New York City Police Department's 'Container Inspection Program', which was implemented on 21 July 2005 to deter and interdict terrorist attacks on the subway which is viewed as a vulnerable 'icon'.[291] The programme established daily inspection checkpoints at selected subway facilities where officers searched bags that met size criteria for containing explosives.

---

[287] (Wyboston, 2008). See previously ACPO, *Interim Practice Advice on Stop and Search in relation to the Terrorism Act 2000* (Centrex, 2005); Metropolitan Police, *Section 44 Terrorism Act 2000: Standard Operating Procedures* (2005); National Centre for Policing Excellence, *Practice Advice on Stop and Search* (Wyboston, 2006).

[288] For earlier versions, see Circulars 038/2004 and 22/2006 (Home Office, London).

[289] Note also the power under s 15 for soldiers which was enforced from 1976 to 1977.

[290] [1994] 1 IR 555.

[291] (2006) 460 F3d 260 at 264 per Straub CJ.

Officers exercised virtually no discretion in determining whom to search but acted according to a selection rate (every fifth or tenth person) set by the supervising sergeant, based on the number of available officers and the passenger volume. The Court affirmed the constitutionality of the programme since preventing a terrorist attack on the subway was a 'special need',[292] which was pressing in the light of recent attacks in Madrid and London. In addition, the Court found that the operation was a reasonably effective deterrent and the intrusion into privacy was minimal.[293] A similar selection method under s 44 could constitute the unlawful fettering of discretion unless a given random stop could evidently contribute to an effective operation.

2.145 Most European countries operate identity check systems, which can partly perform the role of s 44. For example, in France, identity controls can take place anywhere in the country to investigate a crime or to prevent a breach of the peace.[294] More specialist powers were introduced as art 78-2-2 by Law no 2001-1062 of 15 November 2001, art 23, which authorizes the police on order of the district prosecutor to search vehicles for the purpose of investigating terrorism or munitions offences for twenty-four hours.[295] Racial patterning in the application of these powers is evident.[296]

Assessment and conclusions

2.146 The stated purposes of stop and search are 'to deter, disrupt, and detect'.[297] Yet, to stop every pedestrian entering a railway station, for instance, and to search them for a small device is akin to finding a needle in a haystack. One must therefore assume that to 'Pursue' through potential prosecution is not the main aim and, indeed, no prosecution for terrorism offences has ever followed. Instead, other objectives are served: disruption, intelligence-gathering, and public reassurance.

2.147 The exercise of s 44 has been considered at length by the Court of Appeal,[298] and the House of Lords,[299] in *R (Gillan) v Metropolitan Police Commissioner*. The facts were that an Assistant Commissioner of the Metropolitan Police gave an authorization under s 44(4) covering the whole of the Metropolitan Police District. That authorization was confirmed (without any publicity) and was then renewed on a continuous basis. Both applicants were stopped in 2003 near an arms fair being held at the ExCel Centre, Docklands. Nothing incriminating was found; the length of the transaction was up to thirty minutes.

2.148 Both appellants unsuccessfully challenged the police action. Their first argument was that s 44, as an incursion into liberties, should be construed restrictively and had been used excessively. The House of Lords determined that the use of the word 'expedient' in s 44(3)

---

[292] See *Board of Education of Independent School District No 92 v Earls* 536 US 822 (2002); *Chandler v Miller* 520 US 305 (1997).
[293] For application to internal ferries, see *Cabin v Chertoff* 471 F3d 67 (2006).
[294] Criminal Procedure Code art 78-1, 78-2 (Law of 3 September 1986).
[295] There can also be more passive surveillance under 'Pirate Plans' under Law no 2006-64: Cahn, O, 'The fight against terrorism and human rights' in Wade, M and Maljevic, A, *A War on Terror?* (Springer, New York, 2010) p 480.
[296] Open Society Justice Initiative, *Profiling Minorities* (New York, 2009).
[297] National Policing Improvement Agency's *Practice Advice on Stop and Search in Relation to the Terrorism Act* (Wyboston, 2008) p 3.
[298] *R (Gillan) v Metropolitan Police Commissioner* [2004] EWCA Civ 1067 ('*Gillan CA*').
[299] *R (on the application of Gillan) v Metropolitan Police Commissioner* [2006] UKHL 12 ('*Gillan HL*'). See Moeckli, D, 'Stop and search under the Terrorism Act' (2007) 70 *Modern Law Review* 659; Edwards, RA, 'Stop and search, terrorism and the human rights deficit' (2008) 37 *Common Law World Review* 211.

was significant parliamentary language,[300] set alongside the incorporation of other constraints. Taking these contexts together, s 44(3) was taken to mean that an authorization might be expedient if, and only if, the person giving it considered it likely that the stop and search powers would be 'of significant practical value and utility in seeking to achieve . . . the prevention of acts of terrorism'.[301] By contrast, the Home Office's Circular, *Authorisations of Stop and Search Powers under Section 44 of the Terrorism Act 2000*, emphasizes more strictly (and more strictly than the current version of the circular) that: 'Powers should only be authorised where they are absolutely necessary to support a forces [sic] anti-terrorism operations'.[302] Lord Bingham was satisfied that the authorization and confirmation processes had not become a 'routine bureaucratic exercise'[303] though one might argue that their Lordships too easily accepted evidence of vulnerabilities as equivalent to evidence of threats.

The next challenges were that the commander in charge of the police operation had wrongly **2.149** invoked the powers in that place and time and that there was excessive action by the operational officers against the appellants. Lord Bingham emphasized that the implementing constable is not free to act arbitrarily and must not stop and search people who are 'obviously not terrorist suspects'.[304] The lower courts were more pointedly critical of police practices on this score because of lack of direction and briefing.[305] Guidance has since been promulgated, whereby officers are required 'to review fully the intelligence on each authorization and clearly show the link between that intelligence and the geographic extent of the location in which the powers will be used', though a force-wide authorization is still permitted albeit that 'the authorising officer should explain the reasons in detail for rejecting the option of a designated area'.[306]

Turning to implementation questions, though the applicants were not from an ethnic **2.150** minority, some of their Lordships were troubled by the dangers of discrimination inherent in these powers. In Lord Hope's view, 'the mere fact that the person appears to be of Asian origin is not a legitimate reason for its exercise'.[307] While an appearance which suggests that the person is of Asian origin may attract the constable's initial attention, a further factor must be in the mind of the constable. This resolution is commendably in line with international law,[308] but it lacks precision as to prominence of racial considerations and too easily accepts that race or ethnicity is by its nature sufficiently connected to a terrorist suspect benchmark description and that it does not unduly divert attention from more pertinent criteria, such as behavioural and antecedent information. It also remains troublesome to reconcile even this partial reliance upon racial origins as a basis for official action with the absolute ban in the Race Relations Act 1976.[309] Even on the more flexible standard under Article 14 of the European Convention, whether racial or ethnic origins can be said to provide an

---

[300] *Gillan HL*, at paras 14 and 60.
[301] Ibid para 15.
[302] Home Office, *Authorisations of Stop and Search Powers under Section 44 of the Terrorism Act* (Circular 038/2004, 2004) para 9.
[303] Ibid para 18.
[304] Ibid para 35.
[305] See Lord Carlile, *Report on the Operation in 2002 and 2003 of the Terrorism Act 2000* (London, 2004) para 86.
[306] See Home Office Circular 027/2008 (London, 2008).
[307] *Gillan HL*, at para 45.
[308] See *Lecraft v Spain*, G/50 215/51 ESP(99), UN Human Rights Committee, 2009.
[309] See *R (European Roma Rights Centre) v Immigration Officer at Prague Airport* [2005] 2 AC 1.

'objective and reasonable' justification for official action[310] may be doubted since many terrorists do not fit the paradigm of Asian and since 'Asian' does not betoken 'Muslim'.

2.151 Aside from issues of construction and implementation, the House of Lords concentrated heavily on human rights issues. Reflecting a continuing trend in English case law, the House of Lords denied the applicability of Article 5 to police operations where detention is not the primary aim. However, to depict in this way the stop and search process as akin to waiting to board a bus or waiting until the light turns green at a pedestrian crossing[311] is wholly unconvincing for two important reasons. First, s 45 involves the exercise of an official coercive power not a directive power—the person waiting for the bus or for the green light can give up and try another route. Nor is the time of 'non-detention detention' as fleeting as suggested.

2.152 As for Article 8 rights to privacy, the stop and search was readily justified as necessary in a democratic society and proportionate in response to the clear and present danger of terrorism. Indeed, in parallel to his treatment of Article 5, Lord Bingham was 'doubtful whether an ordinary superficial search of the person can be said to show a lack of respect for private life'.[312] Similar arguments applied to Articles 10 and 11.

2.153 As for the standard of legality, relevant to both Articles 5 and 8, their Lordships viewed s 44 as passing the test. Lord Bingham was further seduced into this stance by arguments of security—that 'publishing the details of authorisations . . . would by implication reveal those places where such measures had not been put in place, thereby identifying vulnerable targets'.[313] These latter views confuse legal availability with strategies or tactics of operational implementation across an area as large as London. Given that court cases (and Lord Carlile) have revealed that the sections have been in continuous force throughout London since 2001, only a dim-witted terrorist would be unaware of these powers in general terms. By contrast, the National Policing Improvement Agency emphasizes, in its *Practice Advice on Stop and Search in Relation to the Terrorism Act*,[314] community involvement under s 44, since it will increase confidence, reassure the public, and encourage the flow of intelligence.[315] A role is recognized for police authorities and Community Impact Assessments should always be undertaken.[316] Home Office Circular 27/2008 *Authorisation of Stop and Search Powers under Section 44 of the Terrorism Act 2000* also recommends that a community impact assessment be carried out before any s 44 authorization.

2.154 The judgment of the House of Lords was in part rejected by the European Court of Human Rights in *Gillan and Quinton v United Kingdom*.[317] The complaint was sustained under the rubric of Article 8, while potential claims under Articles 5, 10, 11, and 14 were left aside rather than dismissed. The effect is to uphold the most fundamental assault on s 44, for the power inevitably incurs intrusion onto private life under Article 8 since it is accepted by

---

[310] See *Belgian Linguistics case*, App nos 1474/62 and others, Ser A no 6 (1968) para 10. The same standard has been applied to nationality: *Gaygusuz v Austria*, App no 17371/90, 1996-IV, para 42.

[311] *Gillan HL*, at para 25.

[312] Ibid para 28.

[313] Ibid paras 33, 34.

[314] (Wyboston, 2008) para 1.1, which recognizes a role for police authorities and demands completion of a Community Impact Assessment.

[315] Ibid 12.

[316] Ibid paras 1.4, 3.1.1.

[317] App no 4158/05, 12 January 2010.

the Court that a relatively superficial search will constitute interference.[318] This view contrasts with the House of Lords' position which was that Article 8 was engaged only by exceptional searches extending to personal correspondence or a diary.[319] Engagement of the other rights depends on the vagaries of the extent of the engagement,[320] the travel purpose, and the ethnicity of the traveller. The Strasbourg Court rejected analogies with entry control powers, such as at airports, because of the absence of consent under s 44.[321]

Having established a case to answer under Article 8(1), the Strasbourg Court was not satisfied that s 44 could meet the standards of Article 8(2). Most seriously, it was not 'in accordance with the law' in the sense that it did not afford a measure of legal protection against arbitrary interferences by public authorities. The Court was especially dismayed by reliance upon the word, 'expedient' for the grant of authorization, since it entailed no assessment of the proportionality of the measure.[322] In addition, oversight by the Home Secretary appeared weak, and geographical restrictions were not observed in London (at least until 2009), nor could the Independent Reviewer (Lord Carlile) impact on individual authorizations. The laxity of the power was then compounded by the fact that no reasonable or even subjective suspicion need be formulated by the operational officer,[323] a point further underlined by statistics on use compared to arrests and examples of wayward use, with attendant dangers of discriminatory abuse. Codes and guidance were noted, but they related more to how the officer carried out the search rather than what prompted the stop.

2.155

An attempt to refer the *Gillan and Quinton* decision to the Grand Chamber was rejected on 28 June 2010. In reaction, the operation of s 44 was changed dramatically by ministerial fiat.[324] Under the amended policy, which appeared as an 'advice' from the Home Secretary issued via the Association of Chief Police Officers,[325] individuals on foot may only be stopped under s 43. As for s 44, its usage must be based on 'necessity' and not 'expediency' and be confined to the stopping of vehicles, and officers are only allowed to use the powers on the basis of 'reasonable suspicion'. This attempted mode of fettering discretion is in patent breach of administrative law,[326] but a more sustained review by Lord Macdonald is likely to be followed by legislative confirmation.

2.156

Some dismiss the perceptions or realities of discrimination as hot air, claiming that racial profiling is 'among the most misunderstood and emotionally laden terms in the modern vocabulary of law enforcement and politics'.[327] Nevertheless, the s 44 powers of stop and search are hard to defend on grounds of proportionality. The application of 'all-risks' policing powers, by which the police will treat anyone and everyone as a risk, inevitably encourages reliance upon indicators of involvement and must be drawn in very vague terms, including age, gender, and race, all of which are poor predictors. As a result, many false positives and

2.157

---

[318] Ibid para 63.
[319] *Gillan HL*, at paras 28–29.
[320] See also *Austin v Commissioner of Police of the Metropolis* [2009] UKHL 5.
[321] App no 4158/05, 12 January 2010, para 64.
[322] Ibid para 80.
[323] Ibid para 83.
[324] See Hansard HC vol 513 col 540 (8 July 2010), Theresa May.
[325] *Equality, Diversity and Human Rights Business Area, Section 44 Terrorism Act 2000—Gillan and Quinton v UK* (ACPO, London, 2010).
[326] *R v Metropolitan Police Comr, ex parte Blackburn* [1968] 2 QB 118; *R v Metropolitan Police Comr, ex parte Blackburn (No 3)* [1973] QB 241.
[327] Dershowitz, AM, *Why Terrorism Works* (Yale University Press, New Haven, 2002) p 207.

false negatives are generated, thereby wasting police resources, damaging the legitimacy of the legal system, and perhaps impacting negatively upon 'Prevent'.[328] It is no use being 'data rich but intelligence poor'.[329] Two 9/11 hijackers experienced US traffic stops without impact on their terrorist plans.[330]

2.158 Aside from individual discomforts, there is also the potential to distance minority communities from police when the quest for terrorists impacts unevenly. The House of Commons Home Affairs Select Committee found 'a clear perception among all our Muslim witnesses that Muslims are being stigmatized by the operation of the Terrorism Act: this is extremely harmful to community relations'.[331] Not only does this create social tensions, but it will also hamper the flow of assistance to the police from minority communities.[332] As a result, Lord Carlile has called for much more restrained usage,[333] a call endorsed by senior police officers[334] and backed by more detailed demands for information before authorizations can be confirmed by the Home Office.[335] Added to these national criticisms are accusations of discrimination in international law.[336]

2.159 In conclusion, s 44 exemplifies the dangers of all-risks policing, including the growth of racial profiling in its application, a technique which has increased in acceptability since 11 September 2001 in many parts of the world.[337] Yet, because of the exigencies of the situation (especially limited policing resources), all-risks cannot be applied literally. Therefore, choice will persist and will be based on professional or sectarian cultures as well as rational choice. As a result, like the imaginary American crimes shaped by racial profiling or racial prejudice, such as 'driving while Black'[338] or 'flying while Arab',[339] s 44 may have created the nasty British equivalent of 'perambulating while Muslim'.

2.160 To remedy this situation, s 44 should be substantially redesigned or replaced.[340] There should be adopted a standard of reasonable suspicion for authorization, necessity for application, as well as judicial rather than ministerial oversight. Better still would be to rely primarily on

---

[328] See Harris, DA, 'New risks, new tactics' [2004] *Utah Law Review* 913.

[329] Metropolitan Police Authority, *Report of the MPA Scrutiny on MPS Stop and Search Practice* (London, 2004) p 9.

[330] *National Commission on Terrorist Attacks upon the United States, The 9/11 Commission Report* (GPO, Washington DC, 2004) pp 231, 253.

[331] Home Affairs Committee, *Terrorism and Community Relations* (2003–04 HC 165) para 153. See also Metropolitan Police Authority, *Report of the MPA Scrutiny on MPS Stop and Search Practice* (London, 2004) paras 150–178; House of Lords Select Committee on the Constitution, *Surveillance: Citizens and the State* (2008–09 HL 18) paras 411, 412; Mythen, G et al, '"I", a Muslim, but I'm not a terrorist' (2009) 49 *British Journal of Criminology* 736 at 744; DSTL, *What perceptions do the UK public have concerning the impact of counter-terrorism legislation implemented since 2000?* (Occasional Paper 88, Home Office, London, 2010).

[332] See Lambert, R, 'Salafi and Islamist Londoners' (2008) 50 *Crime, Law and Social Change* 73.

[333] Lord Carlile, *Report on the Operation in 2006 of the Terrorism Act 2000* (Home Office, London, 2007) para 114.

[334] *The Guardian*, 17 February 2006, p 4.

[335] Home Office Circular 27/2008.

[336] *Report of the Special Rapporteur on the promotion and protection of human rights and fundamental freedoms while countering terrorism* (A/HRC/4/26, 2007) Pt II.

[337] See Open Society Justice Initiative, *'I can stop and search whoever I want'* and *Profiling Minorities* (Open Society Institute, New York, 2008 and 2009).

[338] See Harris, DA, *Racial Profiling on Our Nation's Highways* (ACLU, New York, 1999).

[339] See Baker, E, 'Flying while Arab—Racial profiling and air travel security' (2002) 67 *Journal of Air Law and Commerce* 1375.

[340] See Bowling, B and Phillips, C, 'Disproportionate and discriminatory' (2007) 70 *Modern Law Review* 936 at 961. Compare de Schutter, O and Ringelheim, J, 'Ethnic profiling' (2008) 71 *Modern Law Review* 358.

s 43 and to augment it only with blanket security checks for specified listed vulnerable targets or within a short period of an actual or expected incident.[341]

The second reform is to impart more structuring by guidelines about the relationship between racial profile and the professional use of the power, and by clearer narrative about profiling and about the choice of 'special' or 'normal' powers to stop and search. Much more practical operational practice directions have been developed to guide security checks, such as the British Transport Police's Behavioural Assessment Screening System (BASS).[342] Other passenger screening systems include the Screening of Passengers by Observation Techniques (SPOT) and the Visible Intermodal Prevention and Response (VIPR).[343] These should be discussed more openly and promulgated as appropriate. **2.161**

A third consideration is accountability. If a power like s 44 is to remain, then invocation should become subject to confirmation by a judge *ab initio*.[344] There should be a statutory obligation to explain the results, including in local police authorities and neighbourhood forums. The police might also be encouraged to invite community representatives to shadow the exercise of powers. The prerequisite of public involvement has been duly recognized by HM Inspectorate of Constabulary, which emphasizes: **2.162**

> the vital importance of extending the reach of the national security agencies by further utilising the close links between local police and the communities in which they work. This two way linkage, or 'golden thread', is notably absent from the national security structures of some countries but in the UK Special Branch fulfils this role in the course of providing active support both for national agencies and local policing.[345]

Nationally, Parliament must keep under annual review the existence and exercise of s 44.

The repeal of s 44 is now the favoured solution of Lord Carlile,[346] though he calls for the retention of stop and search powers confined to live operations, iconic sites, and critical national infrastructure. **2.163**

Port and border controls

Introduction and background

Another example of the all-risks approach to the policing of terrorism is the universal screening of passengers at airports, based on international standards (which will be considered **2.164**

---

[341] *Report of the Special Rapporteur on the promotion and protection of human rights and fundamental freedoms while countering terrorism* (A/HRC/4/26, 2007) para 61. Compare Moeckli, D, *Human Rights and Non-Discrimination in the 'War on Terror'* (Oxford University Press, Oxford, 2008) p 220; Human Rights Watch, *Without Suspicion: Stop and Search under the Terrorism Act 2000* (New York, 2010).

[342] See British Transport Police, *Embracing Equality, Improving Confidence* (London, 2008) para 3.2.3.

[343] See Transportation Security Administration, *Privacy Impact Assessment for the Screening of Passengers by Observation Techniques (SPOT) Program* (Department of Homeland Security, Washington DC, 2008); Transit Cooperative Research Program *Public Transportation Passenger Security Inspections* (Transportation Research Board, Washington, 2007) p 19; Kölbel, R and Selter, S, 'Hostile intent—the terrorist's Achilles Heel?' (2010) 18 *European Journal of Crime, Criminal Law and Criminal Justice* 237.

[344] See *Newton Report*, para 86; Lord Carlile, *Report on the Operation in 2007 of the Terrorism Act 2000* (Home Office, London, 2008) and *Government Reply* (Cm 7429, London, 2008) para 128.

[345] Her Majesty's Inspectorate of Constabulary, *A Need to Know: HMIC's Thematic Inspection of Special Branch and Ports Policing* (London, 2003) para 2.3. The use of national powers might be preferable on grounds of accountability to private byelaws as under the Railway Act 2005, s 46.

[346] Lord Carlile, *Report on the Operation in 2001–2009 of the Terrorism Act 2000* (Home Office, London) paras 54, 180.

in Chapter 10), with corresponding measures in place relating to maritime security. These international measures are supplemented by the port controls under Pt V and Sch 7 of the TA 2000, which replaced the regime in place since 1974 within the 'Common Travel Area' between the United Kingdom and the Republic of Ireland, where passport controls do not apply.[347] Their purpose is to disrupt possible terrorist planning and logistics and also to gather low level intelligence about movements. The controls also deter attacks on the travel facilities themselves. Further controls were implemented by s 118 of the ATCSA 2001 to travellers through any internal or external port. The port controls supplement the regulation of entry under the Immigration Act 1971, with Sch 2 of that Act acting as a blueprint for Sch 7.

Provisions

2.165   By Sch 1, para 1, an 'examining officer' (meaning a constable, an immigration officer, or a designated customs officer) may question a person for the purpose of determining whether he appears to be a 'terrorist'.[348] Reflecting the 'all-risks' nature of these powers, it is made clear under para 2 that examining officers may exercise their powers whether or not they have grounds for suspicion against any individual. In this way, the 'copper's nose'[349] for wrong-doing may be used, based on intuition rather than overt indicators.[350] This power can be applied to a person entering or leaving Great Britain or Northern Ireland at a port or airport or (under para 3) within one mile of the border between Northern Ireland and the Republic of Ireland or wherever is the first stop of a train from the Republic. By s 118 of the ATCSA 2001, an examining officer may also exercise the controls at other ports in Great Britain or Northern Ireland.

2.166   The TA 2000 travel controls also extend to the Channel Tunnel system by the Channel Tunnel (International Arrangements) (Amendment) Order 2001,[351] made under section 11 of the Channel Tunnel Act 1987. More general arrangements for policing and security in the Channel Tunnel link are covered by the background international agreements[352] which include stop and search powers.[353]

2.167   Under s 114, a constable may not use reasonable force for the purpose of exercising a power under paras 2 and 3. Presumably, unbiddable travellers may give rise to suspicion sufficient for arrest under s 41.

---

[347]   See *Home Office Response to Lloyd Report*, para 11.17.

[348]   Soldiers can no longer act since the repeal of s 97.

[349]   Lord Carlile, *Report on the Operation in 2006 of the Terrorism Act 2000* (Home Office, London, 2007) para 33. See further Norris, C and Armstrong, G, *The Maximum Surveillance Society* (Berg, Oxford, 1999) pp 118–19.

[350]   Lord Carlile, *Report on the Operation in 2004 of the Terrorism Act 2000* (Home Office, London, 2005) para 17.

[351]   SI 2001/178.

[352]   See Protocol between the Government of the French Republic and the Government of the United Kingdom of Great Britain and Northern Ireland concerning Frontier Controls and Policing, Co-operation in Criminal Justice, Public Safety and Mutual Assistance, done at Sangatte on 25 November 1991 (Cm 2366, London, 1993); Agreement with Belgium and France concerning Rail Traffic between Belgium and the United Kingdom using the Channel Fixed Link with Protocol 1993 (Cm 3954, London, 1998); Agreement on the Carrying of Service Weapons by French Officers 2003 (Cm 6604, London, 2005). The Secretary of State does not have unilateral powers to impose requirements for defence and security: *R (Channel Tunnel Group) v Secretary of State for the Environment, Transport and the Regions* [2001] EWCA Civ 1185.

[353]   See Home Affairs Committee, *Fire, Safety and Policing of the Channel Tunnel* (1991–92 HC 23) and *Government Reply* (Cm 1853, London, 1992). See further Channel Tunnel (Security) Order 1994, SI 1994/570; Memorandum of Evidence from Eurotunnel in House of Commons Transport Committee, *Transport Security* (2007–08 HC 191).

To check for persons falling within para 2, an examining officer may under para 7 search a **2.168** ship or aircraft, or anything on it or to be loaded or just unloaded. In order to carry out an examination, an examining officer may under para 6 stop a person or vehicle, authorize the person's removal from a ship, aircraft, or vehicle, or detain a person. The conditions of detention are covered by Sch 8, save that the length of detention must not exceed nine hours; further detention may then be authorized by an arrest but not for port control purposes.[354] Nine hours represents a reduction from twelve in the previous regime, though Lord Lloyd had recommended six hours,[355] and most persons are released within four hours.

A person who is questioned under paras 2 or 3 must, under para 5: (a) give the examining **2.169** officer any information in his possession which the officer requests; (b) give the examining officer on request either a valid passport or another document which establishes his identity; (c) declare whether he has with him documents of a kind specified by the examining officer; or (d) give the examining officer on request any document which he has with him and which is of a kind specified by the officer. The Code of Practice (described later) may unduly extend these powers by including within 'information' passwords to data but not if the data is located elsewhere than in an article in possession of the traveller.[356] No reference is made to the RIPA, s 49, by which the revelation of 'protected information' should only be required under judicial authority.

The compulsory nature of these powers was attacked in *R v Hundal; R v Dhaliwal*,[357] where **2.170** the defendants, accused of membership of the International Sikh Youth Federation, were questioned and searched when held at Dover. The search of their vehicle, which turned up incriminating documents, was held not to breach Article 6 because of the 'clear distinction between requiring someone to answer questions and requiring a person to produce either documents or other information to the prosecution and a case where what the person concerned is compelled to do is to allow the relevant authority to conduct a search'.[358]

The traveller, and the relevant ship or aircraft (or vehicle in Northern Ireland), may also be **2.171** searched under para 8 by an examining officer (or a person authorized under para 10). By amendment under the TA 2006, s 29, there may also be searches within transported vehicles, a power previously confined to the Northern Ireland border. There is also a wide power to search unaccompanied baggage and goods under para 9,[359] though whether postal deliveries are affected is unclear.[360] Section 118(4) of the 2001 Act amends para 9 by applying the powers to examine goods which have arrived in or are about to leave Great Britain or Northern Ireland whether the place they have come from or are going to is within or outside Great Britain or Northern Ireland. Property may be seized for further investigation for a period of seven days under para 11.

To aid the process of scrutiny of traffic, Sch 7 regulates entry and exit points within the **2.172** Common Travel Area (augmenting corresponding restrictions on external ports of entry

---

[354] Compare *Breen v Chief Constable of Dumfries and Galloway* 1997 SLT 826.
[355] *Lloyd Report*, para 10.57.
[356] Para 25.
[357] [2004] EWCA Crim 389 at para 14.
[358] Ibid para 18 per Lord Woolf.
[359] For origins, see PT(AP)A 1996, s 3. For general powers to rummage at borders, see Customs and Excise Management Act 1979, s 27.
[360] Lord Carlile, *Report on the Operation in 2009 of the Terrorism Act 2000 and Part I of the Terrorism Act 2006* (Home Office, London) para 195.

under the Immigration Act 1971). In this way, it becomes more manageable to impose port controls. By para 12, carriers of passengers for reward involved in journeys to or from Great Britain, the Republic of Ireland, Northern Ireland, or any of the Islands, must call at a designated port or in circumstances specifically approved by an examining officer. Aircraft which are not carrying passengers for reward must either call at a designated port or give at least twelve hours' notice in writing to the police,[361] arrangements viewed as lax by Lord Carlile.[362] No regulations apply to non-passenger boat movements, though coastguard monitoring does pertain. A list of designated ports is scheduled. Within designated ports, the Secretary of State may order ship or aircraft operators to allocate 'control areas' (para 13) in which passengers are expected to embark or disembark and may order port managers to provide specified facilities within them (para 14). In practice, formal notice is avoided, and facilities for examining and examination officers are negotiated.[363]

2.173 Operators must routinely ensure that passengers and crew are subject to examination (para 15) and must provide passenger information if an examining officer makes a written request (para 17).[364] Under Sch 7, this provision only applied to the Common Travel Area, but s 119 of the 2001 Act extends the duty to other travel. An order-making power requires the Secretary of State to define the information required, and details are given in Sch 7 to the Terrorism Act 2000 (Information) Order 2002.[365]

2.174 'Carding' is allowed under para 16, so that passengers may be required by an examining officer to complete and produce a card containing information about their identity. The designs of the cards are set out in the Terrorism Act 2000 (Carding) Order 2001.[366] It was hoped that the routine provision of extensive passenger information,[367] plus the desire to encourage the Northern Ireland Peace Process by reducing burdens on Irish travellers, would remove the need for carding.[368] Section 53(2) therefore allows the Secretary of State to order the repeal of 'carding'. If applied, carding must be activated by affirmative order. In the event, the Terrorism Act 2000 (Carding) Order 2001[369] maintains carding in force. Moreover, it is surprising that the facility of low-level intelligence-gathering involved in carding should be given up so readily, given that 'The police have found it to be an extremely useful tool in tackling terrorism' and that there are 'sound strategic reasons to carry out checks at ports'.[370] The possibility of 'back-door' entry by international terrorists is another reason for retention.

---

[361] Compare *Lloyd Report*, para 10.57.
[362] Lord Carlile, *Report on the Operation in 2007 of the Terrorism Act 2000* (Home Office, London, 2008) paras 148, 149.
[363] Home Office Circular 03/01 (London, 2001) para 16.18.
[364] Specified information must not duplicate information under the Immigration Act 1971, sch 2 paras 27(2), 27B. This limit has been criticized (Lord Carlile, *Report on the Operation in 2001 of the Terrorism Act 2000* (Home Office, London, 2002) para 5.18). The police have independent powers to demand passenger and crew information for international journeys (Immigration, Asylum and Nationality Act 2006, s 32), and there is a scheme of information sharing between agencies (ss 36–38; Immigration, Asylum and Nationality Act 2006 (Duty to Share Information and Disclosure of Information for Security Purposes) Order 2008, SI 2008/539). For domestic journeys, see Police and Justice Act 2006, s 14 (not yet implemented).
[365] SI 2002/1945.
[366] SI 2001/426.
[367] *Home Office Response to Lloyd Report*, para 11.20.
[368] Hansard HL vol 613 cols 736–7 (23 May 2000), Lord Bassam.
[369] SI 2001/426.
[370] Hansard HL vol 613, cols 736, 746 (16 May 2000), Lord Bassam.

Further details of the exercise of functions by examining officers are set out in s 115 and Sch **2.175**
14 to the 2000 Act. By para 2 of Sch 14, an officer may enter a vehicle and may, by para 3,
use reasonable force for the purpose of exercising an examining power (apart from paras 2
and 3 of Sch 7). By para 4, any information acquired by an examining officer may be
supplied to immigration, tax, and police authorities or to a person specified by order of the
Secretary of State. Conversely, under para 4(2), information acquired by a customs officer or
an immigration officer may be supplied to an examining officer. No similar powers exist for
freight manifests, and Lord Carlile has long been critical of the accuracy of freight manifest
records under para 17.[371]

Alongside Sch 7, Sch 14, para 6 envisages the issuance of a code of practice for authorized **2.176**
officers.[372] The Code of Practice for Examining Officers under the Terrorism Act 2000 is a
revision in 2009 of a Code issued in 2001.[373] The main difference between the 2001 and
2009 versions arises in relation to clarification and updates (such as mention of Livescan).
Much of the code amounts to no more than a rehearsal of the statutory wording, but there
are some attempts at fuller explanation. Under the 2009 Code, para 6, only in exceptional
circumstances should an immigration officer or customs officer exercise functions under the
Act and only when a police officer is not readily available or if specifically requested to do so
by a police sergeant or higher rank. The powers should only be exercised against persons
believed to be travellers and not against others present at the venue: para 7. In line with the
practice under PACE they should also be provided with a copy of the Code—at least those
detained for more than one hour.

Pursuant to a recommendation of the *Lloyd Report*,[374] and bearing in mind that there is no **2.177**
need for reasonable suspicion, officers are advised about selection of travellers under para 10
as follows:

> Examining officers should therefore make every reasonable effort to exercise the power in such
> a way as to minimise causing embarrassment or offence to a person who is being questioned.
>
> *Note for guidance on paragraph 10:* ... examining officers must take into account that many
> people selected for examination using Schedule 7 powers will be entirely innocent of any
> unlawful activity. The powers must be used proportionately, reasonably, with respect and
> without unlawful discrimination. All persons being stopped and questioned by examining
> officers must be treated in a respectful and courteous manner. Examining officers must
> take particular care to ensure that the selection of persons for examination is not solely
> based on their perceived ethnic background or religion. The powers must be exercised in
> a manner that does not unfairly discriminate against anyone on the grounds of age, race,
> colour, religion, creed, gender or sexual orientation. To do so would be unlawful. It is the
> case that it will not always be possible for an examining officer working at a port to know
> the identity, provenance or destination of a passenger until they have stopped and ques-
> tioned them.

The notes go on to cover how selection for examination might be informed, including factors
such as: known and suspected sources of terrorism; known or suspected individuals;

---

[371] See Lord Carlile, *Report on the Operation in 2007 of the Terrorism Act 2000* (Home Office, London, 2008)
para 156. The police now have extra powers to access freight information: Immigration, Asylum and Nationality
Act 2006, s 33.
[372] *Home Office Response to Lloyd Report*, para 11.14.
[373] See Terrorism Act 2000 (Code of Practice for Examining Officers) Order 2001, SI 2001/427; Terrorism
Act 2000 (Code of Practice for Examining Officers) (Revision) Order 2009 SI 2009/1593.
[374] *Lloyd Report*, para 10.57.

information about terrorist groups and future terrorist activity; the means of travel (and documentation); local trends or patterns of travel. Reflecting the advice in *Gillen*, it is specified that 'A person's perceived ethnic background or religion must not be used alone or in combination with each other as the sole reason for selecting the person for examination'.

2.178　The National Policing Improvement Agency *Practice Advice on Schedule 7 of the Terrorism Act 2000*, contains complementary guidance issued in 2009. The Practice Advice is a much more informative and rounded document than its s 44 counterpart. It especially accords much fuller emphasis to community engagement which it views as 'essential'.[375] Exactly who is the correspondent community derived from what is by definition a transient population is not made clear. But activities might involve: engagement with local advisory and oversight groups, open discussion sessions and meetings, and community impact assessments.

2.179　It is a summary offence under Sch 7, para 18, wilfully to fail to comply with a duty, to contravene a prohibition, or to obstruct or to frustrate a search or examination.[376] To give reassurance to hard-pressed commercial operators, the offence was amended during passage to require wilful default.[377]

Implementation

2.180　Compared to the numbers of passengers passing through the relevant ports, very few examinations are made. For example, in 1995, out of around 170 million travellers, just 720,000 were examined, 60 per cent in the Common Travel Area.[378] During 2000, only 521 persons (mostly Irish) were examined for more than one hour.[379] Examinations under one hour are not centrally recorded,[380] but there were 10,404 examinations for longer than one hour in the period between 1 January 2004 and 30 September 2009; 1,110 persons were detained for the same period, and there were ninety-nine arrests for terrorism-related offences.[381] Of those charges there were forty-three convictions. Many other resultant arrests relate to non-terrorist matters which have been discovered incidentally—such as the possession of stolen goods or drugs or the execution of an outstanding arrest warrant.[382] This suggests that, if there is utility in the exercise, it must primarily be to gather low-level intelligence[383] or to disrupt operations. Stops leading to terrorism convictions for terrorism offences have been made, but the existence of background intelligence as opposed to chance interdiction is not necessarily revealed in court.[384]

2.181　HM Inspectorate of Constabulary was critical of the unduly fragmented nature of ports policing in its 2003 report, *A Need to Know: HMIC's Thematic Inspection of Special Branch and Ports Policing*. Some forces were viewed as too small to provide adequate coverage, and

---

[375] National Policing Improvement Agency, *Practice Advice on Schedule 7 of the Terrorism Act 2000* (London, 2009) para 1.1.
[376] By the Criminal Justice Act 2003, Sch 26, para 55, the penalties are increased for the offence in Sch 7, para 18(2)(a).
[377] Hansard HL vol 614 col 1457 (4 July 2000), Lord Bach.
[378] *Lloyd Report*, paras 10.26, 10.38.
[379] Home Office Statistics.
[380] 2009 Code, para 15.
[381] Hansard HL vol 415 col 35wa (1 December 2009), Lord West.
[382] *Lloyd Report*, para 10.40.
[383] See Home Office, *Regulatory Impact Assessment: Terrorism Act 2000 Passenger Information* (2001) para 3.
[384] See for example: Yassin Nassari *The Times* 14 July 2007, p 4; (Sohail Anjum Qureshi) *Attorney General's Reference (no 7 of 2008)* [2008] EWCA Crim 1054; *R v Sultan Mohammed and Aabid Hassain Khan* [2009] EWCA Crim 2653; Houria Chahed Chentouf *The Times* 3 November 2009, p 18 (Manchester Crown Court); Ishaq Kanmi *The Times* 11 May 2010, p 23.

so HMIC called for stronger regional coordination amongst Special Branches under the supervision of the already established National Co-ordinator of Ports Policing (NCCP).[385] These changes have been implemented. The NCPP post is funded by the Home Office through the Association of Chief Police Officers Council Committee on Terrorism & Allied Matters. The chief role is to coordinate Special Branch activity at all ports as well as providing advice and assistance to Chief Officers and the Home Office on all aspects of border control and port security policing.

Interaction with partners in customs, immigration, and the security services has not always been smooth.[386] A UK Border Agency has been created out of the amalgamation of the border work of the Border & Immigration Agency, UK Visas, and HM Revenue & Customs in order to improve protective security, but not including the police because of the need to maintain integration with domestic police structures.[387] The UK Border Agency operates checks overseas, including watch lists, as well as maintaining controls on arrival. The idea of a border police as part of a wider National Crime Agency has found favour following a change of government.[388] Biometric passports for citizens and e-borders for visitors[389] have long been sought. The system began to be put in place with the Immigration, Asylum and Nationality Act 2002.

Foreign comparisons

All countries have border controls of greater or lesser effectiveness. The US Supreme Court has produced some of the more enlightening jurisprudence. It has accepted routine checkpoints to implement stopping and questioning and visible searching of cars without reasonable suspicion near the Mexican border on the basis of a 'border search' exception to Fourth Amendment rights against unreasonable searches so long as they were not personally intrusive.[390] Selection of those stopped appears in part determined by ethnicity. For instance, Shahid Malik, Member of the UK Parliament and International Development Minister, was stopped at Dulles Airport, Washington DC, as he attempted to return to the United Kingdom after official meetings on tackling terrorism.[391] Dr Sawsaan Tabbaa, a US citizen from Syria, who attended a conference, 'Reviving the Islamic Spirit' in Toronto, was detained on her return to Buffalo as part of a 'random' search along with dozens of other Muslim-Americans who had likewise attended the conference.[392] The US Court of Appeals accepted the Department of Homeland Security argument that there was intelligence that persons with known terrorist ties would be attending that conference and that the Department's procedures were sufficiently narrowly tailored toward achieving a compelling interest.

2.182

2.183

---

[385] See House of Commons Transport Committee, *Transport Security* (2007–08 HC 191), Memorandum from the National Co-ordinator of Ports Policing. There is also a National Ports Office inside the Metropolitan Police. Based at Heathrow Airport, it acts as a clearing house for circulation of wanted terrorist and other suspects who might be using a port.

[386] See HM Inspectorate of Constabulary, *A Need to Know: HMIC's Thematic Inspection of Special Branch and Ports Policing* (Home Office, London, 2003) para 3.24.

[387] Cabinet Office, *Security in a Global Hub* (London, 2007) paras 5.76–5.82. See further UK Borders Act 2007.

[388] Home Office, *Policing in the 21st Century* (London, 2010).

[389] Immigration, Asylum and Nationality Act 2006, ss 31–38. See Home Office, *Secure Borders, Safe Haven* (Cm 5387, London, 2002); House of Commons Home Affairs Committee, *The E-Borders Programme* (2009–10 HC 170).

[390] *US v Martinez-Fuerte* 428 US 543 (1976); *US v Montoya de Hernandez* 473 US 531 (1985); *US v Flores-Montano* 541 US 149 (2004). The search can extend to electronic data: *US v Ickes*, 393 F3d 501 (2005); *US v Arnold* 533 F3d 1003 (2008).

[391] *The Times* 3 November 2007, p 10.

[392] *Tabbaa v Chertoff* 509 F3d 89 (2007).

2.184 The USA Computer-Assisted Passenger Prescreening System (CAPPS) launched in 1998 by the Federal Aviation Administration aims to enable air carriers to identify passengers requiring additional security attention. The Transportation Security Administration then developed CAPPS II in 2002, which draws upon data not only in the airlines' reservation systems but also in government databases and relies upon behavioural characteristics to select passengers for additional screening. The scheme was viewed as unduly intrusive and was replaced in 2004.[393] For domestic flights the TSA operates the Secure Flight programme, while for overseas flights, the Customs and Border Protection Agency operates the Immigration Advisory Program.[394] The systems involve checks against the consolidated terrorist screening database (TSDB) which incorporates the 'No Fly List' and 'Selectee List'. Statutory authority for the scheme is by reference to the Intelligence Reform and Terrorism Prevention Act of 2004.[395] The effectiveness of operation remains debatable, especially after the attempted bombing of an aircraft due to land in Detroit by Umar Farouk Abdulmutallab in 2009,[396] but British equivalents are in the offing.[397]

2.185 Because of the operation of free movement under the Schengen Acquis, comparisons within Europe are less straightforward. Nevertheless, measures have been taken to tighten the monitoring of travellers and foreigners. In Germany, biometrics have been introduced into identity and passport documentation,[398] while new grounds have been granted for the refusal of residence or for expulsion and more information is collected about foreign residents.[399] In France, Law no 2001-1062 of 15 November 2001, arts 25 and 26, allow the police to search travellers, luggage, freight, vehicles, and vessels if present in secure zones. Law no 2006-64 allows for police access to passenger data.

Assessment and conclusions

2.186 Physical controls at ports and airports promote the 'Protect' and 'Pursue' strands of CONTEST. Impacts by way of interdiction and disruption are undoubted gains, though on a scale which is hard to determine. Conversely, there are considerable costs in terms of the delays in transport links. In addition, there may have been displacement of targeting to other transport links, as illustrated in London in 2005.

2.187 As for a rights audit, these checks probably fall within the exception to liberty for a stated legal 'obligation' under Article 5(1)(b) of the European Convention. This verdict was reached by the European Commission in regard to travellers from the Irish Republic in the *McVeigh* case.[400] The same view was adopted in regard to passengers between Britain and Northern

---

[393] See Government Accountability Office, *Aviation Security* (04-285T, Washington DC, 2003, and 04-385, Washington DC, 2004).

[394] See 73 Federal Register 64017 and 64789; Congressional Research Service, *Homeland Security: Air Passenger Prescreening and Counterterrorism* (RL32802, Washington DC, 2005).

[395] PL 108-458.

[396] See Government Accountability Office, *Homeland Security* (GAO 10-401T, Washington DC).

[397] Hansard HC vol 504 col 303 (20 January 2010) Gordon Brown.

[398] Passports Act 1986 (*Passgesetz*) s 4(3); Identity Cards Act 1986 (*Personalausweisgesetz*) s 1(4).

[399] Foreigners Act 2004 (*Ausländergesetz*) ss 8(1)(5), 47(2)(5), 51(3); Central Register of Foreigners Act 1994 (*Ausländerzentralregistergesetz*) s 3.

[400] *McVeigh, O'Neill, and Evans v United Kingdom*, App nos 8022, 8025, 8027/77; DR 18 p 66 (admissibility), DR 25 p 15 (final report). See Warbrick, C, 'The Prevention of Terrorism (Temporary Provisions) Act 1976 and the European Convention on Human Rights: the McVeigh case' (1983) 32 *International & Comparative Law Quarterly* 757; Clayton R and Tomlinson, H, *The Law of Human Rights* (2nd edn, Oxford University Press, Oxford, 2009) para 10.183.

Ireland in *Harkin, X, Lyttle, Gillen, and McCann v United Kingdom*.[401] While these decisions can be doubted both for their reasoning and level of authority,[402] it is notable that the TA 2000 now provides a shorter initial period of detention, though the maximum is considerably more than for stops and searches. It is doubtful that the attempted restrictions in the foregoing code of practice will make much difference, since they are not 'law' under the Convention.[403] Whatever the correct interpretation in regard to liberty, it appears that there can be no complaint in regard to searches on examination under Article 8. In *Gillan and Quinton v United Kingdom*,[404] the European Court viewed the exercise of search powers at ports and airports as being excused by consent.

As well as these extensive powers to check travellers, the trend has been to pre-empt travel altogether. One example has been the ever tightening regulation of foreign students.[405] Entry controls were spotlighted after Operation Pathway in 2009 in which a number of foreign students were arrested and subsequently deported.[406] However, no substantial evidence of terrorism links to any 'bogus' college was uncovered in this or other cases.[407] **2.188**

F. Conclusions

The security authorities have faced many problems in dealing with terrorism since 2001. While their successes in preventing at least twelve attacks are to be commended,[408] they have also suffered reverses. Some are 'inevitable', in the nature of the exercise,[409] but the failures appear greater if it is accepted that many *jihadi* groups are linked and directed.[410] **2.189**

Resource constraints are often cited as a reason for limited impact.[411] But resources should not be increased to a point which produces 'a very different organisation, both in terms of its size and how it operates, which would have huge ramifications for our society and the way we live'.[412] However, whether there is maximum effectiveness with the organizational structures and systems now in place is uncertain, for no comprehensive public review of security structures or their linkages to policing[413] has ever taken place. **2.190**

---

[401] App nos 11539, 11641, 11650, 11651, 11652/85, Ser A 324 (1981).

[402] But the case has not been disowned: *Reyntjens v Belgium*, App no 16810/90, DR 73, 136 (1992); *Novotka v Slovakia*, App no 47422/99, 4 November 2003.

[403] Compare Rowe, JJ, 'The Terrorism Act 2000' [2000] *Criminal Law Review* 527 at 536.

[404] App no 4158/05, 12 January 2010, para 64.

[405] The statement of policy floated the idea of a deduction of points for 'an active disregard for UK values' but this idea has not been implemented: see Home Office, *Earning the Right to Stay* (London, 2009) para 2.11.

[406] See Lord Carlile, *Operation Pathway* (Home Office, London, 2009); *XC v Secretary of State for the Home Department* (SC 02, SC 77-82, 2009).

[407] House of Commons Home Affairs Committee, *Bogus Colleges* (2008–09 HC 595) paras 15, 16 and *Government Reply* (Cm 7766, London, 2009).

[408] Intelligence and Security Committee, *Could 7/7 have been Prevented?* (Cm 7617, London, 2009) para 214.

[409] Lyon, D, *Surveillance after September 11* (Polity, Cambridge, 2003) p 38.

[410] See Hayman, A, *The Terrorist Hunters* (Bantam Press, London, 2009) pp 283–9.

[411] See Pythian, M, 'In the shadow of 9/11' in Moran, J and Phythian, M, *Intelligence, Security and Policing Post-9/11* (Palgrave Macmillan, Basingstoke, 2008).

[412] Intelligence and Security Committee, *Could 7/7 have been Prevented?* (Cm 7617, London, 2009) para 143.

[413] Ibid., para 196. The sharing of intelligence about the Omagh bombing was criticized: Police Ombudsman for Northern Ireland, *Investigation of matters relating to the Omagh Bombing on 15 August 1998* (Belfast, 2001).

2.191   The perception that there is an enhanced state of vulnerability underlines the power of the discourse of risk. Consequently, the all-risks policing approach will have growing cogency to policy-makers and policing bodies.[414]

2.192   Another theme which threads through this chapter is uncertainty about the role of law. It was made clear at the outset that there is much intelligence activity which, while not outside the law, does not produce any transparent legal product. Yet, the inevitably hidden and sensitive nature of intelligence activities has not prevented the judicialization of intelligence, with the broadly beneficial results seen in this chapter and to be discussed in Chapter 7.[415]

---

[414] A power to stop and question has been suggested: Home Office, *Government Discussion Document Ahead of Proposed Counter Terror Bill 2007* (London, 2007).

[415] See further Roach, K, 'When secret intelligence becomes evidence' (2009) 47 *Supreme Court Law Review* 147 at 147; Walker, C, 'The judicialisation of intelligence in legal process' [2011] *Public Law,* forthcoming.

3

DISCLOSURE OF INFORMATION ABOUT TERRORISM

A. Introduction

The disclosure of information about terrorism represents in one sense a continuation of the **3.01** exploration of the laws and practices around terrorism investigations in Chapter 2. Nevertheless, disclosure is a discrete topic for this chapter which goes beyond the previous organizing notion of surveillance. Here, the state demands to know, 'Whose side are you on?' and, rather than leaving individuals to a Manichean debate, imposes a duty to help the state. Consequently, these measures foster a proactive 'informer society' rather than a passive 'surveillance society'.

The 'informer' society still reflects the strategic strands of 'Prevent' and 'Pursue'. There is **3.02** prevention through early intervention and thence the possibilities of aversion, disruption, or prosecution. In this way, private knowledge must become public property, often on a precautionary basis.[1]

This approach does, however, raise distaste for the creation of an informer society which **3.03** would be redolent of the techniques of the German Democratic Republic's *Ministerium für Staatssicherheit*, commonly known as the Stasi.[2] The United Kingdom anti-terrorism legislation has not recreated the Stasi, but it does reflect a degree of permanent distrust and insecurity. Criticisms along these lines were equally raised in 2002 in the US in regard to its Operation TIPS (Terrorism Information and Prevention System), whereby persons such as repair and utility workers, transport operatives, and postal officials were asked to report

---

[1] See Stern, J and Weiner, JB, 'Precaution against terrorism' (2006) 9 *Journal of Risk Research* 393.
[2] See Childs, D and Popplewell, R, *The Stasi* (Macmillan, Basingstoke, 1996); Koehler, JO, *Stasi* (Westview Press, Boulder, 2000).

suspicious activity.[3] Uncontrolled private surveillance proved unacceptable, and TIPS was cancelled and then prohibited.[4] These comparisons do not rule out invitations to report suspected terrorism, whether as a volunteer police informant[5] or for the more venal reasons in the American 'Rewards for Justice Program'.[6] However, the duty to report goes beyond encouragement of voluntary 'peer-to-peer' or 'lateral' surveillance[7] or even the tasking since 7/7 of local communities to combat extremism.[8]

3.04 The next concern about the creation of an 'informer society' is that a proactive public demand conflicts with values of private professionalism. For example, lawyers may resent the commitment to 'a job they consider as extraneous to their profession'[9] and which conflicts with private duties of confidentiality to their clients. The same applies to financial advisers, but their position will be considered in Chapter 9. A different set of conflicting professional values applies to journalists, whose public roles as watchdogs and amplifiers of political speech are counterweights to public duties of disclosure.

3.05 The final concern relates to the speculative basis for intervention, so the dangers are heightened of knowing or unwitting false accusations.

3.06 This chapter will be organized largely according to the scope of the legal duty to disclose information about terrorism. It will first consider general duties of disclosure which affect everyone, including lawyers and journalists. There follows one general duty not to disclose. The later part of the chapter will consider more specialized duties which affect specific public authorities.

B. General Duties Relating to Disclosure

Offence of withholding information

Introduction and background

3.07 An offence is committed under s 38B(2) of the TA 2000 if a person, without reasonable excuse, fails to disclose relevant information about terrorism. This measure revives this offence which subsisted in relation only to Northern Ireland terrorism in s 18 of the PT(TP)A 1989, having been first introduced through back-bench pressure as s 11 of the 1976 Act.[10] The 1989 Act offence was recommended for repeal by the *Lloyd Report*[11] and the subsequent

---

3 See Donohue, LK, *The Cost of Counterterrorism* (Cambridge University Press, Cambridge, 2008) p 251.
4 Homeland Security Act 2002 (PL 107-296), s 880.
5 See <https://tips.fbi.gov/>; <http://www.met.police.uk/so/at_hotline.htm>.
6 See <http://www.rewardsforjustice.net>; Act to Combat International Terrorism 1984 (PL 98-533, 18 USC s 3071). The PATRIOT Act 2001(PL 107-56) increased the maximum reward to $25m (as applies to Osama bin Laden).
7 See Andrejevic, M, 'The work of watching one another' (2005) 2 *Surveillance & Society* 479; Chan, J, 'The new lateral surveillance and a culture of surveillance' in Deflem, M (ed), *Surveillance and Governance* (Emerald, Bingley, 2008).
8 See Home Office, *The Prevent Strategy: A Guide for Local Partners* (London, 2008); Department for Communities and Local Government, *Preventing Violent Extremism: Next Steps For Communities* (London, 2009).
9 See Favarel-Garrigues, G, 'Sentinels in the banking industry' (2008) 48 *British Journal of Criminology* 1 at 17.
10 PT(TP)A 1976, s 10(5). For more distant duties to disclose, see Peace Preservation (Ireland) Act 1870, s 13; Restoration of Order in Ireland Regulation 49 (SR & O 1920 No 1530); Civil Authorities (Special Powers) Act (NI) 1922, s 2(3).
11 *Lloyd Report*, para 14.24.

Home Office Consultation Paper.[12] A much more focused offence dealing with financial institutions, formerly s 18A of the PT(TP)A 1989, is introduced as s 19 of the TA 2000 in line with legislation about money laundering. Despite its considered and principled repeal in 2000, the offence of withholding information was soon revived in almost identical terms (but, given the circumstances of September 11, applicable to all forms of terrorism and not just Irish) by s 117 of the ATCSA 2001, which inserts s 38B into the TA 2000. With issues of citizenship and bonds of allegiance now resurfacing as an antidote to disaffection and radicalization, there is scant prospect of repeal and even interest in revamped treason offences.[13]

Despite the special offence, some lawyers advise against communicating about terrorism **3.08** matters unless a solicitor is present,[14] a stance which has been condemned by the House of Commons Home Affairs Committee as 'disgraceful' and 'reprehensible'.[15] The Law Society is more balanced in its Anti-Terrorism Practice Note of 2007: 'The right of persons suspected of a criminal offence to communicate in confidence with their legal adviser is a fundamental aspect of their right to have a fair trial. . . . Solicitors should never knowingly assist others to commit, or cover up, future crimes.'[16]

No equivalent general duty exists to impart information about crime. As the PACE Code of **3.09** Practice C reflects:[17] 'This Code does not affect the principle that all citizens have a duty to help police officers to prevent crime and discover offenders. This is a civic rather than a legal duty . . .' However, there are some specific duties not to withhold information. The most closely related to the terrorism laws, and discussed further in this chapter, is the offence of misprision of treason—failing to report knowledge that treason is being committed.[18] It is less clear whether failure to inform the authorities where there is foreknowledge of treason amounts to misprision of treason.[19]

The corresponding common law offence of misprision of felony terminated on the abolition **3.10** of the distinctions between felony and misdemeanour by the Criminal Law Act 1967.[20] That Act provided instead for offences involving the more active assistance of offenders. Under s 4(1),[21] where a person has committed an arrestable offence, any other person who, knowing or believing the other to be guilty, acts without lawful authority or reasonable excuse with intent to impede apprehension or prosecution shall be guilty of an offence. Section 5(1)

---

[12] *Home Office Response to Lloyd Report*, para 12.7.

[13] Lord Goldsmith, *Citizenship: Our Common Bond* (Ministry of Justice, London, 2008) para. 4.42.

[14] See <http://www.aranisolicitors.com/know_your_rights.pdf>, 2002.

[15] House of Commons Home Affairs Committee, *Terrorism Detention Powers* (2005–06 HC 910) para 83.

[16] <http://www.lawsociety.org.uk/documents/downloads/dynamic/practicenote_terrorismact2000.pdf>, p 3.

[17] (Home Office, 2008) para 1K. Giving false information in Scotland may be charged as attempting to pervert the course of justice or wasting police time, but it is not a crime to withhold information.

[18] See *Regicides' Case* (1660) 5 State Tr 947; *R v Tonge* (1662) 6 State Tr 225; *R v Walcot* (1683) 9 State Tr 519; *R v Thistlewood* (1820) 33 State Tr 681. The Treason Act 1708 abolished the Scots law of treason and applied the English crime of misprision.

[19] *Sykes v Director of Public Prosecutions* [1962] AC 528 at p 563 per Lord Denning.

[20] See Allen, CK, 'Misprision' (1962) 78 *Law Quarterly Review* 40; Glazebrook, P, 'Misprision of felony' (1964) 8 *American Journal of Legal History* 189, 283, 'How long, then, is the arm of the law to be?' (1962) 25 *Modern Law Review* 301; Criminal Law Revision Committee Seventh Report: *Felonies and Misdemeanours* (Cmnd 659, London, 1965) para 37.

[21] Prior conviction of the principal offender is not a prerequisite: *R v J Donald, R v L Donald* (1986) 83 Cr App Rep 49.

makes it an offence to accept or agree to accept any consideration other than the making good of loss or injury caused by the offence in return for not disclosing information which might be of material assistance in securing the prosecution or conviction. Section 5(2) forbids wasteful employment of police time by knowingly making a false report. The offences are distinct from the withholding of information, since they require active intervention in favour of the suspect, rather than passive non-intervention. By contrast, s 38B catches a bystander, even if knowledge about the terrorism has been attained unwittingly or unwillingly.[22]

3.11   These distinctions dissolve away to a considerable extent in the version of s 5(1) in the Criminal Law Act (Northern Ireland) 1967:

> . . . where a person has committed an arrestable offence, it shall be the duty of every other person, who knows or believes—
>
> > (a)   that the offence or some other arrestable offence has been committed; and
> > (b)   that he has information which is likely to secure, or to be of material assistance in secur-ing, the apprehension, prosecution or conviction of any person for that offence;
>
> to give that information, within a reasonable time, to a constable and if, without reasonable excuse, he fails to do so he shall be guilty of an offence and shall be liable on conviction on indictment to imprisonment according to the gravity of the offence about which he does not give that information . . .

Section 38B remains distinct in that the information must relate to 'terrorism' rather than an 'arrestable offence' and may concern future as well as past activities. Nevertheless, the considerable overlap between s 38B and s 5(1) convinced the *Baker Report* to propose the repeal of s 5(1) in regard to 'terrorist' offences.[23]

3.12   Two other long-established special legal duties, like misprision of treason, underline the citizen's duty to help in overcoming offences against the state, though each requires a greater deal of coaxing on the part of the police than under s 38B. The first is the Explosive Substances Act 1883, s 6, by which the Attorney General may order an inquiry under which a justice may examine on oath any witness where there is reasonable ground to believe that any crime under that Act has been committed.[24] Along the same lines, the Official Secrets Act 1920, s 6, allows a chief officer of police, if satisfied that there is reasonable ground for suspecting that an offence under the Official Secrets Act 1911, s 1, has been committed and for believing that any person is able to furnish information, to apply to a Secretary of State for permission to require the person to divulge any relevant information.

Provisions—the elements of the offence

3.13   The offence is committed under s 38B(2) of the 2000 Act if a person, without reasonable excuse, does not disclose information falling within s 38B(1):

> (1)   This section applies where a person has information which he knows or believes might be of material assistance
> > (a)   in preventing the commission by another person of an act of terrorism, or

---

[22]   See Hansard HC vol 901 cols 931–2 (26 November 1975), George Cunningham; *Colville Report*, para 15.1.2.
[23]   *Baker Report*, para 253.
[24]   See Walker, C, 'Post-charge questioning of suspects' [2008] *Criminal Law Review* 509.

(b) in securing the apprehension, prosecution or conviction of another person, in the United Kingdom, for an offence involving the commission, preparation or instigation of an act of terrorism.

The definition of 'an act of terrorism' is as laid down in s 1 of the TA 2000. So far as information about 'commission' under (a) is concerned, there is an offence even if there is no prospect of a legal process in the United Kingdom, but that possibility must be present under (b). The broad scope of the term 'terrorism', as considered in Chapter 1, may cause some persons to be unaware that their knowledge could be construed as being about 'terrorism', resulting in an unwitting contravention of the offence.

Section 38B(3) lists the officials to whom disclosure should be made: to a constable, or in **3.14** Northern Ireland to a constable or a member of Her Majesty's forces. It is not sufficient to contact other persons in authority, such as magistrates or Members of Parliament, unless perhaps they are requested and agree to pass on the information to an authorized recipient or are known to be certain to do so automatically and promptly.

As for the *actus reus*, a person may commit this offence through total inactivity (by not **3.15** answering police questions or by not volunteering information),[25] through the partial suppression of information, or by relating a false account when the true facts are known.[26] The information must be of a kind which is, or is believed to be, 'of material assistance'. This means that a person reasonably aware of their situation would consider that it ought to be disclosed, whereas information garnered through vague rumour or gossip would not trigger the duty. To prove this issue of fact, the police may have to describe their investigations up to that point, which limits the attractiveness of s 38B at least until their inquiries are exhausted or until a terrorist plot has been completed. Whether or not there is personal benefit from the concealment is not relevant.[27]

The *mens rea*, 'knows or believes', means that it is not enough that the defendant strongly **3.16** suspects the materiality of the assistance flowing from the information or thinks it probable, or that a reasonable person would have been put on inquiry. Belief as an alternative to knowledge is relevant only to the materiality of the assistance which the withheld information might have given.[28] Provided the defendant does genuinely believe the information is relevant, an offence can be committed even if it is neither material nor accurate. In *R v Sherif and others*,[29] the applicants were held to have known or believed that the bombings of 21 July 2005 were to take place and failed to give information under s 38B and even in one case impeded arrest by offering a safe house (contrary to s 4(1) of the Criminal Law Act 1967). In the case of Ali, the judge was entitled in his direction to make it plain 'that it was not sufficient for the prosecution to establish that a defendant had closed his eyes, but that the jury was entitled to conclude, if satisfied that he had deliberately closed his eyes to the obvious because he did not wish to be told the truth, that that fact was capable of being

---

[25] Here it differs from misprision of felony: *R v King* [1965] 1 WLR 706; Hansard HC vol 882 cols 925–6 (28 November 1974), Sam Silkin; Hansard HC vol 964 col 1562 (21 March 1979), George Cunningham.

[26] The relating of false information when the truth is known is forbidden by many other offences: see Law Commission, Report No 96: *Offences Relating to Interference with the Course of Justice* (1979–80 HC 213) Pt III.

[27] Compare *R v Aberg* [1948] 2 KB 143; *Sykes v DPP* [1962] AC 528 at 546; *Moore v Secretary of State for Northern Ireland* [1977] NI 14.

[28] *R v Rock* (NICA, 1990).

[29] [2008] EWCA Crim 2653.

evidence to support a conclusion that that defendant either knew or believed the fact in question'.[30]

3.17 So far as s 38B(1)(b) is concerned, there really must be an existing act of terrorism, whatever the belief of the defendant. In *Attorney General's Reference (No 3 of 1993)*,[31] the defendant believed that a murder of a shopkeeper by shooting was an act of terrorism on the basis that an acquaintance whom she knew to be involved with a proscribed organization had called at her house and arranged with her boyfriend to have the use of his house. She was acquitted on the ground that the Crown had failed to prove that the murder was a terrorist-related offence. The prosecution argued that the word 'believes' in subsection (1) governed the whole of paragraph (b), so that an offence was committed if the defendant believed that an act of terrorism had been committed. Further, if Parliament had intended that a substantive offence should first have been committed, it would have expressly so provided, as is specified under s 5(1) of the Criminal Law Act (Northern Ireland) 1967. The Northern Ireland Court of Appeal rejected these arguments. In line with what were taken to be the intentions of Parliament, the Crown had to prove that an actual terrorist offence had in fact been committed, not merely that the defendant believed such an offence to have been committed nor merely that an offence had been committed. The difference in wording from s 5(1) was explained by the fact that s 38B(1)(a) applies to the withholding of information which might help to prevent the commission of a (future) terrorist offence as well as information which might help to secure the apprehension, prosecution, or conviction of the perpetrator of an actual offence. In the view of Lord Chief Justice Hutton: 'In our opinion Parliament did not intend that a person should be convicted for an offence of failing to give information where it is clear that (contrary to the belief of that person) no crime has ever happened.'[32]

3.18 It is probably correct to understand the *Attorney General's Reference* as being argued on the basis that the defendant's information was about securing apprehension, prosecution, or conviction under the forerunner to s 38(1)(b) and not prevention under s 38(1)(a). In that context, it is consistent to establish an actual offence, otherwise the exercise becomes futile. As regards knowledge or belief relevant to prevention under s 38(1)(a), however, the exercise of demanding prescient information is not futile where no offence has yet been committed or, perhaps thanks to the intervention of the police based on the information, might never be committed; the philosophy is to demand citizen cooperation so as to reduce risk. However, it is still desirable to delimit this potentially draconian offence by interpreting s 38(1)(a) as requiring evidence that, subsequently, an offence related to the knowledge or belief was being committed or would be committed—at least demanding knowledge of the substance of the matters constituting the principal offence but not necessarily the precise or exact legal effect of those matters.[33] Without that link, there is a danger of turning s 38B into a crime affecting the paranoid, and trials would encounter difficulties of establishing links to the mischief of 'preventing . . . an act of terrorism'. This interpretation does, however, considerably reduce the scope of s 38(1)(a) and turns it more into a sanction *ex post facto* than a threat *ex ante*. One might alternatively suggest that the vagueness of the knowledge or belief and uncertainty as to linked action might be left to the defence under s 38(4).

---

[30] Ibid para 27.
[31] [1993] NI 50.
[32] Ibid 56.
[33] *R v Rock* (NICA, 1990).

Provisions—the elements of the defences

By s 38B(4), it is a defence to prove 'a reasonable excuse' for not making the disclosure. The **3.19** reasonable excuse will often relate to fears of reprisal or reaction going beyond the defence of duress.[34] It is unlikely to excuse a person who simply does not wish to 'get involved'. But it was accepted in *R v McLean* that reasonable excuse in the case of a hijacked Northern Ireland taxi driver 'may be constituted by threats or conduct falling short of duress', provided that the fear was 'cogent and well founded. It must in fact be shown to have been specifically directed against and suffered by the particular accused. And it must pass the objective test in which the defendant is required to have the self-control to be expected of an ordinary person in his situation . . .'[35] The operation of this defence gives rise to considerable controversies in four contexts.

The first is where there is a close personal relationship between the person involved in **3.20** terrorism and the person with knowledge of it, such as a husband and wife. Arguably, the sanctity of personal ties should yield to the public interest in safety. Though that prospect caused some anguish in Parliament, the uncompromising view of the sponsor of the original version of the offence[36] and of the government was that 'when dealing with foul and disgusting deeds, someone who knows that someone else is likely to be threatened and imperilled has not only a moral duty to tell the police, but a legal one as well'.[37] However, in order to appease those expressing disquiet, the police were advised by circular in 1989 that:[38]

> A relative of a terrorist who is not involved in terrorism himself should not be put under strain by being reminded in a routine manner of the provisions of [the offence]. This use of section [the offence] can only be justified in extreme cases—where the withholding of information might lead to death, serious injury or the escape of a terrorist offender.

Before 2000, there were few such prosecutions.[39] By contrast, the current Home Office Circular 7/2002 makes no allowance: 'having a legal or familial relationship with someone does not constitute immunity from the obligation to disclose information . . .'.[40] It follows that many recent prosecutions have concerned the spouses or family of terrorists.

Following the suicide attack of Omar Sharif in Tel Aviv in 2003, his wife, Tahira Tabassum, **3.21** his sister, Parveen, and his brother, Zahid, were accused of withholding his plan but were all acquitted in 2004, the siblings after a retrial.[41] Much of the evidence related to e-mails sent by Omar Sharif before the attack in which he asked them to look after his children and dispose of 'problematic' material, plus responses by his sister mentioning 'time . . . slipping away, and . . . no time to be weak and emotional'.[42]

---

[34] It is presumed that the defence of duress can apply, though its relevance to treason remains open: *DPP for Northern Ireland v Lynch* [1975] AC 653 at 672, 707.

[35] [1992] 8 NIJB 1 CA at 6, 8 per Kelly LJ.

[36] Hansard HC vol 882 col 929 (28 November 1974), George Cunningham.

[37] Hansard HC Standing Committee D col 243 (24 November 1983), David Waddington.

[38] Home Office Circular No 90/1983, para 9; see also Home Office Circular No 27/1989, para 7.4. The *Baker Report* was critical of a limited interpretation: para 252.

[39] Three relatives of Sean McNulty, convicted in 1994 of IRA bombings in Tyneside, were discharged: *The Times* 15 November 1994, p 2.

[40] At 5. Compare Home Office Circular No 90/1983, para 9; see also Home Office Circular No 27/1989, para 7.4.

[41] See *The Times* 27 April 2004, p 5, 29 November 2005, p 6.

[42] See <http://news.bbc.co.uk/1/hi/uk/3825765.stm>.

3.22 There were three trials relating to persons who were alleged to have assisted the attempted London bombings of the 21 July 2005. The first convictions were of Yeshiemebet Girma, wife of 21 July bomber, Hussein Osman, Mulumbet Girma (Yeshi's sister) and her former partner Mohammed Kabashi, and Esayas Girma (Yeshi's brother) who were all convicted of withholding information, assisting his escape, and destroying evidence.[43]

3.23 Abdul Sherif and five others were also convicted in connection with the attempted bombings.[44] There were aspects of the treatment of one defendant, Ismael Abdurahman, which were 'undoubtedly troubling'.[45] He was at first treated as a cooperative witness and was therefore not cautioned, though as he accepted the contents of his statement at trial, reliance upon it was viewed as neither unreliable nor unfair. His case also illustrates that it seems to be up to the defendant to volunteer a full and frank disclosure and not up to the police to cajole, threaten, or tease out every detail.

3.24 The other person to be tried in connection with the 21 July bombings was Fardosa Abdullahi, who was previously engaged to a bomber, Yassin Omar. She pleaded guilty to assisting an offender by providing women's clothing as a disguise; a count of failing to disclose information about acts of terrorism was allowed to lie on file.[46]

3.25 Next, Sabeel Ahmed, brother of Kafeel Ahmed who planted car bombs outside London nightclubs and then died following the car bombing of Glasgow Airport in 2007, was convicted under s 38B(1)(b) for failing to disclose e-mails which he discovered the evening after the attack.[47] The e-mail directed Sabeel to online documents containing his statement of involvement, his will, and instructions to mislead investigators by telling them that Kafeel was abroad.

3.26 By contrast, Bouchra El Hor, wife of Yassin Nassari, who was found guilty of possessing terrorism documents in their luggage at Luton airport, was acquitted of the offence.[48] She claimed that a letter to her husband on her computer, citing a religious obligation to fight non-believers and looking forward to their being reunited in heaven, was a piece of creative writing. Cossor Ali, wife of Abdulla Ahmed Ali who was convicted of leading the 2006 plot to blow up transatlantic aircraft, was also acquitted in 2010.[49]

3.27 The second uncertainty within the s 38B(4) defence concerns its impact on privileged relationships, especially as between a lawyer and terrorist client. In *Sykes v Director of Public Prosecutions*,[50] the defendant was convicted of misprision of treason in connection with the supply of firearms to the IRA. In the House of Lords, Lord Denning's view was that a solicitor, doctor, or clergyman who received information in confidence would have a defence but that close personal ties would not suffice.[51]

---

[43] *R v Girma* [2009] EWCA Crim 912. The sentences ranged from fifteen years (for Yeshi Girma) to ten years for the others, with a discount of one year for Mohammed Kabashi who pleaded guilty.
[44] [2008] EWCA Crim 2653. Whabi Mohammed was sentenced to seventeen years, Abdul Sharif, Ismael Abdurahman, and Sirah Ali to ten years, and Muhedin Ali to seven years.
[45] Ibid para 38.
[46] *The Times* 12 July 2008, p 34.
[47] *The Times* 12 April 2008, p 9. The sentence was eighteen months' imprisonment.
[48] *The Times* 14 July 2007, p 4.
[49] *The Times* 6 March 2010, p 37.
[50] [1962] AC 528.
[51] Ibid 564.

The position adopted in *Sykes* should be reproduced in regard to legal privilege under s 38B, **3.28** having regard to the importance of the independent legal advice.[52] The government sought in 1989 to distinguish between (unprivileged) information which may prevent terrorism and (privileged) information which may assist the prosecution of terrorists.[53] This contrast is unwarranted by the wording of s 38B, though it is reflected in guidance in 1999 from the Law Society that a solicitor could reveal information which 'he believes necessary to prevent the client from committing a criminal act that the solicitor believes on reasonable grounds is likely to result in serious bodily harm', but otherwise 'a solicitor is not obliged to disclose confidential or privileged information under this provision other than in wholly exceptional circumstances'.[54] The 1999 Guidance was replaced in 2007 by the Solicitors' Code of Conduct, which refers only to financial provisions in relation to money laundering.[55] However, the Law Society has at the same time issued the Anti-Terrorism Practice Note.[56] In so far as client information is covered by legal professional privilege (relating to advice or litigation),[57] a reasonable excuse to remain silent can be asserted under s 38B since it contains no 'necessary implication'[58] to the contrary. For example: 'It is proper for a lawyer to advise a client on how to stay within the law and avoid committing a crime, or to warn a client that proposed actions could attract prosecution, and such advice will be protected by privilege.'[59] The only exception is where the legal work forms part of a criminal or fraudulent transaction, whether pursued by the client or by a third party.[60] As for information not within the scope of legal professional privilege (which might include attendance notes and personal contact details of clients),[61] the Law Society advises that disclosure contrary to client confidentiality is required by the public interest whenever the information concerns pending serious bodily harm, and so there can be no reasonable excuse under section 38B in those circumstances.[62] This duty goes further than the position in *Sykes* and is yet to be tested.

The third situation to cause misgivings is whether a suspect's own privilege against self- **3.29** incrimination provides a reasonable excuse for non-disclosure. This issue was partly settled for the former PT(TP)A 1989, s 18(1), by an amendment which provided that the information being suppressed must concern terrorist involvement by 'any other person'.[63] This wording

---

[52] See *R v Derby Magistrates, ex parte B* [1996] AC 487; *Three Rivers DC v Bank of England* [2004] UKHL 48.

[53] Hansard HL vol 504 cols 980–1 (28 February 1989).

[54] *The Guide to the Professional Conduct of Solicitors* (8th edn, London, 1999) paras 16.02.3, 16.02.13.

[55] (Solicitors' Regulatory Authority, London, 2007) para 4.06.11. Accountants do not assert privilege: Institute of Chartered Accountants in England and Wales, *Members' Handbook* (London, 2005) para 7.1.2.15.

[56] <http://www.lawsociety.org.uk/documents/downloads/dynamic/practicenote_terrorismact2000.pdf>.

[57] Ibid pp 7–8. It is irrelevant whether the lawyer is aware of the nature of the transaction: *Banque Keyser Ullman v Skandia* [1986] 1 Lloyds Rep 336.

[58] See *B v Auckland District Law Society* [2003] UKPC 38 at para 58.

[59] <http://www.lawsociety.org.uk/documents/downloads/dynamic/practicenote_terrorismact2000.pdf>, p 8. See further *Butler v Board of Trade* [1971] Ch 680.

[60] Ibid pp 8–9; *R v Cox & Railton* (1884) 14 QBD 153; *R v Central Criminal Court, ex parte Francis & Francis* [1989] 1 AC 346. There should be a strong prima facie case of crime or fraud: *O'Rourke v Darbishire* [1920] AC 581. Court advice may be sought: *Finers v Miro* [1991] 1 WLR 35.

[61] *R v Manchester Crown Court, ex parte Rogers* [1999] 1 WLR 832; *R (Miller Gardner Solicitors) v Minshull Street Crown Court* [2002] EWHC 3077 (Admin).

[62] <http://www.lawsociety.org.uk/documents/downloads/dynamic/practicenote_terrorismact2000.pdf>, p 11. See further *Three Rivers District Council and others v Governor and Company of the Bank of England (No 5)* [2004] UKHL 48; *R (on the application of Kelly) v Warley Magistrates Court and another* [2007] EWHC 1836 (Admin).

[63] See *Jellicoe Report*, para 233.

is replicated in s 38B. However, if a person's evidence implicates both himself and another, must it be disclosed when the self-damning details cannot be severed? A broad view in favour of protection against self-incrimination was expressed in relation to the former s 18 in *HM Advocate v Von*.[64] During the interrogation, Von stated that he:[65]

> . . . wished to make a statement and to tell of his own involvement but that he would not name anyone. At this stage police officers, realising that he was about to make a statement implicating himself, advised him that what he said could be used in evidence.

The accused made an inculpatory statement but claimed at trial that it should be inadmissible because he had not been informed that 'he could reasonably be excused from not disclosing information if the information would be self-incriminating'. The presiding judge (Lord Ross) held:[66]

> If . . . the accused had been given the usual full caution or had been informed that he was not obliged to give information which could incriminate himself and he had then made a statement, I would have thought that that statement would have been admissible as being a statement made in response to pressure or inducement or as a result of other unfair means . . . So far as the evidence goes, the accused was left in total ignorance of the fact that he was not obliged to incriminate himself.

Accordingly, the statement was excluded. However, this judgment rested on the premise that Von did not have to make incriminating statements to avoid the commission of an offence under s 18. The reasons given for this assumption will now be examined.

3.30   One argument was that a frequently used statutory duty to disclose, which does impliedly override the right to silence, was deemed distinguishable. By s 172 of the Road Traffic Act 1988, a vehicle owner may be obliged to provide the police with the identity of the driver of it, even if this entails the disclosure of an offence. Lord Ross opined that this was materially different from s 18 since the owner 'is not in normal circumstances even suspect'.[67] However, questioning under s 172 may often lead to the owner being prosecuted for an offence either in that capacity or as the driver. In *Brown v Stott*,[68] statements given under compulsion were admissible under the principle that Article 6 rights to a fair trial allowed limited qualification of the privilege against self-incrimination where necessary to achieve a legitimate aim within the public interest. Since the high incidence of road traffic death and injury could found a necessary and legitimate constraint, surely the investigation of terrorism will found another.

3.31   The second argument adduced by Lord Ross was that 'if Parliament had intended to make statements of suspects admissible against them in the event of their being subsequently charged I would have expected Parliament to have made that clear'.[69] This argument reflects a 'bargain principle' which assumes that a statutory duty to disclose will be accompanied by a grant of immunity from prosecution.[70] However, examples already given, including s 172, demonstrate that the privilege may be impliedly excluded when necessary to avoid frustrating the object of legislation. On that basis, obtaining information about a suspect's

---

[64] 1979 SLT (Notes) 62.
[65] Ibid at 63.
[66] Ibid at 64.
[67] Ibid at 63.
[68] [2000] UKPC D3.
[69] 1979 SLT (Notes) 62 at 64.
[70] Heydon, JD, 'Obtaining evidence versus protecting the accused' [1971] *Criminal Law Review* 13.

own crimes might be just as important as coercing from that person knowledge about others' misdeeds.

Another precedent for recognizing a reasonable excuse defence is that mere silence in response   **3.32**
to incriminating questions did not infringe misprision of felony.[71] However, that offence might be distinguishable from s 38B. The term, 'terrorism' conjures up a picture of an extremely dangerous but limited range of activity. By contrast, misprision of felony covered a wide range of offences, so, if overridden, the privilege against self-incrimination would have been rendered almost worthless.

On balance, the danger of self-incrimination was probably not envisaged by the architects   **3.33**
of the former s 18 as a reasonable excuse. However, given the precedent of *Von's* case, the courts should not curtail the normal right to silence of a witness just because the person's knowledge additionally implicates others. The further argument in favour of protection which now arises is the impact of Article 6 of the European Convention. Though the implied right against self-incrimination is not absolute, as determined in *Brown v Stott*,[72] it is submitted that, on the precedent of cases such as *Saunders v United Kingdom*, a strong steer has been given away from upholding self-incriminatory duties backed directly by the threat of criminal sanction.[73] As for the precedent of *Brown v Stott*, there may be important distinctions concerning the extent of questioning (which was viewed as limited to 'a single, simple question'),[74] the degree of compulsion (given the prior voluntary submission to the regulatory road traffic regime), and the severity of the penalty (which is non-custodial under s 172). Here, the questioning under s 38B will arise in the context of police custody following arrest, safeguards include a confusing caution, and an insufficient response can found an imprisonable offence and not merely an inference from silence in respect of another offence. Likewise, in *R (Malik) v Manchester Crown Court*, the Divisional Court concluded that the TA 2000, Sch 5, para 6 did not oust the privilege in the absence of clear language.[75] Different arguments will apply if s 38B is invoked to obtain documents or other materials existing independently of the will of the subject rather than testimony.[76]

A related complication concerns the inter-relationship between s 38B and laws allowing   **3.34**
inferences to be drawn from silence in response to police questioning, namely, the Criminal Evidence (Northern Ireland) Order 1988[77] and the Criminal Justice and Public Order Act 1994. The inter-relationship is complex. When the suspect has committed an offence and remains silent, there is no infringement of s 38B, but art 3 of the 1988 Order/s 34 of the 1994 Act may penalize silence if a criminal prosecution is mounted. Conversely, where the subject knows about another's wrongdoing but is not personally implicated, an offence may be committed under s 38B. It follows that silence in response to questioning about that offence may also trigger adverse inferences. Consequently, silence could be damning twice

---

[71] *R v King* [1965] 1 WLR 706. Self-incrimination is also a reasonable excuse under the Criminal Law Act (Northern Ireland) 1967: *R v Donnelly and others* [1986] 3 NIJB 48.

[72] See also *Murray v United Kingdom*, App no 18731/91, 1996-I, para 47; *O'Halloran and Francis v United Kingdom*, App nos 15809/02, 25624/02, 29 June 2007.

[73] App no 19187/91, 1996-VI. See Sedley, S, 'Wringing out the fault' (2001) 52 *Northern Ireland Legal Quarterly* 107; Berger, M, 'Compelled self-reporting and the principle against compelled self incrimination' [2006] *European Human Rights Law Review* 25.

[74] [2003] 1 AC 681 at 705 per Lord Bingham.

[75] [2008] EWHC 1362 (Admin) at para 73.

[76] See *R v S* [2008] EWCA Crim 2177.

[77] SI 1988/1987. See *Colville Report*, paras 15.1.5., 15.1.6.

over: it forms the *actus reus* of s 38B and then leads to the adverse inference that the person has suppressed information and is guilty of the offence. Thus, s 38B can pull itself up by its own boot straps with the aid of the other legislation.

3.35 It is regrettable that clear advice is absent from the Home Office Circular 7/2002 or PACE Code H.[78] This problem improved for a time in Scotland since 'the *Von* decision led to the adoption of guidelines to the police which require them to inform a suspect specifically that the provisions of [the terrorism legislation] do not oblige him to incriminate himself'.[79] The dangers of confusion were also reduced by circulars issued to all police forces in 1983 which emphasized the *Jellicoe Report*'s recommendation that the offence of withholding information should only be recited when the police believe that a person possesses information 'which would if revealed prevent acts of terrorism or lead to the apprehension of terrorists offenders'.[80] Thus, the circulars discouraged the duty to disclose being brandished against possessors of very low-level intelligence, but a more apposite reform would be to allow the citation of s 38B whenever it might elicit information but always subject to the special Scottish caution. The prior advice is absent from the Home Office Circular 7/2002, and so the former safeguards in Scotland have lapsed.

3.36 The fourth area of doubt around 'reasonable excuse' arises from the potential pressures on journalists.[81] For example, a reporter may discover information about terrorism by interviewing a terrorist or by witnessing a paramilitary display. Arranging, attending, or reporting such events may breach s 38B, as well as implicating the journalist in other offences (especially under the TA 2006, s 8). Section 38B can create two impacts. Firstly, the offence contributes to a 'chilling' effect on the reporting of terrorism. Correspondents can expect close attention from the police and special restrictions from their own superiors. Thus, reports on Irish terrorism abounded with difficulties and were to some extent suppressed as 'guilty secrets'.[82] The second effect is the direct threat of prosecution. The most serious clashes arose in 1979[83] from an interview with an INLA representative and then the filming (but not transmission) of an IRA road-block in Carrickmore, Northern Ireland. Both events incurred the wrath of the Attorney General, who publicly wrote to the BBC on 20 June 1980 as follows: 'Although I have reached a decision not to institute criminal proceedings in respect of these two incidents I should like to make it clear that I regard conduct of the nature which took place as constituting in principle offences . . .'[84] In response, the BBC Chairman rejected allegations that the BBC had transmitted propaganda or that false statements had been given to the police. However, he was less pugnacious when it came to the offence of withholding information:

> . . . we accept that the law must be obeyed in the difficult area of reporting terrorism in Northern Ireland, and that the journalist has an obligation to disclose to the police anything he may have discovered in the course of an interview with suspected or known terrorists that might be of 'material assistance' . . . There remains, however, one matter which causes us concern . . . [Your

---

[78] Compare Home Office Circular No 90/1983, para 9.

[79] *Jellicoe Report*, para 233.

[80] Home Office Circular No 90/1983, para 9.

[81] See *Report of the Special Rapporteur Mr Ambeyi Ligabo*, submitted in accordance with Commission resolution 2002/48, The right to freedom of opinion and expression (E/CN.4/2003/67, 2002) para 58.

[82] Curtis, L, *Ireland: the Propaganda War* (Pluto Press, London, 1984) p 275.

[83] See for other occurrences before the TA 2000, Walker, CP, *The Prevention of Terrorism in British Law* (2nd edn, Manchester University Press, Manchester, 1992) pp 141–3.

[84] *The Times* 2 August 1980, p 2; Curtis, L, *Ireland—The Propaganda War* (Pluto Press, London, 1984) pp 169–70.

letter] could be read as meaning that the police should be informed, at every turn, of the letter, phone calls, or meetings with go-betweens which are, I have no doubt, necessary if a journalist is ever to acquire information from known or suspected terrorists. If this is really what the law says, then all reporting of who terrorists are and what they say, would, in practice, be halted abruptly.

The exchange was terminated by a final warning from the Attorney General that he would in future take a stricter view of such activities.[85]

There is no exception for the media under s 38B, but the coercion or sanctioning of journalists is now subject to Article 10 of the European Convention which imports two principles of importance. The more general is that the highest priority is given to the encouragement of political speech.[86] Thus, journalists who seek to use 'inside' information about terrorism and counter-terrorism, which by definition are of political relevance, must be accorded some indulgence, since 'freedom of political debate is at the very core of the concept of a democratic society which prevails throughout the Convention'.[87] The same protection has been extended beyond political speech to issues of public concern, such as police illegality.[88] In *Castells v Spain*, it was suggested that 'the dominant position which a government occupies makes it necessary for it to display restraint in resorting to criminal proceedings, particularly where other means are available for replying to the unjustified attacks and criticisms of its adversaries or the media'.[89] **3.37**

The more specific principle of protection is that special scrutiny is given to legal incursions which demand the revelation of sensitive journalistic sources or confidences. Thus, in *Goodwin v United Kingdom*,[90] in the context of the Contempt of Court Act 1981, s 10, the European Court recognized that 'Protection of journalist sources is one of the basic conditions for press freedom'. **3.38**

Implementation

The penalties for the offence are, under s 38B(5) on indictment, imprisonment for up to five years, or a fine or both; or on summary conviction, imprisonment for up to six months or a fine or both. **3.39**

The defendants in *Abdul Sherif and others*[91] appealed against sentence, but the Court of Appeal upheld the application of the maximum of five years. The Court held that 'it will be the seriousness of the terrorist activity about which a defendant has failed to give information which will determine the level of criminality, rather that the extent of the information which could be provided which will affect the sentence'.[92] This approach is troubling. While the sentence should take account of the harm which could have been prevented, the main focus should remain on the culpability of the accused. A harsh outcome also applied since consecutive sentences were imposed on the basis that both limbs of s 38 B (silence before, and after, the crime) were involved. One may again argue that, concentrating on the actions of the defendant rather than the criminals protected by the silence, the culpability was continuous. The only concession was in the case of **3.40**

---

[85] But no threatened prosecution arose from the BBC scoop about an ETA ceasefire: <http://www.bbc.co.uk/news/world-europe-11195595>, 2010.

[86] See *Lingens v Austria*, App no 9815/82, Ser A 103 (1986).

[87] Ibid para 42.

[88] See especially *Castells v Spain*, App no 11798/85, Ser A 236 (1992).

[89] Ibid para 46.

[90] App no 17488/90 (1996) at para 39.

[91] [2008] EWCA Crim 2653.

[92] Ibid para 45. This point is followed in *R v Girma* [2009] EWCA Crim 912 at para 87.

Fardosa Abdullahi, who was the vulnerable fiancée of one of the suicide bombers (though her sentence of three years was not changed), whereas other defendants were young men without remorse. So, vulnerability through age or relationship is a relevant factor.[93] The Court also held that a failure to give information before the terrorism is a more serious offence than a failure afterwards and that several defaults may be charged as distinct offences.[94]

3.41   In the *Girma* case, the maximum penalty of five years was described by Judge Worsley as 'woefully inadequate'.[95] This lament may be justified because the original level was set by reference to the offences of proscription;[96] the maximum for s 11 membership rose from five to ten years in 1989. Offences concerning those offences under s 5 in Northern Ireland carry penalties between seven and ten years. The Court of Appeal upheld two maximum sentences for non-disclosure before and after-the-event for Yeshiemebet Girma but accepted that the sentence for after-the-event non-disclosure could run concurrently with the offence of assisting the offender, a point also taken in respect of the other defendants. For their section 38B offences of non-disclosure after the event, the maximum of five years was also applied to Esayas Girma and Mulumbet Girma; Mohammed Kabashi's sentence was also confirmed at five years (subject to discount for a guilty plea).

3.42   Section 38B(6) allows proceedings for an offence to be taken in any place where the person charged is or has at any time been since the information of material assistance was appreciated. This provision as to venue allows a person present in the United Kingdom to be charged even if abroad at the time when becoming aware of the information: 'For example, information about an act to be carried out in Greece could come to the attention of a UK resident while that person was in Spain—if the information were not disclosed and the act took place, that person could be charged in the UK or elsewhere, if evidence of deliberate non-disclosure were established.'[97]

3.43   In Great Britain, from 1984 until 2001, only fifteen charges were brought, with one conviction.[98] By contrast, the offence figured much more prominently in Northern Ireland, with 140 charges between 1974 and 2001; there were a further 308 charges of withholding information under s 5(1) of the Criminal Law Act (Northern Ireland) 1967.[99] Its higher use there may be attributed to the greater prevalence of terrorist activity and greater familiarity with the concept through the operation of s 5(1). Claims that the revived offence would 'play an important role in countering terrorism and bringing terrorists to justice by reminding the public of their obligation to help protect their fellow citizens'[100] are at best unproven in practice. Since its revival, there has been increasing recourse to s 38B in Britain but a waning of usage in Northern Ireland. The statistical returns, as shown in Table 3.1, are, however, very bare of detail.

3.44   Charges under s 38B can be germane to five situations. The first is where s 38B is used as an additional 'back-stop' count on an indictment, a practice adopted in Northern Ireland

---

[93]   Ibid para 45(c), 53.
[94]   Ibid para 45(b). This point is also followed in *R v Girma* [2009] EWCA Crim 912 at para 87.
[95]   *R v Girma* [2009] EWCA Crim 912 at para 87.
[96]   See Walker, C, *The Prevention of Terrorism in British Law* (1st edn, Manchester University Press, Manchester, 1986) p 92.
[97]   Home Office Circular 7/2002, p 5.
[98]   Home Office Statistics on the Operation of the Prevention of Terrorism Legislation 16/01 (2001) p 12.
[99]   Northern Ireland Office Research and Statistical Bulletin 6/2001 (Belfast, 2001) pp 5, 6.
[100]   Hansard HL vol 629 col 625 (3 December 2001), Lord Rooker.

Table 3.1 Withholding information: charges[a]

	Terrorism Acts charges: GB	Terrorism Acts charges: NI	CLA s 5 charges: NI
2000	0	0	4
2001	0	0	1
2002	0	0	2
2003	6	0	3
2004	0	0	0
2005	10	0	2
2006	6	0	0
2007	5	n/a	n/a

[a] Sources: Home Office, *Statistics on the Operation of the Prevention of Terrorism Legislation 16/01* (2001); Lord Carlile, *Annual Reports on the Terrorism Act*; Northern Ireland Office Statistics and Research Branch, *Northern Ireland Statistics on the Operation of the Terrorism Act 2000.*

though less prevalent in Britain.[101] Secondly, where the police have successfully detected active terrorists, peripheral offenders may be prosecuted under s 38B. Recent examples include Bassiru Gassama, who was convicted under s 38B in connection with the plot by Parvaz Khan and others to kidnap and behead a soldier.[102] The third category is where a police investigation into a terrorist plot has largely failed, but evidence against some minor participants has been unearthed. This pattern was followed in the most important pre-2000 case in Britain. In response to various IRA attacks before Christmas 1978, police inquiries in Essex failed to trace the prime suspects, but the police arrested twenty-three more peripheral players; ten were eventually brought to trial, and seven were convicted under the former s 18.[103] The fourth target, active bystanders who have been coerced into aiding terrorists (especially by loaning their cars),[104] arose in Northern Ireland. It could also arise in kidnap negotiations.[105] The fifth situation affects passive bystanders—persons not accused of terrorism involvement in any degree but who became aware of the plans of terrorists. This category has come to the fore in Britain and affects family members of the prime offender.

Foreign comparisons

Special offences of withholding information are not prevalent[106] but have appeared in some **3.45** European,[107] colonial, and Commonwealth jurisdictions.[108] A set of current comparators

---

[101] See *R v Cubbon and Watt* (1987) *The Times* 19 December p 21, Viscount Colville, *Report on the Operation in 1987 of the Prevention of Terrorism (Temporary Provisions) Acts* (Home Office, London, 1988) para 8.1.

[102] *The Times* 19 February 2008, p 13 (two years' imprisonment with an order for deportation to Gambia).

[103] See *R v Nea*, *The Guardian* 17 September 1980, p 3, *Essex Chronicle* (1980) 17 September, 22 September, 8 December, 15 December. All received suspended sentences for failing to pass on information about a stolen driving licence and car later used by the IRA and (in one case) about the whereabouts of Gerard Tuite (the most wanted suspect).

[104] See *Jellicoe Report*, para 221; *Baker Report*, para 252; *R v Rock* (NICA, 1990).

[105] Consideration arose during the Jennifer Guinness kidnapping: *The Times* 17 April 1986, p 1.

[106] In the USA, misprision of felony is an offence under 18 USC s 4 but has not been applied in terrorist cases.

[107] Picottii, L, 'Expanding forms of preparation and participation' (2009) 78 *International Review of Penal Law* 405. See especially France Criminal Code art 434-1, 434-2 (including an exemption for spouses and relatives).

[108] See especially Internal Security Act 1960, s 60 (Malaysia); Protection of Constitutional Democracy against Terrorism and Related Activities Act 2004, s 12 (South Africa); Prevention of Terrorism (Temporary Provisions) Act 1979, s 5 (Sri Lanka).

exists in the Republic of Ireland, the closest being the offence of withholding information created by s 9 of the Offences against the State Act 1998, but it has not figured in reported litigation.[109] There are also measures which allow adverse inferences from silence, some of which are aimed specifically at terrorism under ss 2 and 5 of the Offences against the State (Amendment) Act 1998.[110] More controversial still have been measures which demand information on pain of a criminal offence. Section 30(6) of the Offences against the State Act 1939 makes it an offence to refuse to give, or to give a false name and address in response to a request by the police under s 30(5). It is also unlawful under s 52 for an arrested person to fail to provide a full, or to give a false, account of his movements and actions during any specified period as well as of all information concerning terrorist offences. Under s 2 of the Offences against the State (Amendment) Act 1972, the person questioned does not have to be arrested but must be found at or near the place and time of the commission of a terrorism-related offence. A member of the Garda Síochána may then demand, on pain of a criminal penalty, name and address and an account of recent movements. Most cases have involved suspects, and the initial purpose is therefore to apply pressure in order to elicit incriminating statements.[111]

3.46   As for constitutionality, the Irish Supreme Court in *Heaney and McGuinness v Ireland*[112] concluded that the state was entitled to encroach on the right to silence. However, the European Court of Human Right disagreed, finding that 'the "degree of compulsion" imposed on the applicants by the application of s 52 of the 1939 Act with a view to compelling them to provide information relating to charges against them under that Act in effect destroyed the very essence of their privilege against self-incrimination and their right to remain silent'.[113] The same point was made in the accompanying European Court case of *Quinn v Ireland*,[114] following which the victorious applicant managed to convince the Irish High Court, in *Quinn v Judge Sean O'Leary*[115] to quash his conviction, but he was refused a declaration that s 52 was unconstitutional or void. It is argued that these Convention judgments 'effectively spell the death-knell for s 52, at least in its present form',[116] and their impact is underlined by later Supreme Court decisions.[117] By contrast, a more indulgent attitude is taken towards adverse inferences.[118]

3.47   The Canadian approach has been judicial, rather than police-based, powers of compulsory disclosure. Under the Anti-Terrorism Act 2001, investigative hearings have been allowed by s 83.28 (inserted into the Criminal Code). A police officer, 'for purposes of an investigation of a terrorism offence', may apply *ex parte* with the consent of the Attorney General to a

---

[109] Repeal was recommended by Prof D Walsh (dissenting) in the (Hederman) *Report of the Committee to Review the Offences against the State Acts, 1939–1998 and Related Matters* (Dublin, 2002) p 258.

[110] As amended by the Criminal Justice Act 2007, s 31.

[111] See generally Hogan, G and Walker C, *Political Violence and the Law in Ireland* (Manchester University Press, Manchester, 1989) p 255.

[112] [1996] 1 IR 580. See Hogan, G, 'The right to silence after National Irish Bank and Finnerty' (1999) 21 *Dublin University Law Journal* 176.

[113] *Heaney and McGuinness v Ireland*, App no 34720/97, 2000-XII at para 55.

[114] App no 36887/97, 21/12/2000, para 56.

[115] [2004] 3 IR 128.

[116] (Hederman) *Report of the Committee to Review the Offences against the State Acts, 1939–1998 and Related Matters* (Dublin, 2002) para 8.48. The Committee opposed the retention of s 52 and s 2 in their present form: para 8.56.

[117] See *In the matter of National Irish Bank Limited* [1999] 3 IR 145; *People (DPP) v Finnerty* [1999] 4 IR 364.

[118] *People (DPP) v Matthews* [2006] IECCA 103; *People (DPP) v Binéad* [2006] IECCA 147; *People (DPP) v Bullman* [2009] IECCA 84.

judge for an order to gather information relevant to that investigation which may precede any formal charges.[119] Where a judge is satisfied that there are reasonable grounds to believe that a terrorism offence has been or will be committed, the judge can order the examination of a material witness to determine what information they possess about a terrorism offence that has been or may be committed. 'Examination' can include the requirement of testimony on oath or the production of materials. The testimony may not be used in criminal proceedings (save for perjury) and legally privileged information need not be disclosed, but the person may not refuse to answer a question or produce an item on the basis that it is incriminating. The power also allowed for the imposition of a recognizance to keep the peace for twelve months. Before its sunset clause took effect in 2007,[120] the power was invoked just once (in British Columbia in connection with the Air India bombings case) and even in that case, an investigative hearing was never held,[121] though the constitutionality of s 83.28 was upheld.[122]

The Australian Security Intelligence Organisation Legislation Amendment (Terrorism) **3.48** Act 2003 is more extreme than the Canadian version.[123] It empowers the Director General of the ASIO, with ministerial consent, to obtain from a judge a warrant issued under s 34D of the *Australian Security Intelligence Organisation Act 1979* to question or detain and question a person who may have information reasonably believed to be important to the gathering of intelligence in relation to terrorism offences. Detention is allowed under s 34F, though questioning must not exceed sixteen hours in total under s 34HB, and detention of twenty-four hours per warrant must not exceed seven days under s 34HC. The person must answer questions under s 34G on pain of an offence, but answers cannot be adduced in criminal proceedings. There are limits on contacts with lawyers, who may not attend questioning under s 34TB. These conditions would make it difficult for this device to meet the standards of Articles 5 and 6 of the European Convention.[124]

The Canadian model is an advance on the archaically constructed *Explosive Substances Act* **3.49** 1883, s 6, in that it is not confined to explosives offences nor to information which relates to specific offences and it is also proactive rather than relying upon sanction. But the experience in Canada suggests there is no pressing need and account must also be taken of the impact of the TA 2000, s 19 as well as 38B. There is also the objection that it leads judges into a partisan investigative role.[125]

---

[119] See Sheldrick, BM, 'Judicial independence and anti-terrorism legislation in Canada' (2006) 10 *International Journal of Evidence and Proof* 75; Roach, K, 'The consequences of compelled self-incrimination in terrorism investigations' (2008) 30 *Cardozo Law Review* 1089.

[120] Extension was suggested by the Special Senate Committee on the Anti-terrorism Act, Fundamental Justice in Extraordinary Times (Ottawa, 2007) rec.16. A bill was tabled (Senate S-3) but failed in 2008. Revival is again proposed by the Combating Terrorism Bill 2010 (C-17).

[121] See Commission of Inquiry into the Investigation of the Bombing of Air India Flight 182, *Air India Flight 182* (Ottawa, 2010).

[122] *In the matter of an application under section 83.28 of the Criminal Code* [2004] 2 SCR 248.

[123] See Palmer, A, 'Investigating and prosecuting terrorism' (2004) 27 *University of New South Wales Law Journal* 373; Carne, G, 'Gathered intelligence or Antipodean exceptionalism' (2006) *Adelaide Law Review* 1; Law Council of Australia, *Anti-Terrorism Reform Project* (Canberra, 2009) para 5.6.4.

[124] See Michaelson, C, 'International human rights on trial—The United Kingdom's and Australia's legal response to 9/11' (2003) 25 *Sydney Law Review* 275 at 283–4; Lynch, A, and Williams, G, *What Price Security?* (UNSW Press, Sydney, 2006) ch 2.

[125] See Sheldrick, BM, 'Judicial independence and anti-terrorism legislation in Canada' (2006) 10 *International Journal of Evidence and Proof* 75.

3.50 An alternative model for the coercion of information is the use of material witness powers in the USA, which exist in state and Federal law, the most often-used source being 18 USC s 3144. The witness is treated as if a criminal defendant under s 3142 but need not be charged or even suspected of a crime. The power was used in seventy terrorist-related cases after September 11, in some cases to achieve detentions for several months as an abusive form of internment and without the live pursuance of depositions for criminal process.[126]

Assessment and conclusions

3.51 Justification for s 38B turns on practice and principle. In practice, the main advantage is that it will 'create an atmosphere in which it [is] respectable to provide . . . information'.[127] Information can then be used to Prevent, Protect, and Pursue in the language of CONTEST. Given these mixed objectives, rates of prosecution are not decisive. The real practical value of the measure is to influence people to volunteer information; the post-incident prosecution of recalcitrant minor participants is a second-best. Two important drawbacks arise from this practical objective. The first is that there is no clear evidence that it has achieved its central goal of increasing the flow of information to the police, and it seems improbable that it will ever do so. It is presumably not claimed that s 38B carries much clout with hardened terrorists, so it must be primarily aimed against those on the periphery of terrorism, whether as minor helpers or true bystanders. Yet, even such soft targets are likely either to be more intimidated by terrorists or more concerned for the plight of their kinfolk than by the remoter threat of s 38B. During past decades, the police have likewise recognized that there is often little advantage in prosecuting bystanders; there is a great deal more to be gained by keeping them under surveillance or in dialogue. The *Jellicoe Report* concluded that 'the section is of significant value to the police service, but that service could operate without it if required to do so'.[128] The second practical drawback concerns the effect of s 38B on the media, where insufficient account has been taken of the value of free reporting and comment on issues as important as terrorism.

3.52 The drawbacks in principle were highlighted by Lord Shackleton[129] who recommended abolition at least in Britain, since 'there are genuine doubts about its implications in principle and about the way it might be used in the course of interviewing someone . . . it has an unpleasant ring about it in terms of civil liberties'. His verdict was rightly attacked in Parliament as hardly 'persuasive rationally',[130] but more precise arguments for and against may be formulated.

3.53 The first justification for s 38B might be that offences involving withholding information are familiar to our legal system, as already outlined. Consequently, in exceptionally dangerous situations, society regularly compels its citizenry to provide succour, and 'in the case of terrorism, which is almost by definition criminal activity aimed at society as a whole, it seems . . . reasonable that there should be more than a merely moral duty to assist the police'.[131]

---

[126] See Boyle, R, 'The material witness statute post September 11' (2003–04) 48 *New York Law School Law Review* 13; Human Rights Watch and ACLU, *Witness to Abuse* (New York, 2005); Cook, JG, 'The detention of material witnesses and the Fourth Amendment' (2006) 76 *Mississippi Law Journal* 585.

[127] Hansard HC vol 882 cols 928–9 (28 November 1974), George Cunningham.

[128] *Jellicoe Report*, para 222.

[129] *Shackleton Report*, paras 132, 133.

[130] Hansard HC vol 969 col 1662 (21 March 1979), George Cunningham.

[131] *Jellicoe Report*, para 101. See also Ministry of Justice, *Rights and Responsibilities* (Cm 7577, London, 2009) para 2.28.

Post-September 11, it is difficult to argue, along the lines adopted by Viscount Colville, that there is nothing 'special' in withholding information about terrorism and so no good reason for a special offence.[132] Thus, our traditional distaste for the enforcement of 'social responsibility'[133] and for creating the sort of 'informer's society which exists in totalitarian states'[134] can be allayed.

Another theoretical objection to s 38B is that the harmful action and the dishonest intent are **3.54** not primarily those of the defendant under s 38B and so the offence should not form part of the criminal law. In reply, if it is acceptable to impose a legal, as well as a moral, duty to help the police to combat terrorism, it follows that an omission to fulfil that duty properly incurs legal sanction. The failure to volunteer information is wicked because of the especially dangerous nature of terrorism.

In conclusion, though good Samaritanism is not a general requirement of English criminal **3.55** law, nor should it become so in a society which encourages policing to be reliant on receptive and cooperative communities rather than imposing a 'police state',[135] s 38B does not fit the model of cooperative policing, but neither does it found a police state. It is confined to the abatement of exceptionally threatening activity, and it demands only a simple, indirect inter-vention which does not involve the commitment of a broad duty to rescue. Without much exploration, the Newton Committee approved the measure.[136] If, as Bobbitt argues, 'market state terrorism' takes as its principal target the citizens of its enemy,[137] then it makes sense to conscript that citizenry to defend themselves. However, to achieve proportionality to other rights, s 38B should be further limited to listed serious offences, and it should deal more explicitly and generously with persons suspected of other offences, with lawyers, and with journalists. Constitutional governance through codes and advice should be reconsidered in the light not only of these issues but also the increasing use against bystander relatives.

Terrorist investigation disclosure notice

Provisions

The Serious Organised Crime and Police Act 2005[138] provides for investigating authorities **3.56** (defined in s 60 as the Director of Public Prosecutions, the Director of Revenue and Customs Prosecutions, and the Lord Advocate, though the power can be delegated to any prosecutor) to compel individuals, whether suspects or otherwise, to produce documents, to answer questions, and to provide information in connection with organized crime, terrorism, or revenue offences. The investigating authority can issue a disclosure notice[139] under s 62 where it appears:

    (a) that there are reasonable grounds for suspecting that an offence to which this Chapter applies has been committed,

---

  [132] *Colville Report*, paras 15.1.3, 15.1.4.

  [133] See Ashworth, A, 'The scope of criminal liability for omissions' (1989) 105 *Law Quarterly Review* 424.

  [134] Hansard HC vol 904 col 475 (28 January 1976), Ian Mikado.

  [135] See further Walker, C, 'Conscripting the public in terrorism policing: towards safer communities or a police state?' [2010] *Criminal Law Review* 441.

  [136] *Newton Report*, B2 para 57.

  [137] *Terror and Consent* (Allen Lane, London, 2008) p 147.

  [138] See Home Office, *One Step Ahead* (Cm 6167, London, 2004) para 6.2.1.

  [139] For details, see Owen, T et al, *Blackstone's Guide to the Serious Organised Crime and Police Act 2005* (Oxford University Press, Oxford, 2005) paras 3.16–3.18.

(b) that any person has information (whether or not contained in a document) which relates to a matter relevant to the investigation of that offence, and

(c) that there are reasonable grounds for believing that information which may be provided by that person in compliance with a disclosure notice is likely to be of substantial value (whether or not by itself) to that investigation . . .

There may be judicial review,[140] but no judicial authorization is required, except where it is decided to proceed under s 66 by forceful entry and seizure under warrant, as when a person has failed to comply with a disclosure notice, or where it is not practicable to issue a disclosure notice, or where giving a notice might seriously prejudice the investigation. An officer of the investigating authority may copy the specified documents and require the recipient of the notice to explain the documents or the location of missing documents (s 63). Retention for the purposes of the investigation can be for so long as is considered necessary, but retention for production in legal proceedings must be justified by reasonable belief (s 66(7) and (8)).

3.57 Failure without reasonable cause to comply with any demand under ss 62 or 63, is a summary offence (s 67(1), (4)). Knowingly or recklessly making a false or misleading statement is an either-way offence (s 67(2), (5)). Wilful obstruction of a warrant under s 66 is a summary offence (s 67(3), (4)).

3.58 Restrictions applying to the material which can be collected are set out under s 64. Exemptions apply to legally privileged material (except that a lawyer may be required to provide the name and address of a client), to 'excluded' material (as defined by PACE, s 11), and confidential banking information unless the person to whom the obligation of banking confidence is owed consents to disclosure or the investigating authority (rather than a circuit judge under PACE) specifically authorizes intrusion. Section 65 also sets out restraints on the use of statements (but not documents)[141] in order to protect Article 6 rights. They cannot be used in evidence in criminal proceedings against the recipient of the notice, other than proceedings for an offence under s 67 (failure to comply), or for an offence of giving a false statement, or where the person seeks in other criminal proceedings to give as evidence an inconsistent statement. This formulation does not restrict reliance for investigatory purposes,[142] but any reliance at trial will be subject to s 78 of PACE.[143]

3.59 Section 61 originally defined the relevant terrorism offences as those in the TA 2000, ss 15 to 18, without any minimum as to financial level. However, this narrow focus was transformed under s 33 of the TA 2006. The disclosure notice powers are thereby extended to any 'terrorist investigation', defined as

an investigation of (a) the commission, preparation or instigation of acts of terrorism, (b) any act or omission which appears to have been for the purposes of terrorism and which consists in or involves the commission, preparation or instigation of an offence, or (c) the commission, preparation or instigation of an offence under the TA 2000 . . . or under Part 1 of the Terrorism Act 2006 other than an offence under section 1 or 2 . . .

---

[140] Compare *R v DPP, ex parte Kebilene* [2000] 2 AC 326; *R v Director of the Serious Fraud Office, ex parte Evans* [2002] EWHC 2304 (Admin).

[141] But Art 6 can still be relevant to the forced disclosure of documents in terrorism cases: *R (Malik) v Manchester Crown Court* [2008] EWHC 1362 (Admin) para 78.

[142] See *R v Hertfordshire County Council, ex parte Green Environmental Industries Ltd* [2000] 2 AC 412.

[143] See *R v Director of Serious Fraud Office, ex parte Smith* [1993] AC 1 at p 15.

Implementation

The powers have not been invoked by the Crown Prosecution Service nor the Director of **3.60** Revenue and Customs Prosecutions up to the end of July 2009.[144]

Foreign comparisons

The comparisons made in connection with s 38B are relevant here. The Canadian model **3.61** incorporating judicial involvement better equates with respect for rights. A closer relation here is the Australian Crime Commission Act 2002,[145] which provides under s 24A for a system of 'examinations' (the 'examiners' are senior lawyers under s 46B) who are tasked by the Board of the Commission which is accountable to an Intergovernmental Committee and a specialist Parliamentary Joint Committee. The Commission has found that it is common practice to refuse to comply with the examination and to accept the statutory sanction.[146] Given that a penalty of up to five years can be imposed, the threat of s 67 may turn out to be inadequate.

Assessment and conclusions

There was virtually no Parliamentary debate to explain the distinct purpose of these measures **3.62** as distinct from TA 2000 measures such as Sch 5, para 13. The judicial oversight in that provision accords more with constitutional governance than the unchecked powers under the 2005 Act.

Security service disclosure

To ensure that any information may be passed on to the intelligence services regardless **3.63** of legal duties of confidentiality, The CTA 2008, s 19, permits such transmission of information,[147] though there is no obligation so created.[148] Information thus obtained can be used for any of the purposes of the security services or for crime-related purposes.[149] Some restraints apply under s 20: the directors of the agencies must strive to ensure observance of their general duties not to act excessively in the collection or disclosure of information; there is particular regard in s 20 to the Data Protection Act 1998 and the RIPA, Pt I, so these cannot be evaded. Of course, whether the Data Protection Act is a restraint depends on what purposes are registered, and there is no equivalent to s 35 of the Serious Organised Crime and Police Act 2005 which restrains onward disclosure from the Serious Organised Crime Agency. The government also rejected as unworkable ongoing review of information held or received by the intelligence services based on whether its collection infringed Article 3.[150]

---

[144] FOIA responses 29 July 2009 (RCPO), 7 October 2009 (Lord Advocate).

[145] See <http://www.crimecommission.gov.au>; <http://www.aph.gov.au/senate/committee/acc_ctte/index.htm>. 895 summonses were issued in 2007–08, all unrelated to terrorism (*ACC Annual Report*, p 38).

[146] Parliamentary Joint Committee on the Australian Crime Commission, *Examination of the Australian Crime Commission Annual Report 2007–08* (Canberra, 2009) para 2.52.

[147] The power to hold such information is considered to lie within the Security Service Act 1989, s 2(2)(a) and the Intelligence Services Act 1994, ss 2(2)(a), 4(2)(a), but this is confirmed by s 19(2) and disclosure is for the wider purposes covered by s 19(3)–(5): Hansard HC Public Bill Committee on the Counter Terrorism Bill col 234 (29 April 2008), Tony McNulty.

[148] Hansard HL vol 704 col 402 (9 October 2008), Lord West.

[149] As a result, Sch 1 amends several information gateways so that the more general rule in s 19 can apply.

[150] Joint Committee on Human Rights, *Government Responses to the Committee's 20th and 21st Reports and other correspondence* (2007–08 HL 127, HC 756) p 28.

Apparently the security services look at these matters in a 'generic fashion' having regard to country and agency provenance.[151]

3.64 No further information is yet available as to implementation or performance. As for foreign comparisons, the most acute debates about the sharing of intelligence have followed the criticisms of the US 9/11 Commission.[152] As a result, the constraints on gathering foreign intelligence for law enforcement purposes have been relaxed by the USA PATRIOT Act,[153] while intelligence sharing is further facilitated by the Intelligence Reform and Terrorism Prevention Act of 2004.[154]

Offences of disclosure of information

Introduction and background

3.65 Most of the measures in this chapter concern the forced disclosure of information. By contrast, s 39 of the TA 2000 is designed to prevent disclosure.[155]

Provisions

3.66 Section 39 enacts two sets of offences to discourage or penalize disclosures that may damage the effectiveness of ongoing terrorist investigations. The offences may affect both 'insiders' who are conducting the investigations and also outsiders who come by the information, such as journalists. Disclosures within the 'regulated sector' are exempted from s 39 since they fall under the strict liability offence of tipping off under s 21D.[156]

3.67 The first set of offences, under s 39(1) and (2), applies whenever a person knows or has reasonable cause to suspect that a constable is conducting or proposes to conduct a terrorist investigation. An offence arises if the person (a) discloses to another anything which is likely to prejudice the investigation, or (b) interferes with material which is likely to be relevant to the investigation, a stricter duty since the material simply has to be relevant without proof that its treatment has been prejudicial.

3.68 The second set of offences, under s 39(3) and (4), applies where, knowing or having reasonable cause to suspect that a disclosure has been or will be made to the authorities under any of ss 19 to 21B or s 38B, a person (a) discloses to another anything which is likely to prejudice an investigation resulting from the disclosure under that section, or (b) interferes with material which is likely to be relevant to an investigation resulting from the disclosure under that section. The same distinction as between prejudice and relevant mentioned for the first set of offences pertains here too. However, the second set of offences is narrower than the first in that the range of investigations is limited to an

---

[151] Hansard HL vol 704 col 408 (9 October 2008), Baroness Manning Buller.

[152] National Commission on Terrorist Attacks upon the United States, *The 9/11 Commission Report* (GPO, Washington DC, 2004).

[153] s 218. See *In re Sealed Case*, 310 F3d 717 (FISA Ct Rev 2002); Kris, DS, 'The Rise and Fall of the FISA Wall' (2006) 17 *Stanford Law & Policy Review* 487; Donohue, LK, *The Cost of Counterterrorism* (Cambridge University Press, Cambridge, 2008) p 234.

[154] PL108-408. See O'Connell, AJ, 'The architecture of smart intelligence' (2006) 94 *California Law Review* 1662.

[155] See formerly PT(TP)A 1989, s 17(2)–(6).

[156] s 39(6A). See Terrorism Act 2000 and Proceeds of Crime Act 2002 (Amendment) Regulations 2007, SI 2007/3398. The regulated sector is as defined by Sch 3A: s 39(9).

investigation resulting from the disclosure to the appropriate authorities rather than any ongoing or even proposed investigation.

Aside from the statement in section 39(8)(a) that 'a reference to conducting a terrorist **3.69** investigation includes a reference to taking part in the conduct of, or assisting, a terrorist investigation', no guidance assists with the interpretation of questions such as the level of likelihood or formality required for a 'proposal' to conduct a terrorist investigation, though police records could provide relevant evidence. However, 'interference' is further defined in section 39(8)(b): 'a person interferes with material if he falsifies it, conceals it, destroys it or disposes of it, or causes or permits another to do any of those things'. Concealment, destruction, and disposal may arise in whole or part in response to an investigator's request or may be action which seeks to ensure that the materials or specific features do not come to the attention of the investigator. Causing another to do something was explained by Viscount Dilhorne in *Alphacell Ltd v Woodward*:[157]

> If a man intending to secure a particular result, does an act which brings that about, he causes that result. If he deliberately and intentionally does certain acts of which the natural consequence is that certain results ensue, may he not also be said to have caused those results even though they may not have been intended by him? I think he can, just as he can be said to cause the result if he is negligent, without intending that result.

Permitting and falsifying involve an element of knowledge and some definite step with respect to the material.[158] In *Alphacell*, Viscount Dilhorne commented that 'There must be a possibility of direction or control by one person over another and therefore inevitably some knowledge of what he is going to do.'[159]

It is a defence under s 39(5) to prove either (a) lack of knowledge or reasonable cause **3.70** to suspect that the disclosure or interference was likely to affect a terrorist investigation, or (b) a reasonable excuse for the disclosure or interference. The defence under (a) alone falls within s 118, by which the burdens placed on the defendant are evidential rather than a persuasive or legal.[160] Disclosures which are made for the purposes of legal advice or proceedings by a professional legal adviser are also excused under s 39(6). Disclosures within the regulated sector which fall under s 21D are exempted from s 39.[161]

Implementation and assessment

The penalties for the offences are (a) on indictment, imprisonment not exceeding five years, **3.71** a fine, or both, or (b) on summary conviction, imprisonment not exceeding six months, a fine, or both. No charges were brought between 2001 and the end of 2007.

These offences under s 39 add to the Official Secrets Act 1989, s 4 of which was raised **3.72** against the disclosure of a Joint Terrorism Analysis Centre document in *R v Thomas Lund-Lack*.[162] A civilian employed by the Metropolitan Police pleaded guilty to 'wilful misconduct in a judicial or public office' by disclosing a document to a journalist; the charge under the

---

[157] [1972] AC 824 at 839.
[158] *Sweet v Parsley* [1970] AC 132; *R v More* [1987] 1 WLR 1578.
[159] [1972] AC 824 at 833.
[160] HL Debs vol 613 col 754 (16 May 2000), Lord Bassam.
[161] s 39(6A). See Terrorism Act 2000 and Proceeds of Crime Act 2002 (Amendment) Regulations 2007, SI 2007/3398. The regulated sector is as defined by Sch 3A: s 39(9).
[162] *The Times* 28 July 2007, p 32.

1989 Act was allowed to remain on file. He was sentenced to eight months' imprisonment. Comparison may next be drawn with the offences of prejudicing investigations contrary to ss 342 and 333A (for the regulated sector) of the Proceeds of Crime Act 2002. Offences of this type are therefore well established, and s 39 has not in practice caused controversy.

C. Specialist Disclosure Powers

Disclosure by public authorities

Introduction and background

3.73 Public authorities and financial institutions are considered two pre-eminent specialist sources of data about terrorism; the latter will be considered in Chapter 9 in the context of terrorism funding. As for the former, the belief is that any notable terrorist group cannot avoid providing information to public bodies whether for national insurance, social security, driving licence, or other purposes. Therefore, Pt III of the ATCSA 2001 authorizes the disclosure of information held by public authorities[163] for law enforcement and intelligence purposes. Though welcomed by the Home Affairs Committee,[164] these powers are not directly linked, nor confined, to 'terrorist investigations'.

3.74 The Pt III powers are, by ss 17(6) and 19(10), additional to existing legal powers of disclosure, such as the powers of disclosure allowed by the Data Protection Act 1998. Section 29 of the 1998 Act provides an exemption to non-disclosure where the disclosure is for the prevention or detection of crime or the apprehension or prosecution of offenders. This exemption was considered inadequate for anti-terrorism purposes for two reasons. First, a pre-disclosure assessment of the legality of disclosing the information is required of the possessor of data, whereas, sometimes, the full picture is held by the requesting authority which will be reluctant to reveal it. Secondly, the Data Protection Act 1998 restrains transfers of data outside the European Economic Area unless the receiving state ensures an adequate level of data protection, whereas terrorism engages several countries which may have inadequate data protection regimes. Whether evasion of this second problem is an effect of s 17 is not clear. The government emphasized during debate that the Data Protection Act 1998 did apply under s 17.[165] However, s 17 is silent (unlike s 19(7) below). In so far as overseas recipients are encountered, one hopes that adequate data protection assurances will be in place. This expectation is not always matched by reality, as illustrated by the exchange of data with the United States relating to (airline) passenger name records and other carrier information[166] which has probably been the most frequent use of the Pt III powers.[167]

---

[163] By s 20(1), 'public authority' has the same meaning as in the Human Rights Act 1998, s 6.

[164] *Report on the Anti-terrorism, Crime and Security Bill 2001* (2001–02 HC 351) para 55.

[165] Hansard HL vol 629 col 418 (28 November 2001), Lord McIntosh.

[166] See Council Directive 2004/82/EC on the obligation of carriers to communicate passenger data; ECJ in C-317/04 and C-318/04, *European Parliament v Council of the European Union and European Parliament v Commission of the European Communities* (2006); Proposal for a Council Framework Decision on the use of Passenger Name Records (PNR) for law enforcement purposes COM (2007) 654 final; Council of the European Union, EU External Strategy on Passenger Name Record (PNR) Data (13986/10, 2010); Communication from the Commission on the global approach to transfers of Passenger Name Record (PNR) data to third countries COM (2010) 492 final; Ntouvas, I, 'Air passenger data transfer to the USA' (2008) 16 *International Journal of Law and Information Technology* 73.

[167] This basis is cited by Performance and Innovations Unit of the Cabinet Office, *Privacy and Data-Sharing: The Way Forward For Public Services* (London, 2002) para 4.30.

As well as the Data Protection Act 1998, there are several other statutory sharing arrangements **3.75** which operate in two directions. The first direction starts with the data holder who is then allowed to transfer data. Thus, the Commissioners for Revenue and Customs Act 2005, ss 17 to 21, grant several powers to transfer information, including for the purposes of the prevention or detection of crime or in relation to public safety or for national security. The handling of information by the social welfare authorities is likewise facilitated under the Social Security Administration Fraud Act 1997 and the Finance Act 1997, s 110. By s 68 of the Serious Crime Act 2007, a public authority may, for the purposes of preventing fraud, disclose information as a member of a specified anti-fraud organization. Otherwise, official bodies must abide by the restraints of the Data Protection Act 1998 as well as the Official Secrets Act 1989.

The second direction of transfer empowers the potential data receiver. For example, the **3.76** Serious Organised Crime and Police Act 2005 ensures that the Serious Organised Crime Agency (SOCA) can use information obtained in connection with any one of its functions to assist in exercising other functions (s 32), while s 33 allows SOCA to disclose information for criminal justice purposes, whether in the United Kingdom or elsewhere, and the exercise of any functions of any intelligence service. Section 34 allows disclosure of information to SOCA. Section 36 even imposes a duty on UK police forces to pass on relevant information. Information obtained under Pts V and VIII of the Proceeds of Crime Act 2002 may also be recycled for other prosecution purposes (s 435).

Provisions

Section 17 of the ATCSA 2001 reinterprets a range of provisions, listed in Sch 4, to have **3.77** effect in relation to the disclosure of information by or on behalf of a public authority, as if the purposes for which the disclosure of information is authorized by each provision includes the purposes of any criminal investigation, actual or contemplated, and whether in the United Kingdom or elsewhere. The information may have been created or gathered before the commencement of the Act (s 17(7)). The list in Sch 4 to the 2001 Act (as amended) comprises forty-one provisions, including, ironically, disclosure by the Information Commissioner and staff under s 59(1) of the Data Protection Act 1998, which was formerly limited to disclosure for the purposes of legal proceedings. By s 17(3), this list may be altered by Treasury order.[168]

Because s 17 authorizes domestic public authorities to aid foreign investigations and **3.78** proceedings, a restraint is inserted by s 18. The implication is that British security interests may not be served by entrusting information to every foreign power that seeks it. The restraint will take the form of a direction from the Secretary of State, who can prohibit a disclosure either absolutely or on conditions. It must appear to the Secretary of State that the overseas proceedings relate or would relate to a matter which could more appropriately be carried out by a court or other authority within the United Kingdom or of a third country. Directions cannot apply to any disclosure by a Minister of the Crown or by the Treasury—they have concurrent authority to make their own decisions as to the public interest. No direction has been published to date. Any person who, knowing of any direction, discloses any information in contravention of that direction shall be guilty of an offence under s 18(6).

---

[168] Orders are subject to affirmative resolution: Delegated Powers and Regulatory Reform Select Committee, *Report on the Anti-terrorism, Crime and Security Bill* (2001–02 HL 45), para 17. No order has been issued, but amendments to s 17 have been made by primary legislation including the Equality Act 2006, the National Health Service Act 2006, and the Wireless Telegraphy Act 2006.

Disclosure by revenue authorities

Introduction and background

3.79 Even more sweeping disclosure powers are granted by s 19 in respect of information held by the Commissioners for Her Majesty's Revenue and Customs within their records of around 32 million individuals and 1.1 million companies or organizations.[169]

Provisions

3.80 Rather than relaxing specific prohibitions on disclosure, s 19(2) simply asserts: 'N[n]o obligation of secrecy imposed by statute or otherwise prevents the disclosure' for the purpose of facilitating the functions of the intelligence services (not mentioned in s 17) or the purposes of criminal investigation, whether in the United Kingdom or elsewhere. Attempts to confine the power to terrorism and security matters were rebuffed.[170]

3.81 Because of privacy concerns, the disclosure must be proportionate to what is sought to be achieved by it (s 19(3)).[171] In addition, there is senior administrative oversight; by s 19(4), the information must be disclosed by the General or Special Commissioners. The Commissioners should also ensure under s 19(5) that there will not be further disclosure except for a purpose mentioned (which does not include intelligence purposes) or by express consent of the Commissioners. There is also a reminder in s 19(7) that nothing in this section authorizes the making of any disclosure that is prohibited by the Data Protection Act 1998. The absence of this reminder from s 17 should not be viewed as a green light for disclosure but reflects its more restrained ambit, though there was a similar phrase in the failed clause 45 of the Criminal Justice and Police Bill of 2000–01.

3.82 According to the HM Revenue and Customs guide of 2002, *Anti-Terrorism, Crime and Security Act 2001: Code of Practice on the Disclosure of Information*,[172] memorandums of understanding will be agreed with correspondent policing organizations. Amongst the guidelines are that agencies which receive information from the Revenue Departments under the criminal investigations and proceedings provisions must not pass that information on to others except with the consent of the relevant Revenue Department and that their ultimate purpose must not be for assisting intelligence-gathering.[173] There should be no disclosure of information to overseas jurisdictions which do not offer an adequate level of protection along the lines of the Data Protection Act 1998 and the Human Rights Act 1998.[174] Only a limited number of staff will be authorized to send or receive requests.[175] Whilst the Code says relatively little about standards of proof for the establishment of 'a legitimate interest'[176] to trigger disclosure, the Code signals greater concern for privacy than under s 17 where there is no equivalent guidance.[177]

---

[169] House of Commons Library, Research Paper 01/98, London, 2001, p 12.

[170] Hansard HC vol 375 col 791 (26 November 2001); Hansard HL vol 629 col 976 (6 December 2001).

[171] See further 'Confidentiality and the duty of disclosure' (2003) 6 *Journal of Money Laundering Control* 248.

[172] <http://www.hmrc.gov.uk/pdfs/cop_at.htm>. See also IDG60150—Procedure for disclosing to others (government): Anti-Terrorism, Crime and Security Act 2001 (ATCSA).

[173] Ibid paras 2.10, 2.11.

[174] Ibid para 3.9.

[175] Ibid paras 3.11, 3.12.

[176] Ibid para 3.11.

[177] See Law Society, *A Memorandum of Evidence to the Committee of Privy Counsellors, Anti-Terrorism, Crime and Security Act 2001 Review* (2002) p 4. There is no mention of the ATCSA 2001 by the Department for Constitutional Affairs in *Public Sector Data Sharing: Guidance on the Law* (London, 2003).

The Association of Chief Police Officers has issued a corresponding *Memorandum of* **3.83**
Understanding – Anti-terrorism, Crime and Security Act 2001. Disclosure of Information by
Inland Revenue.[178] It is the expectation of the police that 'the Inland Revenue will normally
disclose the requested information', but s 19 should not be treated as 'the first option . . .
when seeking information to assist in a criminal investigation or criminal proceedings'.[179]
In terms of the triggering of disclosure, the Memorandum states: 'Each request must include
sufficient information to demonstrate that the requested information is necessary to the
criminal investigation or proceedings for which it was requested. The requesting agency
must show that a failure to disclose the information would prejudice the investigation or
proceedings.'[180] There is no judicial check, and supervision is internal: the request must be
authorized by a senior officer who must be satisfied that disclosure would be made for a
proper purpose, would be 'necessary' within article 8(2) of the European Convention, and
proportionate to the purpose for which the information is requested.[181] There is the further
safeguard that 'Requests must therefore be case specific. General bulk requests and lists will
not be accepted.'[182]

Land Register

Under the terms of the Land Registration Act 2002, s 66, any person can apply to inspect or **3.84**
obtain official copies of various data relating to title, but authorities such as the police can
apply for exempted information (such as related or supporting documentation). The police
are designated as Sch 5 applicants under the Act and can apply under the Land Registration
Rule 140 in a way which is kept closed from public inspection.[183]

Implementation, foreign comparisons, and assessment

Efficiency and effectiveness of ss 17 and 19 are impossible to judge since meagre information **3.85**
has been revealed about the costs of operations or their operational impact. The only insight
has come from the Newton Committee which divulged that between January 2002 and
September 2003, public authorities made 19,909 disclosures of which just 701 (4 per cent)
related to terrorism; the Revenue authorities made an additional 796 disclosures, with 169
(21 per cent) relevant to terrorism.[184]

Though wider in scope, a comparison might be made with the USA PATRIOT Act 2001, **3.86**
s 210, which amended the administrative subpoena power (known as 'National Security
Letters') by which the FBI and other agencies can compel disclosure of sensitive information
held by 'financial institutions', a term which was expanded to include the postal service and
internet service providers.[185] These broad powers allow access to various personal records

---

[178] <http://www.acpo.police.uk/asp/policies/data/inland_revenue_mou.doc>, 2002.
[179] Ibid p 3, para 1.1.5.
[180] Ibid para 1.6.3.
[181] Ibid para 1.7.4.
[182] Ibid para 1.7.2.
[183] SI 2003/1417. See Land Registry, *Practice Guide 43–Applications in connection with court proceedings,*
insolvency and tax liability for further information (2008).
[184] *Newton Report*, D, paras 157, 158.
[185] PL 107-56. The range of issuing agencies was expanded by the Intelligence Authorization Act for the
Fiscal Year 2004 (PL 108-177) s 374. See Nieland, AE, 'National Security Letters and the amended PATRIOT
Act' (2007) 92 *Cornell Law Review* 1201; Office of the Inspector General of the US Department of Justice,
A Review of the Federal Bureau of Investigation's Use of National Security Letters (<http://www.usdoj.gov/oig/
special/s0703b/final.pdf>, 2007).

if they may assist in the investigation of international terrorism, and recipients are gagged from disclosing the fact of a request. Neither probable cause nor judicial authorization applies. The gagging feature was successfully challenged by an internet service provider in *Doe v Ashcroft*.[186] This finding of unconstitutionality was set aside[187] as a result of amendments in the USA PATRIOT Improvement and Reauthorization Act of 2005, which allows for legal advice to be taken.[188] But the amended version was again condemned as unconstitutional in so far as it affected the speech rights of a library manager in *Doe v Gonzales*.[189] National Security Letters have been used annually in their tens of thousands, but, as of 30 March 2005, the more restrained s 215, by which a judicial order may be issued requiring any person or entity to turn over 'any tangible thing' in connection with an international terrorism investigation,[190] had been exercised on thirty-five occasions and never to secure library, bookstore, gun sale, or medical records.[191]

3.87 There may be two lessons derived from this comparison. One is the value of a power to 'pull' information. At present, ss 17 and 19 are designed as a voluntary 'push' which may be hampered by conflicting policy or bureaucratic costs. The second is the need for independent oversight,[192] since administrative arrangements between bureaucracies cannot be trusted to give sufficient weight to individual rights to privacy.

3.88 These disclosure powers fall within the 'Prevent' and 'Pursue' elements of CONTEST. However, the absence of information about operations raises criticisms on the grounds of accountability and constitutional governance. The mixing of 'normal' and security situations reduces scrutiny and safeguards across the board.[193] The Newton Committee called for greater oversight by the Information Commissioner and the publication of statistics, while authorizations should be granted by a judge except in terrorist cases when senior internal authorization should be required.[194]

3.89 The Information Commissioner has commented generally that:[195]

> In a world of rapid change—political, social, economic, and technological—it is vital that we articulate the values of personal privacy and public openness. These values cannot simply be abandoned in the face of threats—whether from terrorism, serious crime, international instability or anti-social conduct on our streets. . . . Equally, the values of privacy and openness are not absolutes. Both require delicate and proportionate balances to be drawn in the face of both threat and opportunity.

3.90 Likewise, the Surveillance Studies Network has warned that 'surveillance, especially that associated with high technology and antiterrorism, distracts from alternatives and from

---

[186] 334 F Supp 2d 471 (2004).
[187] 449 F3d 415 (2006).
[188] PL 109-177, s 116.
[189] 500 F Supp 2d 379 (2007).
[190] See *American Civil Liberties Union v US* 321 F Supp 2d 24 (2004); *Muslim Community Association of Ann Arbor v Ashcroft* 459 F Supp 2d 592 (2006).
[191] Doyle, C and Yeh, BT, *Libraries and the USA PATRIOT Act* (RS21441, Library of Congress. Congressional Research Service, Washington DC, 2006).
[192] The USA PARTIOT Improvement and Reauthorization Act 2005 (PL 109-177) s 118 requires the Attorney General to issue an annual report to Congress and s 119 requires audit by the Inspector General of the Department of Justice.
[193] Newton Report B para 3. See Lyon, D, *Surveillance After September 11* (Polity, Cambridge, 2005).
[194] Ibid B paras 21–3. This proposal was rejected by the *Home Office Response to Newton Report*, Pt II para 25.
[195] Information Commissioner, *Annual Report 2003* (2002–03 HC 727) p 7.

larger and more urgent questions' as well as being applied to an ever-increasing circle of applications away from terrorism.[196] The Information Commissioner's Data Sharing Review emphasizes the need for proportionality with respect to the task in hand and to the amount of data transferred.[197] The blanket measures in the terrorism legislation cannot easily meet these tests. The Home Affairs Committee specifically draws attention to the dangers of data sharing in its report, *A Surveillance Society?*.[198] The measures have evident impact on privacy rights.[199] Part III covers a very wide range of highly confidential information which is often provided under compulsion (a distinction from the financial information dealt with elsewhere in Pt III). Sections 17 and 19 may therefore be questioned on grounds of proportionality as follows.

First, the legislative objective is too widely expressed in terms of 'any criminal investigation whatever' or 'any criminal proceedings whatever', and also without any level of suspicion or belief being reached. How can minor regulatory offences, which may not actually have occurred, warrant serious intrusions into personal informational privacy? The Sch 4 list includes, for example, the Merchant Shipping (Liner Conferences) Act 1982 and the Diseases of Fish Act 1983. The government justified this dragnet approach by arguing that it wanted 'to make it simple for public officials to understand what they are supposed to disclose' by allowing disclosure in virtually all circumstances.[200] The Home Secretary, David Blunkett, further sought to illustrate the need for breadth:[201] **3.91**

> Take an employment agency that is being inspected. The inspectors come across information relating to an individual seeking to take up a particular, sensitive job. It is discovered that that person has claimed large amounts of benefit. Let us call him Mr AQ, just as an example of someone who might seek to do that. According to the framing of the House of Lords proposal [to restrict the power to terrorism], it would not be possible for that information to be shared. No one outside the House would thank us if we so restrained information giving and the sharing of concerns that Mr AQ continued to draw benefits. It would be illegal to pass on the information required.

Of course, it may turn out that Mr AQ is a terrorist and that benefit fraud is a precursor to terrorism and part of the jigsaw of evidence against him. But that is a very long shot and is no more likely than for any motorist stopped for defective tyres or a TV licence defaulter.

Measures very similar to Pt III were encouraged in 2000 by the Performance and Innovations Unit of the Cabinet Office (later published as *Privacy and Data-Sharing*)[202] and by proposals in relation to the proceeds of crime by the Inland Revenue.[203] Yet, these proposals were **3.92**

---

[196] *A Report on the Surveillance Society* (Information Commissioner, Wilmslow, 2006) paras 2.8.3, 9.9.4. See further Thomas, R and Walport, M, *Data Sharing Review* (Ministry of Justice, London, 2008); Home Affairs Committee, *A Surveillance Society?* (2007–08 HC 58, and *Government Reply*, Cm 7449, 2008); House of Lords Select Committee on the Constitution, *Surveillance: Citizens and the State* (2008–09 HL 18, and *Government Reply*, Cm 7616, 2009); Scheinin, M, *Report of the Special Rapporteur on the promotion and protection of human rights and fundamental freedoms while countering terrorism* (A/HRC/13/37, 2009).

[197] Thomas, R and Walport, M, *Data Sharing Review* (Ministry of Justice, London, 2008).

[198] (2007–08 HC 58) para 307. The Government's Reply is Cm 7449, 2008.

[199] Data storage and release is within Art 8: *Leander v Sweden*, App no 9248/81, Ser A 116 (1987) para 69.

[200] Hansard HC vol 375 col 794 (26 November 2001), Ruth Kelly.

[201] Hansard HC vol 376 col 898 (12 December 2001).

[202] (London, 2002) para 4.28.

[203] *Recovering the Proceeds of Crime* (Cabinet Office, London, 2000) p 95.

removed from the Criminal Justice and Police Bill 2000–01.[204] Part III might have made some sense if designed around the concept of 'terrorist investigations' under s 32, but the current wording is explicitly wider and betrays another legislative history and purpose which the 2001 Act should not have been commandeered to serve.

3.93 Other aspects of over-breadth are that information might be disclosed to assist foreign investigations (such as about price-fixing)[205] which are not domestic crimes, that there is no judicial oversight, no comprehensive requirement of senior administrative authorization, and an insufficient evidential standard of proof.[206] Some attempt has been made to answer the first concern by the interpretive clause in s 20(2): 'Proceedings outside the United Kingdom shall not be taken to be criminal proceedings for the purposes of this Part unless the conduct with which the defendant in those proceedings is charged is criminal conduct or conduct which, to a substantial extent, consists of criminal conduct.' In addition, by s 20(3), 'criminal conduct' must comprise either criminal offences under the law of a part of the United Kingdom; or must correspond to conduct which, if it all took place in a part of the United Kingdom, would constitute a crime under domestic law.

3.94 Next, Pt III installs no added safeguards against abuse.[207] Without subsequent notification to those affected,[208] how can existing enforcement mechanisms such as the Data Protection Act 1998 or an action for breach of privacy under the Human Rights Act 1998, s 7, be viable?[209] As a nod in the direction of privacy protection, s 17(5) provides: 'No disclosure of information shall be made by virtue of this section unless the public authority by which the disclosure is made is satisfied that the making of the disclosure is proportionate to what is sought to be achieved by it.'[210] But there is no requirement that the disclosure be considered necessary in the public interest[211] or that it be subjected to prior or subsequent independent oversight. An attempt in the House of Lords to impose prior judicial control was resisted on grounds of practicality: 'If we have delay of the kind involved in prior judicial control, we will lose the scent; we will lose the information; we will lose the opportunity to deal with potential terrorists. It has to be done immediately.'[212] As a result, the Joint Committee on Human Rights condemned these measures.[213]

3.95 Finally, there may be unwanted side-effects, such as reluctance to cooperate with authorities over legitimate information-gathering and their careless handling of data. Another problem is the treatment of self-incrimination. Some of the measures listed in Sch 4, as amended by the Youth Justice and Criminal Evidence Act 1999, ss 58 and 59, do provide restraint on the use of evidence obtained under threat of prosecution but only in respect of those financial offences. The problem does not, however, apply to the disclosing officials since 'There is no

---

[204] 2000–01 HC 31. See Hansard HL vol 625 col 1036 (9 May 2001).
[205] See *Norris v Government of the United States of America* [2008] UKHL 16.
[206] See Hansard HC Standing Committee F, col 412 *et seq* (6 March 2001).
[207] See *Malone v United Kingdom*, App no 8691/79, Ser A 82 (1984) at para 81.
[208] See Binning, P, 'In safe hands?' (2002) 6 *European Human Rights Law Review* 734 at 749.
[209] Compare *Peck v United Kingdom*, App no 44647/98, 2003-I at para 103.
[210] See Hansard HL vol 376 col 1108 (13 December 2001).
[211] Compare the Data Protection Act 1998, s 59.
[212] Hansard HL vol 629 col 390 (28 November 2001), Lord McIntosh.
[213] *Report on the Anti-terrorism, Crime and Security Bill* (2001–02 HL 51, HC 420), para 24.

question of public officials being obliged to make disclosures. It is up to them to decide whether to do so.'[214]

D. Conclusions

The imparting and sharing of intelligence are key elements of responding to terrorism. The **3.96** former has been addressed by s 38B, which demands participation by the public, the most important repository of information about terrorism. The imposition has been marginal, and so the most important relations between general public and authorities remain dependent on consent and respect, though greater burdens apply to professionals. The fact that most information-sharing and special investigative and surveillance techniques are unregulated by judicial supervision not only threatens individual rights and diminishes the opportunity for the production of evidence in a prosecution[215] but also discourages community trust and willingness to cooperate.

The sharing of information within intelligence networks remains legally complex and not **3.97** fully regulated (considered also in Chapter 2).[216] Most limitations on sharing intelligence are not legal but, as discerned by the 9/11 Commission, arise from institutional rivalries and suspicions,[217] or as the *Bichard Report*[218] found, arise from the technical incompatibilities. The Intelligence and Security Committee, in its report *Could 7/7 Have Been Prevented?* likewise found that relations between the Security Service and local police were based on a 'need to know' principle rather than a 'need to share' principle.[219] Its attitude to this state of affairs appears hesitant compared to efforts towards integration in the USA, where the Intelligence Reform and Terrorism Prevention Act 2004, s 1011, created the office of Director of National Intelligence to serve as head of the intelligence community, to act as the principal adviser to the President, to the National Security Council, and to the Homeland Security Council, to set priorities for intelligence agencies, and to coordinate with the National Security Branch within the FBI.[220] The DNI also oversees a National Counterterrorism Center, which analyses and integrates intelligence. Whether this more formal system has altered professional practices and silos more effectively than more limited British reforms remains to be researched, and so a wider inquiry than the promised investigation of intelligence in judicial proceedings[221] within the United Kingdom seems to be warranted.

---

[214] Hansard HL vol 629 col 367 (28 November 2001), Lord McIntosh.

[215] See *Report of the Special Rapporteur on the promotion and protection of human rights and fundamental freedoms while countering terrorism* (A/HRC/10/3. 2009) para 29.

[216] See *Possible Measures for Inclusion in a Future Counter-Terrorism Bill* (Home Office, 2007) para 3.

[217] See National Commission on Terrorist Attacks upon the United States, *The 9/11 Commission Report* (2004) ch 11.

[218] Bichard Inquiry, *Report* (2003–04 HC 653). See further: Home Office, *Bichard Inquiry Recommendations: Progress Report* (Home Office, London, 2004); Bichard Inquiry, *Final Report* (HMSO, London, 2005).

[219] (Cm 7617, London, 2009) para 241.

[220] See <http://www.dni.gov>; <http://www.fbi.gov/hq/nsb/nsb.htm>.

[221] See Hansard HC vol 513 col 175 (6 July 2010).

4

ARREST, DETENTION, AND
TREATMENT OF DETAINEES

A. Introduction

The policing powers in Pt V of the TA 2000, the focus of this chapter, involve arrest and its **4.01** consequences as directed against individuals, rather than powers against places or spaces as related in Chapter 2. This personalized aspect of Pt V is reflected in reliance on the term 'terrorist' in s 40(1), meaning a person who (a) has committed an offence under any of ss 11, 12, 15 to 18, 54, and 56 to 63, or (b) is or has been concerned in the commission, preparation, or instigation of acts of 'terrorism'. By referring to 'preparation or instigation' as well as 'commission', the term covers terrorism which is either 'active' or 'passive' (such as membership of a proscribed organization).[1] The breadth of s 40(1)(b) means that the failure to update this definition with the offences under the TA 2006 is not serious.

The powers in Pt V are not exclusive, but, by s 114, are additional to common law or statutory **4.02** policing powers such as those in PACE.[2] However, terrorism suspects arrested under PACE

---

[1] *McKee v Chief Constable for Northern Ireland* [1984] 1 WLR 1358. See Walker, CP, 'Emergency arrest powers' (1985) 36 *Northern Ireland Legal Quarterly* 145.

[2] See also PACE(NI), SI 1989/1341. In Scotland, powers are more fragmented, but see Police (Scotland) Act 1967, s 17; Criminal Procedure (Scotland) Act 1995, Criminal Justice (Scotland) Act 2003 (asp 7).

cannot then be rearrested under s 41 unless further offences are disclosed.[3] Thus, police officers may be minded to opt initially for the wider Terrorism Act powers, absent also any expressed rule of 'normality'.

B. Arrest

Introduction and background

4.03 At the heart of Pt V is the power of arrest without warrant under s 41. Its lineage can be traced directly back to 1974.[4] A special power of arrest may be founded upon three reasons.

4.04 The traditional purpose is to interrogate suspects so as to uncover admissible evidence sufficient to put before a court, to gather background intelligence information, or simply to disrupt. These objectives are aided by an elongated period of detention and by the fact that no detailed reasons need be adduced at the point of arrest, features which encourage anticipatory police intervention.

4.05 A second and mounting reason is to facilitate searches of two types—the search of premises and forensic testing. Despite occasional and disastrous lapses in standards,[5] explosives analysis, DNA profiling, and the examination of CCTV footage have become the stock in trade of terrorism investigations.

4.06 The third reason for s 41 is to overcome problems posed by jurisdictional boundaries. Investigations which cross the borders of Scotland and England would otherwise entail obscure and complex rules.[6] Therefore, by s 41(9), a constable in one part of the United Kingdom may exercise the power in any other part. Even more troublesome are the complications over proof of identity, translation, and liaison with foreign agencies posed by international terrorism.[7]

Provisions

Core power to arrest

4.07 The core arrest power is s 41(1): 'A constable may arrest without a warrant a person whom he reasonably suspects to be a terrorist.' The standard of reasonable suspicion has been explored in *O'Hara v United Kingdom*.[8] While 'the "reasonableness" of the suspicion on which an arrest must be based forms an essential part of the safeguard against arbitrary arrest and detention', it is accepted that 'facts which raise a suspicion need not be of the same level as those necessary to justify a conviction, or even the bringing of a charge'.[9] In *O'Hara*,

---

[3] See PACE s 41(9). There may be remand back to police custody on charge under the Magistrates' Courts Act 1980, s 128: *R v Cunningham* [2004] NIQB 7.

[4] See Walker, CP, *The Prevention of Terrorism in British Law* (2nd edn, Manchester University Press, Manchester, 1992) ch 8.

[5] See (May Inquiry), *Reports of the Inquiry into the circumstances surrounding the convictions arising out of the bomb attacks in Guildford and Woolwich in 1974* (1989–90 HC 556), (1992–93 HC 296), (1993–94 HC 449); (*Caddy Report*), *Assessment and Implications of Centrifuge Contamination in the Trace Explosive Section of the Forensic Explosives Laboratory at Fort Halstead* (Cm 3491, London, 1996).

[6] See Criminal Justice and Public Order Act 1994, Pt X. See Walker, C, 'Internal cross-border policing' (1997) 56 *Cambridge Law Journal* 114.

[7] See *Jellicoe Report*, paras 13, 23, 75–78.

[8] App no 37555/97, 2001-X.

[9] Ibid paras 34, 36.

the information from four separate informers, who had proved previously reliable and whose information concerning the murder was consistent, amounted to sufficient albeit 'sparse materials'.[10] As for the components of reasonable suspicion, the House of Lords in *O'Hara* decided that it involves both a genuine and subjective suspicion in the mind of the arrestor that the arrestee has been involved in terrorism and also objectively reasonable grounds for forming such a suspicion.[11]

Many arrests will arise in the context of second-hand information via briefings rather than events or information received first-hand by the arresting officer. So long as the two components of reasonable suspicion are present, the arrest can be lawful,[12] but Lord Steyn in *O'Hara* expressed the view that, 'a mere request to arrest without any further information by an equal ranking officer, or a junior officer, is incapable of amounting to reasonable grounds for the necessary suspicion. How can the badge of the superior officer, and the fact that he gave an order, make a difference?'[13] **4.08**

Another recurrent feature associated with s 41 is multiple 'precautionary' arrests, which may rather stretch the bounds of reasonable suspicion.[14] For example, in *Commissioner of Police of the Metropolis v Raissi*,[15] Lotfi Raissi was arrested under s 41 on information from the FBI which alleged links to one of the September 11 hijackers and involvement in flight training in Arizona. His brother and wife were also arrested. Because his wife also had been in Arizona and had worked at an airline check-in, it was reasonable to suspect that the wife was complicit, but the suspicions against the brother, largely based on personal affiliation, were insufficiently 'reasonable', even though that threshold is 'low'.[16] **4.09**

The s 41 formulation next differs from normal arrest powers in that it allows a wider range of activities to be considered because no specific offence need be in the mind of the arresting officer. The result is to afford wider discretion in carrying out investigations. Before 2001, Irish arrests provided the mainstay.[17] Since then, the vast majority in Britain are 'international'. In addition, there have been isolated arrests for domestic causes, such as animal rights and ecological protestors, or Scottish and Welsh nationalism.[18] But there is now a growing trend to arrest right-wing extremists, contrary to the views of previous reviewers.[19] In the separate cases of Martyn Gilleard and Nathan Worrell, neo-Nazis were amongst the first to be arrested under s 41 and then charged and convicted under ss 57 and 58.[20] **4.10**

---

[10] Ibid paras 40, 42.

[11] *O'Hara v Chief Constable of the RUC* [1997] AC 286.

[12] See further Walker, C, 'Emergency arrest powers' (1985) 36 *Northern Ireland Legal Quarterly* 145; Hunt, A, 'Terrorism and reasonable suspicion by "proxy"' (1997) 113 *Law Quarterly Review* 540.

[13] *O'Hara v Chief Constable of the RUC* [1997] AC 286 at 293.

[14] See Metropolitan Police Authority, *Counter-Terrorism: The London Debate* (London, 2007) p 25; Lord Carlile, *Report on the Operation in 2008 of the Terrorism Act 2000* (Home Office, London, 2009) para 125.

[15] [2008] EWCA Civ 1237. See also Leigh, L, 'Arrest: reasonable grounds for suspicion' (2008) 172 *Justice of the Peace* 180. Compensation is being sought by Lotfi Raissi: *R (Raissi) v Secretary of State for the Home Department* [2008] EWCA Civ 72; *Raissi v Secretary of State for Justice* [2010] EWCA 337; *The Times* 24 April 2010, p 2.

[16] Ibid para 20.

[17] See Brown, D, *Detention under the Prevention of Terrorism Act* (Home Office Research and Planning Unit paper 75, London, 1993) p 6.

[18] There were twenty-six arrests between 1980–84: *Colville Report*, para 7.92.

[19] *Jellicoe Report*, para 77; *Colville Report*, paras 7.1.4, 7.1.5.

[20] (Gilleard) *The Times* 26 June 2008, p 20; (Worrell) [2009] EWCA Crim 1431. See also Neil Lewington (*The Times* 16 July 2009, p 23); Terence Gavan (*The Times* 16 January 2010, p 29); Ian and Nicky Davison (*The Times* 15 May 2010, p 31).

Non-terrorist arrest powers and offences could have applied, but a desire for equality with *jihadis* seems to have trumped proportionality.

4.11 Terrorist plots and attacks usually do entail identifiable offences, and this convergence prompted the European Court of Human Rights in *Brogan* to accept 'terrorism' as within the notion of an 'offence' for the purposes of Article 5(1)(c).[21] At the same time, that decision was delivered in the context of indications that specific offences of membership of a proscribed organization were in mind. This limit was emphasized by Lord Lloyd in debates on the Terrorism Bill,[22] and he sought to ensure compliance with Article 5(1)(c) by the enactment of an offence of 'terrorism'.[23] In response, the government cited *Brogan* as authority for the proposition that 'a terrorist arrest power, without an explicit link to a specific offence, is compatible with the ECHR and Article 5(1)(c) in particular'.[24] Overall, the precedents are not favourable to Lord Lloyd's contention, and the tide of legislative development since 2000 is also adverse.

4.12 However, the continued breadth of s 41 is illustrated by Operation Pathway in 2009, which involved twelve arrests, mainly of Pakistani students. No charges were brought, though several of the suspects were then subject to deportation proceedings.[25] The arrests owed more to personal contacts and the use of alleged code words ('Nikkah'—marriage contract) than to any identified offences. This disjunction illustrates the flexibility of s 41 but may breach Article 5(1) of the European Convention, especially as the arrests were prematurely prompted by the inadvertent disclosure of briefing papers to photographers in Downing Street.[26]

Grounds and reasons for arrest

4.13 Because of the basis for arrest, modifications flow to s 28 of PACE (art 30 of PACE(NI)) by which an arrested person must be informed of the arrest and the ground for it. Disclosure could jeopardize police methods or informers or could bolster the anti-interrogation training of suspects. Therefore, detailed reasons are not demanded under s 41. The police must state that an arrest is being imposed and the ground for the arrest, but 'terrorism' covers a multitude of activities, and no specific wrong need be isolated.

4.14 In *R v Officer in charge of Police Office, Castlereagh, ex p Lynch*,[27] a constable arrested Lynch and told him that 'I was arresting him under [the specified statutory power] as I suspected him of being involved in terrorist activities . . . .'. Lynch complained that this recital was inadequate (he was actually suspected of membership of the IRA and the murder of a policeman). Lord Chief Justice Lowry was wary of committing himself to enforcing the recital of substantial reasons, so no specific offence or act need ever be mentioned.[28] It could be argued that the Court confused grounds with authority, but subsequent cases have confirmed that

---

[21] *Brogan v United Kingdom*, App nos 11209, 11234, 11266/84, 11386/85, Ser A 145-B (1988) para 50. See also *Ireland v United Kingdom*, App no 5310/71, Ser A 25 (1978) para 196.

[22] Hansard HL vol 613 col 677 (16 May 2000).

[23] *Lloyd Report*, para 8.16.

[24] Hansard HL vol 613 cols 681–2 (16 May 2000), Lord Bassam. See also Home Office Response to *Lloyd Report*, para 7.16.

[25] See *XC v Secretary of State for the Home Department* (SC 02, SC 77-82, 2009).

[26] Lord Carlile, *Operation Pathway* (Home Office, London, 2009) paras 15–35.

[27] [1980] NI 126 at 128. See Walker, CP, 'Arrest and rearrest' (1984) 35 *Northern Ireland Legal Quarterly* 1.

[28] Ibid 137. The same arguments did not apply to arrests based on s 40(1)(a): ibid 130–1; *Forbes v H.M. Advocate* 1990 SC (JC) 215.

there is no requirement to give detailed reasons at the point of arrest.[29] However, a bare reference to the arrest power was held to be inadequate in *Van Hout v Chief Constable of the Royal Ulster Constabulary.* [30]

The reasons must normally be imparted on arrest but may be delayed under s 28 on grounds **4.15** of impracticability.[31] Article 5.2 of the European Convention allows a few hours' delay with the effect that reasons may be deduced from a later interrogation.[32]

In *Kerr v United Kingdom*,[33] K was arrested and interviewed about a recent bombing, **4.16** membership of the IRA and the contents of his computer. He was charged with the possession of terrorism information (later dropped). The police claimed that the reasons for the arrest were clear from the thirty-nine interviews with Kerr, a point accepted for the purposes of Article 5(2). The same developing picture was sustained in *Sher v Chief Constable of Greater Manchester Police.*[34] It was sufficient to recite to the detainees that they were being arrested under s 41 for terrorism, and more reasons could emerge from the briefing documents which were produced as a prelude to interview sessions.[35]

Purposes of arrest

Since the arrest power is bound up with 'terrorism' and not crime, as stated in *Lynch*,[36] **4.17** 'an arrest is not necessarily . . . the first step in a criminal proceeding against a suspected person on a charge which was intended to be judicially investigated . . . Rather it is usually the first step in the investigation of the suspected person's involvement in terrorism.' Consequently, arrests under s 41 facilitate interviews to gather intelligence as well as the traditional police concern, interrogations to produce admissible evidence. Although this dual purpose is one of the central attractions of s 41, it entails two complications. Firstly, the proactive, intelligence-gathering purpose has predominated, so a relatively low charging rate (described later) has inevitably resulted. This low rate does not mean that most arrests are not based on reasonable suspicion at all, since the criteria and purposes of valid arrests are distinct issues. The second difficulty is that arrests explicitly for intelligence-gathering breach Article 5(1) of the European Convention. Thus, officials have increasingly emphasized that the only legitimate purpose of an arrest is to bring criminal charges.[37]

A further difference from 'normal' arrest powers is that there is no requirement of necessity **4.18** such as arises under PACE, s 24(4). Instead, a looser administrative law standard demands that the power is being used for proper purposes.[38]

---

[29] See *Forbes v HM Advocate* 1990 SC (JC) 215; *Brady v Chief Constable for the RUC* [1991] 2 NIJB 22; *Oscar v Chief Constable of the RUC* [1992] NI 290.

[30] (1984) 28 June (QBD).

[31] The Body of Principles for the Protection of All Persons under Any Form of Detention or Imprisonment (UNGA 43/173, 9 December 1988), Principle 10 requires reasons on arrest.

[32] *Fox, Hartley, and Campbell v United Kingdom*, App nos 12244/86 and 12245/86, Ser A 182 (1990) paras 41–43; *(Margaret) Murray v United Kingdom*, App no 14310/88, Ser A 300-A (1994) para 77.

[33] App no 40451/98, 7 December 1999.

[34] [2010] EWHC 1859 (Admin).

[35] Ibid paras 91, 94.

[36] [1980] NI 126 at 131.

[37] Compare Hansard HC vol 47 col 56 (24 October 1983), Leon Brittan; Hansard HC vol 146 col 67 (30 January 1989), Douglas Hurd; Crawshaw, S, 'Combating terrorism' in Ward, RH and Smith, HE (eds), *International Terrorism* (OICJ, Chicago, 1987) p 20.

[38] *Holgate-Mohammed v Duke* [1984] AC 437.

Legal challenges

4.19   The absence of reasonable suspicion may be challenged after the arrest is over by a civil claim for false imprisonment, as in the *O'Hara* and *Raissi* cases.[39] The courts will demand pursuance of an active reasonable suspicion and will not countenance deprivation of liberty for police administrative purposes such as an unrequested medical examination.[40] In *Connolly v Metropolitan Police Commissioner*,[41] the plaintiff and friends visited the Old Bailey to view the trial of two alleged IRA bombers in 1977. The police were screening visitors, so Connolly, fearing delay because of his Irish name, turned back. The police questioned his friends about his identity; they refused to answer and were arrested. Connolly went to the police station to extricate them, whereupon he was himself arrested. The jury accepted the police claim that they suspected an offence of withholding information (his name), though it was sustained that reasons had not adequately been imparted for which £1 in damages was awarded.

4.20   The High Court specified in *Sher v Chief Constable of Greater Manchester Police*[42] that tort law rather than judicial review should be the vehicle for post-arrest litigation, so as to avoid a 'costs free' civil jurisdiction.

4.21   The remedy for an ongoing detention which is alleged to be unlawful is habeas corpus. In *Re Jacqueline O'Mally*,[43] twenty-four persons, including O'Mally, were arrested on 12 December, 1979 in an operation described by the police as a 'pre-emptive strike'. On 14 December, O'Mally was granted leave to apply for a writ of habeas corpus, but the hearing was adjourned twice until 19 December, which marked the expiration of the statutory detention period. The issue was then resolved, as O'Mally was charged and later pleaded guilty to involvement in a conspiracy to effect the escape from Brixton Prison of an IRA prisoner. Nevertheless, the indulgence shown towards the legality of the arrest is remarkable. In *Re Copeland*,[44] the High Court in Northern Ireland warned against litigation as a disruptive tactic and demanded that even *ex parte* applications be accompanied by affidavit from detainee rather than their lawyer.

Related special powers

4.22   Allied to s 41 is the power under s 42, by which a justice of the peace (or a sheriff in Scotland) may on the application of a constable issue a warrant in relation to specified premises if satisfied that there are reasonable grounds for suspecting that a person whom the constable reasonably suspects to be a 'terrorist' is to be found there. Ancillary search powers under PACE 1984, s 19, might also apply if specific offences are in mind, but not the PACE powers in ss 18 or 32.

4.23   Arrest and search operations may necessitate the incidental detention of all occupants of a household. This practice was approved in *Murray v Ministry of Defence*,[45] at least in connection

---

[39]   See also *Hanna v Chief Constable, RUC* [1986] NI 103; *Moore v Chief Constable, RUC* [1988] NI 456; *Stratford v Chief Constable, RUC* [1988] NI 361; *McKee v Chief Constable for Northern Ireland* [1984] 1 WLR 1358.

[40]   *Petticrew v Chief Constable, RUC* [1988] NI 192; *Davey v Chief Constable, RUC* [1988] 8 NIJB 1.

[41]   (1980) *The Times* 1 May, p 4.

[42]   [2010] EWHC 1859 (Admin) at para 82.

[43]   See *The Times* 13 December 1979, p 1, 15 December, p 2, 18 December, p 4, 19 December, p 4, 20 December, p 2, 4 January 1980, p 2, 4 March 1981, p 3, 6 March, p 4, 12 March, p 2, 18 March, p 2.

[44]   [1990] 5 NIJB 1 (QBD).

[45]   [1988] 1 WLR 692. See further *Murray v United Kingdom*, App no 14310/88, Ser A 300-A (1994); Walker, C, 'Army special powers on parade' (1989) 40 *Northern Ireland Legal Quarterly* 1.

with army searches in Northern Ireland, as a 'reasonable precaution' to stop distractions, warnings to others, or resistance.

Related powers to use force

By the TA 2000, s 114, a constable may 'if necessary use reasonable force' for the purpose **4.24** of exercising a power under the Act (with the exception of the powers to question someone at a port or border area under Sch 7, paras 2 and 3). The underlying common law powers to prevent crime or to act in self-defence or the statutory powers under the Criminal Law Act 1967, s 3, and PACE, s 117[46] can also be invoked in most terrorist policing operations. But s 114 is added since not all security operations are related to specified criminal offences.

Under s 3, the amount of force used to effect arrest such as is 'reasonable in the circum- **4.25** stances' honestly believed to exist.[47] This standard adequately reflects the right to life under Article 2 of the European Convention. In *McCann v United Kingdom*,[48] the killings of three suspected IRA volunteers on a bombing mission in Gibraltar were found to be lawful by the coroner's inquest, and the legal standards applied and procedures for review were sufficiently compliant with the Article 2 standard of absolute necessity. There remains a potential difference that s 3 embodies a partly subjective test in regard to the circumstances in which reasonable suspicion must be exercised (since extended to self-defence by the Criminal Justice and Immigration Act 2008, s 76), whereas the Court in *McCann* demanded that an honest belief must be for 'good reasons'.[49] Aside from this potential discrepancy, the laws on lethal force have generated many controversies when applied to suspected terrorists. There is a lengthy and bitter anthology of lethal shootings by security forces in Northern Ireland,[50] with a majority of those killed being unarmed but only a handful of convictions being sustained.[51]

One controversy is that a breach of Article 2 occurred in *McCann* since the security authorities **4.26** had not designed the operation to minimize loss of life.[52] They had delayed arrest in order to gather evidence and thereby exposed the population to the risk of a car bomb and increased the likelihood of lethal force against the suspects. So Article 2 embodies a positive aspect (a state duty to protect) as well as a negative duty (not to take lives without absolute cause) which is not adequately reflected by s 3.[53]

---

[46] See also Criminal Law Act (Northern Ireland) 1967; *Gillies v Procurator Fiscal, Elgin* [2008] HCJAC 55, para 11.

[47] See Law Commission, *Offences against the Person and General Principles* (No 218, Cm 2370, 1993); Rogers, J, 'Justifying the use of firearms by policemen and soldiers' (1998) 18 *Legal Studies* 486.

[48] App no 18984/91, Ser A 324 (1995). See further *Bubbins v United Kingdom*, App no 50196/99, 17 March 2005; Code of Conduct for Law Enforcement Officials (UNGA 34/169 of 17 December 1979) art 3.

[49] Ibid para 200. Compare *Kelly v MOD* [1989] 3 NIJB 1; *Kelly v United Kingdom*, App no 17579/90, 13 January 1993; *Andronicou v Cyprus*, App no 25052/94, 1997-IV, para 192; *Gül v Turkey*, App no 22676/93, 14 December 2000, para 82.

[50] See Murray, R, *State Violence: Northern Ireland 1969–1997* (Mercier Press, Dublin, 1998); *Operation Banner* (Army Code 71842, London, 2006) para 431.

[51] Ní Aoláin, F, *The Politics of Force* (Blackstaff, Belfast, 1999) p 110.

[52] App no 18984/91, Ser A 324 (1995) para 205. See also the arguments about shooting to wound (para 212) which are not accepted domestic policy.

[53] See *Farrell v Secretary of State for Defence* [1980] 1 WLR 172; *Farrell v United Kingdom*, App no 9013/80, DR 30, p 96 (1982).

4.27 Secondly, potential dissonance with Article 2 arises through the interpretation in the House of Lords in *Reference under section 48A*,[54] whereby lethal force could be used to prevent the escape of a suspected terrorist in South Armagh even though attack was not imminent. Lord Diplock stated that a soldier would be acting unreasonably only if

> no reasonable man (a) with the knowledge of such facts as were known to the accused or reasonably believed by him to exist (b) in the circumstances and time available to him for reflection (c) could be of the opinion that the prevention of the risk of harm to which others might be exposed if the suspect were allowed to escape justified exposing the subject to the risk of the harm to him that might result from the kind of force that the accused contemplated using.

4.28 Thirdly, some commentators have questioned the rejection of a defence of excessive (unreasonable) force which might transform murder into manslaughter. In *R v Clegg*, a soldier who fired lethal shots at a vehicle checkpoint without a reasonable basis for suspecting a terrorist mission or a threat to comrades rather than a joyrider was not excused from the murder conviction until new ballistic evidence raised doubts as to the relevant marksman.[55] A later concession to the plight of the user of lethal force is granted by the Criminal Justice and Immigration Act 2008, s 76. The court is reminded that 'a person acting for a legitimate purpose may not be able to weigh to a nicety the exact measure of any necessary action'.

4.29 To combat some of these potential problems, the Ministry of Defence has issued more detailed advice to soldiers in Northern Ireland by means of the 'Yellow Card'.[56] The Yellow Card gives guidance in accessible, non-legal language which is in places stricter than law, for instance by encouraging prior oral warnings.[57] Other sets of rules have been produced for non-lethal baton rounds[58] and for the response to suicide attacks (Operation Kratos).[59]

4.30 As well as encountering problems in the application of the rules, the procedures for investigating killings have also proven unsatisfactory. Investigations by way of coroners' inquests raise expectations which cannot be satisfied by that circumscribed forum,[60] which is why wider judicial inquiries have been instituted, as outlined in Chapter 2. But the government has struggled to find a forum to its satisfaction—one which will meet the demands of Article 2 for an inquiry which is independent, effective, prompt, and open[61] but at the same time will not reveal sensitive information or become an unwieldy inquisition on government policy.

---

[54] [1977] AC 105 at 137. Compare *Basic Principles on the Use of Force and Firearms by Law Enforcement Officials* (Eighth United Nations Congress on the Prevention of Crime and the Treatment of Offenders, Havana, 1990) Principle 9; (Irish) Law Reform Commission, *Defences in Criminal Law* (LRC 95-2009) para 3.126.

[55] [1995] 2 WLR 80. See further Stannard, JE, 'Excessive defence in Northern Ireland' (1992) 43 *Northern Ireland Legal Quarterly* 147; Standing Advisory Committee on Human Rights, *20th Report for 1994–95* (1994–95 HC 506) ch 2 para 35; *Rowe Report*, paras 173 *et seq*; Yeo, S, *Unrestrained Killings and the Law* (Oxford University Press, Delhi, 1998) ch 3; *R v Martin (Anthony)* [2001] EWCA Crim 2245.

[56] Amnesty International, *Killings by Security Forces and Supergrass Trials* (London, 1988) p 10; Northern Ireland Office, *Guide to the Emergency Powers* (Belfast, 1990) Pt I, para 11.

[57] See Standing Advisory Committee on Human Rights, *19th Report for 1993–94* (1993–94 HC 495) ch 2 para 51. For the 'normal' rules, see National Police Improvement Agency, *Manual of Guidance on the Management, Command and Deployment of Armed Officers* (Wyboston, 2009) para 2.39. See further *Basic Principles on the Use of Force and Firearms by Law Enforcement Officials* (Eighth United Nations Congress on the Prevention of Crime and the Treatment of Offenders, Havana, 1990) Principle 10; *Guerro v Colombia*, 45/1977 HR GAOR 37 Sess Supp 40 (1980) Annex XI.

[58] Association Of Chief Police Officers, *Guidelines on the Use of Baton Rounds and Firearms in Situations of Serious Public Disorder* (see Northern Ireland Human Rights Commission, *Baton Rounds*, Belfast, 2003).

[59] Operation Kratos (Metropolitan Police Service, London, 2005).

[60] See Doherty, F, and Mageen, P, *Investigating Lethal Force Deaths in Northern Ireland* (NIHRC, Belfast, 2006).

[61] See *Jordan v United Kingdom*, App nos 24746/94, 28883/95, 30054/96, 37715/97, 4 May 2001.

Ministers do not accept that the traditional inquest can overcome the 'insurmountable difficulty',[62] even though evidence can be kept confidential on public interest grounds.[63] The alternative blueprint of a model of inquests in secret, without a jury, and headed by a specially appointed, vetted coroner, under the Counter-Terrorism Bill 2007–08, Pt VI,[64] was eventually abandoned.

Prime reliance is to be placed on the public inquiry under the Inquiries Act 2005, albeit that   **4.31** it is denigrated on grounds of independence and secrecy.[65] Additionally, the Coroners and Justice Act 2009, s 11 and Sch 1, allows for the suspension of the normal inquest.[66] By s 41 and Sch 10, the Lord Chief Justice may nominate a High Court or Circuit judge to conduct an investigation into a person's death. By s 45(3), Coroners Rules may provide for the exclusion of all persons in the interests of national security.[67]

As well as disputes about the format of the inquiry, grievous delays have occurred.[68] These   **4.32** delays, the narrow nature of inquests in Northern Ireland, and the policy of leaving investigations wholly in the hands of the police resulted in multiple complaints where breaches of Article 2 were sustained.[69] The principal remedies have included the establishment in 2005 of the Historical Enquiries Team,[70] investigations by the Police Ombudsman for Northern Ireland, and work by coroners to reduce substantially the backlog of cases.[71]

The most recent dispute concerned the shooting of Jean Charles de Menezes in 2005,[72]   **4.33** which resulted in 2007 in the conviction of the Metropolitan Police for failing to ensure safe systems of work under the Health and Safety at Work etc Act 1974. No individual officer faced criminal or disciplinary charges, but there were criticisms of the management of operations and of media manipulation. Reviews into the use of firearms remained as an

---

[62] Joint Committee on Human Rights, *Government Responses to the Committee's 20th and 21st Reports and other correspondence* (2007–08 HL 127, HC 756) p 19.

[63] See ibid, para 135. Compare Joint Committee on Human Rights, *Government Responses to the Committee's 20th and 21st Reports and other correspondence* (2007–08 HL 127, HC 756) p 17. For case law see *McKerr v Armagh Coroner* [1990] 1 WLR 649; *Devine v Attorney General for Northern Ireland* [1992] 1 All ER 609; *Re Wright* [2003] NIQB 17; *Re McKerr* [2004] UKHL 12; *Re Jordan* [2004] NICA 29.

[64] See Joint Committee on Human Rights, *Counter-Terrorism Policy and Human Rights: Counter Terrorism Bill* (2007–08 HL 172, HC 1077) para 116; House of Lords Constitution Committee, *Counter Terrorism Bill: The role of ministers, Parliament and the judiciary* (2007–08 HL 167) para 57; McGahey, C, 'Jury out on terror bill' (2008) 158 *New Law Journal* 508.

[65] See Chapters 1 and 11.

[66] See Hansard HC vol 492 col 68ws (15 May 2009), Jack Straw; Joint Committee on Human Rights, *Legislative Scrutiny: Coroners and Justice Bill* (2008–09 HL 94/HC 524).

[67] An inquest is public even if evidence is given behind a screen: *R v Newcastle upon Tyne Coroner, ex parte A* (1998) *The Times* 19 January.

[68] See Ní Aoláin, F, *The Politics of Force* (Blackstaff, Belfast, 1999) p 152.

[69] See *McKerr, Shanahan, Jordan, Kelly v United Kingdom*, App nos 28883/95, 37715/97, 24746/94, 30054/96, 4 August 2001; *McShane v United Kingdom*, App no 43290/98, 28 August 2002; *Finucane v United Kingdom*, App no 29178/95, 1 October 2003; *Brecknell, McCartney, McGrath, O'Dowd, and Reavey v United Kingdom*, App nos 32457, 34575, 34651, 34622, 34640/04, 27 November 2007.

[70] See House of Commons Northern Ireland Committee, *Policing and Criminal Justice in Northern Ireland* (2007–08 HC 333).

[71] See Ministers' Deputies, 1020th DH Meeting (Council of Europe, Strasbourg, 2008).

[72] Independent Police Complaints Commission, *Stockwell One: Investigation into the shooting of Jean Charles de Menezes at Stockwell underground station on 22 July 2005* (London, 2007), *Stockwell Two: An investigation into complaints about the Metropolitan Police Service's handling of public statements following the shooting of Jean Charles de Menezes on 22 July 2005* (London, 2007). See Kennison, P and Loumanksy, A, 'Shoot to kill' (2007) 47 *Crime, Law & Social Change* 151; Neyland, D, 'Surveillance, accountability and organisational failure' in Goold, BJ and Neyland, D, *New Directions in Surveillance and Privacy* (Willan, Cullompton, 2009).

administrative level and outcomes mainly took the form of modified command and training structures.[73]

4.34 Finally, an emergent area of debate around lethal force concerns the targeted killings of terrorists. One such technique involves the assignment by agents who seek out and kill their target, such as the killing (probably by Israeli agents) in Dubai in 2010 of Mahmoud al-Mabhouh, a Hamas official. The criticism of the United Kingdom government was forthright because some of the assault team used fake British passports. The Foreign Secretary of the day, David Miliband, condemned the abuse of the passports but not the operation itself.[74] The other tactic of targeted killings, unmanned aircraft system (drone) attacks, involves an ally whose handiwork cannot so easily be disowned even when it exceeds the bounds of the lawful use of force.[75]

Implementation

4.35 Arrest rates are modest in volume compared to 'normal' powers under which 1,458,347 arrests were made for recorded crime in 2008–09.[76] Compared to data given previously by Lord Carlile for 2001 to 2007, the column for charging is related to terrorism arrests, whether under s 41 or not, which may have inflated the charging rate (which was 31 per cent in Lord Carlile's data). The rates for 'normal' arrests were 43 per cent for charges plus 14 per cent for cautions in 1997.[77] Lord Carlile's data for 2001–05 also revealed that the type of terrorism suspected was mainly 'international' (80%), compared to Irish (15%) or domestic (5%). The location for arrest during that period was a port in just 11 per cent of cases, underlining the indigenous nature of terrorism. Further analysis of the period from 2005/06 to 2008/09 reveals that males accounted for 94 per cent of arrests and 96 per cent of charges. Age groups are similar to criminal activity: 15% were under 18, 24% were 18–20 years, 26% were 21–24, 24% were 25–29, and 20% were 30 and over.[78] As for ethnicity, Whites were 20% of arrests, 25% of arrests resulting in a charge, and 22% of those charged; Blacks were 14%, 37%, and 22%, Asians 41%, 24%, and 43% (see Tables 4.1 and 4.2).

4.36 Northern Ireland rates are similar but reflect Irish counter-terrorism.

4.37 A key role in the operation of Pt V powers in Britain is played by the National Joint Unit situated at New Scotland Yard, which is the police group made up of officers from the Metropolitan Police Counter Terrorism Command plus seconded officers from elsewhere.[79] The NJU provides advice,[80] monitoring, and filtering for government Ministers of applications

---

[73] See Metropolitan Police Authority, *Stockwell Scrutiny* (London, 2008); Metropolitan Police Service, *Response to the MPA Stockwell Scrutiny* (London, 2009); HMIC, *Stockwell–MPS Progress* (Metropolitan Police Authority, London, 2009). The sufficiency of these responses is being questioned in *da Silva v the United Kingdom*, App no 5878/08.

[74] Hansard HC vol 508 cols 133, 138 (23 March 2010).

[75] See Kretzmer, D, 'Targeted killing of suspected terrorists' (2005) 16 *European Journal of International Law* 171; Gross, E, *The Struggle of Democracy Against Terrorism* (University of Virginia Press, Charlottsville, 2006) ch 8; Murphy, J and Radsan, AJ, 'Due process and the targeted killing of terrorists' (2009) 32 *Cardozo Law Review* 405.

[76] Povey, D et al, *Police Powers and Procedures England and Wales 2008/09* (Home Office 06/10, London, 2010) p 11.

[77] See Phillips, C, and Brown, D, *Entry into the Criminal Justice System* (Home Office Research Study 185, London, 1998).

[78] 37 per cent were under 21 in 2007/08: ibid p 15.

[79] HC Debs vol 193 col 369, 24 June 1991, Kenneth Baker. There were then seventeen assigned officers.

[80] See Lord Carlile, *Report on the Operation in 2001 of the Terrorism Act 2000* (Home Office, London, 2002) para 5.28.

Table 4.1 Arrests under s 41 in Great Britain[a]

Date	Terrorism arrests			Charged (% of arrests)	Convictions (% of charged)	Other action: eg deport or control (% of arrests)
	s 41	*Other*	*Total*			
2001/02	95	14	109	38 (35%)	12 (32%)	13 (12%)
2002/03	236	38	274	94 (34%)	34 (36%)	40 (15%)
2003/04	178	13	191	90 (47%)	21 (23%)	20 (10%)
2004/05	156	12	168	47 (28%)	21 (45%)	11 (7%)
2005/06	273	12	285	78 (27%)	39 (50%)	15 (5%)
2006/07	191	22	213	102 (48%)	47 (46%)	17 (8%)
2007/08	156	75	231	76 (54%)	27 (36%)	19 (8%)
2008/09	123	67	190	73 (38%)	16 (22%)	18 (9%)
Total	1,408	253	1,661	598 (36%)	217 (36%)	153 (9%)

[a] Source: Home Office Statistical Bulletins.

Table 4.2 Arrests under s 41 in Northern Ireland[a]

Year	Arrests	Charges (% of arrests)
2001/02	239	62 (26%)
2002/03	240	97 (40%)
2003/04	339	102 (30%)
2004/05	231	77 (33%)
2005/06	273	72 (26%)
2006/07	177	57 (32%)
2007/08	130	34 (26%)
2008/09	174	40 (23%)
2009/10	169	36 (21%)
Total	1,972	577 (29%)

[a] Source: NIO Statistics & Research Branch. Note: 2001 from 19 February.

for the exercise of policing powers. It also receives security inquiries from ports and checks suspects against databases (there were 51,956 such checks in 1998).[81] These roles are undertaken elsewhere by the Police Service of Northern Ireland.

The implementation of arrest operations has implications for media and community **4.38** relations. Undue media manipulation may prejudice both the effectiveness and fairness of an investigation. An illustration is Operation Pathway, which was billed as 'a very big terrorist plot' by Prime Minister Gordon Brown, in turn condemned by Lord Carlile as 'an unwelcome distraction'.[82] At the same time, community impacts must also be considered since early release of facts can contribute to community assurance. Police briefings about the arrests of Mohammed Abdulkahar and Abul Koyair in Forest Gate in 2006 were criticized as

---

[81] See (Rowe) *Report of the Operation in 1998 of the Prevention of Terrorism (Temporary Provisions) Acts* (Home Office, 1999) Appendix F.

[82] Lord Carlile, *Operation Pathway* (Home Office, London, 2009) para 40. See also House of Commons Home Affairs Committee; *Police and the Media* (2008–09 HC 75) para 13.

self-serving by the House of Commons Home Affairs Committee, which advised the issuance of detailed and enforceable guidelines to govern briefings by police officers or civil servants.[83] Following the de Menezes shooting, the Metropolitan Police responded through the work of the Communities Together Strategic Engagement Team.[84] Lord Carlile contributed the further suggestion that the police should consider the release of information through some vetted senior local officials.[85]

Foreign comparisons

4.39   Under the Republic of Ireland's Offences against the State Act 1939, s 30,[86] the police officer may

> without warrant . . . arrest any person . . . whom he suspects of having committed or being about to commit or being or having been concerned in the commission of an offence under any section or sub-section of this Act or an offence which is for the time being a scheduled offence . . . or whom he suspects of carrying a document relating to . . . or . . . being in possession of information relating to . . . any such offence as aforesaid.

Arrest solely for the possession of information may take the power beyond the confines of Article 5(1).[87] In line with s 41, the suspicion often derives from information provided by superiors,[88] and technical precision is not required for the reasons given on arrest.[89]

4.40   One notable feature is the extent to which the power has been applied in non-terrorism situations, such as 'gangsterism', a practice which was accepted as constitutional in *People (DPP) v Quilligan*.[90] This invitation to promiscuity may undercut the arguments for reliance upon the concept of scheduled offences rather than the promethean term 'terrorism'. However, much of the fault lies within the ill-designed scheduling power in s 36, which simply allows loosely related offences such as malicious damage to be listed by order.[91] As argued in Chapter 1, scheduled offences must be set alongside a factual context—group action and a prolonged campaign—so as to avoid these problems. Another problem under s 30 is that any precision of reference to specific offences is compromised by the requisite level of suspicion which need be just '*bona fide* held and not unreasonable'.[92] By contrast, the link to offences does reduce the opportunities for general intelligence-gathering, which has been held to be wrongful in *People (DPP) v Shaw*.[93]

---

[83]   House of Commons Home Affairs Committee; *Police and the Media* (2008–09 HC 75) paras 12, 28.
[84]   Metropolitan Police Authority, *Stockwell Scrutiny* (London, 2008); Metropolitan Police Service, *Response to the MPA Stockwell Scrutiny* (London, 2009).
[85]   Lord Carlile, *Operation Pathway* (Home Office, London, 2009) paras 109–112.
[86]   See (Hederman) *Report of the Committee to Review the Offences against the State Acts, 1939–1998 and Related Matters* (Dublin, 2002) ch 7; Hogan, G, and Walker, CP, *Political Violence and the Law in Ireland* (Manchester University Press, Manchester, 1989) p 192.
[87]   See ibid para 7.45; *Maloney v Ireland* [2009] IEHC 291.
[88]   *People (DPP) v O'Shea* [1990] 8 ILT 158; *People (DPP) v Cahill* [2001] 3 IR 494; *People (DPP) v Tyndall* [2005] 1 IR 593; *Walshe and Belfode v Fennessy* [2005] 3 IR 516.
[89]   *People (DPP) v Byrne* [1998] 2 IR 417.
[90]   [1986] IR 495 at 509–10. See also *People (DPP) v Walsh* [1986] IR 722; *People (DPP) v Byrne* [1998] 2 IR 417.
[91]   See Offence against the State Act 1939 (Scheduled Offences) Orders 1972 (SI 1972/142, SI 1972/282).
[92]   [1986] IR 495 at 507. See (Hederman) *Report of the Committee to Review the Offences against the State Acts, 1939–1998 and Related Matters* (Dublin, 2002) para 7.68.
[93]   [1982] IR 1.

Assessment and conclusions

4.41 Most arrestees under s 41 arouse suspicion of specific arrestable offences (including conspiracy or special preparatory offences under the terrorism legislation) and are detained with possible prosecution in mind, similar to ordinary suspects but with less focus on offences rather than deeds. Consequently, it may be inferred that the special consequences of arrest under s 41 are of prime distinction. These features afford the opportunity to gather information or to disrupt dangerous activities. The gathering of intelligence is said to be a 'crucial' strategy in dealing with terrorism,[94] and it may in any event be difficult to disentangle intelligence-gathering from forensic interrogation.[95] The low ratio of arrests to ensuing criminal charges in terrorism cases compared to 'normal' arrests does seem to corroborate that intelligence-gathering and also disruption are important objectives. In this way, special arrest powers evidently are meant to serve the interests of 'Pursue' by allowing pre-emptive arrests but also serve 'Protect'.

4.42 The police verdict is that special arrest powers have proven the most 'critical' measure in successive anti-terrorist legislation.[96] The validity of this police endorsement could only be proven through in-depth studies of the uniqueness of the s 41 power in given cases. Aside from the detailed glimpse in Operation Pathway, there is insufficient data to be conclusive.

4.43 An alternative view of s 41 is that it affords excessive and oppressive powers. Several disadvantages can flow from this. First, there is damage to the legitimacy of the criminal justice system through miscarriages of justice.[97] A direct causal effect might be traced through those cases which depended on confessions. The *May Inquiry Final Report*, following the case of the Guildford Four, acutely observed that 'If all the safeguards of PACE are necessary to avoid miscarriages of justice then it must be recognized that in terrorist cases greater risks of injustice are accepted than in the ordinary course of criminal cases.'[98] Fortunately, the reliance on confessions has diminished in recent years.

4.44 The second danger is to community relations, which derives from concern about how suspects from a given community are targeted for arrest and then treated in detention. The perception of police targets is said to be that they are detained 'primarily because they are Irish'[99] or, one might say now, because they are perceived as 'Muslim'. In this way, the legislation is said to have 'constructed a suspect community' and amounts to institutionalized racism.[100] The Equality Impact Assessment carried out in relation to the Counter-Terrorism Bill[101] unearthed strong impressions that the powers were unfairly targeted against Muslims, as a result of which they were less willing to volunteer help to the police. An acute example concerns the arrests in Forest Gate in 2006. The police claimed they were working on a reliable

---

[94] Wilkinson, P, *Terrorism versus Democracy* (Frank Cass, London, 2000) p 105.
[95] *Rowe Report*, 126.
[96] *Lloyd Report*, para 4.14.
[97] See Walker, C (ed), *Miscarriages of Justice* (Oxford University Press, Oxford, 1999) ch 2.
[98] May, Sir John, *Report of the Inquiry into the circumstances surrounding the convictions arising out of the bomb attacks in Guildford and Woolwich in 1974, Final Report* (1993–94 HC 449) para 21.8.
[99] Hillyard, P, *Suspect Community* (Pluto Press, London, 1993) p 7.
[100] Ibid 257, 258.
[101] (Home Office, London, 2008) pp 4, 5. Compare Defence Science and Technology Laboratory, *What Perceptions do the UK Public have Concerning the Impact of Counter-terrorism Legislation Implemented since 2000?* (Home Office Occasional Paper 88, London, 2010) p 18 which reports growing opposition to extension of detention periods.

intelligence report that Abul Koyair and Mohammed Abdul Kahar were manufacturing a chemical weapon. In the raid, the elder brother, Kahar, was shot in the shoulder. The Independent Police Complaints Commission recommended that the police should apologize to the families involved as well as recognize the impact on their communities.[102] Yet, this claim of community disenchantment is not clear-cut, and the 'suspect community' thesis may not be replicable[103] since Muslims do not form such a homogenous and concentrated community as nationalists in Northern Ireland, nor does the scale of security operations resemble the Irish experience.

4.45 Adopting a rights audit, one should uphold as proportionate a special initial power to arrest so as to allow for a broad inquiry and for intelligence-gathering or disruption, which secures public safety and may lead to further criminal investigations or may trigger executive disposals such as control or deportation orders. However, any security gains from s 41 under Article 5(1)(c) of the European Convention must be set against effective guarantees against the abuse of liberty. The basis in reasonable suspicion is one such guarantee, compared to the Irish equivalent. In other respects, the guarantees against abuse are lacking. There is no guidance equivalent to PACE Code G (for the statutory power of arrest by police officers). Another deficiency is that s 41 is not limited by the 'necessity criteria', as specified by PACE, s 24(4).[104] 'Necessity' here should also require the prioritization of PACE powers ahead of s 41. Next, the excessive use of s 41 for intelligence-gathering could be curbed by a 'scheduled' offence approach, as was argued in Chapter 1. Even more radical would be the abolition of s 41 as a power to arrest, leaving only special extensions to PACE periods of detention.

4.46 On the standard of accountability, there are many deficiencies. The level of information provision about what is crucial for arrest, charging, or extended detention is very limited. Subject to the obscurity of the processes, Parliament has tried to apply close scrutiny, as has the Independent Police Complaints Commission which has called in all complaints relating to terrorism arrests and also suggested that they be filmed.[105] The performance of the judiciary is more variable, though *Raissi* suggests a growing willingness to delve deeper.

C. Detention Following Arrest

Introduction and background

4.47 The detention power subsequent to arrest under s 41 affords the police the widest opportunities for investigations and departs considerably from the PACE norms (Scottish laws are more restrictive still). Section 41(3) allows for police-sanctioned detention of up to forty-eight hours. The detention period may then be extended for further judicially authorized periods which can last up to twenty-eight days from arrest, as laid down in Sch 8. The person can be detained pending the relevant applications: s 41(5), (6). A refusal of an extension (unless no grounds then exist for arrest) does not mean immediate release if there is unexpired time

---

[102] IPCC, *Independent Investigations into Complaints made following the Forest Green counter-terrorist operation on 2 June 2006* (London, 2007) p 8.

[103] Greer, S, 'Human Rights and the struggle against terrorism in the United Kingdom' [2008] *European Human Rights Law Review* 163.

[104] See Serious Organised Crime and Police Act 2005, s 110; Police and Criminal Evidence (Amendment) (Northern Ireland) Order 2007, SI 2007/288, art 15.

[105] See *The Times* 18 January 2005, p 2.

already allowed: s 41 (7), (8). Lord Lloyd recommended four days as the maximum.[106] The maximum period stood at seven days from 1974 until 2003.

Provisions

Judicial scrutiny at forty-eight hours—warrant of further detention

The first important waypoint in the process of review of the need for prolonged detention **4.48** arises at forty-eight hours. The authorization rules are set out in Pt III of Sch 8. The process involves an application for a 'warrant of further detention' under Sch 8, para 29 which may be made by a police superintendent or higher rank or, following amendments in the TA 2006, s 23, a Crown Prosecutor in England and Wales, the Lord Advocate or a procurator fiscal in Scotland, or the Director of Public Prosecutions for Northern Ireland. Even before the changes in the 2006 Act, there existed in Scotland a protocol between police and prosecution whereby applications are made only with the agreement of the procurator fiscal who will also attend the relevant hearing and speak to the application.[107] However, applications elsewhere within fourteen days are left to the police,[108] and prosecutors take the lead after fourteen days.[109] Up to 2007, just two applications under the TA 2000 were refused in England and Wales; seven others were granted for a period shorter than requested.[110]

If granted, a warrant of further detention shall expire not later than the end of the period of **4.49** seven days from arrest or a lesser specified period.[111] If a lesser period is granted and more time is needed, the next application should be under para 36 (below) rather than a repeat application under para 29 (as used to be case under the formulation of para 36(1) before amendment in 2006). The form of warrant is set out in the Magistrates' Courts (Forms) (Amendment) Rules 2001.[112]

The application is to 'a judicial authority', so as to comply with Article 5(3) of the European **4.50** Convention. The definition of a 'judicial authority' is (a) in England and Wales, a designated district judge (magistrates' court); (b) in Scotland, the sheriff; and (c) in Northern Ireland, a county court judge, or a designated resident magistrate. The involvement of judicial personnel departs appreciably from the position under the PT(TP)A 1989, pursuant to which the Home Secretary or Northern Ireland Secretary reviewed these applications. This absence of judicial oversight sparked a successful challenge under Article 5(3) before the European Court of Human Rights in *Brogan and others v United Kingdom*.[113] Even the shortest of the four periods of detention concerned, namely four days and six hours, fell outside the requirement of being 'brought promptly before a judge'. The legal consequence was recourse to derogation under Article 15 which was upheld in *Brannigan and McBride v United Kingdom*.[114]

---

[106] *Lloyd Report*, paras 9.10, 9.22.
[107] Hansard HL vol 677 cols 1206–7 (25 January 2006), Baroness Scotland.
[108] Crown Prosecution Service, *Scrutiny of Pre-Charge Detention in Terrorist Cases* (London, 2007) para 11.
[109] Hansard HC vol 478 col 81 (23 June 2008), Tony McNulty.
[110] Crown Prosecution Service, *Scrutiny of Pre-Charge Detention in Terrorist Cases* (London, 2007) para 12.
[111] See TA 2006, s 23.
[112] SI 2001/166.
[113] *Brogan v United Kingdom*, App nos 11209, 11234, 11266/84, 11386/85, Ser A 145-B (1988). See further *McEldowney and others v United Kingdom*, App no 14550/89, Res DH(94) 31; *O'Hara v United Kingdom*, App no 37555/97, 2001-X.
[114] App nos 14553/89, 14554/89, Ser A 258-B (1994). See further *Marshall v United Kingdom*, App no 41571/98, 10 July 2001; *Kerr v United Kingdom*, App no 40451/98, 10 July 2001; Marks, S, 'Civil liberties at the margins' (1995) 15 *Oxford Journal of Legal Studies* 69.

4.51 The desire to avoid continued reliance upon the palliative of derogation was resolved by the TA 2000 with the judicial involvement at forty-eight hours.[115] The notice of derogation was withdrawn when the Act came into force. A less heralded outcome of the reforms has been to extend the permissible period of detention for international terrorist suspects. Since the derogation notice was justifiable only in the case of the situation of Northern Ireland, it was the practice not to detain international suspects for more than four days.[116] However, given the insertion of judicial oversight, the seven-day detention power can be applied to all categories of suspects.

4.52 The insertion of independent judicial scrutiny and the determination to live without derogation should be welcomed, but not all applauded the change. The Official Opposition felt:[117]

> . . . unconvinced that it is legitimately a judicial function, rather than an Executive one. The decision to extend detention under existing legislation is usually based on intelligence material in the hands of the Executive that cannot be considered appropriate for judicial consideration. The information is often of such a sensitive nature that it cannot be disclosed to a detainee or his legal adviser without compromising the source of the intelligence, thus endangering lives or impeding an investigation. By giving that power to a judicial authority, the judiciary would inevitably be seen as part of the investigation and prosecution process, which could bring its independence into question.

4.53 These views correlate closely with the arguments of the UK government in *Marshall v United Kingdom*,[118] when it was opposing a challenge to the then executive-based system of detention review. However, the proposition that judges cannot handle sensitive intelligence evidence and cannot operate without sufficient disclosure to the accused is belied by their deployment as reviewers in other security contexts (such as the Special Immigration Appeal Commission Act 1997) and by the compromises made under the doctrine of public interest immunity.

4.54 Mechanisms by which a warrant of further detention at this first waypoint may be obtained are further related in Pt III of Sch 8. By para 30, an application for a warrant, which may be written or oral, must be made within the initial forty-eight hours or within six hours of the end of that period (if not reasonably practicable to make it within forty-eight hours). Consideration by the judicial authority must likewise take place within those time limits save for adjournments to enable legal representation (para 35), so in practice an application will often commence well within the 48-hour mark. When making an application, a notice must be given to the detainee, and it must state the grounds upon which further detention is sought (para 31). The reference to 'grounds' rather than 'reasons' means that set formulae are cited which do not reveal the details of the investigation.[119] The discretion of the judicial authority to grant an extension is limited by para 32. The judicial authority must be satisfied that (a) there are reasonable grounds for believing that the further detention of the person to whom the application relates is necessary to obtain relevant evidence (relating to proof that he is a 'terrorist' within s 40) whether by questioning him or otherwise or to preserve relevant

---

[115] *Lloyd Report*, para 9.20.
[116] Hansard HC Standing Committee D, cols 182, 183 (25 January 2000), Charles Clarke.
[117] Hansard HC vol 341 col 172 (14 December 1999), Ann Widdecombe.
[118] App no 41571/98, 10 July 2001, p 8.
[119] See *R v Officer in charge of Police Office, Castlereagh, ex parte Lynch* [1980] NI 126.

evidence or pending the result of an examination or analysis of any relevant evidence or of anything the examination or analysis of which is to be or is being carried out with a view to obtaining relevant evidence;[120] and (b) the investigation in connection with which the person is detained is being conducted diligently and expeditiously.

The statement of these criteria is an improvement over the predecessor legislation (which **4.55** contained none). However, they remain opaque compared to the 'Colville criteria'—a listing of reasons originally appearing in the *Colville Report* of 1987[121] and then promulgated to police forces as a guide.[122] They were never comprehensive (interrogation of the detainee is not mentioned) but include:

1. Checking of fingerprints.
2. Forensic tests.
3. Checking the detainee's replies against intelligence.
4. New lines of enquiry.
5. Interrogation to identify accomplices.
6. Correlating information obtained from one or more other detained person in the same case.
7. Awaiting a decision by the DPP.
8. Finding and consulting other witnesses.
9. Identification parade.
10. Checking an alibi.
11. Translating documents.
12. Obtaining an interpreter and carrying out the necessary interview with his assistance.
13. Communications with foreign police forces sometimes across time zones and language difficulties.
14. Evaluation of documents once translated and further investigated.

It follows that lengthy abeyances between interviews will not necessarily be interpreted by the courts as lack of due diligence since other forms of inquiry may still be ongoing. In *Oscar v Chief Constable of the RUC*,[123] a lull in interviews for over three hours was accepted as consistent with a *bona fide* investigation.

A further procedural improvement in the 2000 Act, and one again in keeping with Article **4.56** 5(3) of the European Convention, is that by para 33, the detainee shall be given an opportunity to make oral or written representations to the judicial authority and shall be entitled to be legally represented at the hearing, if necessary following an adjournment.[124] However, the right to make representations does not necessarily entail a hearing. Under para 33(3), the judicial authority may exclude the detainee or any representative from any part of the

---

[120] The ground relating to forensic testing added under the TA 2006, s 24, was added in response to challenge by judicial review in Northern Ireland: Hansard HC vol 832 col 918 (2 November 2005), Charles Clarke.

[121] *Colville Report*, para 5.16.

[122] Home Office Circular No 27/1989: Prevention of Terrorism (Temporary Provisions) Act 1989, para 4.11.

[123] [1992] NI 290.

[124] See Legal Advice and Assistance (Scope) Regulations 2001, SI 2001/179; Legal Advice and Assistance (Amendment) Regulations 2001, SI 2001/191; Criminal Defence Service (General) (No 2) Regulations 2001, SI 2001/1437, para 4(k); Criminal Defence Service (General) (No 2) (Amendment) Regulations 2002, SI 2002/712; Advice and Assistance (Assistance by Way of Representation) (Scotland) Amendment (No 2) Regulations 2001, SSI 2001/43, as consolidated in the Advice and Assistance (Assistance by Way of Representation) (Scotland) Regulations 2003, SSI 2003/179.

hearing. The judicial authority may also, if there are reasonable grounds established under para 34, on an application from the police or prosecution, withhold information from either or both of the detainee or any representative. Relevant grounds are that disclosure could lead to evidence being interfered with or harmed, relevant property (subject to possible investigation or forfeiture or confiscation) being removed or lost, other suspects being alerted, and other persons being interfered with or injured; the prevention of an act of terrorism becoming more difficult as a result of a person being alerted, or the gathering of information about terrorism being interfered with. Yet more grounds relate to the possible benefit from criminal conduct where the recovery of the value of the property constituting the benefit would be hindered if the information were disclosed.[125]

4.57 The detainee and any representative are automatically excluded from the hearing of an application under para 34. This blanket rule may be inconsistent with an effective judicial hearing under Article 5(3) whereby the judicial officer has 'the obligation of hearing himself the individual brought before him'.[126]

4.58 The courts take seriously the right to make representations. In *Re Quigley*,[127] the Northern Ireland High Court warned that failure to take account of representations might result in the quashing of a decision to extend detention.

4.59 In *Ward v Police Service for Northern Ireland*,[128] the House of Lords upheld the exercise of the power under para 33 to exclude the detainee and lawyer from sensitive aspects of police representations—such as an indication of the issues they wanted next to explore or the formulation of questions. Even so, their Lordships warned that judges who allow exclusion must shoulder an enhanced duty to check the police application. However, scepticism should be shown to Lord Bingham's flourish that the suppression of evidence is 'conceived in the interests of the detained person and not those of the police'.[129] Though the absence of the suspect may encourage the 'careful and diligent' judge to push the police as to their grounds, the judges have no independent means of scrutiny nor do they later review whether the police followed the lines of inquiry delineated to the judge.

4.60 Arising from Operation Pathway, the length of detentions (up to fourteen days) was upheld in *Sher v Chief Constable of Greater Manchester Police*.[130] It was evident that close scrutiny has been given to the grounds for loss of liberty, with the review District Judge imposing strict limits.[131] The more general argument that the Sch 8 scheme breached Article 5(4) of the European Convention was rejected on the ground that, although there could be secret hearings, the judge was an active participant.[132]

4.61 The prospect of appearance in person was further reduced by s 75 of the Criminal Justice and Police Act 2001. The judicial authority may direct that the hearing and all representations be effected by communications links and not in the physical presence of the detainee or of any

---

[125] As amended by the Proceeds of Crime Act 2002, Sch 11, para 39.
[126] *Schiesser v Switzerland*, App no 7710/76, Ser A 34 (1979) para 31.
[127] [1997] NI 202.
[128] [2007] UKHL 50.
[129] Ibid para 27.
[130] [2010] EWHC 1859 (Admin).
[131] Ibid para 58.
[132] Ibid para 123.

legal representative. Video links are now used in 80 per cent of cases[133] and are encouraged by para 33(9), whereby, 'If in a case where it has power to do so a judicial authority decides not to give a direction under sub-paragraph (4), it shall state its reasons for not giving it.' This presumption should be reversed, as it fails to pay sufficient weight to liberty where inconvenience of production is minimal.[134] A video link is not as effective a safeguard for discerning oppression or physical welfare as appearance in person.[135] When a video link is used, the police must arrange for a secure and distinct area within the police station to serve as a courtroom (including no photography).

Judicial reviews of extensions beyond seven days—extensions of warrants

The second waypoint in the detention power occurs at seven days. To authorize detention beyond this point, a warrant of further detention must be issued under para 36, two versions of which have prevailed since 2003. By the Criminal Justice Act 2003, s 306, the specified period could be extended by the same judicial authorities as under para 29 to a period ending not later than the end of the period of fourteen days beginning with the arrest. This extension, which came into force on 20 January 2004, was barely debated in Parliament. The main arguments for the change were marshalled by Lord Carlile[136] and related to the difficulties of identifying and interpreting foreigners, as well as arranging specialist legal advice and religious observances, plus the delays in forensic testing and computer analysis.   **4.62**

The provisions in s 306 were trumped by the extension to twenty-eight days by s 23 of the TA 2006 which came into force on 25 July 2006. For applications which take the detention period up to fourteen days, there remains an echo of s 306 since the decision is by the same judicial authority as under para 29 provided no application has previously been made to a senior judge in respect of that period. However, whenever the application for extension takes the period beyond fourteen days, it must be heard by 'a senior judge', meaning a judge of the High Court or of the High Court of Justiciary (para 36(7)).[137] At this point, the Crown Prosecution Service's Counter-Terrorism Division will become involved in the application process.[138] The application will involve open source and sensitive material, and the defendant will be given a summary of lines of inquiry to date and in the future, subject to sensitivity.[139] The court should consider the lines of inquiry, the timetable, the nexus to the charging decision, and evidence of due diligence such as hours worked.[140]   **4.63**

---

[133] Joint Committee on Human Rights, *Counter-Terrorism Policy and Human Rights: 28 Days, Intercept and Post-charge Questioning* (2006–07 HL 157/HC 394) para 75.

[134] *Allen v United Kingdom*, App no 18837/06, 30 March 2010 para 46.

[135] See *R v Chief Constable of Kent Constabulary, ex parte Kent Police Federation Joint Branch Board* (1999) *The Times* 1 December; *Report to the United Kingdom Government on the Visit to the United Kingdom carried out by the European Committee for the Prevention of Torture and Inhuman and Degrading Treatment* (CPT/Inf (2008) 27) para 8 and *Response of the United Kingdom Government* (CPT/Inf (2008) 28) para 14; Joint Committee on Human Rights, *Counter-Terrorism Policy and Human Rights: 28 days, Intercept and Post-charge Questioning* (2006–07 HL 157/HC 394) para 79.

[136] Hansard HL vol 653 cols 957–9 (15 October 2003); Lord Carlile, *Report on the Operation in 2002 and 2003 of the Terrorism Act 2000* (Home Office, London, 2004) para 111. Since 2001, 16 out of 212 detentions had lasted for six days or more: Hansard HL vol 654 col 1296 (11 November 2003).

[137] See Hansard HC vol 439 col 326 (9 November 2005), Charles Clarke. For arguments about recourse to a judge, see Lord Carlile, *Proposals by Her Majesty's Government for Changes to the Laws against Terrorism* (Home Office, London, 2005) paras 64, 67; Hansard HL vol 676 col 1157 (13 December 2005), Lord Lloyd.

[138] See Crown Prosecution Service, *Scrutiny of Pre-Charge Detention in Terrorist Cases* (London, 2007) para 1.

[139] Ibid para 6.

[140] Ibid paras 8, 9.

4.64 Each grant of further detention cannot endure more than seven days (subject to the twenty-eight-day maximum) from the expiration of the previously granted period (para 36(3)(b)). A shorter period than seven days may either be requested or imposed by the senior judge, but it must be inappropriate for the normal seven days to apply (para 36(3AA)). The procedural rules in paras 30 to 34 apply here.

4.65 A further safeguard instituted in 2006 is that the extraordinary extra power of detention was enacted for just one year under s 25 of the TA 2006, but it has so far been renewed by affirmative order.[141] In default of the tabling or approval of an order, the maximum period will revert to fourteen days.

4.66 Challenges to decisions to extend detention might be possible by way of judicial review or habeas corpus within fourteen days. Thereafter, a decision of a High Court judge cannot be reviewed in these ways.[142]

Police reviews

4.67 As well as the judicial authorizations, a police 'review officer'[143] must keep the validity of the detention under constant review under Pt II of Sch 8. There are parallels with PACE, s 40, but also some key differences.

4.68 By para 24, the review officer shall be an officer not directly involved in the investigation. For reviews within the first twenty-four-hour period, the review officer shall be an officer of at least the rank of inspector (but, under para 25, if an investigative officer of a higher rank gives disputed directions, the matter of review shall be referred to a superintendent or higher rank). After twenty-four hours, a superintendent or higher rank must act as reviewer. The reviews must be carried out in person by an officer present at the location of detention.[144] In practice, officers of lower rank are not allowed to 'act up' in these functions.[145]

4.69 By para 21, the first police review shall be carried out as soon as is reasonably practicable after the time of the person's arrest. Subsequent reviews shall be carried out at intervals of not more than twelve hours. The reviews may be postponed where an interviewing officer is satisfied that an interruption would prejudice the inquiry, or while no review officer is readily available, or while it is otherwise not practicable for any other reason to carry out the review (para 22).

4.70 To authorize continued detention, the officer must be satisfied that it is necessary under para 23: (a) to obtain relevant evidence (that the person is a 'terrorist') whether by questioning him or otherwise; (b) to preserve relevant evidence; (ba) to await the result of an examination or analysis of any relevant evidence;[146] (c) pending a decision whether to apply to the Secretary of State for a deportation notice to be served on the detained person; (d) pending the making of an application to the Secretary of State for a deportation notice to be served on the detained

---

141 SI 2007/2181, SI 2008/1745, SI 2009/1883. See Joint Committee on Human Rights, *Counter-Terrorism Policy and Human Rights: Annual Renewal of 28 Days* (2007–08 HL 32/HC 825, 2008–09 HL 132/HC 825).

142 See *R (Hussain) v Collins* [2006] EWHC 2467 (Admin).

143 Para 21. See further PACE Code H, para 14.

144 There is no equivalent to the Criminal Justice and Police Act 2001, s 73.

145 But there may be a power to do so under PACE, s 107, which refers to 'any other Act under which a power in respect of the investigation of offences or the treatment of persons in police custody is exercisable'.

146 See TA 2006, s 24.

person; (e) pending consideration by the Secretary of State whether to serve a deportation notice on the detained person; or (f) pending a decision whether the detained person should be charged with an offence. The review officer must also be sure that the investigations (under (a) or (b)) or the processes (under (c) to (f)) are being conducted diligently and expeditiously. Grounds (a) and (b) have in the past been in practice the most common.[147] By s 41(4), if the review officer does not authorize continued detention, the person shall be released, unless detained under other powers and subject to any application for judicial extension.

Various procedural rights must be observed during the review. First, a review officer shall grant **4.71** an opportunity to make representations (para 26).[148] Secondly, by para 27, where a review officer decides to authorize continued detention, the detained person shall be informed of rights to legal advice and to notify an outsider of his whereabouts. By para 28, the review officer shall make a written record of the outcome of the review and other relevant details in the presence of the detained person and inform him whether continued detention has been authorized, and, if so, of his grounds. There are exceptions when the detainee is incapable of understanding what is said to him, violent, or in urgent need of medical attention.

Formal police reviews terminate under para 21(4) after a judicial warrant extending deten- **4.72** tion has been issued under Pt III of Sch 8. Thus, the TA 2000 does not recognize the need for formal police vigilance beyond forty-eight hours. However, it is considered good practice that police 'welfare' checks, usually by a custody officer, should continue.[149] Furthermore, in view of the lengthier detention times now possible, para 37 (inserted by the TA 2006, s 23) requires that, beyond the forty-eight-hour limit, where it appears to the custody officer in charge of the detained person's case that any of the grounds in para 32 which were relied upon by the judicial authority or senior judge who last authorized his further detention no longer apply, the officer must arrange for the immediate release of the detainee.

Relationship to PACE rules

Several important PACE rules do not apply under the Terrorism Act detention, as is made **4.73** clear by PACE, s 51(b).

First, ss 34 and 37 of PACE are not applicable since s 41 does not involve arrest for an **4.74** offence. One result is that there is no power for the police to release on bail.[150] Given that the range of offences of terrorism now encompass peripheral involvement, it would be helpful to make a power of police bail available.[151] In *R (I) v City of Westminster Magistrates' Court*,[152] Mr Justice Collins considered whether this absence of bail breached Article 5 of the European Convention. Formal reviews at, and after, forty-eight hours were considered to meet the requirements of Article 5. It was even suggested that a police review officer could impose

---

[147] 88 per cent according to Brown, D, *Detention under the Prevention of Terrorism Act* (Home Office Research and Planning Unit paper 75, London, 1993) p 47.
[148] 6 per cent of detainees had a solicitor: ibid 47.
[149] See ibid 46.
[150] PACE Code H, para 1.6. After fourteen days, a High Court judge has common law powers to grant bail: *R v Spilsbury* [1892] 2 QB 615.
[151] Joint Committee on Human Rights, *Counter-Terrorism Policy and Human Rights, Counter-Terrorism Bill* (2007–08 HL 108/HC 554) para 54; HL Hansard vol 704 col 585 (13 October 2008); Lord Carlile, *Operation Pathway* (Home Office, London, 2009) para 94; Joint Committee on Human Rights, *Counter-Terrorism Policy and Human Rights: Bringing Human Rights Back In* (2009–10 HL 86/HC 111) para 89.
[152] [2008] EWHC 2146 (Admin).

conditions on continued detention for specific terrorist offences,[153] though it is unclear how this squares with PACE, s 51.

4.75 Another result of s 51(b) is that there is no need to end pre-charge detention because there is sufficient evidence for a charge—as is further clarified by s 41(7). However, any detention which goes beyond that point may breach Article 5(1)(c) of the European Convention, since it can no longer be said that detention is necessary 'for the purpose of bringing him before the competent legal authority'.

4.76 Next, difficulties might arise with terrorist detainees who are ill. Examples include Mohammed Abdul Kahar, who was shot by police during arrest in 2006,[154] and Dr Kafeel Ahmed, who was severely burnt (and later died) in the attack on Glasgow Airport in 2007.[155] If the person is so ill that there is no formal police arrest, the clock does not run, but the police may choose to arrest so as to impose security. Another scenario is where a suspect is arrested but becomes unfit for interview. Rules allowing the suspension of the detention clock while in hospital, under PACE, s 41(6), do not apply. Assimilation of PACE and the Terrorism Act would seem advisable here.

4.77 Finally, in *ex parte Lynch*, Lord Chief Justice Lowry could foresee no bar on arrest 'twice in quick succession under the same provision . . .'.[156] The practice has been complacently described as 'disquieting [but not] oppression'.[157] However, these assertions that serial arrests can lawfully be undertaken involving s 41 should be rejected as threatening individual liberty and negating the detention scheme in Sch 8, save perhaps in three situations. The first is when the first arrest was by a soldier under the JSA 2007, s 22 (described in Chapter 11); Parliament expressly envisaged that rearrest by the police could follow this short spell of detention. The second is when the later arrest is carried out to charge the person immediately with an offence; this sequence does not negate the statutory limitations on detention. The third is where the subsequent arrest is based on substantially fresh evidence—equivalent to PACE, ss 41(9), 42(11), 43(19).

Implementation

4.78 The use of extended detention (beyond twenty-four hours) far exceeds the rate under PACE, which is below 1 per cent,[158] but most detentions under s 41 still persist for less than forty-eight hours. Arguably the closest scrutiny should focus on detentions between twenty-four hours and seven days, which have a low rate of charging compared to later segments and compared to the charging rate of 71 per cent under PACE (in 2008/09) for those held on warrants of further detention beyond twenty-four hours (see Table 4.3).

4.79 Before the era of the TA 2000, and mainly therefore focused upon Irish terrorist suspects, the total average interviewing time in Britain was 3 hours 8 minutes and the total average detention length

---

[153] Ibid paras 9, 22.

[154] IPCC, *Independent Investigations into Complaints made following the Forest Green counter-terrorist operation on 2 June 2006* (London, 2007).

[155] Lord Carlile, *Report on Proposed Measures for Inclusion in a Counter-Terrorism Bill* (Cm 7262, London, 2007) para 43.

[156] [1980] NI 126 at 128. See Walker, CP, 'Arrest and rearrest' (1984) 35 *Northern Ireland Legal Quarterly* 1.

[157] *Colville Annual Report for 1987*, para 3.6.

[158] Povey, D et al, *Police Powers and Procedures England and Wales 2008/09* (Home Office 06/10, London, 2010) p 27.

Table 4.3 Detention periods in Britain 2001/02–2008/09[a]

Detention less than 24 hours (% within this period)		% of total detentions
Released without charge	452 (70%)	
Charged	128 (20%)	
Other disposal eg caution, bailed, immigration	62 (10%)	
Total	642	46%
Detention between 24 and 48 hours		
Released without charge	171 (65%)	
Charged	66 (25%)	
Other disposal eg caution, bailed, immigration	27 (10%)	
Total	264	19%
Detention between 48 hours and 7 days		
Released without charge	132 (35%)	
Charged	185 (50%)	
Other disposal eg caution, bailed, immigration	51 (14%)	
Total	368	26%
Detention between 7 and 14 days		
Released without charge	34 (25%)	
Charged	95 (69%)	
Other disposal eg caution, bailed, immigration	9 (7%)	
Total	138	10%
Detention beyond 14 days		
Released without charge	3 (27%)	
Charged	8 (73%)	
Other disposal eg caution, bailed, immigration	0 (0%)	
Total	11	1%
Overall		
Released without charge	792 (56%)	
Charged	482 (34%)	
Other disposal eg caution, bailed, immigration	149 (10%)	
Total	1,423	100%

[a] Source: Home Office Statistical Bulletins.

was 28 hours 23 minutes,[159] with 22 per cent being held for more than forty-eight hours. These rates are much longer than PACE 1984, where the average detention is around six hours.[160]

In Northern Ireland, old habits die hard, and no detention lasted beyond seven days until 2008 (see Table 4.4). Most charges are brought within forty-eight hours. During the above period, just two applications for extension were refused. One related to Colin Duffy and others, arrested in 2009 for the murder of two soldiers in Antrim;[161] Duffy was immediately rearrested and charged.   **4.80**

---

[159] Brown, D, *Detention under the Prevention of Terrorism Act* (Home Office Research and Planning Unit paper 75, London, 1993) pp 31, 50.
[160] Brown, D, *PACE 10 Years On* (HORS no 155, London, 1997); Bucke, T and Brown, D, *In Police Custody* (HORS no 174, London, 1998).
[161] *Re Duffy* [2009] NIQB 31.

Table 4.4 Detention periods in Northern Ireland 2001–2008[a]

Year	Arrests	Extended detention (% of arrests)	Extended detention (days)		Charged (% of arrests)	Time of charge (a) up to 48 hrs (b) beyond 48 hrs
			48 hrs –7 days	*7–14 days*		
2001	179	9 (5%)	9	n/a	50 (28%)	(a) 45 (b) 5
2002	236	12 (5%)	12	n/a	80 (34%)	(a) 74 (b) 6
2003	359	23 (6%)	23	n/a	121 (34%)	(a) 112 (b) 9
2004	230	16 (7%)	16	0	69 (30%)	(a) 60 (b) 9
2005	249	24 (10%)	24	0	73 (29%)	(a) 61 (b) 12
2006	215	14 (7%)	14	0	62 (29%)	(a) 54 (b) 8
2007	145	2 (1%)	2	0	43 (30%)	(a) 41 (b) 2
2008	150	24 (16%)	22	2	28 (19%)	(a) 14 (b) 14
Total	1,763	124 (7%)	122	2	526 (30%)	(a) 461 (b) 65

[a] Source: Northern Ireland Office Research and Statistics Branch.

4.81 The controversy around the period beyond fourteen days under the TA 2006 elicited the following more detailed information, which shows a restrained usage and a high rate of charging (Table 4.5). All occurred in Britain in relation to international terrorism. No convictions were sustained against any of the three detainees held for the full twenty-eight-day period arising out of the 'Liquid Bomb' plot.[162]

4.82 There is no evidence that the overall rate of charging is increased by the use of special powers, but the rate has improved compared to the last decade,[163] and the elongation of detention periods does correlate with charging. Following PACE arrests, 52 per cent are charged and 17 per cent are cautioned.[164] Thus, the ratios have remained significantly lower for terrorism arrests, despite the exhaustive investigations and enhanced resources in play. At the

Table 4.5 Detentions beyond fourteen days from 25 July 2006 to 31 March 2009[a]

Period of detention	No of detainees	Charged
14 to 15 days	1	1
18 to 19 days	1	1
19 to 20 days	3	3
27 to 28 days	6	3
Total	11	8

[a] Home Office Statistical Bulletin 18/09, p 21.

---

[162] Sidhu, J, 'Twenty-eight days—what's the verdict?' (2010) 174 *Criminal Law & Justice Weekly* 103; Bajwa, AN, and O'Reilly, B, 'Terrorising the innocent' (2010) 160 *New Law Journal* 481.

[163] Brown, D, *Detention under the Prevention of Terrorism Act* (Home Office Research and Planning Unit paper 75, London, 1993) p 49 gives a rate for charging and other action of 31 per cent.

[164] Phillips, C and Brown, D, *Entry into the Criminal Justice System* (Home Office Research Study 185, 1998) p 82.

same time, it has already been argued that one of the main purposes of s 41 arrests is intelligence-gathering, and so the lower rate of charging may be expected. This claim makes it very difficult to judge 'productivity'. Intelligence is not made public in courts, and the police do not vouchsafe disclosure of the gains to the amount or quality of intelligence.

The lessons from Operation Pathway for the handling of detention powers relate to the **4.83** rigour of the review and the need to involve the Crown Prosecution Service as soon as possible, perhaps with the clarification of a protocol.[165] The CPS were of the opinion that there was insufficient evidence to justify an extension beyond fourteen days, a view not shared by the police, who perhaps were unaware that, as highlighted in *Re Duffy*, the judge's scrutiny will extend to substance as well as to the efficiency of the process.[166]

Foreign comparisons

Comparative law exercises are fraught with danger because of explicit and subtle differences **4.84** in laws and practices. However, no other country within Western Europe, nor comparable common law jurisdiction elsewhere, matches the United Kingdom's grant of twenty-eight days' police detention.[167]

For instance, police pre-charge detention in Australia can extend for twenty-four hours of **4.85** questioning time (Crimes Act 1914, ss 23CA, 23DA, as amended by the Anti-Terrorism Act 2004).[168] The person can be held further during 'Dead Time' (during which no questioning is permitted: s 23CB). Following the Glasgow Airport bombing Dr Mohamed Haneef, cousin of Kafeel Ahmed who died later from burns during the attack, was held for twelve days in 2007. The absence of any cap on dead time was criticized by the Clarke Inquiry into his case.[169] Less comparable to s 41 are Federal 'preventative detention orders' which endure for up to forty-eight hours in connection with an imminent terrorist attack or to preserve evidence after an attack but not for the purposes of questioning (Criminal Code Act 1995, Division 105, as inserted by the Anti-Terrorism Act (No 2) 2005).[170]

In the Republic of Ireland, terrorist suspects can be detained for forty-eight hours under the **4.86** Offences against the State Act 1939, s 30(3). The initial period of detention is twenty-four hours, but it can be extended for another twenty-four hours by a chief superintendent (or a superintendent if expressly authorized). The period was extended by a further twenty-four hours (to a total of seventy-two hours) under the Offences against the State (Amendment) Act 1998, s 10, by warrant of a District Court judge.[171] Rearrest for the same offence is only

---

[165] Lord Carlile, *Operation Pathway* (Home Office, London, 2009) paras 48–51, 76, 91; Joint Committee on Human Rights, *Counter-Terrorism Policy and Human Rights: Bringing Human Rights Back In* (2009–10 HL 86/HC 111) para 70.

[166] Ibid paras 81–88.

[167] See further Foreign & Commonwealth Office, *Counter-Terrorism Legislation and Practice: A Survey of Selected Countries* (London, 2005); JUSTICE, *From Arrest To Charge In 48 Hours* (London, 2007); Russell, J, *Charge or Release: Terrorism Pre-Charge Detention Comparative Law Study* (Liberty, London, 2007).

[168] The initial four hours is extended by application to a magistrate. Note also state laws which can be used for detention: Terrorism (Police Powers) Act 2002 (NSW); Terrorism (Community Safety) Act 2004 (Qld); Terrorism (Community Protection) Act 2003 (Vic).

[169] *Report of the inquiry into the case of Dr Mohamed Haneef* (Canberra, 2008) p 248 (suggesting seven days). See also *Haneef v Minister for Immigration and Citizenship* [2007] FCA 1273. See also Law Council of Australia, *Anti-Terrorism Reform Project* (Canberra, 2009) para 5.4.4; *Attorney General's National Security Legislation Discussion Paper* (Canberra, 2009) p 114.

[170] See Lynch, A, and Williams, G, *What Price Security?* (UNSW Press, Sydney, 2006) ch 3.

[171] See *Finnegan v Member in Charge, Gantry Garda Station* [2007] 4 IR 62.

allowed under judicial warrant under s 11, a clearer pathway than under s 41. An even longer period (seven days, consisting of two days on police authority followed by periods of three and then two days on judicial authority) applies to specified offences, including murder involving the use of firearms or explosives (Criminal Justice Act 2007, s 50). The extra than 'normal' period of detention is not discriminatory since it applies without invidious selection.[172] Some latitude has been afforded to the police to move the detainee from the lawful place of detention under s 30(3) (normally a police station) so as to assist with the investigation[173] but not if done in bad faith for the purposes of harassment or to negate access rights.[174]

4.87   The US Supreme Court stated in *County of Riverside v McLaughlin*[175] that detention based on probable cause is allowed for forty-eight hours and may endure further in emergency or other extraordinary circumstances. Aliens suspected of terrorism may be detained for seven days under the USA PATRIOT Act (8 USC s 1226(a)(5)). Other immigration powers[176] and powers to detain 'material witnesses'[177] have been stretched to the point of abuse in relation to terrorism suspects.

4.88   As well as these statutory powers, Presidential authority to detain 'unlawful combatants' was invoked in 2001.[178] As a result, various detention facilities sprang up, above all at Guantánamo Bay where 759 persons have been held.[179] This parallel system of detention and adjudication is now heavily compromised by adverse US Supreme Court interventions[180] as well as rejection by the Obama administration.[181] It has also been repudiated by successive British Ministers.[182] The war on terror model does not fit guiding principles such as respect for the rule of law and international humanitarian and human rights law,[183] and so will not be dissected further.

4.89   Turning to European examples, pre-charge police detention (*garde à vue*) in France is limited to six days (Criminal Procedure Code, art 706-88).[184] Two days are granted on police authority, followed by two twenty-four-hour judicial extensions (by the prosecutor,

---

[172]   *People (DPP) v Quilligan (No 3)* [1993] 2 IR 305.

[173]   *People (DPP) v Farrell* [1978] IR 13. See also *State (Walsh) v Maguire* [1979] IR 372.

[174]   *People (DPP) v Kelly* [1983] IR 1.

[175]   500 US 44 (1991).

[176]   8 USC ss 1226, 1531–37. A system of detention of foreign terrorism suspects under s 1226a has not been implemented. See Lawyers Committee for Human Rights, *Assessing the New Normal* (Washington DC, 2003) ch 3.

[177]   18 USC s 3144. See *al-Kidd v Ashcroft* (2010) US App LEXIS 5604; Chesney, R, 'The Sleeper Scenario' (2005) 42 *Harvard Journal on Legislation* 1; Human Rights Watch and ACLU, *Witness to Abuse* (New York, 2005); Cook, JG, 'The detention of material witnesses and the Fourth Amendment' (2006) 76 *Mississippi Law Journal* 585.

[178]   Military Order of 13 November 2001, *Detention, Treatment, and Trial of Certain Non-Citizens in the War Against Terrorism* (66 Fed Reg 57, 833, 2001). See Yoo, JC, *The Powers of War and Peace* (University of Chicago Press, Chicago, 2003); Wittes, B, *Law and the Long War* (Penguin, New York, 2008) chs 1–6.

[179]   <http://www.dod.mil/pubs/foi/detainees/detaineesFOIArelease15May2006.pdf>.

[180]   See especially *Rumsfeld v Padilla* 542 US 426 (2004); *Rasul v Bush* 542 US 466 (2004); *Hamdi v Rumsfeld* 542 US 507 (2004); *Hamdan v Rumsfeld* 548 US 557 (2006); *Boumediene v Bush* 533 US 723 (2008).

[181]   Executive Orders 13492 and 13493 (74 FR 4897 and 4901); Detention Policy Task Force, *Memorandum for the Attorney General and for the Secretary of Defense* (Washington DC, 2009).

[182]   See Rose, N, 'Goldsmith calls for US to close down Guantanamo and back the rule of law' (2006) *Law Society Gazette* 21 September, p 6; Miliband, D, '"War on terror" was wrong' (2009) *The Guardian* 15 January 2009, p 29.

[183]   See Bianchi, A (ed), *Enforcing International Norms Against Terrorism* (Hart, Oxford, 2004) chs 1–4; Pejic, J, 'Terrorist acts and groups' (2004) 75 *British Yearbook of International Law* 71; Zerrougui, C et al, *Situation of Detainees in Guantanamo Bay* (E/CN.4/2006/120, New York, 2006).

[184]   See Law 86-1020 of 9 September 1986, as amended by Law 2006-64 of 23 January (by 2006. The detention scheme was upheld in *Bulent* (2010/31 QPC).

investigating magistrate, or the *juge des libertés et de la détention*) plus two further which may be authorized without meeting the detainee by the *juge*. Thereafter, judicial authorities take control of the investigation which can involve up to four years' detention for serious terrorist crimes (article 145-2).[185] In Spain, arrest under police authority is for a maximum of forty-eight hours additional to the normal seventy-two hours (Criminal Procedure Law, s 520*bis*)[186] or ten days if there is a state of emergency (Law 4/1981 art 16). Investigating magistrates can take up to four years to prepare the case for trial. This period of detention during the inquisition is not comparable to police detention.

In conclusion, all these jurisdictions have operated shorter police detention periods than the **4.90** United Kingdom. The same applies even to jurisdictions facing more extreme circumstances, such as Sri Lanka,[187] Turkey,[188] or Zimbabwe.[189] However, this finding is subject to the civil law practice of prolonged judicial investigation and to common law substitute approaches, such as judicial examination and military detention.

Assessment and conclusions

Accountability and constitutional governance of the detention powers presents a mixed **4.91** picture. On the one hand, the Parliamentary debates in 2000, 2006, and 2008 (though not in 2003) were exhaustive. On the other hand, the level of statistical information has been scantier than data for pre-2000 legislation.[190]

The key criticisms within a rights audit are based on incursion upon liberty, and assessments **4.92** may be conducted on grounds of productivity in terms of results, proportionality, the wider drawbacks to society, and the sufficiency of safeguards.

As for productivity, the claim is made that 'the Parliamentary decision to increase pre charge **4.93** detention limits from 14 to 28 days has been justified. We have been able to bring forward prosecutions that otherwise would not have been possible.'[191] But hard evidence that the charging rate is increased by special powers or by the elongation of detention periods could only be discerned by more detailed case studies than currently available, as already discussed in relation to implementation.

Next is the argument from common sense rather than proof—that more incriminating **4.94** evidence is likely to be uncovered if more time is afforded to investigators.[192] Of course, it is always possible that some evidence will emerge at a later date, but on that argument, police detention should be unlimited and liberty should be abolished. As Lord Carlile states, there is 'no logical answer' to setting a maximum which might be required for

---

[185] For breaches of art 5, see *Morgain v France*, App no 17831/91, 30 November 1994; *Debboub v France*, App no 37786/97, 9 November 1999; *Bernard v France*, App no 27678/02, 26 September 2000; *Mouesca v France*, App no 52189/99, 3 June 2003.

[186] Organic Law 4/1998 of 25 May 1998. Police detention for ten days without judicial authorization after seventy-two hours was declared unconstitutional: STC 199/1987 of 16 December 1987.

[187] Prevention of Terrorism (Temporary Provisions) Act 1979, s 7 (72 hours).

[188] Code of Criminal Procedure, arts 250, 251: 5 days 12 hours or 7 days 12 hours in a state of emergency.

[189] Criminal Procedure and Evidence (Amendment) Act 2004 (twenty-one days).

[190] See Joint Committee on Human Rights, *Counter-Terrorism Policy and Human Rights: Annual Renewal of 28 Days* (2007–08 HL 32/HC 825) para 19.

[191] Home Office, *Possible Measures for Inclusion into a Future Counter-Terrorism Bill* (London, 2007) para 12.

[192] Ibid pp 6, 7.

operational reasons.[193] Yet, the entire sacrifice of societal values for chance operational gains is neither lawful under the European Convention (as shall be discussed below) nor the wish of Lord Carlile.

4.95 In summary, the extension of detention beyond the four-day norm is yet to be empirically justified, and there is no compelling factual case for an extension beyond fourteen days. Probably the best one can say is that police experience does show that arrest up to fourteen days has been constantly valued, but there are alternatives in terms of control orders or continued surveillance.

4.96 Regarding the proportionality of any gains to the objective of 'Pursue' set against the infringement of liberty, comparisons with PACE and with other jurisdictions have already been drawn. One might next consider proportionality in the context of the posited problems to be overcome.

4.97 First, there is the amount of evidence generated by the complex and multiple attacks such as those on 21 July 2005 (when there were 38,000 exhibits, 80,000 CCTV videos, 1,400 fingerprints, and 160 crime scenes).[194] But the generation of a large amount of evidence does not demonstrate that it was impossible within fourteen days to amass sufficient evidence for a prosecution to succeed on the basis of serious charges. A surfeit of evidence is not a reason for more detention time. Another case in point is the 2006 airline plot,[195] which did result in acquittals on some of the most serious charges. But one problem was the early police intervention being precipitated by the arrest of Rashid Rauf in Pakistan.[196] Any amount of extra post-arrest time could not make up for lost pre-arrest covert evidence-gathering. Nor has it been alleged that released arrestees have engaged in further terrorism.

4.98 A second aspect of complexity concerns the investigation of computer evidence and especially the difficulties posed by the sheer volume of data and also encrypted evidence. However, voluminous evidence can be sifted post-charge so long as some can be pinpointed for a charge, while encryption has been encountered in very few cases and does not appear to be a pressing operational concern, as already outlined in Chapter 2.

4.99 A third complexity argument relates to foreign linkages. But the lackadaisical response of some foreign governments (as alleged in Operation Springbourne—'the ricin plot' which spread over twenty-six jurisdictions) must be set against subsequent improvements in relations within Europe (described later in this chapter and in Chapter 6). Cooperation with Pakistan may be more uneven. The Pakistani courts refused to extradite Rashid Rauf (mentioned above), and later he escaped from custody. However, other cases have shown cooperation, such as the conviction of Rangzieb Ahmed and Habib Ahmed following the former's arrest in Pakistan.[197] In any event, to set British liberty according to the timetable of the most inefficient or corrupt foreign regime is not desirable.

---

[193] Lord Carlile, *Report on Proposed Measures for Inclusion in a Counter-Terrorism Bill* (Cm 7262, London, 2007) para 46.

[194] Hansard HC vol 438 col 341 (26 October 2005), Charles Clarke. See also Carlisle, D, 'Dhiren Barot' (2007) 30 *Studies in Conflict & Terrorism* 1057.

[195] Home Office, *Options for Pre-Charge Detention in Terrorist Cases* (London, 2007) p 5.

[196] See *The Guardian* 10 September 2008, p 11.

[197] *The Times* 19 December 2008, p 17.

Factual justifications for lengthy detention were devised in 2005 by a letter to the Home **4.100** Office from Assistant Chief Constable Andy Hayman[198] and also in a briefing note to the Home Affairs Committee.[199] But there was no public demand from the police beyond some senior officers,[200] or from the Director of Public Prosecutions,[201] or from Lord Carlile,[202] though he warned that a situation where twenty-eight days are inadequate can be expected.[203] But just one case has been put forward as actually warranting more than twenty-eight days.[204] In the 'ricin plot' of 2003 (Operation Springbourne), one alleged lead conspirator had to be allowed to leave the country, and charges against the rest did not adequately reflect the severity of the plot. At the same time, convictions were sustained for serious offences. Conversely, some practitioners in several key cases claim that fourteen days should have sufficed.[205]

The wider drawbacks to society relate again to the generation of miscarriages of justice and **4.101** also community distrust, as already discussed.

As for the sufficiency of safeguards, several other devices could be conceived in terms of **4.102** shorter time limits, a presumption of detainee presence at review hearings (and special advocates if not allowed), and fuller disclosure of evidence. The greater structuring of hearings beyond fourteen days would also be helpful with more explicit checklists to encourage judicial involvement.[206] There should also be verification of any application beyond seven days by a higher police officer such as an Assistant Chief Constable.[207] Finally, police reviews should formally continue after forty-eight hours, and police bail should be available.

As for whether the special detention regime complies with Article 5 of the European **4.103** Convention, it is true that no time limit is set in Article 5(1)(c) of the European Convention. But it would be misleading to assert that therefore there is no limit, subject to occasional judicial review to satisfy Article 5(3).[208] This interpretation assumes the infallibility of the police's reasonable suspicion and would invite them to find a conveyor belt of new reasons for suspicion or to refuse to accept that old reasons have been satisfactorily dispelled.

---

[198] (Home Office, London, 2005). See Hayman, A, *The Terrorist Hunters* (Bantam Press, London, 2009) ch 4, where the 90-day plan is said to reflect the 7 July investigation (Operation Theseus).

[199] House of Commons Home Affairs Committee, *Detention Powers* (2005–06 HC 910) Appendix.

[200] Compare Home Office, *Options for Pre-Charge Detention in Terrorist Cases* (London, 2007) p 8; Report of the Joint Committee on Human Rights, *Terrorism Policy and Human Rights* (2006–07 HL 157, HC 394) para 22; HC Hansard vol 474 col 658 (1 April 2008), Jacqui Smith; HC Hansard Public Bill Committee on the Counter-Terrorism Bill, Evidence from Sir Ian Blair and Bob Quick, 22 April 2008.

[201] HC Hansard Public Bill Committee on the Counter-Terrorism Bill, Evidence from Sir Ken MacDonald, col 58 (22 April 2008).

[202] Lord Carlile, *Report on Proposed Measures for Inclusion in a Counter Terrorism Bill* (Cm 7262, 2007) para 46.

[203] Lord Carlile, *Report on the Operation in 2008 of the Terrorism Act 2000* (Home Office, London, 2009) para 128.

[204] *R v Bourgass* [2005] EWCA Crim 1943, [2006] EWCA Crim 3397.

[205] Bajwa, AN and Duke, B, 'Pre-trial detention in terrorism cases' (2006) 156 *New Law Journal* 1578.

[206] See Lord Carlile, *Report on the Operation in 2007 of the Terrorism Act 2000* (Home Office, London, 2008) para 105.

[207] Joint Committee on Human Rights, *Counter-Terrorism Policy and Human Rights: Terrorism Bill and related matters* (2005–06 HL 75, HC 561) para 102.

[208] Compare Dickson, B, 'Article 5 of the ECHR and 28-day pre-charge detention' (2009) *Northern Ireland Legal Quarterly* 231; Stevens, L, 'Pre-trial detention' (2009) 17 *European Journal of Crime, Criminal Law and Criminal Justice* 165.

4.104 The better view is that the European Court would place a strong value on liberty and would notice the important fact that the detainee remains in police hands under Sch 8 rather than under the 'competent legal authority', as reflected in the Continental inquisitorial model. Where the tolerance for genuine police endeavours ends will be determined on a case-by-case basis.[209] But a police-led investigation, even under judicial audit, cannot be tolerated just because reasonable suspicion persists since that amounts to detention without trial beyond Article 5.

4.105 The detention powers are even more vulnerable to challenge under the remainder of Article 5. Article 5(2) requires prompt disclosure of the reasons for the arrest and the charges against the detainee.[210] If the latter is taken literally, as requiring charges to be laid promptly, then the reasoning in *Brogan* might suggest that police detention without charge for more than a few days cannot be acceptable, despite longer judicially directed detentions in civil law systems.

4.106 As for Article 5(3), the European Court held in *McKay v United Kingdom*[211] that there must be review which is prompt, automatic, and without requiring action by the detainee, conducted by an independent officer who can order release, and examining the lawfulness of the detention as well as due diligence. The mechanisms under Sch 8 go a long way to meeting these criteria. However, whether this judicial inquiry in a context going on well beyond seven days is sufficiently regular, sufficiently extensive, and sufficiently open[212] remains to be tested. In addition, the absence of bail places a reliance on habeas corpus which is a detriment compared to ordinary police detainees, though a habeas corpus hearing might be an acceptable alternative to bail under Article 5(3) and (4).[213]

4.107 Other problems arise under Article 5(4). The form of judicial hearings is not fully adversarial since disclosure is limited and might be conducted *ex parte*.[214] Nor are they based on a full review of the merits of the detention,[215] although the terms of para 32 are broad enough for the matter to be raised, and the decision by the Northern Ireland High Court in *Re Duffy* asserts that it would amount to 'neglect' if the lawfulness of the basis for the arrest was not considered.[216]

4.108 Given the doubts raised about the proportionality or even legality of existing detention powers, would it be possible to justify a period of forty-two days (as embodied in the

---

[209] The Joint Committee on Human Rights, Criminal Justice Bill (2002–03 HC 724, HL 119) advised that the extended period did not per se breach Article 5 of the European Convention (para 102).

[210] Joint Committee on Human Rights, *Counter-Terrorism Policy and Human Rights: Counter-Terrorism Bill* (2007–08 HL 50, HC 199) para 18.

[211] App no 543/03, 3 October 2006.

[212] See Joint Committee on Human Rights, *Counter-Terrorism Policy and Human Rights: 42 Days* (2007–08 HL 23/HC 156) paras 83, 84 (in three out of seventeen cases of detention beyond fourteen days the suspect was excluded); Joint Committee on Human Rights, *Counter-Terrorism Policy and Human Rights, Counter-Terrorism Bill* (2007–08 HL 108/HC 554) paras 31–33.

[213] See *Fox, Hartley, and Campbell v United Kingdom*, App nos 12244/86 and 12245/86, Ser A 182 (1990) para 45.

[214] See HC Hansard Public Bill Committee on the Counter-Terrorism Bill, Evidence from Susan Hemming, col 56 (22 April 2008). The use of *ex parte* hearings is said to be very limited: col 56.

[215] See *Garcia Alva v Germany*, App no 23541/94, 13 February 2001, para 39; Joint Committee on Human Rights, *Counter-Terrorism Policy and Human Rights, Counter-Terrorism Bill* (2007–08 HL 108/HC 554) para 21.

[216] [2009] NIQB 31 at para 26. Compare *R (Hussain) v Collins* [2006] EWHC 2467 (Admin) at para 16.

Counter-Terrorism Bill 2007–08)[217] or ninety days (as in the Terrorism Bill 2005–06)?[218] Since both versions were defeated in Parliament, it is not necessary to examine them in detail. The only further point which is worth raising and which proved influential in debates is that more apposite reforms should be undertaken. First, concentration should be upon widening the available criminal charges, a notion which has largely been achieved by the offences of engaging in preparatory actions under the TA 2006 (covered in Chapter 5). Next, there could be a widening of admissible evidence through changes in the rules relating to intercept evidence, as discussed in Chapter 2. Thirdly, there should be encouragement to rely upon the Threshold Test for prosecutions which demand reasonable suspicion based on admissible evidence at the point of charge where a serious or complex investigation is continuing and there is a reasonable expectation of further identifiable evidence becoming available within a reasonable time to meet the Full Code Test.[219] It is frequently used in terrorist cases.[220] Fourthly, there could be greater opportunities for post-charge questioning. The CTA 2008 has now implemented this tactic, which will be described later in this chapter. Fifthly, since the availability of defence lawyers can be a factor which produces delays, it is therefore highly counter-productive that changes in legal aid funding arrangements are decimating the number of available solicitors.[221]

Finally, beyond the extraordinary detention powers in the TA 2000 are precautionary **4.109** measures such as control orders and the Civil Contingencies Act 2004.[222] The triple lock of the Civil Contingencies Act 2004 was superior to any proposed for terrorism detentions, not only because of the mechanisms by which there are checks[223] but also because of the fundamental requirement of the recognition of an emergency under Pt II.[224] Whether Pt II encompasses police detention powers in a terrorism emergency became the subject of debate during the passage of the CTA 2008.[225] The contention that detention without trial can be

---

[217] See Home Office, *Options for Pre-Charge Detention in Terrorist Cases* (London, 2007); Joint Committee on Human Rights, *Counter-Terrorism Policy and Human Rights: 42 Days and Public Emergencies* (2007–08 HL 116/HC 635); House of Commons Home Affairs Committee, *The Government's Counter-Terrorism Proposals* (2007–08 HC 43); House of Lords Constitution Committee, *Counter-Terrorism Bill: The role of ministers, Parliament and the judiciary* (2007–08 HL 167).

[218] See Joint Committee on Human Rights, *Counter-Terrorism Policy and Human Rights: Terrorism Bill and related matters* (2005–06 HL 75, HC 561) and *Government Response* (2005–06 HL114/HC 888); House of Commons Home Affairs Committee, *Terrorism Detention Powers* (2005–06 HC 910).

[219] Code for Prosecutors (Crown Prosecution Service, London, 2010) para 5 (which represents a tighter formulation in so far as it requires identifiable evidence). See House of Commons Home Affairs Committee, *Detention Powers* (2005–06 HC 910) para 112; Joint Committee on Human Rights, *Counter-Terrorism Policy and Human Rights: Prosecution and Pre-Charge Detention* (2005–06 HL 240, HC 1576) para 131.

[220] See Joint Committee on Human Rights, *Counter-Terrorism Policy and Human Rights: Counter-Terrorism Bill* (2007–08 HL 50, HC 199) para 77; House of Commons Home Affairs Committee, *The Government's Counter-Terrorism Proposals* (2007–08 HC 43) para 67.

[221] There is also the problem that legal aid is not available for barristers at hearings under Schedule 8: Joint Committee on Human Rights, *Counter-Terrorism Policy and Human Rights: 42 Days* (2007–08 HL 23/HC 156) para 97.

[222] See Home Office, *Options for Pre-Charge Detention in Terrorist Cases* (London, 2007) pp 7, 11; Joint Committee on Human Rights, *Counter-Terrorism Policy and Human Rights: 42 Days* (2007–08 HL 23/HC 156) paras 54–55.

[223] See Joint Committee on Human Rights, *Counter-Terrorism Policy and Human Rights: 42 Days and Public Emergencies* (2007–08 HL 116/HC 635) paras 30–33.

[224] Home Office, *Options for Pre-Charge Detention in Terrorist Cases* (London, 2007) p 11; HC Hansard vol 474 col 658 (1 April 2008), Jacqui Smith.

[225] Joint Committee on Human Rights, *Counter-Terrorism Policy and Human Rights: 42 Days* (2007–08 HL 23/HC 156) paras 54–55.

authorized under civil emergency legislation has never been confirmed by the courts.[226] The sponsor of the 2004 Act understandably refused to rule out the possibility of detention without trial.[227] As for the limitations in s 23 of the 2004 Act, there is a difference between creating an offence punishable at a criminal trial (expressly disallowed under s 23(4)(d)) and a power of detention without trial which can then be enforced through disciplinary offences tried in the usual way (and so also avoiding the alteration for criminal proceedings). Only if 'criminal proceedings' under s 23(4)(d) can be held to include pre-trial policing powers is the use of the 2004 Act ruled out,[228] but this interpretation is not easy to sustain where one does not impact on the other.

4.110   It would be a welcome reform to clarify further these powers under Pt II of the Civil Contingencies Act 2004. The Counter-Terrorism Bill sought to exclude application of the 2004 Act, but this refinement was lost along with the forty-two-day proposal. Instead, the government's reaction was a petulant gesture by the Home Secretary[229] who flourished a draft Bill within hours of defeat of the forty-two-day proposal in the House of Lords.[230] The Counter-Terrorism (Temporary Provisions) Bill 2008, reviving forty-two-day detention but embodying few of the earlier safeguards (only an application by the Director of Public Prosecutions and an independent review of every case), was to be tabled as and when necessary.

4.111   Following the change of government in 2010, the twenty-eight-day detention power was extended only for six months, pending a fuller review by Lord Macdonald.[231]

D. The Treatment of Detainees

Introduction and background

4.112   The humane and fair treatment of terrorist suspects has long generated bitter litigation, whether in Northern Ireland[232] or in Guantánamo Bay.[233] In the light of the experience in Northern Ireland, the UK government declared in 1972 that any methods contrary to Article 3 of the European Convention were not to be countenanced.[234] It would be naïve to assume that this edict has secured universal observance, but the gradual refinement of laws and administrative rules and procedures, especially those rolled out initially in Northern Ireland pursuant to the *Bennett Report*,[235] did eventually reduce physical malpractices by the police. Further safeguards have followed in the wake of PACE and its weak emulation in Scotland.

---

[226] Compare *R v Halliday, ex parte Zadig* [1917] AC 260; *Attorney-General of St Christopher, Nevis and Anguilla v Reynolds* [1980] AC 637.

[227] Letter from Douglas Alexander to the Joint Committee on the Draft Civil Contingencies Bill, 31 October 2003. See further Walker, C and Broderick, J, *The Civil Contingencies Act 2004: Risk, Resilience and the Law in the United Kingdom* (Oxford University Press, Oxford, 2006) ch 5.

[228] See Joint Committee on Human Rights, *Counter-Terrorism Policy and Human Rights: 42 Days* (2007–08 HL 23/HC 156) para 55.

[229] See HC Hansard vol 480 col 620 (13 October 2008).

[230] See HL Hansard vol 704 col 491 (13 October 2008), Lord Dear.

[231] SI 2010/1909.

[232] See *Ireland v UK*, App no 5310/71, Ser A 25 (1978).

[233] See Duffy, H, *The 'War on Terror' and the Framework of International Law* (New York, Cambridge University Press, 2005).

[234] Hansard HC vol 832 col 743 (2 March 1972), Edward Heath.

[235] See also *Body of Principles for the Protection of All Persons under Any Form of Detention or Imprisonment* (UNGA Res 43/173 of 9 December 1988).

Part I of Sch 8 of the TA 2000 provides the contemporary framework for the treatment of **4.113** detainees. Alongside, there are supplementary guides[236] which have been largely consolidated as PACE Code H in Connection with the Detention, Treatment and Questioning by Police Officers of Persons under s 41 of, and Sch 8 to, the TA 2000.[237] PACE Code D (identification) can also apply to terrorism cases.[238]

An equivalent PACE Code H was issued in Northern Ireland in 2008.[239] In the absence of an **4.114** equivalent to PACE in Scotland, the details are contained in the Terrorism (Interviews) (Scotland) Order 2001.[240] The Lord Advocate and the Minister for Justice issued further guidelines in 2006 to Scottish Chief Constables about the detention of terrorist suspects.[241]

The regime under the codes is largely redolent of PACE. Accordingly, the detailed rules in **4.115** Code H rehearse the central role of custody officers,[242] cell accommodation, and physical needs (including special emphasis upon the need to facilitate reading materials, religious observances, and exercise);[243] cautions;[244] interviewing processes (including special efforts to explain when there are extended periods without interviews, with a heightened need to allow visits, exercise, and reading materials if the intermission is twenty-four hours or more);[245] and the taking of statements.[246]

Provisions

Location

The permissible places of detention are designated under para 1. In England and Wales, the **4.116** designated places comprise any police station[247] or prison or (additionally for persons under 18) any young offender institution, secure training centre, or other place of safety.[248] In practice, Paddington Green Police Station in London and Govan in Scotland have been specially adapted,[249] and further facilities are situated in the north of England. High security prisons are used outside Scotland for persons held for more than fourteen days, unless the detainee specifically requests otherwise and that request can be accommodated, or the transfer would hinder the investigation.[250] In Northern Ireland, the Serious Crime Suite in Antrim Police Station serves as the prime venue.

---

[236] See Hansard HL vol 684 col 311 (5 July 2006), Baroness Scotland.

[237] See Home Office Circular 23/2006. The Code does not apply to: detainees under the PTA 2005, s 5 (likely to result in short detentions only); detainees for examination under Sch 7 (a separate code under Sch 14 applies); or detainees under stop and search powers (PACE Code A applies): para 1.4. Compare *Report of the Special Rapporteur on Torture and other Cruel, Inhuman or Degrading Treatment or Punishment* (A/HRC/13/39, Geneva, 2010) paras 51–54.

[238] But see para 2.17(iii).

[239] Police and Criminal Evidence (Northern Ireland) Order 1989 (Codes of Practice) (No 4) Order 2008, SR (NI) 2008/408. Other PACE Codes are authorized by SR (NI) 2007/58. The authority is PACE(NI), art 65.

[240] SI 2001/428.

[241] Guidelines on the detention, treatment, and questioning by police officers of persons arrested under s 41 and Sch 8 of the Terrorism Act 2000 (Crown Office, Edinburgh, 2006).

[242] See PACE Code H, paras 1.15, 1.19, 2.1.

[243] Ibid, para 8.

[244] Ibid, para 10.

[245] Ibid, paras 11, 12.

[246] Ibid, Annex D.

[247] The same applies in Scotland: Guidelines 2006, para 3.

[248] Terrorism Act 2000 (Places of Detention) Designation 2006.

[249] Hansard HL vol 684 col 314 (5 July 2006), Baroness Scotland. The adaptations in Paddington Green include enhanced cell facilities (such as video entertainment), varied diet, and exercise.

[250] PACE Code H, para 14.5. Persons transferred are treated according to the Prison Rules.

4.117   Persons may be removed from the designated place only for the purposes of examination (or to establish nationality or to arrange removal from the country) under Sch 7. Once at the designated place of detention, Sch 8, Pt I, provides for routine processing, investigation, and rights to fair treatment.

Interviews and interrogation

4.118   One purpose of arrest is to allow for the interrogation of suspects. No special guides have been disclosed on the interview techniques which are profitable against terror suspects, but attempts to establish dialogue and the avoidance of challenges to self-justification may be appropriate.[251] Arising from Operation Pathway, it is revealed in *Sher v Chief Constable of Greater Manchester Police*[252] that it is the practice of the police to produce a 'Pre-Interview Briefing Document' as a basis for each session, an excellent device to encourage professionalism and transparency.

4.119   Interviews serve three objectives. The first is to uncover admissible evidence sufficient to put before a court. Though historically important, this objective has become less important because of improvements in forensic testing, the frequent legal advice to remain silent,[253] and the difficulties of extracting statements from suspects with strong motivations and in some cases anti-interrogation training.[254] Secondly, and more commonly in the light of the low charging rate, the task is to gather background intelligence information. Thirdly, there may be public safety concerns, such as the need to ensure that any bombs are located.

4.120   The differences of approach in terrorist interviews from 'ordinary' policing are narrower than in pre-2000 regimes because of various factors. One is the pervasive and incremental influence of the mainstream police practices under PACE. The police have become used to working under detailed rules of treatment, such as tape-recording and the presence of lawyers at interviews. A second is that the standards for the admissibility of the products of interviews, under PACE, ss 76 and 78, are fully applied in terrorism cases. Divergent rules in Northern Ireland, latterly set out in the TA 2000, s 76, were withdrawn in 2002.[255] As a result, the United Kingdom law reflects fully the position of international law that terrorism does not allow for any relaxation of the normal standards against ill-treatment. As stated in *Ireland v United Kingdom*:[256] 'The Convention prohibits in absolute terms torture and inhuman or degrading treatment or punishment, irrespective of the victim's conduct . . . there can be no derogation therefrom even in the event of a public emergency threatening the life of the nation.'

4.121   The absolute ban is further reflected in the offence in the Criminal Justice Act 1988, s 134, which is committed by any public official or person acting in an official capacity in the United Kingdom or elsewhere who 'intentionally inflicts severe pain or suffering on another

---

[251] See Gelles, MG et al, 'Al-Qaeda related subjects' in Williamson, T (ed), *Investigative Interviewing* (Willan, Cullompton, 2006).

[252] [2010] EWHC 1859 (Admin).

[253] Lord Carlile, *Proposals by Her Majesty's Government for Changes to the Laws against Terrorism* (Home Office, London, 2005) para 60.

[254] See *Brogan v United Kingdom*, App nos 11209, 11234, 11266/84, 11386/85, Ser A 145-B (1988) para 56; *Re Quigley* [1997] NI 202.

[255] Terrorism Act 2000 (Cessation of Effect of Section 76) Order 2002 SI 2002/2141.

[256] App no 5310/71, Ser A 25 (1978) para 163.

in the performance or purported performance of his official duties'.[257] Even as an intelligence-gathering exercise, any form of torture will be an offence under the Criminal Justice Act 1988, s 134, as well as a civil law assault.

The clearest political signal of intolerance was the issuance by Prime Minister Heath of the **4.122** Directive on Interrogation by the Armed Forces in Internal Security Operations 1972,[258] forbidding the five techniques of interrogation (hooding, wall-standing, sleep deprivation, noise disorientation, and starvation) at issue in *Ireland v United Kingdom*.

Refusal to admit evidence obtained through third party torture was sustained in *A v Secretary* **4.123** *of State for the Home Department (No 2)*,[259] which was given based on common law rules of inadmissibility of statements and abuse of process. But their Lordships did not rule out the executive taking account of torture statements for the initiation of action such as arrests or securing public safety. Further, it was left uncertain as to whether the same rules extend to inhuman and degrading treatment. Finally, while the victim need only advance some plausible evidence to raise the issue of torture, and then it is for the prosecution or tribunal to inquire, where the tribunal is left in a state of suspicion about whether torture was used, the evidence can be admitted, which could be seen as giving the benefit of the doubt to torturers.

Even assuming that forms of ill-treatment are not to be countenanced, constant vigilance is **4.124** required. Neither legal nor pragmatic doubts have prevented British agencies from resorting to torture and inhuman and degrading treatment against terrorists during colonial campaigns,[260] and inhuman and degrading treatment in Northern Ireland,[261] and in current conflicts.[262] The *Aitken Report 2008*[263] into abuse and killings in Iraq found that the 1972 Directive had 'come to be lost' by the Army. Only in 2005, with the issuance of the Ministry of Defence's document, JDN 3/05 *Tactical Questioning, Debriefing and Interrogation*,[264] were there clear new guidelines. Ongoing allegations from Iraq are being investigated by the Iraq Historic Allegations Team and two public inquiries.[265]

---

[257] See United Nations Convention against Torture and Other Cruel, Inhuman or Degrading Treatment or Punishment 1984 (1465 UNTS 85).

[258] See Hansard HC vol 832 col 743 (2 March 1972).

[259] [2005] UKHL 71. See Hickman, TR, 'Between human rights and the rule of law' (2005) 68 *Modern Law Review* 655; Lester, A and Beattie, K, 'Risking torture' (2005) 6 *European Human Rights Law Review* 565; Rasiah, N, '*A v Secretary of State for the Home Department (No 2)* Occupying the moral high ground?' (2006) 69 *Modern Law Review* 995; Human Rights Watch, '*No Questions Asked*' (New York, 2010).

[260] See (Devlin) *Report of the Nyasaland Commission of Inquiry* (Cmnd 814, London, 1959); *Report of Mr Roderic Bowen QC on Procedures for the Arrest, Interrogation and Detention of Suspected Terrorists in Aden* (Cmnd 3165, London, 1966).

[261] (Compton) *Report of an Enquiry into allegations against the security forces of physical brutality in Northern Ireland arising out of arrests on the 9 August 1971* (Cmnd 4828, London, 1972); (Parker) *Report of the Committee of Privy Counsellors appointed to consider authorised procedures for the interrogation of persons suspected of terrorism* (Cmnd 4901, London, 1972); *Bennett Report*.

[262] (Aitken) *Investigation into cases of Deliberate Abuse and Unlawful Killing in Iraq in 2003 and 2004* (Ministry of Defence, London, 2008).

[263] *An Investigation into Cases of Deliberate Abuse and Unlawful Killing in Iraq in 2003 and 2004* (Ministry of Defence, London, 2008) para 19.

[264] It is now part of JDP 2-10.1, *Human Intelligence in 2008*. See Ministry of Defence, *Joint Doctrine Publication 1-10* (London, 2006) para 209 which specifically forbids the Five Techniques.

[265] See Hansard HC vol 506 col 93ws (1 March 2010) Bill Rammell; Baha Mousa Inquiry under Sir William Gage (<http://www.bahamousainquiry.org>, following *R (Al-Skeini) v Secretary of State for Defence* [2007] UKHL 27); Al-Sweady Inquiry under Sir Thayne Forbes (<http://www.alsweadyinquiry.org>, following *R (Khuder and al-Sweady) v Secretary of State for Defence* [2009] EWHC 1687 (Admin) (No 2) [2009] EWHC 2387 (Admin)).

4.125 With all these safeguards in place, can British security authorities deal effectively with the 'ticking bomb' scenario? Leaving aside the spuriousness of the hypothetical, the dilemma has in policy been answered for the police by 'safety interview'—an off-the-record interview in order to protect life or against serious property damage under Code H paras 6.7 and 11.2. In *R v Ibrahim*,[266] the defendant, one of those charged with the attempted attacks in London on 21 July 2005, wanted to exclude as unfair evidence under PACE, s 78, the fact that he had not mentioned in the safety interview his later defence that he had been engaged in a political stunt. During the safety interview, the police had warned that his statements would be recorded and used in evidence, though, at trial, they were not the prime evidence of the offence. The court admitted the evidence, even though legal advice had also been improperly refused.[267] These safety interviews are to be welcomed as a response to the pressures to torture, but, so as to uphold the good work undertaken since the *Bennett Report*, such statements should be treated as being without evidential merit, as in *R v Caraher*.[268] In that case, convictions were based on incriminating statements which had been recorded alongside informal notes made at the repeated request of the defendant (McGinn), who wanted to conceal the fact from other defendants and even from his own solicitor that he was offering to collaborate. In contrast to *Ibrahim,* no cautions were given, and so the court could more easily form a reasonable doubt as to whether McGinn would have made those admissions if he had been cautioned and other provisions in relation to the conduct of interviews had been observed.

4.126 Aside from the legal position, both the utility and morality of torture remain contested. As for utility, some refute the idea that any useful information can be obtained, though some might distinguish information given at the point of application of pain from coerced conditioning over time.[269] As for morality, some commentators remain shockingly open to the argument that Article 3 treatment may be an inevitable feature of counter-terrorism policy[270] rather than an occasional human failing in extraordinary circumstances where even the European Court of Human Rights can find some room for mitigation of penalty.[271]

Identification and searches

4.127 The identification and search powers in the TA 2000, Sch 8, are variants on those in Pt V of PACE.[272] The power to take steps reasonably necessary to identify the individual (Sch 8, para 2) may be accomplished by photographing, measuring, or otherwise identifying the detained person. The 'other steps' could include voice recognition tests but expressly do not

---

[266] [2008] EWCA Crim 880. See Mendelle, P, and Bajwa, A, 'How safe are safety interviews? (2009) *Justice of the Peace* 132.

[267] Ibid para104. Compare *Report to the United Kingdom Government on the Visit to the United Kingdom carried out by the European Committee for the Prevention of Torture and Inhuman and Degrading Treatment* (CPT/Inf (2008) 27) para 12 and *Response of the United Kingdom Government* (CPT/Inf (2008) 28) para 19.

[268] [2000] NICA (NICC3072).

[269] See Hoare, I, *Camp 020* (Public Records Office, Richmond, 2000) pp 19, 57; Jessberger, F, 'Bad torture—good torture?' (2005) 3 *Journal of International Criminal Justice* 1059; Rumney, P, 'The effectiveness of coercive interrogation: Scholarly and judicial responses' (2006) 44 *Crime, Law & Social Change* 465.

[270] See Gross, O, 'Are torture warrants warranted?' (2004) 88 *Minnesota Law Review* 1481; Dershowitz, A, *Why Terrorism Works* (Yale University Press, New Haven, 2002) ch 4; Ignatieff, M, *The Lesser Evil* (Edinburgh University Press, Edinburgh, 2004) p 140; Waldron, J, 'Torture and positive law' (2005) 105 *Columbia Law Review* 1681; Posner, EA and Vermeule, A, *Terror in the Balance* (Oxford University Press, Oxford, 2007) ch 6.

[271] *Gäfgen v Germany*, App no 22978/05, 1 July 2010, paras 69–70. But compare *Jalloh v Germany*, App no 54810/00, 11 July 2006.

[272] PACE Code H, paras 4, 16.

include fingerprints, non-intimate samples, or intimate sampling since they are dealt with in para 10 (with records being required under para 11). The equivalent provisions in Scotland are in para 20.

Fingerprints and non-intimate samples may be taken with the appropriate consent in **4.128** writing, or without consent where a superintendent authorizes the fingerprints or samples to be taken or where the person has been convicted of a recordable offence. The fingerprints must be taken by a constable—civilian support officers may not act in these cases.[273] In the case of intimate samples, there must be written consent from the detainee,[274] as well as authorization by a superintendent under para 10. The intimate sample (aside from urine) must be taken by a registered medical practitioner or, for dental impressions, a registered dentist (para 13). Under para 12, if two or more non-intimate samples taken for the same means of analysis prove insufficient for forensic purposes, an authorization for an additional intimate sample may be given in respect of a person since released from detention, provided again that the person also consents to the sampling. Under para 11, the detainee shall be informed of the purposes of the process and the reasons for taking it by consent or the grounds on which an authorization has been given. Where consent is refused without good cause, adverse inferences may be drawn from the refusal in later proceedings (para 13).

The establishment of identity is also addressed by the ATCSA 2001, s 89 which specifies that **4.129** fingerprints can be taken from those detained under the TA 2000 in order to ascertain their identity for a wider range of purposes than those already specified in Sch 8, para 10, such as other, non-criminal, forms of disposal. Accordingly, sub-paras (6A) and (6B) to Sch 8 allow a superintendent or higher rank to authorize the taking of fingerprints without consent if the person has refused to identify himself, or the officer reasonably believes that he has given a false identity. Subsection (3) also allows the police, under sub-s (4), to examine fingerprints or DNA samples retained under TA 2000 powers when investigating a crime that is apparently non-terrorist. 'For example, a van may be stolen for use as a bomb, but recovered without any evidence of its intended terrorist use.'[275] Before this change, those records could be searched by the police for terrorism purposes, so there arose 'a risk that they will miss connections between ordinary criminal offences, which may be committed as precursors to terrorist activity, and terrorist suspects'.[276]

Along the same lines, ss 90 (England and Wales) and 91 (Northern Ireland) extend other **4.130** 'normal' search powers under PACE, s 54, to establish identity.[277] By an added s 54A, such searches may also relate to 'any mark that would tend to identify him' or 'for the purpose of facilitating the ascertainment of his identity' where the person has refused to identify himself or the officer has reasonable grounds for suspecting that a false identity has been provided. Photographs may be taken of such marks (meaning bodily features and injuries). In effect, what might otherwise have been considered an intimate search (a search of body orifices

---

[273] See Lord Carlile, *Report on the Operation in 2004 of the Terrorism Act 2000* (Home Office, London, 2005) para 82.
[274] See British Medical Association and the Faculty of Forensic and Legal Medicine, *Guidelines and Advice: Doctors asked to perform intimate body searches* (London, 2007).
[275] Hansard HL vol 629 col 711 (4 December 2001), Lord Rooker.
[276] Hansard HC vol 375 col 742 (26 November 2001), Beverley Hughes.
[277] This use of anti-terrorism legislation was criticized by the *Newton Report*, para C334.

other than the mouth) under s 55 of PACE 1984 can now be undertaken for purposes of identification rather than the investigatory or safety purposes allowed under s 55. It is expressly forbidden to use s 54A for the purposes of intimate searches within s 55 (s 54A(8)), but then it is expressly permitted under s 54A(9) to use or disclose a photograph taken under this section for any purpose related to the prevention or detection of crime, the investigation of an offence, or the conduct of a prosecution. There is no corresponding power for Scotland because of an allegedly lukewarm reaction by the Association of Chief Police Officers in Scotland.[278]

4.131 Next, s 90(2) amends PACE ss 27 and 61 regarding fingerprints taken from an arrested person to establish or check their identity.[279] It allows the taking of fingerprints without consent where, *inter alia*, there are reasonable grounds to suspect their involvement in a criminal offence and that fingerprints would tend to confirm or disprove that involvement. Where fingerprints are authorized to be taken to confirm or disprove a person's involvement in a crime, the prints can only be taken if a police inspector[280] authorizes them to be taken. Fingerprints could not previously be taken where the question is about identity.

4.132 In further pursuance of the establishment of identity, s 92 (s 93 in Northern Ireland) inserts a new s 64A after s 64 of PACE 1984 which affords a power to photograph a person who is detained at a police station with or without consent. Section 92(2) expressly allows the police to require the removal of any item or substance, such as face paint, worn on or over the whole or any part of that person's face or head and if the person does not comply, may use force under s 117 of PACE 1984. While the purpose of the measure is mainly identification, sub-s (4) does allow for photographs to be used for criminal justice purposes and for them subsequently to be retained and used for a related purpose. The taking of photographs for these purposes does not infringe Article 8.[281]

4.133 The photographing of suspects outside a police station or otherwise is not closely regulated. Suspects targeted for surveillance may fall within the RIPA, Pt II, otherwise only the loose protections of 'private life' apply under Article 8 of the European Convention.[282] In line with ss 92 and 93 inside the police station, ss 94 and 95 (in Northern Ireland) replace s 60(4A) of the Criminal Justice and Public Order Act 1994 allowing the removal of face coverings worn for the purpose of concealing identity. Sections 94 and 95 provide that in relation to the power to require the removal of face coverings only, an authorization (in the form required by sub-s (6)) may be given (under s 60AA) where an inspector reasonably believes offences may take place in that locality and that it is expedient to give such an authorization. The authorization lasts for twenty-four hours, extendable for twenty-four hours by a superintendent. It is an offence to refuse to comply. Even in Northern Ireland, there is no revival of the offence, formerly in the EPA 1996, s 35, of wearing a mask or hood in a public place for the purpose of concealing identity.

---

[278] HC Debs vol 375 col 764 (26 November 2001).

[279] Presumably because of the lesser threat from international terrorism, the measure no longer applies in Northern Ireland: Criminal Justice (Northern Ireland) Order 2004, SI 2004/1500, Sch 3. The Police, Public Order and Criminal Justice (Scotland) Act 2006, s 82 also allows the taking of fingerprints to establish identity but they may not be retained.

[280] Criminal Justice and Police Act 2001, s 78.

[281] See *(Margaret) Murray v United Kingdom*, App no 14310/88, Ser A 300-A (1994); *Kinnunen v Finland*, App no 24950/94, 15 May 1996 (Comm).

[282] See *Friedl v Austria*, App no 15225/89, Ser A 305-B (1995); *Wood v Commissioner of Police of the Metropolis* [2009] EWCA Civ 414.

Section 60 of the 1994 Act allows a blanket power to stop and search for offensive weapons **4.134**
and dangerous implements in a given locality and for a given period, provided an authorization
is given by a senior officer on the basis of a reasonable belief that incidents of serious violence
may take place in the locality and that it is expedient to give an authorization to prevent their
occurrence. Section 60 did not extend to Northern Ireland, so, using the 'valuable opportunity'
of the 2001 Act but also in the light of the use of knives in the 11 September hijackings,[283]
s 96 first inserts a new art 23B into the Public Order (Northern Ireland) Order 1987[284]
(the retention of things seized being dealt with under art 23C, inserted by s 97).

The police are expected[285] to heed the warning not to confuse the wearing of coverings **4.135**
intended as disguises with the fact that 'Many people customarily cover their heads or faces
for religious reasons—for example, Muslim women, Sikh men, Sikh or Hindu women, or
Rastafarian men or women.' The Forum against Islamophobia and Racism was not reassured and objected to these powers.[286] The Newton Committee argued that these extra
powers to remove disguises should be confined to terrorism cases.[287] It is admitted that the
motivation behind the legislation is not terrorism but 'because the police believe that the
tactic of wearing face coverings has become increasingly widespread during all kinds of events
that could lead to public disorder'.[288] Thus, the 2001 Act was used as a sly vehicle of wider
public order law reform, though the Minister of State argued that it would be impractical
to categorize in advance trespassers as terrorists or otherwise.[289]

Information sharing and retention

Several special powers have already been noted whereby the police can take prints and bodily **4.136**
samples from detainees. To secure maximum benefit from the exercise, the Home Office
proposed new powers to share these forensic materials as well as to clarify the basis for their
storage.[290]

Though the powers to take and retain fingerprints and samples are wider than under PACE, **4.137**
the purposes for which they can be utilized were originally limited by para 14 in that they could
be used only for the purpose of a terrorist investigation and not for routine criminal checks
under s 63A(1) of PACE 1984. However, the position was changed by s 84 of the Criminal
Justice and Police Act 2001 which allows the subsequent use not only for the purposes of
a terrorist investigation but also for purposes related to the prevention or detection of crime,
the investigation of an offence, or the conduct of a prosecution. Secondly, the exclusion of
checks against the fingerprints or samples under s 63A or its Northern Ireland equivalent is
diminished since the purposes of the prevention or detection of crime, the investigation of
an offence, or the conduct of a prosecution are again allowed. Thirdly, the criminal investigations
may relate to extra-jurisdictional offences.

---

[283] HC Debs vol 375 col 765 (26 November 2001), Jane Kennedy.

[284] SI 1987/463 (NI 7).

[285] PACE Code A, note 4. See Hansard HC vol 375 col 761 (26 November 2001), Beverley Hughes;
Hansard HL vol 629 col 736 (4 December 2001), Lord Rooker; Home Office Circular 32/2002: *Anti-terrorism,
Crime and Security Act 2001: Section 94 Removal of Disguises.*

[286] Submission to the Home Affairs Committee, London, 2001, para 6. See also Joint Committee on
Human Rights, *Report on the Anti-terrorism, Crime and Security Bill* (2001–02 HL 37, HC 372), para 62.

[287] *Newton Report*, para B47, C352. The reform proposal was rejected: *Home Office Response to Newton
Report*, para II.127.

[288] Hansard HC vol 375 col 760 (26 November 2001), Beverley Hughes.

[289] Ibid col 749.

[290] Home Office, *Possible Measures for Inclusion into a Future Counter-Terrorism Bill* (London, 2007) para 23.

4.138 Further data-sharing is facilitated by the CTA 2008 both by further allowing exchanges of data and also by providing legality for the collection of certain types of data. In pursuance of the latter objective, s 18 brings the personal identification data held by law enforcement organizations, such as on the Counter-Terrorism DNA Database though not confined to it, within legal regulation in regard to fingerprints or DNA samples. Without this basis, there may be challenge under Article 8.[291] These samples derive from discarded cigarettes or drinks containers while acting under Pt III of the Police Act 1997, while conducting surveillance under Pt II of the RIPA, or otherwise lawfully obtained (such as from international partners).[292] Once legally grounded in this way, the materials can be used for national security, criminal justice, or identification purposes.

4.139 Having brought all material within a legal footing whether in police criminal databases, the Counter-Terrorism DNA Database, or security services databases, the next step is to allow disclosure between these databases and with foreign agencies. This goal is achieved by ss 14 to 18 of the 2008 Act.

4.140 Section 14 allows for samples and prints obtained under PACE (s 15 applies in Northern Ireland, but Scotland awaits devolved legislation) to be utilized beyond the current purposes in ss 63A and 64 of PACE in the interests of national security,[293] or for criminal justice, or identification purposes. The police will thereby be allowed to check their PACE material, or counter-terrorism material, against the databases of the security services and vice versa.

4.141 The same trick is applied by s 16 to samples taken under Sch 8 of the TA 2000. The wording of para 14 is amended to allow cross-checking against PACE material, security service material, or material under s 18 (s 16). This means that police Terrorism Act samples can be entered on the National DNA Database.[294] It remains unlikely, however, that the security database materials will be used in court since that would require explanations of the provenance of the materials, much of which was not governed by PACE Codes.[295] Section 17 applies the same rules to Scotland.

4.142 The final aspect of the changes returns to s 18. The material covered there can be utilized by allowing a check against it or disclosing it between UK law enforcement or security agencies or indeed to 'any person' (s 18(4)), so long as it is used for proper purposes. The effect is to allow exchanges of this data with foreign policing or security agencies.[296]

4.143 Whether the gains from these changes will be amongst the principal great advances to be achieved by the Counter-Terrorism Act[297] is dubious. Most of the limitations are not legal but, as raised in Chapter 3, are based on institutional rivalries and suspicions or technical incompatibilities or the failure to invest. Nevertheless, the measures represent a worthy attempt at imparting legality and certainty.

---

[291] HC Hansard Public Bill Committee on the Counter-Terrorism Bill col 225 (29 April 2008), Tony McNulty.

[292] Hansard HL vol 704 cols 396, 397 (9 October 2008), Lord West.

[293] See Security Service Act 1989, s 1.

[294] House of Commons Public Bill Committee on the Counter Terrorism Bill col 222 (29 April 2008), Tony McNulty.

[295] Ibid col 220.

[296] Arrangements are being made for the sharing of police data under the Prüm Convention 2005 which was signed by the UK government in 2007 and is being further implemented by the Prüm Council Decision: 2008/615/JHA, Decision 2008/616/2008.

[297] Home Office, *Possible Measures for Inclusion into a Future Counter-Terrorism Bill* (London, 2007) paras 3, 23.

Accountability for the retention of data samples obtained and stored under the foregoing **4.144** rules was very weak. The system was subject only to police guidelines.[298] Oversight is by the Information Commissioner and the Forensic Science Regulator,[299] but the former is essentially responsive while the latter deals with systems not people. The Information Commissioner has called for 'data minimisation'.[300] There may also be overreach in terms of the failure to regulate the weeding out of information which might have been obtained in breach of Article 3.[301] The absence (beyond Scotland) of legal regulation of the retention of data breached Article 8 of the European Convention in *S and Marper v United Kingdom*,[302] and a remedy has now been provided by the Crime and Security Act 2010.[303]

The TA 2000, Sch 8 para 14 (which allows retention without reference to a retention period) **4.145** is amended by the Crime and Security Act 2010, s 17, which substitutes new paras 14 to 14I.[304] The retention periods are set out in paras 14B to 14E and depend on the age of the suspect, the seriousness of the offence, and whether there is a conviction (and whether it is a first conviction). For adults, fingerprints, impressions of footwear, and DNA profiles can be retained indefinitely if convicted and for six years if not convicted. Variant rules apply to persons under eighteen. Under para 14A, the physical samples, must be destroyed within six months or as soon as a DNA profile has been derived. In addition, the rules as to destruction of data are subject to a proviso, whereby a chief officer of police can determine that it is necessary to retain that material for the purposes of national security for up to two years (renewable) (para 14G). The amendments made by the CTA 2008, s 16, are preserved by para 14I, whereby retained material may be applied not only in the interests of a terrorist investigation, but also for national security, for the investigation of crime, or for identification-related purposes. Once the requirement to destroy material applies, the material cannot be used in evidence against the person to whom it relates or for the purposes of the investigation of any offence.

Finally, for material under the CTA 2008, s 18 (where covertly acquired or supplied by **4.146** overseas authorities and held on the police 'counter-terrorism database'), the current indefinite retention period is altered by the Crime and Security Act 2010, s 21. Physical samples should be destroyed within six months (s 18(3A)). Retention periods are set at three years for individuals aged under sixteen (s 18(3B)) and six years for persons over sixteen (s 18 (3C)), unless the person has been convicted of a recordable offence, in which case the material need not be destroyed. There is the usual proviso that data need to be destroyed after a further two years unless the 'responsible officer' determines that it is necessary to retain that material for the purposes of national security (s 18(3E) and (3F)).

Criticisms of these schemes during Parliamentary passage (all rejected) were broadly **4.147** threefold.[305] First, the Opposition argued that the periods were too long and suggested

---

[298] See ACPO, *Retention Guidelines for Nominal Records on the Police National Computer* (London, 2006). No policy statement has been issued by the security services.

[299] Hansard HL vol 704 col 384 (9 October 2008), Lord West.

[300] *Annual Report 2007/08* (2007–08 HC 670) p 8.

[301] See Joint Committee on Human Rights, *Counter-Terrorism Policy and Human Rights: 42 Days and Public Emergencies* (2007–08 HL 116, HC 635) paras 67, 73.

[302] App nos 30562/04, 30566/04, 4 December 2008. See also *Rotaru v Romania*, App no 28341/95, 2000-V.

[303] See Home Office, *Keeping the Right People on the DNA Database* (London, 2009).

[304] For Scotland, the Crime and Security Act 2010, s 18 amends TA 2000, Sch 8, para 20.

[305] Hansard HC Public Bill Committee on the Crime and Security Bill cols 210, 226, 256, 262 (2, 4 February 2010).

instead a retention limit of three years. Second, extensions of two years should be referred to the Crown Court and should not refer to national security. Third, the offences under the TA 2006, ss 1 and 2, should not be qualifying offences for retention since they relate to expression.

Record-taking

4.148 The keeping of full and accurate records of the treatment of a detainee is a vital element of ensuring propriety and humanity. Reflecting PACE rules, a custody record must be kept for every detainee.[306] However, the normal requirement of identification of officers is modified so that only warrant numbers and police stations are revealed.[307] Another modification is that risk assessments do not form part of the custody record and should not be shown to the detained person or their legal representative, so as to secure sensitive contingency procedures.[308]

4.149 As for records of interviews, Sch 8, para 3, deals with the audio and video recording provided they take place in a designated police station (which means that interviews at ports will not necessarily be taped). Statutory orders and codes of practice must be issued for audio recording, but the making of an order and code requiring the video recording is a matter of discretion. The Terrorism Act 2000 (Code of Practice on Audio Recording of Interviews) Order 2001[309] allows for a code of practice in connection with the audio recording. The Terrorism Act 2000 (Code of Practice on Audio Recording of Interviews) (No 2) Order 2001[310] demands that any interview shall be audio recorded in accordance with the audio code. By para 2.1 of the issued Code, the audio recording of interviews shall be carried out openly. By para 3.3, the whole of each interview shall be audio recorded, including the taking and reading back of any statement. In this way, there is no provision for 'off-the-record' conversations, though there is no definition of 'interview' and 'public safety interviews' apparently do not count.[311] Under para 5, an accurate record must also be made of each interview with a detained person, and the person interviewed must be given the opportunity under tape-recorded conditions to read the interview record and to sign it as correct or to indicate inaccuracies. By para 8, at the conclusion of criminal proceedings, or in the event of a direction not to prosecute, the working copy of the tape shall be erased.

4.150 In response to the history of abuses of prisoners, video-recording first applied in Northern Ireland, beginning with overhead silent videos under the EPA 1996, s 53. A power in relation to full video recording in Northern Ireland subsisted in s 100 of the TA 2000, but this power was never activated and has now been repealed.[312] The Terrorism Act 2000 (Video Recording of Interviews) Order 2000[313] provides for interviews only in Northern Ireland to be recorded by video with sound, and then the current Terrorism Act 2000 (Code of Practice on Video Recording of Interviews) (Northern Ireland) Order 2003[314] allows for a detailed code of

---

[306] PACE Code H, para 2.
[307] Ibid, para 2.8.
[308] Ibid, para 3.8.
[309] SI 2001/159. See *Home Office, Code of Practice for the audio recording of interviews under The Terrorism Act 2000* (Stationery Office, London, 2001).
[310] SI 2001/189. PACE Code E is not applicable: para 3.2.
[311] *R v Ibrahim* [2008] EWCA Crim 880.
[312] T(NI)A 2006, s 2.
[313] SI 2000/3179.
[314] SI 2003/110, replacing SI 2001/402.

practice. The source for these orders is paras 3 and 4 of Sch 8 and not s 100. There is no requirement for routine video recording of interviews elsewhere in Britain, though custody areas may be recorded,[315] and the police now regularly favour the routine video-recording of interviews.[316]

Access to outsiders

Aspects of the PACE regime are applied without significant change to s 41 detainees, **4.151** including the rules about appropriate adults[317] and persons responsible for the welfare of juveniles,[318] as well as interpreters.[319] Foreigners (including, for these purposes, Irish citizens detained in Britain) also have rights to contact and consult with consular officials.[320] Some consulates will even be informed automatically.[321] These rights arise pursuant to the Vienna Convention on Consular Relations 1963,[322] Article 36.1, as implemented by the Consular Relations Act 1968.[323]

Code H requires a medical check at least daily after detention of ninety-six hours.[324] **4.152** The Scottish Guidelines of 2006 demand that there must be a medical check 'towards the end of the initial 48 hour or any extended period of detention, or where the senior investigating officer indicates that s/he is considering releasing a detainee from a period of detention'.[325] The strictest rules are in Northern Ireland where medical checks are arranged on arrival, before any interview, every twenty-four hours, and on release.[326] In a study in England and Wales before 2001, it was found that 46 per cent of terrorism detainees saw a doctor; delay was authorized in 26 per cent of cases.[327] Doctors should consider not only medical fitness for interview and any signs of injury but also diet and exercise.[328]

Independent custody visitors may attend under the usual rules,[329] a scheme extended to **4.153** Northern Ireland in 2005 after the summary abolition of the Independent Commissioner for the Holding Centres.[330] Code H also envisages the possibility of other 'official' visitors, including accredited faith representatives, Members of Parliament, and public officials

---

[315] PACE Code H, para 3.11; PACE Code F, para 3.2.

[316] Joint Committee on Human Rights, *Counter-Terrorism Policy and Human Rights: 28 Days, Intercept and Post-charge Questioning* (2006–07 HL 157/HC 394) para 81.

[317] PACE Code H, paras 1.13, 3.17.

[318] Ibid para 3.15.

[319] Ibid para 13.

[320] See ibid paras 3.3, 7; *Colville Report*, paras 6.2.1, 6.2.2; *Colville Annual Report on the Operation in 1990 of the Prevention of Terrorism (Temporary Provisions) Acts* (Home Office), para 4.2.

[321] PACE Code H, Annex F.

[322] Cmnd 2113, London, 1963.

[323] See Brown, D, *Detention under the Prevention of Terrorism Act* (Home Office Research and Planning Unit paper 75, London, 1993) pp 38–9.

[324] PACE Code H, para 9.

[325] Ibid, para 23.

[326] Ibid paras 9.2, 9.3. See Joint Committee on Human Rights, *Counter-Terrorism Policy and Human Rights: 28 Days, Intercept and Post-charge Questioning* (2006–07 HL 157/HC 394) paras 88, 91.

[327] Brown, D, *Detention under the Prevention of Terrorism Act* (Home Office Research and Planning Unit paper 75, London, 1993) p 35.

[328] Faculty of Forensic and Legal Medicine, *Medical Care of Persons Detained under the Terrorism Act 2000* (<https://fflm.ac.uk/upload/documents/1189093340.pdf>, 2004).

[329] Police Reform Act 2002, s 51; *Code of Practice on Independent Custody Visiting* (Home Office, 2003).

[330] See Dickson, B and O'Loan, N, 'Visiting Police Stations in Northern Ireland' (1994) 45 *Northern Ireland Legal Quarterly* 210; Independent Commission on Policing for Northern Ireland, *A New Beginning: Policing in Northern Ireland* (Northern Ireland Office, Belfast, 1999) para 8.16; <http://www.nipolicingboard.org.uk/cv06_antrim-2.pdf>.

(such as from the security services) needing to interview the prisoner in the course of their duties.[331] There is no right of access in these cases, and custody officers 'should have particular regard to the possibility of suspects attempting to pass information which may be detrimental to public safety, or to an investigation'.[332]

4.154 Next, rights to have a person informed of the detention and to have access to a legal adviser are granted by paras 6 and 7 of Sch 8 of the TA 2000.[333] The detainee must also be told clearly about the existence of these rights, but risk assessments of those to be contacted will be carried out by the police.[334] Guidance as to the right not to be held incommunicado places greater emphasis than normal on the grant of family visits which should be allowed where possible or, if not possible, more visits from independent custody visitors (who will be notified of the presence of prisoners).[335] At Paddington Green, family visits are infrequent but telephone contacts are daily.

4.155 The primary legal right of access comprises not only private consultation but also securing the presence of the lawyer during the interview (para 7).[336] In Scotland, the relevant rights are set out in paras 16 and 19, with details in the Terrorism (Interviews) (Scotland) Order 2001.[337]

4.156 Delays to the exercise of these rights may be authorized by a superintendent under para 8 (para 17 in Scotland) for up to forty-eight hours, rather than the normal PACE (ss 56, 58) limit of thirty-six hours. The grounds for doing so are equivalent to those in the PACE legislation, save that extra grounds are added to take account of the basis of the arrest in terrorism and not crime.[338] Thus, the extra grounds are: interference with the gathering of information about terrorism or of evidence about serious crimes; interference with, or physical injury to, any person; the alerting of a person and thereby making it more difficult to prevent an act of terrorism or to secure a person's apprehension, prosecution, or conviction in connection with an act of terrorism or to arrest for a serious crime; hindering the recovery of property related to serious crime or for which a forfeiture order could be made. Writing materials and access to the telephone may be refused on similar grounds.[339] Contrary to the views of the Northern Ireland courts,[340] writing materials are allowed in the Code of Practice[341] only for the purpose of making representations about continued detention. Where delay is authorized, the detained person shall be told the reason for the delay as soon as is reasonably practicable, and the reason shall be recorded. Any decision to delay should

---

[331] PACE Code H, para 5C.
[332] Ibid, para 5G.
[333] Ibid, paras 5, 6.
[334] Ibid para 3.8. See further Home Office Circular 32/2000 *Detainee Risk Assessment & Revised Prisoner Escort Request (PER) Form*.
[335] PACE Code H, para 5.4, 5B. Compare Joint Committee on Human Rights, *Counter-Terrorism Policy and Human Rights: 28 Days, Intercept and Post-charge Questioning* (2006–07 HL 157/HC 394) para 101, and *Government Reply* (Cm 7215, London, 2007) p 8.
[336] Compare at common law: *R v Chief Constable of the Royal Ulster Constabulary, ex parte Begley* [1997] 1 WLR 1475; *HM Advocate v McLean* 2009 HCJAC 97.
[337] SI 2001/428. These rights were until recently more extensive than those for non-terrorist detainees: see *Cadder v HM Advocate* [2010] UKSC 43; Criminal Procedure (Legal Assistance, Detention and Appeals) (Scotland) Act 2010.
[338] Amended by the Proceeds of Crime Act 2002 and the Serious Organised Crime and Police Act 2005.
[339] PACE Code H, para 5.6.
[340] *Re Floyd* [1997] NI 414.
[341] See Terrorism Act 2000, s 99; Code of Practice 2006, para 3G.

be considered in the light of an actual request and the circumstances then prevailing; it would be wrong to lay down any blanket policy of denial or to deny in anticipation of a request.[342] To deny family notification even within the forty-eight-hour limit may breach Article 8.[343]

A lawyer who is considered to impede the interviewing process by preventing proper **4.157** questioning may be excluded under Code H, though such a 'serious step' should be reported to the Law Society.[344] Other concerns about the presence of a given lawyer may give rise to a further residual exclusion power. In *Malik v Chief Constable of Greater Manchester*,[345] the police excluded Malik's solicitor because of evidence from a video of a public meeting relating to recruitment for a terrorist organization. The video made reference to the solicitor's presence at the event. The police justifiably excluded that solicitor on the basis that he could be called as a witness to the nature of the meeting. The action could be explained as sanctioned by para 8 as avoiding an interference with, or harm to, evidence. After forty-eight hours, the arguments would have to rest on broad common law powers to prevent interferences with the administration of justice. By contrast, the court emphasized that issues such as conflicts of interest in representing multiple defendants were for the solicitor to address rather than the police. The same approach should apply to the level of experience and number of attendant lawyers.[346]

A further problem sometimes arises with the physical unavailability of lawyers even after access **4.158** has been formally granted with a resultant loss of valuable time on the detention clock.[347] However, the proposal by the Independent Commissioner for the Holding Centres in Northern Ireland to institute a full time Legal Advice Unit at the centres where terrorism suspects were held did not find favour.[348] The problem has been solved administratively at Paddington Green, where schedules of interviewing and attendance are agreed with the lawyers.

Legal advice was declared in *Cullen v Chief Constable of the Royal Ulster Constabulary*[349] to be **4.159** 'a quasi-constitutional right of fundamental importance in a free society'. The establishment of this quasi-right did not found any action for damages, but its breach may impact on the fairness of any later trial. In *(John) Murray v United Kingdom*,[350] the European Court of Human Rights concluded that it would be incompatible with the right to a fair trial to base a conviction solely or mainly on the accused's silence. In addition, inferences drawn in unfair circumstances, such as where there had been a denial of access to a lawyer for forty-eight hours, would contravene Article 6(1) in conjunction with Article 6(3)(c).[351]

---

[342] *Cullen v Chief Constable of the Royal Ulster Constabulary* [2003] UKHL 39.

[343] 45 hours' delay was a breach in *McVeigh, O'Neill, and Evans v United Kingdom*, App nos 8022, 8025, 8027/77; DR 25 p 15 (1981).

[344] PACE Code H, paras 6.10–6.12. See also Home Office Circular 03/01: *Terrorism Act 2000*, London, 2001, para 17.24.

[345] [2006] EWHC 2396 (Admin).

[346] *Re Campbell* [2010] NIQB 9.

[347] See further PACE Code H, para 6A.

[348] *Delayed Choice or Instant Access?* (Northern Ireland Office, Belfast, 1994). See Walker, C and Fitzpatrick, B, 'Holding Centres in Northern Ireland, the Independent Commissioner and the rights of detainees' [1999] *European Human Rights Law Review* 27.

[349] [2003] UKHL 39 at para 67 per Lord Millett.

[350] App no 18731/91, Reports 1996-I. See further Flaherty, MS, 'Interrogation, legal advice and human rights in Northern Ireland' (1997) 27 *Columbia Human Rights Law Review* 1.

[351] Ibid para 66. The Court emphasized the right of access even when there was no adverse inference from silence, but the unfairness of denial would be irretrievable if there were inferences: *Salduz v Turkey*, App no 36391/02, 12 November 2008, paras 52, 55.

4.160   Breaches were also sustained in *Averill v United Kingdom*[352] and *Magee v United Kingdom*,[353] where reliance was placed upon a confession or on silence after the refusal of legal advice. If no admissions or inferences result from the period of refusal, as in *Brennan v United Kingdom*,[354] then Article 6 rights are less jeopardized. Nevertheless, the government expects deferment to be limited to 'exceptional cases'.[355] PACE Code H further advises that the total exclusion of legal advice means that adverse inferences from silence cannot be drawn.[356]

4.161   A special qualification to the exercise of the right of access to a lawyer is that a direction may be given under para 9 (para 17 in Scotland) that a detained person may consult a solicitor only in the sight and hearing of a 'qualified officer' (an inspector).[357] This serious intrusion must be authorized by an officer of at least the rank of Commander or Assistant Chief Constable and only if the officer giving it has reasonable grounds for believing that the unfettered exercise of the right by the detained person will have any of the consequences specified as for delay. Even with these restraints, it is very doubtful whether access to legal advice under these conditions can ever meet the standards of Article 6 of the European Convention. In *Brennan v United Kingdom*,[358] the presence of the police during a consultation session with the detainee's solicitor triggered a breach of Article 6: '. . . the Court cannot but conclude that the presence of the police officer would have inevitably prevented the applicant from speaking frankly to his solicitor and given him reason to hesitate before broaching questions of potential significance to the case against him'. Covert surveillance may also be conducted under the RIPA, Pt II, but is now subject to regulation as a form of intrusive surveillance.[359]

4.162   Subsequent to *Brennan*, the Home Office issued Circular 42/2003,[360] in which it is emphasized that para 9 remains viable only in 'limited circumstances'. Two factors considered to be of particular relevance to indicating the need for legal advice are whether the suspect has been cooperative and answering questions and whether the suspect could be considered vulnerable, not only in terms of mental or physical attributes but also because of restricted language ability and cultural differences or even 'overwhelming or prolonged emotional distress'.[361] It would have been more straightforward to abolish para 9. Instead, any unacceptable lawyer should be excluded to the extent justifiable in *Malik*.

4.163   As well as the express powers under para 9, it was accepted in *Re C*[362] that the police can lawfully refuse to give assurances not to engage in covert surveillance. Objections may also arise when the surveillance affects Members of Parliament, as discussed in Chapter 2.

---

[352] App no 36408/97, 2000-VI.
[353] App no 28135/95, 2000-VI.
[354] App no 39846/98, 2001-X.
[355] Hansard HC vol 346 col 375 (15 March 2000), Charles Clarke.
[356] PACE Code H, para 6.7(b).
[357] As amended by the CTA 2008, s 82.
[358] App no 39846/98, 2001-X, para 62. *The Body of Principles for the Protection of All Persons under Any Form of Detention or Imprisonment* (UNGA Res 43/173 of 9 December 1988) Principle 18.4 does not allow for overhearing in any circumstances.
[359] Regulation of Investigatory Powers (Extension of Authorisation Provisions: Legal Consultations) Order 2010 SI 2010/461. See further Chapter 2.
[360] (Home Office, London, 2003) paras 9, 12.
[361] Ibid para 15.
[362] [2007] NIQB 101.

Implementation

Around 49 per cent of detainees in England and Wales availed themselves of legal advice in the early 1990s, a higher rate than under PACE and one which rises with the seriousness of the charges and length of detention.[363] The notification rate was 43 per cent.[364] Current rates are not disclosed, but indications are that legal advice is even more prevalent. During the early 1990s in England and Wales, delay of legal access was authorized in 26 per cent of cases, a far higher figure than under PACE, and the average length of delay was sixteen hours.[365] In notification cases, delay ran at 30 per cent.[366] However, access was not deferred in any terrorist case from 1997 to 1999. Though figures have not been released since that time, deferment of rights to legal advice is now assumed to be very uncommon, probably because of the transference of 'normal' practices under PACE. The direction of oversight power is also reputed to be dormant in England and Wales.

4.164

In Northern Ireland, notification to family was delayed in the 1990s in 9 per cent of cases, a figure which has since decreased over the decade. There has also been a major shift in practice in regard to access to solicitors (see Table 4.6). A refusal rate of 59 per cent from 1987 to 1990[367] subsided to close to zero in 2000 and thereafter, with access also granted during the interview. As well as the contributing factor of PACE, pressure from watchdogs such as the Standing Advisory Committee on Human Rights,[368] the European Committee for the Prevention of Torture,[369] and the UN Committee against Torture[370] has been even more manifest. Another contributing factor has been legal challenges, none of which was successful but which did serve to prompt police reflection on their practices.[371] The current positive attitude[372] contrasts with previous hostility, which is alleged to have resulted in police collusion in the murders of two prominent Northern Ireland lawyers, Pat Finucane in 1989[373] and Rosemary Nelson in 1999.[374] Principle 18 of the UN Basic Principles on the Role of Lawyers 1990 states that lawyers must not be identified with their clients or their clients' causes as a result of discharging their functions.

4.165

---

[363] Brown, D, *Detention under the Prevention of Terrorism Act* (Home Office Research and Planning Unit paper 75, London, 1993) pp 9–10, 21–2.

[364] Ibid p 23.

[365] Ibid pp 9–10, 17–18, 21–3, 28.

[366] Ibid p 28.

[367] See Walker, CP, *The Prevention of Terrorism in British Law* (2nd edn, Manchester University Press, Manchester, 1992) p 172.

[368] *24th Report for 1998–99* (1998–99 HC 265) p 5.

[369] See *Report to the UK Government on the Visit to Northern Ireland carried out by the European Commission for the Prevention of Torture etc. 1993* (CPT/Inf (94) 17, 1994); *Response of the UK Government* (CPT/Inf (94) 18, 1994).

[370] See, for example, United Nations Committee against Torture, *4th Report under Article 19 by the United Kingdom of Great Britain and Northern Ireland* (CAT/C/67/Add.2, 2004) para 85.

[371] See *Moore v Chief Constable, Royal Ulster Constabulary* [1988] NI 456; *R v Harper* [1990] NI 28; *Re Duffy* [1991] 7 NIJB 62; *R v Chief Constable, ex parte McKenna and McKenna* [1992] NI 116; *R v Chambers* [1994] NI 170; *R v Cosgrove and Morgan* [1994] NI 182; *In re Russell*, [1996] NI 310; *R v McWilliams* [1996] NI 545; *In re Begley* [1997] 1 WLR 1475; *Re Floyd* [1997] NI 414.

[372] Police Ombudsman for Northern Ireland, *A Study of the Treatment of Solicitors and Barristers by the Police in Northern Ireland* (Belfast, 2003). Compare Murphy, MR, 'Northern Ireland policing reform and the intimidation of defence lawyers' (2000) *Fordham Law Review* 1877.

[373] See *Cory Collusion Inquiry Report, Pat Finucane* (2003–04 HC 470).

[374] See *Cory Collusion Inquiry Report, Rosemary Nelson* (2003–04 HC 473); Rosemary Nelson Inquiry (<http://www.rosemarynelsoninquiry.org>).

Table 4.6 Access to lawyers and family in Northern Ireland[a]

	Lawyer		Family	
	Granted (% of detainees)	*Delayed*	*Granted (% of detainees)*	*Delayed*
2001	124 (69%)	1	32 (18%)	0
2002	232 (98%)	0	130 (55%)	0
2003	354 (99%)	0	167 (47%)	1
2004	223 (97%)	4	102 (44%)	3
2005	246 (99%)	0	81 (33%)	0
2006	213 (99%)	0	114 (53%)	3
2007	142 (98%)	0	65 (45%)	3
2008	148 (99%)	1	54 (36%)	0
Total	1,682 (95%)	6	745 (42%)	10

[a] Source: NIO Statistics & Research Branch.

4.166 As for access to consular officials, few diplomats (other than Irish officials) actually respond to the calls from terrorist suspects. In a study in England and Wales, it was found that the police often do not inform the detainee or embassy in relevant Irish cases (perhaps because of doubts over nationality), and few detainees wish to exercise the right. Delay was authorized in 26 per cent of cases, the grounds often being multiple, and the average length of delay was sixteen hours.[375]

Foreign comparisons

4.167 A similar regime in Ireland of access to a lawyer was applied by the Criminal Justice Act 1984, s 5, to a person held under the Offences against the State Act 1939, s 30.[376] While there is no specific right to have the solicitor present during interviews, the Criminal Justice Act 1984 (Treatment of Persons in Custody in Garda Síochána Stations) Regulations 1987,[377] art 12(6), forbid the taking of a written statement until a consultation has taken place. A further safeguard is that juries must be warned if there is no corroborating evidence for a confession: Criminal Procedure Act 1993, s 10. In practice, s 10 has limited impact in so far as contested confessions are heard in the no-jury Special Criminal Court.[378]

4.168 Contacts with defence lawyers and family members have been less generously afforded in most Continental jurisdictions. In France, extensions to detention during the police *garde à vue* have been accompanied by lengthier exclusion of access to lawyers. Access to a lawyer under art 706-88 of the Code of Criminal Procedure is limited to thirty minutes and without access to the case file after 72, 96, and 120 hours, a level of protection held to be unconstitutional.[379]

---

[375] Brown, D, *Detention under the Prevention of Terrorism Act* (Home Office Research and Planning Unit paper 75, London, 1993) pp 38–9. The symbolic importance of the privilege for diplomats is underlined by the case of *Avena v US* [2004] ICJ 12 (but see *Medellín v Texas* 552 US 491 (2008)).

[376] See *People (DPP) v Shaw* [1982] IR 1; *People (DPP) v Healy* [1990] 2 IR 73; *Ward v Minister for Justice, Equality and Law Reform* [2007] IEHC 39.

[377] SI 1987/119. See *Lavery v Member in Charge, Carrickmacross Garda Station* [1999] 2 IR 390 at 396.

[378] See *People (DPP) v Connolly* [2003] 2 IR 1.

[379] Laws 86-1020 of 9 September 1986, 93–2 of 4 January 1993, 2004-204 of 9 March 2004, 2006-64 of 23 January 2006. For the ruling, see Conseil d'Etat Decision 2010-14/22 QPC, 30 July 2010.

In Spain, Organic Law 15/2003 of 25 November 2003 allows incommunicado detention for thirteen days but provides instead for an assigned lawyer.[380]

Allegations of collusion and disruption in Germany by lawyers acting for Red Army Faction detainees produced several restraints.[381] The Anti-Terrorism Act of 20 December 1974 inserted s 138a into the Code of Criminal Procedure, which allows the exclusion of a lawyer on suspicion of involvement in crime or security breaches. The number of lawyers acting for any suspect was limited to three, with no lawyer acting for more than one person in a group, and the choice of lawyer can exceptionally be overridden by the court (ss 137, 142, 146).[382] The Anti-Terrorism Act of 18 August 1976 (inserting s 148(2)) allowed for written communications to be subjected to judicial control.[383] Most draconian was the Blockage of Contact Act (*Kontaktsperregesetz*) of 2 October 1977,[384] which allows isolation from lawyers for thirty days to avoid danger to life, limb, or freedom of a person if there are definite suspicions arising from a terrorist association; the order is issued by a Minister but must be confirmed by a judge within fourteen days. An amendment allowed contact with an assigned lawyer.[385]

4.169

Some countries have officially experimented with harsh interrogation techniques. In Israel, the (Landau) Commission of Inquiry into the Methods of Investigation of the General Security Service regarding Hostile Terrorist Activity (1987) claimed that some forms of harsh treatment could be justified under a common law defence of necessity, including 'a moderate measure of physical pressure'.[386] The subsequent regime was challenged in *Public Committee against Torture in Israel v State of Israel*.[387] Techniques such as shaking, crouching, face covering, cuffing causing pain, loud noise, and prolonged sleep deprivation were all prohibited.

4.170

The US Presidential detention regime also included techniques such as threatening dogs, isolation, sleep deprivation, prolonged standing, and the removal of clothing.[388] After the shock of revelations at Abu Ghraib prison, the Detainee Treatment Act 2005 prohibited cruel, inhuman, and degrading treatment and punishment for persons held by the Department of Defense or in the custody or control of the US government anywhere in the world.[389] Title X of the Act specifies the United States Army Field Manual on Intelligence Interrogation as the standard for persons in the custody or under the effective control of the Department of Defense or its agencies. However, the Act also limits prosecutions of US officials to grave

4.171

---

[380] See Oehmichen, A, *Terrorism and Anti-Terror Legislation* (Intersentia, Antwerp, 2009) p 224; Catena, VM and Benavente, MC, 'Limiting fundamental rights in the fight against terrorism in Spain' in Wade, M and Maljevic, A, *A War on Terror?* (Springer, New York, 2010).

[381] Oehmichen, A, *Terrorism and Anti-Terror Legislation,* p 243.

[382] See *Croissant v Germany*, App no 13611/88, Ser A 237-B (no breach of Art 6).

[383] See *Erdem v Germany*, App no 38321/97, 2001-VII (no breach of Art 8).

[384] The measure was upheld in *Ensslin, Baader and Raspe v Germany*, App nos 7572, 7586, 7587/76 DR 14, p 91 (1978). See Oehmichen, A, 'Incommunicado Detention in Germany' (2008) 9 *German Law Journal* 855.

[385] *Einführungsgesetz zum Gerichtsverfassungsgesetz*, s 34a (4 December 1985).

[386] Paras 3.15, 4.7. See Zamir, I, 'The rule of law and the control of terrorism' (1988) 8 *Tel Aviv Studies in Law* 81.

[387] (1999) 53(4) PD 817. See Gross, E, *The Struggle of Democracy Against Terrorism* (University of Virginia Press, Charlottesville, 2006) ch 3.

[388] See Levinson, S, *Torture* (Oxford University Press, New York, 2004); Danner, M, *Torture and Truth* (New York Review Books, New York, 2004); Greenberg, KJ and Dratel, JL, *The Torture Papers* (Cambridge University Press, Cambridge, 2005); Wittes, B, *Law and the Long War* (Penguin, New York, 2008) ch 7.

[389] PL 109-148.

breaches and allows the President to specify the meaning of 'grave'.[390] The Military Commissions Act 2009[391] allows for involuntary statements to be adduced at hearings.

Assessment and conclusions

4.172 As underlined by the Code of Conduct for Law Enforcement Officials,[392] 'exceptional circumstances such as a state of war or a threat of war, a threat to national security, internal political instability or any other public emergency' cannot justify torture or other cruel, inhuman, or degrading treatment. One should question whether the TA 2000 has met this challenge.

4.173 Several other safeguards can be conceived which would aid claims to proportionality. One would involve special rules of evidence, such as special warnings, as in Ireland, or inadmissibility of any statements or silences if made after the normal PACE detention period of four days.[393] The second suggestion, floated during debates on extended detention, is to pay compensation to anyone held for more than four days and not charged. Thirdly, more detailed rules are needed as to living conditions, such as clothing, reading and writing materials, exercise, natural light, and clocks. PACE Code H's solution is simply a transfer to prison detention after fourteen days.[394] In London, the transfer is to Belmarsh Prison, though there will be a transfer back for interviewing purposes.

4.174 Fourthly, the independent oversight of detention conditions could be made more effective by reviving the office of the Independent Commissioner for Detained Terrorist Suspects.[395] This work was discontinued in 2005. It was partially then taken up by the Independent Custody Visiting Scheme of the Northern Ireland Policing Board.[396] Although the lay visitors are allowed to witness interviews,[397] they do not review the rules nor meet with detainees.

4.175 The concept of an Independent Commissioner was conceded by the government in debates on the Counter-Terrorism Bill.[398] However, the government later reneged on this promise because of feared delays to investigations.[399] Instead, by the Coroners and Justice Act 2009, s 117, two changes are put in place.

---

[390] Common Article 3 has since been adopted as a baseline: Executive Order 13,491, *Ensuring Lawful Interrogation* (74 Fed Reg 4893, 2009).

[391] PL 111-84.

[392] (UNGA 34/169 of 17 December 1979) art 5. See also UN Standard Minimum Rules for the Treatment of Prisoners 1955, para 95; Body of Principles for the Protection of All Persons under Any Form of Detention or Imprisonment 1988 (UNGA 43/173).

[393] At present, the courts assess the impact on Art 6 case by case: *Latimer v United Kingdom*, App no 12141/04, 31 May 2005.

[394] The Council of Europe Committee for the Prevention of Torture and Inhuman and Degrading Treatment argues that transfer should be compulsory: *Report to the United Kingdom Government on the Visit to the United Kingdom carried out by the European Committee for the Prevention of Torture and Inhuman and Degrading Treatment* (CPT/Inf (2008) 27, para 7) and *Response of the United Kingdom Government* (CPT/Inf (2008) 28, paras 6, 9).

[395] See *Body of Principles for the Protection of All Persons under Any Form of Detention or Imprisonment* (UNGA 43/173 of 9 December 1988) Principle 29; Walker, C and Fitzpatrick, B, 'Holding Centres in Northern Ireland, the Independent Commissioner and the rights of detainees' [1999] *European Human Rights Law Review* 27; Independent Commission on Policing for Northern Ireland, *A New Beginning: Policing in Northern Ireland* (Northern Ireland Office, Belfast, 1999), para 8.16.

[396] *Human Rights Annual Report 2006* (Belfast, 2006) pp 116–24.

[397] Lay Visitors' Reports Order 2005 SR (NI) 420.

[398] HL Hansard vol 705 col 158 (4 November 2008), Lord Lloyd. Lord Lloyd has also suggested an operational role of scrutinizing closed evidence at extension hearings and reporting to the judge: Hansard HL vol 712 col 994 (13 July 2009), Lord Tunnicliffe. See Horne, A, *An Independent Commissioner for Terrorist Suspects* (House of Commons Library, London, 2009).

[399] Hansard HL vol 714 col 867 (11 November 2009), Lord Tunnicliffe.

First, the remit of the Independent Reviewer of Terrorism Legislation under the TA 2006, **4.176**
s 36, is modified to make explicit that the officer may 'in particular' investigate the treatment
of persons detained under s 41 for more than forty-eight hours, including by real time
observation. This scheme suffers from several limits. The additional burden is placed upon
the single, part-time independent reviewer. Even the government expects attendance at no
more than 'the odd extension hearing' and 'the most serious investigations'.[400] A full review
system to match that formerly in Northern Ireland was estimated to require the appointment
of five persons.[401] In addition, the exclusion of scrutiny during the first forty-eight hours puts
beyond reach around a half of detentions.

Secondly, s 117 places a duty on police authorities under the Police Reform Act 2002, s 51, **4.177**
to ensure that independent custody visitors can access audio and video recordings of police
interviews and that copies of their visit reports are submitted to the Independent Reviewer.
However, there is still no direct contact with the detainee, and no review of dealings beyond
interviews. Furthermore, an inspector may deny access to recordings on grounds to be
specified by a code of practice.

E. Post-Charge Questioning and Detention

Introduction and background

Post-charge questioning was proposed by the Home Office in its paper, *Possible Measures for* **4.178**
Inclusion in a Future Counter-Terrorism Bill.[402] Post-charge questioning in terrorism cases
happens 'very rarely' at present.[403] But the impetus for change resides again in the development of the Threshold Test[404] on the basis that new facts become more likely to arise after
charge. In evidence to the Joint Committee on Human Rights, Sue Hemming, head of the
Crown Prosecution Service Counter-Terrorism Division, stated that much new evidence
becomes available after charge and that there could be advantage in obtaining an explanation
from the accused or an adverse inference in the event of silence.[405] The government did not
proffer post-charge questioning as a way of avoiding the prolongation of detention powers,
though critics did present it as one technique of avoidance.

Provisions

Section 22 provides that a Crown Court judge may authorize questioning of a person charged **4.179**
with a terrorist offence (as defined by reference to a fixed list of offences in s 27)[406] or an
offence with a terrorist connection (as defined by s 93). The latter possibility creates

---

[400] Ibid col 872.
[401] Hansard HL vol 712 col 1000 (13 July 2009), Lord Brett.
[402] (London, 2007) para 35. See Walker, C, 'Post-charge questioning of suspects' [2008] *Criminal Law Review* 509.
[403] Lord Carlile, *Report on Proposed Measures for Inclusion in a Counter-Terrorism Bill* (Cm 7262, London, 2007) para 22.
[404] The Joint Committee on Human Rights, *Counter-Terrorism Policy and Human Rights: Counter-Terrorism Bill* (2007–08 HL 50, HC 199) para 77 reveals that the test has been invoked against four out of eight detainees charged after detention for more than fourteen days.
[405] Joint Committee on Human Rights, *Counter-terrorism Policy and Human Rights: 42 Days* (2007–08 HL23 HC156) q 210. See also HC Hansard Public Bill Committee on the Counter-Terrorism Bill, Evidence from Sir Ken MacDonald, col 49, 22 April 2008.
[406] See HC Hansard Public Bill Committee on the Counter-Terrorism Bill col 355 (8 May 2008), Tony McNulty.

uncertainty—it must be shown that the offence is, or takes place in the course of, an act of terrorism, or is committed for the purposes of terrorism. Lengthy preliminary hearings might be entailed where terrorist suspects are charged with ancillary offences such as fraud. The matter would naturally arise at the order for a preparatory hearing,[407] but s 22 does not forbid applications before then for fear of creating a potential gap.[408] The result is to encourage the police to charge a listed terrorist offence to avoid these arguments.[409] Applications may be made by police or prosecutors. The wording of s 22(2) strongly suggests that the application must relate only to 'the offence' which has been charged. If novel offences are uncovered, then a further pre-charge arrest would be viable.

4.180 The judge must be satisfied under s 22(6) that further questioning is necessary in the interests of justice, that the investigation is being conducted diligently and expeditiously, and that questioning will not interfere unduly with the preparation of the person's defence. The judge must specify the period for questioning, but there is an absolute limit of forty-eight hours for any given authorization, though there may be repeated authorizations. Aside from the time limit, the judge may also impose such conditions as appear to be necessary in the interests of justice. They may include conditions as to the place where the questioning is to be carried out, including removal from prison to a police station. It is not expressly ruled out that there can be questioning after the trial commences, but the second criterion for the grant suggests strongly that it would not normally be allowed as it could readily be deemed unfair under PACE, s 78.[410] There are severe dangers in terms of interference with the processes of disclosure, infringement upon legal privilege, or even the production of a 'dry run for cross-examination by the prosecution'.[411]

4.181 Given that many terrorist suspects will be advised to remain silent in response to police questioning, s 22(9) applies s 34(1) of the Criminal Justice and Public Order Act 1994 to allow for adverse inferences, and ss 36 and 37 can also apply. A failure to respond in the courtroom to the evidence for the prosecution will allow adverse inferences under s 35 of the Criminal Justice and Public Order Act 1994. Whether the judge should be able to direct the questioning was doubted by the government as being too redolent of the mantle of an investigative magistrate as well as creating practical problems in oversight.[412] It would be in keeping with legislative intention for a judge to specify as a condition in the interests of justice what cannot be raised at interview. As for the legitimacy of drawing adverse inferences, the European Court of Human Rights in *Murray (John) v United Kingdom* held that the privilege against self-incrimination under Article 6 is not absolute[413] but can be overborne provided there is a strong element of judicial supervision of the questioning and warnings at trial to the jury. However, the fraught circumstances of terrorists facing complex prosecutions will often raise contra-indications.

---

[407] Criminal Procedure and Investigations Act 1996, s 29.

[408] HL Hansard vol 705 col 171 (4 November 2008), Lord West.

[409] See Joint Committee on Human Rights, *Government Responses to the Committee's 20th and 21st Reports and other correspondence* (2007–08 HL 127, HC 756) p 5.

[410] House of Commons Public Bill Committee on the Counter Terrorism Bill col 341 (8 May 2008), Tony McNulty.

[411] Joint Committee on Human Rights, *Counter-Terrorism Policy and Human Rights: 42 Days* (2007–08 HL23 HC156) q 222 (Ali Bajwa).

[412] HL Hansard vol 705 cols 171, 172 (4 November 2008), Lord West.

[413] App no 18731/91, 1996-I, at para 47. See also *Saunders v United Kingdom*, App no 19187/91, 1996-VI; *Shannon v United Kingdom*, App no 6563/03, 4 October 2005.

Another side-effect which will be encouraged by post-charge questioning is plea-bargaining **4.182** and deal-making. It offers a golden opportunity for such discussions which have been also encouraged by the courts[414] and by the Serious Organized Crime and Police Act 2005, Pt II, ch 2.

These rules apply in Northern Ireland, except that a District Judge (Magistrates' Court) takes **4.183** the decision (s 24). In Scotland, the application for post-charge questioning is by a prosecutor and is made to a sheriff under s 23. No inference from silence can be drawn. These judicial designations were made before the switch to Crown Court judges in England and Wales.[415]

Implementation

Post-charge questioning is not yet in force. One reason for delay is that, by s 25, a code of **4.184** practice must be issued under the 2008 Act to take account of the need for the recording of post-charge interviews by video recording with sound and of the dangers of questioning after the commencement of trial.[416] It is difficult to conceive how oppression could be avoided if the defendant were to be subjected to the ordeal of trial by day, and then police interrogation in the evening.[417] The code will also cover access to lawyers, but this important safeguard was not put on the face of the Act for the odd reason that it would give a veto to the suspect.[418]

Foreign comparisons

No other jurisdiction has comparable instruments for post-charge questioning about new **4.185** evidence by the police or at trial. However, both Australia and Canada have forms of judicial examination which can be pre-charge or post-charge and applicable against suspects or witnesses. These have been described in Chapter 3, as has the United Kingdom's Explosives Act 1883, s 6, which allows a form of judicial examination in relation to explosives offences.

Assessment and conclusions

The Home Office accepts that post-charge questioning is not the foremost answer to problems **4.186** encountered by the investigators of terrorism.[419] Because of the weight accorded to silence, it will at best augment rather than found a prosecution.[420]

A striking feature of the debate about post-charge questioning is that it was bereft of detailed **4.187** argument or detailed consideration of relevant principles or practicalities. The impression was fostered by executive policy-makers that their espousal of post-charge questioning was unproblematic.[421] In response, one might contend that the principled position is that the police should desist from questioning after charge for two reasons. The first is that, after charge, the suspect

---

[414] See *R v Goodyear* [2005] EWCA Crim 888.

[415] Hansard HL vol 704 col 768 (15 October 2008), Lord West.

[416] HC Hansard Public Bill Committee on the Counter-Terrorism Bill col 341 (8 May 2008), Tony McNulty. The Lord Advocate will publish guidelines: HL Hansard vol 705 col 183 (4 November 2008), Lord West.

[417] Joint Committee on Human Rights, Counter-Terrorism Policy and Human Rights, Counter-Terrorism Bill (2007-08 HL 108/HC 554) paras. 62, 64.

[418] HC Hansard vol 476 col 196 (10 June 2008), Tony McNulty.

[419] Home Office, *Pre-Charge Detention of Terrorist Suspects* (London, 2007) p 8.

[420] In terrorist cases, the likely effect is to persuade defendants to give evidence at trial (up from 36 per cent to 75 per cent) rather than to affect the conviction rate by filling any large evidential gap in the prosecution case. See Jackson, J, Wolfe, M, and Quinn, K, *Legislating Against Silence* (NIO Research and Statistical Series: report no 1, Belfast, 2000).

[421] See Home Office, *Summary of Responses to the Counter-Terrorism Bill Consultation* (Cm 7269, London, 2007) para 36.

falls under the sway of the court and further actions in pursuance of the case should be governed by the court.[422] The second reason is to guard against oppressive treatment and questioning.

4.188   The first reason, the transfer of authority to the courts, can be evidenced by the Criminal Procedure Rules 2010[423] which set the overriding objective that criminal cases be dealt with justly (rule 1.1) and specify further that the court must advance that overriding objective by actively managing the case (rule 3.2). This transfer of authority from the police is also underlined by the institution of the charging scheme under the Criminal Justice Act 2003, s 28, by which charging decisions and the gathering of furthering evidence in connection with charges become functions for the Crown Prosecution Service. The first point is reflected by the requirement of judicial management under s 22, but the scheme falls short of a system of judicial examination in which the judge remains wholly in charge.

4.189   As regards the second reason for limiting post-charge questioning, possible unfairness to the accused, powers to question post-charge suffer from a long and dismal history. As stated by Lord Mustill in *R v Director of Serious Fraud Office, ex parte Smith*:[424] '. . . there is a long history of reaction against abuses of judicial interrogation'. This second point awaits redress by the new PACE Codes. So, it is impossible to complete a rights audit until the details are revealed. The ruling out of incriminating statements and inferences from silence would be the clearest signal of the exceptionally oppressive nature of this power, but Parliament has agreed otherwise. Nevertheless, there remains the distinct danger that compelled questioning in circumstances of detention and a looming trial may contravene Article 6 of the European Convention.[425] A hostile approach to post-charge police questioning was adopted by the Court of Appeal in *R v Walters*.[426] The defendant was accused of throwing petrol bombs. While on remand, he asked to see a specified police officer. The police officer asked, after caution, whether he was admitting the offence, which he did. No contemporaneous record was made of the conversation. The Court was of the view that there should have been no questioning after charge and excluded the statement, regardless of the problems surrounding the record.

4.190   Assuming that post-charge questioning is to be encouraged, then, despite the misgivings of Lord Mustill, the preferred approach should be to build an enhanced role for the presiding judge[427] rather than the police. The intervention of the judge would reduce concerns about voluntariness and fairness. In this way, there might be a case for adapting the power of judicial examination under the Explosive Substances Act 1883, s 6, by which, on the initiative of the Attorney General, there may be questioning after charge.[428]

4.191   A judicial examination is not, however, equivalent to the institution of a civil law examining magistrate system. The complexities of transplantation, involving new skills and resources, and the doubts concerning efficacy[429] weigh against that idea.

---

[422]   See HL Hansard vol 704 col 745 (15 October 2008), Lord Lloyd.

[423]   SI 2010/60.

[424]   [1993] AC 1 at 31.

[425]   Compare *Shannon v United Kingdom*, App no 6563/03, 4 October 2005.

[426]   [1989] Crim LR 62.

[427]   See TA 2006, s 16.

[428]   The idea is rejected by Lord Carlile, *Report on Proposed Measures for Inclusion in a Counter-Terrorism Bill* (Cm 7262, London, 2007) para 23.

[429]   See Home Office, *Terrorist Investigation and the French Examining Magistrates System* (London, 2007) p 11; Home Office, *Options for Pre-Charge Detention in Terrorist Cases* (London, 2007) p 11; Joint Committee on Human Rights, *Counter-Terrorism Policy and Human Rights: Prosecution and Pre-Charge Detention* (2005–06 HL 240, HC 1576) paras 72, 76, 117.

F. International Arrest and Investigation

International policing cooperation

Formal processes

A mounting willingness by states to partake in mutual policing aid over terrorism has **4.192** developed in the wake of longer-standing mechanisms which facilitate court processes, such as extradition, which will be outlined in Chapter 6. Closer cooperation between law enforcement agencies reflects the internationalization of terrorist movements. Nevertheless, the assertion of national sovereignty and doubts about the standards of foreign protection for nationals remain dominant influences, so the legal implements tend to be qualified and somewhat ponderous.

That progress has been slow may be illustrated by the fact that the United Kingdom did not **4.193** bring into force the European Convention on Mutual Assistance in Criminal Matters of 1957[430] until the Criminal Justice (International Co-operation) Act 1990. Much of the 1990 Act has now been replaced by the Criminal Justice (International Co-operation) Act 2003 which also brings into force for the United Kingdom several other instruments. One is the mutual legal assistance provisions of the Schengen Implementing Convention of 14 June 1985.[431] As applied to the United Kingdom, hot pursuit is not allowed under the Schengen Acquis (including across the Irish border),[432] but there may be requests for pan-European surveillance and even unaccompanied surveillance for up to five hours in exceptional circumstances under s 83. Second is the Convention on Mutual Assistance in Criminal Matters 2000,[433] including the gathering of evidence through television or telephone links under ss 28 to 31 and the transfer of prisoners to assist investigations under ss 47 and 48. Next are the evidence-freezing provisions of the Framework Decision on the execution in the European Union of orders freezing property or evidence adopted by the Council of the European Union on 22 July 2003.[434] Fourth is the 2001 Protocol to the Convention on Mutual Assistance in Criminal Matters[435] which creates obligations to respond to requests for assistance with banking information.

As can be seen, most of this legislation relates to crimes in general rather than terrorism, but **4.194** cooperation on terrorism has also been aided by the Council Framework Decision 2002/475/ JHA of 13 June 2002 which seeks to ensure a common core legal definition of the term 'terrorism' within criminal codes of Member States. Further details of the Schengen Acquis and the Prüm Treaty have been given in Chapter 2.

Inter-state arrests had largely been confined in history to those intertwined neighbours, **4.195** the United Kingdom and the Republic of Ireland.[436] However, the 'backing of arrest warrants' mutual recognition model is now embodied in the European Arrest Warrant (EAW), based on a Council Framework Directive in 2002 which was accelerated by the

---

[430] ETS 30. See also Commonwealth Scheme for Mutual Assistance in Criminal Matters 1986.
[431] See Council of the European Union, *Manual on Cross Border Operations* (10505/2/09 Rev 2, 2009).
[432] House of Commons Northern Ireland Affairs Committee, *Cross-border co-operation between the Governments of the United Kingdom and the Republic of Ireland* (2008–09 HC 78) para 31.
[433] 2000/C197/01.
[434] 2003/577/JHA, L196, 02/08/2003, 45.
[435] 2001/C326/01.
[436] See Hogan, G and Walker, CP, *Political Violence and the Law in Ireland* (Manchester University Press, Manchester, 1989) ch 14.

events of 11 September 2001.[437] Implementation in the United Kingdom is through the Extradition Act 2003.

4.196 To some extent, the EAW replaces extradition proceedings but goes beyond their remit. The level of proof required is simply that specified for arrest rather than criminal process. Immunity based on political motives is wholly removed as are other 'technicalities' such as double criminality. However, extradition bars under s 11 still include persecution or punishment or prejudicial treatment in trial, punishment, detention, or personal restrictions[438] because of 'extraneous considerations' such as the person's political opinions under s 13. Extradition can also be halted under s 21 if it would be incompatible with Convention rights, or if under s 25 it would be unjust or oppressive because of the person's physical or mental condition. Fast-track processes are set in place,[439] removing the stage of ministerial consideration, and by focusing on offence type and documentation but not the weight of evidence. The EAW applies in relation to any offence of a specified type (including 'terrorism')[440] which is punishable under the law of the requesting state by at least twelve months' imprisonment or, where conviction has been secured, a sentence of at least four months has been imposed.

4.197 The implementation of the EAW has not been trouble-free. Various European countries encountered constitutional objections (mainly because of application to nationals),[441] and the drafting of the 2003 Act has been criticized.[442] But there have been successes, and the House of Lords European Union has concluded that 'The EAW has a key role to play in the fight against terrorism . . .'.[443] The EAW enabled the transfer of Hussain Osman, a suspect in the 21 July 2005 attempted London bombings. He fled to Italy, was arrested on 29 July 2005, and was returned to the United Kingdom on 22 September 2005. The EAW has equally delivered transfers of terrorist suspects from the United Kingdom.[444]

4.198 For the purposes of implementation of mutual assistance, the Home Office acts as the 'Central Authority'[445] and the Serious Organised Crime Agency acts as the National Central

---

[437] Council Framework Decision of 13 June 2002 on the European arrest warrant and the surrender procedures between Member States, 2002/584/JHA, [2002] OJ L190/1. See House of Lords European Union Committee, *Counter-Terrorism: The European Arrest Warrant Procedure* (2001–02 HL 34), The European Arrest Warrant (2001–02 HL 89), *European Arrest Warrant—Recent Developments* (2005–06 HL 156); Sievers, J, 'Too difficult to trust?' in Guild, E and Geyer, F, *Security Versus Justice?* (Ashgate, Aldershot, 2008).

[438] There must be proof of a link between the prejudice and criminal justice processes: *Hilali v Central Court of Criminal Proceedings Number 5 of the National Court of Madrid* [2006] EWHC 1239 (Admin).

[439] Compare the delays over extradition in *Ramda v Secretary of State for the Home Department* [2005] EWHC 2526 (Admin).

[440] See Case C-303/05, *Advocaten voor de Wereld VZW v Leden van de Ministerraad* (3 May 2007).

[441] See *Report from the Commission based on Article 34 of the Council Framework Decision of 13 June 2002 on the European arrest warrant and the surrender procedures between Member States* COM (2006) 8 final; Nohlen, N, 'Germany: The European Arrest Warrant case' (2008) 6 *International Journal of Constitutional Law* 153.

[442] See *Office of the King's Prosecutor, Brussels v Cando Armas* [2005] UKHL 67.

[443] *European Arrest Warrant—Recent Developments* (2005–06 HL 156) para 17.

[444] See *Castillo v Spain* [2004] EWHC 1672 (Admin); *Boudhiba v Central Examining Court No 5 of the National Court of Justice, Madrid* [2006] EWHC 167 (Admin); *Hilali v Central Court of Criminal Proceedings Number 5 of the National Court of Madrid* [2006] EWHC 1239 (Admin), *Hilali v Governor of HMP Whitemoor* [2008] UKHL 3 and *R (Hilali) v City of Westminster Magistrates' Court* [2008] EWHC 2892 (Admin); *Dabas v High Court of Justice, Madrid, Spain* [2007] UKHL 6; *Jaso v Central Criminal Court No 2 Madrid* [2007] EWHC 2983 (Admin); *Ignaoua v Judicial Authority of the Courts of Milan* [2008] EWHC 2619 (Admin); *Spain v De Juana Chaos* [2010] NICty 1; *Spain v Arteaga* [2010] NIQB 23. For an unsuccessful application, see *Criminal Court at the National High Court 1st Division v Murua* [2010] EWHC 2609 (Admin).

[445] See Home Office, *Mutual Legal Assistance Guidelines for the United Kingdom* (7th edn, London, 2009).

Bureau for Interpol and the UK Liaison Bureau for Europol.[446] The extension of the purview of Europol to terrorism was approved by the European Union Justice and Home Affairs Council in 1998 and began to be implemented in 1999.[447] Europol operates primarily as an intelligence gathering and exchange agency[448] and does not have a direct operational role. Police operations across borders can take the form of Joint Investigation Teams (JITs).[449] The JIT is set up in the Member State in which investigations are expected to be predominantly carried out and consists of members from the cooperating states and seconded members from third states. Where the JIT needs investigative measures to be taken in one of the Member States, members seconded to the team may request their own competent authorities to take those measures, which avoids more formal requests for mutual legal assistance. The JIT scheme and Europol more generally have achieved modest impact because of the processual complexities and also the reluctance to invest trust on a multilateral basis.[450]

Informal processes

Alongside the expanding methods of legal rendition, the informal or extraordinary rendition **4.199** of terrorism suspects is alleged to have occurred for the purposes of executive detention or for 'torture by proxy'. There are at least three relatively well-documented instances perpetrated by US authorities. One concerns Maher Arar, a Canadian citizen who was detained in New York en route to Canada and transported to Syria.[451] Second was Khaled El Masri, a German citizen, who was arrested in Macedonia and taken to Kabul.[452] Third was Abu Omar who was abducted from Milan to Egypt in 2003; two Italian agents and twenty-three CIA agents were convicted of involvement.[453] These are said to be part of a 'spider's web' of CIA detentions and renditions.[454]

The United Kingdom government has denied complicity in torture by proxy,[455] though **4.200** there are up to nine alleged cases of torture in Pakistan involving British nationals.[456] It also denies extraordinary rendition, whether by hosting 'ghost' prisons or allowing CIA flights through British territory, including the case of Diego Garcia, save for a handful of

---

[446] See Serious Organised Crime and Police Act 2005, s 5.

[447] See Convention based on Article K.3 of the Treaty on European Union, on the Establishment of a European Police Office (Europol Convention) with Declarations (Cm 4837, London, 2000) and Council Decision of 6 April 2009 establishing the European Police Office (Europol) (2009/371/JHA); Deflem, M, 'Europol and the policing of international terrorism' (2006) 23 *Justice Quarterly* 336; Bures, O, 'Europol's fledgling counterterrorism role' (2009) 20 *Terrorism & Political Violence* 498.

[448] Information sharing is required by the 'Swedish' Council Framework Decision 2006/960/JHA.

[449] Convention on Mutual assistance in criminal matters between the Member States of the EU 2000 (OJ [2000] C197/1) art 13; Council of the European Union, Joint Investigation Teams Manual (13598/09, Brussels, 2009). For UK enforcement, see Police Reform Act 2002, ss 103, 104; Crime (International Cooperation) Act 2003, s 16; Serious Organised Crime and Police Act 2005, ss 30, 57. See Placher, M, 'Joint investigation teams', (2005) 13 *European Journal of Crime, Criminal Law & Criminal Justice* 284.

[450] See House of Commons Justice Committee, *Justice Issues in Europe* (2009–10 HC 162).

[451] See Commission of Inquiry into the Actions of Canadian Officials in relation to Maher Arar, *Report of the Events Relating to Maher Arar* (Ottawa, 2007); *Arar v Ashcroft* 585 F 3d 559 (2009).

[452] See *El-Masri v US* 479 F 3d 296 (2007).

[453] See Pollari and others, *The Times* 5 November 2009, p 57.

[454] Council of Europe, Parliamentary Assembly, *Alleged Secret Detentions and Unlawful Inter-State Transfers involving Council of Europe Member States* (AS/JUR (2006) 16, Strasbourg, 2006) Part III. See further, Council of Europe, *CIA Above the Law?* (Strasbourg, 2009).

[455] *Government Reply to the Joint Committee on Human Rights* (Cm 7714, London, 2009) p 3.

[456] See Joint Committee on Human Rights, *Allegations of UK complicity in torture* (2008–09 HL 152/ HC 230) para 7. One case was Rangzieb Ahmed: see *The Times* 19 December 2008, p 17; Hansard HC vol 495 col 940 (7 July 2009), David Davis.

exceptions,[457] including two cases in Iraq.[458] Yet, without wishing to be complicit, block permissions are granted to the US military for aircraft movements in the United Kingdom,[459] and the National Air Traffic Services has revealed hundreds of movements of CIA chartered aircraft for purposes unknown.[460]

4.201 The most protracted disputes have arisen from allegations by Binyam Mohamed, who has sought discovery concerning his treatment in Pakistan and Morocco so as to defend military commission proceedings (dropped in 2009 when he was released from Guantánamo but without prejudice to future charges).[461] Seven former detainees (including Binyam Mohamed) are also seeking civil damages for British complicity in their detention at Guantánamo.[462]

4.202 The assessment of the Intelligence and Security Committee is that the United Kingdom authorities were slow to appreciate the changed practices around 'extraordinary' rendition beyond criminal justice of the US authorities and that guidelines as to involvement were not adequate.[463] The All Party Parliamentary Group on Extraordinary Rendition has called for criminal law prohibitions of facilitation or the use of facilities.[464] Though connivance-complicity in torture is denied,[465] the judicial inquiry was established in 2010.[466] The government has also published the Consolidated Guidance to Intelligence Officers and Service Personnel on the Detention and Interviewing of Detainees Overseas, and on the Passing and Receipt of Intelligence Relating to Detainees. A system of reference up to a Minister applies whenever risk of serious abuse is present.[467]

Detention and treatment of terrorist suspects held abroad

4.203 European Convention rights can apply where there is effective control by British forces, such as through actual custody, subject to any overriding regime applied by the UN Security Council.[468] In *R (Al-Skeini) v Secretary of State for Defence*,[469] combat situations in Iraq were beyond the domestic rights regime, but persons in custody at a British military base benefited at least from the right to life. Thus, Baha Mousa, who died from physical injuries while held in British military custody in Basrah in 2003, fell within this right. Subsequently, the British

---

[457] See Intelligence and Security Committee, *Rendition* (Cm 7171, London, 2007) and *Government Response* (Cm 7172, London, 2007); ACPO, *Extraordinary Rendition* (<http://www.liberty-human-rights.org.uk/news-and-events/pdfs/er-acpo-response-june-07.pdf>, 2007); Hansard HC vol 472 col 547 (21 February 2008), David Miliband.

[458] Hansard HC vol 488 col 394 (26 February 2009), John Hutton.

[459] House of Commons Foreign Affairs Committee, *Human Rights Annual Report 2005* (2005–06 HC 574) para 45.

[460] See Amnesty International, *Below the Radar* (London, 2006).

[461] *Mohamed v Secretary of State for the Foreign and Commonwealth Office* [2008] EWHC 2048, 2100, 2159 (Admin), [2009] EWHC 152, 2048, 2549, 2973 (Admin), [2010] EWCA Civ 65, 158. See also *R (Aamer) v Secretary of State for the Foreign and Commonwealth Office* [2009] EWHC 3316 (Admin).

[462] See *Al-Rawi v Security Service* [2009] EWHC 2959 (QB).

[463] *Rendition* (Cm 7171, London, 2007) para 77.

[464] *Extraordinary Rendition: Closing the Gap* (London, 2009).

[465] *The Times* 29 October 2010, p 16 (Sir John Sawers).

[466] Hansard HC vol 513 col 175 (6 July 2010), David Cameron.

[467] *Consolidated Guidance to Intelligence Officers and Service Personnel on the Detention and Interviewing of Detainees Overseas, and on the Passing and Receipt of Intelligence Relating to Detainees and Note of Additional Information* (Cabinet Office, London, 2010).

[468] See *R (al-Jedda) v Secretary of State for Defence* [2007] UKHL 58; *R (al-Saadoon) v Secretary of State for Defence* [2009] EWCA Civ 7; *al-Jedda v Secretary of State for Defence* [2010] EWCA Civ 758.

[469] [2007] UKHL 27. See *Banković v Belgium*, App no 52207/99, 2001-XII; *Issa v Turkey*, App no 31821/96, 16 November 2003; *Ilaşcu v Moldova and Russia*, App no 48787/99, 8 July 2004.

government admitted to 'substantial breaches' of rights and paid compensation, while a number of soldiers were prosecuted under the International Criminal Court Act 2001 and subjected to courts martial; an inquiry by Sir William Gage is ongoing.[470] However, the application of domestic rights abroad remains uncertain and case-specific. The government has released the rules about treatment by the military[471] but has been more reticent about the rules governing attendance at foreign places of detention by intelligence agents or the reception and use of intelligence obtained by outlawed methods.[472] It has also refrained from ratification of the International Convention for the Protection of All Persons from Enforced Disappearance 2006.[473]

Operational involvement in Iraq ended in 2008. The final two internees (out of 651) were **4.204** then transferred to Iraqi custody pending trial. The legality of their transfer was disputed in *R (Al-Saadoon and Mufdhi) v Secretary of State for Defence*, but it was concluded that there remained no viable legal basis for British detentions in Iraq.[474] However, the transfer unduly risked the death penalty and breached Article 3.[475]

British military practice as to detainees in Afghanistan is to arrange a transfer to Afghan **4.205** authorities within ninety-six hours under a bilateral memorandum of understanding of 2005 (see Table 4.7).[476] The agreement forbids further transfer to a third country or the death penalty. Though this phase of the conflict has moved away from international humanitarian legal rules, it remains the practice to inform the International Committee of the Red Cross field workers of any detention within twenty-four hours and to submit a report to the ICRC in Geneva every seven days.[477]

Table 4.7 Individuals detained by conventional UK forces in Afghanistan[a]

Period	Detained	Released	Transferred to Afghans	Deceased	Detainees at year end
Apr 06 to April 07	51	26	22	3	0
Apr 07 to Oct 07	89	48	38	3	0
Oct 07 to Apr 08	96	56	39	1	0
Apr 08 to Oct 08	128	39	88	1	0
Oct 08 to Dec 08	115	48	67	0	0
Totals	479	217	254	8	0

[a] Ministry of Defence, Statistics on Afghanistan and Iraq Detentions (FOI request 20090710).

---

[470] See <http://www.bahamousainquiry.org/>. See also *Mousa v Secretary of State for Defence* [2010] EWHC 1823 (Admin); Al-Sweady Inquiry (<http://www.alsweadyinquiry.org>).
[471] Ministry of Defence, *Joint Doctrine Publication 1–10* (London, 2006).
[472] Intelligence and Security Committee, *The Handling of Detainees by UK Intelligence Personnel in Afghanistan, Guantánamo Bay and Iraq* (Cm 6469, London, 2005) and *Government Reply* (Cm 6511, London, 2005).
[473] (GA Res 61/177, 20 December 2006) art 9(b) applies on a nationality basis. Ratification is called for by the *Report of the Working Group on Enforced or Involuntary Disappearances* (A/HRC/13/31, Geneva, 2009) para 606. The Convention builds upon the Declaration on the Protection of all Persons from Enforced Disappearance (UNGA Res 47/133, 18 December 1992).
[474] [2009] EWCA Civ 7.
[475] App no 61498/08, 2 March 2010.
[476] See House of Commons Foreign Affairs Committee (2006) *Visit to Guantanamo Bay* (2006–07 HC 44) App 3.
[477] Hansard HL vol 679 col 149W (9 March 2006), Lord Drayson.

4.206 There have been no public inquiries into British army behaviour in Afghanistan, but concerns have been voiced about the conditions of Afghani custody.[478] As a result, the High Court in *R (Evans) v Secretary of State for Defence* ruled out transfers to specified Afghani detention facilities where there was a high risk of maltreatment.[479]

4.207 As for terrorist suspects detained abroad by non-British authorities, the British courts will not order the Foreign Office to help British citizens but can review whether inaction breaches administrative law. This jurisdiction was invoked by Guantánamo detainees seeking governmental intervention with the US authorities.[480] The final British detainees were released in January 2005,[481] though some former British residents remain. The House of Commons Foreign Affairs Committee has warned against the assumption of responsibility for non-citizens.[482]

G. Conclusions

4.208 The *Jellicoe Report* concluded in 1983 that 'there can be no clear proof that the arrest powers in the Prevention of Terrorism Act are, or are not, an essential weapon in the fight against terrorism'.[483] Nevertheless, the Report recommended their continuance 'while a substantial threat from terrorism remains . . .'.[484] In many ways that refuge in faith and risk aversion has barely altered during subsequent decades. Whether such equivocal support should so impact on personal liberty may be questioned, but the special terrorism powers have attracted even more champions since 11 September 2001, though patterns of usage and outcomes have not altered substantially.

4.209 The maxim of UK Prime Minister, Tony Blair, in response to the 7 July 2005 London bombing was to 'Let no one be in any doubt, the rules of the game are changing'.[485] Yet the pursuit of this 'game' can easily entail damage to the legitimacy and fairness of criminal justice systems and can thereby prove counter-productive in trying to engage the support of communities. That outcome threatens the very goal of the government's counter-terrorism strategy, which is 'to reduce the risk from international terrorism, so that people can go about their daily lives freely and with confidence'.[486] Freedom cannot be delivered by legislation which substantially diminishes civil, political, economic, or social life. Confidence cannot be secured if people are fearful of the arbitrary and ineffective impact of security measures.

---

[478] Amnesty International (2007) *Afghanistan: Detainees transferred to torture: ISAF complicity?* London.
[479] [2010] EWHC 1445 (Admin).
[480] See *R (Abassi) v Secretary of State for the Foreign and Commonwealth Office* [2002] EWCA Civ 1598; *R (Al Rawi) v Secretary of State for Foreign and Commonwealth Affairs* [2006] EWCA Civ 1279. Compare *Prime Minister of Canada v Khadr* [2009] FCA 246, *Khadr v Canada* [2010] FC 715, *Prime Minister of Canada v Khadr* [2010] FCA 199.
[481] See Center for Constitutional Rights, *Composite Statement: Detention in Afghanistan and Guantánamo Bay* (New York, 2004); Begg, M, *Enemy Combatant* (Free Press, New York, 2006); Worthington, A, *The Guantanamo Files* (Pluto Press, Cambridge, 2007).
[482] Visit to Guantánamo Bay (2006–07 HC 44) para 92.
[483] *Jellicoe Report*, para 55.
[484] Ibid para 79.
[485] *The Times* 6 August 2005, p 1.
[486] Home Office, *Pursue, Prevent, Protect, Prepare: The United Kingdom's Strategy for Countering International Terrorism* (Cm 7547, London, 2009) para 0.17.

PART III

CRIMINAL LAW AND CRIMINAL PROCESS

5

CRIMINAL OFFENCES AND TERRORISM

A. Introduction

Ever since the implementation of the *Diplock Report* after 1972, the government has **5.01** reiterated that 'prosecution is—first, second, and third—the government's preferred approach when dealing with suspected terrorists'.[1] The criminalization approach, which is the subject of this chapter, logically demands that terrorists should not be treated as offenders or prisoners with political motivations which mark them out as deserving special status. Consistent with this policy, many relevant offences are not contained in specialist anti-terrorism legislation. The criminalization approach, which embodies an appeal to legitimacy, might also be seen as logically demanding priority for established offences such as homicides, offences against the person, and explosives and firearms offences, which are indeed the common fare of major terrorist trials.

A criminal justice approach embodies individual responsibility, equality, system legality, and **5.02** due process. Consequently, it embodies ethical advantages over executive or administrative disposals or any full-blown 'war on terror'.[2] Thus, successive British governments have been right to maximize criminal justice and to reject the contention that 'it is not enough to serve our enemies with legal papers'.[3]

Yet, forbearance from interference with the solemn stages of criminal justice was never **5.03** absolute and has continued to be compromised. Thus, the anti-terrorism legislation has long

---

[1] Hansard HC vol 472 col 561 (21 February 2008), Tony McNulty.
[2] UN Office on Drugs and Crime, *Handbook on Criminal Justice Responses to Terrorism* (New York, 2009) p 3; Zedner, L, *Security* (Routledge, Abingdon, 2009) p 137.
[3] President Bush, State of the Union Address 2004, *The Washington Post* 21 January 2004, p A18.

added to the criminal catalogue. Aside from offences outlined in this chapter, it has generated offences which aid investigation (such as withholding information, as in Chapter 3), offences which curtail extreme speech (Chapter 8), and offences against the use of weapons of mass destruction (Chapter 9).

5.04 Broadly, six substantial functions can be identified for the criminal law in counter-terrorism. First, criminal law can allow for prescient intervention before a terrorist crime is completed. Secondly, there can be net-widening. Thirdly, criminal law can set a lowest common denominator of rights and so reduce obstructive 'technicalities'. Fourthly, the criminal law can be used to mobilize the population against terrorism, a particular function of the crime of withholding information. Fifthly, the criminal law can serve a denunciatory function, as with offences against the state and as also reflected in pronouncements of 'guilt' and in sentencing (Chapter 6). Thus, this chapter concentrates upon offences against the state and its citizens—'anti-systemic' crimes—rather than systemic crimes of terrorism on behalf of the state.[4] State collusion in terrorism and the state use of deadly force have been covered in Chapters 2 and 4. Sixthly, the criminal law can bolster symbolic solidarity with the state's own citizens and with the international community, as reflected by internationally devised crimes and extensions of jurisdiction.

5.05 The first three functions are those principally served by the special crimes in the anti-terrorism laws. The first function, anticipatory intervention, is reflected in precursor crimes which interdict possession or preparation. The peril of attack from Al-Qa'ida, characterized by wanton mass attacks on civilians, demands intervention at an anticipatory stage of the criminal enterprise. The response can be found in offences such as the TA 2000, ss 57 and 58, and the TA 2006, s 5. These extend the reach of the criminal law to a point where, often based on equivocal evidence, the prospect of harm is uncertain and where the only immorality has been the imagining of wickedness rather than its infliction or a fair imputation that it will occur. An almost inevitable companion is furtherance of the third function—imposing a lowest common denominator of rights so that, for example, burdens of proof are abridged.

5.06 The second function is net-widening, which is achieved in three ways. One is through the use of the term 'terrorism', a term discussed in Chapter 1. Its definition deliberately exceeds the bounds of any single offence, though it remains grounded within the notion of criminality.[5] One can perhaps understand and accept that security and policing agencies should be tasked through arrest and surveillance powers in terms wider than a concentration upon crimes. But this argument is harder to sustain regarding criminal offences where the terminology increases the danger of penalising political motives rather than violence. The second aspect of net-widening is guilt by association, such as through proscription offences (in Chapter 8) or by engaging in training. The third aspect arises from the extension of the anti-terrorism laws to foreign terrorism. This trend is reflected in the definition of 'terrorism' itself and is also implemented by jurisdictional extensions (also serving the sixth function). Thus, 'terrorism' activities directed against foreign governments become forbidden, even against those whose unworthiness for office is manifest. A rash of recent cases about Libya is testament to these

---

[4] Ross, JI, *The Dynamics of Political Crime* (Sage, Thousand Oaks, 2003) p 8. An example of an offence only commissionable by an official is torture contrary to the Criminal Justice Act 1988, s 134.

[5] *Ireland v United Kingdom*, App no 5310/71, Ser A 25 (1978) para 196; *Brogan v United Kingdom*, App nos 11209, 11234, 11266/84, 11386/85, Ser A 145-B (1988) para 50.

dangers, but in *R v F*,[6] the Court of Appeal concluded that Parliament wished to restrict political violence even against foreign despots.[7]

B. Criminal Offences Within the Anti-Terrorism Laws

The special offences of terrorism can be categorized by content (rather than the foregoing analysis of purpose). First, there are preparatory offences designed to permit early intervention. Secondly, there are extra-territorial offences, some based on international law and some reflective of national resolve to condemn terrorism worldwide.   **5.07**

Arguably the most problematic offences fall into the first category. Thus, the Joint Committee on Human Rights noted that:[8]   **5.08**

> The criminal law has not traditionally been a preventive tool in the UK. One of the central challenges for counter-terrorism policy is how to deploy the criminal process in support of a preventive strategy in a way which does not undermine the very essence of the due process guarantees which are both a part of our traditional common law and a central part of our international human rights obligations.

Several inherent procedural and evidential obstacles against their usage in the terrorism context arise from admissibility, standards and burdens of proof, timeliness, and secrecy and disclosure of evidence.[9] Imprecision of formulation is another difficulty, and Parliament has permitted offences which lack 'proper and convenient certainty'.[10] All these problems will be mentioned either in this chapter, as inherent in the special offences, or in Chapter 6, as impacting on criminal processes.   **5.09**

Training for terrorism

Introduction and background

Section 54, engagement in weapons training, is the first 'precursor offence' within Pt VI of the TA 2000. The offence previously appeared in Northern Ireland (latterly as s 34 of the EPA 1996). The offence was extended to Britain despite the recommendation otherwise by Lord Lloyd.[11] Perhaps the conviction of David Copeland, who carried out bombings in London in 1999 out of racist and homophobic motives, strengthened the case for extension.[12] He had obtained bomb-making information from the internet, though he could not actually assemble the necessary ingredients. Library books have long supplied such data.[13]   **5.10**

Fearful of incidents such as the use of sarin by the Aum Shinrikyo cult in Tokyo in 1995 as well as scares about anthrax following the 11 September attacks, the offence has been extended beyond conventional munitions.[14] The additions are described in s 55 of the TA   **5.11**

---

[6] [2007] EWCA Crim 243.

[7] Ibid paras 11, 38.

[8] Joint Committee on Human Rights, *Counter-Terrorism Policy and Human Rights: Prosecution and Pre-Charge Detention* (2005–06 HL 240/HC 1576) para 12.

[9] Ibid para 28.

[10] *O'Connell v R* (1844) 8 ER 1061 at 1093 per Tindal LCJ.

[11] *Lloyd Report*, para 14.28.

[12] See *The Times*, 1 July 2000, p 1; Wolkind, M and Sweeney, N, '*R v David Copeland*' (2001) 41 *Medicine Science & Law* 185.

[13] See Grivas-Dighenis, G, *Guerrilla Warfare and EOKA's Struggle* (Longmans, London, 1964).

[14] *Home Office Response to Lloyd Report*, para 12.13.

2000, as amended by s 120(2) of the ATCSA 2001. The offence applies to training in any 'biological weapon', 'chemical weapon', and 'radioactive material'. The definition of 'nuclear weapon', which used to appear in s 55 (by reference to the Nuclear Material (Offences) Act 1983) is now omitted, since the meaning of 'radioactive material' is wider still.

Provisions

5.12   A person commits an offence under s 54(1) by providing instruction or training in the making or use of (a) firearms, (aa) radioactive material or weapons designed or adapted for the discharge of any radioactive material, (b) explosives, or (c) chemical, biological, or nuclear weapons.

5.13   It is correspondingly an offence under s 54(2) to receive instruction or training, or, under s 54(3) to invite another to receive instruction or training contrary to sub-s (1) or (2) even if the activity is to take place outside the United Kingdom. In this way, the offence pertains to recruitment for training as well as the training itself, a response to attempts to recruit British Muslims for military training in Afghanistan, Pakistan, or elsewhere. Under s 54(4), 'instructions' and 'invitations' can be general (such as by a pamphlet or via the internet) or issued to specific persons. Quite why this offence could not be translated into regular explosives and firearms codes is unclear, save for one reference to 'terrorism' in s 54(5).

5.14   It is a defence to prove that one's action or involvement was wholly for a purpose other than assisting, preparing for, or participating in terrorism. This formulation is curiously wide. The defence would seem to apply, for example, to a non-terrorist gangster who trains confederates in how to blow off a safe door.[15] Section 118 applies an evidential burden of proof to the defence, as explained more fully later in this chapter.

5.15   Offences around training are amplified by the TA 2006, ss 6 and 8. These expand on s 54 by capturing techniques other than specified weaponry. The justification for s 6 was the Council of Europe Convention on the Prevention of Terrorism 2005,[16] Article 7, but s 8 does not derive directly from that source.

5.16   By s 6(1), an offence arises through providing instruction or training with knowledge that the person receiving it intends to use the skills in terrorism. The intention of the recipient is important—an earlier version included suspicion of future use, which could have closed down university classes in chemistry and military studies collections of public libraries.[17] Receiving instruction or training with intent is forbidden by s 6(2). Aside from overlap with s 54, similar conduct may breach ss 1 or 2 of the 2006 Act.

5.17   Section 6(3) describes the relevant skills which are the subject of the instruction or training. They must relate to: (a) the making, handling, or use of a noxious substance (defined by s 6(7)); (b) the use of any method or technique for doing anything else that is capable of being done for the purposes of terrorism, in connection with terrorism or Convention offences (as listed in Sch 1); or (c) the design or adaptation, for the purposes of terrorism or Convention offences, of any method or technique. Illustrations of each include:[18] (a) instruction about a bomb to disperse a virus; (b) a technique for causing a stampede in a crowd;

---

15   Compare *R v G and J* [2009] UKHL 13.
16   ETS 196.
17   See Hansard HL vol 676 col 716 (7 December 2005), Baroness Scotland.
18   See Home Office Circular 8/2006 (London, 2006) para 17.

or (c) giving instructions about the placing of a bomb to cause maximum disruption. The skills themselves might have a lawful purpose, especially under (b) (training in anti-surveillance techniques to avoid a stalker) and (c) (learning to fly an aircraft). The absence of a defence of reasonable excuse or lawful purpose comparable to s 54(5) reduces the pretexts which can be raised,[19] though these excuses could negative the *mens rea* under s 6.

Under s 6(4), the instruction or training can be provided to a target audience or to the world at large (such as through the internet) where the identities of the recipients are unknown. However, it will then be difficult to prove *mens rea* since the intention of the recipient(s) will also be hard to gauge.[20] By s 6(4)(b), the forms of terrorism or Convention offences can be specific or agglomerations. **5.18**

An offence under s 8(1) arises when a person attends at any place, whether in the United Kingdom or abroad, where instruction or training within s 6 or s 54(1) of the 2000 Act is being provided. This broad *actus reus* does not require participation by the perpetrator (confirmed by s 8(3)(a)), nor does it require the delineation of specific offences (confirmed in s 8(3)(b)). But the instruction or training must be 'live'. Visiting a camp during vacation breaks to talk with instructors or participants would not be an offence. By s 8(6), there need be no evidence of anyone paying heed, but there should be participants other than the instructors. **5.19**

As for the *mens rea*, by s 8(2), the person in attendance must know or believe that instruction or training is being provided for purposes connected with terrorism or Convention offences, or the circumstances are such that a reasonable person would have realized the nature of the activity. Under the second, objective formula, persons may breach this standard if the penny drops after a reasonable person would have realized what was going on and would have withdrawn beforehand. It is also not part of the *mens rea* that the offender intends or condones the training. Guilt is assigned by association rather than involvement. **5.20**

The main debate about s 8 was whether there should be a reasonable excuse for mere observation, such as by a journalist.[21] The government was steadfast against creating exceptions and viewed such investigative journalism or research as a step too far.[22] The same would apply to the deliverers of groceries[23] or even to would-be peace envoys. **5.21**

Given the allegation that most *jihadi* attacks in Britain are prepared in Pakistan,[24] s 8 could be invoked to cast suspicions on persons attending some *madrasses*. A more beneficial effect might be to displace control orders (described in Chapter 7) which have been repeatedly applied to those travelling abroad in suspicious circumstances.[25] **5.22**

---

[19] See Joint Committee on Human Rights, *Counter-Terrorism Policy and Human Rights: Prosecution and Pre-Charge Detention* (2005–06 HL 240/HC 1576) para 59.

[20] See Leigh, LH, 'The Terrorism Act 2006–a brief analysis' (2006) 170 *Justice of the Peace* 364.

[21] Lord Carlile, *Proposals by Her Majesty's Government for Changes to the Laws against Terrorism* (Home Office, 2005) para 39.

[22] Hansard HC vol 438 col 1015 (3 November 2005), Paul Goggins; *Government Reply to the Joint Committee on Human Rights* (2005–06 HL114/HC 888) p 10.

[23] Jones, A, Bowers, R, and Lodge, HD, *The Terrorism Act 2006* (Oxford University Press, Oxford, 2006) para 3.20.

[24] Cabinet Office, *The National Security Strategy of the United Kingdom: Update 2009—Security for the Next Generation* (Cm 7590, London, 2009) para 2.30.

[25] See the case of Habib Ahmed, *The Times* 21 September 2006, p 11.

Implementation

5.23 The penalty under s 54 is up to ten years' imprisonment, and the court may also forfeit items connected with the offence.[26] The maximum penalty under ss 6 and 8 is ten years, and materials under s 6 can be forfeited under s 7.

5.24 Sulayman Balal Zainulabidin, a chef from Greenwich, was charged under s 54 in 2001 arising from his promotion of the Sakina Security Services, which offered to internet customers 'The Ultimate Jihad Challenge' (some of which was to occur at a facility called Ground Zero in Alabama).[27] He was acquitted. There was no evidence to link him to Al-Qa'ida and, over a period of two years, only one person had applied for the course. The vaguer offence under s 6 might now offer a more suitable charge.

5.25 Next, Mohammed Hamid (the self-styled 'Osama bin London') was convicted with six others for attendance at meetings and some outdoor events (in the New Forest and Berkshire).[28] The Court of Appeal held that, so far as followers of training were concerned, s 8 did not require proof of intent to implement the training, albeit that the person knows or could not fail to understand that the training has a terrorist purpose. In this way, though s 8 refers to training under s 6(1) and though s 6(1) requires proof of intent to put the skills into commission, there is no transmission of that intent into s 8, otherwise proof of s 8 would always require proof of s 6 too. So, s 8 is to be interpreted as referring to the character of the training rather than to the state of mind of the provider of the training. This interpretation left for s 6(2) the situation of a person who receives training with intent to action it. The Court of Appeal also rejected the argument that the skills outlined in s 6(3)(b) were so broad as to lack for certainty in breach of Article 7 of the European Convention. Certainty was ensured by the requirements in s 6(1)(b) that a defendant had to have known that at least one of those he was training had the intention of putting the training to terrorist use.

5.26 Next, Waheed Ali and Mohammed Shakil were convicted of conspiracy to engage in attendance at terrorist training in Pakistan contrary to s 6 of the TA 2006.[29] The somewhat equivocal evidence, albeit from newspaper reports, was their attempt to board an aircraft to Pakistan and their admitted attendance at camps before s 6 came into force. They were sentenced to seven years' imprisonment.

Foreign comparisons

5.27 Under the Australian Anti-terrorism Act 2004 (inserting s 102.5 of the Criminal Code 1995), the offence of training a terrorist organization or receiving training from a terrorist organization is instituted. Proof of knowledge as to the provenance of the training is not required.[30] The Australian government proposes a ministerial scheme to authorize humanitarian aid.[31]

---

[26] See further s 120A, inserted by the TA 2006, s 37, to ensure consistency with s 7.
[27] *The Guardian* 10 August 2002, p 6.
[28] *R v Da Costa* [2009] EWCA Crim 482.
[29] *The Times* 30 April 2009, p 12 (Kingston Crown Court).
[30] See Senate Legal and Constitutional Affairs Legislation Committee, *Anti-Terrorism Laws Reform Bill 2009* (Canberra, 2009) para 2.15; Law Council of Australia, *Anti-Terrorism Reform Project* (Canberra, 2009) para 4.4.3.
[31] Attorney General's Department, *National Security Legislation* (Canberra, 2009) p 67.

Terrorist training in US law may be penalized as a 'material support' offence, discussed later **5.28** in this chapter. According to Combatant Status Review Tribunal hearings at Guantánamo, 317 detainees 'took military or terrorist training in Afghanistan'.[32]

Assessment and conclusions

The policy purpose of these offences is to bring forward the impact of the criminal law and **5.29** thereby secure the CONTEST element of 'Pursue'. Reliance on these special offences, as well as other public order reforms, allowed for the repeal of the Unlawful Drilling Act 1819 by the Statute Law Repeals Act 2008. However, it was retained for Northern Ireland because of unspecified and unexplained 'differences in public order law between Northern Ireland and the remainder of the United Kingdom'.[33]

A grey area which remains is the private military company sector. Proposals for regulation **5.30** by the Foreign and Commonwealth Office began in 2002.[34] However, no action has been taken. In a paper issued in 2009,[35] the government rejects national licensing and adopts self-regulation via a code of conduct. Military equipment is, however, regulated under the Export Control Act 2002.[36]

The legislative objective of avoiding the dissemination of information which makes terrorism **5.31** more prevalent or proficient is sufficiently important to justify limiting associational and expressional rights. However, it may be doubted whether s 8 strikes a proper balance between the gains for the policy purpose and the incursion into individual rights when applied to *bona fide* journalists on whom it is 'incumbent . . . to impart information and ideas on matters of public interest'.[37]

As for accountability, there was full Parliamentary debate about these offences, especially s 8. **5.32** They do not present any acute problems of vagueness, though the Australian proposal for authorizations could improve certainty for charities working in conflict zones.

Directing a terrorist organization

Introduction and background

The next special precursor offence is directing a terrorist organization contrary to s 56 of the **5.33** TA 2000. Section 56 derives from the mounting apprehension in Northern Ireland in the late 1980s about terrorist 'godfathers' who avoided involvement at the sharp end of death and destruction.[38] The first appearance was as s 27 of the EPA 1991 (latterly s 29 of the EPA 1996), but s 56 now applies to all organized terrorism (and not just proscribed organizations) throughout the United Kingdom.

---

[32] Wittes, B, *Law and the Long War* (Penguin, New York, 2008) p 81. Compare 18 USC s 2339D (Intelligence Reform and Terrorism Prevention Act 2004, PL 108-458) which demands a link to a designated foreign terrorist organization.

[33] Law Commission and Scottish Law Commission, Statute Law Repeals (Eighteenth Report) Draft Statute Law (Repeals) Bill (Cm 7303, London, 2008) para 3.9.

[34] *Private Military Companies: Options for Regulation* (2001–02 HC 577). See Walker, C and Whyte, D, 'Contracting out war?' (2005) 54 *International & Comparative Law Quarterly* 651.

[35] Foreign & Commonwealth Office, *Promoting High Standards of Conduct by Private Military and Security Companies (PMSCs) Internationally* (London, 2009) para 24.

[36] See Export Control Order 2008, SI 2008/3231.

[37] *Observer and Guardian v United Kingdom*, App no 13585/88, Ser A 216 (1991) para 59.

[38] See Walker, C and Reid, K, 'The offence of directing terrorist organisations' [1993] *Criminal Law Review* 669.

Provisions

5.34 It is an offence under s 56(1) to direct, at any level, the activities of an organization which is concerned in the commission of acts of terrorism.

5.35 All 'directions' are penalized, even if lawful and, indeed, desirable. For example, it would be an offence for an IRA commander to direct others to surrender, to observe a ceasefire, or to help in fund-raising for prisoners' wives. Another example might be the IRA commander who orders the IRA quartermaster to buy a gross of balaclavas. The underling might commit a Pt II or III offence under the TA 2000; the director would additionally infringe s 56. Evidence of 'predicate crimes' such as these will be powerful aids to prosecution under s 56 but are not essential.

5.36 'Directing' has its ordinary, common-sense meaning, and the reference to 'any level' is designed to catch not so much minor members of the terrorist group as regional and local (as well as headquarters) leaders.[39] Thus, it is not a fair criticism that the concept, 'directs', is contradicted by the qualification, 'at any level', or that the IRA's kitchen staff would be guilty under s 56 by 'directing' the washing up of the IRA's dirty dishes.[40] In law, to 'direct' has been defined more narrowly than is implied by such examples and seems to embody the attributes of being able to order other people and of commanding some obedience from them.[41] Thus, direction 'embraces the notion of a controlling influence on the activities in question'.[42]

Implementation

5.37 Section 56 imposes up to life imprisonment, a level of severity matched only by the TA 2000, s 5.

5.38 Very few convictions have been secured, but the Home Office maintains that they had 'a major impact'.[43] The most notable prosecution in Northern Ireland involved Johnny Adair, the Loyalist gang leader.[44] The only reported British case concerns Rangzieb Ahmed,[45] who was convicted of directing terrorism on behalf of Al-Qa'ida through cells in Dubai and Saudi Arabia. His life sentence tariff was ten years.

Foreign comparisons

5.39 The Canadian Anti-terrorist Act 2001 inserts s 82.22 into the Criminal Code which involves instructing the carrying out of terrorist activities, while s 83.21 involves the instruction of activities to enhance the abilities of terrorist groups.[46]

Assessment and conclusions

5.40 One criticism of s 56 is that it is too widely worded by catching organizations which are not proscribed[47] and that it penalizes all directions, even if lawful and, indeed, even if desirable. Other criticisms surround the severe penalty, which appears disproportionate compared to

---

[39] Hansard HC vol 187 col 404 (6 March 1991).

[40] Hansard HL vol 528 col 1394 (13 May 1991).

[41] See *Bolton Engineering v T.J. Graham* [1957] 1 QB 159; *Dudderidge v Rawlings* (1912) 108 LT 802.

[42] Hansard HL vol 528 col 1396 (13 May 1991), Lord Belstead.

[43] *Home Office Response to Lloyd Report*, para 12.9.

[44] See *The Irish Times* 7 September 1994, p 8.

[45] *The Times* 19 December 2008, p 8 (Manchester Crown Court).

[46] See Roach, K, 'The new anti-terrorism offences and the criminal law' in Daniels, RJ et al, *The Security of Freedom* (University of Toronto Press, Toronto, 2001).

[47] See Hansard HC vol 187 col 403 (6 March 1991).

homicides. The most important practical criticism is that the offence is unnecessary. Proof of it will almost inevitably require proof of other serious offences.

In reply, it may be argued that the offence may ensnare those who influence but do not **5.41** participate. An example might be Danny Morrison of Sinn Féin, who described himself as 'walking on egg shells' to avoid being implicated in an ongoing IRA operation arising from a kidnapping.[48] Yet, the more specific and detailed the direction (features necessary to prove the offence), the less s 56 becomes vital, since it will then become possible to link the director to more specific crimes such as indirect incitements and preparatory acts.

Possession for terrorist purposes

The next two precursor offences, of possession for terrorist purposes in the TA 2000, one **5.42** relating to items (s 57) and one to information (s 58), are the most important of all.

Possession of items—s 57

(i) Introduction and background   The offence of possession of items for terrorist purposes **5.43** began life as s 30 of the EPA 1991, though the notion was there confined to possession in public places.[49] Then, the Criminal Justice and Public Order Act 1994, s 63, enacted the offence in Britain by way of the PT(TP)A 1989, s 16A. Continuance and extension throughout the United Kingdom was supported by Lord Lloyd.[50]

(ii) Provisions   Section 57(1) is contravened by possession of an article in circumstances **5.44** which give rise to a reasonable suspicion that the possession is for a purpose connected with terrorism. The 'terrorism' is not confined to the activities of proscribed organizations. 'Article' is further defined in s 121 to include 'substance and any other thing'. The articles possessed will often be lawful in themselves and even commonplace. Section 57 is not invoked against those caught red-handed in possession of explosives and firearms, where more specific offences apply.[51] Rather, items such as wires, batteries, rubber gloves, scales, electronic timers, overalls, balaclavas, agricultural fertilizer, and gas cylinders, especially in conjunction, form the diet of s 57. The collection may be highly equivocal—persons with overalls and balaclavas may be preparing for an attack on a police patrol or on a rabbit warren.[52]

Where multiple use articles, such as computer disks or cars, are possessed for several **5.45** purposes, it is submitted that s 57(1) only requires 'a' purpose to be nefarious, not a main or sole purpose.[53] In *R v Omar Altimini*,[54] it was held that materials held on computer by a 'sleeper' contravened s 57. The immediate purpose might be safe storage, but an ultimate purpose included terrorism whether by the defendant or another.

The intent required for s 57 requires that the defendant has knowledge of the presence of, **5.46** and control over, the article.[55] Based on that possession and control, the Crown must prove beyond reasonable doubt that those circumstances give rise to a reasonable suspicion of a

---

[48] *R v Martin and Morrison* [1992] 5 NIJB 1. He was later acquitted: *R v Morrison* [2009] NICA 1.
[49] See *Review of the Northern Ireland (Emergency Provisions) Acts 1978 and 1987* (Cm 1115, London, 1990) para 2.9.
[50] *Inquiry into Legislation against Terrorism* (Cm 3420, London, 1996) para 14.6.
[51] See Explosive Substances Act 1883, s 4; Firearms Act 1968, ss 16–21.
[52] See *R v Lanigan* [1987] NI 367; *R v Murray* [1993] NI 105.
[53] Compare *R v Zafar* [2008] EWCA Crim 184 at para 22.
[54] [2008] EWCA Crim 2829.
[55] *R v G and J* [2009] UKHL 13 at para 53.

terrorist purpose. Proof of possession for a terrorist purpose requires examination of the circumstances of possession, but the Crown does not need to prove the precise, subjective purpose harboured by the defendant—'something which might well be impossible to prove'.[56]

5.47   The connection between the content of the article and the implementation of terrorism was clarified in *R v Zafar*.[57] The prosecution had sought a guilty verdict on the basis that the relevant purposes of the articles related to travelling to Pakistan, training in Pakistan, and fighting in Afghanistan. At the time, only the last item on the list was unlawful, which suggests a requirement not only of a link to terrorism in some passive sense but a link to active terrorist offending. To fulfil the phrase 'for a purpose in connection with', there must be proven 'a direct connection between the objects possessed and the acts of terrorism. The section should be interpreted as if it reads . . . he intends it to be used for the purpose . . .'[58] An indirect connection between possession of the item and potential terrorist acts is not enough. So, there was nothing inherent in travel to Pakistan which directly connected to the incitement amongst the group to engage in terrorism. Any further actions in Pakistan were conditional on later intentions and actions.[59] Thus, the convictions were unsound.

5.48   Proof of 'possession' is aided by sub-s (3): if it is proved that an article (a) was on any premises at the same time as the accused; or (b) was on premises of which the accused was the occupier or which he habitually used otherwise than as a member of the public, the court may assume that the accused possessed the article. In response, it is open to the defendant to show he did not know of the presence of the item on the premises or had no control over it.

5.49   Recognizing the possible overreach of this offence from the phrase 'circumstances which give rise to a reasonable suspicion', s 57(2) offers a defence by proof that possession of the article was not for a purpose connected with the commission, preparation, or instigation of an act of terrorism. In *Mohammed Atif Siddique v HM Advocate*, it was emphasized that the trial judge should direct on the 'crucial relationship' between the breadth of s 57(1) and the defence in s 57(2).[60] According to *R v G (Gardner) and J (Jobe)*, the defence does not nullify the elements already proven but provides an excuse for them, which the prosecution can then challenge beyond reasonable doubt.[61] In response, and as already mentioned, the Crown does not, however, have to prove beyond reasonable doubt that the defendant's possession of the article was for a purpose connected with terrorism—that would be to go beyond the defence and add elements to the formulation of the offence.[62] For example, if the evidence concerns the possession of fertilizer, and the defendant shows sufficiently, under s 118, a non-terrorist purpose connected with gardening, the prosecution must show beyond reasonable doubt that the defence is untrue:[63]

> . . . for instance, by leading evidence that the garden had been consistently neglected, that there were no gardening tools in the house, and that the quantity of fertiliser was more than would be required for the garden in question. . . . There is no need whatever for the Crown to

---

[56]   Ibid para 55.
[57]   [2008] EWCA Crim 184.
[58]   Ibid para 29.
[59]   Ibid para 45.
[60]   [2010] HCJAC 7 at para 81.
[61]   [2009] UKHL 13 at paras 63, 66.
[62]   Ibid para 67.
[63]   Ibid para 68.

go further . . . and prove, beyond reasonable doubt, that the defendant actually possessed the fertiliser for a purpose connected with the commission etc of an act of terrorism. That would be to impose on the Crown a requirement that is not to be found in section 57(1).

The meaning of the offence and its possible breach of Article 6(2) of the European Convention, **5.50** by switching the burden of proof onto the defence contrary to the presumption of innocence, has been considered in *R v Director of Public Prosecutions, ex parte Kebilene*.[64] The Divisional Court condemned a 'blatant and obvious' breach of Article 6(2).[65] The House of Lords ultimately decided the case on the technical ground of the non-reviewability of prosecution decisions. Nevertheless, drawing upon s 3 of the Human Rights Act 1998, Lord Hope devised a modified meaning which complied with Article 6(2):[66]

> It is necessary in the first place to distinguish between the shifting from the prosecution to the accused . . . the 'evidential burden', or the burden of introducing evidence in support of his case, on the one hand and the 'persuasive burden,' or the burden of persuading the jury as to his guilt or innocence, on the other. A 'persuasive' burden of proof requires the accused to prove, on a balance of probabilities, a fact which is essential to the determination of his guilt or innocence. It reverses the burden of proof by removing it from the prosecution and transferring it to the accused. An 'evidential' burden requires only that the accused must adduce sufficient evidence to raise an issue before it has to be determined as one of the facts in the case. The prosecution does not need to lead any evidence about it, so the accused needs to do this if he wishes to put the point in issue. But if it is put in issue, the burden of proof remains with the prosecution. The accused need only raise a reasonable doubt about his guilt.

Flowing from this distinction, an 'evidential' burden, as under s 57(2), does not necessarily **5.51** breach the presumption of innocence under Article 6(2), which, though a fundamental right, does allow some manipulation where important social concerns are involved and where the defendant has ready access to the information required for the defence.[67] Once the issue is raised, the burden is met, and the prosecution must disprove any defence and discharge the final burden of proof of guilt beyond reasonable doubt of all essential facts (possession and reasonable suspicion of a terrorist purpose). By contrast, statutory presumptions which transfer the legal or 'persuasive' burden to the accused, or, even more starkly, a 'mandatory' presumption of guilt relating to an essential element of the offence would more probably breach Article 6(2).

In reaction to *Kebilene*, s 118 was added to the 2000 Act and affects s 57(2) and (3). By s 118, **5.52** if evidence is adduced which is sufficient to raise an issue, the court shall treat it as proved unless the prosecution disproves it beyond reasonable doubt. This formula was intended to be merely declaratory.[68] It certainly prevents s 57 from placing any 'legal' or 'persuasive' burden upon the defendant. It may also slightly ease the 'evidential' burden placed on the defendant by requiring simply the issue to be raised for it to negate the presumption in the statute unless the prosecution can prove otherwise.[69] Certainly, the courts have been

---

[64] [2000] 2 AC 326.
[65] Ibid 344 per Lord Bingham.
[66] [2000] 2 AC 326 at 378–9.
[67] See *Salabiaku v France*, App no 10519/83 Ser A 141-A (1988); *Sheldrake v Director of Public Prosecutions; Attorney General's Reference (No 4 of 2002)* [2004] UKHL 43; Trechsel, S, *Human Rights in Criminal Proceedings* (Oxford University Press, Oxford, 2005) pp 168–71.
[68] Hansard HL vol 613 col 754 (16 May 2000), Lord Bassam.
[69] See Rowe, JJ, 'The Terrorism Act 2000' [2000] *Criminal Law Review* 527 at 540.

receptive to defendants. In *R v Boutrab*,[70] a bare claim that 'curiosity' was the reason for possession was sufficient to switch the burden back to the prosecution, though in *Kebilene*, Lord Hope warned that 'It should not be thought that proof to this standard will be a formality.'[71]

5.53   Some commentators suggest that the dispute is misconceived because the prosecution must prove beyond reasonable doubt not only the possession of the items relevant to s 57 but also reasonable suspicion of the terrorist purpose, so that the burden of proof is not shifted at all.[72] A comparison is made with other offences relating to preparatory stages, such as going equipped for theft (Theft Act 1968, s 25) or possession of an offensive weapon (Prevention of Crime Act 1953, s 1). Yet, the presence of items under s 57 is far less suggestive of blameworthy conduct than under those offences. Being in charge of false identity documents, counterfeit credit cards, and a three band radio, as in the case of *Meziane*,[73] is much less determinative of terrorism purposes than is possession of a knife or a jemmy in a public place suggestive of an intended assault or burglary. Proof beyond reasonable doubt of a reasonable suspicion harboured in the minds of the forces of law and order (and not even a guilty mindset on the part of the accused) is a long way away from proof, in classical Millian terms of harm being actually perpetrated by a wrongdoer. Rather, the presence of items will be linked, for example, to associations or expressed beliefs to weave a charge. Thus, s 57 might be said to trivialise the prosecution's burden, especially as, in addition, it requires no direct proof of a terrorist purpose. The fact that the defendant has to respond to such a relatively light burden is surely not much different to a criticism that at the end of the day the burden of proof is shifted. It is true that an offence has to be proven at the outset by the prosecution, but if that takes no great effort, then the real task in court is for the defence, which of course was always the legislative intent.

5.54   A further argument to be considered is that the real argument is about the formulation of criminal offences rather than burdens of proof.[74] Yet, this worthy insight does not absolve s 57 from unfairness. It is true that elements of criminal liability are substantive rather than procedural and so fall outside English conceptions of the presumption of innocence. But the European Convention sense of fairness does seem to be much wider in that it is concerned with the overall fairness of process.[75]

5.55   Adding to the debate is the decision in *Sheldrake v Director of Public Prosecutions; Attorney General's Reference (No 4 of 2002)*.[76] Here, the reverse burden of proof in s 11(2) of the 2000 Act was again read down as an evidential and not legal burden, even though Lord Bingham believed that Parliament's intention was otherwise, especially because it was not listed in s 118.[77] The result would seem to be three levels of reactions to reverse burdens. First, the measure might be interpreted on its face or by reference to s 118 as imposing an evidential burden. Second, where s 118 does not apply and even where the burden is expressed to be

---

[70]   [2005] NICC 30 at paras 80, 84.

[71]   [2000] 2 AC 326 at 387.

[72]   Roberts, P, 'The presumption of innocence brought home?' (2002) 118 *Law Quarterly Review* 41 at 54.

[73]   *The Times* 2 April 2003, p 11. See *R v Meziane* [2004] EWCA Crim 1768.

[74]   Buxton, R, 'The Human Rights Act and the substantive criminal law' [2000] *Criminal Law Review* 331 at 332.

[75]   See *(John) Murray v United Kingdom*, App no 18731/91, 1996-I, at paras 45, 47.

[76]   [2004] UKHL 43.

[77]   Ibid para 50.

legal, then unless the offence is also expressed to overrule Article 6(2), the *Attorney General's Reference (No 4 of 2002)* will ride to the rescue where it is felt that the legal burden would be unfair, which will be judged according to the effects of the reverse burden, including how easily the accused can discharge the burden or how difficult it would be for the prosecution to establish the facts, bearing in mind the seriousness of the offences and the level of penalties.

It should be part of the prosecution's burden to show direct proof of a terroristic purpose in **5.56** the mind of the accused as opposed to reasonable suspicion in the mind of the police or prosecutor. There has latterly been some movement in this direction, as will be described in the commentary about s 58. It should also be realized that there are alternative inchoate offences aplenty in this field. Perhaps it is fairer and more convincing to prove 'conspiracy' rather than 'possession' along with a specific offence, such as causing explosions, rather than a penchant for terrorism.

(iii) Implementation The maximum penalty was increased by the TA 2006, s 13, from **5.57** ten to fifteen years' imprisonment, following criticisms in *R v Rowe*.[78] The appellant was sentenced to seven-and-a-half years' imprisonment on each count consecutive (total sentence, fifteen years' imprisonment). On appeal,[79] it was accepted that s 57 offences are not as culpable as attempting to commit, or actually committing, the terrorist acts in question. However, the forseeability of harm could justify the consecutive sentence for the possession of notes about a mortar as well as a substitution code, but given that it had been possessed for some years without implementation, two-and-a-half years sufficed for that offence (reaching a total of ten years).

Since 2006, sentences have included seven years for a car loaned for terrorist purposes.[80] **5.58** In *R v Sultan Mohamed and Aabid Hassain Khan*,[81] convictions meriting twelve years arose from the possession by the second accused of propaganda and instructional material which had been promoted to others, including through a website, and he had also conducted observations of security at Manchester Airport. Eight-year concurrent sentences were imposed on Omar Khyam for two counts of possessing aluminium powder and fertilizer.[82] Krenar Lusha was sentenced to seven years for five counts under s 57 by collecting information on how to make explosives and suicide belts, alongside a large quantity of petrol and two kilograms of potassium nitrate.[83]

Collection of information—s 58

(i) Introduction and background Offences of collecting, recording, or possessing **5.59** information in a document or record of a kind likely to be useful to terrorism under s 58 of the TA 2000 first existed in Northern Ireland (latterly in the EPA 1996, s 33). They were translated into Britain by the Criminal Justice and Public Order Act 1994, s 63, as s 16B of the PT(TP)A 1989.

(ii) Provisions Section 58(1) contains two variants of *actus reus*: collecting or making a **5.60** record of information likely to be useful in terrorism or possessing a document or record

---

[78] *The Guardian* 24 September 2005, p 7.
[79] [2007] EWCA Crim 635.
[80] See *R v Harkness* [2008] NICA 51.
[81] [2009] EWCA Crim 2653.
[82] [2008] EWCA Crim 1612.
[83] *Derby Evening Telegraph* 16 December 2009, p 2 (Preston Crown Court).

containing information of that kind. A 'record' includes photographic or electronic formats as well as writings and drawings (s 58(2)), but mental notes and knowledge which are not recorded are not covered. It is unnecessary to show that the information was obtained or held in breach of other laws. The possession of army manuals was the basis for conviction in *R v Lorenc*.[84]

5.61   The meaning of 'possession' was considered in *R v McMurray*.[85] M was sentenced to six months, suspended for two years, for possessing nine documents, when his thumbprint was discovered on one of the documents which were found in the house of another. M alleged that he was only invited to have a look. The Northern Ireland Court of Appeal held that possession must be voluntary and must involve actual or potential physical control. The accused must have knowledge of the nature (the contents) of what is possessed. The length of time of possession is not material to guilt, though the sentence reflected his brief period of possession.

5.62   As for *mens rea*, s 58 does not contain any equivalent to s 57(3), regarding the assumption of possession of the articles in certain circumstances. Therefore, the Crown must prove beyond a reasonable doubt that there is knowledge as to the presence of, and control over, the document or record.[86] A further element is that the defendant must be aware of the nature of the information—measures of concealment will be good evidence of such knowledge.[87]

5.63   There is no element in s 58(1) that requires the Crown to show that the defendant had a terrorist purpose. In *R v K*, the defendant, Khalid Khaliq, mounted the bold argument that s 58 was insufficiently certain to comply with Article 7 of the European Convention. In response, the Court of Appeal sought to remedy any imprecision by reading in the require-ment of a purpose useful to terrorism. In this case, it is the purpose of the information rather than the possessor which is at stake—it intrinsically 'calls for an explanation'.[88] The information (without regard to its surrounding circumstances, unlike under s 57) must be of an intrinsic kind which gives rise to a reasonable suspicion on its face that it is likely to provide practical assistance to a person committing or preparing terrorism rather than simply encouraging the commission of terrorism. To illustrate, the A-Z of London could be of use to a terrorist in order to find a target, but that use would not place it under s 58 since that document does not intrinsically arouse suspicion unless one looked at the circumstances of its usage. It fol-lows that the value of extrinsic evidence about the documentation is of very limited value.[89]

5.64   The ruling in *R v K* was applied in *R v Samina Malik*.[90] The defendant, known by her pen-name as the 'Lyrical Terrorist', was convicted under s 58, not for her crass doggerel such as 'How to Behead' but for possession of documents about military techniques, along with other documents of a propagandist nature. She was acquitted on appeal since the judge's summing up had failed to isolate those documents capable of founding a conviction under s 58 by satisfying the test of inherent practical utility. The House of Lords in *R v G and J*[91]

---

[84]   [1988] NI 96.
[85]   [1996] 8 BNIL n 30.
[86]   *R v G and J* [2009] UKHL 13 at para 46.
[87]   Ibid paras 47, 48.
[88]   [2008] EWCA Crim 185 at para 14. See further *R v G and J* [2009] UKHL 13 at para 44 on reliance upon extrinsic explanations.
[89]   *R v G and J* [2009] UKHL 13 at para 44.
[90]   [2008] EWCA Crim 1450.
[91]   [2009] UKHL 13 at para 43. The terrorist may be the defendant or a third party: para 49.

endorsed that 'the aim was to catch the possession of information which would typically be of use to terrorists, as opposed to ordinary members of the population . . . the information must, of its very nature, be designed to provide practical assistance'. The usage need not be unique to terrorists—a manual on explosives might also benefit bank robbers but would still raise suspicions of a terrorist purpose.

This formula was applied in *R v Sultan Mohamed*.[92] The defendant was convicted under s 58 **5.65** for possession of a document which described ways of avoiding surveillance and detection. The defence that avoiding detection was distinct from the perpetration of terrorism was rejected as an unnecessary distinction in the spectrum of preparatory activities. Equally, the fact that the material might be useful to criminals other than terrorists did not exclude it from s 58.

By s 58(3), it is a defence when the prosecution has proven all elements of the offence[93] for **5.66** the defendant to prove a 'reasonable excuse'. As with s 57(2), the defence does not nullify the elements already proven but provides an excuse for them, which the prosecution can then challenge beyond reasonable doubt but without also proving beyond reasonable doubt that the defendant's possession of the article was for a purpose connected with terrorism.[94]

Here, relevant extrinsic evidence can be adduced, and it should be left to the jury to divine **5.67** its reasonableness.[95] Suppose a defendant raises a defence of reasonable excuse regarding the possession of a computer disk containing the *Al Qa'eda Training Manual* that he had found it on a train minutes earlier and was going to hand it in to the police when stopped under s 44.[96] If the Crown proved beyond a reasonable doubt that the defendant's story was untrue—maybe he had phoned a contact to pass on the disk—the defence is defeated, but the Crown do not also have to show the precise terrorist purpose for which the information was really to be used. In *R v McLaughlin*,[97] a hobby radio enthusiast had a reasonable excuse for possessing a list of police radio frequencies, though the Court of Appeal in that case did seem to take account of purpose, which is not sound law under s 58.

Once again, the main controversy surrounding s 58 concerns the equivocal nature of the **5.68** actions involved and the fact that the defendant shoulders the burden of proof of reasonable excuse under s 58(3), subject to s 118. The indeterminate range of the offence causes alarm to journalists: 'What journalist worth his or her salt does not have a contacts book? A cuttings file? A file on the activities and personal details of prominent public figures?'[98] Terrorism scholars might also skirt s 58.

(iii) Implementation   The penalties equate to those for s 54. Forfeiture may be ordered of **5.69** any document or record containing the impugned information.

According to *R v Mansha*,[99] 'a person convicted of a terrorist offence must expect a substantial **5.70** sentence . . . to serve as a deterrent to others and to mark the extreme seriousness of the criminality'. A sentence of six years' imprisonment was imposed.

---

[92] [2010] EWCA Crim 227.
[93] Ibid para 60.
[94] *R v G and J* [2009] UKHL 13 at paras 63, 69.
[95] *R v AY* [2010] EWCA Crim 762 at paras 21, 25.
[96] *R v G and J* [2009] UKHL 13 at para 69.
[97] [1993] NI 28. See further *R v G and J* [2009] UKHL 13 at para 84.
[98] Hickman, L, 'Press freedom and new legislation' (2001) 151 *New Law Journal* 716.
[99] [2006] EWCA Crim 2051 at para 11 per Forbes J.

5.71 Yet, following the foregoing judicial revisions, some toning down in the severity of sentences has occurred for the possession of extremist literature. For example, the court applied a nine-month suspended sentence and community service in *R v Samina Malik* (later acquitted on appeal).[100] In *R v Sultan Mohammed and Aabid Hassain Khan*,[101] the first accused possessed bomb-making materials but had not shown them to others. The appropriate sentence was reduced from ten to eight years. The case returned to the courts in relation to one of counts in *R v Muhammed*; since the offence comprised accessible information, the sentence was lowered from four to two years.[102] Next, Houria Chahed Chentouf was discovered in possession of an explosives manual as well as a document which explained the military applications of household electronics.[103] She was sentenced to two years. Nicky Davison was convicted of three charges and was sentenced to two years' youth detention, recognizing the malign influence of his father, Ian Davison who, by contrast, was sentenced to six years even though the materials comprised readily available works such as *The Anarchist Cookbook* and *The Mujahideen Explosives Handbook*.[104] Akin to Ian Davison, Abdul Patel was likewise sentenced to just six months owing to his naivety in holding materials for an associate of his father.[105] Even Mohammed Shamin Uddin, who collected information about hydrogen peroxide in connection with the 'Liquid Bomb' airline plot, was sentenced to just fifteen months.[106]

Litigation about ss 57 and 58

5.72 Two principal disputes have arisen in recent litigation which cut across both offences. The first controversy is whether ss 57 and 58 are mutually exclusive, which was the unexpected verdict in *R v M*.[107] The defendants (Malik, Zafar, and others) were subject to three sets of 'mirror image' counts under ss 57 and 58. The prosecution sought to justify the dual charges on two grounds: that s 57 refers to an 'instigation' which is not covered by s 58; and that s 58 criminalizes the collection of information or the making of a record of information, which is 'likely to be useful' to terrorism, whereas s 57 demands a reasonable suspicion that that is the case. The foregoing differences were not sufficient to convince Lord Justice Hooper to accept the duality on the basis that it had rendered redundant s 58 since any 'document or record' will be an 'article' under s 57.[108]

5.73 These conclusions were rightly rejected shortly afterwards by the Court of Appeal in *R v Rowe*.[109] Rowe had been convicted under s 57 for the possession of notes on mortar bombs and of a code about possible targets, but he argued that he should have been prosecuted under s 58. However, the earlier decision was rejected. It was accepted that vaguely worded anti-terrorism offences overlap, an intended feature of the sweeping legislation. The overlapping provisions are not, however, redundant since there remain important differences between ss 57 and 58.[110] First, s 57 applies to possession, while s 58 applies not only to

---

[100] *The Times* 6 December 2007, p 31.
[101] [2009] EWCA Crim 2653. A third defendant, Hammaad Munshi, who was sixteen at the time of his arrest, was sentenced to two years' youth detention.
[102] [2010] EWCA 227.
[103] *The Times* 3 November 2009, p 18 (Manchester Crown Court).
[104] *The Times* 15 May 2010, p 31 (Newcastle Crown Court).
[105] *The Times* 27 September 2007, p 13 and 27 October 2007, p 17 (Central Criminal Court).
[106] *The Times* 10 December 2009, p 13 (Woolwich Crown Court).
[107] [2007] EWCA Crim 218.
[108] Ibid paras 33, 34.
[109] [2007] EWCA Crim 635, as applied in *R v Boutrab* [2007] NICA 23.
[110] See further *R v G and J* [2009] UKHL 13 at paras 57–59.

possession but also to collecting or making. Secondly, s 57 covers 'articles' which are widely defined, whereas s 58 covers only 'documents or records' which are a sub-set of articles. Thirdly, s 57 applies where the circumstances give rise to a reasonable suspicion of a terrorist purpose (which may be dispelled by a defendant without specific intent), whereas s 58 focuses on the nature of the information without regard to circumstances or purpose. This ruling was applied to Malik, Zafar, and others in *R v M (No 2)*.[111] Nevertheless, while overlapping offences are possible, there must be regard to the possible confusion of juries if both are run together.[112]

The second principal dispute relates to the bounds of 'reasonable excuse' as a defence under **5.74** ss 57(2) and 58(3). Can plotting terrorism aggressively or defensively against a tyrannical regime be excused as the noble cause of 'freedom fighters' or 'defenders of the people'? In *R v F*,[113] concerning a refugee from Libya who was charged under s 58, the Court of Appeal concluded, correctly in technical terms, that, as a matter of legislative history of s 1, Parliament had decided to restrict political freedoms even for freedom fighters against foreign despots.[114] This line of interpretation was presented as upholding values of democracy and the right to life.[115] Just as the challenge to the interpretation of s 1 failed, so the related argument under s 58(3) was rejected.[116]

The Court of Appeal maintained its hostility to this line of defence in *R v Rowe*, where the **5.75** defendant's purpose under s 57(2) was claimed to be the defence of Muslims in Croatia and Chechnya.[117] A more general right of self-defence beyond ss 57(2) and 58(3), to resist unlawful attack by state forces on one's co-religionists or one's tribe, may also be doubted on the precedent of *R v Jones* (where a 'crime of aggression' was under scrutiny),[118] unless, perhaps, the objective was purely the private protection of kith and kin rather than broader political purposes.

This thread of decisions has been compromised by *R v AY*.[119] The Court of Appeal upheld **5.76** a preliminary ruling that s 58(3) allowed the defendant to argue that the Somali people (a category going beyond kith and kin) had been the victims of unlawful and disproportionate force and required armed assistance in that country for their self-defence and that the documents possessed contrary to s 58(1) furthered that purpose. The Court held this argument to be capable of being a reasonable excuse. No mention was made of the case of *R v Jones* which emphasized that individuals are not allowed to act as if they were 'the sheriff in a Western, the only law man in town' though that dictum was made in the context of 'a democratic society with its own appointed agents for the enforcement of the law'.[120] Rather, the Crown did not dismiss the proposition that self-defence (albeit making no distinction between public and private defence, nor between s 58(3) and a free-standing right to self defence), while the Court itself distinguished *R v F* as 'a case concerned with what was unarguably *offensive*

---

[111] [2007] EWCA Crim 970.
[112] *R v Samina Malik* [2008] EWCA Crim 1450 at para 43.
[113] [2007] EWCA Crim 243.
[114] Ibid para 11.
[115] Ibid para 29.
[116] Ibid para 38.
[117] [2007] EWCA Crim 635 at paras 46, 48.
[118] See *R v Jones* [2006] UKHL 16.
[119] [2010] EWCA Crim 762.
[120] [2006] UKHL 16 at para 74.

purpose and not with a contention that there was a purpose confined solely to lawful *defence*. Presumably, the boundaries between offensive and defensive and public and private within the complex social and political setting of Somalia are to be drawn by the juries. It is submitted that the courts should draw some boundaries, perhaps by ensuring that there is no condonation of international crimes, such as the bombing of civilians.

5.77 The meaning of 'reasonable excuse' under s 58(3) was next examined in *R v G and J*,[121] where the Court of Appeal rejected the prosecution contention that a 'reasonable excuse' under s 58(3) could not be based on an 'illegitimate reason' (such as to 'wind up' prison officers by collecting materials about munitions). This indulgence might appear startling, but it rules out only charges under s 58 and not prison disciplinary charges for possessing objectionable materials.[122] The House of Lords reversed this interpretation and emphasized that the excuse must be reasonable, based on the intrinsic nature of the information.[123] Collections of information to cause annoyance to prison officers were not reasonable. Equally, a defence claim that the information was for the purpose of burgling for private gain, rather than bombing the Home Secretary's house for public purposes, could not amount to a reasonable excuse. The effect is to draw into the scope of the anti-terrorism legislation actions which are 'ordinary decent criminality' rather than terrorism. The House of Lords has thus extended the boundaries of s 58 because society is not prepared to take the risk of discerning for sure between crime and terrorism. The defendant is thrown back on arguments about the intrinsic nature of the information and whether it relates to terrorism, handicapped by not being able to show wider circumstances or purposes or even mental delusions. This interpretation in *R v G and J* is not so startling as to contravene Article 7 of the European Convention, given the impact on the accused of legal rulings arising from a preliminary hearing.[124]

5.78 The same interpretation against nefarious purposes does not apply under s 57(2) since its focus is the purpose of the defendant without reference to its reasonableness: 'So it would indeed be a defence to a section 57(1) charge for a defendant to show, for instance, that his actual purpose for having an explosive was to blow open a bank vault.'[125] The court could feel sanguine about this outcome because other offences, such as under the Explosive Substances Act 1883, s 4, would then be made out.

5.79 Overall, the courts have stopped a trend whereby ss 57 and 58 were becoming akin to offences of the possession of 'terrorism pornography'. When the prosecution can assert without ridicule that the London A–Z is a terrorist document, it is indeed time to slam on the judicial brakes. There was also much public animus against what appeared to be the persecution of the adolescent fantasists. The connection between the content of the article and the implementation of terrorism under s 57 was clarified in *R v Zafar*[126] and *R v K*.[127] But there remains no element in s 58(1) that requires the Crown to show that the defendant had a terrorist purpose, since the information is judged intrinsically (without regard to its surrounding circumstances), with the effect that not only terrorists may be convicted of

---

[121] [2008] EWCA Crim 922.
[122] See Prison Rules 1999, SI 1999/728, r 43.
[123] [2009] UKHL 13 at paras 75, 77.
[124] Compare Hodgson, J, and Tadros, V, 'How to make a terrorist out of nothing' (2009) 72 *Modern Law Review* 984.
[125] Ibid para 74.
[126] [2008] EWCA Crim 184.
[127] [2008] EWCA Crim 185.

terrorism offences. It would have been helpful to read in a requirement of proof of a purpose of emulation in existing circumstances, akin to the TA 2006, s 1.

Though these judgments reduce the scope of sections 57 and 58, the offences are far from **5.80** 'almost redundant'.[128] They remain top of the list for charges, with s 57 by far the most common of all (see below).

Information about the security forces—s 58A

(i) Introduction and background   Section 76 of the CTA 2008 inserted s 58A into the **5.81** 2000 Act. It concerns eliciting, publishing, or communicating information about members of the security forces. In the background was the expiration in Northern Ireland of s 103 of the TA 2000.[129] Enactment was also prompted by two recent convictions for collecting information about soldiers, of Mohammed Abu Bakr Mansha[130] and of Parviz Khan.[131] Yet, the fact that convictions were sustained in those cases (for s 58 possession and s 5 preparation respectively and resulting in sentences of six and fourteen years) suggests that there was no serious legal gap.

(ii) Provisions   By s 58A(1),[132] it is an offence to elicit or attempt to elicit information **5.82** about a member of Her Majesty's forces, a member of any of the intelligence services, or a constable,[133] which is of a kind likely to be useful to a person committing or preparing an act of terrorism, or to publish or communicate such information. By comparison, s 103 applied to soldiers, police officers, judges, and court officers, and prison staff, but not members of the intelligence services.

The list gives rise to dispute as to whether office holders should be privileged at all and which **5.83** office holders should be selected as privileged. On the first point, it may be said that some people in public life are 'specially at risk',[134] and it is in the interests of society to counter any disincentive from terrorism to take part in public life. The second point is more contentious. For example, an attempt was made in 1987 to extend its ambit to Members of Parliament, the Northern Ireland Assembly, and district councils. Following the self-effacing criticism from Northern Ireland representatives that this created 'a privileged political class',[135] the idea was rejected. The inclusion of politicians could also be justified as promoting democracy and safeguarding prime targets of violence. However, the larger the list becomes, the more it might invite over-intrusive police reaction or else become a paper tiger.

Under s 58A(2) (which is subject to s 118), it is a defence for a person charged with an offence **5.84** to prove a reasonable excuse for their action. Recent judicial interpretations of s 58 should apply here too, so that photographs must be intrinsically likely to be useful to terrorism, 'a high bar'.[136] Equally, the isolated media photographing of overt security operations should

---

[128]   Tadros, V, 'Crime and security' (2008) 71 *Modern Law Review* 940 at 968.
[129]   See Home Office, *Possible Measures for Inclusion into a Future Counter-Terrorism Bill* (London, 2007) para 32.
[130]   [2006] EWCA Crim 2051.
[131]   [2009] EWCA Crim 1085.
[132]   Note also Sch 8 of the 2008 Act regarding jurisdiction over information society services.
[133]   Community support officers do not hold the office of constable: Police Reform Act 2002, s 38.
[134]   Hansard HC Debs Standing Committee D col 405 (3 March 1987) Nicholas Scott.
[135]   Ibid col 144 (3 February 1987) Enoch Powell.
[136]   Lord Carlile, *Report on the Operation in 2001–2008 of the Terrorism Act 2000* (Home Office, London) para 197.

escape criminalization.[137] Nevertheless, there is no prosecution burden of proving specific intent, and so there remains a chilling effect.

5.85 How does s 58A add to s 58? The *actus reus* of s 58 includes collecting, recording, or possessing, so that all that appears exclusive to s 58A(1)(a) is eliciting or attempting to elicit, though attempting to collect under s 58 could already be an offence. Publishing or communicating under s 58A(1)(b) could also fall within ss 39 or 57 of the 2000 Act or ss 1, 2, and 5 of the 2006 Act.

5.86 **(iii) Implementation** This offence has been cited by the police for banning photography in public places—especially of the police. This usage, often combined with stop and search under ss 43 or 44, has caused much furore amongst journalists. Therefore, the Home Office issued Circular 012/2009, *Photography and Counter-Terrorism Legislation*, which advises the police that: 'Legitimate journalistic activity (such as covering a demonstration for a newspaper) is likely to constitute such an excuse. Similarly an innocent tourist or other sight-seer taking a photograph of a police officer is likely to have a reasonable excuse.'

Assessment and conclusions on possession offences

5.87 These possession offences anticipate terrorism and facilitate pre-emptive intervention by way of 'Pursue', given 'a new and urgent emphasis upon the need for security, the containment of danger, the identification and management of any kind of risk'.[138] The logic of pre-emption was underlined by US Vice President Dick Cheney in November 2001 who called for action against terrorism based on a 'one percent chance'.[139] The then Director of the Security Service, Dame Eliza Manningham-Buller, has made a similar point: 'We may be confident that an individual or group is planning an attack but that confidence comes from the sort of intelligence I described earlier, patchy and fragmentary and uncertain, to be interpreted and assessed. All too often it falls short of evidence to support criminal charges to bring an individual before the courts, the best solution if achievable.'[140]

5.88 By contrast, criminal justice traditionally demands proof of harmful conduct and not just association with dangerousness.[141] Departures from the Millian standard of harm to the others are troubling in liberal democracies for several reasons.[142] First, the more remote the harm, the less certain it is that harm will actually occur. Secondly, some of the more remote harms, such as the glorification of terrorism, become harms because of the intervening agency of others, rather than the speaker per se, who influence a climate of opinions rather than underwrite an outcome.[143] Thirdly, the expanded purview of the criminal law can impinge on desired constitutional activities such as expressive and associational rights.[144]

---

[137] See Joint Committee on Human Rights, *Demonstrating respect for rights?* (2008–09 HL 47/HC 320) para 95; Hansard HL vol 704 col 1072 (21 October 2008), Lord West; case of Malcolm Sleath (*The Times* 16 April 2009, p 23).

[138] Garland, D, *The Culture of Control* (Oxford University Press, Oxford, 2001) p 12.

[139] Suskind, R, *The One Percent Doctrine* (Simon & Schuster, New York, 2006) p 62.

[140] <https://www.mi5.gov.uk/output/director-generals-speech-to-the-aivd-2005.html>.

[141] See Chesney, R and Goldsmith, J, 'Terrorism and the convergence of criminal and military detention models' (2008) 60 *Stanford Law Review* 1079 at 1084, 1088.

[142] Wallerstein, S, 'Criminalising remote harm and the case of anti-democratic activity' (2007) 28 *Cardozo Law Review* 2697.

[143] See von Hirsch, A, 'Extending the Harm Principle' in Simester, AP and Smith, ATH (eds), *Harm and Culpability* (Clarendon Press, Oxford, 1996) p 267.

[144] See Feinberg, J, *Moral Limits of the Criminal Law: Harm to Others* (Oxford University Press, New York, 1984) pp 187–217.

Yet, compromise might be warranted where the potential harm is extreme and where the interests protected (the lives of others) are vital. As a result, it may be simplistic to say that merely preparatory acts, such as the collection of information useful to terrorism, are never worthy of moral criticism or legal reaction.[145]

The main controversy has been the extent to which the burden of proof has shifted unduly **5.89** to the defendant contrary to Article 6. This argument has been fully canvassed in the courts, so that accountability has been adequately serviced, despite some disinclination by Lord Carlile to investigate reverse burdens of proof.[146] At the same time, it cannot be claimed that ss 57 and 58 meet standards of constitutional governance since it has taken many court cases to clarify and refine their meanings. The unintended consequences of restrictions of photography under s 58A also await fuller scrutiny.

Acts preparatory

Introduction and background

The culmination of the trend favouring precursor offences is the offence of acts preparatory **5.90** to terrorism in the TA 2006, s 5. The Home Office had raised in 2004 the possibility of a broadly drawn offence along these lines,[147] and the idea was endorsed by Lord Carlile as an alternative to executive detention.[148] The *Newton Committee Report*, however, remarked that nobody had pointed to the absence of available offences as being the core obstacle to prosecution,[149] and this assessment has been echoed by the Joint Committee on Human Rights.[150] In part, s 5 responds to the European Convention for the Prevention of Terrorism 2005, Article 6, by which action should be taken against 'recruitment for terrorism', including to solicit another person to participate in the commission of a terrorist offence. However, the correspondence is partial, and so s 5 does not mention 'Convention offences'.

While there is now an offence of facilitation of terrorism, there is no offence of solicitation of **5.91** terrorism. Solicitation (or encouragement) could be treated as an inchoate offence to the proscription offences, but, as far as other solicitations are concerned, they must fall under 'normal' offences.[151]

Provisions

By s 5(1), an offence arises if, with the intention of (a) committing acts of terrorism; or **5.92** (b) assisting another to commit such acts, a person engages in any conduct in preparation for giving effect to that intention.

The scope of possible preparatory acts is deliberately broad, save that the object of atten- **5.93** tion must be 'acts' rather than, say, the continued existence of a proscribed organization.

---

[145] Compare Tadros, V, 'Justice and terrorism' (2007) 10 *New Criminal Law Review* 658 at 675; Special Rapporteur on the promotion and protection of human rights and fundamental freedoms while countering terrorism, *Report to the General Assembly* (A/61/267, 2006) para 11.

[146] Lord Carlile, *Report on the Operation in 2001–2008 of the Terrorism Act 2000* (Home Office, London) para 194.

[147] Home Office, *Counter-Terrorism Powers* (Cm 6147, London, 2004) para 48.

[148] Lord Carlile, *Anti-terrorism, Crime and Security Act 2001 Part IV Section 28, Review 2003* (Home Office, 2004) para 101.

[149] *Newton Report*, para 207.

[150] Joint Committee on Human Rights, *Review of Counterterrorism Powers* (2003–04 HL 158/HC 713) paras 66, 67.

[151] See Serious Crime Act 2007, Pt II.

Acts of terrorism are also distinct from acts of terrorists, the assistance of whom might comprise, say, shopping. The modes of involvement in connection with those 'acts' can be distinct from conspiracies (requiring an agreement with others)[152] or attempts (the very definition of which demands action which is 'more than merely preparatory').[153] In addition, attempts and conspiracies are in relation to specific 'normal' offences rather than 'terrorism'.

5.94 There must be intent to commit or assist the acts. The person must entertain the further intent that the act or assistance must further terrorism. By s 5(2), it is expressly irrelevant whether the intention and preparations relate to one or more particular acts of terrorism, acts of terrorism of a particular description, or acts of terrorism generally.

5.95 It is tricky to pin down which activities might fall distinctly within s 5. The *Explanatory Memorandum* for the 2006 Act, after claiming wholly erroneously that 'At the moment the law does not cover preparatory acts . . .',[154] gave as an example 'if a person possesses items that could be used for terrorism even if not immediately'[155]—a fair recital of s 57. Lord Carlile more cogently mentions the provision of accommodation or credit card fraud to raise living expenses,[156] though offences of withholding information, helping proscribed organizations, and terrorism financing may then apply. As for the latter, a government Minister contended that 'simply making a financial donation would not be caught by the offence' and went on to claim that the true meaning of the *actus reus* demands 'active engagement in planning to carry out an act of terrorism'.[157] This reasoning does not sit easily with s 5(2) but may perhaps be justified by reference to the word 'engages' and its sense of activity rather than, say, a donation or simply agreeing to belong to a group.

Implementation

5.96 The penalty is up to life imprisonment, which, as under s 56, is not mandatory.[158]

5.97 An illustration is Sohail Anjum Qureshi, who pleaded guilty to preparing for the commission of terrorist acts.[159] He was arrested at Heathrow Airport, en route to Pakistan. His luggage included night-vision binoculars, medical provisions, two British passports, and nearly £9,000 in cash. He also possessed computer materials of an extremist and military nature. With discount for a guilty plea, he was sentenced to four-and-a-half years' imprisonment, a level considered lenient but not unduly so.

5.98 In *R v Tabbakh*,[160] the defendant was sentenced under s 5 to seven years for assembling bomb-making instructions and some ingredients (but not a detonator). It was indicated that eight years would have been proper, but there was leniency because of his mental condition following torture in Syria.

---

[152] See Joint Committee on Human Rights, *Counter-Terrorism Policy and Human Rights: Prosecution and Pre-Charge Detention* (2005–06 HL 240/HC 1576) para 54.
[153] Criminal Attempts Act 1981, s 1(1).
[154] Para 49.
[155] (Home Office, London, 2006) para 49.
[156] Lord Carlile, *Proposals by Her Majesty's Government for Changes to the Laws against Terrorism* (Home Office, London, 2005) para 30.
[157] Hansard HC vol 438 cols 1000–1 (3 November 2005), Paul Goggins.
[158] Hansard HL vol 676 col 715 (7 December 2005).
[159] *Attorney General's Reference (No 7 of 2008)* [2008] EWCA Crim 1054.
[160] [2009] EWCA Crim 464.

At the other end of the scale was *R v Parviz Khan*,[161] who was preparing to behead a soldier **5.99** (but lacked any agreement with others for a charge of conspiracy); the sentence was fourteen years. Linked to Parviz Khan, Mohammed Nadim, Shahid Ali, and Shabir Mohammed pleaded guilty to sending items such as balaclavas and thermal clothing, as well as computer software and night-vision binoculars to insurgents fighting on the Afghan/Pakistan border.[162] They received sentences of between two and three years. Abdul Raheem, 32, pleaded guilty to failing to disclose information about these activities and was jailed for a year. Nabeel Hussain, who provided logistical and financial support to the 'Liquid Bomb' airline plot in 2006 was sentenced to eight years.[163] Another case treated with severity involved the founder of the 'Aryan Strike Force', Ian Davison, who not only prepared terrorism but also produced a chemical weapon (ricin) contrary to the Chemical Weapons Act 1996, and possessed materials contrary to s 58 and a prohibited weapon. He was sentenced to ten years for the s 5 offence.[164]

The relationship of s 5 to other offences was raised in the prosecution of another neo-Nazi, **5.100** Martyn Gilleard, who was convicted and sentenced to sixteen years under s 5 and s 58 in connection with possession of nail bombs and *The Anarchist Cookbook*.[165] The overlap in the offences was elucidated in the case of Nicholas Roddis, convicted of leaving a hoax bomb on a bus in Rotherham and collecting items and materials to make explosives contrary to s 5.[166] A note in Arabic was found with the device, saying 'Britain must be punished' and signed 'The al Qaida organisation in Iraq'. He was sentenced to two years for the hoax bomb, with five years consecutive for the s 5 offence. The argument was raised that s 5 should be construed as involving more than simple possession to distinguish it from ss 57 and 58. The Court of Appeal concluded that some overlap between offences exists, and there can be preparation through possession since possession is often part of conduct in preparation for giving effect to a terrorist intention. However, this case was not left to the jury on the basis of simple possession but also involved acts of acquisition of ingredients, documents, and knowledge about explosive devices. Collecting information and materials was undoubtedly 'preparation'.

Assessment and conclusions

In the view of Lord Carlile, s 5 amounts to 'a fair yet robust canon of counter-terrorism **5.101** law'.[167] The offence fits with the 'Pursue' strands of CONTEST and has quickly gained momentum as a favoured charge. It might even displace some control orders, as in the case of Mohammed Abushamma, who was arrested at Heathrow, having attempted to fight in Afghanistan, and was sentenced to three-and-a-half years' imprisonment.[168] The passage of this offence engendered much debate, and so accountability is fulfilled.

It sits less happily with the demands of a rights audit. It avoids express reliance on reverse **5.102** burdens of proof, but the vague extension of the boundaries of criminal law is another way

---

[161] [2009] EWCA Crim 1085.
[162] *The Times* 10 March 2009, p 4 (Central Criminal Court).
[163] *The Times* 10 December 2009, p 13 (Woolwich Crown Court).
[164] *The Times* 15 May 2010, p 31 (Newcastle Crown Court).
[165] *The Times* 26 June 2008, p 22 (Leeds Crown Court).
[166] [2009] EWCA 585.
[167] Lord Carlile, *Proposals by Her Majesty's Government for Changes to the Laws against Terrorism* (Home Office, 2005) para 31.
[168] *The Times* 29 November 2008, p 24 (Croydon Crown Court).

of putting the defendant on the back foot. It might be argued that the concept of preparation is too vague for the purposes of Article 7. The broad nature of 'preparations' comes close to penalizing 'criminal thoughts'[169] rather than harms and leaving no possibility for withdrawal. While there must be some acts and conduct, the 'exact plans are unknown',[170] and there is no list of outlawed activities, and no set level of commitment to the enterprise or of threshold as to its viability. Acts of charity, such as providing accommodation or transport, could become viewed as guilt by association or inadvertence after a guest is found to be involved in terrorism.[171]

5.103   One might reflect on the case of Saajid Badat.[172] He pleaded guilty to conspiring to destroy aircraft and the possession of explosives, when the police discovered in 2003 the parts for a shoe bomb in a box in his bedroom. Badat had withdrawn from the enterprise (unlike his companion, Richard Reid) two years earlier. Changing these facts, what if Badat had withdrawn before collecting the explosives from Pakistan, at a point when his 'preparation' had been to designate a suitable box to store the explosive materials and to write 'Danger: Explosives!' on the lid? Here are acts preparatory, but without harm or even potential harm.

Foreign comparisons with precursor offences

5.104   Following the Council of Europe Convention on the Prevention of Terrorism 2005, several other countries have implemented preparatory offences.[173] For instance, three offences were added to the German Criminal Code by the Act on the Prosecution of the Preparation of Serious Violent Acts Endangering the State (*Gesetz zur Verfolgung der Vorbereitung von schweren staatsgefährdenden Gewalttaten*) 2009. First, s 89a provides that criminal liability is incurred for preparing a serious violent act endangering the state such as by instructing another person or receiving instructions regarding, *inter alia*, the manufacture or use of firearms, explosives, or CBRN material; manufacturing, procuring, storing, or making available weapons, substances, or equipment; or collecting, accepting, or making available assets. Under s 89b, it is an offence to enter into relationships in order to commit a serious act of violence that endangers the state (such as by attending a training camp). Next, s 91 relates to instructions in the commission of a serious act of violence that endangers the state. Whilst the concept of these offences is the same as offences under, for example, the TA 2006, s 5 (and s 6 in the case of s 91), there is greater precision in the delineation of the *actus reus* which is by reference to specified activities and specified crimes of violence.

5.105   In other respects, the Continental approach has been to avoid special offences and to adopt the 'scheduled offence' approach. In France, various offences are listed as 'terrorism' in art 421-1 of the Penal Code if connected with an individual or collective operation aimed at seriously disturbing public order by intimidation or terror. Articles 421 and 422 then criminalize any form of conspiracy or incitement, funding, or failure to account for resources. Aggravated penalties are applied.

---

[169] Jones, A, Bowers, R, and Lodge, HD, *The Terrorism Act 2006* (Oxford University Press, Oxford, 2006) para 3.05.

[170] Hansard HC vol 438 col 999 (3 November 2005), Paul Goggins.

[171] See Joint Committee on Human Rights, *Counter-Terrorism Policy and Human Rights: Prosecution and Pre-Charge Detention* (2005–06 HL 240/HC 1576) para 94.

[172] *The Times* 1 March 2005, p 1 (Central Criminal Court) (13 years).

[173] See Picotti, L, 'Expanding forms of preparation and participation' (2009) 78 *International Review of Penal Law* 405.

In Spain, terrorist offences, as specified by Organic Law 10/1995 of 23 November 1995, are **5.106** set in the Code of Criminal Law, arts 571 to 580, and are mainly based upon belonging to, acting for, or collaborating with armed groups who aim to subvert the constitutional order or to seriously disturb the public peace by the commission of specified offences.[174] A special feature is that Organic Law 6/1985 of 1 July 1985 grants universal jurisdiction over terrorism offences.

Turning to common law jurisdictions, there has been a greater willingness to devise broad **5.107** precursor offences. For example, the Canadian Anti-terrorism Act 2001 inserts into the Criminal Code s 83.19, which forbids the facilitation of a terrorist activity. Along the same lines, the Australian Anti-terrorism Act (No 2) 2004 amends the Criminal Code 1995 by adding as s 102.8 an offence of intentionally associating with another person who is a member of, or a person who promotes or directs, the activities of, a listed terrorist organization. An interesting exclusion, in contrast to s 38B of the TA 2000, is that the offence does not apply if the association is with a close family member and relates only to a matter that could reasonably be regarded as a matter of family or domestic concern. This offence was recommended for repeal by the (Sheller) *Report of the Security Legislation Review Committee.*[175]

Broader still are the 'material support' offences in US Federal law which allow preventive **5.108** prosecutions of those engaged in training camps, money-raising, and service provision.[176]

An offence to provide 'material support' with intent or knowledge to carry out or facilitate **5.109** any of a list of some thirty-six predicate offences was added as 18 US Code s 2339A in 1994.[177] The offence catches the facilitators of amorphous terrorism-related action, such as attending a terrorist training camp in Pakistan.[178] Hemant Lakhani, a British-based businessman, was convicted and sentenced to forty-seven years in New Jersey for attempting to broker the sale to the Ogaden Liberation Front of shoulder-launched missiles to be used in the US as well as in Somalia.[179] However, the offences in the TA 2000, ss 57 and 58, and also in the 2006 Act, ss 5 and 6, are broader still. They do not require proof of a predicate crime, and the proof of intent is reduced because of the statutory presumptions.

Next, 18 US Code s 2339B, passed in 1996,[180] makes it an offence to provide 'material **5.110** support' to a designated 'Foreign Terrorist Organization'.[181] The defendant does not have to be proven to have known or intended that the support would be used for any particular purpose, which avoids difficulties in the case of donations to organizations such as Hamas or

---

[174] See STC 89/1993 of 12 March 1993.
[175] (Canberra, 2006) para 10.77.
[176] See Richman, DC and Stuntz, WJ, 'Al Capone's Revenge' (2005) 105 *Columbia Law Review* 583; Chesney, RM, 'Beyond Conspiracy?' (2007) 80 *Southern California Law Review* 425; Ward, JJ, 'The root of all evil' (2008) 84 *Notre Dame Law Review* 471.
[177] Violent Crime Control and Law Enforcement Act of 1994, PL 103-322. Predicate offences include destruction of aircraft (18 USC s 32), explosives offences (s 844), conspiracy to attack persons or property outside the US (s 956), the murder of US employees (s 1114), the use of weapons of mass destruction (s 2332a), violent attacks inside the US involving transnational planning (s 2332b).
[178] *US v Hayat* 2007 US Dist LEXIS 40157.
[179] 480 F 3d 171 (2007).
[180] Anti-terrorism and Effective Death Penalty Act 1996, PL 104-132.
[181] For designation, see Immigration and Nationality Act 1952 (PL 82-414) s 219 (8 USC s 1189). The current list is at <http://www.state.gov/s/ct/rls/other/des/123085.htm>. Designation may also be achieved in relation to threats to the 'Middle East Peace Process' under the International Emergency Economic Powers Act 1977 (50 USC s 1701, Exec Order No 12947, 3 CFR 319, 1995).

Hezbollah which have social and military wings. The constitutionality of the offences was upheld against challenges based on free speech and vagueness in *Holder v Humanitarian Law Project*.[182] As far as British emulation is concerned, there again appears to be little that is not already covered more explicitly by Pts II and III of the TA 2000, plus ss 5 to 8 of the TA 2006.

5.111   Another foreign precedent of interest is the French Penal Code, art 450-1, which specifies that 'A criminal association consists of any group formed or any conspiracy established with a view to the preparation, marked by one or more material actions, of one or more felonies, or of one or more misdemeanours punished by at least five years' imprisonment.' This offence was delineated in terrorist-related terms through art 421-2-1 in 1996, by which 'The participation in any group formed or association established with a view to the preparation, marked by one or more material actions, of any of the acts of terrorism provided for under the previous articles shall in addition be an act of terrorism'.[183] It is often rendered as the offence of '*association de malfaiteurs en relation avec une entreprise terroriste*' (criminal association in relation with a terrorist undertaking). This offence of criminal association is broader than conspiracy in that it is the association rather than any agreed outcome which is key, though the police must still establish a terrorism link and some concrete action.[184]

5.112   Would this looser form of associational offence be a useful extension to the United Kingdom special criminal code by moving even further backwards in the terrorism process from preparatory acts to the mere disposition of hanging around with the wrong people? One might argue again that membership offences and the preparatory offence in s 5 of the TA 2006 cover much of the same ground. In so far as the French Code goes further, it must be on account of excessively vague charges and vague evidence which have been the subject of criticism in France as 'a catch-all offence which in practice is found to be proved on a minimum of objective, independent evidence and a maximum of speculation, innuendo and inference, some of which is supplied by sources of questionable impartiality and integrity'.[185]

Threats and hoaxes

Introduction and background

5.113   Hoaxes were used by the IRA as a disruptive and diversionary tactic, and they were emulated from the 1970s onwards by animal rights protestors. The common law offence of public nuisance can apply, provided there is impact on the community and a series of linked acts.[186] Because of its uncertainty, statutory alternatives are preferred.

5.114   Under s 51 of the Criminal Law Act 1977, it is an offence to place or send any article intending to make another person believe that it is likely to explode or ignite and thereby cause personal injury or damage to property. It is also an offence under s 51 to communicate any

---

[182] 561 US _ (2010).

[183] See Law no 96-647 of 22 July 1996, art 2. The maximum penalty increased from ten to twenty years by Law no 2006-64 of 23 January 2006. See Mayaud, Y, *Le Terrorisme* (Dalloz, Paris, 1997) pp 27–9; Garapon, A, 'The oak and the reed' (2006) 27 *Cardozo Law Review* 2041.

[184] See Home Office, *Terrorist Investigations And The French Examining Magistrates System* (London, 2007) p 4.

[185] McColgan, M, and Attanasio, A, *France: Paving the Way for Arbitrary Justice* (FIDH, Paris, 1999) p 35. See also Human Rights Watch, *Preempting Justice: Counter-Terrorism Laws and Procedure in France* (New York, 2008) Part IV.

[186] *R v Rimmington and Goldstein* [2005] UKHL 63 at para 76.

hoax information along these lines.[187] Corresponding offences exist in Scotland (s 63) and in Northern Ireland.[188]

A related offence is contamination or interference with goods, or making it appear, or making threats or claims, that goods have been contaminated or interfered with, with intent to cause alarm, injury, or loss, contrary to s 38(1) of the Public Order Act 1986.[189] Further offences involve making threats or claims (s 38(2)) or possessing materials with a view to commission (s 38(3)). These measures responded to incidents of 'consumer terrorism'. In *R v Cruickshank*,[190] the appellant pleaded guilty to two offences under s 38 arising from the insertion of needles and a pin into supermarket foodstuffs, which injured several customers. The appellant had no rational motive and was sentenced to three years' imprisonment. **5.115**

By the Wireless Telegraphy Act 2006, s 47, it is an offence to send or attempt to send false distress messages 'likely to prejudice the efficiency of a safety of life service or to endanger the safety of a person or of a ship, aircraft or vehicle'.[191] **5.116**

These 'normal' offences were considered deficient after the anthrax attacks in the USA in late 2001 which were believed to be Al-Qa'ida inspired but later were attributed to a rogue scientist.[192] Section 51 relates only to hoax devices 'likely to explode or ignite'. Section 38 protects only the integrity of goods in the consumer chain and not other forms of contact or distribution. Therefore, the ATCSA 2001 adds further offences. **5.117**

Provisions

Just as the offence of weapons training has been extended to cover chemical, biological, and nuclear weapons and materials, so ss 113 to 115 of the ATCSA 2001 extend offences relating to threats and hoaxes from firearms and explosives to chemical, biological, and nuclear weapons and materials. **5.118**

By s 113(1), it is an offence to use a noxious substance or thing to cause serious harm in a manner designed to influence the government or to intimidate the public. The serious harm is defined further by sub-s (2), in terms which reflect s 1(2)(a) to (d) (but not disruption to electronic systems) of the TA 2000, including by the induction of fear of serious danger or risk. The latter caters for the situation where the attack has been disrupted, 'for example, where the police intercept a package of anthrax spores designed to kill the recipient before it reaches its target'.[193] By s 113(3), it is an offence to threaten an action which constitutes an offence under sub-s (1) with the intention of inducing fear in a person anywhere in the world. Conduct of these kinds outside the United Kingdom may fall within s 113A. Offences carry sentences of up to fourteen years and a fine on indictment and up to six months and a fine on summary process. **5.119**

Section 113 has not displaced the common law offence of causing a public nuisance. The manufacture of ricin and cyanide was the basis for public nuisance in *R v Bourgass*.[194] **5.120**

---

[187] There is no need to be specific about time or place: *R v Webb* (1995) *The Times* 19 June.
[188] Criminal Law (Amendment) (Northern Ireland) Order 1977, SI 1977/1249, art 3.
[189] See Watson, S, 'Consumer terrorism' (1987) 137 *New Law Journal* 84.
[190] [2001] EWCA Crim 98.
[191] See *R v Judge* [2008] EWCA Crim 1820.
[192] US Fort Detrick scientist, Bruce Ivins, committed suicide in 2008 while charges were pending.
[193] Hansard HL vol 629 col 1162 (10 December 2001), Lord Rooker.
[194] *R v Bourgass* [2005] EWCA Crim 1943, [2006] EWCA Crim 3397.

The Court of Appeal rejected the argument that s 113 should be preferred and also held that its maximum penalty (fourteen years) was not an appropriate yardstick sentence for the common law offence (up to life).

5.121 Section 114 addresses hoaxes with reference to 'a noxious substance or other noxious thing'. It is an offence under sub-s (1) to place or send 'any substance or article intending to make others believe that it is likely to be or contain a noxious substance or thing which could endanger human life or health'. Relevant actions might include 'scattering white powder in a public place or spraying concentrated water droplets around in an Underground train'.[195] By sub-s (2), it is an offence for a person falsely to communicate any information to another person anywhere in the world that a noxious substance or thing is or will be in a place and so likely to cause harm or to endanger human life or health. The penalty for s 114 is up to seven years' imprisonment, equivalent to s 51 but less than the ten years under s 38.

5.122 Relevant to both ss 113 and 114, s 115 clarifies that 'substance' includes any biological agent and any other natural or artificial substance. The word 'noxious' is not defined. The meaning under s 23 of the Offences against the Person Act 1861 (to administer a noxious thing to endanger life) requires the jury to consider 'quality and quantity' and to decide as a question of fact and degree whether that thing was noxious.[196] Section 115 also specifies that no particular victim need be in mind. So, threats and hoaxes issued at large, such as via the internet, are forbidden.

Implementation

5.123 The *Newton Report* recorded just a handful of prosecutions for these offences (three under s 114).[197] Hoaxes have been regularly prosecuted under the 'normal' offences and have been condemned with increasing severity.

5.124 Public transport facilities are especially vulnerable to disruption. A sentence of four years on a guilty plea was applied in *R v Doherty*, whose hoax affected Victoria Railway Station two days after a prior IRA bombing.[198] In *R v Mason*,[199] the defendant was sentenced to four years when, during a flight from Zurich to London, he threatened a flight attendant and shouted that he was hijacking the aircraft. In *R v McMenemy*,[200] the appellant was sentenced to two years' imprisonment for a hoax affecting Heathrow Airport. In *R v Walters*,[201] the defendant made a telephone call about a hoax bomb at an airport. There was recognized a need for a deterrent sentence, but, taking into account the defendant's difficult social and psychological circumstances, a sentence of two years' youth detention was halved on appeal. A hoax about a bomb on a bus (and in a library) merited eighteen months' imprisonment after a guilty plea in *R v Bird*.[202]

5.125 Hoaxes which are part of a political campaign also rate deterrent sentences. In *R v Webber and Paton*, conspiracy to cause death threats and hoaxes in connection with the Scottish

---

[195] Home Office Circular 7/2002, p 4. There is no retrospective effect: Home Affairs Committee, *Report on the Anti-terrorism, Crime and Security Bill 2001* (2001–02 HC 351) para 64.
[196] Archbold, *Criminal Pleading, Evidence and Practice* (56th edn, Sweet & Maxwell, London, 2008) para 19-230.
[197] See *Newton Report*, para 428.
[198] (1993) 14 Cr App R (S) 541.
[199] [2001] EWCA Crim 1138.
[200] [2009] EWCA Crim 42.
[201] [2002] EWCA Crim 1114.
[202] (1993) 14 Cr App R (S) 721.

National Liberation Army merited three years and eighteen months respectively.[203] Three years was the penalty for an Animal Liberation Front hoax bomb sent to Glaxo by Niel Hansen.[204] Nicolas Roberts was sentenced to thirty months for a public nuisance consisting of sending fake anthrax (flour) to the Welsh First Minister.[205]

If the hoax impacts on other public facilities or places, then more varied sentences have been handed down.[206] In *R v Dunbar and Johnson*,[207] a telephone bomb hoax in a department store merited twelve months' imprisonment on a guilty plea in 1987. A similar case, *R v Wilburn* in 1991,[208] incurred two years' youth detention. In 2008 in *R v Philipson*,[209] a hoax affecting a car park at a shopping centre produced a sentence of six months on appeal. In *R v Harris (Phillip Geoffrey)*,[210] the defendant serially placed a hoax bomb in a police station and then in a restaurant in each case in open view. A sentence of three years was imposed (two consecutive sentences of eighteen months). In *R v Harrison*,[211] the appellant made several telephone calls to a theatre about the planting of a terrorist bomb nearby and was sentenced to four years, taking account of previous convictions. In *R v Cann*, repeated hoaxes merited twenty-one months' imprisonment.[212] In *R v Cook*,[213] the appellant, who had mental problems, pleaded guilty to a bomb hoax at Canary Wharf and was sentenced to two years' imprisonment. **5.126**

Foreign comparisons

The Australian Criminal Code Amendment (Anti-Hoax and Other Measures) Act 2002 amended the Criminal Code Act 1995 to insert offences directed at the use of postal and similar services to perpetrate hoaxes, make threats, and send dangerous articles. **5.127**

Assessment and conclusions

These offences have relevance to the tactic of 'Pursue'. They raise few issues of a normative nature. This speech is not of a kind which attracts protection on a rights audit—it is the essence of shouting 'fire' in a crowded theatre. The main criticism which might be levelled is that so little account has been provided—meagre debate and disinterest in their subsequent application. In practice, sophisticated telephonic tracing and food packaging technology have mounted the main deterrent against hoaxes. **5.128**

External jurisdiction offences

Introduction and background

The jurisdiction of the United Kingdom criminal courts traditionally relies upon the principle of territoriality. There have long been some exceptions to this general rule, and Victorian-era foreign dissidents were subjected to the offence of solicitation of murder under the Offences against the Person Act 1861, s 4. However, the growing internationalization of contemporary terrorism has now boosted the proliferation of extra-jurisdictional offences **5.129**

---

[203] *The Times* 22 August 1995, p 3 (Stirling High Court).
[204] *The Times* 10 February 1995, p 3 (Luton Crown Court).
[205] *The Times* 9 April 2002, p 10, 17 July p 7 (Cardiff Crown Court).
[206] See also *R v McClennon* (1993) 15 Cr App R (S) 17; *R v Rung-Ruangap* (1993) 15 Cr App R (S) 326.
[207] (1987) 9 Cr App R (S) 393.
[208] (1991) 13 Cr App R (S) 309. See also *R v Donnelly* (1992) 14 Cr App R (S) 684.
[209] [2008] 2 Cr App R (S) 110.
[210] [2005] EWCA Crim 775.
[211] [1997] 2 Cr App R (S) 174.
[212] [2004] EWCA Crim 1075.
[213] [2006] EWCA Crim 780.

based on three factors. The first is to disabuse any foreign group or state of the impression that the United Kingdom is a 'safe haven' for terrorism.[214] This factor was underlined by lobbying by foreign states (Algeria, Egypt, France, India, Saudi Arabia, and Tunisia amongst others) who wished to secure the curtailment of political opposition by their nationals who were exiled in the United Kingdom.[215] An example was Mohammed al Masari, the Saudi dissident whose attempted deportation to Yemen and then Dominica failed in 1994 and 1996.[216] The second factor is that the extension of jurisdiction is no longer seen as aggression but as a reflection of international solidarity,[217]positively encouraged by UNSCR 1373 and specific international treaties. The third factor is foreboding about case law which suggested that while claims of terrorists to asylum could be rejected, it might not be possible thereafter simply to deport the trouble-makers because of fears of persecution in the receiving state.[218]

5.130 Changes include the Criminal Jurisdiction Act 1975, which ensures overlapping jurisdiction for several terrorism offences between Northern Ireland and the Republic of Ireland. This provision will be considered in Chapter 11.

5.131 Next, the Suppression of Terrorism Act 1978, s 4, allows for prosecution in the United Kingdom in lieu of the grant of an extradition request for a specified range of offences which have been committed in a Convention state. Similar measures apply in relation to India.[219]

5.132 Thirdly, the growing sentiment against foreign terrorism was translated into action as part of the package responding to the Omagh bombing in 1998 under the Criminal Justice (Terrorism and Conspiracy) Act 1998.[220] The Act is not limited to foreign dissidents, and there is no exemption for British citizens. Accordingly, ss 5 to 7 confer jurisdiction over activities in the United Kingdom relating to conspiracy to commit offences committed or intended to be committed abroad, provided the act or event would constitute an offence in the foreign country or territory as well as being an offence within the jurisdiction of England and Wales if the act were to have been committed here. The 1998 Act covers all offences and is not confined to 'terrorism' offences, contrary to the views of the *Lloyd Report*.[221] There remains some protection for political asylum in that the 1998 Act does not breach the principle of extra-territoriality: if the conspiracy as well as the substantive offence takes place outside the jurisdiction, the conspirators cannot be prosecuted. Proceedings also require the consent of the Attorney General (in England and Wales and in Northern Ireland). It is envisaged that one relevant factor to be taken into account by the Attorney General will be the human rights situation in which the offence is to be committed, the United Kingdom's international obligations (including those to act against terrorism), and 'other appropriate considerations'.[222]

5.133 Building on the foregoing, several offences in Pt VI of the TA 2000 relate to the establishment or extension of jurisdiction.

---

[214] See *Lloyd Report*, para 1.12; *Home Office Response to Lloyd Report*, para 4.19.
[215] See *The Guardian* 20 November 1997, p 19, 26 August 1998, p 3.
[216] See *The Guardian* 1 December 1994, p 1, 7 November 1996, p 11.
[217] See Hansard HC Debs vol 317 col 835 (2 September 1998), Adam Ingram.
[218] *Chahal v UK*, App no 22414/93, 1996-V.
[219] See Suppression of Terrorism Act 1978 (Application of Provisions) (India) Order 1993, SI 1993/2533.
[220] See Walker, CP, 'The bombs in Omagh and their aftermath' (1999) 62 *Modern Law Review* 879; Campbell, C, 'Two steps backwards' [1999] *Criminal Law Review* 941.
[221] *Lloyd Report*, paras 12.39, 12.40. See also Hansard HL Debs vol 593 col 34 (3 September 1998).
[222] Hansard HC Debs vol 317 col 902 (2 September 1998), Alun Michael.

Inciting terrorism overseas

Sections 59 to 61 of the TA 2000 grant in turn English, Northern Irish, and Scottish courts **5.134** jurisdiction over offences of incitement of terrorism abroad where the act would, if committed within the jurisdiction, constitute any offence listed in sub-s (2).[223] The listed offences are meant to equate roughly to s 1 of the TA 2000 but are inevitably more precise since there is reference to specified offences. However, the government Minister, Lord Bach, denied that there is any substantial difference:[224]

> Our intention in this provision, which essentially fills in gaps in UK law, is to outlaw the incitement here of very serious acts with a terrorist motive overseas. So, in relation to property crime, the relevant offence is to incite the endangering of life by damaging property. It is not a case of one definition of 'terrorism' for here and a narrower one for abroad; it is the same definition for all acts, whether here or abroad. We are applying the definition in Clause 1 to specify existing offences, to ensure that incitement here to commit certain acts abroad— which, if committed here, would constitute one of those specified offences—will be caught.

There is no need for any corresponding offence of solicitation of murder overseas. The Offences against the Person Act 1861, s 4, is sufficient.

By sub-s (4), it is immaterial whether or not the person incited is in the United Kingdom at **5.135** the time of the incitement. By sub-s (5), any person acting on behalf of, or holding office under, the Crown cannot be liable—members of the security services are still allowed to play fast and loose with foreign codes.[225] The penalty is to correspond to that applicable if the incitement had occurred in the United Kingdom.

Sections 59 to 61 turn selected offences into universal crimes even when they are not so **5.136** recognized in international conventions or under the Suppression of Terrorism Act 1978, s 4. In the official view, this prohibition should extend universally: 'There is no obvious justification for incitement to commit murder in Turkey or India to be an offence in the UK [under s 4], whereas incitement to commit murder in Japan or Australia is not an offence.'[226] But the incitement of many designated terrorist offences (hijacking and so on) already carries universal jurisdiction. Further, no cases of incitement have resulted in prosecution instead of extradition under the 1978 Act.[227] There will also arise evidential difficulties for dissident groups who are seeking to establish their true nature and intentions.[228] By contrast, despotic regimes can seek protection alongside liberal democracies, though prosecutions will be open to challenge under Article 10 of the European Convention.[229]

It is suggested that the offences should at least be confined in two ways. First, in terms of **5.137** persons, the scope should relate to either the activities of British citizens or incitements to persons who are in the United Kingdom. Given the indiscriminate nature of the internet and other modern means of communication, a wide offence would remain. Secondly, in terms of actions, the list of offences should be more clearly politically related and should not go much beyond internationally recognized offences.

---

[223] *Home Office Response to Lloyd Report*, paras 4.18, 4.19.
[224] Hansard HL vol 613 col 760, 16 May 2000.
[225] See Home Office, Circular 03/01: *Terrorism Act 2000* (Home Office, London, 2001) para 6.7. Otherwise, the Criminal Justice Act 1948, s 31 might apply.
[226] Hansard HC vol 341 col 163 (14 December 1999), Jack Straw.
[227] Hansard HC Standing Committee D, col 262 (1 February 2000), Charles Clarke.
[228] See JUSTICE, *Response to Legislation against Terrorism* (London, 1999), paras 3.6, 3.7.
[229] See *Castells v Spain*, App no 11798/85, A 236; *Incal v Turkey*, App no 22678/93, 1998-IV, (2000).

5.138 An illustration is *R v Younis Tsouli* who, under the tag of 'Irhabi007', was convicted of inciting terrorism abroad (as well as fraud) arising from his websites which carried praise for beheadings and other terrorist violence.[230] In *R v Saleem*,[231] the defendants, including Abu Izzadeen (Trevor Brooks), were charged with inciting terrorism overseas under s 59 (and also offences under s 15) arising from DVDs of speeches in 2004 which encouraged support for the *mujahideen* in Fallujah and elsewhere in Iraq. Since there was no evidence that funds had been collected or terrorism committed, a sentence of three-and-a-half years was awarded.

United Nations terrorist bombing and finance offences

5.139 Over several decades, international treaties have responded to specific forms of terrorism such as hijacking and hostage-taking (described later in this chapter). That list has been augmented by two broader UN Treaties, the UN International Convention for the Suppression of Terrorist Bombings[232] and the UN Convention for the Suppression of the Financing of Terrorism.[233] Sections 62 to 64 of the TA 2000 allow for prosecution in the United Kingdom for, or the extradition in respect of, terrorism activities committed abroad and which fall within the terms of these Conventions. However, there is no strict congruence with the UN measures.

5.140 Pursuant to Articles 4 and 6 of the UN Bombing Convention, if a person does anything outside the United Kingdom as an act of terrorism or for the purposes of terrorism, and his action would have constituted the commission of a specified offence (the Explosive Substances Act 1883, ss 2, 3, or 5; the Biological Weapons Act 1974, s 1; or the Chemical Weapons Act 1996, s 2)[234] if it had been done in the United Kingdom, the offence of terrorist bombing under s 62(1) applies. The relevant penalty from the United Kingdom Act will apply. There is no need for any special designation of the foreign territory. Extradition (Art 9) or more or less universal criminal jurisdiction (Art 6) can apply automatically. It follows that terrorists can be tried in the United Kingdom even though the action was conceived, prepared, and perpetrated abroad and involved no British citizens whether as perpetrators or victims. As a limit on s 62, expressed government policy is that extradition should be preferred to extra-territorial prosecution wherever possible.[235] Section 62 exceeds the mandatory terms of the UN Bombing Convention, which, by Article 2, relates to bombings in official or specified public places, though Article 6(5) does not preclude wider domestic law. In particular, the specified s 62 offences are not limited to targets or victims.

5.141 Section 62 arose in *R v McDonald, Rafferty, and O'Farrell*, who were convicted in 2002 of attempting to acquire weaponry for the Real IRA after being lured to a meeting in Slovakia with Security Service agents, pretending to represent the Iraqi government.[236] The broader result of these offences is that terrorist 'facilitators' who have frequent contacts with foreign terror groups and offer advice about their activities overseas can be prosecuted. This position might contrast with, say, events in 1999, when Abu Hamza was linked by communications

---

[230] *Attorney General's References (Nos 85, 86, and 87 of 2007) R v Tsouli* [2007] EWCA Crim 3300.
[231] [2009] EWCA Crim 920.
[232] A/RES/52/164, Cm 4662, London, 1997. See Witten, SM, 'The International Convention for the Suppression of Terrorist Bombings' (1998) 92 *American Journal of International Law* 774.
[233] A/RES/54/109, Cm 4663, London, 1999.
[234] See further Extradition (Terrorist Bombings) Order 2002, SI 2002/1831.
[235] Hansard HC Standing Committee D, col 309 (8 February 2000), Charles Clarke.
[236] [2005] EWCA Crim 1945, [2005] EWCA Crim 1970.

to a group (including his son) involved in kidnappings in Yemen.[237] By contrast, a 'spiritual leader' whose weapons are fiery words of a generalized nature still commits no offence under Pt VI, but such intemperance may contravene the TA 2006, s 1.

Next, the UN Terrorism Financing Convention has also been implemented by the TA 2000. **5.142** Its enforcement subsequently became the mainstay of the work of the Counter-Terrorism Committee which was established under UN Security Resolution 1373 and which demands universal ratification.[238]

Section 63 allows for jurisdiction over forms of financial activities which would fall under ss **5.143** 15 to 18 of the TA 2000 if they had been perpetrated in the United Kingdom but are actually performed outside the jurisdiction. Section 63 exceeds the confines of the UN Terrorism Financing Convention in that the definition of 'terrorism' used in ss 15 to 18 is wider than the definition in Article 2 of the Convention. In this way, action can be taken against non-proscribed groups which are engaged in Pt III offences outside the United Kingdom. The penalties are those for the TA 2000 offences.

By s 64 of the TA 2000, and reflecting Article 9 of the UN Bombing Convention and Article **5.144** 11 of the UN Terrorism Financing Convention, the foregoing Conventions may serve as general extradition arrangements and the relevant offences are added to established bilateral extradition arrangements (now under the Extradition Act 2003). Under the general rules of the Extradition Act 2003, there is no longer any need for the s 64 provision that they are not to be regarded as offences of a political character, in accordance with Article 11 of the UN Bombing Convention and Articles 6 and 14 of the UN Terrorism Financing Convention.

The UN Bombing Convention, Article 15, demands that states parties shall cooperate in the **5.145** prevention of the offences in Article 2, by exchanging information and by consultations on the development of standards for marking explosives, by exchanging information on preventive measures, and by the transfer of technology, equipment, and related materials. Corresponding forms of cooperation are required by Articles 12 and 18 of the UN Terrorism Financing Convention.

External jurisdiction for terrorism offences

The Criminal Justice (International Cooperation) Act 2003, Pt II, extends the jurisdiction **5.146** of several offences in the TA 2000 and the ATCSA 2001. Section 52 inserts a new s 63A into the TA 2000—the effect is to bring within jurisdiction offences under ss 54 and 56 to 61 if committed outside the United Kingdom by a UK national or resident. This extension reflects the Council Framework Decision of 13 June 2002 on Combating Terrorism.[239]

Next, s 63B covers various non-terrorist legislation offences against the person and property **5.147** if committed by a UK national or resident for the purposes of terrorism. If those offences are committed by a non-national/resident against a UK national/resident or a 'protected person' related to British diplomatic services, then criminal jurisdiction can again be assumed under s 63C. The welfare of diplomatic 'protected persons' linked to the United Kingdom is the subject of s 63D. Attacks on their property or vehicles anywhere in the world fall within jurisdiction (attacks on the person already contravene the Internationally Protected Persons Act 1978).

---

[237] See *Mustafa (Hamza) v Government of the United States of America* [2008] EWHC 1357 (Admin).
[238] <http://www.un.org/sc/ctc>.
[239] 2002/475/JHA, OJ [2002] L164, art 9.

5.148 Section 53 of the 2003 Act inserts a new s 113A, relating to the use of noxious substances for the purpose of advancing a political, religious, or ideological cause. There is universal jurisdiction if (i) an act is done by a UK national/resident; or (ii) perpetrated against them or a protected person; or (iii) against the premises or vehicle of a protected person.

5.149 Next, the TA 2006, s 17, further extends jurisdiction for offences contained in ss 1, 6, and 8 to 11 of the TA 2006 and ss 11(1) and 54 of the TA 2000. Section 17 gives effect to Article 14 of the Council of Europe Convention on the Prevention of Terrorism in regard to the offences in ss 1 and 6. Section 8 is included since it is notorious that much terrorist training occurs in Pakistan. Article 9 of the International Convention for the Suppression of Acts of Nuclear Terrorism[240] is the basis for the extension in respect of the offences in ss 9 to 11. Offences of conspiracy, incitement, and attempt in respect of the specific listed offences are also within s 17.

5.150 The offence of conspiring to cause explosions or possessing explosives with intent to endanger life or to cause serious injury to property under s 3 of the Explosive Substances Act 1883, a common charge in terrorist cases, is also amended by s 17.[241] The activities, if committed by a foreigner, must still take place in the United Kingdom or its dependencies (for British citizens, there is already universal jurisdiction), but instead of requiring the explosion to be intended to occur in the United Kingdom or the Republic of Ireland, it may be planned for anywhere. The amendment applies in terrorism or non-terrorism cases, but in Scotland, as a reserved matter, it relates to terrorism alone.[242] Lord Carlile argues this measure is necessary in the absence of jurisdiction for the international criminal court.[243] Yet, there is a major difference between being an active supporter of the application of international criminal law to despots and seeking to impose British domestic values on other situations where there may be justification for violence, such as 'any freedom fighter in Iraq before the overthrow of the Iraqi regime in Kurdistan'.[244]

Foreign comparisons

5.151 Many foreign laws derive from implementation of the same international conventions as mentioned hitherto. It is not necessary to repeat the implementing legislation, but instead attention will be given to national initiatives.

5.152 The United States has probably been most active and inventive in assuming extra-territorial jurisdiction.[245] The trend began with the Omnibus Security and Anti-Terrorism Act 1986[246] which established in 18 US Code s 2332 the offence of homicide or attempts or conspiracies to commit murder or serious bodily injury against US nationals abroad. The Antiterrorism and Effective Death Penalty Act of 1996,[247] s 702, inserts as 18 US Code s 2332b offences which cover a wider range of acts of terrorism transcending national boundaries. Conspiracy to harm people and property abroad is dealt with by s 704 (18 US Code s 956). The breadth of these offences is further increased by the perilous interplay of extra-territorial conspiracy

---

[240] A/59/766, Cm 7301, London, 2008.
[241] See also TA 2000, s 62.
[242] Hansard HL vol 676 col 732 (7 December 2005), Baroness Scotland.
[243] Lord Carlile, *Proposals by Her Majesty's Government for Changes to the Laws against Terrorism* (Home Office, 2005) para 46.
[244] Hansard HC vol 438 col 1045 (3 November 2005), Dominic Grieve.
[245] See Blakesley, C, *Terror and Anti Terrorism* (Transnational, New York, 2006) ch 4.
[246] PL 99-399.
[247] PL 104-132.

offences with broad precursor offences, as in *US v Padilla*.[248] José Padilla was arrested in 2002 as a material witness relating to the 11 September 2001 attacks. A Presidential Order was then issued to detain Padilla as an 'enemy combatant', and he was transferred to a military brig in South Carolina. After protracted litigation about his status,[249] he was transferred to the Federal criminal system in 2006 and was found guilty on three counts of conspiracy to breach s 956 and material support offences. The conspiracy was essentially to engage in a 'violent jihad'.

This legislation raises difficulties in international law which concern the jurisdiction of the **5.153** United States both to make laws and to enforce laws. As regards the jurisdiction to make such a law, there can be no clear justification under the protective principle, so that the passive personality principle, not commonly invoked by common law jurisdictions, must be the basis, given also that the offences concerned are not universally condemned in international law. As regards the jurisdiction of the United States to enforce such laws, possible interference in the affairs of other states is encouraged, for example, by abductions or covert actions. For example, the subject in *US v Fawaz Yunis*[250] was wanted for hijacking and was lured from Lebanon to a boat in the Mediterranean by a promise of a drugs deal. The counter-argument is that threatened intervention by the United States is to encourage local action, including local prosecution.[251] There is also the issue of the technical capability to pursue such difficult and sensitive operations on a worldwide basis, more easily fulfilled by a superpower than by the United Kingdom.

Assessment and conclusions

The transnational nature of contemporary terrorism does require the tactic of 'Pursue' to be **5.154** conceived on an international scale. However, the danger of enforcing United Kingdom expectations and standards in situations which are not at all correspondent is that rights will not be adequately observed. There are safeguards—one is consent to prosecution, which will be described in Chapter 6 and is especially stringent for overseas activities. The other is the jury which is, as ever, expected to show common-sense justice in the application of these offences. Nevertheless, the wider assumption of jurisdiction beyond any international foundation should be treated with reserve.

Assessment and conclusions relating to special criminal offences

The policy relevance and impact of these special offences is based primarily upon 'Pursue', **5.155** though the predominance of precursor offences also addresses 'Prevent' by seeking to set boundaries to involvement in political activity. As to the achievement of these goals, the statistics in Tables 5.1 and 5.2 reveal the frequent use of ss 57 and 58 and the TA 2006 offences, but other offences are symbolic rather than efficient. The statistics in Table 5.3 reveal that the sustaining of convictions in comparison to the effort of arrest and charge is modest, even when account is taken not only of principal and precursor terrorism and terrorism-connected offences but also 'pretext charges' (detailed later in Tables 5.4. and 5.5).[252]

---

[248] See 2006 US Dist LEXIS 63248, 2006 US Dist LEXIS 84497, 2007 US Dist LEXIS 26077.
[249] See *Rumsfeld v Padilla* 542 US 426 (2004); *Padilla v Hanft*, 547 US 1062 (2006).
[250] 681 F Supp 909 (1988).
[251] See Heymann, PB and Gershergorn, IH, 'Pursuing justice, respecting the law' (1991) 3 *Criminal Law Forum* 1.
[252] See Chesney, R, 'The sleeper scenario' (2005) 42 *Harvard Journal on Legislation* 1 at 32.

Table 5.1 Terrorism offence convictions in Great Britain[a]

Date of conviction	Possessing materials – s 57	Possessing information – s 58	Training & Directing – ss 54, 56	Inciting overseas – s 59	Incitement – ss 1, 2 2006 Act	Preparatory act – s 5	Training – ss 6, 8	Total
2001/02	0	0	0	0	–	–	–	0
2002/03	5	1	0	0	–	–	–	6
2003/04	2	0	0	0	–	–	–	2
2004/05	1	1	0	0	–	–	–	2
2005/06	5	2	0	3	–	–	–	10
2006/07	8	5	0	1	1	5	5	25
2007/08	1	2	1	3	3	4	0	14
Total	22	11	1	7	4	9	5	59

[a] Source: *Reports of Lord Carlile.*

Table 5.2 Charges for terrorism offences after arrest under the TA 2000, s 41: Northern Ireland[a]

Date of charge	Possessing materials – s 57	Possessing information – s 58	Weapons training – s 54	Directing terrorism – s 56	Information – s 103	Total
2001	6	7	0	0	0	13
2002	17	17	0	0	6	40
2003	32	10	1	0	5	48
2004	24	1	0	0	1	26
2005	10	3	0	0	3	16
2006	7	0	0	0	0	7
2007	9	3	0	0	–	12
2008	3	0	0	0	–	3
Totals	108	41	1	0	15	165

[a] Source: Northern Ireland Office Statistics & Research Bulletins.

5.156 As for the official British statistics, 62 per cent of those convicted were British citizens and 91 per cent classified themselves as Muslim.[253] However, religion and race/ethnicity are not closely matched. Since 1 April 2005, 42 per cent of arrested suspects and 51 per cent of prisoners were of Asian ethnic appearance, 23 per cent of whom were charged with a terrorism-related offence; 29 per cent of arrestees were of White ethnic appearance while 37 per cent were of Black ethnic appearance. Forty-three per cent of arrested suspects and 38 per cent of those convicted were aged over 30. Independent studies suggest that almost all were male, around 31 per cent had attended higher education, 48 per cent were London residents, and only 31 per cent claimed to have received terrorist training.[254] Between 11 September 2001 and 31 December 2009, 235 persons had been convicted of terrorism-related offences, with 131 in prison and 22 awaiting trial.[255]

---

[253] Lord Carlile, *Report on the Operation in 2008 of the Terrorism Act 2000* (Home Office, London, 2009) p 66.
[254] Simcox, R et al, *Islamist Terrorism* (Centre for Social Cohesion, London, 2010).
[255] Hansard HC vol 513 col 800 (13 July 2010), Theresa May.

Table 5.3 Terrorism prosecutions in Great Britain 11 September 2001 to 31 March 2008[a]

Date	Arrests			Charges					Convictions			Other action				
	TA s 41	Other	Total	Release without charge	TA crimes	Other terrorism crimes	Non-terrorism crimes	Total (% of arrests)	TA crimes	Other crimes	Total (% of charges)	Police caution	Immig'n	Mental health	Transfer to other police	Other total (% of arrests)
2001/02	94	14	108	58	15	7	16	38 (35%)	6	6	12 (32%)	0	13	0	0	13 (12%)
2002/03	237	38	275	141	38	26	30	94 (34%)	9	25	34 (36%)	3	34	2	0	39 (14%)
2003/04	178	13	191	81	34	18	38	90 (47%)	6	15	21 (23%)	3	9	5	2	21 (11%)
2004/05	157	11	168	109	15	20	12	47 (28%)	2	16	18 (38%)	4	5	1	1	13 (8%)
2005/06	273	12	285	193	36	14	25	75 (26%)	24	14	38 (51%)	1	11	2	1	16 (6%)
2006/07	191	22	213	101	60	21	22	103 (48%)	33	12	45 (44%)	0	5	1	1	10 (5%)
2007/08	156	75	231	136	43	12	19	74 (32%)	22	6	28 (38%)	2	11	5	0	19 (8%)
Total	1,286	185	1471	819	241	118	162	521 (35%)	102	94	196 (38%)	13	88	16	5	131 (9%)

[a] Source: Home Office, *Statistics on Terrorism Arrests and Outcomes Great Britain 11 September 2001 to 31 March 2008* (04/09, Home Office, London, 2009). There were an additional thirty-eight arrests following a terrorist investigation from 19 February 2001 to 10 September 2001. Compare Simcox, R et al, *Islamist Terrorism* (Centre for Social Cohesion, London, 2010).

5.157 Applying a rights audit, there are three foremost areas of disharmony. The first relates to the uncertainty inherent in many special offences, which struggle to meet a standard of 'lawfulness' set by the European Convention.[256] The offences enacted in 2006 create not only dangers of unfairness under Article 6 but possible chilling effects under Articles 10 and 11. The second concern is whether the right to fair trial under Article 6 of the European Convention has been adequately respected.[257] This point has already been examined in the context of ss 57 and 58. The third problem is extra-territorial jurisdiction. Comity with Council of Europe and related states, already achieved by the Suppression of Terrorism Act 1978, is certainly acceptable. Otherwise, universal jurisdiction is better serviced by offences within international conventions or by international courts.[258] Beyond those spheres, the imposition of British domestic values may blunder into overseas situations where justification for some crimes against oppressive states may be strong.[259]

5.158 Three practical responses have been made to these problems. The most potent is a proportionate policing. This trait has been evidenced, for example, by restraint in the policing of Tamil demonstrators in London, some of whom showed open support for the Liberation Tigers of Tamil Eelam.[260] Indulgence continues to be shown to Hamas and Hizballah, so that both are only partially proscribed and latitude is given to political activities such as the Al-Manar broadcasts.[261] Against this restraint must be set the prosecution of excessively curious students under ss 57 and 58 and the invocation of these powers against unsophisticated right wing extremists.[262]

5.159 The next response is the filter of consent on prosecution. The involvement of law officers is a 'safety valve'[263] and could offer some antidote to the trend, evident in *R v F*, that the government values friendship with oil-owning despots more highly than the political freedoms of refugee underdogs. Assessments of all manner of delicate disputes arise, such as the decision not to prosecute Boris Beresovsky under s 59 for allegedly plotting 'a new Russian revolution'.[264]

5.160 Thirdly, juries are thought to be unsympathetic towards oppressive prosecutions and are reluctant to take sides in what happens in Sri Lanka, Libya, or Baluchistan.

5.161 As for constitutional governance and accountability, scrutiny through judicial challenge has been fulsome and intense. Rather less care has been shown by Parliament. The data about the application of offences is also patchy and uneven.

---

[256] See *Steel v United Kingdom*, App no 24838/94, 1998-VII, para 54.

[257] *Report of the Special Rapporteur on the promotion and protection of human rights and fundamental freedoms while countering terrorism* (A/63/223, 2008) para 12.

[258] Compare Lord Carlile, *Proposals by Her Majesty's Government for Changes to the Laws against Terrorism* (Home Office, 2005) para 46.

[259] Hansard HC vol 438 col 1045 (3 November 2005), Dominic Grieve.

[260] See *The Times* 8 April 2009, p 20.

[261] Associated journalists such as Ibrahim Moussawi have been banned from entry (*The Times* 14 March 2009, p 14), but there have been no prosecutions for providing satellite television services, unlike the US conviction of Javed Iqbal (*The New York Times* 24 April 2009, p A22).

[262] See the cases of Martyn Gilleard (*The Times* 26 June 2008, p 20); Nathan Worrell ([2009] EWCA Crim 1431); Neil Lewington (*The Times* 16 July 2009, p 23); Terence Gavan (*The Times* 16 January 2010, p 29); Ian and Nicky Davison (*The Times* 15 May 2010, p 31).

[263] Lord Carlile, *Proposals by Her Majesty's Government for Changes to the Laws against Terrorism* (Home Office, London, 2005) para 49.

[264] <http://www.cps.gov.uk/news/press_releases/138_07>.

Despite all the inherent dangers, would the logical next step to the development of special **5.162**
offences in relation to aspects of terrorism be a general offence of terrorism? An example is
the South African Internal Security Act 1982, s 54,[265] whereby a person is guilty of the
offence of terrorism if he or she, *inter alia*, commits (or threatens to commit) an act of
violence or incites, aids, advises, or encourages another person to commit an act of violence
with the intent to: overthrow or endanger the state authority in South Africa; to achieve,
bring about, or promote any constitutional, political, industrial, social, or economic aim or
change in the country; or to induce the government to do or to abstain from doing any act
or to adopt or abandon any particular standpoint. Despite the bitter controversy engendered
by s 54, a replacement offence of terrorism was enacted as the Protection of Constitutional
Democracy against Terrorism and Related Activities 2004, s 2.[266]

An offence of terrorism has been resisted within the United Kingdom. The (Gardiner) *Report of* **5.163**
a Committee to consider, in the context of civil liberties and human rights, measures to deal
with terrorism in Northern Ireland did advocate this measure to catch terrorism 'godfathers'.[267]
However, the government opposed 'catch-all' crimes[268] and settled instead for the directing
offence now in s 56.

The concept raises problems of uncertainty,[269] as experienced in South Africa, and breaches **5.164**
the official policy of 'criminalization' of terrorism by encouraging an inevitable emphasis
upon political motives rather than violence. In any event, the reason why organizers escape
prosecution is not a lack of appropriate and serious charges but a dearth of evidence, which
the proposal cannot remedy. Lord Lloyd[270] adduced another argument for the offences—
that it was a logical consequence of having a power to arrest for terrorism under s 41 and that
the absence of an offence was an anomaly. The government rightly resisted this reasoning,
mainly on the ground that the European Court accepted the term 'terrorism' as akin to a
criminal offence.[271] Of course, the TA 2000 and TA 2006 have now delivered offences which
outlaw important aspects of the proposed offence of terrorism.

The main conceivable gain from a general terrorism offence is jurisdictional—to ensure **5.165**
the domestic prosecution of foreign participants in terrorism, especially those at the
fringes. However, in line with the verdict on similar US models, a universal offence of
terrorism lacks legitimacy in international law, which might hamper international
cooperation and create conflicting jurisdictions.[272] Terrorism is specified as a war crime,[273]
but it was omitted as an express ground for the exercise of the International Criminal

---

[265] No 74. See Mathews, AS, 'The terrors of terrorism' (1974) 91 *South African Law Journal* 381; (Rabie)
Report of the Commission of Inquiry into Security Legislation (RP90/1981, Pretoria, 1981) paras 7.46–7.48,
8.3.5, 9.21–9.22.3.
[266] See South Africa Law Commission, *Project 105: Report on Review of Security Legislation* (Pretoria, 2002)
para 13.152.
[267] (Cmnd 5847, London, 1975) para 70.
[268] Hansard HC Debs vol 893 col 891 (27 June 1975), Mr Rees.
[269] Criminal Law Revision Committee, *14th Report, Offences Against the Person* (Cmnd 7844, London,
1980) para 125.
[270] *Lloyd Report*, para 8.16.
[271] Hansard HL Debs vol 611 col 1487 (6 April 2000), Lord Bassam.
[272] See Duffy, H, *The 'War on Terror' and the Framework of International Law* (Cambridge University Press,
Cambridge, 2005) ch 2.
[273] Third Geneva Convention, Art 119; Fourth Geneva Convention, Art 33; Protocol I, Art 51; Protocol II,
Arts 4, 13. See Pejic, J, 'Terrorist acts and groups' (2004) 75 *British Yearbook of International Law* 71.

Court,[274] and it is doubtful whether it is a customary international law crime.[275] Attempts to legislate for a general international law crime of terrorism have failed, subject to the exception of the League of Nations' Geneva Convention for the Prevention and Punishment of Terrorism 1937, which was never implemented. The task was assigned in 1996 to the Ad Hoc Working Group under the Sixth Committee (legal) of the General Assembly.[276] It has elaborated some important international conventions (on terrorist bombings, finance, and nuclear materials) but has not devised an acceptable comprehensive convention.[277] The reasons which have militated against progress include the political convenience of retaining a flexible definition so that it can be ascribed for political reasons, the difficulty of distinguishing legitimate uses of force in the service of self-determination/liberation struggles, and the unease that state military actions will be tarred with the same brush.

C. Criminal Offences Beyond the Anti-Terrorism Laws

Introduction

5.166 As noted at the outset of this chapter, many of the offences commonly applied in terrorism prosecutions derive from 'normal' law. This categorization is somewhat misleading since some of these 'normal' offences are designed with terrorism in mind, albeit not exclusively so. Accordingly, those offences will be the focus of this section. Some are of long standing and predate the concept of 'terrorism', such as offences against the state. Most of the offences of the contemporary era are based around international terrorism and derive from international treaties. Somewhere in between are the domestic offences against the use of explosives.

5.167 Beyond these, many other offences are applied to terrorists. Of utmost importance are homicides, including the solicitation of murder[278] and threats to kill,[279] other offences against the person, and also criminal damage (especially destroying or damaging property with intent or being reckless as to the endangerment to life).[280] For instance, Kamel Bourgass was convicted of the murder with a kitchen knife of DC Stephen Oake and attempted murder and wounding in relation to four other officers.[281] Dhiren Barot was convicted of conspiracy to murder, including by his 'Gas Limos Project' and 'Radiation (Dirty Bomb) Proposal'.[282] Four of the attempted bombers of 21 July 2005 were convicted of conspiracy to murder.[283]

---

[274] See Arnold, R, 'Terrorism as a crime against humanity under the ICC Statute' in Nesi, G (ed), *International Cooperation in Counter-Terrorism* (Ashgate, Aldershot, 2006).

[275] Compare Cassese, A, 'The multifaceted notion of terrorism in international law' (2006) 4 *Journal of International Criminal Justice* 933.

[276] UNGA Res 51/210 of 17 December 1996. For the most recent affirmation of its mandate, see UNGA Res 64/118 of 16 December 2009. See Nesi, G (ed), *International Cooperation in Counter-Terrorism* (Ashgate, Aldershot, 2006) chs 1–3.

[277] See for drafts <http://www.un.org/law/terrorism/index.html>.

[278] See *R v Most* (1881) 7 QBD 244; *R v Antonelli and Barberi* (1905) 70 JP 4. For more recent cases, see *R v El-Faisal* [2004] EWCA Crim 343, [2004] EWCA Crim 456; *R v Abu Hamza* [2006] EWCA Crim 2918; *R v Saleem, Muhid, and Javed* [2007] EWCA Crim 2692; *R v Rahman* [2008] EWCA Crim 2290.

[279] Offences against the Person Act 1861, s 16.

[280] Criminal Damage Act 1971, s 1(2)(b).

[281] [2005] EWCA Crim 1943, [2006] EWCA Crim 3397.

[282] [2007] EWCA Crim 1119.

[283] *R v Ibrahim* [2008] EWCA Crim 880.

The leading players convicted of the 2006 transatlantic aircraft 'Liquid Bomb' plot were found guilty of conspiracy to murder.[284] Bilal Talal Samad Abdullah was convicted of conspiracy to murder in connection with his attack on Glasgow International Airport in 2007.[285] Attempted murder was sustained against Mohammad Abdulaziz Rashid Saeed-Alim (Nicky Reilly), a white Muslim convert with mental difficulties who attempted to set off a nail bomb in a restaurant.[286]

The Bribery Act 2010 will wholly replace and repeal the ATCSA 2001, ss 108 to 100, so **5.168** measures against corruption will also be omitted.

Offences against the state

Offences of treason as applied to political violence may feature three principal attractions **5.169** compared to less venerable crimes. First, they emphasize the public denunciation of the conduct. Secondly, they have a broader sweep than explosives or firearms offences. Thirdly, treason carried the death penalty long after it was abolished for all other offences, though this lure was removed by the Crime and Disorder Act 1998, s 36.[287] It should be noted that offences of sedition and seditious libel were abolished by the Coroners and Justice Act 2009, s 73.

Various headings of the Treason Act 1351[288] could apply to contemporary terrorism, but **5.170** the most apposite charge is where 'a man do levy war against our Lord the King in his realm'. A substantial campaign of terrorism can amount to 'an insurrection raised to reform some national grievance . . . or for any . . . purpose which usurps the Government in matters of a public and general nature'.[289] Moreover, while the levying of war traditionally required 'a forcible disturbance that is produced by a considerable number of persons',[290] trials in the late nineteenth century involving Fenian activities in England demonstrated that 'a mustering of forces or an irregular mass of men'[291] was no longer necessary and that a mere handful of rebels armed with powerful modern munitions could levy war.

The application of these treason laws to contemporary terrorism was explored in South **5.171** Africa during the *apartheid* era. Overt acts of levying war can include causing explosions in public places or attacks on security forces.[292] Even non-violent aid, such as supplying information and delivering messages to, or rousing support on behalf of, terrorist groups,

---

[284] *R v Abdullah Ahmed Ali, The Times* 9 September 2008, p 1 (Woolwich Crown Court).

[285] *The Times* 17 December 2008, p 1 (Woolwich Crown Court).

[286] *The Times* 31 January 2009, p 18 (Central Criminal Court). He was awarded a minimum sentence for public protection of eighteen years.

[287] Protocol No 6 to the Convention for the Protection of Human Rights and Fundamental Freedoms concerning the abolition of the death penalty (ETS 114, 1983).

[288] The Act applies in Northern Ireland and Scotland; Poyning's Law 1495; Treason Act (Ir) 1537; Crown of Ireland Act 1542; Treason Act 1708.

[289] East, 1 PC 72. See also *R v Dammaree* (1710) 15 St Tr 521; *R v Gordon* (1781) 21 St Tr 485.

[290] Cecil Turner, JW, *Kenny's Outlines of Criminal Law* (19th edn, Cambridge University Press, Cambridge, 1966) para 406. See *R v Smith O'Brien* (1849) 3 Cox CC 360; *R v Burke* (1867) 10 Cox CC 519; *R v McCafferty* (1869) 10 Cox CC 603.

[291] *R v Gallagher* (1883) 15 Cox CC 291 at 317. See also *R v Deasey* (1883) 15 Cox CC 334. These were prosecutions for treason felony.

[292] *S v Mange* 1980 (4) SA 613 (AD); *S v Lubisi* 1982 (3) SA 113 (AD); *S v Tsotsobe* 1983 (1) SA 856 (AD); *S v Gaba* 1985 (4) SA 734 (AD); *S v Ramgobin* 1986 (1) SA 68 (NPD).

was held to suffice.[293] The first treason trial since the reformation of South Africa, commencing in 2003, relates to the 'Boeremag' ('Boer Force') conspirators.[294]

5.172 Though the foregoing survey demonstrates the availability of high treason, many of the prosecutions of rebels in Ireland during the nineteenth century encountered difficulties.[295] Not only were there procedural hitches such as time limits (generally three years)[296] and proof of 'overt acts' matching the indictment,[297] there were also obscurities about the substance of the offence with archaic and obscure terminology affecting elements such as allegiance, residence, territoriality,[298] and the impact of words alone.[299] In any event, the invocation of ancient offences against the state may serve the purpose of ringing condemnation, but in equal part it marks the offence as political and may stir 'robust political opposition'.[300] As the Law Commission recognized, '. . . from the practical point of view it is normally found more expedient to charge ordinary criminal offences than to imply that importance is being attached to the activities by treating them as treasonable, or that there could be any political justification for the conduct, even in the mind of the offenders'.[301]

5.173 Some of these problems were addressed by the Treason Felony Act 1848, s 3:

> If any person . . . compass, imagine, invent, devise or intend to deprive or depose . . . the Queen from the style honour, or royal name of the imperial crown of the United Kingdom . . . or to levy war against her Majesty . . . in her . . . measures or counsels, or in order to put any force or constraint upon or in order to intimidate or overawe both Houses or either House of Parliament, or to move or stir any foreigner or stranger with force to invade the United Kingdom . . . and such compassings, imaginations, inventions, devices, or intentions, or any of them, shall express, utter, or declare, by publishing any printing or writing . . . by any overt act or deed, [he] . . . shall be liable . . . [to imprisonment for life or any shorter term] . . .

5.174 In *R v Dowling*,[302] it was decided that depriving the Queen of her title includes any attempt to substitute a new form of government or to dismember the United Kingdom, while the levying of war need only entail the use of force or intimidation against the state and not actual conflict. Consequently, proceedings have been brought successfully against Irish Republicans during the past century. Thus, thirteen participants in an IRA 'court-martial' were convicted in Belfast in 1936,[303] and eight volunteers were imprisoned after an attack on Omagh Barracks in 1954.[304] In 1972, Callinan, Quinn, and Marcartonio, who had tried to

---

293 *S v Hogan* 1983 (2) SA 46 (WLD). See also *S v Mayekiso* 1988 (4) SA 738 (WLD).
294 See *S v Du Toit* (CC91/03) [2004] ZAGPHC 1, 2004 (2) SACR 584 (T); *S v Vorster* (CC91/2003) [2008] ZAGPHC 172; *Pretorius v Minister of Justice* (North Gauteng High Court, 26 August 2010). Note also the charge of 'sabotage' under the General Law Amendment Act (Sabotage Act) 1962 (No 76) which was applied to Nelson Mandela in 1963 and to opponents of the ANC in *S v Peacock* (A12/2004) [2006] ZAFSHC 136.
295 See McBain, GS, 'Abolishing the crimes of treason' (2007) 81 *Australian Law Journal* 94.
296 See the Treason Act 1695, s 5; the Treason Act 1708, s 1; the Treason (Ireland) Act 1821; the Administration of Justice (Miscellaneous Provisions) Act 1933, s 2(8), Sch 2, para 1.
297 *Mulcahy v R* (1866) IR 1 CL 12 (affd (1868) LR 3 HL 306); *R v Meany* (1867) 10 Cox CC 506; *R v Davitt* (1870) 11 Cox CC 676; *R v Deasy* (1883) 15 Cox CC 334.
298 *Jagar v Natal* [1907] AC 326; *R v Casement* [1917] 1 QB 98; *R v Joyce* [1946] AC 347.
299 *R v Mitchel* (1848) 3 Cox CC 2.
300 Mathews, AS, *Freedom, State Security and the Rule of Law* (Juta, Cape Town, 1988) p 219.
301 Law Commission, *Working Paper No 72: Treason, Sedition and Allied Offences* (London, 1977) para 58.
302 (1848) 3 Cox CC 509.
303 See Bowyer Bell, J, *The Secret Army* (Rev edn, Academy Press, Dublin, 1979) p 125.
304 See Edwards, JL1J, 'Special powers in Northern Ireland' (1956) *Criminal Law Review* 7 at p 14.

recruit in Hyde Park volunteers for the 'Northern Ireland Minority Defence Force', were charged with treason felony, though this count was dropped.[305]

Whatever the present relevance of treason to terrorism, few would deny the need for reform as a prelude to any resurrection. Indeed, this course has been followed whenever the United Kingdom government wished to utilize offences against the state in wartime or colonial crises during the past century.[306] The Law Commission has likewise proposed the redrawing of treason and treason felony,[307] as has a further review by Lord Goldsmith, *Citizenship: Our Common Bond*.[308] **5.175**

Most comparable jurisdictions have likewise abolished, reformulated, or proposed to remodel these crimes. For example, the Irish Republic's Offences against the State Act 1939, Pt II, includes a series of offences relating to the usurpation or obstruction of the functions of government, interference with the military or other employees of the state, engaging in unauthorized military exercises or training, setting up secret societies in the army or police, and administering unlawful oaths. Treason is defined by art 39 of the Constitution and supported by the Treason Act 1939. These offences have excited little usage and therefore impetus to reform.[309] **5.176**

Offences against the state were considered by the Australian Law Reform Commission, which called for substantial reform.[310] Treason has been threatened in the US.[311] In 2006, a Federal grand jury issued an indictment for treason, charging Adam Yahiye Gadahn with involvement in Al-Qa'ida videos.[312] Seditious conspiracy was charged in the US against Sheikh Omar Abdel Rahman arising from the 1993 World Trade Center attack and other plans.[313] **5.177**

By contrast, offences against the state have lain dormant in Britain. Even as against those IRA bombers who sought at Brighton in 1983 to kill the Prime Minister and members of the Cabinet, the Attorney General remained disinclined to contemplate treason charges: '. . . there are substantial problems in bringing a prosecution based on the language of a statute designed for the different circumstances of more than six centuries ago. The common law remedy of murder, coupled with legislation on explosives and firearms, has proved both appropriate and effective for all recent cases.'[314] Likewise, treason charges were allegedly put into the frame but not pursued during the attack in London of July 2005.[315] The courts have also displayed an inclination to let sleeping dogs lie as regards treason felony.[316] **5.178**

---

[305] *The Times* 20 January 1973, p 2.

[306] See: Treachery Act 1940 (terminated by 1946 SR & O No 893).

[307] Law Commission, *Working Paper No 72: Treason, Sedition and Allied Offences* (London, 1977).

[308] (Ministry of Justice, London, 2008) paras 4.39–4.41.

[309] See (Hederman) *Report of the Committee to Review the Offences against the State Acts 1939–1998* (Dublin, 2002) ch 6.

[310] Australian Law Reform Commission, *Fighting Words* (Report 104, Canberra, 2006) chs 8, 9.

[311] See Babb, SK, 'Fear and loathing in America' (2003) 54 *Hastings Law Journal* 1721; Bell, TW, 'Treason, technology and freedom of expression' (2005) 37 *Arizona State Law Journal* 999; Larson, CFW, 'The forgotten constitutional law of treason and the enemy combatant problem' (2006) 154 *University of Pennsylvania Law Review* 863.

[312] See Kash, DA, 'The United States v. Adam Gadahn: A case for treason' (2008) 37 *Capital University Law Review* 1.

[313] *United States v Rahman* 189 F3d 88 (1999) at 94.

[314] Hansard HC Debs vol 98 col 14 (19 May 1986).

[315] *The Times* 8 August 2005, p 6; *The Guardian* 10 August 2005, p 21.

[316] *R (Rusbridger) v Attorney General* [2003] UKHL 38.

Explosives and firearms offences

5.179   The purpose of this section is to explain and review munitions offences especially relevant to terrorism with the focus on the Explosive Substances Act 1883, which was designed in response to Fenian activities in Britain. The Act has broad extra-territorial extent. But no proceedings may be brought without the consent of the Attorney General under s 7. Protective measures regarding munitions will be considered in Chapter 10.

5.180   First, by s 2, the causing of an explosion of a nature likely to endanger life or to cause serious injury to property shall, whether any injury to person or property has been actually caused or not, be an offence which carries imprisonment for life.[317]

5.181   Participation at an earlier stage is encompassed by s 3(1),[318] which relates to (a) actions with intent to cause, or conspiring to cause, by an explosive substance an explosion of a nature likely to endanger life, or to cause serious injury to property or (b) making or possessing an explosive substance with intent by means thereof to endanger life or cause serious injury to property. The offence again merits imprisonment for life. This offence differs from s 2 in that no explosion need occur, nor need the threat to life or property be immediate, thereby allowing timely intervention by the police. The offences are also broadened by the definition of 'explosive substances' which includes all their ingredients and any apparatus used for causing or aiding an explosion.[319]

5.182   Section 4(1) takes a step further back and criminalizes the possession of ingredients giving rise to a reasonable suspicion that possession or control is not for a lawful object, whereupon it is for the defendant to show a lawful object. This forerunner to the approach of s 57 of the TA 2000 was challenged in *R v Berry*.[320] It was accepted that the Crown must first discharge its burden of a 'conduct crime', namely possession giving rise to a reasonable suspicion that it did not have a lawful object; only then need the defendant show on balance a lawful object.[321] In *Re Hardy*, [322] the defendant was arrested on disembarkation at Rosslare from Cherbourg for the possession of sodium chlorate and mercury tilt switches. The Irish Supreme Court concluded that the prosecution was required to prove the essential elements of the offence under s 4, inferring that the accused must simply raise a point of substance to detract from that proof. This idea roughly equates to a 'persuasive' burden of proof. Subsequently, the European Commission of Human Rights[323] considered that the onus rested sufficiently on the prosecution to found guilt initially and ultimately. It might be preferable if proof was required of a reasonable suspicion of possession, not for any unlawful purposes, but only for purposes unlawful under ss 2 and 3.

5.183   These offences remain commonplace in major terrorism cases. For example, Omar Khyam was convicted of conspiracy to cause explosions likely to endanger life or cause serious injury to property, contrary to s 3(1)(a).[324] One of the attempted bombers of 21 July 2005 pleaded

---

[317]   See *R v Ellis* (1991) 95 Cr App Rep 52.
[318]   See Law Commission, *Report No 29, Offences of Damage to Property* (1970–71 HC 91) paras 62–66, 97.
[319]   S 9. See *R v Downey* [1971] NI 224; *R v Wheatley* [1979] 1 WLR 144; *R v Bouch* [1983] QB 246; *R v O'Reilly* [1989] NI 120; *R v Berry (No 3)* (1994) 99 Cr App R 88.
[320]   [1985] AC 246. See also *Berry (No 2)* (1991) 92 Cr App R 147; *Berry (No 3)* (1994) 99 Cr App R 88.
[321]   As in *R v Fegan* [1972] NI 80; *AG's Reference (No 2 of 1983)* [1984] QB 456.
[322]   [1994] 2 IR 550. The description 'evidential' was used by Flood J in the High Court (p 559).
[323]   App no 23456/94, 29 June 2004.
[324]   [2008] EWCA Crim 1612.

guilty to conspiracy to cause an explosion or explosions likely to endanger life or property, after the jury had been unable to agree on a verdict of conspiracy to murder.[325] The 1883 Act can also be used against 'lone wolves' who do not necessitate the full might of anti-terrorism laws. For example, Miles Cooper was convicted under ss 2 and 4 of sending seven letter bombs during his campaign against the state surveillance.[326]

As for firearms offences, the most apposite charge is s 16 of the Firearms Act 1968—to **5.184** possess any firearm or ammunition with intent to endanger life, whether any injury has been caused or not. The offence can apply to threats by terrorists to foreign persons, such as a plot by a Moroccan to kidnap a French police officer.[327]

International convention offences

Over several decades, international treaties have tackled those aspects of terrorism which **5.185** excite universal condemnation, beginning with hijacking. These multilateral instruments follow a common pattern.[328] They delineate and condemn as an international crime a specific form of terrorism. Each state is then obliged to pass domestic measures which ensure it is a crime and is extraditable between party states without any exception for political offenders. Any offender should be considered for extradition or prosecution—*aut dedere aut iudicare*. Cooperation between national authorities will also be required. Most of the offences overlap with existing criminal law, so that the real impact of the measures is to put political pressure on states to recognize international comity. In so far as they operate as legal instruments, the legislation is piecemeal, lacks enforcement, and largely lies dormant. Nevertheless, ratification of the relevant conventions is a constant theme of contemporary international organizations.

Aviation security

Some of the earliest legislation against foreign terrorism combats hijacking and other attacks **5.186** on aircraft and at airports and ports.[329] The relevant offences will be outlined here, with protective security left for Chapter 10.

The first such measure was the Tokyo Convention Act 1967, now mostly consolidated as the **5.187** Civil Aviation Act 1982 (ss 92 to 96).[330] This legislation is aimed at 'offenders and trouble-makers'[331] rather than terrorists. It extends the jurisdiction of UK law to British-controlled aircraft wherever situated and confers powers on aircraft commanders to quell disturbances. More directed against terrorists are the Hijacking Act 1971,[332] the Protection of Aircraft Act 1973,[333] and the Policing of Airports Act 1974. These Acts have been incorporated within

---

[325] *R v Asiedu* [2008] EWCA Crim 1725.
[326] *The Times* 28 September 2007, p 33, 29 September, p 27. An indeterminate sentence with a minimum of four years 149 days was awarded (Oxford Crown Court).
[327] *R v El-Hakkaoui* [1975] 2 All ER 146.
[328] See Kolb, R, 'The exercise of international jurisdiction over international terrorism' in Bianchi, A (ed), *Enforcing International Norms Against Terrorism* (Hart, Oxford, 2004); Sambei, A et al, *Counter-Terrorism Laws and Practice* (Oxford University Press, Oxford, 2009) ch 3.
[329] See Wilkinson, P and Jenkins, B, *Aviation Terrorism and Security* (2nd edn, Routledge, Abingdon, 2007).
[330] Convention on Offences and Certain Other Acts Committed on Board Aircraft, signed at Tokyo on 14 September 1963 (Cmnd 4230, London, 1969).
[331] Hansard HC Debs vol 738 col 885 (16 December 1966), Robert MacLennan.
[332] Convention for the Suppression of Unlawful Seizure of Aircraft, signed at The Hague on 16 December 1970 (10 ILM 133) (Cmnd 4956, London, 1972).
[333] Convention for the Suppression of Unlawful Acts against the Safety of Civil Aviation, signed at Montreal on 23 September 1971 (10 ILM 1151) (Cmnd 5524, London, 1974).

the Aviation Security Act 1982, in turn amended by the Aviation and Maritime Security Act 1990.[334]

5.188　Proceedings for offences under ss 1 to 3 of the 1982 Act can be instituted only with the consent of the Attorney General (s 8), and the maximum penalty is life imprisonment. There are offences of hijacking in s 1 which apply to an aircraft in flight (within s 38). Exceptions affect aircraft used for military, customs, or police service purposes and situations without any United Kingdom or international connections. The courts have not accepted as a defence the motive of fleeing from political persecution,[335] though duress of circumstances was available to Shia Muslims fleeing from Iraq[336] and potentially to Afghani refugees.[337] The destruction, damaging, or endangerment of aircraft so as to render it incapable of flight or so as to endanger its safety is an offence under s 2. An attempt to commit this offence by Nezar Hindawi resulted in a sentence of forty-five years for 'as foul and as horrible a crime as could possibly be imagined'[338] and the breaking of diplomatic relations with Syria. Other acts endangering aircraft safety are covered under s 3. The possession of dangerous articles is dealt with by s 4 (the maximum penalty is five years on indictment). Hoaxes are forbidden under s 3(3) but may also be dealt with under the more generalist offences previously outlined.[339] These offences are supplemented by the Aviation and Maritime Security Act 1990, ss 1 and 5, relating to the protection of aerodromes.

Maritime security

5.189　Shocked by the Achille Lauro incident in 1985[340] the international community responded with the International Maritime Organisation's Convention for the Suppression of Unlawful Acts against the Safety of Maritime Navigation and Protocol for the Suppression of Unlawful Acts against the Safety of Fixed Platforms on the Continental Shelf.[341] These instruments were modelled on the aircraft conventions and have been implemented for ships and harbours by the Aviation and Maritime Security Act 1990. There are several extraditable offences in ss 9 to 13. The maximum penalty is life imprisonment. Extraterritoriality is conferred under s 14. The ship's master is empowered under s 15 to deliver a person to an appropriate officer. Prosecution must be with the consent of the Attorney General under s 16.

5.190　The chaotic situation in Somalia has spawned piracy as a serious threat over the past decade. Though criminal rather than political motives predominate, there are suspicions that some pirates are either financed or 'taxed' by insurgent groups. The English courts have jurisdiction

---

[334] Protocol for the Suppression of Unlawful Acts of Violence at Airports serving International Civil Aviation, supplementary to the Convention for the Suppression of Unlawful Acts against the Safety of Civil Aviation, signed at Montreal on 24 February 1988 (27 ILM 627) (Cm 1470, London, 1991). Note also the ICAO's Convention on the Suppression of Unlawful Acts Relating to International Civil Aviation and the Supplementary Protocol (Beijing, 2010) which contain proposed international offences of using civilian aircraft as weapons and using dangerous materials to attack aircraft or ground targets.

[335] *R v Moussa Membar* (1983) Crim LR 618.

[336] *R v Abdul Hussein* (1999) Crim LR 570.

[337] *R v Safi* [2003] EWCA Crim 1809. See also *S v Secretary of State for the Home Department* [2006] EWCA Civ 1157.

[338] (1988) 10 Cr App R (S) 104. See also *Balfour v Foreign & Commonwealth Office* [1994] 2 All ER 588.

[339] See *R v Mason* [2001] EWCA Crim 1138.

[340] See Cassesse, A, *Terrorism, Politics and Law* (Polity Press, Cambridge, 1989).

[341] (1988) 27 ILM 672, 685. See Ronzitti, N (ed), *Maritime Terrorism and International Law* (Nijhoff, Dordrecht, 1990).

to try piracy *jure gentium*.[342] The Merchant Shipping Act 1997, s 26 and Sch 5, refers the courts to the definition of piracy in the UN Convention of the Law of the Sea 1982, Articles 101 and 102, as constituting the law of nations. There is also a statutory offence under the Piracy Act 1837, s 2, covering attacks associated with piracy. Despite offences aplenty, the affected states have responded by practical, rather than legal, enforcement measures.[343] The United Kingdom has agreed with Kenya and the Seychelles for captured pirates to be detained and processed in those jurisdictions,[344] but most are not taken into formal custody so as to avoid claims to asylum and rights.

Diplomats

Diplomats have featured in several international law initiatives against terrorism in recognition that they are 'by virtue of their duties . . . particularly susceptible to terrorist attacks'.[345] Pursuant to the UN Convention on the Prevention and Punishment of Crimes against Internationally Protected Persons, including Diplomatic Agents of 1973,[346] the Internationally Protected Persons Act 1978 grants them special protection. Thus, s 1 creates wide offences involving attacks on, or threats to, diplomats and governmental officials. There is wide extra-territorial jurisdiction and the offences are extraditable, subject to the political offence exception. Protection along similar lines has been established by the United Nations Personnel Act 1997[347] and the Geneva Conventions and United Nations Personnel (Protocols) Act 2009.[348]

5.191

The enforcement of the Convention arose against Al-Fawwaz, Eidarous, and Bary whose extradition for the East African embassy bombings was granted to the US.[349] The extra-territorial jurisdiction assumed by it was recognized in international law though other offences laid against further conspirators could not apply.

5.192

Diplomats are accorded many concessions by the Vienna Conventions on Diplomatic Relations 1961 and on Consular Relations 1963,[350] some of which have been abused in the furtherance of terrorism. Egregious floutings of diplomatic privileges include shootings from the Libyan People's Bureau in 1984, which killed police officer Yvonne Fletcher,[351] and the kidnapping in a shipping crate of Umaru Dikko by the Nigerian High Commission in

5.193

---

[342] *Re Piracy Jure Gentium* [1934] AC 586.

[343] See Fink, MD and Galvin, RJ, 'Combating pirates off the coast of Somalia' (2009) 56 *Netherlands International Law Review* 367; Kontorovich, E, 'A Guantánamo on the sea' (2010) 98 *California Law Review* 243; Guilfoyle, D, 'Counter-piracy law enforcement and human rights' (2010) 59 *International & Comparative Law Quarterly* 141; House of Lords European Union Committee, *Combating Somali Piracy* (2009–10 HL 103).

[344] See <http://www.fco.gov.uk/en/global-issues/conflict-prevention/piracy/prisoners>.

[345] Hansard HL Debs vol 392 col 397 (17 May 1928), Lord Garner.

[346] (13 ILM 41) (Cmnd 6176, 1977). See Craig Baker, J, *The Protection of Diplomatic Personnel* (Ashgate, Aldershot, 2006) ch 5.

[347] See Convention on the Safety of United Nations and Associated Personnel adopted by the General Assembly of the United Nations on 9 December 1994 (Cm 4803, London, 2000).

[348] Optional Protocol to the Convention adopted by the General Assembly of the United Nations on 8 December 2005 (Cm 7733, London, 2009).

[349] See *Re Al-Fawwaz* [2001] UKHL 69; *R (Bary and Fawwaz) v Secretary of State for the Home Department* [2009] EWHC 2068 (Admin).

[350] See the Diplomatic Privileges Act 1964; Consular Relations Act 1968; the Diplomatic and Consular Premises Act 1987.

[351] See House of Commons Foreign Affairs Committee, *The Abuse of Diplomatic Immunities and Privileges* (1984–85 HC 127) para 95.

1984.[352] Two Israeli diplomats were expelled in 1988 after the conviction of Ismael Sowan, a Mossad double agent who stored a Palestine Liberation Organisation arms cache.[353] The Third Secretary of the Vietnamese embassy, Khang Than Nhan, was expelled in 1988 for brandishing a gun at protestors.[354] An Iraqi attaché, Khamis Khalaf al-Ajili, was expelled in 1995 for collecting information about dissident students.[355] Four Russian diplomats were expelled in 2007 over the failure to assist in the extradition of Andrey Lugovoy for the murder of Alexander Litvinenko.[356] The abuse of British passports in connection with the killing of a Hamas official in Dubai resulted in the expulsion of an Israeli diplomat in 2010.[357] However, extradition to Argentina of a former Iranian diplomat, Hade Soleimanpour, for a bombing in 1994 was turned down on grounds of insufficient evidence in 2003,[358] thereby avoiding any dispute about the continuation of privileges under Article 39 of the Vienna Convention.[359]

5.194   The state reaction has mainly comprised tighter enforcement of sanctions under the Diplomatic Privileges Act 1964 and the Diplomatic and Consular Premises Act 1987. However, neither this legislation nor the UN Convention fosters practical security measures. The United Kingdom government has treated 'Protect' as an administrative issue, but other states have passed more comprehensive legislation for the protection of their diplomats.[360] Attacks on British diplomats include the bombing of the Istanbul consulate in 2003, causing the death of the consul, Roger Short,[361] and the attempted suicide bombing of the ambassador in Yemen in 2010.[362]

Hostage-taking

5.195   The UN's International Convention against the Taking of Hostages of 1979[363] suffers from substantive limits. For example, a demand must be made on a third party, and its enforcement may be hampered by exceptions for political offences or asylum. There is no criminalization of threats or acts preparatory. Consequently, the Taking of Hostages Act 1982, by which the Convention is implemented through an offence of detention for political motives, is mainly designed to resolve jurisdictional and extradition problems.

Assessment and conclusions

5.196   'Normal' offences have been the staple of terrorism trials until the past decade when precursor offences began to make inroads into the criminal code.

---

352 See ibid Pt IV; Ashman, CR, and Trescott, P, *Outrage* (WH Allen, London, 1986).
353 *The Times* 17 June 1988.
354 *The Guardian* 12 September 1988.
355 *The Times* 26 October 1995.
356 Hansard HC vol 463 col 21 (16 July 2007).
357 Hansard HC vol 508 col 133 (23 March 2010).
358 *The Times* 14 November 2003, p 15.
359 Compare *S v Berlin* (1997) 115 ILR 597 (German Constitutional Court) (summarized in 92 *American Journal of International Law* 74 (1998)); *R v Bow Street Metropolitan Stipendiary Magistrate, ex parte Pinochet Ugarte (No 3)* [2000] 1 AC 147.
360 Compare Omnibus and Diplomatic Security and Anti-Terrorism Act 1986 (22 USC s 54801). See Craig Baker, J, *The Protection of Diplomatic Personnel* (Ashgate, Aldershot, 2006) ch 4.
361 See for earlier incidents, Hickman, K, *Daughters of Britannia* (Flamingo, London, 2000).
362 *The Times* 27 April 2010, p 3.
363 (18 ILM 1456) Cmnd 7893, London, 1979. See Morgan, EM, *International Convention against the Taking of Hostages* (Commonwealth Secretariat, London, 1989).

Table 5.4 Non-terrorism offence convictions where considered as terrorism-related in Great Britain[a]

Date of conviction	Homicide related	Offences against person, kidnap, intimidation	Property, blackmail, arson, drugs offences	Munitions offences	Hoax	Total
2001/02	0	0	0	5	0	5
2002/03	2	0	17	2	3	24
2003/04	1	0	7	7	0	15
2004/05	1	0	5	10	0	15
2005/06	4	0	0	1	0	5
2006/07	4	0	0	1	0	5
2007/08	2	0	0	2	0	4
Totals	14	0	29	28	3	73

[a] Source: *Reports of Lord Carlile*. Other offences (twenty-one in the whole period) are omitted.

Table 5.5 Charges for non terrorism offences after arrest under the TA 2000 s 41: Northern Ireland[a]

Date of charge	Homicide related	Offences against person, kidnap, intimidation	Property, blackmail, arson, drugs offences	Munitions offences	Hoax	Total
2001	14	0	5	43	1	63
2002	10	3	18	61	1	93
2003	21	17	49	104	1	192
2004	3	26	23	90	0	142
2005	19	20	32	46	0	117
2006	7	8	6	47	1	69
2007	10	23	6	28	1	68
2008	6	9	7	24	0	46
Totals	90	100	146	443	5	790

[a] Source: *Northern Ireland Office Statistics & Research Bulletins*. Other offences are omitted; none reaches a total beyond ten in the whole period except possession of offensive weapons (thirteen).

The foregoing data reflects the application not only of offences at the severe end of the criminal law scale but also an interest in pretextual prosecutions of terrorists, akin to the Al Capone strategy by which tax laws were used to catch mobsters.[364] For instance, several associates of Kamel Bourgass were convicted of passport fraud.[365] However, the benefits of this strategy can be exaggerated.[366] The availability of such charges is not predictable, and terrorists are not endemically amateurish in their *modus operandi*, as illustrated by the technical and logistical sophistication of IRA attacks at the Brighton Grand Hotel in 1984 or the mortar attacks on Downing Street in 1991. The 9/11 attacks also involved an impressive amount of **5.197**

---

[364] See Richman, DC and Stuntz, WJ, 'Al Capone's revenge' (2005) 105 *Columbia Law Review* 583; Chesney, R, 'The sleeper scenario' (2005) 42 *Harvard Journal on Legislation* 1 at 32.

[365] See *R v Bourgass* [2005] EWCA Crim 1943, [2006] EWCA Crim 3397; *Re Kadre* [2005] EWHC 1712 (Admin).

[366] As by Hamm, MS, *Terrorism as Crime* (New York University Press, New York, 2009) pp 16, 221.

planning and coordination. Furthermore, terrorism may be committed by self-starters with 'clean skins' and no predicate crimes are necessary to facilitate or finance their terrorism, as was largely true of the July 7 bombers.[367] Even if there is a criminal background, it may not be linked to terrorism. For example, Muktar Said Ibrahim had a criminal record consisting of indecent assaults in 1993 and robbery in 1995, but this background could not point to, or avert, attempted terrorist attacks on 21 July 2005. In any event, police officers who deal with 'normal' crimes cannot routinely avail themselves of the language, computing, and international liaison facilities necessary for terrorism investigation.

D. Conclusions

5.198 The agenda of the anti-terrorism legislation has expanded markedly within the criminal code. The consequent dangers to individual rights to fair trial and to collective perceptions of legitimacy have also grown. Nevertheless, this focus on the Old Bailey rather than Belmarsh is welcomed. The idea that justice can be better achieved by executive measures is implausible given their standards and structures.

5.199 Yet, there is the danger that the policy of criminalization will be jeopardized because the siren voice of security will demand convergence between executive measures and criminal justice and a slide towards minimum standards of due process. In this way, the promulgation of special offences represents 'false and extravagant presumptions about the ability of harsh criminal law to stop terrorism'.[368] The tactic more evidently serves symbolic, denunciatory functions.[369]

5.200 To avoid undermining the criminalization project, four checks are suggested. First, prosecutors should consider as a priority charges under 'normal' offences—a principle of 'normalcy'. Secondly, there should be much finer data about the processes and results of prosecution, so that its impact can be better understood. Thirdly, the security services should be trained further to produce and present evidence for criminal courts.[370] Further progress of criminalization demands a reassertion of the primacy of prosecution even if the Security Service retains the lead in intelligence-gathering. Finally, the courts should recognize that they are on their own patch where their expertise exceeds that of the Minister. They must act as prime guardians against unwarranted intrusions on the individual rights of suspects and detainees and against resultant miscarriages of justice.

---

[367] See Kirby, A, 'The London bombers as "self starters"' (2007) 30 *Studies in Conflict & Terrorism* 415.

[368] Roach, K, 'Anti-terrorism and militant democracy' in Sajo, A (ed), *Militant Democracy* (Eleven International, Utrecht, 2004) p 186.

[369] See Roach, K, 'The criminal law and terrorism' in Ramraj, VV, Hor, M, and Roach, K, *Global Anti-terrorism Law and Policy* (Cambridge University Press, Cambridge, 2005) p 136; Drumbi, MA, 'The expressive value of prosecuting and punishing terrorists' (2007) 75 George Washington Law Review 1165.

[370] See Starmer, K, 'Setting the record straight: human rights in an era of international terrorism' [2007] *European Human Rights Law Review* 123 at 131. Compare *MK v Home Secretary* (SIAC Appeal No SC/29/2004, 5 September 2006, para 6.

6

COURT PROCESSES, PUNISHMENT, AND TERRORISM

A. Introduction

The obligation to bring terrorists to justice is specified by Article 2(e) of the UNSCR 1373.[1] **6.01** In pursuance of this objective, criminal justice processes have been remoulded, though not as far as the criminal offences outlined in Chapter 5, except for the special scheme in Northern Ireland (in Chapter 11). The adjustments reflect the shifting of the high bar set by the criminal burden and standard of proof, as well as loosening of normal jurisdictional limitations. They also reflect the enhanced security interests and keen public interest in the management and outcome of state trials.

Alongside criminal justice adaptations, a distinctive penology of terrorists has emerged, **6.02** comprising adjustments to punishments and penal regimes. This issue forms the second part of this chapter.

---

[1] See Betti, S, 'The duty to bring terrorists to justice and discretionary prosecution' (2006) 4 *Journal of International Criminal Justice* 1104.

B. Court Processes

Preliminary issues

Introduction and background

6.03 The primacy of criminal justice prosecution has been endorsed as an ideal since the *Diplock Report* in 1972 sought to deliver a path out of internment without trial.[2] The replacement package in Northern Ireland, which included juryless 'Diplock courts' and an associated package of pre-trial, trial, and post-trial special measures[3] was not a clarion call for a return to mainstream criminal justice, but it did assure the gist of a fair trial within Article 6 of the European Convention on Human Rights. It took until the end of 1975 for internment to be phased out and for 'police primacy' to commence.[4] But, from then on, in the government's words, 'prosecution is—first, second and third–the government's preferred approach when dealing with suspected terrorists'.[5]

6.04 While criminal prosecution has pride of place, there have always been fallbacks, as indicated by Lord Rooker in 2001:[6] 'Our aim throughout has been that our first priority would be to prosecute alleged terrorists; secondly, if we cannot prosecute them, to remove them; and thirdly, failing the opportunity, wherewithal and appropriate circumstances to remove such people, to detain them.' In the aftermath of the 11 September 2001 attacks, there was a partial swing away from prosecution in the forms of detention without trial under the ATCSA 2001 and then control orders under the PTA 2005. In reaction to the London bombings of 7 July 2005, hostility to the traditions of criminal justice were voiced by Prime Minister, Tony Blair, who warned: 'Let no one be in any doubt, the rules of the game are changing.'[7] His message attained traction in respect of foreign terror suspects, whereby the Immigration, Asylum and Nationality Act 2006 and the Criminal Justice and Immigration Act 2008 increased the executive powers in those fields. However, the trend on the domestic front, reflecting the emergence of 'neighbour terrorists'[8] who are British citizens, has been a reinvigoration of criminal prosecution.

6.05 This domestic trend may be evidenced by two indicators. One is the emphasis in recent anti-terrorism legislation—the TA 2006 and the CTA 2008—upon criminal justice, sentencing, and post-conviction management, and away from executive measures. As a result, the Joint Committee on Human Rights felt able to 'welcome the renewed emphasis on prevention in counter-terrorism policy' which it saw as emerging in the context of 'possible adaptations of the criminal justice system which are capable of facilitating the effective criminal prosecution of terrorist suspects in ways compatible with the UK's human rights obligations'.[9]

---

[2] See further Jackson, JR and Doran, S, *Judge without Jury* (Clarendon Press, Oxford, 1995); Donohue, LK, *Counter-Terrorism Law* (Irish Academic Press, Dublin, 2001) p 123.

[3] See Hogan, G and Walker, C, *Political Violence and the Law in Ireland* (Manchester University Press, Manchester, 1989) ch 4.

[4] See Walker, C, 'The role and powers of the Army in Northern Ireland' in Hadfield, B (ed), *Northern Ireland Politics and the Constitution* (Open University Press, Buckingham, 1992) pp 112, 114–15.

[5] Hansard HC vol 472 col 561 (21 February 2008), Tony McNulty.

[6] HL Debs vol 629 col 459 (29 November 2001), Lord Rooker.

[7] <http://webarchive.nationalarchives.gov.uk/+/http://www.number10.gov.uk/Page8041>.

[8] See Walker, C, '"Know thine enemy as thyself": Discerning friend from foe under anti-terrorism laws' (2008) 32 *Melbourne Law Review* 275.

[9] Joint Committee on Human Rights, *Counter-Terrorism Policy and Human Rights: Prosecution and Pre-Charge Detention* (2005–06 HL 240/HC 1576) paras 4, 7.

The second indicator is the divergent application of prosecution compared to executive **6.06** measures. On the one hand, there is a statistical gathering of pace for criminal prosecution, especially in 2005–06, though not markedly so and not with manifest success (as shown in Chapter 5). On the other hand, a paltry number of control orders has been issued (considered further in Chapter 7). This rate is not for a want of customers but because these executive measures are neither as effective nor as legally certain compared to criminal prosecution.

Jurisdiction

Under common law, a substantial part of the activities constituting a criminal offence must **6.07** take place within the jurisdiction in which the court trying the offence is located. Following the Glasgow Airport bombing in 2007, committed by a group which also planted two car bombs in London the previous day, the prospect arose that the attacks could not be tried conveniently together in either Scotland or England.[10]

Therefore, the CTA 2008, s 28, states that for specified terrorism offences committed in the **6.08** United Kingdom, proceedings may be undertaken at 'any place'. The list of terrorism legislation offences includes even relatively low-level offences[11] and may be amended by affirmative statutory order. This power is applied only to offences committed on or after the coming into force of s 28.[12]

For Scotland, pursuant to a Parliamentary promise,[13] there is the Joint Statement by Her **6.09** Majesty's Attorney General and the Lord Advocate, *Handling of Terrorist Cases where Jurisdiction is shared by Prosecuting Authorities with the UK*, 2009. The statement pinpoints the relevant factors in choice of jurisdiction: capacity, resources, and expertise. However, the possibility of multiple proceedings is not entirely discounted. Where there are multiple investigations, then a coordinated case handling structure is recommended, though the (police) Senior National Coordinator (Counter Terrorism) does not cover Scotland. Scotland's stricter pre-trial custody limit[14] and absence of inferences from silence at trial will probably result in transfers south rather than north.

As for Northern Ireland, the fear was that ceding an English or Scottish case to Northern **6.10** Ireland would trigger non-jury trials under the JSA 2007. Section 28(6) therefore specifies that the Director of Public Prosecutions for Northern Ireland may not issue a certificate in respect of transferred proceedings on the basis that the offence was committed in circumstances of religious or political hostility. Thus, non-jury trials are reserved for offences which are connected to a terrorist organization proscribed in connection with the affairs of Northern Ireland where there is a risk that the administration of justice might be impaired by jury trial.

Consent to prosecution and charging

The Crown Prosecution Service has sought to improve its handling of terrorism cases by setting **6.11** up in 2005 a Counter Terrorism Division (CSD). Severe strains can arise from handling

---

[10] Lord Carlile, *Report on Proposed Measures for Inclusion in a Counter-Terrorism Bill* (Cm 7262, London, 2007) para 9.
[11] Hansard HC Public Bill Committee on the Counter Terrorism Bill col 361 (8 May 2008), Tony McNulty.
[12] Hansard HC vol 477 cols 226–7 (10 June 2008), Tony McNulty.
[13] Hansard HL vol 704 col 776 (15 October 2008), Lord West.
[14] Criminal Procedure (Amendment) (Scotland) Act 2004, s 6. See Hansard HC Public Bill Committee on the Counter-Terrorism Bill cols 89–90 (22 April 2008), Elish Angiolini.

multi-defendant, highly complex prosecutions. For example, the trial of Khyam and nine others was said to be the most expensive trial ever at £50m.[15] A report in 2009 by HM Crown Prosecution Service Inspectorate[16] praised the CSD for case preparation and decision-making as well as communications with victims and witnesses. However, the report does not cover in detail the proportionality of terrorism charges,[17] the pathology of cases where there have been repeated failures to convict, nor non-prosecution of control order subjects.[18]

6.12 The Crown Prosecution Service's *Code for Crown Prosecutors* allows for charges on the basis of the 'Threshold Test',[19] which tessellates with the notion of anticipatory police action. The Test applies where: the Full Code Test standard that there is sufficient evidence to provide a realistic prospect of conviction is not met, but there are reasonable grounds to believe, beyond mere speculation, that such an accumulation of evidence will become available within a reasonable time; the seriousness of the circumstances of the case justify immediate charge (so as to avoid release from custody); and there are substantial grounds to object to bail. The evidential standard to be met is a reasonable suspicion, based (unlike police arrests) on admissible evidence, that the person has committed the offence. The decision to charge must be kept under review, and the Full Code Test must be met by the end of the custody time limit.

6.13 Given the sensitivity and potential oppression arising from special offences in the anti-terrorism legislation, the consent of the relevant Director of Public Prosecutions is required in England and Wales or Northern Ireland by s 117 of the TA 2000 for the prosecution of any offence under the Act (save for specified less serious offences under ss 36 and 51 and some of the schedules). The previous PT(TP)A 1989, s 19, relied upon the Attorney General, but there remains an intention that the Director of Public Prosecutions will consult the Attorney General.[20] Under the Prosecution of Offences Act 1985, s 1(7), consent (in writing) may derive from the Director, the Law Officers of the Crown, or from Crown Prosecutors.

6.14 By amendments in s 37 of the TA 2006 and s 29 of the CTA 2008,[21] the Attorney General (or Advocate General for Northern Ireland) must act where it appears to the Director of Public Prosecutions that relevant prosecutions relate to offences committed either outside the United Kingdom or for a purpose connected with the affairs of a foreign country. Proceedings for extra-territorial offences specifically fall under this rule by s 63E. To obtain consent, a detailed pre-charge submission should be made to the Legal Secretariat to the Law Officers. This gateway was applied in *R v Goldan Lambert*,[22] where the defendant was charged under s 12 of the 2000 Act with membership of the Liberation Tigers of Tamil Eelam. Since the consent of the Attorney General was given after the plea before venue hearing, the defendant argued that prior proceedings were therefore a nullity. This plea was sustained,

---

[15] *The Times* 1 May 2007, p 10.

[16] HM Crown Prosecution Inspectorate, *Report of the Inspection of the Counter Terrorism Division of CPS Headquarters* (London, 2009).

[17] The Report says the correct charges were made: para 3.14. See further CPS, *Prosecuting Strategy concerning violent extremism and related criminal offences* (London, 2007).

[18] See further Dandurand, Y, 'Strategies and practical measures to strengthen the capacity of prosecution services in dealing with transnational organised crime, terrorism and corruption' (2007) 47 *Crime, Law & Social Change* 225.

[19] (London, 2010) para 5.

[20] Hansard HC Standing Committee D, col 295 (3 February 2000), Charles Clarke.

[21] See Lord Carlile, *The Definition of Terrorism* (Cm 7052, London, 2007) para 81.

[22] [2009] EWCA Crim 700.

but the Court of Appeal immediately remedied the defect by holding a new plea before venue hearing.

These two levels of filter are next applied by the TA 2006, s 19,[23] to the offences in Pt 1 of the 2006 Act. **6.15**

In Scotland, the Lord Advocate will always prosecute, so filters are unnecessary.[24] **6.16**

The involvement of law officers is a 'safety valve'[25] and some antidote to the trend, evident in *R v F*, that the government might elevate diplomacy above the political freedoms of refugees. The breadth of terrorism offences will certainly entail assessments of all manner of delicate disputes, such as the decision not to prosecute Boris Beresovsky for inciting revolution in Russia.[26] As discussed in Chapter 5, the problem arises because the extra-jurisdictional impact of special terrorism offences goes beyond comity with Council of Europe and related states, already achieved by the Suppression of Terrorism Act 1978, s 4, and beyond international convention offences.[27] Outside those bases, the imposition of British domestic values may blunder into overseas situations where justification for opposional crimes may be strong.[28] **6.17**

Defence resources

There are pressures on the equality of arms through a comparative lack of defence resources.[29] In addition, the high security detention arrangements[30] surrounding the defendants, associated with constant searching, may also affect their ability to give effective instructions.[31] There may also be instances of hostility between assigned lawyers and clients.[32] No special rules affect these problems. **6.18**

Pre-trial processes

Introduction and background

This part will cover pre-trial adaptations to the exigencies of terrorism trials, leaving aside the case of Northern Ireland for Chapter 11. **6.19**

Provisions

One of the few special procedures is s 16 of the TA 2006 which makes mandatory preparatory hearings under s 29 of the Criminal Procedure and Investigations Act 1996.[33] The objective **6.20**

---

[23] As amended by the CTA 2008, s 29.

[24] Hansard HL vol 676 col 736 (7 December 2005), Baroness Scotland.

[25] Lord Carlile, *Proposals by Her Majesty's Government for Changes to the Laws against Terrorism* (Home Office, London, 2005) para 49.

[26] <http://www.cps.gov.uk/news/press_releases/138_07/index.html>.

[27] Compare Lord Carlile, *Proposals by Her Majesty's Government for Changes to the Laws against Terrorism* (Home Office, 2005) para 46.

[28] Hansard HC vol 438 col 1045 (3 November 2005), Dominic Grieve.

[29] See Bajwa, AN, 'Learn by trial and terror' (2007) 151 *Solicitors' Journal* 7; *Report of the Special Rapporteur on the promotion and protection of human rights and fundamental freedoms while countering terrorism* (A/63/223, 2008) paras 17, 30, 35.

[30] See HM Prison Service, *Revised Arrangements for Defendants in Custody Awaiting Trial in Terrorism Cases at the High Security Unit at Belmarsh Prison* and *Access to Justice for Prisoners charged with Terrorisr Related Offences* (London, 2006). Compare the Secure Administrative Measures (28 CFR ss 501.3, 540, 2005); *US v Sattar* (2005) 395 F Supp 2d 79; Dratel, JL, 'Ethical issues in defending a terrorism case' (2005) 30 *Canada-United States Law Journal* 81.

[31] For an extreme example, see *R v Benbrika* [2008] VSC 80.

[32] Cooke, MG et al, 'Trying cases related to allegations of terrorism' (2008) 77 *Fordham Law Review* 1 at 13.

[33] See s 16(3) for the variant impact on serious fraud cases under Criminal Justice Act 1987.

is to ensure that there is enhanced judicial management of terrorism indictments. The rule applies not only where at least one person in the case is charged with a terrorism offence (as defined in s 16(5)) but also where at least one person in the case is charged with an offence that carries a penalty of a maximum of at least ten years' imprisonment and it appears to the judge that the offence has a terrorist connection (defined in s 16(8)). The enhanced judicial management so applied is meant to improve process by identifying issues, by resolving representation, disclosure, severance, and joinder issues, and by expediting the timetable.

6.21 Section 16 has been applied through the Protocol on the Management of Terrorism Cases issued by the President of the Queen's Bench Division.[34] Every indictable only 'terrorism case' will be managed by senior, experienced judges via the 'terrorism cases list', involving the Presiding Judges of the South Eastern Circuit and other nominated judges of the High Court, and will be tried by the same nominated judge.[35] The defendant must be brought before Westminster Magistrates' Court as soon as is practicable and in any event not later than the first sitting after charge.[36] Next, there follows a brisk timetable and close management. The court should normally order a preliminary hearing about fourteen days after charge, three days prior to which the prosecution must serve a preliminary summary of the case and other information, including possible disclosure issues, while the defence should indicate plea and the general nature of the defence at least one day in advance.[37] In view of the concerns expressed in Chapter 4 about ill-treatment, it is disappointing that 'Unless a judge otherwise directs, all Crown court hearings prior to the trial will be conducted by video link for all defendants in custody.'[38]

Implementation

6.22 In practice, around 50 per cent of trials are placed before High Court judges while remaining cases are 'de-listed'. In *R v Khyam*,[39] it was questioned whether a judge who was required to make inquiries about a postponement of a trial date at the behest of the Lord Chancellor should have recused himself. However, the Court of Appeal felt that the scrutiny was in the interests of the parties and the public. More generally, it commended the operation of the Protocol for tackling 'a culture of adjournment' and concluded that 'None of these measures interfere with the due administration of justice, rather they enhance it.'[40]

Foreign comparisons

6.23 One might compare these relatively light-touch administrative prosecution and judicial arrangements with the channelling in the USA of terrorism prosecutions by US Attorney Offices through the Department of Justice Counterterrorism Section in the National Security Division.[41]

6.24 Greater concentration of terrorism cases is achieved in France by Law no 86-1020 of 9 September 1986, which sets up a *Cour d'Assises* of seven judges without a jury within the Paris Regional Court under the Code on Criminal Procedure, art 706-25. Prosecutions are

---

[34] (2nd edn, Courts Service, London, 2007).
[35] Ibid paras 1–3. See further *R v I(C)* [2009] EWCA Crim 1793.
[36] Ibid para 6.
[37] Ibid paras 9, 11.
[38] Ibid para 17.
[39] [2008] EWCA Crim 1612.
[40] Ibid paras 24, 152.
[41] *United States Attorneys' Manual* (Department of Justice, Washington DC, 1997) para 9-2.136.

assigned to the Central Counterterrorism Department of the Prosecution Service in the 14th Division of Paris under art 706-17. The result is said to be 'dangerously intimate and privileged relations between this small group of Magistrates, their colleagues in the Court and the special (6th) division of the *police judiciaire*, with whom they clearly work hand-in-glove'.[42]

Centralization in Spanish terrorism procedures is imposed by Organic Laws 11/1980 and **6.25** 4/1988, which grant exclusive competence to the Central Investigations Chamber (*Juzgado Central de Instrucción*) with investigation by the Central Examining Magistrate and thence to the *Audiencia Nacional de España*. It tries cases by a panel of three professional judges. The system has been criticized for its absence of local links and hostility to habeas corpus applications.[43]

Other changes abroad include restrictions on the grant of bail.[44]   **6.26**

Assessment and conclusions

The imposition of centralized and senior judicial management is generally to be welcomed[45] **6.27** and should help to avert more risky reforms such as the appointment of investigative magistrates.[46] Its potential detriment to trial by peers is diminishing as more provincial trial venues are chosen. However, strenuous efforts must be made to maintain the appearance of impartiality in the face of judicial activism.

Evidentiary rules

Introduction and background

The rules of evidence have not been altered substantially in the terrorism codes, aside from **6.28** in Northern Ireland, though account must be taken of the burden of proof provisions in the special offences and also that terrorism pressures have in part motivated changes to the privilege against self-incrimination.[47] Litigation suggests that the conviction should not rest on silence alone, that effective legal advice should be available,[48] and that compulsion through criminal sanctions for silence not be allowed.[49] Likewise, the use of informant evidence is important, but, unlike during the period from 1981 to 1985 when the testimony of 'supergrasses' dominated the Northern Ireland criminal justice scene, its forensic prominence has receded.[50]

---

[42] McColgan, M and Attanasio, A, *France: Paving the Way for Arbitrary Justice* (FIDH, Paris, 1999) p 35. See also Human Rights Watch, *Preempting Justice: Counter-Terrorism Laws and Procedure in France* (New York, 2008) Part III; Cahn, O, 'The fight against terrorism and human rights' in Wade, M and Maljevic, A, *A War on Terror?* (Springer, New York, 2010).

[43] See Vercher, A, *Terrorism in Europe* (Clarendon Press, Oxford, 1992) ch 10.

[44] (Australia) Anti-Terrorism Act 2004 (Crimes Act 1914, s 15AA).

[45] See Lord Carlile, *Report on the Operation in 2007 of the Terrorism Act 2000* (Home Office, London, 2008) para 309.

[46] See Joint Committee on Human Rights, *Counter-Terrorism Policy and Human Rights: Prosecution and Pre-Charge Detention* (2005–06 HL 240/HC 1576) paras 76, 109, 138.

[47] See JUSTICE, *The Right of Silence Debate: The Northern Ireland Experience* (London, 1994); Jackson, JD, 'Interpreting the silence provisions' [1995] *Criminal Law Review* 587; Jackson, J, Wolfe, M, and Quinn, K, *Legislating Against Silence* (NIO Research and Statistical Series Report No 1, Belfast, 2000).

[48] *(John) Murray v United Kingdom*, App no 18731/91, Reports 1996-I; *Averill v United Kingdom*, App no 36408/97, 2000-VI; *Magee v United Kingdom*, App no 28135/95, 2000-VI.

[49] *Heaney and McGuinness v Ireland*, App no 34720/97, 2000-XII; *Quinn v Ireland*, App no 36887/97, 21 December 2000.

[50] See Greer, SC, *Supergrasses* (Clarendon Press, Oxford, 1995); *McKevitt v DPP* [2003] IESC9/03 and *Breslin v McKenna* [2005] NIQB 18 (involving FBI agent, David Rupert); *R v Stewart and Stewart* [2010] NICC 8.

6.29 Other special departures from evidential norms in the Criminal Justice (Terrorism and Conspiracy) Act 1998, ss 1 and 2, proved to be unworkable and have been dropped.

Provisions

6.30 One source of evidence which haunts terrorism cases concerns the admissibility of evidence derived from torture. Within the context of a Special Immigration Appeals Commission (SIAC) hearing, it was concluded in *A v Secretary of State for the Home Department (No 2)*[51] that while a conventional approach to the burden of proof was inappropriate in proceedings where the appellant might not know the full details of adverse evidence, there was a burden on the appellant to go beyond a generalized and unsubstantiated allegation of torture and to advance some plausible reason why evidence might have been procured by torture. At that point, SIAC must then initiate an inquiry and decide whether, on the balance of probabilities, the information against the appellant was obtained under torture. But the state authority was not required to prove ultimately that there was no real risk that it was obtained by torture. There are three main criticisms of this judgment. The first is that the standard of proof is insufficiently demanding of state authorities[52] and too demanding of the appellant. The second is that no equivalent ruling is made against inhuman and degrading treatment. The third is that the evidence is banned from forensic use but can still impel executive action.

6.31 Torture has been encountered in two recent terrorist criminal trials. In the conspiracy headed by Omar Khyam,[53] Salahuddin Amin alleged that he was questioned repeatedly by two British security officers, while being tortured in custody by the Inter-Services Intelligence agency (ISI) in Pakistan. However, the Court of Appeal concluded that the Crown had not relied on admissions made in Pakistan,[54] and it also rejected any abuse of process which might arise from a joint security agency operation. In *R v Rangzieb Ahmed and Ahmed*,[55] the defendant, who was found guilty of directing terrorism, claimed mistreatment (including the removal of fingernails) by the ISI shortly before being questioned by two United Kingdom Security Service officers and that the British authorities had passed questions to the ISI. This information was withheld from the jury at Manchester Crown Court following a closed hearing which presumably rejected claims of collusion or that the treatment in Pakistan affected the evidence presented to the Court.

6.32 A second recurrent evidential issue is disclosure. The first problem is that the Criminal Procedure and Investigations Act 1996 does not require the disclosure of material held by private or public collaborating entities overseas, though the Attorney General's Guidelines on Disclosure of 2005[56] assume an obligation on the Crown to obtain material that may be held by third parties. Such efforts may be made either informally (agency to agency) or through the Crime (International Co-operation) Act 2003, s 7. British prosecutors' requests

---

⁵¹ [2005] UKHL 71. See Joint Committee on Human Rights, *Counter-Terrorism Policy and Human Rights: Terrorism Bill and Related Matters* (2005–06 HL 75/HC 561, at para 48); Grief, N, 'The exclusion of foreign torture evidence' [2006] *European Human Rights Law Review* 200; Rassiah, N, '*A v Secretary of State for the Home Department (no. 2)*' (2006) 69 *Modern Law Review* 995. For the American position, see the Detainee Treatment Act of 2005, PL 109-148, ss 1001–1006; US Presidential Executive Order 13491: *Ensuring Lawful Interrogations*, 22 January 2009.

⁵² Compare *Selmouni v France*, App no 25803/94, 1999-V (1999) para 101.

⁵³ *R v Khyam* [2008] EWCA Crim 1612 at paras 43, 74.

⁵⁴ Ibid para 68.

⁵⁵ *The Times* 19 December 2008, p 8.

⁵⁶ <http://www.attorneygeneral.gov.uk/Publications/Documents/disclosure.doc.pdf>, para 51.

may not always prevail against foreign security interests,[57] but assistance may be sought from Eurojust (described later) in a European context.

The second disclosure problem is the suppression of evidence through public interest **6.33** immunity (PII).[58] For information held by the security agencies, a ministerial certificate will be issued, which the prosecutor (or counsel for the agencies) will then assert in court. The procedure will be *ex parte*, and even the fact of application may not be revealed to the defence. The normal PII tests ask (i) whether it is really necessary in the interests of justice for documents to be disclosed, (ii) whether there would be 'substantial harm' to the public interest if the documents were disclosed, (iii) if so, whether the interests in the administration of justice outweigh the harm to the public interest, and (iv) where the interests of justice favour non-disclosure, whether the materials can be furnished in less damaging (redacted) format.[59] These tests are altered for procedures in the SIAC Rules and in the High Court in relation to control orders, as will be described in Chapter 7. However, developments have also occurred in criminal and civil proceedings.

As for criminal proceedings, evolution has been modest and the basic rule remains that if a **6.34** prosecution PII claim succeeds in relation to material evidence, then the prosecution may have to terminate. There has been no attempt to allow the evidence into closed proceedings. A more minor point arose in *R v Botmeh and Alami*[60]—whether the Court of Appeal could consider a PII application by the Crown even though the same evidence was not subject to PII in the original trial. It did so, and in the view of the European Court of Human Rights, the intervention of the Court of Appeal was actually helpful.[61] PII also arose in Scottish proceedings for the first time in connection with the appeal against conviction for the Lockerbie bombing.[62]

PII claims in civil cases have been asserted in the context of a malicious prosecution suit for **6.35** the Stalker/Sampson reports into police collusion with paramilitaries in Northern Ireland,[63] for intelligence information about stop and search operations being sought in applications for judicial review,[64] for materials about the withdrawal of security vetting in employment proceedings,[65] and for national security information in applications for judicial review of refusals of applications for British nationality.[66] In all but the first case, special advocate procedures have been offered, a facility which may shift the balance in favour of non-disclosure. The appearance of special advocates and closed hearings in civil process is disturbing. Whilst a statutory inquisitorial process such as SIAC or control order reviews can cope, the executive should not otherwise be allowed to reformulate basic standards of justice.

The issues in a civil context were most fully rehearsed in the claim of Binyam Mohammed in **6.36** which he sought discovery of documents relating to his treatment by British and US agents

---

[57] See *R v Alibhai* [2004] EWCA Crim 681; *R v Flook* [2009] EWCA Crim 682.

[58] See Joint Committee on Human Rights, *Counter-Terrorism Policy and Human Rights: Prosecution and Pre-Charge Detention* (2005–06 HL 240/HC 1576) paras 72, 106. Prosecutors seek to minimize problems by reliance upon academic experts for background information based on open sources: United Nations Office on Drugs and Crime, *Digest of Terrorist Cases* (New York, 2010) para 194.

[59] See *R v Chief Constable of West Midlands Police, ex parte Wiley* [1995] 1 AC 274.

[60] [2001] EWCA Crim 2226.

[61] *Botmeh and Alamhi v United Kingdom*, App No 15187/03, 7 June 2007.

[62] *Al-Megrahi v HM Advocate* [2008] HCJAC 15.

[63] *Taylor v Anderton* [1995] 2 All ER 420.

[64] *Gillan v Commissioner of the Metropolitan Police* [2006] UKHL 12 at para 64.

[65] *Home Office v Tariq* [2010] EWCA Civ 462.

[66] *Secretary of State for the Home Department v AHK* [2009] EWCA Civ 287.

in Guantánamo and Morocco, pursuant to potential proceedings before a military commission (later vacated) and also for tortious damages.[67] Some of the documentation in the hands of the British government originated from US agencies who had transmitted on a strict policy of no further disclosure—the 'control principle'. The High Court adopted a balancing exercise between the public interests in disclosure versus national security and healthy international relations, as well as alternatives means to disclosure (such as an inquiry by the Intelligence and Security Committee[68]). The High Court ordered disclosure, judging that the US threats to withhold security cooperation were empty. The Court of Appeal endorsed this assessment, relying on the further factor that a US Federal Court had already granted disclosure to the claimant, and it also rejected that the 'control principle' was an immutable legal requirement.[69] The judgment was also notable for the comment by Lord Neuberger that 'some SyS officials appear to have a dubious record when it comes to human rights and coercive techniques, and indeed when it comes to frankness about the UK's involvement with the mistreatment of Mr Mohammed by US officials'.[70] Police and judicial inquiries have flowed from this litigation, as well as a promised Green Paper,[71] and potential governmental demands for special rules to nullify any 'quixotic' judge who creates a 'material risk' to security.[72]

6.37   A further systemic factor potentially affecting the legal system is the primacy of the Security Service over the police in terrorism investigation, as signalled by the Home Secretary in 1992, by the Security Service Act 1996, and by executive order in 2007 in respect of Northern Ireland.[73] This primacy may reduce the availability of formal court processes against individuals for the sake of enhanced collective security. As Mr Justice Newman has observed: 'The Security Service material . . . is not recorded and prepared for the purposes of being presented and used as evidence in an adversarial hearing.'[74]

Implementation

6.38   Disclosure can be a major undertaking in terrorism cases, not only because of the quantity of evidence but also because of the fact that it is held across different agencies. On the latter point, there may be a Disclosure Agreement Document to set out the responsibilities of the agencies involved or it may form part of a wider Operational Memorandum of Understanding. Contact by investigators or prosecutors with government departments, including the Treasury Solicitor, is via 'Inquiry Points'. These arrangements do not include the security agencies who are not 'investigators' within the Criminal Procedure and Investigations Act 1996. When materials are sought from them, investigators and prosecutors will specify on-site inspection, which will necessitate security clearance and arrangements for the storage of notes and advice.

---

[67]   *R (Binyam Mohammed) v Secretary of State for the Foreign & Commonwealth Office* [2008] EWHC 2048, 2100, 2519, 2549, 2973 (Admin), [2009] EWHC 152 (Admin). See Joint Committee on Human Rights, *Allegations of UK complicity in torture* (2008–09 HL 152/HC 230) and *Government Reply* (Cm 7714, London, 2009).

[68]   See *The handling of detainees by UK intelligence personnel in Afghanistan, Guantánamo Bay and Iraq* (Cm 6469, London, 2005).

[69]   [2010] EWCA Civ 65.

[70]   [2010] EWCA Civ 158 at para 17.

[71]   See *The Times* 27 March 2009 p 8; Hansard HC vol 513 col 175 (6 July 2010).

[72]   Privy Council Review of intercept as evidence, *Report to the Prime Minister and the Home Secretary* (Cm 7324, London, 2008) paras 63, 90.

[73]   See Lord Carlile, *First Annual Review of Arrangements for National Security in Northern Ireland* (Northern Ireland Office, Belfast, 2008).

[74]   *MK v Home Secretary* (SIAC Appeal No SC/29/2004, 5 September 2006) para 6.

Foreign comparisons

The handling of sensitive evidence has troubled several jurisdictions. A relatively extreme **6.39**
response is the (Australian) National Security Information (Criminal and Civil Proceedings)
Act 2004 (as amended). By s 26 and s 38F (for criminal and civil proceedings), the Attorney
General can issue a non-disclosure certificate because the disclosure of information will be
prejudicial to national security; the prosecution or defence must themselves alert the Attorney
General under s 24, if they are aware of that potential. Defence lawyers can apply for security
clearance under s 39, in the absence of which they will not be allowed to view all the evidence; they generally refuse to comply and thereby cannot operate under the legal aid system.
In response to the certificate of non-disclosure, the court must hold a closed hearing to determine
whether to uphold the ban. The defendant and the defendant's legal representatives can be
excluded from this hearing. The court must consider the certificate of non-disclosure as
carrying the 'greatest weight' under ss 31(8) and 38L(8) but will also take into account
whether an order would have a substantial adverse effect on the defendant's right to a fair
hearing. These mechanisms tilt the balance too far in favour of secrecy.[75] As a result, the Law
Council recommends repeal,[76] but the Attorney General concedes only clarification.[77]

Australia has also faced an equivalent to Binyam Mohamed in Mamdouh Habib, who was **6.40**
detained in Pakistan in October 2001 and then in Egypt, Afghanistan, and Guantánamo.
After release in 2005, he sought damages against the Commonwealth for the tort of misfeasance
in public office and the intentional infliction of harm because of alleged Australian agency
collusion. It was held in *Habib v Commonwealth of Australia*[78] that common law act of state
doctrine cannot exclude the exercise of jurisdiction because of the need to determine the
unlawfulness of acts of agents of foreign states within their own territory. There was still a
need to review whether Australian officials had acted beyond their authority under
Commonwealth law, though subject to limited discovery of documentation which might
affect national security and international relations.[79]

A similar system to the 2004 Act operates in Canada under the Anti-terrorism Act 2001, **6.41**
s 43, which amends ss 37 and 38 of the Canada Evidence Act.[80] Under s 37, a ministerial
certificate can be issued (usually after an alert by a litigant) in respect of 'potentially injurious
information' under s 38.

In the US, the Classified Information Procedures Act[81] specifies procedures and safeguards **6.42**
which involve the presiding judge more closely in the oversight of disclosure through *in
camera* review but do not alter the basic rules of disclosure of relevant material evidence. If
the prosecutor objects to the disclosure, then the court enters a non-disclosure order and
must consider a sanction for the government's failure to disclose (such as the dropping of
some charges or allegations). Otherwise, the judge will give further directions in private for
how the classified evidence can be used in court subject to substitutions—pseudonyms and

---

[75] A challenge on grounds of constitutionality was rejected in *Lodhi v R* [2007] NSWCCA 360. See
Lynch, A, et al, *Law and Liberty in the War on Terror* (Federation Press, Sydney, 2007) chs 8, 9.
[76] See Law Council of Australia, *Anti-Terrorism Reform Project* (Canberra, 2009) para 6.2.3.
[77] *Security Legislation Discussion Paper* (Canberra, 2009) ch 4.
[78] [2010] FCAFC 12. See also [2009] FCA 228; *Habib v Nationwide News* [2010] NSWCA 34.
[79] See *Secretary, Department of Prime Minister v Haneef* [2010] FCA 928.
[80] See Commission of Inquiry into the Investigation of the Bombing of Air India Flight 182, *Air India Flight
182* (Ottawa, 2010).
[81] PL 96-456 of 1980, 18 USC App III. ss 1–16.

paraphrasing—which must not reduce the ability of the defendant to contest the evidence. Assessments suggest that the Act has offered a suitable reaction to the interests of security,[82] though some breaches of due process have occurred.[83]

6.43 The US faces more problems than most jurisdictions over disclosure because of the international spread of its intelligence and military agencies, but the potential obstacles have not been insuperable.[84] A key test case was *US v Moussaoui*[85] when defence access was sought to the testimony of 'high value' prisoners such as Khalid Sheikh Mohammed. The Court of Appeals robustly declared: 'The need to develop all relevant facts in the adversary system is both fundamental and comprehensive.'[86] But access was by adequate substitutions—Moussaoui's counsel could be provided with summaries from intelligence reports that would be read to the jury, so as to convey the essence of any exculpatory information. There could also remain difficulties where a defendant (such as Moussaoui) seeks to represent himself and so circumvents the temperance of a security cleared lawyer.[87] Other problems arise where the court demands that a foreign agent is produced, or where the evidence links to conspirators yet to be charged.[88]

6.44 A less wholesome picture emerges in US civil process. State secrets privilege[89] has been increasingly invoked to exclude evidence based on an affidavit by the government and without any closed hearing or examination by the court. It arose to prevent the civil action of Khalid el-Masri, a German citizen who was allegedly rendered from Macedonia to Afghanistan in 2003.[90] Likewise, the civil claims of Maher Arar, a Canadian citizen who was detained in New York and sent to Syria whilst en route to Canada,[91] were rejected in *Arar v Ashcroft*, though on other grounds.[92] Finally, the claims of Binyam Mohammed and others against Jeppesen Dataplan, an air carrier acting on behalf of the CIA, were halted because of state secrets privilege.[93]

Assessment and conclusions

6.45 As was established in the *Diplock Report* and as will be shown in Chapter 7 in relation to executive processes, the European Convention, Article 6, demands a minimum level of due

---

82 Chesney, RM, 'State secrets and the limits of national security litigation' (2007) *George Washington Law Review* 1249; Zabel, RB and Benjamin, JJ, *In Pursuit of Justice: Prosecuting Terrorism Cases in the Federal Courts* (Human Rights First, New York, 2008) 9, 77–90; Cooke, MG et al, 'Trying cases related to allegations of terrorism' (2008) 77 *Fordham Law Review* 1; Vladeck, SI, 'The case against national security courts' (2009) 45 *Willamete Law Review* 505.

83 See *US v Koubriti* (2007) 509 F 3d 746.

84 Zabel, RB and Benjamin, JJ, *In Pursuit of Justice* (Human Rights First, New York, 2008) p 10.

85 (2004) 382 F 3d 453 (cert den 161 L Ed 2d 496, 2005).

86 Ibid 47–8 per Wilkins CJ.

87 This problem was resolved by the forced appointment of standby counsel. See Bloom, M, 'I did not come here to defend myself' (2007) 117 *Yale Law Journal* 70.

88 See *US v Rahman* (1999) 189 F 3d 88; McCarthy, AC, 'Terrorism on trial: The trials of al Qaeda' (2004) 37 *Case Western Reserve Journal of International Law* 513 at 520.

89 See *US v Reynolds* (1953) 345 US 1.

90 *El-Masri v Tenet* 437 F Supp 2d 530 (2006), 479 F 3d 296 (2007) (cert den 169 L Ed 2d 258; 2007). See Chesney, RM, 'State secrets and the limits of national security litigation' (2007) 75 *George Washington Law Review* 1249.

91 See Commission of Inquiry into the Actions of Canadian Officials in relation to Maher Arar (Ottawa, 2007).

92 (2008) 532 F 3d 157. See Craddock, E, 'Tortuous consequences and the case of Maher Arar' (2008) 93 *Cornell Law Review* 621.

93 614 F 3d 1070 (2010).

process which must not be sacrificed for the sake of national security. Thus, the inventiveness of the courts with devices such as special advocates should be held in check in formal court process.

Trial processes

Introduction and background

Anti-terrorism laws have been relatively reticent about intrusions into trial processes, **6.46** save for the jurisdiction of Northern Ireland. However, there are signs that this for-bearance is waning not just in terrorism prosecutions but also in the handling of other difficult or dangerous offenders such as serious fraudsters, sex offenders, drug traffickers, and gangsters.[94] In this way, precautionary logic pressures criminal justice to deliver risk-averse results and thereby produces convergence between executive and criminal justice processes.[95]

Provisions—Juries in terrorism trials

The selection of jurors in terrorism cases may involve official checks going beyond criminal **6.47** records either to avert improper use of *in camera* material or where 'political beliefs are so biased as to go beyond those reflecting the broad spectrum of views and interests in the com-munity or reflect the extreme views of an interest or pressure group to a degree which might interfere with his fair assessment of the facts of the case or lead him to exert improper pressure on his fellow jurors'.[96] No further investigation should be undertaken unless a chief officer of police has reason to believe that an authorized check may be desirable and proper, in which case the matter is referred to the DPP who then seeks the authority of the Attorney General. Though judges give some leeway to the defence,[97] general questioning about attitudes is not approved in Scotland,[98] though instances have arisen in England where questions have been allowed about whether members of the panel (or close family) have been personally affected by terrorism or maintain views hostile to Muslims.

As for the reliance upon jurors as deciders of fact, the exceptional non-jury trials in Northern **6.48** Ireland are being eased into oblivion while the special non-jury Scottish trial (in the Netherlands) of those accused of the Lockerbie bombing[99] is not easily replicable nor unproblematic in outcome. Both are described further in Chapter 11. Calls for a new security court[100] have not yet been seriously pursued. Instead, the judges have praised juries[101] and treated jurors and witnesses as resilient against extraneous pressures.[102]

---

[94] See Criminal Justice Act 1987; Youth Justice and Criminal Evidence Act 1999, Pt II; Drug Trafficking Act 1994; Criminal Justice Act 2003, Pt VII; Serious Organised Crime and Police Act 2005.

[95] See Chesney, R and Goldsmith, J, 'Terrorism and the convergence of criminal and military detention models' (2008) 60 *Stanford Law Review* 1079.

[96] *Attorney General's Guidelines, Exercise by the Crown of its Right of Stand-By* [1989] 88 Cr App R 123; Juries (Northern Ireland) Order 1996, art 26C(5).

[97] See *R v Jalil* [2008] EWCA 2910.

[98] *M v HM Advocate* 1974 *Scottish Law Times (Notes)* 25. Compare in the US: Cooke, MG et al, 'Trying cases related to allegations of terrorism' (2008) 77 *Fordham Law Review* 1 at 20.

[99] *HM Advocate v Al-Megrahi* 2002 JC 99, [2008] HCJAC 58. See further Chapter 12.

[100] *The Times* 22 November 2003, p 4, 9 February 2005, p 2, 6 August 2005, p 1. See Weisselberg, CD, 'Terror in the courts' (2008) 50 *Crime, Law & Social Change* 25.

[101] As in the trial of Omar Khyam: *The Times* 1 May 2007, p 10.

[102] See *R v Kinsella (Denis), R v MacFhloinn (Pairic)* [1995] Crim LR 731. In the UVF gun-running trial of Lindsay Robb in 1995, Alexander McKinley was convicted of attempting to intimidate a witness: *The Scotsman* 28 March 1997, p 9.

6.49   However, signs of discontent have emerged. Non-jury terrorist trials were mooted by Home Secretary, David Blunkett, in 2004,[103] but his advocacy was quickly refuted by the Director of Public Prosecutions, Ken Macdonald, who said

> criminal trials must remain routinely open and take place before independent and impartial tribunals. In Britain, people have great affection for trial by jury. There must be disclosure of the state's case and equality of arms, fairness between prosecution and defence. There can be no criminal convictions in the face of reasonable doubt. Public faith in public justice will not survive abandonment of these fundamental principles.[104]

The idea was resurrected after the acquittals on the principal charges in Operation Overt following the first 'Liquid Bomb' trial in September 2008 which represented what the police 'believed to be the strongest terrorism case ever presented to a court',[105] though the Metropolitan Police Deputy Assistant Commissioner, Peter Clarke, did also say there is 'no need for military commissions or the juryless Diplock courts of Northern Ireland'.[106] But the press complained of trial by jury being 'broken'.[107] However, a third trial did result in three convictions for conspiracy to murder.[108]

6.50   Where problems of intimidation loom, the Criminal Justice Act 2003, s 44, allows for a non-jury trial. The Court of Appeal gave a strong signal against ready resort to this mode of trial in *R v Twomey*[109] by requiring the criminal standard of proof that the statutory conditions are fulfilled. Perhaps an adverse economic climate may encourage s 44(5) to come more into play in expensive terrorism cases.

Provisions—secrecy in terrorism trials

6.51   The prioritisation of criminal process incurs the drawback of the public airing of sensitive sources, techniques, and data since precautionary prosecutions involve reliance upon intelligence-gathering rather than overt acts. As argued by the *Shackleton Report* in relation to the executive response of exclusion orders:[110]

> It is intelligence information, whose disclosure may involve unacceptable risks. Information which is specific about a person's participation in an act of terrorism may be known to only two or three people. It could, without difficulty, be traced back to its source if it became known to the subject of the exclusion order or to a wider circle of his associates and friends. From this might follow the death of the informant. The flow of information which can lead, and in many cases has led to convictions in the courts would be endangered.

The inevitable pressure for secrecy emanates in several distinct aspects at trial, adding to the pre-trial problems of PII.

6.52   There is the secrecy of witnesses, such as domestic or foreign secret agents, informants, or apprehensive members of the public.[111] The reaction has typically been decided case-by-case,

---

103   *The Times* 22 November 2004, p 4.
104   *The Sunday Times* 29 November 2004, p 4.
105   *The Times* 9 September 2008, p 1.
106   Ibid, p 7.
107   *The Times* 15 September 2008, p 26.
108   *The Times* 9 July 2010, p 13.
109   [2009] EWCA 1035. See also *R v JSM* [2010] EWCA Crim 1755; *R v KS* [2010] EWCA Crim 1756.
110   *Shackleton Report*, para 52, quoted with approval in *R v Secretary of State for Home Affairs, ex parte Stitt* (1987) *The Times* 3 February (QBD).
111   See van Harten, G, 'Weaknesses of adjudication in the face of secret evidence' (2009) 13 *International Journal of Evidence and Proof* 1.

subject to the demand for open justice under Article 6 of the European Convention. For instance, in *R v Murphy and Maguire*,[112] the appellants were convicted of the murder of two soldiers who had been captured after driving into the cortege of a paramilitary funeral in west Belfast. It was held that the judge had properly permitted media witnesses to give evidence anonymously and from behind screens. Those witnesses feared for their safety but their evidence was formal—confirming the nature of filming which had taken place but not directly implicating the accused. Security agents have also been allowed to be heard behind screens,[113] and anonymity has also arisen in extradition[114] and inquests and inquiries.[115] The *Rowe Report* considered that this piecemeal approach did not offer sufficient protection of witnesses,[116] and codification for criminal trials has eventually been imparted by the Criminal Evidence (Witness Anonymity) Act 2008, as replaced by the Coroners and Justice Act 2009, Pt III. There are plenty of European precedents allowing anonymous witnesses as well as ruling out their testimony if significant but not challengeable.[117] Evidence may even be heard in private under common law and the Official Secrets Act 1920, s 8(4).

The postponement of reports of terrorism trials under the Contempt of Court Act 1981, s 4, has arisen occasionally in the context of large terrorism conspiracies for the sake of the administration of justice in later linked cases.[118] Public access was restricted when allegations were made about Security Service involvement in torture in the trial of Salahuddin Amin.[119] Next, virtually all of the judgment in the acquittal on appeal of Danny Morrison[120] remains suppressed under s 11 of the 1981 Act. Disquiet has conversely been expressed about law reports that reveal bomb-making techniques.[121] **6.53**

The impetus towards secrecy ensures that the device of special advocates is constantly extolled and expanded but does not yet reach criminal trials.[122] Their role is to 'represent the interests' of a relevant party excluded from the proceedings. This role will comprise, first, the normal representation work of an advocate, and, second, the handling of disclosure[123] and the testing of the need for closed sessions and closed evidence. **6.54**

---

[112] [1990] NI 306. See also *AM v United Kingdom*, App no 20657/92, 2 December 1992 (inadmissible).

[113] See JUSTICE, *Secret Evidence* (London, 2009) para 302.

[114] *R (Al-Fawwaz) v Governor of Brixton Prison* [2001] UKHL 69.

[115] See *R (A) v Lord Saville of Newdigate* [2001] EWCA Civ 2048; *Re Donaghy* [2002] NICA 25; *Re Meehan* [2003] NICA 34; *Re Officer L* [2007] UKHL 36.

[116] *Rowe Report*, para 169.

[117] See especially *Al-Khawaja and Tahery v United Kingdom*, App nos 26766/05, 22228/06, 20 January 2009; *AM v UK*, App no 20657/92, 2 December 1992; Ormerod, D et al, 'The "witness anonymity" and "investigation anonymity" provisions' [2010] *Criminal Law Review* 368.

[118] See *R v Meziane* [2004] EWCA Crim 1768; *R v Kazi Nurur Rahman* <http://news.bbc.co.uk/1/hi/uk/6206886.stm>, 2007; *R v Khyam* [2008] EWCA Crim 1612. An application was rejected in *R v Barot* [2006] EWCA Crim 2692. See also *R (Malik) v Central Criminal Court* [2006] EWHC 1539 (Admin) (bail hearing).

[119] See *R v Central Criminal Court, ex parte A* [2006] EWCA Crim 4.

[120] *R v Morrison* [2009] NICA 1.

[121] Todd, C, 'Terrorist trials—"then" and "now" ' (2008) 48 *Medicine, Science and the Law* 188 at 190.

[122] See House of Commons Constitutional Affairs Committee, *The operation of the Special Immigration Appeals Commission (SIAC) and the use of Special Advocates* (2004–05 HC 323-I); Bonner, D, *Executive Measures, Terrorism and National Security* (Ashgate, Aldershot, 2007) ch 8; Ip, J, 'The rise and spread of the special advocate' [2008] *Public Law* 717; JUSTICE, *Secret Evidence* (London, 2009) Pt IV; Chamberlain, M, 'Update on procedural fairness in closed proceedings' (2009) 28 *Civil Justice Quarterly* 448; Tooze, J, 'Deportation with assurances' [2010] *Public Law* 362.

[123] Not all material is automatically disclosed even to the special adviser: ibid, para 61.

6.55 The impact of the fifty or so special advocates, experienced barristers, who are appointed in practice by the Solicitor General,[124] has been the subject of extensive debate. Lord Carlile has expressed approbation.[125] Some judges have also delivered positive verdicts, especially Lord Hoffman.[126] In *A v United Kingdom*, the European Court of Human Rights accepted that the device provides an important safeguard, but special advisers are not a panacea to remedy the loss of process rights.[127] A more critical view, expressed by Lord Steyn, is that 'the special advocate procedure undermines the very essence of elementary justice'.[128]

6.56 Undoubtedly, the special advocate works under extra hindrances compared to normal advocates. First, the special advocate cannot be instructed by, or be legally liable to, the suspect. A code of ethics could be helpful.[129] Second, and the most serious hindrance, is their limited ability to consult with the suspect which is only allowed before they have inspected closed materials, unless authorized on application to the court.[130] Applications are rare since they would reveal confidential tactics to the Home Office. The possibility of an *ex parte* application to the High Court would be helpful.[131] Suspects should also be encouraged to give evidence before the closed sessions to keep open the channels of communication as long as possible.[132] A third disadvantage is lack of support in that special advocates do not have instructing solicitors. To remedy this deficiency, the special advocates are supported by the Special Advocates Support Office within the Treasury Solicitor's Office.[133] Its small band of lawyers plays the role of instructing solicitors, but there is no research cadre as the government felt they would be bureaucratic and expensive.[134] Fourthly, special advocates are limited in their ability to cross-examine[135] or to call expert security witnesses.[136] The government will not permit other serving security agents to offer competing narratives, though it has no objections to independent experts.[137]

6.57 To date the impact of special advocates has been felt most in special tribunals and in civil process. As for civil cases, the Court of Appeal in *al-Rawi v Security Service*[138] distinguished

---

[124] Ibid para 69.

[125] Lord Carlile, *Second Report of the Independent Review Pursuant to Section 14(3) of the Prevention of Terrorism Act 2005* (Home Office, London, 2007) para 49.

[126] *Re MB and AF* [2007] UKHL 46 at paras 51, 54. See also *MT (Algeria) v Secretary of State for the Home Department* [2007] EWCA Civ 808.

[127] App no 3455/05, 19 February 2009, paras 219, 220.

[128] *R v Roberts* [2005] UKHL 45 at para 88 (dissenting).

[129] Boon, A and Nash, S, 'Special advocacy' (2006) 9 *Legal Ethics* 101 at 121.

[130] See Joint Committee on Human Rights, *Counter-Terrorism Policy and Human Rights: 28 days, intercept and post-charge questioning* (2006–07 HL 157/HC 394) para 193.

[131] Joint Committee on Human Rights, *Counter-Terrorism Policy and Human Rights, Counter-Terrorism Bill* (2007–08 HL 108/HC 554) para 104.

[132] *Re Bullivant* [2007] EWHC 2938 (Admin).

[133] Constitutional Affairs Committee, *The Operation of the Special Immigration Appeals Commission (SIAC) and the Use of Special Advocates* (2004–05 HC 323-I) paras 108, 109, 112. See Treasury Solicitor's Department, *A Guide to the Role of Special Advocates and the Special Advocates Support Office* (London, 2006).

[134] *Reply to the Constitutional Affairs Committee* (Cm 6596, London, 2005) para 12.

[135] The government has promised to amend the rules: Joint Committee on Human Rights, *Counter-Terrorism Policy and Human Rights: Annual Renewal of Control Orders Legislation 2009* (2008–09 HL37/HC382) para 23.

[136] Joint Committee on Human Rights, *Counter-Terrorism Policy and Human Rights, Counter-Terrorism Bill* (2007–08 HL 108/HC 554) para 110; *Government Reply* (Cm 7344, London, 2008) p 8.

[137] Constitutional Affairs Committee, *The Operation of the Special Immigration Appeals Commission (SIAC) and the Use of Special Advocates* (2004–05 HC 323-I) paras 29, 77, 93; *Reply to the Constitutional Affairs Committee* (Cm 6596, London, 2005) para 10.

[138] [2010] EWCA Civ 482.

between cases in which a 'triangulation of issues' is involved, meaning issues affecting the two parties plus the public, and cases where only the two parties before the courts have interests.[139] Only in these triangulated cases might it be necessary to imply the power to hold closed sessions, including the use of special advocates. In *Raissi v Metropolitan Police Commissioner*,[140] the claimant, the brother of Lotfi Raissi who had been arrested on suspicion of involvement in the September 11 attacks, successfully claimed damages for wrongful arrest and false imprisonment on the basis of a lack of reasonable grounds for suspicion for arrest (as described in Chapter 4). In an interlocutory judgment, the Commissioner had sought to adduce statements from two police officers whose evidence might, on an agreed hypothesis, have derived from intercept evidence. However, the statements were excluded by the RIPA, s 17, and were anyway unlikely to be relevant.

The *Diplock Report* envisaged the possibility of hearings in camera but argued that 'we our- **6.58** selves could find no practical way of keeping [witnesses'] identity secret if they gave evidence under any procedure which would fulfil the minimum requirements of trial. . .'.[141] The House of Lords has ventured that special advocates would be unobjectionable in principle for criminal proceedings.[142] But the later precedent of *R v Davis*[143] strongly suggests that the courts will prefer a statutory foundation to succumbing to the 'melancholy truth' of function creep.[144]

Provisions—the media and terrorism trials

Police relations with the media have been considered in Chapter 2. As for the media and the **6.59** courts, the intense and often hostile publicity attracted by major terrorism trials can threaten fair process,[145] despite the occasional restrictions on comments about subjudice litigation imposed by the Contempt of Court Act 1981.[146]

This threat can be compounded by governmental Ministers who make prejudicial statements. **6.60** Prime Minister Gordon Brown's comment that Operation Pathway had thwarted 'a very big terrorist plot' was understated by Lord Carlile as 'an unwelcome distraction'.[147] Its consequences might have been much worse if criminal proceedings had been instituted.

In *R v McCann and others*,[148] the defendants were alleged to be IRA members who had been **6.61** found near to the home of Secretary of State for Northern Ireland (Tom King). They were charged with conspiracy to murder but declined to give evidence at trial. After closing submissions, the Home Secretary announced the proposal to permit adverse inferences from silence, which drew comments in favour from the Secretary of State for Northern Ireland

---

[139] Ibid paras 35, 36.

[140] [2007] EWHC 2842 (QB) at para 7. See further [2008] EWCA Civ 1237.

[141] *Diplock Report*, para 20.

[142] *R v H* [2004] UKHL 3 at para 22. But no use has occurred: JUSTICE, *Secret Evidence* (London, 2009) para 315.

[143] [2008] UKHL 36.

[144] *al Rawi v Security Service* [2010] EWCA Civ 482 at para 69.

[145] See Qureshi, T, 'Adverse publicity' (2007) 157 *New Law Journal* 969; Bajwa, AN, 'Learn by trial and terror' (2007) 151 *Solicitors' Journal* 7; Cooke, MG et al, 'Trying cases related to allegations of terrorism' (2008) 77 *Fordham Law Review* 1 at 8–10; Intelligence and Security Committee, *Annual Report 2006–2007* (Cm 7299, London, 2008) para 70.

[146] See *Attorney General v Independent Television News* [1995] 1 Cr App Rep 204; *Attorney General v Associated Newspapers Limited* (LEXIS, 31 October 1997). See also *Attorney General v Random House Group* [2009] EWHC 1727 (QB).

[147] *Operation Pathway* (Home Office, London, 2009) para 40.

[148] [1991] 92 Cr App Rep 239. See also *R v Vermette* (1988) 50 DLR 4th 385 (SCC).

and the former Master of the Rolls (Lord Denning). On appeal, Lord Justice Beldam commented that 'We are left with the definite impression that the impact which the statements in the television interviews may well have had on the fairness of the trial could not be overcome by any direction to the jury, and that the only way in which justice could be done and be obviously seen to be done was by discharging the jury and ordering a retrial.'[149]

6.62 The trial judge will be even more unwise to make extraneous comments. In *R v Batth and Sunder*,[150] charges of homicide arose from faction fighting amongst Sikhs. The trial judge (Sir James Miskin) was reported as referring to 'murderous Sikhs', thereby creating an apprehension of bias.

6.63 Trenchant comment by a lawyer after a terrorist trial was the subject of censure in the case of Aamer Anwar. He declared from the steps of the High Court in Glasgow that:[151]

> This verdict is a tragedy for justice and for freedom of speech and undermines the values that separate us from the terrorist, the very values we should be fighting to protect. This prosecution was driven by the State with no limit to the resources used to secure a conviction and it was carried out in an atmosphere of hostility after the Glasgow Airport attack and ending in the week of 9/11.

The High Court concluded that no contempt had been committed but warned that lawyers must 'display the highest professional standards. In particular, we consider that they have a duty to ensure, first, that their public utterances, whether critical or not, are based upon an accurate appreciation of the facts of those proceedings and, second, that their comments are not misleading.'[152] In the Court's view, while an advocate must be 'discreet, honest and dignified',[153] the applicant was entitled under Article 10 of the European Convention to make forceful public statements in his clients' interest, even outside the courtroom. By contrast, in *Coutant v France*,[154] the European Court of Human Rights accepted as within Article 10 the fining of a lawyer acting in a terrorist trial who had, during the trial, accused the police of brutality and also called the investigating magistrates and trial court an insult to justice. The vituperative nature of the comments and the failure to voice them at trial took them beyond any protection.

6.64 However, complaints of abuse of process in the face of media comment have largely been rejected, though the trial of police officers for perverting the course of justice in the case of the Guildford 4 was halted in *R v Bow Street Metropolitan Stipendiary Magistrate, ex parte DPP*.[155] By contrast, in *R v Meziane*,[156] Lord Justice Tuckey held that, even in the context where two jurors had been discharged because of extraneous publicity, 'the assumption is that the trial process will normally remove the risk of prejudice and it will only be in an exceptional case that this cannot reasonably be expected to be done'. An endorsement of the jury's ability 'to focus exclusively on the evidence and to ignore anything they may have heard or read out of court' was expressed in *R v Barot*.[157] In *R v Abu Hamza*,[158] it was concluded

---

[149] Ibid 253.
[150] (1990) *The Times* 11 April.
[151] [2008] HCJAC 36. See further *Mohammed Atif Siddique v HM Advocate* [2010] HCJAC 7.
[152] [2008] HCJAC 36 at para 45.
[153] Ibid para 51.
[154] App no 17155/03, 24 January 2008.
[155] [1992] 95 Cr App Rep 91. Compare in Scotland: *McAlister v Associated Newspapers* 1954 SLT 14 (order against publication); *Kemp, Petitioners* 1982 JC 29 (convictions quashed).
[156] [2004] EWCA Crim 1768 at para 47.
[157] [2006] EWCA Crim 2692 at para 31.
[158] [2006] EWCA Crim 2918 at para 92.

that adverse publicity may have risked prejudicing a fair trial but those adverse circumstances should not halt the trial where the judge concludes that, with his assistance, the jury can perform its job. The *McCann* case was distinguished as arising from 'extraordinary circumstances'.[159] Thus, the media obsession with terrorism represents 'a sad reality of contemporary existence' which must be tolerated.[160]

Implementation

Offence types and conviction rates have already been detailed in Chapter 5.   **6.65**

Foreign comparisons

Variants of special courts for terrorism cases have emerged in many other jurisdictions, with   **6.66**
the removal of the jury and, as already detailed, the centralization of jurisdiction as common ploys.

As for bespoke criminal courts, a prime example is the Special Criminal Court (SCC) in the   **6.67**
Republic of Ireland.[161] The SCC is constitutionally anticipated by Article 38.3.1 of the Constitution. The Offences against the State Act 1939, Pt V, provides the framework for when, under s 35(1), 'the Government are satisfied that the ordinary courts are inadequate'. The SCC has sat from 1939 to 1946, 1961 to 1962, and from 1972 to date. The justification relates to the vulnerability of the jury to intimidation.[162]

Since 1972, SCC judicial personnel have been drawn from the ranks of permanent judges,   **6.68**
in contrast to military officers who previously served, but the appointees still do not enjoy the same security of tenure under art 35 of the Constitution as those judges who sit on the ordinary bench since they are removable at will. The trial, which under s 39 is by an uneven number of judges not fewer than three (but in practice always three), must observe the 'due course of law' under art 38.1 The practice and procedure of the SCC is to follow under s 41, so far as practicable, the normal rules relating to trial on indictment. The decision is by a majority under s 40, but no dissent may be disclosed. There is a right to appeal under s 44.

The constitutionality of the SCC has survived several challenges around its previous   **6.69**
military character[163] and modified security of tenure.[164] Another problem has been the tendency to excessive use, which currently encompasses organized crime prosecutions, though the annual numbers of persons charged are modest.[165] The discretion of the DPP to refer cases under ss 45 to 47 has been repeatedly questioned, but the courts have decisively concluded that the DPP's powers are not reviewable unless in bad faith.[166] The UN Human Rights Commission has sustained a breach of rights to equal treatment because of the

---

[159] Ibid para 88.
[160] *R v Elomar (No 27)* [2009] NSWSC 985 at para 28.
[161] See Davis, FF, *The History and Development of the Special Criminal Court, 1922–2005* (Four Courts Press, Dublin, 2007).
[162] Dail Debs vol 261 col 1764 (15 June 1972).
[163] *Re McCurtain* [1941] IR 83.
[164] *Eccles v Ireland* [1985] IR 545. See further *Eccles v Ireland*, App no 12839/87, DR 59, 212 (1988).
[165] For 1972–86 see Hogan, G and Walker C, *Political Violence and the Law in Ireland* (Manchester University Press, Manchester, 1989) p 243. Between 2000 and 2008, there were 208 persons charged, of whom seventy-six (37%) were convicted after a plea of not guilty and ninety-four (45%) were convicted after a guilty plea: Courts Service, *Annual Reports 2000–2008* (Dublin).
[166] *Kavanagh v Ireland* [1996] 1 IR 321. See also *DPP (Ward) v Special Criminal Court and DPP* [1998] IEHC 48; *Gilligan v Ireland* [2000] 4 IR 579; *People (DPP) v Birney* [2007] 1 IR 337.

breadth and range of scheduled offences, the absence of reasons from the DPP, and the unreviewability of the DPP's decision.[167]

6.70 The majority of the Hederman Committee supported the SCC because of the dangers of intimidation by paramilitaries[168] and endorsed its use against organized crime. But it supported some reforms, including annual review and triennial parliamentary confirmation, security of tenure for judges, scheduling on the facts of the case, a review of the DPP's referral decision, a requirement of unanimity, the giving of full reasons for conviction, and a full right of appeal. However, the government was unwilling to introduce any hobbles: '. . . it is simply not good enough to expose the throat of the Irish State and our democratic institutions to those who would quite willingly slit it'.[169] Now, the Criminal Justice (Amendment) Act 2009, s 8, declares the inadequacy of the ordinary courts to cope with several organized crime offences and invokes the SCC for twelve months at a time.

6.71 Though military courts have not been revived in contemporary Ireland, this most extreme of trial solutions has featured within the military commission established by the US Presidential Order in 2001[170] pursuant to 'the first war of the twenty-first century'.[171] It is not intended to explain these courts in detail. Though the US Supreme Court and Congress have generally sustained the President's imperious claims to broad war powers, the system has experienced constant condemnation and disruption through litigation, which has necessitated successive amendments.[172] The expectation was that the commissions would fall into an unregulated 'legal black hole',[173] but this expectation was misplaced according to *Hamdi v Rumsfeld*[174] and *Rasul v Bush*.[175]

6.72 In response to those decisions, the Defense Department set up the Combatant Status Review Tribunal (CSRT) to check on the assignment of 'enemy combatant' status.[176] There was also set up an annual review under Administrative Review Procedures for Enemy Combatants in the Custody of the Department of Defense at Guantánamo Bay Naval Base, Cuba,[177] to check whether the detainees still posed sufficient threat to justify detention.

6.73 In the meantime, Congress passed the Detainee Treatment Act 2005[178] to confine judicial review to one court circuit and to limit review to the procedures and not the merits of

---

[167] See CCPR/C/71/D/819/1998, 26 April 2001. But the Supreme Court held there was no impact in Irish law: [2002] 3 IR 97.

[168] *Report of the Committee to Review the Offences against the State Acts 1939–1998* (Dublin, 2002) para 9.29.

[169] Dail Debates vol 569 col 786 (25 June 2003), Michael McDowell.

[170] Military Order for the Detention, Treatment and Trial of Certain Non-Citizens in the War against Terrorism (66 Fed Reg 57, 2001); Department of Defense, Military Commission Order No 1 (Washington DC, 2002).

[171] *The Guardian* 14 September 2001, p 5.

[172] See Yoo, JC, *The Powers of War and Peace* (University of Chicago Press, Chicago, 2003); Berkowitz, P (ed), *Terrorism, the Laws of War and the Constitution* (Hoover Institution Press, Stanford, 2005); Duffy, H, *The 'War on Terror' and the Framework of International Law* (Cambridge University Press, Cambridge, 2005) ch 8; Tushnet, M (ed), *The Constitution in Wartime* (Duke University Press, Durham, 2005), Wittes, B, *Law and the Long War* (Penguin, New York, 2008).

[173] Steyn, J, 'Guantanamo Bay' (2003) 53 *International & Comparative Law Quarterly* 1.

[174] (2004) 542 US 507.

[175] (2004) 542 US 466.

[176] Deputy Secretary of Defense Order of July 7, 2004; Implementation of Combatant Status Review Tribunal Procedures, Department of Defense, 30 July 2004.

[177] See Administrative Review Procedures for Enemy Combatants, Department of Defense, 11 May 2004.

[178] Department of Defense Appropriations Act, 2006, Title X (PL 109-148).

the CSRT. The US Supreme Court in *Hamdan v Rumsfeld*[179] limited the impact of this legislation to future cases only and found that the military commissions under the 2001 Presidential Order were illegal under both the Uniform Code of Military Justice[180] and the Geneva Convention common Article 3.

On 7 July 2006 the Secretary of Defense issued a memo, 'Application of Common Article 3 **6.74** of the Geneva Conventions to the Treatment of Detainees in the Department of Defense'. It was followed on 11 July 2006 by an executive statement that all detainees at Guantánamo Bay and in US military custody everywhere are entitled to humane treatment under the Geneva Conventions. Partly to improve regulation and partly because 'black' prisons were being revealed anyway, around fourteen 'high value' prisoners were transferred to Guantánamo.

The Military Commissions Act of 2006[181] responded to *Hamdan*. It invested the President **6.75** with broad discretion to determine whether a person may be designated an 'unlawful enemy combatant' as well as reasserting military commissions to try them.[182] The procedures did not allow access to civilian lawyers or full disclosure of evidence, but admitted hearsay and statements obtained by torture prior to the 2005 Act. Around thirty detainees were informed they would be tried. Its procedures were in turn contested by way of group litigation—*In re Guantanamo Detention Litigation*[183]—until the applications were dismissed as moot since all had been released.

The Supreme Court in *Boumediene v Bush*[184] affirmed as applicable the constitutionally **6.76** guaranteed right of habeas corpus review and found that the Detainee Treatment Act 2005 and the Military Commissions Act 2006 had failed to provide adequate substitutes. But the basic power to detain what are described in the Military Commissions Act 2009[185] as 'unprivileged enemy belligerents' has been upheld.[186]

Despite this huge legal effort, just a handful of detainees have been charged with offences and **6.77** entered guilty pleas, including Khalid Sheikh Mohammed, with just three completed cases (Ali Hamza al-Bahlul, Salim Hamdan, and David Hicks). The military commissions system was suspended in 2009,[187] and five 'high value' prisoners (including Khalid Sheikh Mohammed) were transferred to the Federal criminal courts. There is now a drive by the administration of President Obama to close down the 'war on terror',[188] though the preference for regular courts is not exclusive and the Military Commissions Act 2009 reasserts the possibility of military trials, albeit on a basis more akin to that applicable to US soldiers, but

---

[179] (2006) 548 US 557.
[180] 10 US Code ss 801–941.
[181] PL 109-366, 10 US Code s 948a. See Bradley, CA, 'The Military Commission Act, habeas corpus and the Geneva Conventions' (2007) 101 *American Journal of International Law* 322; Hewitt, MA, 'Hearsay at Guantanamo' (2008) 96 *Georgetown Law Journal* 1375.
[182] ss 948a(1), 950v(24).
[183] US Dist LEXIS 32507 (2010).
[184] (2008) 553 US 723. See also *Boumediene v Bosnia*, App nos 38703, 40123, 43301/06, 18 November 2008.
[185] PL 111-84.
[186] *Al-Bihani v Obama* (2010) 590 F 3d 866.
[187] Executive Order 13492: Review and Disposition of Individuals Detained at the Guantanamo Bay Naval Base and Closure of Detention Facilities, s 7.
[188] Executive Order 13491: Ensuring Lawful Interrogations; Executive Order 13492: Review and Disposition of Individuals Detained at the Guantanamo Bay Naval Base and Closure of Detention Facilities; Executive Order 13493: Review of Detention Policy Options (22 January 2009) (74 FR 4897 and 4901); Detention Policy Task Force, Memorandum for the Attorney General (Washington DC, 2009).

still with significant regressions from normal trial standards, including the admission of involuntary statements and the use of hearsay. The Guantánamo Review Task Force has recommended that 126 inmates be transferred and 36 be prosecuted by Federal court or military commission, leaving seventy-eight detainees in executive detention (48 for an indefinite period).[189] The Commissions resumed operation in 2010 with the trial of Omar Khadr.[190]

6.78 Because of their dubious status in international law,[191] their patent procedural unfairness, their discriminatory impact,[192] as well as their limited practical impact, these military style adjudicative processes present a dysfunctional model for terrorism adjudication.[193] For its part, the United Kingdom government has rejected the 'war on terror' concept, which is said to have given 'ammunition to America's enemies, and pause to America's friends' as well as being 'misleading and mistaken'.[194] Conversely, the language of 'counter-insurgency' is applied when armed forces are committed to action in Afghanistan and Iraq.[195] The shadowy and intermittent activities of terrorism groups will rarely meet the criteria of 'armed conflict' or the conditions for the use of lawful force in that context.[196] In any event, most Guantánamo detainees were not captured in Afghanistan, still less on a battlefield.[197] To designate as terrorist any category of 'combatant' or 'belligerent' gives them a status which bolsters the legitimacy of their cause and their use of lethal force.

Assessment and conclusions

6.79 The criminal trial represents the culmination of the policy of 'Pursue' and delivers it by means which may be viewed as both convincing and legitimate. A criminal justice approach entails individual responsibility, equality, and system legality and due process. Thus, successive governments have been right to seek to maximize criminal justice and to reject the contention that 'it is not enough to serve our enemies with legal papers'.[198] The countervailing dangers include increased miscarriages of justice and the contamination thesis—that special procedures will corrode standards in normal law.

6.80 Certainly, the essence of the traditional criminal process has been retained to the exclusion of more radical and risky departures such as the appointment of investigative magistrates[199] or non-jury security courts. Express modifications to criminal justice in the

---

[189] *Final Report* (Department of Justice, Washington DC, 2010).

[190] See <http://www.defense.gov/news/commissions.html>.

[191] See especially Zerrougui, C et al, *Situation of detainees in Guantanamo Bay* (E/CN.4/2006/120, New York, 2006); Rona, G, 'An appraisal of US practice relating to "enemy combatants"' (2007) 10 *Yearbook of International Humanitarian Law* 232.

[192] US citizens could not be held indefinitely as enemy combatants: *Hamdi v Rumsfeld* (2004) 542 US 507. Prosecutions were mounted for example against John Walker-Lindh (227 F Supp 2d 565 (2002)) and James Ujaama (see *US v Kassir* 2009 US Dist LEXIS 83075).

[193] See also the (Israeli) Incarceration of Unlawful Combatants Law 2002.

[194] Donohue, LK, *The Cost of Counterterrorism: Power, Politics, and Liberty* (Cambridge University Press, Cambridge, 2008) p 2.

[195] Home Office, *Pursue, Prevent, Protect, Prepare* (Cm 7547, London, 2009) para 7.16.

[196] Duffy, H, *The 'War on Terror' and the Framework of International Law* (Cambridge University Press, Cambridge, 2005) ch 6.

[197] Denbeaux, J et al, The Meaning of 'Battlefield' An Analysis of the Government's Representations of 'Battlefield Capture' and 'Recidivism' of the Guantanamo Detainees (<http://law.shu.edu/publications/guantanamoReports/meaning_of_battlefield_final_121007.pdf>, 2007).

[198] President Bush, State of the Union Address 20 January 2004 (<http://georgewbush-whitehouse.archives.gov/news/releases/2004/01/20040120-7.html>).

[199] See Joint Committee on Human Rights, *Counter-Terrorism Policy and Human Rights: Prosecution and Pre-Charge Detention* (2005–06 HL 240/HC 1576) paras 76, 109, 138.

anti-terrorism legislation have been peripheral, as signalled by the title of Part VI of the TA 2000—'Miscellaneous'. However, beyond the express measures, the very incorporation of the term 'terrorism' into the formulation of police powers and crimes inevitably emphasizes that the offender has a political or ideological motivation to cause harm which is redolent of anti-systemic political crimes.[200] As found in previous eras, persons subjected to special policing powers, special crimes, and special disposals will not readily accept their depiction as 'common' criminals, nor will the communities to which they belong.

The official caution shown towards more decisive departures from 'normal' court process is **6.81** therefore warranted, even though devices such as juryless trials cannot be impugned head-on under Article 6 of the European Convention. Nor does the government accept the need for any distinctly British constitutional recognition.[201] A distinct system would not necessarily amount to unreasonable discrimination—reasons can readily be found for objective and reasonable divergence in terms of local conditions.[202] But the establishment of any special security court may affect the appearance of impartiality,[203] and the European Court of Human Rights has found that military trials of civilians will undercut the independence of the judiciary unless there are compelling reasons for that mode of trial.[204]

Three further factors will pressure future developments. One is reticence about public revelation **6.82** of intelligence and surveillance information in normal process. The principal causes of tension will be, first, evidence from intelligence agencies (including foreign partners) and, second, the introduction of communications intercept data and reversal of the rule in the RIPA, s 17 (already discussed in Chapter 2).

A second issue relates to prosecution charging policy, and the need, as in serious fraud litiga- **6.83** tion, to keep terrorism within the bounds of manageable time and comprehension levels for jurors.[205] Implementation of this policy may sometimes require the refinement of charges and also the dropping of charges,[206] thereby adding to the prosecutor's terrorism dilemma— namely, the impetus to intervention prior to the tipping point between bad thoughts and bad deeds.

The third pressure emanates from the intense media interest in terrorism cases. The dangers **6.84** were demonstrated by the momentary carelessness of revealing secret documents to prying photographers in Downing Street, as with Metropolitan Police Assistant Commissioner, Bob Quick, whose resignation duly followed.[207] Another aspect of that episode is the threat to constabulary independence. One hopes that the briefing of politicians was confined to general operational matters rather than individual exercises of police powers which should not be the business of politicians.

---

[200] Ross, JI, *The Dynamics of Political Crime* (Sage, Thousand Oaks, 2003) p 4.
[201] Ministry of Justice, *Rights and Responsibilities: developing our constitutional framework* (Cm 7577, London, 2009) paras 3.30, 3.31.
[202] See *Magee v United Kingdom*, App no 28135/95, 2000-VI, para 50.
[203] *Öcalan v Turkey*, App no 46221/99, 2005-VI.
[204] See *Denmark, Norway, Sweden and the Netherlands v Greece* (1969) 12 YBEC 186; *Incal v Turkey*, App no 22678/93, 1998-IV; *Martin v United Kingdom*, App no 40426/98, 24 October 2006; *Ergin v Turkey (No 6)*, App no 47533/99, 2006-VI.
[205] See Roskill Committee, *Report of Fraud Trials Committee* (HMSO, London, 1986).
[206] This occurred in Operation Overt: *The Times* 2 November 2006, p 4.
[207] *The Times* 9 April 2009, pp 1, 8.

6.85 Profound dissatisfaction with a military commission model combined with reflection on the foregoing pressures faced by normal courts has engendered debate in the US about the value of a 'national security court'. Uncertainties will be raised around the process of establishment (such as discriminatory choices between different classes of defendant) and possible compromises to evidential standards (including the admission of coerced statements)[208] and the handling of sensitive security evidence. There are commentators on both sides of the argument.[209]

6.86 Special courts for terrorists are constitutionally permissible, but the requirements of Article 6 offer 'a minimum floor of due process' which is essentially non-derogable.[210] However, the international obligations of a fair trial are rather less uncompromising in interpretation.[211] If all that is 'special' about a national security court is that the judges have been given extra training on handling intelligence and inhabit facilities with extra physical security, then the result is not far from the Protocol and places the project as special in administrative but not legal terms. More dubious and threatening to the desired attributes of fairness and legitimacy would be trials in a national security court only for foreigners, closed to the public, with a modified standard of proof, or with military judges. When the normal criminal courts do not seem to measure up to the enormity of terrorism offences, then internationalization rather than militarization seems a more promising avenue to avoid the label of 'victor's justice'.[212]

6.87 No national security court has emerged within Great Britain. On the basis of a rights audit, the criminal prosecution of terrorists still involves access to independent and impartial trial and appeal courts. Departure from this standard has been apparent mainly in the specialist context of inquests, perhaps as a way of testing the water for the future abolition of juries in the criminal courts. An attempt to curtail juries and the local appointment of coroners via the Counter-Terrorism Bill 2007–08, Pt VII, and later renewed by the Coroners' Bill 2008–09, cl 11, ended in defeat.[213] Instead, reliance is placed, under the Coroners and Justice Act 2009, s 11 and sch 1, on the Inquiries Act 2005.[214] Otherwise, the standards of

---

[208] See Armed Services Committee, Inquiry into the treatment of detainees in US custody (US Senate, Washington DC, 2008).

[209] See Wittes, B, *Law and the Long War* (Penguin, New York, 2008) ch 6; Zabel, RB and Benjamin, JJ, *In Pursuit of Justice: Prosecuting Terrorism Cases in the Federal Courts* (Human Rights First, New York, 2008); Weisselberg, CD, 'Terror in the courts' (2008) 50 *Crime, Law & Social Change* 25; Vladeck, SI, 'The case against national security courts' (2009) 45 *Willamette Law Review* 505; Sulmasy, G, *The National Security Court System* (Oxford University Press, Oxford, 2009).

[210] See Stavros, S, 'The right to a fair trial in emergency situations' (1992) 41 *International & Comparative Law Quarterly* 343 at 344; Weissbrodt, DG, *The Right to a Fair Trial under the Universal Declaration of Human Rights and the International Covenant on Civil and Political Rights* (Kluwer, The Hague, 2001) ch 5.

[211] See Special Rapporteur on the promotion and protection of human rights and fundamental freedoms while countering terrorism, *4th Report to the General Assembly* (A/63/223, 2008). Compare the better documented Weissbrodt, D, *The Right to a Fair Trial under the Universal Declaration of Human Rights and the International Covenant on Civil and Political Rights* (Kluwer, The Hague, 2001).

[212] Compare Peacey, J (ed), *The Regicides and the Execution of Charles I* (Palgrave, Basingstoke, 2001); Robertson, G, 'Fair trial for terrorists?' in Wilson, RA (ed), *Human Rights in the 'War on Terror'* (Cambridge University Press, Cambridge, 2005) p 169.

[213] See Joint Committee on Human Rights, *Counter-Terrorism Policy and Human Rights: Counter Terrorism Bill* (2007–08 HL 108, HC 554), *Government Responses to the Committee's 20th and 21st Reports and other correspondence* (2007–08 HL 127, HC 756); House of Lords Constitution Committee, *Counter Terrorism Bill: The role of ministers, Parliament and the judiciary* (2007–08 HL 167); McGahey, C, 'Jury out on terror bill' (2008) 158 *New Law Journal* 508.

[214] See Hansard HC vol 492 col 68ws (15 May 2009), Jack Straw; Joint Committee on Human Rights, *Legislative Scrutiny: Coroners and Justice Bill* (2008–09 HL 94/HC 524).

Article 6 can better be realized in the context of a criminal process than in the context of an executive disposal or in the moral and legal debacle of a 'war on terror'. Lord Diplock's policy of criminalization was valid in 1972 and remains valid now.

C. International Aspects of Criminal Process

Introduction and background

International cooperation around terrorism was hampered for many decades by sensitivities **6.88** about national sovereignty and a reluctance to take sides in foreign disputes. These factors were exemplified by the political offence doctrine in extradition.[215] But the international spread of terrorism after the 1960s encouraged new attitudes more favourable to mutual support. Since these developments are not confined to terrorism cases, a selective outline only will be offered here.[216]

Provisions

Mutual assistance

Mutual assistance in investigation has already been detailed in Chapter 4. As for judicial **6.89** cooperation, the most advanced systems affecting the United Kingdom are found within the context of two institutional arrangements within the European Union.

First, Eurojust, a cross-border public prosecutions unit, was established in 2002.[217] Its func- **6.90** tions include improving coordination and cooperation between national authorities by facilitating international mutual legal assistance and investigations such as through coordinated evidence-gathering and enforcement action. On terrorism, it assists with prosecutions which have transborder aspects (there were thirty-nine in 2008, with eight in the financial field).[218] Each country must appoint a 'national correspondent for Eurojust for terrorism matters',[219] who must inform Eurojust of all terrorist proceedings in their country. Once received, the information is analysed by the Case Management Team and issued as a quarterly 'Terrorism Convictions Monitor'. Eurojust does not have operational responsibility,[220] but a Counter-Terrorism Team was set up in 2004 after the Madrid attacks. The CT Team supports casework, such as through tactical meetings, and holds annual strategic meetings.

Other aspects of transborder judicial cooperation are bolstered by the Council Framework **6.91** Decision on Combating Terrorism of 13 June 2002,[221] which establishes parameters for the constituent elements of criminal acts and penalties. In this way, there is constituted an EU

---

[215] See Gilbert, G, *Transnational Fugitive Offenders in International Law* (Nijhoff, The Hague, 1998) ch 6.
[216] See further Home Office, *Mutual Legal Assistance Guidelines for the United Kingdom* (7th edn, London, 2009). The European Convention on the Transfer of Proceedings in Criminal Matters (ETS 73, 1972) has not been signed by the UK.
[217] Decision 2000/799/JHA, as amended by 2002/187/JHA, 2003/659/JHA, 2005/671/JHA, and 2009/426/JHA. See Vlastnik, J, 'Eurojust' in Guild, E and Geyer, F, *Security Versus Justice?* (Ashgate, Aldershot, 2008).
[218] *Annual Report 2008* (The Hague, 2009) p 23.
[219] See House of Lords Select Committee on the European Union, *Judicial Cooperation in the EU: the role of Eurojust* (2003–04 HL 134) para 98. The UK national correspondent is the Senior National Co-ordinator, Counter Terrorism Command, Metropolitan Police Service.
[220] An office of European Public Prosecutor is mentioned in Art 69E of the Treaty of Lisbon.
[221] 2002/475/JHA. See Nuotio, K, 'Terrorism as a catalyst for the emergence, harmonization and the reform of the criminal law (2006) 4 *Journal of International Criminal Justice* 998 at 1010.

common understanding of the term 'terrorism' which facilitates cross-border cooperation, though it also embodies problems of vagueness.[222] Unlike most European countries without anti-terrorism laws, major changes were not required to British law, but the Crime (International Cooperation) Act 2003 ensured compliance.

Transfer for trial

6.92   The growing consensus against terrorism in western Europe, as shared by its close allies, was marked by the European Convention on the Suppression of Terrorism 1977.[223] The Convention is implemented in the United Kingdom via the Suppression of Terrorism Act 1978,[224] which attempts to remove restraint on extradition for scheduled offences based on the political offence extradition.[225] However, even within Europe, alternative constitutional objections were raised in the Republic of Ireland,[226] while, beyond Europe, extradition often remained problematic, including with the United States.[227] Not only was there the barrier of the political offence exception but also procedures remained complex and slow. However, barriers began to tumble in the early 1990s. It became widely accepted that the perpetration of indiscriminate violence was not to be favoured as a 'political offence'.[228]

6.93   Extradition schemes are now set out in the Extradition Act 2003. Part I deals with the fast-track process for Category 1 countries which are within the European Arrest Warrant (EAW) scheme (covered in Chapter 4). Part II covers bilateral or other multilateral[229] treaty arrangements. Arrangements with the USA, now in a 2003 treaty, follow the European precedent by requiring on the UK side only a statement of information rather than prima facie proof.[230] Pt III covers processes for applying for extradition to the United Kingdom from Category 1 territories, but processes for Category 2 countries are left largely to treaties as an exercise of the Royal Prerogative. Corresponding to the position under the EAW, immunity based on political motives is wholly removed for extradition, as are several other 'technicalities'. Extradition bars remaining for Category 2 countries correspond to those under Pt I (ss 11, 79) and include persecution[231] or punishment for 'extraneous' political opinions (ss 13, 81).[232] Extradition can also be halted (ss 21, 87) if it would be incompatible

---

[222]   See Bures, O, 'EU counter terrorism policy: a paper tiger? (2006) 18 *Terrorism & Political Violence* 57.

[223]   ETS no 90. See also Protocol of 2003 (ETS no 190) which adds to the listed offences (art 1) and reduces the scope for reservations (art 16).

[224]   See Lowe, AV and Young, JR, 'Suppressing terrorism under the European Convention' (1978) 25 *Netherlands International Law Review* 305; Gal-Or, N, *International Cooperation to Suppress Terrorism* (Croom Helm, London, 1985) chs 6–12.

[225]   In the Republic of Ireland, see *State (Magee) v O'Rourke* [1971] IR 205; *Bourke v AG* [1972] IR 36.

[226]   *Sloan v Callaghan* [1992] ILRM 194; *McKee v Culligan* 1992 ILRM 186; *Magee v O'Dea* [1994] ILRM 540; *Larkin v O'Dea* [1995] 2 ILRM 1. See Delaney, H and Hogan, G, 'Anglo-Irish extradition viewed from an Irish perspective' [1993] *Public Law* 93; Forde, M, *Extradition Law in Ireland* (2nd edn, Round Hall, Dublin, 1995) ch 5.

[227]   See *Re Doherty* 599 F Supp 270 (1984); *In re McMullen* 788 F 2d 591 (1986); *Quinn v Robinson* 783 F 2d 776 (1986); Holland, J, *The American Connection* (Poolbeg, Dublin, 1989) ch 5.

[228]   *T v Secretary of State for the Home Department* [1996] 2 WLR 766 HL; (Irish) Extradition (Amendment) Act 1994; McElrath, K, *Unsafe Haven* (Pluto, London, 2000). Extradition was granted in *Fusco v O'Dea* [1998] 3 IR 470 and *Quinlivan v Conroy* [2000] 3 IR 154; *Re McGrory* [2000] NI 487.

[229]   See Scheme relating to the Rendition of Fugitive Offenders within the Commonwealth (Cmnd 3008, London, 1966); European Convention on Extradition 1957 (ETS 24).

[230]   Cm 5821, London, 2003, SI 2003/3334. See *Norris v Government of the United States of America* [2008] UKHL 16.

[231]   Police maltreatment is not 'persecution' (but see ss 21, 87): *Higson v Doherty* 2004 SCCR 63.

[232]   See *Emilia Gomez v Secretary of State for the Home Department* [2000] INLR 549; *Asliturk v Turkey* [2002] EWHC 2326 (Admin). It is for the defendant to show there is a 'reasonable chance': *Lodhi v Governor of Brixton Prison* [2001] EWHC 178.

with Convention rights,[233] or (ss 25, 91) if it would be unjust or oppressive because of the person's physical or mental condition.

The EAW has addressed the traditional problems within extradition both of exception and **6.94** procedure. Even before its coming into force, relations in Europe improved. For example, in *Re Kadre*,[234] the applicant was charged in France with an offence of participation in an association established with a view to the preparation of acts of terrorism (French Penal Code, art 421.2.1). The alleged conspiracy occurred in Germany but the intended explosion was at the Christmas market in Strasbourg in 2000. It was emphasized that the function of the district judge was not to ascertain whether there was a case to answer but to determine whether the alleged conduct would, if perpetrated in the United Kingdom, have amounted to extradition offences. On the facts, English charges around conspiracy to cause an explosion could apply.

A comparison might be made with the older case of Rachid Ramda, who was arrested in **6.95** 1995 in connection with financing the attacks on the Paris Metro. His extradition was not achieved until December 2005.[235] Evidence of police ill-treatment of a witness was not sufficient to block extradition but was left for the French courts to consider. The possibility of ill-treatment of Ramda was discounted since there was no intention to interrogate him. Further, the Court was not disturbed by acknowledged 'procedures in French law in cases of extreme urgency, under which some Algerians convicted of terrorist acts have been expelled to Algeria, despite the risk of a breach of Article 3'.[236] The case was hardly one of extreme urgency and future treatment was speculative.

Beyond the EAW context, extradition is still far from assured. For instance, in *R (Al-Fawwaz)* **6.96** *v Governor of Brixton Prison*,[237] Al-Fawwaz, Abdel-Bary, and Eidarous were part of the Advice and Reform Committee, a body based in London and associated with Al-Qa'ida which had contacts with those alleged to be involved in the bombings of the US embassies in East Africa in 1998. The United States government sought extradition on a charge of conspiracy to murder. It was disputed whether any acts in furtherance of the conspiracy had occurred there, though evidence was given of telephone communications through the United States and concurrence in the issuing in the United States of *fatawa* exhorting *jihad*. The House of Lords held in 2001 that US jurisdiction over the appellants had been established since extradition could arise from extraterritorial jurisdiction, provided an equivalent offence would be triable under the extraterritorial jurisdiction of the United Kingdom courts (as under the Internationally Protected Persons Act 1978).

Nevertheless, these fugitives still remain in the jurisdiction. In 2006 the Secretary of State **6.97** decided not to surrender Eiderous because of serious ill-health; he died in 2008. The other two were informed in 2008 that the Secretary of State had issued warrants for their return to the US, whereupon they applied for judicial review[238] on the basis of a potential breach of

---

[233] The inherent impact on family rights is not a bar: *Norris v Government of United States of America* [2010] UKSC 9. Discriminatory selection for prosecution was allowed in *Damir Travica v Croatia* [2004] EWHC 2747 (Admin).

[234] [2005] EWHC 1712 (Admin).

[235] *Ramda v Secretary of State for the Home Department* [2005] EWHC 2526 (Admin). See also *Bensaid v United Kingdom*, App no 44599/98, 6 February 2001.

[236] Ibid para 57. Compare *Re Faraj* [2004] EWHC 2950 (Admin).

[237] [2001] UKHL 69.

[238] *R (Bary and Al Fawwaz) v Secretary of State for the Home Department* [2009] EWHC 2068 (Admin).

Article 3 which might arise from detention under 'special administrative measures' (SAMs) at the United States Penitentiary Administrative Maximum Facility (ADX), Florence, Colorado, and the likelihood of life imprisonment without parole. They also raised concerns about trial in the United Kingdom being considered as a viable alternative, about refoulement to a third country, and about the reliability of US assurances as to treatment. All complaints were dismissed. The test for a real risk of treatment in violation of Article 3 was a stringent one and the burden of proof had not been met. Neither SAMs nor a life sentence without parole would quite cross the Article 3 threshold, though they were near to the borderline. Overall, the importance of international cooperation over terrorism, especially with friendly states, was championed, and so the courts should avoid decisions based on differences in domestic standards which would allow the claimants to escape justice.

6.98 A brisker pace in mutual aid has since emerged. In *Barbar Ahmad v Government of the United States of America*,[239] the applicant was charged with material support for terrorism arising out of US-based websites supporting Chechen and Taliban causes. The troubling background was that the British authorities refused to prosecute on the same evidence in 2003. Nevertheless, extradition was ordered, on the back of diplomatic assurances of prosecution in a Federal court and not before a military commission. An application is pending to the Strasbourg Court.[240]

6.99 The choice of jurisdiction in cases such as *Ahmad* resulted in an attempted legislative amendment to the Police and Justice Bill 2005–06 so as to require US authorities to establish a *prima facie* case.[241] The amendment failed, but there was issued in 2006 the *Guidance for handling criminal cases with concurrent jurisdiction between the United Kingdom and the United States of America*.[242] The CPS is advised to liaise with the US Office of International Affairs and to refer matters upwards in the event of disagreement. In addition, an amendment was carried in Sch 13 para 4 of the 2006 Act to allow the court to stop extradition where (a) a significant part of the conduct alleged to constitute the extradition offence occurred in the United Kingdom, and (b) in view of that and all the other circumstances, it would not be in the interests of justice for trial to take place in the requesting territory. This bar is not yet in force but is under Home Office consideration.

6.100 In *Hashmi v Government of the United States of America*,[243] whilst resident in New York, the appellant became a member of Al-Muhajiroun. This group was not proscribed in the United Kingdom until 2010 but was designated a 'foreign terrorist organization' for funding purposes in the US. In 2000, the appellant recruited another member who was subsequently convicted of material support to an Al-Qa'ida member in the US while staying with the appellant in London. The appellant sought to avoid extradition on the basis that the request was an exercise of an exorbitant jurisdiction and that he should have been tried in England so as to protect his rights under Article 8. The appeal was dismissed. The notion of 'exorbitant jurisdiction' was subsumed within human rights considerations. Thus, it retained relevance only for weighing proportionality under Article 8 of the Convention, on which ground there was no bar.

---

[239] [2006] EWHC 2927 (Admin).

[240] *Ahmad v United Kingdom*, App nos 24027/07, 11949/08, 36742/08, 8 July 2010. US assurances were endorsed in *Al Moayad v Germany*, App no 35865/03, 20 February 2007.

[241] See Broadbridge, S, *The UK/US Extradition Treaty* (SN/HA/2204, House of Commons Library, London, 2009).

[242] <http://www.publications.parliament.uk/pa/ld200607/ldlwa/70125ws1.pdf>. But the guideline did not apply retrospectively: *R (Ahsan) v DPP* [2008] EWHC 666 (Admin).

[243] [2007] EWHC 564 (Admin).

Extradition to the USA was also ordered (pending Strasbourg review) for Abu Hamza **6.101** (*Mustafa v Government of the United States of America*)[244] in respect of hostage-taking offences allegedly committed against tourists in Yemen in 1998 by the Islamic Army of Aden-Abyan, involvement in terrorism organizing and training in Oregon between 1999 and 2000,[245] and raising money for fighters in Afghanistan from 1999 to 2001. The extradition proceedings were suspended when the appellant was convicted of soliciting murder, but they resumed in 2007. The appellant resisted the orders on the grounds of prejudicial delay. He also argued that part of the evidence against him was obtained indirectly by torture and that his extradition to the United States incurred the risk of Article 3 breaches despite diplomatic assurances given by the United States government. The appeals were dismissed.

It was accepted by the European Court of Human Rights in *Chraidi v Germany*[246] that **6.102** delays may occur in extradition proceedings because of their international complexity. In that case, the applicant was extradited to Germany to face charges relating to a terrorist bomb attack on a discotheque in Berlin in 1996. He was convicted in 2001.

As illustrated by these cases, as the possibility of extradition increases in 'political' cases, so **6.103** will the resort to 'safety' arguments as a bar under Article 3 of the European Convention. The trend was established in *Chahal v United Kingdom*,[247] and challenges to that doctrine have been rebuffed.[248] As well as the danger of Article 3 treatment, *Soering v United Kingdom* confirms that a reasonable prospect of a flagrant denial of justice will also be a bar to extradition under Article 6.[249] These potential pitfalls are regularly avoided by seeking diplomatic notes or assurances from the receiving state (also applicable to the death penalty under Article 2).[250]

Additional to bars arising from individual human rights considerations, the Court of Appeal **6.104** in *R v Mullen*[251] emphasized that an abuse of process, by engineering the return of the fugitive from Zimbabwe through an unlawful deportation during which he was denied legal advice so as to stand trial for IRA explosives offences, would result in his conviction for conspiring to cause explosions being set aside, especially as details of the arrangements had not been disclosed at trial. Such a degradation of the lawful administration of justice demanded that the gravity of the offence had to be weighed against the conduct of the prosecuting and security authorities.

Because of the practical barriers to international cooperation, other forms of resolution **6.105** remain in operation. These alternatives include the conferment of extra-territorial jurisdiction

---

[244] [2008] EWHC 1357 (Admin). See also *Ahmad v United Kingdom*, App nos 24027/07, 11949/08, 36742/08, 8 July 2010.

[245] See also *Aswat v Government of the USA* [2006] EWHC 2927 (Admin), *Ahmad v United Kingdom*, App nos 24027/07, 11949/08, 36742/08, 8 July 2010; *US v Kassir* 2009 US Dist LEXIS 83075.

[246] App no 65655/01.

[247] App no 22414/93, 1996-V. Compare *Suresh v Canada (Minister of Citizenship and Immigration)* [2002] SCC 1.

[248] *Saadi v Italy*, App no 37201/06, 28 February 2008; *NA v United Kingdom*, App no 25904/07, 17 July 2008.

[249] App no 14038/88, Ser A 161 (1989). See further *Mamatkulov and Askarov v Turkey*, App nos 46827/99 and 46951/99, 4 February 2005; *Ismoilov v Russia*, App no 2947/06, 1 December 2008; *Baysakov v Ukraine*, App no 54131/08, 18 February 2010; *Klein v Russia*, App no 24268/08, 1 April 2010; *Khodzhayev v Russia*, App no 52466/08, 12 May 2010.

[250] See Tooze, J, 'Deportation with assurances' [2010] *Public Law* 362.

[251] [2000] QB 520. Compare *Öcalan v Turkey*, App no 46221/99, 12 May 2005.

such as under the 1978 Act, s 4, and under the Criminal Jurisdiction Act 1975.[252] The United States has been conspicuously active in assuming extra-territorial jurisdiction.[253]

6.106 Rather less palatable as an alternative is rendition avoiding judicial process, though the United Kingdom government denies any use or involvement in the practice.[254]

Mutual assistance and mutual recognition in evidence gathering

6.107 Various mutual legal assistance instruments have long been in currency, including the Council of Europe's European Convention on Mutual Assistance in Criminal Matters 1959[255] and the EU Mutual Legal Assistance Convention of 2000.[256] The letter of request is the enforcement instrument specified in the Crime (International Co-operation) Act 2003, s 7, though direct applications to foreign jurisdictions remain possible and arrangements can be made within jurisdiction for video links for the testimony of witnesses under the Criminal Justice Act 1988, ss 29 to 32.

6.108 Mutual recognition was bolstered by the Council Framework Decision of 18 December 2008 on the European evidence warrant for the purpose of obtaining objects, documents, and data for use in proceedings in criminal matters.[257] The Framework Decision of the European Evidence Warrant (EEW) is designed to apply the principle of mutual recognition, with procedures which are similar to the EAW, to judicial decisions for the purpose of obtaining physical evidence held in another Member State. In the first phase of the instrument, it addresses pre-existing evidence, whereas phase two will cover evidence-gathering including the taking of witness statements. During the interim period the EEW (which is to be implemented by 2011) and mutual legal assistance procedures will run in parallel.

6.109 The Council of the European Union has proposed a more ambitious 'European investigation order'.[258] The proposal would replace the EEW, the Framework Decision on freezing orders, and the relevant portions of the Council of Europe and EU Convention on mutual assistance. It would demand mutual recognition of orders for most forms of 'investigative measure' (but not Joint Investigation Team or the interception of telecommunications) although without specifying mutual admissibility.

6.110 Several parliamentary select committees[259] have warned that rights have not been adequately safeguarded within these initiatives.

Assessment and conclusions

6.111 Cross-border cooperation is increasingly relevant to terrorism litigation. Its complexity and political sensitivity, heightened in terrorism cases, means that it remains a patchwork of arrangements which are more impressive on paper than in action.

---

[252] See *R v Governor of Belmarsh Prison, ex parte Martin* [1995] 1 WLR 412.

[253] See especially 18 USC s 2331.

[254] See Intelligence and Security Committee, *Rendition* (Cm 7171, London, 2007); Walker, C, 'Foreign terror suspects' (2007) 70 *Modern Law Review* 427.

[255] ETS 30. See also the Additional Protocols of 1978 and (ETS 99 and 182).

[256] OJ [2000] C197/1.

[257] 2008/978/JHA. See Vervaele, JAE (ed), *European Evidence Warrant* (Intersentia, Antwerp, 2005). Note also Council Framework Decision 2003/577/JHA of 22 July 2003 for freezing orders.

[258] Council Documents 9145/10, 9288/10, 11842/10. Compare the more ambitious COM (2009) 624 final. The UK government has decided to opt in: Hansard HC vol 514 col 881 (27 July 2010).

[259] House of Lords European Union Committee, *Procedural Rights in EU Criminal Proceedings* (2008–09 HL 84); House of Commons Justice Committee, *Justice Issues in Europe* (2009–10 HC 162-I) para 60.

D. Penology of Terrorism

Sentencing

Introduction and background

A potential limitation of criminal prosecution is that the expected deterrent impacts of criminal justice may not be secured in the face of perpetrators intent on killing themselves in the act of terrorism.[260] However, most terrorist acts are not suicide operations, and Dershowitz argues that terrorism is more calculated and goal-oriented than crimes commonly driven by impulse or passion.[261] In addition, a failure to deter might suggest not a departure from criminal justice but its reformulation towards incapacitation. In fact, both deterrence and incapacitation for the sake of public security are manifest in the penology of terrorism.[262] Enhanced deterrence and incapacitation arise not only because of harm to multiple victims.[263] Terrorism also undermines state security, and so the denunciatory function of criminal justice is to the fore. Aside from whether sentencing policy is appropriately designed to achieve both deterrence and incapacitation, a second issue for penal initiatives is whether they can offer telling incentives out of terrorism.

6.112

As well as the design of sentences, the conditions of imprisonment also impact on deterrence, incapacitation, and the possibility of rehabilitation. Terrorists are potentially dangerous prisoners. They may subvert other prisoners or the prison regime. All will be counterproductive to the aims of the penal system.

6.113

Provisions—general sentencing laws applied to terrorism

To date, most laws affecting the sentencing of terrorist prisoners were found beyond the anti-terrorism legislation in either policy statements about tariffs in life sentences[264] or in court sentencing decisions. The analysis to follow will adopt a categorization by offence group and also over time. To avoid further complications, only adult offenders will be considered, and repeat offending and extended sentences will also be ignored.[265] Four types of sentence of imprisonment commonly affect terrorist cases.[266]

6.114

There are mandatory life sentences for murder, as well as discretionary life sentences which apply, for example, to some explosives offences. Then, there are determinate (fixed-term) sentences which are subject to release before the end of the term on parole. Under the Criminal Justice Act 2003, s 225, if the person is convicted of an offence for which the maximum penalty is life, then a life sentence must be imposed; if the offence does not carry life imprisonment, then it may be imposed where the culpability of the offender is particularly high or the offence itself particularly serious.[267]

6.115

---

[260] *Report of the Official Account of the Bombings in London on 7 July 2005* (2005–06 HC 1087) para 7.

[261] Dershowitz, A, *Why Terrorism Works* (Yale University Press, New Haven, 2002) p 22.

[262] See Wattad, M S-A, 'Is terrorism a crime or an aggravating factor in sentencing?' (2006) 4 *Journal of International Criminal Justice* 1017.

[263] See Sentencing Guidelines Council, *Overarching Principles: Seriousness* (London, 2004) para 1.23.

[264] See Criminal Justice Act 2003, Sch 21; Amendment No 6 to the Consolidated Criminal Practice Direction [2004] 2 Cr App R 24 IV.49.33.

[265] Criminal Justice Act 2003 ss 225, 227, Sch 15A.

[266] See Murder (Abolition of the Death Penalty) Act 1965; Criminal Justice Act 2003, Pt XII; Parole Board Rules 2004; Directions to the Parole Board issued by the Secretary of State under Section 32(6) of the Criminal Justice Act 1991 or Section 239(6) of the Criminal Justice Act 2003; Prison Service Order 4700, *Indeterminate Sentence Manual* (Home Office, London, 2009).

[267] See Criminal Justice and Immigration Act 2008, s 13.

6.116 Next, there are determinate sentences for offences committed on or after 4 April 2005 which are subject to the Criminal Justice Act 2003, s 224. These fixed-term sentences become subject to 'Imprisonment for Public Protection' (IPP) for 'dangerous offenders' convicted of a 'serious offence' and who pose a significant risk of serious harm.[268] A specified offence (which must be punishable with a maximum of life imprisonment or imprisonment for ten years or more) under Sch 15 becomes a 'serious offence' because it is a 'specified violent offence'.[269] The specified 'violent offences' were amended by the Coroners and Justice Act 2009, ss 138 and 139 (not in Scotland) to expressly mention a wide range of terrorism legislation offences. The list now includes: soliciting murder and threats to kill, various explosives and firearms offences, hostage-taking and hijacking, and offences under ss 54, 56, 57, and 59 of the TA 2000 (but not s 58), offences under ss 47, 50, and 113 of the ATCSA 2001, and offences under ss 5, 6, 9, 10, and 11 of the TA 2006.

6.117 Life sentence prisoners will be subjected to a 'minimum term' (formerly a 'tariff') which must now be set by the court[270] as an estimate of when the punitive elements (retribution and deterrence) of the sentence will have been satisfied. When setting a minimum term, the court should normally set one half of the notional determinate sentence. For IPP sentences, the notional determinate sentence should not be greater than the maximum penalty for the offence. When that time has passed, the case can be referred to the Parole Board which presumes that release will not be directed unless the level of risk is acceptable.[271] From time to time, guidelines have been issued and have always treated terrorism as an especially serious factor. The 1983 version adopted a 20-year period for mandatory life prisoners in terrorist cases.[272] The Practice Statement (Crime: Life Sentences) 2002[273] still depicts some offences, including terrorism, as so grave that a 'minimum term' of twenty years and upwards could be appropriate.

6.118 Various sentencing practices as applied to terrorism reached a degree of maturity around the late 1980s. Conspiracy to murder and attempted murder commonly merited determinate sentences of between twenty and twenty-five years.[274] Cases of international terrorism have often attracted even heavier determinate sentences.[275] Forty-five years was imposed in *R v Hindawi*,[276] where the appellant had attempted to blow up a plane by hiding a bomb in the suitcase of his unwitting girlfriend. In *R v Al-Banna*,[277] sentences of up to thirty-five years were imposed for a Palestine National Liberation Movement attempt to assassinate the Israeli ambassador. In *R v Basra*, the Court awarded thirty-five years for arranging the murders of two political opponents within Sikh political factions.[278] However, in contrast to contemporary

---

[268] Sentencing Guidelines Council, *Dangerous Offenders* (London, 2008) para 6.1.2. For Scotland, see Criminal Justice (Scotland) Act 2003, s 1(1); Risk Management Authority, *Risk Management of Offenders Subject to an Order for Lifelong Restriction* (Paisley, 2007).

[269] See also Criminal Justice (Northern Ireland) Order 2008, SI 2008/1216.

[270] See Criminal Justice Act 2003, s 269 for mandatory life sentences.

[271] See the Crime Sentences Act 1997, s 28 (as amended).

[272] Hansard HC vol 49 cols 505–7 (30 November 1983), Leon Brittan; *In re Findlay* [1985] AC 318; *Pierson v Secretary of State for the Home Department* [1998] AC 539.

[273] [2002] 1 WLR 1789 (see now Amendment No 6 to the Consolidated Criminal Practice Direction [2004] 2 Cr App R 24 IV.49.33). For Northern Ireland, see *R v McCandless* [2004] NICA 1.

[274] See *R v Murphy and McKinley* [1993] 4 NIJB 42; *R v Secretary of State for the Home Department, ex parte McCartney* (1994) *The Times* 25 May 1994; *R v Murray* [1995] 6 BNIL n 88; *R v Magee and O'Hagan* [1996] 5 BNIL n 94.

[275] But see *R (Nejad) v Secretary of State for the Home Department* [2004] EWCA Civ 33 (22 years).

[276] (1988) 10 Cr App R (S) 104.

[277] (1984) 6 Cr App R (S) 426.

[278] (1989) 11 Cr App R (S) 527.

practices, the Court overturned a life sentence since the risk was not viewed as indeterminate. The minimum sentence for Al Megrahi's involvement in the Lockerbie bombing was twenty-seven years (under appeal when he was released).[279]

Explosives and firearms offences eventually attracted equally severe determinate sentences. Early sentences, such as in *R v Al-Mograbi and Cull*[280] (twelve years for an attack outside the Iraqi embassy), and *R v Assali*[281] (nine years) were soon surpassed. In *R v Anderson*,[282] Patrick Joseph Magee, the leader of the IRA group responsible for the bombing of the Grand Hotel, Brighton, in 1984 and later bombings, was sentenced to eight concurrent life terms with a recommendation that he serve a minimum of thirty-five years. More common sentences were in the environs of twenty years, with sentences in Northern Ireland[283] being slightly lighter than those in Britain.[284] Towards the end of the Irish Republican campaign in Britain, the Court of Appeal stated in *R v Martin*[285] that a twenty to thirty-year minimum term was normal for murder in aggravated form and that it was proper to consider equivalence to murder. So a conspiracy not designed to take life should be distinguished; twenty-eight years was the substituted sentence. Lord Bingham stated that 'In passing sentence for the most serious terrorist offences, the object of the court will be to punish, deter and incapacitate; rehabilitation is likely to play a minor (if any) part.'[286]   **6.119**

Sentences for criminal damage by animal welfare extremists are usually lower down the scale. Keith Mann[287] was sentenced to fourteen years' imprisonment for activities which 'often bore the hallmark of terrorism' and were committed by 'a determined and dangerous fanatic'. However, the 'lone wolf' racist, David Copeland, who planted bombs in public spaces in 1999, killing three and injuring 129, received six concurrent life sentences.[288] Mr Justice Burton described the bombings as a 'really exceptional case of deliberate, multiple murder' and doubted that it would ever be safe to release Copeland. The recommendation was a minimum of thirty years. After a reconsideration of that tariff under the Criminal Justice Act 2003, the judge set a minimum term of fifty years because of 'exceptional gravity'.[289]   **6.120**

---

[279] *The Times* 25 November 2003, p 8; <http://www.sccrc.org.uk/ViewFile.aspx?id=293>.
[280] (1980) 70 Cr App R 24.
[281] (1986) 8 Cr App R (S) 364. See further [2005] EWCA Crim 2031.
[282] [1988] QB 678. Compare *R v Gallagher The Times* 25 February 1998, p 2 (20 years for helping the IRA to attack Downing Street in 1991).
[283] *R v O'Reilly* [1989] NI 120 (17 years); *R v Payne* (1989) 9 NIJB 28 (19 years); *R v Cunningham and Devenny* (1989) 9 NIJB 12 (18 years); *R v Breslin and Forbes* [1990] 3 NIJB 96 (18 years); *R v McCorley* [1991] 4 NIJB 70 (22 years); *R v Carroll and Carroll* [1992] NIJB 93 (22 years); *R v McCaugherty and Gregory* [2010] NICC 35 (20 years).
[284] *R v Mullen* (1991) 12 Cr App R (S) 754 (30 years—conviction overturned on appeal: [2000] QB 520); *R v O'Dhuibir and McComb The Times* 7 December 1990, pp 1, 3 (30 years); *R v John William Kinsella* [1995] 16 Cr App R (S) 1035 (16 years); *R v McNulty The Times* 22 August 1994, pp 1, 3, 23 August 1994, p 7 (25 years); *R v Makin and Doherty, The Times* 22 October 1994, p 6 (25 years); *R v Felim O'Hadhmaill* [1996] Crim LR 509 (25 years); *R v Taylor, R v Hayes* (1995) 16 Cr App R (S) 873 (30 years); *R v Fryers and Jack, The Times* 21 January 1995, p 7 (25 years); *R v Cruickshank and O'Donnell* (1995) 16 Cr App R (S) 728 (16 years); *R v McGonagle and Heffernan* [1996] 1 Cr App R (S) 90 (25 years); *R v Mulholland and Grogan, The Times* 22 May 1999, p 11 (25 years); *R v Hulme* [2005] EWCA Crim 1196 (22 years); *R v McDonald* [2005] EWCA Crim 1945 (28 years).
[285] [1999] 1 Cr App Rep (S) 477. See also *R v McKinley and McCardle, The Times* 11 February 1998, p 3, 21 February 1998, p 2 (25 years); *R v Larmour* [2004] NICC 4 (15 years: mitigation arose through immaturity, a guilty plea, and illness).
[286] [1999] 1 Cr App Rep (S) 480.
[287] [1996] 2 Cr App R (S) 28 at 30.
[288] See Wolkind, M and Sweeney, N, 'R v David Copeland' (2001) 41 *Medicine, Science and the Law* 185.
[289] *Re Copeland* [2007] EWHC 368 (QB) at para 10.

6.121 Moving to the contemporary era, sentences have been severely ratcheted up in two directions: lengthier determinate sentences, plus more indeterminate life sentences.

6.122 In *R v Bourgass*,[290] the offender was convicted of the murder of a police officer, DC Stephen Oake, and was sentenced to life imprisonment for murder, with a minimum term fixed at twenty years and six months. He was also convicted of conspiracy to commit a public nuisance from the production of ricin (seventeen years).

6.123 In *R v Barot*,[291] the Court of Appeal held that discretionary life sentences will often be justified in terrorism cases since they involve 'A terrorist who is in the grip of idealistic extremism to the extent that, over a prolonged period, he has been plotting to commit murder of innocent citizens [and] is likely to pose a serious risk for an indefinite period if he is not confined'. As for the appropriate length of the minimum term, *R v Martin* (as above) was considered to be inadequate for terrorist conspiracies incurring the potential for mass injury and death.[292] The life sentence was upheld, with a minimum reduced from forty to thirty years because of a guilty plea and doubts about the certainty and viability of the 'Gas Limos Project'. A minimum term of forty years should be reserved for the terrorist convicted after trial, of a serious attempt to commit mass murder by a viable method. Thus, a minimum of forty years should represent the maximum for a terrorist who seeks mass murder but is not successful.[293] Where the offence is conspiracy, and the acts of the defendant fall short of imminent attempt, the sentence should be lower.[294] Where the seriousness of the offence is 'particularly high' but not exceptionally high, the starting point is a minimum term of thirty years.[295] In a case of 'merciless and extreme crimes', as with the 21 July bombers, life with a minimum of forty years can be merited.[296] Where mass murder flows from the actions of the offenders, whole life terms will be imposed.

6.124 In *R v Abdul Aziz Jalil*,[297] the three accomplices of Barot pleaded guilty to conspiring to cause explosions of a nature likely to endanger life. The principal conspirator pleaded guilty in separate proceedings to conspiracy to murder and was sentenced to life imprisonment with a minimum term of thirty years. The appellants were sentenced to extended sentences ranging from twenty-six years down to fifteen years with an extension period in each case of five years. The sentence of twenty-six years presupposes a starting point of around thirty to thirty-three years after trial—in other words, approximately double that served nowadays by the worst kind of murderers and certainly exceeding the figures canvassed in *Martin*.

6.125 These guidelines were further applied in *R v Asiedu* to another conspirator to murder in the 21 July 2005 attempted bombings.[298] A 33-year minimum following a guilty plea was upheld. The Court also diverted from the suggestion in *Barot* that leaders would merit longer

---

[290] See [2005] EWCA Crim 1943, [2006] EWCA Crim 3397.
[291] [2007] EWCA Crim 1119 at para 37.
[292] But *Martin* may still be relevant for more directed terrorism in Ireland: *R v McKenna* [2009] NICC 55.
[293] [2007] EWCA Crim 1119 at para 60.
[294] See Criminal Justice Act 2003, Sch 21; *Attorney General's References (Nos 85, 86 and 87 of 2007)*, *R v Tsouli* [2007] EWCA Crim 3300 at para 41; *R v Timlin* [2007] EWHC 1225 (QB) (25 years); *R v Khyam* [2008] EWCA Crim 1612 (20 years).
[295] [2007] EWCA Crim 1119 at para 56.
[296] See *R v Ibrahim* [2008] EWCA Crim 880 at para 166.
[297] [2008] EWCA Crim 2910.
[298] [2008] EWCA Crim 1725 at para 33. Other minimum tariffs were: 40 years (Abdulla Ahmed Ali), 36 years (Assad Sarwar); 32 years (Tanvir Hussain), 24 years (Umar Islam) and 20 years (Arafat Waheed Khan, Ibrahim Savant, Waheed Zaman): *The Times* 10 September 2009, p 8, 13 July 2010, p 4.

sentences than followers; no distinction was drawn on the basis that the offenders had acted independently at the point of attack.[299]

There is occasional leniency, if a person has turned away from terrorism and prevented an **6.126** attack. A rare example is Saajid Badat,[300] a colleague of Richard Reid and also equipped with a shoe bomb. Unlike Reid, he cut his ties with the *jihadis* and left the bomb components hidden in his parents' house in Gloucester. After a guilty plea, the sentence was thirteen years.[301]

These policies of extraordinarily severe sentences for terrorists raise issues about differential **6.127** treatment under Articles 5 and 14. In *R (Hindawi) v Secretary of State for the Home Department*,[302] it was stated that a long-term determinate prisoner should be released when it was judged safe to release him. Neither the public interest nor the interest of the offender was well served by continuing to detain a prisoner until the end of his publicly pronounced sentence on the basis of general deterrent policy rather than individual circumstances. The exclusion of Hindawi's case from consideration by the Parole Board because he was liable to deportation was also not justifiable.

Aside from the most serious terrorism cases, a range of other offences have been examined in **6.128** sentencing terms. For example, the rate for solicitation of murder by *jihadis* was at first around seven years.[303] However, a step change occurred in *R v Tsouli*.[304] Sentences imposed for conspiring to incite murder under the TA 2000, s 59, through the creation of *jihadi* websites and internet forums, following guilty pleas after the trial had lasted for nine weeks, were considered unduly lenient. The leading sentence was increased to sixteen years from ten years.

Next, in *R v Da Costa*,[305] two appellants were convicted of, or pleaded guilty to, solicitation **6.129** of murder through meetings and trips for the purpose of training. The appellants appealed against their sentences of IPP with a minimum term of seven-and-a-half years, derived from a notional determinate sentence of fifteen years, and a determinate sentence of seven-and-a-half years, based on an appropriate determinate sentence after trial of ten years' imprisonment, respectively. The earlier sentences in *El Faisal* and *Abu Hamza* were viewed as inadequate, and the appeals were rejected.

Provisions—enhanced sentences

Despite any scintilla of leniency revealed by the foregoing narrative, several reviewers have **6.130** sought to impart stronger statements of deterrence in terrorist sentences.[306] The idea was eventually translated into action by the CTA 2008.[307]

Section 30 allows enhanced sentencing in England and Wales in relation to specified offences **6.131** which have or may have a 'terrorist connection'. The specified offences in Sch 2, which can be amended by affirmative order under s 33, are outside the terrorism legislation and include

---

[299] *R v Ibrahim* [2008] EWCA Crim 880 at para 165.
[300] *The Times* 1 March 2005, pp 1, 6.
[301] <http://news.bbc.co.uk/1/hi/uk/4474307.stm>.
[302] [2006] UKHL 54.
[303] *R v El-Faisal* [2004] EWCA Crim 343, [2004] EWCA Crim 456; *R v Abu Hamza* [2006] EWCA Crim 2918 (seven years); *R v Saleem, Muhid, and Javed* [2007] EWCA Crim 2692 (six years).
[304] [2007] EWCA Crim 3300.
[305] [2009] EWCA Crim 482.
[306] See *Lloyd Report*, ch 15; *Newton Report*, para 44.
[307] Home Office, *Government Discussion Document Ahead of Proposed Counter Terrorism Bill 2007* (Home Office, London, 2007) para 9 and *Possible Measures for Inclusion into a Future Counter-Terrorism Bill* (London, 2007) para 38.

homicides, explosives offences, and offences relating to weapons of mass destruction. Section 31 applies in Scotland (and without requiring more than one witness); service cases fall under s 32. However, the measures do not affect Northern Ireland, presumably because of political sensitivity about terrorism sentencing. Penalties for terrorism legislation offences are of course already set appropriately for that context.

6.132 In applying s 30, the court must first determine whether there is a terrorist connection. This deliberation is treated as a sentencing issue (s 30(3)), so the criminal standard of proof will apply but the decision is judicial.[308] Any dispute over evidence will entail further consideration of the trial evidence or evidence adduced after a guilty plea in a Newton hearing.[309] If a terrorist connection is established, then the court must treat it as an aggravating factor and must so state in open court but not before a jury.

6.133 Given the sentencing history adduced earlier, this provision is of marginal impact. The Home Office somehow believed that the fact that many terrorists are charged with offences other than those under the anti-terrorism legislation prevented enhanced sentences.[310] It is arguable that the non-appearance of an offence in Sch 2 might in future dissuade the court from an enhanced sentence. Perhaps the objective was also to forestall any judicial reversal of the policy of draconian sentences, the sole sign of which emerged in *R v Rahman, R v Mohammed*,[311] where it was feared that excessive sentences would 'inflame rather than deter extremism'.

6.134 Another criticism is that the designation of a case as 'terrorist connected' is a matter for the judge rather than the jury. Thus, it may be unfair to apply an extra penalty where a terrorist connection cannot be sustained beyond reasonable doubt before a jury, especially in situations where 'pretext' offences are charged.[312]

Provisions—incentives

6.135 Sentencing law and policy next arises in the guise of an incentive to end terrorism. It has been so used in two contexts within the United Kingdom and elsewhere.

6.136 One is to grant incentives for cooperation, as in the case of 'supergrasses' in Northern Ireland in the 1980s, with counterparts in Italy (*pentiti*), Spain, and elsewhere.[313] However, this tactic will not be explored further. The nature and scale of the tactic became discredited in Northern Ireland, and the laws relating to incentives for witnesses have now been translated (except in Scotland) into the Serious Organised Crime and Police Act 2005, ss 71 to 75.[314]

6.137 The second aspect of incentives is the grant of an amnesty or concessions on sentences to convicted terrorist prisoners. Given that in a mature and organized campaign of terrorism, much of the leadership will in time reside in prison, this tactic is of crucial impact. Certainly, early release was critical to the Northern Ireland 'Peace Process', whereby the concessions under the Northern Ireland (Remission of Sentences) Act 1995 and the Northern Ireland

---

[308] Hansard HC Public Bill Committee on the Counter-Terrorism Bill col 381 (8 May 2008), Tony McNulty.

[309] See Lord Carlile, *Report on Proposed Measures for Inclusion in a Counter-Terrorism Bill* (Cm 7262, London, 2007) para 27.

[310] The measure also links to notification (Home Office, *Possible Measures for Inclusion into a Future Counter-Terrorism Bill* (London, 2007) para 39) but does not have to be dependent.

[311] [2008] EWCA Crim 1465 at para 8.

[312] Home Affairs Committee, *The Government's Counter-Terrorism Proposals* (2007–08 HC 43) para 97.

[313] See Greer, SC, *Supergrasses* (Clarendon Press, Oxford, 1995). The policy is endorsed by Council Framework Decision 2002/475/JHA of 3 June 2002, art 6.

[314] See Joint Committee on Human Rights, *Counter-Terrorism Policy and Human Rights: Prosecution and Pre-Charge Detention* (2005–06 HL 240/HC 1576) para 110.

(Sentences) Act 1998 aided the success of the enterprise, allied to immunity from prosecution under the Northern Ireland Arms Decommissioning Act 1997. These initiatives will be considered in Chapter 11.

Imprisonment of terrorists

Regime

At the height of 'The Troubles' in Northern Ireland, terrorists formed the bulk of high-risk prisoners.[315] Their reactions to imprisonment included escapes,[316] disturbances,[317] and litigation.[318] By contrast, terrorist prisoners in Britain are fewer in number and have been less resistant to security regimes.[319] Techniques used to maintain security have included searching, bugging, and rotation.[320]

6.138

As well as security, a policy of sanitization has also been pursued to prevent the subversion of other Muslim prisoners by the one hundred or so convicted *jihadis*.[321] Problems have been reported at HMP Whitemoor[322] and HMP Belmarsh.[323] These problems cause difficulties for staff from different cultures who then apply undiscerning treatment to all Muslim prisoners[324] and fail to distinguish threats to security from legitimate demands for religious autonomy or social solidarity.[325] Tough prison regimes designed to achieve security and the isolation of *jihadis* from young Muslim prisoners, were held not to breach Articles 3 and 8 in *R (Bary) v Secretary of State for Justice*.[326] Similar challenges about isolation, bodily searches, and surveillance have failed in most cases before the European Court of Human Rights.[327]

6.139

---

[315] See Von Tangen Page, M, *Prisons, Peace and Terrorism: Penal Policy in the Reduction of Political Violence in Northern Ireland, Italy and the Spanish Basque Country, 1968–97* (St Martin's Press, London, 1998); Crawford, C, *Defenders or Criminals? Loyalist Prisoners and Criminalisation* (Blackstaff Press, Belfast, 1999); Ryder, C, *Inside the Maze* (Methuen, London, 2000); McEvoy, K, *Paramilitary Imprisonment in Northern Ireland* (Oxford University Press, Oxford, 2001).

[316] See especially *Report of an Inquiry by HM Chief Inspector of Prisons into the security arrangements at HM Prison, Maze relative to the escape on Sunday 25th September 1983* (Cmnd 203, HMSO, London, 1984); *Report of the Inquiry into the Escape of Six Prisoners from the Special Security Unit at Whitemoor Prison, Cambridgeshire on Friday 9th September 1994* (Cmnd 2741, HMSO, London); *Report of an inquiry into the escape of a prisoner from HMP Maze on 10 December 1997 and the shooting of a prisoner on 27 December 1997* (1997–98 HC 658).

[317] See Coogan, TP, *On the Blanket* (Palgrave Macmillan, Basingtoke, 2003).

[318] See Livingstone, S et al, *Prison Law* (4th edn, Oxford University Press, Oxford, 2008).

[319] See *The Times* 12 August 2005, p 7 (a 'firecracker'); *R v G* [2009] UKHL 13 (materials).

[320] See Bates-Gaston, J, 'Terrorism and imprisonment in Northern Ireland' in Silke, A (ed), *Terrorists, Victims and Society* (Wiley, Chichester, 2003); Warnes, R and Hannah, G, 'Meeting the Challenge of Extremist and Radicalized Prisoners' (2008) 2 *Policing* 402; Spalek, B, El Awa, S, and Lambert, R, 'Preventing violent extremism in prison' (2008) 180 *Prison Service Journal* 45.

[321] See Pluchinsky, DA, 'Global jihadist recidivism' (2008) 31 *Studies in Conflict and Terrorism* 182; Home Office, *The United Kingdom's Strategy for Countering International Terrorism Annual Report 2010* (London: Cm 7833, 2010) para 3.07. As at July 2007, there were fifty-eight on remand, forty-three convicted, eleven held for deportation, and eleven for extradition (fifty-eight in HMP Belmarsh): Constitutional Affairs Committee, *Towards Effective Sentencing* (2007–08 HC 184-II) Q256.

[322] HM Chief Inspector of Prisons, *Report on an unannounced full follow-up inspection of HMP Whitemoor* (London, 2008) para 3.79.

[323] HM Chief Inspector of Prisons, *Report on a full announced inspection of HMP Belmarsh 8–12 October 2007* (London, 2008).

[324] HM Chief Inspector of Prisons, *Muslim Prisoners' Experiences* (London, 2010).

[325] See Beckford, JA, Joly, D, and Khosrokhavar, F, *Muslims in Prison* (Palgrave Macmillan, Basingstoke, 2005).

[326] [2010] EWHC 587 (Admin).

[327] *Ensslin, Baader and Raspe v Germany*, App nos 7572/76, 7586/76 and 7587/76, DR 14, p 64 (1978); *Kröcher and Möller v Switzerland*, App no 8463/78, DR 34, p 24 (1982); *Öcalan v Turkey*, App no 46221/99, 12 May 2005; *Sanchez v France*, App no 59450/00, 4 July 2006; *Frérot v France*, App no 70204/01, 12 June 2007; *A v United Kingdom*, App no 3455/05, 19 February 2009.

6.140 Responses include the appointment of Prison Service Imams and a mentoring programme for those Muslim prisoners 'potentially susceptible to radicalisation or extremist views and which supports them upon their release from prison to integrate back into their local community'.[328] An Extremism Unit was formed in 2007 to address risks of extremism and radicalization affecting offenders both in custody and under supervision in the community.[329]

6.141 At the same time, there is a refusal to grant special privileges or political status for terrorism prisoners, following the withdrawal of special status for paramilitary prisoners in Northern Ireland in 1976 and then the bitter resistance, culminating in Republican hunger strikes in 1981.[330] Further challenges arose from Loyalist prisoners around the segregation of prisoners.[331]

6.142 As for rehabilitation, no de-radicalization programme has emerged either in Northern Ireland or in British prisons.[332] Its absence was underlined in *R (Botmeh and Alami) v Parole Board*.[333] Parole Board decisions to refuse to release convicted bombers on licence were lawful given the majority view of experts that clinical psychology could offer little guidance on risk assessment for politically motivated offenders. In addition, the bombers continued to deny their guilt in bombing Israeli targets.

6.143 Despite the continued perception of risk,[334] whether now or in the past in Northern Ireland, there is a low reconviction rate. In Northern Ireland, only 9 per cent of persons convicted of scheduled offences were convicted of similar offences within two years.[335] The explanation is probably not any genuine recantation of political views but the creation of a security risk from the designation as a convict.

Provisions—transfers

6.144 The location of imprisonment for terrorist convicts provided another dispute for Republican prisoners, who sought transfer from Britain to prisons in Northern Ireland under the Criminal Justice Act 1961, s 26.[336] Following the (Earl Ferrers) *Interdepartmental Working Group Review of provisions for the transfer of prisoners between United Kingdom jurisdictions, 1992*,[337] the policy of almost blanket refusals was modified, and transfers were granted, albeit on a temporary basis so as to retain remission periods.[338]

---

[328] See Home Office, *Countering International Terrorism* (Cm 6888, London, 2006) para 51.

[329] Hansard HL vol 714 col 229wa (12 November 2009).

[330] See Walker, C, 'Irish Republican prisoners' (1984) 19 *Irish Jurist* 189; Williams, J, 'Hunger-strikes: A prisoner's right or a "wicked folly"?' (2001) 40 *Howard Journal of Criminal Justice* 285; McEvoy, K, *Paramilitary Imprisonment in Northern Ireland* (Oxford University Press, Oxford, 2001) ch 4.

[331] (Colville) *Report on the Operational Policy in Belfast Prison for the Management of Paramilitary Prisoners from Opposing Factions* (Cmnd 1860, London, 1992); (Ramsbotham) *HM Prison The Maze (Northern Ireland): Report of a Full Inspection* (1997–98 HC 369).

[332] See Brandon, J, *Unlocking Al-Qaeda* (Quilliam, London, 2009); Neumann, PR (ed), *Prisons and Terrorism* (ICSR, London, 2010).

[333] [2008] EWHC 1115 (Admin).

[334] See Dwyer, C, 'Risk, politics and the "scientification" of political judgement' (2007) 47 *British Journal of Criminology* 779.

[335] *Baker Report*, para 455.

[336] See *R v Secretary of State for the Home Department, ex parte McComb* (QBD, 1990); *Re Grogan* (NI QBD, 1993); *R v Secretary of State for the Home Department, ex parte McLaughlin* (CA, 1996).

[337] See Hansard HC vol 214 cols 476–7 (23 November 1992), Peter Lloyd.

[338] See *Re O'Dwyer and Quigley* (NI CA, 1996); *Re Kavanagh* [1997] NI 368.

Foreign transfer (including to the Republic of Ireland) depends on either a multilateral or **6.145** bilateral treaty,[339] as enforced by the Repatriation of Prisoners Act 1985. A notable example is the transfer of Al Megrahi—convicted of the Lockerbie bombing—back to Libya in 2009, albeit on compassionate grounds.[340] In Australia, the International Transfer of Prisoners Amendment Act 2004 allows for transfer of Australian citizens convicted by a US military tribunal to serve out the imprisonment in Australia. But those returned from Guantánamo to the United Kingdom have all been released without charge after initial detention, though some have had passports withdrawn.[341]

Release conditions

For released prisoners (including Lifers and Indeterminate Public Protection Sentence **6.146** Offenders), the Multi-Agency Public Protection Arrangements (MAPPA) are set out under the Criminal Justice Act 2003, ss 325–327.[342] MAPPA requires the 'Responsible Authority', the police, National Probation Service, and prisons service, to work together to make arrangements for assessing and managing risks posed by (Category 2) violent offenders who have received a custodial sentence of twelve months or more and (Category 3) persons who pose a risk of serious harm to the public.

Terrorist convicts may become eligible for MAPPA arrangements in various ways.[343] Within **6.147** IPP arrangements, specified 'violent offences' under s 224 mention, following the Coroners and Justice Act 2009, s 138, a wide range of terrorism offences which make terrorists automatically eligible as MAPPA Category 1 or 2 offenders. For other terrorist offenders, the nature of their offence and the risk they pose to the public must be assessed as exceptional, qualifying them as Category 3 offenders. Management plans (devised by Multi-Agency Public Protection Panels) might relate to residence, supervision, meetings, movements, associations, and duties to report and to engage in counselling.[344] Many 'domestic extremism' offenders will not automatically be included in MAPPA due to the nature of the offences they committed, but consideration must be given to the impact on the victim and the offender's attitude towards their offending behaviour which may result in designation as a Category 3 offender.[345]

Foreign comparisons

The severity of terrorist imprisonment is reflected abroad. For example, the Organic Law **6.148** 7/2003 of 30 June 2003 in Spain increased the maximum sentence to forty years and made 'social reinsertion' conditional on abandonment of terrorist aims and cooperation with the authorities.[346] In Australia, the Anti-Terrorism Act 2004 (as s 19AG of the Crimes Act 1914) specifies extended non-parole periods for terrorism convicts.

---

[339] See <http://www.fco.gov.uk/en/about-us/publications-and-documents/treaties/treaty-texts/prisoner-transfer-agreements>.

[340] *The Times* 21 August 2009, p 1. See further Chapter 11.

[341] *The Guardian* 17 February 2005, p 10.

[342] See also Management of Offenders etc (Scotland) Act 2005 and the Criminal Justice (NI) Order 2008, SI 2008/1216, which sets up the Public Protection Arrangements Northern Ireland (PPANI).

[343] Note that 'Potentially Dangerous Persons' may also be monitored: ACPO, *Guidance on Protecting the Public: Managing Sexual and Violent Offenders* (2007).

[344] See National Offender Management Service Public Protection Unit, *MAPPA Guidance* (Version 3.0, 2009) para 16.2.

[345] Ibid para 15.4.

[346] Oehmichen, A, *Terrorism and Anti-Terror Legislation* (Intersentia, Antwerp, 2009) p 219.

6.149 However, there is European disengagement from the death penalty under the influence of Protocols 6 and 13 of the European Convention on Human Rights. The final vestige in terrorism cases in the United Kingdom ended with the EPA 1973, s 1.[347] No execution related to terrorism had been carried out since 1942. Past episodes in history, such as the suppression of the Easter Rising in Dublin in 1916, were telling episodes against its revival, as well as the more recent experiences of grievous miscarriages of justice in terrorism cases.[348] Likewise, the death penalty was abolished in the Republic of Ireland by the Criminal Justice Act 1990.[349] However, terrorist homicides remain prime candidates for capital punishment in the US. After the Oklahoma bombing, the Antiterrorism and Effective Death Penalty Act 1996 was passed to ease its use.[350]

6.150 Penal regimes abroad, in Egypt, Saudi Arabia, Yemen, and Indonesia, have devised de-radicalization programmes, though their effectiveness remains a matter of conjecture.[351]

6.151 Other forms of sentence applied to terrorist offenders include disqualification for seven years from public office following conviction for scheduled offences by the Special Criminal Court under the Irish Offences against the State Act 1939, s 34. Following successful challenge in *Cox v Ireland*[352] on grounds of disproportionality and discrimination, the Hederman Commission has recommended repeal.[353]

Assessment and conclusions

6.152 The penology of terrorism in the United Kingdom reflects above all retribution and public protection, with the latter growing in importance. Thus, 'Pursue' is to the fore with little 'Prevent' work by way of de-radicalization programmes.

6.153 Decisions on sentencing have been judicialized under the influence of Article 6 of the European Convention, so that a more effective rights audit has been put in place. Nevertheless, the judges have presided over a severe ratcheting up of punishments since 2001.

6.154 Accountability and constitutional governance have been less well delivered. The policies are piecemeal and not scrutinized by the independent reviewer. A study of sentencing in terrorism is overdue, though HM Inspector of Prisons has commendably begun to apply close attention to penal regimes.

6.155 A future agenda item for discussion is the development of an alternative social control of terrorism so as to make available a range of interventions by way of assessment, counselling, and assimilation for those on the threshold of political violence or those who have committed

---

[347] See Hogan, G and Walker, C, *Political Violence and the Law in Ireland* (Manchester University Press, Manchester, 1989) p 154.

[348] See Walker, CP and Starmer, K (ed), *Miscarriages of Justice* (Blackstone Press, London, 1999); Roach, K and Trotter, G, 'Miscarriages of justice in the war against terrorism' (2005) 109 *Penn State Law Review* 967.

[349] See also Twenty-first Amendment of the Constitution of Ireland 2001; *Whelan v Minister for Justice, Equality and Law Reform* [2008] 2 IR 142.

[350] PL 104-132.

[351] Counter-Terrorism Implementation Task Force, *First Report of the Working Group on Radicalisation and Extremism that Lead to Terrorism: Inventory of State Programs* (UNICRI, Rome, 2008); Ashour, O, *The De-Radicalization of Jihadists* (Routledge, Abingdon, 2009); Bjørgo, T, and Horgan, J, *Leaving Terrorism Behind* (Routledge, Abingdon, 2009) chs 10–13; Horgan, J, *Walking Away from Terrorism* (Routledge, Abingdon, 2009); Horgan, J and Braddock, K, 'Rehabilitating the terrorists?' (2010) 22 *Terrorism & Political Violence* 267.

[352] [1992] 2 IR 503. See also *Murphy v Ireland* [1996] 3 IR 307; *McDonnell v Ireland* [1998] 1 IR 134.

[353] *Report of the Committee to Review the Offences against the State Acts 1939–1998* (Dublin, 2002) para 6.190.

minor infractions.[354] The Home Office has latterly recognized the need to apply a layered approach to counter-terrorism.[355] A prime example is 'Project Channel' whereby responsible citizens in Muslim communities provide an early warning system for the identification of extremists.[356] Social intervention in the forms of counselling and engagement in approved activities are then applied. Though this non-security label is put upon the project, there arise attendant dangers of loose labelling and net-widening by 'self-appointed busybodies'.[357]

E. Post-Punishment

Introduction and background

The realms of risk management of offenders are taken to the next stage by Pt IV of the CTA **6.156** 2008. Though 'administrative justice', the requirements are backed by criminal offences in the event of default under s 54.

Provisions—notification

Notification is modelled on other 'punishment-plus' measures, especially the sex offender **6.157** registration now under the Sexual Offences Act 2003, Pt II.[358] This same idea applies via MAPPA to 'dangerous' violent and sexual offenders by the Criminal Justice Act 2003. By comparison, Pt IV is a more formalistic system which seeks to monitor without the more positive social intervention aspects under MAPPA. More schemes of notification, for violent offenders and persons with designated special immigration status, are in the Criminal Justice and Immigration Act 2008, Pts VII and X.[359] Orders in that context are of shorter duration (two to five years) and must be expressly applied by a court.

Notification applies to a person aged over 16 and sentenced to imprisonment for one year or **6.158** more (ss 44, 45, and 46) for a terrorism legislation offence (as listed in s 41) or for an offence with a terrorism connection (as described in s 42 and relying on the list in Sch 2).[360] In Northern Ireland, only offences under s 41 are relevant. Service court sentences fall under Sch 6. The obligation of notification is automatically imposed, though the existence of a terrorist connection can be appealed against under s 42(2).

Initial notification under s 47 demands the transmission of details about identity, residence, **6.159** and travel to the police, to be delivered in person within three days of release from detention (s 50). There follow two subsequent duties—notification of changes (s 48) and periodic re-notification (s 49). Changes are defined to include staying at an address in the United Kingdom for a period of seven days or for a combined period of seven days within twelve months. Periodic re-notification is annual, regardless of changes. Complex rules under ss 55 and

---

354 See Allen, CA, 'Alternatives to prosecution for war crimes in the war on terrorism' (2008) 17 *Transnational Law & Contemporary Problems* 121.

355 Home Office, *From the Neighbourhood to the National* (Cm 7448, London, 2008) paras 1.49–1.51.

356 Home Office, *Channel: Supporting individuals vulnerable to recruitment by violent extremists* (London: 2010).

357 Siddiqui, H, 'Muslim-bashing dilutes our democratic values', *Toronto Star* 11 June 2006, p A17.

358 Hansard HC Public Bill Committee on the Counter-Terrorism Bill col 408 (13 May 2008), Tony McNulty. For detailed implementation, see Home Office, *Guidance on the Notification Requirements under Part 4 of the Counter Terrorism Act 2008 and Associated Orders* (London, 2009).

359 See Home Office, *Saving Lives, Reducing Harm, Protecting the Public* (London, 2008) pp 6, 43, *A Guide to Violent Offender Orders* (London, 2009).

360 See s 43 for offences committed before commencement.

56 deal with the impact of absence abroad. The police must issue a written acknowledgment of receipt of the details and, on attendance, may take fingerprints and photographs.[361]

6.160 The duration of notification is regulated by s 53. For persons over 18 at the time of conviction and sentenced to life imprisonment or imprisonment for ten years or more, the period is thirty years. A period of fifteen years applies to those sentenced to five to ten years. Otherwise, the period is ten years (including for all offenders aged 16 and 17). These lengthy periods arise because the government believed that it would not secure renewals of orders: 'The fact that a person has not reoffended is not sufficient to establish the absence of such a risk.'[362]

6.161 Notification can also be applied under s 57 and Sch 4 to persons convicted of terrorism offences abroad. Applications may be made by the chief police officer for the area where the individual resides or is landing. Schedule 4, para 2(4), deems that the foreign offence corresponds to an offence to which Pt IV applies unless disputed by the defendant. If the conditions are met, then the High Court must make an order (para 3). It is denied that this requires proof to a criminal standard.[363] One might argue in response that notification denounces the character of the person and paves the way for prohibition and so should be proven to a high standard. No appeal route is offered, but para 3(3) excepts notification where the foreign conviction involved a flagrant denial of the right to a fair trial.[364]

Provisions—overseas travel restrictions

6.162 Overseas travel restrictions not only prevent wrongdoing abroad but may also further criminal processes.[365]

6.163 As a sub-set of measures within notification, compulsory foreign travel notification can arise under s 52.[366] The power is to be triggered by statutory order. It will be easier to apply the power in all cases of notification so as to firm up the impression that these orders are regulatory rather than selectively punitive and therefore within Article 6(3). If applicable, the person must notify to the police details of departure, destination, and return. Detailed rules limit the obligations to travel for three days or more, but require notice between twenty-four hours and seven days of the due date, and notice of return within three days.[367]

6.164 Next, foreign travel restriction orders are instituted by s 58 and Sch 5.[368] A court can prohibit a person from travelling abroad to any specified country or all countries where it is necessary to prevent engagement in terrorism abroad. The conditions to be met are in para 2: the person must be subject to the notification requirements and must, since being sentenced, have behaved in a way that makes it necessary to prevent him from taking part in

---

[361] It is not clear whether 'photograph' includes an iris scan. Compare Immigration and Asylum Act 1999, s 144; Nationality, Immigration and Asylum Act 2002, s 126; Asylum and Immigration (Treatment of Claimants, etc) Act 2004, s 35; Identity Cards Act 2006, s 42.

[362] Hansard HL vol 704 col 795 (13 October 2008), Lord West.

[363] Hansard HC Public Bill Committee on the Counter-Terrorism Bill col 425 (13 May 2008), Tony McNulty.

[364] See *EM (Lebanon) v Secretary of State for the Home Department* [2008] UKHL 64.

[365] Home Office, *Government Discussion Document Ahead of Proposed Counter Terrorism Bill 2007* (Home Office, London, 2007) para 14 and *Possible Measures for Inclusion into a Future Counter-Terrorism Bill* (London, 2007) para 50.

[366] Home Office, *Possible Measures for Inclusion into a Future Counter-Terrorism Bill* (London, 2007) para 50.

[367] Counter Terrorism Act 2008 (Foreign Travel Notification Requirements) Regulations 2009, SI 2009/2493.

[368] Ibid para 51. See further Magistrates' Courts (Counter Terrorism Act 2008) (Foreign Travel Restriction Orders) Rules (Northern Ireland) 2010, SR NI 2010/13.

terrorism abroad. As under Sch 4, the application must be made by a chief officer of police but in this case to a magistrates' or sheriff's court. The standard of proof in respect of the behaviour will be the heightened civil standard described in *R v Crown Court of Manchester, ex parte McCann*.[369] The magistrates' court has discretion as to its response (para 2(5)) and is subject to appeal to the Crown Court (paras 12 to 14). Breach of an order is an offence under para 15. A person subject to an order prohibiting all foreign travel must surrender all their passports to the police (whether UK or foreign, under s 60). The order lasts for a fixed period of up to six months at a time (para 7).

The device of foreign travel restriction is proliferating and has been imposed on football **6.165** hooligans,[370] sex offenders,[371] drug traffickers,[372] and violent offenders.[373] It may even be consistent with Magna Carta of 1215, para 42, which excludes from free movement persons 'that have been imprisoned or outlawed'. It might also avoid disproportionate resort to control orders and certainly avoids reliance on archaic measures such as the writ of *ne exeat regno*.[374] But the measure may encourage a net-widening impact since it involves far less scrutiny than for control orders, not least because it falls within mere restriction on freedom of movement rather than liberty.

Implementation

The measures do not yet have any published track record.   **6.166**

Assessment and conclusions

Notification orders are designed to aid the detection of crime and act as a deterrent through **6.167** the creation of a prolonged stigma within 'Pursue'.[375] They are preventative in nature but still depend on a prior conviction, unlike for control orders.

The automatic application of notification creates extra workload for the police, takes no **6.168** proportionate heed of individual circumstances of privacy,[376] and signals the failure of criminal justice penal process to avert risk.[377] Notification and especially travel restrictions may also breach European Union law (European Directive 2004/38) as applied to foreigners since the restrictions on movement should be based on public policy grounds and not simply on previous convictions.[378] A prolonged order is simply an admission that there is no specific suspicion of involvement at any given point. The system lacks clarity as to the bounds of lawful requirements, and the extension to overseas crimes could amount to an endorsement of discrimination and procedural unfairness. Different countries have very different conceptions of terrorism.

---

[369] [2002] UKHL 39.

[370] Football Spectators Act 1989; Football (Offences and Disorder) Act 1999.

[371] Sexual Offences Act 2003, s 114.

[372] Criminal Justice and Police Act 2001, s 33.

[373] Criminal Justice and Immigration Act 2008, Pt VII. Note also the more general serious crime prevention order under the Serious Crime Act 2007 (see Chapter 7).

[374] Ministry of Justice, *The Governance of Britain: Review of the Executive Royal Prerogative Powers: Final Report* (London, 2009) p 34. For contemporary usage, see *R v Home Secretary, ex parte Muboyayi* [1992] 1 QB 244 at 258.

[375] Home Office, *Possible Measures for Inclusion into a Future Counter-Terrorism Bill* (London, 2007) paras 47, 48.

[376] Compare *R (Wright) v Secretary of State for Health* [2009] UKHL 3; *R (F) v Secretary of State for Justice* [2010] UKSC 17.

[377] Compare Northern Ireland (Sentences) Act 1998, s 9.

[378] See European Parliament and Council Directive 2004/38/EC of 29 April 2004, art 28, as implemented by Immigration (European Economic Area) Regulations 2006, SI 2006/1003.

6.169 As for accountability and constitutional governance, no formal review mechanisms are put in place, but the independent reviewer has promised to address these measures.[379]

F. Conclusions

6.170 The prime focus of United Kingdom anti-terrorism policy and laws in the aftermath of 9/11 seemed to be on Belmarsh rather than the Old Bailey—in other words, upon detention without trial and latterly on control orders. However, this era of executive measures was never exclusive and is fading, and the emphasis in later legislation has involved a reinvigoration of a criminal justice approach to terrorism which is generally to be welcomed.

6.171 Consistent with normative values, criminal prosecution highly prizes individual responsibility, through solemn and open process. Next, there are also gains for system legality through the 'expressive justification' of prosecution and punishment not only to participants but also to onlookers, especially those from communities from which accused persons are drawn.[380] Thirdly, criminal prosecution secures compliance with international law. This chapter commenced with the demand of UNSCR 1373, art 2(e), and other international instruments also call for the application of criminal justice.[381]

6.172 However, the focus on criminal justice engenders a set of new dangers. The main concerns for the individual defendant are procedural rather than institutional—the pressures on open justice and equality of arms.[382] Other drawbacks relate to collective rather than individual impacts. There might arise the troubling collective perception of the courts protecting the state and not victims. But the appearance is surely worse with more secretive executive measures.

6.173 The complications of prosecuting terrorists have been shown to be less severe than initially feared when, in an early Al-Qa'ida-related trial in Leicester, 'Two juries were discharged after members said they were either too scared to try the case or had been so prejudiced by reports of terrorism and asylum seekers that they could not return a fair verdict.'[383] Nevertheless, the fundamental paradox of proof beyond doubt in a climate of precautionary logic encourages a slide towards minimum standards of due process. The trend should be countered by the courts acting as expert guardians in their own domain. They should contend that the old methods are tried and tested and better avoid hunger strikes, a loss of legitimacy, minority community disenchantment, and miscarriages of justice. One must be more sceptical, however, about the current effectiveness of the penology of terrorism other than as a form of incapacitation.[384]

---

[379] Lord Carlile, *Report on the Operation in 2001–2008 of the Terrorism Act 2000* (Home Office, London) para 264.

[380] See Drumbl, MA, 'The expressive value of prosecuting and punishing terrorists' (2007) 75 *George Washington Law Review* 1165 at 1170.

[381] See Special Rapporteur on the promotion and protection of human rights and fundamental freedoms while countering terrorism, *First Report to the Human Rights Commission, Promotion and Protection of Human Rights* (E/CN.4/2006/98, 2005).

[382] See *Report of the Special Rapporteur on the promotion and protection of human rights and fundamental freedoms while countering terrorism* (A/63/223, 2008) paras 17, 30, 35.

[383] *The Daily Telegraph* 2 April 2003, p 12. See *R v Meziane* [2004] EWCA Crim 176.

[384] Roach, K, 'Anti-terrorism and militant democracy' in Sajo, A (ed), *Militant Democracy* (Eleven International, Utrecht, 2004) p 186 and 'The criminal law and terrorism' in Ramraj, VV, Hor, M, and Roach, K, *Global Anti-terrorism Law and Policy* (Cambridge University Press, Cambridge, 2005) p 136.

PART IV

OTHER LEGAL CONTROLS

7

EXECUTIVE POWERS OVER INDIVIDUALS

A. Background[1]

Policy background

Having preached the virtues of criminalization in Chapter 6, this chapter will explore the **7.01**
alternative of executive powers applied to individuals primarily in the form of control orders.
Three reasons conduce towards these substitutes.

First, executive powers allow for greater executive direction and input. In criminal process, **7.02**
the executive must respect prosecutorial and judicial independence, which brings into play
a clash of priorities—national security versus individual fairness. The courts' traditionally
deferential stance has been modified, as described in Chapter 1. Secondly, the state places an
emphasis upon anticipatory risk of terrorism. Criminal justice outcomes mostly follow the
crime. However, the anticipatory risk of mass terrorism casualties demands pre-emption.[2]
The third reason is to depart further still from the normal standards of criminal process than
the changes encountered in Chapters 5 and 6. The advantage of executive measures is
that they count as 'civil' and so do not have to subsume the more exacting standards of
criminal process under Article 6 of the European Convention in terms of open process and
disclosure, standards and burden of proof and admissibility, and independence of the
tribunal. The purpose is to secure an outcome favourable to the executive and better to
protect the assets of the state and the safety of the population.

---

[1] For footnotes in this chapter, '*Secretary of State for the Home Department*' is omitted from case names.
[2] See further Dershowitz, A, *Preemption* (WW Norton, New York, 2006); Furedi, F, *Invitation to Terror*
(Continuum, 2007).

7.03 These reasons entail a 'crucial' focus on the gathering and rehearsal of intelligence.[3] Intelligence arises because of the sophisticated, secretive, and committed nature of terrorist groups and also because of the drive to pre-empt the future rather than to gather solid evidence of the past. As mentioned in Chapter 2, reliance upon intelligence as the basis for executive action incurs doubts about the reliability of the data and the competence of decision-making in the hands of government Ministers. At the same time, there are no fundamental objections to reliance upon intelligence for legal outcomes. Moreover the boundaries between 'intelligence' and 'evidence' are not fixed.

Legislative background

7.04 Specialist executive restraint orders so as to avert terrorism have long been honed by United Kingdom governments not only at home but also abroad in colonial campaigns.[4]

7.05 Forerunners in Britain include the Prevention of Violence (Temporary Provisions) Act 1939, which reacted to Irish Republican Army attacks with exclusion, prohibition, and registration orders.[5] By the time the Act ended in 1954, there had been 190 expulsion orders, seventy-one prohibition orders, and twenty-nine registration orders. Exclusion orders against Irish terror suspects (around 500 of them) were revived under the Prevention of Terrorism Acts from 1974 to 1998. No new orders were made after 1996, and all twelve remaining orders were revoked in 1997. The system lapsed in 1998, by which time it was considered to be 'of limited utility' and 'wrong on policy grounds'.[6] Exclusion orders were abolished within the TA 2000 reforms.

7.06 The executive power which dominated in Northern Ireland history was internment (detention without trial). It was last invoked from 1971 to 1975 and remained on the statute book until 1998.[7] Around 600 suspects were held during the period, and the mechanism was associated with an escalation of terrorism, compounded by occasional brutal treatment of detainees, as related in *Ireland v United Kingdom*.[8] Like exclusion, it was recommended for abolition by the *Lloyd Report*.[9] His recommendation accorded with Labour government policy—'internment is the terrorist's friend'.[10] The power was terminated by the EPA 1998, and attempts to revive it in 2000 were firmly resisted. While '[the government] does not rule out for all time the introduction of the power to intern . . .'[11] it would be 'a significant backward step at a time when we are normalising the security situation in Northern Ireland'.[12]

7.07 These precedents had little apparent influence over the designs which resulted in the PTA 2005. Instead, control orders grew in reaction to the latest incarnation of detention without

---

[3] Wilkinson, P, *Terrorism versus Democracy* (Frank Cass, London, 2000) p 105. See further Walker, C, 'Intelligence and anti-terrorism laws in the United Kingdom' (2005) 44 *Crime, Law & Social Change* 387.

[4] See Simpson, AWB, *Human Rights and the End of Empire* (Oxford University Press, Oxford, 2004); Bonner, D, *Executive Measures, Terrorism and National Security* (Ashgate, Aldershot, 2007).

[5] See Walker, C, *The Prevention of Terrorism in British Law* (2nd edn, Manchester University Press, Manchester, 1992) ch 4, 'Constitutional governance and special powers against terrorism' (1997) 35 *Columbia Journal of Transnational Law* 1.

[6] Hansard HC vol 327 col 1002 (16 March 1999), Jack Straw.

[7] See Donohue, LK, *Counter-Terrorism Law* (Irish Academic Press, Dublin, 2001).

[8] App no 5310/71, Ser A 25 (1978).

[9] *Lloyd Report*, para 16.8.

[10] HC Debs Standing Committee A col 73 (25 November 1997), Adam Ingram.

[11] *Home Office Response to Lloyd Report*, para14.2.

[12] Hansard HL vol 613 col 1054 (16 May 2000), Lord Falconer.

trial under Pt IV of the ATCSA 2001. Its details have been fully related elsewhere.[13] The ATCSA 2001 was in turn shaped by the judgment of the European Court of Human Rights in *Chahal v United Kingdom*,[14] and the resultant Special Immigration Appeals Commission Act 1997. Since total freedom for foreign *jihadi* terrorist suspects was not an acceptable alternative,[15] detention under Pt IV offered an adjunct to deportation once the public safety danger became acute after September 11.

Just seventeen detention orders were issued under Pt IV. Nevertheless, the emergence of **7.08** detention without trial and the accompanying derogation under Article 15 of the European Convention were politically unpalatable. Opposition culminated in condemnation by the *Newton Report* in 2003.[16] The *Home Office Response to the Newton Report* anticipated no urgent reform. However, this insouciance was terminally shaken because of the intervention of the House of Lords in *A v Secretary of State for the Home Department* (the *Belmarsh* case) in late 2004.[17] While a majority deferentially accepted that a public emergency existed sufficient to warrant derogation under Article 15, Pt IV was not 'strictly necessary' on the grounds of disproportionality and discrimination. There were two troubling features within Pt IV. One was that it only affected deportable aliens and ignored 'neighbour' terrorists.[18] The other was the creation of a 'prison with three walls'—the absent fourth wall allowing foreign terrorists to depart the jurisdiction and plot abroad. This House of Lords verdict was endorsed in 2009 by *A v United Kingdom*.[19] As well as the prompting of the Newton Committee and the House of Lords judgment, detention without trial became increasingly problematic as a long-term policy. At some stage, doubts would surely have grown about the persistence of the 'emergency'. Furthermore, the conditions of potentially perpetual detention would eventually have conflicted with Article 3 standards.

Responding to the *Belmarsh* judgment, detention under Pt IV was repealed and replaced by **7.09** control orders under the PTA 2005. Control orders avoided the identified shortcomings but created a catalogue of further problems as shall now be explored.

B. Control Orders—the System

Legislative background

The PTA 2005 came into force on 11 March 2005, just seventeen days after its introduction **7.10** into Parliament.[20] This rapid legislative delivery was the subject of highly rancorous debate

---

[13] See Walker, C, *The Anti-Terrorism Legislation* (1st edn, Oxford University Press, Oxford, 2002) (ch 8). For reviews, see Joint Committee on Human Rights, *Continuance in Force of Sections 21 to 23 of the Anti-terrorism, Crime and Security Act 2001* (2002–03 HC 462/HL 59), *Statutory Review: Continuance of Pt IV* (2003–04 HL 38/HC 381); Lord Carlile, *Reviews of Pt IV of the Anti-terrorism, Crime and Security Act 2001–2005* (Home Office, London, 2002–06).

[14] *Chahal v United Kingdom*, App no 22414/93, 1996-V.

[15] *Home Office Response to Newton Report*, p ii.

[16] *Newton Report*.

[17] [2004] UKHL 56. See Dickson, B, 'Law versus terrorism: can law win?' [2005] *European Human Rights Law Review* 1; Walker, C, 'Prisoners of "war all the time"' [2005] *European Human Rights Law Review* 50; Feldman, D, 'Proportionality and discrimination in anti-terrorism legislation' (2005) 64 *Cambridge Law Journal* 271.

[18] See Walker, C, '"Know thine enemy as thyself" Discerning friend from foe under anti-terrorism laws' (2008) 32 *Melbourne Law Review* 275.

[19] App no 3455/05, 19 February 2009.

[20] Drafting was conducted by Treasury Counsel (<http://www.cabinetoffice.gov.uk/media/210692/draftsmanscontract1.pdf>) and not by MI5 (Tham, J-C, 'Parliamentary deliberation and the National Security Executive' [2010] *Public Law* 79 at 84).

which 'demeaned' Parliament[21] as well as becoming the catalyst for the most severe bout of disagreement between the Houses of Commons and Lords in modern history. The opposition complained about the lack of debating time, the deficient safeguards, the failure to boost prosecution, and weak review mechanisms. These disagreements have been subdued on later renewals.

7.11 The essence of the legislation is to permit the issuance of 'control orders' which regulate and restrict individuals suspected of being involved in terrorism. They fit the pattern of dealing with anticipatory risk, and so the basis for the orders is intelligence-led and the mechanism for the trigger is executive-based. Many of the former detainees were subjected to control orders, though, following the July 2005 bombings in London; nine such control orders were then revoked and deportation orders issued.[22]

7.12 The instruments for review draw from Pt IV, though the extension to suspect citizens meant that the Special Immigration Appeals Commission (SIAC) Act 1997,[23] as deployed under Part IV, was no longer the appropriate venue. Jurisdiction has instead been vested in the High Court or Court of Session (for Scotland) under s 15. The government's view was that the seriousness of the process merited High Court attention rather than of magistrates or sheriffs,[24] as suggested by Lord Carlile.[25] A more fundamental objection was that judicial involvement would bring disrepute because control orders involved 'a risk assessment' and 'not a decision'.[26] These views were shared by some senior judges[27] but should be rejected. The precedent of SIAC has been firmly established, and judges are involved every day in risk assessment when taking bail and sentencing decisions.

7.13 Besides extending to citizens as well as foreigners and therefore not being dependent on deportation, control orders are distinct from Pt IV in that they do not necessarily rely upon a derogation notice. Derogation from rights to liberty (within the terms of Article 5 of the European Convention) remains possible, and such orders would require a corresponding derogation notice to be issued and can only be made by the courts (s 4). Non-derogating control orders (always expected to be the norm) must be confirmed by the courts (s 3). This distinction between derogating and non-derogating should be understood in light of the jurisprudence of the European Court of Human Rights in *Guzzardi v Italy*, where the Court declared that Article 5:[28]

> . . . is not concerned with mere restrictions on liberty of movement . . . In order to determine whether someone has been 'deprived of his liberty' within the meaning of Art 5, the starting point must be his concrete situation and account must be taken of a whole range of criteria such as the type, duration, effects and manner of implementation of the measure in question.

---

[21] Hansard HC vol 431 col 774 (28 February 2005), Dominic Grieve.

[22] See *Q* [2006] EWHC (Admin) 2690; *RB (Algeria) and OO* [2009] UKHL 10.

[23] It is a court of record under the ATCSA 2001, s 35. This status confers powers at least as great as judicial review (Hansard HC vol 376 col 919, (12 December 2001), David Blunkett.

[24] Hansard HL vol 670 col 671 (8 March 2005), Lord Falconer.

[25] Hansard HL vol 670 col 372 (3 March 2005), Lord Carlile.

[26] Hansard HL vol 670 col 163 (1 March 2005), Lord Lloyd.

[27] Hansard HC vol 431 col 1576 (9 March 2005), Charles Clarke.

[28] App no 7367/76, Ser A 39 (1980) at para 91.

Thus, there is no 'bright line' between liberty and restriction.[29] An important further implication of non-derogating control powers is that they can address sources of terrorism which are not specific to a derogation notice.[30]

Control orders—contents

A control order is defined by s 1(1) as 'an order against an individual that imposes obligations   **7.14**
on him for purposes connected with protecting members of the public from a risk of
terrorism'. By s 1(3), the obligations imposed must be considered 'necessary for purposes
connected with preventing or restricting involvement by that individual in terrorism-related
activity'.[31] Under s 1(5), the meaning of 'terrorism' is taken from the TA 2000, s 1. Section
1(9) defines 'involvement in terrorism-related activity' (which may relate to specific acts
or to terrorism in general) as comprising: (a) the commission, preparation, or instigation
of acts of terrorism; (b) conduct which facilitates or is intended to facilitate such acts;
(c) conduct which gives encouragement or is intended to give encouragement to such acts; or
(d) conduct which gives support or assistance to others known or believed to be involved
in terrorism-related activity. The final leg (d) differs from the others in that it demands an
element of *mens rea* as to outcomes. The government resisted an amendment to insert
'knowingly' in (a) to (c), suggesting that the need to protect the public would not be triggered
by the unwitting.[32]

The original formulation of s 1(9) was excessive. It could encompass individuals who, while   **7.15**
not knowingly assisting terrorism, had intentionally provided, say, accommodation to someone who was believed by the government to be supporting terrorism. There could be any
number of links in this chain of association.[33] Therefore, the CTA 2008, s 79, adds reference
in (d) to activity 'by the individual concerned' which it defines by reference to (a) to (c).

The meaning of terrorism-related 'activity' in s 1(9) was considered further in *AR*.[34] AR's   **7.16**
control order was based on membership of the Libyan Islamic Fighting Group, but his
membership had not been active since proscription. The control order could not stand, since
s 1(5) of the TA 2000, by which 'a reference to action taken for the purposes of terrorism
includes a reference to action taken for the benefit of a proscribed organization', excused
prior activity. However, a control order can be established on a more general view of past
activity, whereby past membership could raise an inference of a future propensity to engage
in terrorism. In *AT and AW*,[35] the Home Secretary was entitled to take a cautious view as to
future involvement. In *AU*, a control order based wholly on previous convictions would not
be sufficient to show current 'activity', but an order was valid where there was also evidence
of a continuing propensity to commit terrorism.[36] In *GG* and *NN*,[37] well-founded suspicions of involvement in terrorism two years previously were balanced against evidence of
the subject settling down with a family, and his order was quashed.

---

[29] *JJ* [2007] UKHL 45 at para 17 per Lord Bingham.
[30] Compare *AU* [2009] EWHC 49 (Admin).
[31] For the standard to be applied, see *AM* [2009] EWHC 3053 (Admin) at para 21.
[32] Hansard HC vol 670 cols 459–60 (3 March 2005), Lord Falconer.
[33] Hansard HC Public Bill Committee on the Counter-Terrorism Bill col 493 (15 May 2008), Tony McNulty.
[34] [2008] EWHC 3164 (Admin).
[35] [2009] EWHC 512 (Admin) at para 29.
[36] [2009] EWHC 49 (Admin) at para 6.
[37] [2009] EWHC 142 (Admin) at para 23.

7.17 Section 1(4) next sets out an extensive list of obligations that may be imposed pursuant to a control order. It includes: (a) a prohibition or restriction on the possession or use of specified articles or substances (such as a computer); (b) a prohibition or restriction on the use of specified services or facilities (banking facilities or a telephone will be in mind here); (c) a restriction with respect to work, occupation, or business; (d) a restriction on associations or communications; (e) restrictions in respect of place of residence or on visitors to it; (f) a prohibition on presence at specified places or areas at specified times or days; (g) a prohibition or restriction on movements; (h) a requirement to comply with such prohibitions or restrictions on movements as may be imposed, for a period not exceeding twenty-four hours; (i) a requirement to surrender a passport or other documents or things; (j) a requirement to give access to a place of residence or to other premises; (k) a requirement to allow searches for the purpose of checking on the contravention of obligations; (l) a requirement to allow specified persons to remove objects and to subject them to tests or to retain them; (m) a requirement to submit to photographing; (n) a requirement to cooperate with arrangements for monitoring by electronic or other means; (o) a requirement to comply with a demand to provide information; (p) a requirement to report to a specified person at specified times and places. Under s 1(8), an obligation may be worded so that it can be waived by the authorities provided prior approval is sought.

7.18 The foregoing list appears comprehensive, and most requirements are applied in combination.[38] An exception in practice is the prohibition on leaving the country which is often not applied to foreigners in the hope that they might opt for self-deportation. Claims of disproportionality, along the lines raised against the 'prison with three walls' under Pt IV, are reduced by the fact that the Home Office usually seizes travel documents such as passports and so can determine their destination.

7.19 The CTA 2008 has responded to an operational need for non-consensual powers of entry into premises.[39] The deficiency related to s 1(4)(j) which allows the imposition of a requirement on the controlled person to give access to specified persons to his place of residence or to other premises to which he has power to grant access. On the original wording, it was arguable that if a controlled person is out of the residence or has gone missing, the police cannot require him to grant access. Arguably, the power should be restricted in this way—to offer a safeguard that the suspect should always be aware of intrusions into privacy unless the police wish to revert to formal search powers. However, the CTA 2008 grants entry powers, applicable also to control orders made before 2008. Obstruction is an offence under s 9.

7.20 So, by s 7A, where a police officer reasonably suspects that the controlled person has absconded, the constable may enter and search relevant premises[40] for the purpose of determining whether the person has absconded or for material that may assist in the tracking and arrest of the controlled person. 'Abscond' is not defined, which suggests that ordinary meanings, such as 'to hide oneself, to go away hurriedly and secretly', should apply.[41] Aside from absconding, other facets of breach of a control order can be checked by entry and search under s 7B.

---

[38] See Lord Carlile, *Fourth Report of the Independent Review Pursuant to Section 14(3) of the Prevention of Terrorism Act 2005* (Home Office, London, 2009) Annexes 1, 3–5.

[39] See Home Office, *Possible Measures for Inclusion into a Future Counter-Terrorism Bill* (London, 2007) para 57.

[40] The formula protects subsequent owners or tenants: Hansard HL vol 705 col 935 (17 November 2008), Lord West.

[41] See *Re M* [2001] EWCA Civ 458 at para 28.

As an alternative to the use of these summary powers, under s 7C, the constable may apply to a justice of the peace or sheriff for a warrant to check on compliance with obligations under a control order.

The CTA 2008 has also amended s 1(4)(m), in line with the general policy in Pt I of the CTA **7.21** 2008 of expanding the storage and sharing of forensic data. Sections 10 to 12 grant a power for a constable to take, in addition to photographs, fingerprints and non-intimate samples from individuals subject to control orders. The sampling can also be for security or criminal investigative purposes as well as preventative purposes.[42] In Scotland, samples from controlled persons may be used only for the purposes of a terrorist investigation or in the interests of national security and not crime detection (since that is a matter within devolved competence), and the sampling must be authorized by an inspector in the case of non-intimate samples of non-pubic hair or nail samples and external body fluid samples (but not fingerprints).[43]

Under the Crime and Security Act 2010, s 14, the retention of fingerprints and DNA profiles **7.22** taken from persons subject to a control order can last for two years after the control order ceases to have effect (PACE, s 64ZC). The same is applied in Scotland by s 20, which amends the CTA 2008, s 11 and adds s 11A which ensures that the foregoing restrictions as to purposes apply also to retained data.

As for s 1(4)(p), it was held in *R v AD*[44] that the Home Office may involve a third party in **7.23** monitoring the reporting obligations, and the third party is not confined to a 'passive role'. Thus, a police inspector could act as an assigned 'contact officer' and be conferred with the power to vary the reporting hours, though there was also a specified 'Control Order Contact Officer' at the Home Office to deal with queries.

There are some limits to s 1(4), including submission to a personal search. The court in *GG* **7.24** and *NN* was unwilling to read in such an incursion into personal liberty.[45] It could also be argued that if obligations are imposed outside the express headings of s 1(4), then they will not be 'prescribed by law' for the purposes of the European Convention.[46] Other attempts during legislative passage to curtail the discretion in s 1(4) (such as through restraints on the taking of legal advice or being required to provide self-incriminating or confidential information) were resisted. However, the government accepted that imposing an obligation to leave the United Kingdom would be an improper usurpation of deportation powers and that legal privilege could only be taken away by express words.[47] The legislators also posited a distinction between the improper asking for information for the purposes of securing a conviction and legitimately asking for information to prevent terrorism. This distinction is not convincing. If a person refuses to answer the question 'Where is the bomb?', then an offence under s 9(1) might arise for contravening an obligation under s 1(4)(o) to provide information.

Obligations are further explained in s 1(5), which emphasizes the restriction of movement **7.25** and thereby allows curfews or exclusion zones. Controlled persons may also be required

---

[42] Hansard HL vol 704 col 393 (9 October 2008), Lord West.
[43] See Criminal Procedure (Scotland) Act 1995.
[44] [2007] EWCA Crim 1009.
[45] [2009] EWHC 142 (Admin) at para 59, as affirmed in *GG* [2009] EWCA Civ 786 and *BH* [2009] EWHC 2938 (Admin).
[46] Joint Committee on Human Rights, *Prevention of Terrorism Bill: Preliminary Report* (2004–05 HL 61/ HC 389) para 17.
[47] Hansard HL vol 670 cols 444–50 (3 March 2005), Lord Falconer.

under s 1(6) to cooperate with practical arrangements for monitoring control orders, such as wearing and maintaining apparatus (such as tags). The controlled person may further be required under s 1(7) to provide information, including advance information about proposed movement or other activities.

Control orders—issuance

7.26 There are two types of control orders. The issuance of a 'non-derogating' control order is by the Home Secretary and with the confirmation of a court under ss 2 and 3. If an order involves any obligation which is incompatible with the liberty under Article 5 of the European Convention on Human Rights—a 'derogating obligation'—it must instead be made by the court on application by the Secretary of State under s 4. Such an order must be justified by reference to a designation order (under s 14(1) of the Human Rights Act 1998). The derogation should relate under ss 1(2)(a) and 1(10) to rights to liberty under Article 5, and no power is granted to issue obligations that derogate from other rights, including Article 6.[48]

Non-derogating control orders

7.27 Section 15 provides the unhelpful definition that a non-derogating control order 'means a control order made by the Secretary of State'. This formulation made sense in the initial drafts of the Act (before court involvement was inserted). In contrast, under s 15, a derogating control order is defined as 'a control order imposing obligations that are or include derogating obligations' (as defined by s 1(10)). One might better define a non-derogating control order as an order which does not contain derogating obligations.

7.28 The Home Secretary may make a non-derogating control order under s 2(1) if she: (a) has reasonable grounds for suspecting that the individual is or has been involved in terrorism-related activity; and (b) considers that it is necessary, for purposes connected with protecting members of the public from a risk of terrorism, to make a control order imposing obligations on that individual. The procedures under s 2(2) allow the Secretary of State to impose a control order on an individual already subject to a control order imposed by the court where the court has decided to revoke a control order (under s 3 below) but has postponed that revocation in order to allow the Secretary of State to consider whether to impose a fresh order. A new order can also be issued after a previous order has expired or has been quashed without postponement by the courts.

7.29 Examining in further detail the two tests in s 2(1), the first test is expressly objective, though 'activity' can cover a wide range. In *AL*,[49] a British citizen was subjected to a control order since he intended to travel to Afghanistan to engage in radicalization activities. The control order was upheld by the High Court. Any net-widening towards the encouragement, rather than the doing, of terrorism might be said to be the fault of the TA 2006, s 1. A more restrictive view was taken in *Bullivant*, whereby 'Expressions of support for Islamic extremists . . . the sharing of extremist views or keeping company with extremists will not suffice, but will obviously provide support for suspicion of intended involvement in such activities.'[50] The Joint Committee on Human Rights has suggested that there should be evidence of direct support for terrorism activity.[51]

---

[48] For arguments that Article 6 is non-derogable, see Chapter 6.
[49] [2007] EWHC 1970 (Admin).
[50] [2008] EWHC (Admin) 337 at para 14 per Collins J.
[51] Joint Committee on Human Rights, *Counter-Terrorism Policy and Human Rights: Counter-Terrorism Bill* (2007–08 HL 50/HC 199) para 39.

The second test of necessity is apparently subjective, though the modern practice is to set an **7.30** objective standard.[52] Necessity will arise from the seriousness and persistence of activity and also the inability of other techniques of surveillance to avert danger.

The proof threshold is set at a low level, consistent with the dynamic of anticipatory risk and **7.31** lower even than required for the issuance of a civil injunction.[53] In response to demands that the legislature adopt a balance-of-probabilities test, the Home Secretary feared that to accede would mean that 'potentially dangerous individuals could simply slip away'.[54] In assessing the level of proof, consideration may be given to the statement of Lord Hoffmann in *Rehman* (a deportation case), in which he stated that 'the question in the present case is not whether a given event happened but the extent of future risk. This depends upon an evaluation of the evidence of the appellant's conduct against a broad range of facts with which they may interact.'[55] This position was echoed in cases decided under Pt IV. In *M*, Lord Woolf stated: 'Although, therefore, the test is an objective one, it is also one which involves a value judgment as to what is properly to be considered reasonable in those circumstances.'[56] In *A (No 2)*, the Court of Appeal regarded as 'unfortunate' a statement by SIAC that the formula was 'not a demanding standard'.[57] Nevertheless, Lord Justice Laws concluded that 'The nature of the subject-matter is such that it will as I have indicated very often, usually, be impossible to prove the past facts which make the case that A is a terrorist.'[58]

By s 2(4), a non-derogating control order expires after twelve months but may be renewed. The **7.32** date must be specified under s 2(5), and there is no express power to vary the period from twelve months. On renewal under s 2(6), the Secretary of State must find that the order would protect members of the public from a risk of terrorism and must deem necessary any obligations imposed by the renewed order. These grounds differ from those pertaining to the original imposition in that there is no need to review the evidence for the original suspicion of involvement in terrorism activity. In this way, the case for renewal may differ entirely from the case for imposition.

In the original draft of the legislation, non-derogating control orders could be instituted **7.33** by the Secretary of State without any involvement of the courts. This feature was one of the major bones of contention in Parliament.[59] After much jousting on the issue, a compromise was reached that there should be an early judicial check by way of an *ex parte* application for leave to make the order. Consequently, the Home Secretary, and not the court, remains the author of the order but only if an application has been made to the court for permission to issue it under s 3(1)(a). There are two exceptional procedures. By s 3(1)(b), the Secretary of State can state in the control order that the urgency of the case requires the making of an order without court permission. Alternatively, s 3(1)(c) allows an order to be made on the Secretary of State's authority alone if issued before 14 March 2005 against a detainee under Pt IV of the 2001 Act. For these exceptional cases, the Secretary of State must still refer the control order to the court immediately under s 3(3) and (4).

---

[52] *Youssef v Home Office* [2004] EWHC 1884 at para 62.
[53] Hansard HL vol 670 col 371 (3 March 2005), Lord Carlile.
[54] Hansard HC vol 431 col 1588 (9 March 2005), Charles Clarke.
[55] [2001] UKHL 47 at para 56.
[56] [2004] EWCA (Civ) 324 at para 16.
[57] [2004] EWCA (Civ) 1123 at para 49 per Pill LJ.
[58] Ibid para 231.
[59] See Joint Committee on Human Rights, *Prevention of Terrorism Bill: Preliminary Report* (2004–05 HL 61/ HC 389).

7.34 On application under s 3(1)(a), provided the court concludes that the relevant decisions are not 'obviously flawed', directions will be given for a full hearing as soon as reasonably practicable. The same rule applies under s 3(3) and (6) after a referral under (b) and (c), but there are two added possibilities for court intervention (again on the 'obviously flawed' standard) in those situations.

7.35 First, s 3(6)(b) allows (in relation to orders issued under sub-ss (3)(1)(b) and (3)(1)(c)) the court to quash a particular obligation within the order, whereas an order under (a) is on an 'all or nothing' basis under s 3(2)(a). However, it is possible that the same review power applies to an order under (a) pursuant to s 2(9). If treated as a proviso guiding action at the later stage of court hearings, it makes sense that obligations can then be imposed as the court considers necessary to prevent involvement in any terrorism activity and not just the activity which originally gave rise to the grounds for the Secretary of State's suspicion.

7.36 Second, in relation to (b) only, the court may quash the 'certificate' of urgency under s 3(8). The wording here betrays the haste of drafting, for a 'certificate' is relevant to a referral under (c) and not under (b). While the 'certificate' can be quashed if flawed, the order itself is not expressly quashed as a result, and the phrase 'certificate contained in the order' suggests a severance of the issues. However, if there was no power under s 3(1)(b) to issue the order in the first place, then the provisions of (a) should have been followed. Thus, in that case, without a court's permission, there can be no valid order, and the Home Secretary must apply to the court for a decision under s 3(2).

7.37 By contrast, it would appear that a case under (a) entails more court discretion in one aspect. Section 3(2)(b) states that the court 'may' grant permission for an order which is not obviously flawed— 'may' suggests some residual discretion, perhaps based on an abuse of process or some other fundamental defect. Under s 3(6)(c), the court 'must' confirm the order if it is not obviously flawed.

7.38 The sensitive nature of these intelligence-led procedures in court is highlighted by s 3(5). The initial hearings in connection with non-derogating control orders, in which the court will decide whether to grant permission for the order to be made under procedure (a) or will consider the Secretary of State's decision to impose the order without the court's permission under procedure (b) or (c) may be made in the absence of, without the knowledge of, and without representation for the subject of the order. However, the court must ensure under s 3(9) that the controlled person is notified of its decision on a reference under sub-s (3)(a). Furthermore, when the court orders a full hearing, the court must make arrangements under s 3(7) within seven days for the suspect to be given an opportunity to make representations *inter partes* about the directions already given or the making of further directions. This seven-day limit has caused problems in practice because delays sometimes occur so that arrangements can be put in place to enforce the order.[60] The CTA 2008, s 80, therefore recalibrates the clock to run from the service of the order on the suspect.

7.39 Assuming there is a full hearing on a non-derogating control order and the suspect does not ask for desistance of proceedings under s 3(14), the court must determine under s 3(10) whether the decisions of the Secretary of State were 'flawed' in terms of the factual grounds

---

[60] Compare Lord Carlile, *First Report of the Independent Reviewer pursuant to Section 14(3) of the Prevention of Terrorism Act 2005* (Home Office, London, 2006) para 49; Joint Committee on Human Rights, *Counter-Terrorism Policy and Human Rights: Counter-Terrorism Bill* (2007–08 HL 50/HC 199) para 39.

or of the necessity for each obligation.[61] Though the term 'flawed' rather than 'obviously flawed' is used here, there is no legal difference: s 3(11) defines both by reference to 'the principles applicable on an application for judicial review'. Hence, the full hearing is not a *de novo* consideration, and the courts should not substitute their own judgment on the merits,[62] which is a narrower role than that exercised by SIAC under Pt IV.[63] However, the boundary of review has been amplified in one respect—evidence which becomes available in time for a s 3(11) hearing but after an order is imposed must still be considered by the court.[64]

As well as the limited basis for review, the court's scrutiny must reflect that the decision only **7.40** requires a 'reasonable suspicion'.[65] Parliamentary challenges to this lowly level of proof, and attempts to insert a balance-of-probabilities test or even the criminal standard of proof were all rebuffed.[66]

If the court decides in a full hearing order that a decision of the Secretary of State was **7.41** flawed, it must under s 3(12): (a) quash the control order; (b) quash one or more of the obligations contained in the order; or (c) give directions to the Secretary of State to revoke or modify the order. Otherwise, under s 3(13), it must uphold the order, and no residual discretion is mentioned. The quashing of an order may be stayed pending appeal under s 15(2); alternatively, the Secretary of State may proceed to make a new order (Sch, para 8). Otherwise, unless a viable order is affected by change of circumsatnces, the order is quashed *ab initio*.[67] Compensation may arise under the Human Rights Act 1998, s 8. Whether common law damages arise is less clear since there may be no infringement of liberty at any point.[68]

Lord Carlile has suggested that the courts should be granted a power to amend orders so as **7.42** to avoid the complications of making and serving a new order.[69] However, a discretion of such breadth may infringe the separation of powers doctrine.

Derogating control orders

Section 4 envisages orders which are so draconian in their impact on liberty that they must **7.43** be justified by reference to a derogation notice under Article 15. The most palpable obligation will be 'house arrest'—confinement within a specified place for a substantial portion of the time. Whether a derogating order could even allow internment may be doubted. Section 1(4) only allows restrictions in respect of a 'place of residence' and restrictions on movement only for up to twenty-four hours. Furthermore, s 1(2)(a) only allows derogations in relation to Article 5, and internment will inevitably negate other rights such as family life.

Reflecting the dire impact on liberty,[70] the courts are more heavily involved in the issuance **7.44** of derogating control orders, though the standard of proof and procedures still respond to anticipatory risk and diverge from criminal process. In contrast to non-derogating orders,

---

[61] This procedure is preferred to judicial review: *BX* [2010] EWCA Civ 481.
[62] *MB* [2006] EWHC (Admin) 1000 at para 79.
[63] *A* [2005] EWHC 1669 (Admin) at para 16.
[64] *Bullivant* [2008] EWHC 337 (Admin) at para 11.
[65] The standard is that set out for police arrests: *AM* [2009] EWHC 3053 (Admin) at para 20.
[66] Hansard HL vol 670 col 152 (1 March 2005) and col 482 (7 March 2005).
[67] *AF (No 4)* [2010] EWCA Civ 869.
[68] *AN* [2010] EWCA Civ 869.
[69] Lord Carlile, *Special Report of the Independent Reviewer in relation to Quarterly Reports under section 14(1) of the Prevention of Terrorism Act 2005* (Home Office, London, 2006) para 24.
[70] Hansard HL vol 670 col 121 (3 March 2005), Lord Falconer.

the courts issue the s 4 order, and the civil standard of proof applies. Next, the production of these orders must be predicated upon the lawful issuance of a notice of derogation under Article 15 and a designation order under the Human Rights Act 1998, s 14(1)(b).

7.45 As mentioned, under s 4(1), the order must be made by the court. The court must convene an immediate preliminary hearing on an application from the Secretary of State to decide whether to make a derogating control order. No time limit is specified for what is to count as 'immediate'. Once again, this preliminary hearing may occur under s 4(2) in the absence of, without the knowledge of, and without representation for, the subject of the order. At the preliminary hearing, the court may make the order if, by s 4(3), it appears that: (a) there is material which is capable of establishing involvement in terrorism-related activity; (b) there are reasonable grounds for believing that the imposition of obligations is necessary to protect the public; (c) the risk is linked to a public emergency in respect of which there is a designated derogation in respect of Article 5; and (d) the obligations being imposed are derogating obligations. The test in (a) is suggestive of a *prima facie* case, intentionally more searching than for a non-derogating order. Even the test in (b) requires the court positively to satisfy itself rather than asking in the negative whether the Secretary of State is obviously wrong. As with s 3(2)(b), there is also some suggestion of a residual discretion. If the court decides to make the order, then it must give directions for a full hearing.

7.46 Pending a full hearing, the court may impose interim obligations under s 4(4), no doubt on promptings from the Home Office. At the full hearing, the court may confirm, modify, or revoke the control order under s 4(5) and (13). The tests to be applied by the court are much more searching than the 'flawed' test under s 3. Under s 4(7), the court may confirm the order only if: (a) it is satisfied, on the balance of probabilities, of involvement in terrorism-related activity; (b) it considers that the imposition of obligations is necessary to protect the public; (c) the risk is linked to a designated derogation from Article 5; and (d) the obligations include derogating obligations. At the same time, there is no explicit basis on which to review the necessity for the derogation order itself. In the *Belmarsh* case, some judges were of the view that review of derogation in the context of detention without trial was only possible because of the express grounds for review in s 30 of the 2001 Act.[71] Another limitation concerns the standard of proof, set at the 'balance of probabilities'. Here, however, the courts might be expected to adapt the civil standard to the circumstances, and, where the allegations and consequences are serious, the standard of proof rises.[72]

7.47 The mechanics of a derogating control order include that it will last for six months under s 4(8), unless revoked or because it would otherwise continue beyond the period provided for in s 6 (linking it to the term of the relevant derogation notice). Under s 6, the Secretary of State declares that it remains necessary for him to have the power to impose derogating obligations under the original derogation. Assuming the derogation remains operative, a derogating control order can be renewed under s 4(10). Its wording differs subtly from the criteria for the original order. The balance-of-probabilities standard is not repeated; instead, a test of necessity is applied. It is likely, however, that courts will apply the same standard of proof as before. A temporary extension pending the decision in the renewal hearing can be allowed under s 4(11) and (12).

---

[71] [2004] UKHL 56 at para 164 per Lord Rodger.
[72] *R (McCann) v Manchester Crown Court* [2002] UKHL 39 at para 83; Hansard HL vol 670 col 507 (7 March 2005), Lord Falconer.

The government made it clear from the outset that derogating orders were an embellishment **7.48** to the legislation which will be, and has in fact been, locked in the trophy cabinet. The Home Office views non-derogating notices as proportionate to the operational needs of the security forces. As for the political and legal reasons for this reticence, derogating notices involve the bother of proof of an 'emergency' which might be disputed if based on the threat from just one or two individuals, and the debates about them would also raise evident conflicts in constitutional roles and dangers of prejudice to individual rights. Nevertheless, the government asserted that as a matter of principle the 'threat that we currently face' allowed for a derogation.[73] The Joint Committee on Human Rights' contention that it is a breach of human rights law to sponsor a provision dependent upon a derogation when no derogation is in force[74] is mistaken in principle and contrary to European jurisprudence.

Processes

Jurisdiction to handle control orders is conferred under the Schedule, para 10, on the Queen's **7.49** Bench Division of the High Court or the Outer House of the Court of Session in Scotland. The procedures in these courts are, however, profoundly modified towards a version of the SIAC. The hearings are sensitive because they will involve not only open material, relating facts about the suspect such as movements and meetings, but also closed material, such as intercept data, intelligence assessments, and statements from security sources or third parties. Accordingly, s 11(1) and 11(2) provide that control order decisions and derogation matters are not to be questioned in any other legal proceedings, including for Human Rights Act purposes. The scope of appeals is reduced by s 11(3), which states that appeals can only be on a question of law. Lord Carlile has expressed the view that an appeal court should be able to raise factual error or factual change of circumstances.[75] A further restriction is set out in s 11(4), whereby only the Secretary of State can appeal against a judgment on an application under s 3(1)(a) (seeking permission to impose a non-derogating control order) or on a reference under s 3(3)(a) (seeking confirmation of a non-derogating control order made without court permission). In these cases, the controlled person is still able to challenge the decision in the full hearing following directions.

Additional procedural issues are addressed in the Act's schedule.[76] More detailed court rules **7.50** can be devised by the normal channels, though, by para 3, outside of Scotland, the first set of rules was delivered by the Lord Chancellor.[77]

Under para 2, there is a general duty on persons exercising the relevant powers to have regard **7.51** to the need to secure the proper review of control orders. At the same time, there is equally a duty to have regard to the need to ensure that disclosures of information are not made contrary to the public interest.

By para 4(2), the rules may provide for proceedings in the absence of the controlled person **7.52** or his legal representative (though there may be provided a summary of the evidence taken in closed proceedings) and for the withholding of full particulars of the reasons for decisions.

---

[73] Hansard HC vol 431 col 153 (22 February 2005), Charles Clarke.
[74] Joint Committee on Human Rights, *Prevention of Terrorism Bill: Preliminary Report* (2004–05 HL 61, HC 389) para 9.
[75] Lord Carlile, *Third Report of the Independent Review Pursuant to Section 14(3) of the Prevention of Terrorism Act 2005* (Home Office, London, 2008) para 82.
[76] For legal assistance, see Community Legal Service (Financial) (Amendment No 2) Regulations 2005, SI 2005/1097, r 2. For legal costs, see *E* [2009] EWHC 597 (Admin).
[77] See Delegated Powers and Regulatory Reform Committee, *Twelfth Report* (2004–05 HL 63) para 14, *Thirteenth Report* (2004–05 HL 80) annex 4.

At the same time, under para 4(3), all 'relevant material' (as defined in sub-para (5)) must be disclosed; thus, exculpatory material must be disclosed even if the Home Office does not wish to rely on it.[78] However, application may be made (always in the absence of the controlled person and his legal representative) for evidence to be treated as 'closed' and so be disclosed only to the court and to a person appointed under para 7 as the special advocate. If the Secretary of State elects not to disclose relevant material or provide a summary, the court may prevent the Secretary of State from relying on that material. The court may also require the Secretary of State to withdraw any allegation or argument to which that material relates.

7.53 Paragraph 5 deals with an application by the controlled person or the Secretary of State for an order mandating the anonymity of the controlled person. Anonymity has become the norm and is worthwhile to avoid harassment and prejudice to any subsequent trial.[79] It was held in *Times Newspapers*[80] that even though the principles of open justice could encompass control orders, anonymity was justified, though it should not be applied automatically, primarily to secure the effective operation of the control order. Monitoring and enforcement could become more difficult through intrusive media and community involvement. Privacy and family rights under Article 8 could also be affected by the stigma of being labelled a terrorist. The application for anonymity may be made even before court proceedings have commenced, such as following an arrest under s 5. Similar arguments were rehearsed in *AP (No 2)*,[81] alongside the fear of racist attack under Article 3. The CTA 2008, s 81, also allows for anonymity provided, under para 5 to the Schedule, an application for a control order has been made to the High Court.[82]

7.54 Paragraph 6 allows for the court to call for assistance from lay advisers, appointed for this purpose by the Lord Chancellor.[83] These advisers are likely to be experts in security and terrorism.

7.55 Further special court rules are contained in Pt 76 of the Civil Procedure Rules (CPR).[84] Rule 76.2(2) requires the court to give effect to the overriding objective in para 2 of the Schedule to the 2005 Act to 'ensure that information is not disclosed contrary to the public interest'. This stance contrasts with the balancing and consideration of alternatives under Public Interest Immunity. In *AH*,[85] the applicant sought to present evidence of twelve meetings with security service agents who were to be called as witnesses. The Home Secretary objected to this manoeuvre by reference to the 'Neither Confirm Nor Deny' policy in regard to security information.[86] Given that the Home Office was not relying upon the meetings as adverse evidence, the court had little difficulty in translating NCND to mean that the security agents would, if called, have no obligation to answer questions about the meetings.

---

[78] See Hansard HL vol 670 col 692 (8 March 2005).

[79] Lord Carlile, *Special Report of the Independent Reviewer in relation to Quarterly Reports under section 14(1) of the Prevention of Terrorism Act 2005* (Home Office, London, 2006) paras 10, 11, 22; Lord Carlile, *Third Report of the Independent Review Pursuant to Section 14(3) of the Prevention of Terrorism Act 2005* (Home Office, London, 2008) para 20.

[80] [2008] EWHC 2455.

[81] [2010] UKSC 26.

[82] Joint Committee on Human Rights, *Counter-Terrorism Policy and Human Rights: Counter-Terrorism Bill* (2007–08 HL 50, HC 199) para 39.

[83] This allows for payment: Hansard HL vol 670 col 702 (8 March 2005), Lord Falconer.

[84] SI 2005/656, Pt 76, as amended by SI 2009/2092 which allows special advocates to adduce evidence and cross-examine. For Scotland, see Rules of the Court of Session chap 89 (Act of Sederunt (Rules of the Court of Session Amendment No 4) (Prevention of Terrorism Act 2005) 2005, SSI 2005/153).

[85] [2008] EWHC 1045 (Admin).

[86] See *Re Scappaticci* [2003] NIQB 56.

CPR 76.22 allow the court to conduct hearings in private and to exclude the controlled **7.56** person and his representatives. The controlled person may choose not to provide evidence, but silence should not entail adverse inferences though it might affect the weight of other evidence[87] and it might also affect the level of disclosure.[88] CPR 76.26 enables the court to 'receive evidence that would not, but for this rule, be admissible'. One controversy here was whether the rules should exclude evidence emanating from torture. In *A (No 2)*,[89] the House of Lords directed that SIAC could not receive evidence obtained by the use of torture, as explored in Chapter 6. The same rules can be expected to apply to control orders. Less controversial is the submission of evidence previously submitted in a criminal trial. In *Bullivant*,[90] Mr Justice Collins felt uneasy about any attempt to refute evidence accepted at a criminal trial, but this approach was rightly not followed in *AU*, aside from the fact of conviction.[91]

Other evidential rules are in CPR 76.27, by which the Secretary of State must make a **7.57** reasonable search for relevant material (even if exculpatory) and file and serve that material. By CPR 76.28 and 76.29, the Secretary of State must apply to the court for permission to withhold closed material and file a statement explaining the reasons for withholding that material. The material is then scrutinized by a Special Advocate (below) who may challenge the need to withhold all or any of the closed material. If the court finds in favour of the Secretary of State, it must next consider whether to direct the Secretary of State to serve a summary of that material.

A key safeguard for the controlled person is the appointment of vetted lawyers as 'special **7.58** advocates' under para 7 and CPR 76.24. Their role is to 'represent the interests' of a relevant party in control order proceedings where that party and his legal representative are excluded from the proceedings. This role will comprise, first, the normal representation work of an advocate as applied in closed sessions. Their second job relates to disclosure and the testing of the need for closed sessions and closed evidence. There may be a further facet of the disclosure role, which is to ensure that all material evidence has been disclosed under CPR 76.27, whether closed or not.[92]

As already considered in Chapter 6, the value of special advocates remains controversial. **7.59** In control order litigation, they are assigned after sounding out the views of the legal representatives of the controlled person, but the special advocate is not 'responsible' under para 7(5) to the controlled person. The most serious hindrance is their limited ability to consult with the suspect which is only allowed before they have inspected closed materials, unless authorized on application under CPR 76.25 to the court. As mentioned in Chapter 6, applications are rare mainly because the Home Office would object on security grounds but also because they would compromise legal privilege.

Aside from the utility of special advocates, there are other disadvantages of process secrecy, **7.60** especially the absence of public understanding and over-reliance upon the executive as the

---

[87] *GG* [2009] EWHC 142 (Admin) at para 29.
[88] *AS* [2009] EWHC 2564 (Admin) at para 18.
[89] [2005] UKHL 71 at para 52.
[90] [2008] EWHC 337 (Admin) at para 8.
[91] [2009] EWHC 49 (Admin) at paras 7, 8 (as required by the Civil Evidence Act 1968, s 11(2)).
[92] See Constitutional Affairs Committee, *The Operation of the Special Immigration Appeals Commission (SIAC) and the Use of Special Advocates* (2004–05 HC 323-I) para 61.

font of data.[93] The latter problem is underlined by the practice on the part of intelligence services of destroying data when their own purposes are served.[94]

Criminal prosecution

7.61   Despite the dynamic of anticipatory risk, the government claims that prosecution is 'our preferred approach'.[95] Section 8 reflects this assertion and applies when it appears to the Secretary of State that (a) an individual's suspected involvement in terrorism-related activity may have involved the commission of an offence relating to terrorism, and (b) that the commission of that offence is being or would fall to be investigated by a police force. The latter prong presumably rules out criminal consideration where an alleged foreign offence is of a nature alien to the English legal system (such as slandering the state or officials) or where the foreign offence would not fall within any extra-jurisdictional provision. Before making a control order, s 11(2) requires the Secretary of State to consult with the relevant chief police officer (as defined in s 8(7)) to consider whether evidence is available that could realistically be used for the purposes of a prosecution. If a control order is made, sub-s (3) requires the Secretary of State to inform that chief police officer, and, thereafter, sub-s (4) requires the chief police officer to keep the feasibility of prosecution under review. It has been argued that the formula in s 8 excludes cases where public interest grounds have predetermined that there should be no investigation with a view to prosecution.[96] However, the better view is that s 8 requires consideration, no matter how hopeless the prospects.

7.62   The Act's reliance on the police (and not the Crown Prosecution Service) as the agency empowered to make judgments about prosecution seems obtuse. Admittedly, s 11(5) requires the chief police officer to consult the relevant prosecuting authority, but only when a control order has been made and only to the extent that it is considered appropriate to do so. Subsection (6) even provides that the chief police officer's duty to consult the relevant prosecuting authority may be satisfied by a consultation that took place before the Act was passed. The government sought to justify the secondary role of the prosecution by reference to the need to maintain its independence.[97] Why the prosecution should be more deserving than the constabulary of symbolic independence is not apparent. It is equally unclear why prosecutors would sacrifice independence when their professional judgment is reported to the Home Secretary rather than a court.

7.63   Other ideas for the facilitation of prosecution (and therefore the reduction or avoidance of reliance on control orders) occupied lengthy debates on the Bill.[98] Most prominent was the proposal that evidence from the interception of communications should be available in criminal proceedings, thereby amending the current exclusionary rule in the RIPA, s 17, and bringing it into line with the inclusionary rule applicable in control order proceedings (Sch, para 9). This debate was considered in Chapter 2. The *Chilcot Report*[99]

---

[93] See van Harten, G, 'Weaknesses of adjudication in the face of secret evidence' (2009) 13 *International Journal of Evidence and Proof* 1 at 15–17.

[94] The practice was condemned in *Charkaoui v Canada (No 2)* [2008] SCC 38.

[95] Hansard HC vol 431 col 339 (23 February 2005), Charles Clarke.

[96] Lord Carlile, *First Report of the Independent Reviewer pursuant to Section 14(3) of the Prevention of Terrorism Act 2005* (Home Office, London, 2006) para 55.

[97] Hansard HL vol 670 cols 442, 539 (3 March 2005), Baroness Scotland.

[98] See also Joint Committee on Human Rights, *Counter-Terrorism Policy and Human Rights: Prosecution and Pre-Charge Detention* (2005–06 HL 240/HC 1576).

[99] *Privy Council Review of intercept as evidence* (Cm 7324, London, 2008) paras 53, 58.

downplays any change for terrorist cases, and Lord Carlile concurs that decisive impact will be 'rare'.[100]

The prioritization of prosecution does not preclude later resort to control orders. For **7.64** example, Rauf Abdullah Mohammad was charged under the TA 2000, s 57, with making a video which extolled the killing of Western political leaders. The jury returned a not-guilty verdict, but he was immediately subjected to a control order—dubbed 'conviction lite' by one commentator.[101] In *AY*,[102] acquittal in the airline bomb plot did not preclude a control order on the same evidence, even if a retrial was still under consideration, provided that suspicions had not been entirely dispelled by the trial process. It was also suggested that the Home Secretary is not bound to follow the advice of the police and prosecutors under s 8.

Ancillary issues

Section 5(1) allows for arrest and detention pending the issuance of a derogating control **7.65** order where the Secretary of State has applied to the court. The power has several unusual features (including up to ninety-six hours of detention), which probably breach Article 5 of the European Convention. Section 5(9) admits this breach but authorizes it by reference to the designated derogation which will thereby serve a dual purpose. By contrast, there is no specific power to arrest and detain in connection with non-derogating control orders. The prime explanation is that a control order may be made as a matter of urgency by the Home Secretary under s 3(1)(b). In many cases, arrest will already have taken place under s 41 of the TA 2000.

Modification or revocation of orders falls under s 7. There is no need for prior notice or to **7.66** hear representations.[103] Appeals relating to non-derogating control orders are covered by s 10. Paragraph 8(2) to the Schedule allows the Secretary of State to make a new control order to the same or similar effect and can rely on the same matters.

The next ancillary issue concerns breaches of orders under s 9, which cites offences of (1) **7.67** contravening an obligation without reasonable excuse, (2) failing without reasonable excuse to report on entering or leaving the country, and (3) intentionally obstructing the delivery of a notice (the latter is a summary only offence). Indulgence is often shown in the application of s 9, and numerous minor infractions are not prosecuted.[104] In *Bullivant*, a prosecution under s 9 for failure to report at the police station failed on the basis that the defendant was mentally ill.[105] Where a control order or obligation is quashed, s 12 allows a person convicted of a related offence under s 9(1) or (2) to obtain the quashing of the conviction. This result follows from para 8(1) of the Schedule, whereby where an order or obligation is quashed, it shall be treated as never having been made. In consequence, s 12(8) permits compensation to be awarded.

---

[100] *Third Report of the Independent Reviewer pursuant to Section 14(3) of the Prevention of Terrorism Act 2005* (Home Office, London, 2008) para 38.
[101] *The Times* 30 August 2006, p 4 (quoting Gareth Crossman).
[102] [2010] EWHC 1860 (Admin).
[103] *BX* [2010] EWCA Civ 481.
[104] Lord Carlile, *First Report of the Independent Reviewer pursuant to Section 14(3) of the Prevention of Terrorism Act 2005* (Home Office, London, 2006) para 63.
[105] [2008] EWHC 337 (Admin).

C. Control Orders—Review Mechanisms

Review by Parliament and the executive

7.68 So as to aid future parliamentary review, s 13 provides that ss 1 to 9 expire after twelve months (from 11 March 2005). They may then be renewed for a period not exceeding one year at a time by affirmative order (unless urgent), subject to the Secretary of State consulting with the independent reviewer appointed under s 14 (discussed below), the Intelligence Services Commissioner, and the Director-General of the Security Service. Only the views of the independent reviewer are published.[106] Opponents of the legislation asked for a sunset deadline to be imposed, as well as a review by Privy Counsellors. The government rejected these demands and even offered the disquieting anti-democratic interpretation that sunset clauses would in fact 'send the message to terrorists . . . that we are uncertain'.[107] The government also promised that another anti-terrorism Bill would be forthcoming in the following session when amendments or repeals could be tabled.[108] In fact, when the TA 2006 emerged, no changes were made to the 2005 Act.

7.69 Further assistance to parliamentary scrutiny is secured under s 14, by which the Secretary of State must report to Parliament on a tri-monthly basis on the exercise of the powers. In practice, the Secretary of State has lodged a ministerial written answer, thereby foreclosing debate.[109]

7.70 As mentioned, also under s 14, the Secretary of State must appoint an independent person to review the operation of the Act after nine months and every twelve months thereafter. These reports must be laid before Parliament. Lord Carlile was appointed as independent reviewer. He has accepted that all control orders to date were properly made but has raised a number of important systemic deficiencies.

7.71 Lord Carlile called for the establishment of a Home Office-led procedure whereby officials and representatives of the control authorities meet to monitor each case.[110] Consequently, the government established a Home Office Review Group, including law enforcement and intelligence representatives (but there is again no mention of prosecutors). It considers on a quarterly basis and in private all extant orders.[111] Lord Carlile later argued that the Control Order Review Group should give more attention to proactive measures to achieve exit from the regime.[112] The idea was then underlined by a proposal that orders should normally expire after two years,[113] a proposal which will be considered later.

---

[106] See Joint Committee on Human Rights, *Counter-Terrorism Policy and Human Rights: Annual Renewal of Control Orders Legislation 2010* (2009–10 HL64/HC395) para 13.

[107] Hansard HC vol 431 col 1626 (9 March 2005), Hazel Blears.

[108] Hansard HL vol 670 col 1058 (10 March 2005), Lord Falconer.

[109] See Lord Carlile, *Special Report of the Independent Reviewer in relation to Quarterly Reports under section 14(1) of the Prevention of Terrorism Act 2005* (Home Office, London, 2006) para 27.

[110] Ibid para 46.

[111] See *Fourth Report of the Independent Review Pursuant to Section 14(3) of the Prevention of Terrorism Act 2005* (Home Office, London, 2009) para 56.

[112] *Second Report of the Independent Review Pursuant to Section 14(3) of the Prevention of Terrorism Act 2005* (Home Office, London, 2007) para 43.

[113] *Fourth Report of the Independent Review Pursuant to Section 14(3) of the Prevention of Terrorism Act 2005* (Home Office, London, 2009) para 58.

As regards s 8, Lord Carlile has revealed that letters from chief officers of police in relation to **7.72** each controlled person are woefully thin on explanations. Accordingly, he has repeatedly asked for more detail and also suggested that the letters be disclosed to the suspects.[114]

The Joint Committee on Human Rights has delivered more policy-oriented scrutiny, **7.73** covering compliance with Articles 5 and 6 of the European Convention, greater judicial involvement, higher standards of proof,[115] and the boosting of prosecution.

Judicial review

Court scrutiny of executive measures has considerably increased in intensity over the past **7.74** decade. Operative influences include, first, the strong signal of activism imparted by the Human Rights Act, as seized upon by the House of Lords in the *Belmarsh* case. Secondly, judicial interference with control orders seems less dramatic than springing a suspected terrorist from Belmarsh Prison. Thirdly, the legislative scheme signals encouragement to judicial intervention. The review role is vested in courts of record and not government Ministers, with the High Court or Court of Session operating within the mainstream of the legal system.[116] The results of the judicial review will now be explored, especially the triptych of judgments from the House of Lords, delivered on 31 October 2007.

Impact on liberty

In the absence of ratification, there is no concern about the impact of control orders on rights **7.75** to movement in Article 2 of Protocol 4. However, Lord Carlile criticized in his *First Report* the severity of curfew obligations which 'fall not very far short of house arrest, and certainly inhibit normal life considerably'.[117] This prescient hint was taken up by the judicial House of Lords.

In *JJ*,[118] the control orders imposed on the respondents an eighteen-hour curfew confined to **7.76** their small flats, the wearing of electronic tags, and the authorization of visitors. Beyond their residences, they were confined to movements within seventy-two square kilometres, not including any area in which they had previously lived, and were forbidden to meet unauthorized persons. There were prohibitions on communications equipment. The House of Lords held that the cumulative effect breached Article 5 since their lives were 'wholly regulated by the Home Office'.[119] The majority even opined that an analogy with detention in an open prison was apt, though the fate of the suspects was bleaker still since 'controlled persons did not enjoy the association with others and the access to entertainment facilities which a prisoner in an open prison would expect to enjoy'.[120] It was emphasized by Lord Bingham that the line between compliance and non-compliance with Article 5 could not be treated as mechanical and that operative factors went beyond physical restraints.[121] Compatibility with Article 5 must therefore embrace the type, duration, effects, and manner of implementation of the obligations. Other cases have suggested that account must also be taken of the impact of the

---

[114] Ibid para 78. See *Government Reply* (Cm 7367, London, 2008) p 6.

[115] Joint Committee on Human Rights, *Counter-Terrorism Policy and Human Rights: Draft Prevention of Terrorism Act 2005 (Continuance in force of sections 1 to 9) Order 2006* (2005–06 HL 122, HC 915).

[116] But note that SIAC could reach its own conclusions rather than being confined to review: *A* [2005] EWHC 1669 (Admin) at paras 15, 16.

[117] Lord Carlile, *First Report of the Independent Reviewer pursuant to Section 14(3) of the Prevention of Terrorism Act 2005* (Home Office, London, 2006) para 43.

[118] [2007] UKHL 45.

[119] Ibid para 24.

[120] [2007] UKHL 45 at para 24.

[121] Ibid para 16. Lords Hoffmann and Carswell dissented.

restrictions in the light of the mental state of the affected individual.[122] This broad interpretation was justified by the jurisprudence of the European Court, and the subsequent decision in *A v United Kingdom*[123] likewise urges a strict interpretation of exceptions to Article 5 which also seems consistent with Lord Bingham's approach.

7.77 By comparison, a similar complaint raised by *AF*, who was subject to a curfew for fourteen hours in a flat occupied with his father, was rejected. Likewise, controlled person *E*, subject to a curfew for twelve hours which he had to spend with his wife and family, was not adjudged to have been subjected to a breach of his liberty.

7.78 Despite Lord Bingham's stricture against mechanical tests, Lord Brown in *JJ* took pity on the practical difficulties facing the Home Office and pronounced that sixteen hours would normally be an acceptable maximum limit, though he warned that it could be excessive in given circumstances.[124] Since then, orders have been reissued with 16-hour curfews as a maximum[125] and with an average of thirteen hours.[126]

7.79 The courts have continued to insist on taking account of all restrictions and not just curfew terms. The impact on family life of an obligation requiring physical location on seven-day notice[127] was linked back to Article 5 in *AP*.[128] A Somali refugee had been granted indefinite leave to remain in 1999 but became subject to a control order in 2008. One obligation required him to relocate 150 miles from his family home and other established social ties in London, producing in his perception a form of 'internal exile'.[129] The Court of Appeal depicted these impacts as entirely affecting family and private life, and they were as such excused as proportionate under Article 8(2) because his family could also relocate or they could avail themselves of 'cheap train and coach fares'.[130] That approach is in line with earlier stances on exclusion orders.[131] It was overturned by the Supreme Court.[132] The impact on family life was not only a relevant issue to the determination of Article 5 but was capable of being decisive. The totality of conditions were destructive of the freedom to family life.

7.80 This case history suggests that the Home Office did not view *JJ* as fundamentally undermining the viability of control orders. However, the later judgment in *AP* is troubling not only because it restricts discretion but also because it reintroduces uncertainty into the Article 5 litigation, moving away from a quantitative argument about hours into qualitative arguments about social life.

Processes and fairness

7.81 The House of Lords considered issues of process under the standard of Article 6 in *MB* and *AF*.[133] The material which justified MB's control order included open and closed statements. The open

---

122 *E* [2007] EWCA Civ 459 at para 55; *Rideh* [2007] EWHC 2237 (Admin) at para 60; *AP* [2010] UKSC 24 at para 28.

123 App no 3455/05, 19 February 2009 para 171.

124 [2007] UKHL 45 at paras 105, 106.

125 Hansard HC vol 469 col 38ws (12 December 2007), Tony McNulty.

126 Lord Carlile, *Fourth Report of the Independent Review Pursuant to Section 14(3) of the Prevention of Terrorism Act 2005* (Home Office, London, 2009) para 15.

127 *Government Reply* (Cm 7856, London, 2010) p 3.

128 [2009] EWCA Civ 731.

129 *AP* [2008] EWHC 2001 (Admin) at para 97.

130 [2009] EWCA Civ 731 at para 40. See also *BX* [2010] EWHC 990.

131 Compare *McCullogh v United Kingdom*, App no 24889/94, 12 September 1997. See also *Ryan v United Kingdom*, App no 9202/80; *Mooney v United Kingdom*, App no 11517/85, 3 March 1986.

132 [2010] UKSC 24.

133 [2007] UKHL 46.

statement contained specific allegations about links to extremists and attempted travel to Iraq to fight against coalition forces.[134] These open allegations were admitted to be 'relatively thin' so that 'it is difficult to see how, in reality [MB] could make any effective challenge'.[135] The position of AF was even worse. AF was suspected of active links with the proscribed Libyan Islamic Fighting Group. The essence of the Secretary of State's case against AF was in the closed material.[136]

The House of Lords accepted that these proceedings fell within the less demanding civil limb **7.82** of Article 6(1) since they did not involve the determination of a criminal charge. The Secretary of State's suspicions did not have to disclose any criminal offence, and the order was preventative in purpose, not punitive or retributive.[137] Next, the disclosure of all relevant evidence was not an absolute right even in criminal proceedings against terrorism.[138] Applying these general principles, there was a breach of Article 6 since neither suspect had enjoyed a substantial measure of procedural justice. Yet, the court did not issue a declaration of incompatibility since the legislation did not impose an unacceptable level of secrecy. A majority of their Lordships read down under s 3 of the Human Rights Act 1998 so that the procedures take effect 'except where to do so would be incompatible with the right of the controlled person to a fair trial'.[139]

This outcome was not wholly in favour either of the controlled persons or the Home Office. **7.83** The Home Office secured two clear victories—acceptance of the lower civil standard under Article 6(1) with the prediction that breaches of it would be 'wholly exceptional'[140] and avoidance of a declaration of incompatibility under s 4 of the Human Rights Act 1998. At the same time, Lord Bingham accepted that 'the application of the civil limb of art 6(1) does in my opinion entitle such person to such measure of procedural protection as is commensurate with the gravity of the potential consequences'.[141] By the time the case had been fully argued, taking into account open material, closed material, and the impact of the special advocate, the High Court will have to assess whether 'a substantial measure or degree of procedural justice'[142] has been accorded. However, aside from Lord Hoffmann,[143] the majority concluded that the special advocate system is not a panacea which can automatically wipe clean the slate of any grave disability under Article 6.

In this way, the outcome on Article 6 is inherently more uncomfortable for the Home Office **7.84** than the position on liberty. Article 6 is a less dispositive concept. Fairness cannot readily be measured in a quantum of hours or conversant relatives. The Home Office faces a stark choice as to whether to compromise compelling security arguments in favour of disclosure, or to avoid reliance on sensitive information and hope that less sensitive submissions will be compelling, or to abandon the control order application.[144] The result may be described as a

---

[134] Ibid para 20.
[135] Ibid paras 39, 66.
[136] Ibid para 42.
[137] Ibid para 24. Compare Joint Committee on Human Rights, *Counter-Terrorism Policy and Human Rights: Draft Prevention of Terrorism Act 2005 (Continuance in force of sections 1 to 9) Order 2006* (2005–06 HL 122/HC 915) para 50.
[138] See *Botmeh and Alami v United Kingdom*, App no 15187/03, 7 June 2007.
[139] [2007] UKHL 46 at para 72.
[140] Ibid para 90 per Lord Brown.
[141] Ibid para 24.
[142] Ibid para 32.
[143] [2007] UKHL 46 at paras 51, 54.
[144] See *AF (No 3)* [2009] UKHL 28; *BM* [2009] EWHC 1572 (Admin); *AN* [2009] EWHC 1966 (Admin); *AE* [2008] EWHC 132 (Admin); *AS* [2009] EWHC 2564 (Admin).

teasing dance involving the shedding of intelligence veils, as the coy Home Office reluctantly reveals tantalizing flashes of its dossier but will not lay everything bare from the outset.[145] It is fortunate that the dance can be played out in the High Court which has offered to allow the Home Office to remedy any defect by further revelation after the close of the arguments in both open and closed hearings.[146] The courts have also assisted by offering to assume the validity of findings made on an earlier hearing under s 3(10), subject to any differences in the evidence relevant to those issues before the court on each of those hearings.[147] The courts have also assisted the Home Office by allowing it to impose confidentiality undertakings in relation to disclosed materials, so long as they do not hamper the legitimate pursuit of the suspect's case.[148]

7.85 This process of to and fro has raised another complaint of unfairness, namely, whether a judge who had decided issues in relation to detainees under the 2001 Act should then sit under the 2005 Act in relation to the same suspects.[149] Lord Justice Kennedy stated that no 'sweeping conclusion'[150] could be reached either to disqualify or to affirm competence. In *AF (No 2)*,[151] it was questioned whether a High Court judge who had previously rejected submissions in control order hearings, which had been reversed by the House of Lords and remitted back, should hear the case again. The Court of Appeal held that there was no appearance of bias and justice was served by employing a judge who was familiar with the case.

7.86 As expected, it has proven tricky to apply the *MB* judgment.[152] The most notable dispute returned to the House of Lords in *AF (No 3)*.[153] The question was whether suppression of even the gist of evidence meets Article 6 standards where, as stated by Lord Brown in *AF*,[154] 'no possible challenge could conceivably have succeeded'. The House of Lords concluded that *MB* had not set any 'core irreducible minimum' for the level of disclosure.[155] However, any complacency about this outcome was dispelled by the Strasbourg Court. In *A v United Kingdom*, a decision delivered just weeks previously, it endorsed the idea that there can be restrictions upon adversarial process in the interests of national security,[156] but it sustained breaches of Article 6 where disclosure had been insubstantial or non-existent.[157] The House of Lords treated this judgment as a damning retort to the Home Office's advocacy of total suppression. The test is now that[158]

> . . . the controlee must be given sufficient information about the allegations against him to enable him to give effective instructions in relation to those allegations. Provided that this requirement is satisfied there can be a fair trial notwithstanding that the controlee is not provided with the detail or the sources of the evidence forming the basis of the allegations.

---

145 Its attitude is criticized by the Joint Committee on Human Rights, *Counter-Terrorism Policy and Human Rights: Annual Renewal of Control Orders Legislation 2010* (2009–10 HL64/HC395) para 51.

146 *Bullivant* [2007] EWHC 2938 (Admin).

147 *AF* [2007] EWHC 2828 (Admin) para 17. Findings of SIAC are not binding: *AR* [2008] EWHC 3164 (Admin) at para 4.

148 *M* [2009] EWHC 425 (Admin).

149 *A* [2005] EWHC 1669 (Admin); *AF (No 2)* [2008] EWCA Civ 117.

150 Ibid para 22.

151 [2008] EWCA Civ 117. See further [2008] EWHC 453 (Admin).

152 See *Abu Rideh* [2008] EWHC 1993 (Admin); *AE* [2008] EWHC 132 (Admin); *AH* [2008] EWHC 1018 (Admin); *AN* [2008] EWHC 372 (Admin).

153 [2009] UKHL 28.

154 [2007] UKHL 46 at para 90.

155 [2009] UKHL 28 at paras 21, 38.

156 App no 3455/05, 19 February 2009, para 205.

157 Ibid paras 223, 224.

158 [2009] UKHL 28 para 59. Compare *A v United Kingdom*, App no 3455/05, 19 February 2009, para 220.

Where, however, the open material consists purely of general assertions and the case against the controlee is based solely or to a decisive degree on closed materials the requirements of a fair trial will not be satisfied . . .

Paragraph 4(3)(d) of the Schedule to the 2005 Act was therefore 'read down' under the Human Rights Act. In *AS*, the disclosure level required by *AF (No 3)* meant that all 'significant' allegations must be sufficiently disclosed.[159] Four orders were revoked after *AF (No 3)*, but two were replaced.[160]

Several control orders were subsequently abandoned by the Home Office. But control was **7.87** not rendered unworkable since substantial non-disclosure is still flexibly allowed. More positively, *MB* recognizes the human agency of suspects and their potential to correct error, the potential feelings of resentment of their relatives and community, and the need for public confidence in the application of draconian powers. It also recognizes that common law doctrines of natural law and of Article 6 demand fair process no matter whether the outcome is supportable or not. The outcome also encourages some degree of adversarial contest, as intended by the Schedule to the PTA 2005.

An attempt was later made to evade the strictures of Article 6 through orders which amounted **7.88** to 'control lite' and mainly limited movement and associations rather than imposing a curfew. In *BC* and *BB*, the High Court still viewed the order as involving restrictions which were 'the marks of a totalitarian regime'.[161] The extent of obligations was held not to alter the basic rule in *AF (No 3)* which applies to all control orders.[162]

A further suggestion along these lines by Lord Carlile is that there should be an alternative **7.89** 'Travel Restriction Order', similar to the orders under the CTA 2008, s 58, but for persons who have not been convicted.[163] The government doubted the utility of another distinct and narrow system, especially as the effectiveness of the restriction would depend on the ability to restrict communications about travel arrangements.[164]

Prosecution

In contrast to the foregoing achievements, the courts have been less insistent upon the **7.90** prioritization of prosecution. In *E*,[165] a non-derogating control order was challenged because the Secretary of State breached s 8. E, a Tunisian and former detainee under the 2001 Act, was suspected of involvement in the Tunisian Fighting Group, though it was not a proscribed organization and there was no evidence that E had directly engaged in violence. His claim that the realistic prospects of prosecuting him had not been properly pursued under s 8 arose from prosecutions of associates in Belgium in 2003 and 2005. Yet, no serious inquiry appeared to have been conducted by the English authorities, and E had not been interviewed by the police.[166]

The House of Lords accepted that the duty to consider prosecution under s 8(2) before an **7.91** initial control order is imposed was not a mandatory precondition to the initial making of a

---

[159] [2009] EWHC 2564 (Admin) at para 9.
[160] *Government Reply* (Cm 7856, London, 2010) p 4.
[161] [2009] EWHC 2927 (Admin) para 25.
[162] Ibid para 57.
[163] Lord Carlile, *Fifth Report of the Independent Reviewer pursuant to Section 14(3) of the Prevention of Terrorism Act* (Home Office, London, 2010) para 27.
[164] *Government Reply* (Cm 7855, London, 2010) p 4.
[165] [2007] UKHL 47.
[166] [2007] EWHC (Admin) 233 at para 124.

control order. To require otherwise could emasculate the preventative intent behind control orders. Nevertheless, s 8(2) was found to be 'expressed in strong mandatory terms . . . Plainly this duty is to be taken seriously.'[167] Furthermore, if prosecution was not properly considered, then the High Court could find the making of the order to be unnecessary or to be flawed under s 3. In this case the Secretary of State had consulted the chief officer of police, who had consulted the Crown Prosecution Service, and the advice had been negative.

7.92   The next argument was that the Secretary of State failed under s 8(4) to ensure that prosecution was kept under effective review after the control order was first made. The expressed view of the Home Office, that s 8(4) required no more than asking the police from time to time whether the prospect of successful prosecution had increased, was wrong, and Lord Bingham demanded a meaningful continuing review. Moreover, the Home Office must fulfil its duty to supply any relevant materials which came into its possession.[168] Adverse findings similar to s 8(2) could flow under s 3 in the event of non-observance of these duties.

7.93   After all these warnings, the case ended with a whimper, for the House of Lords dismissed the materiality of the new information about E. Rather like the position on Article 5, the more diligent consideration of prosecution might require more resources to be expended but does not present any insuperable practical problem for the Home Office or police. This judgment was a mere shot across the bows of the Home Office, and efforts to comply have been rather perfunctory, as evidenced by Lord Carlile's concerns. The government claims that more careful scrutiny has been instituted,[169] but no person subject to a control order has ever been prosecuted (aside from breaches of the order). The ruling out of prosecution should be a legal precondition, and the legislation should specify the frequency of review, the duty on relevant agencies to share information, and the duty to give reasons.[170]

Other legal challenges

7.94   Challenges were also raised in lower court litigation in *E* about the impact of control orders on family life (Article 8), an issue which was also taken up at one stage by his wife and children as third parties. The restrictions on computers and telephones raised issues under Article 10 (freedom of expression) but were not pursued. A further complaint was the damage to the mental health of his children (Article 3). The judges paid close attention to the psychological impacts, which caused depression for E himself and stress for his children. There was also information about hindrances to religious observances and child-care arrangements and, more generally, social isolation and stresses. However, national security interests provided justification within Article 8(2). As for Article 3, the control order restrictions were held not to pose a risk of such significant impact on the children's mental health that they were sufficiently 'humiliating and debasing them and possibly breaking their moral resistance'.[171] No specific conclusion was reached about E himself as the complaint was not pursued. It seems unlikely that control orders will regularly breach Article 3, given its 'high threshold' of damaging treatment.[172]

---

[167] Ibid para 15 per Lord Bingham.
[168] Ibid para 18.
[169] *Government Reply* (Cm 7194, London, 2007) p 12.
[170] Joint Committee on Human Rights, *Terrorism Policy and Human Rights: Annual Review of Control Orders Legislation 2008* (2007–08 HL 57/HC 356) paras 67, 72, 73; Joint Committee on Human Rights, *Counter-Terrorism Policy and Human Rights, Counter-Terrorism Bill* (2007–08 HL 108/HC 554) paras 73, 80. Compare Hansard HL vol 705 col 611 (11 November 2008), Lord West; *Government Reply* (Cm 7368, London, 2008) p 9.
[171] [2007] EWHC 233 (Admin) at para 309; [2007] EWCA Civ 459 at para 121.
[172] *A v United Kingdom*, App no 3455/05, 19 February 2009, para 134.

Mental health issues were further raised by Abu Rideh.[173] The applicant experienced a par-   **7.95**
ticular aversion to the process of reporting to the police. The court accepted that the mental
stress did not remove the need for a control order—mentally disturbed people can still
commit terrorism. But the Home Secretary was ordered to find alternatives to the mechanism of
reporting to the police in person and, in a second hearing, was ordered to reduce the frequency of reporting by telephone.

Challenges are of course regularly made both to the evidential sufficiency for the suspicion of ter-   **7.96**
rorism activity[174] or the necessity of an obligation and as to the formulation of an obligation.[175]

Conclusions

This morass of cases reveals that despite continued professions of 'due deference',[176] there is   **7.97**
applied an 'intense'[177] and sustained level of judicial vigilance and regular defeats for the
government. But, unlike in the *Belmarsh* case, a declaration of incompatibility has been
avoided. Perhaps the judges wished to avoid another spectacular show-down with the politicians. Perhaps control orders are objectively a lower order threat to basic rights. Either way,
the subtle effect of the judgments is to assert case-by-case resolution which is unpredicatble
in outcome. Thus, the control order system may be 'largely unscathed' but the courts have
hardly 'beaten a retreat' or confined their role to 'major irritant'.[178] There are regularly over
thirty hearings per year, they are heard in primary courts of justice, and their superintendence
has required justification and regular reassessment by the Home Office. A fair proportion of
control orders have not survived the process, and there have been squeals of anguish along
the way from Home Secretaries, bemoaning that control orders 'have got holes all through
them'[179] or that adverse court decisions are 'extremely disappointing'.[180] Yet, the Home
Office continues to prefer the nuanced case law to statutory restatement.[181]

In this way, the Prevention of Terrorism Act provides a platform for intervention by the High   **7.98**
Court, whose authority and ability to face down the securitocracy has unquestionably surpassed the deferential approach adopted in response to previous executive security measures,
whether exclusions orders[182] or Pt IV detention.[183] An important jurisprudence of executive
security is emergent through frequent and demanding court review. Far from being 'futile'
gestures, the human rights challenges have secured genuine transformations in the lives of
individuals.[184] At the same time, further reforms are needed to achieve more than minimalist

---

[173] *A* [2008] EWHC 1382 (Admin); *Rideh* [2008] EWHC 2019 (Admin). See also Liberty, *Renewing the Prevention of Terrorism Act 2005* (London, 2006) Annex 2.

[174] See *AV* [2009] EWHC 902 (Admin).

[175] See *E* [2007] EWHC 2232 (Admin); *AR* [2008] EWHC 2789 (Admin) and [2008] EWHC 3164 (Admin); *AE* [2008] EWHC 1743 (Admin); *AP* [2008] EWHC 2001 (Admin); *M* [2009] EWHC 572 (Admin); *AR* [2009] EWHC 1736 (Admin).

[176] *AM* [2009] EWHC 3053 (Admin) at para 185.

[177] *M* [2009] EWHC 572 (Admin) at para 7.

[178] Compare Ewing, KD and Tham, J-C, 'The continuing futility of the Human Rights Act' [2008] *Public Law* 668 at 668, 691.

[179] *The Times* 25 January 2007, p 2 (John Reid).

[180] *The Times* 11 June 2009, pp 6, 7 (Alan Johnson).

[181] See *Government Reply to the Joint Committee on Human Rights* (Cm 7625, London, 2009).

[182] Compare *Gallagher* (1994) *The Times* 16 February, [1996] 1 CMLR 557; *Adams* (1994) *The Times* 29 July, [1995] All ER (EC) 177 and *Adams and Benn v United Kingdom*, App nos 28979/95, 30343/96, 88A D & R 137 (1997); *McQuillan* [1995] 4 All ER 400.

[183] For the sole overturning of a Pt IV order, see *M* [2004] EWCA (Civ) 324.

[184] See for *AF* <http://news.bbc.co.uk/1/hi/uk/8240997.stm>, 2009.

fairness—changing the standard of proof to make it commensurate with restrictions imposed, setting a minimum standard of disclosure, and issuing reasons for making an order.[185]

7.99   For its part, the Home Office has put a brave face on the curtailment of control orders. They remain viable but only for a small number of cases.[186] The government's case for continuance is that control orders offer valuable protection where neither prosecution nor deportation is immediately viable and are more cost-effective than surveillance.[187]

Parliamentary review

7.100   Renewal debates have been disappointing—they are short and ill-attended. Much more detailed and persistent scrutiny has been undertaken by the Joint Committee on Human Rights. Its reports are fully referenced throughout this chapter.

D. Control Orders—Implementation

7.101   Three trends are evidenced in Table 7.1. First, the absolute numbers are low. There were dire predictions that control orders could affect 'hundreds—thousands, who knows'.[188] The actual number of orders in force has averaged 13.2, a rate similar to detention without trial even though there is no requirement of a derogation notice. This paltry total also starkly contrasts with the analysis in 2007 of Jonathan Evans, the Director of the Security Service, that there were 2,000 specific people who posed a direct threat to national security, plus as many again yet to be identified.[189] The meagre number of control orders is not for a want of customers but relates to their lack of security effectiveness and legal certainty compared to criminal prosecution.

Table 7.1 Control orders in force and by nationality[a]

Year end to 10 Dec	Control orders in force at year end		
	British citizen	*Foreigner*	*Total*
2005	1	8	9
2006	7	9	16
2007	8	6	14
2008	4	9	15
2009	9	3	12
Ave total	5.8	7	13.2

[a] Sources: Home Office Statements to Parliament; *Carlile Reports*

---

[185] Joint Committee on Human Rights, *Counter-Terrorism Policy and Human Rights: Counter-Terrorism Bill* (2007–08 HL 50, HC 199) para 64; Joint Committee on Human Rights, Counter-Terrorism Policy and Human Rights, *Counter-Terrorism Bill* (2007–08 HL 108/HC 554) paras 101, 107.

[186] Lord Carlile, *Fifth Report of the Independent Reviewer pursuant to Section 14(3) of the Prevention of Terrorism Act* (Home Office, London, 2010) para 96.

[187] Home Office, *Memorandum to the Home Affairs Committee, Post Legislative Assessment of the Prevention of Terrorism Act 2005* (Cm 7797, London, 2010); *Government Reply* (Cm 7856, London, 2010) p 14. Compare Joint Committee on Human Rights, *Counter-Terrorism Policy and Human Rights: Annual Renewal of Control Orders Legislation 2010* (2009–10 HL64/HC395) para 112.

[188] Gearty, C, 'Human rights in an age of counter-terrorism' (2005) 58 *Current Legal Problems* 25 at 43.

[189] *Manchester Evening News*, 5 November 2007.

The second feature is that orders against British citizens have become a growing proportion. **7.102**
Yet, the total of orders in force would have been higher and more oriented towards foreigners
were it not for an aggressive policy of deportations after July 2005. Deportation notices were
served on ten persons previously subject to control, and six have been deported.[190] Orders
against foreigners will persist, especially because of the occasional willingness to grant bail
pending deportation.[191]

A third feature (disclosed by the sources for the tables) is that all subjects are male and suspected **7.103**
of international terrorism. Irish republican dissidents have not been candidates, a reflection
of the origins of control orders.

Table 7.2 qualifies the picture just presented. The cumulative total of orders issued and **7.104**
persons affected far exceeds the figure for detention without trial. At the same time, even if
the figure for control orders is higher than for detention without trial, it is much lower than the
rate of prosecution for terrorist-related offences; from 2005 to 2008, over 100 prosecutions
have been mounted. The dynamic nature of the system is also reflected in modifications—in
the period 2008–09, there were 372 modifications (not including those refused).

Table 7.2 Control orders issued and persons affected[a]

Year end to 10 Dec	Control orders issued	Cumulative total persons affected
2005	18	18
2006	19	19
2007	7	31
2008	9	38
2009	13	45

[a] Sources: Home Office Statements to Parliament; *Carlile Reports*.
For individual profiles, see Simcox, R, *Control Orders* (Centre for
Social Cohesion, London, 2010).

Another quantitative indicator which has sparked comment is the rate of breaches and **7.105**
absconders. A seventh absconder was reported in 2007 but none since then.[192]

E. Control Orders—Foreign Comparisons

Expressly borrowing from British precedents, the (Australian) Anti-Terrorism Act (No 2) **7.106**
2005,[193] Sch 4 (inserting Division 104 into the Criminal Code Act 1995), allows for a senior
Australian Federal Police officer, subject to permission from the Attorney General, to apply
ex parte to a Federal court to issue an interim control order for up to twelve months. The
court must be satisfied, on the balance of probabilities that: making the order would substantially assist in preventing a terrorist act, or the person has provided training to, or received

[190] *Government Reply* (Cm 7855, London, 2010) p 19.
[191] See *Al-Saadi* [2009] EWHC 3390 (Admin).
[192] *Government Reply* (Cm 7855, London, 2010) p 7. There have been eight prosecutions, with one
conviction and three awaited: p 8.
[193] See Jaggers, B, *Anti-Terrorism Control Orders in Australia and the United Kingdom* (RP28, Parliamentary
Library, Canberra, 2008).

training from, a listed terrorist organization; and that all impositions under the order are reasonably necessary and appropriate to protect the public from a terrorist act. For a full order, there must be a confirmation hearing at which both parties appear, though material may be withheld to avoid prejudice to national security or police operations. The legislation is subject to a sunset clause of ten years.

7.107   The first control order was issued in 2006 against Joseph Terrence ('Jihad Jack') Thomas because of his training and links with Al-Qa'ida.[194] The High Court upheld the constitutionality of Division 104 under various headings of s 51 of the Federal Consitution. The High Court also dismissed separation of powers challenges; control orders were not incompatible with judicial involvement in terms of their procedure or preventative substance. Thomas' control order, which followed the overturning of a conviction,[195] included conditions such as a five-hour curfew, restrictions on communications (including specifically with Osama bin Laden), and a ban on foreign travel. Thomas was retried in 2008 but was convicted only of possessing a forged passport.[196] Pending that trial, the control order was lifted, though equivalent bail conditions were imposed.

7.108   An equally contentious control order was issued in 2007 against David Hicks, pending his release after being convicted of terrorist training before a military commission in Guantánamo Bay and then, after transfer, being imprisoned in Australia. The order imposed a four-hour curfew[197] but expired in 2008.

7.109   Another former Guantánamo resident, Mamdouh Habib, was not subjected to control, but his passport was cancelled.[198]

7.110   The USA PATRIOT Act 2001 allows for the drastic executive response of detention for up to six months at a time of non-citizens who are certified as suspected terrorists.[199] This power has not been invoked, though, as described in Chapter 6, there remains the alternative system of military detention and commissions for foreigners in Guantánamo. Two US citizens (Yaser Hamdi and José Padilla) were initially detained without trial (and held in military custody on the mainland), but their cases were resolved by prosecution in one case and expulsion after withdrawal of citizenship in the other.[200] Control orders have not been seriously considered, though restrictions of liberty for foreigners on grounds of national security were countenanced in *Zadvydas v David*.[201]

F. Control Orders—Assessment and Conclusions

7.111   The policy objectives behind control orders are prevention and disruption, though the measure formally falls within 'Pursue' within 'CONTEST'. On a quantitative basis, its impact appears modest, though controlled persons are often presented as exceedingly dangerous individuals.

---

[194]   *Thomas v Mowbray* [2007] HCA 33.
[195]   *R v Thomas* [2006] VSCA 165.
[196]   See *R v Thomas (No 3)* [2006] VSCA 300, *(No 4)* [2008] VSCA 107.
[197]   See *Jabbour v Hicks* [2008] FMCA 178; *Hicks v Ruddock* [2007] FCA 299.
[198]   See *Habib v Director of National Security* [2009] FCAFC 48.
[199]   PL 107-56, s 412.
[200]   See *Hamdi v Rumsfeld* (2004) 542 US 507; *Rumsfeld v Padilla* (2004) 542 US 426 (2004); *Padilla v Hanft* (2006) 542 US 1062; *US v Hassoun* [2007] US Dist LEXIS 85720.
[201]   (2001) 533 US 678 at 696.

Turning to qualitative assessments, levels of constitutional governance are good, with detailed **7.112** rules as to the working of the system. Accountability has already been assessed in regard to reviews by Parliament and by the independent assessor.

Audit on the basis of individual rights by the courts has also been explored. Control orders **7.113** reflect a more judicialized approach than prior executive models but still fail abysmally by the standards of criminal process. The legal regulation of security intelligence remains at nascent stage compared to traditional rules of evidence. There is little legal guidance about targeting, despite the known dangers of skewing the objects of investigative attention through police cultures.[202] What is counted as 'quality' or 'valid' intelligence is barely structured, a concept which was summarily rejected in *GG* and *NN*[203] but which is a developing theme in criminal intelligence.[204]

Outcomes based on intelligence also await smarter delimitation. In particular, without the **7.114** high standard of proof as in judicial contexts, there should be time limits on orders. To this end, control orders should persist for no more than twelve months, without the possibility of renewal on the same grounds.[205] A time limit could transform the landscape by turning a control order away from the warehousing of suspects into a provisional charge or a provisional deportation pending the compilation of a dossier which proves or dispels the state's suspicions. Either way, the Home Office would put on notice that control orders cannot be relied on for what one government Minister called (with inimitable logic), 'an identifiable, limited period . . . on a continuous basis'.[206] Lord Carlile has endorsed a time limit, though with a modified period of two years and without imposing it as an absolute boundary.[207] As at the end of 2008, five suspects had been controlled for longer than two years.[208] The government responds that there is nothing 'magical' about any set period,[209] though indefinite reliance is 'probably not appropriate'.[210] The judicial viewpoint is that an order can continue so long as the terrorist activity persists.[211] However, the effluxion of time was decisive in *Al-Saaadi*,[212] where a control order was imposed in 2008 following attempts to deport the subject, who had been detained from 2002 until 2007. Given that the period had passed without observed terrorist activities, any terrorist links had 'atrophied' and so a control order became unnecessary.[213] The court accepted as a guide that a control order should not persist for more than two years,[214] also endorsed in *AT* and *AW*.[215]

---

[202] See Gill, P, *Rounding Up the Usual Suspects?* (Ashgate, Aldershot, 2000) pp 130, 249.
[203] [2009] EWHC 142 (Admin) at para 41.
[204] See National Centre for Policing Excellence, *National Intelligence Model* (Home Office, London, 2005); NPIA, *Guidance on the Management of Police Information* (2nd edn, Wyboston, 2010) App 2.
[205] See Walker, C, 'Keeping control of terrorists without losing control of constitutionalism' (2007) 59 *Stanford Law Review* 1395 at 1458.
[206] Hansard HL vol 670 col 515 (7 March 2005), Baroness Scotland.
[207] See *Fourth Report of the Independent Review Pursuant to Section 14(3) of the Prevention of Terrorism Act 2005* (Home Office, London, 2009) para 58. See also Joint Committee on Human Rights, *Terrorism Policy and Human Rights: Annual Review of Control Orders Legislation 2008* (2007–08 HL 57/HC 356) para 84.
[208] Hansard HC vol 488 col 738 (3 March 2009).
[209] Hansard HC vol 477 col 211 (10 June 2008), Tony McNulty. See further *Government Reply* (Cm 7367, London, 2008) p 4; *Government Reply to the Report by Lord Carlile* (Cm 7624, 2009) p 8.
[210] Hansard HC vol 472 cols 566, 584 (21 February 2008), Tony McNulty.
[211] *Rideh* [2008] EWHC 2019 (Admin) at para 24; *GG and NN* [2009] EWHC 142 (Admin) at para 50.
[212] [2009] EWHC 3390 (Admin).
[213] [2009] EWHC 3390 (Admin) at para 186.
[214] Ibid para 182.
[215] [2009] EWHC 512 (Admin) at para 29.

7.115   What will or what should become the future fate of control orders? One may simply concur that control orders are 'odious' and wish them gone.[216] Two arguments contend against this preferred outcome. First, the imperative of responding to anticipatory risk of terrorism has not dissipated. Secondly, the factual persistence of special anti-terrorism executive measures since 1974 in Britain for all but eleven months in 2001 equally conduces against their summary abandonment.

7.116   A more sophisticated analysis is that whilst prosecution is an ethically superior pathway towards 'Pursue' as explained in Chapter 6, control orders can be conceptually justifiable as distinctive preventive measures, joining the legal landscape further populated by anti-social behaviour orders, sex offender orders, serious crime prevention orders, and violent offender orders.[217] Given the evident trend towards preventative quasi-crime devices, it is not plausible to exempt terrorism from this approach.[218]

7.117   The prospects for Parliament calling time on control orders will strengthen when the number of extant orders has been sufficiently depressed through a combination of factors—court challenges and an increase in prosecutions with intercept evidence. Limited action against Al-Qa'ida suspects could alternatively be taken via the travel ban pursuant to listing under UNSCR 1390, though it is arguably more monstrous an imposition than control orders, as described in Chapter 9. In the meantime, attention to minimizing the role of control orders should be taken more seriously if freedoms, such as the right to due process in para 39 of Magna Carta in 1215, are to represent more than archaic sentiments.

G. Other Executive Powers Relevant to Terrorism

Civil and social control

7.118   Various measures have been suggested instead of control orders. Lord Carlile proposed that anti-social behaviour orders or civil injunctions might be deployed.[219] The government is sceptical, presumably because of their limited impact and their open procedures.[220] Nevertheless, a tiered pyramid of responsive social regulation to terrorism should be considered. Instead of the limited repertoire of prosecution or control, various social interventions could handle those merely 'at risk' of terrorism.[221] A prime example might be 'Project Channel', as delineated in Chapter 6.

Detention without trial

7.119   Far less appealing prospects than control orders have been contemplated, including the reversal of the abandonment of detention without trial which is claimed to have been based on 'egregious mistakes'.[222] However, this viewpoint is based upon shallow research into relevant case law, a caul of gullibility about the facts of executive policy and intentions, and

---

[216]   Bates, E, 'Anti terrorism control orders' (2009) 29 *Legal Studies* 99 at 119, 125.

[217]   Crime and Disorder Act 1997, Pt I; Serious Crime Act 2007, Pt I; Criminal Justice and Immigration Act 2008, Pt VII.

[218]   Zedner, L, 'Preventive justice or just pre-punishment?' (2007) 60 *Current Legal Problems* 174 at 203.

[219]   Lord Carlile, *Third Report of the Independent Review Pursuant to Section 14(3) of the Prevention of Terrorism Act 2005* (Home Office, London, 2008) para 26.

[220]   *Government Reply* (Cm 7367, London, 2008) p 2; Hansard HC vol 472 col 566 (21 February 2008), Tony McNulty.

[221]   See Home Office, *From the Neighbourhood to the National* (Cm 7448, London, 2008) paras 1.49–1.51.

[222]   Campbell, D, 'The threat of terrorism and the plausibility of positivism' [2009] *Public Law* 501 at 505.

a failure to appreciate the law/fact interface at the heart of the dispute in the *Belmarsh* case.[223] The proposal would also revive the problems of 'neighbour' terrorists who were ignored by Pt IV and the even more fundamental quandary of wrapping security laws within the cloak of immigration detention. In short, continued support for foreigner detention without trial ignores the inconvenient truths which persist today just as they existed in 2007. These problems do not evaporate if a new system of detention without trial could be established separate from deportation and apply to citizen and foreigner alike. While the persistence of a *jihadi* terrorism 'emergency' for the next thirty years[224] no more rules out a valid notice of derogation than did the persistence for decades of an Irish terrorism 'emergency', the era of judicial acquiescence to long-term detention is waning on the evidence of the *Belmarsh* case. Furthermore, long-term detention could give rise to viable complaints under Article 3.[225]

A variant of this demand for detention without trial is that it might be revived under Pt II of the **7.120** Civil Contingencies Act 2004.[226] The definition of 'emergency' in s 19(1)(c) expressly refers to terrorism, ensuring that the legislation is potentially relevant.[227] Yet, even the government decided against resort to the 2004 Act as an alternative to 42-day detention during debates on the Counter-Terrorism Bill 2007–08.[228] Factors against the Civil Contingencies Act include doubts over whether any form of detention would be *intra vires*, despite the breadth of s 22(3).[229] If invoked, there would be debates in Parliament about the application of powers to individuals, contrary to the principle of the separation of powers.[230] Next, the details of the measures to be implemented by Pt II would be revealed only during a feverish emergency period when the guard of Parliament is down. Thus, a foreseeable risk such as terrorism should be tackled within standing primary legislation while emergency regulations remain a last resort when planning has failed.

Entry, immigration, and nationality controls

Introduction and background

The *Belmarsh* case effectively dislodged a security detention regime from the panoply of **7.121** immigration law. However, it did not stop the continued securitization of immigration laws against foreigners. A resolution within immigration law affords several attractions for the state. Compared to criminal prosecution and even control orders, Article 6 safeguards are reduced.[231] Compared to control orders, the 'exit model'[232] offers a cleaner and surer method of eliminating risk, as well as again eliminating many human rights requirements. At the same time, whether it makes sense in policing terms to lose sight of one's enemies was one of the doubts voiced by the Newton Committee.[233] The government promised that 'we shall

---

[223] See further Walker, C, 'The threat of terrorism and the fate of control orders' [2010] *Public Law* 3.

[224] House of Commons Defence Select Committee, *UK national security and resilience* (2007–08 HC 718) 21 October 2008 q 63 Lord West.

[225] Compare *A* [2008] EWHC 1382 (Admin); *Rideh* [2008] EWHC 2019 (Admin); *Léger v France*, App no 19324/02, 11 April 2006.

[226] Campbell, D, 'The threat of terrorism and the plausibility of positivism' [2009] *Public Law* 501 at 515.

[227] See Walker, C and Broderick, J, *The Civil Contingencies Act 2004* (Oxford University Press, Oxford, 2006) ch 5.

[228] See Home Affairs Committee, *The Government's Terrorism Proposals* (2007–08 HC 43) para 74; Joint Committee on Human Rights, *Counter-Terrorism Policy and Human Rights: 42 days* (2007–08 HL 116/HC 635) paras 24–31.

[229] Home Office, *Pre-charge Detention of Terrorist Suspects* (Home Office, London, 2007) p 7. Compare the restrictive approach in *GG* [2009] EWCA Civ 786.

[230] See House of Lords Select Committee on the Constitution, *Counter-Terrorism Bill: The Role of Ministers, Parliament and the Judiciary* (2007–08 HL 167).

[231] See *Y* (SC/36/2005, 2006) para 72; *Al-Sirri* [2009] EWCA Civ 222 at para 25.

[232] See Walker, C, 'The treatment of foreign terror suspects' (2007) 70 *Modern Law Review* 427.

[233] *Newton Report*, Pt D, para 195.

not use the powers to export risk'.[234] Policy contradictions notwithstanding, a number of tactics are being adopted to enhance the exit model.

Provisions—deportation and exclusion

7.122 Section 8B of the Immigration Act 1971 (inserted by s 8 of the Immigration and Asylum Act 1999) specifies refusal of entry for 'excluded persons', including persons listed pursuant to UN or EU instrument as linked to Al-Qa'ida or the Taliban.[235]

7.123 Deportation can arise automatically following a period of imprisonment of at least twelve months under the UK Borders Act 2007, s 32, unless in breach of fundamental rights under s 33.[236] Discretionary deportation on grounds of national security is of greater relevance. Under the Immigration Act 1971, s 3(5)(a), 'A person who is not a British citizen is liable to deportation from the United Kingdom if the Secretary of State deems his deportation to be conducive to the public good . . .' SIAC accepted in the 'singular' case of *T* that the Algerian terror suspect had put terrorism behind him and wanted to live quietly with his family.[237]

7.124 These powers are limited for non-British European Union state citizens who qualify for free movement as workers or other protected categories under the Citizens Directive 2004/58/EC, as implemented by the Immigration (European Economic Area) Regulations 2006.[238] Curtailment of freedoms under 'the public policy proviso' must be based on current personal conduct and not mere suspicions or past associations or misdeeds.[239] Under art 28 (2006 Regulation 21(6)), a Member State must to take into account factors such as length of residence (with tighter rules applying after ten years), other personal circumstances, and social and cultural integration. However, these may be proportionately overriden by the need to disrupt terrorist communications and cohesion by deportation.[240]

7.125 The Nationality, Immigration and Asylum Act 2002, s 82, provides for a right of appeal against a decision to deport, but a special system of challenge against public good or national security grounds is afforded when the Secretary of State issues a certificate under ss 97 and 98. This triggers the Special Immigration Appeals Commission Act 1997, as implemented by the the Special Immigration Appeals Commission (Procedure) Rules 2003.[241] The processes of SIAC formed the basis of the Schedule to the PTA 2005 and CPR 76, and so have largely been described. SIAC occasionally rejects the determination of the government on the threat to national security[242] but does recognize the expertise of the security and governmental authorities.[243] In *XC*,[244] SIAC suggested that the security assessment should be 'clearly wrong' before it could be overturned.

---

234 House of Commons Standing Committee E col 271 (25 October 2005), Tony McNulty.
235 See Immigration (Designation of Travel Bans) Order 2000, SI 2000/2724 (as amended by SI 2001/2377 and SI 2003/3285).
236 For Irish nationals, see Hansard HC vol 457 col 3ws (19 February 2007); UK Border Agency, *Enforcement Instructions and Guidance* (2008) para 12.3.1.
237 (SC/31/2005, 22 March 2010) para 28.
238 SI 2006/1003.
239 See *Rutili v Minister for the Interior* [1975] ECR 1219, [1976] 1 CMLR 140; Case C-503/03, *European Commission v Spain* [2006] ECR I-1097.
240 *MK* (SC/29/2004, 2006).
241 SI 2003/1034, as amended by SI 2007/1285.
242 See *Sihali* (SC/38/2005, 2007).
243 *Y* (SC/36/2005, 2006) para 324.
244 (SC 77-82, 2009) para 2.

The expulsion of aliens was held in RB (*Algeria*) not to engage rights to a judicial hearing **7.126** under Article 6, but any detention must be subject to review by a 'court' under Article 5(4) and if any appeal is granted then it must be fair, a standard met by SIAC.[245] The decisions in *MB* and *AF (No 3)* do not have direct application to deportation decisions.[246] Once again, procedural protections are strengthened for those persons falling within the Citizens Directive 2004/58/EC (Articles 30 and 31). In *Rutili*, the immigrant had to be given (in terms redolent of *AF (No 3)* 'a precise and comprehensive statement of the grounds for the decision' to enable effective steps to prepare a defence.[247]

The exit strategy for terrorists under these rules was considered in a Consultation document **7.127** issued by the Home Office in August 2005, *Exclusion or Deportation from the UK on Non-Conducive Grounds*. The grounds of 'not conducive to the public good' were extended from reasons related to, *inter alia*, national security or good relations with a third country to include 'unacceptable behaviours' as follows:[248]

> To express views which the Government considers:– Foment terrorism or seek to provoke others to terrorist acts; Justify or glorify terrorism; Foment other serious criminal activity or seek to provoke others to serious criminal acts; Foster hatred which may lead to intra community violence in the UK; Advocate violence in furtherance of particular beliefs . . .

Related work was undertaken to compile 'lists of extremist bookshops etc, engagement of which would trigger deportation' and 'to identify extremists overseas who pose a threat to the UK [and] a similar list of individuals in the UK'.[249] A total of twenty-two persons were initially put on the list.[250] Persons affected include 'preachers of hate' and persons allegedly linked to terrorist groups. The highest profile casualty was Geert Wilders, the Dutch MP who made the film, *Fitna*. He successfully appealed against his ban in 2009.[251] The views which the government considers to be 'unacceptable' are formulated in very broad and vague terms and so, despite the envisaged restrictions in Article 16 of the European Convention, may raise objections under Articles 10 or 14.[252]

An associated issue is detention pending deportation under the Immigration Act 1971, **7.128** Sch 3 para 2. There were 2,595 detainees under Immigration Act powers at the end of 2009, and all bar 735 were held for more than twenty-eight days.[253] There is no set statutory limit on detention, but the courts have imposed constraints to comply with Article 5(1)(f).[254] The detention must serve the genuine and live purpose of deportation; the purpose must be pursued with reasonable diligence and expedition; and the period must be reasonable in all the cir-

---

[245] [2009] UKHL 10 at para 105. See further *Maaouia v France* App no 39652/98, 5 October 2000.
[246] Ibid paras 178, 226, 255, 264. But compare Lord Philips at para 88. SIAC expressly rejected the notion of gisting: *OO* (SC/51/2006, 2007) para 20; *ZZ* (SC/63/2007, 2008) para 14; *IR* (SC/70/2008, 2009). The common law position on fairness is displaced by the clear rules of the SIAC system: *W* [2010] EWCA Civ 898.
[247] *Rutili v Minister for the Interior* [1975] ECR 1219, [1976] 1 CMLR 140 at para 39.
[248] (Home Office, 2005) para 7.
[249] HC Deb vol 440 col 167ws (15 December 2005), Charles Clarke.
[250] *The Times* 6 May 2009, p 5.
[251] [2009] UKAIT 00050.
[252] Compare *Piermont v France* App nos 15773/89; 15774/89, Ser A 314 (1995); *Farrakhan* [2002] EWCA Civ 606.
[253] Home Office, *Control of Immigration: Quarterly Statistical Summary, United Kingdom—Fourth Quarter 2009* (London, 2010) p 54.
[254] *Saadi v United Kingdom*, App no 13229/03, 29 January 2008, para 70; *A v United Kingdom*, App no 3455/05, 19 February 2009, para 164.

cumstances, so that the deportation is foreseeable within a reasonable timeframe.[255] Bail can be granted (under the Immigration Act 1971, Sch 2, paras 22 and 34 and under the SIAC Act 1997, s 3) but is not very common in national security cases.[256] If granted, bail conditions can be stricter than control obligations.[257] The stance on bail was altered significantly in late 2009, when the Administrative Court in *R (Cart) v Upper Tribunal; U v SIAC* decided that the same minimum standard of procedural fairness applies in the case of SIAC bail hearings with respect to Article 5(4) as applies in the case of control orders under Article 6.[258]

Provisions—refining exceptions to non-refoulement

7.129 A foreign terror suspect may claim asylum under the (Geneva) Convention relating to the Status of Refugees 1951 as a persecuted freedom fighter or political dissident. If the claim is valid, then refoulement will be forbidden, subject to Articles 32 and 33 which provide exceptions on grounds of danger to national security or where danger to the community arises on account of having been convicted of a particularly serious crime. A 'serious crime' is further defined by the Nationality, Immigration and Asylum Act 2002, s 72. The offences listed in the Nationality, Immigration and Asylum Act 2002 (Specification of Particularly Serious Crimes) Order 2004[259] include many terrorism-related offences and carry the presumption of seriousness.

7.130 The Immigration, Asylum and Nationality Act 2006, s 54, seeks to deny that some claims to asylum can be denied. A claimant under Article 1F of the 1951 Convention will fail if:

> (a) he has committed a crime against peace, a war crime, or a crime against humanity, as defined in the international instruments drawn up to make provision in respect of such crimes;
> (b) he has committed a serious non-political crime outside the country of refuge prior to his admission to that country as a refugee; (c) he has been guilty of acts contrary to the purposes and principles of the United Nations.

These terms are to be interpreted under s 54 as including acts of committing, preparing, or instigating terrorism (whether or not the acts amount to an actual or inchoate offence) and acts of encouraging or inducing others to commit, prepare, or instigate terrorism. 'Terrorism' has the meaning given by s 1 of the TA 2000 (s 54(2)), and no account can be taken of the justifiability of the political violence.[260] The term was interpreted in *KK*[261] as not applying to every political crime within United Kingdom law but referring to acts which are the subject of intense disapproval by the governing body of the entire international community. It followed in *MH (Syria) v Secretary of State for the Home Department* that involvement in political and humanitarian work for the PKK did not fall within Article 1F.[262] In *R (JS) (Sri Lanka)*,[263] an asylum claim by a long-term officer of the LTTE could not be denied on a joint enterprise argument that as the LTTE was tainted with crimes against humanity and war crimes, so were its members, regardless of their specific contribution. Mere membership was not sufficient under Article 1F.

---

[255] *R v Governor of Durham Prison, ex parte Hardial Singh* [1984] 1 WLR 704; *I* [2002] EWCA Civ 888; *HXA v Home Office* [2010] EWHC 1117 (QB).

[256] UK Border Agency, *Enforcement Instructions and Guidance* (2008) ch 57.5.1.

[257] See *VV* (SC/59/2006, 2007); *O* (SC/15/2005, 2008).

[258] [2009] EWHC 3052 (Admin) at para 112. See further *A v United Kingdom*, App no 3455/05, 19 February 2009, para 217; *U* (SC32/2005, SC/77, 80/2009) para 7.

[259] SI 2004/1910.

[260] Joint Committee on Human Rights, *Counter-Terrorism Policy and Human Rights: Terrorism Bill and related matters* (2005–06 HL75, HC 561) para 176.

[261] [2004] UKIAT 101.

[262] [2009] EWCA Civ 226. See Chapter 8 for details of the PKK.

[263] [2010] UKSC 15. See Chapter 8 for details of the LTTE.

A further complication is Council Directive 2004/83/EC of 29 April 2004 on minimum   **7.131**
standards for the qualification and status of third country nationals or stateless persons
as refugees or as persons who otherwise need international protection and the content of
the protection granted, as implemented by the Refugee or Person in Need of International
Protection (Qualification) Regulations 2006.[264] Article 12 reflects Article 1F of the
Convention. In *Al-Sirri*,[265] the forbidden actions formulated in art 12 were viewed as narrower than the TA 2000, s 1. As a result, the adoption by s 54(2) of the meaning of terrorism
in s 1 must be read down where necessary.

Provisions—nationality and terrorism

The next move against terrorism is the denial of nationality by naturalization under the   **7.132**
British Nationality Act 1981, s 6 and Sch 1, on the grounds that the Secretary of State is not
satisfied of 'good character'. Article 6 rights do not apply to any dispute.[266]

The Immigration, Asylum and Nationality Act 2006, ss 56 and 57, allow for the deprivation   **7.133**
of British nationality or rights of abode on the further ground that it is conducive to the
'public good'. 'Public good' replaces the previous narrower criterion in s 40 of the 1981 Act
that the applicant had done something which was 'seriously prejudicial to the vital interests
of the United Kingdom'. Since there is no intention to create statelessness,[267] this measure
will inevitably discriminate against persons of minority racial or ethnic origins who have
dual nationality.[268]

These provisions followed litigation over David Hicks, an Australian citizen who had been   **7.134**
detained at Guantánamo Bay. He sought British citizenship so as to force the Foreign and
Commonwealth Office to lobby for his release.[269] Based on the pre-2006 version of s 40, the
Home Secretary accepted his claim to registration, but his claims that there existed an overriding power to refuse on public interest grounds or that there was a power to instantaneously
withdraw citizenship were rejected.[270] The Secretary of State would have to conduct an assessment of Hick's actions and intentions after he became a citizen to found lawful grounds.

The final aspect of policy development regarding nationality was accomplished by the   **7.135**
Immigration, Asylum and Nationality Act 2006, s 58, which requires applicants for British
nationality by registration (unless on the basis of statelessness) to satisfy the Secretary of State
that they are 'of good character'. The change has been now reformulated by the Borders,
Citizenship and Immigration Act 2009, s 47. The measure was cited in *AHK* where the
refusal was on non-disclosed grounds relating to extremist views or terrorist associations.[271]

Provisions—safety on return and deportation with assurances

Even when the path to removal has been cleared, the authorities must still contend with   **7.136**
the doctrine against creating a risk of Article 3 treatment, as pronounced in *Chahal v*

---

[264] SI 2006/2525.

[265] [2009] EWCA Civ 222 at para 29.

[266] *MH (Syria)* [2008] EWHC 2525 (Admin), [2009] EWCA Civ 226.

[267] See *Al-Jedda* (SC/66/2008, 2009).

[268] Joint Committee on Human Rights, *Counter-Terrorism Policy and Human Rights: Terrorism Bill and related matters* (2005–06 HL75, HC 561) para 163 and *Government Response* (2005–06 HL 114, HC 888) p 17.

[269] See *R (Abbasi) v Secretary of State for Foreign and Commonwealth Affairs* [2002] EWCA Civ 1598.

[270] *Hicks* [2006] EWCA Civ 400. In the Immigration, Asylum and Nationality Act 2006, s 56, public good factors are decoupled from allegiance.

[271] [2009] EWCA Civ 287.

United Kingdom.[272] This ruling can benefit a suspected terrorist, no matter how 'undesirable or dangerous' and national security cannot be balanced against Article 3.[273] Added to this potential obstacle, the Court also has pronounced against removal which risks a flagrant breach of liberty or due process.[274] Thus, a legal limbo can be created for terror suspects—subject to deportation (and possibly detention too)[275] but going nowhere in reality.

7.137 Possible responses include control orders or encouraging another state to seek extradition.[276] However, a more direct response has been to secure assurances from the receiving state as to safety on return.[277] This device has been explored for some time[278] and builds on the precedent of assurances from US authorities not to apply the death penalty in extradition cases.[279] Yet, assurances in the context of the death penalty are easier to monitor since the death penalty will normally be applied with official approval and will be announced and perhaps witnessed. The same device applied to torture stumbles over the ability to secure credible assurances against practices which are often denied, hidden, ignored, or embedded despite the best of official intentions.[280] Furthermore, the transfer of the issue into the diplomatic sphere means that human rights are no longer the sole or perhaps predominant issue.

7.138 Negotiations have been pursued with several states, culminating in an agreement with Jordan on 10 August 2005.[281] Procedural safeguards require, *inter alia*, treatment in a humane and proper manner and in accordance with international standards, pre-trial legal assistance, prompt processes, and a fair and public hearing. Visits will be made by the representative of a jointly nominated independent body. On the other hand, consular visits are not permitted after arrest. Nor is there provision for the recording of interrogations, regular and independent medical checks, or unannounced access by the independent body. Nor is there any specific guarantee against the death penalty. No suspect has as yet been rendered back to Jordan on the basis of this agreement. A second Memorandum of Understanding was signed with Libya on 18 October 2005.[282] Notable extra clauses here include the promise of retrial where, before deportation, a person has been convicted in absentia and also

---

[272] App no 22414/93, 1996-V at para 97. The doctrine has been reaffirmed, most notably in the face of UK third party intervention in *Saadi v Italy*, App no 37201/06, 28 February 2008. It also avows the United Nations Convention against Torture and Other Cruel, Inhuman or Degrading Treatment or Punishment 1984, art 3(1).

[273] Ibid paras 76, 80.

[274] See *EM (Lebanon)*[2008] UKHL 64 at para 38.

[275] See *Q* [2006] EWCA Civ 2690 (Admin); Lord Carlile, *First Report of the Independent Reviewer pursuant to Section 14(3) of the Prevention of Terrorism Act 2005* (Home Office, London, 2006) paras 22, 23.

[276] As in the request of the US government following *Naseer* (SC/77, 80-83/2009, 18 May 2010).

[277] See Jones, K, 'Deportation with assurances' (2008) 57 *International and Comparative Law Quarterly* 183; Tooze, J, 'Deportation with assurances' [2010] *Public Law* 362 (forty-three persons have been affected since August 2005: p 377).

[278] See *Lloyd Report*, para 18.14; *Home Office Response to Newton Report*, para 38.

[279] See *Soering v United Kingdom*, App no 14038/88, Ser A 161 (1989).

[280] See especially *Youssef v Home Office* [2004] EWHC 1884 (QB); Human Rights Watch, *Still at Risk: Diplomatic Assurances No Safeguard Against Torture* (New York, 2005); Amnesty International, *Dangerous Deals* (London, 2010).

[281] Memorandum of Understanding Between the Government of the United Kingdom of Great Britain and Northern Ireland and the Government of the Hashemite Kingdom of Jordan Regulating the Provision of Undertakings in Respect of Specified Persons Prior to Deportation (2005).

[282] Memorandum of Understanding Between the Government of Libya and the Government of the United Kingdom Concerning the Provision of Assurances in Respect of Persons Subject to Deportation (2005).

an assurance that the death penalty will not be carried out. The monitoring body in Libya can order medical examinations. A third Memorandum of Understanding was agreed with Lebanon on 23 December 2005.[283] A fourth memorandum relates to Ethiopia.[284] As regards Algeria,[285] the more oblique arrangements involved pledges in governmental correspondence during 2005, bolstered by a bilateral agreement on the Circulation of Persons and Readmission and on Extradition signed in 2006, but without any ongoing monitoring or protections.[286]

The European Court of Human Rights[287] has applied a strict scrutiny to assurances; some **7.139** have been accepted,[288] while others have been rejected as insufficiently impacting on the degree of risk under Article 3.[289] Despite these misgivings, the device of diplomatic assurances should not be discarded. It may serve wider policy goals of education and standard-setting for foreign states in transition towards criminal justice reforms. Furthermore, it is overly 'dogmatic' to assert that there can never be any circumstances whereby diplomatic assurances can afford sufficient practical protection.[290]

The record of the United Kingdom courts on the acceptance of diplomatic assurances **7.140** relating to terrorist suspects has been just as variable in outcome. The tests suggested by SIAC in *BB* are that: '(i) the terms of the assurances must be such that, if they are fulfilled, the person returned will not be subjected to treatment contrary to Article 3; (ii) the assurances must be given in good faith; (iii) there must be a sound objective basis for believing that the assurances will be fulfilled; (iv) fulfilment of the assurances must be capable of being verified'.[291]

Assurances on extradition from the United States about the death penalty and the avoidance **7.141** of Guantánamo Bay processes have been accepted and in reality fully observed.[292] By contrast, assurances by the Russian Federation concerning the treatment of Ahkmed Zakayev, a leading Chechen separatist whose return was sought for homicide and levying war, were rejected.[293] In *AS*, the courts refused to sanction a return to Libya.[294] Next, qualms about assurances relating to deportations to Algeria and Jordan, including the use of torture evidence in Jordanian proceedings, were rejected in *RB (Algeria) and OO*.[295]

---

[283] Memorandum of Understanding Between the Government of the United Kingdom of Great Britain and Northern Ireland and the Government of the Lebanese Republic concerning the provision of Assurances in respect of Persons Subject to Deportation (2005).

[284] Memorandum of Understanding between the Government of the United Kingdom of Great Britain and Northern Ireland and the Government of the Federal Democratic Republic of Ethiopia (2008).

[285] SIAC accepted the assurances in *Y* (SC/36/2005, 2006) and *Y* (SC/32, 36, 39/2005, 2007). See also *Saoudi v Spain*, App no 22871/06, 8 September 2006; *Daoudi v France*, App no 19576/08, 3 December 2009.

[286] Cm 6926 and 6928, London, 2006.

[287] See also *Ahmed Agiza and Mohammed al-Zari v Sweden* CAT/C/34/D/233/2003, 24 May 2005.

[288] *Mamatkulov and Askalov v Turkey* App nos 46827/99; 46951/99, 4 February 2005; *Abu Salem v Portugal* App no 26844/04, 9 May 2006.

[289] *Saadi v Italy*, App no 37201/06, 28 February 2008; *A v Netherlands*, App no 4900/06, 20 July 2010.

[290] Lester, A and Beattie, K, 'Risking torture' (2005) 6 *European Human Rights Law Review* 565 at 569.

[291] (SC/39/2005, 2006) para 5. See further *XX* (SC/61/2007, 2010).

[292] *Ahmad v Government of the USA* [2006] EWHC 2927 Admin. But see *Ahmad and Aswat v United Kingdom*, App no 24027/07. US assurances were endorsed in *Al Moayad v Germany*, App no 35865/03, 20 February 2007.

[293] *The Times* 14 November 2003, p 15.

[294] [2008] EWCA Civ 289.

[295] [2009] UKHL 10. See also *VV* (SC/59/2006, 2007).

The latter appellant (who is Abu Qatada) awaits the verdict of the European Court of Human Rights.[296]

7.142 A set of precepts has been devised by the Council of Europe Committee of Ministers in their guidelines on forced returns,[297] designed to ensure legality, transparency, due process, and respect for liberty and humanity. It is submitted that two conditions should generally be emphasized. First, the receiving state should demonstrate sustained and practical reforms, preferably both legal and political. Secondly, there should be a degree of verification of the receiving state's criminal justice and penal processes which goes well beyond what has been on offer to date—including effective record-keeping and independent legal and medical access.

Provisions—miscellaneous

7.143 A rump of measures survive under Pt IV of the 2001 Act to block the consideration of the substance of an asylum claim made by persons whose removal from the United Kingdom has already been deemed to be conducive to the public good (ss 33 and 34). The Immigration, Asylum and Nationality Act 2006 and the Criminal Justice and Immigration Act 2008, Pt X, have since repealed and replaced s 33.

7.144 Finally, fingerprints taken in asylum and certain immigration cases can be retained under s 36.

Implementation

7.145 Between July 2005 and the end of 2008, 153 persons were excluded from entry on national security grounds and eighty-seven for unacceptable behaviour.[298] In the aftermath of the July 2005 bombings, thirty-eight persons were detained on deportation grounds, but only two were deported within a year.[299] By 2009, there had been three deprivations of citizenship and eight deportations (plus twelve subject to appeal).[300]

Foreign comparisons

7.146 Executive powers over individuals are commonplace in the emergency laws of many other states too numerous to mention.[301] Therefore, this section will be confined to a few key comparisons as to the extent to which immigration is directly utilized for security functions and the consequent tolerance of indefinite detention.[302]

7.147 The High Court of Australia claimed that detention under the Migration Act 1958 may persist as a 'tragic' fate even when there is 'no real likelihood or prospect of [the alien's] removal in the reasonably foreseeable future'.[303] Thus, indefinite detention by implied

---

[296] App no 8139/09. See Garrod, M, 'Deportation of suspected terrorists with "real risk" of torture' (2010) 73 *Modern Law Review* 631.

[297] Committee of Ministers, *Forced Returns* (925th Meeting of the Ministers' Deputies, Strasbourg, 4 May 2005).

[298] Home Office, *Pursue, Prevent, Protect, Prepare* (Cm 7547, London, 2009) para 8.19.

[299] Home Office, *Countering International Terrorism* (Cm 6888, London, 2006) para 73.

[300] Home Office, *Pursue, Prevent, Protect, Prepare* (Cm 7547, London, 2009) paras 8.22, 8.28.

[301] See Country Reports at <http://www.un.org/en/sc/ctc/resources/countryreports.html>.

[302] See Ip, J, 'Comparative perspectives on the detention of terrorist suspects' (2007) 16 *Transnational Law & Contemporary Problems* 773.

[303] *Al Kateb v Godwin* [2004] HCA 37 at para 31 per McHugh J and at para 230 per Hayne J. See Curtin, J, 'Never Say Never' (2005) 27 *Sydney Law Review* 355; McHugh, MH, 'The need for agitators—the risk of stagnation' (<http://www.hcourt.gov.au/speeches/mchughj/mchughj_12oct05.pdf>, 2005).

operation of immigration laws was upheld in *Al Kateb v Godwin* in the case of a stateless Palestinian on the basis that the Minister claimed to be expending *bona fide* effort to attain deportation even though there was no reasonable prospect of success.[304]

The (Canadian) Immigration and Refugee Protection Act 2001 allows preventive detention **7.148** of foreigners involved in terrorism[305] and removal on the basis of a ministerial security certificate issued under s 77.[306] A court must consider the reasonableness of the certificate under s 78. Detention may be ordered of a certified person under ministerial warrant under s 81, subject to six-monthly review under s 82. If a security certificate is issued, then, by s 83, sensitive information must be protected at hearings under ss 78 and 82, including by the exclusion of the suspect and lawyers.

The Canadian Supreme Court in *Charkaoui v Canada*[307] condemned these processes as **7.149** unconstitutional in 2007, but on grounds of procedural unfairness and without addressing any need for finite limits on detention nor the discriminatory setting within immigration law.[308] The Canadian system was reformed in the year afforded by the Court so as to insert (in s 85) a system of special advocates modelled on SIAC.[309]

Nevertheless, mounting doubts have emerged as to whether indefinite detention can be **7.150** factually justified where involvements have grown cold (reflecting similar arguments about time limits in control order cases). Accordingly, all detentions pursuant to security certificates have terminated,[310] though some of their erstwhile subjects remain subject to conditions of residence under s 82(5), akin to British control orders, and to eventual deportation.

Another notable feature of Canadian jurisprudence is the stance taken on safety on return. **7.151** In *Suresh v Canada*,[311] it was held that the risk of torture, an obstacle to removal under s 115, is not an absolute bar to removal. Canada's interest in combating terrorism may be balanced against the refugee's interest in not being deported to torture. Therefore, the legislation leaves open the possibility of deportation to torture in 'exceptional circumstances', though this 'Suresh exception' has never been imposed.[312]

In US Federal law, material witness statutes[313] and detention for minor immigration **7.152** violations[314] deliver some of the same ends as control orders. In total, 1,182 persons were detained after 9/11 (mainly for immigration violations), and there was a call-in

---

[304] [2004] 219 CLR 562. See also *B* [2004] EWCA Civ 1544.

[305] The meaning is taken from the (UN) International Convention for the Suppression of the Financing of Terrorism 1999: *Suresh v Canada* [2002] 1 SCR 2.

[306] See Diab, R, *Guantánamo North* (Fernwood, Halifax, 2008) ch 2.

[307] [2007] 1 SCR 350.

[308] Duffy, MT and Provost, R, 'Security Detention in Practice' (2009) 40 *Case Western Reserve Journal of International Law* 531 at 547.

[309] Immigration and Refugee Protection Act 2008. See Roach, K, 'Charkaoui and Bill C-3' (2008) 42 *Supreme Court Review* 281.

[310] See *Re Charkouri* 2009 FC 1030; *Re Mahjoub* 2009 FC 1220, 2010 FCJ 900; *Re Almrei* 2009 FC 1263; *Re Harkat* 2009 FC 1266; *Re Jaballah* 2010 FC 507.

[311] [2002] 1 SCR 2. See also *Suresh* [2001] EWHC Admin 1028.

[312] See *Mahjoub v Canada* (2005) 261 FTR 95, [2007] 4 FCR 247; *Almrei v Canada* (2005) 262 FTR 7.

[313] 18 USC s 3144. See *US v Awadallah* (2003) 349 F 3d 42; Boyle, R, 'The Material Witness Statute Post September 11' (2003) 48 *New York Law School Law Review* 13.

[314] See Cole, D, *Enemy Aliens* (New Press, New York, 2003) ch 2.

process by which 82,000 foreigners who had entered the jurisdiction within two years from around forty-five countries viewed as having an Al-Qa'ida presence were subject to identification screening and questioning.[315] Regulatory changes allowed detention to be increased from twenty-four to forty-eight hours and to be unlimited in an emergency.[316] That detention pending removal cannot proportionately persist for ever on the basis of a forlorn hope of removal without negating the refugee's liberty has been accepted by the US Supreme Court, though with an open question as to its application to national security cases.[317]

7.153　When one adds in the Guantánamo regime, which is wholly aimed at foreigners, it is evident that US policy has blatantly 'sacrificed the rights of a minority for the majority's security interests'.[318] The attendant dangers are overreaction, the encouragement of similar incursions into the rights of citizens, reduced cooperation from minority communities, and ignorance of 'homegrown' terrorists.

Assessment and conclusions

7.154　As with control orders, though immigration powers are being deployed in a preventative mode against terrorism, these measures are formally counted as 'Pursue' within 'CONTEST'.[319] Do they achieve that policy goal? Terrorism threats and refugee protection often amount to 'unwarranted linkages',[320] and the same applies to migrant workers.[321] But to deny that foreigners in those categories never imperil national security is not supported by instances in Chapters 8 and 9 of émigré incitement and financing of terrorism nor by the received wisdom of UNSCR 1373, which by art 2(f) demands that states 'Deny safe haven to those who finance, plan, support, or commit terrorist acts'.[322] However, this source of danger should not lead to the assumption that every right of non-citizens can be lightly dismissed via immigration laws. The non-citizen's freedoms from arbitrary detention or from inter-ferences with family life, privacy, or expression are not more liable to infringement than those of citizens, save during the actual process of removal within Article 5(1)(f).[323] By contrast, several jurisdictions in 2001 sought to confuse residence and liberty either in the belief that there was no 'neighbour terrorism' to worry about or as a cynical ploy to reduce the electorate's vigilance about repressive responses. However, the House of Lords in the *Belmarsh* case astutely decoupled detention without trial from the cloak of immigration law. Those who advocate the lesser toleration of risk from non-citizens[324] fail to appreciate the universality

---

[315] See Lawyers' Committee for Human Rights, *A Year of Loss* (Washington DC, 2002) ch 3, *Assessing the New Normal* (Washington DC, 2003) ch 3.

[316] 8 CFR s 287.3 (66 FR 48335). There is an automatic stay on any release on bond (8 CFR s 3.19(i)(2), 66 FR 54907; *Bezmen v Ashcroft* 245 F Supp 2d 446 (2003)). Restrictions are also applied on access to lawyers: (28 CFR s 501.3, 66 Fed Reg 55062). The application of secrecy to the detention process (8 CFR s 236.6, 67 Fed Reg 19508) was upheld in *Center for National Security Studies v Department of Justice* 331 F 3d 918 (2003).

[317] *Zadvydas v Davis* (2001) 533 US 678 at 696.

[318] Cole, D, *Enemy Aliens* (New Press, New York, 2003) p 5.

[319] See Home Office, *Pursue, Prevent, Protect, Prepare* (Cm 7547, London, 2009) ch 8.

[320] *Report of the Special Rapporteur on the promotion and protection of human rights and fundamental freedoms while countering terrorism* (A/62/263, 2007) para 34.

[321] *Report of the Special Rapporteur on the Rights of Migrant Workers* (E/CN.4/2003/85) para 37.

[322] Compare Harvey, C, 'And fairness for all?' in Ramraj, VV, Hor, M, and Roach, K (eds), *Global Anti-terrorism Law and Policy* (Cambridge University Press, Cambridge, 2005).

[323] Weissbrodt, DS, *The Human Rights of Non-Citizens* (Oxford University Press, Oxford, 2008) p 50.

[324] Finnis, J, 'Nationality, alienage and constitutional principle' (2007) 123 *Law Quarterly Review* 417 at 438; Campbell, D, 'The threat of terrorism' [2010] *Public Law* 459 at 462.

of rights and overvalue nationality and raw majoritarian power. Any purported justification based on sweeping prerogative powers[325] must also be set in a contemporary context of international human rights law and, where applicable, of European citizenship.

The immigration measures described here undoubtedly reflect a waning of tolerance for **7.155** foreign dissent within the United Kingdom. While security officials had already recognized the threat of 'home-grown' terrorism,[326] the attacks of July 2005 triggered a political epiphany in the form of a fundamental revaluation of the dangers of *jihadism* at home and a decisive legal policy switch away from 'Londonistan'[327]—a watchful tolerance of provocative *jihadis*.[328] That approach is now in sharp decline, as demonstrated not only by laws in this chapter but also extradition measures in Chapter 6 and the amplified repression of expressive rights to be detailed in Chapter 8. Official endorsement of intolerance[329] and the devaluation of the humanity of outsiders[330] now prevail.

H. Executive Powers—Conclusions

Whatever might be the chosen mechanism of executive intervention, there remains to be **7.156** addressed the positivist viewpoint that the executive knows best in an emergency. A lucid and strong version of this argument is put forward by Posner and Vermeule[331] who adopt both a 'trade-off thesis', involving a balance between liberty and security and also a 'deference thesis', that judges should be submissive towards executive action because of need for secrecy, speed, and flexibility. They suggest that the appropriate locus for emergency decision-making should reside with the executive which has access to the fullest information and expertise and is well-intentioned.[332] By contrast, judges are said to be 'amateurs playing at security policy'.[333] In reply, the primacy of the executive and legislature in policy initiative and invocation should be endorsed. However, the application of policy to individuals in situations which affect absolute or unqualified rights, such as liberty or due process, should appropriately fall for the ultimate determination of the courts as 'a cardinal feature of the modern democratic state, a cornerstone of the rule of law itself'.[334] The application of unreconstructed positivism is neither a plausible normative stance in the era of the Human Rights Act 1998 nor a more promising way of achieving the accurate or fair determination or distribution of risk, including in the appliance of control orders.

In contrast to the judicial record in the context of control orders, two recent holders of **7.157** the office of Home Secretary have been disarmingly but abjectly apologetic about their expertise. Jacqui Smith (2007–09) expressed the fear that she was not adequately trained for office and opined that if she had performed well, 'it was more by luck than by any kind

---

[325] See *Johnson v Pedlar* [1921] 2 AC 263.
[326] Clarke, P, 'Learning From Experience—Counter Terrorism in the UK since 9/11' (Colin Cramphorne Memorial Lecture, London, 2007).
[327] See Phillips, M, *Londonistan* (Gibson Square, London, 2006).
[328] See O'Neill, S and McGrory, D, *The Suicide Factory* (HarperCollins, London, 2006).
[329] Compare Popper, KR, *The Open Society and Its Enemies* (5th edn, London, Routledge, 1966) p 265 (warning that 'Unlimited tolerance must lead to the disappearance of tolerance').
[330] See further Butler, J, *Precarious Life* (Verso, London, 2004).
[331] Posner, EA and Vermeule, A, *Terror in the Balance* (Oxford University Press, Oxford, 2007).
[332] Ibid 30.
[333] Ibid 31.
[334] *A* [2004] UKHL paras 29, 42 per Lord Bingham.

of development of those skills'.[335] Her successor, Alan Johnson (2009–10), likewise downplayed his credentials: '. . . I am not legally trained—I am not a lawyer or a barrister; I am a hack politician—I can only go by the advice that I receive from lawyers in the Attorney-General's Department. . . .'[336] Politicians are perfectly suited to representing and being accountable to the public in the policy sphere. Yet, few can claim to match the technical training, detachment,[337] and understanding of pre-committed transcendental values such as fairness and justice[338] of the standard High Court judge when it comes to the treatment of individuals.

---

[335] <http://news.bbc.co.uk/go/pr/fr/-/1/hi/uk_politics/8155454.stm>, 2009.

[336] *Hansard* HC vol 496 col 331 (15 July 2009).

[337] See *Lord Atton* (PC/02/2006, 30 November 2007) para 360 and [2008] EWCA Civ 443; *R (Al-Sweady) v Secretary of State for Defence* [2009] EWHC 1687 (Admin) at para 22.

[338] See House of Lords Constitution Committee, *Counter Terrorism Bill: The role of ministers, Parliament and the judiciary* (2007–08 HL 167) para 22; Dyzenhaus, D, *The Constitution of Law* (Cambridge University Press, Cambridge, 2006) ch 1; Bellamy, R, *Political Constitutionalism* (Cambridge University Press, Cambridge, 2007).

8

EXTREMIST ORGANIZATIONS, EXPRESSIONS, AND ACTIVITIES

A. Introduction

If assailed by political violence, then legal systems must both counter 'violence' and **8.01** address the 'political ends' behind it. The contemporary duality of this threat is illustrated by the pronouncement in 1981 of Danny Morrison, a leader of Sinn Féin: 'Who here really believes we can win the war through the ballot box? But will anyone here object if, with a ballot paper in this hand and an Armalite in the other, we take power in Ireland?'[1] Responsive measures to be discussed in this chapter are particularly directed towards the 'Prevent' element of the CONTEST strategy (described in Chapter 1). They strive to nullify extremist narratives, also in line with UNSCR 1456 of 20 January 2003 which requires states to 'take urgent action to prevent and suppress all active and passive support to terrorism'. The 'Pursue' strand is less effectively secured, for few prosecutions have occurred.

In pursuance of these objectives, this chapter will address a wide range of measures. It **8.02** begins with bans on organizations linked to political violence and then considers how extremist expressions and political activities are directly regulated, by methods ranging from criminal law, through to the regulation of political channels and social intervention.

---

[1] McAllister, I, '"The Armalite and the ballot box": Sinn Fein's electoral strategy in Northern Ireland' (2004) 23 *Electoral Studies* 123 at 124.

B. Proscription of Organizations

Introduction

8.03 Part II of the TA 2000 deals with the proscription of organizations. Under the TA 2000, s 121, the interpretation of 'organization' includes any association or combination of persons, a phrase wide enough to encompass an affinity group or even an anarchistic 'disorganization'. Diffuse networks such as Al-Qa'ida and self-generating combinations inspired by their ideologies could therefore qualify as 'organizations'. However, the looser the network, the more difficult will become proof of group membership, rather than loyalty to personal confederates. In the signal prosecutions of Brahmin Benmerzouga and Baghdad Meziane, the funding charges were sustained, but the charges of Al-Qa'ida membership were dropped.[2]

Proscribed groups—Irish

Provisions

8.04 Organizations designated as concerned in Irish terrorism have long been proscribed. Under the TA 2000, Pt II, proscription is remodelled by being promulgated nationwide,[3] so that Loyalist groups become banned in Britain.[4] The listings under the TA 2000 are established in two ways. First, groups which were mentioned in prior legislation are listed afresh in Sch 2. Extra groups may be added under s 3(3) by order, but no Irish group has been listed (nor, as yet, de-listed) since 2000.

Implementation

8.05 It was suggested during debates on the 2000 Act that some of the foregoing listed in Table 8.1 are at any one time dormant but that proscription should continue so as to deny historically resonant titles to dissidents.[5] Titles of Irish paramilitary organizations can indeed become both emotive and thorny. For example, the government hoped that the title, the 'Irish Republican Army', as it appears in Sch 2, should be considered sufficiently all-purpose to encompass the Provisional IRA, the Official IRA, the Real IRA, and the Continuity IRA (also listed for the sake of comprehensive cover as the Continuity Army Council). In favour of the government's interpretation appears to be s 3(1)(b), by which an organization is proscribed if it operates under the same name as an organization listed in that Schedule. The interpretation was tested on charges of membership of the Real IRA and rejected by the Belfast Crown Court in *R v Mullen, Dillon, Murphy and O'Connor*. That judgment was reversed in *R v Z* by the Northern Ireland Court of Appeal and House of Lords.[6]

8.06 There are two main grounds for supporting the House of Lords' decision. The first is that it was Parliamentary intent to cover 'the whole gambit'[7] of Irish Republican paramilitary

---

[2] *The Times* 2 April 2003, p 11.

[3] For pre-2000 history, see Walker, C, *The Prevention of Terrorism in British Law* (2nd edn, Manchester University Press, Manchester, 1992) ch 5.

[4] Prior practice involved broad conspiracy charges: *Hamilton v HM Advocate* 1980 SC 66; *Sayers v HM Advocate* 1982 JC 17; *Walker v HM Advocate*, *The Times* 14 March 1986, p 2; *HM Advocate v Copeland* 1987 SCCR 232; *Forbes v HM Advocate* 1990 SCCR 69; *Reid v HM Advocate* 1990 SCCR 83. See Cusak, J and McDonald, H, *UVF* (Poolbeg, Dublin, 1997) ch 7.

[5] Hansard HC Standing Committee D, Pt 2 (25 January 2000), Adam Ingram.

[6] [2004] NICC 15, [2004] NICA 23, [2005] UKHL 35. See Bennion, F, 'Is the Real IRA a proscribed organization? (2004) 168 *Justice of the Peace* 472, 'The Real IRA is proscribed after all' (2004) 168 *Justice of the Peace* 694.

[7] Hansard HC Standing Committee D, Pt 3 (25 January 2000), Adam Ingram.

Table 8.1 Proscribed organizations: Northern Ireland[a]

Continuity Army Council	Formed in 1994 in opposition to the 'Peace Process' as the armed wing of Republican Sinn Féin, it also spawned the Continuity IRA.
Cumann na mBan	The 'Union of Women' was founded as an auxiliary to the IRA.
Fianna na hEireann	The 'Warriors of Ireland' are the auxiliary youth section of the IRA.
Irish National Liberation Army	The INLA emerged in 1974 from former Official IRA members.
Irish People's Liberation Organisation	A title adopted by dissident INLA members.
Irish Republican Army	The leading Republican paramilitary group formed in 1918. A split in 1969 spawned the Official IRA (observing a ceasefire since 1972) and the Provisional IRA (the main source of Republican terrorism until a ceasefire in 1996).
Loyalist Volunteer Force	It formed in 1996 out of the mid-Ulster Ulster Volunteer Force unit.
Orange Volunteers	Several Loyalist groups have adopted this label since the early 1970s.
Red Hand Commando	A Loyalist group formed in 1972 and linked to the Ulster Volunteer Force.
Red Hand Defenders	A Loyalist paramilitary group, formed in 1998 from dissidents in other paramilitary groups who oppose the 'Peace Process'.
Saor Eire	'Free Ireland' has appeared intermittently since 1931.
Ulster Defence Association	The Loyalist UDA began in 1971 as a militant mass movement to support Unionism.
Ulster Freedom Fighters	The Loyalist UFF emerged from the Ulster Defence Association in the early 1970s, often as a cover-name.
Ulster Volunteer Force	The Loyalist UVF was formed initially in 1912 but was reconstituted in 1966.

[a] Source: TA 2000, Sch 2. For descriptions, see the reports of the Independent Monitoring Commission under the Northern Ireland (Monitoring Commission etc) Act 2003.

groups which choose to adopt a title resonating with the historical body, the Irish Republican Army, to avoid circumvention of proscription by minor name changes. Lords Bingham and Woolf treated s 3(1)(a) (an organization listed in Sch 2) and s 3(1)(b) as a composite whole (it being sufficient that a part or emanation of the group operates under the name of a scheduled organization). Under this view, no organization at present falls directly under the term 'Irish Republican Army' in s 3(1)(a), but all those mentioned are within s 3(1)(b). Lords Rodger, Carswell, and Brown treated paragraphs (a) and (b) of s 3(1) as mutually exclusive, whereby, if the Real IRA were not comprised within the name 'the IRA' and thus scheduled, they could not be said to be operating under 'the same name' under s 3(1)(b) unless the name of the new group was identical to a listed group.[8] It is submitted that the approach of Lords Bingham and Woolf is preferable. Thus, any organization using an identical name should fall within s 3(1)(a)—all are to be condemned whether original or mainstream or neither. After all, no IRA group is able to register a trade mark and claim exclusivity over upstarts. Lord Brown's interpretation is exacerbated in the case of Al-Qa'ida, a name which

---

[8] [2005] UKHL 35 at para 68 per Lord Brown.

can be assumed as a *nom de guerre* by whomsoever is stirred. All become Al-Qa'ida for legal purposes, whether Saudi compatriots of Osama bin Laden or autonomous bombers from Leeds. Thus, 'the same' does not mean 'identical', and it is sufficient that the proscribed name is exactly reproduced by the later group, even if it does not comprise the full extent of its name.

8.07 The second argument arises from the mention of the Real IRA in the (Northern Ireland (Sentences) Act 1998 (Specified Organisations) Order 1998.[9] The Sentences Act provides for the accelerated release of prisoners who fulfil various conditions, including the disavowal of violence and of support for any 'specified' organization. By s 3(8) of the Sentences Act, a specified organization is (a) involved in Northern Irish terrorism but (b) has not established or is not maintaining a complete and unequivocal ceasefire. A listing in the Sentences Act does not undermine the foregoing assertions in relation to the 'global family' meaning of proscription under the Terrorism Act for the following reasons. The purpose of the 1998 Act is to discern which factions are on ceasefire. It was recognized that the definition of 'proscribed' organization would not be sufficiently discriminate. Thus, the legislative purpose is different and so the listings are different. The fact that some groups are not specified does not mean that the law distinguishes 'good' from 'bad' terrorists,[10] since groups such as the Irish Republican Army remain proscribed. Thus, an absence of specification does not imply that proscription should fall away.

8.08 For practical purposes, this problem of name changes has been solved by the TA 2006, s 22, described later.

Proscribed groups—other domestic

8.09 Beyond the Irish context, it was announced during the passage of the TA 2000 that there were no plans to proscribe any (non-Irish) domestic groups.[11] Aside from the sporadic activities of Welsh and Scottish extremists,[12] animal rights and environmental militants were thought to be possible candidates for proscription, but none possesses the sophistication, threat to persons, or overall strength to warrant suppression. In *Animal Rights Extremism*, the Home Office expressed itself as unpersuaded that proscription would assist[13] and recommended alternatives.[14]

8.10 Though proscription has not been applied to Combat 18 or Redwatch,[15] some (but not all) neo-Nazis have been arrested and convicted under anti-terrorism laws.[16] These reactions appear attractive in creating symmetry with the *jihadis*, but such individuals generally lack the sophistication, the scale, and the international linkages to make proportionate this application of anti-terrorism laws.

---

[9] See SI 2008/1975.

[10] Hansard HC vol 317, col 885 (2 September 1998), William Ross.

[11] Hansard HC vol 341, col 227 (14 December 1999), Charles Clarke.

[12] Wayne Cook and Steven Robinson were convicted of threats to kill on behalf of the Scottish National Liberation Army (*The Times* 26 January 2008, p 2). The police stated that 'these men are terrorists' (*Manchester Evening News* 18 January 2008, p 2).

[13] (London) para 3.7.5.

[14] Ibid para 3.4.2.

[15] Hansard HC Standing Committee D (25 January 2000), David Maclean; Hansard HL vol 656 col 169 (7 January 2004), Lord Greaves.

[16] See Chapter 5.

Proscribed groups—foreign

Provisions

Reflecting the growing threat from international terrorism,[17] s 3 can also apply to groups pri- **8.11** marily based abroad. London is a magnet for foreign groups because of its media outlets, large foreign communities (including students), and tradition of sheltering peripatetic dissidents, from Karl Marx and Guiseppe Mazzini to Abu Qatada. In the prelude to the TA 2000, several foreign governments lobbied for the curtailment of opposition émigré groups.[18] The stance of the United Kingdom government began to alter as it pursued more vigorously international cooperation against terrorism. In September 1998, arrests were made of Al-Qa'ida activists in the 'Advice and Reform Committee' in London in connection with the bombing of the US embassies in East Africa.[19] Next, Shafiq Ur Rehman became the first case heard under the Special Immigration Appeals Commission Act 1997 after the issuance of a deportation order relating to involvement in Lashkar e Tayyaba.[20] Finally, prosecutions (ultimately unsuccessful) for terrorist preparations were mounted against four Algerians who had been arrested in 1997 and 1998.[21]

Proscription also offers protection when deportation cannot be secured because of risks of **8.12** torture[22] even when claims to asylum can be rejected.

Implementation

By the Terrorism Act 2000 (Proscribed Organisations) (Amendment) Order 2001,[23] twenty- **8.13** one foreign organizations were listed when the Act came into force. *Jihadi* groups predominate in this list, but it also includes selective nationalist movements (Basque, Kashmiri, Khalistani, and Kurd) and even one Marxist group (November 17). The list has now grown to forty-three, as detailed in Table 8.2.

There has been one de-proscription order—concerning the Mujaheddin e Khalq, founded **8.14** in 1965 as an Iranian dissident group. It is also known as the People's Mujahedin Organisation of Iran. (PMOI). It renounced violence in 2003, and, following litigation described below, was de-listed in 2008.[24]

The factors which originally shaped this list were enumerated by Lord Bassam:[25] **8.15**

> First, we would have to consider carefully the nature and scale of the group's activities; secondly, we would have to look at the specific threat that it posed to the United Kingdom and our citizens abroad, which is clearly a very important consideration, as well as the extent of its presence in this country. . . . Thirdly, we would also have to consider our responsibility to support other members of the international community in the global fight against terrorism.

They were then tabulated in a Home Office press release of 28 February 2001 which **8.16** accompanied the first proscription statutory Order:

(a) The nature and scale of an organization's activities.
(b) The specific threat that it poses to the United Kingdom.

---

[17] *Home Office Response to Lloyd Report*, para 4.14, 4.16.
[18] See *The Guardian* 20 November 1997, p 19; 26 August 1998, p 3.
[19] *Al Fawwaz v Governor of Brixton Prison* [2001] UKHL 69.
[20] *Secretary of State for the Home Department v Rehman* [2001] 3 WLR 877.
[21] *R v Director of Public Prosecutions, ex parte Kebilene* [1999] 3 WLR 972.
[22] *Chahal v United Kingdom*, App no 22414/93, 1996-V.
[23] SI 2001/1261.
[24] SI 2008/1645. See Hansard HC vol 478, col 98 (23 June 2008).
[25] Hansard HL vol 613, col 252 (16 May 2000).

Table 8.2 Proscription: international organizations[a]

Abu Nidal Organisation	This Palestinian group split from the PLO in 1974 and also includes the Fatah Revolutionary Council.
Abu Sayyaf Group	The Abu Sayyaf Group ('Bearer of the Sword') has been active in Mindanao, where it seeks an autonomous Islamic state.
Al-Gama'at al-Islamiya	The Egyptian Islamic Group (GI) has existed since the late 1970s when it split from the EIJ (below). Its attacks included the killing of 58 tourists (including six British citizens) in Luxor in 1997.
Al-Ittihad Al-Islamia	The 'Islamic Union' is based in Somalia. Some of its leaders have left to form the Islamic Court Union.
Al-Qa'ida	'The Base' aims to unite Muslims, to eliminate Western presence in the Middle East, and to replace Arab governments with a Caliphate. Osama bin Laden is the figurehead. The movement is responsible for the East African embassy bombings in 1998 and the 11 September 2001 attacks as well as UK activities.[b] Since 2001, it mainly operates as a dispersed ideological vanguard.
Al-Shabaab	The group is the military 'youth' wing of the Islamic Courts Union. In conflict in Somalia, it has been responsible for the killing of a British journalist in 2005 and two British teachers in 2008. British supporters have engaged in logistical activity as well as travelling to fight in Somalia.
Ansar Al-Islam	The 'Supporters or Partisans of Islam' is a Kurdish Sunni Islamist group, based in northern Iraq.
Ansar Al-Sunna	Jamaat Ansar Al-Sunna or Group of the Protectors of the Sunna is an Islamist group in Iraq.
Armed Islamic Group (Groupe Islamique Armée)	The GIA seeks to install an Islamist state in Algeria. The GIA began in early 1992 after the government prevented the election of the Islamic Salvation Front (FIS).
Asbat Al-Ansar	Asbat Al-Ansar ('the League of the Partisans') consists of Sunni Islamists based in southern Lebanon.
Babbar Khalsa	The group fights for the liberation of Khalistan, the Sikh homeland in Punjab, which declared its independence in 1987. External attacks culminated in the bombing of Air India Flight 182 in 1985.
Baluchistan Liberation Army	The organization is dedicated to fighting for the independence of Baluchistan, currently split between Iran, Pakistan, and Afghanistan.
Basque Homeland & Liberty (Euskadi ta Askatasuna)	ETA was founded in 1959 to fight for an independent Basque homeland mainly in Spain.
Egyptian Islamic Jihad	The group has existed since 1973 and, aside from activities in Egypt, is alleged to have bombed the East African US embassies in 1998.
Groupe Islamique Combattant Marocain	The Moroccan Islamic Combattant Group (Groupe Islamique Combattant Marocain, or GICM) is an Islamist group which carried out an attack in Casablanca in 2003 and was involved in the Madrid bombing of 2004.
HAMAS-Izz al-Din al-Qassem Brigades	Various groupings coalesced in the late 1980s to pursue the goal of establishing an Islamic Palestinian state. HAMAS is the acronym for Harakat al-Muqawama al-Islamiyya or Islamic Resistance Movement. The Izz el-Din al-Qassam (IDQ) Brigades are its military wing. HAMAS controls Gaza.
Harakat ul Mujahideen (HK)	HK is a group based in Pakistan and operating primarily in Kashmir, having formed in 1993 (as Harakat ul-Ansar).
Harakat-ul-Jihad-ul-Islami (HUJI)	The aim of HUJI is to achieve accession of Kashmir to Pakistan. HUJI has targeted Indian security positions in Kashmir and in India.

Harakat-ul-Jihad-ul-Islami (Bangladesh) (HUJI-B)	HUJI-B seeks the creation of an Islamist regime in Bangladesh. Three persons were convicted in 2008 of attempting to kill British diplomat, Anwar Choudhury, in 2004.
Harakat-ul-Mujahideen/ Alami (HuM/A)	The aim of HuM/A seeks to establish a Caliphate based on Sharia law, and to incorporate Kashmir within Pakistan.
Hezb-e Islami Gulbuddin	The Hezb-e-Islami Gulbuddin is a fundamentalist faction of Afghanistan's Hezbi Islami Party. It was founded in 1977 by Gulbuddin Hekmatyar.
Hizballah Military Wing	Hizballah (The Party of God) is the Lebanese-based Islamist movement founded after the Israeli invasion in 1982. Since Hizballah is a major political party in Lebanon, proscription is confined to its military wing, Jihad Council (listed in 2008) and the Hizballah External Security Organization.
International Sikh Youth Federation	Also involved in the Khalistan conflict and drawing support from overseas Sikh communities. ISYF was founded in the UK in 1984 but may have dissolved after proscription with some of its political aims being assumed in 2003 by the Sikh Federation (UK).
Islamic Army of Aden	The group fights principally in Yemen. It is involved in the formation of the Aden-Abyan Islamic Army and attacks on Western tourists.
Islamic Jihad Union	The Islamic Jihad Movement in Palestine (Harakat al-Jihād al-Islāmi fi Filastīn) is a Palestinian group. The PIJ's armed wing, the Al-Quds brigades, has claimed responsibility for numerous attacks in Israel.
Islamic Movement of Uzbekistan	The Islamic Movement of Uzbekistan (IMU), also known as the Islamic Movement of Turkestan (IMT) and the Islamic Party of Turkestan (IPT), aims to establish an Islamic State. The IMU kidnapped four US citizens in 2000 and attempted to bomb embassies in 2004.
Jaish e Mohammed	The 'Army of Mohammed' is an Islamist group based in Pakistan and is concerned with attacks in Kashmir.
Jamaat ul-Furquan (JuF)	The aim of JuF is to unite Kashmir with Pakistan and to establish a radical Islamist state in Pakistan.
Jammat-ul Mujahideen Bangladesh	The group has claimed responsibility for numerous fatal bomb attacks across Bangladesh in recent years, including suicide bomb attacks in 2005.
Jemaah Islamiyah	The 'Islamic Group' or 'Islamic Community' is based in South-east Asia. It has also attacked Western targets, through bombings at Bali in 2002 (which killed 24 British tourists) and in Jakarta in 2003 and 2004.
Jundallah	Jundallah ('Army of God') is an Islamist organization based in Waziristan, Pakistan and in Iran's Sistan and Baluchistan Provinces. The group seeks an independent Baluchistan under a Sunni Islamist government.
Khuddam ul-Islam (KuI)	The aim of KuI is to unite Kashmir with Pakistan and to establish a radical Islamist state in Pakistan.
Kurdistan Workers' Party (Partiya Karkeren Kurdistan, PKK)	The PKK was founded in 1974 and seeks an independent Kurdish state in south-eastern Turkey. It engaged in armed attacks from 1984 until after the capture of its leader, Abdullah Öçalan in 1999. Ceasefires have been observed from 2000–2004. The names, Kongra Gele Kurdistan and KADEK, are treated as other names for the group according to a further order in 2006.
Lashkar e Tayyaba	This Pakistani-based group (the 'Army of the Righteous') supports the decoupling of Kashmir from India. It also operates as Jama'at ud Da'wa.
Lashkar-e Jhangvi	Lashkar i Jhangvi (Army of Jhang) is a Sunni group in Pakistan. It attacked US oil workers in 1997, attempted to kill Pakistani Prime Minister Nawaz Sharif in 1999, and kidnapped and killed US journalist Daniel Pearl in 2002.

(continued)

Table 8.2 *Continued*

Liberation Tigers of Tamil Eelam (LTTE)	The LTTE was founded in 1972 and is the most powerful group in Sri Lanka fighting for a distinct Tamil state. Armed conflict began in 1983, but it was militarily defeated in 2009.
Libyan Islamic Fighting Group (LIFG)	The LIFG aims to establish an Islamic state in Libya. Its attempted assassination of al-Qadhafi in 1996 was allegedly part funded by the UK.
Palestinian Islamic Jihad – Shaqaqi (PIJ)	A variety of Shia groups formed in the 1970s and based in the Gaza Strip committed to the creation of an Islamic Palestinian state and the destruction of Israel. Like HESO, PIJ is pro-Iranian.
Revolutionary Peoples' Liberation Party – Front (DHKP-C)	The DHKP-C (Devrimci Halk Kurtulus Partisi-Cephesi) is a Marxist Turkish group with origins going back to the 1970s and whose operations have been mainly confined to Turkish targets in Turkey. The DHKP-C had an office in London which engaged in overt political activity.
Salafist Group for Call and Combat	The GSPC (Groupe Salafiste pour la Prédication et le Combat—also called the Hassan Hattab faction) emerged from the GIA in 1998 and aims to create an Islamic state in Algeria.
Sipah-e Sahaba Pakistan	Sipah-e-Sahaba Pakistan (also known as Millat-E Islami Pakistan) targets the minority Shia Muslims in Pakistan. Lashkar i Jhangvi is a splinter group.
Tehrik Nefaz-e Shari'at Muhammadi.	Tehrik Nefaz-e Shari'at Muhammadi regularly attacks Coalition and Afghan government forces in Afghanistan.
Teyrebaz Azadiye Kurdistan (TAK)	TAK is a Kurdish group which is suspected of killing UK nationals in a July 2005 minibus bombing in Kusadasi, Turkey.
17 November Revolutionary Organisation (N17)	A Marxist group established in 1975 in Greece and opposing the government and Western interests. In June 2000, N17 murdered Brigadier Stephen Saunders, the British Defence Attaché, which triggered several arrests.

[a] See Terrorism Act 2000 (Proscribed Organisations) (Amendment) Orders 2001–10, SI 2001/1261; SI 2002/2724; SI 2005/2892; SI 2006/1919; SI 2006/2016; SI 2007/2184; SI 2008/1931; SI 2010/611. Explanations are given at Hansard HC vol 391 col 875 (30 October 2002); vol 437 col 466 (13 October 2005); vol 462 col 1369 (10 July 2007); vol 479 col 193 (15 July 2008); vol 506 col 1035 (4 March 2010). For further descriptions, see Staniforth, A, *Blackstone's Counter-Terrorism Handbook* (2nd edn, Oxford University Press, Oxford, 2010) App 2.

[b] See Home Office, *Pursue, Prevent, Protect, Prepare: The United Kingdom's Strategy for Countering International Terrorism* (Cm 7547, London, 2009) para 2.01.

(c) The specific threat that it poses to British nationals overseas.

(d) The extent of the organization's presence in the United Kingdom.

(e) The need to support other members of the international community in the global fight against terrorism.

The last factor allows a very wide discretion but reflects the UN Convention for the Suppression of Terrorist Bombings of 1997[26] which demands under Article 15 that states take all practicable measures to prevent and counter terrorist preparations. This requirement is backed by UNSCR 1373 of 28 September 2001: states are required by Article 2(c) and (d) to deny safe haven and to prevent terrorist acts. Nevertheless, it remains controversial that cosmopolitan protection should be applied equally not only to liberal and democratic allies against whom violence for political ends may be said to be 'specious'[27] but also to the 'axis of evil'.[28]

---

[26] A/RES/52/164 (Cm 4662, London, 1997).

[27] *Lloyd Report*, vol II p 4.

[28] <http://georgewbush-whitehouse.archives.gov/news/releases/2002/01/20020129-11.html>, 2001.

Another drawback with this policy is its apparent partiality, as the UK government attempts **8.17** to turn itself into the arbiter between 'terrorist' and 'freedom fighter' and tries to keep pace with the fluidity of factions.[29] Examples of unproscribed groups which seem to fit the 'Bassam' criteria include Fuerzas Armadas Revolucionarias de Colombia (FARC), formed in 1964. James Monaghan, Niall Connolly, and Martin McCauley were convicted in 2004 of training FARC personnel in IRA bomb-making techniques. Another example is Dhamat Houmet Daawa Salafia (DHDS) which broke away from the GIA in Algeria in 1996 and now supports Al-Qa'ida; one senior member, Mustapha Taleb was alleged to be involved in the ricin plot headed by Kamel Bourgass.[30] It is also unclear why it took until 2010 to proscribe Al-Shabaab. The fluidity of threat reinforces Lord Carlile's assessment that the police remain 'equivocal' about proscription.[31] Nevertheless, the listings are ever widening, perhaps also bolstering trade relations and diplomacy.

Mechanisms and procedures of proscription

Executive implementation and review

The TA 2000 applies a steadfastly executive approach to the activation of proscription. By **8.18** s 3(3), the Secretary of State may by order (a) add an organization to Sch 2; (b) remove an organization from that schedule; (c) amend that schedule in some other way (such as in relation to notes within it which may be used to explain or qualify proscription orders, as in the case of the 'Orange Volunteers'). Furthermore, the criteria remain subjectively worded—by s 3(4), orders can be made against a group if 'he believes that it is concerned in terrorism', a belief which may be derived under s 3(5) if an organization (a) commits or participates in acts of terrorism; (b) prepares for terrorism; (c) promotes or encourages terrorism; or (d) is otherwise concerned in terrorism. While subjective on paper, in *Lord Alton of Liverpool & others (In the Matter of The People's Mojahadeen Organization of Iran) v Secretary of State for the Home Department* (hereinafter the '*Alton* case'),[32] the test in s 3(4) has been interpreted as applying in two stages.

The first stage is whether the Secretary of State has an honest belief on reasonable grounds **8.19** to satisfy the statutory test in s 3(4). Then a second stage addresses whether discretion should be used to apply proscription on policy grounds. An honest belief on reasonable grounds can only be formed through materials known to the decision-maker—the decision is personal and cannot be delegated.[33] That case also demanded 'current, active steps' by way of proof of being 'concerned in' terrorism; the mere contemplation of the possibility of some future violence is not enough.[34] Thus, the Court of Appeal distinguished between a group that has temporarily ceased terrorism 'for tactical reasons' with one that has decided to resile from violence, 'even if the possibility exists that it might decide to revert to terrorism in the future'.[35]

Once an order has been made, there is no statutory time-limit for review or reissuance, **8.20** though the Home Secretary has reassured that 'We do not put their names in a filing cabinet

---

[29] As predicted in the *Lloyd Report*, para 4.16.
[30] *Y v Secretary of State for the Home Department* (SC/36/2005, 2006).
[31] *Report on the Operation in 2001 of the Terrorism Act 2000* (2002) para 2.2; *Report on the Operation in 2002 and 2003 of the Terrorism Act 2000* (Home Office, 2004) para 29.
[32] PC/02/2006, 30 November 2007 at paras 67, 68; *Secretary of State for the Home Department v Lord Alton of Liverpool* [2008] EWCA Civ 443 at para 22.
[33] Ibid para 130.
[34] Ibid paras 124, 128.
[35] *Secretary of State for the Home Department v Lord Alton of Liverpool* [2008] EWCA Civ 443 at para 38.

and forget about them.'[36] Proscription orders for international groups are kept under rolling review every twelve months by a working group within the Home Office and Northern Ireland Office, with Foreign & Commonwealth Office support.[37] The *Alton* case considered that regular review is a requirement of administrative law.[38]

8.21 Reflecting the disputes over the title of the Real IRA, the TA 2006, s 22 inserts for the sake of 'important flexibility'[39] further powers into s 3(6). Where the Secretary of State believes that an organization listed in Sch 2 is operating wholly or partly under a name that is not specified in that Schedule but is for all practical purposes the same as one so listed, an order may provide that the extra name is to be treated as another name for the listed organization. Of course, if it can be shown that the new activities are really committed under an alias on behalf of a proscribed organization, then a prosecution under that original name could still be mounted.[40] Under s 3(3) the negative resolution procedure is used for parliamentary scrutiny of adaptation orders and the affirmative resolution procedure for initial bans under s 123 of the TA 2000. This power has been applied to two aliases of the PKK and one of the Lashkar e Tayyabi.[41]

8.22 While the Secretary of State retains the whip-hand, two procedures within the TA 2000 allow for challenge. One envisages an application to the Secretary of State for setting aside an order. If refused (and no application has ever been granted),[42] the second step is an application for review by the Proscribed Organisations Appeal Commission (POAC). Direct application to POAC is not allowed—the government wishes to consider the matter first and also to save possible expense.[43] The procedures may be used to contest the initial order for proscription and to challenge the continuing propriety of an order.[44]

8.23 Applications to the Secretary of State for deproscription arise under s 4(1). The applicant may be either the proscribed organization or any person affected by the proscription order. The phrase 'person affected' was interpreted in *R v Broadcasting Standards Commission, ex parte British Broadcasting Corporation*[45] to allow a complaint about an unwarranted infringement of the privacy of a body corporate on its own behalf arising from its employees being secretly filmed. An action by a group leader would most evidently fall within s 4(1),[46] but a minority faction, or even just one group member, may also conceivably bring an application, even where the majority favour a new group and prefer the old group to remain banned.

8.24 The only successful deproscription application, the *Alton* case,[47] was in the name of the Liberal peer, Lord Alton, joined by eighteen other members of the House of Lords (including

---

[36] HC Standing Committee D, col 65 (18 January 2000), Charles Clarke.

[37] Lord Carlile, *Report on the Operation in 2007 of the Terrorism Act 2000* (Home Office, London, 2008) para 42; *Report on the Operation in 2008 of the Terrorism Act 2000* (Home Office, London, 2009) paras 53, 55.

[38] PC/02/2006, 30 November 2007 at para 73.

[39] Hansard HL vol 676, col 1144 (13 December 2005), Baroness Scotland.

[40] See Jones, A, Bowers, R, and Lodge, HD, *The Terrorism Act 2006* (Oxford University Press, Oxford, 2006) para 6.40.

[41] Proscribed Organisations (Name Changes) Orders, SI 2006/1919 and SI 2009/578.

[42] The latest was an application by the LTTE: Lord Carlile, *Report on the Operation in 2007 of the Terrorism Act 2000* (Home Office, London, 2008) para 45.

[43] Hansard HL vol 613, col 262 (16 May 2000), Lord Bassam.

[44] Ibid col 261.

[45] [2000] 3 WLR 1327.

[46] See *R v Broadcasting Complaints Commission, ex parte Owen* [1985] 1 QB 1153.

[47] PC/02/2006, 30 November 2007. Unsuccessful applications were made by the Baluchistan Liberation Army, the LTTE and the PKK in 2009: Lord Carlile, *Report on the Operation in 2009 of the Terrorism Act 2000* (Home Office, London, 2010) para 68.

a former Lord of Appeal in Ordinary) and sixteen members of the House of Commons, none of whom claimed PMOI membership. Their status as 'persons affected' derived simply from their wish to support the PMOI and was not contested.[48] While the great and the good were evidently sincere, such indulgence could allow busybodies to meddle, with attendant dangers of ill-argued or inappropriate disputes. The phrase has 'a wide and ill-defined catchment',[49] but it should not be applied with abandon.

Regulations relating to these proceedings must be made under s 4(3) and (4) and must **8.25** include the giving of reasons. The Proscribed Organisations (Applications for Deproscription) Regulations 2001[50] require an application to be made in writing and with a statement of the grounds (r 3). Where the application is being made by the organization, the application must also state under r 4 the name and address of the person submitting the application and the position held in the organization or his authority to act on behalf of the organization. Where the application is made by a person affected by the organization's proscription, the application must detail, under r 5, the manner in which the applicant is affected. By r 8, the Secretary of State shall determine an application within ninety days from receipt of the application. Where the Secretary of State refuses an application, the applicant shall be informed immediately in writing (r 9).

The Proscribed Organisations Appeal Commission

The POAC is established under s 5 and is modelled on the Special Immigration Appeals **8.26** Commission Act 1997.[51] By s 5(3), the POAC shall allow an appeal against a refusal to deproscribe if it considers that the decision to refuse was 'flawed when considered in the light of the principles applicable on an application for judicial review'. This phrase was meant to avoid review of the factual merits. Where an order is made in favour of an applicant, the Secretary of State shall as soon as is reasonably practicable (a) lay before Parliament the draft of an order under s 3(3)(b) removing the organization from the list in Sch 2 or (b) make an order removing the organization from the list in that schedule. By s 9 and the Proscribed Organisations Appeal Commission (Human Rights Act Proceedings) Rules 2001,[52] the POAC is also the appropriate tribunal for the purposes of litigation based on s 7 of the Human Rights Act 1998 arising from a refusal by the Secretary of State to deproscribe.

The constitution and procedures of the POAC are related in Sch 3 and in the Proscribed **8.27** Organisations Appeal Commission (Procedure) Rules 2007.[53] By Sch 3 para 1, appointments shall be made by the Lord Chancellor. Given that members 'shall hold and vacate office in accordance with the terms of his appointment', there is no guarantee of statutory independence for the purposes of Article 6 of the European Convention.[54] It is specified that each POAC panel must comprise three persons, at least one of whom holds, or has held, high judicial office (as defined by the Appellate Jurisdiction Act 1876). The membership in 2008

---

[48] Ibid para 20.
[49] *Huntingdon Life Sciences Group plc and others v Stop Huntingdon Animal Cruelty* [2007] EWHC 522 (QB) at para 43 per Holland J regarding the Civil Procedure Rules, Pt 19.6.
[50] SI 2001/107, as amended by the Proscribed Organisations (Applications for Deproscription etc) Regulations 2006, SI 2006/2299.
[51] See *Lloyd Report*, para 13.32.
[52] SI 2001/127.
[53] SI 2007/1286 as amended by SI 2007/3377.
[54] See *Khan v United Kingdom*, App no 35394/97, 2000-V; *Millar v Dickson* [2001] UKPC D4.

consisted of two judicial members, Sir Harry Ognall (chair) and Sir Charles Mantell, plus four other lawyer members and five lay members.

8.28 Under the supplementary r 6, an appeal must be lodged within forty-two days. Where proceedings are lodged by an organization, it may designate an individual to conduct those proceedings under para 6, so as to avoid rival factions causing duplication or confusion. By para 5, the Lord Chancellor shall make procedure rules, including for determining without an oral hearing in specified circumstances, for determining the burden of proof and admissibility of evidence, and for securing that information, including reasons for decisions,[55] is not disclosed contrary to the public interest. Though legal representation is to be allowed, the rules may provide for full particulars to be withheld from the organization or applicant and from any representative, and the POAC shall be empowered to exclude persons (including representatives) from proceedings. Under para 7, the relevant law officer may appoint a 'special advocate' to represent the interests of an organization or other applicant. No matter what is withheld from the appellant and his legal representative, the POAC and special advocate must be provided under supplementary rules 12 and 14 by the Secretary of State with a summary of the reasons and facts relating to the decision, and the grounds (and evidence in support) for opposing the appeal. Communications surveillance is likely to be an important source of evidence, and it can exceptionally be heard according to the RIPA, s 18, but must not be disclosed to the applicant, the organization, or their representatives. Under supplementary r 25, the POAC may receive other evidence that would not normally be admissible.

8.29 Section 6 of the TA 2000 preserves a right of further appeal on a question of law to (depending on jurisdiction) the Court of Appeal, the Court of Session, or the Court of Appeal in Northern Ireland. An appeal may be brought only with the permission of the POAC or the appeal court.[56]

8.30 If an appeal under s 5 is successful, then by s 7 of the 2000 Act, compensation shall be payable under s 133(5) of the Criminal Justice Act 1988 for any conviction sustained in relation to activity which took place on or after the date of the refusal to deproscribe.

8.31 The establishment of the POAC under s 5 of the TA 2000 is in principle desirable and offers some antidote to executive dominance. However, the system suffers from considerable weaknesses.

8.32 First, it reflects an unwillingness to put sensitive security evidence before the courts[57] and thereby perpetuates the unfairness inherent in secret hearings which cannot necessarily be overcome by the device of special advocate.[58] Lord Carlile has suggested that the quality of review could improve were POAC to be provided with a security-cleared case assistant.[59]

8.33 Next, though the wide interpretation given to 'person affected' encourages challenges, it will still involve considerable courage to take a stance as a supporter and risk being labelled as

---

[55] See TA 2006, s 22(11).

[56] r 30. See further Court of Appeal (Appeals from Proscribed Organisations Appeal Commission) Rules 2002, SI 2002/1843; Proscribed Organisations Appeal Commission (Procedure) (Amendment) Rules 2007, SI 2007/3377; Civil Procedure Rules Practice Direction 52 r 21.11.

[57] Hansard HC Standing Committee D, col 86 (25 January 2000), Charles Clarke.

[58] See *Secretary of State for the Home Department v MB* [2007] UKHL 46.

[59] Lord Carlile, *Report on the Operation in 2004 of the Terrorism Act 2000* (Home Office, London, 2005) para 47.

a sympathizer or even a terrorist. Not surprisingly, few have dared. Aside from PMOI, notices of appeal have been lodged but not pursued by Lashkar e Tayyaba and the International Sikh Youth Federation. Immunity is granted by s 10 from criminal proceedings for an offence under any of ss 11 to 13, 15 to 19, and 56 of the 2000 Act arising from any submissions in an application. But this half-hearted concession does not relate to other offences or rule out other retribution such as immigration proceedings:[60]

> The clause does not provide general immunity, and it would be wrong to do so. If, for instance, it emerged during proceedings that an individual had been involved in a bombing attack or had incited an act of terrorism abroad, immunity in respect of criminal proceedings would not apply. That strikes the right balance. Offences involving weapons, articles, information and so on are omitted from the immunity provided in the clause because they do not relate directly to proscription.

The review system could be enhanced if the POAC took the role not only of appeal tribunal but also proactive review commission, so that each proscribed group undergoes independent annual scrutiny,[61] alongside the systemic review by the government's independent reviewer (Lord Carlile). The Home Office review working group's scrutiny is not public, not published, and not independent. The Independent Monitoring Commission comes close to performing this function but for the Northern Ireland groups alone.

Another problem with the POAC is that (contrary to the marginal note to s 5—'Deproscription: **8.34** appeal') it is confined to the principles of judicial review: s 5(3). Furthermore, under general administrative law, POAC procedures will have to be exhausted before turning to the Divisional Court.[62] This point was sustained in *R (on the application of the Kurdistan Workers' Party and others) v Secretary of State for the Home Department*.[63] The People's Mujahedin Organisation of Iran (PMOI), the Kurdistan Workers' Party (PKK), and Lashkar e Tayyabah (LT) sought to challenge the lawfulness of their proscriptions and the lawfulness of the regime of offences laid down by the 2000 Act. The PMOI and LT had also applied to the POAC for review (no decision had by then been given), but the PKK had not challenged at POAC level. The challenges were viewed as arguable on the grounds of procedural fairness (since so many organizations had been outlawed together in one fell swoop, suggesting a lack of attention), on the grounds of proportionality (in the cases of the PMOI and LT), and on the ground of breach of rights. The High Court also took into account that the PMOI had successfully challenged its proscription in the USA on procedural grounds,[64] and it expressed some attraction for the idea that a group should be warned in advance before a ban comes into force.[65] However, all these arguable challenges failed on the threshold procedural ground that 'Parliament . . . intended the POAC to be the forum of first resort'.[66] The special features of the POAC—the secret hearings, the availability of intercept evidence, and its designation as the forum to hear arguments about the Human Rights Act 1998—provide a rationale for this viewpoint. Thus, there was 'no reason why POAC should be any less able than the Administrative Court to provide effective scrutiny of the matters under challenge'.[67]

---

[60] Hansard HC Standing Committee D col 111 (25 January 2000), Charles Clarke.
[61] See *Lloyd Report*, para 13.32.
[62] *R v Chief Constable of Merseyside, ex parte Calveley* [1986] 2 WLR 144.
[63] [2002] EWHC 644 (Admin).
[64] This decision was later overturned: *PMOI v Department of State* 327 F 3d 1238 (2003).
[65] [2002] EWHC 644 (Admin) at para 65.
[66] Ibid para 75 per Richards J.
[67] Ibid para 84.

8.35 Yet, the Administrative Court does enjoy three advantages. It can quash forthwith a proscription by statutory order (but probably not a listing under the original Sch 2), whereas the POAC can only demand a further deproscription order; but s 7 means that there is little practical difference. Secondly, the POAC does not have the power to grant a declaration of incompatibility under s 4 of the Human Rights Act or to award damages under s 8. Thirdly, the POAC is also unable to entertain challenges to the appurtenances of proscription, such as the penalties under Pt II (which formed part of the PKK's claim).

8.36 Assuming the POAC is the prime remedy for those suffering a loss of rights because of proscription, will its standard of judicial review be sufficient to satisfy Articles 6, 10, 11, and 13 of the European Convention? There is a long history of judicial deference to challenges to national security restrictions on organizations, as demonstrated by cases such as *McEldowney v Forde* (rejecting in 1969 a direct challenge to a proscription order).[68] Has the era of the Human Rights Act 1998, as well as indicators of a less executive-dominated process in the Terrorism Act, encouraged more adventure?

8.37 The first indication was negative. In *Re Williamson*,[69] the applicant sought review of the decision in 1999 under the Northern Ireland (Sentences) Act 1998 by the Northern Ireland Secretary of State not to 'specify' the Provisional IRA even though the Secretary of State was satisfied that the Provisional IRA was involved in arms smuggling from the United States and a murder during 1999. The Northern Ireland Court of Appeal accepted that the Secretary of State possessed a high degree of knowledge and expertise and that decisions required political judgment as well as analytical skills. Lord Chief Justice Carswell concluded:[70]

> The area with which the 1998 Act is concerned is delicate and sensitive, and it is hardly surprising that strong views should be held on it or that decisions within this area should give rise to serious differences of opinion. It is part of the democratic process that such decisions should be taken by a Minister responsible to Parliament, and so long as the manner in which they are taken is in accordance with the proper principles the courts should not and will not step outside their proper function of review.

8.38 However, a more assertive outcome was sustained in the *Alton* case before the POAC. The PMOI claimed to have ceased all military activity in 2003. While doubting the need for any hearing before the order is made,[71] the POAC demanded regular Home Office reviews thereafter as a matter of law[72] and expressed itself as willing to apply 'intense scrutiny' to the material before it,[73] albeit that at the second stage of review of discretion based on national security and foreign policy considerations there would be some deference.[74] The Court of Appeal confirmed the need for an 'intense and detailed scrutiny'.[75] On the basis of that review (the open materials alone ran to fifteen volumes), POAC concluded that the Home Secretary's decision had been flawed at the first stage and had confused current involvement in terrorism with 'a secret mental reservation' about eschewing violence for ever as well as

---

[68] [1971] AC 632.
[69] [2000] NI 281.
[70] Ibid 304.
[71] PC/02/2006, 30 November 2007 at para 63.
[72] Ibid para 73.
[73] Ibid para 113.
[74] Ibid para 119.
[75] [2008] EWCA Civ 443 at para 43.

seeking explicit renunciation as an absolute requirement.[76] At the second stage, the POAC graciously accepted that the Minister had not refused to deproscribe as a diplomatic sop either to Iraqis or Iranians. But the Court of Appeal reserved some harsh words for the Minister: 'It is a matter for comment and for regret that the decision-making process in this case has signally fallen short of the standards which our public law sets and which those affected by public decisions have come to expect.'[77] Whilst one case should not be depicted as a judicial revolution, the PMOI case displayed judicial assertiveness over proscription without precedent.

Proscription offences

Provisions

Three offences complete Pt II of the TA 2000. Proscription here serves the purpose of short-circuiting the process of proof—criminalization is through linkage to an organization rather than to specific activities.[78] It may also amount to a positive assumption of vulnerability which excludes a defence of duress for other more serious offences.[79] **8.39**

By s 11(1) of the TA 2000, a person commits an offence by belonging or professing to belong to a proscribed organization. The term, 'profess' is uncertain in its ambit according to Lord Bingham in *Sheldrake v Director of Public Prosecutions; Attorney General's Reference (No 4 of 2002)*:[80] 'it is far from clear, in my opinion, whether it should be understood to denote an open affirmation of belonging to an organization or an acknowledgment of such belonging, and whether (in either case) such affirmation or acknowledgment, to fall within section 11(1), would have to be true'. However, the concerns about political stability and public order which provide foundations for this offence suggest that both affirmation and acknowledgment could be caught, and the truth of the assertion is beside the point since it is dangerous even to pretend that a proscribed organization is tolerable. At the same time, some expressions are uttered in circumstances of such frivolity or abstract debate that they should not be counted as an affirmation or acknowledgment at all, a possibility which was not, however, applied to the defendant in the *Reference*, even though he was described as 'some latter day Walter Mitty or Billy Liar'.[81] Following the TA 2006, s 17, where a person does anything outside the United Kingdom that would amount to an offence under s 11(1) if done in any part of it, liability will arise. The maximum penalties are: (a) on indictment, imprisonment not exceeding ten years, a fine, or both; or (b) on summary conviction, imprisonment not exceeding six months, a fine, or both. **8.40**

A defence is provided in s 11(2) where membership has been shown to have lapsed since the date of proscription. The prosecution must, of course, first establish membership,[82] but then the defendant must assert the defence on the balance of probabilities and s 118[83] does not apply here. In *R v Hundal; R v Dhaliwal*,[84] the relevant organization (the International Sikh Youth Federation) was not proscribed in this country at the time that appellants joined it in **8.41**

---

[76] Ibid paras 338, 342.
[77] Ibid para 57.
[78] See *Home Office Response to Lloyd Report*, para 4.6. Compare *Sayers v HM Advocate* 1982 JC 17.
[79] *R v Payne, McCullogh and Aitken* [1989] 9 NIJB 28 (CA) at 35; *R v O'Neill* [1991] 9 NIJB 13 (CA).
[80] [2004] UKHL 43 at para 48. See also *R v Keogh* [2007] EWCA Crim 528.
[81] Ibid.
[82] Hansard HC Standing Committee D, col 117 (25 January 2000), Charles Clarke.
[83] See Chapter 6.
[84] [2004] EWCA Crim 389.

Germany, but it was proscribed when they continued to undertake activities with the organization and arrived at Dover in 2002 with various ISYF paraphernalia. Both appellants admitted membership of the ISYF in Germany. Mr Hundal claimed that he had renounced membership in April 2001. Mr Dhaliwal claimed that he had not been a member of the ISYF since October 2000. It was accepted that neither appreciated that it was proscribed in the United Kingdom, though that mistake of law would affect sentence rather than conviction.[85] But the Court was clear that, after proscription, activities anywhere in the world could incriminate, otherwise the device of joining a foreign branch would 'enable a coach and horses to be driven through the objects of the legislation'.[86]

8.42 The relationship of ss 11 and 118 was further considered in *Attorney General's Reference (No 4 of 2002)*, arising from charges of membership of the Hamas-Izz al-din al Qassem Brigades.[87] The starkest evidence against the accused was that, on 28 September 2001, he announced to his college class-mates that 'my family name is Bin Laden' and 'I am a member of Hamas'.[88] After arrest, he admitted that he had been a member of Hamas from around 1997 but said that he had left in 1999. At trial, the Crown conceded that s 11(2) imposed only an evidential burden on the defendant, but the Court of Appeal viewed s 11(2) either as not relating to any element of the offence or as imposing a legal burden on the accused to prove the defence.[89] Nevertheless, the Court of Appeal upheld s 11(2) as justified and proportionate under Articles 6(2) and 10 of the European Convention.

8.43 In the House of Lords,[90] Lord Bingham set down the parameter that 'Security concerns do not absolve member states from their duty to observe basic standards of fairness.'[91] His conclusion was that s 11(1) created a real risk that blameless conduct could be penalized. Bearing in mind that participation in the activities of a proscribed organization was not an ingredient of the s 11(1) offence, a defendant could encounter substantial difficulties in proving the elements of s 11(2) (amounting to proof of negative inactivity).[92] Consequently, the imposition of a legal burden upon the defendant was not a proportionate response. Even though Parliament had intended to impose a legal burden by not listing s 11(1) in s 118,[93] the words should be read down under the Human Rights Act 1998, s 3, and should be read as imposing an evidential burden only. This reading reduces the chance that purely passive membership can suffice for conviction, and Lord Bingham welcomed that outcome.[94] At the same time, Lord Bingham ventured that s 11(2) is 'proportionate, for article 10 purposes, whether subsection (2) imposes a legal or an evidential burden'.[95]

8.44 Persons who cannot be shown directly to be members but have provided support to the organization commit an offence under s 12 of the TA 2000. Amongst the distinct forms of involvement forbidden by s 12(1) is the act of inviting support. It is declared that the support

---

[85] Ibid para 8. The sentence was reduced from thirty months to twelve.
[86] Ibid para 12.
[87] [2003] EWCA Crim 762 (regarding Adnan Abdelah, a Palestinian at N Tyneside College).
[88] Ibid para 6.
[89] Ibid paras 23, 42.
[90] *Sheldrake v Director of Public Prosecutions; Attorney General's Reference (No 4 of 2002)* [2004] UKHL 43.
[91] Ibid para 21.
[92] Ibid para 51.
[93] Ibid para 50.
[94] Ibid para 52.
[95] Ibid para 54. Lords Rogers and Carswell dissented, since they preferred this reasoning.

is not restricted to the provision of money or other property (such activity is expressly within s 15). Thus, the provision of labour and services, such as digging a hole for weapons, could fall under s 12.

Secondly, by s 12(2) of the TA 2000, a person commits an offence by arranging, managing, **8.45** or assisting in arranging or managing a meeting which is known (a) to support a proscribed organization; (b) to further the activities of a proscribed organization; or (c) to be addressed by a person who belongs or professes to belong to a proscribed organization.[96] There is a defence under s 12(4) to charges under sub-s (2)(c) if it can be shown that he had no reasonable cause to believe that the address mentioned in sub-s (2)(c) would support a proscribed organization or further its activities: '. . .[t]hat provides sufficient protection for arranging genuinely benign meetings while still ensuring that subsection (2)(c) will serve its basic purpose'.[97] 'Benign' meetings might include meetings between government representatives and paramilitary leaders in order to end violence. The defence under s 12(4) is expressly confined to private meetings. In the words of the government Minister:[98]

> We accept that there could be a genuinely benign private meeting to be addressed by a member of a proscribed organization . . . However, we cannot accept the arranging of public meetings to be addressed by members of proscribed organizations, even when the person arranging the meeting does not think that the address will support the organization.

Because of concerns about Article 6 of the European Convention, this defence must be read subject to s 118(4): if evidence is adduced which is sufficient to raise an issue, the court shall treat it as proved unless the prosecution disproves it beyond reasonable doubt. This express declaration secures that an evidential rather than legal burden is placed on the defence.[99]

Thirdly, by s 12(3) of the TA 2000, a person commits an offence by addressing a meeting **8.46** where the purpose of the address is to encourage support for a proscribed organization or to further its activities. For these purposes, a 'meeting' must involve three or more persons, whether or not the public are admitted, and a meeting is 'private' if the public are not admitted.

The maximum penalties under s 12 are (a) on indictment, imprisonment not exceeding ten **8.47** years, a fine, or both; or (b) on summary conviction, imprisonment not exceeding six months, a fine, or both. The intention behind s 12 is to condemn any public statement on behalf of a proscribed organization—'to drive it down, drive it down, drive it down'.[100] However, a proposed offence of addressing a meeting which is known to be addressed by 'a person who belongs or professes to belong to a proscribed organization' was dropped in 2000.[101]

Perhaps the most flagrant breach of a proscription order (though not the most serious) is to **8.48** display public allegiance with, or support for, an impugned group. Under s 13(1), a person in a public place commits an offence if he (a) wears an item of clothing; or (b) wears, carries, or displays an article, in such a way or in such circumstances as to arouse reasonable suspicion that he is a member or supporter of a proscribed organization. In *Rankin v Murray*,[102] the

---

[96] See *R v Goldan Lambert* [2009] EWCA Crim 700.
[97] Hansard HL vol 614 col 1453 (4 July 2000), Lord Bassam.
[98] Hansard HC vol 353 col 655 (10 July 2000), Charles Clarke.
[99] Hansard HL vol 613 col 754 (16 May 2000), Lord Bassam.
[100] Hansard HC Standing Committee D, col 137 (25 January 2000), Charles Clarke.
[101] Hansard HL vol 614 col 182 (20 June 2000), Lord Bach.
[102] [2004] SCCR 422.

defendant was convicted for wearing a ring inscribed with the initials, 'UVF', when embarking from the Belfast-Troon ferry terminal. The offence plugs gaps in s 1 of the Public Order Act 1936 which is confined to the concept of a 'uniform'.[103] The offence can only be tried summarily, with maximum penalties of imprisonment not exceeding six months, a fine not exceeding level 5, or both. A distinct power to arrest without warrant is granted in Scotland.

Implementation

8.49 Much of the purpose of proscription is symbolic[104]—to express society's revulsion at violence as a political strategy as well as its determination to stop to it. This purpose is especially evident in Britain, where, as shown in Table 8.3, there were no convictions from 1990 to 2001, and few since that time. It takes a crass admission, such as assuming the role of the 'emir' in Britain of Osama bin Laden, to prove affiliation to a body as amorphous as Al-Qa'ida.[105] In contrast, membership charges are more constant in Northern Ireland, often as an added charge,[106] and there were ninety convictions between 1991 and 1998.

Table 8.3 Charges under Part II of the TA 2000[a]

Year	GB	NI
2001	5	2
2002	8	4
2003	13	34
2004	4	9
2005	3	11
2006	15	23
2007	7	n/a
Total	55	83

[a] Sources: Home Office, Northern Ireland Office, *Reports of Lord Carlile*. Figures are from 19 February 2001.

Foreign comparisons

8.50 Constitutional protections for free speech and association restrict proscription in many jurisdictions, save for financial purposes as described in Chapter 9. This situation prevails in the USA, where the advocacy of ideas is protected against criminal sanction,[107] though civil restrictions on associations are allowed.[108]

8.51 Nonetheless, most 'old' Commonwealth jurisdictions have deployed proscription. In Australia, a new scheme was enacted as the Security Legislation Amendment (Terrorism) Act 2002 (as amended by the Criminal Code Amendment (Terrorist Organisations) Act 2004),

---

[103] See *O'Moran v DPP, Whelan v DPP* [1975] QB 864; Walker, C, 'Paramilitary displays and the PTA' [1992] *Juridical Review* 90.

[104] See the view of Home Secretary, Roy Jenkins, *IRA Terrorism in Great Britain* (C(74)139, National Archives, London, 1974) para 3.

[105] See the case of Ishaq Kanmi, *The Times* 11 May 2010, p 23 (Manchester Crown Court).

[106] See Hogan, G and Walker C, *Political Violence and the Law in Ireland* (Manchester University Press, Manchester, 1989) ch 11; *R v McCaugherty and Gregory* [2010] NICC 35 (10 years).

[107] See *Dennis v US* 341 US 494 (1951); *Scales v US* 367 US 203 (1961); *Noto v US* 367 US 290 (1961); *Yates v US* 354 US 298 (1957).

[108] Compare *Communist Party of US v Subversive Activities Control Board* 367 US 1 (1961); *US v Robel* 389 US 258 (1967). See Stone, GR, *Perilous Times* (WW Norton, New York, 2005) ch 5.

allowing for proscription under the Criminal Code 1995 (Division 102) by two pathways.[109] There may be a finding of the court on conviction for a terrorist offence. Alternatively, the Governor General may promulgate a regulation when the Attorney General is satisfied that an organization has been listed by the United Nations Security Council or is a terrorist organization engaged in a terrorist act. Regulations last for two years and are reviewed by the Parliamentary Joint Committee on Intelligence and Security. There are currently eighteen listed organizations (including al Shabaab). Once an organization is listed, various support offences apply, including, as amended by the Anti-Terrorism Act (No 2) 2004, intentional association on two or more occasions with the organization, or its members or leadership. Under the first pathway, these offences can apply against unlisted entities within the definition of 'terrorist organisation' in s 102(1). The advantage is that self-created *jihadi* cells can be prosecuted, but the disadvantages are uncertainty of application, the conferment of wide discretion on police and prosecutors, and the absence of parliamentary endorsement.

Forty groups are proscribed under s 83.05 of the Canadian Criminal Code (inserted by the **8.52** Anti-Terrorism Act 2001), including Aum Shinrikyo, Fuerzas Armadas Revolucionarias de Colombia (FARC), and Sendero Luminoso.[110] Any 'entity' (thus encompassing relatively informal groupings) may be listed by regulation by the Governor in Council when, on the recommendation (based on reasonable grounds) of the Minister of Public Safety and Emergency Preparedness, the Governor is satisfied that there are reasonable grounds to believe that the entity is involved in, or associated with, terrorism. The power is subject to judicial review within sixty days, subject to special rules as to evidence disclosure and admissibility. Any listing must be confirmed by the Minister every two years. Once listed, offences of participation and facilitation apply (ss 83.18–23).

The European Council Framework Decision on Combating Terrorism of 2002[111] **8.53** demands the national implementation of offences of directing and participating relating to a 'terrorist group' (meaning 'a structured group of more than two persons, established over a period of time, and acting in concert to commit terrorist offences'). Consequently, some European jurisdictions have forms of proscription (a few predating the European initiative),[112] but they tend to be more closely linked to criminal activity than in the United Kingdom.

For example, by s 129a of the German Criminal Code, it is unlawful to form, lead, or **8.54** support a terrorist organization whose objectives or activities are directed towards the commission of specified crimes. Organizations based abroad are covered under s 129b if the offence was committed by an activity within the jurisdiction or if the offender or the victim is German or is found within Germany.

Action against terrorist groups in France was taken by Law no 96-647 of 22 July 1996 **8.55** which inserted art 421-2-1 of the Penal Code to designate as 'terrorism' the participation

---

[109] See (Sheller) *Report of the Security Legislation Review Committee* (Canberra, 2006) (which proposes the repeal of the association offence); Attorney General, *National Security Legislation Discussion Paper* (Canberra, 2009); Law Council of Australia, Anti-Terrorism Reform Project (Canberra, 2009) para 4.4.3; Lynch, A et al, 'The Proscription of Terrorist Organisations in Australia' (2009) 37 *Federal Law Review* 1.

[110] See Roach, K, 'The new terrorism offences and the criminal law' in Daniels, RJ, Macklem, P, and Roach, K, *The Security of Freedom* (University of Toronto Press, Toronto, 2001).

[111] 2002/475/JHA, art 2.

[112] See Nuotio, K, 'Terrorism as a catalyst for the emergence, harmonisation and reform of the criminal law' (2006) 4 *Journal of International Criminal Justice* 998.

in any group formed or association established with a view to the preparation of acts of terrorism. Article 421.2.3 (inserted by Act no 2003-239 of 18 March 2003) also includes a 'lifestyle offence' of being unable to account for resources corresponding to one's lifestyle when habitually in close contact with a person or persons who engage in terrorist activities.

8.56   The closest parallel to United Kingdom law is proscription of 'unlawful organisations' in the Republic of Ireland's Offences against the State Act 1939, Part III.[113] The High Court hears objections to suppression orders issued by the government under s 19 and is not confined under s 20 to scrutiny on the basis of judicial review.[114] In furtherance of the Council Framework Decision, the Criminal Justice (Terrorist Offences) Act 2005, s 5, deems a group falling within its scope to be an unlawful organization for the purposes of the 1939 Act.

8.57   Special features of the Irish code relate to evidence and to penalties. Some evidential points have been covered in Chapter 3, but note should also be taken of the shifting of the evidential burden by the proof of possession of incriminating documents under s 24[115] and of the admissibility of statements of opinion about membership from a police chief superintendent under the Offences against the State (Amendment) Act 1972, s 3(2).[116] As for penalties, s 25 of the 1939 Act (as amended by s 4 of the Criminal Law Act 1976) allows a chief superintendent to order the closure of any building for twelve months.[117] In addition, a person convicted by the Special Criminal Court will be disqualified for seven years from public office and pensions under s 34 of the 1939 Act. The constitutionality of s 34 was successfully challenged in *Cox v Ireland*.[118]

Assessment and conclusions

8.58   Policy relevance to the CONTEST strategy has been considered at the outset of this chapter.

8.59   As for a rights audit, the objectives of security and the protection of life appear compelling. Challenges under European Convention standards will be answered either under Article 17 or under the limitations to Articles 9 to 11 by the depiction of expressive and associational rights as being instrumental to democracy and pluralism rather than goods in themselves.[119] Thus, the banning of bodies which seek to impose *sharia* law has been sustained.[120] Any association with violent methods will produce condemnation, even if the ultimate policy

---

[113] See (Hederman) *Report of the Committee to Review the Offences against the State Acts 1939–1998* (Dublin, 2002) ch 6.

[114] See *Sloan v Special Criminal Court* [1993] 3 IR 528.

[115] See *O'Leary v Attorney General* [1995] 1 IR 254.

[116] See *People (DPP) v Kelly* [2006] IESC 20; *People (DPP) v Donohue* [2007] IECCA 97; Heffernan, L, 'Evidence and national security' [2009] *European Public Law* 65.

[117] See *Hederman Report* (above) para 6.129.

[118] [1992] 2 IR 503. See *Murphy v Ireland* [1996] 3 IR 307; *McDonnell v Ireland* [1998] 1 IR 134. See further Chapter 6.

[119] *German Communist Party v Germany*, App no 350/57, 1 YBEC 222; *Retimag v Germany* App no 712/60, 4 YBEC; *Norwood v United Kingdom*, App no 23131/03, 2004-XI. See Brems, E, 'Freedom of political association and the question of party closures' in Sadurski, W (ed), *Political Rights Under Stress in 21st Century Europe* (Oxford University Press, Oxford, 2006).

[120] *Refah Partisi v Turkey*, App nos 41340/98, 41342/98, 41343/98, and 41344/98, 2003-II. The level of political support is not crucial where groups unequivocally espouse violence; compare Cram, I, *Terror and the War on Dissent* (Springer, Heidelberg, 2009) p 61.

goals are acceptable;[121] conversely, those with peaceful ambitions to change constitutional foundations should not be debarred.[122]

Proscription powers under the TA 2000 have been held to be compatible with the European **8.60** Convention. In *R v Hundal; R v Dhaliwal*,[123] the fact that the membership had started before the organization was proscribed did not breach Article 7 (retrospective penalties) since the bite of the offence was on arrival in the United Kingdom, in 2002. The bolder challenges, that the proscription of an entire organization or the criminalization of plain membership infringe expressive rights under Articles 10 or 11, were fleetingly raised in *O'Driscoll v Secretary of State for the Home Department*[124] (considered further in Chapter 3) but were not pursued.[125] In *Sheldrake v Director of Public Prosecutions; Attorney General's Reference (No 4 of 2002)*,[126] it was stated in the House of Lords without argument that s 11(1) interferes with exercise of the right of free expression but that it is justifiable under Article 10(2). The courts have also accepted partial restrictions, such as broadcast bans[127] and physical exclusion.[128]

Next, the proportionality of banning an organization, as opposed to interdicting funding or **8.61** prosecuting specific activities, may be questioned. Proscription has often been of marginal utility in combating political violence, to which the survival of the IRA since 1918 in the teeth of almost continuous proscription bears witness. Paramilitary organizations cannot be abolished by legislative fiat, and proscription increases the difficulties of infiltration and monitoring. Next, Pt II is disproportionate in extent and impact—for example, bans cannot be confined to one territory, such as Northern Ireland (as applied in many cases before 2001). There should also be caution about the special offences, when similar outcomes can be achieved by ordinary offences such as the possession of weapons, conspiracy to carry out attacks, or public order offences.[129] Displays of political uniforms and the management of quasi-military organizations are contrary to ss 1 and 2 of the Public Order Act 1936, charges sustained against IRA sympathizers in *O'Moran v DPP; Whelan v DPP*.[130] These public order law alternatives may be sufficient to answer any rationale for proscription based on the 'presentational'[131]—that it expresses the condemnation of the community and 'averts the

---

[121] See further *Gündüz v Turkey*, App no 59745/00, 2003-XI.
[122] See *United Communist Party of Turkey and Others v Turkey*, App no 19392/92, 1998-I; *Socialist Party v Turkey*, App no 21237/93, 1998-III; *Partidul Comunistilor (Nepeceristi) and Ungureanu v Romania*, App no 46626/99, 2005-I.
[123] [2004] EWCA Crim 389 at para 14.
[124] [2002] EWHC 2477 (Admin).
[125] Ibid para 14.
[126] [2004] UKHL 43 at para 54 per Lord Bingham.
[127] See *In re McLaughlin* [1989] 8 NIJB 83; *R v Secretary of State for the Home Department, ex parte Brind* [1991] AC 696; *Brind and McLaughlin v United Kingdom*, App nos 18714/91, 18759/91, 77-A DR 42 (1994); *Purcell v Ireland*, App no 15404/89, 70 DR 262 (1991); *Hogefeld v Germany*, App no 35402/97, 20 January 2000.
[128] *Adams and Benn v United Kingdom*, App nos 28979/95; 30343/96, 88A D & R, 137 (1997).
[129] In Scotland, see *Loyal Orange Lodge No 493, Hawick First Purple v Roxburgh D.C.* 1981 *Scottish Law Times* 33; *Aberdeen Bon-Accord Loyal Orange Lodge v Grampian RC* 1988 *Scottish Law Times* (Sh Ct) 58; *Aberdeen Bon Accord Loyal Orange Lodge 701 v Aberdeen City Council* 2002 *Scottish Law Times* (Sh Ct) 52; *Wishart Arch Defenders Loyal Orange Lodge 404 v Angus Council* 2002 *Scottish Law Times* (Sh Ct) 43. See also the Public Processions (Northern Ireland) Act 1998.
[130] [1975] QB 864. The Scottish offence of breach of the peace was used in *Duffield and Crosbie v Skeen* 1981 SCCR 66; *McAvoy v Jessop* 1989 SCCR 301; Subhaan Younis (*The Times* 29 September 2005, p 3). See also Public Order (Northern Ireland) Order 1987, SI 1987/463, art 21.
[131] *Jellicoe Report*, para 207.

danger of public outrage being expressed in public disorder'.[132] However, the government has called in aid three bases for proscription in total:[133]

> First, it has been, and remains, a powerful deterrent to people to engage in terrorist activity. Secondly, related offences are a way of tackling some of the lower-level support for terrorist organisations. . . . Thirdly, proscription acts as a powerful signal of the rejection by the Government—and indeed by society as a whole—of organisations' claim to legitimacy. . . . The legislation is a powerful symbol of that censure and is important.

8.62 The precept of accountability is much less securely attained. There is no system for the production of a detailed factual case for proscription, nor for the original ban to be determined by a judge,[134] nor for periodic review, unlike under the Australian model. A further problem concerns multiple proscriptions within a single order, meaning that the listed groups are condemned on an indiscriminate 'take it or leave it' basis.[135]

8.63 As for constitutional governance, the work of the POAC has improved upon prior processes. But the restoration of normal constitutional life is not sufficiently pressing. Few have disputed the banning of Al-Qa'ida, though the activities within the United Kingdom of most other *jihadi* groups remain obscure. As for the Irish organizations, a distinction must be drawn between those observing ceasefires since 1998 and those dissenting from that stance. Regarding the former, there must come a time when their indisputable past involvement in violence becomes historical. The Independent Monitoring Commission has confirmed that by 2008 the Provisional IRA was withering away.[136] Yet, the government seems unwilling as yet to offer deproscription in return for anticipated desistance.

C. Extremist Expressions and Activities

Group glorification

Introduction and background

8.64 Commitment to legislation on glorification had been promised in the Labour Party's 2005 election manifesto[137] but became acute after the London bombs of July 2005. Fear of the radicalization of young Muslim men by foreign extremists drew from the Prime Minister a 12-point plan which included the banning of organizations which encourage extremism.[138] In the background, international intolerance of foreign dissidents was marked after 11 September 2001 by UNSCR 1373 of 28 September 2001, art 3(f), which calls for action against asylum-seekers involved in terrorism. International law took more definite shape, with Article 5 of the Council of Europe Convention on the Prevention of Terrorism of 2005 demanding domestic offences to outlaw the public provocation of terrorism offences.[139]

---

[132] *Baker Report*, para 414.
[133] Hansard HC Standing Committee D, col 56 (18 January 2000), Charles Clarke.
[134] Compare Report of the Special Rapporteur, *Protection of Human Rights and fundamental freedoms while countering terrorism* (A/61/267, Geneva, 2006)) para 26.
[135] See Hansard HC vol 462, col 1369 (10 July 2007), Tony McNulty.
[136] *Nineteenth Report* (Cm 7464, London, 2008) ch 2.
[137] *Britain forward not back* (London, 2005) p 53.
[138] *The Times*, 6 August 2005, p 1.
[139] CETS No 196. See further Committee of Experts on Terrorism, '*Apologie du Terrorisme*' and '*Incitement to Terrorism*' (CODEXTER, Strasbourg, 2004); Joint Committee on Human Rights, The Council of Europe Convention on the Prevention of Terrorism (2006–07 HL 26/HC 247); Hunt, A, 'The Council of Europe Convention on the Prevention of Terrorism' (2006) 4 *European Public Law* 603.

Further impetus for action was provided by the UNSCR 1624 of 14 September 2005, calling upon states to 'Prohibit by law incitement to commit a terrorist act or acts'. The TA 2006 is the British retort.

Provisions

The first measure is to extend proscription to group glorification. Though s 3(5)(c) of the **8.65** 2000 Act already allows proscription where an organization promotes or encourages terrorism, the link to action is even less direct under the 2006 Act since its emphasis is on speech and not deeds. Furthermore, the thrust of the power is aimed against domestic-based non-Irish groups.

Powers to proscribe organizations which glorify terrorism are inserted by the TA 2006, s 21. **8.66** A new s 3(5A) inserted in the TA 2000 specifies that the power to proscribe under s 3(5)(c) shall encompass the 'unlawful glorification of the commission or preparation (whether in the past, in the future, or generally) of acts of terrorism'. 'Glorification' requires the reasonable expectation that the audience will emulate terrorism in present circumstances (s 3(5B)), and it comprises any form of praise or celebration (s 3(5C)). The boundaries of glorification are uncertain and threatening to free speech since they exceed the encouragement of crime,[140] but changes made in the drafting to Pt I of the 2006 Act (considered later) were reflected here too. As a result, the Minister was sure that the final formula would distinguish 'cultural events or those that celebrate a part of our collective memory, such as Guy Fawkes and bonfire night, and people who glorify acts of terror to try to encourage similar acts here and now in existing circumstances'.[141] The same distinction would apply to Irish celebrations of the past deeds of Michael Collins or William of Orange, depending on whether the praise relates to an heroic history or future emulation.

A potential problem might be to ascribe responsibility to an organization. Must every remark **8.67** by every member be taken as 'official' policy, or must impugned statements emanate from prominent or multiple members?[142] The same point could arise with unsanctioned activities, but violent acts probably require joint planning and often evince formal claims of responsibility. It is easier to make a wayward impulsive remark than to carry out an impromptu bombing.

Implementation

As detailed in Table 8.4, two groups (Al-Ghurabaa and The Saved Sect) were banned in July **8.68** 2006.[143] Five more were listed in January 2010 as reflecting variant names of the first two, though in terms of organizational history, the founding group was al-Muhajiroun.[144]

One element of evidence against Al-Ghurabaa concerned the following comments by a repre- **8.69** sentative about the London bombings of 2005: 'What I would say about those who do suicide operations or martyrdom operations is that they're completely praiseworthy. I have no allegiance to the Queen whatsoever or to British society; in fact if I see mujahideen attack the UK I am always standing with the Muslims.'[145]

---

[140] Hansard HC vol 438 col 985 (2 November 2005).
[141] Hansard HC vol 438, col 994 (3 November 2005), Paul Goggins.
[142] Saul, B, 'Speaking of terror' (2005) 28 *University of New South Wales Law Review* 868 at 880.
[143] SI 2006/2016, Hansard HC vol 449, col 490 (20 July 2006). See Wiktorowicz, Q, *Radical Islam Rising* (Rowman & Littlefield, Lanham, 2005).
[144] SI 2010/34. See Pantucci, R, 'The Tottenham Ayatollah and the Hook-Handed Cleric' (2010) 33 *Studies in Conflict & Terrorism* 226.
[145] Hansard HC vol 449 col 493 (20 July 2006).

Table 8.4 Proscription of group glorification

Al-Ghurabaa	Al-Ghurabaa ('The Strangers') is an Islamist group. It succeeded Al-Muhajiroun.
Al-Muhajiroun	Al-Muhajiroun ('The Emigrants') was founded by Omar Bakri Muhammad and others in Saudi Arabia in 1983. It was disbanded in 2004 but relaunched in 2009. It is considered a variant name.
Call to Submission	A variant name.
Islam4UK	This Islamist group was led by Anjem Choudary and became prominent for its involvement in public protests. It is considered a variant name.
Islamic Path	A variant name.
London School of Sharia	A variant name. Anjem Choudary adopted the title of 'Judge of the Shari'ah Court of the UK'.
The Saved Sect	The Saved Sect (formerly the Saviour Sect) pursues the mission of speaking out for proper standards for Muslims living in Western countries so as to ensure their salvation.

8.70 The 2010 proscriptions were provoked by the announcement by Islam4UK of a protest march through Wootton Bassett, the location where the corteges of service personnel killed in Afghanistan are informally honoured by the public. The protest was not intended to coincide with any funeral processions, but it was condemned by Prime Minister Gordon Brown as 'abhorrent and offensive'.[146] The Home Secretary, Alan Johnson, initially indicated there might be a ban under the Public Order Act 1986, s 13, though no advance notice was given and, soon after, Islam4UK said it was cancelling any plans.

8.71 Lord Carlile predicted that there could be 'a significant number of additional proscriptions' through 'reducing the opportunity for disaffected young people to become radicalized towards terrorism'.[147] In response, the government has shown restraint in relation to potential candidates,[148] especially Hizb ut-Tahrir,[149] a transnational movement established in 1953 which advocates in Arab countries the establishment of a Caliphate and *sharia* laws. Nevertheless, it 'remains an organization of concern and is kept under close review'.[150] It was even mentioned in the 2010 election manifesto of the Conservative Party.[151] Whether proscription would be a worthwhile venture may be doubted.[152] The profusion of organizational names in 2010 points to an endemic weakness in the mechanism of proscription as applied to *jihadi* movements which are far removed from the historically and geographically

---

[146] *The Guardian* 5 January 2010, p 4.
[147] Lord Carlile, *Proposals by Her Majesty's Government for changes to the laws against terrorism* (Home Office, London, 2005) paras 51, 52. Compare Lord Carlile, *Report on the Operation in 2007 of the Terrorism Act 2000* (Home Office, London, 2008) para 50.
[148] For example, Ahlus Sunnah wal Jamaah, the Muballigh, the Islamic Thinkers Society, the Society of Muslim Lawyers, the Supporters of Sharia, and Tablighi Jama'at: Hansard HC vol 449, col 496 (20 July 2006), Patrick Mercer.
[149] See Ahmed, H and Stuart, H, *Hizb ut Tahrir* (Centre for Social Cohesion, London, 2009).
[150] Hansard HC vol 472 col 588W (19 February 2008), Tony McNulty.
[151] *Invitation to Join the Government of Britain* (London, 2010) p 105.
[152] Lord Carlile, *Report on the Operation in 2009 of the Terrorism Act 2000* (Home Office, London, 2010) para 72.

defined proponents of Irish or other nationalist terror groups whose names are legends in songs and inscribed on gravestones.

Foreign comparisons

The European Council Framework Decision on Combating Terrorism was amended in 2008 so as to require the national implementation of offences against public provocation, recruitment, and training, subject to 'fundamental principles relating to freedom of expression'.[153] **8.72**

Even beyond Europe, other countries are now banning organizations on the basis of advocacy, such as the Australian Anti-Terrorism Act (No 2) 2005. The Act allows listing by the Attorney General and prosecutions for activities where the organization advocates a terrorist act contrary to Div 102(1A) of the Criminal Code. **8.73**

Incitement of terrorism

Introduction and background

The principal and highly controversial changes brought about by the TA 2006 in relation to extremist speech are set out in offences in ss 1 and 2. **8.74**

Provisions—statements

The principal offence in s 1(1) relates to the publication of a statement that is 'likely to be understood by some or all of the members of the public to whom it is published as a direct or indirect encouragement or other inducement to the commission, preparation or instigation of acts of terrorism' or specified offences (referred to as 'Convention offences' and listed in Sch 1, subject to change by affirmative order under s 20(9)). **8.75**

Publication of one's statement is the core of the *actus reus* (s 1(2)(a)). The 'statement' may take many formats under s 20(6), including words, sounds, or images, and, by s 20(4), can be published 'in any manner' such as through an electronic service.[154] A 'statement' may be part of a wider message and need not be confined to terrorism or offences in, or with respect to, the United Kingdom.[155] But s 1(4) demands that account be taken of the contents as a whole and the circumstances and manner of publication. For instance, 'there is a difference in how an academic thesis on an issue and a radical and inflammatory pamphlet are likely to be understood'.[156] The statement must be made to 'members of the public', who must be in the multiple and are distinct from 'persons' in a private conversation.[157] If the statement is made at a meeting, it must be a meeting or other group of persons which is open to the public.[158] By s 20(3), the 'public' can include the public (or any section of it) of any part of the United Kingdom or of a country or territory outside the United Kingdom. Furthermore, in so far as it relates to 'Convention offences', s 1 is within the parameters of s 17 of the Act (discussed below), which means that the offence could be committed by Palestinians in Gaza **8.76**

---

[153] 2008/919/JHA, art 3. See House of Commons European Scrutiny Committee, *Seventeenth Report* (2007–08 HC 16-vii) para 8.14; Boyne, SM, 'Free speech, terrorism, and European security' (2010) 30 *Pace Law Review* 418 at 449.

[154] By s 20(5), providing a service includes making a facility available.

[155] Leigh, LH, 'The Terrorism Act 2006–a brief analysis' (2006) 170 *Justice of the Peace* 364 at 364.

[156] Home Office Circular 8/2006, *The Terrorism Act 2006*, para 3.

[157] Hansard HL vol 676 col 435 (5 December 2005), Baroness Scotland.

[158] s 20(3).

and Pakistanis in Peshawar.[159] The offence does not require that all targeted members of the public are likely to be affected; the influenced sub-set must comprise 'some' which could mean one or more affected recipients.[160] In applying the impact test, juries may face challenging calculations where the statement is confined to a section of the public consisting of 'small cohesive congregations'.[161] The limit in the offence to a public context is odd, given the mischief of radicalization.[162]

8.77 As for the *mens rea*, in s 1(2)(b), the publisher must either intend members of the public to be directly or indirectly encouraged or otherwise induced, by the statement, to commit, prepare, or instigate acts of terrorism or specified offences, or be subjectively reckless as to whether members of the public will be so directly or indirectly encouraged by the statement. The original draft of the offence lacked this element of subjective specific intent—it was sufficient that there was intent as to publication and reasonable belief as to encouragement.[163] There was prolonged opposition to that version,[164] which was seen as reviving the version of inadvertent recklessness in *Metropolitan Police Commissioner v Caldwell*[165] despite its reversal in *R v G*.[166] The other notable aspect of the *mens rea* is that the defendant must seek to affect multiple members of the public, so some of the queries about the extent of publication may become irrelevant. The requirement points again to a strong public order element.

8.78 By s 1(5), it is irrelevant whether the encouragement relates to one or more particular acts of terrorism or specified offences, or those of a particular description, or generally. This provision should not, however, excuse the prosecution from specifying the one or more acts or offences which were relevant.[167] It is also no defence under s 1(5)(b) to show that the dissemination fell on deaf ears—in other words, that no person was in fact encouraged or induced by the statement. The offence considers the objective tendency of the publication. However, where the allegation is of a recklessly made statement, it is a defence under s 1(6) to show that the statement neither expressed the originator's views nor had his endorsement and that it was clear, in all the circumstances of the statement's publication, that it did not express his views and (unless in receipt of a notice under s 3(3)) did not have his endorsement. Thus, the government intended a legal rather than an evidential burden to be placed on the defence,[168] though the precedent of the *Attorney General's Reference (No 4 of 2002)*[169] strongly suggests that the courts might take another view.

---

159 Prosecution is subject to s 19(2).

160 It has been suggested that 'some' requires more than a single person (and compare s 2(6)): Jones, A, Bowers, R, and Lodge, HD, *The Terrorism Act 2006* (Oxford University Press, Oxford, 2006) para 2.18. But see further s 1(2)(b), as discussed below.

161 Ibid, para 2.35.

162 Compare Public Order Act 1986, s 18. See *Review of Public Order Law* (Cmnd 9510, London, 1985) para 6.7.

163 2005–06 HC no 55. See Hansard HC vol 438 col 834 (2 November 2005), Dominic Grieve.

164 Hansard HL vol 676 col 430 (5 December 2005), Baroness Scotland.

165 [1982] AC 341.

166 [2003] UKHL 50 para 45 per Lord Browne-Wilkinson.

167 Compare Hunt, A, 'Criminal prohibitions on direct and indirect encouragement of terrorism' [2007] *Criminal Law Review* 441 at 445.

168 Hansard HL vol 676 col 455 (5 December 2005), Baroness Scotland, vol 678 col 217 (1 February 2006), Lord Goldsmith.

169 [2004] UKHL 43.

The most *controversial* aspect of the offence is indirect encouragement, and so Parliament **8.79** sought to apply further clarifications and limits.[170] By sub-s (3), the indirect encouragement of terrorism includes a statement that 'glorifies' the commission or preparation of acts of terrorism or specified offences (either in their actual commission or in principle) but only if members of the public could reasonably be expected to infer that the glorified conduct should be 'emulated by them in existing circumstances'. The continued mention of 'glorification' reflects a vestige of the pre-parliamentary draft of the Bill, which included an offence of glorification distinct from the offence of encouragement.[171] The impact is on members of the public at large and not a particular audience, as under s 1(1). In this way, a predictive application of 'likely impact' is replaced by a wholly objective test where the jury can put themselves in the shoes of an audience.[172] It follows that it is no defence to show that an actual audience did not believe there was glorification, though this circumstance can be pleaded to direct incitement or other indirect incitements.

The notion of 'emulation' ensures that the words uttered should be understood as more than **8.80** rhetorical. Consequently, praise for historical violence, such as the armed occupation of the General Post Office, Dublin, in 1916, is not an offence, unless the statements can be understood to resonate with the present and to guide future action. The position may be clearer where the speaker glorifies ongoing or future (but not futuristic) acts of terrorism since the possibility of replication is then more palpable and practicable. Thus, a declaration that most devout British Muslims were 'over the moon' about the September 11 attacks refers to an historical act when uttered in 2005, but must sail close to s 1(3) when allied to the statement that 'Ultimately, if your brothers and sisters were being killed in any part of the world, you would make your utmost effort to try to help them.'[173]

'Glorify' is partly defined in s 20(2) as including 'praise or celebration'. An all-embracing **8.81** *working* (non-legal) definition was proffered by a Home Office Minister as follows: 'To glorify is to describe or represent as admirable, especially unjustifiably or undeservedly.'[174] Section 20(7) clarifies that references to conduct to be 'emulated in existing circumstances' include references to conduct that is illustrative of a type of conduct that should be so emulated. For example, a statement glorifying the bombing of a bus at Tavistock Square on 7 July 2005 and encouraging repeat performances may be interpreted as an encouragement to emulate by attacks on the transport network in general. The government's advice for speakers wishing to avoid glorification is that they should 'preface their remarks with the statement that they do not condone or endorse acts of terrorism or encouraging people to kill others. They could express sympathy and even support for the activity, but not in a way that encourages people to commit acts of terrorism.'[175] This 'love-hate' formula—love the cause but hate violent means—is not a magic incantation which wards off all iniquity. Juries may consider the context of words and the sincerity of speakers, as made clear by s 1(4).

---

[170] See Hansard HL vol 679 col 136 (28 February 2006), vol 680 col 241 (22 March 2006).
[171] See Lord Carlile, *Proposals by Her Majesty's Government for changes to the laws against terrorism* (Home Office, London, 2005) para 21; Barendt, E, 'Threats to freedom of speech in the United Kingdom' (2005) 28 *University of New South Wales Law Journal* 895 at 897.
[172] See Jones, A, Bowers, R, and Lodge, HD, *The Terrorism Act 2006* (Oxford University Press, Oxford, 2006) para 2.41.
[173] These words were spoken by Hassan Butt: Taseer, A, 'A British Jihadist' (2005) 113 Prospect (<http://www.prospectmagazine.co.uk/2005/08/abritishjihadist>).
[174] Hansard HL vol 677 col 583 (17 January 2006), Baroness Scotland.
[175] Hansard HC vol 439 col 429 (9 November 2005), Hazel Blears.

8.82   There is no illumination of the meaning of 'indirect incitement' beyond the concept of glorification. Presumably, an incitement is not direct when less than an explicit stimulus but still predictably steering towards an outcome. Within this residue of indirect incitement, any requirement of emulation is absent.

8.83   The overall impact is to criminalize generalized and public encouragements—that terrorism would be a good thing, without stating where or when or against whom. In comparison, the 'normal' law of criminal encouragement in Pt II of the Serious Crime Act 2007 requires the encouragement of an act which would amount to one or more offences and at least with the belief that one or more offences would be committed as a consequence. Section 1 advances these normal boundaries, in the case of direct incitement, by specifying that it is an offence 'to incite people to engage in terrorist activities generally' and extra-territorially.[176] In the case of indirect incitement, it is an offence 'to incite them obliquely by creating the climate in which they may come to believe that terrorist acts are acceptable'.[177] How this differs from 'normal' incitement remains uncertain. The 'normal' law does not use the terms 'direct' and 'indirect' but does occasionally accord a wide meaning to 'encourage', such as in cases of speed trap detection machines or books giving advice on the production of cannabis.[178] Perhaps the absence of any requirement of intended emulation outside of the realm of glorification could be one key difference, though the absence of actual audience reaction is less of a distinction under the 2007 Act.[179]

Provisions—dissemination of statements

8.84   Having dealt with the originators of statements in s 1, s 2(1) deals with the secondary dissemination of terrorist publications with intent or recklessness as to direct or indirect encouragement to acts of terrorism.[180] Closely parallel to s 1(3), the meaning of indirect encouragement is explained in s 2(4). The activity involved in a 'terrorist publication' is distribution, circulation, giving, selling, lending, offering for sale or loan, provision of a service to others that enables them to access or acquire,[181] transmitting electronically, or possessing 'with a view' to the foregoing activities (s 2(2)).[182] Possession was added at the last stage of the Bill and reflects race hatred legislation.[183] It is sufficient that possession is one of the defendant's purposes and not necessarily the prime purpose. The publication may take many formats—it means an article or record[184] which may be read, listened to, looked at, or watched (s 2(13)).

---

[176]   But see Criminal Justice (Terrorism and Conspiracy) Act 1998.
[177]   Hansard HL vol 676 cols 432–3 (5 December 2005), Baroness Scotland. Compare Cohen-Almagor, R, 'Boundaries of free expression before and after Prime Minister Rabin's assassination' in Cohen-Almagor, R, *Liberal Democracy and the Limits of Tolerance* (University of Michigan Press, Ann Arbor, 2000).
[178]   *Invicta Plastics Ltd v Clare* [1976] RTR 251; *R v Marlow* [1998] 1 Cr App Rep (S) 273.
[179]   See Law Commission, *Inchoate Liability for Assisting and Encouraging Crime* (Report no 300, Cm 6878, London, 2006) para 1.3.
[180]   Subjective recklessness was inserted in line with s 1: Hansard HL vol 677 col 551 (17 January 2006), Baroness Scotland.
[181]   An example might be the running of a market stall: Leigh, LH, 'The Terrorism Act 2006—a brief analysis' (2006) 170 *Justice of the Peace* 364 at 364.
[182]   This definition is exclusive to s 2, and so s 20(4) does not apply.
[183]   See Hansard HL vol 678 col 197 (1 February 2006); Public Order Act 1986, s 23 (as suggested by the *Review of Public Order Law* (Cmnd 9510, London, 1985) para 6.8). Lord Carlile also suggested an analogy with paedophile offences as in Criminal Justice Act 1988, s 160 (*Proposals by Her Majesty's Government for changes to the laws against terrorism* (Home Office, London, 2005) para 25), but possession per se is not an offence under s 2.
[184]   See further s 20(2), (8).

In content, a 'terrorist publication' is defined in s 2(3) as containing materials of two distinct **8.85** types. First, it covers matter likely to be understood, by some or all of the persons to whom it is or may become available as a consequence of publication, as a direct or indirect encouragement or other inducement to them to the commission, preparation, or instigation of acts of terrorism. Secondly, it covers matter likely to be useful in the commission or preparation of such acts and to be understood, by some or all of those persons, as contained in the publication, or made available to them, wholly or mainly for the purpose of being so useful to them. This second leg compensates for the fact that 'Convention offences' (as in Sch 1) are not mentioned under s 2(1). The explanation for this distinction is that s 1 is tied more closely to the terms in Article 5 of the Council of Europe Convention, namely, 'public provocations', whereas s 2 is more an artefact of British legislative design.[185] As a result, there is no extra-territorial effect under s 17.

The effect of a terrorist publication can be judged by reference to one or more persons to **8.86** whom it is or may become available as a consequence (s 2(6)). The possibility of affecting a single person contrasts with the position under s 1. In further contrast is the possibility of judging the likely impact not only on persons who were exposed but also on those who may be exposed to the materials. In this way, the audience may in part be determined by the designs of the defendant, but it might also be affected by the choice of medium. For example, it will be difficult to delimit the audience for an internet posting. It is also notable that the offence mentions 'persons' and not members of the public as in s 1, which means that private circulations of public statements can be prohibited. An explanation for the distinction is again that s 2 does not directly derive from Article 5 of the 2005 Convention.

The concept of 'terrorist publication' is explained further by s 2(5). The nature of the publi- **8.87** cations must be determined at the time of the conduct in s 2(2) and having regard both to the entire contents of the publication and to the circumstances in which that conduct occurs. It is irrelevant whether the dissemination relates to particular, generic, or general acts of terrorism (s 2(7)).

The *mens rea* presumably requires intention as to the forms of dissemination in s 2(2)(a) to **8.88** (e), while for the possession offence under s2(2)(f), there must be an intent to possess with future intent to disseminate. In addition, it is specified in sub-s (1) that the person must intend or be reckless that an effect of his conduct (not necessarily the sole or prime effect) amounts to a direct or indirect encouragement or other inducement to the commission, preparation, or instigation of acts of terrorism or assistance in the commission or preparation of such acts.

Parallel to s 1(6), it is a defence under s 2(9) to show that the statement neither expressed the **8.89** publisher's views nor had his endorsement and that this position was clear in all the circumstances (unless in receipt of a notice under s 3(3)).[186] By s 2(10), the defence is again confined to reckless and not intentional actions, and is also confined to encouragement offences and

---

[185] Hunt, A, 'Criminal prohibitions on direct and indirect encouragement of terrorism' [2007] *Criminal Law Review* 441 at 444, 445.
[186] The government intended that the defendant carries a legal burden of proof: Hansard HL vol 678 col 218 (1 February 2006), Lord Goldsmith. Compare Lord Carlile, *Proposals by Her Majesty's Government for changes to the laws against terrorism* (Home Office, London, 2005) para 25. The courts are likely to impose an evidential burden: *Sheldrake v Director of Public Prosecutions; Attorney General's Reference (No 4 of 2002)* [2004] UKHL 43.

not offences relating to useful materials. Of course, it is conceivable that materials will be prosecuted as relating to both types of offence in s 2(3), and if the defence is raised in those circumstances, the jury might find it difficult to disentangle liability.

8.90 The defence can benefit 'all legitimate librarians, academics and booksellers' (and the same applies to news broadcasters) who may have examined the article but still do not endorse the contents.[187] Nevertheless, where an academic officer suspects or believes that a student intends to use the available materials for terrorist purposes rather than scholastic endeavour, she should 'as a good citizen' inform the security authorities.[188]

8.91 This injunction was taken to heart by the University of Nottingham when a student, Rizwaan Sabir, was arrested in 2008 for downloading materials in connection with his postgraduate research, together with his friend and ex-student, Hicham Yezza, to whom he had passed the materials.[189] The offending materials were an Al-Qa'ida training manual which had been published in redacted form on the US Department of Justice website.[190] The Vice Chancellor, Sir Colin Campbell, warned, without much regard for the defences in ss 1 and 2, that it is illegitimate to study the operational or tactical aspects of terrorism, as opposed to its political dimensions.[191] Lord Carlile had rightly cautioned before enactment that there was a danger that academic research into terrorism might be 'turned into samizdat activity'.[192]

8.92 As in s 1, it is no defence that the dissemination fell on deaf ears. By sub-s (8) it is irrelevant whether any person is in fact encouraged or induced or makes use of the materials. However, where under sub-s (10) the offence is one of direct or indirect encouragement only (and so this is not applicable to material useful to terrorists) and the person was not acting intentionally within sub-s (1)(a), there is a defence of unauthorized dissemination under sub-s (9) by which it is a defence to show that the publication neither expressed the defendant's views nor had his endorsement and that this position was clear in all the circumstances (subject to receiving a notice under s 3(3)).

8.93 Section 2 exceeds the 'normal' law of incitement in many respects, though much of its potential impact on third party publishers is moderated by s 2(9). Thus, the important impact is upon sympathetic disseminators or possessors of materials, where the accused is one step away from the original incitement and where it might be difficult to prove the sharing of the same *mens rea* as the author.

Implementation

8.94 The penalties under ss 1 and 2 are, on indictment, imprisonment not exceeding seven years, a fine, or both; on summary conviction in England and Wales, imprisonment not exceeding twelve months[193] (six months in Scotland or Northern Ireland), or a fine, or both.

---

187 Hansard HL vol 676 col 465 (5 December 2005), Baroness Scotland. See also Hansard HL vol 677 col 554 (17 January 2006), Baroness Scotland; *Explanatory Notes to the Terrorism Act 2006* (HMSO, London, 2006) para 27.

188 Hansard HL vol 676 col 629 (7 December 2005), Baroness Scotland.

189 See *The Guardian*, 24 May 2008, p 8; <http://freehicham.co.uk>.

190 <http://www.usdoj.gov/ag/manualpart1_1.pdf>, 2005.

191 Hunt, S, 'Feeding culture of fear won't defend freedom' *Times Higher Educational Supplement* 24 July 2008, p 28.

192 Lord Carlile, *Proposals by Her Majesty's Government for changes to the laws against terrorism* (Home Office, London, 2005) para 28.

193 Subject to the commencement of the Criminal Justice Act 2003, s 154(1).

In *R v Rahman, R v Mohammed*,[194] the conviction of Rahman under s 2(2)(f) arose from an **8.95**
instruction to disseminate to six named persons a letter containing instructions for the distribution of Al-Qa'ida propaganda and a description of fighting. Mohammed sold Islamist
materials at stalls in the North of England, some of which breached s 2. The Court of Appeal
gave guidance that: any reduction in sentence for recklessness rather than intention would be
small; the volume and content of the material disseminated would be relevant; and s 2 offences
are likely to be less serious than breaches of ss 57 and 58 of the TA 2000.[195] The conviction
under s 2 of Shella Roma underlines the sentencing point. A three-year community order
sufficed for seeking to print and distribute an extremist pamphlet.[196] Likewise, the 'Blackburn
Resistance' consisting of Ishaq Kanmi, Abbas Iqbal, and Ilyas Iqbal, were accused of promoting through internet forums martyrdom operations against Prime Ministers Blair and Brown,
as well as filming for propaganda purposes 'military' exercises in a Blackburn public park.[197]

Section 28 provides for an alternative mode of disposal of s 2 materials, modelled on Sch 3 of **8.96**
the Customs and Excise Management Act 1979. A justice of the peace (or sheriff in Scotland),
if satisfied that there are reasonable grounds for suspecting that articles falling within s 2(2)
(a) to (e)[198] are likely to be found on any premises, may issue a search and seizure warrant.
Proceedings for forfeiture may then be taken on an information laid by, or on behalf of, the
Director of Public Prosecutions, except in Scotland where no special process is specified.[199]

Forfeiture procedures are governed by Sch 2. By para 2, the relevant constable must give **8.97**
notice to owners or, in default, occupiers of the premises where the article was seized. Any
person disputing forfeiture may give written notice within one month under para 3 to any
police station in the police area in which the premises where the seizure took place are
located. If no such counter-claim is issued, the article can be treated under para 5 as automatically forfeited at the end of the relevant periods. If there is a counter-claim, the relevant
constable must decide under para 6 whether to proceed. If so, the court can make an order if
it finds that the article was liable to forfeiture at the time of seizure, and it is not satisfied that
its forfeiture would be inappropriate. If either the constable does not take proceedings or the
court is not convinced to order forfeiture, the article must be remitted.[200] The venues can be
either the High Court or a magistrates' court (with appeal to the Crown Court) in England
or Wales, either the Court of Session or the sheriff court in Scotland, and either the High
Court or a summary court (with appeal to the county court) in Northern Ireland.[201]

Disposal by this route follows the pattern of s 3 of the Obscene Publications Act 1959.[202] However, **8.98**
the danger is that this administrative route underplays the value of free expression. An owner or
occupier might conceivably decline to take on the forces of the state and incur a dubious

---

[194] [2008] EWCA Crim 1465. Note also *R v Malcolm Hodges*, where the defendant was convicted in 2008 of
reckless encouragement of jihadis to attack accountancy organizations: <http://www.dailymail.co.uk/news/arti-
cle-516448/Man-urged-terror-attacks-accountancy-institutes—10-years-failing-professional-exams.html>.
[195] Ibid at paras 5, 7, 41. The sentences were five-and-a-half years (Rahman) and two years (Mohammed).
[196] *The Times* 31 March 2009, p 17 (Manchester Crown Court).
[197] Kanmi was sentenced to three years, Abbas Iqbal to two years, and Ilyas Iqbal to fifteen months under
s 58: *The Times* 20 March 2010, p 40, 11 May 2010, p 23.
[198] The private possession covered by s 2(2)(f) is thereby excluded. There is also a saving for legally privileged
materials under PACE, s 19(6): Hansard HL vol 676 col 1244 (7 December 2005), Baroness Scotland.
[199] s 28(5), (10).
[200] It can be disposed of if it is not practicable within twelve months: para 13.
[201] Paras 7, 10.
[202] See Robertson, G, *Obscenity* (Weidenfeld & Nicolson, London, 1979) ch 4.

reputation. Lord Carlile argued that the jurisdiction should be exercised by professional district judges (magistrates' courts) and not magistrates,[203] though a lay element is desirable in principle.

Foreign comparisons

8.99   The notion of *apologie du terrorisme* appeared in some European jurisdictions well before 2001.[204] Thus, the French Law of 29 July 1881 on Freedom of the Press, art 24(4), makes it an offence to utter an *apologie* for attacks on human life or criminal damage which endangers life. Secondly, the Spanish Penal Code, art 578, defines apology as praise of specified (terrorist) offences or bringing about the discredit, contempt, or humiliation of victims or their families. The offence itself, in art 18(2) requires the presentation of ideas or doctrines that praise or justify a crime or its perpetrator, but in a way which, by its nature and circumstances, amounts to a direct incitement to commit an offence. Neither jurisdiction uses the offence frequently,[205] but its deployment in Spain has resulted in the closure of two Basque newspapers.[206] Other jurisdictions have responded to the European Convention of 2005. The German Criminal Code, s 91, passed in 2009, forbids instruction in the commission of a serious act of violence that endangers the state provided the instruction encourages the commission of the act.[207]

8.100   The Canadian House of Commons Standing Committee on Public Safety and National Security called for an offence of glorification in 2007, but it has not been enacted.[208]

8.101   Advocacy offences are constrained by US constitutional law which demands express propagation of immediate law violation which is likely to occur,[209] though less imminent and less explicit 'true threats' may alternatively found a conviction.[210] The US constitutional rejection of speech content offences may also come into play.[211] Yet, as noted in Chapter 5, the Federal offence of 'seditious conspiracy' in 18 USC s 2384 was invoked against Sheik Omar Abdel Rahman who stirred his congregation to 'do jihad with the sword, with the cannon, with the grenades, with the missile'.[212]

8.102   The Australian Law Reform Commission rejected an offence of 'encouragement' or 'glorification' of terrorism as too vague and 'an unwarranted incursion into freedom of expression and the constitutionally protected freedom of political discourse'.[213] However, publications, films,

---

[203] Lord Carlile, *Proposals by Her Majesty's Government for changes to the laws against terrorism* (Home Office, London, 2005) para 75.

[204] See Ribbelink, O, *'Apologie du Terrorisme' and 'Incitement to Terrorism'* (Council of Europe, Strasbourg, 2004) p 7.

[205] Ibid, pp 35, 39.

[206] See Cram, I, 'Regulating the media' (2006) 18 *Terrorism & Political Violence* 335.

[207] See Sieber, U, 'Blurring the categories of criminal law and the law of war' in Manacorda, S and Nieto, MA (eds), *Criminal Law Between War and Peace* (Universidad de Castilla-La Mancha, Cuenca, 2009).

[208] *Rights, Limits, Security* (Ottawa, 2007) p 12.

[209] *Brandenburg v Ohio* 395 US 444 (1969); *Hess v Indiana* 414 US 105 (1972). Interpretation of these terms has become less rigorous: *US v Timimi* (1:04cr385, 2005); Healey, T, 'Brandenburg in time of terror' (2009) 84 *Notre Dame Law Review* 655. Compare Barnum, D, 'Indirect incitement and freedom of speech in Anglo-American law' [2006] *European Human Rights Law Review* 258; Barendt, E, 'Incitement to, and glorification of terrorism' in Hare, I, and Weinstein, J (eds), *Extreme Speech and Democracy* (Oxford University Press, Oxford, 2009).

[210] *Watts v US* 394 US 705 (1969); *Planned Parenthood of the Columbia/Willamette v ACLA* 290 F 3d 1058 (2002); *Virginia v Elton* 538 US 343 (2003).

[211] *RAV v St Paul* 505 US 377 (1992). See Parker, E, 'Implementation of the UK Terrorism Act 2006' (2007) 21 *Emory International Law Review* 711 at 747.

[212] *United States v Rahman* 189 F 3d 88 (1999) at 104, 107. See Cohan, J, 'Seditious Conspiracy, the Smith Act, and prosecution for religious speech advocating the violent overthrow of the government' (2003) 17 *St John's Journal of Legal Commentary* 199. Note also the offence of weapons training: PL 106-54, 18 USC s 842(p); Donohue, LK, 'Terrorist speech and the future of free expression' (2005) 27 *Cardozo Law Review* 233 at 280.

[213] *Fighting Words* (Report 104, Canberra, 2006) para 6.24.

and computer games can be refused classification under the Classification (Publications, Films and Computer Games) Amendment (Terrorist Material) Act 2007 if deemed to advocate the doing of a terrorist act. This system, operated through the Office of Film and Literature Classification, is cumbersome and blunt since it fails to take account of the circumstances of publication and consumption.[214]

Rather than prohibitory and repressive responses, some jurisdictions have sought to challenge extremist speech with more speech, especially on the internet where the chances of actually closing down communications are slim. For instance, the Saudi Ministry of Islamic Affairs' 'Campaign Assakina' focuses on the correct understanding of Islamic doctrines about violence.[215] The impact is untested. **8.103**

Media restrictions

Broadcasting

Formal broadcast bans relating to interviews of representatives of specified organizations such as Sinn Féin were imposed in 1988 but lifted in 1994.[216] Comparable media controls under the Broadcasting Authority Act 1961, s 31, were likewise lifted in the Republic of Ireland.[217] Their compatibility with Article 10 of the European Convention was never fully tested in Strasbourg, but, two decades later in *Kanat and Bozan v Turkey*, the Court strongly indicated that restrictions must be based on a tendency to violence rather than the fact that its source, Abdullah Öçalan, was the leader of the PKK.[218] The Court also emphasized that prior restraints on the press are viewed as particularly draconian.[219] Nevertheless, tight oversight of broadcast programmes about terrorism remains intact. For instance, the 'BBC Editorial Guidelines',[220] refer to 'War, Terror & Emergencies'. Alongside editorial advice about sources, tone, and dignity, including instruction to avoid the term 'terrorism' without attribution, the Guidelines impose a reference up system, with mandatory referrals to Controller Editorial Policy. Where the TA 2000 comes into play (such as under s 38B), the matter must be referred to the Controller Editorial Policy and Programme Legal Advice. **8.104**

These heightened checks and restraints may indirectly 'chill' controversial reports as well as imposing more direct censorship.[221] Examples include the ministerial displeasure in 1977 **8.105**

---

[214] See <http://www.classification.gov.au> for its decisions in 2006 on The Absent Obligation (allowed) and Join the Caravan (refused). Repeal is recommended by the Law Council of Australia, Anti-Terrorism Reform Project (Canberra, 2009) para 6.3.3.

[215] <http://en.assakina.com/index.php>.

[216] See Banwell, C, 'The courts' treatment of the broadcasting bans in Britain and the Republic of Ireland' (1995) 16 *Journal of Media Law & Practice* 21.

[217] See *O'Toole v RTE (No 2)* [1993] 13 ILRM 458; *Brandon Books Publishers v RTE* [1993] ILRM 806; Hogan, G, 'The demise of the Irish broadcasting ban' (1995) 1 *European Public Law* 69.

[218] App no 13799/04, 21 October 2008. Compare *Brind and McLaughlin v United Kingdom*, App nos 18714/91, 18759/91, 77-A DR 42 (1994); *Purcell v Ireland*, App no 15404/89, 70 DR 262 (1991); *Hogefeld v Germany*, App no 35402/97, 20 January 2000.

[219] *Ürper v Turkey*, App no 14526/07, 20 October 2009; *Ürper v Turkey (No 2)*, App no 55036/07, 26 January 2010; *Turgay v Turkey*, App nos 8306, 8340, 8366/08, 15 June 2010 and *(no 2)* App no 13710/08, 21 September 2010.

[220] <http://www.bbc.co.uk/guidelines/editorialguidelines/edguide/war>, Section 11.

[221] See Curtis, L, *Ireland: the Propaganda War* (Pluto Press, London, 1984); Rolston, B (ed), *The Media and Northern Ireland, Covering the Troubles* (Macmillan, Basingstoke, 1991); Paletz, DL and Schmid, AP (eds), *Terrorism and the Media* (Sage, London, 1992); Miller, D, *Don't Mention the War* (Pluto Press, London, 1994); Butler, D, *The Trouble with Reporting Northern Ireland* (Avebury, Aldershot, 1995); Edgerton, G, 'Quelling the "Oxygen of Publicity"' (1996) 30 *Journal of Popular Culture* 115.

which delayed the Thames Television programme, *This Week: Inhuman and Degrading Treatment*, and demanded the inclusion of an unchallenged police statement. There was governmental criticism of the BBC programme, *Real Lives: At the Edge of the Union*, in 1985, in which Martin McGuiness (of Sinn Féin) participated. The Governors postponed its transmission because of concerns about balance and the lack of internal checks. Finally, the Thames Television programme, *Death on the Rock*, about the Gibraltar shootings in 1988, provoked government censure, but its main criticisms were rejected by the *Windlesham-Rampton Report*.[222]

8.106   Broadcasters such as al-Manar (linked to Hizbollah) have been blocked by French authorities from European satellite access.[223]

Cyber-terrorism

8.107   The variants of cyber-terrorism might be comprehended as comprising at least five aspects.[224] The first mode, whereby information technology is the means or object of attack, might be termed 'cyber-attack'. Clear instances are hard to enumerate,[225] but official concern is evidenced by the establishment of various agencies. The National Infrastructure Security Co-ordination Centre was established in 1999 as a cross-departmental body to monitor the risk from electronic attack.[226] It is now incorporated within the Centre for the Protection of the National Infrastructure.[227] The Communications Electronic Security Group is the information assurance branch of GCHQ. The National Technical Assistance Centre is a surveillance advice and interception facility within the Security Services (described in Chapter 2). The Office of Cyber Security & Information Assurance in the Cabinet Office provides strategic direction and coordinates action, while the Cyber Security Operations Centre (based in GCHQ) works with government and agencies on the implementation of programmes.[228]

8.108   Remaining modes of cyber-terrorism amount to 'ancillary cyber-activities' and, some would argue, do not truly constitute 'cyber-terrorism'.[229] The Home Office views these ancillary modes as being used 'to great effect'.[230] One aspect is that the internet offers a widely available, fast, and cheap form of communication for transnational networks. For example, Mohammed Naeem Noor Khan, who was arrested in Pakistan in 2004, admitted that 'most of al-Qaeda's communication was done through the Internet'.[231]

---

[222] Lord Windlesham and Rampton, R, *The Windlesham-Rampton Report on Death on the Rock* (Faber and Faber, London, 1989).

[223] See *CSA v Eutelsat*, French Conseil d'Etat, N° 274757, 13 December 2004). The CSA also warned Eutelsat regarding al-Aqsa TV (linked to Hamas) in 2008.

[224] See Bunt, GR, *Islam in the Digital Age* (Pluto Press, Cambridge, 2003); Weimann, G, *Terror on the Internet* (United States Institute of Peace, Washington, 2006); Walker, C, 'Cyber-terrorism' (2006) 110 *Penn State Law Review* 625; Golumbic, MC, *Fighting Terror Online* (Springer, New York, 2008); Brandon, J, *Virtual Caliphate* (Centre for Social Cohesion, London, 2008); Musawi, MA, *Cheering for Osama* (Quilliam, London, 2010).

[225] See NISCC, *Emerging Electronic Attack Threats to 2010* (London, 2005); Brenner, SW, 'At light speed' (2007) 97 *Journal of Criminal Law & Criminology* 379 at 388.

[226] See NISCC Secretariat, 'NISCC and the Internet security threat' (2001) 12(3) *Computers & Law* 7; Hansard, HL vol 667 col 1075 9 December 2004 (Lord Bassam).

[227] See Walker, C, 'The governance of the Critical National Infrastructure' [2008] *Public Law* 323.

[228] Cabinet Office, *Cyber Security of the United Kingdom* (Cm 7642, London, 2009).

[229] See Weimann, G, 'Cyberterrorism: The Sum of All Fears?' (2005) 28 *Studies in Conflict & Terrorism* 129 at 130–3.

[230] Home Office, *Safeguarding Online* (Home Office, London, 2009) p 2.

[231] See *The Times* 3 August 2004, p 1.

Secondly, there is personnel and logistical support. The web presence increases public **8.109**
consciousness of the group, and may augment recruitment, fund-raising,[232] and weapons
expertise. An example of the latter is *R v Sultan Muhammed and Aabid Hassain Khan*[233]
and *R v Muhammed*,[234] where three defendants were convicted under s 58 of the 2000
Act for amassing, mainly from the internet, especially through involvement in the
website, At-Tibyaan, a vast collection of terrorist-related documentation containing
propaganda and also practical utility items, such as instructions on munitions, poisons,
and the like.

Thirdly, there is the acquisition of target information. US Defense Secretary Donald **8.110**
Rumsfeld observed that an Al-Qa'ida training manual recovered in Afghanistan stated that
'Using public sources openly and without resorting to illegal means, it is possible to gather at
least 80 percent of all information required about the enemy.'[235]

Finally, there are propaganda purposes, by which terrorists can amplify their actions and **8.111**
importance, such as through Al-Qa'ida's As-Sahab operation.[236] An illustration is Younis
Tsouli who, under the tag of 'Irhabi007', was convicted of inciting terrorism abroad by
maintaining a website which carried praise for beheadings and other violence.[237] Examples
of 'propaganda of the deed' have included the webcasting of beheadings, such as of Daniel
Pearl in 2002,[238] and Nick Berg and Ken Bigley in 2004.[239] 'Extremist' websites have
allegedly grown from twelve in 1998 to over 4,000 in 2008.[240]

The most direct legal response is s 3 of the TA 2006, which applies the ss 1 and 2 offences to **8.112**
electronically produced or delivered 'unlawfully terrorism-related' articles or records[241] on
the internet and devises a short-circuit enforcement power. 'Unlawfully terrorism-related'
means, under s 3(7): either material which constitutes either a direct or indirect encouragement or inducement to terrorism or Convention offences, or information which is likely to
be useful to the commission or preparation of such acts.[242] As in ss 1 and 2, indirect encouragement is refined in s 3(8) to include glorification provided that there is a suggestion of
emulation in existing circumstances.

The short-circuit process is that, under s 3(3), where a constable forms the opinion that a **8.113**
statement, article, or record held on the system of the service provider is 'unlawfully terrorism-related', a notice[243] can be issued which requires the provider to arrange for the
material to become unavailable to the public and also warns (by s 3(9)) that a failure to

---

232 See Jacobson, M, 'Terrorism financing and the internet' (2010) 33 *Studies in Conflict & Terrorism* 353.
233 [2009] EWCA Crim 2653.
234 [2010] EWCA 227.
235 Weimann, G, 'www.terrorism.com' (2002) 25 *Studies in Conflict & Terrorism* 317 at 327.
236 See *Eighth Report of the Analytical Support and Sanctions Monitoring Team* (S/2008/324, New York, 14 May 2008) para 13.
237 *Attorney General's References (Nos 85, 86 and 87 of 2007), R v Tsouli* [2007] EWCA Crim 3300.
238 Omar Saeed Sheikh was convicted of murder but has appealed following the confession of Khalid Sheik Mohammed: <http://www.defense.gov/news/transcript_ISN10024.pdf>, p 18.
239 See *The Times* 9 October 2004, p 1.
240 Home Office, *Pursue, Prevent, Protect, Prepare* (Cm 7547, London, 2009) para 5.14.
241 s 3(7). The meaning is by reference to the two categories of matter within s 2(3), with the usual definition of 'indirect incitement' in s 3(8).
242 The phrase in sub-s (7)(a), 'likely to be understood' demands a higher standard of proof than 'capable of being understood': Hansard HL vol 676, col 700 (7 December 2005), Baroness Scotland.
243 See further s 4.

comply within two working days will result in the matter being regarded, under s 3(2) as having his endorsement, and explains the possible liability under sub-s (4). A failure to comply under s 3(4) can equally arise where a person initially complies with the notice but subsequently publishes or causes to be published a statement to the same effect (known as a 'repeat statement').

8.114　There is a defence under sub-ss (5) and (6) if the person can demonstrate to a legal burden of proof[244] that he has 'taken every step he reasonably could' to prevent a repeat statement or took 'every step he reasonably could' to deal with it once aware of it. The phrase is meant to impose a higher duty of attention than 'taking reasonable steps', a standard which may be satisfied overall without taking some reasonable steps. The threat regarding failure to comply is not tantamount to the commission of an offence through endorsement under s 1 or s 2, since other elements of those offences must be proven, nor are all Convention offences covered by s 2. Furthermore, the refusal to comply with a notice is not itself an offence, nor even is there any police power to enforce the take-down of materials.

8.115　Critics felt it to be mistaken that these restrictions on freedom of expression do not engage a judicial officer, who, more likely than a commercial service provider, could be expected to stand up for the principle of expression.[245] The government's retort was that judicial process would cause undue delay in a 'fast moving world'.[246] However, the possibility that an over-enthusiastic police officer might tread too heavily is taken up by the *Home Office Guidance on Notices Issued under Section 3 of the Terrorism Act 2006*, which was promised in response to parliamentary apprehensions.[247] The Guidance advises that notices can be initiated by any constable but in practice ought to be confined to officers of the Metropolitan Police Service Counter-Terrorist Command (SO15) who are trained and experienced in electronic policing. They will apply in writing or electronically, setting out reasons for the giving of the notice, to an authorizing officer of superintendent rank or above. There should also be consultation with the Association of Chief Police Officers Terrorism and Allied Matters policy lead.[248]

8.116　This Guidance, not amounting to formal 'law', may not save the scheme from challenge under Articles 6, 10, and 13 of the European Convention by web publishers. The scheme does not require reasons to be given, does not pay express regard to free expression, and does not encompass any scheme for objections.[249]

8.117　The potential operation of s 3 has to be curtailed by the impact of the Electronic Commerce Directive[250] where an information society service provider acts as an automatic

---

[244] Hansard HL vol 678 col 217 (1 February 2006), Lord Goldsmith. This burden of proof is said to be fair and reasonable: Hansard HL vol 676 col 709 (7 December 2005), Baroness Scotland. Lord Carlile viewed it as an evidential burden: *Proposals by Her Majesty's Government for changes to the laws against terrorism* (Home Office, London, 2005) para 25. The courts may impose an evidential burden: *Sheldrake v Director of Public Prosecutions; Attorney General's Reference (No 4 of 2002)* [2004] UKHL 43.

[245] See Hansard HL vol 679 col 168 (28 February 2006); Lord Carlile, *Proposals by Her Majesty's Government for changes to the laws against terrorism* (Home Office, London, 2005) para 27.

[246] Hansard HL vol 676 col 677 (7 December 2005), Baroness Scotland.

[247] Hansard HC vol 442 col 1472 (15 February 2006), Hazel Blears.

[248] Paras 13–16.

[249] Compare *Zaoui v Switzerland*, App no 41615/98, 18 January 2001.

[250] 2000/31/EC. See Electronic Commerce (European Communities Directive) Regulations 2002, SI 2002/2013.

'conduit' of information (Art 12), provider of a cache for information (Art 13), or host of information without actual knowledge of illegal activity (Art 14). It is also forbidden under Article 15 to impose a general obligation on providers, when providing the services covered by arts 12, 13, and 14, to monitor the information which they transmit or store, nor a general obligation actively to seek facts or circumstances indicating illegal activity. The government conceded during debates on the TA 2006 that UK-based providers who are blocked from taking action against information held on a computer in a third country by the laws of that land will be viewed as having a reasonable excuse under s 3(2).[251] It was also conceded that s 3(5), as applied to repeat statements, should not be interpreted as imposing a duty of general monitoring or prevention.[252] There was also the promise that the police should first act against the webmaster rather than the service provider.[253] The Electronic Commerce Directive (Terrorism Act 2006) Regulations 2007[254] further clarify the relationship to the Electronic Commerce Directive. The government resisted any further, domestic exemption for common carrier services.[255]

No use has yet been made of s 3 since service providers are responsive to police 'advice'.[256] **8.118** Indeed, the Guidance suggests making contact with the service provider before any notice is issued and that a 'voluntary approach' should be adopted where the provider is not viewed as encouraging publication.[257]

A practical enforcement measure in furtherance of s 3 is that the Home Office established in **8.119** 2010 a website which invites members of the public to report web messages of hate, extremism, and terrorism.[258] This follows the initiative of the Internet Watch Foundation which deals with child pornography.[259] The reports are channelled to the police.

Alongside s 3, the download of internet materials may be prosecuted as a possession offence **8.120** under s 58 of the TA 2000. An example is *R v Muhammed*, where the defendant downloaded a vast amount of information from the internet and was involved in the running of the Al-Tibyaan website.[260] Further examples were given in Chapter 5.

The willingness to take all these forms of action may be moderated by the prior needs of **8.121** intelligence-gathering, which may prefer open channels. The network also offers easy evasion, with interchangeable foreign hosts and no international system to replicate British 'take down' measures.[261]

---

[251] Hansard HL vol 676 col 671 (7 December 2005), Baroness Scotland.
[252] Ibid col 672. See also Guidance, para 42.
[253] Ibid col 612. This point is not reflected in the Guidance, para 10.
[254] SI 2007/1550.
[255] Hansard HL vol 677 col 611 (17 January 2006), Baroness Scotland. 'Electronic communications network' is defined in the Communications Act 2003, s 32.
[256] See Lord Carlile, *Report on the Operation in 2007 of the Terrorism Act 2000* (Home Office, London, 2008) para 297.
[257] Paras 20, 27, Annex C.
[258] <https://reporting.direct.gov.uk>. For guidance, see <http://www.direct.gov.uk/en/CrimeJusticeAndTheLaw/Counterterrorism/DG_183993>.
[259] <http://www.iwf.org.uk>.
[260] [2010] EWCA Crim 227.
[261] See Sieber, U and Brunst, PW, *Cyberterrorism* (Council of Europe, Strasbourg, 2007) p 97; Sieber, U, 'Instruments of international law' in Wade, M and Maljevic, A, *A War on Terror?* (Springer, New York, 2010) p 213.

Defence advisory notices

8.122   The Defence, Press and Broadcasting Advisory Committee advises that 'Public discussion of the United Kingdom's defence and counter-terrorist policy and overall national security strategy does not impose a threat to national security and is welcomed by Government.'[262] Nevertheless, DA-Notice 05 covers 'Security and Intelligence Services' and advises against divulging 'specific covert operations, sources and methods'.

Political participation restrictions

Restraints in Northern Ireland

8.123   Sinn Féin was proscribed in Northern Ireland until 1974, but emerged during the prison hunger-strike campaigns in 1981 in response to the electoral success of Bobby Sands. Its participation is mirrored by other nationalist movements, but this strategy is less appropriate for post-sovereignty movements such as Al-Qai'da. Whilst political dialogue with extremist groups is preferable to armed confrontation with them, there arise several dangers that the apologists of terrorism might abuse their political involvement. They may gather information about targets and vulnerabilities. Their presence may incite hatred amongst opponents. They may also use illicitly gathered funds to fund political campaigning beyond the capabilities of legitimate parties. Finally, their very presence feeds the 'oxygen of publicity',[263] giving the impression of the success of terrorism.

8.124   The rise of Sinn Féin produced two legal reactions in Northern Ireland.[264] First, minor changes were made to extended disqualification from council membership following conviction and sentence to not less than three months' imprisonment under the Local Government Act (Northern Ireland) 1972, s 4(1)(d).[265]

8.125   More important was the device of 'Declaration as a condition of office', implemented by the Elected Authorities (Northern Ireland) Act 1989, ss 3 and 5.[266] In relation to candidature for a Northern Ireland District Council or the Northern Ireland Assembly, a candidate's consent to nomination must include the declaration in Schedule 2, not to 'by word or deed express support for or approval of (a) . . . a proscribed organisation . . .; or (b) acts of terrorism (that is to say, violence for political ends) connected with the affairs of Northern Ireland'. Any breach can be sanctioned by application to the High Court for removal from office. Though no removals have resulted, the policy persists and has been applied to membership of policing boards.[267]

Restraints throughout the United Kingdom

8.126   The candidature of prisoners in parliamentary elections was by no means a novel tactic in Ireland, but the election of hunger-striker, Bobby Sands, in 1981 provoked furious state reaction.[268] The Representation of the People Act 1981 disqualifies from nomination for,

---

[262] <http://www.dnotice.org.uk/standing_da_notices.htm>.

[263] Edgerton, G, 'Quelling the "Oxygen of Publicity"' (1996) 30 *Journal of Popular Culture* 115.

[264] Northern Ireland Office, *Elected Representatives and the Democratic Process in Northern Ireland* (Belfast, 1987).

[265] Elected Authorities (Northern Ireland) Act 1989, s 9.

[266] See Walker, C, 'Elected representatives and the democratic process in Northern Ireland' (1988) 51 *Modern Law Review* 605.

[267] Police (Northern Ireland) Act 2003, s 15; s 16 reduces disqualification on conviction to five years.

[268] Walker, C, 'Prisoners in Parliament—another view' [1982] *Public Law* 389.

and membership of, the House of Commons any person convicted of an offence and sentenced to more than twelve months' imprisonment either in the United Kingdom or in the Republic of Ireland.

Various justifications were cited for the Act.[269] Such bans operated in local government **8.127** elections and in many other countries, including the Republic. A second reason was that prisoners would be unable to perform in person most of their duties. Thirdly, their very candidature (hence the disqualification in the 1981 Act from nomination and not just election) was seen as serving propaganda rather than constituency purposes and as exacerbating community tensions. Drawbacks are that the Act limits expressions of opinion and the gauging of political support. Disqualification may also encourage resort to violence rather than politics and allows terrorists to claim that political pathways are blocked.

This ban is unlikely to be impugned under Article 3 of the First Protocol to the European **8.128** Convention on Human Rights as affecting the right to candidature. Restrictions have been upheld on grounds of past conduct.[270]

As for successful candidates, the oath of allegiance still excludes Sinn Féin from House of **8.129** Commons participation.[271]

Foreign comparisons

The regulation of political parties on the basis of support for terrorism has been applied **8.130** against Basque parties in Spain.[272] Organic Law 6 of 2002 allows for the dissolution of political parties which were perceived to support terrorism. The Law was applied to Batasuna in 2002 and to Herritarren Zerrenda in 2004 as well as to individual party candidates. The European Court of Human Rights acknowledged that the ban met a pressing social need which had been fully considered within the national margin of appreciation, especially given the 'international preoccupation with condemning apology of terrorism'.[273]

Corporate targeting

The most frequent cause of property damage from political extremism in the UK derives **8.131** from animal rights extremism, primarily directed at corporate targets.[274] Whilst activists have not faced proscription, the armoury of responses includes the application of 'normal' laws and some new laws.[275]

---

[269] See Finn, J, 'Electoral regimes and the proscription of anti-democratic parties' (2000) *Terrorism & Political Violence* 51.

[270] *Ždanoka v Latvia*, App no 58278/00, 2006-IV, para 115. See also *Glimmerveen and Hagenbeek v Netherlands*, App nos 8348/78, 8406/78, DR 18, p 187.

[271] See *McGuinness v United Kingdom*, App no 39511/98, 8 June 1999; Walker, A and Wood, E, *The Parliamentary Oath* (House of Commons Research Paper 00/17, London, 2000); Gay, O, *Sinn Fein, allowances and access to Commons facilities* (SN/PC/1667, House of Commons Library, London, 2006).

[272] See Cram, I, 'Constitutional responses to extremist political associations' (2008) 28 *Legal Studies* 68; Prado, CV, 'Spain' in Thiel, M (ed), *The 'Militant Democracy' Principle in Modern Democracies* (Ashgate, Aldershot, 2009).

[273] *Herri Batasuna and Batasuna v Spain* App nos 25803/04, 25817/04, 30 June 2009, para 91. Action was taken in France on grounds of foreign funding: *Parti Nationaliste Basque v France*, App no 71251/01, 7 June 2007.

[274] Individuals such as farmers may also be victims, as with the stealing of the body of Gladys Hammond: *R v Ablewhite and others*, *The Times* 12 May 2006, p 37.

[275] See Home Office, *Animal Rights Extremism* (London, 2001); Home Office, *Animal Welfare—Human Rights* (London, 2004).

'Normal' laws

8.132   The array of 'normal' laws includes the mundane use of common law powers relating to breach of the peace,[276] the Public Order Act 1986, the Malicious Communications Act 1988, and, above all, the Protection from Harassment Act 1997.[277] Conspiracy to blackmail has been sustained against groups headed by Gregg Avery and by Sarah Whitehead in relation to their campaigns against business contacts of Huntingdon Life Sciences.[278] Beyond the criminal law are anti-social behaviour orders under the Crime and Disorder Act 1998, s 1, or exclusion orders under s 46 of the Criminal Justice and Courts Services Act 2000. An indefinite ASBO, forbidding the organizing of any demonstration about animal experimentation or any contact with Huntingdon Life Sciences or linked persons or companies, was imposed on Avery and others alongside their sentences of imprisonment for blackmail. Affected companies, traders, or farmers have also resorted to civil law injunctions.

Special provisions

8.133   Amongst the more specialist laws are ss 68 and 69 of the Criminal Justice and Public Order Act 1994 which establishes the offence of aggravated trespass. By s 42 of the Criminal Justice and Police Act 2001, the police are given broad powers to direct protestors away from a private residence where it is reasonably believed that their presence amounts to harassment or is likely to cause alarm or distress.

8.134   The Serious Organised Crime and Police Act 2005 adds offences involving interference with contractual relationships so as to harm animal research organizations (s 145) and the intimidation of persons concerned with animal research organizations (s 146). The latter are very broadly constituted in that they can be committed via the infliction or threat of an act amounting to any criminal offence or any tortious act causing loss or damage of any description.[279] In *R v Harris*,[280] the defendant pleaded guilty to three offences under s 145, involving criminal damage by slashing vehicle tyres and gluing locks of companies which had traded with Huntingdon Life Sciences. Concurrent sentences of two years' imprisonment were imposed. A similar level of offending under s 145 was dealt with in the *Attorney General's Reference (No 113 of 2007)*.[281] The offender pleaded guilty to six counts of blackmail, one count of attempted blackmail and five counts under s 145. Over a period of five years, she sent threatening messages to employees of a bank who provided financial services to Huntingdon Life Sciences and others.

---

[276] The concept of breach of the peace in this context was upheld in *Steel v United Kingdom*, App no 24838/94, 1998-VII.

[277] See: *Silverton v Gravett* [2001] All ER (D) 282 (Oct); *Daiichi UK Ltd v Stop Huntington Animal Cruelty* [2003] EWHC 2337 (QB); *Emerson Developments Ltd v Avery* [2004] EWHC 194 (QB); *Chiron Corpn Ltd v Avery* [2004] EWHC 493 (QB); *Huntingdon Life Sciences Group v Stop Huntingdon Animal Cruelty* [2004] EWHC 1231 (QB), [2004] EWHC 3145 (QB), [2005] EWHC 2233 (QB), [2007] EWHC 522 (QB); *Hall v Save Newchurch Guinea Pigs (Campaign)* [2005] EWHC 372 (QB); *Green v DB Group Services (UK) Ltd* [2006] EWHC 1898 (QB); *Oxford University v Webb* [2006] EWHC 2490 (QB); *Chancellor, Masters and Scholars of the University of Oxford v Broughton* [2006] EWCA Civ 1305, [2006] EWHC 2490 (QB), [2008] EWHC 75 (QB); *Smithkline Beecham plc v Avery* [2007] EWHC 948 (QB), [2009] EWHC 1488 HC; *AGC Chemicals v Stop Huntingdon Animal Cruelty* 2010] EWHC B10 (QB).

[278] [2009] EWCA Crim 2670 (up to 11 years); *The Times* 26 October 2010, p 19 (up to 6 years).

[279] See the criticisms as to necessity and certainty of the Joint Committee on Human Rights, *Scrutiny: Seventh Progress Report* (2004–05 HL 97/HC 496) paras 2.3–2.7.

[280] [2006] EWCA Crim 3303.

[281] [2008] EWCA Crim 22.

Some of the threats were by letters which contained white powder, and one recipient was taken to hospital for decontamination. The offender was sentenced to two years' imprisonment.

Corporate law has also been amended. The Criminal Justice and Police Act 2001, s 45, allows for 'confidentiality orders' to be issued by the Secretary of State (for Trade and Industry) relating to the addresses of company officers on grounds of serious risk of violence and intimidation. Next, following the sending of letters to shareholders of GlaxoSmithKline in 2006, asking them to ensure disinvestment from Huntingdon Life Sciences, the company obtained an injunction against 'persons unknown'.[282] The government then moved to restrict access to shareholder identities. So, by the Companies Act 2006, by s 116(3), any request for shareholder information must be accompanied by an explanation of purpose. If the company declines to grant the request, it may apply for court review. Next, by s 240, persons becoming directors can have their home addresses kept on a separate list to which access will be restricted without proof of serious risk.[283] Thirdly, information about persons with whom the company has business arrangements can be withheld under s 417 so as to avoid, in the opinion of the directors, serious prejudice.

8.135

Foreign comparisons

The Animal Enterprise Protection Act of 1992 and Animal Enterprise Terrorism Act of 2006 have established in the US an offence of causing disruption or damage to an animal enterprise, with enhanced penalties and restitution orders, but subject to a saving for expressive conduct.[284] This offence was upheld as constitutional in the 'SHAC-7' case of *US v Fullmer*[285] because of either the imminence of electronic attacks on the enterprises or the 'true threat' against individual officers. The confinement to animal enterprises has meant that more general offences, such as conspiracy to damage, must be raised against 'eco-terrorism'.[286]

8.136

Implementation and assessment

The gravity of the threat is reflected in specialist policing structures. The National Extremism Tactical Coordination Unit provides tactical advice to businesses. The National Public Order Intelligence Unit gathers and collates intelligence for policing purposes, while the National Domestic Extremism Team helps with investigations. All are headed by the National Coordinator for Domestic Extremism who reports to the Association of Chief Police Officers' Terrorism and Allied Matters Committee. There is no legal definition of 'extremism', but it is operationally understood to mean 'the activity, individuals or campaign groups that carry out criminal acts of direct action in furtherance of a campaign. These people and activities usually seek to prevent something from happening or to change legislation or domestic policy, but attempt to do so outside of the normal democratic process.'[287]

8.137

---

282   *The Times* 10 May 2006, p 44. See *Pelling v Families Need Fathers Ltd* [2001] EWCA Civ 1280.
283   See further Companies (Disclosure of Address) Regulations 2009, SI 2009/214.
284   PL102-346, 109-374; 18 USC s 43. See Goodman, JS, 'Shielding corporate interests from public dissent' (2008) 16 *Journal of Law & Policy* 823.
285   584 F 3d 132 (2009); <http://www.shac7.com>.
286   See *US v McDavid* [2008] US Dist LEXIS 25591; Potter, W, 'The relationship between national security and other fundamental values' (2009) 33 *Vermont Law Review* 671.
287   <http://www.netcu.org.uk/de/default.jsp>.

8.138 The Association of the British Pharmaceutical Industry reports a substantial decline in attacks and intimidation since the peak years of 2003 and 2004.[288] The ABPI contends that improved local policing (bolstered by extra central funding), civil injunctions, and anti-harassment legislation have secured this impact.[289] However, the most targeted company, Huntingdon Life Sciences, still complains that 'insufficient consideration was given to counter-terrorism powers in what was widely considered in practice (but not in name) to be domestic terrorism'.[290]

Social harmony and 'Prevent' campaigns

8.139 The concern that terrorism is both an emanation of, and causes, social disharmony has spawned policies to quell hatred and to prevent extremism.

Racial and religious hatred

8.140 Part V of the ATCSA 2001 addresses racial and religious hatred.[291] The presence of Part V is explained on two grounds: one is to avert Islamophobia, including violent attacks; the other offers a signal that the repression of terrorism, albeit that it impacts unduly upon Muslim communities, is not motivated by racial or religious hatred.[292]

8.141 Offences of stirring up hatred are applied to racial groups abroad under ss 37 and 38 (now repealed). Next, ss 40 and 41 increase the maximum imprisonment for race hatred offences from two to seven years. As for hatred against religious groups, s 39 allows religious motivation to be treated as an aggravating factor in charging under the Crime and Disorder Act 1998, s 28, and then sentencing under s 153 of the Powers of Criminal Courts (Sentencing) Act 2000.[293]

8.142 The additional proof of motive offers a safeguard for the value of free speech,[294] but equally hinders prosecution,[295] as reflected in the modest annual rates of conviction which range from ten in 2003 to twenty-four in 2007.[296]

8.143 The Newton Committee recommended that these issues should be considered in a broader context than terrorism.[297] Following rejection in 2001,[298] an offence of religious hatred has emerged in the Racial and Religious Hatred Act 2006, adding to the equivalent in the Public Order (Northern Ireland) Order 1987, art 13.[299]

---

[288] <http://www.abpi.org.uk>. But there remained seventy instances of damage (146 in 2003; 177 in 2004) and ten 'home visits' (compared to 259 and 179).

[289] See Joint Committee on Human Rights, Demonstrating respect for rights? (2008–09 HL 141/HC 522) Memorandum submitted by the Association of the British Pharmaceutical Industry.

[290] Ibid. Memorandum submitted by Huntingdon Life Sciences.

[291] See Idriss, MM, 'Religion and the Anti-terrorism, Crime and Security Act 2001' [2002] *Criminal Law Review* 890; House of Lords Select Committee on Religious Offences in England and Wales (2002–03 HL 95) chs 8, 9; Addison, N, *Religious Discrimination and Hatred Law* (Routledge-Cavendish, London, 2006) pp 125–6.

[292] HC Debs vol 375 col 703 (26 November 2001), David Blunkett.

[293] Scottish equivalents are the Crime and Disorder Act 1998, s 96, and the Criminal Justice (Scotland) Act 2003, s 74. See *Watts v Procurator Fiscal, Kilmarnock* [2009] HC JAC 59.

[294] Compare House of Lords Select Committee on Religious Offences in England and Wales (2002–03 HL 95) paras 120, 124, 125.

[295] Crown Prosecution Service, Guidance on prosecuting cases of racist and religious crime (2nd edn, <http://www.cps.gov.uk/Publications/prosecution/rrpbcrpol.html>).

[296] Source: Crown Prosecution Service.

[297] *Newton Report*, para 270.

[298] See HC Debs vol 376 col 1112, 13 December 2001; HL Debs vol 629 col 1163, 10 December 2001, Lord Goldsmith; House of Commons Home Affairs Committee, *Report on the Anti-terrorism, Crime and Security Bill 2001* (2001–02 HC 351) para 61.

[299] SI 1987/463 (NI 7); Hadfield, B, 'The prevention of incitement to religious hatred—an article of faith?' (1984) 35 *Northern Ireland Legal Quarterly* 231.

'Prevent' strategy

The London transport bombings of July 2005 were the trigger for a new programme, **8.144** 'Preventing Extremism Together' which has since developed local community, policing, religious, and prison strands of activity.[300] These spurs to vigilance and net-widening mainly range beyond the legal focus of this book. However, they have the potential to impact directly on legal action, as with Project Channel programme, described in Chapter 6.

Assessment and conclusions

Based on a rights audit, expressive speech which encourages violence need not be tolerated.[301] **8.145** In *Zana v Turkey*,[302] the applicant's statement of sympathy for the PKK was regarded as exacerbating a violent situation and could be punished, even though he was a mayor in the region. In *Gündüz v Turkey*,[303] the leader of an Islamic sect criticized moderate Islamic intellectuals and called on his supporters to produce 'one brave man among the Muslims to plant a dagger in their soft underbelly and run them through twice with a bayonet'. Even as a rhetorical flourish, such language did not deserve protection from the European Court of Human Rights, nor, at the extreme end of the margin of appreciation, did a cartoon in praise of the September 11 attacks, published in the Basque country in *Leroy v France*.[304]

But where, as in *Arslan v Turkey*,[305] the Court was sure that the words used did not incite **8.146** violence, then it defended statements which alleged that the Turkish state oppressed the Kurds and so explained Kurdish 'resistance' and 'intifada'. As made clear in *Gerger v Turkey*,[306] broad words such as 'resistance', 'struggle', and 'liberation' do not necessarily constitute an incitement to violence but may do so when reporting the utterances of hunger striking prisoners.[307] Latitude is also accorded to the neutral reporting of the declarations or interviews of terrorist representatives by media professionals, as in *Sürek and Özdemir v Turkey*,[308] to artistic and academic speech,[309] and to demonstrators protesting about genuine issues of public concern.[310] Being one step removed from direct incitement to violence and being uncertain that anyone is roused to action and/or that any offence will result from publication may all cast doubt on the compliance of ss 1 and 2 of the TA 2006 with rights to

---

[300] See Walker, C and Rehman, J, '"Prevent" Responses to Jihadi Extremism' in Ramraj, VV, Hor, M, and Roach, K, *Global Anti-terrorism Law and Policy* (2nd edn, Cambridge University Press, Cambridge, 2011).

[301] See *Arrowsmith v United Kingdom*, App no 7075/75, DR 19, p 5.

[302] App no 18954/91, 1997-VII. See also *Sürek v Turkey (No 1)*, App no 26682/95, 1999-IV; *Sürek v Turkey (No 3)*, App no 24735/94, 8 July 1999; *Falakaoglu and Saygili v Turkey*, App nos 22147/02, 24972/03, 23 January 2007. See Davis, H, 'Lessons from Turkey: anti-terrorism legislation and the protection of free speech' [2005] *European Human Rights Law Review* 75.

[303] App no 59745/00, 2003-XI.

[304] App no 36109/03, 2 October 2008.

[305] App no 23462/94, 8 July 1999, para 48. See also *Ceylan v Turkey*, App no 23556/94, 1999-IV; *Erdoğdu v Turkey* App no 25723/94, 2000-VI.

[306] App no 24919/94, 8 July 1999, para 50. See also *Erdogdu and Ince v Turkey*, App nos 25067/94; 25068/94, 8 July 1999; *Okçuoglu v Turkey*, App nos 24246/94, 8 July 1999; *Polat v Turkey*, App no 23500/94, 8 July 1999.

[307] *Saygılı and Falakaoğlu v Turkey*, App no 38991/02, 17 February 2009.

[308] App nos 23927/94, 24277/94, 8 July 1999. See also *Sürek v Turkey (No 2)*, App no 24122/94, 8 July 1999; *Sürek v Turkey (No 4)*, App no 24762/94, 8 July 1999.

[309] *Başkaya and Okçuoğlu v Turkey*, App nos 23536/94, 24408/94, 1999-IV; *Karataş v Turkey*, App no 23168/94, 1999-IV.

[310] *Yılmaz and Kılıç v Turkey*, App no 68514/01, 17 July 2008.

expression.[311] However, enthusiasm for enforcement in Britain is by no means equivalent to Turkey, as illustrated by the case of Leyla Zana who was convicted in Turkey for a speech delivered at the University of London in 2008 which was not the subject of any British legal action.[312]

8.147 A further criticism of the TA 2006 is its imprecision.[313] However, the English courts have viewed as compatible with Article 10 words such as 'insulting',[314] while the European Court of Human Rights has upheld the term 'breach of the peace'.[315]

8.148 The third test, of proportionality, raises the question whether the myriad of clearer and less contentious offences which already circumscribe extremist speech make irrelevant much of the TA 2006.[316] Offences already within the terrorism legislation include incitement of terrorism abroad.[317] Beyond that category, soliciting murder under the Offences against the Person Act 1861, s 4, can be used even when no victim is specified.[318] Public order offences can apply to outrages such as beheading videos[319] or vituperative protests outside an embassy.[320] The availability of alternative charges was illustrated by the first recorded conviction under the 2006 Act. Arising from materials in his possession when arrested at Glasgow Airport, Mohammed Atif Siddique was convicted not only of collecting and distributing terrorist materials, but also of offences under the TA 2000, ss 54, 57, and 58, plus breach of the peace.[321]

8.149 As for the overall balance in the fourth test of proportionality, a significant factor in the justification of ss 1 and 2 must reside in the element of emulation of action. Subject to the exception of non-glorifying indirect incitements, these are not pure speech crimes, but they do seek to intervene before one extreme speaker generates multiple extreme actors.[322] Nevertheless, there may be four important qualifications to any endorsement.

8.150 First, the application of these offences in the context of foreign regimes (under s 17) is problematic.[323] For example, would this offence criminalize support for the revered Nelson

---

[311] See Joint Committee on Human Rights, Counter-Terrorism Policy and Human Rights: Terrorism Bill and related matters (2005–06 HL 75/HC 561) para 34.

[312] BBC Monitoring Europe, 28 July 2009. She was sentenced to fifteen months' imprisonment under the Anti-Terror Law 1991 (Act 3713), art 7(2) for propaganda on behalf of a terrorist organization.

[313] Joint Committee on Human Rights, Counter-Terrorism Policy and Human Rights: *Terrorism Bill and related matters* (2005–06 HL 75/HC 561) paras 27–28. See also *Report of the Special Rapporteur on the promotion and protection of human rights and fundamental freedoms while countering terrorism* (A/61/267, 2006) para 7.

[314] *Hammond v DPP* [2004] EWHC 69 (Admin) at para 27.

[315] Compare *Steel and others v United Kingdom*, App no 24838/94, 1998-VII; *Hashman and Harrup v United Kingdom*, App no 25594/94, 1999-VIII.

[316] This point is disputed: Joint Committee on Human Rights, Counter-Terrorism Policy and Human Rights: *Terrorism Bill and related matters* (2005–06 HL 75/HC 561) para 25.

[317] *R v Abu Izzadeen*, *The Times* 19 April 2008, p 25.

[318] See *R v el-Faisal* [2004] EWCA Crim 456; *R v Hamza* [2006] EWCA Crim 2918; *R v Saleem, Javed, and Muhid* [2007] EWCA Crim 2692; O'Donoghue, T, 'Glorification, Irish terror and Abu Hamza' (2006) 170 *Justice of the Peace* 291.

[319] See the case of Subhann Younis (Glasgow District Court, *The Times* 29 September 2005, p 3).

[320] See the case of Anjem Choudary (*The Guardian* 22 July 2006, p 14).

[321] *The Times* 18 September 2007, p 31; *The Scotsman* 24 October 2007, p 7. For the views of his lawyer, see *Re Anwar* [2008] HCJAC 36.

[322] See Fiss, O, 'Freedom of speech and political violence' in Cohen-Almagor, R, *Liberal Democracy and the Limits of Tolerance* (University of Michigan Press, Ann Arbor, 2000) p 75.

[323] Joint Committee on Human Rights, *Counter-Terrorism Policy and Human Rights: Terrorism Bill and related matters* (2005–06 HL 75/HC 561) para 12.

Mandela, who condoned acts of political violence against official property,[324] or the statement of Cherie Booth, the wife of Prime Minister Tony Blair, that 'in view of the illegal occupation of Palestinian land I can well understand how decent Palestinians become terrorists'.[325] What if Saddam Hussein were still in power and called upon the British government to take action against any surviving 'terrorists' of Dujail who, in 1982, had attempted to assassinate him (reprisals against whom resulted in his execution in 2006)? Plots against the Libyan regime were possibly encouraged years ago,[326] but now there is rapprochement. Conversely, plots against Syria are openly tolerated.[327] The extension of jurisdiction leads to a slippery slope of judgments which take sides in foreign disputes and sometimes in favour of despots.

The second qualification is that the policy of closing down channels of discourse may be counter-productive in political terms. Whilst much of what violent groups have to say is unpalatable or even reprehensible, their views must be debated so that the extremists, government, and public can be educated and respond without exalting extremist groups[328] or receiving only the hateful bulletins of martyrs such as Mohammed Siddique Khan.[329] In line with these concerns, the European Court of Human Rights has been particularly wary of restraints on the speech of politicians.[330] Likewise, even Lord Lowry recognized membership as a 'political offence' in *R v Adams*.[331]   **8.151**

Thirdly, any gains from reducing the tolerance of extreme speech may be overshadowed by resentment of stigmatization and selective repression, which may hinder policing by reducing flows of intelligence. As stated by the House of Commons Home Affairs Committee,[332] rather than the sole pursuit of suppression, 'the Government must engage British Muslims in its anti-terrorist strategy'.   **8.152**

Fourthly, the offences in the 2006 Act go beyond what is required by the Convention on the Prevention of Terrorism of 2005.[333] The government views this discrepancy as unproblematic,[334] but the consequent curtailments of rights may later be judged excessive in international forums.   **8.153**

Democratic accountability has been adequately engaged during the passage of these controversial offences, though their potential impact on internet expression is not being adequately monitored so as to facilitate future policy debate.   **8.154**

Constitutional governance might also be said to be deficient because of the vague nature of 'incitement' in ss 1 and 2, which are riddled with uncertainties and anomalies.   **8.155**

---

[324] <http://www.law.umkc.edu/faculty/projects/ftrials/mandela/mandelahome.html>, 1964.
[325] Hansard HC vol 438 col 844 (2 November 2005), Bob Marshall-Andrews.
[326] Allegations were made by David Shayler: <http://cryptome.org/shayler-gaddafi.htm>.
[327] See the activities of the 'National Salvation Front': *The Times* 5 June 2006, p 30.
[328] See Ahmed, H and Stuart, H, *Hizb ut-Tahrir* (Centre for Social Cohesion, London, 2009).
[329] <http://news.bbc.co.uk/1/hi/uk/4206800.stm>, 2005.
[330] *Castells v Spain*, App No 11798/85, Ser A 236 (1992); *Association Ekin v France*, App no 39288/98, 2001-VIII; *Isak Tepe v Turkey*, App no 17129/02, 21 October 2008.
[331] [1987] 5 NIJB (BCC).
[332] *Terrorism and Community Relations* (2004–05 HC 165) para 225.
[333] See Joint Committee on Human Rights, *Counter-Terrorism Policy and Human Rights: Terrorism Bill and related matters* (2005–06 HL 75/HC 561) para 41; Joint Committee on Human Rights, *The Council of Europe Convention on the Prevention of Terrorism* (2006–07 HL 26/HC 247) paras 26–39.
[334] Government Response to the Joint Committee on Human Rights, *Counter-Terrorism Policy and Human Rights: Terrorism Bill and related matters* (2005–06 HL 114, HC 888) p 7.

D. Extremism—Conclusions

8.156 The anti-terrorism legislation reflects a long-standing notion of 'militant democracy'[335] in which a state based on legitimate foundations should confront opponents who abuse its tolerance. Even if this stance of militancy is legitimate and its impact has been largely symbolic, consideration should be given as to whether, on a rights audit, less intrusive measures than crimes would better distinguish the legitimacy of extreme speech which seeks the overthrow of the constitutional order and the illegitimate propagation of violence. On the basis of democratic accountability and constitutional governance, significant improvements in proscription processes have been noted. But these must be set alongside the expanded and barely explained invocation of the powers. As for the offences in the 2006 Act, the breadth of the definition of terrorism, including its extra-territorial application, compounds the latitude of these measures. These criticisms do not imply that extreme speech and associations should be endured without reaction, but the main retort in a democracy must be engagement. The 'Prevent' strategies have latterly opened a new front which commendably seeks dialogue but with attendant dangers of net-widening surveillance.

---

[335] Lowenstein, K, 'Militant democracy and fundamental rights' (1937) 31 *American Political Science Review* 417, 638 at 431–2. See also Sajo, A (ed), *Militant Democracy* (Eleven International Publishing, Utrecht, 2004); Thiel, M (ed), *The 'Militant Democracy' Principle in Modern Democracies* (Ashgate, Aldershot, 2009).

9

TERRORIST FUNDING AND PROPERTY

A. Introduction

For many years, the humble lifestyles of terrorists emerging from the ghettos of Belfast did **9.01** not excite financial counter-attack. Yet, terrorist funding has now become a prolific topic for terrorism laws. The initial impetus was sparked by the analogy with legislation against drugs traffickers, whereby Irish terrorists were depicted as venal racketeers. Over the last two decades, it has become a constant refrain that 'money is a crucial factor in the continuance of terrorism'[1] and that 'Money underpins all terrorist activity . . .'.[2] Action against terrorism resources could deter support and divest assets. It could also enhance the delineation and detection of activists. A legislative rejoinder started in earnest in the PT(TP)A 1989, Pt III, with complex variants in the EPA 1991, Pt VII.[3]

The attention to the financing of terrorism has intensified with the prominence of international **9.02** terrorism for two reasons. First, these sources of terrorism outrun local neighbourhoods for recruits and targets and so gather resources through wider and more sophisticated means.

---

[1] *Jellicoe Report*, para 213.
[2] Home Office, *Possible Measures for Inclusion into a Future Counter-Terrorism Bill* (London, 2007) para 54.
[3] As amended by the Criminal Justice Act 1993, Pt IV. See Walker, CP, *The Prevention of Terrorism in British Law* (2nd edn, Manchester University Press, Manchester, 1992) ch 7.

The second reason is that these less parochial forms of terrorism have triggered reaction via international law.

9.03 International action was first signalled by the United Nations Convention for the Suppression of the Financing of Terrorism of 1999.[4] The United Nations Security Council also passed resolutions against the Taleban and Al-Qa'ida from 1999 onwards. This policy became a universal edict with the UNSCR 1373 of 28 September 2001. The European Union has backed these measures. The Council of Europe has in turn contributed the (Warsaw) Convention on the Laundering, Search, Seizure and Confiscation of the Proceeds from Crime and on the Financing of Terrorism,[5] but it has not yet been signed by the United Kingdom.

9.04 The Financial Action Task Force (FATF), an emanation of the G8,[6] has promulgated, in response to the attacks of 2001, nine Special Recommendations on Terrorist Financing.[7] They demand state action on: the implementation of UN instruments; national criminal law; civil law freezing and confiscation of assets; the reporting of suspicious transactions; international cooperation; action to monitor alternative remittance systems, wire transfers, and cash couriers; and tighter regulation of non-profit organizations.

9.05 These approaches to terrorism often underplay the personal commitment which drives terrorism and overplay the criminal racketeering analogy. Yet, the running costs of the largest paramilitary groups in Northern Ireland have recently consumed annual budgets of over £1m, some of which derives from racketeering, including 'the smuggling of drugs, oil and other high value goods, large scale counterfeiting and bank robbery [and] the retail end of larger operations, like the supply of smuggled alcohol to individual pubs'.[8] The pinnacle was reached with the robbery of £26m from the Northern Bank, Belfast in 2004.[9]

9.06 While the worldwide outlay of Al-Qa'ida has been estimated to cost up to $30m per annum,[10] individual operations may entail modest costs derived from lawful sources. The ambitious attacks on 11 September 2001, did consume up to $500,000 in travel and accommodation expenses.[11] However, the 7 July 2005 London bombers left a small financial footprint of around £8,000.[12]

---

[4] (A/RES/54/109, Cm 4663, London, 1999) art 1. See further Bianchi, A, *Enforcing International Norms Against Terrorism* (Hart, Oxford, 2004) chs 8, 15, 16; Schott, PA, *Reference Guide to Anti-Money Laundering and Countering the Financing of Terrorism* (2nd supp edn, World Bank Publications, 2006).

[5] CETS 198. See *Government Reply* (Cm 7718, London, 2009) p 3.

[6] For other international bodies, see Gilmore, WS, *Dirty Money* (3rd edn, Council of Europe, Strasbourg, 2004) ch 5.

[7] <http://www.fatf-gafi.org/document/9/0,3343,en_32250379_32236920_34032073_1_1_1_1,00.html>.

[8] Independent Monitoring Commission, *Third Report* (2003–04 HC 1218) para 5.2. See further Northern Ireland Select Committee, *The Financing of Terrorism in Northern Ireland* (2001–02 HC 978), *Organised Crime in Northern Ireland* (2005–06 HC 886); Organised Crime Task Force, *Annual Report and Threat Assessment 2008* (Belfast, 2008) p 27; Moran, J, *Policing the Peace in Northern Ireland* (Manchester University Press, Manchester, 2008) chs 3, 4, 6.

[9] Independent Monitoring Commission, *Fourth Report* (2004–05 HC 308).

[10] House of Lords European Union Committee, *Money Laundering and the Financing of Terrorism* (2008–09 HL 132) para 9. See Napoleoni, L, *Modern Jihad* (Pluto, 2003); Ehrenfeld, R, *Funding Evil* (Bonus Books, Santa Monica, 2003); Burr, JM and Collins, RO, *Alms for Jihad* (Cambridge University Press, New York, 2006); Naylor, RT, *Satanic Purses* (McGill-Queen's University Press, Montreal, 2006).

[11] National Commission on Terrorist Attacks upon the United States, *Final Report* (USGPO, Washington, DC, 2004) p 172.

[12] Home Office, *Report of the Official Account of the Bombings in London on the 7th July 2005* (2005–06 HC 1087) paras 63, 64.

Consequently, the quantitative prominence of the legislation is not evidently translated **9.07** into quantitative impact.[13] Nevertheless, the policy persists and is translated into the TA 2000, Pt III,[14] comprising several offences, extensive powers of seizure and forfeiture, and civil forfeiture through cash seizures.[15] Part III begins with a definition of 'terrorist property' in s 14, which exceeds the demands of the United Nations Financing Convention since it extends beyond 'money and other property' relating to the purposes of terrorism into 'any resources' which are made available for a proscribed organization.[16] This 'terrorist property' concept captures activities of a proscribed organization which may be lawful in themselves, such as political campaigning or support for relatives of prisoners. The 'money and other property' representing the proceeds of terrorism can be traced into any representative property.

These measures were supplemented by the ATCSA 2001. Part I replaced and extended **9.08** beyond internal or external borders the cash seizure powers in the TA 2000. There were also new measures to extend the scope of investigative and freezing powers, including account monitoring and customer information orders. Freezing powers are further regulated by the CTA 2008.

These changes reflect the strategy set out in the *Action Plan on Terrorist Financing* of **9.09** 2001.[17] Further statements and developments have emphasized the need to regulate underground banking systems and money service businesses, underlined by European Directives,[18] in response to the distinctive methods of finance of Al-Qa'ida. They include reliance upon informal funds transfer systems, notably the hawala system of money remittances,[19] which is singled out by Special Recommendation VI of the FATF. The audit trail of these transactions may be poor, but any blanket restraint would severely affect the flow of innocent remittances from expatriate labourers to the world's poorest countries.[20]

As well as the varieties of municipal laws outlined above, this chapter will also address **9.10** the international aspects of restraints on terrorism finance, especially the special restrictions which are applied by international organisations to individuals. These are mainly set out in UNSCRs, the Terrorist Asset-Freezing etc. Act 2010, and European regulations.

---

[13] See *Lloyd Report*, ch 13; *Home Office Response to Lloyd Report*, ch 6.

[14] Extensive guidance is given by Joint Money Laundering Steering Group, *Guidance on the Prevention of Money Laundering and the Financing of Terrorism for the Financial Services Industry* (British Bankers' Association, London, 2006).

[15] See further (A/RES/54/109, Cm 4663, London, 1999) art 7.

[16] (A/RES/54/109, Cm 4663, London, 1999) arts 1, 2. See Bantekas, I, 'International Law of Terrorist Financing, The Current Development' (2003) 97 *American Journal of International Law* 315.

[17] Hansard HC vol 372 col 940 (15 October 2001), Gordon Brown.

[18] See Third Money Laundering Directive (2005/60/EC; 2007/64/EC); HM Treasury, *The Financial Challenge to Crime and Terrorism* (London, 2007) para 3.66; Money Laundering Regulations 2007, SI 2007/2157; HMRC, *The Money Service Business Action Plan* (London, 2008).

[19] See National Commission on Terrorist Attacks Upon the United States, *Final Report* (GPO, Washington, DC, 2004) pp 171, 533.

[20] See Qorochi, M, Maimbo, SM, and Wilson, JF, *Informal Funds Transfer Systems* (IMF, Washington DC, 2003); McCulloch, J and Pickering, S, 'Suppressing the financing of terrorism' (2005) 45 *British Journal of Criminology* 470; Razavy, M, 'Hawala' (2006) 44 *Crime, Law and Social Change* 277; Passas, N and Maimbo, SM, 'The design, development and implementation of regulatory and supervisory frameworks for informal funds transfer system' in Biersteker, TJ and Eckert, SE (eds), *Countering the Financing of Terrorism* (Routledge, London, 2008).

B. Offences

Introduction and background

9.11   All stages of tangible support for terrorism are forbidden by offences in the TA 2000, ss 15 to 18, reflecting the UN Financing Convention (Article 2) and going beyond in some respects. There are three principal cycles of illicit financing: the compilation of assets; their transmission to suitable recipients and their transformation into suitable formats; and their application towards terrorism. Alongside these participative offences are the crimes of professionals, who, without necessarily endorsing terrorism, aid the flow of finance.

9.12   Alongside these special offences sit relevant 'normal' offences, such as extortion or demanding money with menaces which are crimes under the Theft Act 1968, s 21, and which are treated with severity in a terrorism context,[21] The use of resources in connection with specific acts of terrorism may amount to conspiracy 'with others unknown'.[22] An abduction to collect a ransom for terrorist coffers involves the offence of kidnap, but the proof that the ransom benefits a terrorist group may be difficult, as in cases connected with Somali pirates. In any event, the Home Office has expressed reluctance to punish the family of victims,[23] and guidelines from the Council of Europe do not suggest the freezing of family assets so as to block payments,[24] but UNSCR 1904 does forbid ransom payments which might benefit Al-Qa'ida or the Taleban.[25]

Provisions

9.13   Initial collection or making available through fund-raising or donations is forbidden by three offences of 'fund-raising' in s 15 of the TA 2000, involving (1) the invitation of a contribution, (2) receiving such a contribution, or (3) providing a contribution.[26] The aid can be provided by money or other property being solicited, received, or made available, whether or not for consideration. In this way, a loan would be covered whether it was intended to be repaid or not.

9.14   The *mens rea* for the offences requires, as alternatives, intention as to terroristic purposes or reasonable suspicion of them. The most straightforward instance of reasonable suspicion is where the person knows of the primary facts from which reasonable suspicion can be inferred. More difficult is where the person is ignorant of the primary facts founding the reasonable suspicion, whether because of negligence or otherwise. Section 15 does appear to require that the person really does harbour a reasonable suspicion and so must

---

[21] See *Attorney General's Reference (No 5 of 2006) (Potts)* [2004] NICA 27; *Attorney General's Reference No 5 of 2006 (O'Donnell)* [2006] NICA 38; *R v Lowey and Bennett* [2007] NICA 9; Northern Ireland Affairs Select Committee, *Organised Crime in Northern Ireland* (2005–06 HC 886) para 192.

[22] See *R v Hulme and Maguire* [2005] EWCA Crim 1196.

[23] House of Lords European Union Committee, *Money Laundering and the Financing of Terrorism* (2008–09 HL 132) para 172 and *Government Reply* (Cm 7718, London, 2009) p 18.

[24] Committee of Ministers Rec R (82)14, *On measures to be taken in cases of kidnapping followed by a ransom demand* (Strasbourg, 1982).

[25] (17 December 2009) para 5.

[26] Compare the Terrorism Financing Convention, Art 2, which requires the involvement to be conducted wilfully and has no equivalent to s 15(1)(a): Legal Department of the IMF, *Suppressing the Financing of Terrorism: A Handbook for Legislative Drafting* (IMF, Washington DC, 2003) p 7; Davis, KE, 'The financial war on terrorism' in Ramraj, VV et al, *Global Anti-Terrorism Law and Policing* (Cambridge University Press, Cambridge, 2005) p 182.

have subjective knowledge of the primary facts. A more truly objective standard to cater for the wilfully or carelessly ignorant should not apply in the absence of wording such as that the defendant 'ought to' reasonably suspect or where 'there is' a reasonable suspicion.[27]

Examples of s 15 offences include *R v McDonald, Rafferty, and O'Farrell*,[28] concerning a Real **9.15** IRA team who sought to obtain weapons and money in Slovakia from an agent of the CIA and British Security Service posing as an Iraqi; the maximum sentence was imposed, discounted for a guilty plea. In *R v Kamoka, Bourouag, and Abusalem*, the defendants were convicted of providing funds and false passports to the Libyan Islamic Fighting Group.[29] In the case of Hassan Mutegombwa, money was solicited from another (an undercover officer) for a one-way flight to Nairobi the purpose of which was suggestive of terrorist purposes in Somalia; appeal against sentence (of ten years) was dismissed.[30] Abu Izzadeen (also known as Omar or Trevor Brooks) was convicted of terrorist fund-raising by the sale of a DVD recording of a sermon in Regents Park Mosque in 2004 in which he encouraged resistance to US forces in Fallujah; his sentence was reduced on appeal to eighteen months in the absence of evidence of the collection of funds.[31] The major financier for the Tamil Tigers was Arunachalam Chrishanthakumar, who became President of the British Tamil Association which was set up after proscription of the Liberation Tigers of Tamil Eelam in 2001. He was charged with receiving money for terrorism purposes and the collection and supply of army gear and weapons manuals; the sentence was two years in view of his humanitarian work.[32]

Having assembled terrorist resources, a person commits an offence under s 16(1) by using **9.16** money or other property for the purposes of terrorism. There is no further description of this offence, so it must be assumed that *mens rea* (intent or recklessness) is required for both the use and for the purposes of that use. By contrast, s 16(2) covers the possession of money or other property. In this situation, as well as intent, it is sufficient that the person has reasonable cause to suspect that it may be used for the purposes of terrorism. Thus, the s 16(2) *actus reus* of possession seems to create an offence dependent entirely on *mens rea* in the sense that the money or property may not have been obtained by unlawful means.[33]

Section 16 was tested in *O'Driscoll v Secretary of State for the Home Department*.[34] The **9.17** defendant, arrested at Dover for possession of a magazine associated with a proscribed Turkish group, DHKP-C, argued that s 16 breached Articles 10 and 11 of the European Convention on Human Rights. The Divisional Court noted that proof of the offence required a showing that the defendant had specific intent, and the same mental element was also important in assessing proportionality.[35] Assuming the organization had been properly proscribed, which was not disputed, then a narrowly conceived offence to enforce some financial aspects of

---

[27] Compare Smith, I, Owen, T, and Bodnar, A, *Asset Recovery* (Oxford University Press, Oxford, 2007) para I.3.349.
[28] [2005] EWCA Crim 1945 and [2005] EWCA Crim 1970.
[29] *Birmingham Post* 12 June 2007, p 1.
[30] [2009] EWCA Crim 684.
[31] *R v Saleem and others* [2009] EWCA Crim 920.
[32] Press Association Mediapoint, 12 June 2009.
[33] It exceeds the Convention: Davis, KE, 'The financial war on terrorism' in Ramraj, VV et al, *Global Anti-Terrorism Law and Policing* (Cambridge University Press, Cambridge, 2005) p 182.
[34] [2002] EWHC 2477 (Admin). See also *R v Kazi Nurur Rahman* <http://news.bbc.co.uk/1/hi/uk/6206886.stm>, 2007.
[35] Ibid paras 26, 27.

proscription was not disproportionate. There are two points of weakness for s 16 in this reasoning. The first is that it assumes a close linkage between a publication and the funding of a proscribed organization. In this case, the applicant had not been convicted of an offence of membership. The second weakness is that s 16 can also relate to 'the purposes of terrorism'. This formulation does not founder on grounds of vagueness,[36] but the absence of proscription undermines the assumption that 'there is no question about the terrorist nature of the organization'.[37]

9.18 The stages of transmission and transformation are covered by ss 17 and 18. By s 17 ('Funding arrangements'), a person commits an offence by entering into (in other words, being part of the initiation of), or becoming concerned in (in other words, joining in some existing relationship or transaction), an arrangement by which money or other property is, or will be, made available, with knowledge or reasonable cause to suspect that it will or may be used for the purposes of terrorism.

9.19 The application of s 17 was illustrated by the conviction in 2003 of Benmerzouga and Meziane.[38] These two Algerians raised money through skimming credit card details and sending them to associates, who raised over £200,000.

9.20 By s 18 ('Money laundering'), a person commits an offence by entering into, or becoming concerned in, an arrangement which facilitates the retention or control by or on behalf of another person of terrorist property. The 'arrangements' can involve concealment, by removal from the jurisdiction, by transfer to nominees, or otherwise. Most of the classical transactions of laundering, placement, layering, and integration can be encompassed by these terms. By use of the term 'terrorist property', s 18 catches funding purposes not directly related to terrorism, such as payments to the relatives of paramilitary prisoners.[39] The offence does not therefore depend on 'predicate offences' and so is arguably wider and clearer than the FATF Special Recommendation II.[40] Under s 18(2), proof of *mens rea* is even easier: the burden is switched to the defendant to prove on balance neither knowledge nor reasonable cause to suspect that the arrangement related to terrorist property. Reasonable cause to suspect may be based on information then available, though wilful reluctance to investigate suspicious circumstances will not provide absolution. Section 118 does not apply to this defence. Arguably, this legal burden of proof is beyond 'reasonable limits',[41] at least when imposed beyond the regulated sector or professional actors.[42]

Implementation

9.21 Under s 22, the maximum penalties for the foregoing offences are: (a) on indictment, imprisonment not exceeding fourteen years, a fine, or both;[43] (b) on summary conviction, imprisonment not exceeding six months, a fine, or both. An increased maximum of life

---

[36] Ibid para 24.

[37] Ibid para 26.

[38] *R v Meziane* [2004] EWCA Crim 1768. See also *R v Khan* [2007] EWCA Crim 2331; *R v McCaugherty and Gregory* [2010] NICC 35.

[39] Compare and distinguish *R v Loizou* [2005] EWCA Crim 1579.

[40] See Pieth, M, 'Criminalising the financing of terrorism' (2006) 4 *Journal of International Criminal Justice* 1074 at 1083.

[41] *Salabiaku v France*, App no 10519/83, Ser A 141-1, para 28; *R v Lambert* [2001] UKHL 37 at para 17.

[42] See further Smith, I, Owen, T, and Bodnar, A, *Asset Recovery* (Oxford University Press, Oxford, 2007) para I.3.626.

[43] The maximum was increased in 1989 and 2000: see *R v O'Reilly and Montgomery* [1989] 10 NIJB 20; *R v Quigg* [1991] 9 NIJB 38 (CA).

imprisonment has been mooted,[44] but the courts have already warned that 'substantial deterrent sentences' will be imposed.[45]

The jurisdiction over these offences is extended by s 63 of the TA 2000 to actions outside the **9.22** United Kingdom which would have constituted the commission of an offence under any of ss 15 to 18 if the activities had occurred within jurisdiction.

Finance offences have been the principal charge in thirty-four British cases, producing ten **9.23** convictions, as indicated in Table 9.1.[46]

Table 9.1 Terrorism Act Part III finance
offences charges, ss 15–19[a]

Year	GB	NI
2001	10	4
2002	12	9
2003	7	7
2004	7	4
2005	11	7
2006	5	11
2007	19	n/a
Total	71	42

[a] Sources: Carlile Reports; NIO Statistics & Research Branch. 2001 is from 19 February.

C. Forfeiture

Introduction and background

As demanded by the United Nations Convention for the Suppression of the Financing of **9.24** Terrorism, Article 8, and by the FATF Special Recommendation III,[47] The TA 2000, s 23,[48] contains compendious provisions which allow criminal forfeiture, predicated upon an *ad personam* conviction under ss 15 to 18.[49]

Provisions—the powers of forfeiture

Where a forfeiture order is imposed under s 23(2) regarding an offence under ss 15(1), **9.25** 15(2), or 16, it may extend to money or other property which the convict, at the time of the offence, possessed or controlled, and which, at that time, has in fact been used for terrorism or where there is intent or reasonable cause to suspect its use for the purposes of terrorism. This wording is altered under s 23(3) in relation to s 15(3)—there has in fact been

---

[44] HM Treasury, *The Financial Challenge to Crime and Terrorism* (London, 2007) para 2.9.
[45] *R v Meziane* [2004] EWCA Crim 1768 at para 74 per Lord Justice Tuckey (imposing a sentence of eleven years under s 17). Note also *R v Khan*, *The Times* 18 March 2006, p 41.
[46] *Carlile Report for 2008*, Tables 3(a), 7(a).
[47] See FATF, *International Best Practice: Freezing of Terrorist Assets* (2009), *Money Laundering and Terrorist Financing in the Securities Sector* (2009).
[48] As amended by the ATCSA 2001, Pt II; CTA 2008, ss 34, 35.
[49] See *Lloyd Report*, para 13.24; *Home Office Response to Lloyd Report*, para 6.21; HM Treasury, *The Financial Challenge to Crime and Terrorism* (London, 2007) para 2.9.

use for terrorism purposes or the person subjectively knew or had reasonable cause to suspect the use for the purposes of terrorism.

9.26 For ss 17 and 18 offences, there may be forfeiture under s 23(4) where there has in fact been use for terrorism or where the person intended such use. In addition, s 23(5) allows forfeiture in connection with s 17 where the person subjectively knew or had reasonable cause to suspect the use for the purposes of terrorism. An added rider for s 18 is that it is sufficient under s 23(6) that the arrangement related to that money or property. Thus, there is no burden on the prosecution to show that the money or property was then in the possession of the convicted person or even knowledge or reasonable cause to suspect that it might be used for the purposes of terrorism, though the defendant may have contested these matters under s 18(2).[50]

9.27 By amendments in 2008, forfeiture is allowed of property which has in fact been used for the purposes of terrorism, whether envisaged to any degree or not, and this rule applies to offences under ss 15 to 17 and not just s 18. A case in point might be the forfeiture of a rented flat where bombs are made. The property of an unwitting landlord is thus put in jeopardy.

9.28 Forfeiture under s 23A, also inserted in 2008, arises when there is a conviction for specified offences which comprise specified terrorism legislation offences beyond ss 15 to 18. Listed offences are the TA 2000, ss 54, 57, 58, 58A, 59, 60, and 61, and the TA 2006, ss 2, 5, 6, and 9 to 11, offences ancillary (as defined by s 94 of the 2008 Act), or 'normal' offences beyond the terrorism legislation falling within Sch 2 of the CTA 2008[51] where the court determines under ss 30 or 31 that there exists a terrorist connection (as defined in s 93). The property must be in the possession or control of the convict where it had been used for the purposes of terrorism, or it was intended for such use, or where the court believes that it will be used for such use.[52]

9.29 The court may order under s 23(7) the forfeiture of any money or property which wholly or partly, and directly or indirectly, is received by any person as a payment or reward in connection with offences under ss 15 to 18. So, while a terrorist finance offence must have been committed, it need not have been committed by the person holding the money or property or in relation to that money or property. Thus, where an accountant prepared accounts on behalf of a proscribed organization and was recompensed, the payment can be forfeited even though it was not intended or suspected for use in terrorism.[53]

9.30 By s 23B(2) (inserted by s 36 of the CTA 2008), when considering whether to make an order, a court shall have regard to (a) the value of the property; and (b) the likely financial and other effects on the convicted person.

Provisions—the procedures of forfeiture

9.31 Procedural details are set out in Sch 4 to the TA 2000,[54] Pt I relating to England and Wales, Pt II to Scotland, and Pt III to Northern Ireland. These provisions will be described primarily by reference to England and Wales.

---

[50] Compare Mitchell, AR, Taylor, SME, and Talbot, K, *Mitchell, Taylor and Talbot on Confiscation and the Proceeds of Crime* (3rd edn, Sweet & Maxwell, London, 2002) para 12.005.

[51] The list can be amended by affirmative order for future offences: s 23A(5), (6); Delegated Powers and Regulatory Reform Committee, *Counter-Terrorism Bill* (2007–08 HL 133) para 5.

[52] Compare TA 2000, s 111 (repealed in 2007): Hansard HC Public Bill Committee on the Counter-Terrorism Bill cols 394–5 (13 May 2008), Tony McNulty.

[53] See Home Office, *Explanatory Notes to the Terrorism Act 2000* (London, 2000) para 33.

[54] As amended by the CTA 2008, s 39 and Sch 3 to account for ss 23A, 23B.

Forfeiture orders can be imposed on the initiative of the court handling the prosecution, **9.32** except in Scotland where an order can only be made on the application of the prosecutor under s 23B(3). Schedule 4, paras 2 to 4, detail the court powers of sale and disposal,[55] while payments to third party claimants are under s 23(7).

Section 23B(1) (replacing s 23(7)) allows the court to hear property claims by third parties **9.33** such as family relatives. Third parties in the guise of victims of terrorism are considered by s 37 of the CTA 2008. By Sch 4, para 4A, the court may order that an amount is to be paid to the victim out of the proceeds of forfeiture (after deduction of the costs of disposal, third party property rights, and the fees of a receiver). This type of compensation can be made where an order under s 130 of the Powers of Criminal Courts (Sentencing) Act 2000 would be made but for the inadequacy of the offender's means.

Given that the criminal trial and related forfeiture proceedings may take some time to trans- **9.34** act, para 5 seeks to avert the interim dissipation of assets. Accordingly, the High Court may make a restraint order where a forfeiture order has already been made, or it appears to the High Court that a forfeiture order may arise in ongoing proceedings for the offence.[56] The ATCSA 2001 amends para 5 to bring forward the bite of restraint orders. An application may also apply when a criminal investigation has been started with regard to relevant offences and it appears to the High Court that a forfeiture order may be made in subsequent proceedings.[57] Prosecutors may apply under para 5(4) for a restraint order to a judge in chambers without notice.[58] Lord Lloyd suggested that the restraint order procedure should be handled by the Crown Court so as to reduce the procedural complications for police and prosecutors.[59] The Crown Court judge should be notified of the proceedings, but there is no set rule.[60]

The effect of a restraint order is to prohibit a notified person from dealing with the relevant **9.35** property: para 5(3). To reinforce the powers of restraint, para 7 allows a constable a summary power of seizure of any property subject to a restraint order for the purpose of preventing it from being removed from the jurisdiction, though the seizure should be notified to the High Court. The consequences of restraint orders on registered land are covered by para 8.

Once a restraint order is issued,[61] notice must be given to any person affected by the order, **9.36** and such persons can apply for variation or discharge (para 6). A restraint order shall also be discharged on such an application if the proceedings for the offence are not instituted within such time as the High Court considers reasonable, or, in any event, if the proceedings for the offence have been 'concluded' as defined by para 11 (though a forfeiture order might then be imposed). The court rules also allow for the indemnification of third parties against expenses incurred in complying with the order, and for living and legal expenses of the defendant.[62]

---

[55] As specified under para 4, and amended by the Courts Act 2003.
[56] See further: Civil Procedure Rules, RSC Ord 115 Pt III; Practice Direction: Restraint orders and appointment of receivers in connection with criminal proceedings and investigations; *Re G (restraint order)* [2001] EWHC Admin 606.
[57] Lord Lloyd had sought a limit of five days: *Lloyd Report*, paras 13.26, 13.27.
[58] See Sch 4, para 5(4); RSC Ord 115 r 26. See *Jennings v Crown Prosecution Service* [2005] EWCA Civ 746; *Customs and Excise Commissioners v S* [2004] EWCA Crim 2374.
[59] See *Lloyd Report*, para 13.26.
[60] Compare Criminal Procedure Rules 2010, r 61.14.
[61] It is argued that an order might be resisted by an offer of an undertaking (see Smith, I, Owen, T, Bodnar, A, *Asset Recovery* (Oxford University Press, Oxford, 2007) para II.134), but the public interest in preventing terrorism financing is higher than that in criminal money laundering.
[62] Civil Procedure Rules, RSC Ord 115 r 27; Practice Direction, r 4.

On the latter aspect, the related *Practice Direction: Restraint orders and appointment of receivers in connection with criminal proceedings and investigations*[63] provides that these expenses will be allowed 'normally, unless it is clear that a person restrained has sufficient assets which are not subject to the order . . .'.

9.37 Where a restraint order is discharged because criminal proceedings are not instituted within a reasonable time, or do not result in conviction, or result in conviction which is subsequently pardoned or quashed, affected persons may apply under para 9 to the High Court for compensation. However, the right to compensation is strictly confined by para 9(4), by which the High Court must be satisfied: (a) that there was a 'serious default' by a person concerned in the investigation or prosecution of the offence; (b) that the default is attributable to the police or Crown Prosecution Service; (c) that the applicant has suffered loss in consequence of the forfeiture or restraint order; and (d) that, in all the circumstances, it is appropriate to order compensation.[64] Furthermore, by para 9(5), the High Court shall not order compensation where it appears that proceedings for the offence would have been instituted even if the serious default had not occurred.

9.38 A slightly more generous compensation scheme is granted by para 10, which applies where a forfeiture order or a restraint order is made in, or in relation to, proceedings for a relevant offence, where the conviction is subsequently quashed on an appeal under s 7(2) or (5) and without proof of serious default. A person who had an interest in affected property may receive compensation if the High Court is satisfied the applicant has suffered loss and it is appropriate to order compensation to be paid (by the Secretary of State).[65]

9.39 Forfeiture or restraint orders made in other jurisdictions in the British Islands and in external jurisdictions specified by order may be enforced as Scottish, Northern Ireland, Islands, or external orders in England and Wales under paras 12 to 14. The Terrorism Act 2000 (Enforcement of External Orders) Order 2001[66] includes all European Union and G7 states (plus India). Both restraint and forfeiture orders made elsewhere in the British Islands can be enforced by the High Court. The details for external orders involve either a request for assistance to the Secretary of State, which is transmitted to the Crown Prosecution Service or a direct request to the High Court. The High Court may register an external restraint order if proceedings for forfeiture are to be instituted or are ongoing and have reasonable prospects of success and it is of the opinion that enforcing the order would not be contrary to the interests of justice.[67] The Court may register an external forfeiture order if not subject to an appeal and if of the opinion that enforcing the order would not be contrary to the interests of justice.[68]

9.40 These designation arrangements are to be replaced for European Union states (and others to be designated by order) by the addition of paras 11A to 11G to Sch 4 via the Crime (International Co-operation) Act 2003.[69] The 2003 Act implements the Framework Decision on the execution

---

[63] Practice Direction, para 4.4.

[64] The phraseology derives from the *ex gratia* system (abolished in 2006) of compensation for miscarriages of justice (Hansard HC vol 87 cols 689W (29 November 1985), Douglas Hurd). These restraints are not considered arbitrary: *Andrews v United Kingdom*, App no 49584/99, 26 September 2002; *Capewell v CCE* [2005] EWCA Civ 964.

[65] There may also be a residual discretion to protect third parties under the Human Rights Act 1998: *Re A* [2002] EWHC 611.

[66] SI 2001/3927.

[67] SI 2001/3927, art 10.

[68] SI 2001/3927, art 9(1).

[69] s 90 and Sch 4 (not in force). For other offences, see Serious Organised Crime and Police Act 2005, s 96.

in the European Union of orders freezing property or evidence adopted by the Council of the European Union on 22 July 2003.[70] Relevant offences are those listed in art 3(2) of the Directive (which includes 'terrorism', subject to a minimum custodial sentence of three years) or those prescribed by order. The scheme allows two-way enforcement. Under para 11B, property which is the subject of a restraint order which is to be found in a participating country may be the subject of a certificate by the High Court if there is a 'good arguable case' that it relates to terrorism. These certificates are transmitted to the Secretary of State under para 11C for forwarding to the relevant foreign court or authority. Conversely, a certificate for an overseas freezing order based on criminal proceedings or investigations in a participating country may be transmitted along with the court order under para 11D to the Secretary of State who will send a copy to the High Court and to the Director of Public Prosecutions, who must be given an opportunity to be heard (para 11E). The court may decline enforcement only if its impact would be incompatible with the Human Rights Act 1998 (para 11E). It may also postpone enforcement if it would prejudice domestic proceedings or if the property is already subject to an order in criminal proceedings (para 11F). If the overseas freezing order is to be enforced, it must be registered in the High Court, and notice must be given to any person affected (para 11G).

These attempts to foster cross-border forfeiture in practice encounter many difficulties, including the small value of seizures compared to procedural costs and the unfair division of seized funds.[71] **9.41**

Corresponding forfeiture powers for Scottish courts are set out in Pt II of Sch 4. The powers are conferred principally upon the Court of Session.[72] Applications for restraint orders shall be made by the Lord Advocate. **9.42**

Forfeiture in Northern Ireland is related by Pt III.[73] One special feature is a specific offence under para 37 to contravene a restraint order. This offence is additional to the contempt power of the High Court and allows special pre-trial and trial processes to be applied (now under the JSA 2007). It is a defence to prove that there was a reasonable excuse for the contravention; s 118 does not apply. **9.43**

Finally, Sch 4, Pt IV (which applies throughout the United Kingdom) relates to the impact of forfeiture in the case of 'qualifying insolvency proceedings'. The effect is that an application can be made by an insolvency practitioner within six months of the making of a forfeiture order to remove the property from the impact of the forfeiture order and allow it to be dealt with in the insolvency proceedings. **9.44**

Implementation

In 2008/09, £839k plus $61k was forfeited in London-based investigations.[74] In Northern Ireland in 2009/10,[75] there were 168 cash seizures (151 under POCA) to a value of £1,648,707 (£1,221,591) of which £848,349 was forfeited. Court orders were made against assets to a **9.45**

---

[70] 2003/577/JHA, art 3. For implementation, see Council Document 5937/2/06; *Report from the Commission of 22 December 2008 based on Article 14 of the Council Framework Decision 2003/577/JHA of 22 July 2003 on the execution in the European Union of orders freezing property or evidence* (COM (2008) 885 final).

[71] House of Lords European Union Committee, *Money Laundering and the Financing of Terrorism* (2008–09 HL 132) ch 3.

[72] See Act of Sederunt (Rules of the Court of Session Amendment No 6) (TA 2000) 2001, SSI 2001/494.

[73] Para 36 was repealed by the TA(NI)A 2006. See *Lloyd Report,* para 13.22.

[74] Lord Carlile, *Report on the Operation in 2009 of the Terrorism Act 2000* (Home Office, London, 2010) para 105.

[75] Organised Crime Task Force, *Annual Report and Threat Assessment 2010* (Belfast, 2010) p 44.

value of £18,476,011, and criminal assets recovered amounted to £4,207,852 but the terrorism element is not disclosed.

D. Seizure of Cash

Introduction and background

9.46 The most eye-catching change introduced by the TA 2000 is a power to seize cash, a form of *in rem* civil forfeiture which is not dependent on criminal conviction.[76] The seizure power assumes that the 'criminal economy is more cash intensive than the legitimate economy', based around the needs for liquidity and anonymity.[77] The powers initially in the TA 2000 were confined to seizures at borders (including between Britain and Northern Ireland). In order to remove this limitation,[78] but also to extend the definition of 'cash', s 1 and Sch 1 of the ATCSA 2001 replaced wholesale ss 24 to 31 of the TA 2000.

Provisions

9.47 According to s 1(1) of the ATCSA 2001, the powers of seizure are to enable the forfeiture in civil proceedings before a magistrates' court or (in Scotland) the sheriff of 'terrorist cash'. It is emphasized by s 1(2) that the seizure is exercisable whether or not any criminal proceedings have been brought.

9.48 'Terrorist cash' is defined in s 1(1) as cash which (a) is intended to be used for terrorism purposes; (b) consists of resources of a proscribed organization; or (c) is, or represents, property obtained through terrorism. Under Sch 1, para 1, 'terrorist cash' is assigned a slightly different definition; it means cash within sub-s (1)(a) or (b) of s 1, or 'property earmarked as terrorist property'. 'Earmarking' is described below under paras 11 and 12. Since it basically captures property obtained through terrorism and property which represents property obtained through terrorism, there is no substantial difference from s 1(1), though it would be helpful if the two definitions had matched exactly. In more detail, 'cash' includes under Sch 1, para 1(2), coins and notes in any currency, postal orders, cheques and travellers' cheques, bankers' drafts, bearer bonds and bearer shares, and such monetary instrument as the Secretary of State may specify by order. Any amount, no matter how small, may be seized.[79] Counterfeit 'cash' is not within para 1 but could be held on import and export under ss 20 and 21 of the Forgery and Counterfeiting Act 1981.[80]

9.49 The notion of 'earmarking' is explained further in paras 11 and 12 which ensure that forfeiture can capture property obtained through terrorism and proceeds from that property. By para 11, a person obtains property through terrorism if property is obtained by, or in return for, acts of terrorism (such as carrying out a killing or explosion in return for payment) or acts carried out for the purposes of terrorism (for example, leasing a house to a terrorist cell). It is immaterial whether any money, goods, or services were provided. Thus, property

---

[76] See *Lloyd Report*, para 13.33.
[77] Bell, RE, 'The seizure, detention and forfeiture of cash in the UK' (2003) 11 *Journal of Financial Crime* 134 at 134.
[78] Compare *Webb v Chief Constable of Merseyside Police* [2000] QB 427.
[79] See *Home Office Response to Lloyd Report*, para 6.28. Compare Proceeds of Crime Act 2002, s 303 (currently, £1,000 is specified).
[80] Hansard HL vol 629 col 1049 (6 December 2001), Lord Rooker.

still counts as having been obtained through terrorism regardless of any investment in it: 'So if a person buys guns with honestly come by money, and sells them at a profit, the whole of the proceeds of the sale will count as having been obtained through terrorism, and not just the profit.'[81] It is also unnecessary to show that the property was obtained through a particular act of terrorism if it is proven that the property was obtained through a range of terrorist acts. Therefore, it need not be established that funds are attributable, for example, to extortion, duty evasion, or armed robbery, provided that all are acts of terrorism or are for the purposes of terrorism.

Having established that the property is obtained through terrorism in these ways, it is then **9.50** 'earmarked as terrorist property' under para 12. If earmarked terrorist property is disposed of (as defined by para 18), it remains earmarked if the recipient obtained it on a disposal from the person who obtained the property through terrorism or if the recipient is a person from whom the cash could be directly seized. Conversely, anyone who obtains terrorist property on disposal and does so in good faith, for value, and without notice that it was earmarked is immune from forfeiture (para 16). Thus, a purchaser who paid full value for a car used in terrorism but who was unaware of its terrorist origins escapes forfeiture and the property is no longer earmarked, though the cash paid for the car then becomes earmarked. This immunity also applies to civil damages paid out of terrorist property or to payments of compensation or restitution. If the property remains earmarked, it can be traced through to property which represents the original terrorist cash (para 13). Thus, if a person is given a car in return for carrying out an act of terrorism and then sells it, the cash so obtained will be property earmarked as terrorist property, as will property secured when the cash is spent. Mixed property can also be apportioned, so that only the terrorist cash element is forfeited (para 14). Whilst identified property can be seized, there is no 'terrorism lifestyle' forfeiture reliant upon rebuttable presumptions about ownership of the entire assets held by someone implicated in terrorism.[82] Paragraph 15 provides that any profits accruing from property obtained through terrorism or traceable property are also to be treated as relevant property. All these provisions about earmarked terrorist property apply under para 18 to events occurring before commencement of the Act. This retrospective application does not breach Article 7 of the European Convention since these are civil *in rem* proceedings.[83]

By para 2, an 'authorised officer' may seize and detain terrorist cash on the basis of reasonable **9.51** grounds for suspecting its presence, even if it is not reasonably practicable to split it from a larger stash.[84] The Code of Practice for Authorised Officers Acting under Schedule 1 to the ATCSA 2001 specifies that 'reasonable grounds':[85]

> . . . depend upon particular circumstances and . . . such factors as how the cash was discovered, the amount involved, its origins, intended movement, destination, reasons given for a cash as opposed to normal banking transaction, whether the courier(s) and/or the owners of the cash

---

[81] Home Office, *Explanatory Notes on the Anti-terrorism, Crime and Security Bill* (London, 2001) para 340.
[82] Compare EPA1991, s 51; Proceeds of Crime Act 2002, s 10.
[83] Compare *Welch v United Kingdom*, App no 17440/90, Ser A 307-A (1995). See further *Phillips v United Kingdom*, App no 41087/98, 2001-VII; *McIntosh v Lord Advocate* [2001] UKPC D1.
[84] See Home Office Circular 30/2002: *Guidance for the Police and Public on the implementation of Sections 1–2 of the Anti-terrorism Crime and Security Act 2001*, para 17.
[85] Terrorism Act 2000 (Code of Practice for Authorised Officers) Order 2001, SI 2001/425, para 11. See Delegated Powers and Regulatory Reform Select Committee, *Report on the Anti-terrorism, Crime and Security Bill* (2001–02 HL 45) para 15; Bell, RE, 'The seizure, detention and forfeiture of cash in the UK' (2003) 11 *Journal of Financial Crime* 134 at 138.

(if different) have any links with terrorists or terrorist groups, whether here or overseas. Where the authorized officer has suspicions about the cash he/she should give the person who has possession of it a reasonable opportunity to provide an explanation on the details of its ownership, origins, purpose, destination, and reasons for moving the amount in this way and to provide the authorized officer with supporting documentation. The authorized officer should make clear to the person that anything said will be noted and used in the event that the cash is seized and an application made to the court for its detention or forfeiture.

9.52 Authorized officers are advised under para 15 to give written notification to the possessor of the cash, including a statement of powers exercised, value seized, and rights to challenge in court. The person should also be invited to sign the copy kept by the officer.

9.53 The cohort of 'authorised officers' comprises constables, customs officers, and immigration officers, but the Code of Practice (para 6) advises that the powers should normally be exercised by the police.

9.54 Once seized, the cash must be released not later than forty-eight hours from seizure (counting only working days).[86] An authorized officer or the Commissioners of Customs and Excise (or in Scotland a procurator fiscal) may apply under Sch 1, para 3, to a magistrates' court (or in Scotland, the sheriff) for an extension order. The court must be satisfied that the assets are terrorist cash and that the continued detention of the cash is justified pending investigation or pending a determination whether to institute criminal proceedings; up to three months' extra time can be allowed from the date of the order.[87] On the first application for extension, the hearing may take place without notice and in the absence of the affected persons or their representative (para 3(3A)).[88] The provisional nature of this hearing, the pressing social need of combating terrorism, and the involvement of a judicial officer may perhaps avert a breach of rights to due process, privacy, or property under the European Convention.[89] A court detention order may be renewed further but not beyond two years from the time of the first extension order (para 3(2)). During its detention, the cash shall, under para 4, unless required as evidence of an offence, be held in an interest bearing account.

9.55 Under para 5, a person from whom the cash was seized may apply for a court direction that seized cash be released. An authorized officer, or, in Scotland, the procurator fiscal, may themselves take the initiative to release cash if satisfied that detention is no longer justified (with notice to the magistrates' court or sheriff). But no cash may be released while proceedings on an application for its forfeiture or for its release under paras 6 or 9 (below) or proceedings in the United Kingdom or elsewhere which relate to a person connected with the cash are pending.

9.56 The next stage will normally involve forfeiture procedures under para 6. This process is quite distinct from that under ss 23 or 23A. An authorized officer or the Commissioners of Customs and Excise may apply to a magistrates' court, or, in Scotland, the Scottish Ministers (formerly the procurator fiscal) may apply to the sheriff, for an order to forfeit detained cash. The court must be satisfied on the balance of probabilities that the cash

---

[86] Sch 1, para 3, as amended by the CTA 2008, s 83. See Home Office, *Possible Measures for Inclusion in a future Counter-Terrorism Bill* (London, 2007) para 70.

[87] See Magistrates' Courts (Detention and Forfeiture of Terrorist Cash) (No 2) Rules 2001, SI 2001/4013; Magistrates' Courts (Detention and Forfeiture of Terrorist Cash) Rules (Northern Ireland) 2002, SR 2002/12.

[88] Inserted by TA 2006, s 35(1).

[89] Compare *Crémieux v France*, App no 11471/85, Ser A 256-B (1993); *Chappell v United Kingdom*, App no 10461/83, Ser A 152-A (1989).

is terrorist cash.[90] The forfeiture can apply not only against the seized cash, but also in relation to any accrued profits (para 15). The proceedings are to be treated as civil under s 1(1) of the ATCSA 2001.

Parties with a claim to ownership of detained cash (oddly labelled as 'victims') may apply for release of the cash (or their share of it) (para 9). As well as determining ownership, it must appear to the court that the applicant was deprived of the assets by criminal conduct, that the assets were not, immediately prior to deprivation, property obtained by, or in return for, criminal conduct nor representing such assets. Furthermore, the forfeiture will not apply against an excepted joint owner in circumstances in which it would not (as against the owner) be earmarked as terrorist property (paras 6, 17).   **9.57**

Paragraphs 7 and 7A[91] afford an appeal by a party to the original hearing within thirty days in England and Wales, to the Crown Court, or in Scotland to the Court of Session, or, in Northern Ireland, to the county court. The appeal court does not have to hold a full rehearing and may make any order it thinks appropriate. Public legal services (authorized by s 2(1) of the ATCSA 2001) may be sought.[92]   **9.58**

If the cash is subjected to a forfeiture order, then para 8 requires that it shall be paid into central government coffers. If the cash is not ultimately subjected to a forfeiture order (unless paid over to a third party under para 9), the person to whom it belongs or from whom it was seized may apply for compensation under para 10. Where the cash was not held in an interest-bearing account while detained, the amount of compensation will be the equivalent interest which would have been earned. Beyond taking account of any interest actually paid or which would have been payable, further compensation for loss can only be paid if there are 'exceptional' circumstances and at a rate deemed to be 'reasonable'.   **9.59**

Further enforcement rules concerning the roles of authorized officers are set out in s 115 and Sch 14 to the TA 2000. By paras 2 and 3 of Sch 14, an officer may enter a vehicle or use reasonable force. By para 4, information acquired by an officer may be supplied to specified agencies.   **9.60**

Detailed rules about forms and process for magistrates' courts in relation to cash seizures[93] are provided for under the Magistrates' Courts (Detention and Forfeiture of Terrorist Cash) (No 2) Rules 2001[94] and the Magistrates' Courts (Detention and Forfeiture of Terrorist Cash) Rules (Northern Ireland) 2002.[95] Hearings are to be conducted as in the case of a criminal complaint, but without powers of arrest for failure to appear. The Crown Court (Amendment) Rules 2001[96] establish appeal procedures, including issuing notice of the appeal to persons with an interest in proceedings who may not previously have been joined as parties.   **9.61**

Procedures in the Sheriff Court are dealt with by the Act of Sederunt (Summary Applications, Statutory Applications and Appeals etc Rules) Amendment (Detention and Forfeiture of   **9.62**

---

[90] See *R(K) v Bow Street Magistrates' Court* [2005] EWHC 2271 (Admin).
[91] As substituted by the CTA 2008, s 84. See *Home Office, Possible Measures for Inclusion in a future Counter-Terrorism Bill* (London, 2007) para 70.
[92] Compare *Benham v United Kingdom*, App no 19380/92, 1996-III.
[93] The TA 2000, s 31, was not replaced in 2001 so general rule-making powers apply.
[94] SI 2001/4013, replacing SI 2001/194, and further amended by the Magistrates' Courts (Miscellaneous Amendments) Rules 2003, SI 2003/1236.
[95] SR NI 2002/12, replacing SR NI 2001/65.
[96] SI 2001/193.

Terrorist Cash) 2002.[97] Applications are made by summary application or, where an order has been made, by minute in the process.

9.63 Should the lowest tier criminal courts handle this potentially complex and sensitive civil forfeiture litigation?[98] Attempts to switch proceedings to the Crown Court were defeated in the House of Lords on the basis that the corresponding jurisdiction in respect of drugs-related cash had not encountered any problems.[99] The *Newton Report* deprecated hearings in magistrates' courts, albeit more because of their openness than their level of expertise.[100]

Implementation

9.64 Statistics are disclosed (as in Table 9.2) as to cash seizures under the ATCSA 2001 for the National Terrorist Financial Investigation Unit in the Metropolitan Police but not elsewhere. In a period of two years from April 2006, it seized £1,344,271 in cash,[101] but this total sum also derived from search operations and action other than under the ATCSA 2001, s 1. The most publicized cash seizure was from Loyalist paramilitary leader, Johnny Adair, who, during relocation from Northern Ireland in 2003, was relieved of £70,000 at the Cairnryan ferry terminal.[102]

Table 9.2 Cash seizures under the
ATCSA 2001[a]

	GB: Cash seized £ (no. of cases)
2001	18,500 (n/a)
2002	90,170 (8)
2003	269,396 (14)
2004	16,312 (3)
2005	9,318 (1)
2006	81,818 (n/a)
2007	9,155 (n/a)
Total	494,699

[a] Sources: Carlile Reports 2001 is from
19 February.

9.65 Evidence which might persuade a court to make a seizure order includes the overall amount of cash, a preponderance of low denomination banknotes, avoidance of normal financial channels, previous proceedings against the possessor, tainted associates, a dearth of normal documentation, the presence of other items suggesting wrongdoing, the nature of the travel

---

[97] SSI 2002/129.

[98] Binning, P, '"In safe hands?" Striking the balance between privacy and security–Anti-terrorist finance measures' (2002) 6 *European Human Rights Law Review* 734 at 743.

[99] Hansard HL vol 629 col 305 (28 November 2001) col 1047 (6 December 2001), Lord Rooker.

[100] *Newton Report*, para B15. The idea of a transfer was welcomed: *Home Office Response to Newton Report*, para II4.

[101] Hansard HC vol 473 col 938w (18 March 2008). Other seizures under Sch 5 amount to £650k: HM Treasury, *The Financial Challenge to Crime and Terrorism* (London, 2007) para 2.52.

[102] See Wood, IS, *Crimes of Loyalty* (Edinburgh University Press, Edinburgh, 2006) p 292.

arrangements, and the actions and responses of the applicant including inconsistent statements and attempts at subterfuge.[103] According to *Muneka v Comrs of Customs & Excise* (arising under Part V of the Proceeds of Crime Act 2002),[104] there is no requirement to identify the precise conduct which has given rise to the cash or even the type of activity. However, in *R v W and others*,[105] greater specification was required for criminal recovery under Part VII of the 2002 Act, but *Muneka* was not overruled.[106]

E. Financial Investigations and Oversight

Reporting duties

Introduction

In order to assist the detection process, and in line with FATF Special Recommendation IV, professional financial intermediaries should report their suspicions to the authorities.[107]   **9.66**

Provisions

By s 19(1) of the TA 2000, where a person believes or suspects that another person has committed an offence under either of ss 15 to 18 on the basis of information accruing in the course of a trade, profession, business, or employment, an offence is committed if the information is not disclosed to a police officer or member of the Serious Organised Crime Agency (SOCA) as soon as reasonably practicable. The width of the duty is striking. It is sufficient to have a subjective belief or suspicion which can only be safely suppressed if the intermediary has a 'reasonable excuse' under sub-s (3). This defence is not subject to s 118, but it is arguable that this switch is fair only in the context of professionals who are trained and keep records; the extension to other businesses is more dubious.[108] Under s 19(7), the duty has a global reach to equivalent transactions overseas.   **9.67**

Exceptions are accorded to legally privileged information or the making of a disclosure by an employee to an established higher authority, and the officials in regulatory authorities are also excused.[109] The disclosure defence allows for professional actors to perform collating and channelling functions for police organizations by means of a Suspicious Activity Report (SAR).[110] The intelligence is then stored on the ELMER database of SOCA.   **9.68**

The government emphasized the confinement of s 19 to professionals handling finance, but family and business relations may overlap in the situation of small enterprises. Another concern arises from the fact that journalism also counts as a 'profession'.[111]   **9.69**

---

[103] Bell, RE, 'The seizure, detention and forfeiture of cash in the UK' (2003) 11 *Journal of Financial Crime* 134 at 138.

[104] [2005] EWHC 495 (Admin).

[105] [2008] EWCA Crim 2 at paras 37–38 per Laws LJ.

[106] See Whitelaw, F, 'Prove it!' (2008) 158 *New Law Journal* 812.

[107] As amended by the TA 2000 and Proceeds of Crime Act 2002 (Amendment) Regulations 2007, SI 2007/3398.

[108] See also Smith, I, Owen, T, Bodnar, A, *Asset Recovery* (Oxford University Press, Oxford, 2007) para 1.3.634.

[109] Terrorism Act 2000 (Crown Servants and Regulators) Regulations 2001, SI 2001/192.

[110] The preferred forms are at <http://www.soca.gov.uk/financialIntel/suspectActivity.html>. See further Home Office, Circular 53/2005: Money Laundering (London, 2005).

[111] Hansard HC Standing Committee D, col 155 (25 January 2000), Charles Clarke. A specific exemption was rejected: Hansard HL vol 613 col 653 (16 May 2000), Lord Bassam.

9.70 The reach of s 19 has been supplemented further by the CTA 2008, s 77. This measure arose from allegations that charities are being misused as a vehicle for raising or transferring money to terrorists.[112] Section 77 therefore inserts as s 22A of the TA 2000 a new definition of 'employment' which encompasses both paid and unpaid employment and can even include voluntary work. In this way, the unpaid volunteers who are the trustees of a charity must act with the same insight as professional forensic accountants. The Home Office misleadingly describes the amendment as 'a very minor change to close a possible gap in the current provisions'.[113] The result might be to deter community-spirited individuals, though, as described later, the Charity Commission has sought to offer some guidance.

9.71 An even stricter duty to disclose is imposed on the 'regulated sector'[114] by Sch 2, Pt III, of the ATCSA 2001. This duty is applied instead of, and not additional to, s 19. Most businesses handling substantial financial activity are covered. Under s 21A (inserted into the TA 2000), a person in that sector commits an offence by knowing or suspecting or having reasonable grounds for knowing or suspecting, that another person has attempted[115] or committed an offence under either of ss 15 to 18 (including with extra-territorial effect), unless that information is disclosed to a constable, officer of SOCA, or the employer's nominated officer as soon as practicable. The duty is subject to a reasonable excuse not to disclose and to exceptions for privileged legal advice.[116] The objective standard of liability, which can arise without subjective awareness of any suspicion, is justified by the 'Greater awareness and higher standards of reporting in the financial sector'.[117] Given that objective standard, the court must consider whether there was compliance with guidance by the relevant supervisory authority or professional body. That guidance has to be approved by the Treasury and be published in a manner approved by the Treasury. Guidance is issued via the Joint Money Laundering Steering Group.[118] Though such guidelines are helpful,[119] they do not answer criticisms that the impact of s 21A unfairly applies equally to junior and senior staff,[120] and there are also difficulties in distinguishing between the regulated sector and the non-regulated sector when some businesses (lawyers and accountants) operate in both sectors. Nevertheless, only one offence is recorded up to the end of 2005,[121] suggesting that the offence mainly operates as a reference point and a threat. Under s 21B, any disclosure within s 21A does not breach legal restraints on disclosure.

---

[112] See HM Treasury, *The Financial Challenge to Crime and Terrorism* (London, 2007); Home Office and HM Treasury, *Review of Safeguards to Protect the Charitable Sector (England and Wales) from Terrorist Abuse* (London, 2007).

[113] Home Office, *Possible Measures for Inclusion into a Future Counter-Terrorism Bill* (London, 2007) para 22.

[114] TA 2000, Sch 3A, as substituted by: Terrorism Act 2000 (Business in the Regulated Sector and Supervisory Authorities) Order 2007, SI 2007/3288; Terrorism Act 2000 and Proceeds of Crime Act 2002 (Amendment) Regulations 2007, SI 2007/3398. The duty is required by 2005/60/EC, art 22, and is defined by types of persons rather than by activities.

[115] The element of attempts was added by the Terrorism Act 2000 and Proceeds of Crime Act 2002 (Amendment) Regulations 2007, SI 2007/3398, Sch 1, paras 3, 4, as required by 2005/60/EC, art 22.1.

[116] The Terrorism Act 2000 and Proceeds of Crime Act 2002 (Amendment) Regulations 2007, SI 2007/3398, Sch 1, para 3, as required by 2005/60/EC, art 23.2.

[117] Home Office, *Regulatory Impact Assessment: Terrorist Property* (2001) para 8.

[118] See <http://www.jmlsg.org.uk/content/1/c6/01/18/54/CHX%20JMLSG%20Dec%2007.pdf>, 2007.

[119] See also Wolfsberg Standards (<http://www.wolfsberg-principles.com>); Law Society, *Anti-terrorism practice note: The conflicting duties of maintaining client confidentiality and reporting terrorism* (London, 2007).

[120] See Lord Carlile, *Report on the Operation in 2002 and 2003 of the TA 2000* (Home Office, 2004) para 50.

[121] Hansard HL vol 687 col 264wa (18 December 2006).

As well as disclosure duties, s 21D forbids tipping off in the regulated sector, subject to s 21E **9.72** (disclosures within an undertaking or group), s 21F (other permitted disclosures between institutions or professionals for the purpose only of preventing offences), and s 21G (disclosure to a supervisory authority or for the purpose of dissuading a client from unlawful conduct).[122] The measures place advisers within the regulated sector in a difficult position if their client demands explanations for inaction in response to contractually enforceable instructions.[123] There is no set period for SOCA to reach a decision.[124]

Alongside a duty to disclose, s 20 of the TA 2000 adopts a more permissive approach. A person **9.73** may choose to disclose to a suitable authority a suspicion or belief of the presence of terrorist property or its derivatives or a belief or suspicion that arises in the course of a trade, profession, business, or employment of an offence under ss 15 to 18. The disclosure may be made according to s 20(3) notwithstanding any legal restriction on disclosure, and there may also apply residual common law defences to breach of confidence or of a fiduciary duty. It follows that s 20 encourages disclosures even if based on thin, even irrational facts. The standard of 'reasonable excuse' in section 19(3) is not mentioned here.

The next encouragement for the assistance of law enforcement is contained in s 21 of the TA **9.74** 2000, which allows for ongoing cooperation with the police. A person avoids offences under ss 15 to 18 if acting with express police consent or even where the person acts on his own initiative but discloses as soon as reasonably practicable.[125] Consent should also be sought from SOCA by professional advisers and financial bodies to avoid incurring tipping off penalties. If the police intervene before contact is made, s 21(5) provides for a defence where the person intended to make a disclosure and there is reasonable excuse for the failure to do so up to that point. Section 118 does not apply to this defence. In some instances, consent should also be sought under Pt II of the RIPA for covert human intelligence sources or intrusive surveillance.[126]

The same two provisions in s 21 are applied to contacts with an 'authorised officer' in SOCA **9.75** under ss 21ZA and 21ZB, while s 21ZC grants a defence to anyone with a reasonable excuse for non-disclosure under s 21ZA or 21ZB at any stage.[127] It is also made clear by s 21C that any disclosure to a constable (including by the non-regulated sector) must be relayed to SOCA.

Implementation

The number of SARs has increased considerably—from 18,408 in 2000 to 228,834 in **9.76** 2008–09, though just 703 terrorist-related reports were referred to the National Terrorist Finance Investigation Unit.[128] Problems then arise as to how to sort the wheat from the chaff, to discourage defensive reporting, and to encourage a customer-friendly reaction from the security authorities.[129] *The Newton Report* argued for the destruction of reports unless an

---

[122] TA 2000 and Proceeds of Crime Act 2002 (Amendment) Regulations 2007, SI 2007/3398, Sch 1, para 5. Tipping off is forbidden by 2005/60/EC, art 28.
[123] See *K Ltd v National Westminster Bank* [2006] EWCA Civ 1039.
[124] Compare Proceeds of Crime Act 2002, s 335.
[125] There were 13,618 applications (mainly relating to non-terrorist cases) for consent in 2008–09: SOCA, *The Suspicious Activity Reports Regime Annual Report 2009* (London, 2009) p 14.
[126] See *Teixeira da Castro v Portugal*, App no 25829/94, 1998-IV; *Lambert v France*, App no 23618/94, 1998-V.
[127] Terrorism Act 2000 and Proceeds of Crime Act 2002 (Amendment) Regulations 2007, SI 2007/3398, Sch 1, para 2. These reflect 2005/60/EC, art 24.
[128] SOCA, *The Suspicious Activity Reports Regime Annual Report 2009* (London, 2009) p 14.
[129] KPMG, *Review of the Regime for Handling Suspicious Activity Reports* (London, 2003); *Newton Report*, para D134; Lander, S, *Review of the Suspicious Activity Reports Regime* (Home Office, London, 2006); HM Treasury, *The Financial Challenge to Crime and Terrorism* (London, 2007) paras 2.39, 2.60.

investigation is ongoing,[130] but the Home Office was opposed.[131] Professional bodies have also complained about regulatory costs and the lack of responsiveness to reporters.[132] The *Lander Report* recommended that SOCA should deliver regular reports on the functioning of the regime so as to augment dialogue with reporters and end users. Nevertheless, the Report concluded that 'the regime was clearly delivering benefits in both the terrorist and money laundering contexts'.[133] A House of Lords select committee review in 2009 suggested the exclusion from SARs of minor crimes, some case-specific feedback in selected cases, and more limited scope for data retention (currently ten years) and for accessing by different agencies.[134]

9.77   Disclosure under s 20 is said to be used frequently.[135]

Disclosure duties

Introduction and background

9.78   Further powers to assist financial investigations are granted by way of customer information orders and account monitoring orders, based on precedents in the Proceeds of Crime (Northern Ireland) Order 1996.[136]

Customer information—provisions

9.79   At the core of the TA 2000, Sch 6 (introduced by s 38) is the customer information disclosure order. The application is made under para 2 by a police superintendent (or higher rank) or, in Scotland, by the procurator fiscal. The order can be authorized under para 3 by, in England and Wales, a circuit judge, in Scotland, the sheriff, or, in Northern Ireland, a Crown Court judge.[137] They must be satisfied (not to any objective standard) under para 5 that: (a) the order is sought for the purposes of a terrorist investigation, (b) the tracing of terrorist property is desirable for the purposes of the investigation, and (c) the order will enhance the effectiveness of the investigation.

9.80   If an order is granted, then, by para 1, a named constable may require the financial institution to provide 'customer information' for the purposes of a terrorist investigation, notwithstanding legal restrictions on the disclosure of information. 'Customer information' means, under para 7,

> (a) information whether a business relationship exists or existed between a financial institution and a particular person ('a customer'), (b) a customer's account number, (c) a customer's full name, (d) a customer's date of birth, (e) a customer's address or former address, (f) the date on which a business relationship between a financial institution and a customer begins or ends,

---

[130]   *Newton Report*, para D136.

[131]   *Home Office Response to Lloyd Report*, Pt II para 10.

[132]   House of Lords European Union Committee, *Money Laundering and the Financing of Terrorism* (2008–09 HL 132).

[133]   Lander, S, *Review of the Suspicious Activity Reports Regime* (Home Office, London, 2006) para 2.

[134]   House of Lords European Union Committee, *Money Laundering and the Financing of Terrorism* (2008–09 HL 132) paras 108, 123, 180, 182. The exemption for minor crimes has been rejected: *Government Reply* (Cm 7718, London, 2009) p 11.

[135]   *Report of the Operation in 1998 of the Prevention of Terrorism (Temporary Provisions) Acts* (Home Office, London, 1999), para 66.

[136]   SI 1996/1299, Sch 2.

[137]   The Criminal Procedure Rules 2010, r 6.9 and 6.11, now deal with the application, variation and discharge of orders, including the possibility of witholding information under r 6.12.

(g) any evidence of a customer's identity obtained by a financial institution in pursuance of or for the purposes of any legislation relating to money laundering, and (h) the identity of a person sharing an account with a customer.

In line with restraints under Article 6 of the European Convention, Sch 6, para 9 provides **9.81** that customer information provided by a financial institution under this schedule shall not be admissible in evidence in criminal proceedings against the institution or any of its officers or employees (save for a prosecution for an offence of non-compliance under paras 1 or 8).

Orders can apply against specified financial institutions or as a collective,[138] the latter reflecting **9.82** operational practice of 'general bank circulars' in Northern Ireland.[139] The financial institution only has to say whether it holds accounts in the names given but cannot be required to provide account details. If the police want such information, they would need to seek a production order under Sch 5 or an account monitoring order under Sch 6A. Perhaps because Sch 6 might obviate more costly investigations, the banks were 'generally supportive' of the device.[140] It is arguable that a collective authorization infringes privacy rights.[141]

Customer information—implementation

Most applications have related to bank and credit card details[142] whereby the police have a **9.83** name (and perhaps an address) but are unsure of accounts held. Just one order was sought by the Metropolitan Police in 2007.

The penalty for the offence is a fine not exceeding level 5 on the standard scale (paras 1(5), **9.84** 8(3)). If the offence was committed with the consent or connivance of an officer of the institution, or was attributable to neglect by an officer, that officer, as well as the institution, is guilty of a further offence (para 8(1), (2)). It is a defence (para 1(4)) to prove that the information required was not in the institution's possession or that it was not reasonably practicable to comply with the requirement (such as where there would be an enormous amount of information to convey).[143] No charges arose under s 39 up to the end of 2007.

Account monitoring—provisions

The ATCSA 2001, s 3 and Sch 3, inserted s 38A and Sch 6A into the TA 2000 to allow for **9.85** account monitoring orders. These powers can be activated in relation to 'financial institutions'.[144] They differ from Sch 6 in two major effects: they relate to transactions rather than identity, and they can allow for real-time disclosure rather than disclosure of records.[145]

---

[138] Sch 6, para 1(1A), inserted by the ATCSA 2001, Sch 2, para 6(1), (3). See Home Office Circular 30/2002: *Guidance for the Police and Public on the implementation of Sections 1-2 of the Anti-terrorism Crime and Security Act 2001*, para 72.

[139] See the *Rowe Report*, para 145. There were twenty-three general bank circulars issued between August 1996 and December 2000: Donohue, LK, *The Cost of Counterterrorism* (Cambridge University Press, Cambridge, 2007) p 140.

[140] Hansard HC vol 346 col 329 (15 March 2000), Charles Clarke.

[141] Compare *Chappell v United Kingdom*, App no 10461/83, Ser A 152-A (1989).

[142] Lord Carlile, *Report on the Operation in 2001 of the Terrorism Act 2000* (Home Office, London, 2002) para 4.7.

[143] Hansard HC vol 346 col 331 (15 March 2000), Charles Clarke.

[144] See TA 2000, Sch 6, para 6, Sch 6A, para 1(5), as amended. The definition was based on the Money Laundering Regulations 1993, SI 1992/33 (see now SI 2003/3075, art 2(2)).

[145] See Home Office Circular 30/2002: *Guidance for the Police and Public on the implementation of Sections 1–2 of the Anti-terrorism Crime and Security Act 2001*, para 45.

There are no limits on the information so gathered, including legal matters, for 'we cannot see any occasion when such information would be legally privileged'.[146]

9.86 By Sch 6A, para 2, a judge may, on an application by an appropriate officer, make an account monitoring order if satisfied that: the order is sought for the purposes of a terrorist investigation; the tracing of terrorist property is desirable for the purposes of the investigation; and the order will enhance the effectiveness of the investigation. The test for an order is subjectively worded,[147] since 'the requirement to have reasonable grounds would preclude the use of this investigatory tool at an early stage in the investigation when it might not be possible to establish such reasonable grounds'.[148] These proceedings will (by para 1) be conducted before a circuit judge in the Crown Court or, in Scotland, a sheriff. The judge may hear the application *ex parte* (para 3). The 'appropriate officer' will be a police officer (likely to be a senior detective) or, in Scotland, the procurator fiscal.

9.87 If an order is made, then the financial institution specified in the application for the order will be notified with a copy of the order.[149] The financial institution must then for the period specified in the order (not exceeding ninety days) provide information of the description specified to an appropriate officer. Applications to vary or discharge may be made by an authorized officer or by any person affected by the order, with the possibility of witholding information from a respondent if thought necessary.[150]

Account monitoring—implementation

9.88 If an order is granted,[151] then it takes effect as if it were an order of the court (so its breach would be a contempt of court), and it overrides any legal restriction on the disclosure of information (para 6). Because of its compulsory nature, a statement made by a financial institution under an account monitoring order may not be used in evidence against it in criminal proceedings (para 7), save for proceedings for contempt of court, for forfeiture under s 23, or for a prosecution for an offence where the body makes a statement inconsistent with a prior statement.

Institutional frameworks

Policing

9.89 There are two key organizations in Britain. One is the UK Financial Intelligence Unit, a role conferred upon SOCA, which gathers and analyses intelligence, including via the receipt of SARs, within its specialist Terrorism Finance Team.[152] SOCA's primacy, recommended by the Lander Review,[153] supplanted in 2008 the Assets Recovery Agency, which was deemed an expensive failure.[154] This transfer was not so welcome in Northern Ireland, so the Home

---

146 Hansard HL vol 629 col 345 (28 November 2001), Lord Rooker.
147 Compare *Chappell v United Kingdom*, App no 10461/83, Ser A 152-A (1989) para 60.
148 Hansard HL vol 629 col 344 (28 November 2001), Lord Rooker.
149 Criminal Procedure Rules, 2010, r 6.10.
150 See also ibid r 6.11 and 6.12.
151 In January–July 2008, fewer than ten orders were granted to the Metropolitan Police.
152 Designation of a Unit is required by the FATF Recommendation 26 and by 2005/60/EC, art 21. See House of Lords European Union Committee, *Money Laundering and the Financing of Terrorism* (2008–09 HL 132) paras 56–66.
153 Lander, S, *Review of the Suspicious Activity Reports Regime* (Home Office, London, 2006) Pt IV.
154 See National Audit Office, *The Assets Recovery Agency* (2006–07 HC 253); Home Office, *One Step Ahead* (Cm 6167, London, 2004) para 5.1; Young, SMN (ed), *Civil Forfeiture of Criminal Property* (Edward Elgar, Cheltenham, 2009) chs 7, 8; Serious Crimes Act 2007, Pt III.

Office gave assurances about the maintenance of dedicated resources.[155] Plans were announced in 2010 to incorporate SOCA into a National Crime Agency.[156]

The operational arm of financial policing is the National Terrorist Financial Investigation **9.90** Unit, part of the Metropolitan Police Counter Terrorism Command.[157]

In Northern Ireland alone, an integrated policy unit, the Organised Crime Task Force, was **9.91** established in 2000.[158] It provides strategic direction and a forum for discussion amongst policing, governmental, and business stakeholders. Whether this body has enhanced the strategic steer in Northern Ireland is not clear[159]—if it has, then perhaps it should apply nationally.

Charities

Aside from financial bodies, charities are mistrusted as potential channels for terrorism **9.92** finance, as pointed out by FATF Special Recommendation VIII.[160] The paradigm form of abuse will arise from humanitarian work abroad by minority cultural associations, especially if it involves cash intensity, complex multiple donor patterns, politically committed officials, and the distribution of funds through overseas associates. The Islamic custom of *zakat*—the duty of donating to charity—is felt to enhance vulnerability. In the past, the Irish Northern Aid Committee (NORAID) aided the IRA but was curtailed under the Foreign Agents Regulation Act only when it became politically convenient to do so in the 1980s.[161]

The Charity Commission is reported to have investigated seventeen charities as a result of **9.93** which trustees were removed under the Charities Act 1993, s 20.[162] Most notable is Abu Hamza, removed from the North London Central Mosque (Finsbury Park) in 2003.[163] Next, Sanabel l'il-Igatha was closed in 2006 following international sanctions listing because of links to the Libyan Islamic Fighting Group.[164]

Allegations of terrorist involvement have been raised against several other charities.[165] Persistent **9.94** allegations of links to HAMAS relate to Interpal, the Palestinian Relief and Development Fund, which works in the occupied territories, Lebanon, and Jordan.[166] It was listed by the US Treasury in 2003[167] and investigated by the BBC Panorama programme, *Faith, Hate and Charity*, in 2006. The Charity Commission's report in 2009 was critical of Interpal's due diligence and

---

[155] <http://www.nio.gov.uk/letter_from_home_secretary_to_secretary_of_state_about_asset_recovery_work_in_northern_ireland.pdf>, 2007.

[156] Home Office, *Policing in the 21st Century* (London, 2010).

[157] See 'Investigation and enforcement' (2003) 6 *Journal of Money Laundering Control* 269.

[158] See <http://www.octf.gov.uk>.

[159] See Northern Ireland Select Committee, *The Financing of Terrorism in Northern Ireland* (2001–02 HC 978) para 119.

[160] See further FATF, *International Best Practices: Combating the abuse of non-profit organisations—Special Recommendation VIII* (2002); FATF, *Terrorist Financing* (2008) pp 10, 11; Bjorklund, VB et al, 'Terrorism and money laundering' (2005) 25 *Pace Law Review* 233.

[161] 22 USC s 611. See *AG v Northern Aid Committee* 688 F 2d 159 (1982); *AG v The Irish People* 796 F 2d 520 (1986); Adams, J, *The Financing of Terrorism* (New English Library, London, 1986) ch 6.

[162] Gunning, J, 'Terrorism, charities and diasporas' in Biersteker, TJ, and Eckert, SE (eds), *Countering the Financing of Terrorism* (Routledge, London, 2008).

[163] Charity Commission, *North London Central Mosque Trust* (London, 2004).

[164] *The Guardian* 9 February 2006, p 8 and 25 May 2006, p 4.

[165] See Charity Commission, Sivayogam (London, 2010); Green Crescent Bangladesh (*The Times* 26 March 2009, p 3).

[166] See *Hewitt and others v Grunwald and others* [2004] EWHC 2959 (QB); Levitt, M, *Hamas, Politics, and Charity* (Yale University Press, New Haven, 2006).

[167] No evidence was furnished by the US authorities: Hansard HC vol 492 col 677w (12 May 2009), Ian Pearson.

monitoring procedures, and the Commission also warned about the choice of highly partisan trustees and the need to check thoroughly overseas partners.[168] But Interpal was cleared of promoting terrorist ideology or activities, and the Charities Commission was understanding of the 'challenging' environment in which Palestinian charities inevitably work:[169]

> Humanitarian assistance cannot be denied to people because they support, actively or otherwise, or are sympathetic towards the work or aims of a political body, such as Hamas. However, assistance cannot be given solely on the basis of a person's support for Hamas.

9.95 In response to the perils of terrorist infiltration of charities, the Home Office and HM Treasury in their report, *Review of Safeguards to Protect the Charitable Sector (England and Wales) from Terrorist Abuse*,[170] regard the channelling of funds by charities to terrorists as 'extremely rare'. Nevertheless, they urge the Charity Commission to reinforce awareness of risk factors.

9.96 The Charity Commission has responded by publishing a *Counter-Terrorism Strategy*, which applies 'zero tolerance' to any connections to proscribed organizations, support for terrorist activity, or the fostering of 'criminal extremism'.[171] The Commission has put in place a Proactive Monitoring Unit and a Counter Terrorism Team which forms part of the Intensive Casework Unit in Compliance and Support, as well as issuing Operational Guidance.[172] A specialist Faith and Social Cohesion Unit seeks to engage with faith communities (primarily Muslim). Nevertheless, a 'strong and vibrant sector' should be encouraged,[173] and this understanding stance is welcome since, 'A wholesale blight on the provision of financial support for humanitarian aid . . . could fuel the destabilization of struggling people abroad and enhance the appeal of terrorist groups to these people'.[174] Such upheaval has been caused by the United Nations listing of the Al Barakaat group in Somalia from 2001 to 2009,[175] so it has been suggested that government-approved schemes of aid or a vetted 'safe list' should balance some of the more negative responses. However, government schemes may not attract such voluntary support and governments are wary of abuses by approved groups.

9.97 Another type of sanction against suspect charities, including Interpal, has involved civil litigation to pressure banks to withdraw facilities.[176]

Assessment of financial investigations

9.98 These powers cumulatively enable the objective of 'Pursue' of terrorists, as well as disruption to 'prevent' terrorism. As for accountability, scrutiny and information provision is sketchy. As for constitutional governance, there has been limited case law, and the guides are patchy. The measures do not fall within Lord Carlile's remit. The Criminal Procedure Rules 2010, rr 6.9 and 6.10 deal with the details respectively of both customer information and account monitoring orders.[177]

---

[168] *Inquiry Report: Palestinian Relief and Development Fund (Interpal)* (London, 2009) paras 188–201.
[169] Ibid paras 176, 183.
[170] (London, 2007) para 2.10.
[171] (London, 2008) pp 4, 10.
[172] OG96: *Charities and Terrorism* (2007).
[173] (London, 2008) pp 2, 7.
[174] Crimm, NJ, 'High alert' (2004) 45 *William & Mary Law Review* 1341, at 1450–1.
[175] Scheinin, M, *Reports of the Special Rapporteur on the promotion and protection of human rights and fundamental freedoms while countering terrorism* (A/HRC/6/17, 2007) para 48.
[176] See *Weiss v National Westminster Bank* 2008 US Dist LEXIS 99443 (USDC, EDNY).
[177] See also Act of Adjournal (Criminal Procedural Rules Amendment No 2) (Terrorism Act 2000 and Anti-Terrorism, Crime and Security Act 2001) 2001, SSI 2001/486.

Amongst the issues arising on a rights audit are the subjectively worded powers, and the **9.99** absence of any requirement to consider the impact on third parties of account monitoring, all affecting rights of privacy under Article 8. Next there is considerable overlap with the Proceeds of Crime Act 2002, which allows both customer information (ss 363 and 397) and account monitoring (ss 370 and 404) orders.[178] There are also Financial Reporting Orders in the Serious Organised Crime and Police Act 2005, which permit long-term monitoring as part of sentence at conviction.[179]

F. Crown Servants and Regulators

By s 119(1) of the TA 2000, the Secretary of State may make regulations providing for any **9.100** of ss 15 to 23A and 39 to apply to persons in the public service of the Crown, who may not assert a defence of Crown privilege.[180] Consequently, the TA 2000 (Crown Servants and Regulators) Regulations 2001,[181] r 3, apply ss 15 to 23A and 39 to the Director of Savings and subordinates who carry on relevant financial business. On the other hand, r 4 disapplies s 19 from officers in the following: the Bank of England; the Financial Services Authority; a designated professional body within s 326(2) of the Financial Services and Markets Act 2000; the Council of Lloyds; and the Registrar and Assistant Registrar of Credit Unions for Northern Ireland.

The Secretary of State may also under s 119(2) choose to exempt from duties of disclosure **9.101** under s 19 persons who are in his opinion performing regulatory, supervisory, investigative, or registration functions of a public nature. Those persons are of course expected to tip off where appropriate, but do not require a criminal sanction to encourage them to do so, nor, perhaps, would it be appropriate for them to answer in court for slip-ups.[182]

G. Foreign Comparisons

The pressures of international laws, especially the UN Terrorism Finance Convention of **9.102** 1999, mean that foreign jurisdictions bear marked similarities.[183]

In Australia, the Suppression of the Financing of Terrorism Act 2002 added a new offence to **9.103** the Criminal Code Act 1995, Division 103, by which persons who provide or collect funds and are reckless as to whether those funds will be used to facilitate a terrorist act are guilty of an offence. The maximum penalty is imprisonment for life.

The Canadian Anti-terrorism Act 2002 amended the Criminal Code by adding three terrorism **9.104** financing offences, ss 83.02, 83.03, and 83.04, carrying penalties of up to ten years'

---

[178] The customer information orders under the Proceeds of Crime Act 2002, ss 364(2), 398(2), cover information about other accounts: Smith, I, Owen, T, and Bodnar, A, *Asset Recovery* (Oxford University Press, Oxford, 2007) para I.2.706).

[179] See HM Treasury, *The Financial Challenge to Crime and Terrorism* (London, 2007) para 2.17. But the only specified triggering terrorism offence is the TA 2000, s 56.

[180] Hansard HC Standing Committee D col 297 (3 February 2000), Charles Clarke.

[181] SI 2001/192, as amended by the Financial Services and Markets Act 2000 (Consequential Amendments) Order 2002, SI 2002/1555, art 43.

[182] See Hansard HC Standing Committee D col 297 (3 February 2000), Charles Clarke.

[183] See Muller, WH, Kalin, CH, and Goldsworth, JG, *Anti-Money Laundering: International Law and Practice* (John Wiley, Chichester, 2007).

imprisonment.[184] Not dependent on any criminal conviction, property can be subject to restraint (s 83.13) and then forfeiture (s 83.13) on application by the Attorney General to a Federal Court judge.

9.105 Rather than leaving investigations of charities to a specialist civil agency, the (Canadian) Charities Registration (Security of Information) Act 2001 (enacted within the Anti-terrorism Act, Pt VI) allows ministerial certificates to assert links to terrorism, subject to determination by the Federal Court as to reasonableness.[185] This executive deeming is subject to determination under s 5 by the Federal Court that the certificate is reasonable.

9.106 In Ireland, the principal code relating to money laundering offences and confiscation, primarily prompted by drug trafficking, is the Criminal Justice Act 1994.[186] However, the threat of paramilitary crime combined with organized crime drove the development of the Criminal Assets Bureau Act 1996. The Bureau, a division of the Garda Síochána, has broad criminal and civil law powers and consists of staff from customs and revenue, the civil service, and the police.[187]

9.107 The Criminal Justice (Terrorist Offences) Act 2005, Pt IV,[188] has added two specialist offences (with penalties of up to twenty years' imprisonment) to existing measures under the Criminal Justice Act 1994. The offences, in ss 13(1) and (3), deal with providing, collecting, or receiving funds either to carry out terrorism offences or acts or for the benefit or purposes of a terrorist group. Section 32 of the Act obliges designated bodies to adopt measures to prevent and detect the commission of offences and to train directors, other officers, and employees. Sections 14 and 15 allow for interim and interlocutory freezing orders. In addition, the Minister for Justice, Equality and Law Reform can, under the Offences against the State Amendment Act 1985, require a bank to pay suspected moneys of an unlawful organization into the High Court.

9.108 A particularly determined attempt to securing restraint and forfeiture is provided by Spain's Law for the Prevention and Blocking of Terrorism Finance.[189] The Law created the *Comisión de Vigilancia de Actividades de Financiación del Terrorismo* (Commission for the Surveillance of Terrorist Financing) with powers to freeze accounts and transactions and to prohibit the opening of new accounts. It may aid the criminal courts or act independently. Its composition includes ministerial and civil service appointees and also prosecutors.

9.109 In the USA,[190] 18 USC s 2339A, enacted in 1994,[191] addresses the provision directly or indirectly of financial or other material support or resources knowing or intending their use

---

[184] See Davis, KE, 'Cutting off the flow of funds to terrorists' in Daniels, RJ, Macklem, P, and Roach, K, *The Security of Freedom* (University of Toronto Press, Toronto, 2001).

[185] See Duff, DG, 'Charitable status and terrorist funding' in Daniels, RJ, Macklem, P, and Roach, K, *The Security of Freedom* (University of Toronto Press, Toronto, 2001). Evidence may be withheld from the suspected body; compare *Tebieti Mühafize Cemiyyeti and Israfilov v Azerbaijan*, App no 37083/03, 8 October 2009, para 53.

[186] The Offences against the State (Amendment) Act 1985 allowed the forfeiture of bank deposits on ministerial order. One order was made and then the Act lapsed: Hogan, G and Walker C, *Political Violence and the Law in Ireland* (Manchester University Press, Manchester, 1989) p 272.

[187] See McCutcheon, JP and Walsh, DPJ, *The Confiscation of Criminal Assets* (Round Hall Sweet & Maxwell, Dublin, 1999).

[188] See The Money Laundering Steering Committee, *The Financial Sanctions Regime for Bodies Designated under section 32 of the Criminal Justice Act 1994* (Dublin, 2005).

[189] Law 12/2003 (21 May 2003). See UN Security Council S/2003/628 (New York, 2003).

[190] See Chesney, RM, 'The sleeper scenario' (2005) *Harvard Journal on Legislation* 1 and 'Federal prosecution of terrorism related offences' (2007) 11 *Lewis & Clark Law Review* 851; Cole, D, 'Terror financing, guilt by association and the paradigm of prevention in the "war on terror"' in Bianchi, A and Keller, A, *Counterterrorism* (Hart, Oxford, 2008);Ward, J, 'The root of all evil' (2008) 84 *Notre Dame Law Review* 471.

[191] Violent Crime Control and Law Enforcement Act 1994, PL 103-322, s 120005.

for terrorist activities as being forbidden by thirty-six listed offences. Proof of intent is required that the recipient is a terrorist group (even recklessness is not sufficient and certainly not negligence as in the United Kingdom legislation).[192] By 18 USC s 2339B,[193] it is an offence without any requirement of intent or belief as to the terrorist nature of the acts to be aided[194] to provide material support or resources (including personnel who might comprise oneself) to a designated 'Foreign Terrorist Organization'[195] (Al-Qa'ida was listed in 1999). The constitutionality of the offences was upheld against challenges based on free speech and vagueness in *Holder v Humanitarian Law Project*.[196]

Title III of the USA PATRIOT Act, ss 803 to 815, also known as the International Money **9.110** Laundering Abatement and Anti-Terrorist Financing Act 2001,[197] augmented ss 2339A and 2339B. It widened the notion of 'material support or resources' by including, for example, expert advice or assistance, and included those offences as predicate offences under the Racketeer Influenced and Corrupt Organizations Act (RICO). RICO had already been occasionally used in terrorism cases on the basis of a wide judicial interpretation of the term 'enterprise'.[198] The PATRIOT Act, s 376, modifies 18 USC s 1956, which makes unlawful the laundering of monetary instruments, to include the provision of material support or resources to designated foreign terrorist organizations in its definition of 'unlawful activity'. Aside from offences, forfeiture is also extended (ss 319 and 372). Financial transactions to secure various actions outside the US, such as crimes of violence, are forbidden by s 315.

Next, the Suppression of the Financing of Terrorism Convention Implementation Act **9.111** 2002[199] penalizes under 18 USC s 2339C fund-raising and other financial transactions that support terrorists and their activities. Money service businesses, such as hawala, must be licensed under ss 359 and 373 of the PATRIOT Act.[200]

Many countries require the routine or specific disclosure of banking information. **9.112** A prominent example is the US Bank Secrecy Act 1970 (PL 91-508), which obliges financial institutions to file reports of non-electronic cash transactions of $10,000 or more and to keep records in relation to, and report on, any suspicious transactions.[201] This model is followed in Australia[202] and Canada.[203] The Financial Crimes Enforcement Network (FinCEN)

---

[192] But see *US v Lakhani* 480 F 3d 171 (2007).

[193] Antiterrorism and Effective Death Penalty Act 1996, PL 104-132, s 303.

[194] The Intelligence Reform and Terrorism Prevention Act 2004, PL 108-458, s 6603(c)(2) clarified that knowledge (but still not recklessness or negligence) is confined to the fact that the group is designated or has engaged in terrorism.

[195] 8 USC s 1189(a)(1), inserted by the Antiterrorism and Effective Death Penalty Act 1996, s 302 (see also 31 CFR s 597.101-901).

[196] 561 US _ (2010). Note also *32 County Sovereignty Committee v Department of State* 292 F 3d 797 (2002).

[197] PL 107-56.

[198] See Shipman, D, 'Taking terrorism to court' (2008) 86 *North Carolina Law Review* 526.

[199] PL 107-197 s 301.

[200] See *US v Lakhani* 480 F 3d 171 (2007).

[201] 31 USC ss 5311–5332 and 31 CFR 103, as extended by the Anti-Drug Abuse Act 1986 (PL 100-690), the Housing and Community Development Act 1992 (PL 102-550), and the PATRIOT Act, 311, 317, 318, 326, 351, 356, 365, 371.

[202] The Australian Transaction Reports and Analysis Centre (AUSTRAC) was established under the Cash Transaction Reports Act 1988 (see now the Anti-Money Laundering and Counter-Terrorism Financing Act 2006) and responds to reports under the Financial Transaction Reports Act 1988.

[203] The Financial Transactions and Reports Analysis Centre of Canada (FINTRAC) is the principal financial intelligence unit (see Proceeds of Crime (Money Laundering) and Terrorist Financing Act 2000, as amended by the Anti-terrorism Act 2002).

of the US Treasury Department's Office of Terrorism and Financial Intelligence processes the Currency Transaction Reports and Suspicious Transaction Reports, and the Terrorist Financing Operations Section in the FBI's Counterterrorism Division takes on investigations. The more discerning British approach appears preferable and corresponds with a risk-based approach which avoids unthinking box-ticking.[204]

9.113 The final noteworthy aspect of US policy concerns the data mining of financial information, under the US Terrorist Finance Tracking Program[205] in relation to 'SWIFT'—the Society for Worldwide Interbank Financial Telecommunication. This organization, based in Brussels, holds information for nearly 9,000 financial institutions about the millions of daily electronic financial transactions. After September 11, OFAC obtained unprecedented access to SWIFT data, probably in breach of European data protection laws.[206] The response was a US–EU compromise arrangement agreed in 2007, by which a set of 'Representations' (unilateral assurances) about the processing, disclosure, and retention of personal data were given by the US Treasury, all overseen by an 'eminent European' monitor.[207] This arrangement proved to be unacceptable to the European Parliament, and another agreement took its place in 2010.[208] Another response has been realignment to the architecture of SWIFT, whereby US-related data is partitioned. However, the European Council fears this refinement undermines the purpose of the project and so has called for a European equivalent to the US Terrorist Finance Tracking Program.[209] The safeguards under the 2010 agreement remain weak. There are limits as to the data affected (terrorism and not other forms of criminality), and there is the requirement of a pre-existing 'reason to believe that the subject of the search has a nexus to terrorism or its financing' to justify a search under Articles 5 and 10 (but not including documentary proof). Continuing safeguards, such as obligations to delete and oversight by the eminent monitor and an annual reviewer, are meagre substitutes for independent checks before the transfer takes place and an effective complaints system.

9.114 The regulation and registration of hawaldars has been tightened in countries such as the United Arab Emirates,[210] while Saudi Arabia has sought to confine remittance activity to bank and licensed exchanges.[211] The purpose of these measures may have been to improve the recording of transactions rather than to prevent them,[212] and there are suggestions that incentives as well as sanctions should be applied.[213] This demand for action against

---

[204] See further Commission Directive 2006/70/EC; HM Treasury, *The Financial Challenge to Crime and Terrorism* (London, 2007) para 1.30. For criticism, see Pieth, M, 'Criminalising the financing of terrorism' (2006) 4 *Journal of International Criminal Justice* 1074 at 1077.

[205] The authority is Executive Order 13224 and the United Nations Participation Act of 1945 s 5 (22 USC 287c): <http://www.ustreas.gov/press/releases/reports/legalauthoritiesoftftp.pdf>.

[206] See Council of the EU, *Processing of EU Originating Personal Data by United States Treasury Department for Counter Terrorism Purposes–SWIFT* (10741/2/07 Rev 2, 2007) p 2.

[207] See Committee on Civil Liberties, Justice and Home Affairs, *First ECC report on the implementation of the EU-US SWIFT undertakings* (LIBE/6/73175, 16 February 2009).

[208] Agreement between the European Union and the United States of America on the processing and transfer of Financial Messaging Data from the EU to the US for the purposes of the Terrorist Finance Tracking Program (Brussels, 2010); European Commission, *Proposal for a Council Decision* (COM (2010) 316 final).

[209] Council of the EU, *Interinstitutional File* (11172/10) p 4.

[210] See *Report from UAE to the Counter Terrorism Committee* (S/2005/573) p 8; *Ninth Report of the Analytical Support and Sanctions Monitoring Team* (S/2009/245, 13 May 2009) para 63.

[211] See *Report from Saudi Arabia to the Counter Terrorism Committee* (S/2004/884) p 8.

[212] But see Winer, JW, 'Globalization, terrorist finance, and global conflict' in Peith, M (ed), *Financing Terrorism* (Kluwer, 2002) p 26.

[213] Perkel, W, 'Money laundering and terrorism' (2004) 41 *American Criminal Law Review* 183.

arrangements from another culture may mask some inattention to arrangements embedded in our own culture and practices, such as the lack of information about beneficial ownership under trusts and corporate veils.[214]

H. Assessment and Conclusions on Domestic Measures

Legal responses to terrorism financing fall within the 'Prevent' and 'Pursue' strands of CONTEST. Two broad gains flow from a financial approach to terrorism. First, if finance can be limited, then terrorist groups are forced to choose between violent activities or political and social activities or scaling down their operations. Secondly, monitoring and interventions will constrain and detect the activities of terrorists. There may be direct detection at points of acquisition or dealing. More indirect action arises through forfeitures. **9.115**

The suppression of terrorism finance is a worthy ambition, but it may be questioned whether these schemes to 'follow the money' have delivered more than meagre results.[215] The statistics since 2000 do not suggest quantitative success. Causality cannot be attributed to any legislative inattention but may reside in under-valuation in policing cultures, under-resourcing, and obstacles to inter-agency cooperation.[216] **9.116**

Yet, it may be mistaken to confine attention to quantitative measures.[217] Small sums are seized because small sums are involved, and finance is declining under pressure.[218] For individual actors, financial checks may represent a disruptive factor which offers intelligence leads, as for Rashid Rauf, whose arrest in Pakistan sparked the arrests in the 'Liquid Bomb' airline plot in 2006.[219] The dampening of impacts on the political economy by ensuring insurance cover availability and giving confidence to business investment are also worthwhile goals.[220] **9.117**

Moving from a policy to a rights audit, the courts have been less solicitous of property and family rights compared to liberty and due process. Criminal forfeiture is treated as 'a financial penalty',[221] so Article 6(2) does not apply since the person is not 'charged'.[222] The European Court of Human Rights in *Butler v United Kingdom*[223] found that civil forfeiture was a preventative measure and not a criminal sanction. The Court also accepted the proportionality of the intervention. However, Article 6(1) remains applicable and may require some **9.118**

---

[214] FATF, *Third Mutual Evaluation Report on the United Kingdom* (Paris, 2007).
[215] See Zagaris, B, 'The merging of the anti-money laundering and counter-terrorism financial enforcement regimes after Sept. 11, 2001' (2004) 22 *Berkeley Journal of International Law* 123.
[216] See Northern Ireland Affairs Select Committee, *The Financing of Terrorism in Northern Ireland* (2001–02 HC 978) paras 50, 129, 140, 157; Bullock, K et al, *Examining Attrition in Confiscating the Proceeds of Crime* (Research Report 17, Home Office, London, 2009).
[217] Levi, M, 'Lessons for countering terrorist finances from the war on serious and organised crime' in Biersteker, TJ and Eckert, SE (eds), *Countering the Financing of Terrorism* (Routledge, London, 2008) p 264.
[218] Burr, JM and Collins, RO, *Alms for Jihad* (Cambridge University Press, New York, 2006) p 302.
[219] Acharya, A and Husin, G, 'Countering terrorist financing' *The Business Times Singapore* 25 August 2006.
[220] See Alexander, DC, *Business Confronts Terrorism* (University of Wisconsin Press, Madison, 2004); Enders, W and Sanders, T, *The Political Economy of Terrorism* (Cambridge University Press, New York, 2006) chs 9, 10.
[221] *McIntosh v Lord Advocate* [2001] UKPC D1 at para 25. See also *Phillips v United Kingdom*, App no 41087/98, 2001-VII.
[222] See *R v Briggs-Price* [2009] UKHL 19.
[223] App no 41661/98, 2002-VI. UK courts take the same view: *Butt v HM Customs & Excise* [2001] EWHC Admin 1066; *R v Rezvi* [2002] UKHL 1; *Re Director of the Assets Recovery Agency* [2004] NIQB 21; *R(K) v Bow Street Magistrates' Court* [2005] EWHC 2271 (Admin); *Walsh v Director of the Assets Recovery Agency* [2005] NICA 6; *Belton v Director of the Assets Recovery Agency* [2006] NICA 2.

moderation of the operation of the measures, most likely under ss 15(3), 17, and 18 where there can be a reverse onus presumption.[224] Another aspect where the trial judge should remain guarded concerns the standard of proof, given that forfeiture of property linked to terrorism involves a serious imputation against personal reputation.[225]

9.119 Insufficient attention has been paid to the impact on family members without property rights.[226] There may be yet wider feelings of injustice when humanitarian assistance through charities is blocked or when the remittance of the expatriate's wage is no longer feasible.[227]

9.120 Turning attention to democratic accountability, there is a dearth of information about the operation of forfeiture, and not much detail even regarding the Pt III offences. These aspects of the terrorism legislation are largely ignored during debates in Parliament.

9.121 As for constitutional governance, the main criticism is too many overlapping and complex codes rather than an absence of regulation. The complexity of the terrorism legislation is compounded by overlap and deficiency compared to the Proceeds of Crime Act 2002.[228] Money laundering offences in Pt VII of the 2002 Act produced between 2001 and 2008 three terrorist-related charges, as well as seven charges of conspiracy to defraud, and three charges of money laundering under the Criminal Justice Act 1988.[229] The 2002 Act also allows for the appointment of accredited financial investigators,[230] as previously allowed under the EPA1991, s 57, but no longer within the terrorism code.

9.122 Criminal confiscation is covered by Pts II to IV of the 2002 Act, and substantial seizures have been made by the National Terrorist Financial Investigation Unit under that legislation (£537,000 in 2007 and £597,000 in 2008).[231] The 2002 Act scheme is more ambitious than the terrorism legislation in several respects, such as by providing for presumptions about benefit over six prior years from 'lifestyle'.[232] This lifestyle presumption did formerly exist in the EPA 1991, s 51, until it was dropped by the EPA 1996 in favour of the Proceeds of Crime (Northern Ireland) Order 1996.[233]

9.123 More radical still, civil recovery, going well beyond cash seizure and not necessarily associated with criminal process,[234] is allowed by the 2002 Act, Pt V. The applicability to terrorism is

---

[224] See *R v Rezvi* [2002] UKHL 1 at para 15; Trechsel, S, *Human Rights in Criminal Proceedings* (Oxford University Press, Oxford, 2005) pp 34–5.

[225] See *R (on the application of McCann) v Crown Court at Manchester* [2002] UKHL 39 at para 83; *Assets Recovery Agency v He & Chen* [2004] EWHC 3021 (Admin) at para 66.

[226] See *Director of Assets Recovery Agency v Jackson* [2007] EWHC 2553 (QB) at para 221.

[227] See Crimm, NJ, 'The moral hazard of anti-terrorism financing measures' (2008) 43 *Wake Forest Law Review* 577; Bower, CB, 'Hawala, Money Laundering, and Terrorism Finance' (2009) 37 *Denver Journal of International Law and Policy* 379.

[228] See also the Proceeds of Crime (Scotland) Act 1995.

[229] *Carlile Report for 2009*, Table 3(c). See for example *R v Silcock* [2004] EWCA Crim 408.

[230] See Proceeds of Crime Act 2002 (References to Financial Investigators) Order 2009 SI 2009/975. Compare Financial Investigations (Northern Ireland) Order 2001, SI 2001/1866, arts 3, 6. Article 6 affords a power to require a solicitor to provide information as to whether a specified person was a client and about the nature of any transaction: Donohue, LK, *The Cost of Counterterrorism* (Cambridge University Press, Cambridge, 2007) p 140.

[231] Source: *Carlile Reports*.

[232] Proceeds of Crime Act 2002, ss 6, 75, Sch 2. See *Welch v United Kingdom*, App no 17440/90, Ser A 307-A (1995); *R v Shabir* [2008] EWCA Crim 1809.

[233] SI 1996/1299, art 9, as extended by the Financial Investigations (Northern Ireland) Order 2001, SI 2001/1866. See Bell, RE, 'Confiscation orders under the Proceeds of Crime legislation' (1998) 49 *Northern Ireland Legal Quarterly* 38.

[234] See Leong, AVM, 'Asset recovery under the Proceeds of Crime Act 2002' in Young, SMN, *Civil Forfeiture of Criminal Property* (Edward Elgar, Cheltenham, 2009).

demonstrated by the action against Thomas 'Slab' Murphy, an alleged quartermaster for the IRA,[235] who forfeited (in conjunction with his brothers) €1.2m to agencies in Ireland and Britain and awaits tax evasion charges.[236] Several alleged Loyalist financiers have also faced action.[237] Alongside this civil confiscation, s 317 allows for the issuance of tax demands in relation to gains reasonably believed to derive from crime.

It would be overly simplistic to abolish the terrorism legislation and rely solely on the 2002 **9.124** Act. For terrorist finance, 'It is not their criminal origins that makes them "tainted" but their use . . .'[238] However, the Proceeds of Crime Act 2002 offers a blueprint for thorough revision and some simplification.

As well as learning from the 2002 Act, more emphasis could be invested in private governance **9.125** in order to reduce funds at source. The device is being tested in Northern Ireland through the appointment of specialist auditors, Independent Private Sector Inspectors General, within the construction and charitable sectors.[239]

While the policy of 'following the money' appears to lead participants on a merry dance, the **9.126** Treasury remains determined to persevere,[240] on the basis that intelligence-based investigation will involve a huge amount of patient sifting.

I. International Freezing Orders

Introduction and background

Legal action originating in the United Kingdom now represents only part of the story against **9.127** terrorism finance. The admixture of international and state-sponsored terrorism has also prompted the United Nations and European Union to react to terrorist finances by general international law and specific sanctions. The general measures include the United Nations Convention for the Suppression of the Financing of Terrorism,[241] as already described. The added device of sanctions against individuals amounts to a remarkable new form of international financial outlawry against specified persons and organizations which are not dependent on criminal conviction[242] and yet inflict direct impact based on constitutionally inappropriate foreign and political mechanisms.

United Kingdom freezing orders

Introduction and background

Part II of the ATCSA 2001 represents a bridging measure between the domestic measures **9.128** and internationally imposed measures. Whereas remaining legal weapons detailed in this chapter are placed initially in the hands of international organizations, Pt II allows for

---

[235] See *Murphy v Times Newspapers* [2000] 1 IR 522.
[236] See *The Times* 18 October 2008, p 28. Note also the interim receiving order against Sean Gerard Hughes: *Belfast Telegraph* 10 November 2009, p 1.
[237] See *Re Warnock* [2005] NIQB 16; *R v Benson* [2005] NICC 31; *Re Armstrong* [2007] NIQB 20.
[238] See Legal Department of the IMF, *Suppressing the Financing of Terrorism: A Handbook for Legislative Drafting* (IMF, Washington DC, 2003) p 49. See further Alexander, R, 'Money laundering and terrorist finance' (2009) 30 *Company Lawyer* 200.
[239] See Goldstock, R, *Organised Crime in Northern Ireland* (Northern Ireland Office, Belfast, 2004).
[240] HM Treasury, *The Financial Challenge to Crime and Terrorism* (London, 2007).
[241] (A/RES/54/109, Cm 4663, London, 1999).
[242] See *Third Report of the Monitoring Group* (S/2002/1338, 17 December 2002) para 17.

unilateral and summary action by domestic authorities where there is a foreign element. Where action is taken to impose sanctions pursuant to a European Community decision or under a UNSCR, as described later in this chapter, 'it would not be appropriate to use the power'.[243]

Provisions

9.129   By s 4 of the ATCSA 2001, the Treasury may make a freezing order: either to deny funds and assets to foreign terrorists where they may pose a threat to the life or property of UK nationals or residents (categories defined in s 9); or, to prohibit financial transactions by foreign governments or persons who are deemed to be threatening the national economy.[244]

9.130   It was expressly asserted during enactment, in the teeth of opposition,[245] that the breadth of the second leg went beyond terrorism and reached into other emergencies and threats to security, thereby replacing pre-existing powers derived from wartime regulations.[246] The previous recorded instance of their use was against the Iraqi government after its invasion of Kuwait in 1990.[247] Future applications within official contemplation include 'kleptocrats', rogue states, and illegal funds from the proceeds of crime.[248]

9.131   The power is exercisable under s 10 by statutory instrument which must be laid before Parliament and is subject to the requirement of affirmative resolution within twenty-eight days. The Bank of England will draw the attention of banks to such orders.[249] Orders can be amended or revoked under ss 11 and 12.

9.132   The contents of freezing orders are specified in ss 5, 6, and Sch 3. A freezing order is an order which prohibits persons from making funds available to, or for the benefit of, persons specified in the order. 'Funds' are defined as 'financial assets and economic benefits of any kind'. By Sch 3, para 4, the order must allow for the granting of licences authorizing funds to be made available, such as for basic living expenses or legal fees. Paragraph 7 envisages a range of offences. By para 10, an order may include provision for the award of compensation where a person has suffered loss as a result of an order or the refusal of a licence.

9.133   By s 7, the Treasury must keep a freezing order under review, and, in any event, by s 8, it must cease after two years. However, the ATCSA 2001 does not explicitly provide for substantive challenge or appeal or review, though, by para 11, the specified person can demand written reasons from the Treasury.[250] An application for judicial review would be possible.[251] Challenge may also be mounted on the basis of Article 6 and Article 1 of Protocol 1 under the Human Rights Act 1998.

9.134   The Treasury announced in 2007 that it wished to use closed source evidence and would not object to the use of special advocates.[252] 'Financial restrictions proceedings' (s 65) are now

---

243   Hansard HL vol 629 col 353 (28 November 2001), Lord McIntosh.
244   See further Lennon, G and Walker, C, 'Hot money in a cold climate' [2008] *Public Law* 37.
245   Hansard HL vol 629 col 600 (3 December, 2001), Baroness Symons; Hansard HL vol 629 col 353 (28 November 2001), Lord McIntosh.
246   See Emergency Laws (Re-enactments and Repeals) Act 1964, s 2; Finance Act 1968, s 55.
247   Hansard HL vol 704 col 1054 (21 October 2008).
248   Hansard HC vol 375 col 34 (19 November, 2001), David Blunkett.
249   Hansard HL vol 629 col 362 (28 November 2001), Lord McIntosh.
250   These are qualified by the CTA 2008, s 70, by which disclosures are limited by Pt VI (see below).
251   Hansard HL vol 629 col 1060 (6 December 2001), Lord McIntosh.
252   HM Treasury, *The Financial Challenge to Crime and Terrorism* (London, 2007) para 2.33.

allowed by the CTA 2008, Pt VI, and apply to orders passed before and after the Act. An application to set aside an order may be made (under s 71) to the Queen's Bench Division of the High Court or the Court of Session in Scotland which will apply under s 63(3) the principles of judicial review.[253]

Closed source materials are then handled under the special procedures of Pt VI of the CTA 2008. The prime features are the appointment of special advocates (s 68) and the admission of intercept evidence (s 69). Detailed rules of court are required under s 66, having regard to the need to secure both (a) that the impugned decisions are properly reviewed; and (b) that disclosures of information are not made contrary to the public interest. The ongoing controversy over control order procedures (described in Chapter 7) prompted more detailed guidance for court rules on disclosure under s 67. The Treasury may apply to withhold sensitive material from disclosure. If their application is unsuccessful, the Treasury may elect not to disclose, in which case the court may direct either that the Treasury may not rely on the material or must make such concessions as the court specifies. If the material can be suppressed, the court can still order a summary of the material to be provided. By s 67(6), no rule of court is to be read as requiring the court to act in a manner inconsistent with Article 6 of the European Convention on Human Rights. **9.135**

Part 79 of the Civil Procedure Rules (CPR), Proceedings under the CTA 2008, offers further detail.[254] The overriding objective of achieving justice (CPR 1.1) is modified by the demand under s 66(2) to take account of two predominant interests: the need for a proper review of the decision subject to challenge, and the need to ensure that disclosures are not made where this would be contrary to the public interest (CPR 79.2(2)). It is regrettable that no priority is set between these two interests, but, in the absence of any derogation notice, the courts have demanded that a fundamental level of procedural justice must be observed, even if the effect is to curtail the available evidence which the government is able to adduce.[255] **9.136**

Any application must be started and heard in the Administrative Court (CPR 79.4) and will be followed by a directions hearing within fourteen to twenty-eight days (CPR 79.7). The appointment and functions of the special advocate are covered by CPR 79.18–21.[256] **9.137**

Whether these procedures satisfy the demands of Article 6 will be decided on a case-by-case basis. To take an example, s 67(3)(d) states that 'if permission is given by the court not to disclose material, it must consider requiring the Treasury to provide a summary of the material' to parties. Even if a summary is provided, it may not be enough; if it is not, then objections will surely be raised.[257] **9.138**

Implementation

The power in s 4 rested in obscurity for several years, but its first invocation was spectacular. Prompted by the severe banking crisis in Iceland and a threat by the Icelandic government to leave British depositors at the back of the queue for compensation, the Landsbanki Freezing **9.139**

---

[253] See Hansard HL vol 704 col 1048 (21 October 2008).

[254] For Scotland, see Rules of the Court of Session, ch 96.

[255] *Bank Mellat v HM Treasury* [2010] EWCA Civ 483, citing *Re AF (No 3)* [2009] UKHL 28. Compare Rees, G and Moloney, T, 'The latest efforts to interrupt terrorist supply lines' [2010] *Criminal Law Review* 127 at 134.

[256] This office will be explained in connection with control orders in Chapter 7.

[257] See HC Hansard Public Bill Committee on the Counter-Terrorism Bill, *Memorandum from JUSTICE*, para 108.

Order 2008[258] prevented the British branch of that bank from 'repatriating' assets back to Iceland.[259] The Icelandic Prime Minister, Geir Haarde, complained that Britain had performed an 'unfriendly act'.[260] The Order was revoked in 2009 after an agreement to reimburse the guarantee payments made to British creditors by the United Kingdom government.[261] However, the Icelandic President refused to sign the implementing Bill, and a referendum in March 2010 rejected the deal, resulting in renewed inter-governmental negotiations.

Assessment and conclusions

9.140 Given the breadth of s 4, the Newton Committee recommended that the measures should be translated into the Civil Contingencies Act 2004.[262] The proposal was rejected by the government on the basis that s 4 allowed 'rapid emergency action if and when UK interests are, or could be threatened'.[263]

FATF enforcement by United Kingdom law

Introduction and background

9.141 The role of the FATF has already been outlined. Added as an afterthought as Pt V of the CTA 2008[264] in the form of '23 pages of fresh legislation that is only tangentially related'[265] is a further platform for international financial restrictions which can be applied unilaterally by the United Kingdom government. But there is not the same degree of freedom of action as under Pt II freezing orders since legal action is made dependent on initial advice from the FATF. As happened in 2001, these measures were explained and debated with a lamentable degree of attention, even though they apply beyond terrorism and overlap with the ATCSA 2001 scheme. The rationale is to ensure the rapid translation into law of FATF demands. The Treasury is empowered to direct, regulate, or prohibit transactions by financial and credit institutions with persons in non-EEA countries in order to stop criminal money laundering, terrorist financing, or weapons proliferation. The Schedule then outlines a supervisory regime, including civil and criminal penalties for non-compliance.

9.142 The urgency behind enactment of Pt V, unless simply to avoid close scrutiny, was justified by the government in terms of an FATF statement on 16 October 2008 which warned of the involvement of Iran in terrorism financing and of Uzbekistan in money laundering.[266] However, neither danger was wholly novel, other FATF missives have been ignored,[267] and other regulatory powers already existed to ensure restraints.[268] Possibly, there was US pressure for such action, especially because British banks were being sanctioned for trading with Iran, most notably Lloyds TSB which was fined $350m in 2009.[269]

---

[258] SI 2008/2668, as amended by SI 2008/2766.
[259] See Hansard HL vol 704 col 1548 (28 October 2008); Hansard HC vol 481 col 775w (27 October 2008). Iceland had adopted the EU Directive on Deposit Guarantee Schemes (94/19/EC).
[260] *The Times* (London) 10 October 2008, p 7.
[261] SI 2009/1392. See *The Times* 29 August 2009, p 1.
[262] *Newton Report*, para B20.
[263] *Home Office Response to Newton Report*, paras 12–13.
[264] Hansard HL vol 705 col 576 (11 November 2008).
[265] Ibid col 936 (17 November 2008), Lord Marksford.
[266] Ibid col 577 (11 November 2008), Lord Myners.
[267] Ibid col 587 (11 November 2008), Baroness Miller.
[268] The Money Laundering Regulations 2007, SI2007/2157, were claimed to be too limited (ibid col 578), but no mention was made of the Export Control Act 2002 or sectoral regulatory powers.
[269] See Kittrie, OF, 'New sanctions for a new century' (2009) 30 *University of Pennsylvania Journal of International Law* 789; *Blue Sky One v Mahan Air* [2010] EWHC 631 (Comm).

Provisions

The additional power is introduced by s 62, with copious details in Sch 7. The core conditions **9.143** for the exercise of powers in Sch 7, para 1, are that (a) the FATF has called for measures to be taken against a country because of the risk it presents of money laundering or terrorist financing; (b) the Treasury reasonably believe that a country poses a significant risk to national interests because of the risk of money laundering or terrorist financing there; or (c) the Treasury reasonably believe that a country poses a significant risk to national interests because of involvement with nuclear, radiological, biological, or chemical weapons.

Directions may be issued under para 3 to designated persons in the financial sector (which is **9.144** defined in paras 4 to 7, subject to change by affirmative order) on an individual, categorical, or universal basis.

The contents of directions are delineated by para 9. The Treasury can impose requirements **9.145** or restraints over transactions or relationships with private businesses, governmental bodies, or individual residents. Some of the kinds of directions which may be imposed are set out in paras 10 (customer due diligence), 11 (ongoing monitoring), 12 (systematic reporting), and 13 (limiting or ceasing business). In all instances, the direction must be proportionate to the risks or national interests (para 9(6)). Paragraph 17 allows for the issuance of licences to exempt acts.

The procedures governing directions to all persons in the sector demand issuance by a **9.146** statutory order which must be affirmative if it curtails business transactions; a direction to a particular person need not be contained in an order (para 14). Directions expire after one year (renewable) and notice of directions issued to a particular person should be served on them, while general directions should be publicized (paras 15, 16, and 42).

In the exercise of their functions, enforcement authorities (defined, under s 18, as the **9.147** Financial Services Authority, the Revenue and Customs, the Office of Fair Trading, and the Department of Enterprise, Trade and Investment in Northern Ireland—but not the police) may demand information or documents (para 19), and may enter and inspect with and without warrant (paras 20 and 21). Paragraph 22 seeks to protect legal professional privilege.

Civil penalties may be imposed for default or breach by the enforcement authorities under **9.148** paras 25 to 27, subject to appeal under para 28. Criminal offences for non-compliance or false information are set out in paras 30 and 31, with coverage under paras 32 and 34 of conduct outside the United Kingdom.

As the responsible ministry, the Treasury must report annually to Parliament on their exercise **9.149** of powers (para 38). Enforcement authorities must also take appropriate measures to monitor persons operating in their financial sectors, and the Treasury shall assist by drawing up guidance (paras 39 and 40).

Some minor amendments to these measures are to be made by the Terrorist Asset-Freezing **9.150** etc. Act 2010, Pt II. The Act clarifies the institutional structures within a company which can be affected by a direction (ss 48 and 49) and introduces an offence of circumventing the requirements of a direction (s 50). There is also a transfer to the Treasury of some enforcement functions of the Department of Enterprise, Trade and Investment in Northern Ireland (s 51).

Implementation, assessment, and conclusions

9.151   The Treasury issued a warning about Iran and Uzbekistan in 2009,[270] followed by the Financial Restrictions (Iran) Order 2009.[271] The Order arises from Iran's alleged nuclear weapons programme and affects for one year at first instance the Bank Mellat and the Islamic Republic of Iran Shipping Lines. A challenge to the Order by the Bank Mellat resulted in a ruling that the government has to disclose the gist of the case against the applicant, along the lines specified for control orders (as discussed in Chapter 7) but with the distinction that there must be disclosed sufficient evidence to allow the applicant not just to deny but to refute the basis for the order.[272] This distinguishing line was not explained further, and the procedural rules which apply to these applications (discussed later in this chapter) do allow for closed sessions, the security of which can be rigorously enforced such as by checking the mobile phone of a witness.[273] The subsequent challenge by Bank Mellat to the Order failed; there was no requirement for representations prior to issuance, and the Order was reasonably grounded and proportionate in extent.[274]

9.152   The same criticisms of an absence of constitutional governance can be made about Pt V as were made about the ATCSA 2001. Indeed, the House of Lords' Select Committee on the Constitution[275] picked Pt V as a prime example of the late tabling of amendments nullifying the input of legislators and public experts. The lack of transparency of the FATF itself deepens the disapproval.

Al-Qa'ida and Taliban listings

9.153   Moving into the financial sanctions which are more fully controlled by international organizations, the process began with the UNSCR 1267 on 15 October 1999.[276] The sanctions included: an arms embargo; the closure of Taliban (non-diplomatic) offices overseas; the closure of Afghan flights, and a freeze on Taliban funds. UNSCR 1333 of 19 December 2000 added a travel ban on Taliban officials and restrictions on the financial assets of bin Laden and listed associates. Some of the governmental restrictions began to be lifted by UNSCRs 1388 and 1390 of 15 and 16 January 2002. At the same time, UNSCR 1390 imposed a more general travel ban.[277] However, implementation of travel bans has faltered because of inadequate border security,[278] and so by mid-2007, just eighteen listed individuals had been extradited, expelled, deported, or repatriated from one state to another.[279] Interpol has

---

[270] See <http://www.hm-treasury.gov.uk/press_26_09.htm>.

[271] SI 2009/2725. Note also the Iran (Financial Sanctions) Order 2007, SI 2007/281 (under the United Nations Act 1946); EU Regulations 423/2007, 1110/2008, 961/2010; Iran (European Communities Financial Sanctions) Regulations 2007, SI 2007/1374 and 2010, SI 2010/2613. Bank Mellat was listed in the US under EO 13382 in 2007.

[272] *Bank Mellat v HM Treasury* [2010] EWCA Civ 483 at para 21.

[273] *Bank Mellat v HM Treasury* [2010] EWHC 498 (QB).

[274] *Bank Mellat v HM Treasury* [2010] EWHC 1332 (QB).

[275] *Fast-track Legislation* (2008–09 HL 116–I) paras 100, 101.

[276] UNSCR 1267. See Legal Department of the IMF, *Suppressing the Financing of Terrorism: A Handbook for Legislative Drafting* (IMF, Washington DC, 2003) p 22.

[277] *Third Report of the Monitoring Group* (S/2002/1338, 17 December 2002), para 53; *First Report of the Monitoring Team* (S/2004/679, 25 August 2004) para 71; *Third Report of the Monitoring Team* (S/2005/572, 9 September 2005) para 122. See Betti, S, 'A member of al Qaida shows up at your border' (2009) 17 *European Journal of Crime, Criminal Law and Criminal Justice* 23.

[278] *Ninth Report of the Analytical Support and Sanctions Monitoring Team* (S/2009/245, 13 May 2009) para 73.

[279] *Seventh Report of the Monitoring Team* (S/2007/677, 20 November 2007) para 91.

sought to assist in this effort since 2005 by issuing INTERPOL-United Nations Security Council Special Notices to police.[280]

9.154 By way of financial implementation, there is the Al-Qaida and Taliban Sanctions Committee (the 1267 Committee)[281] which is supported by an expert Analytical Support and Sanctions Monitoring Team.[282] The 1267 Committee can designate or de-list persons at the request of governments,[283] and governments are obliged by UNSCR 1455 of 17 January 2003 to notify the Committee of persons against whom national action has been taken or persons known to be involved with Al-Qa'ida or the Taliban. The Committee does not appraise the information, and the process is held in private, without notice, disclosure, or reasoned decisions being provided.[284] UNSCR 1452 of 20 December 2002 modified the enforcement regime so that individual states can administer exemptions for living expenses, so long as the 1267 Committee is informed.[285] The UNSCR 1617 of 29 July 2005 demands from states fuller statements for proposed listings and clearer identification of subjects.

9.155 These diplomatic processes are wholly unsuitable for the fair treatment of individuals. Working guidelines in November 2002 invited listed individuals to petition their government of residence or citizenship to request a review. But the government has no obligation to support the petition, and the 1267 Committee requires consensus. Following official criticism,[286] the Security Council agreed that, instead of listed persons having to lobby their own governments to take up their case with the 1267 Committee, UNSCR 1730 of 19 December 2006 establishes a de-listing procedure whereby those listed may petition the Committee, though there is still no right of appearance or disclosure. UNSCR 1735 of 22 December 2006 specifies the procedures and forms that states must complete for proposals and notification. All orders must be reviewed, if not already reviewed within three years, but few de-listings have been secured.[287]

9.156 The Analytical Support and Sanctions Monitoring Team has expressed alarm that the mounting level of review will disturb the sensitive sharing of information.[288] Its preferred reforms include (a) a quasi-judicial review panel; (b) an ombudsman; or (c) review by the Monitoring Team.[289] The Office of Ombudsperson was established by UNSCR 1904 of 17 December 2009, art 20, to assist with de-listing requests and to liaise with affected individuals and entities. As for the quasi-judicial panel, the intervention by national and regional courts is now established and offers more convenience and likely rigour as to disclosure, evidence, and proof.

---

[280] See S/1699/2006; <http://www.interpol.int/public/NoticesUN/Default.asp>.

[281] <http://www.un.org/sc/committees/1267/index.shtml>.

[282] UNSCR 1526 of 30 January 2004. It replaced an earlier Monitoring Group (UNSCR 1363 of 30 July 2001). The system was affirmed by UNSCR 1822 of 30 June 2008. See <http://www.un.org/Docs/sc/committees/1267/1267mg.htm>.

[283] See 1267 Committee, Guidelines of the Committee for the Conduct of its Work (<http://www.un.org/sc/committees/1267/pdf/1267_guidelines.pdf>, 2002–07).

[284] See Radicati di Brocolo, LG and Meghani, M, 'Freezing the assets of international terrorist organisations' in Bianchi, A, *Enforcing International Norms Against Terrorism* (Hart, Oxford, 2004) p 398.

[285] Many states do not comply: *Tenth Report of the Analytical Support and Sanctions Monitoring Team* (S/2009/502, 2 October 2009) para 55.

[286] Fassbender, B, *Targeted Sanctions and Due Process* (United Nations Office of Legal Affairs, New York, 2006). See also S/2005/83 and S/2005/572.

[287] UNSCR 1888, 30 September 2009. By 30 July 2010, 443 out of 488 entries had been renewed. A specific review of listed deceased individuals is ongoing under UNSCR 1904, 17 December 2009.

[288] *Ninth Report* (S/2009/245, 2009) para 22.

[289] *Tenth Report* (S/2009/502, 2009) para 39.

General international listings

9.157   Responding to the events of 11 September 2001, the UNSCR 1373 of 28 September 2001[290] demands that states should curtail terrorism financing and sets up a Counter-Terrorism Committee to chivvy state action. Its remit is not confined to terrorism finance, and so it implements a wider remit of encouraging compliance with other international conventions and measures against terrorism.[291] The breadth of this promulgation has been problematic. There is a lack of clarity as to its focus, and so some states have abused their powers by directing anti-terrorism measures against political dissenters.[292] Attempts have since been made to improve state observance by the setting up under UNSCR 1535 of 26 March 2004 of a Counter-Terrorism Committee Executive Directorate which deals with capacity-building, inspections, and advice.

9.158   As for abuses of counter-terrorism activity, UNSCR 1456 of 20 January 2003 reiterated the need for states to enforce international law against terrorism but also reminded them of their obligations in international human rights, refugee, and humanitarian law. UNSCR 1617 of 29 July 2005 offers some guidelines on the degree of affiliation to the Taliban or Al-Qa'ida. UNSCR 1566 of 8 October 2004, albeit long after state legislation had been put in place, provided in art 3 a wide definition of terrorism. UNSCR 1566 also called for the creation of a working group to inflate the listing system beyond UNSCR 1267. In the event, no consensus was reached in the working group as to an expanded listing system.[293] For more general oversight the UN Commission on Human Rights Resolution 2005/80 appointed the Special Rapporteur on the promotion and protection of human rights and fundamental freedoms while countering terrorism.[294]

European Union measures

UNSCR 1267 in European Union law

9.159   Added to this complex picture, the European Union has underwritten the international obligations under UNSCR 1267 so as to ensure consistency in application. In practice the listings are precisely copied across as a 'mandatory duty'.[295] There are two tiers of implementation under Article 301 of the European Community Treaty. First, the Council issues a decision to take action under the Second Pillar (Common Foreign and Security Policy), then there is direct enforcement under a First Pillar Community Regulation, with national measures being necessary for criminal sanction. Thus, Council Common Position 1999/727/CFSP of 15 November 1999 specified that UNSCR 1267 should be implemented in EU law.[296] The details were delivered in Council Regulation (EC) 337/2000 of

---

[290] See Legal Department of the IMF, *Suppressing the Financing of Terrorism: A Handbook for Legislative Drafting* (IMF, Washington DC, 2003) p 14; Counter-Terrorism Committee Executive Directorate, *Technical Guide to the Implmentation of Security Council Resolution 1373 (2001)* (New York, 2009).

[291] For example, UNSCR 1624, 14 September 2005, para 6. See Biersteker, TJ et al, 'International initiatives to combat the financing of terrorism' in Biersteker, TJ and Eckert, SE (eds), *Countering the Financing of Terrorism* (Routledge, London, 2008).

[292] Scheinin, M, *Reports of the Special Rapporteur on the promotion and protection of human rights and fundamental freedoms while countering terrorism* (E/CN.4/2006/98, 2005) para 63; Marschik, A, 'The Security Council's role' in Nesi, G (ed), *International Co-operation in Counter-Terrorism* (Ashgate, Aldershot, 2006).

[293] See S/2005/789, para 34.

[294] The Rapporteur has called for the replacement of existing resolutions: A/65/259, 6 August 2010.

[295] Case T-306/01, *R, Aden and others v Council and Commission* [2002] ECR II-2387, para 70. See further Eckes, C, *EU Counter-Terrorist Policies and Fundamental Rights: The Case of Individual Sanctions* (Oxford University Press, Oxford, 2009) ch 5.

[296] See also 2001/154/CFSP.

14 February 2000 which allowed for the freezing of the assets of entities designated by the 1267 Sanctions Committee. A Council Regulation (EC) 467/2001 of 6 March 2001 implemented UNSCR 1333 and replaced Council Regulation (EC) 337/2000. In turn, Council Regulation (EC) 881/2002 of 27 May 2002 implemented UNSCR 1390 (2002) and replaced Council Regulation (EC) 467/2001.[297]

Under Council Regulation (EC) 881/2002, 'funds' means financial assets and economic **9.160** benefits of every kind while 'economic resources' means assets of every kind, whether tangible or intangible, movable or immovable, which are not funds but can be used to obtain funds, goods, or services (art 1). These assets and resources of designated persons or groups can be frozen under art 2. No funds must then be made available, and military assets or training are forbidden under art 3. National authorities should be willing to share information (arts 5 and 8). By Council Regulation (EC) 561/2003 and following UNSCR 1452, art 2a was inserted in Regulation (EC) 881/2002 in order to disapply freezing orders where any of the competent authorities of the Member States has decided to allow access to funds or resources on the basis that they are (i) necessary to cover basic expenses; (ii) intended exclusively for payment of reasonable professional fees and reimbursement of incurred expenses associated with the provision of legal services; (iii) intended exclusively for payment of fees or service charges for the routine holding or maintenance of frozen funds or frozen economic resources; or (iv) necessary for extraordinary expenses.

UNSCR 1373 in European law

The European Union has chosen to bolster UNSCR 1373 autonomously, beginning with **9.161** Council Common Position 2001/931/CFSP, which required a further listing and asset freezing system to address terrorism extending beyond the borders of one member state, leaving national authorities alone to deal with local terrorism.[298] For these purposes, an extensive definition of 'terrorism' is adopted in Article 1(3), dependent on specified intentional acts, in the context of a structured terrorist group. The listing under Article 1(4) should be based on 'precise information or material in the relevant file which indicates that a decision has been taken by a competent authority', but it is not demanded that 'competent authority' shall always mean a judicial authority. As with UNSCR 1267, the Common Foreign and Security Policy listings are political declarations as to future action. They do not entail direct legal impact in terms of freezing assets, but there is evident stigma from listing, the practical detriment of being subject to operational scrutiny under the Third Pillar, and little judicial protection.[299] To allay complaints, especially from those who are not subjected to subsequent regulatory action, the 'Working Party on implementation of Common Position 2001/931/CFSP on the application of specific measures to combat terrorism' (CP 931 Working Party) was established in 2007 to provide a less political setting for examination of proposals for listings and de-listings.[300] But the final decision (which must be unanimous) still rests with the Council in secret session and without consulting the European Parliament. There is a review every six months, but it relates to the entire list which makes an individual amendment 'unpalatable'.[301]

---

[297] For differences from earlier regulations, see Case T-253/02, *Ayadi v Council* [2006] ECR II-2139).

[298] See also 2001/930/CPSP, 27 December 2001.

[299] See Case C-354/04P, *Gestoras Pro Amnistía v Council of the European Union* 27 February 2007); Case C-355/04, *Segi v Council* [2007] ECR I-1657.

[300] Council Document 10826/07, 21 June 2007.

[301] Hansard HL vol 703 col 1651 (22 July 2008), Lord Malloch-Brown. See further Case T-284/08, *Organisation des Modjahedines du Peuple d'Iran v Council* 4 December 2008.

9.162   Since the list is not intended to duplicate those covered by UNSCR 1267[302] and since no listing is specified under UNSCR 1373 itself, the subjects of CFSP decisions[303] have rehearsed a mixture of familiar European terrorist groups, including specified Irish organizations, Basque groups, a range of Leftist revolutionaries from Greece (including Revolutionary Organisation 17 November) and Italy (including the Brigate Rosse), plus international groups with a presence in Europe such as Hamas-Izz al-Din al-Qassem, Palestinian Islamic Jihad, European-based Islamist groups, the International Sikh Youth Federation, the LTTE, the PKK, and the Peruvian Sendero Luminoso.

9.163   Those listed should present a threat to the European Community and beyond the borders of one member state in order to fall within European competence under Articles 60, 301, and 308.[304] However, there is no published fact-finding by which the threats are established in Council. The list is compiled following private (secret) discussions in Council.[305] Article 3 goes on to impose a general duty to ensure that funds, financial assets, or economic resources or financial or other related services will not be made available to those on the list. Article 4 demands mutual cooperation between member states.

9.164   Full enforcement of the European scheme is imparted by Council Regulation (EC) 2580/2001 of 27 December 2001.[306] It covers, by art 1(1), 'Funds, other financial assets and economic resources', but the definition of terrorism is as given in the Common Position 2001/931/CFSP. The list is compiled on nomination by a state's 'Competent Authority' (HM Treasury) or a third state (through the President),[307] the CFSP instrument constituting a prerequisite for adoption. Once someone is listed, all funds should be frozen, and no funds or financial services shall be provided (art 2). Circumvention must be prohibited (art 3), and financial institutions must pass on information to enable the enforcement of the regulations (art 4). Sanctions for breach should be 'effective, proportionate and dissuasive' (art 9). Applications may be made under art 6 to unfreeze all or part of the funds, and any grant should be notified to other member states, the Council, and the Commission. Orders may also be challenged under art 230, and art 238 might found an application for damages.

9.165   As at 12 July 2010,[308] twenty-five persons and twenty-seven entities were listed with reference to Council Regulation (EC) 2580/2001, a much shorter compendium than that for Common Foreign and Security Policy purposes and not including specified Irish organizations.

European Union law litigation about international listings

9.166   These European systems have provoked much litigation. Under UNSCR 1267, a person can apply to a national authority to ask it to request a 'specific authorisation' to unfreeze. If the national authority rejects the application, there are two possibilities for legal action: challenge under Article 230(4) of Treaty of Rome, provided the regulation or decision can be viewed as of 'direct and individual concern';[309] or challenge under national law against the state on

---

[302]   But overlap occurs: *A, K, M, Q and G v HM Treasury* [2008] EWHC 869 (Admin) at para 1.
[303]   The latest statement is 2009/1004/CFSP.
[304]   Doubts about competence are allayed by the Lisbon Treaty, Arts 75, 215.
[305]   But a 'national substratum' of scrutiny is required: T-348/07, *Stitching Al-Aqsa v Council*, 9 September 2010.
[306]   See Eckes, C, *EU Counter-Terrorist Policies and Fundamental Rights: The Case of Individual Sanctions* (Oxford University Press, Oxford, 2009) ch 6.
[307]   See for the latest (EU) 610/2010 (12 July 2010).
[308]   Ibid.
[309]   The Lisbon Treaty, Art 230(4) requires that the regulatory act be of direct concern but not necessarily individual concern.

human rights grounds or even against the financial institution which holds the money and refuses to pay over, leaving the bank to defend by reference to the European Regulation. There have been many challenges under the first procedure.[310]

The European Court of Justice recognizes that the Council has broad competence but is not **9.167** allowed to make a 'manifest error' of fact[311] or to disregard fundamental rights. The key decision on the latter, arising from a European listing in pursuance of UNSCR 1267, was delivered by the Grand Chamber of the Court of Justice in *Kadi and Al Barakaat International Foundation v Council of the EU*.[312] The Court asserted that even the faithful implementation of UNSCR 1267 may not contradict European law constitutional principles, which include respect for fundamental rights.[313] The following reasons were cited: that the Community was based on the rule of law, and the basic constitutional charter in this case was the EC Treaty; that United Nations resolutions could not affect the exclusive jurisdiction of the Court or the autonomy of the Community legal system; that respect for human rights was a condition of the lawfulness of Community acts; and that a finding against a Community measure implementing a UNSCR did not challenge the primacy of that resolution in international law. Therefore, the fundamental rights inherent in the lawfulness of Community acts rather than just *jus cogens*, the line taken by the Court of First Instance, came into play. Such rights include the right to an effective hearing, the right to a remedy before a court, and the right to property. All had been breached by the Council, which had neither communicated to the appellants the evidence invoked against them nor effectively allowed them to be heard. Equally, the right to property had been infringed since the freezing order was a disproportionate interference. The result was an annulment, subject to a stay for three months to allow the Council to remedy the defects. The Council is placed in a quandary when listing is at the secretive behest of a national government (not necessarily European) and the Security Council.

Due process rights have also been applied to the European Union listings and procedures **9.168** pursuant to UNSCR 1373, which are in any event more autonomous. Though not a criminal process within Article 6, decisions as to listing and the procedures have also been found to be wanting.[314]

The Council has formalized its procedures in response to these strictures by providing a **9.169** statement of reasons to affected parties and inviting representations (but not a hearing), but these processes are also subject to challenge. Following its successful challenge under previous procedures, the People's Mojahedin Organization of Iran has successfully applied to set aside

---

[310] See Almqvist, J, 'A human rights critique of European judicial review: counter-terrorism sanctions' (2008) 57 *International & Comparative Law Quarterly* 303; Eckes, C, *EU Counter-Terrorist Policies and Fundamental Rights: The Case of Individual Sanctions* (Oxford University Press, Oxford, 2009); Cardwell, PJ et al, 'European Court of Justice' (2009) 58 *International & Comparative Law Quarterly* 299.

[311] Case T-228/02, *Organisation des Modjahedines du Peuple d'Iran v Council* 12 December 2006, para 159. See also Cases T-157/07, T-256/07, 23 October 2008; T-284/08, 4 December 2008.

[312] Cases T-315/01, 21 September 2005, C-402/05, 415/05, 3 September 2008, [2008] ECR I-6351. The attempt to reimpose listing was struck down in T-85/09, 30 September 2010.

[313] Cases C-402/05, 415/05, 3 September 2008 at paras 348, 349, 352, 370. On retrospectivity, see Case C-550/09, *Reference from the Oberlandesgericht Dusseldorf* 29 June 2010.

[314] See Cases T-228/02, *Organisation des Modjahedines du Peuple d'Iran v Council* 12 December 2006, T-157/07, T-256/07, 23 October 2008, T-284/08, 4 December 2008; Case T-327/03, *Stichting al-Asqa v Council* 11 July 2007; Cases C-229/05, *Ocalan, Kurdistan Workers Party (PKK) and Kurdistan National Congress (KNK) v Council* 18 January 2007, T-229/02, 15 February 2005, 3 April 2008; Case T-253/04, *Kongra-Gel v Council* 3 April 2008.

its listing on grounds that, while rights of defence were sufficiently observed, insufficient reasons were given for its continued outlawry in the light of the lifting of the United Kingdom national ban by the Proscribed Organisations Appeals Commission.[315] Likewise, in *Sison v Council of the European Union*,[316] Sison, who was listed for involvement in the Philippines Communist Party, secured the annulment of his listing in 2007, whereupon the Council adopted a new decision to freeze his assets. The Court of Justice annulled the further listing, demanding that there should be divulged 'actual and specific reasons'[317] with a judicial review on the basis of 'serious and credible evidence' and not just the legality of the decision, while the Council should act on 'precise information or material'.[318]

United Kingdom implementation

9.170 The domestic implementation of UNSCRs 1267 and 1373 has also operated separately. But United Kingdom implementation is not a mirror image of United Nations or European Union listings since there is a power of independent action under the implementation of UNSCR 1373.

Initial enforcement of UNSCRs 1267 and 1373

9.171 UNSCR 1267 was primarily implemented under the United Nations Act 1946, s 1, initially by the Afghanistan (United Nations Sanctions) Orders of 1999 and 2001,[319] and then by the Al-Qaida and Taliban (United Nations Measures) Orders 2002 and 2006.[320] Affected persons or organizations comprised those designated by the Sanctions Committee or anyone designated by a Treasury direction based on reasonable grounds for suspecting. The 2002 Order restricted the supply and export of restricted goods.[321] Restrictions on funding and economic resources of specified designated persons were set out in the 2006 Order.

9.172 The UK government reacted to UNSCR 1373 by the passage of the Terrorism (United Nations Measures) Order 2001,[322] issued under the authority of the United Nations Act 1946, a basis selected because of doubts about European Union competency. The European-led aspects began to be implemented by the Terrorism (United Nations Measures) Order 2001 (Amendment) Regulations 2003,[323] under the authority of s 2(2) of the European Communities Act 1972. There was an attempt to consolidate these two strands by the Terrorism (United Nations Measures) Order 2006, issued under the United Nations Act 1946.[324] The Terrorism (United Nations Measures) Order 2009[325] in turn replaced the 2006 Order in order to amend some details, to respond to case law, and to allow for future changes of European regulations (as specified by the Legislative and Regulatory Reform Act 2006, s 28). The 2006 Order thus affected designated persons as identified either by European Council Regulation (in other words, Regulation 2580/2001) or by a unilateral Treasury direction

---

[315] Cases T-157/07, T-256/07, *People's Mojahedin Organization of Iran v Council* 23 October 2008.
[316] Case T-341/07, 30 September 2009.
[317] Ibid para 60.
[318] Ibid para 93.
[319] SI 1999/3133; SI 2001/396 and 2557. Regulation (EC) 881/2002 is directly enforceable, aside from criminal sanctions *R (M) v HM Treasury* [2006] EWHC (Admin) 2328 at para 41.
[320] SI 2002/111, 251; SI 2006/2952. See Hansard HC vol 450 col 11WS (10 October 2006).
[321] See Export Control (Security and Para-military Goods) Order 2006, SI 2006/1696.
[322] SI 2001/3365.
[323] SI 2003/1297. See further the amending orders at SI 2003/2209, SI 2003/2430, SI 2004/2309, SI 2005/1525.
[324] SI 2006/2657.
[325] SI 2009/747. See also the consequential amendments at SI 2009/1912.

(limited to twelve months). The list was not intended to duplicate those covered by UNSCR 1267, but there was some duplication.[326]

Some of the procedural deficiencies at domestic level, remedies for which were promised in 2006,[327] were belatedly addressed for both schemes by 'Financial restrictions proceedings' (s 65) under the CTA 2008, Pt VI.[328] An application to set aside financial restrictions under the United Nations Orders (defined by s 64)[329] can be made under s 63. These procedures were described earlier in this chapter. Their ability to deliver due process remains problematic in the context of UNSCR 1267 listings. In *HM Treasury v Ahmed* (described below),[330] there was recognition that United Nations UNSCRs might take precedence over European Convention obligations, perhaps subject to *jus cogens* norms.[331] **9.173**

Post-2006 litigation

The restraints on listing were held to be 'deliberately draconian' in *R (M) v HM Treasury*.[332] In that case, the female partners of the listed persons encountered problems from curtailed access to social benefits for themselves and their children. The Treasury did issue a licence for these exceptional payments,[333] but the claimants sought to avoid the scheme altogether. The House of Lords made a preliminary reference to the European Court of Justice,[334] whereupon the latter ruled that social welfare benefits paid to a partner were not within the remit of Regulation 881/2002, art 2a, even if there is indirect benefit to a listed person.[335] The European Court of Justice viewed the objective of the Regulation as being the interdiction of economic resources which could be used to support terrorist activities,[336] so passive or reflected benefit alone was not enough. **9.174**

In the meantime, further complaints, in *A, K, M, Q, and G v HM Treasury*,[337] produced wholesale condemnation in the High Court on grounds of breach of the fundamental principles of European Union law, disproportionality in comparison to UNSCR 1373, and also *ultra vires* the parent United Nations Act 1946 since the Order was not 'necessary and expedient'. The Court of Appeal reversed in part, with Lord Justice Sedley in dissent. The Order implementing UNSCR 1373 was only *ultra vires* in so far as it allowed Treasury designation of those who 'may be' involved in terrorism.[338] However, procedural safeguards could be sufficiently achieved on a case-by-case basis,[339] and the criminal sanctions under Articles 7 and 8 were also adequately certain and proportionate, including by the licensing scheme under Art 11 and the operation of the *de minimis* principle.[340] On similar reasoning, the 1267 Order and the designation under it were also upheld, though only by implying a 'merits based review'.[341] **9.175**

---

[326] See *A, K, M, Q and G v HM Treasury* [2008] EWHC 869 (Admin) at para 1.
[327] See Hansard HC vol 450 col 11ws (10 October 2006).
[328] Hansard HL vol 704 col 1048 (21 October 2008).
[329] The Financial Restrictions Proceedings (UN Terrorism Orders) Order 2009, SI 2009/1911, specifies the Terrorism (United Nations Measures) Order 2009 for these purposes.
[330] [2010] UKSC 2 at para 71. See also *R (al-Jedda) v Secretary of State for Defence* [2007] UKHL 58.
[331] Ibid para 151. See Qureshi, K, 'A major first' (2010) 160 *New Law Journal* 423
[332] [2006] EWHC (Admin) 2328 at para 64. See also [2007] EWCA Civ 173, [2C
[333] For differences in wording, see [2006] EWHC (Admin) 2328 at paras 48–50.
[334] [2008] UKHL 28.
[335] Case C-340/88, *M(FC) v HM Treasury* 14 January 2010.
[336] Ibid para 56.
[337] [2008] EWHC 869 (Admin), [2008] EWCA Civ 1187.
[338] [2008] EWCA Civ 1187 at para 53.
[339] Ibid para 78.
[340] Ibid paras 87–101.
[341] Ibid paras 119, 121.

CASES (handwritten)

9.176   Another designation under the 1267 Order was, however, condemned in *Hay v HM Treasury*.[342] The applicant, an Egyptian, had been listed by the 1267 Committee on the request of another country which the Foreign & Commonwealth Office sought to remove. The result was that there was no effective access to the United Kingdom courts for challenging the listing, and such a scheme was held to be *ultra vires* the 1946 Act since it interfered with fundamental rights without express Parliamentary authority.

9.177   The appeal from *A, K, M, Q, and G v HM Treasury* reached the UK Supreme Court in *HM Treasury v Ahmed*.[343] Three of the appellants had been listed under the Terrorism (United Nations Measures) Order 2006 (based on UNSCR 1373); two were named in the Consolidated list under UNSCR 1267 and so were automatically listed under the Al-Qaida and Taliban (United Nations Measures) Order 2006 (as it was then) even though HM Treasury was actively seeking the de-listing of one them (Hay) who had been selected by another government. The Supreme Court accepted that these Orders were *ultra vires* the United Nations Act 1946, s 1, because of the absence of express Parliamentary approval for them as 'necessary or expedient'. The Terrorism (United Nations Measures) Order 2006 was condemned because it was not based on any detailed system of United Nations listing but nevertheless inflicted grave intrusions into the fundamental rights of property, family, and due process. Some judges viewed the Order as an unwarranted departure from UNSCR 1373 by relying upon a lowly standard of reasonable suspicion as the basis for the decision to freeze. As a result, the whole of the Terrorism (United Nations Measures) Order 2006 was quashed, and there were firm indications that the same would apply to the Terrorism (United Nations Measures) Order 2009 which had replaced the 2009 Order during the currency of the litigation. The Al-Qaida and Taliban (United Nations Measures) Order 2006 was viewed as faithful to the mandatory requirements of UNSCR 1267 and so was not quashed in its entirety, but the process for listing and the absence of effective legal challenge were so unfair that the treatment of the appellants had been unlawful.

9.178   The Court was conscious of its overt challenge to government policy and, as in the *Belmarsh* judgment in 2004, raised the constitutional shield of the protection of democracy rather than asserting judicial superiority per se. In summary, Lord Phillips was keen to assert that 'Nobody should conclude that the result of these appeals constitutes judicial interference with the will of Parliament. On the contrary it upholds the supremacy of Parliament in deciding whether or not measures should be imposed that affect the fundamental rights of those in this country.'[344] Lord Hope ventured a more sweeping assertion that 'Even in the face of the threat of international terrorism, the safety of the people is not the supreme law. We must be just as careful to guard against unrestrained encroachments on personal liberty.'[345]

9.179   One consequential matter was a challenge to the anonymity of the applicants made in *Re Guardian News and Media*.[346] It was decided that by suppressing their names in pursuance of privacy and family interests, the courts unduly denied the public information which is relevant to debate about the merits of the freezing order system, and the press were 'being

---

[342] [2009] EWHC 1677 (Admin).

[343] [2010] UKSC 2. See Qureshi, K, 'A major first' (2010) 160 *New Law Journal* 423.

[344] Ibid para 157. But note that Parliament had chosen not to react to the call for primary legislation by the *Newton Report*, para 149.

[345] Ibid para 6.

[346] [2010] UKSC 1.

prevented from publishing a complete account of an important public matter'.[347] Those rights to expression outweighed privacy, especially because of the speculative degree of the accusations.[348]

Another consequential issue concerned the impact of the judgment. A further HM Treasury **9.180** application to postpone the application of the quashing order for six or eight weeks (from the original judgment of 28 January 2010) was rejected (on 4 February 2010), subject to the dissent of Lord Hope.[349] The Orders were void *ab initio* (giving rise also to potential compensation claims), and that legal effect should not become obfuscated. This second judgment placed the government under the whip to respond, especially as Lord Rodger had described the CTA 2008, Pt VI procedure as a 'palliative'.[350]

Legislation in 2010

The first legislative response was the Terrorist Asset-Freezing (Temporary Provisions) Act **9.181** 2010, which was introduced in the House of Commons on 5 February 2010 and passed four days later. This fast-track process prevented, on the one hand, the removal of assets or access to fresh assets and, on the other hand, allowed new orders to be made. Radical amendments were all rejected, including the adoption of procedures akin to control orders whereby a ministerial order would have to be confirmed by the High Court within a month. The Attorney General was determined that freezing orders must remain a bastion of executive action.[351] Equally, reliance upon alternative tactics such as control orders and forfeiture of cash was not enough; control orders cannot affect third parties and forfeiture requires a higher degree of proof. Freezing via the ATCSA 2001, Pt II, is confined to foreign based threats.

The Terrorist Asset-Freezing (Temporary Provisions) Act 2010 ensures by s 1 that the **9.182** Terrorism (United Nations Measures) Orders 2001, 2006, and 2009 (as well as actions taken under them under s 2, such as by financial institutions) are deemed to have validity under the 1946 Act from 4 February until 31 December 2010. Independent grounds of challenge are preserved under s 2(4) and (5). The start date does not avert the possibility of a claim for breach of rights beforehand; it also means that there was a period from 27 January to 4 February when no lawful restraint applied, though whether this was apparent to asset owners is another matter.[352] The end date allowed for more permanent and comprehensive legislation to be forthcoming. Aside from these dates, there was much antagonism about the 'reasonable suspicion' standard for designation. Though no standard is set out in UNSCR 1373, the government claimed that its formula was endorsed by the FATF.[353] In fact, there is discretion under FATF guidelines which allow designation 'based on reasonable grounds, or a reasonable basis to suspect or believe'.[354] The Act applies to the whole of the United Kingdom, but only s 1 is applied to the British Islands and territories (s 3) because of the limited impact of the UK Supreme Court judgment.

---

[347] Ibid paras 69, 73.
[348] Ibid paras 58, 78.
[349] *HM Treasury v Ahmed* [2010] UKSC 5.
[350] [2010] UKSC 2 at para 174.
[351] Hansard HL vol 717 col 671 (9 February 2010), Baroness Scotland.
[352] Lord Myners wrongly claimed that the Supreme Court judgment impacted from 4 February: Hansard HL vol 717 col 629 (9 February 2010). The same point is reflected in HM Treasury, *Publication in Draft of the Terrorist Asset-Freezing Bill* (Cm 7806, London, 2010) para 8.
[353] Hansard HC vol 505 col 713 (8 February 2010), Sarah McCarthy-Fry.
[354] FATF, *International Best Practices: Freezing of Terrorist Assets* (2009) para 18.

9.183 No mention is made in the Terrorist Asset-Freezing (Temporary Provisions) Act 2010 of the impugned Order pursuant to UNSCR 1267. It was not quashed entirely, and the European Communities Act 1972, s 2(2), provided an alternative mode of enforcement,[355] though the European Regulations require national backing on criminal sanctions so a new Order was required.[356] Consequently, two months later, the Al-Qaida and Taliban (Asset Freezing) Regulations 2010[357] replaced the Al-Qaida and Taliban (United Nations Measures) Order 2006. Since the United Nations Act 1946 was deemed an inadequate parent, the 2010 Regulations emanate from the European Communities Act 1972, s 2(2), and so are wholly dependent on the enforcement of Regulation 881/2002.

9.184 Under the 2010 Order, reg 2 defines a designated person as any person named in Annex I to the Council. Unlike under the 2006 Order, there is no independent action allowed under this measure—any non-European listing would have to take the UNSCR 1373 pathway. Attending to the issue of enforcement, regs 3 and 4 provide that an offence is committed where a person contravenes the prohibitions, while r 6 includes an offence of circumvention. Because the Order is European-based, the maximum penalty has been reduced from seven to two years' imprisonment (r 10) in line with the European Communities Act 1972, s 1(1)(d). Exceptions to the prohibitions are provided by r 5 in line with the Council Regulation, including interest and payments due under contracts and prior obligations. Licensing to enable funds and economic resources to be exempted from the prohibitions is allowed under r 7, and in practice, the Treasury will seek to exercise some flexibility for the sake of family members so that there is 'very little, if any impairment' of their rights.[358] Schedule 1 provides powers for the Treasury to obtain and disclose information. Schedule 2 ensures that a person affected can avail themselves of legal challenge under s 63 of the CTA 2008, though there may be recourse also to the European Court of Justice regarding the listing.

9.185 This fruit of the *Ahmed* decision confirms that the judges may have done the right thing for the wrong people. The hope that Parliament would apply effective scrutiny was forlorn. There was forty minutes of debate on the affirmative 2010 Order in a House of Lords Grand Committee and thirty-six minutes in the Delegated Legislation Committee in the Commons but none on the floor of the House.[359]

9.186 The next upshot of the *Ahmed* decision was the Terrorist Asset-Freezing Bill, issued on 5 February 2010 as a draft for pre-legislative scrutiny,[360] and designed to replace the Terrorist Asset-Freezing (Temporary Provisions) Act 2010 and the respective Orders relevant to UNSCR 1373. The title directs the measures towards 'terrorists' which reflects that, though entities may also be addressed under UNSCR 1373, the United Kingdom-initiated practice has selected only individuals, leaving proscription or cash forfeiture to deal more readily with groups. The second version of the draft Bill was presented to Parliament in March 2010[361] and was passed as the Terrorist Asset-Freezing etc. Act 2010.[362] Since the scheme depends on UNSCR 1373,

---

[355] Hansard HC vol 488 col 54ws (27 February 2009).
[356] Hansard HC vol 505 col 663 (8 February 2010), Liam Byrne.
[357] SI 2010/1197.
[358] See *R (K) v HM Treasury* [2009] EWHC 1643 (Admin) para 63.
[359] Hansard HL vol 718 col 452GC (25 March 2010); Hansard HC Delegated Legislation Committee (30 March 2010), vol 508 col 942 (6 April 2010).
[360] HM Treasury, *Publication in Draft of the Terrorist Asset-Freezing Bill* (Cm 7806, London, 2010).
[361] HM Treasury, *Public Consultation: Draft Terrorist Asset-Freezing Bill* (Cm 7852, London, 2010).
[362] The 'etc.' was added because of Pt II: Hansard HL vol 720 col 1285 (27 July 2010).

HM Treasury may by s 47 lay an order to repeal Pt I should the resolution be repealed. Part II has already been considered. The legislation extends to the whole United Kingdom under s 53; s 54 allows application by Order to the British Islands and overseas territories, but the temporary legislation is also extended to 31 March 2011 to allow instead for local legislation.

Part I of the Terrorist Asset-Freezing etc. Act 2010 deals with designation. Under s 1, 'designated persons' are those who are designated on the initiative of HM Treasury or are listed under Article 2(3) of Council Regulation 2580/2001. Designation by HM Treasury is controlled by ss 2 and 6, and may arise in two steps. A final designation order can be issued under s 2 where there are reasonable grounds for believing (a) that the person is or has been involved in terrorist activity, and (b) that it is considered necessary for purposes connected with protecting members of the public from terrorism that financial restrictions should be applied in relation to the person. When required by circumstances, an interim order may be issued under s 6, and only reasonable suspicion of (a) and (b), akin to arrest powers,[363] need then be established. Interim orders will be avoided if there is sufficient evidence to do so.[364] One distinction from the 2009 Order is that the order may relate entirely to past activities. It is claimed that this is not a departure in practice,[365] but it should have been specified that if past activities are the sole basis for an order, then the order cannot persist for more than a specified time period since the last known involvement—perhaps two years. As with control orders, stale information should not justify an order. **9.187**

A Treasury designation must be notified under s 3 (s 7 for an interim order) by written notice to the designated person and must be publicized more generally (in practice by web listing and notices to financial institutions), but secrecy can apply to protect individuals under eighteen and public interests in national security, justice, or serious crime detection. There are no secret designations at present. The Treasury can also demand under s 10 that information is kept confidential for partial notifications. By s 4, a Treasury final designation expires after one year (or may be expressly varied or revoked sooner under s 5) but may then be renewed. Because of their lesser evidential standard, interim s 6 orders may only last for thirty days (s 8, and are subject to variations under s 9), and a second interim order is not allowed on the basis of the same, or substantially the same, evidence (s 6(3)). **9.188**

The prohibitions which flow from designation and European listings are set out in ss 11 to 15. Section 11 brings about the freezing of funds and economic resources (defined in s 39), ss 12 and 13 forbid the making available of funds or financial services, and ss 14 and 15 forbid the making available of economic resources. Breaches of these prohibitions are offences which require as *mens rea* that the perpetrator knows or reasonably suspects the purpose, in contrast to the absolute liability under the 2009 Order. There is also a broader offence under s 18 of circumventing the prohibitions. The penalties for the main offences in ss 11 to 15 and 18 are set by s 32 and range up to seven years' imprisonment, but lesser penalties apply to the more regulatory offences under ss 10, 17, 19, and 22 (with the latter two also being subject to a time limit under s 36). The offences are conferred with extra-territorial application under s 33 when committed by a UK national or corporation. Prosecutions must be consented to under s 37 by the Attorney General or Advocate General for Northern Ireland. **9.189**

---

[363] HM Treasury, *Public Consultation: Draft Terrorist Asset-Freezing Bill* (Cm 7852, London, 2010) paras 4.2–4.4.
[364] Hansard HL vol 721 col 1057 (25 October 2010) Lord Sassoon.
[365] Ibid para 4.31.

9.190 The prohibitions are subject to exceptions in s 16. These relate to crediting a frozen account with accrued interest but also add the important new standing exception (reflecting the Court of Justice decision in *M(FC) v HM Treasury)* of welfare benefits. That new exception is from s 13 only and covers receipt of benefits payable to linked persons other than the designated person and also payment of benefits due to a designated person but which are received by a non-designated person such as a family member. In either event, those funds must still not be passed on to the designated person contrary to s 9. The Treasury also claims that the benefits must not confer a substantial benefit under s 13, but this view appears doubtful since s 16 gives exemption from s 13.[366]

9.191 The prohibitions are next subject to licences granted by the Treasury under s 17 (which also serve as authorizations under art 6 of Regulation 2580/2001). 'General' licences are routinely issued for personal insurance cover (but not payments under the policy), legal aid and expenses, and for money earned as prisoners.[367] Specific licences may be granted by negotiation for purchases such as cars and holidays.[368] It is an offence knowingly or recklessly to provide information that is false or misleading to obtain a licence. There could be far greater flexibility and avoidance of referral back if more inventive forms of licensing were to be considered—such as forms of trusteeship—but the government prefers to maintain active stewardship over the designated person.

9.192 To assist with designation and enforcement, relevant financial institutions (defined by s 40) must under s 19 inform the Treasury, first, of any customer whom it 'knows, or has reasonable cause to suspect' is a designated person and the details of their account and, secondly, must inform as soon as practicable of information which came to it in the course of carrying on its business and which it 'knows, or has reasonable cause to suspect' amounts to an offence against the scheme by a designated person. The Treasury may also request information, including on a continuous basis, from the designated person and other persons resident in the United Kingdom under s 20. It is specified that s 20 is exercisable against the designated person only where HM Treasury 'believe that it is necessary for the purpose of monitoring compliance with or detecting evasion'. There is no express saving against self-incrimination, though a prosecutor would have to show for the offence under s 22 that the refusal to comply with the request was without reasonable excuse. In addition, s 25(3) protects legally privileged information. The production of documents may likewise be demanded under s 21, including a supplementary demand for an explanation thereof. Failures to comply with a request for information without reasonable excuse, knowingly or recklessly giving false information, or obstructing the request are offences under s 22. More positively, HM Treasury is empowered under s 23 to disclose information to policing and governmental authorities within the British Islands or an overseas territory, to legal and financial services officials, to United Nations and European Union bodies, and for the purposes of legal proceedings. There may also be cooperation under s 24 for the purposes of assisting investigations by other bodies. For these purposes, s 25 ensures that rules of confidentiality are not breached, but the Data Protection Act 1998 and Pt 1 of the RIPA must still be observed.

---

[366] See Bill HL 15 Explanatory Notes, para 36.
[367] <http://www.hm-treasury.gov.uk/fin_sanctions_general_licences.htm>. As well as the general licence for legal aid, there will be another general licence to allow third parties to pay legal expenses: Hansard HL vol 721 col 1062 (25 October 2010) Lord Sassoon.
[368] HM Treasury, *Public Consultation: Draft Terrorist Asset-Freezing Bill* (Cm 7852, London, 2010) para 5.14.

Legal challenge to designation powers is envisaged by s 26, by which any person affected by **9.193** any decision of HM Treasury to make, vary, or revoke an interim or final designation order (or to refuse to do so) or to renew a final designation may apply to the High Court or, in Scotland, the Court of Session. The court will hear a full appeal and not just apply judicial review standards as originally envisaged by the Bill, though judicial review only is available under s 27 for other complaints, such as regarding the granting of specific licences. The appeal jurisdiction allows wide remedial powers: 'the court may make such order as it considers appropriate' (s 26(3)), whereas the Bill originally specified that any decision to set aside a designation must result in it being quashed. Damages for breach of the Human Rights Act 1998 can also be awarded. The court processes are further explained in s 28 by which intercept evidence can be admitted. Otherwise, the provisions of ss 66 to 68 of the CTA 2008 are applied, including the supplementary provisions relating to rules of court and special advocates, and the possibility of further court rules under s 29.

Other checks and balances involve the formalization in s 30 of the quarterly Treasury reports **9.194** to Parliament, to which is added under s 31 the appointment of an independent reviewer who will report annually to the Treasury which must lay a copy before Parliament.

The Terrorist Asset-Freezing etc. Act 2010 represents an improvement over the previous **9.195** Orders, but criticisms persist.[369] One is that the reform is partial, and there is no attempt to consolidate even the UNSCR 1267 measures, let alone the several other financial powers covered in this chapter. As a result, there remains great complexity, with overlapping powers which have different quirks. One can appreciate the technical distinctions between the two United Nations sources. UNSCR 1267 applies to those named terrorist sources only, whereas UNSCR 1373 is at large. UNSCR 1267 has global reach through UN listing whereas UNSCR 1373 encourages national or European listing only and so demands initiative rather than replication. Yet there can be overlap of restricted persons between the two, as arose in *Ahmed* and in Operation Overt (the freezing of £160,000 under UNSCR 1373 and £210,000 under UNSCR 1267).[370] More generally, divergence between the systems creates complication, potential unfairness, and uneven scrutiny.[371]

The next problem concerns the threshold standard for Treasury designation under the **9.196** UNSCR 1367 scheme. This standard was first set at 'reasonable suspicion' but was raised during parliamentary passage for final orders to 'reasonable belief'.[372] It remains debatable whether any standard below criminal charge or prosecution, as noted in *Ahmed*,[373] is required by the UNSCR 1373, but a tenable argument is that a wider power is necessary to deal with foreign-based entities and individuals rather than persons within the jurisdiction.[374]

---

[369] Many are rehearsed in HM Treasury, *Draft Terrorist Asset Freezing Bill: Summary of Responses* (Cm 7888, London, 2010); House of Lords Select Committee on the Constitution, *Terrorist Asset-Freezing etc Bill* (2010–11 HL 25); Joint Committee on Human Rights, *Legislative Scrutiny: Terrorist Asset-Freezing etc. Bill* (2010–11 HL 41/HC 535).

[370] HM Treasury, *Public Consultation: Draft Terrorist Asset-Freezing Bill* (Cm 7852, London, 2010) para 4.6.

[371] [2010] UKSC 2 at para 223.

[372] For differences between the standards, see *Wills v Bowley* [1983] 1 AC 57 at 103; *Johnson v Whitehouse* [1984] RTR 38; *R v Hall (Edward Leonard)* (1985) 81 Cr App R 260. It is unclear whether even 'reasonable belief' amounts to proof on the balance of probabilities: Joint Committee on Human Rights, *Legislative Scrutiny: Terrorist Asset-Freezing etc. Bill* (2010–11 HL 41/HC 535) para 1.16.

[373] [2010] UKSC 2 at paras 137, 199–200.

[374] See Hansard HL vol 721 col 1041 (25 October 2010) Lord Sassoon.

9.197 Next, the standard of review and accountability has improved but, to emulate the position for control orders, there should be the issuance of the final order by the court rather than an appeal process. Arguments that only Ministers can handle security-based decisions are, as noted in Chapter 6, rather outdated.[375] There should also be consideration of the priority for prosecution and a final time limit to the duration of freezing orders.

9.198 Finally, there is every reason to suppose that the systems are vulnerable to further challenge under Article 6 standards. Rather obtusely, the government refused to accede to demands that the disclosure standards for control orders be written into the legislation and prefers to takes its chance in litigation that the different rights primarily affected will encourage the courts to permit a less demanding standard of process.[376] In addition, the permanent nature of the system may give rise to challenges under Article 8 and Protocol 1 Article 1, though the flexibility allowed under ss 12 and 13 is helpful, especially for family members.

Foreign comparisons

9.199 The counter-measures required by international law require very similar responses in all national jurisdictions. Many have struggled to meet any semblance of fair procedures. For example, in Ireland, the Criminal Justice (Terrorist Offences) Act 2005, s 42, empowers the Minister for Finance to make regulations in respect of UN listings or EU Regulations or even unilaterally.[377] Sections 14 and 15 of the Criminal Justice (Terrorist Offences) Act 2005 empowers the Garda Siochána to apply to the High Court for interim and interlocutory orders freezing funds. Rather apologetically, the government commentary on the Act states that 'New legislation providing for more proportionate, dissuasive and effective penalties is due to be introduced in the near future.'[378]

9.200 Some of the most extensive measures are implemented in the US, which also drove 'smart' sanctions in the United Nations. The International Emergency Economic Powers Act 1977[379] allows for Presidential declarations of emergency in response to any 'unusual and extraordinary' external threat to national security, foreign policy, or the economy of the United States by issuing executive orders which impose economic restrictions and seizures of assets. The 1977 Act was adapted in 1995 to apply to non-state groups and persons who were identified as 'Specially Designated Terrorists' under Executive Order 12947 as seeking to sabotage the Middle East peace process. The powers were extended to bin Laden by Executive Order 13099 in 1998 and to the Taliban by Executive Order 13129 in 1999.[380] A further emergency Executive Order 13224 was declared on 23 September 2001 in relation to persons who commit, threaten to commit, or support terrorism and created a 'Specially Designated Global Terrorists' list.[381] The 1977 Act allows official

---

[375] Compare Hansard HL vol 721 col 135 (6 October 2010), Lord Sassoon and col 1051 (25 October 2010), Lord Lloyd. There are 36 orders against foreign-based persons and 27 orders against persons (6 not convicted) within the jurisdiction: ibid col 149, Lord Wallace.

[376] Hansard HL vol 721 col 1077 (25 October 2010), Lord Wallace. See also Hansard HC vol 520 col 865 (14 December 2010) Mark Hoban.

[377] See <http://www.finance.gov.ie/publications/legi/sanctions.htm>.

[378] Money Laundering Steering Committee. *Guidance on the offence of financing of terrorism and the financial sanctions regime for bodies designated under section 32 of the Criminal Justice Act, 1994* (Dublin, 2005) p 20.

[379] PL 95-223, 50 USC s 1701. There must be a declaration of emergency under the National Emergencies Act (50 USC s 1601). EO 13224 is also based on the United Nations Participation Act 1945 (PL 79-264).

[380] 31 CFR 595.101-901.

[381] 31 CFR s 594.101-901. For challenges to designation, see *Islamic American Relief Agency v Gonzales* 477 F 3d 728 (2007).

action against passive membership and general terrorism support. The PATRIOT Act, s 106, bolstered these measures by allowing in camera and ex parte hearings as well as the interim freezing of assets.

The seizure of money is handled by the Office of Foreign Assets Control (OFAC) in the US Treasury. **9.201**

These powers have been the subject of constant judicial review on grounds of infringement of speech, reputational, and due process rights.[382] Amongst the reforms suggested are time limits on interim freezes and listings and fuller disclosure.[383] **9.202**

Implementation

Responsibility for domestic enforcement shifted to the Asset Freezing Unit of the Financial Crime Team in the Treasury in 2007.[384] **9.203**

After 9/11, around £90m was seized under UNSCR 1267, but much of it was returned to the successor Afghan government.[385] As at 24 August 2010, there were at UN level 135 listed individuals (and no entities) associated with the Taliban; 258 listed individuals associated with Al-Qa'ida, plus ninety-two entities and other groups and undertakings.[386] By the end of June 2010, 202 UK-based accounts containing just under £360,000 were frozen, mostly under UNSCR 1267;[387] there were then thirty-nine persons designated under both UNSCR 1267 and 1373 plus 459 persons designated under only the UNSCR 1267 (1999) regime.[388] **9.204**

Under UNSCR 1373, fifty-one designations have been made in total with thirty-three remaining by early 2010; twenty-seven of those had been charged with criminal offences (twenty-two convicted, four awaiting trial and one for whom charges were dropped and who is being considered for de-listing).[389] Only six had been affected by closed evidence. Thus, UNSCR 1373 tackles 'home-grown terrorists' who have been subjected to criminal process.[390] The practice seems to leave to enforcement under EU regulation those who are listed on the basis of their trans-border activities but who are not so active within the United Kingdom as to be prosecuted. This linkage to prosecution suggests that the Proceeds of Crime Act 2002 regime might be invoked in some cases. **9.205**

---

[382] See *Global Relief Foundation v O'Neill* 315 F 3d 748 (2002); *Benevolence International Foundation v Ashcroft* 200 F Supp 2d 935 (2002); *Holy Land Foundation for Relief and Development v Reno* 219 F Supp 2d 64 (2003); *Islamic American Relief Agency v Gonzales* 477 F 3d 728 (2007); *Al-Aqeel v Paulson* 568 F Supp 2d 64 (2008).

[383] See Donohue, LK, 'Anti-terrorist Finance in the United Kingdom and United States' (2006) 27 *Michigan Journal of International Law* 303; Ortblad, V, 'Criminal Prosecution in Sheep's Clothing' (2008) 98 *Journal of Criminal Law & Criminology* 1439; O'Leary, RE, 'Improving the terrorist finance sanctions process' (2010) 42 *New York University Journal of International Law and Politics* 549.

[384] <http://www.hm-treasury.gov.uk/fin_sanctions_afu.htm>. An Asset Freezing Working Group deals with policy and coordination, while the Terrorist Finance Action Group is the coordinating body for providing a framework for 'Pursue' activity: HM Treasury, *The Financial Challenge to Crime and Terrorism* (London, 2007) paras 3.25, 3.106.

[385] Binning, P, 'In safe hands? Striking the balance between privacy and security—Anti-terrorist finance measures' (2002) 6 *European Human Rights Law Review* 734 at 741.

[386] <http://www.un.org/sc/committees/1267/consolidatedlist.htm>.

[387] Hansard HC vol 514 col 56ws (26 July 2010), Mark Hoban.

[388] HM Treasury, *Draft Terrorist Asset Freezing Bill: Summary of Responses* (Cm 7888, London, 2010) para 5.30.

[389] Hansard HL vol 717 col 616 (9 February 2010).

[390] Hansard HL vol 718 col 453GC (25 March 2010), Lord Myners.

Assessment and conclusions relating to international measures

9.206 These international measures are as much vaunted as domestic law as being 'at the heart of the international effort against terrorism'.[391] That effort is consistent with the 'Prevent' strategy and allows disruption on low levels of proof. Another notable strategic gain for the UK government is the ability to foist upon European and even global audiences its own condemnation of domestic groupings,[392] allowing several Irish groups to become European pariahs. At the same time, the effectiveness of enforcement capacity in many countries is questionable. Concerted action has been hampered either because of technical shortcomings or because of lack of will from countries which do not perceive themselves as threatened.[393]

9.207 In grave doubt are the accountability and the constitutional governance of international listings. Parliamentary scrutiny is abysmal, though quarterly reporting was instituted in 2006 by HM Treasury,[394] and fifteen factual reports have ensued.[395] Yet, they are delivered as written statements, so that there can be no debate. Even the independent commissioner has shown a meagre amount of interest—understandably so, as the measures are beyond his remit. Those affected are left beyond democratic governance and are subject primarily to political spheres of influence at international level.

9.208 Next, 'smart' sanctions lack due process and amount to significant incursions into property rights and family life.[396] The listing systems are contemporary revivals of outlawry, whereby people are condemned without legal process or protection. The systems of review and the appointment of an ombudsperson and more assertive national and European judicial review have all had some impact. But the claim that 'great strides'[397] have been made in standards of fairness is highly fanciful. The UK Supreme Court views the subjects of listing as 'effectively prisoners of the state'.[398]

---

[391] HM Treasury, *Public Consultation: Draft Terrorist Asset-Freezing Bill* (Cm 7852, London, 2010) para 1.1.
[392] Ibid para 3.12.
[393] See Enders, W and Sanders, T, *The Political Economy of Terrorism* (Cambridge University Press, New York, 2006) p 158.
[394] Hansard HC vol 450 col 11ws (10 October 2006), Ed Balls.
[395] Hansard HC vol 514 col 56ws (26 July 2010), Mark Hoban.
[396] See *Report of the Special Rapporteur on the promotion and protection of human rights and fundamental freedoms while countering terrorism* (A/61/267, 2006) paras 31–41.
[397] Hansard HC Delegated Legislation Committee col 5 (30 March 2010), Sara McCarthy-Fry.
[398] *HM Treasury v Ahmed* [2010] UKSC 2 at para 60 per Lord Hope.

10

PROTECTIVE SECURITY

A. Introduction

The title of this chapter reflects the 'Protect' strand of the CONTEST strategy,[1] but 'Prepare' is an equal companion. 'Protect' seeks to reduce vulnerability to a terrorist attack, including by target-hardening against the forms or objects of attack. The 'Prepare' strand is concerned with identifying and assessing terrorism risk, and preparing for the consequences of terrorism by ensuring resilience. **10.01**

The implementation of 'Protect' and 'Prepare' will be related in this chapter at several levels. First, there are measures of general application. The detailed implementation will then be **10.02**

---

[1] Home Office, *Pursue, Prevent, Protect, Prepare: The United Kingdom's Strategy for Countering International Terrorism* (Cm 7547, London, 2009).

reflected by concentrating on specialist sectors: explosives and firearms; biological and chemical; nuclear; transportation; the critical national infrastructure; and others. The chapter will end with analysis of the protection for victims of terrorism.

B. General Measures of 'Protect' and 'Prepare'

Introduction and background

10.03 The state's protection of individual rights to life, liberty, and property are amongst its most fundamental political duties. These normative considerations translate into duties in domestic law under the broad reach of the Royal Prerogative.[2] They also feature in international law especially within the right to life under Article 2 of the European Convention on Human Rights and Fundamental Freedoms of 1950, though no absolute guarantee of safety is demanded.[3]

10.04 The response of the United Kingdom state to these general duties will be considered at an organizational level and then with reference to operational activities.

Policing and security counter-terrorism organizations

Provisions and implementation

10.05 (i) **Policing** Within policing history, the prime counter-terrorism intelligence-gathering organization has been the Metropolitan Police's Special Branch (MPSB),[4] a unit which has been replicated in other local forces. The MPSB maintains a National Joint Unit[5] which liaises between police and Home Office, and a National Ports Office at Heathrow. There also appeared in 1970 a Metropolitan Police Bomb Squad, renamed the Anti-Terrorist Squad in 1976, with a more operational focus.

10.06 This policing profile remained in place while Irish terrorism was the principal threat. However, restructuring took place once international terrorism rose to the fore. Policing policy development, entirely on a non-statutory basis, has been headed by the Association of Chief Police Officer's Terrorism and Allied Matters business area (ACPO (TAM)). Under the guidance of ACPO (TAM), an impressive police counter-terrorism structure network has emerged. This structure is headed by the Counter-Terrorism Command (CTC) of the Metropolitan Police Service,[6] incorporating the Anti-Terrorism Branch and most of the former Special Branch. The chief of the CTC acts nationally as the Senior National Coordinator, Counter-Terrorism, and there is also within CTC the National Co-ordinator of Terrorist Investigations. Outside London, there are four Counter-Terrorism Units (CTUs) located in the North East, North West, West Midlands, and Thames Valley, together with

---

[2] *Calvin's case* (1609) 77 ER 377; *Mutasa v Attorney General* [1980] QB 114; *R (Abassi) v Secretary of State for the Home Department* [2002] EWCA Civ 1598.

[3] See *X v Ireland*, App no 6040/73, 16 YB 388 (1973); *W v UK*, App no 9348/81, 32 DR 190 (1983); *X v UK*, App no 9825/82, 8 EHRR 49 (1985); *M v UK and Ireland*, App no 9837/82, 47 DR 27 (1986); *K v UK and Ireland*, App no 9839/82, 4 March 1986; *McCann, Savage and Farrell v United Kingdom*, App no 18984/91, Ser A 324 (1995).

[4] See Bunyan, T, *The Political Police in Britain* (Quartet Books, London, 1983); Allason, R, *The Branch* (Secker & Warburg, London, 1983); Porter, R, *The Origins of the Vigilant State* (Weidenfeld & Nicolson, London, 1987); Home Office, *Guidelines on Special Branch Work in Great Britain* (London, 1994).

[5] See (Rowe) *Report on the operation in 1998 of the Prevention of Terrorism (Temporary Provisions) Act 1989* (Home Office, London, 1999) Appendix F.

[6] There remains a MPS Royalty Protection Branch and Diplomatic Protection Group.

four Counter-Terrorism Intelligence Units (CTIUs) in Scotland, Wales, the South West, and East Midlands.[7] These units have again subsumed most Special Branch work but are much larger and more firmly linked to intelligence agencies. Provincial Special Branches are increasingly regionalized[8] and concentrate on borders and special protective duties. The work of the counter-terrorism police network is coordinated by a Joint Counter Terrorism Oversight Group, overseen by a Police Counter Terrorism Board, chaired by the Home Secretary.[9]

In addition to the Units, around 300 officers spread across twenty-four forces work on the Prevent Strategy and Delivery Plan, launched in 2008.[10] The National Coordinator for Community Engagement, appointed by the ACPO, oversees the work.   **10.07**

The other specialist policing body of prime importance to protective security is the National Counter-Terrorism Security Office (NaCTSO), established in 2002 under the aegis of ACPO (TAM). Its work involves the protection of vulnerable sites, delivered mainly through local police Counter-Terrorism Security Advisers (CTSAs).   **10.08**

Other structures handle what is indistinctly called 'domestic extremism', in practice comprising elements within animal welfare, anti-globalization, anti-capitalism, anti-war, environmental protection, and anarchist activities. The precise boundaries of this policing are controversial, since they are not always evidently related to a propensity towards violent action. Some of this policing effort has been considered in Chapter 8. A degree of separation from counter-terrorism is reflected in organizational terms. The National Extremism Tactical and Co-ordination Unit (NETCU) acts as the central protective service. The National Domestic Extremism Team (NDET) assists local police with investigations. The National Public Order Intelligence Unit (NPOIU) liaises with Special Branches and CTUs to maintain a strategic overview of domestic extremism-related public order issues. A National Coordinator Domestic Extremism was appointed in 2004.   **10.09**

Several further specialist policing bodies are of relevance to protective security and will be covered later in this chapter. Others potentially include the Serious Organised Crime Agency and the UK Border Agency. These will not be discussed since their roles do not substantially affect terrorism. The Home Office announced in 2010 plans to incorporate these agencies and possibly also the CTUs into a National Crime Agency.[11]   **10.10**

Despite this growing list of specialist policing counter-terrorism organizations, a rider is that counter-terrorism is firmly on the agenda of non-specialist policing bodies. The CTUs themselves have sought closer and fuller community relations, though the converse problem is greater fears of spying.[12] In addition, the growing recognition that 'neighbour terrorism' emanates from neighbourhood problems has encouraged the introduction of terrorism and extremism as a topic within local policing plans and neighbourhood policing, based   **10.11**

---

[7] See Staniforth, A, *Blackstone's Counter-Terrorism Handbook* (2nd edn, Oxford University Press, Oxford, 2010) ch 3.

[8] See Her Majesty's Inspectorate of Constabulary, *A Need to Know: HMIC's Thematic Inspection of Special Branch and Ports Policing* (Home Office, London, 2003).

[9] See Home Office, *Pursue, Prevent, Protect, Prepare* (Cm 7547, London, 2009) para 14.30.

[10] Ibid para 9.16.

[11] *Policing in the 21st Century* (London, 2010) paras 4.32, 4.38.

[12] See House of Commons Home Affairs Committee, *The Home Office's Response to Terrorist Attacks* (2009–10 HC 117) para 17; *Government Reply* (Cm 7788, London, 2010) p 7.

on the relatively novel assumption that communities can play a part in the countering of terrorism.[13]

10.12 (ii) **Intelligence** The intelligence agencies have historically been less affected in organizational terms by terrorism.[14] The functions of the prime domestic agency, the Security Service (SyS), have expressly related to terrorism since the Security Service Act 1989, s 1(2). Attention to that mandate is on the rise, as indicated by three factors.

10.13 First, SyS became the lead British agency for the gathering of intelligence about Irish Republicanism in 1992.[15] Northern Ireland followed suit in 2007.[16] There are three questions arising from this prioritization. One concerns the policy implications for criminalization. It has been argued in Chapters 2 and 6 that the ownership and disposition of information about terrorism affects the balance between collective public safety and criminal justice purposes. The second and third questions are whether the lead of the security service successfully delivers the collaboration between agencies and effective counter-terrorism outcomes. Answers are uncertain since no public inquiry has ever been conducted.[17]

10.14 The second feature of increasing attention to terrorism is that the intelligence agencies have received and mobilized greater resources within counter-terrorism. These increases are reflected by a regionalization programme since 2005.[18] The Security Service has opened eight British regional offices, including in West Yorkshire, the West Midlands, and Greater Manchester, often sited alongside the new policing units.[19]

10.15 The Secret Intelligence Service (SIS) provides intelligence regarding foreign targets under the Intelligence Services Act 1994, s 1(2). Protection against international terrorism has again become a top priority.

10.16 Next, the Government Communications Headquarters (GCHQ), recognized under the Intelligence Services Act 1994, s 3, deals with communications intelligence. Its remit is in corresponding terms to SIS, but its jurisdiction can be domestic as well as international.

10.17 To encourage intelligence collaboration between the relevant agencies, thereby avoiding the major failure highlighted later by the US National Commission on Terrorist Attacks upon the United States,[20] the Joint Terrorism Analysis Centre (JTAC) was set up in 2003 within the SyS. As mentioned in Chapter 2, JTAC is a body consisting of personnel from security, policing, and governmental agencies. The products of JTAC include the setting of threat levels from terrorism and analysis of terrorist trends, groupings, and capabilities.[21] The data

---

[13] Home Office, *From the Neighbourhood to the National* (Cm 7448, London, 2008) paras 1.49–1.51. See Pickering, S et al, *Counter Terrorism Policing* (Springer, New York, 2008).

[14] See Lustgarten, L and Leigh, I, *In from the Cold* (Clarendon Press, Oxford, 1994); Gill, P, *Policing Politics* (Frank Cass, London, 1994); Hollingsworth, M and Fielding, N, *Defending the Realm* (Andre Deutsch, London, 1999); Moran, J and Pythian, M, *Intelligence, Security and Policing Post 9/11* (Palgrave MacMillan, Basingstoke, 2008); Andrew, C, *The Defence of the Realm* (Allen Lane, London, 2009) pp 600, 644, 683, 734, 773, 799, 813.

[15] Hansard HC vol 207 col 297 (8 May 1992), Kenneth Clarke. See further ATCSA 2001, s 116.

[16] See Hansard HC vol 431 col 62ws (24 February 2005), Paul Murphy.

[17] But see Lord Carlile, *First Annual Review of Arrangements for National Security in Northern Ireland* (Northern Ireland Office, Belfast, 2008).

[18] An office has existed in Northern Ireland since 1969: Andrew, C, *The Defence of the Realm* (Allen Lane, London, 2009) p 604.

[19] <https://www.mi5.gov.uk/output/who-we-are.html>.

[20] *Report* (GPO, Washington DC, 2004).

[21] See Intelligence and Security Committee, *Annual Report 2002–03* (Cm 5837, London, 2003) para 62 and *Annual Report 2003–04* (Cm 6240, London, 2004) para 92.

is fed from security services and police, as well as governmental and private sources. Its intelligence products go to intelligence and policing agencies and governmental departments, as well as to the Joint Intelligence Committee (JIC) within the Cabinet Office where the process of translation into policy priorities and responses begins.

(iii) Military The military provide elements of intelligence-gathering (for example, **10.18** through the Defence Intelligence Staff). As for policing, three contributions can arise under the generic heading of Military Assistance to the Civil Authorities (MACA), though in all cases as a 'last resort'.[22] One comprises Military Aid to the Civil Power (MACP), where the military assists the civil power in the maintenance or restoration of order. Soldiers have been deployed in Northern Ireland in this way (described in Chapter 11). More commonplace MACP involves the disposal of explosive ordnance. Military Aid in the Civil Community (MACC) involves support in emergencies, such as disaster relief after bombings. At the other end of the scale is the RAF Quick Reaction Alert force which protects against airborne threats, such as a hijacked plane.[23] Military Aid to Other Government Departments (MAGD) comprises urgent work of national importance or in maintaining essential supplies and services.[24]

Foreign comparisons

Many of the changes encountered by the British counter-terrorism organizations have been **10.19** experienced in those of comparable states. For instance, the US 'fusion center' network reflects the needs for collaboration. Concerns have equally arisen about their effectiveness and mission creep.[25] Changes higher up the chain of command, including the National Counterterrorism Center, have been mentioned in Chapter 3. However, comparisons will not be taken further since their agenda ranges far beyond counter-terrorism.

Assessment and conclusions

'Amplification' and 'Melding' are posited as the two themed trends experienced in counter- **10.20** terrorism agencies since 11 September 2001.

Amplification in policing involves increased funding for counter-terrorism policing.[26] The **10.21** Special Branches increased from 1,638 officers in 1978 to 4,247 in 2003.[27] The increase is continuing, with a rise in funding by £240m (around a quarter) between 2007/08 and 2010/11.[28] Terrorism has also grown in prominence as a police strategic priority. In the First National Policing Plan for 2003–06, terrorism was mentioned briefly as a matter for 'Metropolitan Police and national agencies'.[29] By the Second National Policing Plan 2004–07,[30] counter-terrorism becomes an 'underpinning theme' for all forces. Under the

---

[22] See Ministry of Defence, *Operations in the UK: the Defence Contribution to Resilience* (2nd edn, London, 2007) para 205. See for laws and procedures: Walker, C and Broderick, J, *The Civil Contingencies Act 2004* (Oxford University Press, Oxford, 2006) ch 8; Tebbit, K, 'Countering international terrorism' in Hennessy, P, *The New Protective State* (Continuum Books, London, 2007).
[23] Hansard HC vol 511 col 95w (8 June 2010).
[24] See Emergency Powers Act 1964, s 2.
[25] German, M and Stanley, J, *Fusion Center Update* (ACLU, Washington DC, 2007).
[26] See Home Office, *Pursue, Prevent, Protect, Prepare* (Cm 7547, London, 2009) para 14.26.
[27] See Gregory, F, 'Police and counter-terrorism in the UK' in Wilkinson, P (ed), *Homeland Security in the UK* (Routledge, London, 2007) p 212.
[28] Home Office, *Pursue, Prevent, Protect, Prepare* (Cm 7547, London, 2009) para 0.67.
[29] Home Office, National Policing Plan 2003–2006 (Home Office, London, 2002) paras 3.37, 4.37–4.40.
[30] Home Office, *National Policing Plan 2004–2007* (Home Office, London, 2003) para 3.3.

successor statement, the Home Secretary's Strategic Policing Priorities 2009–10, one of four such priorities is: 'Work with and through partners and local communities to tackle terrorism and violent extremism in line with the counter terrorism strategy . . .'.[31]

10.22 Amplification in the security agencies is even more marked. The complement of 1,800 staff in the SyS in 2001 grew to 3,000 by the end of 2007, with plans for 4,000 by the end of 2011. The budget for all security and intelligence work has more than doubled since 11 September 2001.[32] However, this organizational growth has not generated such a radical quantitative re-orientation for the security services. Thus, 70 per cent of the work of the SyS was focused on counter-terrorism in 1993,[33] though amplification is detectable, since the proportion reached 91 per cent in 2009.[34]

10.23 The concept of melding challenges the long-standing analysis that counter-terrorism involves 'high' policing (covert, specialized, and serving executive purposes) whereas combating crime involves 'low' policing (consensual, general, and serving community purposes).[35] This demarcation has become dynamic in counter-terrorism policing, whereby CTUs seek links to neighbourhood policing,[36] and also by SyS agents making appearances in court as witnesses, especially in executive order proceedings. Melding of structures has also occurred,[37] as illustrated by the JTAC and also the Centre for the Protection of the National Infrastructure (CPNI), discussed later in this chapter.

10.24 As mentioned previously, the effectiveness of these policy changes[38] is hard to assess, especially when the objective is negative prevention.[39] The limited reviews of specific events—the Bali bombing,[40] irregular detentions[41] and renditions,[42] and the 7 July 2005 bombings[43]—were highly circumscribed 'narratives'.[44] Some analysis suggests successful interdiction on specific occasions,[45] but other indicators point to an inability to contain the

---

[31] Hansard HC vol 485 col 40WS (8 December 2008), Jacqui Smith.

[32] Home Office, *Pursue, Prevent, Protect, Prepare* (Cm 7547, London, 2009) para 13.08.

[33] Clutterbuck, L, 'The United Kingdom' in Jackson, BA et al, *Considering the Creation of a Domestic Intelligence Agency in the United States* (RAND, Santa Monica, 2009) p 129.

[34] <https://www.mi5.gov.uk/output/major-areas-of-work.html>.

[35] See Brodeur, J-P, 'High and low policing in post 9/11 times' (2007) 1 *Policing* 25. Compare Gregory, F, 'The police and the intelligence service' in Harfield, C et al, *The Handbook of Intelligent Policing* (Oxford University Press, Oxford, 2008).

[36] See Thiel, D, *Policing Terrorism* (Police Foundation, London, 2009) p 37.

[37] See Sheptycki, J, 'Organisational pathologies in police intelligence systems' (2004) 1 *European Journal of Criminology* 307.

[38] The expectations are set by ACPO, *Protective Services Minimum Standards* (London, 2007).

[39] Her Majesty's Inspectorate of Constabulary and the Audit Commission, *Preventing Violent Extremism: Learning and Development Exercises* (London, 2008).

[40] Intelligence and Security Committee, *Inquiry into Intelligence, Assessments and Advice prior to the Terrorist Bombings on Bali 12 October 2002* (Cm 5724, London, 2002).

[41] Intelligence and Security Committee, *The Handling of detainees by UK Intelligence Personnel in Afghanistan, Guantanamo Bay and Iraq* (Cm 6469, London, 2005) and *Government Response* (Cm 6511, London, 2005).

[42] Intelligence and Security Committee, *Report into Rendition* (Cm 7171, London, 2007) and *Government Response* (Cm 7172, London, 2007).

[43] Home Office, *Report of the Official Account of the Bombings in London on the 7th July 2005* (2005–06 HC 1087); Intelligence and Security Committee, Inquiry into Intelligence, *Report into the London Terrorist Attacks on 7 July 2005* (Cm 6785, London, 2005) and *Government Reply* (Cm 6786, London, 2006); Intelligence and Security Committee, *Could 7/7 have been Prevented?* (Cm 7617, London, 2009).

[44] See Institute for Public Policy Research, *Commission on National Security in the 21st Century* (London, 2009) ch 10.

[45] See Klausen, J, *Al-Qaeda-affiliated and 'Homegrown' Jihadism in the UK: 1999–2010* (Institute for Strategic Dialogue, London, 2010).

threat. The official threat level[46] has been pitched at 'severe' or 'critical' since 1 August 2006. It reduced to 'substantial' on 20 July 2009 but was raised again on 22 January 2010. Another negative performance indicator might be the increase in the number of terror suspects, though the upturn might alternatively be interpreted as reflecting greater proficiency in detection. Another indicator is that, since 11 September 2001, there have been several terrorist attacks, though they are outweighed by the greater number of plots which have resulted in premature termination and successful prosecution. The sharing of information with community representatives has been troublesome.[47] Finally, there are conflicting priorities within the policy agendas. One obvious conflict arises from the emphasis on covert practices, such as infiltration and surveillance, set against efforts to befriend and mobilize communities.

The next problem is the oversight of intelligence agencies. Even the government has recog- **10.25**
nized that current mechanisms for intelligence agencies, including the Intelligence and Security Committee, are weak.[48] Most of the new policing bodies are also oversight-deficient.

There is also a threat to individual rights. The gathering of intelligence particularly affects **10.26**
privacy rights, as already explored in Chapter 2.

General duties of planning and resilience

Provisions and implementation

General duties of planning and resilience are posited by the Civil Contingencies Act 2004 **10.27**
and other sectoral legislation. The legislation is too complex and detailed for full coverage here, and in any event much of its working is motivated by potential emergencies from flooding or disease rather than terrorism.[49]

In outline, Pt I of the 2004 Act relates to local planning for civil protection against emergencies **10.28**
(the definition of which in s 1 includes terrorism). Schedule 1 lists those bodies—called 'Responders'—which are subject to duties under Pt 1. The Act imposes direct duties on mainly local authority bodies ('Category 1 responders') while 'Category 2 responders'— selected utilities, transport undertakers, and health bodies—must cooperate together in multi-agency Local Resilience Forums. The Cabinet Office circulates to responders a National Risk Register as to the types and strength of risks which responders should reflect in planning processes. Terrorism figures prominently within the section on 'Malicious attacks'.[50] The local bodies liaise with regional government offices. Within central government, the Civil Contingencies Committee, chaired by the Home Secretary, is the key Cabinet Committee. The Civil Contingencies Secretariat within the Cabinet Office is the pivotal executive organization, but emergencies are in practice allocated to specified 'Lead Government Departments'.

Part II of the 2004 Act confers ministerial powers to issue regulations in response to a wide **10.29**
range of 'live' emergencies (including terrorism under s 19). Safeguards are included which reflect the 'triple lock' principles—that restraints will be imposed on the triggering definitions by reference to seriousness, necessity, and geographical proportionality. These measures have never yet been activated.

---

46 <https://www.mi5.gov.uk/output/threat-levels.html>.
47 See Cabinet Office, *Emergency Preparedness: Guidance on Part 1 of the Civil Contingencies Act 2004, its associated Regulations and non-statutory arrangements* (London, 2005) para 3.39.
48 See *The Governance of Britain* (Cm 7170, London, 2007) paras 89–96.
49 See Walker, C and Broderick, J, *The Civil Contingencies Act 2004* (Oxford University Press, Oxford, 2006).
50 2010 edition, para 2.77.

Foreign comparisons

10.30 The Department for Homeland Security and the Federal Emergency Management Agency (FEMA) in the USA provide a much more prominent and centralized structure than the British concept of 'Lead Government Department'. Conferring responsibility on a single central department and executive agency helps to develop policy and to assert audit.[51] It might also assist with the implementation of European regulations and rapid alert systems under EPCIP—the European Programme for Critical Infrastructure Protection.[52] Yet, the US models represent extremes of size and centralization which have proven far from assured in delivery.

Assessment and conclusions

10.31 Many of the mundane failings in the delivery structure for civil contingency planning and response were highlighted by the Pitt Review into flood response.[53] The feasibility of 'partnership' in the co-production of the far more sensitive issue of security planning remains challenging, though the Pitt Review praised the work of the CPNI (discussed later).[54] Since most infrastructure rests within the hands of Category 2 private sector responders, their willingness to share commercially sensitive information becomes crucial, as is the effectiveness of sectoral regulators.

C. Protective Security for Explosives and Firearms

Introduction and background

10.32 The current regulation of explosives and firearms is a far cry from the bold promise of the right to possess arms for defence in the Bill of Rights 1689, article 7. Regulatory and criminal controls have been substantially tightened, not only because of anti-social usage (including terrorism, as reflected in the Explosive Substances Act 1883 considered in Chapter 5), but also to control dangerous industrial processes.

Provisions

10.33 The Firearms Acts 1968–97 impose amongst the tightest controls in the world. Many weapons are prohibited from private possession under s 5 of the 1968 Act, including automatic weapons and also handguns.[55] It was argued unsuccessfully that these latter restrictions breached human rights to property.[56] The acquisition of firearms by terrorists has principally derived from foreign government suppliers (like Libya), foreign dealers (especially in the US), and latterly suppliers in Europe where arms controls are much laxer.

---

[51] See Department for Homeland Security, *National Infrastructure Protection Plan* (Washington DC, 2006); Moteff, J, *Critical Infrastructures: Background, Policy, and Implementation* (Washington DC: RL30153, Congressional Research Service, 2007).

[52] See COM (2006) 786 and 787 final. Note also the *Communications from the Commission, Preparation and Consequence Management in the Fight against Terrorism* (COM (2004) 701 final), *Critical Infrastructure Protection in the fight against terrorism* (COM (2004) 702 final).

[53] Pitt, M, *Learning Lessons from the 2007 Floods Final Report* (Cabinet Office, London, 2008).

[54] Ibid para 99.

[55] See Lord Cullen, *The Public Inquiry into the Shootings at Dunblane Primary School on 13 March 1996* (Cm 3386, 1996).

[56] *Ian Edgar (Liverpool) Ltd v United Kingdom*, App no 37683/97, 2000-1; *Andrews v United Kingdom*, App no 37657/97, 26 September 2000 (twelve other applications were decided on the same date).

The control of explosives is primarily a health and safety issue, now falling under the Manufacture **10.34** and Storage of Explosives Regulations 2005.[57] The (Montreal) Convention on the Marking of Plastic Explosives for the Purpose of Detection 1991 has been implemented by the Marking of Plastic Explosives for Detection Regulations 1996.[58] Advice is also given to suppliers and users (principally farmers) of nitrate materials commonly incorporated into home-made bombs.[59]

Foreign comparisons

The same broad notion of conspiracy to use explosions also appears in the US Code.[60] More **10.35** controversial, since it abuts into First Amendment rights to free speech, is an offence of demonstrating or teaching the use of explosives or weapons of mass destruction, knowing or intending implementation through a crime of violence.[61]

International enforcement is boosted by the Communication from the European Commission **10.36** on Enhancing the Security of Explosives in 2007.[62] It proposes a mutual alert system in the event of loss or theft, restricting explosive precursors, a European Explosive Ordnance Disposal Network, forensic assistance from Europol, and requirements as to vetting. The UK government is awaiting elaboration.[63]

Assessment and conclusions

Despite the European activity, there is no consensus as to the appropriate levels of control, **10.37** and the availability of weapons from Europe remains a threat.

There is also a disinclination to have any ongoing debate. The Firearms Consultative **10.38** Committee, under Firearms Act 1988, s 22, has been disbanded,[64] perhaps because it reflected strong elements of regulatory capture rather than constructive debate.

D. Protective Security for Biological and Chemical Materials

Introduction and background

Within the sphere of biological agents and toxins and chemical weapons,[65] the overall aim, even **10.39** of the offences which are rarely prosecuted, is 'to reduce the likelihood of a CBRN attack and, if an attack should occur, respond quickly to minimise harm and restore public confidence'.[66] Threats and hoaxes about these types of materials have already been explored in Chapter 6.

---

[57] SI 2005/1082.

[58] SI 1996/890. In Northern Ireland, see SR 1996/262.

[59] <http://www.secureyourfertiliser.gov.uk>. See also Directive 76/769/EEC.

[60] 18 USC s 844.

[61] Act for the relief of Global Exploration and Development Corporation 1999 (PL 106-54) adding 18 USC s 842.

[62] COM (2007) 651 final.

[63] House of Commons Select Committee on European Scrutiny, *Fifth Report* (2007–08 HC 16-v) para 18.13. Implementation has begun through: Council Framework Directive 2008/919/JHA of 28 November 2008; COM-Directive 2008/43/EC; Explosives Ordnance Disposal units network (EEODN).

[64] See *Twelfth Annual Report* (2003–04 HC 1082) para 1.6.

[65] See Kellman, B, *Bioviolence* (Cambridge University Press, New York, 2007); Bellany, I (ed), *Terrorism and Weapons of Mass Destruction* (Routledge, Abingdon, 2007); Clunan, AL, Lavoy, PR, and Martin, SB (eds), *Terrorism, War, or Disease?* (Stanford University Press, Stanford, 2008); Fidler, DP and Goston, LO, *Biosecurity in the Global Age* (Stanford University Press, Stanford, 2008).

[66] Home Office, *The United Kingdom's Strategy for Countering Chemical, Biological, Radiological and Nuclear (CBRN) Terrorism* (London, 2010) p 3.

10.40 Various measures have been included in the ATCSA 2001, Pts VI to IX, in reaction to intelligence about Al-Qa'ida interest in weapons of mass destruction (WMD).[67] The threat became more pressing, after letters containing anthrax were posted in the US during late 2001, albeit that the attacks later probably transpired to be the work of an insider scientist.[68] The terrorist interest in WMD has a longer history. Nineteenth-century anarchists contrived to spread diseases.[69] In contemporary times, Georgi Markov was killed by Bulgarian agents in London in 1978 by ricin poisoning,[70] and the Aum Shinrikyo sect in Japan executed sarin gas attacks in 1994 and 1995. The perception of heightened risk has been affirmed by the Home Office[71] and by UNSCR 1540 of 28 April 2004 which demands action against non-state actors.

10.41 The ATCSA 2001, Pt VI,[72] builds upon controls already set out in the Biological Weapons Act 1974 and the Chemical Weapons Act 1996. That legislation is based on international treaties, namely the Convention on the Prohibition of the Development, Production and Stockpiling of Bacteriological (Biological) and Toxin Weapons and on their Destruction 1972 (BWC)[73] and the Convention on the Prohibition of the Development, Production, Stockpiling and Use of Chemical Weapons and on their Destruction 1993 (CWC).[74]

10.42 The Biological Weapons Act 1974 implements the BWC. The BWC is generally considered to suffer from weak verification mechanisms, a characteristic which flows from the stance of the United States which fears that inspection could compromise biotechnology trade secrets and security. This stance was affirmed in the Sixth Review Conference in 2006, though it was agreed then to establish an Implementation Support Unit.[75] Otherwise, the United Nations Security Council can order expert investigations on request of a state,[76] and a 1540 Committee is mandated to promote implementation.[77] The World Health Organization also assists states.[78] Domestically, the Department of Energy and Climate Change undertakes responsibility.

10.43 The CWC bans the development, production, stockpiling, transfer, and use of chemical weapons, as overseen by an inspection and verification regime through the Organisation for the Prohibition of Chemical Weapons.[79] At national level, the Department of Energy and Climate Change acts as the Chemical Weapons Convention National Authority.[80]

Biological and chemical materials: offences

Provisions

10.44 The Biological Weapons Act 1974 is amended by the ATCSA 2001, s 43, to make it an offence to transfer biological agents or toxins outside the United Kingdom or to assist another

---

[67] See National Commission on Terrorist Attacks upon the United States, *The 9/11 Commission Report* (GPO, Washington DC, 2004) pp 117, 128, 151.

[68] The chief suspect, Bruce Ivins, committed suicide: *The Times* 2 August 2008, p 37.

[69] Quail, J, *The Slow Burning Fuse* (Paladin, London, 1978) p 169.

[70] Bereanu, V and Todorov, K, *The Umbrella Murder* (TEL, Bury St Edmunds, 1994).

[71] See Home Office, *Pursue, Prevent, Protect, Prepare* (Cm 7547, London, 2009) p 126.

[72] See further Home Office Circular 16/2002: *Part 6 of the Anti-Terrorism, Crime & Security Act 2001—Weapons of Mass Destruction.*

[73] Cmnd 5053, London 1972.

[74] Cm 2331, London 1993.

[75] See <http://www.unog.ch/bwc/isu>.

[76] BWC, art 6.

[77] See <http://www.un.org/sc/1540>.

[78] See <http://www.who.int/csr/outbreaknetwork/en>.

[79] <http://www.opcw.org>.

[80] See *Annual Report for 2009* (2009–10 HC 307).

person to do so, if undertaken with knowledge or reason to believe that the biological agent or toxin is likely to be kept or used (whether by the transferee or any other person) otherwise than for prophylactic, protective, or other peaceful purposes. This offence is added as s 1(1A), and it supplements offences already in s 1:

(1) No person shall develop, produce, stockpile, acquire or retain—
    (a) any biological agent or toxin of a type and in a quantity that has no justification for prophylactic, protective or other peaceful purposes; or
    (b) any weapon, equipment or means of delivery designed to use biological agents or toxins for hostile purposes or in armed conflict.
(2) In this section 'biological agent' means any microbial or other biological agent; and 'toxin' means any toxin, whatever its origin or method of production.

There is no corresponding alteration to the Chemical Weapons Act 1996 because it is an **10.45** offence under s 2 to 'participate in the transfer of a chemical weapon' (which includes precursors under s 1):

(1) No person shall—
    (a) use a chemical weapon;
    (b) develop or produce a chemical weapon;
    (c) have a chemical weapon in his possession;
    (d) participate in the transfer of a chemical weapon;
    (e) engage in military preparations, or in preparations of a military nature, intending to use a chemical weapon.

Next, s 44 extends jurisdiction over offences under s 1 of the Biological Weapons Act 1974 **10.46** carried out overseas by a United Kingdom person (defined by s 56). The corresponding measure in relation to chemical weapons already exists under s 3 of the 1996 Act. In addition, under s 50, it becomes an offence for a United Kingdom person outside the United Kingdom to assist a foreigner to do an act which would (for a United Kingdom person) be contrary to s 1 of the Biological Weapons Act 1974 or s 2 of the Chemical Weapons Act 1996. This phraseology would not extend to a United Kingdom-resident foreigner, who, while abroad, commits an act that, if committed by a British person, would be an offence.[81] However, the TA 2000, s 62, would cover this deficiency.[82]

Further incidental matters are dealt with in ss 45 and 46 (except in Scotland). The **10.47** Customs and Excise Commissioners can enforce offences under the Biological Weapons Act 1974 and the Chemical Weapons Act 1996 (or under s 50 of the ATCSA 2001 relating to biological weapons), in cases of the development or production outside the United Kingdom of relevant materials or the movement of a biological or chemical weapon across a border. The Attorney General must consent to prosecution under s 2 of the 1974 Act and s 31 of the 1996 Act.

Implementation

Severe penalties apply to these offences—life imprisonment under both the 1974 and **10.48** 1976 Acts.

Some post-2001 criminal charges have emerged—the first since enactment of the WMD **10.49** legislation. For instance, the 'Wood Green plot' comprised an alleged chemical attack on the

---

[81] Hansard HC vol 375 col 719 (26 November 2001), Ben Bradshaw.
[82] See *Newton Report*, para 280.

London tube, and castor oil beans were found with recipes (but no ricin). Arrests followed in London, Bournemouth, Norfolk, and Manchester where Detective Constable Stephen Oake was killed in 2003. Kamel Bourgass was convicted of murder and public nuisance, but the charges under the Chemical Weapons Act 1993 were not sustained.[83] Public nuisance through chemical and radiological attacks was alleged against Dhiren Barot but not pursued.[84] In the next case, Abdurahman Kanyare was acquitted of conspiracy to possess terrorism materials through the attempted purchase of 'red mercury' from an undercover *News of the World* journalist.[85] Allegations against two brothers, Mohammed Abdul Kahar and Abdul Koyair, arrested in Forest Green in June 2006, likewise came to naught. The only recorded conviction concerns Ian Davison, who was found guilty of producing a chemical weapon (ricin) contrary to s 2(1)(b) of the Chemical Weapons Act 1996, as well as other offences. He was sentenced to ten years in total.[86]

Foreign comparisons

10.50 Since these measures closely reflect international conventions, many other jurisdictions have implemented comparable measures.

Biological and chemical materials: facilities controls

Provisions

10.51 There are reasons to be especially fearful of biological weapons. The substances can be more readily obtained or produced than chemical or radiological materials. The urban environment facilitates transmission and hinders containment. Detection of the perpetrators is difficult when there may be no immediate impact. Prevention and containment are therefore vital.

10.52 Domestic controls are considered by the Advisory Committee on Dangerous Pathogens (ACDP),[87] based within the Department of Health. It advises the Health and Environment Departments, the Health and Safety Executive, and their devolved counterparts, on all aspects of hazards from work exposure to pathogens. Its guides cover the running of laboratories and healthcare premises in the light of the Control of Substances Hazardous to Health Regulations 2002.[88]

10.53 The Home Office has issued guidance and provided equipment to deal with deliberate releases and decontamination,[89] while the Department of Health has formulated its broad-ranging NHS Emergency Planning Guidance 2005. The Health Protection Agency (HPA)[90] also provides a service through its Centre for Emergency Preparedness and Response, Centre for Infections, and Centre for Radiation, Chemical, and

---

[83] See *R v Bourgass* [2005] EWCA Crim 1943, [2006] EWCA Crim 3397.

[84] See *R v Barot* [2007] EWCA Crim 1119; Carlisle, D, 'Dhiren Barot' (2007) 30 *Studies in Conflict & Terrorism* 1057. Compare Home Office, *The United Kingdom's Strategy for Countering Chemical, Biological, Radiological and Nuclear (CBRN) Terrorism* (London, 2010) para 1.10.

[85] *The Times* 26 July 2006, p 14.

[86] *The Times* 15 May 2010, p 31 (Newcastle Crown Court).

[87] See <http://www.dh.gov.uk/ab/ACDP/index.htm>.

[88] SI 2002/2677, as amended by SI 2004/3386.

[89] Home Office, *The Decontamination of People Exposed to Chemical, Biological, Radiological or Nuclear (CBRN) Substances or Material* (London, 2003), *The United Kingdom's Strategy for Countering Chemical, Biological, Radiological and Nuclear (CBRN) Terrorism* (London, 2010) paras 2.38–2.44.

[90] See Walker, C, 'Biological attack, terrorism and the law' (2004) 17 *Terrorism and Political Violence* 175.

Environmental Hazards. Plans exist to deal with more specific threats, including smallpox and anthrax.[91]

Implementing the advisory standards in the workplace is the responsibility of the Health **10.54** and Safety Executive (HSE). There is guidance on laboratories from its Occupational Health Services Advisory Committee.[92] Laboratories handling pathogens must first notify the HSE (2002 Regulations, Sch 3) and must then have suitable facilities for containment under reg 7. The Regulations (Sch 3, para 2) define four levels of hazard, and there are corresponding containment levels for laboratory work (Sch 3, para 3), which are matched to the hazard levels in the Approved List of Biological Agents, published by the ACDP.[93]

While extensive, these controls focus mainly on health and safety in the workplace rather **10.55** than on physical or personnel security.[94] Hence, security concerns lie at the heart of Pt VII of the ATCSA 2001. Its regulatory scheme proceeds not by licensing but by compulsory audit.[95] The pathogens and toxins within its scheme are defined as 'dangerous substances' in s 58 and listed in Sch 5. The list of 'Pathogens and Toxins' in Sch 5 was chosen by reference to their degree of hazard as well as their availability and usefulness to terrorists. As well as natural substances, the Schedule covers micro-organisms which have been 'genetically modified by any means' (Notes 1(b)).[96] Orders in 2002 and 2007 exclude substances held as a medicine, or for clinical or diagnostic purposes (provided there is disposal after the diagnosis), or in a form that will not allow propagation, or as food or feeding stuff, or where toxins are held in very small quantities.[97] Though no specific exemption is granted, the listing is not considered to include vaccine strains derived from listed micro-organisms, such as attenuated Yellow Fever virus vaccine strain 17D, since they are not seriously harmful to health.[98] If listed material is stably modified by the deletion of genes involved in pathogenicity, then it can be exempted.[99] The possession of a gene library or viral replicons derived from listed materials is not covered so long as an infectious agent cannot be generated.[100]

The Secretary of State may, by affirmative order under s 73(2), modify the list, provided the **10.56** material is not simply dangerous but 'could be used in an act of terrorism to endanger life or cause serious harm to human health' (s 58(3)). The same process may be used under s 75 to apply Pt VII to a wider range of substances, namely: (a) toxic chemicals (within the meaning

---

[91] *Smallpox Mass Vaccination* (Department of Health, London, 2005); *Aide-Memoires on the Deliberate Release of Anthrax* (Department of Health, London, 2004).
[92] *Safe Working and the Prevention of Infection in Clinical Laboratories and Similar Facilities* (HSE Books, Sudbury, 2003).
[93] (HSE, Norwich, 2004). See further Importation of Animal Pathogens Order 1980, SI 1980/212; Specified Animal Pathogens Order 1998, SI 1998/463; Plant Health (England) and (Scotland) Orders 2005, SI 2005/2530 and SSI 2005/613.
[94] See Home Office, Regulatory Impact Assessment: Security of Pathogens and Toxins (2001), para 2.
[95] Hansard HL vol 629 col 650 (3 December 2001), Lord Bassam.
[96] See further Genetically Modified Organisms (Contained Use) Regulations 2000, SI 2000/2831; National Counter-Terrorism Security Office, *Pathogens and Toxins Guidance* (London, 2007) para 19.
[97] Security of Pathogens and Toxins (Exceptions to Dangerous Substances) Regulations 2002, SI 2002/1281; Security of Animal Pathogens (Exceptions to Dangerous Substances) Regulations 2007, SI 2007/932.
[98] National Counter-Terrorism Security Office, *Pathogens and Toxins Guidance* (London, 2007) para 12.
[99] Ibid para 13.
[100] Ibid paras 16, 17.

of the Chemical Weapons Act 1996), provided the Secretary of State is satisfied that the chemical could be used in terrorism to endanger life or cause serious harm to human health; or (b) animal pathogens, plant pathogens, and pests, provided the Secretary of State is satisfied that there is a risk that the pathogen or pest could be used in an act of terrorism to cause widespread damage to property, significant disruption to the public, or significant alarm to the public.

10.57 The 2001 version of Sch 5 derived from the intergovernmental 'Australia Group' which had worked since 1985 to contain state proliferation of chemical and biological materials.[101] The government was not satisfied with the focus of the Australia list[102] and circulated after 2001 a wider 'Salisbury Group' list with which it encouraged voluntary compliance.[103] Legislative enforcement has followed in two steps. First was the addition of animal pathogens by order under s 75 in 2007.[104] Secondly, changes were issued to the original list,[105] urged not only by the cross-governmental 'Salisbury Group' review,[106] but also by the Science and Technology Select Committee and the *Newton Report*. The relevant considerations for inclusion on the list are as follows: the extent to which the UK population is vulnerable to infection by the pathogen; how infectious the pathogen is when spread airborne or through contamination of food or water supplies; the extent to which the disease caused by the pathogen is transmitted from person to person; the availability of measures, such as vaccines, to deal with potential incidents; the severity and duration of illness caused by the pathogen, including the availability of treatment; how long the pathogen is able to survive in the environment; and how easy it is to grow and store the pathogen.[107] The animal pathogens were added in a distinct Sch 5, with the strange result that there are two discrete Sch 5s to the Act, one for 'Pathogens and Toxins' and another for 'Animal Pathogens'. The reason for this convoluted drafting is to allow separate 'Notes' sections for each schedule. A representation of key impacts of Sch 5 is set out in Table 10.1.

10.58 Further amendment is under consideration in 2010 following a review by the HPA.[108] It has suggested: three categories of regulation according to security risk to achieve better proportionality; two yearly reviews; changes to the list (including the omission of plant pathogens).

10.59 Having set the parameters, s 59 obliges the occupiers of premises to notify the Secretary of State within one month before keeping or using any dangerous substance. Further information can be demanded by the police under ss 60 and 61 about the substances, security arrangements, and personnel involved. Section 61 also requires occupiers to exclude outsiders. Where occupiers intend to give access to anyone else, notification must be given to the

---

[101] See <http://www.australiagroup.net>.

[102] Hansard HL vol 690 col 914 (15 March 2007), Lord Bassam.

[103] *Home Office Response to Newton Report*, Pt II para 68. The name derives from the Centre for Applied Microbiology and Research, Porton Down.

[104] Pt 7 of the Anti-terrorism, Crime and Security Act 2001 (Extension to Animal Pathogens) Order 2007, SI 2007/926.

[105] Sch 5 to the Anti-terrorism, Crime and Security Act 2001 (Modification) Order 2007, SI 2007/929. See NaCTSO, *Pathogens and Toxins Guidance* (London, 2007).

[106] See Regulatory Impact Assessment, para 10.1.

[107] Ibid para 1.3.

[108] Home Office, *Amendment to the Anti-terrorism, Crime and Security Act 2001* (London, 2010).

Table 10.1 Examples of dangerous substances under Pt VII [a]

Nature	Substance	Hazard group
VIRUS (an organism that can only reproduce within other organisms' cells which are affected by the process)	Dengue fever virus	3
	Ebola virus	4
	Herpes simiae (B virus)	4
	Influenza viruses (pandemic strains)	3
	Lassa fever virus	4
	Polio virus	2
	Rabies virus	3
	Variola virus (smallpox)	4
	Yellow fever virus	3
RICKETTSIAE (bacteria which cannot survive outside the cells of animals)	Rickettsia prowazeki (typhus)	3
	Rickettsia rickettsii (typhus)	3
BACTERIA (single celled organisms that multiply by cell division and do not possess a nucleus)	Bacillus anthracis (anthrax)	3
	Clostridium botulinum	2
	Mycobacterium tuberculosis	3
	Salmonella paratyphi A, B, C and typhi	3
	Shigella boydii, dysenteriae and flexneri	2, 3, 2
	Vibrio cholerae	2
	Yersinia pestis (Plague)	3
FUNGI (organisms which share some characteristics of animals as well as plants)	Cladophialophora bantiana	3
	Cryptococcus neoformans	2
TOXIN (a poisonous agent or substance, such as proteins from bacteria, produced by a living organism)	Botulinum toxins (Botulism)	2
	Ricin	None
	Staphylococcus aureus toxins	2
ANIMAL PATHOGENS (biological agents which cause diseases in animals derived from animals)	Foot and mouth disease virus	None
	Highly pathogenic avian influenza (HPAI)	None
	Rabies and rabies-related Lyssaviruses	3

[a] See Ghosh, TK et al (eds), *Science and Technology of Terrorism and Counterterrorism* (Marcel Dekker, New York, 2002); Zubay, G et al (eds), *Agents of Bioterrorism* (Columbia University Press, New York, 2005).

police, and access must be denied for thirty days following the notification unless otherwise agreed by the police. The police can also, under s 65, enter relevant premises, on at least two days' notice, accompanied by any other persons, to assess security measures. In addition (for example, when there is urgency), a justice of the peace or sheriff may issue a search warrant under s 66.

10.60 Having carried out checks on the premises and relevant personnel, the police can, under s 62, require the occupier to improve security arrangements. More drastic enforcement powers are given to the Secretary of State, who can require under s 63 the disposal of any dangerous substances where security arrangements are unsatisfactory, and, under s 64, can require that any specified person be denied access to dangerous substances or the premises where exclusion is necessary in the interest of national security or public safety. It is assumed that 'national security' embraces 'international security'.[109]

10.61   By s 67, it is an offence (punishable by up to five years' imprisonment) for occupiers of premises to fail, without reasonable excuse, to comply with any duty or directions. Sections 68 and 69 deal with offences by bodies corporate, partnerships, and unincorporated associations.

10.62   In view of the constraints on personal property and privacy imposed by these measures, appeal mechanisms are available but to date have stood idle. The Pathogens Access Appeal Commission (PAAC) is established under s 70 to receive appeals by any person denied access on the direction of the Secretary of State under s 64. By s 70(3), the Commission must allow an appeal if it considers that the decision to give the directions was flawed when considered under judicial review principles. A further appeal on law may be made with permission under s 70(4) to the Court of Appeal or Court of Session.

10.63   Schedule 6 deals with the constitution and procedures of the PAAC. The Commissioners are appointed by the Lord Chancellor and shall hold and vacate office in accordance with the terms of the appointment (para 1); whether this is sufficient independence for European Convention purposes is doubtful.[110] The PAAC shall normally sit as a panel of three, including one person who holds, or has held, high judicial office (defined by para 4). By para 5, in line with the Proscribed Organisations Appeal Commission (described in Chapter 8), the rules of procedure may provide for the denial of reasons and evidence from the applicant and from any representative or their exclusion from all or part of proceedings. Where evidence is kept secret, Schedule 6 follows the patterns established in the Special Immigration Appeals Commission Act 1997. More detailed rules are in the Pathogens Access Appeal Commission (Procedure) Rules 2002[111] and the Court of Appeal (Appeals from Pathogens Access Appeal Commission) Rules 2002.[112]

10.64   Appeals aside from persons denied access (such as from occupiers of premises against compliance with security directions, the disposal of dangerous substances, or the provision of information about security arrangements) are provided for by s 71. Appeal must be lodged within one month to a magistrates' court (with a further appeal to the Crown Court) on the ground that the direction or act is unreasonable. In Scotland, the route is from the sheriff's court, to sheriff principal, to the Court of Session.

Implementation

10.65   Initial surveys suggested that around a half of affected laboratories required some work.[113] No prosecutions or closures have been reported, but health and safety legislation transgressions have occurred.[114]

10.66   Enforcement is by the NaCTSO. CTSAs will conduct inspection visits, informed by two Home Office guidelines (which have restricted access), *Security of Pathogens* and

---

[109]   Hansard HL vol 629 col 676 (3 December 2001), Lord Rooker.
[110]   The position is preserved by the Tribunals, Courts and Enforcement Act 2007, s 59. But note the requirement to consult the Lord Chief Justice (Constitutional Reform Act 2005, Sch 4, para 300).
[111]   SI 2002/1845.
[112]   SI 2002/1844, r 4.
[113]   Hansard HC vol 375 col 723 (26 November 2001), Beverley Hughes.
[114]   See *HSE v Imperial College* (Blackfriars Crown Court, 2 March 2001) Health and Safety Executive Press Release E031:01–2 March 2001.

Toxins and Personnel Security Measures for Laboratories. Much emphasis is rightly placed on 'personnel security and the insider threat',[115] but no individual has been barred from access.[116]

Of the 395 sites under the Act,[117] around 100 (diagnostic laboratories) are exempted under **10.67** the 2002 Order,[118] though they still receive visits; an extra ten sites holding animal pathogens were added in 2007.[119]

Foreign comparisons

Corresponding developments have taken place in the USA. The criminal law was tightened **10.68** by the USA PATRIOT Act 2001, s 817, which makes it an offence knowingly to possess any biological agent, toxin, or delivery system. The Public Health Security and Bioterrorism Preparedness and Response Act 2002,[120] Title II, requires all entities which handle any of a list of pathogens and toxins to register with the Centers for Disease Control and Prevention[121] and to implement safety and security measures.

Assessment and conclusions

The balance of legal attention in favour of protective security rather than criminal law is **10.69** sound. The domestic regulatory scheme seems to work passably well and without dispute. Yet vulnerabilities remain. First, no security standards are set in Pt VII, so the CTSAs lack waypoints[122] and must rely either upon general guidance[123] or even on the advice of the technicians being audited. Secondly, the absence of a counterpart international convention compromises the UK regime.[124] It has been suggested that the UN Security Council should build upon the 1540 Committee to set up further structures around biological security.[125] A third gap is that the regulations do not apply to substances in post or transit[126] or to supplies of DNA part sequences of pathogens.[127]

The House of Commons Foreign Affairs Committee has proffered the idea of a central **10.70** authority for the control of dangerous pathogens,[128] covering not only laboratories but also the proliferation of human expertise. The real threat lurks not so much in identified laboratories, which often store just a few microgrammes of toxins, but mail order imports or

---

[115] *Explanatory Memorandum to Part 7 of the Anti-terrorism, Crime and Security Act 2001 (Extension to Animal Pathogens) Order 2007*, para 4.1.

[116] House of Commons Science and Technology Committee, *The Scientific Response to Terrorism* (2003–04 HC 415) para 289.

[117] Home Office, *Amendment to the Anti-terrorism, Crime and Security Act 2001: Regulatory Impact Assessment* (London, 2010) para 4.2.

[118] But see *Newton Report*, para 295; *Home Office Response to Newton Report*, Pt II para 70.

[119] Explanatory Memorandum to Part 7 of the Anti-terrorism, Crime and Security Act 2001 (Extension to Animal Pathogens) Order 2007, paras 4.2, 4.3.

[120] PL 107–188.

[121] <http://www.cdc.gov>.

[122] See House of Commons Science and Technology Committee, *The Scientific Response to Terrorism* (2003–04 HC 415) para 191; *Newton Report*, para 288.

[123] See *Home Office Response to Newton Report*, Pt II, para 71.

[124] Foreign Affairs Committee, *Biological Weapons*, Green Paper (2003–03 HC 150) para 34. Note also the World Health Organization, *Laboratory Biosafety Manual* (3rd edn, Geneva, 2004).

[125] Kellman, B, *Bioviolence* (Cambridge University Press, New York, 2007) p 226; Fidler, DP and Goston, LO, *Biosecurity in the Global Age* (Stanford University Press, Stanford, 2008) p 253.

[126] See *Newton Report*, para 296; *Home Office Response to Newton Report*, para 75.

[127] See Aldhous, P, 'The bioweapon is in the post' (2005) *New Scientist* 9 November, p 8.

[128] Foreign Affairs Committee, *Biological Weapons, Green Paper* (2003–03 HC 150) para 32.

knowledge transfer to dangerous individuals who can access materials abroad. The spectre of unethical scientists on the loose is exemplified by Huda Salih Mahdi Ammash ('Mrs Anthrax' in the popular press) who, after studying in US universities, became the head of the Iraqi biological weapons programme. Next, Rihab Taha ('Dr Germ') obtained a doctorate in plant toxins from the University of East Anglia in 1984. Dr Taha's team produced several pathogens and toxins in Iraq. Both women were detained in Iraq by US forces from 2003 to 2005.

10.71 The dangers of the subversion of research have been recognized in several ways. First, there was the Voluntary Vetting Scheme of potential students in around thirty higher education institutes within the United Kingdom. Those institutes were advised of concerns about proliferation and technology transfer whenever the student applicant came from one of ten target countries and was interested in one of twenty-one disciplines.[129] That scheme was replaced in 2007 by the Academic Technology Approval Scheme (ATAS), covering forty-one disciplines and potentially all countries.[130]

10.72 A second academic restriction was announced by the Medical Research Council, the Wellcome Trust, and the Biotechnology and Biological Sciences Research Council in 2005.[131] Their joint policy statement demands that applications for research funding and their assessment should specifically consider risks of misuse. There has also been heightened vigilance by scientific journals to filter out information about dual uses.[132]

10.73 The threats of bioterrorism are worthy of headlines but should not become 'a political obsession . . . a phantasm'.[133] Excessive restraints will affect not only the relatively weak rights to privacy and property but also benign technological development.

E. Protective Security for Nuclear Materials

Introduction

10.74 The proliferation of nuclear materials has been the subject of intense international attention, with the International Atomic Energy Agency to the fore.[134] Domestically, the Department for Energy and Climate Change oversees nuclear regulation, while the executive authority is the United Kingdom Atomic Energy Authority (UKAEA) which delivers the UK Safeguards Programme. Compliance with the international regimes is vested in the Nuclear Directorate of the Health and Safety Executive, though there are plans to establish an independent Office for Nuclear Regulation.[135]

---

[129] See House of Commons Science and Technology Committee, *Scientific Response to Terrorism* (2003–04 HC 415) para 200.

[130] <http://www.fco.gov.uk/en/about-us/what-we-do/services-we-deliver/atas/>.

[131] <http://www.mrc.ac.uk/Utilities/Documentrecord/index.htm?d=MRC002538>.

[132] See Aldhous, P, 'The accidental terrorists' *New Scientist* 10 June 2006, p 24; Lindes, MS, 'Censuring science' in Gerstmann, E and Streb, MJ, *Academic Freedom at the Dawn of a New Century* (Stanford University Press, Stanford, 2006) p 90.

[133] Sarasin, P, *Anthrax: Bioterror as Fact and Fantasy* (Harvard University Press, Cambridge, 2006) p 6.

[134] See Allison, G, *Nuclear Terrorism* (Henry Holt, New York, 2004); Levi, M, *On Nuclear Terrorism* (Harvard University Press, Cambridge, 2007).

[135] See Department for Business and Regulatory Reform, *Meeting the Energy Challenge* (Cm 7296, London, 2008).

Nuclear materials: offences

Provisions

Whilst terrorist usage of nuclear weapons would undoubtedly inflict serious offences against **10.75** the person and against property, crude devices—'dirty bombs'—and the preparatory stages of manufacturing a weapon were not so clearly covered by any offence prior to the ATCSA 2001. Consequently, by s 47(1), it is an offence (punishable by life imprisonment) if a person (a) knowingly causes a nuclear weapon explosion; (b) develops or produces, or participates in the development or production of, a nuclear weapon; (c) has a nuclear weapon in his possession; (d) participates in the transfer of a nuclear weapon; or (e) engages in military preparations, or in preparations of a military nature, intending to use, or threaten to use, a nuclear weapon. Section 48 makes exceptions for actions carried out in the course of an armed conflict or for actions authorized by the Secretary of State.[136] Section 49 sets out defences for the absence of knowledge that an object was a nuclear weapon or for an attempt to inform the Secretary of State or a police officer as soon as practicable after discovering that an object was a nuclear weapon. The term, 'nuclear weapon' does not readily cover radiological or 'dirty' bombs.[137] Therefore, by s 47(6), 'nuclear weapon' is defined to include nuclear explosive devices not intended for use as a weapon—for example, nuclear material from the nuclear power industry may be released as a 'dirty' bomb where the explosive material is non-nuclear and the nuclear material is a contaminant. The offences under s 47 apply to acts outside the United Kingdom by a United Kingdom person. Furthermore, s 50 applies to a s 47 offence, so it becomes an offence for a United Kingdom person outside the jurisdiction to assist a foreigner to do an act which would (for a United Kingdom person) contravene s 47.

By s 47(9), the offence of knowingly causing a nuclear weapon explosion will cease to have **10.76** effect on the coming into force of the Nuclear Explosions (Prohibitions and Inspections) Act 1998. Because it contains a similar, internationally approved offence, it will replace s 47(1)(a). The relevant offence is in s1(1) of the 1998 Act and applies to 'Any person who knowingly causes a nuclear weapon test explosion or any other nuclear explosion …'. The 1998 Act will become operative following the entry into force of the Comprehensive Test Ban Treaty.[138] Though ratified by the United Kingdom in 1998, the Treaty awaits ratification by China and the USA.[139] The Comprehensive Nuclear-Test-Ban Treaty Organization Preparatory Commission[140] engages in remote monitoring but not site monitoring.

The TA 2006 has added further offences to implement the UN Convention for the **10.77** Suppression of Acts of Nuclear Terrorism, which the United Kingdom signed in 2005.[141] These add to, and overlap with, existing offences, not only those under the ATCSA 2001 but also under the Nuclear Material (Offences) Act 1983, the Radioactive Substances Act 1993, and even the common law offence of causing a public nuisance.

So as to allow early intervention against someone who possesses the material for a weapon **10.78** rather than a weapon itself (as under s 47 of the 2001 Act), s 9 forbids the making or possession

---

[136] See Hansard HC vol 375 col 721 (26 November 2001), Ben Bradshaw. See further s 54.
[137] Hansard HL vol 629 col 643 (3 December 2001), Baroness Symons.
[138] Comprehensive Nuclear-Test-Ban Treaty adopted in New York on 10 September 1996 and the Protocol to that Treaty (Cm 3665 and 4675, London, 1997, 2000).
[139] An Additional Protocol (Cm 4282, London, 1999) is implemented by the Nuclear Safeguards Act 2000.
[140] <http://www.ctbto.org>.
[141] Cm 7301, London, 2008. See Joyner, CC, 'Countering nuclear terrorism' (2007) 18 *European Journal of International Law* 225.

of radioactive devices or materials with the intention of use in terrorism. The 'terrorism' may be a particular act or an unformulated general inclination. The penalty is up to life imprisonment.[142] The meaning of a 'radioactive device' can range under s 9(4) from a nuclear weapon through to radioactive dispersal or radiation emission devices. Radioactive material must be of sufficient strength to cause serious danger to personal life or injury (presumably, including the possessor's own life or bodily integrity), serious damage to property, or danger to the health or safety of the public (including a foreign public under s 20(3)). Thus, very low level radioactive material, which might otherwise be covered by the 'radiation-emitting device' mentioned in s 9(4), cannot give rise to the offence, even if a scientifically challenged terrorist believes, for example, that a handful of lithium batteries or ionizing-based smoke detectors can cause harm.[143] On the meaning of 'public', s 20(3)(b) states that 'except in s 9(4)', that term can extend to 'a meeting or other group of persons which is open to the public (whether unconditionally or on the making of a payment or the satisfaction of other conditions)'. The result is that the court should be satisfied that the threat from radioactivity is to the public at large, including innocent victims at a public meeting, and not just to a gathering of plotters.[144]

10.79 Section 10 forbids the misuse of radioactive devices or materials (s 10(1)), or the misuse or damage of nuclear facilities (including reactors, plant, transportation, or storage) so as to cause release of radioactive material or its risk (s 10(2)). In either case, the action must be for the purposes of 'terrorism'. But this attendant condition could conceivably be met by protestors who engineer damage resulting in the release of radioactivity and amounting to property damage designed to influence a government within s 1 of the TA 2000. The penalty is up to life imprisonment.

10.80 Section 11(1) relates to demands backed by the threat of action for supply or access relating to radioactive devices or materials or to nuclear facilities for the purposes of terrorism. This offence is akin to demanding with menaces.[145] Section 11(2) relates to threats alone not backed by 'menaces', covering also the ground of hoax offences. In both cases, the *actus reus* must relate to existing acts of terrorism or more broadly for the purposes of terrorism which might include preparatory stages.[146]

10.81 By s 11A (added by the CTA 2008, s 38, as a simpler alternative to s 23A of the TA 2000), the court may order forfeiture on conviction under ss 9 to 10.

10.82 Section 14 increases the penalty from fourteen years to up to life imprisonment for s 2 of the Nuclear Material (Offences) Act 1983 (offences involving preparatory acts and threats).

10.83 Further changes to the Nuclear Material (Offences) Act 1983 are implemented by the Criminal Justice and Immigration Act 2008, s 75 and Sch 17. The choice of this Act as the vehicle for change, rather than the CTA 2008, appears capricious. Section 75 follows up the ratification of the Amendment to the Convention on the Physical Protection of

---

[142] See Hansard HL vol 676 col 723 (7 December 2005).
[143] But see Silverstein, K, *The Radioactive Boy Scout* (Random House, New York, 2004).
[144] Hansard HL vol 676 col 723 (7 December 2005) and ibid col 725 and vol 677 col 1200 (25 January 2006), Lord Bassam.
[145] See Theft Act 1968, s 21.
[146] Compare Jones, A, Bowers, R, and Lodge, HD, *The Terrorism Act 2006* (Oxford University Press, Oxford, 2006) para 4.11.

Nuclear Material 2005,[147] which amends the Convention on the Physical Protection of Nuclear Material 1980,[148] as implemented mainly by the Nuclear Material (Offences) Act 1983. The main impact of the amendment is to create extra criminal offences with universal jurisdiction within the 1983 Act, and the opportunity has also been taken to increase penalties to life imprisonment in that Act and under the Customs and Excise Management Act 1979. In accordance with the Convention, the 1983 Act does not apply to nuclear materials or facilities for military or non-peaceful purposes.[149]

10.84 As for the body of Sch 17, s 1 offences in relation to nuclear material are added to by s 1(1A) (causing death, injury, or damage resulting from the emission of ionizing radiation, or from the release of radioactive material, or from an act interfering with the operation of, a nuclear facility), s 1B (receiving, holding, or dealing nuclear material or doing an act in relation to a nuclear facility for the purpose of causing damage to the environment), and s 1C (unlawfully importing or exporting nuclear material). Section 2 offences involving preparatory acts and threats are reworked and are added to by s 2A (providing for extended jurisdiction for inchoate and secondary offences).

Implementation

10.85 Section 51 of the ATCSA 2001 allows the venue for trial for offences under ss 47 and 50 to be anywhere in the United Kingdom.

10.86 By s 52, powers of entry and search under a justice's or sheriff's warrant can be granted to officers of the Secretary of State. The police cannot obtain a warrant directly (presumably these are considered to be matters beyond their expertise), but they may be permitted to accompany authorized officers. It was intended to preserve legal privilege under the order-making power in s 124,[150] but no order has appeared.

10.87 By s 53, the Customs and Excise Commissioners can enforce ss 47 and 50 in cases involving offences outside the United Kingdom or the movement of a nuclear weapon across a border. Officers of the Commissioners can institute offences in England and Wales and Northern Ireland (assuming the Attorney General gives consent under s 54).

10.88 By s 55, the Attorney General's consent is required for prosecutions under ss 47 and 50 in England and Wales and Northern Ireland.

10.89 Trade in these materials can also be restricted. Importation can be forbidden under the Import of Goods (Control) Order 1954.[151] The Export Control Act 2002[152] imposes corresponding controls over exports, including for the purpose of preventing terrorism anywhere in the world (Sch, para 3(2)E).

Foreign comparisons

10.90 It is not profitable to undertake detailed comparison since these offences largely derive from international conventions.

---

[147] <http://www.iaea.org/Publications/Documents/Conventions/cppnm.html>.
[148] Cmnd 8112, London, 1983.
[149] See further ss 3A, 6.
[150] Hansard HL vol 629 col 640 (3 December 2001), Baroness Symons.
[151] SI 1954/23, amended by SI 1954/627, SI 1975/2117, SI 1978/806. See Export and Customs Powers (Defence) Act 1939; Import and Export Control Act 1990.
[152] See Export Control Order 2008, SI 2008/3231; Department for Trade and Industry, *Export Control Act 2002. 2007 Review of export control legislation* (London, 2007); Yihdego, Z, and Savage, A, 'The UK arms export regime' [2008] *Public Law* 546.

Assessment and conclusions

10.91 Individual liberty does not exert any strong normative pull in this field. The state has a duty to protect the right to life, whereas there can be no conceivable right to dabble with substances which are horrendously dangerous to fellow humans.

10.92 What is more in doubt is the utility of the domestic effort beyond symbolism and reassurance. Given the absence of prosecutions, it might be helpful to consider the alternative approach of *in rem* forfeiture of materials and equipment on grounds of reasonable suspicion, as applies under the Chemical Weapons Act 1993, ss 4 to 10.

Nuclear materials: security of sites

Introduction

10.93 Part VIII of the ATCSA 2001 addresses the security of the nuclear industry. Its focus is organizations, installations, and information rather than the materials themselves, as under Pt VII.

Provisions: protective nuclear policing

10.94 The Civil Nuclear Constabulary (CNC) is the lead protective force. As constituted by the Energy Act 2004, s 52,[153] CNC officers enjoy full constabulary powers under s 56 and are tasked to provide physical protection at non-defence nuclear sites and at non-designated defence sites. The largest contingent (from a total of around 750 officers and staff) is based at Sellafield. Its jurisdiction is confined to seventeen civil nuclear sites, a five-kilometre radius around them, plus the transportation of nuclear materials. 'Nuclear material' is defined in s 71 as including only fissile material in the form of uranium or plutonium or as prescribed,[154] but not other radioactive material. Aside from its remote system of accountability and the fact that it is funded by the industry, the other notable feature of the CNC is that its officers are routinely armed.

10.95 To assist counter-terrorism work, s 57 of the 2004 Act confers on the CNC the power to stop and search under s 44 of the TA 2000. The Home Office Circular 26/2005, *Coordinated Policing Protocol between the Civil Nuclear Constabulary and Home Office Police Forces/Scottish Police Forces*, deals with policing cooperation. It directs notice of external armed patrols, confers prime authority for the policing of anti-nuclear and environmental protests on the local Chief Constable, and requires consultation before s 44 is used.[155]

Provisions: security of installations

10.96 By s 77 of the ATCSA 2001,[156] the civil nuclear industry is subjected to augmented security obligations, replacing earlier powers in the Nuclear Installations Act 1965 and the Atomic Energy Authority Act 1971. The Secretary of State may make regulations under s 77(1) (after consultation with the HSE and subject to negative resolution) for the security of nuclear sites, premises, material, and equipment, including material in transport, other radioactive material, and sensitive nuclear information. The regulations may require under s 77(2) the

---

[153] See Department for Trade and Industry, *Managing the Nuclear Legacy* (Cm 5552, London, 2002); Simpson, J, 'The UK and the threat of nuclear terrorism' in Wilkinson, P (ed), *Homeland Security in the UK* (Routledge, Abingdon, 2007). These arrangements replaced those in the ATCSA 2001 s 76.

[154] See Nuclear Industries Security Regulations 2003, SI 2003/403, art 3.

[155] Paras 14, 18, 29. See Civil Nuclear Police Authority, *Annual Report and Accounts 2007/08* (2007–08 HC 817) p 14.

[156] As amended by the Energy Act 2004, s 77.

production of satisfactory security plans, compliance with any directions, and the creation of criminal offences. They can apply under s 77(4) to acts done outside the United Kingdom by United Kingdom persons. For these purposes, 'sensitive nuclear information' means under s 77(7)(a) information relating to, or capable of use in connection with, the enrichment of uranium; or (b) information relating to activities carried out on or in relation to nuclear sites or other nuclear premises which appears to the Secretary of State to be information which needs to be protected in the interests of national security.

The Nuclear Industries Security Regulations 2003[157] are partly based on the authority **10.97** of s 77, especially Pt III (transportation arrangements and the use of approved carriers) and Pt IV (sensitive information), and partly on the Health and Safety at Work etc Act 1974. Part II requires an approved Site Security Plan, covering the physical environment and also the suitability of staff. For other nuclear sites, directions can be issued under the Atomic Energy Act 1954, s 3, and the Nuclear Installations Act 1965.

The Office of Civil Nuclear Security (OCNS), made part of the Health and Safety Executive's **10.98** Nuclear Directorate in 2007, is the principal security regulator, though non-security aspects are for the Nuclear Installations Inspectorate.[158] Within the setting of the 2003 Regulations, the OCNS sets security standards and inspects for compliance. It covers site, transport, information, and personnel security, the latter through a Vetting Office.[159] It works with the Department for Business, Enterprise and Regulatory Reform's Nuclear Consultations and Liabilities Directorate and with operators and security personnel via the Nuclear Industry Security Forum. The Nuclear Emergency Planning Liaison Group in the Department of Energy and Climate Change produces the Nuclear Emergency Planning Liaison Group Consolidated Guidance on planning, testing, response, and recovery.[160] Emergency preparedness for other radiological emergencies is the subject of the Radiation (Emergency Preparedness and Public Information) Regulations.[161] The lead regulator is the Environment Agency. There is less regulation for non-licensed sites, such as universities and hospitals.[162]

Further oversight and standard-setting is provided at an international level by the Convention **10.99** on the Physical Protection of Nuclear Material[163] which came into force in 1987 under the sponsorship of the UN's International Atomic Energy Agency. The UK Safeguards Office, also within the Nuclear Directorate, handles compliance with its international safeguards obligations.

The next special measure regarding nuclear security is the TA 2006, s 12, which deals with **10.100** trespass upon nuclear sites. Section 12 amends ss 128 and 129 (for Scotland) of the Serious Organised Crime and Police Act 2005 so as to extend that legislation to include all licensed

---

[157] SI 2003/403, as amended by SI 2006/2815.

[158] <http://www.hse.gov.uk/nuclear/ocns>. The Nuclear Directorate deals with military facilities. See Simpson, J, 'The UK and the threat of nuclear terrorism' in Wilkinson, P (ed), *Homeland Security in the UK* (Routledge, Abingdon, 2007).

[159] See *The State of Security in the Civil Nuclear Industry and the Effectiveness of Security Regulation April 2007 to March 2008* (<http://www.hse.gov.uk/nuclear/ocns/ocns0708.pdf>, 2008) para 5.

[160] Department for Business Enterprise and Regulatory Reform, London, 2008.

[161] 2001 SI/2975, implementing 96/29/Euratom. See also Health and Safety Executive, *Guide to the Radiation (Emergency Preparedness and Public Information) Regulations 2001* (HSE Books, Sudbury, 2001); Mobbs, S et al, *UK Recovery Handbook for Radiation Incidents* (Health Protection Agency, Chilton, 2005).

[162] See *Newton Report*, para 310; *Home Office Response to Newton Report*, para 76.

[163] Cm 2945, London, 1995.

nuclear sites (both civil and defence).[164] It is an offence to enter or to be on a nuclear site as a trespasser. These 'protected sites' do not have to be designated by order, unlike others within the 2005 Act.[165] The 'protected' nuclear site is defined, in s 128(1B), as (a) so much of premises in respect of which a nuclear site licence (within the meaning of the Nuclear Installations Act 1965) is in force as lies within the outer perimeter of the protection provided for those premises (meaning the outermost fences, walls, or other obstacles provided or relied on for protecting those premises from intruders); and (b) so much of any other premises falling within that outer perimeter of protection. In this way, where the area covered by the outer perimeter fence goes beyond the area of the licensed site, it is still an offence to be within the outer perimeter fence. Conversely, where there is land that is part of a licensed nuclear site, but which falls beyond the outer perimeter fence, it is not an offence to trespass; if it is not a secure area, then trespass is not an immediate threat. Extra powers arise under s 130 to make arrests. Trespassers may assert the defence that they did not know, nor had reasonable cause to suspect, that the site was a protected site (s 128(4)); but ignorance of the designation as trespass is no defence.

10.101   The 2005 Act has been criticized as an undue brake on public protest,[166] and equivalent powers under s 132 which affect the vicinity of Parliament are to be removed.[167] However, preventive measures against the exercise of expression or association are not *per se* an infringement of rights.[168] The government claims justification on the basis that protest might be used as a cover for entry by terrorists or to distract guards.[169]

10.102   Beyond the anti-terrorism legislation, other measures taken after the September 11 attacks to enhance nuclear safety related to aircraft overflights.[170] Aircraft are prohibited from flying below a specified height and within a specified radius of Sellafield and five other sites.[171] The restrictions are specified in the Air Navigation (Restriction of Flying) (Nuclear Installations) Regulations 2007.[172]

Provisions: security of information

10.103   Licensed companies working in the nuclear industry are already subjected to security regimes. The Nuclear Industries Security (Amendment) Regulations 2006[173] substitute a new reg 22 within the 2003 Regulations. Licensed operators must maintain appropriate security standards to minimize risk of loss, theft, or unauthorized disclosure of nuclear information or uranium enrichment equipment or software. They must also ensure that

---

[164] For a listing, see Home Office Circular 018/2007: *Trespass on Protected Sites—Sections 128–131 of the Serious Organised Crime and Police Act 2005*, Annex B.

[165] See Serious Organised Crime and Police Act 2005 (Designated Sites under Section 128) Order 2007, SI 2007/930.

[166] See *DPP v Haw* [2007] EWHC 1931. Compare Lord Carlile, *Proposals by Her Majesty's Government for Changes to the Laws against Terrorism* (Home Office, London, 2005) para 42.

[167] See Ministry of Justice, *The Governance of Britain: Constitutional Renewal* (Cm 7342, London, 2008) para 29.

[168] See *Christians against Fascism and Racism v United Kingdom*, App no 8440/78, DR 21, p 138 (1980); *Steel v United Kingdom* App no 24838/94, 1998-VII; *R (Laporte) v Chief Constable of Gloucestershire Constabulary* [2006] UKHL 55; *Austin v Commissioner of Police of the Metropolis* [2009] UKHL 5.

[169] Hansard HC vol 438 col 1027 (3 November 2005), Paul Goggins.

[170] See Edwards, E, 'What would happen if a passenger jet ploughed into a nuclear plant', *New Scientist*, 13 October 2001, p 1010.

[171] Hansard HC vol 374 col 540w (12 November 2001).

[172] SI 2007/1929.

[173] SI 2006/2815.

their officers, employees, contractors, and consultants observe the relevant security standards. The Secretary of State can issue specific directions about security and should be informed of any loss or threat. OCNS Information Security Inspectors advise operators.[174]

Section 79 of the ATCSA 2001[175] adds to the regulations by making it an offence for anyone, **10.104** whether falling under the regulations or not,[176] to disclose any information or thing where disclosure might prejudice the security of any nuclear site or material either with intent to prejudice security or being reckless as to prejudice. Section 79 extends to activities committed outside the United Kingdom if done by a United Kingdom person. For these purposes, the relevant nuclear material is that held on a nuclear site within the United Kingdom or nuclear material anywhere in the world which is being transported to or from a nuclear site or carried on board a British ship. The penalty is up to seven years' imprisonment. This broad offence makes no reference to whether the information is in the public domain or whether it might be in the public interest to disclose it. Battles fought over the Official Secrets Act 1989 might have to be resumed here.[177] However, the government offered the following reassurance:[178]

> . . . there is a great deal of information on nuclear transport that has no security implications. This is not in any way intended to be an attack on monitoring by environmental groups on where nuclear matter is moved around the country. People standing and observing on bridges and railway lines can hardly be prejudicing security because they are collecting public information. The same applies to the disclosure of information already in the public domain. The dissemination of that information is very unlikely to fall within the offence here . . . I reiterate that it will not cover environmental monitoring or whistle-blowing on health and safety matters. It is about giving advance notice of transport movements that leaves them open to attack.

Next, s 80 allows the Secretary of State to make regulations (by the affirmative procedure) to **10.105** prohibit the disclosure of information about the 'enrichment' of uranium (meaning any treatment of uranium that increases the proportion of the isotope 235 in the uranium). Like s 79, s 80 extends to individuals as well as regulated companies.[179] The regulations may provide for prohibitions to apply to acts done outside the United Kingdom by United Kingdom persons because 'this technology is highly attractive to proliferators'.[180] Breach of the regulations is an offence under s 80(3), and the penalty is up to seven years' imprisonment. The Enrichment Technology (Prohibition on Disclosure) Regulations 2004[181] prohibit the disclosure of equipment, software, and information. Regulation 2 applies to both intentional and reckless disclosures and to disclosures within the United Kingdom as well as disclosures by United Kingdom persons abroad. The test of recklessness replicates the formulation of

---

[174] See *The State of Security in the Civil Nuclear Industry and the Effectiveness of Security Regulation April 2007 to March 2008* (<http://www.hse.gov.uk/nuclear/ocns/ocns0708.pdf, 2008>) para 45.
[175] As amended by the Energy Act 2004, s 69.
[176] See Home Office, *Regulatory Impact Assessment: Security of Nuclear Industry, Security of Pathogens and Toxins* (2001) para 41.
[177] See also Joint Committee on Human Rights, *Report on the Anti-terrorism, Crime and Security Bill* (2001–02 HL 51/HC 420) para 26.
[178] Hansard HL vol 629 cols 1277, 1279 (11 December 2001), Lord Rooker.
[179] Home Office, *Regulatory Impact Assessment: Security of Nuclear Industry, Security of Pathogens and Toxins* (2001) para 25.
[180] Hansard HL vol 629 col 685 (3 December 2001), Lord Sainsbury.
[181] SI 2004/1818.

inadvertent recklessness in *Metropolitan Police Commissioner v Caldwell* .[182] Some exemptions are granted in reg 3, while the Secretary of State has 'override' powers in regs 4 and 5.

10.106 Section 80A is inserted by the Energy Act 2008, s 101. It allows the Secretary of State to designate as a 'prohibited place' for the purposes of s 3(c) of the Official Secrets Act 1911 a site which holds equipment, software, or information connected to the enrichment of uranium, no matter whether it is Crown property or not. Two issues are addressed by this amendment. First, following the restructuring of the nuclear industry under the Energy Act 2004, sensitive information about uranium enrichment may be stored away from licensed sites (for example, at research facilities). Secondly, the only offences protecting information at premises that are not licensed to undertake uranium enrichment are 'normal' offences such as burglary, theft, or receiving. So as to impose more severe sanctions, s 80A brings the Official Secrets Act 1911, s 1, into play, along with its penalty of not less than three and not more than fourteen years' imprisonment.[183] Further, s 1(2) of the Official Secrets Act 1911 allows conviction without proof that a person entered a 'prohibited place' for a purpose which would adversely affect the security interests of the state.[184]

10.107 Finally, s 81 provides that the offences under ss 79 and 80 may only be prosecuted by, or with the consent of, the relevant Attorney General. The same applies to s 80A under the Official Secrets Act 1911, s 8.

Foreign comparisons

10.108 Since there is an underlying framework of international conventions behind many of the foregoing measures, foreign jurisdictions evince little novelty.[185]

Assessment and conclusions

10.109 Overall, the system is 'comprehensive and incisive'.[186] It would appear to have helped to avoid proliferation to terrorists,[187] though scant information is divulged about application.

F. Protective Security for the Aviation, Maritime, and Other Transportation Sectors

Introduction

10.110 The entire transportation sector is considered in this section, but aviation is the most prominent target in the sector. Aviation is a recurrent terrorist target for several reasons. It involves an emblematic representation of state interests and Western modernity. There is vulnerability because of its complex operations and its need for public access. The drama of attack is also empathetic—onlookers can readily appreciate the experiences, so there is strong media and political attention.

---

[182] [1982] AC 341. Compare *R v G* [2003] UKHL 50.
[183] Official Secrets Act 1920, s 8(1).
[184] See further *Chandler v DPP* [1964] AC 763.
[185] See for example in the USA: Atomic Energy Act 1954 PL 83-703, 42 USC s 2274 , and 18 USC ss 831, 2332a; Levin, B and Austin, SE, 'An analysis of the legal issues relating to the prevention of nuclear and radio-logical terrorism' (2003) 46 *American Behavioral Scientist* 845.
[186] Simpson, J, 'The UK and the threat of nuclear terrorism' in Wilkinson, P (ed), *Homeland Security in the UK* (Routledge, Abingdon, 2007) p 177.
[187] See Home Office, *Pursue, Prevent, Protect, Prepare* (Cm 7547, London, 2009) para 12.08.

Aviation

Provisions

In the aftermath of the hijackings on 11 September, Pt IX of the ATCSA 2001 supplements **10.111** the substantial body of international laws relating to aviation security.[188]

Within domestic law, the most relevant measures are the Tokyo Convention Act 1967[189] **10.112** which was replaced by the Civil Aviation Act 1982, s 92 (as supplemented by the Civil Aviation (Amendment) Act 1996), the Hijacking Act 1971,[190] the Protection of Aircraft Act 1973,[191] and the Policing of Airports Act 1974, all three replaced by the Aviation Security Act 1982, and the Aviation and Maritime Security Act 1990.[192] Their impacts fall into three parts.

(i) **Aviation offences**   First, Pt I of the Aviation Security Act 1982 contains broad offences **10.113** with wide jurisdiction dealing with hijacking, the destruction or endangerment of aircraft, and the possession of dangerous articles. These offences have been considered in Chapter 5. Further offences of endangering the safety of an aircraft are set out in the Air Navigation Order 2009, art 137.[193] There is a specific power under the Aviation Security Act 1982, s 7, to prevent a person from embarking on an aircraft or to remove the person from the aircraft and to arrest and detain the person for so long as may be necessary for that purpose. In addition, the Civil Aviation Act 1982, s 94, allows the commander of an aircraft in flight to use force against persons on board whose actions jeopardize the safety of the aircraft or other persons on board, and police officers may use these powers with the authority of the commander.

(ii) **Aviation protective measures**   Protective measures for aircraft and aerodromes are **10.114** required by directive from the Secretary of State for Transport or the Director of the Transport Security and Contingencies Team (TRANSEC)[194] under Pt II of the 1982 Act. The measures imposed include the supply of information, restrictions on access, restrictions on flights, technical equipment, searches of persons and premises, alterations to buildings, and powers to inspect and test.[195] It is an offence under s 5 of the 1990 Act to make false statements in response to baggage or identity checks or to enter restricted zones without authority. These measures reflect the International Civil Aviation Organization's Standards and Recommended Practices (SARPs). The SARPs relating to civil aviation security are contained in Annex 17[196] to the (Chicago) Convention on International Civil Aviation 1944. The emphasis is upon ground security, the scrutiny of passengers, and passenger-baggage matching.[197]

---

[188] See Tan, AK-J, 'Recent developments relating to terrorism and aviation security' in Ramraj, VV, Hor, M, and Roach, K, *Global Anti-terrorism Law and Policy* (Cambridge University Press, Cambridge, 2005); Clarke, RV and Newman, GR, *Outsmarting the Terrorists* (Praeger, Westport, 2006) ch 4; Wilkinson, P, 'Enhancing UK aviation security post 9/11' in Wilkinson, P (ed), *Homeland Security in the UK* (Routledge, Abingdon, 2007).
[189] Convention on Offences and certain other Acts committed on board aircraft (Cmnd 2261, London, 1961).
[190] Convention for the Suppression of Unlawful Seizures of Aircraft (Cmnd 4577, London, 1971).
[191] Convention for the Suppression of Unlawful Acts against the Safety of Civil Aviation (Cmnd 4822, London, 1971).
[192] Protocol for the Suppression of Unlawful Acts of Violence at Airports Serving International Civil Aviation (Cm 378, London, 1988).
[193] SI 2009/3015.
[194] See <http://www.dft.gov.uk/pgr/security/about>.
[195] <http://www.ukaepg.org>.
[196] (8th edn, Montreal, 2006), as subject to Amendment 10 (ICAO Doc 7300/8, 2001).
[197] See also EU Regulation 300/2008 (replacing 2320/2002); Commission Regulations (EC) 622/2003, 1217/2003, 1486/2003, 68/2004, 849/2004, 1138/2004, 781/2005, 857/2005, 65/2006, 1546/2006, 358/2008, 820/2008, 272/2009, 1254/2009, 18/2010. The Council of the EU has sought the phasing out of the ban on liquids by 2014 (13974/09).

10.115 The processes by which protective security is applied locally have been strengthened by the Policing and Crime Act 2009, Pt VII. Security planning is dealt with under s 79, which adds Pt IIA to the Aviation Security Act 1982. Risk Advisory Groups (RAG) and Security Executive Groups (SEG) must be established by managers of those aerodromes under s 24AA which are the subject of a direction by the Secretary of State under ss 12, 13, or 14 of the Aviation Security Act 1982 on the basis that the aerodrome is within the National Aviation Security Programme (covering around sixty public airports). Other airports can be brought within the scheme by order. The RAGs (which take the place of around thirty-five groups which operated the Multi-Agency Threat and Risk Assessment (MATRA) process) comprise, under s 24AB, airport and police members as well as others. The duty of the RAGs under ss 24AC and 24AD is to produce a comprehensive risk assessment which must reflect the security directions and national threat assessments issued by the Minister. This Airport Security Plan (ASP) is transmitted to the SEG, consisting under s 24AG of airport, police, airline representatives, cargo agents, and airport retailers. The SEG must under ss 24AH and 24AJ decide on implementation and monitoring, with TRANSEC dealing with disputes and able to impose measures. Aerodrome stakeholders outside the SEG may object under s 24AI, and those on the SEG may refer the matter to the Secretary of State under s 24AN who will follow a dispute resolution procedure under s 24AP and 24AQ. Any party affected by a declaration, determination, or order of the Secretary of State has a right to appeal to the High Court (s 24AR).

10.116 The Secretary of State may also issue directions under the Airports Act 1986, s 30, to the operators of airports in the interests of national security.[198] Under the Transport Act 2000, s 93, the Secretary of State may give directions to air traffic and transport operators in any time of great national emergency or even, under s 94, seize possession of aerodromes, aircraft, and other assets.

10.117 The ATCSA 2001, s 86 (inserting s 20B into the Aviation Security Act 1982), extends further the powers of 'authorized persons' (meaning officials in TRANSEC).[199] They may issue a written direction to detain aircraft, if necessary by force, not solely to carry out an inspection of airworthiness (as permitted by s 60 of the Civil Aviation Act 1982 and Art 24 of the Air Navigation Order 2005)[200] but also if 'of the opinion' that the standard of security uncovered by inspection is inadequate or because of threats or potential acts of violence. The operator may appeal to the Secretary of State and must be allowed to make representations. There are no recorded uses of s 86,[201] but flights have been grounded by operators on security advice.[202]

10.118 Further protective security measures are contained in ss 85 and 87 of the 2001 Act. Section 85 inserts s 20A into the Aviation Security Act 1982 in order to extend powers under s 21F of that Act. Under s 21F, the Secretary of State for Transport maintains a list of approved air cargo agents who meet the security standards pursuant to the Aviation Security (Air Cargo Agents) Regulations 1993.[203] These arrangements are applied by s 85 to other parts of the

---

[198] See also DfT/ODPM Circular 1/2003.
[199] Compare Aviation and Maritime Security Act 1990, s 21; Channel Tunnel (Security) Order 1994, SI 1994/570, art 27.
[200] SI 2005/1970.
[201] *Newton Report*, para 319.
[202] See *The Times* 2 January 2004, p 1 (Washington), 3 January 2004, p 1 (Riyadh), 13 February 2004, p 1 (Washington and Riyadh).
[203] SI 1993/1073, as amended by SI 1996/1607, SI 1998/1152.

industry which provide security services to civil aviation—'for example companies contracted by airports and airlines to provide passenger and baggage screening services, and companies and individuals who provide aviation security training services'.[204] Section 87 also tightens the regulations relating to air cargo agents themselves to prevent fraud.[205] It creates a level 5 summary offence of issuing a document which falsely claims to come from a security-approved air cargo agent. Three cases have arisen, resulting in a caution and warnings.[206]

(iii) Aviation policing   The third element of protective security, the policing of airports, is implemented by Pt III of the Aviation Security Act 1982. Airports may be 'designated' under s 25 so that the local police force may freely enter what is otherwise private property. Section 28 confers extra powers to stop and question, and bylaws under the Airports Authority Act 1972 can also restrict or prohibit access to airports.[207] Most ominous of all, airport managers may be directed to inform the local Chief Officer of Police that the Secretary of State considers it appropriate that the police at airports should carry weapons.[208]   **10.119**

These policing arrangements have been substantially amended under s 80 and Sch 6 of the Policing and Crime Act 2009. The main impact is that the sixty or so major airports are regulated fully and not just nine major designated airports. The system of designation is repealed, since, under s 25B (as inserted in the 1982 Act), all relevant aerodromes must have a Police Services Agreement (PSA) between the manager of the aerodrome, the relevant police authority, and the chief officer of police. There is also an amendment to s 26 so that a relevant police constable is entitled to enter any regulated aerodrome. Where there is a dispute about PSAs, the Secretary of State can make a determination under ss 29A–E, subject to appeal to the High Court.   **10.120**

Further policing changes have been effected by Pt IX of the ATCSA 2001.[209] Extra powers of summary arrest were granted under s 82 for offences relating to unauthorized presence in the restricted zone of an airport or on an aircraft (the Aviation Security Act 1982, ss 21C(1) and 21D(1)) and trespassing on a licensed aerodrome (the Civil Aviation Act 1982, s 39(1)). These powers were replaced by the Police Reform Act 2002, Sch 6, which in turn has been overtaken by the Serious Organised Crime and Police Act 2005, s 110.[210] In Scotland, a statutory power of arrest without warrant remains in force under s 82(3), and a further Scottish summary power is granted[211] for offences relating to the contravention of an offence under an order in council made under the Civil Aviation Act 1982, s 60, where the offence relates to specified behaviour by a person in an aircraft towards a crew member or which is likely to endanger an aircraft, or a person in an aircraft.[212]   **10.121**

Other relatively minor policing changes include, by s 83, an increase in the penalty (from level 1 to level 3) for the offence of trespass on an aerodrome contrary to s 39(1) of the Civil Aviation Act 1982,[213] and by s 84, the conferment of a specific power for the police or   **10.122**

204 Home Office, *Explanatory Notes to the Anti-terrorism, Crime and Security Bill* (London, 2001) para 189.
205 Home Office, *Regulatory Impact Assessment: Aviation Security* (London, 2001) para 36.
206 *Newton Report*, para 325.
207 s 9. See also Civil Aviation Act 1982, ss 18, 27–40.
208 1990 Act, s 15(5). Compare 1982 Act, s 16(1).
209 See also the Police and Justice Act 2006, ss 12, 14.
210 See also PACE (NI) Order 2007, SI 2007/288, art 15.
211 Added by the Aviation (Offences) Act 2003, s 1(3).
212 See especially Air Navigation Order 2005, SI 2005/1970, arts 73–78.
213 It must be an aerodrome licensed under the Air Navigation Order 2005, SI 2005/1970, art 128.

aviation authority employees to use force to remove intruders whose presence is unauthorized under s 21C of the Aviation Security Act 1982 (equivalent to s 31(4) of the Aviation and Maritime Security Act 1990, as amended, for ports areas and under art 31 of the Channel Tunnel Security Order 1994).[214] While the purported aim of these measures is to ensure the security of airports, they could be used against environmental protesters. It was also threatened that they would be used against journalists who 'probe' airport security.[215] There are around seventy incidents per year,[216] but the *Newton Report* recorded just one conviction under ss 82 to 84.[217]

Implementation

10.123   Aviation security policy is overseen by the Department of Transport's National Aviation Security Committee.[218] The National Aviation Security Programme and Handbook[219] is applied at each airport by the processes already outlined. Private sector air transport planning occurs in the United Kingdom Flight Safety Committee and United Kingdom Airlines Emergency Planning Group.

10.124   After the attacks of September 11, increased security involved the random searching of hold baggage, increased searching of passengers, and an expanded list of prohibited articles.[220] Sky marshals were insisted upon by US authorities in late 2003,[221] despite long-standing opposition from British pilots.[222]

10.125   The possibility of shooting down a hijacked passenger aircraft also arose before the German Constitutional Court. It concluded that the empowerment of state authorities under the *Luftsicherheitsgesetz* of 2005 (Air Security Act) was an unconstitutional infringement of the right to life of passengers.[223] The position in criminal law self-defence or arrest, especially if undertaken by the air crew, was not considered. There has been no announced British policy, but an incident in late 2001 has been revealed by former Prime Minister Tony Blair in which he claims that he was close to ordering an airborne fighter jet to shoot down an airliner over London.[224]

Foreign comparisons

10.126   In the USA, the Transportation Security Administration (TSA) was created under the Aviation and Transportation Security Act 2001[225] but was brought within the Department for Homeland Security in 2003. The TSA certainly provides a focus and entails the ability to

---

[214] SI 1994/570.

[215] Home Office, *Regulatory Impact Assessment: Aviation Security*, 2001, para 8. For examples, see *The Independent* 3 November 2001, p 5 (*The Mirror*); *The Independent* 7 January 2002, p 9 (*Sunday People*); *Daily Telegraph* 6 January 2004, p 9 (BBC).

[216] Home Office, *Regulatory Impact Assessment: Aviation Security* (London, 2001) para 9.

[217] *Newton Report*, para 316. There were thirteen arrests.

[218] House of Commons Transport Committee, *Transport Security* (2007–08 HC 191).

[219] See Sir John Wheeler, *Report on Airport Security* (Department for Transport, London, 2002) paras 1.3, 3.28.

[220] See ibid para 1.19.

[221] See Government Accountability Office, *Federal Air Marshal Service* (GAO-09-273, GAO-09-903T, Washington DC).

[222] See Air Navigation Order 2005, SI 2005/1970, art 69; Hansard HC vol 416 col 161 (6 January 2004).

[223] *Entscheidungen des Bundesverfassungsgerichts*, BVerfGE 118 (2006). See Hornle, T, 'Hijacked airplanes' (2007) 10 *New Criminal Law Review* 582.

[224] *A Journey* (Hutchinson, London, 2010) pp 350–1.

[225] PL 107–71.

set more unified standards in a Federalised state, though the transition took time.[226] But British aviation systems have always been more uniformly regulated, and the existence of TRANSEC plus effective changes in airport policing mean that the TSA has few lessons to offer.

Assessment and conclusions

It would be difficult to devise on paper a more stringent security system, though one impact **10.127** may be displacement to other civilian targets.[227] Nonetheless, incidents have affected British aircraft and airports,[228] including after 2001 the attack on Glasgow Airport in 2007.[229] Other notable plots have been thwarted by incompetence or interdiction, including the shoe bomber, Richard Reid in 2001 and the 'Liquid Bomb' plot in 2006.[230] Further restrictions could always be imagined, but for air travel to grind to a halt because of security restrictions would itself be a 'victory' for terrorism.[231]

More telling criticisms point to limited accountability and constitutional governance. **10.128** Piecemeal reviews have included the *Wheeler Review of Airport Security, 2002*,[232] the (Boys Smith) *Independent Review of Airport Policing in 2006*,[233] and the (Boys Smith) *Independent Review of Personnel Security across the Transport Sector*.[234] In response, the Department of Transport paper, *Airport Policing Funding and Security Planning*,[235] promised to implement changes, and they appeared in the Policing and Crime Act 2009.

The main threat to personal rights from aviation security has been to privacy. One aspect **10.129** concerns physical privacy. Bodily searches at airports are the only occasion when most people encounter counter-terrorism laws. There is a remarkable degree of tolerance to screening, but rights against privacy and discrimination are at risk, as discussed in Chapter 2. Anxiety was heightened by the summary introduction of body scanners in early 2010, in response to the failed attempt by Umar Farouk Abdulmutallab to blow up a Detroit-bound aircraft.[236] The Home Affairs Committee estimated the privacy concerns as 'overstated',[237] a strange assessment considering the evidently intrusive nature of the imaging and also the fact that images can be recorded (though this is currently forbidden).

The other aspect where privacy arises concerns the sharing of passenger data. The United **10.130** States government demanded in November 2001, pursuant to the Aviation and Transportation Security Act,[238] full disclosure of the passenger name record (PNR)—the airline's

---

[226] See Government Accountability Office, *Aviation Security* (GAO-04-285T, GAO-06-864T, GAO-06-597T, GAO-10-650T, Washington DC).

[227] See Hainmuller, J and Lemnitzer, JM, 'Why do Europeans fly safer?' (2003) 15 *Terrorism and Political Violence* 1; Enders, W and Sandler, T, *The Political Economy of Terrorism* (Cambridge University Press, Cambridge, 2006) chs 3, 5.

[228] See Malik, O, *The Analysis of Terrorist Attacks on Aviation* (RIIA, London, 2000) p 16.

[229] See Hansard HC vol 467 col 667 (14 November 2007).

[230] *R v Abdulla*, *The Times* 17 December 2008, p 3; *US v Reid* 369 F 3d 619 (2004).

[231] See House of Commons Transport Committee, *Passengers' experience of air travel* (2006–07 HC 435).

[232] Department for Transport, London, 2002, para 5.37.

[233] Department for Transport, London, 2006.

[234] Department for Transport, London, 2008.

[235] Department for Transport, London, 2008.

[236] Department for Transport, *Interim Code of Practice for the Acceptable Use of Advanced Imaging Technology (Body Scanners) in an Aviation Security Environment* (London, 2010). The code warns against ethnic profiling: p 5.

[237] House of Commons Home Affairs Committee, *Counter Terrorism Measures in British Airports* (2009–10 HC 311) para 30. Compare COM (2010) 311/4.

[238] 49 USC s 44909(c)(3); 8 CFR 231; 19 CFR 122.31.

reservation file for each passenger journey. This automatic transfer of data raised objections under the European Data Protection Directive 95/46/EC. Consequently, the bilateral EU–US agreement for transfer in 2004[239] was condemned before the European Court of Justice.[240] A subsequent agreement was devised in 2006.[241] The idea of passenger data transfer for air travel between Europe and destinations other than the US is now being advanced by the draft Framework Decision on the Use of Passenger Name Records for Law Enforcement Purposes 2007.[242] The UK government has criticized the draft as inadequate, preferring it to apply to all travel formats (including rail) and to journeys inside the European Union.[243]

10.131 As mentioned in Chapter 2, the TSA operates the Secure Flight programme for domestic flights, while the Customs and Border Protection agency operates the Immigration Advisory Program for overseas flights.[244] The systems involve checks against the consolidated terrorist screening database which incorporates the 'No Fly List' and 'Selectee List'.[245] Statutory authority for the scheme is provided by the Intelligence Reform and Terrorism Prevention Act of 2004.[246] The effectiveness of operation remains debatable,[247] but British equivalents are in the offing.[248]

Maritime

Introduction and background

10.132 Attention to ports and shipping has been laggardly compared to aviation security.[249] Port controls have been described in Chapter 2, but these are confined largely to the scrutiny of passenger transits rather than transportation security. International law has been a greater driver of change. Following the Achille Lauro incident in 1985,[250] the (Rome) Convention for the Suppression of Unlawful Acts against the Safety of Maritime Navigation,[251] and the (Rome) Protocol for the Suppression of Unlawful Acts Against the Safety of Fixed Platforms Located on the Continental Shelf[252] were agreed. They have been implemented by the

---

[239] See Council Decision 2004/496/EC of 17 May 2004.

[240] See Cases C-317/04 and C-318/04, *European Parliament v Council of the European Union and European Parliament v Commission of the European Communities* (2006).

[241] Agreement between the European Union and the United States of America on the processing and transfer of passenger name record (PNR) data by air carriers to the United States Department of Homeland Security (13668/06) and Annexes (11304/07); House of Lords European Union Committee, *The EU/US Passenger Name Record (PNR) Agreement* (2007–08 HL 108).

[242] COM (2007) 654 final.

[243] See House of Lords European Union Committee, *The Passenger Name Record (PNR) Framework Decision* (2007–08 HL 106) and *Government Reply* (Cm 7461, London, 2008); House of Commons European Scrutiny Committee, *Seventh Report* (2007–08 HC 16-vii).

[244] See 73 Federal Register 64017 and 64789; Government Accountability Office, *Aviation Security* (GAO-07-346, GAO-08-456T, Washington DC, 2007).

[245] See Florence, J, 'Making the no fly list fly' (2006) 115 *Yale Law Journal* 2148; Government Accountability Office, *Aviation Security* (GAO-08-1136T, GAO-09-292, Washington DC).

[246] PL 108–458.

[247] See Government Accountability Office, *Homeland Security* (GAO 10-401T, Washington DC).

[248] Hansard HC vol 504 col 303 (20 January 2010).

[249] See Beckman, RC, 'International responses to combat maritime terrorism' in Ramraj, VV, Hor, M, and Roach, K, *Global Anti-terrorism Law and Policy* (Cambridge University Press, Cambridge, 2005); Greenberg, MD et al, *Maritime Terrorism* (RAND, Santa Monica, 2006); Lehr, P, 'Port security in the UK' in Wilkinson, P, (ed), *Homeland Security in the UK* (Routledge, Abingdon, 2007).

[250] See Cassese, A, *Terrorism, Politics, and Law* (Blackwell, Oxford, 1989).

[251] 27 ILM 668, 1988.

[252] 27 ILM 685, 1988.

Aviation and Maritime Security Act 1990. Part II contains offences such as hijacking, while Pt III deals with protective security.

Provisions

The Aviation and Maritime Security Act 1990, ss 18(1) and 26(5), are concerned with the physical protection of ships and ports in the United Kingdom or British ships anywhere. As under the Aviation Security Act 1982, the Secretary of State is empowered under ss 19–25, 28–32, 36–39, and 41 to demand information, to designate 'restricted zones', to direct searches, to specify numbers of guards and security apparatus, and to inspect and test. These powers apply to ships and harbours. Fixed platforms have received some protection since the passage of the Continental Shelf Act 1964 (now the Petroleum Act 1987),[253] by which a 'safety zone' may be imposed. **10.133**

After the bombings of the USS Cole in 2000 and the French tanker, Limburg, in 2002, the International Maritime Organization produced an International Ship and Port Facility Security Code 2004 (ISPS) as Chapter XI-2 to the Safety of Life at Sea Convention 1974.[254] The Code requires ports and specified ships to be certified as having adequate security plans, training, personnel, and identification and tracking equipment. TRANSEC oversees the application of ISPS. The system is enforced through the Ship and Port Facility (Security) Regulations 2004,[255] and it is also enforceable through insurance requirements. Further security measures going beyond the ship/port interface are imposed through the Port Security Regulations 2009.[256] **10.134**

As befits the unique status of the development, a separate legal regime has been created by the Channel Tunnel Act 1987. For policing purposes, the Tunnel is integrated within the Kent Constabulary, and its security is overseen by an Intergovernmental Commission and Safety Authority.[257] One of the reasons for choosing a tunnel was that it is inherently least vulnerable to terrorism,[258] but extensive bylaws akin to those at airports are issued under s 9. **10.135**

Implementation

The Department for Transport has established the National Maritime Security Committee to enable consultation, plus a Shipping Panel and a Ports Panel.[259] Maritime Security Compliance Inspectors are appointed within TRANSEC to scrutinize ports and passenger ships, while the Maritime and Coastguard Agency covers security compliance by cargo and freight ships. The National Coordinator of Ports Policing coordinates Special Branch activities. One wonders whether a unified organization might achieve more.[260] **10.136**

Other domestic implementation measures include the Home Office's Programme Cyclamen—radiation screening at ports and airports.[261] **10.137**

---

[253] See Offshore Installations (Safety Zones) Orders.
[254] See further Regulation (EC) 725/2004 of 31 March 2004. See Robertson, S, 'Shipping and terrorism' (2004) 154 *New Law Journal* 388.
[255] SI 2004/1495 (as amended by SI 2005/1434).
[256] SI 2009/2048. See further Directive 2005/65/EC of 26 October 2005.
[257] ss 14, 17. Hermitage, P, 'Light on the start of the Tunnel' (1984) 5 *Policing* 121.
[258] *The Channel Fixed Link* (Cmnd 9735, 1986) para 23, Annex B.
[259] See House of Commons Transport Committee, *Transport Security* (2007–08 HC 191).
[260] Compare the Malaysian Maritime Enforcement Agency Act 2004.
[261] Hansard HC vol 442 col 957W (6 February 2006), Hazel Blears.

10.138 In the US, the ISPS as well as other security regulations are implemented under the Maritime Transportation Security Act of 2002.[262] An ambitious Container Security Initiative was launched in 2002 which includes the pre-screening of containers and is enforced under the SAFE Port Act of 2006.[263] The European Union states agreed to cooperate in this programme in 2004.[264]

10.139 The US has also pursued an aggressive policy of the boarding of suspect vessels under its Proliferation Security Initiative.[265] The UK government is a party to these arrangements and British intercessions have also occurred.[266]

Assessment and conclusions

10.140 The maritime sector has been boosted mainly through international law and US demands. The next stage might be ratification of the 2005 Protocol to the Convention for the Suppression of Unlawful Acts against the Safety of Maritime Navigation.[267]

Other transportation sectors

10.141 The Madrid and London transportation bombings in 2004 and 2005 raised the priority for protective security for railways. Experiments with entry checks have not been pursued but better communications links have been implemented. There is a National Rail Security Programme led by TRANSEC.[268]

10.142 The Secretary of State retains powers under the Railways Act 1993, s 118, to issue directions 'in time of hostilities, whether actual or imminent, severe international tension or great national emergency' and under s 119 to demand protective measures.

Transportation policing—the British Transport Police

Introduction and background

10.143 The British Transport Police (BTP) is constituted under the Railways and Transport Safety Act 2003, Pt III.[269] The Act establishes a national police authority and clarifies powers and jurisdiction. The BTP focus of operations under s 31 is primarily confined to railway property but can venture beyond for a purpose connected to the railway. The BTP does not extend to Northern Ireland but does take responsibility for some light railways, including the London Underground. There are around 2,800 officers, spread across seven divisions. Their prime work arises from public order, assaults, and property offences, but terrorism has become a headline activity.

---

[262] PL 107–295.

[263] Security and Accountability for Every Port Act 2006 (PL 109-347, 6 USC s 945). There is also the voluntary Customs-Trade Partnership Against Terrorism (C-TPAT) scheme: s 961. See Dominguez-Mates, R, 'From Achille Lauro to the present day' in Fernandez Sanchez, P (ed), *International Legal Dimension of Terrorism* (Nijhoff, Leiden, 2009).

[264] See L 304/34, 30 September 2004; Council Decision 2004/634/EC of 30 March 2004.

[265] See Byers, M, 'Policing the High Seas' (2004) 98 *American Journal of International Law* 526; Guilfoyle, D, 'Maritime interdiction of weapons of mass destruction' (2007) 12 *Journal of Conflict and Security Law* 1.

[266] See *The Independent* 28 December 2001, p 5.

[267] See Hansard HC vol 497 col 1619w (22 October 2009).

[268] House of Commons Transport Committee, *Transport Security* (2007–08 HC 191) para 8.

[269] See Department for Transport, *Modernising the British Transport Police* (London, 2001).

Provisions and implementation

By Pt X of the ATCSA 2001, specific counter-terrorism powers are conferred. Section 100 **10.144** allows the BTP to act outside their railways jurisdiction. According to the government memorandum accompanying the 2001 Bill:[270]

> . . . BTP officers are frequently called upon to intervene in incidents outside their 'railways' jurisdiction. It is estimated that some such 8,000 incidents occur each year. In these circumstances BTP officers only have the powers of an ordinary citizen, despite being police officers fully trained to the standards of a Home Office force, and despite routinely dealing with the same range of incidents in the course of their railway activities.

Therefore, s 100(1) permits a BTP officer to assist other forces (and with the full powers of that force) on request in relation to a 'particular' incident, investigation, or operation. The power can be exercised without request in an emergency. Next, the ATCSA 2001, Sch 7, paras 29–34, allows the BTP to use powers under the TA 2000 including cordons and stop and search.

A protocol guides good relations with local police. The BTP must inform the local Chief **10.145** Constable of any crime of terrorism and should consult before any authorization under the TA 2000, s 44, but their assistance should not be routinely requested.[271]

Since 2001, the BTP has engaged in protective security checks through the widespread use **10.146** of stop and search powers under s 44.[272] The BTP has also encountered many bomb threats and seeks to handle them with a minimum of disruption; over 10,000 threats from 2000 onwards have resulted in fewer than seventy station closures.[273]

Assessment and conclusions

Many of these extensions of the jurisdiction revived plans announced in 1998. **10.147** Consequently, the familiar criticism arose of the ATCSA 2001 being used as a vehicle for unpalatable changes without time for proper consideration.[274] The refusal to tie down the extensions to terrorism connections was valiantly addressed by the Defence Minister, Lord Bach:[275]

> . . . what is it reasonable to assume is terrorism? . . . Perhaps I may cite as an example an individual acting suspiciously and tampering with a vehicle. He may be attempting simply to steal it, which would not be an act of terrorism. Alternatively, he may be seeking to place a bomb under the car. Clearly that would be such an act.

Aside from the extent of the roles of the BTP, the effectiveness of policing institutions **10.148** at ports and airports may be questioned. The forces, including the BTP, several small bands of ports police,[276] Special Branches, and the UK Border Agency, remain highly

---

[270] London, 2001, para 254.
[271] Home Office Circular 25/2002: *A protocol between British Transport Police and Home Office Police Forces*, paras 4, 12, 15.
[272] 66,000 stops were carried out in 2007–08: *Annual Report 2007–08* (London, 2008) p 3.
[273] Ibid p 25.
[274] Joint Committee on Human Rights, *Report on the Anti-terrorism, Crime and Security Bill* (2001–02 HL 37/HC 372) para 68.
[275] HL Debs vol 629 col 643, 4 December 2001; see also cols 1466, 1533, 13 December 2001.
[276] Harbours, Docks and Piers Clauses Act 1847, ss 79, 83, and the Port of London Act 1968, ss 154, 160, 170; Hansard HC vol 442 col 72w (7 June 2004).

fragmented.[277] Local accountability is also limited. Proposals to incorporate some, but by no means all, of these bodies into a National Crime Agency have already been mentioned.[278]

G. Protective Security for Critical and Other Sectors, Activities, Sites, and Events

Introduction

10.149 The almost infinite agenda of protective security suggested by the foregoing title might be said to betray excessive paranoia.[279] Boundless reaction to every imaginable risk would indeed be folly, but it is worthwhile to protect from terrorist risk both societal infrastructures which support widely shared basic necessities and those more specific facilities which, if attacked, would result in maximum casualties or financial loss to an extent amounting to the destabilization of society. The application of protective security at different tiers of vulnerability will now be considered.

Critical national infrastructure (CNI)

Provisions

10.150 Two problems arise with protective security for the CNI.[280] First, how is the CNI to be defined and what does it comprise? Second, how can protective security be delivered effectively and fairly within a disparate set of highly complex enterprises many of which are owned and operated for private profit rather than in the public interest?

10.151 The definition of the CNI remains extra-legal but, in practice, is outlined for tasking purposes by the Centre for the Protection of the National Infrastructure (CPNI) as 'those facilities, systems, sites and networks necessary for the delivery of the essential services upon which daily life in the UK depends and which ensure the country continues to function socially and economically'.[281]

10.152 This identification of vulnerability feeds into the Cabinet Office's Key Capabilities Programme, consisting of twenty-two capability 'workstreams', each undertaken by a designated Lead Government Department.[282] The workstreams fall into three groups: four are structural, six deal with essential services; and twelve relate to functional sectors.

Implementation

10.153 Various legal offences and powers afford protection to the elements within the CNI. Overall, there is the Civil Contingencies Act 2004, as already related. A large ragbag of other measures

---

[277] Home Affairs Committee, *Policing in the 21st Century* (2007–08 HC 364) para 265. See further ACPO and UKBA, *Memorandum of Understanding: Police and UK Border Agency Engagement to Strengthen the UK Border* (2008).

[278] Home Office, *Policing in the 21st Century* (London, 2010) paras 4.32, 4.38.

[279] See Furedi, F, *Invitation to Terror* (Continuum Press, London, 2007).

[280] See Walker, C, 'The governance of the Critical National Infrastructure' [2008] *Public Law* 323.

[281] See <http://www.cpni.gov.uk/About/whatIs.aspx>.

[282] See <http://www.ukresilience.info/preparedness/ukgovernment/capabilities.aspx>. See further Cabinet Office, *Sector Resilience Plans for Critical National Infrastructure* (London, 2010) which identifies nine national infrastructure sectors.

comprises trespass offences,[283] the regulation of industrial sites,[284] and the maintenance of power and fuel industries.[285]

Communications networks are a CNI component and are vital during emergency response. **10.154** Various powers allow for emergency directions to be issued, including for broadcasts[286] and the suspension of telecommunications services to prevent overload in an emergency via the GTPS (Government Telephone Preference Scheme) and ACCOLC (ACCess OverLoad Control scheme).[287] A National Emergency Plan for the UK Telecommunications Sector is overseen by a Telecommunications Industry Emergency Planning Forum.[288] Concerns over the security and robustness of emergency communications networks have spurred the development of 'Airwave'.[289]

The resilience of the internet features as another prominent part of the CNI agenda. Threats **10.155** are monitored by the Serious Organised Crime Agency's e-Crime Unit.[290] As noted in Chapter 8, the Office of Cyber Security & Information Assurance in the Cabinet Office provides strategic direction and coordinates action, while the Cyber Security Operations Centre (based in GCHQ) works on implementation.[291]

Though the legal list is cumulatively broad and sometimes potentially conflicts with rights to **10.156** political assembly, it is far from a rational code. Why, for instance, is it considered more important to punish trespass on the Castleford to Pontefract rail line than, say, the Easington, East Yorkshire, gas terminus or the London Internet Exchange (LINX)? Why is the focus often on criminal offences for wrongful activity which has been perpetrated rather than on policing powers to avert intrusion?

The task of implementing protective security falls upon the CPNI, which was formed in **10.157** 2007. The CPNI provides security advice to relevant businesses and organizations, mainly disseminated via specialist CTSAs. Its key features include special access to intelligence and close working relationships with the private sector. However, compared to previous arrangements, the CPNI operates on a broader scale, across all CNI sectors. In addition, it has adopted a more public interface, evidenced by the populist trumpeting of its 'top ten security guidelines'.[292] All aspects of the CPNI are said to operate under the Security Service Act 1989 and to be formally accountable to the Security Service. However, neither the establishment

---

[283] Railway Regulation Act 1840, s 16; Harbours, Docks and Piers Clauses Act 1847, s 83; Military Lands Act 1892, s 14; Civil Aviation Act 1982, s 39; Serious Organised Crime and Police Act 2005, s 128.

[284] Control of Major Accident Hazards Regulations 1999 (COMAH), 1999 SI/743 as amended by 2005 SI/1088. See also Planning (Hazardous Substances) Act 1990; Dangerous Substances (Notification and Marking of Sites) Regulations 1990, SI 1990/304.

[285] See Energy Act 1976. See Bonner, D, *Emergency Powers in Peacetime* (Sweet & Maxwell, London, 1985) p 220.

[286] See Agreement Dated the 25th Day of January 1996 Between Her Majesty's Secretary of State for National Heritage and the British Broadcasting Corporation, para 8; Communications Act 2003, ss 5, 132.

[287] See Telecommunications Act 1984, s 94; Home Office, *Addressing Lessons from the Emergency Response to the 7 July 2005 London Bombings* (London, 2006) paras 55–62.

[288] <http://www.ofcom.org.uk/static/archive/oftel/ind_groups/emer_plan/index.htm>.

[289] See Home Office, *Addressing Lessons from the Emergency Response to the 7 July 2005 London Bombings* (London, 2006) paras 63–72.

[290] See House of Lords Science and Technology Committee, *Personal Internet Security* (2006–07 HL 165) paras 7.38 and 7.39.

[291] Cabinet Office, *Cyber Security of the United Kingdom* (Cm 7642, London, 2009).

[292] <http://www.cpni.gov.uk/About/topTen.aspx>.

nor the operation of the CPNI has been explained in any consultation paper or debated in Parliament.

Foreign comparisons

10.158 The US equivalent formula for defining the CNI offers no clearly superior model for solving these problems, save that constitutional governance is better secured through the establishment of an explicit legal basis, the Critical Infrastructure Protection Act 2001 (part of the USA PATRIOT Act 2001).[293] A visible and comprehensive National Infrastructure Protection Plan was produced by the Department for Homeland Security in 2006 and updated in 2009.[294] Sector-Specific Plans have also been prepared.[295]

10.159 The European Commission has faced the same definitional quandary in its Council Directive of 8 December 2008 on the identification and designation of European critical infrastructures and the assessment of the need to improve their protection.[296] It seeks to concentrate on 'European Critical Infrastructure', meaning vital infrastructures the disruption or destruction of which would significantly affect two or more Member States. This intervention into national security is viewed with great suspicion by United Kingdom authorities.[297] The Directive therefore places duties on Member States, rather than the Commission, to assess operator security plans.

Assessment and conclusions

10.160 The governance of the CNI poorly reflects constitutional normative standards. The problem is compounded by the lack of formal structure in central government and reliance on prerogative emergency powers.[298] A principal target of added regulation should be the central government.[299] The Joint Committee on the Draft Civil Contingencies Bill likewise proposed a centralized system of enforcement and inspection, delivered through a national Civil Contingencies Agency, headed by a Civil Contingencies Commissioner.[300]

10.161 As for the operational regulation of protective security, the preferred mode of governance should rely on a light-touch benchmarking approach.[301] A regulatory approach to CNI, including in the field of counter-terrorism, is not a novel departure.[302] Regulatory approaches, which are built on networks of governance and are sensitive to the interests and cost burdens of the private sector, have been long established in counter-terrorism.[303]

---

[293] 42 USC s 5195(c). See Bagley, N, 'Benchmarking, critical infrastructure security, and the regulatory war on terror' (2006) 43 *Harvard Journal on Legislation* 47.

[294] <http://www.dhs.gov/files/programs/editorial_0827.shtm>, based on the Homeland Security Act 2002 (PL 107-296), s 101(b)(2). See Moteff, J, *Critical Infrastructure Protections* (RL32531, Congressional Research Service, Washington DC, 2005).

[295] See <http://www.dhs.gov/xprevprot/programs/gc_1179866197607.shtm>.

[296] 2008/114/EC. See Olsson, S (ed), *Crisis Management in the European Union* (Springer, Dordrecht, 2009).

[297] HC European Scrutiny Committee, *Fifteenth Report* (2006–07 HC 41-xv); *Second Report* (2010–11) HC 428) para 27.10.

[298] See Ministry of Justice, *The Governance of Britain—War Powers and Treaties: Limiting Executive Powers* (Cm 7239, London, 2007).

[299] See Walker, C, and Broderick, J, *The Civil Contingencies Act 2004* (Oxford University Press, Oxford, 2006) ch 8.

[300] Draft Civil Contingencies Bill (2002–03 HC 1074, HL 184), paras 257, 260.

[301] Bagley, N, 'Benchmarking, critical infrastructure security, and the regulatory war on terror' (2006) 43 *Harvard Journal on Legislation* 47 at 50.

[302] Compare Posner, EA, 'Fear and the regulatory model of counterterrorism' (2002) 25 *Harvard Journal of Law & Public Policy* 681 at 681–683; Ogus, A, 'Responding to threats of terrorism: how the law can generate appropriate incentives' (2007) 19 *Journal of Interdisciplinary Economics* 35 at 36.

[303] See Frey, BS, *Dealing with Terrorism: Stick or Carrot?* (Edward Elgar, Cheltenham, 2004).

In addition, legal protections for CNI facilities should reflect greater consistency. The emphasis **10.162** should be on protection rather than criminalization. Thus, there might be power to make directions about search on entry and restrictions on movement after entry, forced removal or the exclusion of persons, and the issuance of regulations for the control of nearby highways. Consideration should also be given to the appropriate policing structures, as described next.

CNI policing—the Ministry of Defence Police (MDP)

Introduction and background

The history of the MDP does not suggest that it should be conceived as the 'CNI police', but **10.163** it has been so deployed in recent years. The MDP was constructed in 1971 from the unification of distinct service constabularies and now subsists under the Ministry of Defence Police Act 1987. The MDP is a civilian (but armed) police force with around 3,500 officers in five divisions and exercising full constabulary powers.[304] Its jurisdiction is confined to around 200 Ministry of Defence establishments. The MDP is part of the Ministry of Defence Police and Guarding Agency, created by merger in 2004 with the Ministry of Defence Guard Service. That Service, with around 3,900 personnel, was formed in 1992 after Irish Republican attacks on military targets in England.[305] Other defence security needs are met by the Military Provost Guard Service and by private security firms.[306]

Provisions

The MDP's counter-terrorism work is enhanced by Pt X of the ATCSA 2001. By s 98(3), **10.164** which amends s 2 of the Ministry of Defence Police Act 1987, the MDP's jurisdiction in relation to defence personnel within the United Kingdom is extended from the alleged commission of offences by defence personnel to offences against defence personnel as well as the incitement or corruption of soldiers (such as to reveal confidential information).

By s 98(4), the MDP is enabled to operate beyond defence property and with full constabulary **10.165** powers whenever a constable of a Home Department police force, the Police Service of Northern Ireland, the British Transport Police, or the Civil Nuclear Constabulary requests assistance. The intervention must relate to 'a particular incident, investigation or operation', and the powers will then be exercisable within the requesting police force area. In an emergency, an MDP officer in uniform (or with proof of office, such as a warrant card), may act on reasonable suspicion of an offence or where action is reasonably believed necessary to save life or prevent or minimize personal injury, and on the reasonable belief that awaiting a request would frustrate or seriously prejudice the purpose of the action. It is expected that such emergency circumstances will be narrowly conceived: 'Given the availability of modern radio communications, the effect will restrict its use to circumstances of genuine emergency when a virtually instant reaction is needed.'[307] Examples might be where 'Intelligence is received that a possible terrorist is near a defence base—perhaps a US base . . .' or even where '. . . an MDP officer in a street adjacent to defence property is approached by a woman who says, "Stop that man, he has taken my purse"'.[308]

---

[304] The Guard Service (and the Northern Ireland Security Guard Service) can be given special constable status under the Emergency Laws (Miscellaneous Provisions) Act 1947, Sch 2.

[305] See Walker, CP, *The Prevention of Terrorism in British Law* (2nd edn, Manchester University Press, Manchester, 1992) ch 11.

[306] See *Ministry of Defence Police and Guarding* (1995–96) HC 189.

[307] Hansard HC vol 375 col 775 (26 November 2001), Lewis Moonie.

[308] Ibid col 776.

10.166 Additional to s 98, s 99 (inserting a new s 2A into the 1987 Act) envisages that the MDP may also swing into action where another police force requires extra resources to meet a special burden (similar to the Police Act 1996, s 24(3). Corresponding Scottish measures are in Sch 7, paras 1 to 7.

10.167 Another aspect of counter-terrorism deployment of the MDP since 2001 has involved the exercise of stop and search powers under s 44 of the TA 2000. The amendment by the ATCSA 2001, Sch 7, para 31, allows the MDP, through an Assistant Chief Constable, themselves to authorize its use. The MDP is also allowed to exercise cordoning powers under the TA 2000, s 34 (under Sch 7, para 30).

Implementation

10.168 The MDP regularly undertakes patrols in the Government Security Zone in Whitehall and Westminster under Metropolitan Police authority.[309] There were 5,236 such searches during 2007–08. Similar assistance has also been given to the British Transport Police and at demonstration sites, such as Menwith Hill.[310]

10.169 Another prominent aspect of MDP counter-terrorism deployment has comprised protective security for gas processing sites under Operation Vintage.[311] The MDP's national coverage and armed capability make it ideal for these purposes, and this role, which presumably falls within s 99 rather than amounting to 'a particular incident' under s 98(4), had become semi-permanent by 2008 even though Home Office guidelines state that assistance should not be 'routinely requested'.[312]

10.170 This demand on MDP resources for CNI purposes has begun to be officially recognized by the CTA 2008, ss 85 to 90,[313] though not confined to terrorism risk.[314] The CTA 2008 allows recovery from gas transporters of the costs of the 'extra police services' incurred by the MDP or local forces at gas installations where their deployment is considered by the Secretary of State to be: '(a) . . . necessary because of a risk of loss of or disruption to the supply of gas connected with it, and (b) that the loss or disruption would have a serious impact on the United Kingdom or any part of it'.

10.171 So as to avoid confusion, especially when firearms are involved, a protocol has been agreed between the MDP and local police. The MDP must inform the local Chief Constable of any crime of terrorism, so that the investigation can be taken over, and any armed deployment should be the subject of prior notification for escorts and agreement for patrols.[315] There should also be consultation before authorization under s 44.[316]

---

[309] See Ministry of Defence Police and Guarding Agency, *Annual Report and Accounts 2007–2008* (2007–08 HC 699) p 29. The total for all sites was 6,127, all on the basis of non-MDP authorizations: p 40.

[310] During 2007–08, 415 stops were made under s 44: ibid p 31.

[311] See Walker, C, 'The governance of the Critical National Infrastructure' [2008] *Public Law* 323 at 338.

[312] Home Office Circular 24/2002: *A protocol between the Ministry of Defence Police and Home Office Police Forces*, para 11.

[313] *Possible Measures for Inclusion in a Future Counter-Terrorism Bill* (London, 2007) para 67.

[314] Hansard HC Public Bill Committee on the Counter-Terrorism Bill col 497 (15 May 2008), Tony McNulty.

[315] Home Office Circular 24/2002: *A protocol between the Ministry of Defence Police and Home Office Police Forces*, paras 4, 22, 24.

[316] Ibid para 14.

Assessment and conclusions

Reflecting the history of BTP's expanded role, similar ideas for MDP development had **10.172** appeared in the Armed Forces Bill 2000–01 but had been withdrawn because of criticisms about the pre-emption of local police forces, lack of training to interface with the public, and limited local public accountability.[317] None of these concerns was addressed by the ATCSA 2001, but the Defence Select Committee supported the 2001 reforms as sensible and practicable despite the remaining defects.[318] Subsequently, three independent members have been added to the Ministry of Defence Police Committee,[319] and complaints and inspection systems are addressed by the Police Reform Act 2002, Pt V.[320]

The government has robustly asserted that the MDP and other specialist forces should be **10.173** entrusted with wider protective duties:[321]

> Anyone would think that members of the MDP police only ever deal with people in uniform. That is simply not the case; they police housing estates . . . They undergo the same basic training as any other constable. Their primary role is, in fact, to deal with civilians, dependants, contractors, trades people and visitors to our sites. The MDP police service football and rugby matches. They police public events, garrison areas, such as Colchester, Salisbury Plain, Aldershot and Catterick, and public roads open to and widely used by the general public. They run community initiatives in defence areas . . . They are not amateurs; they are highly trained civilian police officers. They are not a military police force.

Seemingly, the MDP is stumbling towards the assumption of the mantle of CNI police. **10.174** However, a comprehensive vision, encompassing consolidation with other specialist policing bodies and effective local and national accountability structures, is lacking. Consideration should also be given to the potential role of private security personnel. The Association of Chief Police Officers has suggested that, in the event of an emergency, a legal duty should be imposed on private security personnel to follow the directions of the police and thereby deliver extra trained capacity.[322] Arrangements under the accreditation provisions of the Police Reform Act 2002 could be invoked.

Other sectors, activities, sites, and events

General provisions

Measures of general application to protective security against terrorism include the manage- **10.175** ment of traffic. First, the TA 2000, s 48, allows a uniformed constable to impose prohibitions or restrictions on the parking of vehicles on a road as specified in an authorization. The authorization must be given by an Assistant Chief Constable or Metropolitan commander who 'considers it expedient for the prevention of acts of terrorism'. The authorization must be confirmed in writing, though the document need not be published or notified. The roads affected should be marked by signs under s 49. The authorization must not exceed twenty-eight days under s 50 but may then be renewed. Parking in contravention of a prohibition or restriction is a summary offence under s 51. As well as bans on movement, there are also protective traffic controls in Sch 2 of the Civil Contingencies Act 2004.

---

[317] Select Committee on the Armed Forces Bill, (2000–01 HC 154-I), xvi and paras 36, 39, 40, 46, 52.

[318] Defence Select Committee, *The Ministry of Defence Police* (2001–02 HC 382) paras 23, 28, 34, 36.

[319] Hansard HC vol 375 col 779 (26 November 2001), Lewis Moonie.

[320] See for Scotland, Police, Public Order and Criminal Justice (Scotland) Act 2006 (Consequential Provisions and Modifications) Order 2007, SI 2007/1098, art 4.

[321] Hansard HC vol 375 cols 778–9 (26 November 2001), Lewis Moonie.

[322] Association of Chief Police Officers, Press Release 55/05, 2005.

Provisions specific to activities, sites, and events

10.176 Several protective security measures relating to the restriction of entry onto sensitive sites have already been mentioned. Others include protection for 'prohibited places' under the Official Secrets Act 1911, s 3,[323] or 'protected sites' under the Serious Organised Crime and Police Act 2005, s 128.[324] By comparison, in South Africa, the National Key Points Act 1980 allows for the designation by a Minister, the effect of which is to impose protective duties upon owners and an offence of hindrance or obstruction. Equally permissive is the Control of Access to Public Premises and Vehicles Act 1985, by which private owners can undertake security measures, including by imposing conditions of entry such as identification and, subject to ministerial determination, search.

10.177 Political conferences are next singled out for special treatment. After the Brighton Bombing of 1984, central government made *ad hoc* payments to the extra policing costs of party conferences in Britain.[325] These grants were formalized by the Criminal Justice and Public Order Act 1994, s 170, provided the party has two MPs or one MP plus 150,000 votes.

10.178 As well as legal frameworks, much activity has consisted of non-legal guidance, the issuance of which became a deluge after the *Review of the Protection of Crowded Places, Critical National Infrastructure and Transport Infrastructure*, and the *Protective Security Review relating to Hazardous Substances* were undertaken by Lord West in 2007 and 2008.[326] Details were not revealed, but the emphasis was placed on local partnerships, involvement of CTSAs, consideration at planning processes, training for business, hotel, and retail staff under Project Argus,[327] and the issuance of guidelines by the NaCSTO[328] and by the Home Office.[329]

10.179 These planning processes have been most evident in the preparations for the Olympic Games in London in 2012, with funding for safety and security set at £600 million.[330] The Olympics represent a prime target for terrorism as symbols of national power, as well as attracting huge crowds. Attacks have occurred at previous games venues, in Munich in 1972 and in Atlanta in 1996. In response, the London 2012 Olympic and Paralympic Security Strategy was concluded by the Home Office in 2009. The foremost organization is the Olympic and

---

[323] See Official Secrets (Prohibited Place) Order 1955, SI 1955/1497, and 1994, SI 1994/968.

[324] See Serious Organised Crime and Police Act 2005 (Designated Sites under Section 128) Orders 2005, SI 2005/3447 and 2007, SI 2007/930 and SI 2007/1387; Home Office Circular 18/2007, *Trespass on protected sites—sections 128–131 of the Serious Organised Crime and Police Act 2005*; Ministry of Justice, *The Governance of Britain* (Cm 7170, London, 2007) paras164–166.

[325] Hansard HC vol 102 col 614w (25 July 1986), Margaret Thatcher.

[326] See Hansard HC vol 467 col 44ws (14 November 2007); Hansard HL vol 703 col 153ws (22 July 2008).

[327] <http://www.nactso.gov.uk/OurServices/Argus.aspx>.

[328] See *Secure in the Knowledge; Expecting the Unexpected, Counter Terrorism Protective Security Advice for General Aviation; Security at General Aviation Aerodromes; Counter Terrorism Protective Security Advice for Bars, Pubs and Nightclubs; Counter Terrorism Protective Security Advice for Cinemas and Theatre; Counter Terrorism Protective Security Advice for Commercial Centres; Counter Terrorism Protective Security Advice for Higher and Further Education; Counter Terrorism Protective Security Advice for Major Events; Counter Terrorism Protective Security Advice for Health; Counter Terrorism Protective Security Advice for Hotels and Restaurants; Counter Terrorism Protective Security Advice for Shopping Centres; Counter Terrorism Protective Security Advice for Stadia and Arenas; Counter Terrorism Protective Security Advice for Visitor Attractions* (London, 2009). Note also CPNI, *Protecting Against Terrorism* (3rd edn, London, 2010).

[329] *Working Together to Protect Crowded Places* (London, 2009 and 2010), *Safer Places* (London, 2009), *Crowded Places: The Planning System and Counter Terrorism* (London, 2010), *Protecting Crowded Places: Design and Technical Issues* (London, 2010).

[330] See House of Commons Committee of Public Accounts, *The budget for the London 2012 Olympic and Paralympic Games* (2007–08 HC 85).

Paralympic Security Directorate which is a unit within the Home Office's Office for Security and Counter-Terrorism. Head of operations is the National Olympic Security Co-ordinator, who works alongside the Assistant Commissioner for Specialist Operations in the Metropolitan Police. They are linked to the National Olympic Co-ordination Centre.

Such work may be assisted by the UN International Permanent Observatory on Security **10.180** during the Major Events programme.[331] Its remit covers assistance to national agencies with major sports and political meetings, Expos, and other mass events.

H. Victims of Terrorism: Compensation and Redress

Introduction and background

The next application of 'Protect' concerns the treatment of the victims of terrorism. Three **10.181** approaches have been adopted over time. The first approach was largely to ignore them. For many years, this stance prevailed in Great Britain but is now on the wane, whereas the collective nature of the threat and serious scale of loss has been recognized in Northern Ireland for centuries. Schemes particular to Northern Ireland will be considered in Chapter 11. The second approach has been to develop state compensation schemes. The third approach has been to encourage civil litigation—self-help but with state facilitation.

Special state compensation schemes

Introduction and background

Of the three schemes of special state compensation, two have related to commercial victims— **10.182** property owners or occupiers and airlines. The latter has expired and so will not be discussed.[332] The other, more recent and more modest, benefits victims of terrorism abroad.

Provisions: commercial property

(i) Introduction and background   Terrorism against commercial targets may be tempting in **10.183** order to impact upon the political economy through not only direct costs of repair but also more enduring signifiers of economic vitality such as business confidence.[333] Within that strategic setting, financial and media concentrations, such as the City of London, have become prized targets for terrorism because of their symbolic and practical importance.[334] An IRA source revealed the following assessment: 'It's really about getting their attention. London is one of the major cities in Europe and when we make it unstable that's when the talking begins.'[335]

The IRA's strategy was not entirely coherent from the outset.[336] Nevertheless, it was calcu- **10.184** lated and became concerted, with two large truck-bomb attacks on City of London targets, St Mary Axe in 1992 and Bishopsgate in 1993. Though four people died and hundreds were

---

[331] E/2006/28, <http://www.unicri.it/news/Background_IPO.pdf>.

[332] For details of Troika (which expired in 2003), see Walker, C, 'Political violence and commercial risk' (2004) 56 *Current Legal Problems* 531. A more ambitious US scheme appeared in the Air Transportation Safety and System Stabilization Act 2001 (PL 107-42).

[333] See ibid, Enders, W and Sanders, T, *The Political Economy of Terrorism* (Cambridge University Press, New York, 2006) chs 2, 9, 10; Jackson, BA et al, *Economically Targeted Terrorism* (RAND, Santa Monica, 2007); Buesa, M and Baumert, T (eds), *The Economic Repercussions of Terrorism* (Oxford University Press, Oxford, 2010).

[334] See Graham, S (ed), *Cities, War and Terrorism* (Blackwell, Oxford, 2004).

[335] Dillon, M, *25 Years Of Terror: The IRA's War Against The British*, (Bantam, London, 1995) p 271.

[336] Mallie, E and McKittrick, D, *The Fight For Peace*, (Heinemann, London, 1996) p 148.

injured, the financial costs, estimated at more than £300 million in the second event, secured greater legal impact.[337] The end of the first Provisional IRA cease-fire in February 1996 was marked by a resumption of this economic campaign,[338] with bombs at Canary Wharf, London, and the Arndale Shopping Centre, Manchester.

10.185 The bomb at St Mary Axe began to precipitate a crisis in the reinsurance market. The issuance of a model terrorism exclusion clause by the Association of British Insurers (ABI) to its members on 12 November 1992 confirmed that, effective from 1 January 1993, terrorism cover for commercial property would not be available.[339] In response, on 21 December 1992, the Secretary of State for Trade and Industry announced that the government would act as insurer of last resort.[340]

10.186 (ii) **Provisions**   The vehicle for government intervention is a reinsurance company, Pool Re, which offers reinsurance for buildings, contents, computers, engineering, and business interruption related to commercial insurance policies. A later amendment applied the scheme to blocks of flats owned by commercial companies and insured for a sum in excess of £2.5 million. Insurers within the scheme may not select which properties are insurable for terrorism cover or offer stand-alone terrorism cover. Terrorism cover is by default excluded in customer policies[341] but can be bought back for an additional premium which is remitted into the mutual pool, managed, and staffed by insurance industry personnel on behalf of over 200 insurance companies and almost 100 Lloyd's of London syndicates within the scheme. The government agrees to meet 90 per cent of any subsequent claims not covered by the pool fund, and insurance companies meet the remaining 10 per cent.

10.187 Reflection upon the attacks of September 11 prompted some revisions.[342] Cover has extended from 'fire and explosion' to an 'all risks basis', to ensure cover for commercial property against biological or nuclear contamination, impact by aircraft, or flood damage. However, exclusion remains for war risks and for computer hacking and virus damage (because of difficulties of proof). The rates of retention have been capped per event, and insurers are allowed to set the premiums for the underlying policies according to normal commercial considerations. These changes are designed to encourage commercial reinsurance to cover these retentions. Changes to the governance arrangements include the appointment of a Public Interest Director on the board of Pool Re, who reports annually to the Treasury.

10.188 The scheme was accorded a legal framework by the Reinsurance (Acts of Terrorism) Act 1993,[343] though the body of the design remains in the Retrocession Agreement between the Secretary of State for Trade and Industry and the Pool Reinsurance Company. The following points should be noted from the 1993 Act itself. Section 1 confers the reinsurance powers on the Secretary of State, backed by public moneys, though Pool Re is not mentioned as such.

---

[337] City of London Police, *Annual Report for 1993* (London, 1994) p 32.

[338] Craig, T, 'Sabotage!' (2010) 25 *Intelligence and National Security* 309.

[339] Souter, G, 'London Reinsurers Expect Restrictions Due to Catastrophes' (1992) 26(43) *Business Insurance* 10.

[340] *The Times* 22 December 1992, p 1.

[341] Exclusions in personal injury claims arising from the 7/7 attacks were not enforced as a concession by some insurers.

[342] HC Debs vol 389 col 960w (23 July 2002), Ruth Kelly. See further <http://www.hm-treasury.gov.uk/newsroom_and_speeches/press/2002/press_73_02.cfm>.

[343] See Bice, WB, 'British government reinsurance and acts of terrorism' (1994) 15 *University of Pennsylvania Journal of International Business Law* 441.

Section 2 outlines the reinsurance arrangements to which the Act applies, namely, loss **10.189**
or damage (direct and consequential) to property in Great Britain resulting from acts of
terrorism. The Act does not closely define 'damage' or 'property', but personal injury and
losses to vehicles or the equipment of utilities are not covered. The geographical bounds are
confirmed by s 3(2); Northern Ireland is omitted because alternative arrangements apply
(described in Chapter 11).

By s 2(2), 'acts of terrorism' means 'acts of persons acting on behalf of, or in connection **10.190**
with, any organisation which carries out activities directed towards the overthrowing or
influencing, by force or violence, of Her Majesty's government in the United Kingdom or
any other government *de jure* or *de facto*'. This definition is narrower than the TA 2000, s 1,
standard since it delimits the perpetrator to an 'organisation' which, by s 2(3) includes 'any
association or combination of persons'. It has not been decided whether, for example, a
collective of anarchists, such as have from time to time attempted to 'Stop the City', could
constitute an organization. The 1993 Act definition is also narrower in that the purpose
is confined to the terrorizing of governments and not the public. In practice, the application
of the definition to a given event is settled by a certificate from HM Treasury.

(iii) **Implementation**   The scheme has operated since 1992, building up a financial reserve **10.191**
which was more than adequate to meet the commercial losses from the bombings in 1996.[344]
A total of twelve incidents have been certified, with losses (not including the July 2005
bombings) of £611m.[345] However, those events highlighted the limits in Pool Re. Losses
sustained by non-commercial property and utilities, plus the costs of extra policing, were
met by local councils who in turn sought extraordinary central government grants.[346]

(iv) **Foreign comparisons**   The US Terrorism Risk Insurance Act 2002[347] reflects many **10.192**
similar features. In return for a deductible from direct earned premiums, all commercial
insurers of buildings are required to offer terrorism coverage, but the Federal government
must pay 90 per cent of the cost of an attack in the US by foreign terrorists once losses reach
more than $10 billion, up to a total of $100 billion. The government will pay a smaller
amount for losses of less than $10 billion. The Act was set to expire at the end of 2004 but
has been extended to 2014.[348] It does not cover losses from WMD.[349]

Several European countries also operate public-private schemes of insurance or reinsur- **10.193**
ance.[350] In France, Law no 86-1020 of 9 September 1986 combines both insurance cover
and compensation for victims. The insurance scheme involves insurance companies being
required to offer terrorism damage and casualty cover. Following the September 11 attacks
and also the suspected terrorist bombing of the AZF chemical factory in Toulouse later in the
same month, the prospect of catastrophic loss resulted in an indemnity from the GAREAT

---

[344] It was reported as £1.5bn in 2002: *The Times* 6 June 2002, p 3.
[345] <http://www.poolre.co.uk/HistoryOfPool.html>.
[346] Various sources contributed, including the 'Bellwin scheme': Local Government and Housing Act 1989,
s 155; Hansard HC vol 367 col 750w (3 May 2001).
[347] PL 107-297. See Stempel, JW, 'The insurance aftermath of September 11' (2002) 37 *Tort & Ins.
Law Journal.* 817; Jerry, RH, 'Insurance, terrorism, and 9/11' (2002–03) 9 *Connecticut Insurance Law
Journal* 397.
[348] Terrorism Risk Insurance Program Reauthorization Act of 2007 (PL110-160).
[349] See Governmental Accountability Office, *Terrorism Insurance* (GAO09-39, Washington DC, 2009).
[350] See Koch, B (ed), *Terrorism, Tort Law and Insurance* (Springer, Vienna, 2004); OECD, *Terrorism Risk
Insurance in OECD Countries* (Policy Issues 12, Paris, 2005).

(*Gestion de l'Assurance et de la Réassurance contre les Attentats*) Pool. The government will meet loss above €2 billion.

10.194   **(v) Assessment and conclusions**   The queries surrounding policy impacts include, first, the take-up of terrorism cover. Availability at a substantial premium means that many property owners, especially small and medium enterprises, decide against coverage, leaving economies vulnerable to dereliction. Secondly, the private insurance path exalts private over public recovery. Consequently, where the loss is to an important public space, such as a shopping centre, state grants will still be required. A third issue is that the opportunity to insist on greater resilience as a condition of insurance has not been systematically imposed.[351] A fourth problem is disruption to private insurance mechanisms and lack of incentives to resurrect a commercial market.[352] However, the possibility of purposive catastrophic loss renders this risk potentially not as self-correcting as with losses from hurricanes and earthquakes. So, the prospect is for continuance and proliferation of these schemes rather than redundancy.

10.195   As for efficiency, Pool Re has operated at modest outlay to government. New state infrastructure is minimal, and the mechanism has covered all claims without state subvention. Furthermore, the premiums charged to larger commercial enterprises are sustainable, and there has been no exodus from the City of London. Of course, any supposed achievements of Pool Re must be set within the security and political contexts which have developed since 1992. The political contexts include IRA cease-fires in 1994 and 1996. The security context is the application of added policing powers under the Criminal Justice and Public Order Act 1994, s 81, and the PT(AP)A 1996 (now translated into the TA 2000), plus an application of closed circuit television and automatic number-plate recognition technology to form a 'Ring of Steel'.[353] One consequence is displacement to equally alluring targets within striking distance, such as Heathrow (attacked by mortars in 1994) or Docklands in 1996.

10.196   The Pool Re system can be said to be largely unsuccessful in terms of accountability and constitutional governance. The working of Pool Re is conducted on the basis of corporatist rather than legal relations. Parliament has shown no interest whatever.

10.197   As for fairness, it has been argued that '. . . the insurance industry has much to offer in the battle against terrorism'.[354] Special mechanisms have spread liability in a way which has maintained property interests and commerce. However, the mechanisms reflect unfairness in the distribution of security, with the rich occupants of the City of London securing the greatest protection at potential cost to the taxpayer. The taxpayer's rights are also affected by enhanced surveillance, much of which resides in private corporate hands.

Provisions: individual compensation

10.198   **(i) Introduction and background**   Owners of the opulent towers of the City of London hardly comprise the needy poor, but compensation for personal injury caused by terrorism has been far less forthcoming, as shall now be explained.

---

[351] See Ericson, RV et al, *Insurance as Governance* (University of Toronto Press, Toronto, 2003) ch 8.

[352] See Dixon, L et al, *Trade Offs Among Alternative Government Interventions in the Market for Terrorism Insurance* (RAND, Santa Monica, 2007).

[353] Kelly, O, 'The IRA threat to the City of London' (1993) 9 *Policing* 88; Coaffee, J, 'Recasting the "Ring of steel"' in Graham, S (ed), *Cities, War and Terrorism* (Blackwell, Oxford, 2004).

[354] Rappe, G, 'The role of insurance in the battle against terrorism' (1999) 12 *De Paul Business Law Journal* 351 at 353.

(ii) Provisions The standard Criminal Injuries Compensation Scheme, administered by **10.199** the Criminal Injuries Compensation Authority under the Criminal Injuries Compensation Act 1995 is available to terrorism victims. Its nature and shortcomings are considered further in the context of its counterpart in Northern Ireland in Chapter 11. The main complaints in Britain are that it is dilatory and ungenerous.[355]

The other deficiency is that the scheme did not apply to terrorism inflicted overseas on **10.200** British citizens. Though 141 British citizens have been killed abroad by terrorism since 2001,[356] the government resisted statutory support,[357] though it has donated to the British Red Cross Relief Fund for UK Victims of Terrorism Overseas[358] and also offers assistance through embassies.[359] This meagre sustenance was highlighted by British victims of attacks in Bali in 2002, Sharm al-Sheikh in 2005, and Mumbai in 2008. This accumulation of tragic cases eventually promoted a change in policy by way of the 'Victims of Overseas Terrorism Compensation Scheme' which was added as an afterthought to the Crime and Security Act 2010.

By s 47, the Secretary of State may make arrangements for payments for injuries (including **10.201** fatal injuries) as a result of a 'designated' terrorist act. Designation is made by the Secretary of State for Foreign and Commonwealth Affairs for a relevant act which took place outside the United Kingdom, which occurred on or after 18 January 2010 (the date when the scheme was first announced),[360] which, in the view of the Secretary of State, constitutes 'terrorism' within the meaning of the TA 2000, s 1, and in respect of which, having regard to all the circumstances (such as whether a Foreign Office travel advisory had warned against a visit),[361] the Secretary of State considers that it would be appropriate to designate. For injuries sustained before the start date, the government conceded that *ex gratia* payments will be made for continuing injuries (but not deaths) inflicted back to 1 January 2002.[362]

Eligibility to apply under s 49 may be determined by nationality, place, or length of residence, **10.202** and any other factor considered appropriate. As for nationality, eligibility for compensation will certainly extend to nationals of the European Union and European Economic Area with a sufficient connection to the United Kingdom.

Detailed arrangements for the scheme are made under s 48 and Sch 2. Procedures and **10.203** payments mirror the standard Criminal Injuries Compensation Scheme, and the Criminal Injuries Compensation Authority handles applications under s 51. Payments under s 50 are calculated by reference to the nature of the injury, loss of earnings, and expenses incurred. The standard scheme adopts a tariff-based approach and a maximum payment of £500,000. Decisions of a claims officer may be contested internally under s 52 with appeal to the First-tier Tribunal; judicial review also applies.

An annual report to Parliament is required under s 53, and major alterations to the scheme **10.204** must be approved by the affirmative resolution procedure under s 54.

---

[355] See Home Office, *Addressing Lessons from the Emergency Response to the 7 July 2005 London Bombings* (London, 2006) paras 30–35.
[356] Hansard HC vol 481 col 249WH (29 November 2008), Tessa Jowell.
[357] See Victims of Terrorism (Compensation) Bill 2006–07 (HC no 23).
[358] See <http://www.redcross.org.uk/news.asp?id=70137>. The maximum payment is £15,000.
[359] Hansard HC vol 481 col 253WH (29 November 2008), Tessa Jowell.
[360] Hansard HC vol 504 col 25 (18 January 2010), Alan Johnson.
[361] Hansard HC Public Bill Committee col 438 (23 February 2010), David Hanson.
[362] Ibid col 439.

10.205 (iii) **Foreign comparisons** Further afield, the picture is variable.[363] A compensation scheme for personal loss from violent crime within European Union states is required by the EU Council Directive relating to Compensation to Crime Victims of 2004 and applies to injuries after 1 July 2005.[364] Beyond Europe, many states maintain no scheme or maintain systems which do not recognize non-nationals or offer very modest payments.

10.206 A marked exception is the USA, where there are several munificent special relief schemes for terrorism victims. The Antiterrorism and Effective Death Penalty Act of 1996, Title II,[365] as amended by the USA PATRIOT Act in 2001, provides for compensation for victims of terrorism, including for terrorism abroad under the International Terrorism Victims Compensation Program (ITVERP). Implementation is undertaken by the Terrorism and International Victims Unit in the US Department of Justice's Office for Victims of Crime.[366] Available funding includes: Crisis Response Grants and Consequence Management Grants (to rebuild capacities and help victims to adapt), Criminal Justice Support Grants (to allow victim participation in proceedings), Crime Victim Compensation Grants (to reimburse expenses), and Training and Technical Assistance.

10.207 As for business and property loss, the Federal Emergency Management Agency (FEMA)[367] coordinates emergency planning and response and issues Federal disaster grants to assist state governments.

10.208 Added to these standing schemes is the *ad hoc* September 11th Victim Compensation Fund.[368] The Fund offers no-fault Federal compensation on a generous tort-based scale for personal and economic loss and administered through a Special Master. The Fund was justified as avoiding the hurdles of civil litigation and also as a strong political signal of social solidarity with victims and of collective determination to recover from 'an insult to the body politic' and from 'exposed feelings of vulnerability'.[369] The Fund was a success by averting most (but not all) litigation and by incurring low process costs. But even its Special Master doubted whether it should be repeated since it unduly discouraged risk and responsibility and unduly empowered government.[370]

10.209 (iv) **Assessment and conclusion** The shortcomings of United Kingdom compensation and assistance are evident when set alongside US provision. The Victims of Overseas Terrorism Compensation Scheme is a welcome concession. However, aside from reflecting the shortcomings of the standard scheme, it is surprising that the tactic of insurance cover, so

---

[363] See Greer, DS (ed), *Compensating Crime Victims* (IUSCRIM, Freiburg, 1996); Albrecht, HJ and Kilching, M, 'Victims of terrorism protection' in Wade, M and Maljevic, A, *A War on Terror?* (Springer, New York, 2010).

[364] 2004/08/EC. See also the European Convention on the Compensation of Victims of Violent Crimes 1983 (ETS 116); Katsoris, CN, 'The European Convention on the Compensation of Victims of Violent Crime' (1990–91) 14 *Fordham International Law Review* 186.

[365] 42 USC s 10602. See also the Victims of Trafficking and Violence Protection Act 2000 (PL 106-386) and the Victims of Terrorism Tax Relief Act 2002 (PL 107-134).

[366] <http://www.ojp.usdoj.gov/ovc/publications/factshts/tivu/welcome.html>.

[367] See <http://www.fema.gov>; Robert T. Stafford Disaster Relief and Emergency Assistance Act 1988 (PL 100-707, 42 USC ss 5121–5206).

[368] Air Transportation Safety and Safety Stabilization Act 2001, Title IV. See Shapo, MS, *Compensation for Victims of Terror* (Oceana, New York, 2005) ch 6; Rabin, RL and Sugarman, SD, 'The case for specially compensating victims of terrorist attacks' (2007) 35 *Hofstra Law Review* 901.

[369] Shapo, MS, *Compensation for Victims of Terror* (Oceana, New York, 2005) p xvi.

[370] Feinberg, KR, *What is Life Worth?* (Public Affairs, New York, 2005) p 178.

prominent in the commercial sphere, was not part of the reform package. Only a third of travel insurance covers terrorism risk,[371] and 19 per cent of travellers do not purchase travel insurance.[372]

Civil litigation

Introduction and background

The incorporeal nature of many terrorist organizations, the frugal existence of many terrorists, delays, costs, and complexity render civil litigation an unappealing option. Yet, there may be some situations where civil law can help victims.[373] One is where a defendant of substance can be located—not the terrorists themselves but culpable governments or third party aides. The second is where the victim pursues an action for non-financial reasons—to secure a public account and condemnation or to exert pressure for official action.

10.210

Provisions and implementation

Litigation against government has often arisen from the application of excessive or mis-directed lethal force applied by the security forces in terrorism operations (described in Chapter 4). Rather less straightforward is to sustain governmental fault for terrorism attacks. The first such instance was *Donaldson v Chief Constable of the Royal Ulster Constabulary*.[374] The widow of a police chief inspector killed in the IRA mortar bombing of Newry police station in 1985 sued the Chief Constable and Police Authority for negligence based on the assertion that the police premises were inadequately protected. The litigation was settled in 1991, though the perils of legal action were highlighted by the issuance of a public interest immunity certificate relating to security measures.[375] More typically, the relative of a victim of the Omagh bombing in 1998 was not allowed in *Rush v Chief Constable of the PSNI* to claim against the police on the ground that no exceptional relationship had been established[376] and that access to sensitive evidence would not be allowed.[377]

10.211

Actions against third party aides can encompass many different players. Transportation carriers may be sued for failing to provide safe systems. Action against the Pan American airline for the Lockerbie bombing contributed to its bankruptcy.[378] Legal action has also been mounted against British financial institutions for holding accounts of bodies (such as charities) which are implicated in terrorism funding.[379]

10.212

Finally, frustrations with the lack of progress in criminal investigations of the Omagh bombing encouraged victims to mount direct civil action against the alleged perpetrators. Judgment was given in *Breslin v McKenna* in 2009 against four individuals (McKevitt,

10.213

---

[371] Hansard HC Public Bill Committee col 446 (23 February 2010), David Hanson.
[372] <http://www.fco.gov.uk/en/news/latest-news/?id=22548119&view=News>.
[373] See generally, Walker, C, 'Liability for acts of terrorism' in Koch, B (ed), *Terrorism, Tort Law and Insurance* (Springer, Vienna, 2004).
[374] 1990 4 BNIL n 106 (QBD).
[375] *The Guardian* 19 and 20 November 1991. See also *Re Savage* [1991] NI 103.
[376] See *Hill v Chief Constable of West Yorkshire* [1989] AC 53; *X v Bedfordshire County Council* [1995] 2 AC 633; *Osman v United Kingdom*, App no 23452/94, 1998-VIII; *Keenan v United Kingdom*, App no 27229/95, 2001-III; *TP and KM v United Kingdom*, App No 28945/95, 2001-V.
[377] [2010] NI Master 6.
[378] See *Re Lockerbie Air Disaster* (1992) *The Times* 20 May (CA).
[379] See *Weiss v National Westminster* 453 F Supp 2d 609 (2006).

Campbell, Murphy, and Daly) plus the Real IRA in the sum of £16m.[380] The suit is controversial in several ways. It seems to contradict the criminal justice system in the case of Colm Murphy, who had been acquitted in the Republic of Ireland. In addition, the government took sides by granting special legal aid funding to the victims but not to the defendants, an apparent bias upheld in *Murphy and Daly v Lord Chancellor*.[381] The litigation was also affected by rulings on disclosure of sensitive security information which may be less favourable to the defendant than in criminal cases (as discussed in Chapter 6).[382]

Foreign comparisons

10.214   Civil terrorism litigation has been a pronounced tactic of victim support in the US. It is encouraged by the Alien Tort Claims Act of 1789 (assuming jurisdiction over torts committed in violation of the laws of nations),[383] the Antiterrorism Act of 1990 (allowing US citizens affected by 'an act of international terrorism' except by a foreign state the right to seek threefold damages),[384] and amendments in 1996 and 1999 to the Foreign Sovereign Immunities Act 1977 (PL 94-583) (removing the immunity of states which are designated as sponsors of terror).[385]

10.215   As for suits against foreign states, there have been numerous successful suits, usually by default judgment.[386] Their enforcement remains problematic, for foreign state property remains within sovereign immunity. Furthermore, it has been held that amendments to the Foreign Sovereign Immunities Act 1977 do not create any private right of action, so plaintiffs must identify foreign officials or agents who bear personal responsibility under independent causes of action.[387]

10.216   In *Re Terrorist Attacks on September 11, 2001*,[388] an ongoing action by relatives of victims seeks damages from hundreds of named defendants (mainly linked to Saudi Arabia) who had allegedly funded Muslim charities which had helped Al-Qa'ida. The US Foreign Sovereign Immunities Act[389] was invoked in favour of four Saudi princes as well as the Saudi High Commission for Relief to Bosnia and Herzegovina.

10.217   By contrast, sustained litigation against Libya[390] was an element of pressure (admittedly less powerful than UN sanctions) which resulted in the Libyan government accepting before the UN Security Council responsibility for the actions of its officials in relation to the Lockerbie bombing and agreeing to pay compensation.[391]

---

[380] [2008] NIQB 50.

[381] [2008] NICA 34. Compare *R (Patel) v Lord Chancellor* [2010] EWHC 2220 (Admin).

[382] See *Breslin v McKenna* [2005] NIQB 18, [2008] NIQB 49, 51, 120, [2008] IESC 43.

[383] 28 USC s 1350.

[384] PL 101-519 as amended by PL 102-572, 18 USC s 2333, subject to s 2337.

[385] 28 USC s 1605(a)(7). The states are listed at 22 CFR Pt 126(1)(d) (2004).

[386] See Elsea, JK, *Lawsuits against state supporters of terrorism* (CRS 22094, Washington DC, 2005); Shapo, MS, *Compensation for Victims of Terror* (Oceana, New York, 2005) ch 3.

[387] See *Flatlow v Iran* 999 F Supp 1 (1998); *Cicippio-Puelo v Islamic Republic of Iran* 353 F 3d 1024 (2004).

[388] (2008) 538 F 3d 71.

[389] 28 USC ss 1602–11.

[390] See *Smith v Socialist People's Libyan Arab Jamahiriya*, 101 F 3d 239 (1996), *cert. denied*, 520 US 1204; *Rein v Socialist People's Libyan Arab Jamahiriya* (1998) 162 F 3d 748.

[391] S/RES/1506 (2003). For implementation, see: US-Libya Agreement of 14 August 2008; Libyan Claims Resolution Act 2008 (PL 110-301).

Turning to non-state defendants, actions have been mounted against financial institutions, **10.218** as noted previously.[392] In addition, transport carriers have been challenged, including the owners of the Achille Lauro[393] and Pan American for wilful misconduct (thus avoiding the limits on liability under the Warsaw Convention 1929).[394]

Assessment and conclusions

The transfer of responsibility for counter-terrorism represented by civil litigation seems **10.219** fitting in principle for a late modern society, though the public interest may be overlooked by placing foreign policy in private hands by allowing actions against states. Its execution in practice remains highly problematic. In any event, private litigation cannot be a sufficient response to terrorism, where the destruction and injury is symbolic and the real impact is to be on the state. These features call for a state response which protects collective economic and political interests and which promotes, in the words of the Preamble to the European Convention on the Compensation of Victims of Violent Crimes 1983, 'equity and social solidarity'. However, the state has struggled to find a comprehensive and consistent response to terrorism victimization. The inclination of the late modern state is to manage risk rather than to resolve it, as illustrated by the insurance interventions.

I. Conclusions

In service of the strategic purposes of 'Protect' and 'Prepare', the resources and efforts devoted **10.220** to the realm of protective security have been impressive and far exceed those for police investigation and criminal prosecution. The outcomes represent a mixed success. The security of air travel has seemingly interdicted or deterred most attacks upon British airlines or airports. Sadly, other transportation systems and crowded places have been less secure, as evidenced by the bombings on 7 July 2005,[395] though most mass transit systems and public venues more generally cannot successfully operate if treated like air travel. Therefore, much of the emphasis must be on 'Prepare', especially under the Civil Contingencies Act 2004, though the July bombings again underlined shortcomings.

Issues of human rights appear less prominently in this chapter than in others. One reason is **10.221** that some of the counter-measures are remote from ordinary lives and impact on constituencies which are content with their corporatist relationships. The second, less excusable, reason is that the threat to rights is insidious. Thus, target-hardening through mass surveillance is imposed without individual notice or judicial oversight but with consequent threat to privacy, expressive freedoms, and rights against discrimination, as outlined in Chapter 2 and in this chapter.

Doubts about accountability have already been raised in relation to the specialist policing **10.222** forces, and most of the relevant agencies, such as TRANSEC, are also guilty of 'Spartan'

---

[392] See also *Linde v Arab Bank* 384 F Supp 2d 571 (2005); *Almog v Arab Bank* 471 F Supp 2d 257 (2007); *Goldberg v UBS* 690 F Supp 2d 92 (2010). Examples of more direct action include: *Boim v Quranic Literacy Inst.* 291 F 3d 1000 (2002).
[393] *Klinghoffer v Achille Lauro and the PLO* 921 F 2d 21 (1991), 937 F 2d 44, 50 (1991).
[394] *Pescatore v Pan American* 97 F 3d 1 (1996). See also *Sakaria v TWA 8 F 3d 164* (1993); *Shah v Pan Am* 148 F 3d 84 (1999).
[395] Hansard HL vol 467 col 44ws (14 November 2007), Lord West.

reports.[396] Parliament has generally performed feebly, while the Independent Reviewer has no jurisdiction over much of this agenda.[397]

10.223 Regarding constitutional governance, the protective security landscape appears highly fragmented and indistinctly revealed, littered with extra-legal bodies such as CTU, NaCSTO, and the CPNI, and subject to unpublished reviews.[398] Attempts to engage with science and technology, industry, and academia are made only to generate innovation around the application of protective security rather than its governance.[399]

10.224 How a liberal democracy cohabits with the endemic risk created by the dark side of its technological progress is a challenge yet to be fully resolved. Progress will depend to a greater extent than for other areas covered in this book upon resource allocation and also corporatist and international cooperation. Another unresolved problem is the displacement impact of protective security in one state, undertaken with the best of intentions, resulting in transference of terrorism risk to less willing or wealthy states.[400]

---

[396] House of Commons Transport Committee, *UK Transport Security* (2005–06 HC 637) para 37.

[397] See *Newton Report*, paras 295, 311.

[398] See Hansard HC vol 467 col 44ws (14 November 2007); Hansard HL vol 703 col 153ws (22 July 2008).

[399] Home Office, *The United Kingdom's Science and Technology Strategy for Countering International Terrorism*, and *Countering the Terrorist Threat: Ideas and Innovation: How Industry and Academia can Play their Part* (London, 2009).

[400] Enders, W and Sandler, T, *The Political Economy of Terrorism* (Cambridge University Press, Cambridge, 2006) chs 4, 6.

PART V

OTHER JURISDICTIONS

11

REGIONAL VARIATIONS
IN NORTHERN IRELAND
AND SCOTLAND

A. Introduction

This chapter is primarily devoted to Northern Ireland which has been the crucible of many **11.01** special laws against terrorism. The Sinn Féin President, Gerry Adams, in the aftermath of the Provisional IRA ceasefire in 1994, reassured constituents that 'They haven't gone away, you know'.[1] The same sentiment applies to the province's anti-terrorism legislation, despite the 'Peace Process' which was heralded by the 1994 ceasefire (suspended in 1996 but reinstated in 1997) and cemented by a permanent cessation on 28 July 2005. The Belfast Agreement 1998[2] has resulted in a dramatic improvement in security, including ceasefires by Loyalist groups, as evidenced by Table 11.1.

Yet, the most striking reduction is revealed in the shooting match between security forces and paramilitaries, while other violence persists and with no promise of paramilitary disbandment. In particular, Republican dissidents remain capable of violence, as shown by the

---

[1] *The Guardian* 14 August 1995, p 1. See Tonge, J, 'They haven't gone away, you know' (2004) 16 *Terrorism & Political Violence* 671.
[2] Cm 3883, London, 1998. See Wilford, R (ed), *Aspects of the Belfast Agreement* (Oxford University Press, Oxford, 2001).

Table 11.1 **Security trends in Northern Ireland 1968–2010**[a]

Year period	Shootings		Bombings		Deaths				
	Incidents	*Incidents ave. p.a.*	*Devices*	*Devices ave. p.a.*	*Police*	*Military*	*Civilian*	*Total*	*Ave. p.a.*
1969–1979	27,175	2,470	9,740	885	131	429	1,445	2,005	182
1980–1994	7,883	526	5,143	343	165	223	795	1,183	79
1995–1998	611	153	585	117	6	3	92	101	25
1999–2010	2,001	182	1,363	124	1	2	86	89	8
Whole period	37,670	919	16,831	411	303	657	2,418	3,378	82

[a] Sources: Police Service of Northern Ireland; Independent Monitoring Commission. The year ending varies between 31 December and 31 March.

killings of two soldiers and one police officer in February 2009.[3] Therefore, anti-terrorism laws persist to counter this 'severe' threat.[4]

11.02 The British government committed itself in the Belfast Agreement to 'normal security arrangements'.[5] The dismantling of the British Army presence has followed.[6] The process of demilitarization on both sides has been scrutinized by the Independent Monitoring Commission.[7] Its work has been attacked by Sinn Féin as unfair, but the courts have rejected any breach of administrative law standards.[8]

11.03 Special laws in Northern Ireland have been constructed at a prodigious rate. Their lineage can be traced back to the Civil Authorities (Special Powers) Acts (Northern Ireland) 1922–43 and beyond, which were followed by the Northern Ireland (Emergency Provisions) Acts 1971–98, and then the TA 2000.[9] That Act contained a distinct Pt VII, which was renewed and reviewed annually under s 112[10] until its expiration on 18 February 2006. Then, the T(NI) A 2006 extended Pt VII until 31 July 2007, subject to some repeals and modifications.

11.04 A further tranche of normalization measures was notified to the Independent Monitoring Commission in early 2006, including a commitment to repeal Pt VII in 2007.[11] The JSA 2007 has duly replaced Pt VII.[12] Its advent was marked by the end of Operation

---

[3] Independent Monitoring Commission, *Twenty-First Report* (2008–09 HC 496) paras 2.5, 4.9. See also Lord Carlile, *First Annual Review of Arrangements for National Security in Northern Ireland* (Northern Ireland Office, Belfast, 2008) para 44.

[4] Whalley, R, *Second Report of the Independent Reviewer: Justice and Security (Northern Ireland) Act 2007* (Northern Ireland Office, Belfast, 2009) para 219.

[5] Cm 3883, London, 1998, Security para 2.

[6] See Independent Monitoring Commission, *Ninth Report* (2005–06 HC 969).

[7] Northern Ireland (Monitoring Commission etc) Act 2003. The *First Report* is at (2003–04 HC 516).

[8] *Re Sinn Fein* [2005] NIQB 10; *R (Sinn Féin) v Secretary of State for Northern Ireland* [2007] EWHC 12 (Admin).

[9] See Hogan, G and Walker C, *Political Violence and the Law in Ireland* (Manchester University Press, Manchester, 1989); Donohue, LK, *Counter-Terrorism Law* (Irish Academic Press, Dublin, 2001).

[10] See SI 2002/365, 2003/427, 2004/431, 2005/350; Lord Carlile, *Reports on the Operation in 2001–2005 of Part VII of the Terrorism Act 2000* (Home Office, London).

[11] Independent Monitoring Commission, *Ninth Report* (2005–06 HC 969) para 5.1.

[12] See also Terrorism (Northern Ireland) Act 2006 (Transitional Provisions and Savings) Order 2007, SI 2007/2259.

Banner—military intervention in support of the civil authorities in Northern Ireland, which began in 1969.[13] Now, the military provide only specialist support under Operation Helvetic.

Several important aspects of the Pt VII package were terminated by the JSA 2007, including **11.05** the special offences of collecting information under s 103 (subject to s 58A, as described in Chapter 5) and the offence of wearing a hood in public places under s 35 (subject to powers to remove face coverings in Chapter 4). Many of the rules responding to the Omagh bombing[14] about 'specified organizations', originally contained in the Criminal Justice (Terrorism and Conspiracy) Act 1998 and then translated into ss 107 to 111 of Pt VII, were also dropped as a futile dead-letter.[15]

More changes occurred within the sphere of pre-trial criminal justice process. Special **11.06** restrictions on bail (under s 67 of the 2000 Act) were ended, alongside special rules about the pre-trial detention of young persons (ss 70 and 71), rules about time limits on the length of the pre-trial process (ss 72 and 73—dormant in any event),[16] special evidential rules about the admissibility of confessions (s 76),[17] and the switching of proof for the possession of munitions (s 77) have also been culled.[18] Post-conviction, a variety of special penal measures (ss 78 to 80) also terminated.

Since the passage of the JSA 2007 the main legislative development has been the termin- **11.07** ation of its special regulation of the private security industry (ss 48, 49, and Sch 6). The Northern Ireland Office accepted in 2006 as the best solution[19] the application of normal regulation by the Security Industry Authority under the Private Security Industry Act 2001.[20] The interim scheme in the JSA 2007 ended in 2010.

After analysing the regional variations in Northern Ireland, brief attention will be paid **11.08** to terrorism laws in Scotland.[21] However, no foreign comparisons will be offered in this chapter. Northern Ireland measures do emanate from the same history of 'coercion' as terrorism laws in the Republic of Ireland. However, comparisons have already been under-taken in previous chapters, especially in Chapter 6 where the Republic's Special Criminal Court was examined.

---

[13] *Operation Banner* (Army Code 71842, London, 2006). For the continued role of the army, see Bass, C and Smith, MLR, 'The war continues?' in Dingley, J (ed), *Combating Terrorism in Northern Ireland* (Routledge, Abingdon, 2009).

[14] See further Walker, CP, 'The bombs in Omagh and their aftermath' (1999) 62 *Modern Law Review* 879; Campbell, C, 'Two steps backwards' [1999] *Criminal Law Review* 941; Kent, KD, 'Basic rights and anti-terrorism legislation' (2000) 33 *Vanderbilt Journal of Transnational Law* 221.

[15] See *R v Hoey* [2007] NICC 49; Police Ombudsman for Northern Ireland, *Investigation of Matters relating to the Omagh Bombing on 15 August 1998* (Belfast, 2007); Policing Board for Northern Ireland, *Omagh Bomb Investigation* (Belfast, 2008); *A Review of the Science of Low Template DNA Analysis* (Home Office, London, 2008); Northern Ireland Affairs Committee, *The Omagh Bombing* (2008–09 HC 873), (2009–10 HC 374), (2009–10 HC 440).

[16] See *Re Shaw* [2003] NIQB 68. See now Criminal Justice (Northern Ireland) Order 2003, SI 2003/1247, Pt III (not in force). The average for the period 2001 to the end of June 2007 from remand to trial is sixty-eight weeks: Source: Northern Ireland Office Statistics & Research Agency; *Carlile Reports*.

[17] See Terrorism Act 2000 (Cessation of Effect of Section 76) Order 2002, SI 2141.

[18] See *R v Shoukri* [2003] NICA 53.

[19] Northern Ireland Office, *Regulating the Private Security Industry in Northern Ireland* (Belfast, 2006) para 36. See also Security Industry Authority, *Northern Ireland Research* (London, 2009).

[20] See SI 2009/644, 2009/3048. For the impact of previous convictions, see *Re McComb* [2003] NIQB 47.

[21] For the remainder of the British Islands, see Terrorism and Crime (Bailiwick of Guernsey) Law 2002; Terrorism (Jersey) Law 2002; (Isle of Man) Anti-Terrorism and Crime Act 2003; and Terrorism (Finance) Act 2009.

B. Special Criminal Process

11.09   Between 1973 until 2007, a distinct special anti-terrorism criminal process was maintained. The centrepiece was the non-jury trial and arranged around it were extraordinary rules as to pre-trial processes, evidence, and punishment. The JSA 2007 maintains the core feature of juryless trials, but most of the outliers have been discarded, as already noted. More constant are the rules in 'normal' law which have been readily applied to terrorist trials. These include the drawing of adverse inferences from silence under the Criminal Evidence (Northern Ireland) Order 1988.[22] Likewise, the use of informant evidence is vital, but, unlike during the period from 1981 to 1985 when the testimony of 'supergrasses' dominated the criminal justice scene,[23] this type of evidence has largely receded into the background.[24]

Trial without jury

Background

11.10   The major modification brought about by the EPA 1973 was a policy of criminalization through a special court. The device was championed by the *Diplock Report*,[25] and, taking its name from that report's chairman, began life in 1973 as the 'Diplock courts'. The prime reasons for removing the jury were based upon, first, the sectarian bias, real or perceived, arising from what were then juries composed mainly of Protestants and, secondly, the prospect of intimidation of jurors by paramilitaries.[26]

11.11   There has been a commitment to phase out the Diplock courts since 1998,[27] and it was reaffirmed by the Northern Ireland Office's consultation paper, *Diplock Review: Report*, published in May 2000.[28] Yet, the time was not then considered ripe for change,[29] although three factors favoured some modification.

11.12   First, the number of Diplock trials declined sharply.[30] By 2006, just ninety-one out of 1,543 (6 per cent) defendants in the Crown Court that year fell within the Diplock system, down from a rate of around 20 per cent during the previous decade (see Table 11.2).[31]

11.13   Secondly, there arose a viable alternative in the shape of the Criminal Justice Act 2003, Pt VII.[32] A Crown Court judge may proceed without a jury where satisfied that there is a real and present danger of jury tampering and the likelihood that such tampering would take place is

---

[22] SI 1988/1987. See *Murray (John) v United Kingdom*, App no 18731/91, Reports 1996-I; *Averill v United Kingdom*, App no 36408/97, 2000-VI; *Magee v United Kingdom*, App no 28135/95, 2000-VI; Jackson, JD, 'Interpreting the silence provisions' [1995] *Criminal Law Review* 587.

[23] See Greer, SC, *Supergrasses* (Clarendon Press, Oxford, 1995). Note the concessions in the Serious Organised Crime and Police Act 2005, ss 71–75; Criminal Appeal (Offenders Assisting Investigations and Prosecutions) Rules (Northern Ireland) 2008 (SR(NI) 2008/23).

[24] But see *McKevitt v DPP* [2003] IESC9/03; *Breslin v McKenna* [2005] NIQB 18; *R v Stewart and Stewart* [2010] NICC 8.

[25] See Twining, WL, 'Emergency powers and the criminal process' [1973] *Criminal Law Review* 406.

[26] See Jackson, JD, Quinn, K, and O'Malley, T, 'The jury system in contemporary Ireland' (1999) 62 *Law & Contemporary Problems* 203; Donohue, L, 'Terrorism and trial by jury' (2007) 59 *Stanford Law Review* 1321 at 1329.

[27] *Home Office Response to Lloyd Report*, para 13.8.

[28] (Belfast, 2000) p 2.

[29] Ibid pp 6, 16.

[30] See Northern Ireland Office, *Replacement Arrangements for the Diplock Court System* (Belfast, 2006) para 2.5.

[31] Source: Northern Ireland Court Service, *Judicial Statistics 2006*, Table C.6.

[32] See Home Office White Paper, *Justice for All* (Cm 5563, London, 2002) paras 4.32, 4.33.

Table 11.2 Trials without a jury 2001–2009[a]

Year	Total defendants disposed of	Found guilty or guilty plea to at least one count	Not guilty all charges	Other, eg not proceed
2001	62	52	8	2
2002	113	97	11	5
2003	111	101	10	0
2004	77	52	23	2
2005	90	66	18	6
2006	91	83	8	0
2007	113	101	12	0
2008	35	29	6	0
2009	35	29	6	0
Total	727	610	102	15

[a] Source: Northern Ireland Court Service, Judicial Statistics.

so substantial as to make it necessary in the interests of justice to dispense with a jury. As noted in Chapter 6, the Court of Appeal gave a strong signal against non-jury trial in *R v Twomey*.[33] Nevertheless, s 50 applies the Act to Northern Ireland,[34] albeit on a basis which is mutually exclusive with Diplock trials. It was applied in *R v Mackle*, a case of evasion of duty where a juror had been approached by two partly masked men.[35] In *R v Clarke and McStravick*,[36] concerning a 'tiger kidnapping' and armed robbery, the jury was discharged at the end of the prosecution case after the foreperson had been intimidated. The trial judge proceeded with the hearing under what was stated to be the general (but not inflexible) rule to do so.[37]

11.14 Though the Criminal Justice Act 2003 is available, the government does not view it as a total solution for Northern Ireland,[38] primarily because of the levels of information required for triggering the measures and also the relatively open processes by which the issue is considered. The government has accepted that the 2003 Act can effectively apply where tampering arises after the trial has commenced, a situation where the evidence will be clear, whereas the JSA 2007 should be used proactively to deal with earlier threats.[39] This demarcation is reflected in s 2 of the JSA 2007, which requires intervention before arraignment.

11.15 The third factor impelling a return to jury trials is the desire for normalization. Thus, the commitment to jury trial was repeated in 2006 in a Northern Ireland Office paper, *Devolving Police and Justice in Northern Ireland*.[40] The government also rebuffed the absolute rejection of jury trials by the House of Commons Northern Ireland Affairs Committee.[41] The Northern

---

[33] [2009] EWCA 1035.

[34] See Criminal Appeal (Trial without jury where danger of jury tampering and trial by jury of sample counts only) Rules (Northern Ireland) 2006, SR (NI) 2006/487; Crown Court (Amendment) Rules (Northern Ireland) 2008 (SR (NI) 2008/505).

[35] [2007] NICA 37.

[36] [2010] NICC 7. See also [2010] NICC 13, [2010] NICC 21.

[37] Ibid para 27 per McCloskey.

[38] Lord Carlile, *Report on the Operation in 2004 of Part VII of the Terrorism Act 2000* (Home Office, London, 2005) para 2.7.

[39] Hansard HC vol 454 col 896 (13 December 2006), Peter Hain.

[40] (Belfast, 2006) para 18.10.

[41] Northern Ireland Affairs Committee, *Organised Crime in Northern Ireland* (2005–06 HC 886) para 222 and *Government Reply* (2005–06 HC 1642) para 59.

Ireland Office then formulated its considered views in a consultation paper, *Replacement Arrangements for the Diplock Court System.*[42] The government pledged itself to a presumption in favour of jury trial but asserted a fall-back position of non-jury trials.[43] The opportunity was also to be taken to reform jury practices to offer more protection,[44] including proactive criminal record checks, restricted access to juror information, the abolition of peremptory challenge and the restriction of the Crown's right to stand-by, and the physical screening and separation of the jury from other court users and the public.[45] These sensible proposals[46] have largely been enacted by the JSA 2007, ss 10 to 13 for all trials. But the Crown's right to stand-by survives, an apparent breach of equality of arms though one which persists in England too.[47] Under Attorney General guidelines[48] (which closely mirror the English version),[49] routine background checks will not be confined to criminal convictions but will also consider whether potential jurors can be entrusted with *in camera* evidence and whether their political beliefs are unacceptably biased.

11.16   The respective treatment of defence and prosecution under the JSA 2007 was considered in *Re McPartland*.[50] The complaint was that the removal of the protections afforded by peremptory challenge and the right to know the identity of jurors compromised the fairness of the trial, especially having regard to the continued rights of the prosecution. Lord Chief Justice Kerr endorsed the Act's policy of protection against 'malevolent individuals'.[51] The Court accepted that anonymization reduced the value of challenge for cause but was essential to reassure jurors and preserve the integrity of trials.[52]

11.17   At the same time, these reforms do not eradicate with sufficient certainty all paramilitary pressure. Though proven cases of jury tampering are few,[53] the ability to threaten and the perception of threat are appreciably greater than in Britain. Therefore, the 2006 consultation paper proposed a system whereby the Director of Public Prosecutions should be able to apply for a non-jury trial on defined statutory grounds, with challenge via judicial review.[54]

11.18   Lord Carlile largely endorsed this blueprint but argued that certification should be reviewed by a High Court judge on application[55] and that the English reforms on eligibility for service,

---

[42]   Belfast, 2006.

[43]   Ibid paras 1.2, 2.7, 2.8.

[44]   See also Criminal Evidence (Northern Ireland) Order 1999, SI 1999/2789, Pts II–IV.

[45]   Ibid paras 3.5, 3.7, 3.11, 3.16, 3.18, 3.19. Juries are regulated by the Juries (Northern Ireland) Order 1996 (SI 1996/1141) and the Juries (Northern Ireland) Regulations 1996 (SR(NI) 1996/269).

[46]   Such suggestions were made also in the *Rowe Report*, ch 14.

[47]   See Joint Committee on Human Rights, Legislative Scrutiny: *Third Progress Report* (2006–07 HL 46/ HC 303) para 1.51; *Attorney General's Guidelines, Exercise by the Crown of its Right of Stand-By* [1989] 88 Cr App R 123.

[48]   Hansard HL vol 690 col GC138 (19 March 2007), Lord Goldsmith. The authority for non-criminal checks is shifted to the Advocate General for Northern Ireland by the Northern Ireland Act 2009, s 3.

[49]   *Attorney General's Guidelines on Jury Checks on the Use of the Prosecution of Stand-By* (London, 2007).

[50]   [2008] NIQB 1.

[51]   Ibid para 38.

[52]   Ibid paras 41, 43.

[53]   See Joint Committee on Human Rights, Legislative Scrutiny: *Third Progress Report* (2006–07 HL 46/HC 303) para 1.11.

[54]   Northern Ireland Office, *Replacement Arrangements for the Diplock Court System* (Belfast, 2006) paras 4.5, 4.12.

[55]   Ibid App A, para 23; Lord Clyde, *6th Report of the Justice Oversight Commissioner* (NIO, Belfast, 2006) para 8.51.

which have included police officers and prosecutors,[56] should extend to Northern Ireland,[57] contrary to the Northern Ireland Office's queasiness about 'perception issues'.[58]

Without Lord Carlile's variations, these proposals were largely enacted as the JSA 2007. The **11.19** Independent Monitoring Commission implausibly sought to distance the new arrangements from the past, claiming 'a very different focus'.[59] In reality, the 'I can't believe it's not Diplock' courts represent a continuum, which the JSA 2007 recognizes by placing a two-year time limit under s 9, though this period can be extended by affirmative order for further two-year periods, as duly happened in 2009.[60]

Certification

The JSA 2007, s 1, allows the Director of Public Prosecutions for Northern Ireland to issue **11.20** a certificate so that a trial on indictment can be conducted in the Crown Court without a jury. Thus, the default position is jury trial, though there is no expressed presumption, just as there is not under the Criminal Justice Act 2003. The choice of Director rather than Attorney General (as under Pt VII) signals a more judicial and locally based process.[61] Under s 2, the certificate must be lodged with the magistrates' court prior to committal or prior to arraignment—after that time, the Criminal Justice Act 2003 comes into play, as already described.

There is a two-part statutory test under s 1 for the exercise of the power. The formulae are **11.21** more explicit and comprehensive than under Pt VII but, compared to the 2003 Act, set a lower standard of proof and take account of factors other than jury-tampering.

First, any one of four conditions must be suspected by the Director under s 1(3) to (6). **11.22** Condition 1 is that the defendant has a link to a proscribed organization as an existing or former member or through an 'associate' (defined in s 1(9) as an existing or former spouse, civil partner, enduring family partner, friend, or relative). The term 'associate' is very broad, and the government accepted that the spirit of the legislation demands that the Director will consider the quality of relationships going beyond formal blood ties in the case of relatives. After all, 'one could be estranged from one's parents but very close to a second cousin'.[62] Condition 2 is that an offence is committed with involvement by, or on behalf of, a proscribed organization. Condition 3 is that an attempt is made to interfere with the investigation or prosecution with involvement by, or on behalf of, a proscribed organization. The intimidation of witnesses might be a ready indication of a willingness to threaten a juror. Equally, interference with physical evidence[63] would be relevant. It should be noted that Conditions 3 and 4 do not require paramilitary membership to be proven.[64] Condition 4 is that the indictable offence occurred as a result of, or in connection with, sectarianism (defined in s 1(7) as hostility

---

[56] Criminal Justice Act 2003, Sch 33. See *R v Abdroikov* [2007] UKHL 37; *R v Khan* [2008] EWCA Crim 531.

[57] Northern Ireland Office, *Replacement Arrangements for the Diplock Court System* (Belfast, 2006) App A, para 32.

[58] Ibid para 3.25.

[59] Independent Monitoring Commission, *Sixteenth Report* (London, 2007) para 5.8.

[60] SI 2009/2090.

[61] Hansard HL vol 690 col GC108 (19 March 2007), Lord Goldsmith.

[62] Hansard HL vol 689 col 1056 (20 February 2007), Lord Rooker.

[63] The buildings of the Forensic Science Service of Northern Ireland were damaged by a van bomb: *The Guardian* 25 September 1992, p 25. There was forensic cleansing following the murder of Robert McCartney in 2005: Independent Monitoring Commission, *Fifth Report* (2004–05 HC 46) ch 4.

[64] Hansard HC vol 456 col 757 (6 February 2007), Paul Goggins.

based to any extent on religious belief or political opinion, whether real or supposed, or its absence, and applying under s 1(8) even if the sectarianism was not shared by the defendant or was viewed as the fault of the victims). Only proscribed groups connected to Northern Ireland are relevant to any condition (s 1(10)).

11.23 Secondly, because of one of the foregoing conditions being satisfied, the Director must also under s 1(2) be 'satisfied that . . . there is a risk that the administration of justice might be impaired if the trial were to be conducted with a jury'. The Director is not asked also to consider whether lesser restrictions (including under ss 10 to 13 or in addition under the Contempt of Court Act 1981 or the Criminal Evidence (Northern Ireland) Order 1999) would suffice.[65]

11.24 This system of certification is undoubtedly superior to the Pt VII scheme (in Sch 9 of the TA 2000), which relied upon the trigger of an offence within the indictment falling within a listed schedule—the 'scheduled offence' approach. The relevant conditions under s 1 embody a more explicit and clear connection to interferences with trials. By contrast, under Pt VII, the presumption was for juryless trial, subject to certifying out by the Attorney General. The Attorney General applied a non-statutory test which, as approved in *Re Shuker*,[66] stated 'that it is his policy not to deschedule an offence unless he is satisfied that it is not connected with the emergency'.[67] The Attorney General's decision was based on background intelligence information and advice from the police, plus an assessment of descheduling, submitted by prosecutors through the Director of Public Prosecutions.[68] Between 2001 and the end of June 2007, the rate of certifying out was 84 per cent.[69] The same bundle now appears before the Director of Public Prosecutions.[70]

11.25 The lack of certain connection between the scheduled offence and terrorism became acute where the scheduled offence was an ancillary offence, such as robbery, which might be committed by paramilitaries or 'ordinary decent criminals'.[71] The result was the overuse of the Diplock courts,[72] especially as the certifying out power did not apply to all offences until the enactment of the T(NI)A 2006, s 3. By contrast, the JSA 2007 system allows for flexibility—any offence with a terrorism connection can be assigned to juryless trial. This switch to certifying in may incidentally assist with the ability to leave aside cases involving international terrorism which otherwise would be tried by jury in Britain but not in Northern Ireland. Earlier objections to certifying in fell away by 2007, especially as the rate of descheduling had risen to 90 per cent.[73]

11.26 The main point of contention remaining about certification under the JSA 2007 relates to limits on challenge. Certification is presented as no more than a mode of trial decision.[74] But if it is maintained that jury trial is superior, as is contended by 77 per cent of the Northern

---

[65] Joint Committee on Human Rights, Legislative Scrutiny: *Third Progress Report* (2006–07 HL 46/HC 303) para 1.26.
[66] [2004] NIQB 20 at para 14.
[67] *Explanatory Memorandum to the Justice & Security Act 2007* (Stationery Office, London, 2007) para 5.
[68] Ibid para 15.
[69] Sources: Northern Ireland Office Statistics & Research Agency; *Carlile Reports*.
[70] *Re Arthurs* [2010] NIQB 75 at para 9.
[71] *Baker Report*, para 136.
[72] See Walsh, DPJ, *The Use and Abuse of Emergency Legislation in Northern Ireland* (Cobden Trust, London, 1983); *Rowe Report*, para 36; *Lloyd Report*, para 16.16.
[73] Northern Ireland Office, *Replacement Arrangements for the Diplock Court System* (Belfast, 2006) para 2.5.
[74] *Replacement Arrangements for the Diplock Court System* (Belfast, 2006) para 4.5.

Ireland population,[75] then those who are being selected for non-jury trial are suffering a perceived detriment. They should only suffer this detriment if their fate is demonstrably proportionate to societal interests in a fair trial. But how will fairness be demonstrated if the decision of the DPP is taken, even if with the advice of counsel,[76] behind closed doors and taking account of 'national security interests'[77] and not just those of immediate parties to the trial? Consequently, there is much to commend Lord Carlile's suggestion of the involvement of special advocates and the testing of the certificate before a High Court judge in procedures similar to the Special Immigration Appeal Commission.[78] This check would still fall well short of the process in the Criminal Justice Act 2003, by which an application is made to the judge at a preparatory hearing at which both parties can make representations (s 50(3)). In the format actually adopted, the 2007 Act affords neither hearings nor reasons because of fears about intelligence 'spilling out'[79] and about delays.[80]

Section 7(1) confines challenges to the grounds of dishonesty, bad faith, or other exceptional circumstances.[81] The courts will decide what constitutes 'exceptional circumstances', a phrase taken from *Kebilene*.[82] In addition, s 7(1)(c) interprets the phrase as 'including in particular exceptional circumstances . . . lack of jurisdiction or error of law'.[83] There may also be challenge under the Human Rights Act 1998 (s 7(2)). The government justified s 7(1) as at least equivalent to what the judges had considered appropriate for review of the Attorney General's decision not to deschedule a Diplock case under Pt VII of the TA 2000 in *Re Shuker*,[84] which rejected the full range of judicial review and accepted review only within limited categories of exceptions.[85]   **11.27**

The extent of challenge on judicial review of s 7 has been explored in *Re Arthurs*,[86] in which the certification was attacked as substantively flawed, in breach of Article 6 of the European Convention, and procedurally flawed. As for the first ground, the exclusion of jury trial infringes common law rights and must be strictly construed. Nevertheless, s 1 unambiguously restricts the right, and its tests are 'set at a modest level' of proof.[87] Thus, there was ample material relied on by the Director for this claim to be rejected. Secondly, the Court rejected the applicability of Article 6. Certification is a matter of public law rather than 'civil rights', since Convention rights are not determined at this preliminary stage.[88] Though not considered in this case, it could be argued that where the process is discriminatory, then Article 6 is   **11.28**

---

[75] *Review of the Criminal Justice System in Northern Ireland* (NIO, Belfast, 2000) para 7.62.

[76] Northern Ireland Office, *Replacement Arrangements for the Diplock Court System* (Belfast, 2006) para 4.18. Lord Carlile suggested an automatic referral for opinion by a special advocate: App A, para 20.

[77] Ibid para 4.12.

[78] Ibid App A, para 23.

[79] Hansard HC vol 454 col 969 (13 December 2006), Paul Goggins.

[80] HC Hansard Public Bill Committee on the Justice and Security Bill col 18 (16 January 2007), Paul Goggins.

[81] The absence of a full appeal is criticized by the UN Human Rights Committee, *Concluding Observations* (CCPR/C/GBR/CO/6, 2008) para 18.

[82] *R v DPP, ex parte Kebilene* [2000] 2 AC 326 at 371 per Lord Steyn.

[83] These meanings were viewed as already implicit: Hansard HL vol 690 col GC125 (19 March 2007), Lord Goldsmith.

[84] [2004] NIQB 20. See also *Re Rooney* [1995] NI 398; *Re Adams* [2001] NI 1.

[85] The House of Lords Constitution Committee, *Justice and Security (Northern Ireland) Bill* (2006–07 HL 54) paras 4 and 5 viewed s 7 as unnecessary and preferred a case-based approach.

[86] [2010] NIQB 75.

[87] *Re Arthurs* [2010] NIQB 75 at para 32.

[88] Ibid para 29.

engaged,[89] and it remains to be seen whether the s 7 review categorizes discrimination as an exceptional circumstance. It could in any event fall within the Human Rights Act 1998. A further certificate under the Northern Ireland Act 1998, s 90, might then arise, diverting the litigation into the s 91 tribunal. As for procedural unfairness at common law, the Court held that the Director need not consult or make materials available but had to 'act fairly in the sense of making a dispassionate decision'.[90]

Trial process

11.29 When a certificate is issued, the key feature is trial by Crown Court judge sitting without a jury under s 5.[91] Otherwise, the court can exercise the same powers and jurisdiction as if a jury were present, including conviction on alternative lesser charges. An exception, under s 8, is that a jury must still decide issues of fitness for trial, even if a certificate has been issued. Rules of court can be made under s 6.

11.30 As under the previous regime, there are some subsidiary special features. First, by s 5(4), the trial court may not draw any adverse inferences from the fact that a certificate has been issued. Secondly, s 5(6) requires the court to provide a reasoned verdict for conviction (but not acquittal) on any count. This requirement facilitates the bringing of an appeal. Thirdly, s 5(7) and (9) remove restrictions on the right of appeal that would otherwise apply under ss 1 and 10(1) of the Criminal Appeal (Northern Ireland) Act 1980. A defendant can appeal against sentence or conviction, and the prosecution can appeal against sentence directly to the Court of Appeal, without seeking the leave of the Court of Appeal or a certificate of the trial judge. Fourthly, the juryless trial will normally be held in the Crown Court buildings in Belfast, but s 4 allows the Lord Chief Justice of Northern Ireland to direct other venues. Terrorist trials have always been located in Belfast, for reasons of security and convenience. However, alternatives are allowed with a view to reducing delays.[92]

Comment

11.31 The continuance of juryless trials furthers the tactic of 'Pursue' of terrorists in a way which does not inherently breach Article 6 of the European Convention, since no jury trial is guaranteed therein.[93] Nor does a distinct system amount to unreasonable discrimination—reasons can readily be found for objective and reasonable divergence in terms of local conditions.[94] The further assessment of Diplock courts depends principally upon delivery in practice through the performance of the judge and the practical impact of the absence of the jury.

11.32 The government's view is that 'there is nothing to show that the system has produced perverse judgments or that it has lowered standards'.[95] The independence and legal competence of assigned judges from the county court or High Court is assured. It is some forty years since

---

[89] *Tinnelly and McElduff v United Kingdom*, App nos 20390/92; 21322/92, 1998-IV, para 61. See also *Devlin v United Kingdom*, App no 29545/95, 30 October 2001; *Devenney v United Kingdom*, App no 24265/94, 19 March 2002.

[90] *Re Arthurs* [2010] NIQB 75 at para 33.

[91] See further Crown Court Rules (Northern Ireland) 1979, SR(NI) 1979/90; Magistrates' Courts (Amendment) Rules (Northern Ireland) 2008, SR(NI) 2008/251.

[92] See *Baker Report*, paras 173–187.

[93] See Jackson, JD and Kovalev, N, 'Lay adjudication and human rights in Europe' (2006–07) 13 *Columbia Journal of European Law* 83.

[94] See *Magee v United Kingdom*, App no 28135/95, 2000-VI, para 50.

[95] Hansard HC vol 301 col 173 (18 November 1997), Adam Ingram. See also Ministry of Justice, *Rights and Responsibilities* (Cm 7577, London, 2009) para 3.28.

military officers have sat in trials in either part of Ireland.[96] Next, some defendants may even prefer the more detailed and reasoned verdict of a judge to that of the Delphic jury verdict.[97] Moreover, there have been few claims of breaches of fundamental rights or miscarriages of justice,[98] though this vindication may need reassessment after the emergence of quashed verdicts on referral from the Criminal Cases Review Commission,[99] and with more than 200 cases reportedly pending.[100] The judges sometimes fell short in areas such as legal advice and police treatment during interviews.

11.33 Amongst the possible discontents arising from non-jury trials is prejudice from the enhanced role of 'case-hardened' judges.[101] Given the preponderance of non-Catholic judges, these misgivings have been more keenly felt by Republican defendants. The effective acquittal rate (percentage pleading not guilty found not guilty) has been variable (ranging from 29 per cent in 1993 to 100 per cent in 1998, reflecting low numbers of defendants who plead not guilty). It has generally fallen below the rate for non-scheduled trials. Another detriment is the diminution of community confidence, input of standards, and education through jury service.[102] Thirdly, there is the problem of overreach—that non-terrorist cases are drawn into the system.[103]

11.34 The absence of the jury has other impacts. Judicial primacy seems to encourage more interventions and questioning but without becoming inquisitorial; the tendency is also to focus more on legal issues rather than on advocacy.[104] There is also a heightened reliance upon silence as evidence.[105]

11.35 Given that there are at least some perceived drawbacks, could they be avoided by alternative designs? One compromise would be to employ a judge accompanied by three lay assessors of fact, who would retain the elements of common sense and freshness normally imparted by a jury.[106] There is less enthusiasm for a three-judge court because of staffing difficulties[107] and because, in principle, it is no nearer to a jury.[108] During the current period of normalization, any interim reforms could even be seen as 'provocative' or 'mere tinkering'.[109] The official

---

[96] See *Eccles v Ireland* [1985] IR 545.

[97] It seems to comply more fully with *Taxquet v Belgium*, App no 926/05, 13 January 2009, para 48.

[98] See Dickson, B, 'Miscarriages of justice in Northern Ireland' in Walker, C, and Starmer, K, *Miscarriages of Justice* (Blackstone Press, London, 1999); Jackson, JD, 'Many years on in Northern Ireland: the Diplock legacy' (2009) 60 *Northern Ireland Legal Quarterly* 213 at 215.

[99] See *R v Gorman* (NICA, 29 October 1999); *R v Magee* [2001] NI 17, [2007] NICA 34; *Re Boyle* [2004] NIQB 63, [2008] NICA 35; *R v Hindes and Hanna* [2005] NICA 36; *R v Adams* [2006] NICA 6; *R v Mulholland* [2006] NICA 32; *R v McCartney* [2007] NICA 10, [2009] NIQB 62; *R v McMenamin* [2007] NICA 22; *R v Morrison* [2009] NICA 1; *R v Walsh* [2010] NICA 7. For convictions upheld after referral, see *R v Latimer* [2004] NICA 3; *Re McCrory* [2007] NIQB 93.

[100] *The Guardian* 12 October 2010, p 12.

[101] *Lloyd Report*, paras 16.16–16.18.

[102] Matthews, R, Hancock, L, and Briggs, D, *Jurors' perceptions, understanding, confidence and satisfaction in the jury system* (Findings 277, Home Office, London, 2004).

[103] Walsh, DPJ, *The Use and Abuse of Emergency Legislation in Northern Ireland* (Cobden Trust, London, 1983).

[104] See Jackson, JD and Doran, S, *Judge without Jury* (Clarendon Press, Oxford, 1995); Jackson, JD, Quinn, K, and O'Malley, T, 'The jury system in contemporary Ireland' (1999) 62 *Law & Contemporary Problems* 203.

[105] Jackson, JD, Quinn, K, and Wolfe, M, *Legislating against Silence* (Northern Ireland Office, Belfast, 2001).

[106] See Greer, S and White, A, *Abolishing the Diplock Courts* (Cobden Trust, London, 1986); *Baker Report*, paras 108–129.

[107] Ten extra judges would be needed: Hansard HC Standing Committee E col 25 (8 November 2005).

[108] *Rowe Report*, paras 62–64.

[109] Lord Carlile, *Report on the Operation in 2002 of Part VII of the Terrorism Act 2000* (Home Office, London, 2003) para 5.16.

preference is simply for the existing model to 'wither on the vine'.[110] Early indications are promising as shown by Table 11.1. Nonetheless, a lingering tail of business might arise from the Historical Enquiries Team (for deaths from 1969 until 1998)[111] and the Retrospective Murder Review Unit (1998 to 2004, when the Crime Operations Division was established).[112]

11.36 Accountability is signally lacking. During the passage of the JSA 2007, Ministers undertook to make a statement to Parliament each year on the volume of non-jury trial cases but have not done so. There is no ongoing independent review.[113] Constitutional governance is, however, much better secured under the certain terms of this scheme than under Pt VII of the TA 2000, subject to the limits of s 7.

Pre-trial special processes

11.37 One lingering pre-trial special rule under s 3 concerns requests for a preliminary inquiry before a magistrates' court[114] rather than a preliminary investigation. When a s 1 certificate is being returned, the court must grant the request unless a preliminary investigation is considered to be in the interests of justice (sub-s (4)(b)) or there is an extra-territorial offence under the Criminal Jurisdiction Act 1975 (sub-s (4)(c)). The normal need for agreement from the defence can be dispensed with so as to avoid delays due to the non-recognition of the court system by Republican defendants[115] or, more pertinent nowadays, to avoid the calling of witnesses who might then be intimidated.

11.38 This measure inflicts a lost opportunity for the defence to challenge evidence. Whether it is unfair in the context of a trial will depend on the extent of later disclosure and cross-examination.[116] Nevertheless, it is surely wrong for the courts to extend preliminary inquiries for the sake of convenience (such as where soldier-witnesses are in Afghanistan) or to allow anonymity for such witnesses.[117]

C. Special Police and Military Powers

11.39 Vestiges of a startling array of special powers, granted to soldiers as well as police officers, remain in the JSA 2007. Their retention was far less debated than the juryless trials, though they affect thousands more people. The commitment to normalization and police primacy[118] must be curtailed by recognition that the British Army must still be involved in munitions disposals and manpower reinforcement at the policing of parades.[119] So, special powers for

---

[110] Hansard HL vol 689 col 1052 (20 February 2007), Lord Rooker.

[111] See Northern Ireland Affairs Committee, *Policing and Criminal Justice in Northern Ireland* (2007–08 HC 333 and *Government Response* HC 1084).

[112] See Moran, J, *Policing the Peace in Northern Ireland* (Manchester University Press, Manchester, 2008) ch 6.

[113] There was an internal 'light touch' review, *Non-Jury Trial—Decision For Extension*, in 2009 which, on disclosure under freedom of information legislation, was almost entirely blacked out.

[114] See Magistrates' Courts (Northern Ireland) Order 1981, SI 1981/1675.

[115] See *Report of a Committee to consider, in the context of civil liberties and human rights, measures to deal with terrorism in Northern Ireland* (Cmnd 5847, London, 1975).

[116] See *Re Kerr* [1997] NI 225.

[117] See *DPP v McKenna* [2008] NI MAG 1.

[118] See Walker, C, 'The role and powers of the Army in Northern Ireland' in Hadfield, B (ed), *Northern Ireland Politics and the Constitution* (Open University Press, Buckingham, 1992) pp 112, 114–15.

[119] See Northern Ireland Office, *Devolving Police and Justice in Northern Ireland* (Belfast, 2006) para 18.10; Public Processions (Northern Ireland) Act 1998; *Strategic Review of Parading in Northern Ireland, Interim Consultative Report* (Northern Ireland Office, Belfast, 2008).

soldiers are required.[120] Fewer special police powers remain, though some have alternatively been translated into permanent laws, including the CTA 2008. Several powers were dropped entirely in 2007. The departed include s 81, by which a constable could enter and search any premises to look for a 'terrorist',[121] and the police power of arrest for scheduled offences in s 82.[122]

Reasonable force may be used under s 33 in the execution of the provisions which follow. **11.40** This extra power is necessary since not all circumstances will involve crime prevention or enforcement for the purposes of the Criminal Law Act (Northern Ireland) 1967, s 3. The application of this rule to lethal force and plastic baton rounds has been an enduring controversy.[123]

These special policing powers (and also the powers to undertake security operations described **11.41** in the next part of the chapter) are additional under s 33(2) to any under the royal prerogative[124] or under the common law.

Stop and question

Broad powers are granted both to soldiers and police officers under s 21 (formerly s 89 in **11.42** Pt VII) to stop and question any person, including the power to stop a vehicle. The purpose under s 21(1) is to ascertain 'his identity and movements'. Additional powers are granted under s 21(2) to soldiers to question the person about what he knows about a recent explosion or another recent incident endangering life, or what he knows about a person killed or injured in a recent explosion or incident. These additional powers are no longer granted to the police, presumably because they are conferred with sufficient other powers to engage the public, including under s 43 of the TA 2000. The incidental detention may persist 'for so long as is necessary'. It will normally amount to a matter of minutes, but a detention of one hour twenty-five minutes was deemed lawful in *Mooney v Ministry of Defence*.[125] This phrase must be read as subject to reasonably connected purposes, but an attempt to impose a specific time limit (such as fifteen minutes) has failed during successive parliamentary debates.[126] It is an offence (punishable only by fine) to fail to stop, to refuse to answer a question, or to fail to answer to the best of one's knowledge and ability.[127]

The breadth of s 21—without any requirement of pre-authorization or operational reason- **11.43** able suspicion or necessity[128]—will probably evade liability under Articles 5 and 8 of the

---

[120] The Minister claimed just eight out of forty-eight: Hansard HC vol 454 col 899 (13 December 2006), Peter Hain.

[121] See Hansard HC Standing Committee B col 162 (30 January 1996), Sir John Wheeler.

[122] See alternatively SI 2007/288, art 15.

[123] See especially *Reference under s 48A Criminal Appeal (Northern Ireland) Act 1968 (No 1 of 1975)* [1977] AC 105; *R v Clegg* [1995] 1 AC 482; *Re McBride*, 17 April 2002 (QBD); *McCann v United Kingdom*, App no 18984/91, Ser A 324 (1995).

[124] See Walker, C and Broderick, J, *The Civil Contingencies Act 2004* (Oxford University Press, Oxford, 2006) para 2.24.

[125] [1994] 8 BNIL n 28.

[126] Hansard HC Standing Committee D col 282 (3 February 2000), Adam Ingram; Hansard HL vol 690 col GC216 (21 March 2007).

[127] As suggested by the *Rowe Report*, para 93.

[128] The government resisted such conditions as unnecessary and creating uncertain change from the Part VII formulae and possible delay: Joint Committee on Human Rights, Legislative Scrutiny: *Third Progress Report* (2006–07 HL 46/HC 303) para 1.79; HC Hansard Public Bill Committee on the Justice and Security Bill cols 107–8 (18 January 2007), Paul Goggins.

European Convention provided the length and extent is kept short.[129] In addition, the breadth of the possible questioning, the absence of any legal advice, and the possible serious-ness of the issues involved would surely cast doubt on whether the reliance in court upon answers produced under s 21(2) could withstand challenge under Article 6(2).[130] However, the more likely scenario for questioning is where the military undertake explosive ordnance disposal work and seek information to conduct a search or to clear the area.[131]

Military arrest

11.44 In peacetime, soldiers have no special legal powers but are, literally, citizens in uniform. Given their enhanced policing function in Northern Ireland, it has been necessary to bolster their legal armoury. So, s 22 (based on s 83 in Pt VII) provides that a member of the armed forces on duty may arrest and detain a person for up to four hours if reasonably suspected of committing, being about to commit, or having committed any offence. The detention power of four hours is to afford sufficient time for a handover to a police officer who can then arrest under, say, s 41. Premises (as defined by s 42) where that person is or is reasonably suspected to be may be entered and searched for the purposes of the arrest. This broad power can apply even to trivial offences, but wide (perhaps disproportionate) latitude is afforded because of the lack of legal training of soldiers. While an individual arrest would be too fleeting to come within Article 5 of the European Convention, repeated arrests might breach Articles 5 or 8.

11.45 Equally reflecting a deficiency in legal expertise is s 22(2), by which a soldier making an arrest is deemed to comply with any rule of law requiring him to state the ground of arrest 'if he states that he is making the arrest as a member of Her Majesty's forces'. But the requirements of Article 5(2) of the European Convention are preserved under s 22(5).[132] This requirement at first glance negates s 22(2). However, the European Court in *Fox* accepted that reasons can be inferred from later questions put to a suspect; in other words, it might still be possible to comply with Article 5(2) without giving a formal recitation of reasons. The House of Lords also accepted in *Murray v Ministry of Defence*[133] that the reason-giving process can be postponed until the scene is made secure. It should have been possible to require the recitation of the triggering facts (as is the common practice),[134] even if legal reasons (in terms of offences) would be more difficult for untutored soldiers.[135]

11.46 There are supplementary powers of entry and search for the purpose of making an arrest under s 22(3) (theoretically narrower than the previous version because entry is on the basis

---

[129] See *R (Gillan) v Commissioner of the Police of the Metropolis* [2006] UKHL 12; *Austin v Commissioner of Police of the Metropolis* [2009] UKHL 5. Compare: *McVeigh, O'Neill and Evans v United Kingdom*, App nos 8022, 8025, 8027/77, DR 25 p 15 (1981); *Murray (Margaret) v United Kingdom*, App no 14310/88, Ser A 300-A (1995).

[130] See *Murray (John) v United Kingdom*, App no 18731/91, Reports 1996-I.

[131] *Explanatory Memorandum to the Justice and Security (Northern Ireland) Act 2007* (Stationery Office, London, 2007) para 61; Whalley, R, *Second Report of the Independent Reviewer: Justice and Security (Northern Ireland) Act 2007* (Northern Ireland Office, Belfast, 2009) paras 136–137.

[132] *Fox, Campbell, and Hartley v United Kingdom*, App nos 12244, 12245, 12383/86, Ser A 182 (1990) paras 40–42. See Finnie, W, 'Anti-terrorist legislation and the European Convention on Human Rights' (1991) 54 *Modern Law Review* 288.

[133] [1988] 2 All ER 521. See Walker, CP, 'Army special powers on parade' (1989) 40 *Northern Ireland Legal Quarterly* 1; *Murray (Margaret) v United Kingdom*, App no 14310/88, Ser A 300-A (1994).

[134] Hansard HL vol 690 col GC223 (21 March 2007), Lord Rooker.

[135] Joint Committee on Human Rights, Legislative Scrutiny: *Third Progress Report* (2006–07 HL 46/HC 303) paras 1.88, 1.89.

of an offence rather than a 'terrorist'). There is also granted by s 22(3) a power of seizure of items for a period not exceeding four hours of anything which he reasonably suspects is being, has been, or is intended to be used in the commission of an offence under ss 31 and 32 (described below).

Powers of entry

Section 23(1) (formerly s 90 of Pt VII) allows to police officers or soldiers a power of entry **11.47** onto premises, including vehicles under s 42, if considered necessary in the course of operations for the preservation of peace or the maintenance of order. Because of the possible need for a rapid response, this wording does little to discourage disproportionate intrusions into property and privacy by specifying an objective standard or requiring a link to terrorism.[136] The absence of reasonable suspicion and judicial oversight must render the power vulnerable to challenge under Article 8 of the European Convention.

Unlike under s 90, a constable may not enter a building without written authorization from **11.48** an officer of the rank of superintendent or above under s 23(2). However, oral authorization from an inspector or above will suffice where it is not reasonably practicable to obtain written authorization. If it is not reasonably practicable to obtain either written or oral authorization, then the constable may still lawfully enter. A record shall be made of each entry as soon as reasonably practicable, with details as specified in s 23(6); central record-keeping has improved under pressure from the Whalley Review.[137] Copies of records or authorizations must be given to the owners or occupiers as soon as reasonably practicable. But there are no corresponding demands for authorization or record-keeping for soldiers. To require formalities was viewed as endangering operations.[138]

Search powers

Searches for unlawful munitions and transmitters are covered by s 24 and Sch 3 (formerly in **11.49** s 84 and Sch 10 of Pt VII). Any materials found may be seized, retained, and destroyed under Sch 3, para 5.

By para 2 of Sch 3, police officers or soldiers may enter property to conduct searches on a **11.50** random or routine basis. In the case of the police only, they can be accompanied by other persons, such as civilian Scenes of Crime Officers. Authorization of team members must be explicit, if not precise.[139] Dwellings may only be entered based on a reasonable suspicion that there are munitions or wireless apparatus unlawfully present. There must also be prior authorization: for soldiers by a commissioned officer; for police officers by an officer of inspector rank or above. Authorization can be verbal as well as written, and the members of the search team do not have to be personally selected by authorizing officer.[140]

Paragraph 3 bestows on the police and military supplementary powers which may be **11.51** exercised if reasonably believed to be necessary in order for the search to be carried out or to

---

[136] See HC Hansard Public Bill Committee on the Justice and Security Bill col 126 (18 January 2007), Paul Goggins.

[137] Whalley, R, *Second Report of the Independent Reviewer: Justice and Security (Northern Ireland) Act 2007* (Northern Ireland Office, Belfast, 2009) para 109.

[138] HC Hansard Public Bill Committee on the Justice and Security Bill col 127 (18 January 2007), Paul Goggins.

[139] *Kirkpatrick v Chief Constable of the RUC* [1988] NI 421.

[140] *Doonan (Superintendent of Police) v Darcy* [1995] NI 378.

stop the search from being frustrated. These measures react to case law in which preventative tactics were challenged.[141] The officer may require any occupier or visitor to remain in the building in general or in a specified part or to go from one part to another. An officer may also stop someone who does not live in the building from entering it. No requirement can last for more than four hours, unless it is extended for up to a further four hours (which is only allowed once) by a superintendent (in the case of the police) or a major (in the case of the army). An extension may only be granted on grounds of reasonable necessity to carry out the search or to prevent the search being frustrated. It is an offence under para 8 knowingly to fail to comply with requirements under para 3 or to wilfully obstruct or to seek to frustrate searches of premises. The detention may be justifiable under Article 5(1)(b) of the European Convention by reference to the offence in Sch 3 para 8.[142] Paragraph 4 allows persons found in dwellings (as defined by s 42) entered under para 2 to be searched.

11.52 Unless it is not reasonably practicable, records must be made of searches of premises under para 6, and, under para 7, a copy shall be supplied as soon as possible to the occupier. In practice, records are also made of any damage caused by the search, and the owner is asked to sign these records.[143]

11.53 Paragraph 4 also allows stop and search powers in a public place on a random or routine basis in order to establish whether a person unlawfully possesses munitions or wireless apparatus. For individuals not in a public place, the officer must have reasonable suspicion. Failure to stop is an offence under para 9.

11.54 Next, search powers under s 25 (formerly in s 86 of Pt VII) are granted to soldiers to enter and search any premises in which they reasonably believe a person has been unlawfully detained and whose life is endangered. No warrant or authorization is normally required because of the critical danger to life. However, if entry is into a dwelling, there must be a prior authorization by a commissioned officer. There is still no requirement for reasonable suspicion in relation to the detained person being located in the premises to be searched—it follows that area searches are possible. There are no corresponding police powers because the PACE (Northern Ireland) Order 1989, art 19(1)(e), allows a constable to enter and search any premises for the purpose of 'saving life or limb'. The absence of reasonable suspicion or judicial oversight raises questions under Article 8 of the European Convention.

11.55 Powers to search premises in ss 24 and 25 also include, under s 42, vehicles, which may be stopped by order. Section 26 explains further that, where necessary or expedient, the vehicle may be taken away for searching. An offence of failing to stop a vehicle is contained in s 26. When searching a vehicle for munitions and transmitters, the officer may under s 26(5) require a person to remain with the vehicle or to go to any place the vehicle is taken where the searcher reasonably believes it necessary for carrying out the search. The requirement as to presence may only last as long as the search, or for four hours (extendable to eight hours as under Sch 3), whichever is shorter. A record must be made and a copy given to the owner or driver of the vehicle.

---

[141] See *Murray v Ministry of Defence* [1988] 2 All ER 521; *Murray (Margaret) v United Kingdom*, App no 14310/88, Ser A 300-A (1995). See also *Connor v Chief Constable of Merseyside Police* [2006] EWCA Civ 1549.

[142] Hansard HL vol 690 col GC227 (21 March 2007), Lord Rooker. See Joint Committee on Human Rights, *Legislative Scrutiny: Third Progress Report* (2006–07 HL 46/HC 303) para 1.96.

[143] See Walker, CP, 'Army special powers on parade' (1989) 40 *Northern Ireland Legal Quarterly* 1.

These powers have been applied on an enormous scale in the past, though the operations **11.56** have now been scaled back. Section 24 is additional to police powers under ss 43 and 44 of the TA 2000. Section 44 has been invoked around ten times more frequently than ss 21 and 24 since 2007, and its rapidly increasing usage has outstripped the rate of usage of s 44 for every other police area except London.[144] It was not explained during debates in 2007 why extra stop and search powers were needed beyond ss 43 and 44, but the PSNI have since claimed that authorization procedures (themselves viewed as inadequate in *Gillan v United Kingdom*)[145] would be an 'inhibition'.[146] It is further argued that s 21 allows questioning in a way which s 44 does not.[147] However, as the main purpose is disruption,[148] the loss of interrogatory powers should not imperil the success of the powers. It would also be misleading to infer that the police stand mute during s 44 searches. The potential operational confusion between s 21 and s 44 has been the subject of police guidance, record-keeping, and training, as prompted by the Whalley Review,[149] but the details are not disclosed nor is there attention to overlap with s 24.

This rapid increase in resort to s 44 has, as noted in Chapter 2, been summarily halted by the **11.57** Northern Ireland Policing Board in 2010, and then by the Secretary of State who now refuses to issue authorizations unless 'necessary' and only allows stops to be conducted in relation to vehicles and on reasonable suspicion.[150] Following this decision, one might predict further resort to ss 21 and 24.

The governance arrangements for ss 21, 24, and 26 compare unfavourably with s 44, which **11.58** imposes pre-authorization and a time limit on enforcement.

Document examinations

Exceptional powers are granted under s 27 (formerly s 87 of Pt VII and applying to both **11.59** police and soldiers) to soldiers only, who are conducting a search under ss 24 to 26 in order to ascertain whether information contained in documents or records is likely to be useful for terrorism, and if necessary or expedient, to remove them for up to forty-eight hours. There is an exemption where there is reasonable cause to believe legal privilege applies. It is an offence to obstruct the soldier. Under s 28, the documents may not be photographed or copied. A written record of examinations must be made as soon as reasonably practicable, and a copy supplied to the person who had custody or to the occupier of the building. The power is now wider than the version in s 87, which was confined to evidence of just two specified offences. This extension, added to the absence of any requirement of reasonable suspicion or judicial oversight, may again give rise to challenges of a breach of privacy rights.

Section 27 does not extend to the police because they are granted permanent powers under **11.60** the Policing (Miscellaneous Provisions) (Northern Ireland) Order 2007,[151] art 13, to examine

---

[144] See Table 2.5 in Chapter 2. Data is not kept about the religion of those stopped.
[145] App no 4158/05, 12 January 2010.
[146] Whalley, R, *First Report of the Independent Reviewer: Justice and Security (Northern Ireland) Act 2007* (Northern Ireland Office, Belfast, 2008) para 84.
[147] Ibid para 84.
[148] Whalley, R, *Second Report of the Independent Reviewer: Justice and Security (Northern Ireland) Act 2007* (Northern Ireland Office, Belfast, 2009) para 107.
[149] Ibid para 95. But there is no specific record or document devised by the PSNI in response: Northern Ireland Office, F-2010-02098.
[150] Hansard HC vol 513 col 540 (8 July 2010).
[151] SI 2007/912.

documents and electronic records in order to find evidence of a serious crime. The documents and records can be taken away and examined for up to forty-eight hours (extendable to ninety-six hours). It has already been noted in Chapter 4 that further powers have been granted to the police to remove documents for examination under the CTA 2008, s 1.

Statistics as to use

11.61   Table 11.3 displays the dwindling of special powers, save for powers to stop and search. The 'peace dividend' is evident in the downward trend, especially for the military. Between 1990 and 1994, there were 362 military arrests; from 1995 to 2000, there were forty-nine. There have been eighteen since 2003. By contrast, police stops are still widely used, especially when s 44 stops are added.

Table 11.3 Special powers[a]

Year	Army arrest: s 83/ s 22	Army search: s 83/ s 22	Police entry: s 90/ s 23	Premises search: s 84/s 24 (police/ army)	Premises search: s 25	Stop and search: s 84/ s 24	Vehicle search: s 26	Document: s 87/s 27	Stop and question: s 89/s 21 (police/army)
2001 (part)	44	6	n/a	266/359	n/a	166	n/a	46	99/6,223
2002	23	106	n/a	591/283	n/a	3,957	n/a	51	2,448/9,873
2003	5	72	n/a	565/1,686	n/a	2,621	n/a	101	1,368/10,921
2004	6	22	n/a	322/361	n/a	2,984	n/a	83	1,962/5,156
2005	6	79	n/a	388/239	n/a	3,925	n/a	106	2,473/3,101
2006	1	125	n/a	232/104	n/a	2,071	n/a	36	1,104/24
2007–08	0	0	n/a	210/0	0	406	210	0	61
2008–09	0	0	57	223/0	0	356	239	0	829

[a] Sources: Northern Ireland Office Statistics & Research Agency, *Carlile Reports*, PSNI.

D. Security Operations

11.62   The JSA 2007 preserves various provisions which range well beyond the concept of policing powers. Their purpose is to permit security operations, as well as more permanent installations relating to the offensive or defensive capabilities of the security forces. Part VII of the TA 2000 is the font of this collection, but some former powers have been dropped.[152] Rights to private property under Article 1 of Protocol 1 of the European Convention are subject to limitations for public goods, and so it is unlikely that the proportionate use of these security measures could be impugned, and the same applies to privacy and family rights. No local consultation or judicial oversight is required, but police guidance specifies approval by an Assistant Chief Constable except in an emergency.[153]

11.63   Section 29 allows the Secretary of State, if considered necessary for the preservation of the peace or the maintenance of order, to authorize a person to take possession of land or other property or to carry out works on land (or even to destroy property). This power allows the

---

[152] See Northern Ireland (Emergency Provisions) Regulations 1991, SI 1991/1759; Lord Carlile, *Report on the Operation in 2005 of Part VII of the Terrorism Act 2000* (Home Office, London, 2006) para 99.

[153] PSNI, *Service Procedure: Orders restricting the use of roads and property* (SP40/2008).

building of military structures (such as watchtowers), the dismantling of structures which threaten military bases, the provision of protection for residents at sectarian interfaces, and the reinforcement of security barriers at contentious parades.[154]

More specific powers are granted by s 30 to soldiers or persons authorized by the Secretary of State in order to implement road restrictions, diversions, and closures. The diversion or closure may be ordered by any soldier or person authorized by the Secretary of State for the immediate preservation of the peace or the maintenance of order. Directions for closure in calmer circumstances must be issued by the Secretary of State under s 32. These interventions are undertaken for defensive purposes (both to benefit the security forces and vulnerable communities) or to make movement more detectable, such as around the border with the Republic. In that setting, there has been considerable discord, because of inconvenience for local inhabitants. Some residents have therefore sought physically to remove the barriers or to fill in cratered roads. An array of offences relating to interferences and the creation of by-passes is therefore set out in ss 31 and 32. Section 31 deals with interferences to works, s 32(2) deals with interferences with closures, and s 32(3) forbids the execution of by-passes and even the possession of construction equipment within 200 metres of road closure works. It is a defence to show reasonable excuse, but s 118 does not apply. **11.64**

Police officers are not empowered by s 30 but enjoy alternative and permanent powers under the Policing (Miscellaneous Provisions) (Northern Ireland) Order 2007, art 12. Article 12 allows police to wholly or partly close or divert roads or prohibit or restrict the exercise of a right of way or the use of a waterway, if necessary for the preservation of the peace or the maintenance of public order. It also makes it an offence to interfere with works, apparatus, or equipment. **11.65**

E. Penal and Release Schemes

Successive waves of special penal measures have pertained to Northern Ireland. The most dramatic changes affected the imprisonment of paramilitary prisoners, as outlined in Chapter 6. The regimes have varied from 'special status' up to 1976, followed by an attempt to apply normalization.[155] The proportion of paramilitary prisoners is now much reduced, and standard prison regimes[156] are more prevalent, especially after the closure of HMP Maze in 2000. Nevertheless, a rump of paramilitaries have exerted control through separation at HMP Maghaberry[157] and conduct protests redolent of earlier decades, including attacks on staff and 'dirty' protests in 2003[158] and 2010.[159] There were thirty-one Republicans and thirty-four Loyalist prisoners in 2007.[160] **11.66**

---

[154] See Lord Carlile, *Report on the Operation in 2002 of Part VII of the Terrorism Act 2000* (Home Office, London, 2003) para 11.4.

[155] See McEvoy, K, *Paramilitary Imprisonment in Northern Ireland* (Oxford University Press, Oxford, 2001).

[156] See Prison Act (Northern Ireland) 1953; Prison and Young Offenders Centres Rules (Northern Ireland) 1995, SR(NI) 1995/8.

[157] See Northern Ireland Prison Service, *Compact and Information Booklet* (Belfast, 2006).

[158] See House of Commons Northern Ireland Affairs Committee, *The Separation of Paramilitary Prisoners at HMP Maghaberry* (2003–04 HC 302 and *Government Reply* 2003–04 HC 583).

[159] See *Belfast Telegraph* 19 July 2010, p 26 (involving thirty-seven Republicans). The resolution was by an agreement to end the protest at Roe House in Maghaberry Prison on 12 August 2010.

[160] House of Commons Northern Ireland Affairs Committee, *The Northern Ireland Prison Service* (2007–08 HC 118) para 87.

11.67   The reason for these modest totals is that most paramilitary offenders have been released under special schemes in furtherance of the 'Peace Process'. Under the terms of the Northern Ireland (Sentences) Act 1998,[161] a Sentence Review Commission is established under s 1 to review whether a declaration for eligibility for release should be issued for scheduled offences committed in Northern Ireland before 10 April 1998 where the person has been sentenced to life or five years or more.[162] Terrorism offences in Britain are correspondingly under s 17 and Sch 3. A series of sentences served consecutively must include one of five years or more. Prisoners must show that they are not supporters of 'terrorism'[163] or of 'specified organisations',[164] are unlikely, if released, to become involved in specified organizations or terrorism, and (only if serving a life sentence) would not be a danger to the public.[165] The Prison Service will respond to these issues, after liaison with the police and psychiatric experts. Under s 14, evidence adduced before the Commission cannot be admitted in criminal proceedings for pre-2000 special terrorism offences.

11.68   In order to constrict eligibility and also to encourage the shift to peace, the 1998 Act creates the concept of the 'specified organisation'. Members cannot claim eligibility for early release under the 1998 Act. A 'specified terrorist organisation' is so declared by the Secretary of State on the basis of a 'belief' under s 3(8) that it is concerned in, or promoting or encouraging terrorism, and is failing to observe 'a complete and unequivocal ceasefire'. In applying this test, the Secretary of State shall take particular account under s 3(9) of whether an organization (a) is committed to the use of purely democratic and peaceful means to achieve its objectives; (b) has ceased to be involved in any acts of violence or preparation for violence; (c) is directing or promoting acts of violence by other organizations; and (d) is cooperating fully with the Northern Ireland Arms Decommissioning Act 1997 regime (described later). Listed 'specified organisations' at present are the Continuity Irish Republican Army, the Loyalist Volunteer Force, Óglaigh na hEireann, the Orange Volunteers, the 'Real' Irish Republican Army, and the Red Hand Defenders.[166] The courts were highly reluctant to interfere with the judgment of a Minister not to specify the Provisional IRA in 1999; the judges felt inferior in knowledge and expertise, despite the Minister's verbal errors.[167]

11.69   Life sentence prisoners qualify for release (subject to confirmation by the Commission) for sentences imposed before the date of enactment (28 July 1998) whichever is the earlier of either two years from date of enactment (s 10—accelerated release) or a date which represents at least two-thirds of the period which the prisoner would have been likely to spend in prison under the sentence according to the belief of the Commission (s 6). For fixed sentence prisoners sentenced before 28 July 1998, the choice is between is one-third of the sentence under s 4

---

[161] See also in the Republic the Criminal Justice (Release of Prisoners) Act 1998.

[162] For procedures, see Northern Ireland (Sentences) Act 1998 (Sentence Review Commissioners) Rules 1998, SI 1998/1859.

[163] Defined in s 11 as the use of violence for political ends, and includes any use of violence for the purpose of putting the public or any section of the public in fear.

[164] A declaration suffices unless contradicted: <http://www.sentencereview.org.uk/articles.htm>.

[165] The Commissioners interpret 'danger' as meaning death or serious personal injury, whether physical or psychological, resulting from further offences: <http://www.sentencereview.org.uk/articles.htm>. See *R v Sheridan* [2004] NIQB 4.

[166] Northern Ireland (Sentences) Act 1998 (Specified Organisations) Orders, SI 2008/1975 (see previously SI 1998/1882, 1998/2869, 1999/1152, 2001/3411, 2004/3009, 2005/2558).

[167] See *Re Williamson* [2000] NI 281.

or, more likely, two years from the date of enactment under accelerated release under s 10. Those sentenced for qualifying offences after 28 July 1998 must serve two years from the date of sentence.[168]

Release is subject to conditions, but only those listed under s 9: (a) that he does not support **11.70** a 'specified organisation', (b) that he does not become concerned in the commission, preparation, or instigation of acts of terrorism connected with the affairs of Northern Ireland, and (c) in the case of a life prisoner, that he does not become a danger to the public. The Secretary of State may suspend a licence on the belief that the person has broken, or is likely to break, a condition.[169] The Secretary of State may also intervene under s 8 to inform the Commissioners of new or changed circumstances or evidence. Victims may request statements about release under s 15, but they will not be issued if to do so would create a danger to the safety of any person.

In total, 444 qualifying prisoners were released in the North, and fifty-seven in the South by **11.71** 14 July 2001.[170] The scheme is a decisive element of the Peace Process but is not an amnesty. Life sentence prisoners remain under indefinite licence, while determinate sentence prisoners are under licence during the extra remission.

Beyond changes to terms of imprisonment, remission rates have also been an instrument **11.72** for the deterrence or encouragement of paramilitary prisoners. By the TA 2000, s 79, the remission in respect of a sentence of imprisonment for five years or more for a scheduled offence was set at a maximum of 33 per cent of the term (instead of 50 per cent, which applied from 1976 to 1989).[171] The ceasing of s 79 in 2007 brought into play the Northern Ireland (Remission of Sentences) Act 1995,[172] which restores 50 per cent. Whilst on licence, prisoners may be recalled up until the two-thirds point of sentence if they are thought likely to commit further offences or they would pose a threat to public safety. After the two-thirds point, they may be granted remission. The 50 per cent rule was ended by the Criminal Justice (NI) Order 2008, Pt II,[173] for offences committed on or after 1 April 2009 in respect of sentences of twelve months or more. Part II creates a new type of prison sentence by which the first half of the sentence will be served in custody followed by a licence period to the end of the sentence as set by the court. Prisoners given these sentences will not receive remission on custody.

Rates of conviction for scheduled offences during remission are relatively low but reflect **11.73** resurgent dissident activity. Between 2005 and 2008, 266 persons were convicted of scheduled offences, peaking at 101 in 2007 and falling to twenty-eight in 2008.[174]

---

[168] See *R v McArdle* [2000] NI 390.

[169] See *Re McClean* [2004] NICA 13; *Re Mullan* [2007] NICA 47; *Re McCafferty* [2009] NIQB 59; *Re Knights* [2010] NIQB 30. See also the possibility of denial of release after the decision of the Commissioners: Northern Ireland (Sentences) Act 1998 (Amendment of Section 10) Order 2000, SI 2000/2024; *Re McClean* [2004] NICA 14.

[170] See Dwyer, CD, 'Risk, Politics and the scientification of political judgement prisoner release and conflict transformation in Northern Ireland' (2007) 47 *British Journal of Criminology* 423; Shirlow, P and McEvoy, K, *Beyond the Wire* (Pluto Press, London, 2008); McAuley, JW et al, 'Conflict, transformation and former Loyalist paramilitary prisoners in Northern Ireland' (2009) 22 *Terrorism & Political Violence* 22.

[171] See Treatment of Offenders Act (NI) 1968, s 26.

[172] See *R v McArdle* [2000] NI 390.

[173] SI 2008/1261.

[174] Source: NIO Statistics and Research Branch.

11.74   The employment prospects of former prisoners are hampered because no special concessions have been granted on criminal records disclosure,[175] though disqualification from service on police boards has been eased.[176]

11.75   A next incentive to peaceful behaviour is the Northern Ireland Arms Decommissioning Act 1997.[177] This scheme grants 'a tightly defined and narrow amnesty'[178] period during which firearms, ammunition, and explosives may be decommissioned under s 3 by (a) transfer for destruction to the Independent International Commission on Decommissioning set up under s 7 or to a designated person; (b) depositing for collection and destruction; (c) provision of information for the purpose of collection and destruction; or (d) destruction by persons in unlawful possession. A scheme can apply to munitions in Britain under s 8. If dealt with in these ways, no proceedings may be brought for a list of specified offences (not including international treaty offences) for actions taken under a decommissioning scheme (s 4). In addition, a decommissioned article, or information derived from it or the scheme in general, shall not be admissible in evidence in criminal proceedings (s 5), nor shall forensic tests be conducted (s 6). However, the person may be prosecuted for an offence involving the weapon, and the government promised prosecutions 'to the utmost degree'.[179] The Commission's life was extended until February 2010, by which time it had overseen decommissioning by the UDA, UVF, Provisional and Official IRA, and the INLA.[180]

F. Assessment and Conclusions on Special Powers

11.76   In terms of the CONTEST strategy, these measures mainly perform similar roles to s 44 of the TA 2000. Though 'Pursue' may result, the main impact is to 'Prevent' through disruption and intelligence gathering.[181] Some assert great success,[182] but intelligence impacts remain too shadowy to assess with certainty. As for drawbacks, several design aspects pay insufficient consideration to individual rights, though actual challenges have been relatively few and have produced 'a relatively easy ride',[183] probably reflecting the street level of their application. There is also a question mark against the entire existence of some powers as unnecessary duplications, especially the police stop and search powers. As for the remaining military powers, some have suggested that military aid should be replaced by mutual police aid from Britain,[184] but that prospect raises unpalatable political drawbacks as well as training and

---

[175]   See Independent Monitoring Commission, *Twenty Second Report* (2008–09 HC 1085) para 6.5.

[176]   See Police (Northern Ireland) Act 2003, ss 15, 16.

[177]   In the Republic, see Decommissioning Act 1997. The initiative follows the (Mitchell) *Report of the International Body on Decommissioning* (Belfast, 1996).

[178]   Hansard HC vol 287 col 24 (9 December 1996), Patrick Mayhew.

[179]   Ibid col 85, John Wheeler.

[180]   Hansard HC vol 505 col 624 (8 February 2010), Gordon Brown. See Northern Ireland Arms Decommissioning Act 1997 Amnesty Period Order 2009, SI 2009/281, Northern Ireland (Miscellaneous Provisions) Act 2006, SI 2009/281.

[181]   Whalley, R, *First Report of the Independent Reviewer: Justice and Security (Northern Ireland) Act 2007* (Northern Ireland Office, Belfast, 2008) para 82.

[182]   Dingley, J (ed), *Combating Terrorism in Northern Ireland* (Routledge, Abingdon, 2009) pp 3, 188.

[183]   Morgan, A, 'Northern Ireland terrorism' in Dingley, J (ed), *Combating Terrorism in Northern Ireland* (Routledge, Abingdon, 2009) p 172.

[184]   Whalley, R, *First Report of the Independent Reviewer: Justice and Security (Northern Ireland) Act* 2007 (Northern Ireland Office, Belfast, 2008) para 100.

logistical complexities.[185] In any event, the military are 'highly unlikely'[186] to be needed to assist with public order (with no call out since 2006). Their remaining focus on munitions disposal points towards continuing military special powers confined to that purpose.

As for accountability, the JSA 2007 reflects the oversight mechanisms in the main body of **11.77** the TA 2000. Thus, unlike for Pt VII, there is no fixed life span, on the basis that the threat may remain 'for a considerable time'.[187] But there is a partial annual review. By s 40, the Secretary of State must appoint a reviewer to report on the operation of ss 21 to 32, and the report must be laid before Parliament. This review is markedly less effective than under Pt VII, since the remit does not extend to juryless trials, even though they are the most temporary and exceptional of all.

To assist the review, and accountability in general, s 37 (formerly s 104) requires the police **11.78** to keep records of the exercise of the powers in ss 21 to 26. This requirement follows a recommendation of the Patten Commission,[188] but it is subject to the proviso that it must be reasonably practicable to implement in the circumstances.

The reviewer under s 40 must additionally report on the procedures adopted by the armed **11.79** forces in Northern Ireland for receiving, investigating, and responding to complaints, a function formerly exercised by the Independent Assessor of Military Complaints Procedures (first instituted on a non-statutory basis following Viscount Colville's report in 1990[189] and latterly under s 98 and Sch 11 of Pt VII).[190] The reviewer may not receive or investigate complaints, but stands one step back and audits the process. The closest this comes to direct intervention is that the reviewer may require the General Officer Commanding to review a particular case (under s 40(6)(d)). The reviewer's impact cannot therefore match that of the Ombudsman under the Police (Northern Ireland) Act 2000, Pt VIII. Most complaints nowadays relate to helicopter overflights which arise as much from training for missions in Afghanistan as from security missions in Northern Ireland.[191] The decline in military patrolling makes the absence of more interventionist powers less troubling.

The Secretary of State may also under s 40 direct the reviewer to conduct a review into other **11.80** specified matters. No request has yet been made.

The first review, by Robert Whalley, appeared in 2008. It may be criticized as lacking an **11.81** appreciation of the interplay with TA 2000 powers (especially s 44),[192] though this failing was less marked in the *Second Report*.[193] Next, the statistical information is more limited

---

[185] See Whalley, R, *Second Report of the Independent Reviewer: Justice and Security (Northern Ireland) Act 2007* (Northern Ireland Office, Belfast, 2009) para 158.

[186] Ibid para 191.

[187] HC Hansard Public Bill Committee on the Justice and Security Bill col 147 (18 January 2007), Paul Goggins.

[188] Independent Commission on Policing for Northern Ireland, *A New Beginning: Policing in Northern Ireland* (Northern Ireland Office, Belfast 1999) para 8.14.

[189] *Review of the Northern Ireland (Emergency Provisions) Acts 1978 and 1987* (Cm 1115, London, 1990) ch 5.

[190] The first annual report of the assessor was at (1993–94 HC 369).

[191] Whalley, R, *First Report of the Independent Reviewer: Justice and Security (Northern Ireland) Act 2007* (Northern Ireland Office, Belfast, 2008) para 131; *Second Report of the Independent Reviewer: Justice and Security (Northern Ireland) Act 2007* (Northern Ireland Office, Belfast, 2009) paras 171, 174.

[192] *First Report* paras 30, 183.

[193] *Second Report* paras 88–95.

than that issued under Pt VII, though some effort is reflected in the *Second Report* to improve data collection and to energize the Northern Ireland Police Board.[194] The review also lacks any firm grounding in principle. There is recitation of the notion of 'balance'[195] between operational effectiveness and the need for a transition to normality, but no detailed rights audit. There is now better liaison with Lord Carlile's reviews,[196] but a more comprehensive review panel could better handle all these inquiries together and should extend oversight to the Diplock courts.

11.82 The review and the impetus towards normalization are reflected in s 41, by which the Secretary of State may by affirmative order repeal ss 21 to 40. However, that impetus is contradicted by the *Whalley Report* which has advocated the threat of organized crime as a subject for the 2007 Act,[197] without explaining why 'normal' laws such as the Proceeds of Crime Act 2002 and the Serious and Organised Crime and Police Act 2005 cannot suffice. The extension of special powers to normal criminality has proven unwelcome in the past in Northern Ireland, as already explained, and reflects a parallel controversial trend in the Republic of Ireland.[198]

11.83 Remaining aspects of constitutional governance rely upon the trend set by the PACE legislation. Thus, the various security powers may be subjected under s 34 to regulation by codes of practice, as issued under s 36. The hesitant 'may' appears because the government may conclude that PACE codes are sufficient.[199] No specific 2007 Act code has appeared, in breach of a ministerial promise and in contrast to earlier times.[200] According to s 35, the status of the codes follows the PACE model. A failure to comply shall not create criminal or civil liability, but it shall be admissible in evidence and taken into account.

11.84 Another control is that any offence arising under ss 21 to 32 (except under Sch 4, para 12) can only be prosecuted with the consent of the Director of Public Prosecutions under s 39, with the added permission of the Attorney General where the offence has been committed for a purpose connected with the affairs of a foreign country. This extra restraint is in line with the CTA 2008, s 29.

11.85 Accountability for Northern Ireland special powers has been poor compared to the main body of the Terrorism Acts. Pre-legislation consultation papers were confined to juryless trials and private security services. Debates in the parliamentary chambers have been short and poorly attended. The legislation has been largely ignored by select committees and by the Northern Ireland Human Rights Commission.[201] Perhaps the devolving of policing and justice under the Northern Ireland Act 2009 and the Department of Justice Act (Northern Ireland) 2010 will encourage more attention.

---

[194] Ibid paras 109, 119, 225.

[195] *First Report* para 17.

[196] *Second Report* para 23.

[197] *Second Report* para 77.

[198] See *People (DPP) v Quilligan* [1986] IR 495; *People (DPP) v Walsh* [1986] IR 722; *People (DPP) v Byrne* [1998] 2 IR 417; Criminal Justice (Amendment) Act 2009.

[199] Hansard HC Standing Committee D col 284 (3 February 2000), Adam Ingram.

[200] Hansard HL vol 689 col 1058 (20 February 2007), Lord Rooker. Compare the Northern Ireland Office's *Guide to the Emergency Powers* in 1990 which was superseded by statutory codes in 1994 and 1996 (SI 1993/2788, SI 1996/1698) under the EPA 1991, s 61.

[201] See Northern Ireland Act 1998, s 68.

G. Compensation, Protection, and Victims

Terrorism legislation compensation schemes

Compensation is provided under s 38 and Sch 4, para 1, whenever '(a) real or personal property **11.86**
is taken, occupied, destroyed or damaged, or (b) any other act is done which interferes with
private rights of property' in exercising powers under ss 21 to 32. The nature of 'private
rights' has been explained in *R (McCreesh) v County Court Judge of Armagh*[202] and in
R (Secretary of State for Northern Ireland) v County Court Judge for Armagh.[203] The cases
demonstrate that special loss (such as to business profits) arising from interference with a
public right (such as a road closure) is not recoverable.

Under para 3, claims must be brought within twenty-eight days, subject to a discretion to **11.87**
allow applications within six months on written request, with appeal to the county court if
refused. Claims are determined at the first instance by the Secretary of State (para 4); no
reasons need be given.[204] Appeals can again be taken to the county court (para 5), where there
is a full hearing.[205] Where a claim is allowed, then costs are payable under para 7. Compensation
may be refused or reduced because of false statements or incomplete disclosure (para 6—these
actions may also be offences of deception under para 12). In addition, compensation may be
refused on public policy grounds under para 9 in respect of an act done in connection with,
or revealing evidence of, an offence for which the claimant is convicted.[206] The width of this
disqualification is disproportionate under Art 1 of Protocol 1 of the European Convention.
Those whose houses are damaged in searches which reveal hidden explosives or firearms
should attract no sympathy. But why should a person who has been fined for an offence of
attempting to create a by-pass additionally be refused compensation for land occupied as a
result of the road blocks?

Under the Peace Process, military and security installations were dismantled, and many **11.88**
border crossings have reopened. Thus, requisitions and compensation payments are also
diminishing, as demonstrated by Table 11.4:

Table 11.4 Requisition and compensation[a]

Year	Requisition order	De-requisition order	Compensation (£m)
2001	12	13	2.16
2002	14	15	4.57
2003	14	22	2.20
2004	14	14	0.47
2005	15	16	0.18
2006	2	2	0.20
2007	2	26	0.10
2008	1	5	0.13

[a] Source: Northern Ireland Office Statistics & Research Agency.

---

[202] [1978] NI 164.
[203] [1981] NI 19.
[204] See *Adams v Secretary of State for Northern Ireland* [1990] NI 183 (criminal injuries rules).
[205] Ibid.
[206] Compare (under criminal injuries rules) *Re McCallion* [2001] NI 401; *Re Creighton*, 23 April 2001 (QB).

There remains the 'Terrorism Act Compensation Scheme' administered by the Compensation Agency which also deals with property damage from search operations under special powers. There were thirty-four claims in 2006–07, twenty-nine in 2007–08, and thirty-eight in 2008–09; the annual cost ranges between £100k and £200k.[207]

Property damage from terrorism

11.89   Several other schemes provide financial recompense for terrorism victims in Northern Ireland. Compensation for personal injury, where the scheme applies to crimes in general and Northern Ireland follows English norms, has been considered in Chapter 10. In addition, and without counterpart in England, there has been a long tradition of state compensation for criminal damage to private property arising from political violence, based upon social solidarity with victims and local communities as well as the unavailability or unaffordability of private insurance cover.[208] The contemporary legislative response in Northern Ireland is the Criminal Damage (Compensation) (Northern Ireland) Order 1977.[209]

11.90   Under the 1977 Order, the Secretary of State is liable to pay under arts 4 to 6 for financial loss above £200 in respect of property affected by the following circumstances. The first is looting—the unlawful removal of property from a building in the course of a riot involving three or more persons tumultuously[210] and riotously assembled. The second category is property unlawfully, maliciously, or wantonly damaged where three or more persons are unlawfully, riotously, or tumultuously assembled together.[211] The third category is property unlawfully, maliciously, or wantonly damaged as a result of an act committed maliciously by a person acting on behalf of, or in connection with, an unlawful association.[212] In this case, the Chief Constable issues a certificate under the Schedule that he believes an unlawful association was implicated; this certificate is sufficient evidence unless there is proof to the contrary. The fourth category is malicious and wanton damage caused to agricultural buildings and property.[213] This 'special treatment'[214] for farmers avoids proof of involvement of three or more persons or an unlawful association. Finally, an amendment in 2009 applies a similar rule to community (mainly Unionist) halls.[215]

11.91   It was the government's intention to provide compensation for 'damage' to property, rather than for 'loss' of property.[216] By art 3(1): 'compensation shall be payable by the Secretary of

---

[207] Source: Compensation Agency Annual reports. There was a spike of claims in 2002–03 which resulted mainly from lax procedures: Northern Ireland Affairs Committee, *The Compensation Agency* (2003–04 HC 271) para 42.

[208] See (Macrory) *Report of the Review Body on Local Government in Northern Ireland* (Cm 546, Belfast, 1970) para 74; (Waddell) *Report of a Committee to Review the Principles and Operation of the Criminal Injuries to Property (Compensation Act) (Northern Ireland)* (Belfast, 1971).

[209] SI 1977/1247. For details, see Greer, DS and Mitchell, VA, *Compensation For Criminal Damage* (SLS, Belfast, 1982); Walker, C, 'Political violence and commercial risk' (2004) 56 *Current Legal Problems* 531.

[210] See *Fosters of Castlereagh v Secretary of State for Northern Ireland* [1978] NI 25.

[211] See *McGuinness v Secretary of State for Northern Ireland* [1981] 9 NIJB; *Wells v Secretary of State for Northern Ireland* [1981] NI 233; *WAC McCandless (Engineers) Ltd v Secretary of State* [1986] NI 155; *McGeown v Secretary of State for Northern Ireland* [1987] NI 262; *Gilmore v Secretary of State* [1995] NI 46.

[212] An 'unlawful association' is any organization engaged in terrorism, including any organization proscribed under the ambit of what is now the TA 2000, Pt I: Art 2.

[213] As for the meaning of 'agricultural property', see *McAvoy v Down CC* [1958] NI 183; *Stewart v Secretary of State for Northern Ireland* [1983] NI 335; *Gillespie v Secretary of State for Northern Ireland* [1990] NI 392.

[214] Hansard HC vol 935 col 1520 (20 July 1977), Don Concannon.

[215] SI 2009/884. Twenty-eight were attacked in 2007: Hansard HL vol 708 col 814 (4 March 2009), Lord Browne.

[216] Ibid.

State for damage caused . . . or for . . . unlawful removal . . .'. Thus, claims may relate to the cost of repairs or reinstatement or reduction in market value of property, fixtures and fittings and also damage to vehicles and other goods such as stock. Nevertheless, compensation for consequential loss (such as loss of profits or rental of alternative accommodation or bank interest arising from extra costs) continues to be available, provided it can be related to damage. Thus, in *Public Works (Belfast) Limited v Secretary of State for Northern Ireland*,[217] the High Court would allow compensation for losses directly flowing from the bombing of a canteen at a construction site, such as delay in the work programme owing to delays for meal breaks, but would not allow disruption arising from shock or fear on the part of employees. Where compensation is payable, applicants will also be entitled under art 12 to reasonable costs (for lawyers and loss assessors) incurred in the claims process. Compensation is expressly not available under arts 6 and 10 for any damage to, destruction, or theft of coins, bank notes, foreign currency, postal orders, money orders, or any postage stamps; or any articles of personal adornment, including watches and jewellery unless part of stock in trade; or property taken from a damaged vehicle or building except from a damaged building in the course of a riot.

The scheme is not confined to commercial property, but most claims relate to commercial or communal property since they are the predominant targets and since domestic property and contents can be insured. Where property is insured, the insurance company pays the applicant based on the insurance cover, and compensation awards are paid by the Compensation Agency to the insurers. **11.92**

The claims process begins under art 7 with service within ten days of a 'Notice of Intention to Claim Compensation' upon the Secretary of State, the local divisional police commander, and other persons prescribed. A claim form (C1) has been devised by the Compensation Agency which has administered the scheme on behalf of the Northern Ireland Office since 1992.[218] The time limit is extendable under arts 7 and 15 for up to six months at the Secretary of State's discretion or by the court on appeal.[219] **11.93**

The full application by compensation form (C2) must be made within four months (subject to extension up to a year under arts 8 and 15). The information in the compensation form, together with additional forms if applicable—notice for particulars (property) or[220] motor vehicle—forms the initial basis for assessing compensation. **11.94**

Applicants must show under art 9 that they have taken all reasonable precautions to reduce or avoid loss and that they have complied with statutory requirements as to safety. An example would be the proper regulation and storage of flammable materials.[221] The Compensation Agency will also take into account any unlawful use of the property and any provocative or negligent behaviour which contributed directly or indirectly to the loss or which increased the chances of it being sustained. **11.95**

---

[217] [1987] NI 322. See also *McCaughey v Secretary of State for Northern Ireland* [1975] NI 133; *Gilmurray v Secretary of State for Northern Ireland* [1976] NI 28; *Harkness (John) & Co v Secretary of State for Northern Ireland* [1978] NI 43.

[218] See <http://www.compensationni.gov.uk>.

[219] See *Stewarts Supermarkets v Secretary of State for Northern Ireland* [1982] 8 NIJB; *Bank of Ireland Finance v Secretary of State for Northern Ireland* [1982] 15 NIJB.

[220] See *Electronic Sales (Ulster) v Secretary of State for Northern Ireland* [1979] NI 151.

[221] Hansard HC vol 935 col 1521 (20 July 1977), Don Concannon.

11.96 A further important limit under art 10(3) is that no present or past member of an unlawful association, or anyone who has, or is, engaged in terrorist activity, even if wholly unrelated to the damage, may receive compensation.[222] The Secretary of State may override this limit where considered to be in the public interest under art 12(5). This discretion will take account of (but is not limited to) the 'Bloomfield criteria'—the seriousness of the terrorist convictions, age at the time of the offences, the time that has elapsed, subsequent behaviour in terms of criminal record or community work, whether compensation was paid in respect of any offence committed, whether there was any connection between the criminal behaviour and the damage sustained, and the circumstances that gave rise to the claim.[223] The width of this disqualification is potentially disproportionate to the needs of public policy under Article 1 of Protocol 1 of the European Convention.

11.97 As might be expected, compensation is also not payable under arts 10(8) and 12(2) where the applicant planned, assisted in, or actively and willingly facilitated the act which resulted in the damage (or looting), or was associated with the person(s) who caused it, or where the applicant fails to cooperate with the police in identifying and apprehending offenders.

11.98 Compensation is also not payable under art 10(1) where the loss has been, or can be, recovered under other statutory provision or common law. One possibility here is where the loss is related to terrorism but arises from security operations under the JSA 2007.

11.99 Terms for the repair or reinstatement of buildings are covered by art 11.[224] The aim here is to plug a loophole which had facilitated abuse of the scheme by some property owners and effectively allowed them to take compensation payments without using the moneys to repair or reinstate buildings. Effectively they were making profit from the scheme, thus running contrary to the principles of indemnity and restoration. It was alleged that the former loophole had allowed paramilitary organizations to profit.[225]

11.100 The appeals procedure under art 15 allows resort within six weeks to the county court.[226] Articles 16 and 17 provide for the recovery of moneys from the offender and from the applicant if he or she is subsequently awarded damages or compensation by a court or even if a court case is settled with payment to the claimant.

11.101 In 2000–01, £9.3 million was paid in compensation for criminal damage, with a further £4.9 million to meet claims under the Terrorism Act (and the previous anti-terrorism legislation).[227] By 2008–09, £12.3m was paid.[228] These figures are much lower than in previous years owing to paramilitary ceasefires. In 1972–73, the figure was £26.6m, in 1982–83 £31.1m, and in 1992–93 £75.9m (the highest annual total).

11.102 The scheme for compensation for property damage and loss reflects a 'Protect' purpose in terms of ensuring community resilience through providing business confidence and physical

---

[222] See *Re Mahood* [2009] NIQB 100.
[223] Ibid para 4.
[224] See *Greenan Lodge Co v Secretary of State* [1979] NI 65; *Traynor v Secretary of State* [1980] 4 NIJB.
[225] Hansard HC vol 935 col 1524 (20 July 1977), John Biggs-Davison.
[226] See further *Tansey v Secretary of State for Northern Ireland* [1981] NI 193; *Coyle v Secretary of State for Northern Ireland* [1987] NI 64.
[227] *Annual Report 2000–01*, p 38.
[228] Source: Compensation Agency Annual reports.

restoration. Faced with provincial 'acts of war',[229] central government must assume the costs. But one of the problems created by this protective embrace of the state is that it squeezes out private insurance arrangements. Cover for terrorism damage of commercial property declined sharply after 1969.[230] After the passage of the 1977 Order, the British Insurance Association announced 'an overriding exclusion clause designed to free insurance companies from any liability in cases which came within the 1977 Order'.[231] The situation has barely improved since 1998.[232]

Physical protection

Other support for the potential victims of terrorism has involved the Key Persons Protection Scheme, which was funded by the Northern Ireland Office. Protection was granted on two stated grounds: (i) a threat risk assessment from the Chief Constable which shows that the applicant is under a serious or significant threat; and (ii) that the subject is the holder of a relevant job/occupation/specified role.[233] The cost was £7.1m on average per annum from 1998/99 to 2005/06, with a peak of £13m in 2003/04 (when some 2,000 people were affected by the loss of personal data).[234] The allocation of resources has been a matter of dispute. In *Re Lavery*,[235] protection was denied to a Sinn Féin councillor because of that party's stance on violence. Certiorari was granted because of the need to take account of personal circumstances, but Sinn Féin's support for violence was a relevant consideration. By comparison, in *Re O'Hagan*,[236] a Sinn Féin councillor was properly refused a firearms certificate not because of party membership but because of a previous arrest and alleged paramilitary connections. Even in those circumstances, Art 2 of the European Convention requires suitable protection against threats to life and not just in the context of specified jobs or offices.

11.103

The scheme was replaced with the Limited Home Protection Scheme in 2006, with expenditure of £2.1m in 2007/08 and £1.66m in 2008/09.[237] The selection of subjects involves 'individuals whose death or injury as a result of terrorist attack could damage or seriously undermine the democratic framework of government, the effective administration of government and/or the criminal justice system or the maintenance of law and order'.[238] Where the threat to a candidate is assessed as severe or substantial and where they also fall within a list of specified occupations or public appointments, they are automatically admitted to the Scheme. Otherwise, the Minister exercises discretion, paying due attention to the obligations under Article 2 of the European Convention. The policy is subject to advice from the Northern Ireland Committee on Protection.[239]

11.104

---

[229] Hansard HC (NI) Debs vol 40 col 2617 (1 November 1956).

[230] (Waddell) *Report of a Committee to Review the Principles and Operation of the Criminal Injuries to Property (Compensation Act) (Northern Ireland)* (Belfast, 1971) para 53.

[231] Greer, DS and Mitchell, VA, *Compensation For Criminal Damage* (SLS, Belfast, 1982) p 28.

[232] Northern Ireland Affairs Committee, *The Compensation Agency* (2003-04 HC 271) para 37.

[233] See Northern Ireland Human Rights Commission, *Compatibility of Key Person Protection Scheme with the ECHR* (Belfast, 2002). There are also special schemes within the police and prison services: Northern Ireland Affairs Committee, *The separation of paramilitary prisoners at HMP Maghaberry* (2003–04 HC 302-II) Q800.

[234] <http://www.nio.gov.uk/kpps_foi_request.pdf>; Hansard HC vol 449 col 2400w (13 September 2006).

[235] (1994) 6 BNIL n 2 (QBD).

[236] [1996] 6 BNIL n 17 (QBD).

[237] Hansard HC vol 487 col 22w (26 January 2009).

[238] *Re L* [2009] NIQB 67 at para 10.

[239] Lord Carlile, *Report on the Operation in 2009 of the Terrorism Act 2000 and Part I of the Terrorism Act 2006* (Home Office, London) para 238.

Victim support and reconciliation

11.105   Aside from financial and physical assistance, victim support in several formats has been a major aspect of the Peace Process, with initiatives both narrow and broad. Amongst the narrowly conceived is the Northern Ireland (Location of Victims Remains) Act 1999, which sets up the Independent Commission for the Location of Victims' Remains.[240] The Commission is to receive information about the remains of a victim of violence, meaning under s 1(4) 'a person killed before 10th April 1998 as a result of an unlawful act of violence committed on behalf of, or in connection with, a proscribed organisation'. Any information divulged is not admissible in criminal proceedings (s 3); there are restrictions on forensic tests (s 4) and onward disclosure of information (s 5). However, there is no full amnesty, and prosecution can be based on information from other sources. There are fifteen 'disappeared', and the IRA has announced the location of nine graves,[241] but only seven bodies have been recovered. There is a counterpart, the Criminal Justice (Location of Victims' Remains) Act 1999, in the Irish Republic to allow the Commission to work in both jurisdictions.

11.106   Another specific, and as yet unsolved, legacy concerns fugitives from Northern Ireland who have settled abroad— 'on the run'. Proposed legislation in 2005 to attract them back with a summary trial followed by early release proved abortive.[242]

11.107   At the other end of the scale of measures, the South African Truth and Reconciliation Commission[243] set a powerful precedent which has prompted some echoes in Northern Ireland. The report in 1998, *We Will Remember Them*, of the Northern Ireland Victims Commissioner, Sir Kenneth Bloomfield, was lukewarm about 'truth and justice' models, warning that they can amount to 'a weapon as well as a shield'.[244] One tangible outcome was the establishment in 1999 of the Northern Ireland Memorial Fund to promote peace and reconciliation.[245]

11.108   The closest approach to a truth and reconciliation strategy may be found in the various inquiries which have been conducted into specific killings, as related in Chapter 1. The signal event is the Bloody Sunday Inquiry,[246] set up in 1998 under Lord Saville to re-examine the events considered by the Widgery report on the shootings of thirteen civilians at a demonstration in Londonderry in 1972.[247] The Inquiry reported in 2010, and it seems that its lengthy process of review and exhaustive reporting (plus a Prime Ministerial apology)[248] represents its principal benefit to society by furnishing time for reflection and recognition of wrongdoing. More specific inquiries were conducted under retired Canadian Judge Peter Cory into the deaths of Pat Finucane, Rosemary Nelson, Robert Hamill, and Billy Wright, and, aside from the first named, they have resulted in further ongoing public inquiries under

---

[240] (Mitchell) *Report of the International Body on Decommissioning* (Belfast, 1996) para 52. See Pertile, E, 'Trail of truth' (2007) *Police Review* 16 March, p 30.

[241] Hansard HC vol 331 col 40 (10 May 1999), Adam Ingram. See further <http://www.iclvr.ie>.

[242] See Northern Ireland Office, *Proposal in Relation to On the Runs* (Belfast, 2003); Northern Ireland (Offences) Bill (2005–06 HC 81).

[243] *Final Report* (Pretoria, 1998); Promotion of National Unity and Reconciliation Act 1995 no 34 SA.

[244] Para 5.37.

[245] See http://www.nimf.org.uk/.

[246] *Report of the Bloody Sunday Inquiry* (2010–11 HC 29); <http://www.bloody-sunday-inquiry.org.uk/>.

[247] *Report of a Tribunal appointed to inquire into the events on Sunday 30th January, 1972* (1971–72 HC 220). See Walsh, D, *Bloody Sunday and the rule of law in Northern Ireland* (Macmillan, Basingstoke, 2000).

[248] Hansard HC vol 511 col 739 (15 June 2010), David Cameron.

the Inquiries Act 2005.[249] The Bloody Sunday Inquiry has been criticized for delays of twelve years and costs of £195m, and so 'there will be no more open-ended and costly inquiries into the past'.[250] The future model is the Inquiries Act 2005, despite criticisms that it unduly limits and controls investigations.[251]

The structures for overseeing these policies have also been contested. By the Victims and Survivors (Northern Ireland) Order 2006, the Office of the Commissioner for Victims and Survivors[252] is established to promote the interests of victims and survivors of 'The Troubles' through service delivery, benefits, and the establishment of a forum. An Interim Commissioner for Victims and Survivors had already been appointed in 2005 and produced a review and plan in 2007.[253] That appointment was successfully challenged in court,[254] so a reconstituted Commission for Victims and Survivors Act (Northern Ireland) 2008 arranged for the appointment of four commissioners (three are now appointed).[255] The principal aim of the Commission remains to promote the interests of victims and survivors of the conflict, and it offers advice and strategic assessment to the devolved government. A Victims Unit within the Office of the First Minister and Deputy First Minister aims to raise awareness of, and coordinate activity on, issues affecting victims. Other ideas being pursued[256] include the Victims and Survivors Forum and the Victims and Survivors Service. **11.109**

Beyond government, the Consultative Group on the Past, an independent study, reported in 2009.[257] It proposed complex bureaucracies which would assume the work into pre-1998 crimes being conducted by the Historical Enquiries Team and Police Ombudsman and also grant 'recognition' payments to all 'victims' (including relatives of terrorists shot dead by the security forces). The Northern Ireland Secretary of State ruled out the latter proposal, though consultation is ongoing.[258] The Northern Ireland Affairs Committee was not persuaded by most of these proposals,[259] but the Commission for Victims and Survivors supported a new investigation agency.[260] **11.110**

---

[249] See *Cory Collusion Inquiry Reports*, Billy Wright (2003–04 HC 472) and Billy Wright Inquiry (<http://www.billywrightinquiry.org/> and 2010–11 HC 431); Pat Finucane (2003–04 HC 470); Robert Hamill (2003–04 HC 471) and Robert Hamill Inquiry (<http://www.roberthamillinquiry.org/>); Rosemary Nelson (2003–04 HC 473) and Rosemary Nelson Inquiry (http://www.rosemarynelsoninquiry.org/). There is no further Finucane inquiry owing to family objections: *Finucane v United Kingdom*, App no 29178/95, 2003-VIII; <http://www.patfinucanecentre.org/>. Note also the Police Ombudsman for Northern Ireland, *RUC Investigation of the alleged involvement of the late Father James Chesney in the bombing of Claudy on 31 July 1972* (Belfast, 2010).
[250] Hansard HC vol 511 col 741 (15 June 2010), David Cameron. See further Blom-Cooper, L, 'What went wrong on Bloody Sunday' [2010] *Public Law* 61.
[251] See Joint Committee on Human Rights, *Scrutiny: First Progress Report* (2004–05, HL 26/HC 224) ch 2; Requa, M, 'Truth, transition and the Inquiries Act 2005' [2007] *European Human Rights Law Review* 404; Gay, O, *Investigatory inquiries and the Inquiries Act 2005* (SN/PC/02599, House of Commons, London, 2009).
[252] SI 2006/2953; <http://www.cvsni.org/>. See Northern Ireland Affairs Committee, *Ways of Dealing with Northern Ireland's Past* (2005–06 HC 530).
[253] *Support for Victims and Survivors: Addressing the Human Legacy* (Belfast, 2007).
[254] *Re Downes* [2007] NIQB 1.
[255] See *Re Williamson* [2010] NICA 8.
[256] *Reshape, Rebuild, Achieve* (Belfast, 2002), *Strategy for Victims and Survivors* (Belfast, 2009).
[257] *Report of the Consultative Group on the Past* (<http://www.cgpni.org>, 2009).
[258] Northern Ireland Office, *Dealing with the Past in Northern Ireland* (Belfast, 2009) p 8, *Summary of Responses to Consultation* (Belfast, 2010).
[259] Northern Ireland Affairs Committee, *The Report of the Consultative Group on the Past in Northern Ireland* (2009–10 HC 171).
[260] Commission for Victims and Survivors, *Advice to Government: Dealing with the Past* (Belfast, 2010).

H. Cross-Border Cooperation

Policing

11.111 Aside from the formal arrangements outlined in Chapters 5 and 6, there are reciprocal administrative arrangements with the Republic of Ireland which allow PSNI officers to investigate in the Republic, accompanied by Garda officers.[261]

Judicial

11.112 Prior to the reinterpretation of extradition (or backing of warrant)[262] arrangements between the Republic of Ireland and the United Kingdom which occurred from the 1980s onwards, a solution was sought to fugitive terrorists by the adoption of what the Law Enforcement Commission called the 'extra-territorial method'[263] as follows:[264]

> Under this method each legislature would confer upon its domestic courts jurisdiction to try under domestic law certain offences when committed in the other part of Ireland. . . . The domestic courts of one jurisdiction would not have any judicial power in the other. The only way in which a court would exercise this extra-territorial jurisdiction would be trying [a] person, arrested within its own territorial jurisdiction, for a scheduled offence committed in the other jurisdiction. The extended extra-territorial jurisdiction taken would be without qualification in respect of all the scheduled offences.

The Criminal Jurisdiction Act 1975 and the Criminal Law (Jurisdiction) Act 1976 in the Irish Republic[265] implement this concept.

11.113 By s 1 of the 1975 Act: 'Any act of omission which (a) takes place in the Republic of Ireland and (b) would, if taking place in Northern Ireland, constitute an offence described in Part 1 of Schedule 1 of this Act, shall, for the purposes of the law of Northern Ireland, constitute that offence.' The listed extra-territorial offences are in Sch 1. It is made clear by s 1(4) that liability for an extra-territorial offence 'attaches irrespective of the nationality of the offender'. By s 2, the hijacking of vehicles or ships in Northern Ireland or the Republic is deemed to be a criminal offence, thereby allowing conviction no matter where the hijacking took place. An escape from legal custody in the Republic of Ireland is an offence under s 3, and s 6 covers inchoate offences. The use of written statements as evidence taken in the other jurisdiction is handled by s 9, while s 10 covers the attendance of a witness. Schedule 4, Pt 1, deals with the examination of witnesses in Northern Ireland to assist a court in the Republic; Pt 2 manages their examination in the Republic of Ireland to assist a court in Northern Ireland. Important safeguards are that, under s 4, any offence may not be tried summarily, and, under s 11, no proceedings for an extra-territorial offence shall be instituted except by, or with the consent of, the Advocate General for Northern Ireland.[266]

---

[261] FOI Request, F-2008-03911 (<http://www.psni.police.uk/garda_entering_northern_ireland.pdf>).

[262] See Hogan, G and Walker C, *Political Violence and the Law in Ireland* (Manchester University Press, Manchester, 1989) ch 14.

[263] (PL 3832, Dublin, 1974) p 180. See further Hogan, G and Walker C, *Political Violence and the Law in Ireland* (Manchester University Press, Manchester, 1989) ch 15.

[264] Ibid pp 17–22.

[265] See *In the Matter of Article 26 of the Constitution and In the Matter of the Criminal Law (Jurisdiction) Bill, 1975* [1977] IR 129.

[266] See *R v Smyth* [1982] NI 271.

There is a right to opt for trial in the Republic under Sch 3, art 2. If a person is accused of an **11.114** extra-territorial offence, and a judge of the (Northern Ireland) High Court or the court of trial is satisfied that a warrant has been duly issued in the Republic of Ireland on an information laid by a police officer for a corresponding offence, the judge shall, if the accused so requires, issue an order directing that the accused be delivered as soon as may be into the custody of a member of the police force in the Republic of Ireland and shall be kept in custody in Northern Ireland until thus delivered. The question arises as to whether the Director of Public Prosecutions in the Republic can be compelled to prosecute an accused who is charged with the same offences in Northern Ireland, so as to afford the right to opt for trial in the Republic. In *State (McCormack) v Curran*,[267] it was held that the prosecuting functions of the Director were executive in nature and hence reviewable by the courts only on grounds of bad faith or improper motive or policy. The Irish courts have also decided that there is no right to trial for an extra-jurisdictional offence instead of extradition,[268] but where extra-jurisdictional offences have been pursued, it may be oppressive later to seek extradition for related offences.[269]

The legislation has been sparsely invoked and has been labelled 'a compromise measure **11.115** of doubtful effectiveness'.[270] The foremost obstacle concerns the gathering and collation of evidence and the transportation of witnesses (and possibly also the jurors) between jurisdictions. A flavour of the difficulties is provided by *R v Lambeth Stipendiary Magistrate, ex parte McCoomb*.[271] Gerard Tuite had been convicted by the Special Criminal Court in Dublin for explosives offences in Britain. Tuite had escaped from Brixton Prison in 1980 after his committal for trial, but the English Director of Public Prosecutions supplied evidence to the Dublin court to enable his conviction and imprisonment for the same offences. While Tuite was appealing to the Court of Criminal Appeal, the English Director of Public Prosecutions applied for return of the supplied evidence since a confrere of Tuite, McCoomb, was to be committed for trial in England. The Court of Criminal Appeal agreed to the request, on an undertaking to return the exhibits after the committal proceedings. However, McCoomb wished to inspect these exhibits and commenced proceedings in the English courts seeking to restrain the English Director from returning the exhibits. The English Court of Appeal refused to grant the relief because of the undertaking, but it observed that this decision might cause the exhibits to be 'commuting backwards and forwards across the Irish Sea'[272] with the danger of loss or damage.

By November 1991, the United Kingdom prosecuting authorities had lodged thirty-two **11.116** applications for proceedings in the Republic under the 1976 Act. No applications from the Republic had been made under the 1975 Act, but eighteen persons were prosecuted in the United Kingdom for offences allegedly committed in the Republic.[273] Many early cases related to prison escapees from Northern Ireland where the evidence is clear-cut.[274] While the option of extra-territorial prosecution was at first 'conspicuously more successful' than

---

[267] [1987] ILRM 225.
[268] *Russell v Fanning* [1988] IR 505 at 520.
[269] *Fusco v O'Dea (No 2)* [1998] 3 IR 470.
[270] Rees, M, *Northern Ireland: A personal perspective* (Methuen, London, 1985) p 216.
[271] [1983] QB 551.
[272] Ibid pp 566–7.
[273] Hansard HC vol 198 col 352wa (11 November 1991). The total is thirty-seven persons in 2009: Northern Ireland Affairs Committee, *Cross-border co-operation between the Governments of the United Kingdom and the Republic of Ireland* (2008–09 HC 1031) Evidence q 261 Sir Alasdair Fraser.
[274] See, for example, *Sloan v Culligan* [1992] 1 IR 223; *Fusco v O'Dea* [1994] 2 IR 93.

extradition,[275] the numbers thereafter declined as the possibilities of rendition, always the preferred option, have increased. However, the offences of hijacking still have utility,[276] and there remain some exceptional cases where extradition or arrest warrants are not viable.[277] Despite the absence of activity, the Northern Ireland Affairs Committee advocates the extension of scheduled offences to include money laundering, and the government has promised a review.[278]

I. Conclusions on Northern Ireland

11.117 The decline of political violence in Northern Ireland since 1996 has engaged a wide range of policies. Anti-terrorism legislation has certainly played a part, with the delivery of criminalization through juryless trials being the key achievement. Special powers represent a more mixed blessing, with militarization being part of the reason for conflict by stimulating violent reaction[279] but also as constraining paramilitarism.[280] The legislation has been largely driven by history as well as pragmatism.[281] The main recent innovations comprise the attempts to release paramilitary prisoners and to care for victims. Other major reforms, beyond the scope of this book, have affected policing[282] and criminal justice institutions.[283] All are at best work in progress.[284]

11.118 Lessons to be drawn from 'The Troubles' remain contested, but two might be ventured. One is that human rights abuses fuel further conflict,[285] so it is vital to instil the values of rights, accountability, and constitutionalism. The JSA 2007 improves on its predecessors on these scores but is far from progressive.

11.119 The second lesson is that the reduction of such bitter conflict demands attention to the political aspects of terrorism at least as much as security aspects. The willingness to talk constructively with sworn enemies is an unpalatable but necessary precondition. The Provisional IRA might be withering away,[286] but Northern Ireland remains a deeply fissured society,[287] and the Peace Process is far from its journey's end.[288]

---

[275] Campbell, C, 'Extradition to Northern Ireland' (1989) 52 *Modern Law Review* 585 at 592.

[276] See *Averill v United Kingdom*, App no 36408/97, 2000-VI; *R v O'Neill* [2005] NICC 2; *R v Fulton and Gibson* [2006] NICC 35, [2007] NICC 2; *Kelly v Anderson* [2004] IESC 10; *Scully v DPP* [2005] IESC 11.

[277] See *McElhinney v Ireland*, App no 31253/96, 21 November 2001.

[278] House of Commons Northern Ireland Affairs Committee, *Cross-border co-operation between the Governments of the United Kingdom and the Republic of Ireland* (2008–09 HC 78) para 91 and *Government Reply* (2008–09 HC 1031) p 7.

[279] Campbell, C and Connelly, I, 'Making war on terror?' (2006) 69 *Modern Law Review* 935 at 956.

[280] Irwin, A and Maloney, M, 'The military response' and Morgan, A, 'Northern Ireland terrorism' in Dingley, J (ed), *Combating Terrorism in Northern Ireland* (Routledge, Abingdon, 2009) pp 215, 223.

[281] Compare ibid p 157.

[282] Police (Northern Ireland) Act 2000. See Mulcahy, A, *Policing Northern Ireland* (Willan, Cullompton, 2006).

[283] See Justice (Northern Ireland) Act 2002; Justice (Northern Ireland) Act 2004.

[284] See Northern Ireland Affairs Committee, *Relocation following paramilitary intimidation* (2000–01 HC 59) and Reply of the Northern Ireland Executive (2001–02 HC 461).

[285] See Committee on the Administration of Justice, *War on Terror* (Belfast, 2007).

[286] Independent Monitoring Commission, *Nineteenth Report* (Cm 7464, London, 2008) para 2.12.

[287] For physical segregation, see <http://www.belfastinterfaceproject.org>.

[288] Neumann, PG, *Britain's Long War* (Palgrave, Basingstoke, 2003) p 188.

J. Scotland and Terrorism

Scottish nationalist terrorism has also intermittently arisen,[289] especially the Scottish National Liberation Army, which has used parcel and letter bombs.[290] But this feeble variant of nationalist terrorism has not deserved attention by special laws. Thus, terrorism in Scottish law amounts to adaptations of measures against Irish and international terrorism in national legislation, terrorism being a reserved matter under the Scotland Act 1998, Sch 5. **11.120**

One notable exception has been the trial[291] of the two Libyans accused in 1991[292] of involvement in the planting of bombs on Pan Am Flight 103 which crashed at Lockerbie in 1988.[293] The trial in the High Court of Justiciary was convened in the Netherlands (at Camp Zeist where the defendants were detained) pursuant to the High Court of Justiciary (Proceedings in the Netherlands) Order 1998 made under the United Nations Act 1946.[294] Article 3 allowed for trial of named defendants, Al Megrahi and Fhimah, on the basis of Scots law. Under art 5, the trial was to be conducted before three Lords Commissioners of Justiciary without a jury (the jury was opposed by Libya). Further arrangements were agreed with the Netherlands government.[295] **11.121**

The two defendants were charged with murder and conspiracy to murder of 259 persons on the aircraft and eleven Lockerbie residents and also offences under the Aviation Security Act 1982 (which were not pursued). They argued that the Scottish courts lacked jurisdiction since the conspiracy was transacted outside Scotland. The High Court rejected this initial objection, finding that the conspiracy was a continuing crime, and it also rejected the complaint of the duplicity of charges.[296] Al Megrahi alone was convicted in 2001 and was sentenced to life imprisonment with a later recommendation that he should serve a minimum period of twenty-seven years. On appeal,[297] the appellant argued that the trial court **11.122**

---

[289] For surveys of Scotland and Wales, see Walker, CP, *The Prevention of Terrorism in British Law* (2nd edn, Manchester University Press, Manchester, 1992) ch 3.

[290] Recent convictions have included Adam Busby (the SNLA founder) (*The Irish Times* 15 March 1997; see also *McMahon v Judges of the Special Criminal Court*, High Court 1998); Andrew McIntosh (*McIntosh v HM Advocate* 1997 SCCR 68, 389); Paul Smith (*The Glasgow Herald* 6 September 2003, p 1); Wayne Cook and Steven Robinson (*The Times* 26 January 2008, p 2); Adam Busby Jr, (*The Scotsman* 19 June 2009, p 13).

[291] See also Air Accidents Investigation Branch, *Aircraft Accident Report no 2/90* (EW/C1094); *Fatal Accident Inquiry relating to the Lockerbie air disaster* (1991).

[292] See UN SCR 731 of 21 January 1992, 748 of 31 March 1992, and 888 of 11 November 1993. See also *Libyan Arab Jamahiriya v UK and USA* [1992] ICJ Reports 3, 114, [1998] 26. That case was settled in 2003 in a deal which included compensation to relatives (see S/2003/818) and the lifting of sanctions (UN SCR 1506 of 12 September 2003). Libya had also agreed in 1999 to compensate the family of WPC Fletcher. The Foreign Office has set up a unit to help victims of Libyan-sponsored terrorism: Hansard HC vol 497 col 32 (12 October 2009).

[293] See generally Klip, A and Mackarel, M, 'The Lockerbie trial' (1999) 70 *Revue Internationale de Droit Pénal* 777; Black, R, 'The Lockerbie disaster' (1999) 3 *Edinburgh Law Review* 85; Aust, A, 'Lockerbie' (2000) 49 *International and Comparative Law Quarterly* 278; Wallis, R, *Lockerbie* (Praeger, Westport, 2001); Grant, JP, *The Lockerbie Trial* (Oceana, Dobbs Ferry, 2004).

[294] SI 1998/2251. See UN Security Council, *Letter from the Permanent Representatives of the United Kingdom and the United States of America to the Secretary-General* (S/1998/795).

[295] Agreement between the Government of the United Kingdom of Great Britain and Northern Ireland and the Government of the Kingdom of the Netherlands concerning a Scottish Trial in the Netherlands 1998 (Cm 4378, London, 1999).

[296] *HM Advocate v Al Megrahi (No 1)* [2000] SLT 1393.

[297] *HM Advocate v Al Megrahi (No 4)* 2002 JC 99. See also *HM Advocate v Al Megrahi* 2002 JC 38.

had failed to give adequate reasons for its conclusions, had erred in various respects in its assessment of material evidence, and had failed to call all relevant witnesses. These points were rejected.[298]

11.123 A further appeal arose on referral under s 194B(1) of the Criminal Procedure (Scotland) Act 1995 by the Scottish Criminal Cases Review Commission. The grounds related to the trial court's assessment of evidence concerning the date of purchase of items involved in the bombing and new evidence on that issue, plus the fact that a key identification witness had seen a photograph of the applicant in a magazine before making the identification, plus undisclosed evidence on these points. The appellant sought to introduce further appeal grounds beyond the points supported by the Commission and relating mainly to non-disclosure and the reliability of witnesses,[299] a wider ambit which was upheld by the High Court.[300]

11.124 Before the appeal hearings could begin, it was revealed in 2008 that the prisoner had terminal cancer. He then sought either a formal prisoner transfer[301] (and withdrew his appeal on 18 August 2009 so that the path was cleared of any legal obstacle, though there remained a Crown appeal on sentence) and alternatively sought release on compassionate grounds under the Prisoners and Criminal Proceedings (Scotland) Act 1993, s 3.[302] On 20 August 2009, the Scottish Executive Minister of Justice, Kenny MacAskill, released him on compassionate grounds and he immediately returned to Libya.[303] The United Kingdom government expressed the preference both before and after the release that 'as a matter of policy we were not seeking Al Megrahi's death in Scottish custody'.[304]

11.125 A police investigation into the Lockerbie bombing has been resumed. A public inquiry into the conviction, clearly warranted by the aborted appeal, would probably encounter the suppression of sensitive evidence. Ignoring the sustained doubts about the reliability of the conviction, the US Senate has sought instead to investigate the circumstances of release where the known unknowns are much narrower.[305] The UK government has resisted any inquiry but, in 'violent agreement' with US sentiment, now openly condemns the release and has instituted an internal review of the papers.[306]

11.126 The Lockerbie case encapsulates the dynamics between terrorism and the law. A tragic case triggers extraordinary responses, some justifiable, some damaging to standards of justice.

---

[298] Both trial and appeal were criticized by a member of the Trial Observer Mission (see UN SCR 1192 of 27 August 1998), Hans Kochler: <http://www.i-p-o.org/lockerbie_observer_mission.htm>.

[299] See <http://www.megrahimystory.net/>.

[300] *Al Megrahi v HM Advocate* [2008] HCJAC 58. For PII claims, see [2008] HCJAC 15.

[301] Treaty between the United Kingdom of Great Britain and Northern Ireland and the Great Socialist People's Libyan Arab Jamahiriya on the transfer of prisoners (Cm 7540, London, 2008). The Scottish Executive sought to exclude Al Megrahi: Hansard HC vol 497 col 30 (12 October 2009). The only formal specification about place of imprisonment was by the Libyan government who feared transfer to the US (letter to UN of 19 March 1999: SC/6655).

[302] Scottish Prison Service advice (<http://www.sps.gov.uk//MultimediaGallery/7de51399-f515-4f75-810f-19e49a838cb5.pdf>, 2005) suggests a life expectancy of less than three months.

[303] See Scottish Parliament col 18891 24 August 2009; <http://www.scotland.gov.uk/Topics/Justice/legal/Lockerbie>.

[304] Hansard HC vol 497 col 32 (12 October 2009), David Miliband.

[305] See <http://foreign.senate.gov/hearings/hearing/?id=4af54aa9-5056-a032-52bc-d38201eaa076>.

[306] *The Times* 21 July 2010, pp 1, 7 David Cameron.

The recurrent problems of cross-jurisdictional crime and sensitive evidence arise but are no more surmounted here than elsewhere. In view of the controversial outcomes, there is diminished intention to replicate the Lockerbie trial arrangements or to resort to international courts to try terrorists. Yet, the endeavour to dispense criminal justice should be welcomed. After all, the contemporary alternatives of enemy combatant confinement during 'war all the time'[307] or summary death by drone[308] garner less legitimacy in process or outcome.

---

[307] Thursday, *War all of the time, In the shadow of the New York skyline* (Island Records, 2003).

[308] Murphy, J and Radsan, AJ, 'Due process and the targeted killing of terrorists' (2009) 32 *Cardozo Law Review* 405; Special Rapporteur on extrajudicial, summary or arbitrary executions, *Study On Targeted Killings* (A/HRC/14/24/Add.6, New York, 2010).

BIBLIOGRAPHY

These listings concentrate upon key and substantial post-2000 sources which principally discuss contemporary anti-terrorism legislation in the United Kingdom. Most sources and references are contained in the footnotes of individual chapters.

Barendt, E, 'Incitement to, and glorification of terrorism' in Hare, I and Weinstein, J (eds), *Extreme Speech and Democracy* (Oxford University Press, Oxford, 2009).

Barnum, D, 'Indirect incitement and freedom of speech in Anglo-American law' [2006] *European Human Rights Law Review* 258.

Bates, E, 'A "public emergency threatening the life of the nation"?' (2005) 76 *British Yearbook of International Law* 245.

Bates, E, 'Anti-terrorism control orders' (2009) 29 *Legal Studies* 99.

Bonner, D, *Executive Measures, Terrorism and National Security* (Ashgate, Aldershot, 2007).

Cabinet Office, *Security in a Global Hub* (London, 2007).

Cabinet Office, *The National Security Strategy of the United Kingdom* (Cm7291, London, 2008), *The National Security Strategy of the United Kingdom: Update 2009: Security for the Next Generation* (Cm7590, London, 2009) and *A Strong Britain in an Age of Uncertainty: The National Security Strategy* (Cm 7953, London, 2010).

Campbell, C, '"War in terror" and vicarious hegemons' (2005) 54 *International and Comparative Law Quarterly* 321.

Campbell, C and Connelly, I, 'Making war on terror? (2006) 69 *Modern Law Review* 935.

Campbell, D, 'The threat of terrorism and the plausibility of positivism' [2009] *Public Law* 501.

Chamberlain, M, 'Update on procedural fairness in closed proceedings' (2009) 28 *Civil Justice Quarterly* 448.

(Chilcot) Privy Council Review, *Intercept as Evidence* (Cm 7324, London, 2008).

(Chilcot) Advisory Group of Privy Counsellors, *Intercept as Evidence* (Cm 7760, London, 2009).

Choudhury, T, 'The Terrorism Act 2006: Discouraging terrorism' in Hare, I and Weinstein, J (eds), *Extreme Speech and Democracy* (Oxford University Press, Oxford, 2009).

Cory Collusion Inquiry Reports, Billy Wright (2003–04 HC 472), Pat Finucane (2003–04 HC 470), Robert Hamill (2003–04 HC 471), Rosemary Nelson (2003–04 HC 473).

Cram, I, *Terror and the War on Dissent* (Springer, Heidelberg, 2009).

Crown Prosecution Service, *Scrutiny of Pre-Charge Detention in Terrorist Cases* (London, 2007).

Defence Science and Technology Laboratory, *What Perceptions do the UK Public have Concerning the Impact of Counter-terrorism Legislation Implemented since 2000?* (Home Office Occasional Paper 88, London, 2010).

Delegated Powers and Regulatory Reform Select Committee, *Report on the Anti-terrorism, Crime and Security Bill* (2001–02 HL 45).

Dickson, B, 'Law versus terrorism: can law win?' [2005] *European Human Rights Law Review* 1.

Dickson, B, 'Article 5 of the ECHR and 28-day pre-charge detention' (2009) *Northern Ireland Legal Quarterly* 231.

Dingley, J (ed), *Combating Terrorism in Northern Ireland* (Routledge, Abingdon, 2009).

Donohue, L, 'Terrorism and trial by jury' (2007) 59 *Stanford Law Review* 1321.

Donohue, LK, *The Cost of Counterterrorism: Power, Politics, and Liberty* (Cambridge University Press, Cambridge, 2008).

Duffy, H, *The 'War on Terror' and the Framework of International Law* (Cambridge University Press, Cambridge, 2005).

Eckes, C, *EU Counter-Terrorist Policies and Fundamental Rights: The Case of Individual Sanctions* (Oxford University Press, Oxford, 2009).

Edwards, RA, 'Stop and search, terrorism and the human rights deficit' (2008) 37 *Common Law World Review* 211.

Feldman, D, 'Proportionality and discrimination in anti-terrorism legislation' (2005) 64 *Cambridge Law Journal* 271.

Feldman, D, 'Human rights, terrorism risks: the roles of politicians and judges' [2006] *Public Law* 364.

Fenwick, H, 'The Anti-terrorism, Crime and Security Act 2001' (2002) 65 *Modern Law Review* 724.

Financial Action Task Force, *International Best Practices: Freezing of Terrorist Assets* (Paris, 2009).

Financial Action Task Force, *Money Laundering and Terrorist Financing in the Securities Sector* (Paris, 2009).

Gearty, C, 'Terrorism and morality' [2003] *European Human Rights Law Review* 377.

Gearty, C, 'Human rights in an age of counter-terrorism' (2005) 58 *Current Legal Problems* 25.

Gearty, C, '11 September 2001, counter-terrorism and the Human Rights Act 1998' (2005) 32 *Journal of Law & Society* 18.

Gibson, Sir Peter, *Review of Intercepted Intelligence in relation to the Omagh Bombing of 15 August 1998* (Northern Ireland Office, Belfast, 2009).

Goldstock, R, *Organised Crime in Northern Ireland* (Northern Ireland Office, Belfast, 2004).

Goold, BJ and Lazarus, L, *Security and Human Rights* (Hart, Oxford, 2007).

Gross, O and Ní Aoláin, F, *Law in Times of Crisis* (Cambridge University Press, Cambridge, 2006).

Hickman, TR, 'Between human rights and the rule of law' (2005) 68 *Modern Law Review* 655.

Hiebert, JL, 'Parliamentary review of terrorism measures' (2005) 65 *Modern Law Review* 676.

HM Crown Prosecution Service Inspectorate, *Report of the Inspection of the Counter Terrorism Division of CPS Headquarters* (London, 2009).

HM Inspectorate of Constabulary, *A Need to Know: HMIC's Thematic Inspection of Special Branch and Ports Policing* (Home Office, London, 2003).

HM Treasury, *The Financial Challenge to Crime and Terrorism* (London, 2007).

HM Treasury, *Publication in Draft of the Terrorist Asset-Freezing Bill* (Cm 7806, London, 2010).

HM Treasury, *Public Consultation: Draft Terrorist Asset-Freezing Bill* (Cm 7852, London, 2010).

HM Treasury, *Draft Terrorist Asset Freezing Bill: Summary of Responses* (Cm 7888, London, 2010).

Hodgson, J and Tadros, V, 'How to make a terrorist out of nothing' (2009) 72 *Modern Law Review* 984.

Home Office, *Addressing Lessons from the Emergency Response to the 7 July 2005 London Bombings* (London, 2006).

Home Office, *Amendment to the Anti-terrorism, Crime and Security Act 2001: A Consultation Paper and Regulatory Impact Assessment* (London, 2010).

Home Office, Circular 3/2001: *Terrorism Act 2000*.

Home Office, Circular 2/2002: *International application of the UK law on corruption*.

Home Office, Circular 7/2002: *Guidance for the police and public on the implementation of Section 89; Sections 113–115; Sections 117–120 and Section 121 of the Anti-Terrorism, Crime & Security Act 2001. (Part 13 of the Anti-Terrorism, Crime & Security Act).*

Home Office, Circular 16/2002: *Part 6 of the Anti-Terrorism, Crime & Security Act 2001—Weapons of Mass Destruction.*

Home Office, Circular 24/2002: *A protocol between the Ministry of Defence Police and Home Office Police Forces.*

Home Office, Circular 25/2002: *A protocol between British Transport Police and Home Office Police Forces.*

Home Office, Circular 30/2002: *Guidance for the police and public on the implementation of Sections 1–3 of the Anti-Terrorism, Crime & Security Act 2001.*

Home Office, Circular 32/2002: *Section 94 of the Anti-Terrorism, Crime & Security Act: Removal of Disguises.*

Home Office, Circular 42/2003: *Guidance for the police in the application of 9 of Schedule 8 to the Terrorism Act 2000, subsequent to the ruling of the European Court of Human Rights in the case of Brennan v the United Kingdom.*

Home Office, Circular 26/2005: *Coordinated Policing Protocol between the Civil Nuclear Constabulary and Home Office Police Forces/Scottish Police Forces.*

Home Office, Circular 8/2006: *The Terrorism Act 2006.*

Home Office, Circular 27/2008: *Authorisation of Stop and Search Powers under Section 44 of the Terrorism Act 2000.*

Home Office, *Counter-Terrorism Powers: Reconciling Security and Liberty in an Open Society* (Cm 6147, London, 2004).

Home Office, *Countering International Terrorism* (Cm 6888, London, 2006).

Home Office, *Government Discussion Document Ahead of Proposed Counter Terrorism Bill 2007* (Home Office, London, 2007).

Home Office, *Guidance on Notices Issued under Section 3 of the Terrorism Act 2006* (London, 2006).

Home Office, *Memorandum to the Home Affairs Committee, Post Legislative Assessment of the Prevention of Terrorism Act 2005* (Cm 7797, London, 2010).

Home Office, *Options for Pre-Charge Detention in Terrorist Cases* (London, 2007).

Home Office, *Possible Measures for Inclusion into a Future Counter-Terrorism Bill* (London, 2007).

Home Office, *Pursue, Prevent, Protect, Prepare: The United Kingdom's Strategy for Countering International Terrorism* (Cm 7547, London, 2009).

Home Office, *Report of the Official Account of the Bombings in London on the 7th July 2005* (2005–06 HC 1087).

Home Office, *Summary of Responses to the Counter-Terrorism Bill Consultation* (Cm 7269, London, 2007).

Home Office, *Terrorist Investigations and the French Examining Magistrates System* (London, 2007).

Home Office, *The United Kingdom's Strategy for Countering Chemical, Biological, Radiological and Nuclear (CBRN) Terrorism* (London, 2010).

Home Office, *The United Kingdom's Strategy for Countering International Terrorism* (Cm 7833, London, 2010).

Home Office and Northern Ireland Office, *Legislation against Terrorism* (Cm 4178, London, 1998).

Home Office and HM Treasury, *Review of Safeguards to Protect the Charitable Sector (England and Wales) from Terrorist Abuse* (London, 2007).

Horne, A, *The Use of Intercept Evidence in Terrorism Cases* (SN/HA/5249, House of Commons Library, London, 2009).

House of Commons Constitutional Affairs Committee, *The Operation of the Special Immigration Appeals Commission (SIAC) and the Use of Special Advocates* (2004–5 HC 323-I).

House of Commons Defence Select Committee, *The Ministry of Defence Police: Changes in Jurisdiction Proposed under the Anti-Terrorism, Crime and Security* Bill 2001 (2001–02 HC 382) and *Government Response* (2001–02 HC 621).

House of Commons Home Affairs Committee, *Police and the Media* (2008–09 HC 75).

House of Commons Home Affairs Committee, *Report on the Anti-terrorism, Crime and Security Bill 2001* (2001–02 HC 351).

House of Commons Home Affairs Committee, *Terrorism and Community Relations* (2003–04 HC 165).

House of Commons Home Affairs Committee, *Terrorism Detention Powers* (2005–06 HC 910).

House of Commons Home Affairs Committee, *The Government's Counter-Terrorism Proposals* (2007–08 HC 43).

House of Commons Home Affairs Committee, *The Home Office's Response to Terrorist Attacks* (2009–10 HC 117) and *Government Reply* (Cm 7788, London, 2010).

House of Commons Defence Select Committee, *The Threat from Terrorism* (2001–02 HC 348-I).

House of Commons Transport Committee, *Transport Security* (2007–08 HC 191).

House of Commons Library, 01/101: The Anti-Terrorism, Crime and Security Bill (Introduction and Summary); 01/94 (Parts VI & VII: Pathogens, Toxins and Weapons of Mass Destruction); 01/96 (Parts IV & V: immigration, asylum, race and religion); 01/97 (Part X: Police Powers)); 01/98 (Parts III & XI: Disclosure and Retention of Information); 01/99 (Parts I, II, VIII, IX & XIII: Property, Security & Crime); 02/54 The Anti-terrorism, Crime and Security Act

2001: Disclosure of Information; 02/52 Detention of suspected international terrorists – Part 4 of the Anti-Terrorism, Crime and Security Act 2001; 05/14 The Prevention of Terrorism Bill; 05/66, The Terrorism Bill; 05/70 The Terrorism (Northern Ireland) Bill; 08/20 Counter-Terrorism Bill; 08/52 Counter-Terrorism Bill: Committee Stage Report.

House of Commons Foreign Affairs Committee, *Visit to Guantánamo Bay* (2006–07 HC 44).

House of Commons Northern Ireland Affairs Committee, *Cross Border Cooperation between the Governments of the United Kingdom and the Republic of Ireland* (2008–09 HC 78) and *Government Reply* (2008–09 HC 1031).

House of Commons Northern Ireland Affairs Committee, *Organised Crime in Northern Ireland* (2005-06 HC 886) and *Government Reply* (2005–06 HC 1642).

House of Commons Northern Ireland Affairs Committee, *Policing and Criminal Justice in Northern Ireland* (2007–08 HC 333).

House of Commons Northern Ireland Affairs Committee, *The Financing of Terrorism in Northern Ireland* (2001–02 HC 978).

House of Commons Northern Ireland Affairs Committee, *The Omagh Bombing* (2008–09 HC 873), (2009–10 HC 374), (2009–10 HC 440).

House of Commons Northern Ireland Affairs Committee, *The Report of the Consultative Group on the Past in Northern Ireland* (2009–10 HC 171).

House of Commons Northern Ireland Affairs Committee, *The Separation of Paramilitary Prisoners at HMP Maghaberry* (2003–04 HC 302 and *Government reply* 2003–04 HC 583).

House of Commons Science and Technology Committee, *The Scientific Response to Terrorism* (2003-04 HC 415) and Government Reply (Cm 6108, London, 2004).

House of Commons Transport Committee, *UK Transport Security* (2005–06 HC 637).

House of Commons Transport Committee, *Passengers' experience of air travel* (2006–07 HC 435).

House of Commons Transport Committee, *Transport Security* (2007–08 HC 191).

House of Lords Constitution Committee, *Counter-Terrorism Bill: The role of ministers, Parliament and the judiciary* (2007–08 HL 167).

House of Lords Constitution Committee, *Fast Track Legislation* (2008–09 HL 116).

House of Lords Constitution Committee, *Justice and Security (Northern Ireland) Bill* (2006–07 HL 54).

House of Lords Constitution Committee, *The Prevention of Terrorism Bill* (2004–05 HL 66).

House of Lords European Union Committee, *After Madrid* (2004–05 HL 53).

House of Lords European Union Committee, *Money Laundering and the Financing of Terrorism* (2008–09 HL 132) and *Government Reply* (Cm 7718, London, 2009).

House of Lords Select Committee on the Constitution, *Surveillance: Citizens and the State* (2008–09 HL 18) and *Government Response* (Cm 7616, London, 2009).

House of Lords Select Committee on the Constitution, *Terrorist Asset-Freezing etc Bill* (2010–11 HL 25).

Hunt, A, 'The Council of Europe Convention on the Prevention of Terrorism' (2006) 4 *European Public Law* 603.

Hunt, A, 'Criminal prohibitions on direct and indirect encouragement of terrorism' [2007] *Criminal Law Review* 441.

Independent Assessor of Military Complaints Procedures in Northern Ireland, *Annual Reports* (1993–4 HC 369) and onwards.

Independent Commissioner for Detained Terrorism Suspects, *Annual Reports* (Northern Ireland Office, Belfast).

Independent Monitoring Commission, *1st to 23rd Reports* (2004–10).

Independent Police Complaints Commission, *Stockwell One* (London, 2007) and *Stockwell Two* (London, 2007).

Intelligence and Security Committee, *Could 7/7 have been Prevented?'* (Cm 7617, London, 2009).

Intelligence and Security Committee, *Inquiry into Intelligence, Assessments and Advice prior to the Terrorist Bombings on Bali 12 October 2002* (Cm 5724, London, 2002).

Intelligence and Security Committee, *Inquiry into Intelligence, Report into the London Terrorist Attacks on 7 July 2005* (Cm 6785, London, 2005) and *Government Reply* (Cm 6786, London, 2006).

Intelligence and Security Committee, *The Handling of Detainees by UK Intelligence Personnel in Afghanistan, Guantánamo Bay and Iraq* (Cm 6469, London, 2005) and *Government Reply* (Cm 6511, London, 2005).

Intelligence and Security Committee, *Rendition* (Cm 7171, London, 2007) and *Government Reply* (Cm 7172, London, 2007).

Jackson, JD, 'Many years on in Northern Ireland: the Diplock legacy' (2009) 60 *Northern Ireland Legal Quarterly* 213.

Jackson, JD, Quinn, K, and Wolfe, M, *Legislating against Silence* (Northern Ireland Office, Belfast, 2001).

Joint Committee on Human Rights, *Allegations of UK complicity in torture* (2008–09 HL 152/HC 230) and Government Reply (Cm 7714, London, 2009).

Joint Committee on Human Rights, *Continuance in Force of Sections 21 to 23 of the Anti-terrorism, Crime and Security Act 2001* (2002–03 HC 462/HL 59).

Joint Committee on Human Rights, *Counter-Terrorism Policy and Human Rights: Prosecution and Pre-Charge Detention* (2005–06 HL 240/HC 1576).

Joint Committee on Human Rights, *Counter-Terrorism Policy and Human Rights: Terrorism Bill and related matters* (2005–65 HL 75, HC 561) and *Government Response* (2005–06 HL 114, HC 888).

Joint Committee on Human Rights, *Counter-Terrorism Policy and Human Rights: 28 days, intercept and post-charge questioning* (2006–07 HL 157/HC 394) and *Government Reply* (Cm 7215, London, 2007).

Joint Committee on Human Rights, *Counter-Terrorism Policy and Human Rights: 42 days* (2007–08 HL 23/HC 156).

Joint Committee on Human Rights, *Counter-Terrorism Policy and Human Rights: Annual Renewal of 28 days* (2007–08 HL 32/HC 825).

Joint Committee on Human Rights, *Counter-Terrorism Policy and Human Rights: Counter-Terrorism Bill* (2007–08 HL50/HC 199).

Joint Committee on Human Rights, *Counter-Terrorism Policy and Human Rights: 42 days and public emergencies* (2007–08 HL 116/HC 635).

Joint Committee on Human Rights, *Counter-Terrorism Policy and Human Rights: Counter-Terrorism Bill* (2007–08 HL 172/HC 1077).

Joint Committee on Human Rights, *Counter-Terrorism Policy and Human Rights: Counter-Terrorism Bill* (2007–08 HL 50/HC 199) and *Government Reply* (Cm 7344, London, 2008).

Joint Committee on Human Rights, *Counter-Terrorism Policy and Human Rights, Counter-Terrorism Bill* (2007–08 HL 108/HC 554).

Joint Committee on Human Rights, *Counter-Terrorism Policy and Human Rights: Annual Renewal of Control Orders Legislation 2009* (2008–09 HL 37/HC 382).

Joint Committee on Human Rights, *Counter-Terrorism Policy and Human Rights: Annual Renewal of Control Orders Legislation 2010* (2009–10 HL 64/HC 395) and *Government Reply* (Cm 7856, London, 2010).

Joint Committee on Human Rights, *Counter-Terrorism Policy and Human Rights (Seventeenth Report): Bringing Human Rights Back In* (2009–10 HL 86/HC 111).

Joint Committee on Human Rights, *Demonstrating respect for rights?* (2008–09 HL 47/HC 320).

Joint Committee on Human Rights, *Government Responses to the Committee's 20th and 21st Reports and other correspondence* (2007–08 HL 127, HC 756).

Joint Committee on Human Rights, *Legislative Scrutiny: Third Progress Report* (2006–07 HL 46/HC 303).

Joint Committee on Human Rights, *Legislative Scrutiny: Terrorist Asset-Freezing etc. Bill* (2010–11 HL 41/HC 535).

Joint Committee on Human Rights, *Reports on the Anti-terrorism, Crime and Security Bill* (2001–02 HL 37, HC 372) and (2001–02 HL 51, HC 420).

Joint Committee on Human Rights, *Review of Counterterrorism Powers* (2003–04 HL 158/HC 713).

Joint Committee on Human Rights, *Statutory Review: Continuance of Pt IV* (2003–04 HL 38/ HC 381).

Joint Committee on Human Rights, *Terrorism Policy and Human Rights: Annual Review of Control Orders Legislation* 2008 (2007–08 HL 57/HC 356) and *Government Reply* (Cm 7368, London, 2008).

Joint Committee on Human Rights, *The Council of Europe Convention on the Prevention of Terrorism* (2006–07 HL 26/HC 247).

Jones, A, Bowers, R, and Lodge, HD, *The Terrorism Act 2006* (Oxford University Press, Oxford, 2006).

JUSTICE, *From Arrest to Charge in 48 Hours* (London, 2007).

JUSTICE, *Secret Evidence* (London, 2009).

Kennison, P and Loumanksy, A, 'Shoot to kill' (2007) *Crime, Law & Social Change* 151.

Koch, B (ed), *Terrorism, Tort Law and Insurance* (Springer, Vienna, 2004).

Leigh, LH, 'The Terrorism Act 2006—a brief analysis' (2006) 170 *Justice of the Peace* 364.

Leigh, LH, 'Arrest: reasonable grounds for suspicion' (2008) 172 *Justice of the Peace* 180.

Lennon, G and Walker, C, 'Hot money in a cold climate' [2008] *Public Law* 37.

Lloyd Report, Lord Lloyd and Sir John Kerr, *Inquiry into Legislation against Terrorism* (Cm 3420, London, 1996).

Lord Carlile, *Anti-terrorism, Crime and Security Act 2001 Part IV Section 28*, Reviews 2001–2005 (Home Office, London).

Lord Carlile, *Reports on the Operation in 2001–2005 of Part VII of the Terrorism Act 2000* (Home Office, London).

Lord Carlile, *Proposals by Her Majesty's Government for Changes to the Laws against Terrorism* (Home Office, London, 2005).

Lord Carlile, *Special Report of the Independent Reviewer in relation to Quarterly Reports under section 14(1) of the Prevention of Terrorism Act 2005* (Home Office, London, 2006).

Lord Carlile, *Report on Proposed Measures for Inclusion in a Counter-Terrorism Bill* (Cm 7262, London, 2007).

Lord Carlile, *The Definition of Terrorism* (Cm 7052, London, 2007) and *Government Reply* (Cm 7058, London, 2007).

Lord Carlile, *Reports of the Independent Reviewer pursuant to Section 14(3) of the Prevention of Terrorism Act 2005–2010* (Home Office, London) and *Government Replies* (Cm 7194, London, 2007), (Cm 7367, London, 2008), (Cm 7855, London, 2010).

Lord Carlile, *Report on the Operation in 2001–2009 of the Terrorism Act 2000* (Home Office, London) and *Government Replies* (Cm 7133, London, 2007), (Cm 7429, London, 2008) *(note: later reports also cover Part I of the Terrorism Act 2006)*.

Lord Carlile, *Operation Pathway* (Home Office, London, 2009).

Lord Saville, *Report of the Bloody Sunday Inquiry* (2010–11 HC 29).

McCulloch, J and Pickering, S, 'Suppressing the financing of terrorism' (2005) 45 *British Journal of Criminology* 470.

McEvoy, K, *Paramilitary Imprisonment in Northern Ireland* (Oxford University Press, Oxford, 2001).

McGoldrick, D, 'Security detention—United Kingdom practice' (2009) 40 *Case Western Reserve Journal of International Law* 507.

Moeckli, D, 'Stop and search under the Terrorism Act' (2007) 70 *Modern Law Review* 659.

Moeckli, D, *Human Rights and Non-Discrimination in the 'War on Terror'* (Oxford University Press, Oxford, 2008).

Moran, J, *Policing the Peace in Northern Ireland* (Manchester University Press, Manchester, 2008).

Moran, J, 'Evaluating Special Branch and the Use of Informant Intelligence in Northern Ireland' (2010) 25 *Intelligence & National Security* 1.

Moran, J and Phythian, M, *Intelligence, Security and Policing Post-9/11* (Palgrave Macmillan, Basingstoke, 2008).

National Policing Improvement Agency, *Practice Advice on Schedule 7 of the Terrorism Act 2000* (London, 2009).

Ni Aolain, F, *The Politics of Force* (Blackstaff, Belfast, 2000).

Northern Ireland Office, *Diplock Review: Report* (Belfast, 2000).

Northern Ireland Office, *Regulating the Private Security Industry in Northern Ireland* (Belfast, 2006).

Northern Ireland Office, *Replacement Arrangements for the Diplock Court System* (Belfast, 2006).

Oehmichen, A, *Terrorism and Anti-Terror Legislation* (Intersentia, Antwerp, 2009).

Organised Crime Task Force, *Annual Reports and Threat Assessments 2004–2008* (Northern Ireland Office, Belfast).

Pantazis, C and Pemberton, S, 'From the "old" to the "new" suspect community' (2009) 49 *British Journal of Criminology* 646.

Police Ombudsman for Northern Ireland, *A Study of the Treatment of Solicitors and Barristers by the Police in Northern Ireland* (Belfast, 2003).

Police Ombudsman for Northern Ireland, *Investigation of Matters relating to the Omagh Bombing on August 15 1998* (Belfast, 2007).

Police Ombudsman for Northern Ireland, *Statement by the Police Ombudsman for Northern Ireland on her investigation into the circumstances surrounding the death of Raymond McCord Jr and related matters* (Belfast, 2007).

Police Ombudsman for Northern Ireland, *RUC Investigation of the alleged involvement of the late Father James Chesney in the bombing of Claudy on 31 July 1972* (Belfast, 2010).

Policing Board for Northern Ireland, *Omagh Bomb Investigation* (Belfast, 2008).

Posner, EA and Vermeule, A, *Terror in the Balance* (Oxford University Press, Oxford, 2007).

Privy Counsellor Review Committee, *Anti-Terrorism, Crime and Security Act 2001, Review, Report* (2003–04 HC 100) (*'Newton Report'*).

Ramraj, VV, Hor, M, and Roach, K (eds), *Global Anti-terrorism Law and Policy* (Cambridge University Press, Cambridge, 2005).

Roberts, P, 'The presumption of innocence brought home?' (2002) 118 *Law Quarterly Review* 41.

Rose, Sir Christopher, *Report on two visits by Sadiq Khan MP to Babar Ahmad at HM Prison Woodhill* (Cm 7336, London, 2008).

Rowe, JJ, 'The Terrorism Act 2000' [2000] *Criminal Law Review* 527.

Russell, J, *Charge or release: Terrorism Pre-Charge Detention Comparative Law Study* (Liberty, London, 2007).

Sajó, A (ed), *Militant Democracy* (Eleven International Publishing, Utrecht, 2004).

Sambei, A, du Plessis, A, and Polaine, M, *Counter-Terrorism Laws and Practice* (Oxford University Press, Oxford, 2009).

Sandhill, A, 'Liberty, fairness and UK control order cases' [2008] *European Human Rights Law Review* 119.

Saul, B, 'Speaking of terror' (2005) 28 *University of New South Wales Law Review* 868.

Saul, B, *Defining Terrorism in International Law* (Oxford University Press, Oxford, 2006).

Scheinin, M, *Reports of the Special Rapporteur on the promotion and protection of human rights and fundamental freedoms while countering terrorism* (A/60/370, 2005), (E/CN.4/2006/98, 2005), (A/61/267, 2006), (A/HRC/4/26, 2007), (A/62/263, 2007), (A/HRC/6/17, 2007), (A/63/223, 2008), (A/HRC/10/3, 2009), (A/HRC/13/37, 2009), (A/HRC/14/46, 2010) (United Nations).

Simcox, R, *Control Orders* (Centre for Social Cohesion, London, 2010).

Simcox, R, Stuart, H, Ahmed, H, *Islamist Terrorism* (Centre for Social Cohesion, London, 2010).

Staniforth, A, *Blackstone's Counter-Terrorism Handbook* (2nd edn, Oxford University Press, Oxford, 2010).

Starmer, K, 'Setting the record straight: human rights in an era of international terrorism' [2007] *European Human Rights Law Review* 123.

Strawson, J, *Law After Ground Zero* (Glasshouse Press, London, 2002).

Tadros, V, 'Justice and terrorism' (2007) 10 *New Criminal Law Review* 658.

Tadros, V, 'Crime and security' (2008) 71 *Modern Law Review* 940.

Thiel, D, *Policing Terrorism* (Police Foundation, London, 2009).

Thiel, M (ed), *The 'Militant Democracy' Principle in Modern Democracies* (Ashgate, Aldershot, 2009).

Tierney, S, 'Determining the state of exception' (2005) 68 *Modern Law Review* 668.

Tomkins, A, 'Legislating against terror: The Anti-terrorism, Crime and Security Act 2001' [2002] *Public Law* 205.

Tomkins, A, 'Readings of A v Secretary of State for the Home Department' [2005] *Public Law* 259.

Tooze, J, 'Deportation with assurances' [2010] *Public Law* 362.

Vaughan, B and Kilcommins, S, *Terrorism, Rights and the Rule of Law* (Willan, Cullompton, 2008).

Wade, M and Maljevic, A, *A War on Terror?* (Springer, New York, 2010).

Walker, C and Akdeniz, Y, 'Anti-Terrorism laws and data retention: war is over?' (2003) 54 *Northern Ireland Legal Quarterly* 159.

Walker, C and Broderick, J, *The Civil Contingencies Act 2004: Risk, Resilience and the Law in the United Kingdom* (Oxford University Press, Oxford, 2006).

Walker, C, 'Briefing on the Terrorism Act 2000' (2000) 12(2) *Terrorism & Political Violence* 1.

Walker, C, 'Biological attack, terrorism and the law' (2004) 17 *Terrorism and Political Violence* 175.

Walker, C, 'Terrorism and criminal justice' [2004] *Criminal Law Review* 311.

Walker, C, 'Clamping Down on Terrorism in the United Kingdom' (2006) 4 *Journal of International Criminal Justice* 1137.

Walker, C, 'Cyber-terrorism: Legal principle and the law in the United Kingdom' (2006) 110 *Penn State Law Review* 625.

Walker, C, 'Intelligence and Anti-Terrorism Legislation in the United Kingdom' (2006) 44 *Crime, Law & Social Change* 387.

Walker, C, 'Keeping control of terrorists without losing control of constitutionalism' (2007) 59 *Stanford Law Review* 1395.

Walker, C, 'The legal definition of "Terrorism" in United Kingdom law and beyond' [2007] *Public Law* 331.

Walker, C, 'The treatment of foreign terror suspects' (2007) 70 *Modern Law Review* 427.

Walker, C, '"Know thine enemy as thyself": Discerning friend from foe under anti-terrorism laws' (2008) 32 *Melbourne Law Review* 275.

Walker, C, 'Post-charge questioning of suspects' [2008] *Criminal Law Review* 509.

Walker, C, 'The governance of the Critical National Infrastructure' [2008] *Public Law* 323.

Walker, C, 'Neighbor terrorism and the all-risks policing of terrorism' (2009) 3 *Journal of National Security Law & Policy* 121.

Walker, C, *The Anti Terrorism Legislation* (2nd edn, Oxford University Press, Oxford, 2009).

Walker, C, 'Conscripting the public in terrorism policing: towards safer communities or a police state?' [2010] *Criminal Law Review* 441.

Walker, C, 'The threat of terrorism and the fate of control orders' [2010] *Public Law* 3.

Warbrick, C, 'The principles of the ECHR and the response of states to terrorism' [2002] *European Human Rights Law Review* 287.

Whalley, R, *Reports of the Independent Reviewer: Justice and Security* (Northern Ireland) Act 2007 (Northern Ireland Office, Belfast, 2008, 2009).

Wilkinson, P, (ed), *Homeland Security in the UK* (Routledge, Abingdon, 2007).

Zedner, L, 'Securing liberty in the face of terrorism' (2005) 32 *Journal of Law & Society* 507.

Zedner, L, *Security* (Routledge, Abingdon, 2009).

INDEX

References are to chapter and paragraph number.

.